WordSharp

STUDENT WRITER'S
DICTIONARY

Collins

D1404195

NELSON EDUCATION

NELSON EDUCATION

Text copyright © 2009 HarperCollins Publishers Ltd.

Illustrations and instructional features copyright © 2009 by Nelson Education Ltd.

Printed and bound in Hong Kong
1 2 3 4   11 10 09 08

School distribution by
Nelson Education Ltd.
1120 Birchmount Road, Toronto, Ontario, M1K 5G4
www.nelson.com

Trade distribution by
HarperCollins Canada
2 Bloor Street East,
Toronto, ON M4W 1A8
www.collinsdictionaries.ca

Nelson Education Ltd. is licensed to use the Collins trademark by HarperCollins Publishers Limited.

Collins is one of the world's leading reference publishers. **The Collins Word Web** contains 125 million words of Canadian English and grows at over 1.5 million words per month.

Gage represents a 40-year tradition of Canadian dictionary making. Today, Gage is the reference division of **Nelson Education Ltd.**, Canada's foremost educational publisher.

Library and Archives Canada Cataloguing in Publication

Collins Gage Canadian word sharp student writer's dictionary.
ISBN-13: 978-0-17-635473-2 (pbk.)
ISBN-10: 0-17-635473-5

1. English language--Dictionaries, Juvenile.

PE1628.5.C66 2008   j423
C2008-902179-7

Reviewers
Mary Cairo
Toronto Catholic District School Board

Irene Heffel
Language Arts Centre for Education, Edmonton

Diana Maliszeswki
Toronto District School Board

Linda O'Reilly
Educational Consultant, Vancouver

Kelly Rilley
Windsor-Essex Catholic District School Board

Ruth McQuirter Scott
Brock University

Janet Lee Stinson
Simcoe County District School Board

Chris Wentzell
South Shore Regional School Board

Editorial and Production

Director of Publishing
Kevin Martindale

General Manager, Literacy and Reference
Michelle Kelly

Publishing Consultant
Joe Banel

Publisher, Supplementary Literacy and Reference
David Friend

Managing Editor, Development
Lara Caplan

Senior Program Manager, Supplementary Literacy and Reference
Ann Downar

Project Manager
Maureen de Sousa

Project Editor
Lisa Peterson

Assistant Editor
Adam Rennie

Executive Director, Content and Media Production
Renate McCloy

Director, Content and Media Production
Sujata Singh

Content Production Editor
Linda Cahill

Copy Editor
Sandra Manley

Proofreader
Linda Jenkins

Production Coordinator
Susan Ure

Creative Director
Ken Phipps

Cover Design
Glenn Toddun

Page Design
Glenn Toddun

Compositor
Zenaida Diores

Printer
CTPS

☳ CONTENTS ☰

WordSharp
Walkthrough

Word Sharp doesn't look the same as other dictionaries— because it isn't.

Word Sharp is a Student Writer's Dictionary, and it's packed with information that will increase your word sharpness. Being sharp about words helps you understand

- what a word means and what feelings it can suggest

- how words are put together

- how words are related to each other

- why some words and phrases mean a lot more than they seem to mean

- which words are used much too often

- which words have an interesting story behind them

In Word Sharp, all the special information about words POPS off the page.

That makes it easy for you to bump into interesting details about words that will help you make your writing stronger.

A **sharp** person is quick to notice or understand things.

Keep reading and we'll explain all the special features found in Word Sharp.

They're worth checking out!

SPECIAL FEATURES

Word Sharp has a different approach to words than most dictionaries you've used.

That's because it's good to play with words, to experiment with them, to mix them and mash them to see what happens. But to get the most out of words, you need to understand how they work—and that's where this dictionary can help.

Word Sharp is full of special features that are meant to jump off the page and catch your attention. These features point out interesting and useful things about words. The more you know about words, the more success you'll have with your writing.

Researchers have discovered that word knowledge is linked to a strong vocabulary. Students with a strong vocabulary are better writers and readers, and that helps them do better in every subject.

The expression "Heads Up" tells someone to pay attention to something.

In *Word Sharp* there are Heads Up! boxes to warn you about words that can cause trouble or be confusing. Some of them tell you when **not** to use a word, some provide a language hint, and some give a detail that might save you from a major writing embarrassment.

de-
PREFIX When the prefix *de-* is added to a noun or verb, it changes the meaning to its opposite: *decode*

⚠ HEADS UP
De- usually means *do the opposite*: **de**-*ice*, **de**forest.
Un- means *not*: **un**able, **un**friendly.

Skilled writers are always in search of the specific noun, the amazing adjective, or the vivid verb that will make their writing clear and fun to read.

A thesaurus is a reference book in which words with similar meanings (synonyms) are grouped together.

Word Sharp has a mini-thesaurus feature that can help you find those words. For example, the mini-thesaurus for *big* shows that there are many other words that have a similar meaning but are more interesting—words like *enormous*, *massive*, and *colossal*.

Notice that each synonym is shown in a short phrase, so you get a better idea of how to use it.

an **enormous** building
an **immense** fortune
a **vast** wilderness
a **massive** beast

Instead of **BIG** try…

a **grave** error
a **colossal** statue
a **momentous** occasion
a **significant** difference

If you type the word **kwick** on a computer, a spell-check will underline the word to say, **"Check your spelling!"**

It will even suggest other words that you might have been trying to spell—like *kick*, *wick*, and *quick*. What a spell-check won't do is warn you about words that are spelled correctly but are still wrong.

Spell-Check This! shows you some of the common spelling mistakes that a spell-check won't be able to pick up.

A surprising number of spelling mistakes are like the one shown, where the writer used *by* instead of *buy* because the two words sound the same. Even when two words that look similar don't sound the same it can be easy to use the wrong one by mistake.

SPELL-CHECK THIS!

A computer's spell-check won't catch wrong **homophones** (words that are spelled differently but sound the same).

She went out to by her weekly groceries.

In this sentence, **by** should be **buy**. **By** can mean *beside* or *through*. **Buy** means *purchase*.

NEL

To be word sharp, sometimes you have to slow down and look carefully at words.

BE WORD SHARP!

E17-D3

When you do that, you start to see them in a new way. You notice patterns and similarities you may have missed before. You discover that some words are tricky or unusual.

The more you look at words and learn how they're put together, the better you come

to know them. It becomes easier to figure out the meaning of an unfamiliar word when you're reading.

The Knowing Words boxes will add to your understanding of how words work. You'll have more words at your fingertips when you write, which means you can express yourself more effectively.

Word Building boxes help you take words apart and put them back together. You'll find information about prefixes and suffixes, and you'll see how compound words are constructed. Learn to spot the similarities among words.

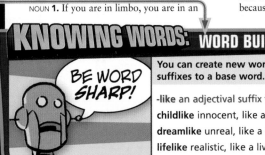

limbo
NOUN **1.** If you are in limbo, you are in an

VERB **1.** If you lim because you have

KNOWING WORDS: **WORD BUILDING**

BE WORD SHARP!

You can create new words by add suffixes to a base word.

-like an adjectival suffix that mean
childlike innocent, like a child
dreamlike unreal, like a dream
lifelike realistic, like a living thing
springlike warm, like springtime

bloodstained
ADJECTIVE covered with blood

NOUN a stain or a patch o
blotchy ADJECTIVE

KNOWING WORDS: **WORD HISTORY**

BE WORD SHARP!

Words are like living things. They grow a

Blog is a shortened form of the compoun meaning a log (or diary) on the World Wi blogs, there were Internet message board people could comment on a single topic the word was coined in the 1990s, people similar words like **artblog**, **photoblog**, an blog). Now many people use blog as a ve are **blogging** when writing a blog.

E17-D3

Word History boxes tell you something interesting about the life story of a specific word or phrase. Knowing where a word came from can help you understand other words that have a similar history.

Idioms boxes list some common expressions and explain what they mean. Many of these meanings are not obvious, so these boxes can really help!

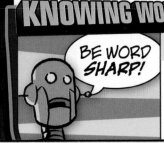

KNOWING WORDS: **IDIOMS**

BE WORD SHARP!

Idioms add colour to language by playi meanings of words.

word a single unit of language
eat your words take back what you hav
in a word briefly
say the word give a signal to do someth
spread the word tell other people a me

THE WRITER'S EDGE

Sharp writers have a number of tricks they use to make their writing more vivid and interesting.

We call these tricks literary devices. Some literary devices, such as puns and irony, make readers smile. Imagery and metaphors help readers create a mental picture of what they're reading.

Every day we read things in traditional formats like books and magazines and in newer formats like blogs and graphic novels. Literary devices are useful in every kind of writing.

> A literary device is a writing technique used to create an effect on the reader.

Here are the different literary devices you'll find in *Word Sharp*:

Throughout *Word Sharp* you'll see pages called The Writer's Edge. Each one has a comic that shows a particular literary device in action. It explains what the literary device is and tells you where to find it in the comic. As you get to know the different literary devices, you can try them out in your own writing.

MY GRAVITY BLAST DIDN'T STOP HIM! HE'S NOT A MAN, HE'S A MOUNTAIN!

Here is where you'll find the definition of the literary device.

This part tells where the literary device was used in the comic.

THE WRITER'S EDGE

METAPHOR

an imaginative way of describing something as another thing, to suggest that it has the typical qualities of that other thing

"He's not a man, he's a mountain!"

Here's the metaphor. It describes the villain in a way that gives the reader the impression that the man is huge and unbreakable.

KANAKO DAMERUM

353

WHAT'S IN A WORD SHARP ENTRY?

An entry word is the word you are looking up.

A definition explains the meaning of a word. Notice that most words have more than one meaning.

A verb form shows you how to spell the verb's different tenses.

Some words have a common phrase associated with them. It's good to know what they mean!

A phrasal verb is a verb used in combination with an adverb or preposition. You can't always work out the meaning of a phrasal verb from the usual meanings of the separate words.

A cross reference tells you to look for the meaning of the word in a different part of the dictionary.

Ii

I
PRONOUN A speaker or writer uses *I* to refer to himself or herself: *I like that colour.*

ibis ibises
NOUN a large wading bird with a long, thin, curved bill that lives in warm countries

-ible
SUFFIX Words that end in *-ible* form adjectives with the meaning *able to* or *causing*: *visible, horrible*

-ic, -ical
SUFFIX Words that end in *-ic* and *-ical* form adjectives from nouns. For example, *historic* or *historical* are formed from *history*.

ice ices icing iced
NOUN **1.** water that has frozen solid **2.** a frozen surface for sports and recreation such as hockey or skating
VERB **3.** If you ice a cake, you cover it with icing.
PHRASE **4.** If you do something to **break the ice**, you make people feel relaxed and comfortable.
ice up
VERB **5.** If something ices up, it becomes covered with a layer of ice.

ice age ice ages
NOUN a period of time lasting thousands of years when much of the earth's surface was covered with ice

iceberg icebergs
NOUN a large mass of ice floating in the sea

icecap icecaps
NOUN a layer of ice and snow that permanently covers the North or South Pole

ice cream ice creams
NOUN a frozen, sweet food made from cream

ice cube ice cubes
NOUN Ice cubes are small cubes of ice put in drinks to make them cold.

ice hockey
NOUN hockey

ice skate ice skates ice skating ice skated
1. the full name for SKATE
VERB **2.** If you ice skate, you move around on ice wearing ice skates.

icicle icicles
NOUN a piece of ice shaped like a pointed stick that hangs down from a surface

Ii

icing

NOUN a mixture of powdered sugar and other ingredients, used to decorate cakes

icon icons

NOUN **1.** a picture on a computer screen representing a program that can be activated by moving the cursor over it and clicking on it **2.** a well-known person or thing that is considered a symbol of something important in a particular culture: *The maple leaf is one Canada's most famous icons.*

ICT an abbreviation for *information and communications technology*

icy icier iciest

ADJECTIVE **1.** Something that is icy is very cold: *an icy wind* **2.** Something that is icy has ice on it: *The icy highway was the cause of many traffic accidents today.*
icily ADVERB

id

NOUN In psychology, your id is your basic instincts and unconscious thoughts.

idea ideas

NOUN **1.** a plan, suggestion, or thought that you have after thinking about a problem **2.** an opinion or belief: *old-fashioned ideas about technology* **3.** An idea of something is what you know about it: *They had no idea of where they were, so they asked for directions.*

ideal ideals

NOUN **1.** a principle or idea that you try to achieve because it seems perfect to you ADJECTIVE **2.** An ideal condition is exactly as you would wish: *ideal weather* **3.** The ideal person or thing is the best possible person or thing for the situation.

idealism

NOUN behaviour that is based on a person's ideals
idealist NOUN
idealistic ADJECTIVE

idealize idealizes idealizing idealized
VERB If you idealize someone or something, you regard that person or thing as being perfect.
idealization NOUN

ideally

ADVERB **1.** If you say that ideally something should happen, you mean that you would like it to happen, but you know that it is not possible. **2.** Ideally means perfectly: *The hotel is ideally placed for business travellers.*

identical

ADJECTIVE exactly the same: *identical twins*
identically ADVERB

A guide word shows the first or last word on a page. A guide word on the left-hand page is the first entry and a guide word on the right-hand page is the last entry.

An example sentence or phrase uses the word to help you understand it.

The part of speech tells you what role the word plays in a sentence. The parts of speech are noun, verb, adjective, adverb, pronoun, preposition, conjunction, and interjection. Many words can be used as more than one part of speech.

A plural form shows you how to spell the word when you refer to more than one of it.

A related word has the same root as the main entry.

Aa

a an
ADJECTIVE The indefinite article *a*, or *an* if the next sound is a vowel, is used when you are talking about one of something: *I ate an apple. There was a car parked in the garage.*

a-
PREFIX **1.** When *a-* comes before an adjective it adds the meaning *without* or *opposite to*. *An-* is the form used before a vowel: *amoral* **2.** When *a-* comes at the beginning of certain words it adds the meaning *toward* or *in the state of*: *ashore, asleep*

aardvark aardvarks
NOUN an African animal with a long snout and a very long, sticky tongue. It eats ants and termites.

aback
ADVERB If you are taken aback, you are very surprised.

abacus abacuses
NOUN a frame with beads that slide along rods, used for counting

abalone abalones
NOUN a shellfish that can be eaten

abandon abandons abandoning abandoned
VERB **1.** If you abandon someone or something, you leave that person or thing for good.
NOUN **2.** If you do something with abandon, you do it in an uncontrolled way: *He began to laugh with abandon.*
abandoned ADJECTIVE
abandonment NOUN

abate abates abating abated
VERB If something abates, it becomes less: *Her anger abated.*

abattoir abattoirs
NOUN a place where animals are killed for meat

abbreviate abbreviates abbreviating abbreviated
VERB To abbreviate something is to make it shorter.

abbreviation abbreviations
NOUN a short form of a word or phrase. An example is *W*, which is short for *West*.

abdicate abdicates abdicating abdicated
VERB If a king or queen abdicates, he or she gives up being a king or queen.
abdication NOUN

abdomen abdomens
NOUN the front part of your body below your chest, containing your stomach and intestines
abdominal ADJECTIVE

abduct abducts abducting abducted
VERB To abduct someone is to take that person away by force.
abduction NOUN

abet abets abetting abetted
VERB If you abet someone, you help that person to do something: *She robbed the bank, but he abetted her by driving the getaway car.*

abhor abhors abhorring abhorred
VERB *a formal word* If you abhor something, you hate it.
abhorrence NOUN
abhorrent ADJECTIVE

abide abides abiding abided
VERB **1.** If you can't abide something, you dislike it very much: *I can't abide liars.*
2. If you abide by a decision or law, you act in agreement with it.

abiding
ADJECTIVE lasting forever: *an abiding interest in history*

ability abilities
NOUN the intelligence or skill needed to do something: *the ability to get along with others*

abject
ADJECTIVE very bad: *abject failure*
abjectly ADVERB

ablaze
ADJECTIVE on fire

able abler ablest
ADJECTIVE **1.** If you are able to do something, you can do it. **2.** Someone who is able is very clever or talented.

-able
SUFFIX **1.** forming adjectives that have the meaning *capable of* an action: *enjoyable, breakable* **2.** forming adjectives with the meaning *able to* or *causing*: *comfortable, miserable*

ably
ADVERB skilfully and successfully: *He is ably supported by the cast.*

abnormal
ADJECTIVE not normal or usual
abnormally ADVERB

abnormality abnormalities
NOUN something that is not normal or usual

aboard
PREPOSITION OR ADVERB on a ship, plane, bus, train, or other vehicle

Aa

abode abodes
NOUN *an old-fashioned word* Your abode is your home.

abolish abolishes abolishing abolished
VERB To abolish something is to do away with it: *the campaign to abolish hunting*
abolition NOUN

abominable
ADJECTIVE very unpleasant or shocking
abominably ADVERB

aboriginal aboriginals
NOUN **1.** An aboriginal is a person who or thing that has existed in a region since the earliest times. **2.** In Canada, an **Aboriginal** is a person who is a member of the Inuit, Métis, or First Nations peoples.

! HEADS UP

First Peoples is a term for *Aboriginal peoples*. It's best to use specific names like **Cree**, **Inuit**, or **Métis**, if possible.

aborigine aborigines
NOUN **1.** An aborigine is a member of the earliest known population of a region. **2.** An **Aborigine** is someone descended from the people who lived in Australia before Europeans arrived.

abort aborts aborting aborted
VERB **1.** If a plan or activity is aborted, it is stopped before it is finished. **2.** If a pregnant woman aborts, the pregnancy ends too soon and the fetus dies.

abortion abortions
NOUN If a woman has an abortion, the pregnancy is ended deliberately and the fetus dies.

abortive
ADJECTIVE unsuccessful: *an abortive bank robbery*

abound abounds abounding abounded
VERB If things abound, there are very large numbers of them.

about
PREPOSITION OR ADVERB **1.** of or concerning **2.** approximately and not exactly
ADVERB **3.** in different directions: *There were some bottles scattered about.*
PHRASE **4.** If you are **about to** do something, you are going to do it very soon.

above
PREPOSITION OR ADVERB **1.** directly over or higher than something: *above the clouds* **2.** greater than a level or amount: *The temperature didn't rise above the freezing point.*

aboveboard
ADJECTIVE completely open and honest: *They made sure the competition was aboveboard by obeying all the rules.*

abrasion abrasions
NOUN an area where your skin has been scraped

abrasive
ADJECTIVE **1.** An abrasive substance is rough and can be used to clean hard surfaces. **2.** Someone who is abrasive is unpleasant and rude.

abreast
ADJECTIVE **1.** side by side: *teens riding their bicycles four abreast*
PHRASE **2.** If you keep **abreast of** a subject, you know all the most recent facts about it.

abroad
ADVERB in a foreign country

abrupt
ADJECTIVE **1.** sudden and quick: *The rain brought our baseball game to an abrupt end.* **2.** not friendly or polite
abruptly ADVERB
abruptness NOUN

abscess abscesses
NOUN a painful swelling filled with pus

absent
ADJECTIVE Something that is absent is not present in a place or situation.
absence NOUN

absentee absentees
NOUN someone who is not present when that person should be

absent-minded
ADJECTIVE forgetful

absolute

Instead of **ABSOLUTE** try...

ADJECTIVE
1. total and complete: *absolute honesty*
2. having total power: *an absolute monarch*
absolutely ADVERB

sheer foolishness
a **complete** success
a grin of **pure** delight
utter chaos everywhere
total amazement in her eyes

absolve absolves absolving absolved
VERB To absolve someone of something is to state that that person or thing is not to blame for it.

Aa

absorb absorbs absorbing absorbed
VERB If something absorbs liquid or gas, it soaks it up.

absorbent
ADJECTIVE Absorbent materials soak up liquid easily.

absorption
NOUN **1.** the soaking up of a liquid **2.** great interest in something: *my brother's absorption in the documentary*

abstain abstains abstaining abstained
VERB **1.** If you abstain from something, you do not do it or have it: *The patient had to abstain from fatty foods.* **2.** If you abstain in a vote, you do not vote.
abstention NOUN

abstinence
NOUN Abstinence is deliberately not doing something you enjoy.

abstract
ADJECTIVE **1.** An abstract idea is based on thoughts and ideas rather than physical objects or events, for example *bravery*. **2.** Abstract art is a style of art that uses shapes that don't resemble people or objects. **3.** Abstract nouns refer to qualities or ideas rather than to physical objects, for example *happiness* or *a question*.
abstraction NOUN

absurd
ADJECTIVE ridiculous and stupid
absurdly ADVERB
absurdity NOUN

abundance
NOUN Something that exists in abundance exists in large numbers: *an abundance of wildlife*

abundant
ADJECTIVE present in large quantities
abundantly ADVERB

abuse abuses
NOUN **1.** cruel treatment of someone: *child abuse* **2.** rude and unkind remarks directed toward someone **3.** the wrong use of something: *an abuse of power, alcohol abuse*

abuse abuses abusing abused
VERB **1.** If you abuse someone, you speak insultingly to that person. **2.** To abuse someone also means to treat that person cruelly. **3.** If you abuse something, you use it wrongly or for a bad purpose.
abuser NOUN

abusive
ADJECTIVE rude and unkind
abusively ADVERB
abusiveness NOUN

abysmal
ADJECTIVE very bad: *an abysmal performance*
abysmally ADVERB

abyss abysses
NOUN a very deep hole or crack in the earth

acacia acacias
NOUN a type of thorny shrub with small yellow or white flowers

academic academics
ADJECTIVE **1.** Academic work is work done in a school, college, or university.
NOUN **2.** someone who teaches or does research in a college or university
academically ADVERB

academy academies
NOUN **1.** a school or college, usually one that specializes in one particular subject: *a dance academy, a military academy* **2.** an organization of scientists, artists, writers, or musicians

accelerate accelerates accelerating accelerated
VERB To accelerate is to go faster.

acceleration
NOUN the rate at which the speed of something is increasing

accelerator accelerators
NOUN the pedal in a vehicle that you press to make it go faster

accent accents
NOUN **1.** a way of pronouncing a language: *She has an Australian accent.* **2.** a mark placed above or below a letter in some languages, which affects the way the letter is pronounced **3.** an emphasis on something: *The accent is on action and special effects.*

accentuate accentuates accentuating accentuated
VERB To accentuate a feature of something is to make it more noticeable.

accept accepts accepting accepted
VERB **1.** If you accept something, you say yes to it or take it from someone. **2.** If you accept a situation, you realize that it cannot be changed: *He accepts criticism as part of his job.* **3.** If you accept a statement or story, you believe it is true: *The teacher accepted my explanation.* **4.** If a group accepts you, they treat you as one of the group.
acceptance NOUN

acceptable
ADJECTIVE good enough to be accepted
acceptably ADVERB

access accesses accessing accessed
NOUN **1.** the right or opportunity to enter a

 **HEADS UP** Abuse is pronounced ab-YOOS when used as a noun and ab-YOOZE when used as a verb.

NEL

place or to use something
VERB **2.** If you access information from a computer, you get it.

accessible
ADJECTIVE **1.** easily reached or seen: *The cottage was accessible only by boat.* **2.** easily understood or used: *guidebooks that present information in a clear and accessible style*
accessibility NOUN

accessory accessories
NOUN **1.** an extra part **2.** someone who helps another person commit a crime

accident accidents
NOUN **1.** an unexpected event in which people are injured or killed **2.** Something that happens by accident happens by chance.

accidental
ADJECTIVE happening by chance
accidentally ADVERB

acclaimed
ADJECTIVE If someone or something is acclaimed, that person or thing is praised enthusiastically.

accolade accolades
NOUN *a formal word* great praise or an award given to someone

accommodate accommodates accommodating accommodated
VERB **1.** If you accommodate someone, you provide that person with a place to sleep, live, or work. **2.** If a place can accommodate a number of things or people, it has enough room for them.

accommodating
ADJECTIVE willing to help and to adjust to new situations

accommodations
PLURAL NOUN a place provided for someone to sleep or live

accompaniment accompaniments
NOUN **1.** The accompaniment to a song is the music played to go with it. **2.** An accompaniment to something is another thing that comes with it: *Ketchup is a good accompaniment to French fries.*

accompany accompanies accompanying accompanied
VERB **1.** If you accompany someone, you go with that person. **2.** If one thing accompanies another, the two things exist at the same time: *severe pain accompanied by fever* **3.** If you accompany a singer or musician, you play an instrument while that person sings or plays the main tune.

accomplice accomplices
NOUN a person who helps someone else to commit a crime

accomplish accomplishes accomplishing accomplished
VERB If you accomplish something, you succeed in doing it.

accomplished
ADJECTIVE very talented at something: *an accomplished cook*

accomplishment accomplishments
NOUN Someone's accomplishments are the skills that person has gained.

accord accords according accorded
VERB **1.** If you accord someone or something a particular treatment, you treat that person or thing in that way: *He was accorded a proper respect for his status.*
NOUN **2.** agreement
PHRASE **3.** If you do something **of your own accord**, you do it willingly and not because you have been forced to do it.

accordance
PHRASE If you act **in accordance with** a rule or belief, you act in the way the rule or belief says you should.

according to
PREPOSITION **1.** If something is true according to a particular person, that person says that it is true. **2.** If something is done according to a plan, that plan is used as the basis for it.

accordion accordions
NOUN a musical instrument like an expanding box. It is played by squeezing the two sides together while pressing the keys on it.

accost accosts accosting accosted
VERB If someone accosts you, especially someone you do not know, that person comes up and speaks to you: *The actor is accosted by fans wherever he goes.*

account accounts accounting accounted
NOUN **1.** a written or spoken report of something **2.** If you have a bank account, you can leave money in the bank and take it out when you need it.
PLURAL NOUN **3.** Accounts are records of money spent and received by a person or business.
PHRASE **4.** If you **take something into account**, you include it in your planning.
5. On account of means because of.
VERB **6.** To account for something is to explain it: *This might account for her strange behaviour.* **7.** If something accounts for a particular amount of something, it is that amount: *The brain accounts for three percent of body weight.*

Aa

accountable
ADJECTIVE If you are accountable for something, you are responsible for it and have to explain your actions: *You are accountable for your behaviour.*
accountability NOUN

accountant accountants
NOUN a person whose job is to keep or inspect financial accounts

accounting
NOUN the keeping and checking of financial accounts

accrue accrues accruing accrued
VERB If money or interest accrues, it increases gradually.

accumulate accumulates accumulating accumulated
VERB If you accumulate things or they accumulate, they collect over time.

accurate
ADJECTIVE completely correct or precise
accurately ADVERB
accuracy NOUN

accuse accuses accusing accused
VERB If you accuse someone of doing something wrong, you say that person has done it.
accusation NOUN
accuser NOUN

accustom accustoms accustoming accustomed
VERB If you accustom yourself to something new or different, you get used to it.

accustomed
ADJECTIVE used to something

ace aces
NOUN **1.** In a pack of cards, a card with a single symbol on it.
ADJECTIVE **2.** *an informal use* good or skilful: *an ace squash player*

acerbic
ADJECTIVE *a formal word* Acerbic remarks are harsh and bitter.

Instead of **ACHE** try...

ache aches aching ached
VERB **1.** If you ache, you feel a continuous dull pain in a part of your body.
2. If you are aching for something, you want it very much.
NOUN **3.** a continuous dull pain

mild **discomfort**

a **pang** of hunger

a **crick** in his neck

a short **twinge** of pain

throb with each heartbeat

achieve achieves achieving achieved
VERB If you achieve something, you successfully do it or cause it to happen.

achievement achievements
NOUN something that you succeed in doing, especially after a lot of effort

acid acids
NOUN **1.** a chemical liquid with a pH value of less than seven and that turns litmus paper red. Strong acids can damage metal.
ADJECTIVE **2.** Acid tastes are sharp or sour.
acidic ADJECTIVE
acidity NOUN

acid precipitation
NOUN rain or snow polluted by acids that have been released into the atmosphere by certain industries

acknowledge acknowledges acknowledging acknowledged
VERB **1.** If you acknowledge a fact or situation, you agree or admit it is true. **2.** If you acknowledge someone, you show that you have seen and recognized that person. **3.** If you acknowledge a message, you tell the person who sent it that you have received it.
acknowledgment NOUN

acne
NOUN pimples, usually on the face

acorn acorns
NOUN the fruit of the oak tree, consisting of a pale oval nut in a cup-shaped base

acoustic
ADJECTIVE **1.** relating to sound or hearing **2.** An acoustic instrument does not use an electric amplifier.

acoustics
PLURAL NOUN The acoustics of a room are its features that are responsible for how clearly you can hear sounds made in it.

acquaintance acquaintances
NOUN someone you know slightly but not well

acquainted
PHRASE If you are **acquainted with** someone, you know that person slightly but not well.

acquire acquires acquiring acquired
VERB If you acquire something, you obtain it.

acquisition acquisitions
NOUN something you have obtained

acquit acquits acquitting acquitted
VERB **1.** If someone is acquitted of a crime, that person has been tried in a court and found not guilty. **2.** If you acquit yourself well on a particular occasion, you behave or perform well.
acquittal NOUN

Aa

acre acres
NOUN a nonmetric unit for measuring an area of land. One acre is equal to about 4047 square metres.

acrid
ADJECTIVE sharp and bitter: *the acrid smell of burning plastic*

acrimony
NOUN *a formal word* bitterness and anger
acrimonious ADJECTIVE

acrobat acrobats
NOUN an entertainer who performs gymnastic tricks
acrobatic ADJECTIVE
acrobatics PLURAL NOUN

acronym acronyms
NOUN a word made up of the initial letters of a phrase. An example of an acronym is *RAM*, which stands for *Random Access Memory*.

across
PREPOSITION OR ADVERB **1.** going from one side of something to the other **2.** on the other side of a road or river

acrylic
NOUN **1.** Acrylic is a type of cloth made from artificial fibres. **2.** Acrylics are thick paints that are used by artists.

act acts acting acted
VERB **1.** If you act, you do something: *It would be irresponsible not to act swiftly.* **2.** If you act in a particular way, you behave in that way. **3.** If a person or thing acts as something else, it has the function or does the job of that thing: *She was able to act as an interpreter.* **4.** If you act in a play or movie, you play a part.
NOUN **5.** a single thing someone does: *It was an act of disloyalty to the prime minister.* **6.** a law passed by the government **7.** In a play, ballet, or opera, an act is one of the main parts it is divided into.

acting
NOUN the profession of performing in plays, movies, and other entertainments

action actions
NOUN **1.** the process of doing something **2.** something that is done **3.** a physical movement

activate activates activating activated
VERB To activate something is to make it start working.

active
ADJECTIVE **1.** full of energy **2.** busy and hard-working **3.** In grammar, a verb in the active voice is one where the subject does the action. For example, *The dog chased the cat* is in the active voice.
actively ADVERB

activist activists
NOUN a person who tries to bring about political and social change

activity activities
NOUN **1.** Activity is a situation in which a lot of things are happening at the same time. **2.** something you do for pleasure: *sport and leisure activities*

Instead of **ACTIVITY** try…

a noble **pursuit**
a casual interest
a part-time hobby
our favourite pastime
a profitable enterprise

actor actors
NOUN a man or woman whose profession is acting

actress actresses
NOUN a woman whose profession is acting

actual
ADJECTIVE real, rather than imaginary or guessed at: *That is the official figure; the actual figure is much higher.*
actually ADVERB

acumen
NOUN the ability to make good decisions quickly: *business acumen*

acupuncture
NOUN the treatment of illness or pain by sticking small needles into specific places in a person's body

acute
ADJECTIVE **1.** severe or intense: *an acute shortage of accommodation* **2.** very intelligent: *an acute mind* **3.** An acute angle is less than 90°. **4.** In French and some other languages, an acute accent is a line sloping upward from left to right placed over a vowel to indicate a change in pronunciation, as in the word *café*.

ad ads
NOUN *an informal word* an advertisement

AD AD is an abbreviation of the Latin words *anno Domini*, which means *in the year of the Lord*. You use *AD* in dates to indicate the number of years after the birth of Jesus Christ. CE is the same thing and is now the more commonly used term in dates: *The village was founded in 966 AD.*

Aa

ad-

PREFIX The prefix *ad-* means *near* or *next to*: *adverb, adjoining*

adage adages

NOUN a saying that expresses some general truth about life

adamant

ADJECTIVE If you are adamant, you are determined not to change your mind.

adamantly ADVERB

Adam's apple Adam's apples

NOUN the larynx, a lump at the front of the neck that is more obvious in men than in women and young boys

adapt adapts adapting adapted

VERB **1.** If you adapt to a new situation, you change so you can deal with it successfully. **2.** If you adapt something, you change it so it is suitable for a new purpose or situation.

adaptable ADJECTIVE

adaptation NOUN

adapter adapters

NOUN a type of device that can be used to connect two or more parts that do not match

add adds adding added

VERB **1.** If you add something to a number of things, you put it with the things. **2.** If you add numbers together or add them up, you work out the total.

adder adders

NOUN a small poisonous snake

addict addicts

NOUN someone who cannot stop taking harmful drugs

addicted ADJECTIVE

addiction NOUN

addictive

ADJECTIVE If a drug is addictive, the people who take it cannot stop.

addition additions

NOUN **1.** something that has been added to something else **2.** the process of adding numbers together

additional

ADJECTIVE extra or more: *They made the decision to take on additional staff.*

additionally ADVERB

additive additives

NOUN something added to something else, usually in order to improve it

address addresses addressing addressed

NOUN **1.** the number of the house where you live, together with the name of the street and the city, town, or village **2.** a speech given to a group of people

VERB **3.** If a letter is addressed to you, it has

your name and address written on it. **4.** If you address a problem or task, you start to deal with it.

adept

ADJECTIVE very skilful at doing something: *She is adept at motivating others.*

adequate

ADJECTIVE enough in amount or good enough for a purpose: *an adequate diet*

adequately ADVERB

adequacy NOUN

adhere adheres adhering adhered

VERB **1.** If one thing adheres to another, it sticks firmly to it. **2.** If you adhere to a rule or agreement, you do what it says. **3.** If you adhere to an opinion or belief, you firmly hold that opinion or belief.

adherence NOUN

adherent adherents

NOUN An adherent of a belief is someone who holds that belief.

adhesive adhesives

NOUN **1.** any substance used to stick two things together, for example glue

ADJECTIVE **2.** Adhesive substances are sticky and able to stick to things.

adjacent

ADJECTIVE *a formal word* **1.** If two things are adjacent, they are next to each other: *a hotel adjacent to the beach* **2.** Adjacent angles share one side and have the same point opposite to their bases.

adjective adjectives

NOUN a word that adds to the description given by a noun. For example, in *They live in a large white house*, *large* and *white* are adjectives.

adjectival ADJECTIVE

 HEADS UP

Avoid vague, overused adjectives like **nice** or **good**. Use a thesaurus to find more vivid adjectives.

adjoining

ADJECTIVE If two rooms are next to each other and are connected, they are adjoining.

adjourn adjourns adjourning adjourned

VERB **1.** If a meeting or trial is adjourned, it stops for a time: *The case was adjourned until September.* **2.** If people adjourn to another place, they go there together after a meeting: *We adjourned to the lounge.*

adjournment NOUN

adjust adjusts adjusting adjusted

VERB **1.** If you adjust something, you change its position or alter it in some other way. **2.** If you adjust to a new situation, you get used to it.

adjustment NOUN

adjustable ADJECTIVE

ad lib ad libs ad libbing ad libbed

VERB **1.** If you ad lib, you say something that has not been prepared beforehand: *The reporter ad libs on TV but uses a script on radio.*

NOUN **2.** a comment that has not been prepared beforehand

administer administers administering administered

VERB **1.** To administer an organization is to be responsible for managing it. **2.** To administer the law or administer justice is to put it into practice and apply it. **3.** If medicine is administered to someone, it is given to them.

administration administrations

NOUN **1.** Administration is the work of organizing and supervising an organization. **2.** Administration is also the process of administering something: *the administration of criminal justice* **3.** The administration is the group of people that manages an organization or a country.

administrative ADJECTIVE

administrator NOUN

admirable

ADJECTIVE very good and deserving to be admired

admirably ADVERB

admiral admirals

NOUN the commander of a navy

admiration

NOUN a feeling of great liking and respect

admire admires admiring admired

VERB If you admire someone or something, you respect and approve of that person or thing.

admirer NOUN

admiring ADJECTIVE

admiringly ADVERB

admission admissions

NOUN **1.** If you are allowed admission to a place, you are allowed to go in. **2.** If you make an admission of something, you agree, often reluctantly, that it is true: *It was an admission of guilt.*

admit admits admitting admitted

VERB **1.** If you admit something, you agree, often reluctantly, that it is true. **2.** To admit someone or something to a place or organization is to allow that person or

thing to enter it. **3.** If you are admitted to a hospital, you are taken there to stay until you are better.

admittedly

ADVERB People use *admittedly* to show that what they are saying contrasts with something they have already said or are about to say, and weakens their argument: *My studies, admittedly only from books, taught me much.*

adolescent adolescents

NOUN a young person who is no longer a child but who is not yet an adult

adolescence NOUN

adopt adopts adopting adopted

VERB **1.** If you adopt a child who is not your own, you take that child into your family as your son or daughter. **2.** *a formal use* If you adopt a particular attitude, you start to have it.

adoption NOUN

adorable

ADJECTIVE sweet and attractive

adore adores adoring adored

VERB If you adore someone, you feel deep love and admiration for that person.

adoration NOUN

adorn adorns adorning adorned

VERB To adorn something is to decorate it: *The table is adorned with flowers and candles.*

adornment NOUN

adrenalin

NOUN a substance that is produced by your body when you are angry, scared, or excited and that makes your heart beat faster

adrift

ADJECTIVE OR ADVERB If a boat is adrift or goes adrift, it floats on the water without being controlled.

adulation

NOUN great admiration and praise for someone

adulatory ADJECTIVE

adult adults

NOUN a mature and fully developed person or animal

adultery

NOUN sexual intercourse between a married person and someone he or she is not married to

adulterer NOUN

adulterous ADJECTIVE

adulthood

NOUN the time during someone's life when that person is an adult

Aa

advance advances advancing advanced
VERB **1.** To advance is to move forward. **2.** To advance a cause or interest is to help it to be successful. **3.** If you advance someone a sum of money, you lend it to that person.
NOUN **4.** Advance in something is progress in it: *a scientific advance* **5.** a sum of money lent to someone
ADJECTIVE **6.** happening before an event: *The event received little advance publicity.*
PHRASE **7.** If you do something **in advance**, you do it before something else happens: *We booked the room well in advance.*

advantage advantages
NOUN **1.** a benefit or something that puts you in a better position
PHRASE **2.** If you **take advantage of** someone, you treat that person unfairly for your own benefit. **3.** If you **take advantage of** something, you make use of it.

advantageous
ADJECTIVE likely to benefit you in some way: *The delay was advantageous as it gave us more time to plan our trip.*

advent
NOUN The advent of something is its start or its coming into existence: *The advent of the submarine changed naval warfare.*

adventure adventures
NOUN an event that is unusual and exciting

adventurer adventurers
NOUN someone who enjoys doing dangerous and exciting things

adventurous
ADJECTIVE willing to take risks and do new and exciting things
adventurously ADVERB

adverb adverbs
NOUN a word that adds information about a verb or a following adjective or other adverb, for example *slowly*, *now*, and *here*, which say how, when, or where something is done
adverbial ADJECTIVE

⚠ **HEADS UP**

Avoid overused adverbs like **really** or **very**. Use a thesaurus to find more precise and colourful adverbs.

adversary adversaries
NOUN someone who is your enemy or who opposes what you are doing

adverse
ADJECTIVE not helpful to you or opposite to what you want or need: *adverse weather conditions*
adversely ADVERB

adversity adversities
NOUN a time of danger or difficulty

advertise advertises advertising advertised
VERB **1.** If you advertise something, you tell people about it, for example in a newspaper or poster, or on TV. **2.** To advertise is to make an announcement, for example in a newspaper or poster, or on TV.
advertiser NOUN
advertising NOUN

advertisement advertisements
NOUN an announcement about something, for example in a newspaper or poster, or on TV

advice
NOUN a suggestion from someone about what you should do

advisable
ADJECTIVE sensible and likely to achieve the result you want: *It is advisable to ask someone to read your report before writing the final version.*
advisably ADVERB
advisability NOUN

advise advises advising advised
VERB **1.** If you advise someone to do something, you tell that person you think he or she should do it. **2.** *a formal use* If you advise someone of something, you inform that person of it.
advisory ADJECTIVE

SPELL-CHECK THIS!

A computer's spell-check won't catch a word that is spelled correctly but used in the wrong way.

▼✕

She went to the school counsellor to get advise.

In this sentence, **advise** should be **advice**.
Advise is a verb that means *give suggestions*.
Advice is a noun that means *guidance*.

NEL

Aa

adviser advisers
NOUN a person whose job is to give advice

advocate advocates advocating advocated
VERB **1.** If you advocate a course of action or plan, you support it publicly.
NOUN **2.** An advocate of something is someone who supports it publicly.
3. *a formal use* a lawyer who represents clients in court
advocacy NOUN

aerial aerials
ADJECTIVE **1.** Aerial means happening in the air: *We watched an aerial display by the Snowbirds.*
NOUN **2.** a radio or TV antenna

aero-
PREFIX The prefix *aero-* means *involving the air, the atmosphere, or aircraft*: aeronautics

aerobics
PLURAL NOUN a type of fast physical exercise, which increases the oxygen in your blood and strengthens your heart and lungs
aerobic ADJECTIVE

aerodynamic
ADJECTIVE having a streamlined shape that moves easily through the air

aerosol aerosols
NOUN a liquid kept under pressure so that it can be forced out as a spray

aerospace
ADJECTIVE involved in making and designing airplanes and spacecraft

aesthetic
ADJECTIVE *a formal word* relating to the appreciation of beauty or art
aesthetically ADVERB

afar
NOUN *a literary or poetic word* From afar means from a long way away: *to admire from afar, to see someone from afar*

affable
ADJECTIVE pleasant and easy to talk to
affably ADVERB
affability NOUN

affair affairs
NOUN **1.** an event or series of events: *The funeral was a sad affair.* **2.** To have an affair is to have a secret sexual or romantic relationship, especially when one of the people is married.
PLURAL NOUN **3.** Your affairs are your private and personal life: *Don't interfere in my affairs.*

affect affects affecting affected
VERB If something affects you, it influences you in some way.

affected
ADJECTIVE Affected behaviour is not genuine but is put on to impress people.

affection
NOUN a feeling of love and fondness for someone

affectionate
ADJECTIVE full of fondness for someone: *an affectionate embrace*
affectionately ADVERB

affiliate affiliates affiliating affiliated
VERB If a group is affiliated with another, larger group, it forms a close association with it: *The local TV station is not affiliated with any of the big networks.*
affiliation NOUN

affinity affinities
NOUN a close similarity or understanding between two things or people: *There are affinities between the two poets.*

affirm affirms affirming affirmed
VERB If you affirm an idea or belief, you clearly indicate your support for it: *The politician affirmed his commitment to helping the homeless.*
affirmation NOUN

affirmative
ADJECTIVE An affirmative word or gesture is one that means yes.

afflict afflicts afflicting afflicted
VERB If illness or pain afflicts someone, that person suffers from it: *She was afflicted by depression.*
affliction NOUN

affluent
ADJECTIVE having a lot of money and possessions
affluence NOUN

afford affords affording afforded
VERB **1.** If you can afford to do something, you have enough money or time to do it.
2. If you cannot afford something to happen, it would be harmful or embarrassing for you if it happened: *You cannot afford to miss this opportunity.*

affordable
ADJECTIVE If something is affordable, most people have enough money to buy it: *the availability of affordable housing*

affront affronts affronting affronted
VERB **1.** If you are affronted by something, you are insulted and angered by it.
NOUN **2.** something that is an insult: *The conditions in some of our prisons are an affront to civilized society.*

 **HEADS UP** Don't confuse **affect** and **effect**. **Affect** means *influence* and **effect** means *result*.

Aa

afield

ADVERB Far afield means a long way away: *Students from as far afield as Russia and China took part in the competition.*

afloat

ADVERB OR ADJECTIVE **1.** floating on water **2.** successful and making enough money: *Many small businesses are struggling hard to stay afloat.*

afoot

ADJECTIVE OR ADVERB happening or being planned, especially secretly: *Plans are afoot to build a new museum.*

afraid

ADJECTIVE **1.** If you are afraid, you are very frightened. **2.** If you are afraid something might happen, you are worried it might happen: *I'm afraid it might rain tomorrow.*

afresh

ADVERB again and in a new way: *I wish I could start today afresh.*

Africa

NOUN Africa is the second largest continent. It is almost surrounded by sea, with the Atlantic on its west side, the Mediterranean to the north, and the Indian Ocean and the Red Sea to the east.

African Africans

ADJECTIVE **1.** belonging or relating to Africa NOUN **2.** someone who comes from Africa

aft

ADVERB OR ADJECTIVE toward the back of a ship or boat

after

PREPOSITION OR ADVERB **1.** later than a particular time, date, or event **2.** behind and following someone or something: *They ran after her.*

afterlife

NOUN The afterlife is a life that some people believe begins when you die.

aftermath

NOUN The aftermath of a disaster is the situation that comes after it: *The aftermath of the hurricane was flooded streets.*

afternoon afternoons

NOUN the part of the day between noon and about six o'clock

aftershave

NOUN an antiseptic liquid that men put on their faces after shaving

afterthought afterthoughts

NOUN something you do or say as an addition to something else you have done or said

afterwards

ADVERB after an event or time

again

ADVERB **1.** happening one more time: *He looked forward to becoming a father again.* **2.** returning to the same state or place as before: *We ran to the lake and back again.*

against

PREPOSITION **1.** touching and leaning on: *I leaned against the wall.* **2.** in opposition to: *We will play against last year's champions in the final game of the season.* **3.** in preparation for or in case of something: *It is important to take precautions against fire.* **4.** in comparison with: *The American dollar is now at its lowest rate against the Canadian dollar.*

age ages aging aged

NOUN **1.** The age of something or someone is the number of years that person has lived or that thing has existed. **2.** Age is the quality of being old: *Some kinds of cheese improve with age.* **3.** a particular period in history: *the Iron Age*

PLURAL NOUN **4.** *an informal use* Ages means a very long time: *He's been talking on the phone for ages.*

VERB **5.** To age is to grow old or to appear older.

aged

ADJECTIVE having a particular age: *people aged 16 to 24*

KNOWING WORDS: WORD HISTORY

BE WORD SHARP!

Words are like living things. They grow and change.

The prefix **a-** can mean *in a particular way or place*. Long ago, people used this prefix to make an adjective or an adverb out of almost any word. **Sleep** was used to make **asleep**, and **ground** was turned into **aground**. We still have lots of these words in modern English. Some of them are on this page. Can you think of any more?

Aa

aged
ADJECTIVE very old: *Her aged grandparents live in a nursing home.*

agency agencies
NOUN an organization or business that provides certain services: *a detective agency*

agenda agendas
NOUN a list of items to be discussed at a meeting

agent agents
NOUN **1.** someone who arranges work or business for other people, especially actors or singers **2.** someone who obtains information for a government, especially in secret

aggravate aggravates aggravating aggravated
VERB **1.** To aggravate a bad situation is to make it worse. **2.** *an informal use* If someone or something aggravates you, that person or thing makes you annoyed.
aggravating ADJECTIVE
aggravation NOUN

aggregate aggregates
NOUN a total that is made up of several smaller amounts

aggression
NOUN violent and hostile behaviour

aggressive
ADJECTIVE full of hostility and violence
aggressively ADVERB
aggressiveness NOUN

aggressor aggressors
NOUN a person or country that starts a fight or a war

aggrieved
ADJECTIVE upset and angry about the way you have been treated

aghast
ADJECTIVE shocked and horrified

agile
ADJECTIVE able to move quickly and easily: *He is as agile as a cat.*
agilely ADVERB
agility NOUN

agitate agitates agitating agitated
VERB **1.** If you agitate for something, you campaign energetically to get it. **2.** If something agitates you, it worries you.
agitation NOUN
agitator NOUN

agnostic agnostics
NOUN OR ADJECTIVE Someone who believes we cannot know definitely that God exists.
agnosticism NOUN

ago
ADVERB in the past: *She bought her guitar three years ago.*

agog
ADJECTIVE excited and eager to know more about an event or situation: *They were agog to hear his news.*

agonizing
ADJECTIVE extremely painful, either physically or mentally: *an agonizing decision*

agony
NOUN very great physical or mental pain

agoraphobia
NOUN the fear of open spaces
agoraphobic ADJECTIVE

agrarian
ADJECTIVE *a formal word* relating to farming and agriculture: *agrarian economies*

agree agrees agreeing agreed
VERB **1.** If you agree with someone, you have the same opinion as that person. **2.** If you agree to do something, you say you will do it. **3.** If two stories or totals agree, they are the same.
PHRASE **4.** Food that doesn't **agree with** you makes you ill.

agreeable
ADJECTIVE **1.** pleasant or enjoyable **2.** If you are agreeable to something, you are willing to allow it or to do it: *She was agreeable to the project.*
agreeably ADVERB

agreement agreements
NOUN **1.** a decision that has been reached by two or more people **2.** Two people who are in agreement have the same opinion about something.

agriculture
NOUN Agriculture is farming.
agricultural ADJECTIVE

aground
ADVERB If a boat runs aground, it becomes stuck on the bottom in shallow water.

ahead
ADVERB **1.** in front: *He looked ahead.* **2.** more advanced than someone or something else: *That video-game company is five years ahead of the competition.* **3.** in the future: *I haven't had time to think far ahead.*

aid aids aiding aided
NOUN **1.** Aid is money, equipment, or services provided for people in need: *food and medical aid* **2.** something that makes a task easier: *teaching aids*
VERB **3.** *a formal use* If you aid people or organizations, you help or support them.

⚠ HEADS UP Aged can be pronounced in two ways: a child EHJD six, an EH-jid uncle.

Aa

aide aides

NOUN an assistant to an important person, especially in the government or the armed forces: *the prime minister's closest aides*

AIDS

NOUN a disease which destroys the body's natural system of immunity to diseases. AIDS is an acronym for *acquired immune deficiency syndrome.*

ailing

ADJECTIVE **1.** sick or ill, and not getting better **2.** getting into difficulties, especially with money: *an ailing company*

ailment ailments

NOUN a minor illness

aim aims aiming aimed

VERB **1.** If you aim an object or weapon at someone or something, you point it at that person or thing. **2.** If you aim to do something, you are planning or hoping to do it.

NOUN **3.** Your aim is what you intend to achieve. **4.** If you take aim, you point an object or weapon at someone or something.

aimless

ADJECTIVE having no clear purpose or plan

aimlessly ADVERB

aimlessness NOUN

air airs airing aired

NOUN **1.** Air is the mixture of oxygen and other gases that we breathe and which forms the earth's atmosphere. **2.** An air someone or something has is the impression that person or thing gives: *an air of defiance* **3.** Air is used to refer to travel in aircraft: *I travelled by air for the first time last summer.*

VERB **4.** If you air your opinions, you talk about them to other people.

airborne

ADJECTIVE in the air and flying: *Once we were airborne we were allowed to unbuckle our seat belts.*

air conditioning

NOUN a system of providing cool, clean air in buildings

air-conditioned ADJECTIVE

air force air forces

NOUN the part of a country's armed forces that fights using aircraft

air gun air guns

NOUN a gun that uses air pressure to fire pellets

airless

ADJECTIVE having no wind or fresh air

airlift airlifts

NOUN an operation to move people or goods by air, especially in an emergency

airmail

NOUN the system of sending letters and parcels by air

air raid air raids

NOUN an attack by enemy aircraft, in which bombs are dropped

airship airships

NOUN a large, light aircraft, consisting of a rigid balloon filled with gas and powered by an engine, with a passenger compartment underneath

airtight

ADJECTIVE not letting air in or out

airy airier airiest

ADJECTIVE full of fresh air and light

airily ADVERB

aisle aisles

NOUN a long narrow gap that people can walk along between rows of seats or shelves of goods

ajar

ADJECTIVE A door or window that is ajar is slightly open.

akin

ADJECTIVE *a formal word* similar: *The taste is akin to chocolate.*

alabaster

NOUN a type of smooth, white, translucent stone

KNOWING WORDS: WORD BUILDING

BE WORD SHARP!

To build a compound word, put two or more base words together.

air the sky

aircraft any vehicle that can fly

airfield a large open area for aircraft to take off and land

airline a company that provides air travel

airplane a flying vehicle with wings and engines

airport a place where people go to catch planes

NEL

Aa

alarm alarms alarming alarmed

NOUN **1.** a feeling of fear and worry: *The cat sprang back in alarm.* **2.** an automatic device used to warn people of something: *a car alarm*

VERB **3.** If something alarms you, it makes you worried and anxious.

alarming ADJECTIVE

alas

INTERJECTION unfortunately or regrettably: *But, alas, the princess would never become queen.*

albatross albatrosses

NOUN a large white sea bird

albeit

CONJUNCTION *a formal word* although: *He was making progress, albeit slowly.*

albino albinos

NOUN a person or animal with very white skin, white hair, and pink eyes

album albums

NOUN a book in which you keep a collection of things such as photographs or stamps

alchemy

NOUN a medieval science that attempted to change ordinary metals into gold

alchemist NOUN

alcohol

NOUN Alcohol is any drink that can make people drunk. It is also the colourless, flammable liquid found in these drinks, produced by fermenting sugar.

alcoholic alcoholics

ADJECTIVE **1.** An alcoholic drink contains alcohol.

NOUN **2.** someone who is addicted to alcohol

alcoholism NOUN

alcove alcoves

NOUN an area of a room that is set back slightly from the main part

ale

NOUN a type of beer

alert alerts alerting alerted

ADJECTIVE **1.** paying full attention to what is happening: *The criminal was spotted by an alert member of the public.*

NOUN **2.** a situation in which people prepare themselves for danger: *A severe weather alert will be in effect until midnight.*

VERB **3.** If you alert someone to a problem or danger, you warn that person of it.

alertness NOUN

algae

PLURAL NOUN plants that grow in water or on damp surfaces

algebra

NOUN a branch of mathematics in which symbols and letters are used instead of numbers to express relationships between quantities

algebraic ADJECTIVE

alias aliases

NOUN a false name: *The blogger's real name is Joanna, but she goes by the alias Carmen.*

! HEADS UP

Online, **alias** can mean a simplified website address, or a name for a group e-mail list.

alibi alibis

NOUN An alibi is evidence proving you were somewhere else when a crime was committed.

alien aliens

ADJECTIVE **1.** not normal to you: *a totally alien culture*

NOUN **2.** someone who is not a citizen of the country in which he or she lives **3.** In science fiction, an alien is a creature from outer space.

alienate alienates alienating alienated

VERB If you alienate someone, you do something that makes that person stop being sympathetic to you: *His sudden mood swings alienated everyone on the team.*

alienation NOUN

alight alights alighting alighted

ADJECTIVE **1.** Something that is alight is burning.

VERB **2.** If a bird or insect alights somewhere, it lands there. **3.** *a formal use* When passengers alight from a vehicle, they get out of it at the end of a journey.

align aligns aligning aligned

VERB **1.** If you align yourself with a particular group, you support it. **2.** If you align things, you place them in a straight line.

alignment NOUN

alike

ADJECTIVE **1.** Things that are alike are similar in some way.

ADVERB **2.** If people or things are treated alike, they are treated in a similar way.

alimony

NOUN money someone has to pay regularly for the support of his or her wife or husband after a divorce

alive

ADJECTIVE **1.** living **2.** lively and active

Aa

alkali alkalis
NOUN a chemical substance that turns litmus paper blue
alkaline ADJECTIVE
alkalinity NOUN

all
ADJECTIVE, PRONOUN, OR ADVERB **1.** used when referring to the whole of something: *Why did he have to say all that? She managed to finish it all.*
ADVERB **2.** *All* is also used when saying the two sides in a game or contest have the same score: *The final score was six all.*

Allah
NOUN the name of the Supreme Being in Islam

allay allays allaying allayed
VERB To allay someone's fears or doubts is to stop that person from feeling afraid or doubtful.

allege alleges alleging alleged
VERB If you allege that something is true, you say it is true but do not provide any proof: *It is alleged that she stole money from several lockers.*
allegation NOUN
alleged ADJECTIVE

allegiance allegiances
NOUN loyal support for a person or organization: *The team's allegiance to their coach was unwavering.*

allegory allegories
NOUN a piece of writing or art in which the characters and events are symbols for something else. Allegories usually make some moral, religious, or political point. For example, George Orwell's novel *Animal Farm* is an allegory in that the animals who revolt in the farmyard are symbols of the political leaders in the Russian Revolution.

allergy allergies
NOUN If you have an allergy to something, you become ill when you eat it or touch it: *an allergy to peanuts*

alleviate alleviates alleviating alleviated
VERB To alleviate pain or a problem is to make it less severe: *The government should take measures to alleviate poverty.*
alleviation NOUN

alley alleys
NOUN a narrow passage between buildings

alliance alliances
NOUN a group of people, organizations, or countries working together for similar aims

alligator alligators
NOUN a large animal, similar to a crocodile

alliteration
NOUN *a literary or poetic word* the use of several words together that all begin with the same consonant sound, for example *around the ragged rock the ragged rascal ran*
alliterative ADJECTIVE

allocate allocates allocating allocated
VERB If you allocate something, you decide it should be given to a person or place, or used for a particular purpose: *The school board allocated funds for new computers.*
allocation NOUN

allot allots allotting allotted
VERB If something is allotted to you, it is given to you as your share: *Space was allotted for visitors' cars.*

allotment allotments
NOUN **1.** a piece of land that a person can rent to grow vegetables on **2.** a share of something

allow allows allowing allowed
VERB **1.** If you allow something, you say it is all right or you let it happen. **2.** If you allow a period of time or an amount of something, you set it aside for a particular purpose: *Allow four hours for the paint to dry.*
allowable ADJECTIVE

allowance allowances
NOUN **1.** money given regularly to someone for a particular purpose: *I always save half of my weekly allowance.*
PHRASE **2.** If you **make allowance** for something, you take it into account: *The school made allowance for the bad weather and didn't require excuses for lateness.*

alloy alloys
NOUN a mixture of two or more metals

all right
ADJECTIVE **1.** If something is all right, it is acceptable. **2.** If someone is all right, that person is safe and not harmed. **3.** You say *all right* to agree to something.

> **! HEADS UP**
>
> **Alright** is sometimes used informally instead of **all right**. Don't use it in formal writing.

allude alludes alluding alluded
VERB If you allude to something, you refer to it in an indirect way.

allure
NOUN The allure of something is an exciting quality that makes it attractive: *the allure of foreign travel*
alluring ADJECTIVE

MAY I PAY WITH A DEBIT CARD?

THE BLUE SCARAB!

MANNERLY AND MAJESTIC, OUR HERO ARRIVES TO DEFROST AND DETHRONE THE SNOW QUEEN!

BLIZZARD! SNOW JOB! PUT HIM ON ICE! MUSH! MUSH!!

ICE DAGGERS, EH!?

AUNTIE FREEZE'S HUSKY HENCHMEN QUICKLY HEED HER COLD CALL AND...

FFUT FFUT FFUT

BOP!

COME NOW, YOU WINTRY WIMPS ARE GONNA HAVE TO DO BETTER THAN THAT!

ALLITERATION ▼×

the use of several words together that all begin with the same consonant sound

"Mannerly and majestic, our hero arrives to defrost and dethrone the snow queen."

Here are two examples of alliteration. Can you find other examples on this page?

Aa

allusion allusions
NOUN a brief reference to something from history, literature, or culture as a way of adding meaning to a piece of writing: *Her new song contains several allusions to different TV shows.*

ally allies allying allied
NOUN **1.** a person or country that helps and supports another
VERB **2.** If you ally yourself with someone, you agree to help and support each other.

almanac almanacs
NOUN a book published every year giving information about a particular subject

almighty
ADJECTIVE very great or serious: *He made such an almighty fuss that I had to take him for ice cream.*

almond almonds
NOUN a pale brown, oval nut

almost
ADVERB very nearly: *Prices have almost doubled in the last five years.*

alms
PLURAL NOUN *an old-fashioned word* Alms are gifts of money, food, or clothing for poor people.

aloft
ADVERB up in the air or in a high position: *The sailor climbed aloft to untangle some ropes.*

alone
ADJECTIVE OR ADVERB not with other people or things: *He just wanted to be alone.*

along
PREPOSITION **1.** moving, happening, or existing continuously from one end to the other of something, or at various points beside it: *Put rivets along the top edge.*
ADVERB **2.** moving forward: *We marched along, singing as we went.* **3.** with someone: *Why could they not take her along?*
PHRASE **4.** All along means from the beginning of a period of time right up to now: *You've known that all along.*

alongside
PREPOSITION OR ADVERB **1.** next to something: *Steer the boat until it is alongside the dock.*
PREPOSITION **2.** If you work alongside other people, you are working in the same place and co-operating with them: *He was thrilled to work alongside the famous actor.*

aloof
ADJECTIVE When you are aloof you are withdrawn or distant from someone or something.

aloud
ADVERB When you speak aloud, you speak loudly enough for other people to hear you.

alphabet alphabets
NOUN a set of letters in a fixed order that is used in writing a language
alphabetical ADJECTIVE
alphabetically ADVERB

alpine
ADJECTIVE existing in or relating to high mountains: *alpine flowers*

already
ADVERB having happened before the present time or earlier than expected: *She has already gone to bed.*

Alsatian Alsatians
NOUN a large wolflike dog

also
ADVERB in addition to something that has just been mentioned

altar altars
NOUN a holy table in a place of worship

alter alters altering altered
VERB If something alters or if you alter it, it changes.
alteration NOUN

altercation altercations
NOUN *a formal word* a noisy disagreement

alternate alternates alternating alternated
VERB **1.** If one thing alternates with another, the two things regularly occur one after the other.
ADJECTIVE **2.** If something happens on alternate days, it happens on the first day but not the second, and happens again on the third day but not the fourth, and so on. **3.** Alternate angles are two angles on opposite sides of a line that crosses two other lines.
alternately ADVERB
alternation NOUN

alternating current alternating currents
NOUN a current that regularly changes its direction, so that the electrons flow first one way and then the other

alternative alternatives
NOUN **1.** something you can do or have instead of something else: *One alternative to prison is community service.*
ADJECTIVE **2.** Alternative plans or actions can happen or be done instead of what is already happening or being done.
alternatively ADVERB

although
CONJUNCTION in spite of the fact that: *He isn't well known in Canada, although he did make a movie here.*

ALLUSION

a brief reference to something from history, literature, or culture as a way of adding meaning to your writing

"To flee or not to flee, that is the question."

Here is the allusion. It's a reference to the famous "To be or not to be" line from William Shakespeare's play *Hamlet*.

KAGAN MCLEOD

Aa

altitude altitudes

NOUN The altitude of something is its height above sea level: *The mountain range reaches an altitude of 1330 metres.*

altogether

ADVERB **1.** entirely: *She wasn't altogether sorry to be leaving.* **2.** in total; used for amounts: *Altogether, I get paid 500 dollars a month from my two part-time jobs.*

aluminum

NOUN a silvery-white, lightweight metal

always

ADVERB all the time or forever: *She's always moaning about the weather.*

am the first person singular, present tense of BE

a.m. The abbreviation a.m. is used to specify times between 12 midnight and 12 noon. It is an abbreviation for the Latin phrase *ante meridiem*, which means *before noon*: *I get up at 6 a.m. and leave for school at 7 a.m.*

amalgamate amalgamates amalgamating amalgamated

VERB If two organizations amalgamate, they join together to form one new organization.
amalgamation NOUN

amass amasses amassing amassed

VERB If you amass something such as money or information, you collect large quantities of it: *He amassed a huge fortune.*

amateur amateurs

NOUN someone who does something as a hobby rather than as a job

amateurish

ADJECTIVE not skilfully made or done
amateurishly ADVERB

amaze amazes amazing amazed

VERB If something amazes you, it surprises you very much.

amazement

NOUN complete surprise

amazing

ADJECTIVE very surprising or remarkable
amazingly ADVERB

ambassador ambassadors

NOUN a person sent to a foreign country as the representative of his or her own government

amber

NOUN **1.** a hard, brownish yellow substance used for making jewellery
NOUN OR ADJECTIVE **2.** brownish yellow

ambi-

PREFIX The prefix *ambi-* means *both*. For example, something that is *ambiguous* can have either of two meanings.

ambidextrous

ADJECTIVE Someone who is ambidextrous is able to use both hands equally skilfully.

ambience

NOUN *a formal word* The ambience of a place is its atmosphere.

ambient

ADJECTIVE **1.** surrounding: *low ambient temperatures* **2.** creating a relaxing atmosphere: *ambient music*

ambiguous

ADJECTIVE A word or phrase that is ambiguous has more than one meaning.
ambiguously ADVERB
ambiguity NOUN

ambition ambitions

NOUN **1.** If you have an ambition to achieve something, you want very much to achieve it: *His ambition is to be an actor.* **2.** a great desire for success, power, or wealth: *She's talented and full of ambition.*

ambitious

ADJECTIVE **1.** Someone who is ambitious has a strong desire for success, power, or wealth. **2.** An ambitious plan is a large one and requires a lot of work: *an ambitious rebuilding schedule*

ambivalent

ADJECTIVE having or showing two conflicting attitudes or emotions
ambivalence NOUN

amble ambles ambling ambled

VERB If you amble, you walk slowly and in a relaxed manner.

ambulance ambulances

NOUN a vehicle for taking sick and injured people to the hospital

ambush ambushes ambushing ambushed

VERB **1.** To ambush someone is to attack that person after hiding and lying in wait for him or her.
NOUN **2.** an attack on someone after hiding and lying in wait for that person

amen

INTERJECTION Amen is said at the end of a Christian prayer. It means *so be it*.

amenable

ADJECTIVE willing to listen to suggestions, or to co-operate with someone: *Both brothers were amenable to the arrangement.*
amenably ADVERB
amenability NOUN

amend amends amending amended

VERB **1.** To amend something that has been written or said is to alter it slightly: *Our constitution had to be amended.*

⚠ **HEADS UP** | **Altogether** means *completely* and **all together** means *together in a group*.

Aa

PHRASE **2.** If you **make amends** for something bad you have done, you try to make up for it by doing something good.
amendment NOUN

amenity amenities
NOUN Amenities are things that are available for the public to use, such as sports facilities or shopping centres.

American Americans
ADJECTIVE **1.** belonging or relating to the United States
NOUN **2.** someone who comes from the United States

amethyst amethysts
NOUN a type of purple semiprecious stone

amiable
ADJECTIVE pleasant and friendly: *The hotel staff was very amiable.*
amiably ADVERB
amiability NOUN

amicable
ADJECTIVE fairly friendly: *an amicable divorce*
amicably ADVERB

amid
PREPOSITION *a formal word* surrounded by: *She found her gloves amid the pile of leaves.*

amiss
ADJECTIVE If something is amiss, there is something wrong.

ammonia
NOUN a colourless, strong-smelling gas or liquid

ammunition
NOUN anything that can be fired from a gun or other weapon, for example bullets and shells

amnesia
NOUN loss of memory

amnesty amnesties
NOUN an official pardon for political or other prisoners

amoeba amoebas
NOUN the smallest kind of living creature, consisting of one cell. Amoebas reproduce by dividing into two.

amok
PHRASE A person or animal that **runs amok** behaves in a violent and uncontrolled way.

among
PREPOSITION **1.** surrounded by: *The bike lay among piles of chains and pedals.* **2.** in the company of: *He was among friends.* **3.** between more than two: *The money will be divided among seven charities.*

amoral
ADJECTIVE Someone who is amoral has no moral standards by which to live.

amorous
ADJECTIVE passionately affectionate: *an amorous relationship*
amorously ADVERB
amorousness NOUN

amount amounts amounting amounted
NOUN **1.** An amount of something is how much there is of it.
VERB **2.** If something amounts to a particular total, all the parts of it add up to that total: *Her vocabulary amounted to only 50 words.*

amp amps
NOUN An amp is the same as an ampere.

ampere amperes
NOUN a unit that is used for measuring electric current

ampersand ampersands
NOUN the character &, meaning *and*

amphetamine amphetamines
NOUN a drug that increases people's energy and makes them excited. It can have dangerous and unpleasant side effects.

amphibian amphibians
NOUN a creature that lives partly on land and partly in water, for example a frog or a newt

amphibious
ADJECTIVE An amphibious animal, such as a frog, lives partly on land and partly in the water.

amphitheatre amphitheatres
NOUN a large, semicircular, open area with sloping sides covered with rows of seats

ample
ADJECTIVE If there is an ample amount of something, there is more than enough of it.
amply ADVERB

amplifier amplifiers
NOUN a piece of equipment in a radio or stereo system that causes sounds or signals to become louder

amplify amplifies amplifying amplified
VERB If you amplify a sound, you make it louder.
amplification NOUN

amplitude
NOUN In physics, the amplitude of a wave is how far its curve moves away from its normal position.

amputate amputates amputating amputated
VERB To amputate an arm or a leg is to cut it off in a surgical operation.
amputation NOUN

 **HEADS UP** Use **amount** for things that can be measured and **number** for things that can be counted.

Aa

amuse amuses amusing amused
VERB **1.** If something amuses you, you think it is funny. **2.** If you amuse yourself, you find things to do that stop you from being bored.
amused ADJECTIVE
amusing ADJECTIVE

amusement amusements
NOUN **1.** Amusement is the state of thinking something is funny. **2.** Amusement is also the pleasure you get from being entertained or from doing something interesting. **3.** Amusements are ways of passing the time pleasantly.

an
ADJECTIVE *An* is used instead of *a* in front of words that begin with a vowel sound.

-an
SUFFIX The suffix *-an* comes at the end of nouns and adjectives that show where or what someone or something comes from or belongs to: *Canadian, Victorian*

anachronism anachronisms
NOUN something that belongs or seems to belong to another time
anachronistic ADJECTIVE

anagram anagrams
NOUN a word or phrase formed by changing the order of the letters of another word or phrase. For example, *triangle* is an anagram of *integral*.

anal
ADJECTIVE relating to the anus

analgesic analgesics
NOUN a substance that relieves pain

analogy analogies
NOUN a comparison showing that two things are similar in some ways
analogous ADJECTIVE

analysis analyses
NOUN the process of investigating something in order to understand it or find out what it consists of: *a full analysis of the problem*

analyst analysts
NOUN a person whose job is to analyze things to find out about them

analytical
ADJECTIVE using logical reasoning: *Planning in detail requires an acute analytical mind.*
analytically ADVERB

analyze analyzes analyzing analyzed
VERB To analyze something is to break it down into parts, or investigate it carefully, so that you can describe its main aspects, or find out what it consists of.

anarchy
NOUN a situation where nobody obeys laws or rules

anatomy anatomies
NOUN **1.** the study of the structure of the human body or of the bodies of animals **2.** An animal's anatomy is the structure of its body.
anatomical ADJECTIVE
anatomically ADVERB

ancestor ancestors
NOUN Your ancestors are the members of your family who lived many years ago and from whom you are descended.
ancestral ADJECTIVE

ancestry ancestries
NOUN Your ancestry consists of the people from whom you are descended: *a Canadian citizen of Greek ancestry*

anchor anchors anchoring anchored
NOUN **1.** a heavy object at the end of a chain or rope, dropped from a boat into the water to keep the boat in one place
VERB **2.** To anchor a boat or another object is to stop it from moving by dropping an anchor or attaching it to something solid.

anchorage anchorages
NOUN a place where a boat can safely anchor

anchovy anchovies
NOUN a type of small edible fish with a very strong salty taste

ancient
ADJECTIVE **1.** existing or happening in the distant past: *ancient Rome* **2.** very old or having a very long history: *an ancient tomb, an ancient civilization*

ancillary
ADJECTIVE The ancillary workers in an institution are the people such as cooks and cleaners, whose work supports the main work of the institution.

and
CONJUNCTION You use *and* to link two or more words or phrases together.

androgynous
ADJECTIVE *a formal word* having both male and female characteristics

android androids
NOUN In science fiction, a robot that looks like a human being.

anecdote anecdotes
NOUN a short, entertaining story about a person or event
anecdotal ADJECTIVE

ANALOGY ▼×

a comparison showing that two things are similar in some ways

"Hip hop is like a tree."

Here is the analogy. Though hip hop and trees don't seem related, the character shows how they both have roots and branches.

KAGAN MCLEOD

Aa

anemia
NOUN a medical condition resulting from too few red cells in a person's blood. People with anemia look pale and feel very tired.
anemic ADJECTIVE

anemone anemones
NOUN a plant with red, purple, or white flowers

anesthetic anesthetics
NOUN a substance that stops you from feeling pain. A general anesthetic stops you from feeling pain in the whole of your body by putting you to sleep, and a local anesthetic makes just one part of your body go numb.

anesthetist anesthetists
NOUN a doctor who is specially trained to give anesthetics

anesthetize anesthetizes anesthetizing anesthetized
VERB To anesthetize someone is to give that person an anesthetic to make him or her unconscious.

anew
ADVERB If you do something anew, you do it again: *They left the city to start life anew in the country.*

angel angels
NOUN Angels are spiritual beings some people believe live in heaven and act as messengers for God.
angelic ADJECTIVE

anger angers angering angered
NOUN **1.** the strong feeling you get when you feel someone has behaved in an unfair or cruel way
VERB **2.** If something angers you, it makes you feel angry.

angina
NOUN a brief but very severe heart pain, caused by lack of blood supply to the heart. It is also known as *angina pectoris*.

angle angles
NOUN **1.** the distance between two lines at the point where they join together. Angles are measured in degrees. **2.** the direction from which you look at something: *He had painted the vase from all angles.* **3.** An angle on something is a particular way of considering it: *the same story from a child's angle*

angler anglers
NOUN someone who fishes with a fishing rod
angling NOUN

Anglophone
NOUN a person whose native language is English

Anglo-Saxon Anglo-Saxons
NOUN **1.** The Anglo-Saxons were Germanic people who settled in England from the fifth century CE. **2.** Anglo-Saxon is another name for OLD ENGLISH.

angora
ADJECTIVE yarn made from the long, silky hair of the **Angora goat** or **Angora rabbit**

angry angrier angriest
ADJECTIVE very irritated or annoyed
angrily ADVERB

angst
NOUN a feeling of anxiety and worry

anguish
NOUN extreme suffering
anguished ADJECTIVE

angular
ADJECTIVE Angular things have straight lines and sharp points: *He has an angular face and a pointed chin.*

animal animals
NOUN any living being except a plant, or any mammal except a human being

animate animates animating animated
VERB To animate something is to make it lively and interesting.

animated
ADJECTIVE lively and interesting: *an animated conversation*

animation
NOUN **1.** a method of filmmaking in which a series of drawings is photographed. When the film is projected, the characters in the drawings appear to move. **2.** Someone who has animation shows liveliness in speaking and acting: *The crowd showed no sign of animation.*
animator NOUN

animosity animosities
NOUN a feeling of strong dislike and anger toward someone

aniseed
NOUN the seed of a Mediterranean plant used as a flavouring in candy, cooking, drinks, and medicine

ankle ankles
NOUN the joint that connects your foot to your leg

annex annexes annexing annexed
NOUN **1.** an extra building that is joined to a larger main building
VERB **2.** If one country annexes another, it seizes the other country and takes control of it.
annexation NOUN

⚠ HEADS UP **Anesthetic** is pronounced an-us-THET-ick and **anesthetist** is pronounced uh-NESS-thuh-tist.

Aa

annihilate annihilates annihilating annihilated
VERB If something is annihilated, it is
completely destroyed.
annihilation NOUN

anniversary anniversaries
NOUN a date that is remembered because
something special happened on that date in a
previous year

announce announces announcing announced
VERB If you announce something, you tell
people about it publicly or officially: *The
team was announced on Friday morning.*

announcement announcements
NOUN a statement giving information about
something

announcer announcers
NOUN someone who introduces programs on
radio and television

annoy annoys annoying annoyed
VERB If someone or something annoys you,
that person or thing irritates you and makes
you angry.
annoyed ADJECTIVE

annoyance
NOUN **1.** a feeling of irritation **2.** something
that causes irritation

annual annuals
ADJECTIVE **1.** happening or done once a year:
their annual fundraiser **2.** happening or
calculated over a period of one year: *the
hockey team's annual budget for ice time*
NOUN **3.** a book or magazine published once a
year **4.** a plant that grows, flowers, and dies
within one year
annually ADVERB

annuity annuities
NOUN a fixed sum of money paid to someone
every year from an investment or insurance
policy

annul annuls annulling annulled
VERB If a marriage or contract is annulled,
it is declared invalid, so that legally it is
considered never to have existed.
annulment NOUN

anoint anoints anointing anointed
VERB To anoint someone is to put oil on that
person as part of a ceremony.
anointment NOUN

anomaly anomalies
NOUN Something is an anomaly if it is
unusual or different from normal.
anomalous ADJECTIVE

anon an abbreviation for ANONYMOUS

anonymous
ADJECTIVE If something is anonymous, nobody
knows who is responsible for it: *The police
received an anonymous phone call.*
anonymously ADVERB
anonymity NOUN

anorak anoraks
NOUN a warm, waterproof jacket, usually
with a hood

anorexia
NOUN Anorexia is a psychological illness in
which a person refuses to eat because he or
she is frightened of becoming fat.
anorexic ADJECTIVE

another
ADJECTIVE OR PRONOUN Another thing or person
is an additional thing or person.

answer answers answering answered
VERB **1.** If you answer someone, you reply
to that person using words or actions or in
writing.
NOUN **2.** the reply you give when you answer
someone **3.** a solution to a problem

answerable
ADJECTIVE If you are answerable to someone
for something, you are responsible for it: *He
must be made answerable for these terrible
crimes.*

answering machine answering machines
NOUN a machine that records telephone calls
while you are out

ant ants
NOUN Ants are small insects that live in large
groups.

-ant
SUFFIX The suffix *-ant* is used to form
adjectives: *important*

antagonism
NOUN hatred or hostility

antagonist antagonists
NOUN an enemy or opponent

antagonistic
ADJECTIVE Someone who is antagonistic
toward you shows hate or hostility.
antagonistically ADVERB

antagonize antagonizes antagonizing
antagonized
VERB If someone is antagonized, that person is
made to feel anger and hostility.

Antarctic
NOUN The Antarctic is the region south of the
Antarctic Circle.

Antarctica
NOUN The Antarctica is the continent covering
the South Pole.

Antarctic Circle
NOUN The Antarctic Circle is an imaginary
circle around the southern part of the world.

HEADS UP The word **annihilate** is pronounced uh-NEYE-uh-late.

Aa

Antarctic Ocean
NOUN the ocean covering the South Pole

ante-
PREFIX The prefix *ante-* means *before*. For example, *antedate* means *come before in time*.

antecedent antecedents
NOUN **1.** An antecedent of a thing or event is something that happened or existed before it and is related to it in some way: *the prehistoric antecedents of the horse* **2.** Your antecedents are your ancestors, the relatives from whom you are descended.

antelope antelopes
NOUN an animal that looks like a deer

antenna antennae *or* antennas
NOUN **1.** The antennae of insects and certain other animals are the two long, thin parts attached to their heads that they use to feel with. The plural is *antennae*. **2.** An antenna is a radio or television aerial. The plural is *antennas*.

anthem anthems
NOUN a hymn written for a special occasion

anther anthers
NOUN in a flower, the part of the stamen that makes pollen grains

anthology anthologies
NOUN a collection of writings by various authors published in one book

anthropo-
PREFIX The prefix *anthropo-* means *to do with human beings*: *anthropology*

anthropology
NOUN the study of human beings and their society and culture
anthropological ADJECTIVE
anthropologist NOUN

anti-
PREFIX The prefix *anti-* means *opposed to* or *opposite to* something: *antiwar marches, antihero*

antibiotic antibiotics
NOUN a drug or chemical used in medicine to kill bacteria and cure infections

antibody antibodies
NOUN a substance produced in the blood that can kill the harmful bacteria that cause disease

anticipate anticipates anticipating anticipated
VERB If you anticipate an event, you are expecting it and are prepared for it: *She had anticipated his visit.*
anticipation NOUN

anticlimax anticlimaxes
NOUN something that disappoints you because it is not as exciting as expected, or because it occurs after something that was very exciting

antics
PLURAL NOUN funny or silly ways of behaving

antidote antidotes
NOUN a chemical substance that acts against the effect of a poison

antihistamine antihistamines
NOUN a drug used to treat an allergy

antipathy
NOUN a strong feeling of dislike or hostility toward something or someone

antiperspirant antiperspirants
NOUN a substance that stops you from sweating when you put it on your skin

antipodes
PLURAL NOUN any two points on the earth's surface that are situated directly opposite each other. Australia and New Zealand are sometimes called the Antipodes by those living in the Northern Hemisphere.
antipodean ADJECTIVE

antiquarian
ADJECTIVE relating to or involving old and rare objects: *antiquarian books*

antiquated
ADJECTIVE very old-fashioned or out of date: *an antiquated method of storing information, antiquated ideas*

antique antiques
NOUN **1.** an object from the past that is collected because of its value or beauty
ADJECTIVE **2.** from or concerning the past: *antique furniture*

antiquity antiquities
NOUN **1.** Antiquity is the distant past.
2. Antiquities are interesting works of art and buildings from the distant past.

anti-Semitism
NOUN hatred of Jewish people
anti-Semitic ADJECTIVE
anti-Semite NOUN

antiseptic
ADJECTIVE Something that is antiseptic kills germs.

antisocial
ADJECTIVE **1.** An antisocial person is unwilling to meet and be friendly with other people.
2. Antisocial behaviour is annoying or upsetting to other people: *Spitting in public is antisocial.*

⚠ **HEADS UP** Don't confuse ante- and anti-. **Ante-** means *before* and **anti-** means *opposed to*.

NEL

antithesis antitheses
NOUN *a formal word* The antithesis of something is its exact opposite: *Work is the antithesis of leisure.*

antivenin antivenins
NOUN a substance that reduces the effect of a venom, especially a snake venom

antler antlers
NOUN A male deer's antlers are the branched horns on its head.

antonym antonyms
NOUN a word that means the opposite of another word. For example, *hot* is the antonym of *cold.*

! HEADS UP

Many antonyms are made by adding the prefixes **dis-**, **un-**, or **mis-**: *discomfort, unfriendly, misbehave.*

anus anuses
NOUN the opening between the buttocks

anvil anvils
NOUN a heavy iron block on which hot metal is beaten into shape

anxiety anxieties
NOUN nervousness or worry

anxious
ADJECTIVE **1.** If you are anxious, you are nervous or worried. **2.** If you are anxious to do something or anxious that something should happen, you very much want to do it or want it to happen: *She was anxious to start school.*
anxiously ADVERB

any
ADJECTIVE OR PRONOUN **1.** one, some, or several: *Do you have any paper clips I could borrow?* **2.** even the smallest amount or even one: *He was unable to tolerate any dairy products.* **3.** whatever or whichever, no matter what or which: *Any type of cooking oil will do.*

anybody
PRONOUN any person

anyhow
ADVERB **1.** in any case **2.** in a careless way: *They were all shoved in anyhow.*

anyone
PRONOUN any person

anything
PRONOUN any object, event, situation, or action

anyway
ADVERB in any case

anywhere
ADVERB in, at, or to any place

aorta
NOUN the main artery in the body, which carries blood away from the heart

apart
ADVERB OR ADJECTIVE **1.** When people or things are apart, there is a space or a distance between them: *Please keep the dog and cat apart. The gliders landed about 70 metres apart.*
ADVERB **2.** If you take something apart, you separate it into pieces.

apartheid
NOUN In South Africa, apartheid was the government policy and laws that kept people of different races apart. It was abolished in 1994.

apartment apartments
NOUN a set of rooms for living in, usually on one floor of a building

apathetic
ADJECTIVE not interested in anything

apathy
NOUN a state of mind in which you do not care about anything

ape apes aping aped
NOUN **1.** Apes are animals with a very short tail or no tail. They are closely related to humans. Apes include chimpanzees, gorillas, and gibbons.
VERB **2.** If you ape someone's speech or behaviour, you imitate it.

aphid aphids
NOUN a small insect that feeds by sucking the juices from plants

apiece
ADVERB If people have a particular number of things apiece, they have that number each.

aplomb
NOUN If you do something with aplomb, you do it with great confidence.

apocalypse
NOUN In the Christian religion, the Apocalypse is the end of the world.
apocalyptic ADJECTIVE

apocryphal
ADJECTIVE A story that is apocryphal is generally believed not to have really happened.

apolitical
ADJECTIVE not interested in politics

apologetic
ADJECTIVE showing or saying you are sorry
apologetically ADVERB

Aa

apologize apologizes apologizing apologized
VERB When you apologize to someone, you say you are sorry for something you have said or done.

apology apologies
NOUN something you say or write to tell someone you are sorry

apostrophe apostrophes
NOUN a punctuation mark used to show that one or more letters have been missed out of a word, for example *he's* for *he is*. Apostrophes are also used with -s at the end of a noun to show that what follows belongs to or relates to the noun, for example *my brother's books*. If the noun already has an -s at the end, for example because it is plural, you just add the apostrophe. For example, *my brothers' books* refers to more than one brother.

! HEADS UP

A common mistake is to use **it's** when you mean **its**. **It's** is short for *it is*. **Its** shows possession, like *his* or *her*.

appal appals appalling appalled
VERB If something appals you, it shocks you because it is very bad.

appalling
ADJECTIVE so bad as to be shocking: *She suffered appalling injuries in the car accident.*

apparatus
NOUN The apparatus for a particular task is the equipment used for it.

apparent
ADJECTIVE **1.** seeming real rather than actually being real: *an apparent hit-and-run accident* **2.** obvious: *It was apparent that he had lost interest.*
apparently ADVERB

apparition apparitions
NOUN something you think you see but that is not really there: *a ghostly apparition in the window*

appeal appeals appealing appealed
VERB **1.** If you appeal for something, you make an urgent request for it: *The police appealed for witnesses to come forward.* **2.** If you appeal to someone in authority against a decision, you formally ask that person to change it. **3.** If something appeals to you, you find it attractive or interesting.
NOUN **4.** a formal or serious request: *an appeal for peace* **5.** The appeal of something is the quality it has that people find

attractive or interesting: *the rugged appeal of the Rockies*
appealing ADJECTIVE

appear appears appearing appeared
VERB **1.** When something that you could not see appears, it moves (or you move) so that you can see it. **2.** When something new appears, it begins to exist. **3.** When actors or actresses appear in a movie or play, they take part in it. **4.** If something appears to be a certain way, it seems or looks that way: *He appeared to be searching for something.*

appearance appearances
NOUN **1.** The appearance of someone in a place is that person's arrival there, especially when it is unexpected. **2.** The appearance of something new is the time when it begins to exist: *the appearance of computer technology* **3.** Someone's or something's appearance is the way it looks to other people: *His gaunt appearance had sparked fears for his health.*

appease appeases appeasing appeased
VERB If you appease someone, you calm that person down when he or she is angry. You usually do this by giving the person what he or she wants.
appeasement NOUN

appendage appendages
NOUN a less important part attached to a main part

appendicitis
NOUN a painful illness in which a person's appendix becomes infected

appendix appendices *or* appendixes
NOUN **1.** An appendix to a book is extra information placed after the main text. The plural is *appendices*. **2.** a small closed tube forming part of your digestive system. The plural is *appendixes*.

appetite appetites
NOUN **1.** Your appetite is your desire to eat. **2.** If you have an appetite for something, you have a strong desire for it and enjoyment of it: *She had lost her appetite for air travel.*

appetizing
ADJECTIVE Food that is appetizing looks and smells good, and makes you want to eat it.

applaud applauds applauding applauded
VERB **1.** When a group of people applaud, they clap their hands in approval or praise. **2.** When an action or attitude is applauded, people praise it.

applause
NOUN Applause is clapping by people.

apple apples
NOUN a round fruit with smooth skin and firm flesh

Aa

appliance appliances
NOUN any machine you used to do a job like cleaning or cooking: *kitchen appliances*

applicable
ADJECTIVE Something that is applicable to a situation is relevant to it: *The rules are applicable to everyone.*

applicant applicants
NOUN someone who is applying for something: *My sister was one of many applicants for the job.*

application applications
NOUN **1.** a formal request for something, usually in writing **2.** The application of a rule, system, or skill is the use of it in a particular situation.

apply applies applying applied
VERB **1.** If you apply for something, you formally ask for it, usually by writing a letter. **2.** If you apply a rule or skill, you use it in a situation: *He applied his mind to the problem.* **3.** If something applies to a person or a situation, it is relevant to that person or situation: *Those rules apply only to those students who ride the bus to school.* **4.** If you apply something to a surface, you put it on: *Apply this lotion to your hands.*

appoint appoints appointing appointed
VERB **1.** If you appoint someone to a job or position, you formally choose that person for it. **2.** If you appoint a time or place for something to happen, you decide when or where it will happen.
appointed ADJECTIVE

appointment appointments
NOUN **1.** an arrangement you have with someone to meet at a certain time and place **2.** The appointment of a person to do a particular job is the choosing of that person to do it. **3.** a job or a position of responsibility: *He applied for an appointment in Ottawa.*

apposite
ADJECTIVE well-suited for a particular purpose: *She left before he could think of anything apposite to say.*

appraise appraises appraising appraised
VERB If you appraise something, you estimate the value or quality or it.
appraisal NOUN

appreciable
ADJECTIVE large enough to be noticed: *an appreciable difference*
appreciably ADVERB

appreciate appreciates appreciating appreciated
VERB **1.** If you appreciate something, you like it because you recognize its good qualities: *He appreciates good food.* **2.** If you appreciate a situation or problem, you understand it and know what it involves. **3.** If you appreciate something that someone has done for you, you are grateful to that person: *I really appreciate your coming to visit me.* **4.** If something appreciates over a period of time, its value increases: *The property appreciated by 50 percent in two years.*
appreciation NOUN

appreciative
ADJECTIVE **1.** understanding and enthusiastic: *They were a very appreciative audience.* **2.** thankful and grateful: *I am particularly appreciative of the help my family and friends have given me.*
appreciatively ADVERB

apprehend apprehends apprehending apprehended
VERB *a formal word* **1.** When the police apprehend someone, they arrest that person and take him or her into custody. **2.** If you apprehend something, you understand it fully: *They were unable to apprehend his hidden meaning.*

apprehensive
ADJECTIVE afraid something bad may happen: *I was very apprehensive about flying.*
apprehensively ADVERB
apprehension NOUN

apprentice apprentices
NOUN a person who works for a period of time with a skilled worker in order to learn a skill or trade
apprenticeship NOUN

approach approaches approaching approached
VERB **1.** To approach something is to come near or nearer to it. **2.** When a future event approaches, it gradually gets nearer: *As winter approached, the sale of snow shovels increased.* **3.** If you approach someone about something, you ask that person about it. **4.** If you approach a situation or problem in a particular way, you think about it or deal with it in that way.
NOUN **5.** The approach of something is the process of it coming closer: *the approach of spring* **6.** An approach to a situation or problem is a way of thinking about it or dealing with it. **7.** a road or path that leads to a place
approaching ADJECTIVE

Aa

appropriate appropriates appropriating appropriated
ADJECTIVE **1.** suitable or acceptable for a particular situation: *Shorts are not appropriate attire at a formal dinner.*
VERB **2.** *a formal use* If you appropriate something that does not belong to you, you take it without permission.
appropriately ADVERB
appropriation NOUN

approval
NOUN **1.** Approval is agreement given to a plan or request: *The plan will require approval from the local government.*
2. Approval is also admiration: *She looked at her friend with approval.*

approve approves approving approved
VERB **1.** If you approve of something or someone, you think that thing or person is acceptable or good. **2.** If someone in a position of authority approves a plan or idea, that person formally agrees to it.
approved ADJECTIVE
approving ADJECTIVE

approximate
ADJECTIVE almost exact: *What was the approximate distance between the cars?*
approximately ADVERB

apricot apricots
NOUN a small, soft, yellowish-orange fruit

April
NOUN the fourth month of the year. April has 30 days.

apron aprons
NOUN a piece of protective clothing worn over the front of regular clothing

apt
ADJECTIVE **1.** suitable or relevant: *a very apt description* **2.** having a particular tendency: *They are apt to jump to the wrong conclusions.*

aptitude
NOUN Someone's aptitude for something is that person's ability to learn it quickly and to do it well: *I have a natural aptitude for painting.*

aqua-
PREFIX The prefix *aqua-* means *water.*

aquarium aquariums
NOUN a glass tank filled with water in which fish are kept

aquatic
ADJECTIVE **1.** an animal or plant that lives or grows in water **2.** involving water: *aquatic sports*

aqueduct aqueducts
NOUN a long bridge with many arches carrying a water supply over a valley

arable
ADJECTIVE Arable land is used for growing crops.

arbiter arbiters
NOUN a person with the authority to decide something

arbitrary
ADJECTIVE An arbitrary decision or action is one that is not based on a plan or system.
arbitrarily ADVERB

arbitrate arbitrates arbitrating arbitrated
VERB When someone arbitrates between two people or groups who are in disagreement, that person considers the facts and decides who is right.
arbitration NOUN
arbitrator NOUN

arc arcs
NOUN **1.** a smoothly curving line **2.** in geometry, a section of the circumference of a circle

arcade arcades
NOUN a covered passage, often with an arched roof

arcane
ADJECTIVE mysterious and difficult to understand

arch arches arching arched
NOUN **1.** a structure that has a curved top supported on either side by a pillar or wall **2.** the curved part of bone at the top of the foot
VERB **3.** When something arches, it forms a curved line or shape.

arch-
PREFIX The prefix *arch-* means *most important* or *chief*: *archenemy, archrival*

archaeology
NOUN the study of the past by digging up and examining the remains of buildings, tools, and other things
archaeological ADJECTIVE
archaeologist NOUN

archaic
ADJECTIVE very old or old-fashioned

archbishop archbishops
NOUN a bishop of the highest rank in a Christian church

archeology another spelling of
ARCHAEOLOGY

archer archers
NOUN someone who shoots with a bow and arrow

Aa

archery
NOUN a sport in which people shoot at a target with a bow and arrow

archipelago archipelagos
NOUN a group of small islands

architect architects
NOUN a person who designs buildings

architecture
NOUN the art or practice of designing buildings
architectural ADJECTIVE

archive archives
NOUN Archives are collections of historical documents.

arctic
ADJECTIVE **1.** extremely cold: *arctic conditions*
NOUN **2. The Arctic** is the region north of the Arctic Circle.

Arctic Circle
NOUN The Arctic Circle is an imaginary circle around the northern part of the world.

Arctic Ocean
NOUN the ocean covering the North Pole

ardent
ADJECTIVE full of enthusiasm and passion
ardently ADVERB

ardour
NOUN a strong and passionate feeling of love or enthusiasm

arduous
ADJECTIVE tiring and needing a lot of effort: *the arduous task of rebuilding the country*

are the plural form of the present tense of BE

area areas
NOUN **1.** a particular part of a place, country, or the world: *a built-up area of the city*
2. The area of a piece of ground or a surface is the amount of space it covers.

arena arenas
NOUN **1.** a place where sports and other public events take place **2.** A particular arena is the centre of attention or activity in a particular situation: *the political arena*

arguable
ADJECTIVE An arguable idea or point is not necessarily true or correct and should be questioned.
arguably ADVERB

argue argues arguing argued
VERB **1.** If you argue with someone about something, you disagree with that person about it, sometimes in an angry way. **2.** If you argue that something is so, you give reasons why you think it is so: *She argued that her client had been wrongly accused.*

argument arguments
NOUN **1.** a disagreement between people
2. a point or a set of reasons you use to try to convince people about something

Instead of **ARGUMENT** try...
- a serious **disagreement**
- a **labour** dispute
- a petty **squabble**
- a lovers' **quarrel**
- a **clash** with protesters

argumentative
ADJECTIVE An argumentative person is always disagreeing with other people.

aria arias
NOUN a song sung by one of the leading singers in an opera

arid
ADJECTIVE Arid land is very dry because it gets very little rain.

arise arises arising arose arisen
VERB **1.** When something such as an opportunity or problem arises, it begins to exist. **2.** *a formal use* To arise also means to stand up from a sitting, kneeling, or lying position.

aristocracy aristocracies
NOUN a class of people who have a high social rank and special titles

aristocrat aristocrats
NOUN someone whose family has a high social rank, and who has a title
aristocratic ADJECTIVE

arithmetic
NOUN the part of mathematics to do with the addition, subtraction, multiplication, and division of numbers
arithmetical ADJECTIVE
arithmetically ADVERB

arm arms arming armed
NOUN **1.** Your arm is the part of your body between your shoulder and your wrist.
2. The arms of a chair are the parts on which you rest your arms. **3.** An arm of an organization is a section of it: *the political arm of the armed forces*
PLURAL NOUN **4.** Arms are weapons used in a war.
VERB **5.** To arm someone is to provide that person with weapons.

armada armadas
NOUN a large fleet of warships

armadillo armadillos
NOUN a mammal from South America covered with strong bony plates like armour

Aa

Armageddon

NOUN A huge battle that is seen as likely to destroy the world.

armament armaments

NOUN Armaments are weapons and military equipment.

armchair armchairs

NOUN a comfortable chair with a support on each side for your arms

armed

ADJECTIVE A person who is armed is carrying a weapon or weapons.

armed forces

PLURAL NOUN the army, navy, and air force of a country

armistice armistices

NOUN an agreement in a war to stop fighting in order to discuss peace

armour

NOUN In the past, armour was metal clothing worn for protection in battle.

armoured

ADJECTIVE covered with thick steel for protection from gunfire and other missiles: *an armoured car*

armoury armouries

NOUN a place where weapons are stored

armpit armpits

NOUN the area under your arm where your arm joins your shoulder

army armies

NOUN a large group of soldiers organized for fighting on land

aroma aromas

NOUN a strong, pleasant smell

aromatic ADJECTIVE

aromatherapy

NOUN a type of therapy that involves massaging the body with special fragrant oils

around

PREPOSITION **1.** placed at various points in a place or area: *There are many seats around the building.* **2.** from place to place inside an area: *We walked around the showroom.* **3.** at approximately the time or place mentioned: *The rain began around noon.*

ADVERB **4.** here and there: *His papers were scattered around.*

arouse arouses arousing aroused

VERB If something arouses a feeling in you, it causes you to begin to have this feeling: *Her death still arouses very painful feelings.*

arousal NOUN

arrange arranges arranging arranged

VERB **1.** If you arrange to do something, you make plans for it. **2.** If you arrange

something for someone, you make it possible for that person to have it or do it: *The bank has arranged a loan for her.* **3.** If you arrange objects, you set them out in a particular position: *He started to arrange the books in piles.*

arrangement NOUN

array arrays

NOUN An array of different things is a large number of them displayed together.

arrears

PLURAL NOUN **1.** Arrears are amounts of money you owe: *mortgage arrears*

PHRASE **2.** If you are paid **in arrears**, you are paid at the end of the period for which the payment is due.

arrest arrests arresting arrested

VERB **1.** If the police arrest someone, they take that person into custody to decide whether to charge him or her with an offence.

NOUN **2.** An arrest is the act of taking a person into custody.

arrival arrivals

NOUN **1.** the act or time of arriving: *The arrival of the train was delayed.* **2.** someone or something that has arrived: *I awaited the arrival of my birthday with great anticipation.*

arrive arrives arriving arrived

VERB **1.** When you arrive at a place, you reach it at the end of your journey. **2.** When a letter or a piece of news arrives, it is brought to you: *The card I sent arrived late.* **3.** When a moment, event, or new thing arrives, it begins to happen: *We can hardly wait for summer to arrive.*

PHRASE **4.** When you **arrive at** an idea or decision you reach it.

arrogant

ADJECTIVE Someone who is arrogant behaves as if he or she is better than other people.

arrogantly ADVERB

arrogance NOUN

arrow arrows

NOUN a long, thin stick with a sharp point at one end, shot from a bow

arsenal arsenals

NOUN a place where weapons and ammunition are stored or produced

arsenic

NOUN a very strong poison that can kill people

arson

NOUN the crime of deliberately setting fire to something, especially a building

art arts

NOUN **1.** Art is the creation of objects such as

paintings and sculptures, which are thought to be beautiful or which express a particular idea; also used to refer to the objects themselves. **2.** An activity is called an art when it requires special skill or ability: *the art of cooking*
PLURAL NOUN **3.** The arts are literature, music, painting, and sculpture, considered together.

artery arteries
NOUN **1.** Your arteries are the tubes that carry blood from your heart to the rest of your body. **2.** a main road or major section of any system of communication or transportation

artful
ADJECTIVE clever and skilful, often in a cunning way
artfully ADVERB

arthritis
NOUN a condition in which the joints in someone's body become swollen and painful
arthritic ADJECTIVE

artichoke artichokes
NOUN the flower head of a thistlelike plant. It is made up of clusters of leaves with a soft fleshy part that is eaten as a vegetable.

article articles
NOUN **1.** a piece of writing in a newspaper, magazine, or website **2.** a particular item: *an article of clothing* **3.** In English grammar, *a* and *the* are sometimes called articles: *a* (or *an*) is the indefinite article; *the* is the definite article.

articulate articulates articulating articulated
ADJECTIVE **1.** If you are articulate, you are able to express yourself well in words.
VERB **2.** When you articulate your ideas or feelings, you express in words what you think or feel: *She could not articulate her grief.* **3.** When you articulate a sound or word, you speak it clearly.
articulation NOUN

artifact artifacts
NOUN any object made by a person

artificial
ADJECTIVE **1.** created by people rather than occurring naturally: *artificial colouring* **2.** pretending to have attitudes and feelings that other people realize are not real: *an artificial smile*
artificially ADVERB

artillery
NOUN **1.** Artillery consists of large, powerful guns such as cannons. **2.** The artillery is the branch of an army that uses large, powerful guns.

artist artists
NOUN **1.** a person who draws or paints or produces other works of art **2.** a person who is very skilled at a particular activity

artiste artistes
NOUN a professional entertainer, for example a singer or a dancer

artistic
ADJECTIVE **1.** able to create good paintings, sculpture, or other works of art **2.** concerning or involving art or artists
artistically ADVERB

artistry
NOUN Artistry is the creative skill of an artist, writer, actor, or musician: *a supreme demonstration of his artistry as a cellist*

artsy artsier artsiest
ADJECTIVE *an informal word* interested in painting, sculpture, and other works of art, often in a trendy, snobbish, or superficial way

as
CONJUNCTION **1.** at the same time that: *She waved at fans as she arrived for the concert.* **2.** in the way that: *They had talked as only the best of friends can.* **3.** because: *As band practice runs late tonight, don't bother to cook dinner.* **4.** You use the structure **as ... as** when you are comparing things that are similar: *It was as big as four football fields.*
PREPOSITION **5.** You use **as** when you are saying what role someone or something has: *He worked as a waiter.* **6.** You use **as if** or **as though** when you are giving a possible explanation for something: *She behaves as if she were the person in charge.*

asbestos
NOUN a grey material that does not burn or conduct heat. It was used in the past to make things fireproof.

ascend ascends ascending ascended
VERB *a formal word* To ascend is to move or lead upward: *We finally ascended to the top of a steep hill.*

ascendant
ADJECTIVE **1.** rising or moving upward
PHRASE **2.** Someone or something **in the ascendant** is increasing in power or popularity.

ascent ascents
NOUN an upward journey, for example up a mountain

ascertain ascertains ascertaining ascertained
VERB *a formal word* If you ascertain that something is the case, you find out it is the case: *He ascertained that the flight was on time.*

Aa

⚠ **HEADS UP** The word **artiste** is pronounced are-TEEST.

Aa

ascribe ascribes ascribing ascribed
VERB **1.** If you ascribe an event or state of affairs to a particular cause, you think that it is the cause of it: *His stomach pains were ascribed to his overeating.* **2.** If you ascribe a quality to someone or something, you think that person or thing has it: *Don't ascribe human qualities to animals.*

ash ashes
NOUN **1.** the grey or black powdery remains of anything that has been burnt **2.** a tree with grey bark and hard, tough wood used for timber

ashamed
ADJECTIVE **1.** feeling embarrassed or guilty **2.** If you are ashamed of someone, you feel embarrassed to be connected with that person.

ashen
ADJECTIVE grey or pale: *Her face was ashen with fatigue.*

ashore
ADVERB on land or onto the land

Asia
NOUN Asia is the largest continent. It has Europe on its western side, with the Arctic to the north, the Pacific to the east, and the Indian Ocean to the south. Asia includes several island groups, including Japan, Indonesia, and the Philippines.

Asian Asians
ADJECTIVE **1.** belonging or relating to Asia
NOUN **2.** someone who comes from Asia

aside asides
ADVERB **1.** If you move something aside, you move it to one side.
NOUN **2.** a comment made away from the main conversation or dialogue that all those talking are not meant to hear

ask asks asking asked
VERB **1.** If you ask someone a question, you put a question to that person for him or her to answer. **2.** If you ask someone to do something or give you

Instead of **ASK** try...

something, you tell that person you want him or her to do it or to give it to you. **3.** If you ask someone's permission or forgiveness, you try

plead for mercy
appeal for silence
question a suspect
inquire about a job
beg for more time

to obtain it. **4.** If you ask someone to go somewhere with you, you invite that person there: *Not everybody had been asked to the dance.*

askew
ADJECTIVE not straight

asleep
ADJECTIVE sleeping

asparagus
NOUN a vegetable with long shoots that are cooked and eaten

aspect aspects
NOUN **1.** An aspect of something is one of its features: *Exam results illustrate only one aspect of a school's success.* **2.** The aspect of a building is the direction it faces: *The southern aspect of the cottage faces over fields.*

asphalt
NOUN A black substance used to make road surfaces and playgrounds. It is also called bitumen.

aspiration aspirations
NOUN Someone's aspirations are that person's desires and ambitions.

aspire aspires aspiring aspired
VERB If you aspire to something, you have an ambition to achieve it: *He aspired to work in journalism.*
aspiring ADJECTIVE

Aspirin Aspirins
NOUN *a trademark* a drug used to relieve pain, fever, and colds. Aspirin is the trademark name.

ass asses
NOUN a donkey

assailant assailants
NOUN someone who attacks another person

assassin assassins
NOUN someone who has murdered a political or religious leader

assassinate assassinates assassinating assassinated
VERB To assassinate a political or religious leader is to murder him or her.
assassination NOUN

assault assaults assaulting assaulted
NOUN **1.** a violent attack on someone
VERB **2.** To assault someone is to attack that person violently.

assemble assembles assembling assembled
VERB **1.** To assemble is to gather together. **2.** If you assemble something, you fit the parts of it together.

assembly assemblies
NOUN **1.** a group of people who have gathered

Aa

together for a meeting **2.** The assembly of an object is the fitting together of its parts: *The assembly of this bookcase should be simple.*

Assembly of First Nations
NOUN the political organization that officially represents the First Nations in Canada

assent assents assenting assented
NOUN **1.** If you give your assent to something, you agree to it.
VERB **2.** If you assent to something, you agree to it.

assert asserts asserting asserted
VERB **1.** If you assert a fact or belief, you state it firmly and forcefully.
PHRASE **2.** If you **assert yourself**, you speak and behave in a confident and direct way, so that people pay attention to you.

assertion assertions
NOUN a statement or claim

assertive
ADJECTIVE If you are assertive, you speak and behave in a confident and direct way, so that people pay attention to you.
assertively ADVERB
assertiveness NOUN

assess assesses assessing assessed
VERB If you assess something, you consider it carefully and make a judgment about it.
assessment NOUN

assessor assessors
NOUN someone whose job is to assess the value of something

asset assets
NOUN **1.** a person or thing considered useful: *He will be a great asset to the team.*
PLURAL NOUN **2.** The assets of a person or company are all the things that that person or company owns that could be sold to raise money.

assign assigns assigning assigned
VERB **1.** To assign something to someone is to give it to that person officially or to make that person responsible for it. **2.** If someone is assigned to do something, that person is officially told to do it.

assignment assignments
NOUN a job someone is given to do

assimilate assimilates assimilating assimilated
VERB **1.** If you assimilate ideas or experiences, you learn and understand them. **2.** When people are assimilated into a group, they become part of it.
assimilation NOUN

assist assists assisting assisted
VERB To assist someone is to help that person do something.
assistance NOUN

assistant assistants
NOUN someone whose job is to help another person in his or her work

associate associates associating associated
VERB **1.** If you associate one thing with another, you connect the two things in your mind. **2.** If you associate with a group of people, you spend a lot of time with them.
NOUN **3.** Your associates are the people you work with or spend a lot of time with.

association associations
NOUN **1.** an organization for people who have similar interests, jobs, or aims **2.** Your association with a person or group is the connection or involvement you have with that person or group. **3.** An association between two things is a link that you make in your mind between them: *The place contained associations for her.*

assonance
NOUN the use of similar vowel or consonant sounds in words near to each other or in the same word, for example *a blue mood*

assorted
ADJECTIVE Assorted things are different in size and colour: *assorted swimsuits*

assortment assortments
NOUN a group of similar things that are different sizes and colours: *an amazing assortment of old toys*

assume assumes assuming assumed
VERB **1.** If you assume that something is true, you accept that it is true even though you have not thought about it: *I assumed that he would turn up.* **2.** To assume responsibility for something is to put yourself in charge of it.

assumption assumptions
NOUN a belief that something is true, without thinking about it

assurance assurances
NOUN **1.** something said that is intended to make people less worried: *She was emphatic in her assurances that she wanted to stay.* **2.** Assurance is a feeling of confidence: *He handled the car with ease and assurance.*

assure assures assuring assured
VERB If you assure someone that something is true, you tell that person it is true.

asterisk asterisks
NOUN the symbol (*) used in printing and writing

Aa

astern
ADVERB toward or at the back of a ship or aircraft

asteroid asteroids
NOUN one of the large number of very small planets that moves around the sun between the orbits of Jupiter and Mars

asthma
NOUN a disease of the chest that causes wheezing and difficulty in breathing
asthmatic ADJECTIVE

astonish astonishes astonishing astonished
VERB If something astonishes you, it surprises you very much.
astonished ADJECTIVE
astonishing ADJECTIVE
astonishingly ADVERB
astonishment NOUN

astound astounds astounding astounded
VERB If something astounds you, it shocks and amazes you.
astounded ADJECTIVE
astounding ADJECTIVE

astray
PHRASE **1.** To **lead someone astray** is to influence that person to do something wrong. **2.** If something **goes astray**, it gets lost: *The money had gone astray.*

astride
PREPOSITION with one leg on either side of something: *He is pictured astride his new bicycle.*

astringent astringents
NOUN a liquid that makes skin less greasy or stops bleeding

astro-
PREFIX The prefix *astro-* means *involving the stars and planets.*

astronomical
ADJECTIVE **1.** involved with or relating to astronomy **2.** extremely large in amount: *an astronomical sum of money*
astronomically ADVERB

astute
ADJECTIVE clever and quick at understanding situations and behaviour: *an astute student*

asunder
ADVERB *a literary or poetic word* If something is torn asunder, it is violently torn apart.

asylum asylums
NOUN **1.** *an old-fashioned use* in former times, a hospital for the support and care of the mentally ill **2.** Political asylum is protection given by a government to someone who has fled from his or her own country for political reasons.

asymmetrical
ADJECTIVE unbalanced or with one half not exactly the same as the other half
asymmetry NOUN

at
PREPOSITION **1.** used to say where someone or something is: *My aunt met us at the airport.* **2.** used to mention the direction something is going in: *He threw the ball at the wall.* **3.** used to say when something happens: *The game starts at three o'clock.* **4.** used to mention the rate or price of something: *The car was travelling at 100 kilometres per hour.*

atheist atheists
NOUN someone who believes there is no God
atheistic ADJECTIVE
atheism NOUN

athlete athletes
NOUN someone who is good at sports and takes part in sporting events

athletic
ADJECTIVE **1.** strong, healthy, and good at sports **2.** involving athletes or athletics: *I lost two years of my athletic career because of injury.*

athletics
NOUN Sporting events such as running, jumping, and throwing are called athletics.

KNOWING WORDS: WORD BUILDING

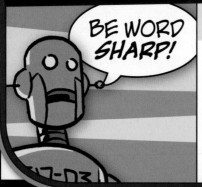

BE WORD SHARP!

You can create new words by adding prefixes and suffixes to a base word.

astro- a prefix that means *involving the stars and planets*
astrology the study of stars and planets to predict the future
astrologer a person who studies astrology
astronaut a person who operates a spacecraft
astronomy the scientific study of stars and planets
astronomer a person who studies astronomy

Aa

Atlantic Ocean
NOUN the ocean separating North and South America from Europe and Africa

atlas atlases
NOUN a book of maps

atmosphere atmospheres
NOUN **1.** the air and other gases that surround a planet; also the air in a particular place: *a musty atmosphere* **2.** the general mood of a place: *a relaxed atmosphere* **3.** the mood created by the writer of a novel or play
atmospheric ADJECTIVE

atom atoms
NOUN the smallest part of an element that can take part in a chemical reaction

atomic
ADJECTIVE relating to atoms or to the power released by splitting atoms: *atomic energy*

atomic bomb atomic bombs
NOUN an extremely powerful bomb that explodes because of the energy that comes from splitting atoms

atone atones atoning atoned
VERB *a formal word* If you atone for something wrong you have done, you do something good to try to make up for it.

atrocious
ADJECTIVE extremely bad

atrocity atrocities
NOUN an extremely cruel and shocking act

attach attaches attaching attached
VERB If you attach something to something else, you join or fasten the two things together.

attaché attachés
NOUN a specialist on the official staff in an embassy: *a cultural attaché*

attached
ADJECTIVE If you are attached to someone, you are very fond of that person.

attachment attachments
NOUN **1.** Attachment to someone is a feeling of love and affection for that person. **2.** Attachment to a cause or ideal is a strong belief in it and support for it. **3.** a piece of equipment attached to a tool or machine to do a particular job **4.** an extra document attached to or included with another document **5.** a file that is attached to an e-mail

attack attacks attacking attacked
VERB **1.** To attack someone is to use violence against that person so as to hurt or kill. **2.** If you attack people or their ideas, you criticize them strongly: *He attacked the government's economic policies.* **3.** If a disease or chemical attacks something, it damages or destroys it: *diseases that attack crops* **4.** In a game such as soccer, to attack is to get the ball into a position from which a goal can be scored. NOUN **5.** An attack is violent physical action against someone. **6.** An attack on people or their ideas is strong criticism of them. **7.** An attack of an illness is a short time in which you suffer badly with it: *an attack of the flu*
attacker NOUN

attain attains attaining attained
VERB *a formal word* If you attain something, you manage to achieve it: *He eventually attained the rank of major.*
attainable ADJECTIVE
attainment NOUN

attempt attempts attempting attempted
VERB **1.** If you attempt to do something, you try to do it or achieve it, but may not succeed: *They attempted to escape.* NOUN **2.** an act of trying to do something: *The player made no attempt to go for the ball.*

attend attends attending attended
VERB **1.** If you attend an event, you are present at it. **2.** To attend school, church, or meetings is to go there regularly. **3.** If you attend to something, you deal with it: *We have business to attend to first.*
attendance NOUN

attendant attendants
NOUN someone whose job is to serve people in a place such as a parking lot or coat check

attention
NOUN Attention is the thought or care you give to something: *The woman needed medical attention.*

attentive
ADJECTIVE paying close attention to something: *an attentive audience*
attentively ADVERB
attentiveness NOUN

attest attests attesting attested
VERB *a formal word* To attest something is to show or declare it is true.
attestation NOUN

attic attics
NOUN a room at the top of a house, immediately below the roof

attire
NOUN Attire is clothing: *You must wear appropriate attire at school.*

attitude attitudes
NOUN Your attitude to someone or something is the way you think about and behave toward that person or thing.

Aa

attorney attorneys
NOUN An attorney is a lawyer.

attract attracts attracting attracted
VERB **1.** If something attracts people, it interests them and makes them want to go to it: *The lake attracts many swimmers on a hot day.* **2.** If someone attracts you, you like and admire that person: *He was attracted to her outgoing personality.* **3.** If something attracts support or publicity, it gets it.

attraction attractions
NOUN **1.** Attraction is a feeling of liking someone or something very much.
2. something people visit for interest or pleasure: *Niagara Falls is a major tourist attraction.* **3.** a quality that attracts someone or something: *the attraction of living in the country*

attractive
ADJECTIVE **1.** interesting and possibly advantageous: *an attractive proposition* **2.** pleasant to look at or be with: *an attractive individual, an attractive personality*
attractively ADVERB
attractiveness NOUN

attribute attributes attributing attributed
VERB **1.** If you attribute something to a person or thing, you believe it was caused or created by that person or thing: *That painting is attributed to Tom Thomson. Water pollution was partly attributed to the use of fertilizers.* NOUN **2.** a quality or feature someone or something has
attribution NOUN
attributable ADJECTIVE

attrition
NOUN Attrition is the constant wearing down of an enemy.

attuned
ADJECTIVE accustomed or well adjusted to something: *His eyes quickly became attuned to the dark.*

aubergine another name for EGGPLANT

auburn
ADJECTIVE reddish brown

auction auctions auctioning auctioned
NOUN **1.** a public sale in which goods are sold to the person who offers the highest price VERB **2.** To auction something is to sell it in an auction.

auctioneer auctioneers
NOUN the person in charge of an auction

audacious
ADJECTIVE very daring: *an audacious escape from jail*
audaciously ADVERB
audacity NOUN

audi-
PREFIX The prefix *audi-* means *involving hearing or sound*: *audible, auditorium*

audible
ADJECTIVE loud enough to be heard: *She spoke in a barely audible whisper.*
audibly ADVERB
audibility NOUN

audience audiences
NOUN **1.** the group of people who are viewing or listening to a performance **2.** the group of people who will be reading or viewing a piece of writing, a movie, an advertisement, and so on **3.** a private or formal meeting with an important person: *an audience with the Governor General*

audio
ADJECTIVE used in recording and reproducing sound: *audio equipment*

audit audits auditing audited
VERB **1.** To audit financial accounts is to examine them officially to check that they are correct.
NOUN **2.** an official examination of an organization's accounts
auditor NOUN

audition auditions
NOUN a short performance given by an actor or musician, so that a director can decide whether that person is suitable for a part in a play or movie or for a place in an orchestra

auditorium auditoriums
NOUN the part of a theatre where the audience sits

augment augments augmenting augmented
VERB *a formal word* To augment something is to add something to it.

August
NOUN the eighth month of the year. August has 31 days.

aunt aunts
NOUN Your aunt is the sister of your mother or father, or the wife of your uncle.

aura auras
NOUN an atmosphere that surrounds a person or thing: *She has a great aura of calmness.*

aural
ADJECTIVE relating to or done through the sense of hearing: *The music exam had two parts: a theory test and an aural test.*

auspices
PLURAL NOUN *a formal word* If you do something under the auspices of a person or organization, you do it with the support of

Aa

that person or organization: *The Sports Day was held under the auspices of the Board of Education.*

auspicious

ADJECTIVE *a formal word* favourable and seeming to promise success: *It was an auspicious start to the month.*

austere

ADJECTIVE plain and simple, and without luxury: *an austere grey office block*

austerity NOUN

Australasia

NOUN Australasia consists of Australia, New Zealand, and neighbouring islands in the Pacific.

Australasian ADJECTIVE

Australia

NOUN Australia is the smallest continent and the largest island in the world. It is situated between the Indian Ocean and the Pacific.

Australian Australians

ADJECTIVE **1.** belonging or relating to Australia
NOUN **2.** someone who comes from Australia

authentic

ADJECTIVE real and genuine

authenticity NOUN

author authors

NOUN The author of a book is the person who wrote it.

authoritarian

ADJECTIVE believing in strict obedience: *an authoritarian government*

authoritarianism NOUN

authoritative

ADJECTIVE **1.** having authority: *his deep, authoritative voice* **2.** accepted as being reliable and accurate: *an authoritative biography of the prime minister*

authoritatively ADVERB

authority authorities

NOUN **1.** Authority is the right to control people: *The police force has the authority to question suspects.* **2.** Someone who is an authority on something knows a lot about it: *She is the world's leading authority on global warming.*
PLURAL NOUN **3.** The authorities are the people who have the right to make decisions: *local health authorities*

authorize authorizes authorizing authorized

VERB To authorize something is to give official permission for it to happen.

authorization NOUN

auto-

PREFIX The prefix *auto-* means *self.* For example, an automatic machine works by itself without needing to be operated by hand.

autobiography autobiographies

NOUN An autobiography is an account of a person's life written by that person.

autobiographical ADJECTIVE

autograph autographs

NOUN the signature of a famous person

automated

ADJECTIVE If a factory or way of making things is automated, it works using machinery rather than people.

automation NOUN

automatic

ADJECTIVE **1.** An automatic machine is programmed to perform tasks without needing a person to operate it: *The plane was flying on automatic pilot.* **2.** Automatic actions or reactions take place without involving conscious thought. **3.** A process or punishment that is automatic always happens as a direct result of something: *The penalty for murder is an automatic life sentence.*

automatically ADVERB

automobile automobiles

NOUN a car

autonomous

ADJECTIVE An autonomous country governs itself rather than being controlled by anyone else.

autonomy NOUN

autopsy autopsies

NOUN a medical examination of a dead body to discover the cause of death

autumn autumns

NOUN the season between summer and winter

autumnal ADJECTIVE

⚠ **HEADS UP**

Autumn is also known as **fall**. Fall is a North American word, named for leaves falling from trees.

---

auxiliary auxiliaries

NOUN **1.** a group of people, usually volunteers, employed to help other members of a staff: *The hospital auxiliary runs the gift shop.*
ADJECTIVE **2.** Auxiliary equipment is used when necessary in addition to the main equipment: *Auxiliary oxygen tanks are necessary when scuba diving for long periods of time.*

Aa

auxiliary verb auxiliary verbs

NOUN In grammar, an auxiliary verb is a verb that forms tenses of other verbs or questions. For example in *He has gone*, *has* is the auxiliary verb and in *Do you understand?*, *do* is the auxiliary verb.

avail

PHRASE If something you do is **of no avail** or **to no avail**, it is not successful or helpful.

available

ADJECTIVE **1.** Something that is available can be obtained: *Artichokes are available in supermarkets.* **2.** Someone who is available is ready for work or free for people to talk to: *I'm only available to work on weekends.*
availability NOUN

avalanche avalanches

NOUN a huge mass of snow and ice that falls down a mountainside

avant-garde

ADJECTIVE extremely modern or experimental, especially in art, literature, or music

avarice

NOUN *a formal word* greed for money and possessions
avaricious ADJECTIVE

avenge avenges avenging avenged

VERB If you avenge something harmful someone has done to you or your family, you punish or harm the other person in return: *He was prepared to avenge the death of his friend.*
avenger NOUN

avenue avenues

NOUN a street, especially one with trees along it

average averages averaging averaged

NOUN **1.** a result obtained by adding several amounts together and then dividing the total by the number of different amounts: *Six students were examined in a total of 39 subjects, an average of 6.5 subjects per student.*
ADJECTIVE **2.** Average means standard or normal: *the average Canadian teenager*
VERB **3.** To average a number is to produce that number as an average over a period of time: *Monthly sales averaged more than 110 000 units.*
PHRASE **4.** You say **on average** when mentioning what usually happens in a situation: *Dogs are, on average, larger than cats.*

averse

ADJECTIVE unwilling to do something: *He was averse to taking painkillers.*

aversion aversions

NOUN If you have an aversion to someone or something, you dislike that person or thing very much.

avert averts averting averted

VERB **1.** If you avert an unpleasant event, you prevent it from happening. **2.** If you avert your eyes from something, you turn your eyes away from it.

aviary aviaries

NOUN a large cage or group of cages in which birds are kept

aviation

NOUN the science of flying aircraft

avid

ADJECTIVE eager and enthusiastic for something
avidly ADVERB

avocado avocados

NOUN a pear-shaped fruit, with dark green skin, soft, greenish yellow flesh, and a large stone

avoid avoids avoiding avoided

VERB **1.** If you avoid doing something, you make a deliberate effort not to do it. **2.** If you avoid someone, you keep away from that person.
avoidable ADJECTIVE
avoidance NOUN

avowed

ADJECTIVE **1.** *a formal word* If you are an avowed supporter or opponent of something, you have declared that you support it or oppose it. **2.** An avowed belief or aim is one you hold very strongly.

avuncular

ADJECTIVE friendly and helpful in manner toward younger people, rather like an uncle

await awaits awaiting awaited

VERB **1.** If you await something, you expect it. **2.** If something awaits you, it will happen to you in the future.

awake awakes awaking awoke awoken

ADJECTIVE **1.** Someone who is awake is not sleeping.
VERB When you awake, you wake up. **2.** If you are awoken by something, it wakes you up.

awaken awakens awakening awakened

VERB If something awakens an emotion or interest in you, you start to feel this emotion or interest.

award awards awarding awarded

NOUN **1.** a prize or certificate for doing

Aa

something well

VERB **2.** If you award someone something, you give it to that person formally or officially.

aware

ADJECTIVE **1.** If you are aware of something, you realize it is there. **2.** If you are aware of something, you know about it.

awareness NOUN

awash

ADJECTIVE OR ADVERB covered with water: *After the downpour the road was awash.*

away

ADVERB **1.** moving from a place: *I saw them walk away.* **2.** at a distance from a place: *The nearest hospital is 12 kilometres away.* **3.** in its proper place: *He put his hockey equipment away.* **4.** not at home, school, or work: *She had been away from home for years.*

awe

NOUN *a formal word* a feeling of great respect mixed with amazement and sometimes slight fear

awesome

ADJECTIVE **1.** Something that is awesome is very impressive and frightening. **2.** *an informal use* Awesome also means excellent or outstanding.

awful

ADJECTIVE **1.** very unpleasant or very bad **2.** *an informal use* very great: *It took an awful lot of courage.*

awfully ADVERB

awkward

ADJECTIVE **1.** clumsy and uncomfortable: *an awkward gesture* **2.** embarrassed or nervous: *He was a shy, awkward young man.* **3.** difficult to deal with: *You seem to be in an awkward situation.*

awning awnings

NOUN a large roof of canvas or plastic attached to a building or vehicle

awry

ADJECTIVE wrong or not as planned: *Why had their plans gone so badly awry?*

axe axes axing axed

NOUN **1.** a tool with a handle and a sharp blade, used for chopping wood

VERB **2.** To axe something is to end it.

axiom axioms

NOUN a statement or saying that is generally accepted to be true

axis axes

NOUN **1.** an imaginary line through the centre of something, around which it moves **2.** one of the two sides of a graph

axle axles

NOUN the long bar that connects a pair of wheels on a vehicle

ayatollah ayatollahs

NOUN a religious leader in Iran

azure

ADJECTIVE *a literary or poetic word* bright blue

Instead of **AWFUL** try…

an **atrocious** way to behave

a **dreadful** accident

a **horrible** mistake

a **nasty** surprise

a **hideous** mask

a **disgusting** smell

ghastly noises in the night

appalling living conditions

Bb

Bb

babble babbles babbling babbled
VERB When someone babbles, that person talks in a confused or excited way.

baboon baboons
NOUN an African monkey with a pointed face, large teeth, and a long tail

baby babies
NOUN a child in the first year or two of its life
babyhood NOUN
babyish ADJECTIVE

babysit babysits babysitting babysat
VERB To babysit for someone means to look after that person's children while that person is out.
babysitter NOUN
babysitting NOUN

bachelor bachelors
NOUN a man who has never been married

back backs backing backed
ADVERB **1.** When people or things move back, they move in the opposite direction from the one they are facing. **2.** When people or things go back to a place or situation, they return to it: *She went back to sleep.* **3.** If you get something back, it is returned to you.
4. If you do something back to someone, you do to that person what he or she has done to you: *I smiled back at them.* **5.** Back also means in the past: *It happened back in the early eighties.*
NOUN **6.** the rear part of your body **7.** the part of something that is behind the front
ADJECTIVE **8.** The back parts of something are the ones near the rear: *an animal's back legs*
VERB **9.** If a building backs onto something, its back faces in that direction. **10.** When a car backs, it moves backwards. **11.** To back a person or organization means to support or finance that person or organization.
back down
VERB **12.** If you back down on a demand or claim, you withdraw and give up.
back out
VERB **13.** If you back out of a promise or commitment, you decide not to do what you had promised to do.
back up
VERB **14.** If you back up a claim or story, you produce evidence to show that it is true.
15. If you back someone up, you help and support that person.

backbone backbones
NOUN **1.** the column of linked bones along the middle of a person's or animal's back **2.** strength of character: *She showed real backbone when standing up for her beliefs.*

backdate backdates backdating backdated
VERB If an arrangement is backdated, it is valid from a date earlier than the one on which it is completed or signed.

backdrop backdrops
NOUN the background to a situation or event: *The visit occurred against the backdrop of the political crisis.*

backer backers
NOUN The backers of a project are the people who give it financial help.

backfire backfires backfiring backfired
VERB **1.** If a plan backfires, it fails. **2.** When a car backfires, there is a small but noisy explosion in its exhaust pipe.

background backgrounds
NOUN **1.** the circumstances that help to explain an event or that caused it to happen **2.** the kind of home you come from and your education and experience: *a rich background* **3.** If sounds are in the background, they are there but no one really pays any attention to them: *She could hear voices in the background.*

backing
NOUN support or help: *The project got government backing.*

backlash
NOUN a hostile reaction to a new development or a new policy: *There has been plenty of backlash to the banning of cellphones in the classroom.*

backlog backlogs
NOUN a number of things that have not yet been done, but that need to be done: *I have a backlog of assignments to complete before class on Monday.*

backpack backpacks
NOUN a bag with straps for carrying it on your back

backside backsides
NOUN *an informal word* the part of your body that you sit on

backward
ADJECTIVE **1.** Backward means directed behind you: *without a backward glance* **2.** slow or behind others in development
backwardness NOUN

backwards
ADVERB **1.** Backwards means behind you: *She looked backwards.* **2.** If you do something

backwards, you do it the opposite of the usual way: *He instructed them to count backwards from ten down to one.*

bacon
NOUN meat from the back or sides of a pig, which has been salted or smoked

bacteria
PLURAL NOUN Bacteria are very tiny organisms that can cause disease.
bacterial ADJECTIVE

bad worse worst
ADJECTIVE
1. Anything harmful or upsetting can be

Instead of **BAD** try...

a painful headache
a faulty program
a mean temper
a rough road

a difficult day
gloomy weather
an evil character
a disobedient dog

described as bad: *I have some bad news. Is the pain bad?*
2. insufficient or of poor quality: *bad roads* **3.** evil or immoral in character or behaviour: *a bad person* **4.** lacking skill in something: *I was bad at sports.* **5.** Bad language consists of swearwords. **6.** If you have a bad temper, you become angry easily.
badness NOUN

bade a form of the past tense of BID

badge badges
NOUN something that you can attach to your clothes to show that you belong to an occupation, organization, school, etc.

badger badgers badgering badgered
NOUN **1.** a wild animal that has a white head with two black stripes on it
VERB **2.** If you badger someone, you keep asking the person questions or pestering him or her to do something.

badly
ADVERB in an inferior or unimpressive way: *He dances badly.*

badminton
NOUN a game in which two or four players use rackets to hit a shuttlecock over a high net

baffle baffles baffling baffled
VERB If something baffles you, you cannot understand or explain it: *The symptoms baffled the doctors.*
baffled ADJECTIVE
baffling ADJECTIVE

bag bags
NOUN a container for carrying things in

baggage
NOUN the suitcases and bags that you take on a journey

baggy baggier baggiest
ADJECTIVE Baggy clothing hangs loosely.

bagpipes
PLURAL NOUN a musical instrument played by squeezing air out of a leather bag through pipes

bail bails bailing bailed
NOUN **1.** Bail is a sum of money paid to a court to allow an accused person to go free until the trial: *He was released on bail.*
VERB **2.** If you bail water from a boat, you scoop it out.

bailiff bailiffs
NOUN a law officer who makes sure that the decisions of a court are obeyed

Baisakhi
NOUN a Sikh festival celebrated every April

bait baits baiting baited
NOUN **1.** a small amount of food placed on a hook or in a trap, to attract a fish or wild animal so that it gets caught **2.** something used to tempt a person to do something
VERB **3.** If you bait a hook or trap, you put some food on it to catch a fish or wild animal.

bake bakes baking baked
VERB **1.** To bake food means to cook by dry heat in an oven. **2.** To bake earth or clay means to heat it until it becomes hard.

baker bakers
NOUN a person who makes and sells bread and cakes

bakery bakeries
NOUN a building where bread and cakes are baked and sold

balaclava balaclavas
NOUN a close-fitting knitted hood that covers every part of your head except your face

balance balances balancing balanced
VERB **1.** When someone or something balances, that person or thing remains steady and does not fall over.
NOUN **2.** Balance is the state of being upright and steady. **3.** Balance is also a situation in which all the parts involved have a stable relationship with each other: *the chemical balance of the brain* **4.** The balance in someone's bank account is the amount of money in it.

Bb

balcony balconies
NOUN **1.** a platform on the outside of a building with a wall or railing around it **2.** an area of seats in the upper level of a theatre or concert hall

bald balder baldest
ADJECTIVE **1.** A bald person has little or no hair on the head. **2.** A bald statement or question is made in the simplest way without any attempt to be polite.
baldly ADVERB
baldness NOUN

bale bales baling baled
NOUN a large bundle of something, such as paper or hay, tied tightly

balk balks balking balked
VERB If you balk at something, you object to it and may refuse to do it: *He balked at the cost.*

ball balls
NOUN **1.** a round object that is thrown, kicked, and bounced, especially one used in games **2.** The ball of your foot or thumb is the rounded part where your toes join your foot or your thumb joins your hand. **3.** a large formal social event at which people dance

ballad ballads
NOUN **1.** a long song or poem that tells a story **2.** a slow, romantic song

ballast
NOUN any heavy material placed in a ship to make it more stable

ballerina ballerinas
NOUN a female ballet dancer

ballet
NOUN Ballet is a type of artistic dancing based on precise steps.

balloon balloons
NOUN **1.** a small bag made of thin rubber that you blow into until it becomes larger and rounder **2.** a large, strong bag filled with gas or hot air that travels through the air carrying passengers in a compartment underneath

ballot ballots balloting balloted
NOUN **1.** a secret vote in which people select a candidate in an election, or express their opinion about something
VERB **2.** When people are balloted, they are asked questions to find out what they think about a particular problem or question.

ballpoint ballpoints
NOUN a pen with a small metal ball at the end that transfers ink onto paper

ballroom ballrooms
NOUN a very large room used for dancing or formal balls

balm
NOUN *an old-fashioned word* a sweet-smelling, soothing ointment used to heal or lessen pain

balmy balmier balmiest
ADJECTIVE mild and pleasant: *balmy summer evenings*

> ⚠ **HEADS UP**
>
> In the words **balm** and **balmy** the letter l is silent, so they're pronounced BOM, like **calm**.

balsa
NOUN Balsa is very lightweight wood.

bamboo
NOUN Bamboo is a tall tropical grass with hard, hollow stems used for making furniture.

ban bans banning banned
VERB **1.** If something is banned, or if you are banned from doing it or using it, you are not allowed to do it or use it.
NOUN **2.** If there is a ban on something, it is not allowed.

banal
ADJECTIVE very ordinary and not at all interesting: *She made some banal remark.*
banality NOUN

banana bananas
NOUN a long curved fruit with a yellow skin

band bands
NOUN **1.** a group of musicians who play jazz or pop music together, or a group who play brass instruments together **2.** a group of people who share a common purpose: *a band of rebels* **3.** a group of First Nations people who live on a reserve and are officially recognized as a unit by the government. A single First Nation may be divided into many different bands. **4.** a narrow strip of something used to hold things together or worn as a decoration: *an elastic band, a wedding band*

bandage bandages bandaging bandaged
NOUN **1.** a strip of cloth wrapped around a wound to protect it
VERB **2.** If you bandage a wound, you tie a bandage around it.

bandit bandits
NOUN a robber, especially a member of an armed gang

Bb

bandstand bandstands
NOUN a platform, usually with a roof, where a band can play outdoors

bandwagon
PHRASE To **jump on the bandwagon** means to become involved in something because it is fashionable or likely to be successful.

bandy bandies bandying bandied
VERB If a name is bandied about, many people mention it.

bane
NOUN *a literary or poetic word* Someone or something that is the bane of a person or organization causes a lot of trouble for that person or organization: *The barking dog upstairs is the bane of my existence.*

bang bangs banging banged
VERB **1.** If you bang something, you hit it or put it somewhere violently, so that it makes a loud noise: *He banged the door shut.*
2. If you bang a part of your body against something, you accidentally bump it.
NOUN **3.** a sudden, short, loud noise **4.** a hard or painful bump against something

bangle bangles
NOUN an ornamental band worn around the wrist or ankle

banish banishes banishing banished
VERB **1.** To banish someone means to send that person into exile. **2.** To banish something means to get rid of it: *We can all help to banish prejudice.*
banishment NOUN

banister banisters
NOUN a rail supported by posts along the side of a staircase

banjo banjos
NOUN a musical instrument, like a small guitar with a round body

bank banks banking banked
NOUN **1.** a business that looks after people's money **2.** a bank of something is a store of it kept ready for use: *a blood bank* **3.** the raised ground along the edge of a river or lake **4.** the sloping side of an area of raised ground
VERB **5.** When you bank money, you pay it into a bank. **6.** If you bank on something happening, you expect it and rely on it.
banker NOUN
banking NOUN

banknote banknotes
NOUN a piece of paper money

bankrupt bankrupts bankrupting bankrupted
ADJECTIVE **1.** People or organizations that go bankrupt do not have enough money to pay their debts.

NOUN **2.** someone who has been declared bankrupt
VERB **3.** To bankrupt someone means to make that person bankrupt: *Restoring the house nearly bankrupted them.*
bankruptcy NOUN

banner banners
NOUN a long strip of cloth, paper, or plastic with a message or slogan on it

bannister another spelling of BANISTER

banquet banquets
NOUN a grand formal dinner, often followed by speeches

banter
NOUN Banter is friendly joking and teasing.

baobab baobabs
NOUN a small fruit tree with a very thick trunk that grows in Africa and northern Australia

baptism baptisms
NOUN a ceremony in which someone is baptized

baptize baptizes baptizing baptized
VERB When people are baptized water is sprinkled on them, or they are immersed in water, as a sign that they have become Christian.

bar bars barring barred
NOUN **1.** a counter or room where alcoholic drinks are served **2.** a long, straight piece of metal **3.** a piece of something made in a rectangular shape: *a bar of soap* **4.** The bars in a piece of music are the many short parts of equal length that the piece is divided into.
VERB **5.** If you bar a door, you place something across it to stop it from being opened. **6.** If you bar someone's way, you stop that person from going somewhere by standing in front of him or her.

barb barbs
NOUN a sharp curved point on the end of an arrow or fishhook

barbarian barbarians
NOUN a member of a people thought to be wild or uncivilized

barbaric
ADJECTIVE cruel or brutal: *a barbaric act of terrorism*
barbarity NOUN

barbecue barbecues barbecuing barbecued
NOUN **1.** a grill or open fire on which you cook food, usually outdoors; also an outdoor party where you eat food cooked on a barbecue
VERB **2.** When food is barbecued, it is cooked over a grill.

⚠ HEADS UP You may see the word **barbecue** written *barbeque* with a *q*. This is incorrect.

barbed

ADJECTIVE A barbed remark is one that seems straightforward but is really unkind or spiteful.

barbed wire

NOUN Barbed wire is strong wire with sharp points sticking out of it, used to make fences.

barber barbers

NOUN a person who cuts hair and shaves or trims beards for pay

barbiturate barbiturates

NOUN a drug that people take to make them calm or to put them to sleep

bar code bar codes

NOUN a small pattern of numbers and lines on something you buy in a store, which can be electronically scanned at a checkout to give the price

bard bards

NOUN *a literary or poetic word* A bard is a poet and singer from long ago. Some people call Shakespeare the Bard.

bare bares baring bared

ADJECTIVE **1.** If a part of your body is bare, it is not covered by any clothing. **2.** If something is bare, it has nothing on top of it or inside it: *a bare floor, a small bare office* **3.** When trees are bare, they have no leaves on them. **4.** The bare minimum or bare essentials means the very least that is needed: *They were fed the bare minimum.*

VERB **5.** If you bare something, you uncover or show it: *The wolf bared its teeth. He bared his true feelings for her.*

barefoot

ADJECTIVE OR ADVERB not wearing anything on your feet

barely

ADVERB only just: *The girl was barely 16.*

bargain bargains bargaining bargained

NOUN **1.** an agreement in which two people or groups discuss and agree what each will do, pay, or receive in a matter that involves them both **2.** something that is sold at a low price and is good value

VERB **3.** When people bargain with each other, they discuss and agree to terms about what each will do, pay, or receive in a matter that involves both.

barge barges barging barged

NOUN **1.** a large boat with a flat bottom used for carrying heavy loads, especially on rivers and canals

VERB **2.** *an informal use* If you barge into a place, you enter it in a rough or rude way.

baritone baritones

NOUN a man with a fairly deep singing voice

bark barks barking barked

VERB **1.** When a dog barks, it makes a short, loud noise, once or several times.

NOUN **2.** the short, loud noise that a dog makes **3.** the tough material that covers the outside of a tree

barley

NOUN a cereal that is grown for food and is also used for making beer and whisky

bar mitzvah

NOUN in Judaism, a ceremony that takes place on a boy's thirteenth birthday, after which he is regarded as an adult; also describes a boy who has reached this age. A Jewish girl of 12 to 14 is known as a *bat mitzvah*.

barn barns

NOUN a large farm building used for storing crops and sheltering animals

barnacle barnacles

NOUN a small shellfish that fixes itself to rocks and to the bottom of boats

barometer barometers

NOUN an instrument that measures air pressure and shows when the weather is changing

baron barons

NOUN in some countries, a member of the lowest rank of the nobility

baronial ADJECTIVE

baroness baronesses

NOUN a woman who has the rank of baron, or who is the wife of a baron

baronet baronets

NOUN a man with an honorary knighthood, which has been passed to him from his father

barracks

PLURAL NOUN a building where members of the armed forces live

barracuda barracudas

NOUN a large, fierce, tropical fish with sharp teeth

barrage barrages

NOUN **1.** A barrage of questions or complaints is a lot of them all coming at the same time. **2.** A barrage is continuous artillery fire, to prevent the enemy from moving.

barrel barrels

NOUN **1.** a wooden container with rounded sides and flat ends **2.** The barrel of a gun is the tube through which the bullet is fired.

barren

ADJECTIVE **1.** Barren land has soil of such poor quality that plants cannot grow on it. **2.** A barren woman or female animal is not able to have babies.

Bb

barricade barricades barricading barricaded
NOUN **1.** a temporary barrier put up to stop people getting past
VERB **2.** If you barricade yourself inside a room or building, you put something heavy against the door to stop people getting in.

barrier barriers
NOUN **1.** a fence or wall that prevents people or animals getting from one area to another **2.** If something is a barrier, it prevents two people or groups from agreeing or communicating, or prevents something from being achieved: *Cost is often a major barrier to going away on vacation.*

barrister barristers
NOUN a lawyer who works in a courtroom

barter barters bartering bartered
VERB **1.** If you barter goods, you exchange them for other goods, rather than selling them for money.
NOUN **2.** Barter is the activity of exchanging goods.

base bases basing based
NOUN **1.** the lowest part of something, which often supports the rest **2.** A place that part of an army, navy, or air force works from. **3.** In chemistry, a base is any compound that reacts with an acid to form a salt.
VERB **4.** To base something on something else means to use the second thing as a foundation or starting point of the first: *The movie was based on one of Shakespeare's plays.* **5.** If you are based somewhere, you live there or work from there.

> ⚠ **HEADS UP**
> Don't confuse **base** and **basis**. A **base** supports real objects, and a **basis** supports opinions or beliefs.

baseball
NOUN Baseball is a game played with a bat and a ball, by two teams of nine players each on a diamond-shaped field with a base at each corner.

basement basements
NOUN a floor of a building built completely or partly below the ground

bases
NOUN **1.** the plural of BASIS **2.** the plural of BASE

base word
NOUN a word to which you can add a prefix or a suffix to make a new word

bashful
ADJECTIVE shy and easily embarrassed

basic basics
ADJECTIVE **1.** The basic aspects of something are the most necessary ones: *the basic necessities of life* **2.** Something that is basic has only the necessary features without any extras or luxuries: *The accommodation is pretty basic.*
PLURAL NOUN **3.** The basics of something are the things you need to know or understand: *the basics of cooking*
basically ADVERB

basin basins
NOUN **1.** a round, wide container that is open at the top **2.** The basin of a river is a bowl of land from which water runs into the river.

basis bases
NOUN **1.** The basis of something is the essential main principle from which it can be developed: *The same colour theme is used as the basis for several patterns.* **2.** The basis for a belief is the facts that support it: *There is no basis for this assumption.*

bask basks basking basked
VERB If you bask in the sun, you sit or lie in it, enjoying its warmth.

basket baskets
NOUN a container made of thin strips of plastic, wood, wire, or other material woven together

basketball
NOUN Basketball is a game in which two teams try to score points by throwing a large ball through one of two circular nets placed high up at each end of the playing area, which is usually indoors.

bass basses
NOUN **1.** a man with a very deep singing voice **2.** a musical instrument with the lowest range in a family of musical instruments

bass basses
NOUN a type of edible fish

bassoon bassoons
NOUN a large woodwind musical instrument

bastard bastards
NOUN **1.** *an offensive use* People sometimes call someone a bastard when they dislike that person or are very angry with him or her. **2.** *an old-fashioned use* A bastard is someone whose parents were not married when he or she was born.

baste bastes basting basted
VERB When you baste food that is roasting, you pour melted fat or oil over it so that it does not become dry while cooking.

Bb

bastion bastions
NOUN *a literary or poetic word* something that protects a system or way of life: *The Charter of Rights is a bastion of freedom.*

bat bats batting batted
NOUN **1.** a specially shaped piece of wood with a handle, used for hitting the ball in a game such as baseball **2.** a small flying animal, active at night, that looks like a mouse with wings
VERB **3.** In some sports, when someone is batting, it is that person's turn to try to hit the ball and score runs.

batch batches
NOUN a group of things of the same kind produced or dealt with together

bated
PHRASE **With bated breath** means very anxiously.

bath baths
NOUN the washing of the body while sitting in a bathtub filled with water

bathe bathes bathing bathed
VERB **1.** When you bathe, you take a bath. **2.** When you bathe a wound, you wash it gently. **3.** *a literary or poetic use* If a place is bathed in light, a lot of light reaches it: *The room was bathed in spring sunshine.*
bather NOUN
bathing NOUN

bathing suit bathing suits
NOUN a garment worn for swimming

bathroom bathrooms
NOUN a room with a bathtub or shower, a sink, and a toilet in it

bathtub bathtubs
NOUN a long container that you fill with water and sit in to wash yourself

baton batons
NOUN **1.** a light, thin stick that a conductor uses to direct an orchestra or choir **2.** A baton is a short stick passed from one runner to another in a relay race.

battalion battalions
NOUN an army unit consisting of three or more companies

batten battens battening battened
NOUN **1.** a strip of wood that is fixed to something to strengthen it or hold it firm
batten down
VERB **2.** If you batten something down, you make it secure by fixing battens across it.

batter batters battering battered
VERB **1.** To batter someone or something means to hit that person or thing many times: *The waves kept battering the dock.*

NOUN **2.** Batter is a mixture of flour, eggs, and milk, used to make cakes or pancakes, or to coat food before frying it.

battery batteries
NOUN **1.** a device, containing two or more cells, for storing and producing electricity, for example in a flashlight or a car **2.** a large group of things or people

battle battles
NOUN **1.** a fight between armed forces or a struggle between two people or groups with conflicting aims: *the battle between town and country* **2.** A battle for something difficult is a determined attempt to obtain or achieve it: *the battle for equality*

battlefield battlefields
NOUN a place where a battle is being or has been fought

battlements
PLURAL NOUN The battlements of a castle consist of a wall built around the top, with gaps through which guns or arrows could be fired.

battleship battleships
NOUN a large, heavily armoured warship

batty battier battiest
ADJECTIVE *an informal word* crazy or eccentric

bauble baubles
NOUN a pretty but cheap ornament or piece of jewellery

bawdy bawdier bawdiest
ADJECTIVE A bawdy joke or song contains humorous but indecent references to sex.

bawl bawls bawling bawled
VERB **1.** *an informal word* To bawl at someone means to shout at that person loudly and harshly. **2.** When a child is bawling, he or she is crying very loudly and angrily.

bay bays baying bayed
NOUN **1.** a part of a sea or lake where the land curves inward **2.** a space or area used for a particular purpose: *a loading bay* **3.** a tree similar to the laurel, with leaves used for flavouring in cooking
PHRASE **4.** If you **keep something at bay**, you prevent it from reaching you: *He believes that eating oranges keeps colds at bay.*
VERB **5.** When a hound or wolf bays, it makes a deep howling noise.

bayonet bayonets
NOUN a sharp blade that can be fixed to the end of a rifle and used for stabbing

bazaar bazaars
NOUN **1.** a sale to raise money for charity **2.** a shopping district, especially in the Middle East

⚠ **HEADS UP** **Bath** is a noun, pronounced BATH. **Bathe** is a verb, pronounced BAYTH.

Bb

BC BC means *before Christ*. BCE is the same thing and is now the more commonly used term in dates: *The fortress was built in 49 BC.*

BCE BCE means *before the Common Era* and is used in preference to BC: *The fortress was built in 49 BCE.*

be am is are; being; was were; been
AUXILIARY VERB **1.** *Be* is used with a present participle to form the continuous tense: *She is attending the game right now. Crimes of violence are increasing.* **2.** *Be* is also used to say that something will happen: *We are hoping to go to Nunavut next month. I am planning to take history next semester.* **3.** *Be* is used to form the passive voice: *The walls were being repaired.*
VERB **4.** *Be* is used to give more information about the subject of a sentence: *Her favourite sport is hockey. Skyscrapers are tall buildings.*

be-
PREFIX **1.** The prefix *be-* is used to form verbs from nouns and adds the meaning *treat as*. For example, to *befriend* someone is to make friends with that person. **2.** The prefix *be-* is also sometimes used to form other verbs from verbs when it is used for emphasis or to mean *covering completely*. For example, to *besmear* means to smear all over.

beach beaches
NOUN an area of sand or pebbles beside the shore of a lake or an ocean

beacon beacons
NOUN A beacon is a light used as a guide or warning signal, especially for ships or aircraft.

bead beads
NOUN **1.** Beads are small pieces of glass, metal, plastic, or wood with a hole through the middle, often strung together to make jewellery. **2.** Beads of liquid are drops of it.

beady
ADJECTIVE Beady eyes are small and bright like beads.

beak beaks
NOUN A bird's beak is the hard part of its mouth that sticks out.

beaker beakers
NOUN a glass container with a lip, used in laboratories

beam beams beaming beamed
NOUN **1.** A beam of light is a band of light that shines from something such as a flashlight. **2.** a long, thick bar of wood or metal, especially one that supports a roof
VERB **3.** If you beam, you smile because you are happy.

bean beans
NOUN Beans are the seeds or pods of a climbing plant that are eaten as a vegetable; also used to name some other seeds, for example the seeds from which coffee is made.

bear bears bearing bore borne
NOUN **1.** a large, strong, wild animal with thick fur and sharp claws
VERB **2.** To bear something means to carry it or support its weight: *The ice wasn't thick enough to bear their weight.* **3.** If something bears a mark or typical feature, it has that feature: *The room bore all the signs of a violent struggle.* **4.** If you bear something difficult, you accept it and are able to deal with it: *He bore his last illness with courage.* **5.** If you can't bear someone or something, you dislike that person or thing very much. **6.** When a plant or tree bears flowers, fruit, or leaves, it produces them.
bearable ADJECTIVE

beard beards
NOUN the hair that grows on the lower part of a man's face
bearded ADJECTIVE

bearer bearers
NOUN The bearer of something is the person who carries or presents it: *the bearer of bad news*

SPELL-CHECK THIS!

A computer's spell-check won't catch wrong **homophones** (words that are spelled differently but sound the same).

I've bean thinking about this for a long time.

In this sentence, **bean** should be **been**. **Bean** is a seed used for food. **Been** is the past participle of the verb *be*.

bearing
NOUN **1.** If something has a bearing on a situation, it is relevant to it. **2.** the way in which a person moves or stands

beast beasts
NOUN **1.** *an old-fashioned use* a large wild animal **2.** *an informal use* If you call someone a beast, you mean that the person is cruel or spiteful.

beastly beastlier beastliest
ADJECTIVE *an old-fashioned word* cruel or spiteful

beat beats beating beat beaten
VERB **1.** To beat someone or something means to hit that person or thing hard and repeatedly. **2.** If you beat someone in a race or game, you defeat that person or do better than him or her. **3.** When a bird or insect beats its wings, it moves the wings up and down quickly. **4.** When your heart is beating, it is pumping blood with a regular rhythm. **5.** If you beat eggs you mix them vigorously. NOUN **6.** The beat of your heart is its regular pumping action. **7.** The beat of a piece of music is its main rhythm. **8.** A police officer's beat is the area that he or she patrols.
beat up
VERB **9.** To beat someone up means to hit or kick that person repeatedly.
beater NOUN
beating NOUN

beautiful
ADJECTIVE very attractive or pleasing: *a beautiful face, beautiful music*
beautifully ADVERB

beauty beauties
NOUN **1.** Beauty is the quality of being beautiful. **2.** *an old-fashioned use* a very attractive person, usually a woman **3.** *an informal use* The beauty of an idea or plan is what makes it attractive or worthwhile: *The beauty of the plan is its simplicity.*

beaver beavers
NOUN an animal with a big, flat tail and webbed hind feet. The beaver is a symbol of Canada.

because
CONJUNCTION **1.** *Because* is used with a clause that gives the reason for something: *I went home because I was tired.*
PHRASE **2. Because of** is used with a noun that gives the reason for something: *He quit playing hockey because of a knee injury.*

beck
PHRASE If you are at someone's **beck and call**, you are always available to do what that person asks.

beckon beckons beckoning beckoned
VERB **1.** If you beckon to someone, you signal with your hand that you want that person to come to you. **2.** If you say that something beckons, you mean that you find it very attractive: *A cool, clear lake beckons us to go swimming.*

become becomes becoming became become
VERB To become something means to start feeling or being that thing: *I became very angry. He became an actor.*

bed beds
NOUN **1.** a piece of furniture that you lie on when you sleep **2.** A bed in a garden is an area of ground in which plants are grown. **3.** The bed of a sea or river is the ground at the bottom of it.

bedlam
NOUN You can refer to a noisy and disorderly place or situation as bedlam: *The delay caused bedlam at the station.*

bedraggled
ADJECTIVE A bedraggled person or animal is in a messy or untidy state.

bedrock
NOUN **1.** Bedrock is the solid rock under the soil. **2.** The bedrock of something is the

KNOWING WORDS: WORD BUILDING

BE WORD SHARP!

To build a compound word, put two or more base words together.

bed a piece of furniture that you lie on when you sleep

bedclothes sheets and covers used on beds

bedpan a container used as a toilet by bedridden people

bedridden unable to get out of bed

bedroom a room used for sleeping

bedspread a cover put on top of sheets and blankets

foundation and principles on which it is based: *His life was built on the bedrock of integrity.*

bee bees
NOUN a winged insect that makes honey and lives in large groups

beech beeches
NOUN a tree with a smooth grey trunk and shiny leaves

beef
NOUN Beef is the meat of a cow, bull, or steer.

beefy beefier beefiest
ADJECTIVE *an informal word* A beefy person is strong and muscular.

beehive beehives
NOUN a container in which bees live and make their honey

beeline
PHRASE *an informal use* If you **make a beeline** for a place, you go there as quickly and directly as possible.

been the past participle of BE

beer beers
NOUN an alcoholic drink made from malt and flavoured with hops

beet beets
NOUN a plant with an edible root and leaves

beetle beetles
NOUN a flying insect with hard wings that cover its body when it is not flying

befall befalls befalling befell befallen
VERB *an old-fashioned word* If something befalls you, it happens to you: *A similar fate befell my cousin.*

before
ADVERB, PREPOSITION, OR CONJUNCTION **1.** *Before* is used to refer to a previous time: *Apply the ointment before going to bed.*
ADVERB **2.** If you have done something before, you have done it on a previous occasion: *Never before had he seen such poverty.*
PREPOSITION **3.** *a formal use* Before also means in front of: *They stopped before a large white house.*

beforehand
ADVERB earlier: *It had been agreed beforehand that they would spend the night there.*

befriend befriends befriending befriended
VERB If you befriend someone, you act in a kind and helpful way and so become friends with that person.

beg begs begging begged
VERB **1.** When people beg, they ask for food or money, because they are very poor. **2.** If you beg someone to do something, you ask that person very anxiously to do it.

beggar beggars
NOUN someone who lives by asking people for money or food

begin begins beginning began begun
VERB If you begin to do something, you start doing it. When something begins, it starts.

beginner beginners
NOUN someone who has just started learning to do something and cannot do it very well yet

beginning beginnings
NOUN The beginning of something is the first part of it or the time when it starts: *The beginning of the movie was scary.*

begonia begonias
NOUN a plant with brightly coloured flowers

begrudge begrudges begrudging begrudged
VERB If you begrudge someone something, you are angry or envious because that person has it: *No one could begrudge him the glory.*

beguiling
ADJECTIVE charming, but often in a deceptive way

behalf
PHRASE To do something **on behalf of** someone means to do it as that person's representative.

behave behaves behaving behaved
VERB **1.** If you behave in a particular way, you act in that way: *They were behaving badly.*
2. To behave yourself means to act correctly or properly.

behaviour
NOUN Your behaviour is the way in which you behave.

behead beheads beheading beheaded
VERB To behead someone means to cut that person's head off.

beheld the past tense of BEHOLD

behind
PREPOSITION **1.** at the back of: *I was seated behind the desk.* **2.** responsible for or causing: *He was the driving force behind the move.* **3.** supporting someone: *Her whole family was behind her.*
ADVERB **4.** If you stay behind, you remain after other people have gone. **5.** If you leave something behind, you do not take it with you.

Bb

behold

INTERJECTION *a literary or poetic word* You say *behold* when you want someone to look at something.

beholder NOUN

beige

NOUN OR ADJECTIVE pale creamy brown

being beings

1. the present participle of BE

NOUN **2.** Being is the state or fact of existing: *The organization came into being in 2005.* **3.** a living creature, either real or imaginary: *alien beings from a distant galaxy*

belated

ADJECTIVE *a formal word* A belated action happens later than it should have: *a belated birthday present*

belatedly ADVERB

belch belches belching belched

VERB **1.** If you belch, you make a sudden noise in your throat because air has risen up from your stomach. **2.** If something belches smoke or fire, it sends it out in large amounts: *Smoke belched from the chimney.*

NOUN **3.** the noise you make when you belch

beleaguered

ADJECTIVE **1.** struggling against difficulties or criticism: *the beleaguered fishing industry* **2.** overpowered or surrounded by an enemy: *the beleaguered garrison*

belief beliefs

NOUN **1.** a feeling of certainty that something exists or is true: *My belief in his innocence is unshakable.* **2.** one of the principles of a religion or moral system: *Her beliefs are different from mine.*

believable

ADJECTIVE possible or likely to be the case

believe believes believing believed

VERB **1.** If you believe that something is true, you accept that it is true. **2.** If you believe someone, you accept that he or she is telling the truth. **3.** If you believe in things such as UFOs and miracles, you accept that they exist or happen. **4.** If you believe in something such as a plan or system, you are in favour of it: *They believe in recycling.*

believer NOUN

belittle belittles belittling belittled

VERB If you belittle someone or something, you make that person or thing seem unimportant: *He belittled my opinions.*

bell bells

NOUN **1.** a cup-shaped metal object with a piece inside that swings and hits the sides, producing a ringing sound **2.** an electrical device that rings or buzzes in order to attract attention

belligerent

ADJECTIVE aggressive and keen to start a fight or an argument

belligerence NOUN

bellow bellows bellowing bellowed

VERB **1.** When an animal such as a bull bellows, it makes a loud roaring noise. **2.** If someone bellows, that person shouts in a loud voice.

PLURAL NOUN **3.** Bellows are a piece of equipment used for blowing air into a fire to make it burn more fiercely.

belly bellies

NOUN **1.** Your belly is your stomach or the front of your body below your chest. **2.** An animal's belly is the underneath part of its body.

belong belongs belonging belonged

VERB **1.** If something belongs to you, it is yours and you own it. **2.** To belong to a group means to be a member of it. **3.** If something belongs in a particular place, that is where it should be: *The hockey bag did not belong in the living room.*

belongings

PLURAL NOUN Your belongings are the things that you own.

beloved

ADJECTIVE A beloved person or thing is one that you feel great affection for.

⚠ HEADS UP

Beloved can be pronounced in two ways: *You are my* be-LUHV-ed. *This is a* be-LUHVD *old movie.*

---

below

PREPOSITION OR ADVERB **1.** If something is below a line or the surface of something else, it is lower down: *six centimetres below soil level* **2.** Below also means at or to a lower point, level, or rate: *The temperature fell below ten degrees Celsius.*

belt belts belting belted

NOUN **1.** a strip of leather or cloth that you fasten around your waist to hold clothing up or as a decoration **2.** In a machine, a belt is a circular strip of rubber that drives moving parts or carries objects along. **3.** a specific area of a country: *Canada's wheat belt* VERB **4.** *an informal use* To belt someone means to hit that person very hard.

bemused

ADJECTIVE If you are bemused, you are puzzled or confused.

bench benches

NOUN **1.** a long seat that two or more people can sit on **2.** a long, narrow table for working at, for example in a laboratory

bend bends bending bent

VERB **1.** When you bend something, you use force to make it curved or angular.
2. When you bend, you move your head and shoulders forward and downward.
NOUN **3.** a curved part of something
bent ADJECTIVE

bene-

PREFIX The prefix *bene-* means *good* or *well*. For example, something *beneficial* makes you well or produces a good result, and a *benevolent* person is kind and good to others.

beneath

PREPOSITION **1.** below or under **2.** If someone thinks something is beneath him or her, that person thinks that it is too unimportant to bother with it.

benefactor benefactors

NOUN a person who helps to support a person or institution by giving money

beneficial

ADJECTIVE Something that is beneficial is good for people: *the beneficial effects of exercise*
beneficially ADVERB

beneficiary beneficiaries

NOUN A beneficiary of something is someone who receives money or other benefits from it.

benefit benefits benefiting benefited

NOUN **1.** The benefits of something are the advantages that it brings to people: *the benefits of relaxation*
PLURAL NOUN **2.** Benefits are payments given by the government or an employer to people who are unemployed or ill.
VERB **3.** If you benefit from something or something benefits you, it helps you.

benevolent

ADJECTIVE kind and helpful
benevolence NOUN
benevolently ADVERB

benign

ADJECTIVE **1.** Someone who is benign is kind and gentle. **2.** A benign tumour is one that will not cause death or serious illness.
benignly ADVERB

bent

1. the past participle and past tense of BEND
PHRASE **2.** If you are **bent on** doing something, you are determined to do it.

bequeath bequeaths bequeathing bequeathed

VERB *a formal word* If someone bequeaths money or property to you in a will, it belongs to you after that person has died.

bequest bequests

NOUN *a formal word* money or property that has been left to someone in a will

berate berates berating berated

VERB *a formal word* If you berate someone, you scold that person angrily: *He berated them for misbehaving.*

bereaved

ADJECTIVE *a formal word* You say that someone is bereaved when a close relative of that person has recently died.
bereavement NOUN

bereft

ADJECTIVE *a literary or poetic word* If you are bereft of something, you no longer have it: *The government seems bereft of ideas.*

beret berets

NOUN a circular, flat hat with no brim

berry berries

NOUN Berries are small, round fruits that grow on bushes or trees.

berserk

PHRASE If someone **goes berserk**, that person loses control and becomes very violent.

berth berths

NOUN **1.** a space in a harbour where a ship stays when it is being loaded or unloaded **2.** In a boat, camper, or train, a berth is a bed.

beseech beseeches beseeching beseeched besought

VERB *a literary or poetic word* If you beseech someone to do something, you ask that person very earnestly to do it: *Her eyes beseeched him to show mercy.*
beseeching ADJECTIVE

beset

ADJECTIVE *a formal word* If you are beset by difficulties or doubts, you have a lot of them.

beside

PREPOSITION If one thing is beside something else, both things are next to each other.

besiege besieges besieging besieged

VERB **1.** When soldiers besiege a place, they surround it and wait for the people inside to surrender. **2.** If you are besieged by people, many people want something from you and continually bother you.

besought a past tense and past participle of BESEECH

best
1. the superlative of **good** and **well**
ADVERB **2.** The thing that you like best is the thing that you prefer to

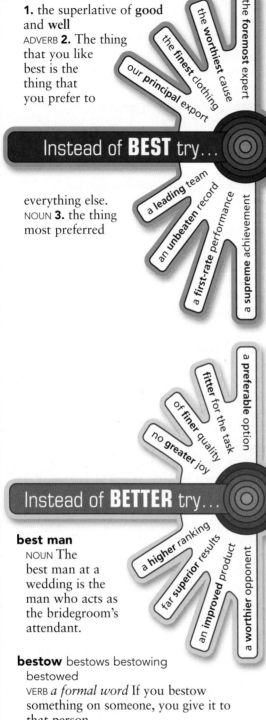

Instead of **BEST** try...

the **foremost** expert
the **worthiest** cause
the **finest** clothing
our **principal** export
a **leading** team
an **unbeaten** record
a **first-rate** performance
a **supreme** achievement

everything else.
NOUN **3.** the thing most preferred

Instead of **BETTER** try...

a **preferable** option
fitter for the task
of **finer** quality
no **greater** joy
a **higher** ranking
far **superior** results
an **improved** product
a **worthier** opponent

best man
NOUN The best man at a wedding is the man who acts as the bridegroom's attendant.

bestow bestows bestowing bestowed
VERB *a formal word* If you bestow something on someone, you give it to that person.

bet bets betting bet
VERB **1.** If you bet on the result of an event, you will win money if something happens and lose money if it does not.
NOUN **2.** the act of betting on something, or the amount of money that you agree to risk
PHRASE *an informal use* **3.** You say **I bet** to

indicate that you are sure that something is or will be so: *I bet the answer is no.*
betting NOUN

betray betrays betraying betrayed
VERB **1.** If you betray someone who trusts you, you do something that harms that person, such as helping his or her enemies.
2. If you betray your feelings or thoughts, you show them without intending to.
betrayal NOUN
betrayer NOUN

betrothal betrothals
NOUN *an old-fashioned word* an engagement to be married
betrothed ADJECTIVE OR NOUN

better
1. the comparative of **good** and **well**
ADVERB **2.** If you like one thing better than another, you like it more than the other thing.
ADJECTIVE **3.** If you are better after an illness, you are no longer ill.

between
PREPOSITION OR ADVERB **1.** If something is between two other things, it is situated or happens in the space or time that separates the two things: *flights between Europe and Canada* **2.** a relationship or difference between two people or things that involves only those two: *What's the difference in price between these two computers?*

beverage beverages
NOUN *a formal word* a drink

bevy bevies
NOUN a small group of people, animals, or things: *a bevy of lawyers, a bevy of quail*

beware
VERB If you tell someone to beware of something, you are warning that person that it might be dangerous or harmful.

bewilder bewilders bewildering bewildered
VERB If something bewilders you, it is too confusing or difficult for you to understand.
bewildered ADJECTIVE
bewildering ADJECTIVE
bewilderment NOUN

bewitch bewitches bewitching bewitched
VERB **1.** To bewitch someone means to cast a spell on that person. **2.** If something bewitches you, you are so delighted by it that you cannot pay attention to anything else.
bewitched ADJECTIVE
bewitching ADJECTIVE

beyond
PREPOSITION **1.** If something is beyond a certain place, it is on the other side of it: *Beyond the hills was the forest.* **2.** If something continues

beyond a particular point, it continues further than that point: *an education beyond the age of 17* **3.** If someone or something is beyond understanding or help, that person or thing cannot be understood or helped.

bi-

PREFIX The prefix *bi-* means *two* or *twice*: *bicycle, biannual*

bias

NOUN Someone who shows bias favours one person or thing unfairly.

biased

ADJECTIVE favouring one person or thing unfairly: *biased attitudes*

bib bibs

NOUN a piece of cloth or plastic that is worn under the chin of very young children when they are eating, to keep their clothes clean

Bible Bibles

NOUN **1.** The Bible is the sacred book of the Christian religion. **2.** Any book that is accepted as an authority in a particular field: *This dictionary is the bible for Canadian spelling and usage.*

biblical ADJECTIVE

bicentenary bicentenaries

NOUN The bicentenary of an event is its two-hundredth anniversary.

biceps

NOUN Your biceps are the large muscles on your upper arms.

bicker bickers bickering bickered

VERB When people bicker, they argue about unimportant things.

bicycle bicycles

NOUN a two-wheeled vehicle that you ride by pushing two pedals with your feet

bid bids bidding bade bidden bid

NOUN **1.** an attempt to obtain or do something: *He made a bid for freedom.* **2.** an offer to buy something for a certain sum of money

VERB **3.** If you bid for something, you offer to pay a certain sum of money for it.

4. *an old-fashioned use* If you bid someone a greeting or a farewell, you say it to that person.

bide bides biding bided

PHRASE If you **bide your time**, you wait for a good opportunity before doing something.

bidet bidets

NOUN a low basin in a bathroom that is used for washing your bottom

big bigger biggest

ADJECTIVE **1.** of a large size **2.** of great importance

biggish ADJECTIVE
bigness NOUN

bigamy

NOUN Bigamy is the crime of marrying someone when you are already married to someone else.

bigamist NOUN

bigot bigots

NOUN someone who has strong and unreasonable opinions that he or she refuses to change

bigoted ADJECTIVE
bigotry NOUN

bike bikes

NOUN *an informal word* a bicycle

bikini bikinis

NOUN a small two-piece bathing suit worn by women

bilateral

ADJECTIVE A bilateral agreement is one made between two groups or countries.

bile

NOUN Bile is a bitter yellow liquid produced by the liver that helps the digestion of fat.

bilge

NOUN the lowest part of a ship, where dirty water collects

bilingual

ADJECTIVE **1.** involving or using two languages: *bilingual street signs* **2.** In Canada, a bilingual person is able to speak both French and English.

bilingualism

NOUN **1.** the ability to speak two languages fluently **2.** In Canada, bilingualism is the ability to speak both French and English.

bill bills

NOUN **1.** a written statement of how much is owed for goods or services **2.** a piece of paper money **3.** a formal statement of a proposed new law that is discussed and then voted on in Parliament **4.** a notice or a poster **5.** A bird's bill is its beak.

Instead of **BIG** try...

an enormous building
an immense fortune
a vast wilderness
a massive beast
a grave error
a colossal statue
a momentous occasion
a significant difference

Bb

billboard billboards
NOUN a large board on which advertisements are displayed

billet billets billeting billeted
VERB When someone is billeted, arrangements are made for that person to stay in a private home.

billiards
NOUN Billiards is a game in which a long stick called a cue is used to move balls on a table.

billion billions
NOUN a thousand million

billow billows billowing billowed
VERB **1.** When things made of cloth billow, they swell out and flap slowly in the wind. **2.** When smoke or a cloud billows, it spreads upward and outward.
NOUN **3.** a large wave

bin bins
NOUN a container for holding loose things like bulk food, toys, and small items

binary
ADJECTIVE The binary system expresses numbers using only two digits, 0 and 1.

bind binds binding bound
VERB **1.** If you bind something, you tie rope or string around it so that it is held firmly. **2.** If something binds you to a course of action, it makes you act in that way: *He was bound by that decision.*

binding bindings
ADJECTIVE **1.** If a promise or agreement is binding, it must be obeyed.
NOUN **2.** The binding of a book is its cover.

binge binges
NOUN *an informal word* a brief period of drinking or eating too much

bingo
NOUN Bingo is a game in which players aim to match the numbers that someone calls out with the numbers on the card that they have been given.

binoculars
PLURAL NOUN Binoculars are an instrument with lenses for both eyes that you look through in order to see objects far away.

bio-
PREFIX The prefix *bio-* means *life* or *living things*. For example, a *biography* is the story of someone's life and *biology* is the study of living things.

biochemistry
NOUN Biochemistry is the study of the chemistry of living things.
biochemical ADJECTIVE
biochemist NOUN

biodegradable
ADJECTIVE If something is biodegradable, it can be broken down into its natural elements by the action of bacteria: *biodegradable cleaning products*

biodiversity
NOUN the existence of a wide variety of plant and animal species in a particular area

biography biographies
NOUN the history of someone's life, written by someone else
biographer NOUN
biographical ADJECTIVE

biology
NOUN Biology is the study of living things.
biological ADJECTIVE
biologically ADVERB
biologist NOUN

biometric
ADJECTIVE relating to biometrics: *a biometric passport*

biometrics
NOUN the use of mathematical measurements to analyze physical characteristics, especially to identify people

bionic
ADJECTIVE having an artificial body part that works electronically

biopsy biopsies
NOUN an examination under a microscope of tissue from a living body to find out the cause of a disease

birch birches
NOUN a tall deciduous tree with thin bark

bird birds
NOUN an animal with two legs, two wings, and feathers

birth births
NOUN **1.** The birth of a baby is when it comes out of its mother's womb at the beginning of its life. **2.** The birth of something is its beginning: *the birth of modern art*

birthday birthdays
NOUN Your birthday is the anniversary of the date on which you were born.

birthmark birthmarks
NOUN a mark on someone's skin that has been there since that person was born

biscuit biscuits
NOUN a small flat cake made of baked dough

bisect bisects bisecting bisected
VERB To bisect a line or area means to divide it in half.

bisexual
ADJECTIVE sexually attracted to both men and women

 **HEADS UP** Knowing the meaning of the prefix helps you figure out words like *biodegradable*.

NEL

Bb

bishop bishops
NOUN **1.** a high-ranking clergyman in some Christian churches **2.** In chess, a bishop is a piece that is moved diagonally across the board.

bison
NOUN a large hairy animal related to cattle

bistro bistros
NOUN a small, informal restaurant

bit bits
1. Bit is the past tense of BITE.
NOUN **2.** A bit of something is a small amount of it: *a bit of homework*
PHRASE *informal* **3.** A bit means slightly or to a small extent: *That's a bit tricky.*

bitch bitches
NOUN a female dog

bite bites biting bit bitten
VERB **1.** To bite something is to cut it or cut through it with the teeth.
NOUN **2.** a small amount that you bite off something with your teeth **3.** the injury you get when an animal or insect bites you

bitter bitterest
ADJECTIVE **1.** If someone is bitter, that person feels angry and resentful. **2.** A bitter disappointment or experience makes people feel angry or unhappy for a long time afterwards. **3.** In a bitter argument or war, people argue or fight fiercely and angrily: *a bitter power struggle* **4.** A bitter wind is an extremely cold wind. **5.** Something that tastes bitter has a sharp, unpleasant taste.
bitterly ADVERB
bitterness NOUN

bivouac bivouacs
NOUN a temporary camp in the open air

bizarre
ADJECTIVE very strange or eccentric

blab blabs blabbing blabbed
VERB *an informal word* When people blab, they give away secrets by talking carelessly.

black blacker blackest; blacks
NOUN OR ADJECTIVE **1.** Black is the darkest possible colour, like tar or soot. **2.** Someone who is black is of African descent.
ADJECTIVE **3.** Black coffee or tea has no milk or cream added to it. **4.** Black humour involves jokes about death or suffering.
blackness NOUN

⚠ **HEADS UP**
When describing a person, terms like **African-Canadian** or **Jamaican-Canadian** are acceptable.

blackberry blackberries
NOUN a small black fruit that grows on a thorny bush

blackbird blackbirds
NOUN a bird with black feathers. Canadian species include the red-winged blackbird and the grackle.

blackboard blackboards
NOUN a dark-coloured board in a classroom that teachers write on using chalk

black box black boxes
NOUN an electronic device in an aircraft that collects and stores information during flights

blackcurrant blackcurrants
NOUN a small, dark purple fruit that grows in bunches on bushes

blacken blackens blackening blackened
VERB To blacken something means to make it black: *The smoke from the chimney blackened the roof.*

blackhead blackheads
NOUN a very small, black spot on the skin caused by a pore being blocked with dirt

blacklist blacklists blacklisting blacklisted
NOUN **1.** a list of people or organizations who are thought to be untrustworthy or disloyal
VERB **2.** When someone is blacklisted, that person is put on a blacklist.

blackmail blackmails blackmailing blackmailed
VERB **1.** If someone blackmails you, that person threatens to reveal an unpleasant secret about you unless you give the person money or do what he or she wants.
NOUN **2.** Blackmail is the action of blackmailing people.
blackmailer NOUN

black market
NOUN If something is bought or sold on the black market, it is bought or sold illegally.

blackout blackouts
NOUN If you have a blackout, you lose consciousness for a short time.

blacksmith blacksmiths
NOUN a person whose job is making things out of iron, such as horseshoes

bladder bladders
NOUN the part of your body where urine is held until it leaves your body

blade blades
NOUN **1.** The blade of a weapon, cutting tool, or ice skate is the sharp part of it. **2.** The blades of a propeller are the thin, flat parts that turn around. **3.** A blade of grass is a single piece of it.

Bb

blame blames blaming blamed
VERB **1.** If someone blames you for something bad that has happened, that person believes you caused it.
NOUN **2.** The blame for something bad that happens is the responsibility for letting it happen.

blameless
ADJECTIVE Someone who is blameless has not done anything wrong.

blanch blanches blanching blanched
VERB If you blanch, you suddenly become very pale.

bland blander blandest
ADJECTIVE tasteless, dull, or boring: *a bland diet, bland pop music*
blandly ADVERB

blank blanker blankest
ADJECTIVE **1.** Something that is blank has nothing on it: *a blank sheet of paper* **2.** If you look blank, your face shows no feeling or interest.
NOUN **3.** If your mind is a blank, you cannot think of anything or remember anything.

blanket blankets
NOUN **1.** a large rectangle of thick cloth that is put on a bed to keep people warm **2.** A blanket of something such as snow is a thick covering of it.

blare blares blaring blared
VERB To blare means to make a loud, unpleasant noise: *The radio blared pop music.*

blaspheme blasphemes blaspheming blasphemed
VERB When people blaspheme, they are disrespectful about religion.

blasphemy blasphemies
NOUN Blasphemy is speech or behaviour that shows disrespect for religion.
blasphemous ADJECTIVE

blast blasts blasting blasted
VERB **1.** When people blast a hole in something they make a hole with an explosive.
NOUN **2.** a big explosion, especially one caused by a bomb **3.** a sudden strong rush of wind or air

blatant
ADJECTIVE If you describe something as blatant, you mean that rather than hide it, those responsible actually seem to be making it obvious: *a blatant disregard for the law*

blaze blazes blazing blazed
NOUN **1.** a large, hot fire **2.** A blaze of light or colour is a great or strong amount of it: *a blaze of red* **3.** A blaze of publicity or

attention is a lot of it.
VERB **4.** If something blazes it burns or shines brightly.

blazer blazers
NOUN a kind of jacket, often in the colours of a school or sports team

bleach bleaches bleaching bleached
VERB **1.** To bleach material or hair means to make it white, usually by using a chemical.
NOUN **2.** Bleach is a chemical that is used to make material white or to clean thoroughly and kill germs.

bleak bleaker bleakest
ADJECTIVE **1.** If a situation is bleak, it is bad and seems unlikely to improve. **2.** If a place is bleak, it is cold, bare, and exposed to the wind.

bleary
ADJECTIVE If your eyes are bleary, they are red and watery, usually because you are tired.

bleat bleats bleating bleated
VERB **1.** When sheep or goats bleat, they make a high-pitched cry.
NOUN **2.** the high-pitched cry that a sheep or goat makes

bleed bleeds bleeding bled
VERB When you bleed, you lose blood as a result of an injury.

blemish blemishes
NOUN a mark that spoils the appearance of something

blend blends blending blended
VERB **1.** When you blend substances, you mix them together to form a single substance.
2. When colours or sounds blend, they combine in a pleasing way.
NOUN **3.** A blend of things is a mixture of them, especially one that is pleasing.
4. a word formed by joining together the beginning and the end of two other words; for example, *brunch* is a blend of *breakfast* and *lunch*

blender blenders
NOUN a machine used for mixing liquids and foods at high speed

bless blesses blessing blessed
VERB When people or things are blessed, they are made holy or sacred.

blessed
ADJECTIVE If someone is blessed with a particular quality or skill, that person has it: *He was blessed with a sense of humour.*
blessedly ADVERB

blessing blessings
NOUN **1.** something good that you are thankful for: *Good health is the greatest*

blessing.
PHRASE **2.** If something is done **with someone's blessing**, that person approves of it and supports it.

blew the past tense of BLOW

blight blights blighting blighted
NOUN **1.** something that damages or spoils other things: *the blight of the recession*
VERB **2.** When something is blighted, it is seriously harmed: *His life had been blighted by sickness.*

blind blinds blinding blinded
ADJECTIVE **1.** Someone who is blind cannot see. **2.** If someone is blind to a particular fact, that person does not understand it.
VERB **3.** If something blinds you, you become unable to see, either for a short time or permanently.
NOUN **4.** a roll of material that you pull down over a window to keep out the light
blindly ADVERB
blindness NOUN

blindfold blindfolds blindfolding blindfolded
NOUN **1.** a strip of cloth tied over someone's eyes so that the person cannot see
VERB **2.** To blindfold someone means to cover that person's eyes with a strip of cloth.

blinding
ADJECTIVE A blinding light is so bright that it hurts your eyes: *There was a blinding flash.*

blindingly
ADVERB *an informal use* If something is blindingly obvious, it is very obvious.

bling blinger blingest *an informal word*
NOUN **1.** jewellery that looks expensive in a vulgar way
ADJECTIVE **2.** flashy; expensive-looking in a vulgar way

blink blinks blinking blinked
VERB When you blink, you close your eyes quickly for a moment.

blinker blinkers
NOUN A blinker is a warning light: *Flash your blinkers to signal that you are turning the corner.*

bliss
NOUN Bliss is a state of complete happiness.
blissful ADJECTIVE
blissfully ADVERB

blister blisters blistering blistered
NOUN **1.** a small bubble on your skin containing watery liquid, caused by a burn or rubbing
VERB **2.** If someone's skin blisters, blisters appear on it as result of burning or rubbing.

blithe
ADJECTIVE casual and done without serious thought: *a blithe disregard for their safety*
blithely ADVERB

blitz blitzes blitzing blitzed
NOUN **1.** a bombing attack by enemy aircraft on a city **2.** an intense campaign, often in advertising or for charitable organizations: *We launched a door-to-door blitz in an attempt to gain more support for our cause.*
VERB **3.** When a city is blitzed, it is bombed by aircraft and is damaged or destroyed.

> ⚠ **HEADS UP**
> **Blitz** is the German word for *lightning*. Other English words are taken from German, like **strudel** and **kindergarten**.

blizzard blizzards
NOUN a heavy snowstorm with strong winds

bloated
ADJECTIVE Something that is bloated is much larger than normal, often because there is a lot of liquid or gas inside it.

blob blobs
NOUN a small amount of a thick or sticky substance

bloc blocs
NOUN A group of countries or political parties with similar aims acting together is often called a bloc: *a voting bloc*

block blocks blocking blocked
NOUN **1.** In a town or city, a block is an area of land with streets on all its sides: *He lives a few blocks down from me.* **2.** A block of something is a large rectangular piece of it.
VERB **3.** To block something, such as a road, means to put a barrier across it so that nothing can get through. **4.** If something blocks your view, it is in the way and prevents you from seeing what you want to see. **5.** If someone blocks something, that person prevents it from happening: *The councillor blocked our plans.*

blockade blockades blockading blockaded
NOUN **1.** an action that prevents supplies or people from reaching a place
VERB **2.** When a place is blockaded, supplies or people are prevented from reaching it.

blockage blockages
NOUN When there is a blockage in an opening, something is clogging it.

Bb

blog blogs
NOUN *an informal word* A blog is a person's online diary that he or she puts on the Internet so that other people can read it.

blogger bloggers
NOUN *an informal word* a person who keeps a blog

blond blonds **blonde** blondes
ADJECTIVE **1.** Blond hair is pale yellow in colour. The spelling *blonde* is commonly used when referring to women and girls.
NOUN **2.** A blond, or blonde, is a person with light-coloured hair.

blood
NOUN **1.** Blood is the red liquid that is pumped by the heart around the bodies of human beings and other mammals.
PHRASE **2.** If something cruel is done **in cold blood**, it is done deliberately and without showing any emotion.

bloodhound bloodhounds
NOUN a large dog with an excellent sense of smell

bloodless
ADJECTIVE **1.** If someone's face or skin is bloodless, it is very pale. **2.** In a bloodless coup or revolution, nobody is killed.

blood pressure
NOUN Your blood pressure is a measure of the force with which your blood is being pumped around your body.

bloodshed
NOUN When there is bloodshed, people are killed or wounded.

bloodshot
ADJECTIVE If a person's eyes are bloodshot, the white parts have become red.

blood sport blood sports
NOUN any sport that involves deliberately killing or injuring animals

bloodstained
ADJECTIVE covered with blood

bloodstream
NOUN the flow of blood through your body

bloodthirsty
ADJECTIVE Someone who is bloodthirsty enjoys using or watching violence.

blood transfusion blood transfusions
NOUN a process in which blood is injected into the body of someone who has lost a lot of blood

blood vessel blood vessels
NOUN Blood vessels are the narrow tubes in your body through which your blood flows.

bloody bloodier bloodiest
ADJECTIVE **1.** A bloody event is one in which a lot of people are killed: *a bloody revolution* **2.** Bloody also means covered with blood: *a bloody gash on his head*

bloom blooms blooming bloomed
NOUN **1.** a flower on a plant
VERB **2.** When a plant blooms, it produces flowers. **3.** When something like a feeling blooms, it grows: *Romance can bloom where you least expect it.*

blossom blossoms blossoming blossomed
NOUN **1.** Blossom is the growth of flowers that appears on a tree before the fruit.
VERB **2.** When a tree blossoms, it produces blossom.

blot blots blotting blotted
NOUN **1.** a drop of ink that has been spilled on a surface **2.** A blot on someone's reputation is a mistake or case of bad behaviour that spoils that person's reputation.

blot out
VERB **3.** To blot something out means to be in front of it and prevent it from being seen: *The smoke blotted out the sky.*

blotch blotches
NOUN a stain or a patch of a different colour
blotchy ADJECTIVE

KNOWING WORDS: WORD HISTORY

BE WORD SHARP!

Words are like living things. They grow and change.

Blog is a shortened form of the compound word **weblog**, meaning a log (or diary) on the World Wide Web. Before blogs, there were Internet message boards, where many people could comment on a single topic or **thread**. Since the word was coined in the 1990s, people have invented similar words like **artblog**, **photoblog**, and **vlog** (a video blog). Now many people use blog as a verb, saying they are **blogging** when writing a blog.

NEL

Bb

blouse blouses
NOUN a light, loosely fitting shirt, worn by a girl or a woman

blow blows blowing blew blown
VERB **1.** When the wind blows, the air moves. **2.** If something blows or is blown somewhere, the wind moves it there. **3.** If you blow a whistle or horn, you make a sound by blowing into it.
NOUN **4.** If you receive a blow, someone or something hits you. **5.** something that makes you very disappointed or unhappy: *Her grandfather's death was a terrible blow.*
blow up
VERB **6.** To blow something up means to destroy it with an explosion. **7.** To blow up a balloon or a tire means to fill it with air.

blubber
NOUN The blubber of animals such as whales and seals is the layer of fat that protects them from the cold.

bludgeon bludgeons bludgeoning bludgeoned
VERB To bludgeon someone means to hit that person several times with a heavy object.

blue bluer bluest
ADJECTIVE OR NOUN **1.** Blue is the colour of the sky on a clear, sunny day.
PHRASE **2.** If something happens **out of the blue**, it happens suddenly and unexpectedly.
ADJECTIVE **3.** Blue films and jokes are about sex.
bluish ADJECTIVE

bluebell bluebells
NOUN a woodland plant with blue, bell-shaped flowers

bluebottle bluebottles
NOUN a large fly with a shiny, dark blue body

blue-collar
ADJECTIVE Blue-collar workers do physical work as opposed to office work.

blueprint blueprints
NOUN a plan of how something is expected to work: *the blueprint for successful living*

blues
NOUN The blues is a type of music that is similar to jazz, but is always slow and sad.

bluff bluffs bluffing bluffed
NOUN **1.** an attempt to make someone wrongly believe that you are in a strong position
VERB **2.** If you are bluffing, you are trying to make someone believe that you are in a position of strength.

blunder blunders blundering blundered
VERB **1.** If you blunder, you make a silly mistake.
NOUN **2.** a silly mistake

blunt blunter bluntest
ADJECTIVE **1.** A blunt object has a rounded end or edge, rather than a sharp one. **2.** If you are blunt, you say exactly what you think, without trying to be polite.

blur blurs blurring blurred
NOUN **1.** a shape or area that you cannot see clearly because it has no distinct outline or because it is moving very fast
VERB **2.** To blur the differences between things means to make them no longer clear: *The dreams blurred confusingly with her memories.*
blurred ADJECTIVE

blurt out blurts out blurting out blurted out
VERB If you blurt something out, you say it suddenly, after trying to keep it a secret.

blush blushes blushing blushed
VERB **1.** If you blush, your face becomes red because you are embarrassed or ashamed.
NOUN **2.** the red colour on someone's face when that person is embarrassed or ashamed

bluster blusters blustering blustered
VERB **1.** When someone blusters, that person behaves aggressively because he or she is angry or frightened.
NOUN **2.** Bluster is aggressive behaviour by someone who is angry or frightened: *Her bluster did nothing to calm the fears of everyone else around her.*

blustery
ADJECTIVE Blustery weather is rough and windy.

boa boas
NOUN **1.** A boa, or a boa constrictor, is a large snake that kills its prey by coiling around it and crushing it. **2.** a long thin scarf of feathers or fur

boar boars
NOUN a wild pig, or a male domestic pig used for breeding

board boards boarding boarded
NOUN **1.** a long, flat piece of wood **2.** the group of people who control a company or organization: *the school board, the board of directors* **3.** Board is the meals provided when you stay somewhere: *The price includes full board.*
VERB **4.** If you board a ship, train, or aircraft, you get on it or in it.
PHRASE **5.** If you are **on board** a ship, train, or aircraft, you are on it or in it.

boarder boarders
NOUN a student who lives at school during term

boarding school boarding schools
NOUN a school where the students live during the term

boardroom boardrooms
NOUN a room where the board of a company meets

boast boasts boasting boasted
VERB **1.** If you boast about your possessions or achievements, you talk about them proudly.
NOUN **2.** something you say that shows you are proud of what you own or have done

boastful
ADJECTIVE tending to brag about things

boat boats
NOUN a small vehicle for travelling across water

 HEADS UP

What's the difference between a **boat** and a **ship**? Well, you can put a boat onto a ship.

bob bobs bobbing bobbed
VERB **1.** When something bobs, it moves up and down.
NOUN **2.** a woman's hair style in which her hair is cut level with her chin

bobbin bobbins
NOUN a small round object on which thread or wool is wound

bode bodes boding boded
PHRASE *a literary or poetic word* If something **bodes ill**, or **bodes well**, it makes you think that something bad, or good, will happen.

bodice bodices
NOUN the upper part of a dress

bodily
ADJECTIVE **1.** relating to the body: *bodily contact*
ADVERB **2.** involving the whole of someone's body: *He was carried bodily up the steps.*

body bodies
NOUN **1.** Your body is either all your physical parts, or just the main part not including your head, arms, and legs. **2.** a person's dead body **3.** the main part of a motor vehicle or aircraft, not including the engine **4.** A body of people is also an organized group.

bodyguard bodyguards
NOUN a person employed to protect someone

bodywork
NOUN the outer part of a motor vehicle

bog bogs
NOUN an area of land that is always wet and spongy

boggle boggles boggling boggled
VERB If your mind boggles at something, you find it difficult to imagine or understand: *The number of stars in the universe is so large, it boggles the mind.*

bogus
ADJECTIVE not genuine: *a bogus doctor*

bohemian
ADJECTIVE Someone who is bohemian does not behave in the same way as most other people in society, and is usually involved in the arts.

boil boils boiling boiled
VERB **1.** When a hot liquid boils, bubbles appear in it and it starts to give off steam.
2. When you boil a kettle, you heat it until the water in it boils. **3.** When you boil food, you cook it in boiling water.
NOUN **4.** a red swelling on your skin

boiler boilers
NOUN a tank that heats water to be used for heating or running equipment

boiling
ADJECTIVE *an informal word* very hot

boisterous
ADJECTIVE Someone who is boisterous is noisy and lively.

bold bolder boldest
ADJECTIVE **1.** confident and not shy or embarrassed: *He was not bold enough to ask them.* **2.** not afraid of risk or danger **3.** clear and noticeable: *bold colours*
boldly ADVERB
boldness NOUN

bolster bolsters bolstering bolstered
VERB To bolster something means to support it or make it stronger: *She relied on others to bolster her self-esteem.*

bolt bolts bolting bolted
NOUN **1.** a metal bar that you slide across a door or window in order to fasten it **2.** a metal object that screws into a nut and is used to fasten things together
VERB **3.** If you bolt a door or window, you fasten it using a bolt. If you bolt things together, you fasten them together using a bolt. **4.** To bolt means to escape or run away. **5.** To bolt food means to eat it very quickly.

bomb bombs bombing bombed
NOUN **1.** a container filled with material that explodes when it hits something or is set off by a timer
VERB **2.** When a place is bombed, it is attacked with bombs.

Bb

bombard bombards bombarding bombarded
VERB **1.** To bombard a place means to attack it with heavy gunfire or bombs. **2.** If you are bombarded with something you are made to face a great deal of it: *I was bombarded with criticism. We are bombarded with advertising.*
bombardment NOUN

bomber bombers
NOUN an aircraft that drops bombs

bombshell bombshells
NOUN a sudden piece of shocking news

bona fide
ADJECTIVE genuine: *We are happy to donate to bona fide charities.*

bond bonds bonding bonded
NOUN **1.** a close relationship between people **2.** *a literary or poetic use* Bonds are chains or ropes used to tie a prisoner up. **3.** a certificate that records that you have lent money to a government or business and that it will repay you the loan with interest **4.** Bonds are also feelings or obligations that force you to behave in a particular way: *the social bonds of community*
VERB **5.** When two things bond or are bonded, they become closely linked or attached.

bondage
NOUN Bondage is the condition of being someone's slave.

bone bones
NOUN Bones are the hard parts that form the framework of a person's or animal's body.
boneless ADJECTIVE

bonfire bonfires
NOUN a large fire made outdoors

⚠ **HEADS UP**

The word **bonfire** comes from an older word, **bonefire**. These types of fires were once used for burning corpses.

bonnet bonnets
NOUN a baby's or woman's hat tied under the chin

bonus bonuses
NOUN **1.** an amount of money added to your usual pay **2.** Something that is a bonus is a good thing that you get in addition to something else: *The view from the hotel was an added bonus.*

bony bonier boniest
ADJECTIVE Bony people or animals are thin, with very little flesh covering their bones.

boo boos booing booed
NOUN **1.** a shout of disapproval
VERB **2.** When people boo, they shout *boo* to show their disapproval.

book books booking booked
NOUN **1.** a number of pages held together inside a cover
VERB **2.** When you book something such as a room, you arrange to have it or use it at a particular time.

bookcase bookcases
NOUN a piece of furniture with shelves for books

booking bookings
NOUN an arrangement to book something such as a hotel room

bookkeeping
NOUN Bookkeeping is the keeping of a record of the money spent and received by a business.

booklet booklets
NOUN a small book with a paper cover

bookmark bookmarks
NOUN a piece of card that you put between the pages of a book to mark your place

boom booms booming boomed
NOUN **1.** a rapid increase in something: *the baby boom* **2.** a loud, deep, echoing sound
VERB **3.** When something booms, it increases rapidly: *Sales are booming.* **4.** To boom means to make a loud, deep, echoing sound.

boomerang boomerangs
NOUN a curved wooden missile that can be thrown so that it returns to the thrower, originally used as a weapon by Australian Aborigines

boon boons
NOUN Something that is a boon makes life better or easier: *Credit cards have been a boon to shoppers.*

boost boosts boosting boosted
VERB **1.** To boost something means to cause it to improve or increase: *The campaign had boosted sales.*
NOUN **2.** an improvement or increase: *a boost to the economy*
booster NOUN

boot boots booting booted
NOUN **1.** Boots are strong shoes that come up over your ankle and sometimes your calf.
VERB **2.** *an informal use* If you boot something, you kick it.
PHRASE **3.** **To boot** means also or in addition: *The story was compelling and well written to boot.*

Bb

booth booths
NOUN a small, partly enclosed area: *a telephone booth, a voting booth*

booty
NOUN Booty is valuable things taken from a place, especially by pirates or soldiers after a battle.

border borders bordering bordered
NOUN **1.** the dividing line between two places or things **2.** a strip or band around the edge of something: *plain tiles with a bright border* **3.** a long flower bed in a garden
VERB **4.** To border something means to form a boundary along the side of it: *Tall poplar trees bordered the fields.*

borderline
ADJECTIVE near the dividing line between two categories: *a borderline pass*

bore bores boring bored
VERB **1.** If something bores you, you find it dull and not at all interesting. **2.** If you bore a hole in something, you make the hole by using a tool such as a drill.
NOUN **3.** someone or something that bores you

bored
ADJECTIVE If you are bored, you are impatient because you do not find something interesting or because you have nothing to do.

boredom
NOUN a lack of interest

boring
ADJECTIVE dull and lacking interest

born
VERB **1.** When a baby is born, it comes out of its mother's womb at the beginning of its life.
ADJECTIVE **2.** You use *born* to mean that someone has a particular quality from birth: *He was a born pessimist.*

borne the past participle of BEAR

borough boroughs
NOUN In former times in Ontario, a borough was an urban community with the status of township rather than a city.

borrow borrows borrowing borrowed
VERB If you borrow something that belongs to someone else, that person lets you have it for a period of time.
borrower NOUN

bosom bosoms
NOUN **1.** A woman's bosom is her breasts.
ADJECTIVE **2.** A bosom friend is a very close friend.

boss bosses bossing bossed
NOUN **1.** Someone's boss is the person in charge of the area where that person works.
VERB **2.** If someone bosses you around, that person keeps telling you what to do.

bossy bossier bossiest
ADJECTIVE A bossy person enjoys telling other people what to do.
bossiness NOUN

botany
NOUN Botany is the scientific study of plants.
botanical ADJECTIVE
botanist NOUN

botch botches botching botched
VERB *an informal word* If you botch something, you do it badly or clumsily.

both
ADJECTIVE OR PRONOUN *Both* is used when saying something about two people or things: *Both of her brothers are very tall. Both cakes are delicious.*

bother bothers bothering bothered
VERB **1.** If you do not bother to do something, you do not do it because it takes too much effort or it seems unnecessary. **2.** If something bothers you, you are worried or concerned about it. If you do not bother about it, you are not concerned about it: *She is not bothered about money.* **3.** If you bother someone, you interrupt that person when he or she is busy.
NOUN **4.** Bother is trouble, fuss, or difficulty.
bothersome ADJECTIVE

bottle bottles bottling bottled
NOUN **1.** a glass or plastic container for

SPELL-CHECK THIS!

A computer's spell-check won't catch wrong **homophones** (words that are spelled differently but sound the same).

▼✕

When we're board on a rainy day, we play bored games.

In this sentence, **board** and **bored** are mixed up. **Bored** means *not excited*. A **board** is a *flat surface*.

Bb

keeping liquids in
VERB **2.** To bottle something means to store it in bottles.

bottleneck bottlenecks
NOUN a narrow section of road where traffic has to slow down or stop

bottom bottoms
NOUN **1.** The bottom of something is its lowest part. **2.** Your bottom is your buttocks. ADJECTIVE **3.** The bottom thing in a series of things is the lowest one.
bottomless ADJECTIVE

bough boughs
NOUN a large branch of a tree

bought the past tense and past participle of BUY

boulder boulders
NOUN a large rounded rock

boulevard boulevards
NOUN a wide street in a city, usually with trees along each side

bounce bounces bouncing bounced
VERB **1.** When an object bounces, it springs back from something after hitting it. **2.** To bounce also means to move up and down: *Her long black hair bounced as she walked.* **3.** If a cheque bounces, the bank refuses to accept it because there is not enough money in the account.

bouncy bouncier bounciest
ADJECTIVE **1.** Someone who is bouncy is lively and enthusiastic. **2.** Something that is bouncy is capable of bouncing or being bounced on: *a bouncy ball, a bouncy mattress*

bound bounds bounding bounded
ADJECTIVE **1.** If you say that something is bound to happen, you mean that it is certain to happen. **2.** If people or vehicles are bound for a place, they are going there. **3.** If someone is bound by an agreement or regulation, that person must obey it. NOUN **4.** a large leap PLURAL NOUN **5.** Bounds are limits that restrict or control something: *Their enthusiasm knew no bounds.* PHRASE **6.** If a place is **out of bounds**, you are forbidden to go there. VERB **7.** When animals or people bound, they move quickly with large leaps: *He bounded up the stairway.* **8.** Bound is also the past tense and past participle of BIND.

boundary boundaries
NOUN something that indicates the furthest limit of anything: *the city boundary, the boundaries of taste*

boundless
ADJECTIVE without end or limit: *her boundless energy*

bountiful
ADJECTIVE *a literary or poetic word* freely available in large amounts: *a bountiful harvest*

bounty
NOUN **1.** *a literary or poetic word* Bounty is a generous supply: *autumn's bounty of fruits* **2.** Someone's bounty is that person's generosity in giving a lot of something.

bouquet bouquets
NOUN an attractively arranged bunch of flowers

bourgeois
ADJECTIVE typical of middle-class people

bourgeoisie
NOUN the middle-class people in a society

bout bouts
NOUN **1.** If you have a bout of something such as an illness, you have it for a short time: *a bout of flu* **2.** If you have a bout of doing something, you do it enthusiastically for a short time. **3.** a boxing or wrestling match

boutique boutiques
NOUN a small shop or department in a store that sells fashionable items

bovine
ADJECTIVE relating to cattle

bow bows bowing bowed
VERB **1.** When you bow, you bend your body or lower your head as a sign of respect or greeting. **2.** If you bow to something, you give in to it: *He bowed to public pressure.* NOUN **3.** the movement you make when you bow **4.** the front part of a ship

bow bows
NOUN **1.** a knot with two loops and two loose ends: *Please help your little sister tie a bow in her hair.* **2.** a long, thin piece of wood with horsehair stretched along it that you use to play a violin **3.** a long, flexible piece of wood used for shooting arrows

bowel bowels
NOUN Your bowels are the tubes leading from your stomach, through which waste passes before it leaves your body.

bowl bowls bowling bowled
NOUN **1.** a round container with a wide, uncovered top, used for holding liquid or for serving food **2.** the hollow, rounded part of something: *a toilet bowl* VERB **3.** To bowl means to play the game of bowling.
bowler NOUN

⚠ HEADS UP **Bow** can be pronounced in two ways: *BOW before the queen! She tied a BO in her hair.*

Bb

bowling
NOUN Bowling is a game in which you roll a ball down a narrow track toward five or ten wooden objects called pins and try to knock them down.

bow tie bow ties
NOUN a man's necktie in the form of a bow

box boxes boxing boxed
NOUN **1.** a container with a firm base and sides and usually a lid **2.** On a form, a box is a rectangular space that you have to fill in. **3.** In a theatre or at a sports event, a box is a small separate area where a few people can watch the performance or event together.
VERB **4.** To box means to fight someone according to the rules of boxing.

boxer boxers
NOUN **1.** a person who boxes **2.** a medium-sized, smooth-haired dog with a flat face

boxing
NOUN Boxing is a sport in which two people fight using their fists, wearing padded gloves.

box office box offices
NOUN the place where tickets are sold for various events such as movies, concerts, and shows

boy boys
NOUN a male child
boyhood NOUN
boyish ADJECTIVE

boycott boycotts boycotting boycotted
VERB **1.** If you boycott an organization or event, you refuse to have anything to do with it.
NOUN **2.** the boycotting of an organization or event: *a boycott of the elections*

boyfriend boyfriends
NOUN Someone's boyfriend is the man or boy with whom that person is having a romantic relationship.

bra bras
NOUN a piece of underwear worn by a woman to support her breasts

brace braces bracing braced
VERB **1.** When you brace yourself, you stiffen your body to steady yourself: *The ship lurched and he braced himself.* **2.** If you brace yourself for something unpleasant, you prepare yourself to deal with it: *The islanders braced themselves for the coming hurricane.*
NOUN **3.** an object fastened to something to straighten or support it: *a neck brace*

bracelet bracelets
NOUN a chain or band worn around someone's wrist as an ornament

bracing
ADJECTIVE Something that is bracing makes you feel fit and full of energy: *the bracing sea air*

bracken
NOUN Bracken is a plant like a large fern that grows on hills and in woods.

bracket brackets
NOUN **1.** Brackets are a pair of written marks, ( ), [ ], or { }, placed around a word or sentence that is not part of the main text, or to show that the items inside the brackets belong together. **2.** a piece of metal or wood fastened to a wall to support something such as a shelf

brag brags bragging bragged
VERB When people brag, they boast about their achievements: *Both leaders bragged they could win by a landslide.*

braggart braggarts
NOUN someone who brags

braid braids braiding braided
NOUN **1.** Braid is a strip of decorated cloth used to decorate clothes or curtains. **2.** a length of hair that has been woven together using three or more strands or bunches and tied
VERB **3.** To braid hair or yarn means to weave it.

Braille
NOUN Braille is a system of printing for blind people in which letters are represented by raised dots that can be felt with the fingers.

> ⚠ **HEADS UP**
>
> Braille is named after Louis Braille, a blind man who invented the system in the 1800s.

brain brains
NOUN **1.** Your brain is the mass of nerve tissue inside your head that controls your body and enables you to think and feel; also used to refer to your mind and the way that you think: *I admired his artistic brain.*
PLURAL NOUN **2.** If you say that someone **has brains,** you mean that that person is very intelligent.

brainchild
NOUN *an informal word* Someone's brainchild is something that that person has invented or created.

brainstorm brainstorms brainstormed
VERB quickly gather as many ideas as possible from a group of people

brainwash brainwashes brainwashing brainwashed
VERB If people are brainwashed into believing something, they accept it without question because they are told it repeatedly.
brainwashing NOUN

brainwave brainwaves
NOUN *an informal word* a clever idea you think of suddenly

brainy brainier brainiest
ADJECTIVE *an informal word* clever

braise braises braising braised
VERB To braise food means to fry it for a short time, then cook it slowly in a little liquid.

brake brakes braking braked
NOUN **1.** a device for making a vehicle stop or slow down
VERB **2.** When a driver brakes, he or she makes a vehicle stop or slow down by using its brakes.

bramble brambles
NOUN a wild, thorny bush that produces blackberries

bran
NOUN Bran is the ground husks that are left over after flour has been made from wheat grains.

branch branches branching branched
NOUN **1.** The branches of a tree are the parts that grow out from its trunk. **2.** A branch of an organization is one of a number of its offices. **3.** A branch of a subject is one of its areas of study or activity: *specialists in certain branches of medicine*
VERB **4.** A road that branches off from another road splits off from it to lead in a different direction.

brand brands branding branded
NOUN **1.** A brand of something is a particular kind or make of it: *a popular brand of chocolate*
VERB **2.** When an animal is branded, a mark is burned on its skin to show who owns it.

brandish brandishes brandishing brandished
VERB *a literary or poetic word* If you brandish something, you wave it vigorously: *He brandished his sword over his head.*

brand new
ADJECTIVE completely new

brandy
NOUN a strong alcoholic drink, usually made from wine

brash brasher brashest
ADJECTIVE If someone is brash, that person is overconfident or rather rude.

brass
NOUN OR ADJECTIVE **1.** Brass is a yellow-coloured metal made from copper and zinc. **2.** In an orchestra, the brass section consists of brass wind instruments such as trumpets and trombones.

brassiere brassieres
NOUN *a formal word* a bra

brat brats
NOUN *an informal word* A badly behaved child may be referred to as a brat.

bravado
NOUN Bravado is a display of courage intended to impress other people.

brave braver bravest; braves braving braved
ADJECTIVE **1.** A brave person is willing to do dangerous things and does not show any fear.
VERB **2.** If you brave an unpleasant or dangerous situation, you face up to it in order to do something: *His fans braved the rain to hear him sing.*
bravely ADVERB

bravery
NOUN the quality of being courageous

bravo
INTERJECTION People shout *Bravo!* to express appreciation when something has been done well.

brawl brawls brawling brawled
NOUN **1.** a rough fight
VERB **2.** When people brawl, they take part in a rough fight.

brawn
NOUN Brawn is physical strength.
brawny ADJECTIVE

bray brays braying brayed
VERB **1.** When a donkey brays, it makes a loud, harsh sound.
NOUN **2.** the sound a donkey makes

brazen
ADJECTIVE When people's behaviour is brazen, they do not care if other people think they are behaving wrongly.
brazenly ADVERB

breach breaches breaching breached
VERB **1.** *a formal word* If you breach an agreement or law, you break it. **2.** To breach a barrier means to make a gap in it: *The river breached its banks.*
NOUN **3.** A breach of an agreement or law is an action that breaks it: *a breach of contract* **4.** a gap or break

bread
NOUN a food made from flour and water, usually raised with yeast, and baked

Bb

breadth
NOUN The breadth of something is the distance between its two sides.

breadwinner breadwinners
NOUN the person who earns the money in a family

break breaks breaking broke broken
VERB **1.** When an object breaks, it is damaged and separates into pieces. **2.** If you break a rule or promise, you fail to keep it. **3.** When a boy's voice breaks, it becomes permanently deeper.
4. When a wave breaks, it falls and becomes foam. **5.** When you break for a short period of time, you rest or do something different: *Let's break for dinner.*
NOUN **6.** a short

period during which you rest or do something different: *Let's take a break for ten minutes.*

break down
VERB **7.** When a machine or a vehicle breaks down, it stops working. **8.** When a discussion or relationship breaks down, it ends because of problems or disagreements

break up
VERB **9.** If a relationship breaks up, it ends: *The marriage broke up after a year.*

breakable ADJECTIVE

breakage breakages
NOUN the act of breaking something or a thing that has been broken

breakaway
ADJECTIVE A breakaway group is one that has separated from a larger group.

breakdown breakdowns
NOUN **1.** The breakdown of something such as a system is its failure: *a breakdown in communications* **2.** If you have a breakdown, you experience a complete loss of health or strength: *a nervous breakdown* **3.** If a driver has a breakdown, that person's vehicle has stopped working.

breaker breakers
NOUN Breakers are big waves.

breakfast breakfasts
NOUN the first meal of the day

Instead of **BREAK** try...

crack through the ice
crumble a cookie
snap a twig
fracture a bone
splinter wood
demolish a wall
breach a contract
shatter a window

break-in break-ins
NOUN the illegal entering of a building, especially by a burglar

breakneck
ADJECTIVE *an informal word* Someone or something that is travelling at breakneck speed is travelling dangerously fast.

breakthrough breakthroughs
NOUN an important development: *a medical breakthrough*

breakwater breakwaters
NOUN a wall extending into a body of water that protects a shoreline or harbour from the force of the waves

breast breasts
NOUN A woman's breasts are the two soft, fleshy parts on her chest that produce milk after she has had a baby.

breath breaths
NOUN **1.** Your breath is the air you take into your lungs and let out again when you breathe.
PHRASE **2.** If you are **out of breath**, you are breathing with difficulty after doing something energetic. **3.** If you say something **under your breath**, you say it in a very quiet voice.

breathe breathes breathing breathed
VERB When you breathe, you take air into your lungs and let it out again.

! HEADS UP

Breath is a noun, pronounced BRETH.
Breathe is a verb, pronounced BREETH.

breathless
ADJECTIVE If you are breathless, you are breathing fast or with difficulty.
breathlessly ADVERB
breathlessness NOUN

breathtaking
ADJECTIVE If you say that something is breathtaking, you mean that it is very beautiful or exciting.

bred the past tense and past participle of BREED

breeches
PLURAL NOUN Breeches are pants reaching to just below the knee, nowadays worn especially for riding.

breed breeds breeding bred
NOUN **1.** A breed of a species of domestic animal is a particular type of it.
VERB **2.** Someone who breeds animals or

plants keeps them to produce more animals or plants with particular qualities. **3.** When animals breed, they mate and produce offspring.

breeze breezes
NOUN a gentle wind

brevity
NOUN *a formal word* Brevity means shortness: *the brevity of his report*

brew brews brewing brewed
VERB **1.** If you brew tea or coffee, you make it in a pot by pouring hot water over it. **2.** To brew beer means to make it, by boiling and fermenting malt. **3.** If an unpleasant situation is brewing, it is about to happen: *Another scandal is brewing.*
brewer NOUN

brewery breweries
NOUN a place where beer is made, or a company that makes it

briar another spelling of BRIER

bribe bribes bribing bribed
NOUN **1.** a gift or money given to an official to persuade that person to make a favourable decision
VERB **2.** To bribe someone means to give that person a bribe.
bribery NOUN

bric-a-brac
NOUN Bric-a-brac consists of small ornaments or knick-knacks of no great value.

brick bricks
NOUN Bricks are rectangular blocks of baked clay used in building.

⚠ HEADS UP

The expression **a few bricks short of a load** means *a bit stupid*. Do you know any similar expressions?

bricklayer bricklayers
NOUN a person whose job is to build with bricks

bride brides
NOUN a woman who is getting married or who has just got married
bridal ADJECTIVE

bridegroom bridegrooms
NOUN a man who is getting married or who has just got married

bridesmaid bridesmaids
NOUN a woman who helps a bride and accompanies her on her wedding day

bridge bridges
NOUN **1.** a structure built over a river, road, or railway so that vehicles and people can cross **2.** the platform from which a ship is steered and controlled **3.** the hard ridge at the top of your nose **4.** Bridge is a card game for four players.

bridle bridles
NOUN a set of straps around a horse's head and mouth that the rider uses to control the horse

brief briefer briefest; briefs briefing briefed
ADJECTIVE **1.** Something that is brief lasts only a short time.
VERB **2.** When you brief someone on a task, you give that person all the necessary instructions and information about it.
briefly ADVERB

briefcase briefcases
NOUN a small flat case for carrying papers

briefing briefings
NOUN a meeting at which information and instructions are given

brier briers
NOUN a dense prickly bush, especially the wild rose

brigade brigades
NOUN an army unit consisting of three battalions

brigadier general brigadier generals
NOUN an army officer of the rank immediately above colonel

bright brighter brightest
ADJECTIVE **1.** strong and startling: *a bright light* **2.** clever: *the brightest student* **3.** cheerful: *a bright smile*
brightly ADVERB
brightness NOUN

brighten brightens brightening brightened
VERB **1.** If something brightens, it becomes brighter: *The weather had brightened.* **2.** If someone brightens, that person suddenly looks happier.
brighten up
VERB **3.** To brighten something up means to make it more attractive and cheerful.

brilliant
ADJECTIVE **1.** A brilliant light or colour is extremely bright. **2.** A brilliant person is extremely clever. **3.** A brilliant career is extremely successful.
brilliantly ADVERB
brilliance NOUN

brim brims
NOUN **1.** the edge of a cup or container **2.** The brim is the wide part of a hat that sticks outward at the bottom.

Bb

brine
NOUN Brine is salt water.

bring brings bringing brought
VERB **1.** If you bring something or someone with you when you go to a place, you take that person or thing with you: *You can bring a friend to the party.* **2.** To bring something to a particular state means to cause it to be like that: *Bring the vegetables to the boil.*
bring about
VERB **3.** To bring something about means to cause it to happen: *We must try to bring about a better world.*
bring up
VERB **4.** To bring up children means to look after them while they grow up. **5.** If you bring up a subject, you introduce it into the conversation: *She brought up the subject at dinner.*

⚠ HEADS UP

Don't confuse the words **bring** and **take**. **Bring** means *carry to*. **Take** means *carry away*.

brink
PHRASE If you are **on the brink of** something, you are just about to do it or experience it.

brisk brisker briskest
ADJECTIVE **1.** A brisk action is done quickly and energetically: *A brisk walk restores your energy.* **2.** If someone's manner is brisk, it shows that that person wants to get things done quickly and efficiently.
briskly ADVERB
briskness NOUN

bristle bristles bristling bristled
NOUN **1.** Bristles are strong animal hairs used to make brushes.
VERB **2.** If the hairs on an animal's body bristle, they rise up because it is frightened.
bristly ADJECTIVE

brittle
ADJECTIVE An object that is brittle is hard but breaks easily.

broach broaches broaching broached
VERB When you broach a subject, you introduce it into a discussion.

broad broader broadest
ADJECTIVE **1.** wide: *a broad smile* **2.** having many different aspects or concerning many different people: *A broad range of issues was discussed.* **3.** general rather than detailed: *the broad concerns of the government*

broadband
NOUN Broadband is a digital system used on the Internet and in other forms of telecommunication that can process and transfer information input from various sources, such as from telephones, computers, or televisions.

broadcast broadcasts broadcasting broadcast
NOUN **1.** a program or announcement on radio or television
VERB **2.** To broadcast something means to send it out by radio waves, so that it can be seen on television or heard on radio.
broadcaster NOUN
broadcasting NOUN

broaden broadens broadening broadened
VERB **1.** When something broadens, it becomes wider: *His smile broadened.* **2.** To broaden something means to cause it to involve more things or concern more people: *The company plans to broaden the scope of this job.*

broadly
ADVERB true to a large extent or in most cases: *There are broadly two schools of thought on this.*

broad-minded
ADJECTIVE Someone who is broad-minded does not disapprove of behaviour or attitudes that many other people disapprove of.

broadsheet broadsheets
NOUN a newspaper with large pages and long news stories

brocade
NOUN Brocade is a heavy, expensive material, often made of silk, with a raised pattern.

broccoli
NOUN a green vegetable, closely related to cauliflower

brochure brochures
NOUN a booklet or leaflet that gives information about a product or service

broke
1. the past tense of BREAK **2.** *an informal use* If you are broke, you have no money.

broken
ADJECTIVE If something is broken, it is in pieces.

broker brokers
NOUN a person whose job is to buy or sell certain items for other people

bronchitis
NOUN Bronchitis is an illness in which the two tubes that connect your windpipe to your lungs become infected, making you cough.

brontosaurus brontosauruses
NOUN a type of very large, plant-eating dinosaur

bronze
NOUN Bronze is a yellowish brown metal that is a mixture of copper and tin; also the yellowish brown colour of this metal.

brooch brooches
NOUN a piece of jewellery with a pin at the back for attaching it to clothes

brood broods brooding brooded
NOUN **1.** a family of baby birds
VERB **2.** If you brood about something, you keep thinking about it in a serious or unhappy way.

brook brooks
NOUN a stream

broom brooms
NOUN a long-handled brush for sweeping

broth
NOUN Broth is the water in which meat, fish, or vegetables have been boiled. It is often used as a thin soup or a base for soup.

brother brothers
NOUN Your brother is a boy or man who has the same parents as you.
brotherly ADJECTIVE

brotherhood brotherhoods
NOUN **1.** Brotherhood is the affection and loyalty that brothers or close male friends feel for each other. **2.** a group of men with common interests or beliefs

brother-in-law brothers-in-law
NOUN Someone's brother-in-law is the brother of that person's husband or wife, or his or her sister's husband.

brought the past tense and past participle of BRING

brow brows
NOUN **1.** Your brow is your forehead. **2.** Your brows are your eyebrows. **3.** The brow of a hill is the top of it.

brown browner brownest
ADJECTIVE OR NOUN Brown is the colour of earth or wood.

brownie brownies
NOUN a small square or bar of rich, dense, chocolate cake

browse browses browsing browsed
VERB **1.** If you browse through a book, you look through it in a casual way. **2.** If you browse in a store, you look at the things in it for interest rather than because you want to buy something.

browser browsers
NOUN a piece of computer software that lets you look at websites on the Internet

bruise bruises bruising bruised
NOUN **1.** a purple mark that appears on your skin after something has hit it
VERB **2.** If something bruises you, it hits you so that a bruise appears on your skin.

brunette brunettes
NOUN a girl or woman with dark brown hair

brunt
PHRASE If you **bear the brunt** of something unpleasant, you are the person who suffers most: *I bore the brunt of the housework.*

brush brushes brushing brushed
NOUN **1.** an object with bristles that you use for cleaning things, painting, or tidying your hair
VERB **2.** If you brush something, you clean it or tidy it with a brush. **3.** To brush against something means to touch it while passing it: *Her lips brushed his cheek.*

brusque
ADJECTIVE Someone who is brusque deals with people quickly and without considering their feelings.
brusquely ADVERB

Brussels sprouts
PLURAL NOUN Brussels sprouts are vegetables that look like tiny cabbages.

brutal
ADJECTIVE Brutal behaviour is cruel and violent: *the victim of a brutal murder*
brutally ADVERB
brutality NOUN

brute brutes
NOUN **1.** a rough and insensitive person
ADJECTIVE **2.** Brute force is strength alone, without any skill: *You have to use brute force to open the gates.*
brutish ADJECTIVE

bubble bubbles bubbling bubbled
NOUN **1.** a ball of air in a liquid **2.** a hollow, delicate ball of soapy liquid
VERB **3.** When a liquid bubbles, bubbles form in it. **4.** If you are bubbling with excitement, you are full of enthusiasm.
bubbly ADJECTIVE

buck bucks bucking bucked
NOUN **1.** the male of various animals, including the deer and the rabbit
VERB **2.** If a horse bucks, it jumps into the air with its feet off the ground.

bucket buckets
NOUN a deep, round container with an open top and a handle

Bb

buckle buckles buckling buckled
NOUN **1.** a fastening on the end of a belt
VERB **2.** If you buckle a belt or strap, you fasten it. **3.** If something buckles, it becomes bent because of severe heat or pressure.

bud buds budding budded
NOUN **1.** a small, tight swelling on a tree or plant that develops into a flower or a cluster of leaves
VERB **2.** When a tree or plant buds, new buds appear on it.

Buddha
NOUN the title of Siddhartha Gautama, a religious teacher living in the sixth century BCE in India and founder of Buddhism. Buddha means *the enlightened one*.

Buddhism
NOUN Buddhism is a religion, founded by Buddha, that teaches that the way to end suffering is by overcoming your desires.
Buddhist NOUN OR ADJECTIVE

budding
ADJECTIVE just beginning to develop: *a budding artist*

budge budges budging budged
VERB If something will not budge, you cannot move it.

budget budgets budgeting budgeted
NOUN **1.** a plan showing how much money will be available and how it will be spent
VERB **2.** If you budget for something, you plan your money carefully, so that you are able to afford it.
budgetary ADJECTIVE

budgie budgies
NOUN *an informal word* A budgie is a small, brightly coloured pet bird. The full name is *budgerigar*.

buff buffs
ADJECTIVE **1.** a pale brown colour
NOUN **2.** *an informal use* someone who knows a lot about a subject: *a hockey buff*

buffalo buffaloes
NOUN an animal like a large cow with curved horns

buffer buffers
NOUN something that prevents something else from being harmed: *keep savings as a buffer against unexpected cash needs*

⚠ HEADS UP

Buffet the meal is pronounced buh-FAY. **Buffet** the action is pronounced BUFF-et.

---

buffet buffets
NOUN a meal at which people serve themselves

buffet buffets buffeting buffeted
VERB If the wind or sea buffets a place or person, it strikes the place or person violently and repeatedly.

bug bugs bugging bugged
NOUN **1.** an insect, especially one that causes damage **2.** a small error in a computer program, which means that the program will not work properly **3.** *an informal use* a virus or minor infection: *a stomach bug*
VERB **4.** If a place is bugged, tiny microphones are hidden there to pick up what people are saying.

bugle bugles
NOUN a brass instrument that looks like a small trumpet
bugler NOUN

build builds building built
VERB **1.** To build something such as a house means to make it from its parts. **2.** To build something such as an organization means to develop it gradually.
NOUN **3.** Your build is the shape and size of your body.
builder NOUN

building buildings
NOUN a structure with walls and a roof

bulb bulbs
NOUN **1.** an electric light bulb **2.** an onion-shaped root that grows into a flower or plant

bulge bulges bulging bulged
VERB **1.** If something bulges, it swells out from a surface.
NOUN **2.** a lump on a normally flat surface

bulk bulks
NOUN **1.** a large mass of something: *The book is more impressive for its bulk than its content.* **2.** The bulk of something is most of it: *the bulk of the world's great poetry*
PHRASE **3.** To buy something **in bulk** means to buy it in large quantities.

bulky bulkier bulkiest
ADJECTIVE large and heavy: *a bulky package*

bull bulls
NOUN the male of some species of animals, including the cow family, elephants, and whales

NEL

Bb

bulldog bulldogs
NOUN a squat dog with a broad head and muscular body

bulldozer bulldozers
NOUN a powerful tractor with a broad blade in front, used for moving earth or knocking things down

bullet bullets
NOUN a small piece of metal fired from a gun

bulletin bulletins
NOUN **1.** a short news report on radio or television **2.** a leaflet or small newspaper regularly produced by a group or organization

bullion
NOUN Bullion is gold or silver in the shape of bars.

bullock bullocks
NOUN a young, castrated bull

bully bullies bullying bullied
NOUN **1.** someone who uses strength or power to hurt or frighten other people
VERB **2.** If you bully someone, you frighten or hurt that person deliberately. **3.** If someone bullies you into doing something, that person makes you do it by using force or threats.

bump bumps bumping bumped
VERB **1.** If you bump or bump into something, you knock it with a jolt.
NOUN **2.** a soft or dull noise made by something knocking into something else **3.** a raised, uneven part of a surface
bumpy ADJECTIVE

bumper bumpers
NOUN **1.** Bumpers are bars on the front and back of a vehicle that protect it if there is a collision.
ADJECTIVE **2.** A bumper crop or harvest is one that is larger than usual.

bun buns
NOUN a small bread roll

bunch bunches bunching bunched
NOUN **1.** a group of people **2.** a number of flowers held or tied

Instead of **BUNCH** try...

together
3. a group of things
4. a group of bananas or grapes growing on the same stem
VERB **5.** When people bunch together or bunch up, they stay very close to each other.

a **mob** of people
a **herd** of cows
a **stack** of books
a **band** of criminals
a **heap** of dirty laundry

bundle bundles bundling bundled
NOUN **1.** a number of things tied together or wrapped up in a cloth
VERB **2.** If you bundle someone or something somewhere, you push that person or thing there quickly and roughly.

bung bungs
NOUN a stopper used to close a hole in something such as a barrel

bungalow bungalows
NOUN a one-storey house

bungle bungles bungling bungled
VERB To bungle something means to fail to do it properly.

bunion bunions
NOUN a painful lump on the first joint of a person's big toe

bunk bunks
NOUN a bed fixed to a wall in a ship or camper, or built in a unit that includes two beds, one above the other

bunker bunkers
NOUN **1.** On a golf course, a bunker is a large hole filled with sand. **2.** A bunker is a storage place for fuel on a ship. **3.** an underground shelter with strong walls to protect it from bombing

bunting
NOUN Bunting is strips of small coloured flags displayed on streets and buildings on special occasions.

buoy buoys
NOUN a floating object anchored to the bottom of the sea, river, or lake marking a channel or warning of danger

buoyant
ADJECTIVE **1.** able to float **2.** lively and cheerful: *She was in a buoyant mood.*
buoyancy NOUN

burble burbles burbling burbled
VERB To burble means to makes a soft bubbling sound: *The water burbled over the gravel.*

burden burdens
NOUN **1.** a heavy load **2.** If something is a burden to you, it causes you a lot of worry or hard work.
burdensome ADJECTIVE

bureau bureaus
NOUN **1.** an office that provides a service: *an employment bureau* **2.** a chest of drawers or a writing desk with shelves and drawers

bureaucracy
NOUN Bureaucracy is the complex system of rules and procedures that operates in government departments.
bureaucratic ADJECTIVE

Bb

bureaucrat bureaucrats
NOUN a person who works in a government department, especially one who follows rules and procedures strictly

burgeoning
ADJECTIVE growing or developing rapidly: *a burgeoning political crisis*

burglar burglars
NOUN a thief who breaks into a building
burglary NOUN

burial burials
NOUN the act of burying a dead person, or a ceremony held when a dead person is buried

burly burlier burliest
ADJECTIVE A burly person has a broad body and strong muscles.

burn burns burning burned
VERB **1.** If something is burning, it is on fire. **2.** To burn something means to destroy it with fire. **3.** If you burn yourself or are burned, you are injured by fire or by something hot.
NOUN **4.** an injury caused by fire or by something hot

burp burps burping burped
VERB **1.** If you burp, you make a noise because air from your stomach has been forced up through your throat.
NOUN **2.** the noise that you make when you burp

burrow burrows burrowing burrowed
NOUN **1.** a tunnel or hole in the ground dug by a small animal
VERB **2.** When an animal burrows, it digs a burrow.

bursary bursaries
NOUN a sum of money given to someone to help fund that person's education

burst bursts bursting burst
VERB **1.** When something bursts, it splits open because of pressure from inside it. **2.** If you burst into a room, you enter it suddenly. **3.** To burst means to happen or come suddenly and with force: *The aircraft burst into flames.* **4.** *an informal use* If you are bursting with something, you find it difficult to keep it to yourself: *We were bursting with joy.*
NOUN **5.** A burst of something is a short period of it: *He had a sudden burst of energy.*

bury buries burying buried
VERB **1.** When a dead person is buried, that person's body is put into a grave and covered with earth. **2.** To bury something means to put it in a hole in the ground and cover it up.

3. If something is buried under something, it is covered by it: *My bag was buried under a pile of old newspapers.*

bus buses
NOUN a large motor vehicle that carries passengers

bush bushes
NOUN a thick plant with many stems branching out from ground level

bushy bushier bushiest
ADJECTIVE Bushy hair or fur grows very thickly: *bushy eyebrows*

business businesses
NOUN **1.** Business is work relating to the buying and selling of goods and services. **2.** an organization that produces or sells goods or provides a service **3.** You can refer to any event, situation, or activity as a business: *This whole business has upset me.*
businessman NOUN
businesswoman NOUN

businesslike
ADJECTIVE dealing with things in an efficient way

busker buskers
NOUN someone who plays music, sings, or provides other entertainment for money in public places

bust busts busting bust
NOUN **1.** a statue of someone's head and shoulders: *a bust of Beethoven* **2.** A woman's bust is her breasts.
VERB **3.** *an informal use* If you bust something, you break it.
ADJECTIVE **4.** *an informal use* If a business goes bust, it becomes bankrupt and closes down.

bustle bustles bustling bustled
VERB **1.** When people bustle, they move in a busy, hurried way.
NOUN **2.** Bustle is busy, noisy activity.

busy busier busiest; busies busying busied
ADJECTIVE **1.** If you are busy, you are in the middle of doing something. **2.** A busy place is full of people doing things or moving about: *a busy farmers' market*
VERB **3.** If you busy yourself with something, you occupy yourself by doing it.
busily ADVERB

but
CONJUNCTION **1.** used to introduce an idea that is opposite to what has gone before: *I don't miss football practice, but I miss the team.* **2.** used when apologizing: *I'm sorry, but I can't come tonight.* **3.** except: *We can't do anything but wait.*

butcher butchers
NOUN a person who cuts up and sells meat for food

butler butlers
NOUN the chief male servant in a rich household

butt butts butting butted
NOUN **1.** The butt of a weapon is the thick end of its handle. **2.** If you are the butt of teasing, you are the target of it.
VERB **3.** If you butt something, you ram it with your head.

butt in
VERB **4.** If you butt in, you join in a private conversation or activity without being asked to.

butter butters buttering buttered
NOUN **1.** Butter is a solid fat made from cream, which is spread on food and used in cooking.
VERB **2.** To butter bread means to spread butter on it.

buttercup buttercups
NOUN a wild plant with bright yellow flowers

butterfly butterflies
NOUN a type of insect with large colourful wings

buttocks
PLURAL NOUN Your buttocks are the part of your body that you sit on.

button buttons buttoning buttoned
NOUN **1.** Buttons are small, hard objects sewn on clothing, and used to fasten two surfaces together. **2.** a small object on a piece of equipment that you press to make it work
VERB **3.** If you button a piece of clothing, you fasten it using its buttons.

buttonhole buttonholes
NOUN a hole that you push a button through to fasten a piece of clothing

buxom
ADJECTIVE A buxom woman is plump and full-bosomed.

buy buys buying bought
VERB If you buy something, you obtain it by paying money for it.
buyer NOUN

buzz buzzes buzzing buzzed
VERB **1.** If something buzzes, it makes a humming sound, like a bee.
NOUN **2.** the sound something makes when it buzzes

buzzard buzzards
NOUN a large brown and white bird of prey

buzzer buzzers
NOUN a device that makes a buzzing sound, to attract attention

by
PREPOSITION **1.** used to indicate who or what has done something: *The statement was issued by his lawyer.* **2.** used to indicate how something is done: *He frightened her by hiding behind the door.* **3.** located next to: *I sat by her bed.* **4.** before a particular time: *It should be ready by next spring.*
PREPOSITION OR ADVERB **5.** going past: *We drove by our school.*

by-election by-elections
NOUN an election held in a riding to choose a new member of parliament after the previous member has resigned or died

bygone
ADJECTIVE *a literary or poetic word* happening or existing a long time ago: *the ceremonies of a bygone era*

bypass bypasses
NOUN a main road that takes traffic around a city or town rather than through it

bystander bystanders
NOUN someone who is not included or involved in something but is there to see it happen

byte bytes
NOUN a unit of storage in a computer

SPELL-CHECK THIS!

A computer's spell-check won't catch wrong **homophones** (words that are spelled differently but sound the same).

She went out to by her weekly groceries.

In this sentence, **by** should be **buy**.
By can mean *beside* or *through*.
Buy means *purchase*.

Cc

cab cabs

NOUN **1.** a taxi **2.** In a truck, bus, subway, train, or tractor, the cab is where the driver sits.

cabaret cabarets

NOUN a show consisting of dancing, singing, or comedy acts

cabbage cabbages

NOUN a large green or reddish purple leafy vegetable

cabin cabins

NOUN **1.** a room in a ship where a passenger sleeps **2.** a small house, usually in the country and often made of wood **3.** the area where the passengers or the crew sit in a plane

cabinet cabinets

NOUN **1.** a small, upright piece of furniture used to hold or display things: *a medicine cabinet, a china cabinet* **2.** The cabinet in a government is a group of ministers who advise the leader and decide policies.

cable cables

NOUN **1.** a strong, thick rope or chain **2.** a bundle of wires with a rubber covering, which carries electricity **3.** in former times, a message sent abroad by using electricity

cable car cable cars

NOUN a vehicle pulled by a moving cable, for taking people up and down mountains or steep hills

cable television

NOUN a television service people can receive from cables that carry the signals

cacao

NOUN A cacao is a type of small tropical evergreen tree, whose seeds are used to produce chocolate and cocoa.

cache caches

NOUN a store of things hidden away: *a cache of weapons, a cache of acorns*

cachet

NOUN *a formal word* Cachet is the status and respect something has: *No-name brands don't have the cachet of designer brands.*

cackle cackles cackling cackled

VERB **1.** If you cackle, you laugh harshly. NOUN **2.** a harsh laugh

cacophony

NOUN *a formal word* a mixture of loud, unpleasant noise: *a cacophony of barking dogs*

cactus cactuses

NOUN a thick, fleshy plant that grows in deserts and is usually covered in spikes

cad cads

NOUN *an old-fashioned word* a man who treats people, especially women, unfairly

CAD an abbreviation for *computer-aided (or -assisted) design*

caddie caddies

NOUN a person who carries golf clubs for a golf player

cadence cadences

NOUN The cadence of someone's voice is the way it goes up and down as that person speaks.

cadet cadets

NOUN a person being trained in the armed forces or police

Caesarean Caesareans

NOUN A Caesarean section is an operation in which a baby is lifted out of a female's womb through a cut in her abdomen.

café cafés

NOUN a place where you can buy light meals and drinks

cafeteria cafeterias

NOUN a restaurant in an institution, store, or office where you serve yourself or are served at a counter

caffeine

NOUN Caffeine is a chemical in coffee, tea, and chocolate that makes you more active.

cage cages

NOUN a box made of wire or bars in which birds or animals are kept

caged ADJECTIVE

cagey cagier cagiest

ADJECTIVE *an informal word* cautious and not open: *She was too cagey to commit to the cause.*

cahoots

PHRASE *an informal use* If you are **in cahoots** with someone, you are working closely with that person on a secret plan.

cairn cairns

NOUN a pile of stones built as a memorial or as a landmark

cajole cajoles cajoling cajoled

VERB If you cajole someone into doing something, you persuade that person to do it by saying nice things to him or her.

cake cakes caking caked

NOUN **1.** a sweet food made by baking flour, eggs, fat, and sugar **2.** a block of a hard substance such as soap

⚠ **HEADS UP** The é in **café** means that you pronounce the word caf-EH.

NEL

Cc

VERB **3.** If something cakes or is caked, it forms or becomes covered with a solid layer: *caked with mud*

calamity calamities
NOUN an event that causes disaster or distress
calamitous ADJECTIVE

calcium
NOUN a soft white substance found in bones and teeth

calculate calculates calculating calculated
VERB If you calculate something, you work it out, usually by doing some arithmetic.
calculation NOUN

calculated
ADJECTIVE deliberately planned to have a particular effect

calculating
ADJECTIVE carefully planning situations to get what you want: *He was always a calculating type.*

calculator calculators
NOUN a small electronic machine used for doing mathematical calculations

calculus
NOUN Calculus is a branch of mathematics concerned with amounts that can change and rates of change.

calendar calendars
NOUN **1.** a chart showing the date of each day in a particular year **2.** a system of dividing time into fixed periods of days, months, and years: *the Islamic calendar*

calf calves
NOUN **1.** a young cow, bull, elephant, whale, or seal **2.** the thick part at the back of your leg below your knee

calibre calibres
NOUN **1.** the ability or intelligence someone has: *a player of her calibre* **2.** The calibre of a gun is the width of the inside of the barrel of the gun.

call calls calling called
VERB **1.** If someone or something is called a particular name, it is that person's or thing's name: *a man called Jeffrey* **2.** If you call people or situations something, you use words to describe your opinion of them: *They called me silly.* **3.** If you call someone, you telephone that person. **4.** If you call or call out something, you say it loudly: *He called out his daughter's name.* **5.** If you call on someone, you pay that person a short visit: *Don't hesitate to call on me.*
NOUN **6.** If you get a call from someone, that person telephones you or visits you. **7.** a cry or shout: *a call for help* **8.** a demand for something: *The call for art*

teachers was small.

call off
VERB **9.** If you call something off, you cancel it.

call up
VERB **10.** If someone is called up, that person is drafted into military service.

call centre call centres
NOUN an office in which most of the staff are employed to answer telephone calls on behalf of a particular company or organization

calling
NOUN **1.** a profession or career **2.** If you have a calling to a particular job or line of work, you have a strong feeling that you should do it.

callous
ADJECTIVE cruel and not concerned with other people's feelings
callously ADVERB
callousness NOUN

calm calmer calmest; calms calming calmed
ADJECTIVE **1.** Someone who is calm is quiet and does not show any worry or excitement. **2.** If the weather or the sea is calm, it is still because there is no strong wind.
NOUN **3.** Calm is a state of quietness and peacefulness: *He liked the calm of the evening.*
VERB **4.** To calm someone means to make that person less upset or excited.
calmly ADVERB
calmness NOUN

calorie calories
NOUN a nonmetric unit of measurement for the energy food gives you: *All chocolate is high in calories.*

calves the plural of CALF

calypso calypsos
NOUN a lively style of music from the West Indies, accompanied by a rhythmic beat, whose words are about something happening at the time

calyx calyxes
NOUN In a flower, a calyx is the covering of outer leaves that protects the developing bud.

camaraderie
NOUN Camaraderie is a feeling of trust and friendship among a group of people.

camber cambers
NOUN a slight downward slope from the centre of a boat's deck to each side of it

camel camels
NOUN a large mammal with either one or two humps on its back. Camels live in hot desert areas and are sometimes used for carrying things.

Cc

cameo cameos
NOUN **1.** a small but important part in a play or movie played by a well-known actor or actress **2.** a brooch with a raised design on a flat surface of another colour

camera cameras
NOUN a piece of equipment used for taking photographs or for filming

camomile
NOUN Camomile is a plant with daisylike flowers that are used to make herbal tea.

camouflage camouflages camouflaging camouflaged
NOUN **1.** Camouflage is a way of avoiding being seen by having the same colour or appearance as the surroundings.
VERB **2.** To camouflage something is to hide it by giving it the same colour or appearance as its surroundings.

camp camps camping camped
NOUN **1.** a collection of buildings for a particular group of people, usually with a program of activities for recreation or for training: *summer camp* **2.** a group of people who support a particular idea or belief: *the liberal camp*
VERB **3.** If you camp, you stay in a tent or trailer.
camper NOUN
camping NOUN

campaign campaigns campaigning campaigned
NOUN **1.** a set of actions aiming to achieve a particular result: *a campaign to educate people*
VERB **2.** To campaign means to carry out a campaign: *He has campaigned against smoking.*
campaigner NOUN

campus campuses
NOUN the area of land and the buildings that make up a university or college

can could
VERB **1.** If you can do something, it is possible for you to do it or you are allowed to do it: *You can go to the movie.* **2.** If you can do something, you have the ability to do it: *I can speak Italian.*

⚠ **HEADS UP**

In formal language, **can** means *able to.* **May** means *be allowed to.* Informally, **can** is used for both meanings.

can cans canning canned
NOUN **1.** a metal container, often a sealed one with food or drink inside
VERB **2.** To can food or drink is to seal it in cans.

Canada
NOUN the second-largest country in the world. Canada occupies most of the northern half of North America.

Canadian Canadians
ADJECTIVE **1.** belonging or relating to Canada
NOUN **2.** someone who comes from Canada

canal canals
NOUN **1.** a long, narrow stretch of water dug across land **2.** a passageway in the body or in a plant: *the birth canal*

canary canaries
NOUN a small, yellow bird

cancan cancans
NOUN a lively dance in which women kick their legs high in the air to fast music

cancel cancels cancelling cancelled
VERB **1.** If you cancel something that has been arranged, you stop it from happening. **2.** If you cancel a cheque or an agreement, you make sure that it is no longer valid.
cancellation NOUN

cancer cancers
NOUN a serious disease in which abnormal cells in a part of the body increase rapidly, causing growths
cancerous ADJECTIVE

candelabra candelabras
NOUN an ornamental holder for a number of candles

candid
ADJECTIVE honest and frank
candidly ADVERB
candour NOUN

candidate candidates
NOUN a person who is being considered for a job, a political office, an honour, or a prize: *There are five candidates running in the election.*
candidacy NOUN

candied
ADJECTIVE covered or cooked in sugar: *candied fruit*

candle candles
NOUN a stick of hard wax with a wick through the middle. The lighted wick gives a flame that provides light.

candlestick candlesticks
NOUN a holder for a candle

Cc

candy candies
NOUN A candy is a sweet snack made with sugar or syrup and flavouring.

cane canes caning caned
NOUN **1.** Cane is the long hollow stem of a plant such as bamboo: *sugar cane* **2.** Cane is also strips of cane used for weaving things such as baskets. **3.** a long narrow stick to help a person walk
VERB **4.** To cane someone means to beat that person with a cane as a punishment.

canine
ADJECTIVE relating to dogs

canister canisters
NOUN a container with a lid, used for storing foods such as sugar or tea

cannabis
NOUN a tall plant with divided, serrated leaves. It is also called marijuana.

canned
ADJECTIVE **1.** Canned food is kept in cans. **2.** Canned music or laughter on a television or radio show is recorded beforehand.

cannibal cannibals
NOUN a person who eats other human beings; also used to describe animals that eat animals of their own type
cannibalism NOUN

cannon cannons
NOUN a large gun, usually on wheels, used in battles to fire heavy metal balls

cannot
VERB Cannot is the same as can not: *She cannot come home yet.*

canny
ADJECTIVE clever and cautious: *canny businesspeople*
cannily ADVERB

canoe canoes
NOUN a light, narrow boat that you move using a paddle
canoeing NOUN

canon canons
NOUN a basic rule or principle: *the canons of polite behaviour*

canopy canopies
NOUN a cover for something, used for shelter or decoration: *a frilly canopy over the bed*

cantankerous
ADJECTIVE Cantankerous people are quarrelsome and bad-tempered.

canteen canteens
NOUN **1.** the part of a workplace, camp, or school where people can go to eat **2.** a small container, especially a flat, round one, for carrying water or other drinks

canter canters cantering cantered
VERB When a horse canters, it moves at a speed between a gallop and a trot.

cantilever cantilevers
NOUN a long beam or bar fixed at only one end of a wall or base, which supports a structure such as a balcony or either end of a bridge

canton cantons
NOUN a political and administrative region of a country, especially in Switzerland

canvas canvases
NOUN **1.** Canvas is strong, heavy cloth used for making things such as sails and tents. **2.** a piece of canvas on which an artist does a painting

canvass canvasses canvassing canvassed
VERB **1.** If you canvass people or a place, you go around trying to persuade people to vote for a particular candidate or party in an election. **2.** If you canvass an opinion, you find out what people think about a particular subject by asking them.

canyon canyons
NOUN a narrow river valley with steep sides

cap caps capping capped
NOUN **1.** a soft, flat hat, often with a peak at the front **2.** the top of a bottle **3.** Caps are small explosives used in toy guns.
VERB **4.** To cap something is to cover it with something. **5.** If you cap a story or a joke that someone has just told, you tell a better one.

capable
ADJECTIVE **1.** able to do something: *a dog capable of learning new tricks* **2.** skilful or talented: *She was a very capable person.*
capably ADVERB
capability NOUN

capacity capacities
NOUN **1.** the maximum amount that something can hold or produce: *a seating capacity of 11 000* **2.** a person's power or ability to do something: *her capacity for learning languages* **3.** someone's position or role: *in his capacity as guidance counsellor*

cape capes
NOUN **1.** a cloak with no sleeves **2.** a large piece of land sticking out into the sea: *the Cape of Good Hope*

caper capers
NOUN **1.** Capers are the flower buds of a spiky Mediterranean shrub, which are pickled and used to flavour food. **2.** a trick or scheme: *They would have nothing to do with such capers.*

Cc

capillary capillaries
NOUN Capillaries are very thin blood vessels.

capital capitals
NOUN **1.** The capital of a country is the city where the government meets. **2.** Capital is the amount of money or property owned or used by a business. **3.** Capital is also a sum of money that you save or invest in order to gain interest. **4.** A capital or capital letter is a larger letter used at the beginning of a sentence or a name.

capitalism
NOUN Capitalism is an economic and political system where businesses and industries are not owned and run by the government, but by individuals who can make a profit from them.
capitalist ADJECTIVE OR NOUN

capitalize capitalizes capitalizing capitalized
VERB **1.** If you capitalize on a situation, you use it to get an advantage. **2.** If you capitalize a letter, you turn it into a capital.
capitalization NOUN

capital punishment
NOUN Capital punishment is legally killing someone as a punishment for a crime he or she has committed.

capitulate capitulates capitulating capitulated
VERB To capitulate is to give in and stop fighting or resisting: *He capitulated when he realized that arguing was useless.*
capitulation NOUN

cappuccino cappuccinos
NOUN coffee made with frothy milk

! HEADS UP

Cappuccino is an Italian word, and we still use the Italian pronunciation: kap-uh-CHEE-no.

capricious
ADJECTIVE often changing unexpectedly: *the capricious weather*

capsize capsizes capsizing capsized
VERB If a boat capsizes, it turns upside down in the water.

capsule capsules
NOUN **1.** a small container, usually of gelatin, with medicine inside, which you swallow **2.** the part of a spacecraft in which astronauts travel

captain captains captaining captained
NOUN **1.** the officer in charge of a ship or airplane **2.** in the army and air force, an officer of the rank immediately above lieutenant and below major **3.** a navy officer of the rank immediately above commander **4.** the leader of a sports team: *captain of the hockey team*
VERB **5.** If you captain a group of people, you are their leader.

caption captions
NOUN an explanation or title printed beside a picture or photograph

captivate captivates captivating captivated
VERB To captivate people is to fascinate or attract them so that they cannot take their attention away: *I was captivated by her.*
captivating ADJECTIVE

captive captives
NOUN **1.** a person who has been captured and kept prisoner
ADJECTIVE **2.** imprisoned or enclosed: *a captive bird*
captivity NOUN

captor captors
NOUN someone who has captured a person or animal

capture captures capturing captured
VERB **1.** To capture someone is to take that person prisoner. **2.** To capture a quality or mood means to succeed in representing or describing it: *That book captures the mood of the time.*
NOUN **3.** The capture of someone is the action of taking that person prisoner: *the fifth anniversary of his capture*

car cars
NOUN **1.** a four-wheeled road vehicle with room for a small number of people **2.** a railway vehicle that carries people or freight, or is used for a particular purpose: *the buffet car*

carafe carafes
NOUN a glass bottle for serving water, coffee, or wine

caramel caramels
NOUN **1.** a chewy candy made from sugar, butter, and milk **2.** Caramel is burnt sugar used for colouring or flavouring food.

carat carats
NOUN a unit for measuring the weight of diamonds and other precious stones

caravan caravans
NOUN a group of people and animals travelling together, especially across a desert

carbohydrate carbohydrates
NOUN Carbohydrate is a substance that gives you energy. It is found in foods like sugar and bread.

Cc

carbon

NOUN Carbon is a chemical element that is pure in diamonds and also found in coal. All living things contain carbon.

carbonated

ADJECTIVE Carbonated drinks contain bubbles of carbon dioxide that make them fizzy.

carbon dioxide

NOUN Carbon dioxide is a colourless, odourless gas that is found in the atmosphere. The air that humans and animals breathe out contains carbon dioxide.

carburetor carburetors

NOUN the part of the engine in a vehicle in which air and gasoline are mixed together

carcass carcasses

NOUN the body of a dead animal

card cards

NOUN **1.** a piece of stiff paper or plastic with information or a message on it: *a birthday card, a social insurance card* **2.** Cards can mean playing cards: *a tattered deck of cards* **3.** When you play cards, you play any game using playing cards. **4.** Card is strong, stiff paper.

cardboard

NOUN Cardboard is thick, stiff paper.

cardiac

ADJECTIVE relating to the heart: *cardiac disease*

cardigan cardigans

NOUN a sweater or knitted jacket that fastens up the front

cardinal

ADJECTIVE extremely important: *a cardinal principle of law*

care cares caring cared

VERB **1.** If you care about something, you are concerned about it and interested in it. **2.** If you care about someone, you feel affection toward that person. **3.** If you care for someone, you look after that person. NOUN **4.** Care is concern or worry. **5.** Care is treatment for someone or something or looking after that person or thing: *the care of the elderly* **6.** If you do something with care, you do it with close attention.

career careers careering careered

NOUN **1.** the series of jobs that someone has in life, usually in the same occupation: *a career in medicine* VERB **2.** To career somewhere is to move very quickly, often out of control: *The car careered off the road.*

carefree

ADJECTIVE having no worries or responsibilities

careful

ADJECTIVE **1.** acting sensibly and with care: *Be careful what you say to him.* **2.** complete and well done: *It needs very careful planning.*
carefully ADVERB

careless

Instead of **CARELESS** try...

ADJECTIVE
1. done badly without enough attention: *careless driving* **2.** relaxed and unconcerned: *careless laughter*
carelessly ADVERB
carelessness NOUN

sloppy editing
reckless driving
neglectful parenting
irresponsible actions
an absent-minded mistake

caress caresses caressing caressed

VERB **1.** If you caress someone, you stroke that person gently and affectionately. NOUN **2.** a gentle, affectionate stroke

caretaker caretakers

NOUN **1.** a person who looks after a large building such as a school ADJECTIVE **2.** having an important position for a short time until a new person is appointed: *The caretaker government will be in place until a new one can be elected.*

cargo cargoes

NOUN the goods carried on a ship, motor vehicle, or plane

caricature caricatures caricaturing caricatured

NOUN **1.** a drawing or description of someone that exaggerates striking parts of that person's appearance or personality VERB **2.** To caricature someone is to make a caricature of that person.

carjack carjacks carjacking carjacked

VERB If a car is carjacked, its driver is attacked and the car is stolen.

carnage

NOUN Carnage is the violent killing of large numbers of people.

carnal

ADJECTIVE *a formal word* desires and pleasures related to the body: *carnal instincts*

carnation carnations

NOUN a plant with a long stem and white, pink, or red flowers

carnival carnivals

NOUN a public festival involving a particular sport, season, or place: *a winter carnival*

Cc

carnivore carnivores
NOUN an animal that eats meat
carnivorous ADJECTIVE

carol carols
NOUN a religious song, especially one sung at Christmas

carousel carousels
NOUN a merry-go-round

carp carps carping carped
NOUN **1.** a large, edible freshwater fish
VERB **2.** To carp means to complain about unimportant things.

carpel carpels
NOUN the seed-bearing female part of a flower

carpenter carpenters
NOUN a person who makes and repairs wooden structures
carpentry NOUN

carpet carpets carpeting carpeted
NOUN **1.** a thick covering for a floor
VERB **2.** To carpet a floor means to cover it with a carpet.

carriage carriages
NOUN **1.** a vehicle for carrying passengers, usually pulled by horses **2.** a machine part that moves and supports another part: *a typewriter carriage* **3.** Carriage is the way people hold their head and body when they move.

carrier carriers
NOUN **1.** anything that is used for carrying things **2.** A carrier of a germ or disease is a person or animal that can pass it on to others.

carrion
NOUN Carrion is the decaying flesh of dead animals.

carrot carrots
NOUN a long, thin, orange-coloured root vegetable

carry carries carrying carried
VERB **1.** To carry something is to hold it and take it somewhere. **2.** When a vehicle carries people, they travel in it. **3.** A person or animal that carries a germ can pass it on to other people or animals: *I still carry the disease.* **4.** If a sound carries, it can be heard far away: *Her voice barely carried over the cheering.* **5.** In a meeting, if a proposal is carried, it is accepted by a majority of the people there: *That motion should easily carry.*

carry away
VERB **6.** If you are carried away, you are so excited by something that you do not behave sensibly.

carry on
VERB **7.** To carry on doing something means to continue doing it.

carry out
VERB **8.** To carry something out means to do it and complete it: *The renovation was carried out by a local builder.*

cart carts
NOUN a vehicle with wheels, used to carry goods and often pulled by horses or oxen

cartilage
NOUN Cartilage is a strong, flexible substance found around the joints and in the nose and ears.

carton cartons
NOUN a cardboard or plastic container

cartoon cartoons
NOUN **1.** a drawing or a series of drawings that are funny or make a point **2.** a movie in which the characters and scenes are drawn
cartoonist NOUN

⚠ HEADS UP

Cartoons printed in newspapers are called **comic strips**, because they're usually laid out in straight lines.

cartridge cartridges
NOUN **1.** a tube containing a bullet and an explosive substance, used in guns **2.** a case containing a refill of some substance, such as toner for a photocopier

cartwheel cartwheels
NOUN an acrobatic movement in which you throw yourself sideways onto one hand and move around in a circle with arms and legs stretched until you land on your feet again

carve carves carving carved
VERB **1.** To carve an object means to cut it out of a substance such as stone or wood. **2.** To carve meat means to cut slices from it.

carving carvings
NOUN a carved object

cascade cascades cascading cascaded
NOUN **1.** a waterfall or group of waterfalls
VERB **2.** To cascade means to flow downward quickly: *Water cascaded from the attic.*

case cases
NOUN **1.** a particular situation, event, or example: *a clear case of mistaken identity* **2.** a container with a handle, designed to carry something: *a camera case* **3.** Doctors sometimes refer to a patient as a case. **4.** Police detectives refer to a crime they are

Cc

investigating as a case. **5.** In an argument, the case for an idea is the reasons used to support it. **6.** In law, a case is a trial or other inquiry. **7.** In grammar, the case of a noun or pronoun is the form of it that shows its relationship with other words in a sentence: *the accusative case*
PHRASE **8.** You say **in case** to explain something that you do because a particular thing might happen: *I didn't want to shout in case I startled you.* **9.** You say **in that case** to show that you are assuming something said before is true: *In that case we won't do anything.*

casement casements
NOUN a window that opens on hinges at one side

cash cashes cashing cashed
NOUN **1.** Cash is money in bills and coins.
VERB **2.** If you cash a cheque, you take it to a bank and exchange it for money.

cashew cashews
NOUN a curved, edible nut

cash flow
NOUN Cash flow is the money that a business makes and spends.

cashier cashiers
NOUN the person that customers pay in a store

cashmere
NOUN Cashmere is very soft, fine wool from goats.

cash register cash registers
NOUN a machine in a store that records sales, and in which the money is kept

casing casings
NOUN a protective covering for something

casino casinos
NOUN a place where people go to gamble

cask casks
NOUN a wooden barrel

casket caskets
NOUN a coffin

casserole casseroles
NOUN a dish made by cooking a mixture of meat and vegetables slowly in an oven; also used to refer to the pot a casserole is cooked in

cassette cassettes
NOUN a small flat container with magnetic tape inside, which is used for recording and playing back sounds

cast casts casting cast
NOUN **1.** all the people who act in a play or movie **2.** an object made by pouring liquid into a mould and leaving it to harden: *the casts of classical sculptures* **3.** a stiff plaster covering put on broken bones to keep them still so that they heal properly
VERB **4.** To cast actors is to choose them for roles in a play or movie. **5.** When people cast their votes in an election, they vote. **6.** To cast something is to throw it. **7.** If you cast your eyes somewhere, you look there: *I cast my eyes down briefly.* **8.** To cast an object is to make it by pouring liquid into a mould and leaving it to harden: *An image of him has been cast in bronze.*

cast off
VERB **9.** If you cast off, you untie the rope fastening a boat to a dock or shore.

castanets
PLURAL NOUN a musical instrument consisting of two small round pieces of wood or plastic that are clicked together with the fingers

castaway castaways
NOUN a person who has been shipwrecked

caste castes
NOUN **1.** one of the four classes into which Hindu society is divided **2.** Caste is a system of social classes decided according to family, wealth, and position.

caster casters
NOUN a small wheel fitted to furniture so that it can be moved easily

castigate castigates castigating castigated
VERB *a formal word* To castigate someone is to criticize that person severely.

cast iron
NOUN **1.** Cast iron is iron that is made into objects by casting.
ADJECTIVE **2.** A cast-iron excuse or guarantee is absolutely certain and firm.

castle castles
NOUN **1.** a large building with walls or ditches around it to protect it from attack **2.** In chess, a castle is the same as a rook.

castoff castoffs
NOUN an item that is thrown away or put aside because it is no longer useful

castor another spelling of CASTER

castor oil
NOUN Castor oil is a thick oil that comes from the seeds of the castor oil plant. It is used as a laxative.

castrate castrates castrating castrated
VERB To castrate a male animal is to remove its testicles so that it can no longer produce sperm.
castration NOUN

Cc

casual

ADJECTIVE **1.** happening by chance without planning: *a casual remark* **2.** careless or without interest: *a casual glance*

Instead of **CASUAL** try…

over his shoulder
3. Casual clothes are suitable for informal occasions. **4.** Casual work is not regular or permanent.
casually ADVERB
casualness NOUN

a **carefree** attitude
an **offhand** remark
an **informal** meeting
an **easygoing** teacher
a **relaxed** atmosphere

casualty casualties
NOUN a person killed or injured in an accident or war: *Many of the casualties were passengers.*

cat cats
NOUN **1.** a small furry animal with whiskers, a tail, and sharp claws, often kept as a pet **2.** any of the family of mammals that includes lions and tigers

catacomb catacombs
NOUN Catacombs are underground passages where dead bodies are buried.

catalogue catalogues cataloguing catalogued
NOUN **1.** a book containing pictures and descriptions of items that you can buy in a store or through the mail **2.** a list of things such as the objects in a museum or the books in a library
VERB **3.** To catalogue a collection of things means to list them in a catalogue.

catalyst catalysts
NOUN **1.** something that causes a change to happen: *the catalyst that provoked a change in policy* **2.** a substance that speeds up a chemical reaction without changing itself

catamaran catamarans
NOUN a sailing boat with two hulls connected to each other

catapult catapults catapulting catapulted
NOUN **1.** an ancient war machine for throwing big rocks **2.** a slingshot
VERB **3.** To catapult something is to throw it violently through the air. **4.** If people are catapulted into a situation, they find themselves unexpectedly in that situation: *She has been catapulted into the limelight.*

cataract cataracts
NOUN **1.** an area of the lens of someone's eye that has become white instead of clear, so that person cannot see properly **2.** a large waterfall

catarrh
NOUN Catarrh is a condition in which you get a lot of mucus in your nose and throat.

catastrophe catastrophes
NOUN a terrible disaster
catastrophic ADJECTIVE

catch catches catching caught
VERB **1.** If you catch a ball moving in the air, you grasp hold of it when it comes near you. **2.** To catch an animal means to trap it: *I caught ten fish.* **3.** When the police catch criminals, they find them and arrest them. **4.** If you catch someone doing something that person should not be doing, you discover him or her doing it: *I caught her using my computer.* **5.** If you catch a bus, plane, or train, you get on it and travel somewhere. **6.** If you catch a cold or a disease, you become infected with it. **7.** If something catches on an object, it sticks to it or gets trapped: *The red fibres caught on the mesh.*
NOUN **8.** a device that fastens something **9.** a problem or hidden complication in something

catch on
VERB **10.** If you catch on to something, you understand it. **11.** If something catches on, it becomes popular: *That show never really caught on in Canada.*

catch out
VERB **12.** To catch someone out is to discover that person doing something wrong.

catch up
VERB **13.** To catch up with someone in front of you is to reach the place where that person is by moving slightly faster than him or her. **14.** To catch up with someone is also to reach the same level or standard as that person.

catching
ADJECTIVE tending to spread very quickly: *Colds are catching.*

catchy catchier catchiest
ADJECTIVE attractive and easily remembered: *a catchy tune*

categorical
ADJECTIVE absolutely certain and direct: *a categorical denial*
categorically ADVERB

categorize categorizes categorizing categorized
VERB To categorize things is to arrange them in different categories.

Cc

category categories
NOUN a set of things with a particular characteristic in common: *The Canada Food Guide divides food into four categories.*

cater caters catering catered
VERB To cater for people is to provide them with what they need, especially food.

caterer caterers
NOUN a person or business that provides food for parties and groups

caterpillar caterpillars
NOUN the larva of a butterfly or moth. It looks like a small, coloured worm and feeds on plants.

catharsis catharses
NOUN *a formal word* Catharsis is the release of strong emotions and feelings by expressing them through drama or literature.

cathedral cathedrals
NOUN an important church with a bishop in charge of it

Catholic Catholics
ADJECTIVE **1.** relating or belonging to the branch of the Christian church that accepts the Pope in Rome as its leader **2.** If a person has **catholic** interests, that person has a wide range of interests.
NOUN **3.** someone who belongs to the Roman Catholic Church
Catholicism NOUN

cattle
PLURAL NOUN Cattle are cows and bulls kept by farmers.

catty cattier cattiest
ADJECTIVE unpleasant and spiteful
cattiness NOUN

catwalk catwalks
NOUN a high, narrow pathway that people walk along, for example over a stage

Caucasian Caucasians
NOUN a person belonging to the race of people with fair or light-brown skin

caught the past tense and past participle of
CATCH

cauldron cauldrons
NOUN a large, round, metal cooking pot, especially one that sits over a fire

cauliflower cauliflowers
NOUN a large, round, white vegetable surrounded by green leaves

cause causes causing caused
NOUN **1.** The cause of something is the thing that makes it happen: *the most common cause of back pain* **2.** an aim or principle that people are working for: *dedication to the cause of peace* **3.** If you have cause for something, you have a reason for it: *They gave us no cause to believe that.*
VERB **4.** To cause something is to make it happen: *Poor weather can cause delays at the airport.*
causal ADJECTIVE

causeway causeways
NOUN a raised path or road across water or marshland

caustic
ADJECTIVE **1.** A caustic chemical can destroy substances: *caustic liquids such as acids* **2.** bitter or sarcastic: *your caustic sense of humour*

caution cautions cautioning cautioned
NOUN **1.** Caution is the great care that you take to avoid danger: *You will need to proceed with caution.* **2.** a warning: *A caution has been posted about the thin ice.*
VERB **3.** If someone cautions you, that person warns you, usually not to do something again: *A man has been cautioned by police.*
cautionary ADJECTIVE

cautious
ADJECTIVE acting very carefully to avoid danger: *a cautious approach*
cautiously ADVERB

cavalcade cavalcades
NOUN a procession of people on horses or in cars or carriages

cavalier
ADJECTIVE arrogant and behaving without sensitivity: *a cavalier attitude to danger*

cavalry
NOUN In the past, the cavalry was the part of the army that used horses.

cave caves caving caved
NOUN **1.** a hollow place that is underground or in the side of a cliff
VERB **2.** If a roof caves in, it collapses inward.

cave dweller
NOUN Cave dwellers were people who lived in caves in prehistoric times.

cavern caverns
NOUN a large cave

cavernous
ADJECTIVE large, deep, and hollow: *a cavernous warehouse*

caviar
NOUN Caviar is the tiny salted eggs of a fish called the sturgeon.

cavity cavities
NOUN a small hole in something solid: *There were cavities in his back teeth.*

Cc

cavort cavorts cavorting cavorted
VERB When people cavort, they jump around excitedly.

caw caws cawing cawed
VERB When a crow caws, it makes a harsh sound.

CD an abbreviation for *compact disc*

CD-ROM CD-ROM is a method of storing video, sound, or text on a compact disc that can be played on a computer using a laser. CD-ROM is an abbreviation for *compact disc read-only memory*.

CE CE means *Common Era* and is used in preference to AD. You use *CE* in dates to indicate the number of years after the birth of Jesus Christ: *The village was founded in 966 CE.*

cease ceases ceasing ceased
VERB **1.** If something ceases, it stops happening. **2.** If you cease to do something, you stop doing it.

ceasefire ceasefires
NOUN an agreement between groups that are fighting each other to stop for a period and discuss peace

ceaseless
ADJECTIVE going on without stopping: *the ceaseless movement of the streets*
ceaselessly ADVERB

cedar cedars
NOUN a large evergreen tree with wide branches and needle-shaped leaves

cede cedes ceding ceded
VERB To cede something is to give it up to someone else: *Haiti was ceded to France in 1697.*

ceiling ceilings
NOUN the top inside surface of a room

celebrate celebrates celebrating celebrated
VERB If you celebrate, or celebrate something, you do something special and enjoyable because of it: *a party to celebrate the end of the exams*

celebrated
ADJECTIVE famous: *the celebrated Canadian athlete*

celebration celebrations
NOUN an event in honour of a special occasion
celebratory ADJECTIVE

celebrity celebrities
NOUN a famous person

celery
NOUN a vegetable with long, pale green stalks

celestial
ADJECTIVE *a formal word* concerning the sky or heaven: *The telescope is pointed at a celestial object.*

celibate
ADJECTIVE Someone who is celibate does not marry or have sex.
celibacy NOUN

cell cells
NOUN **1.** In biology, a cell is the smallest part of an animal or plant that can exist by itself. Each cell contains a nucleus. **2.** a small room where a prisoner is kept in a prison or police station **3.** a small group of people set up to work together as part of a larger organization **4.** a device that converts chemical energy to electricity

cellar cellars
NOUN a room underneath a building, often used to store food or wine

cello cellos
NOUN a large, stringed musical instrument that you play sitting down, holding the instrument upright with your knees
cellist NOUN

cellophane
NOUN *a trademark* Cellophane is thin, transparent, plastic material used to wrap food or other things to protect them.

cellphone cellphones
NOUN a small, portable telephone

cellular
ADJECTIVE Cellular means relating to the cells of animals or plants.

celluloid
NOUN Celluloid is a type of plastic that was once used to make photographic film.

Celsius
NOUN Celsius is a scale for measuring temperature in which water freezes at 0 degrees (0°C) and boils at 100 degrees (100°C). Celsius is the same as *centigrade*.

cement cements cementing cemented
NOUN **1.** Cement is a fine powder made from limestone and clay that is mixed with sand and water to make concrete.
VERB **2.** To cement things is to stick them together with cement or cover them with cement. **3.** Something that cements a relationship makes it stronger: *Their adventures together at summer camp cemented their friendship.*

cemetery cemeteries
NOUN an area of land where people are buried after they die

Cc

cenotaph cenotaphs
NOUN a monument built in memory of dead people, especially soldiers buried elsewhere

censor censors censoring censored
NOUN **1.** a person officially appointed to examine books or movies and to ban parts that are considered unsuitable for the public
VERB **2.** If someone censors a book or movie, that person cuts or bans parts of it that are considered unsuitable for the public.
censorship NOUN

censure censures censuring censured
NOUN **1.** Censure is strong disapproval of something.
VERB **2.** To censure someone is to criticize that person severely.

census censuses
NOUN an official survey of the population of a country

cent cents
NOUN a unit of currency in Canada and some other countries. A cent is worth one-hundredth of a dollar.

centaur centaurs
NOUN a creature in Greek mythology with the top half of a man and the lower body and legs of a horse

centenary centenaries
NOUN the hundredth anniversary of something

centi-
PREFIX The prefix *centi-* is used to form words that have *hundred* or *hundredth* as part of their meaning: *centimetre*

central
ADJECTIVE **1.** in or near the centre of an object or area: *The park is in a central part of town.* **2.** main or most important: *the central idea of the story*
centrally ADVERB
centrality NOUN

central heating
NOUN Central heating is a system of heating a building in which water or air is heated in a tank and then travels through pipes and radiators around the building.

centralize centralizes centralizing centralized
VERB To centralize a system is to bring the organization of it under the control of one central group.
centralization NOUN

centre centres centring centred
NOUN **1.** the middle of an object or area **2.** a building where people go for activities, meetings, or help: *a health centre* **3.** Someone or something that is the centre of attention attracts a lot of attention.
VERB **4.** To centre something is to move it so that it is balanced or at the centre of something else. **5.** If something centres on or around a particular thing, that thing is the main subject of attention: *The discussion centred on his request.*

centrifugal force
ADJECTIVE In physics, centrifugal force is the force that makes rotating objects move outward.

centripetal force
ADJECTIVE In physics, centripetal force is the force that makes rotating objects move inward.

centurion centurions
NOUN a Roman officer in charge of 100 soldiers

century centuries
NOUN a period of 100 years

ceramic ceramics
NOUN **1.** Ceramic is a hard material made by baking clay to a very high temperature.
2. Ceramics is the art of making objects out of clay.

cereal cereals
NOUN **1.** a food made from grain, often eaten with milk for breakfast **2.** a plant that produces edible grain, such as wheat or oats

---

KNOWING WORDS: WORD BUILDING

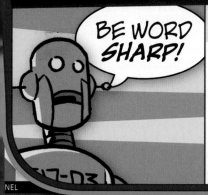

BE WORD SHARP!

You can create new words by adding prefixes and suffixes to a base word.

cent- and **centi-** prefixes that mean *one hundred* or *one hundredth*

centennial lasting one hundred years

centenary a hundredth anniversary

centilitre one-hundredth of a litre

centimetre one-hundredth of a metre

centipede an insect that seems to have hundreds of legs

Cc

cerebral
ADJECTIVE *a formal word* relating to the brain: *a cerebral hemorrhage*

cerebral palsy
NOUN Cerebral palsy is an illness caused by damage to a baby's brain, which makes his or her muscles and limbs very weak.

ceremonial
ADJECTIVE relating to or used in a ritual: *ceremonial dress*
ceremonially ADVERB

ceremony ceremonies
NOUN **1.** a set of formal actions performed at a special occasion or important public event: *a graduation ceremony* **2.** Ceremony is very formal and polite behaviour: *He hung up the phone without ceremony.*

certain
ADJECTIVE **1.** definite or reliable: *She is certain to be at the dance.* **2.** having no doubt in your mind **3.** You use *certain* to refer to a specific person or thing: *certain aspects of the job* **4.** You use *certain* to suggest that a quality is noticeable but not obvious: *There's a certain resemblance to your mother.*

certainly
ADVERB **1.** without doubt: *The doctor was certainly interested.* **2.** of course: *Will you be there? Certainly.*

certainty certainties
NOUN **1.** Certainty is the state of being certain. **2.** something that is known without doubt: *There are no certainties and no guarantees.*

certificate certificates
NOUN a document stating particular facts, for example of someone's birth or death: *a marriage certificate*

certify certifies certifying certified
VERB **1.** To certify something means to declare formally that it is true: *certifying the cause of death* **2.** To certify someone means to declare officially that that person is insane.

cervix cervixes
NOUN the entrance to the womb at the top of the vagina
cervical ADJECTIVE

cessation
NOUN *a formal word* The cessation of something is the stopping of it: *a swift cessation of hostilities*

cf. cf. means *compare*. It is written after something in a text to let the readers know that they should compare what has just been written to something else in the text.

CFC CFCs
NOUN CFCs are manufactured chemicals that are used in aerosol sprays. They damage the ozone layer. CFC is an abbreviation for *chlorofluorocarbon.*

chaff
NOUN Chaff is the outer parts of grain separated from the seeds by beating.

chaffinch chaffinches
NOUN a small European bird with black and white wings

chagrin
NOUN *a formal word* Chagrin is a feeling of annoyance or disappointment.

chain chains chaining chained
NOUN **1.** a number of metal rings connected together in a line: *a bicycle chain* **2.** a number of things in a series or connected to one another: *a chain of restaurants*
VERB **3.** If you chain one thing to another, you fasten them together with a chain: *The protesters had chained themselves to railings.*

chainsaw chainsaws
NOUN a large saw with teeth fixed in a chain that is driven around by a motor

chair chairs chairing chaired
NOUN **1.** a seat with a back and four legs for one person **2.** The chair, or chairperson, is the person in charge of a meeting or the head of a committee.
VERB **3.** The person who chairs a meeting is in charge of it.

chairlift chairlifts
NOUN a line of chairs that hang from a moving cable and carry people up and down a mountain

chairman a male CHAIR

chairwoman a female CHAIR

chalet chalets
NOUN a wooden house with a sloping roof, especially in a mountainous area

chalk chalks chalking chalked
NOUN **1.** Chalk is a soft white rock. Small sticks of chalk are used for writing or drawing on a chalkboard.
VERB **2.** To chalk up a result is to achieve it: *He chalked up his first win.*
chalky ADJECTIVE

challenge challenges challenging challenged
NOUN **1.** something that is new and exciting but requires a lot of effort: *Learning this complicated dance routine was a challenge.* **2.** a suggestion from someone to compete with him or her **3.** A challenge to something is a questioning of whether it is correct or true: *a challenge to authority*
VERB **4.** If someone challenges you, that person suggests that you compete with him

⚠ **HEADS UP** Instead of **chairman**, use gender-free terms like **chair**.

Cc

or her in some way. **5.** If you challenge something, you question whether it is correct or true.
challenger NOUN
challenging ADJECTIVE

chamber chambers
NOUN **1.** a large room, especially one used for formal meetings: *the Senate Chamber* **2.** a hollow place or compartment inside something, especially inside an animal's body or inside a piece of machinery: *the chambers of the heart*

chambermaid chambermaids
NOUN a woman who cleans and tidies rooms in a hotel

chameleon chameleons
NOUN a lizard that is able to change the colour of its skin to match the colour of its surroundings

chamois chamois
NOUN a soft leather cloth used for polishing

champagne champagnes
NOUN Champagne is a sparkling white wine made in France.

champion champions championing championed
NOUN **1.** a person who wins a competition **2.** someone who supports or defends a cause or principle: *a champion of women's causes*
VERB **3.** Someone who champions a cause or principle supports or defends it.

championship championships
NOUN a competition to find the champion of a sport

chance chances chancing chanced
NOUN **1.** The chance of something happening is how possible or likely it is: *There's a chance of rain later.* **2.** an opportunity to do something: *You have a chance to be in the school musical.* **3.** a possibility that something dangerous or unpleasant may happen: *Don't take chances, he's armed.* **4.** Chance is also the way things happen unexpectedly without being planned: *I only found out by chance.*
VERB **5.** If you chance something, you try it although you are taking a risk.

chancellor chancellors
NOUN **1.** the head of government in some European countries **2.** the honorary head of a university

chandelier chandeliers
NOUN an ornamental light fixture that hangs from the ceiling

change changes changing changed
NOUN **1.** a difference or alteration in something: *a change in attitude* **2.** a

replacement of something by something else: *a change of clothes* **3.** Change is money you get back when you have paid more than the actual price of something.
VERB **4.** When something changes or when you change it, it becomes different: *It changed my life.* **5.** If you change something, you exchange it for something else. **6.** When you change, you put on different clothes. **7.** To change money means to exchange it for smaller coins of the same total value, or to exchange it for foreign currency.

changeable
ADJECTIVE likely to change all the time

changeover changeovers
NOUN a change from one system or activity to another: *the changeover from video to DVD*

channel channels channelling channelled
NOUN **1.** a wavelength used to receive programs broadcast by a television or radio station; also the station itself: *I was watching the other channel.* **2.** a passage along which water flows or along which something is carried **3.** a body of water joining two larger ones **4.** a method of achieving something: *We have tried to do things through the proper channels.*
VERB **5.** To channel something such as money or energy means to direct it in a particular way: *Their efforts are being channelled into worthy causes.*

chant chants chanting chanted
NOUN **1.** a group of words repeated over and over again: *The demonstrators made up a chant for the anti-poverty rally.* **2.** a religious song sung on only a few notes
VERB **3.** If people chant a group of words, they repeat them over and over again: *Crowds chanted his name.*

Chanukah another spelling of HANUKKAH

chaos
NOUN Chaos is a state of complete disorder and confusion.
chaotic ADJECTIVE

chap chapping chapped
VERB If your skin chaps, it becomes dry and cracked, usually as a result of cold or wind.

chapel chapels
NOUN a type of small church

chaperone chaperones
NOUN an older woman who accompanies a young unmarried woman on social occasions, or any person who accompanies a group of younger people

Cc

chapter chapters
NOUN **1.** one of the parts into which a book is divided **2.** a particular period in someone's life or in history

char chars charring charred
VERB If something chars, it gets partly burned and turns black.
charred ADJECTIVE

character characters
NOUN **1.** all the qualities that combine to form the personality or atmosphere of a person or place **2.** A person or place that has character has an interesting, attractive, or admirable quality: *an inn of great character and simplicity* **3.** The characters in a movie, play, or book are the people in it. **4.** a person: *an odd character* **5.** a letter, number, or other written symbol

characteristic characteristics
NOUN **1.** a quality that is typical of a particular person or thing: *Silence is a characteristic of libraries.*
ADJECTIVE **2.** Characteristic means typical of a particular person or thing: *He prepared his report with characteristic thoroughness.*
characteristically ADVERB

characterize characterizes characterizing characterized
VERB **1.** A quality that characterizes something is typical of it: *a condition characterized by muscle stiffness* **2.** If you characterize someone or something, you describe the special qualities of that person or thing.
characterization NOUN

characterless
ADJECTIVE dull and uninteresting: *a tiny, characterless apartment*

character sketch
NOUN a brief description of a person or of a fictional character

charade charades
NOUN a ridiculous and unnecessary activity or pretence

charcoal
NOUN Charcoal is a black form of carbon made by burning wood without air, used as a fuel and also for drawing.

charge charges charging charged
VERB **1.** If someone charges you money, that person asks you to pay it for something you have bought or received: *The store charged far too much money for that coat.* **2.** To charge someone means to accuse that person formally of having committed a crime. **3.** To charge a battery means to pass an electrical current through it to make it store electricity. **4.** To charge somewhere means to rush forward, often to attack someone: *The rhino charged at the hyena.*
NOUN **5.** the price that you have to pay for something **6.** a formal accusation that a person is guilty of a crime and has to go to court **7.** To be in charge of someone or something means to be in control of that person or thing. **8.** an explosive put in a gun or other weapon **9.** An electrical charge is the electricity that something carries.

charger chargers
NOUN a device for charging batteries

chariot chariots
NOUN a two-wheeled, open vehicle pulled by horses. Chariots were used in former times in battles, races, and processions.

charisma
NOUN Charisma is a special ability to attract or influence people by your personality.
charismatic ADJECTIVE

charity charities
NOUN **1.** an organization that raises money to help people who are ill, poor, or disabled **2.** Charity is money or other help given to poor, disabled, or ill people: *to help raise money for charity* **3.** Charity is also a kind, sympathetic attitude toward people.
charitable ADJECTIVE

charlatan charlatans
NOUN someone who pretends to have skill or knowledge that he or she does not have

charm charms charming charmed
NOUN **1.** Charm is an attractive and pleasing quality that some people and things have: *a man of great personal charm* **2.** a small ornament worn on a bracelet **3.** a magical spell or an object that is supposed to bring good luck
VERB **4.** If you charm someone, you use your charm to please that person.

charmer charmers
NOUN someone who uses his or her charm to influence people

Instead of **CHARMING** try...

a **delightful** companion
a **lovable** character
a **charismatic** leader
a **captivating** speaker
a **magnetic** entertainer

charming
ADJECTIVE very pleasant and attractive: *a charming man*
charmingly ADVERB

Cc

chart charts charting charted
NOUN **1.** a diagram or table showing information: *He noted the score on his chart.* **2.** a map of the sea or stars
VERB **3.** If you chart something, you observe and record it carefully.

charter charters chartering chartered
NOUN **1.** a document stating the rights or aims of a group or organization, often written by the government: *the Canadian Charter of Rights and Freedoms*
VERB **2.** To charter transport such as a plane or boat is to hire it for private use.
chartered ADJECTIVE

chase chases chasing chased
VERB **1.** If you chase people or things, you run after them in order to catch them. **2.** If you chase someone, you force that person to go somewhere else.
NOUN **3.** the activity of chasing someone or something: *a high-speed car chase*

chasm chasms
NOUN **1.** a deep crack in the earth's surface **2.** a very large difference between two ideas or groups of people: *the chasm between rich and poor in our country*

chassis chassis
NOUN the frame on which a vehicle is built

chaste
ADJECTIVE *an old-fashioned word* not having sex with anyone outside marriage
chastity NOUN

chastise chastises chastising chastised
VERB *a formal word* If someone chastises you, he or she criticizes you or punishes you for something that you have done.

chat chats chatting chatted
NOUN **1.** a friendly talk with someone, usually about things that are not very important
VERB **2.** When people chat, they talk to each other in a friendly way.
chat up
VERB **3.** *an informal use* If you chat up someone, you talk to that person in a friendly way, because you are attracted to him or her.

château châteaux
NOUN a large country house or castle in France

chat room chat rooms
NOUN an Internet site where users have group discussions using e-mail

chatter chatters chattering chattered
VERB **1.** When people chatter, they talk very fast. **2.** If your teeth are chattering, they are knocking together and making a clicking

noise because you are cold.
NOUN **3.** Chatter is a lot of fast, unimportant talk.

chatty chattier chattiest
ADJECTIVE talkative and friendly

chauffeur chauffeurs
NOUN a person whose job is to drive another person's car

chauvinist chauvinists
NOUN a person who thinks his or her nation, sex, cause, or group is always superior or right: *A male chauvinist believes that men are superior to women.*
chauvinistic ADJECTIVE
chauvinism NOUN

cheap cheaper cheapest
ADJECTIVE **1.** costing very little money **2.** inexpensive but of poor quality **3.** A cheap joke or cheap remark is unfair and unkind.
cheaply ADVERB

cheat cheats cheating cheated
VERB **1.** If someone cheats, that person does wrong or unfair things to win or get something that he or she wants. **2.** If you are cheated out of something, you do not get what you are entitled to.
NOUN **3.** a person who cheats

check checks checking checked
VERB **1.** To check something is to examine it in order to make sure that everything is all right. **2.** To check the growth or spread of something is to make it stop: *a plan to check the spread of disease*
NOUN **3.** an inspection to make sure that everything is all right **4.** Checks are different coloured squares that form a pattern.
PHRASE **5.** If you keep something **in check**, you keep it under control: *She kept her emotions in check.*
check out
VERB **6.** To check out items from a store is to bring them to a cashier and pay for them. **7.** If you check something out, you inspect it and find out whether everything about it is right.

checked
ADJECTIVE Checked means marked with a pattern of squares: *a checked design*

checkered
ADJECTIVE **1.** covered with a pattern of squares **2.** A checkered career is a career that has both good and bad parts.

⚠ **HEADS UP** The word **château** is pronounced sha-TOE.

Cc

checkmate
NOUN In chess, checkmate is a situation where one player cannot stop his or her king from being captured and so loses the game.

checkout checkouts
NOUN a counter in a supermarket or store where the customers pay for their goods

checkpoint checkpoints
NOUN a place where traffic has to stop in order to be checked

checkup checkups
NOUN an examination by a doctor to see if you are healthy

cheek cheeks
NOUN **1.** Your cheeks are the sides of your face below your eyes. **2.** Cheek is speech or behaviour that is rude or disrespectful: *She wouldn't put up with her daughter's cheek.*

cheeky cheekier cheekiest
ADJECTIVE rather rude and disrespectful

cheer cheers cheering cheered
VERB **1.** When people cheer, they shout with approval or in order to show support for a person or team.
NOUN **2.** a shout of approval or support
cheer up
VERB **3.** When you cheer up, you feel more cheerful.

cheerful
ADJECTIVE **1.** happy and in good spirits: *I had never seen her so cheerful.* **2.** bright and pleasant: *a cheerful and charming place*
cheerfully ADVERB
cheerfulness NOUN

cheery cheerier cheeriest
ADJECTIVE happy and cheerful: *He gave me a cheery nod.*

cheese cheeses
NOUN a hard or semi-solid food made from milk

cheesecake cheesecakes
NOUN a dessert usually made with cream cheese, eggs, and sugar, often with a crumb crust on the bottom

cheetah cheetahs
NOUN a wild animal like a large cat with black spots

chef chefs
NOUN a head cook in a restaurant or hotel

chemical chemicals
NOUN **1.** Chemicals are substances manufactured by chemistry.
ADJECTIVE **2.** involved in chemistry or using chemicals: *chemical pesticides*
chemically ADVERB

chemist chemists
NOUN a scientist who does research in chemistry

chemistry
NOUN Chemistry is the scientific study of substances and the ways in which they change when they are combined with other substances.

chemotherapy
NOUN Chemotherapy is a way of treating diseases such as cancer by using chemicals.

cheque cheques
NOUN a printed form on which you write an amount of money. You sign the cheque and your bank pays the money from your account to the person or company whose name is on the cheque.

cherish cherishes cherishing cherished
VERB **1.** If you cherish something, you care deeply about it and want to keep it or look after it lovingly. **2.** If you cherish a memory or hope, you have it in your mind and care deeply about it: *I cherish the good memories I have of him.*

cherry cherries
NOUN **1.** a small, juicy fruit with a red or black skin and a hard stone in the centre **2.** a tree that produces cherries

cherub cherubs
NOUN an angel, shown in pictures as a plump, naked child with wings
cherubic ADJECTIVE

chess
NOUN Chess is a board game for two people in which each player has 16 pieces and tries to move his or her pieces so that the other player's king cannot escape.

chessboard chessboards
NOUN A chessboard is a board divided into 64 squares of two alternating colours on which chess is played.

chest chests
NOUN **1.** the front part of your body between your shoulders and your waist **2.** a large, wooden box with a hinged lid

chestnut chestnuts
NOUN **1.** Chestnuts are reddish brown nuts that grow inside a prickly green outer covering. **2.** a tree that produces these nuts
ADJECTIVE **3.** Something that is chestnut is reddish brown.

chest of drawers chests of drawers
NOUN a piece of furniture with drawers in it, used for storing clothes and other items that can be folded

Cc

chew chews chewing chewed

VERB When you chew something, you use your teeth to break it up in your mouth before swallowing it.

Instead of CHEW try...

crunch ice cubes

gnaw tough meat

munch carrots

nibble small snacks

chomp potato chips

chewy
ADJECTIVE

chewing gum
NOUN Chewing gum is a kind of sweet substance that you chew for a long time, but which you do not swallow.

chic
ADJECTIVE elegant and fashionable: *a chic restaurant*

chick chicks
NOUN a young bird

chicken chickens chickening chickened
NOUN **1.** a bird kept on a farm for its eggs and meat; also the meat of this bird: *roast chicken*
VERB **2.** *an informal use* If you chicken out of something, you do not do it because you are afraid.

chicken pox
NOUN Chicken pox is an illness that produces a fever and blister-like spots on the skin.

chicory
NOUN Chicory is a plant with bitter leaves that are edible. They are sometimes used in salads or can be roasted and used as a coffee substitute.

chide chides chiding chided
VERB *an old-fashioned word* To chide someone is to tell that person off.

chief chiefs
NOUN **1.** the leader of a group or organization
ADJECTIVE **2.** most important: *the chief source of oil*
chiefly ADVERB

chieftain chieftains
NOUN the leader of a tribe or clan

chiffon
NOUN Chiffon is a very thin, lightweight cloth made of silk or nylon.

chihuahua chihuahuas
NOUN a breed of very small dog with short hair and pointed ears

chilblain chilblains
NOUN a sore, itchy swelling on the hands or feet, caused by long exposure to cold

child children
NOUN **1.** a young person who is not yet an adult **2.** Someone's child is that person's son or daughter.

childbirth
NOUN Childbirth is the act of giving birth to a child.

childhood childhoods
NOUN Someone's childhood is the time when he or she is a child.

childish
ADJECTIVE immature and foolish: *I don't have time for childish arguments.*
childishly ADVERB
childishness NOUN

childless
ADJECTIVE having no children

childlike
ADJECTIVE like a child in appearance or behaviour: *childlike enthusiasm*

chili chilies
NOUN the red or green seed pod of a type of pepper, which has a very hot, spicy taste

chill chills chilling chilled
VERB **1.** To chill something is to make it cold: *Chill the cheesecake.* **2.** If something chills you, it makes you feel worried or frightened: *The thought chilled her.*
NOUN **3.** a feverish cold **4.** a feeling of cold: *the chill of the night air*

chilly chillier chilliest
ADJECTIVE **1.** rather cold: *the chilly November breeze* **2.** unfriendly and without enthusiasm: *a chilly reception*

! HEADS UP

Don't confuse **chilly** and **chilling**.
Chilly means *uncomfortably cold*.
Chilling means *frightening*.

chime chimes chiming chimed
VERB When a bell chimes, it makes a clear ringing sound.

chimney chimneys
NOUN a vertical pipe or other hollow structure above a fireplace or furnace through which smoke from a fire escapes

chimpanzee chimpanzees
NOUN a small ape with dark fur that lives in forests in Africa

chin chins
NOUN the part of your face below your mouth

china
NOUN China is items like cups, saucers, and plates made from very fine clay.

Cc

chink chinks
NOUN **1.** a small, narrow opening: *a chink in the roof* **2.** a short, light, ringing sound, like one made by glasses touching each other

chintz
NOUN Chintz is a type of brightly patterned cotton fabric.

chip chips chipping chipped
NOUN **1.** a small or thin piece of food: *chocolate chips, a potato chip* **2.** a French fry: *fish and chips* **3.** In electronics, a chip is a tiny piece of silicon inside a computer, which is used to form electronic circuits. **4.** a small piece broken off an object, or the mark made when a piece breaks off **5.** In some gambling games, chips are counters used to represent money.
VERB **6.** If you chip an object, you break a small piece off it.

chipboard another name for PARTICLEBOARD

chipmunk chipmunks
NOUN a small rodent with a striped back

chiropodist chiropodists
NOUN a person whose job is treating people's feet
chiropody NOUN

chirp chirps chirping chirped
VERB When a bird chirps, it makes a short, high-pitched sound.

chisel chisels chiselling chiselled
NOUN **1.** a tool with a long metal blade and a sharp edge at the end, which is used for cutting and shaping wood, stone, or metal
VERB **2.** To chisel wood, stone, or metal is to cut or shape it using a chisel.

chivalry
NOUN Chivalry is polite and helpful behaviour, especially by men toward women.
chivalrous ADJECTIVE

chive chives
NOUN Chives are grasslike, hollow leaves that have a mild onion flavour.

chlorine
NOUN Chlorine is a poisonous, greenish yellow gas with a strong, unpleasant smell. It is used as a disinfectant for water, and to make bleach.

chloroform
NOUN Chloroform is a colourless liquid with a strong, sweet smell used in cleaning products.

chlorophyl
NOUN Chlorophyl is a green substance in plants that enables them to use the energy from sunlight in order to grow.

chocolate chocolates
NOUN **1.** Chocolate is a sweet food made from cacao seeds. **2.** a candy made of chocolate
ADJECTIVE **3.** dark brown

choice choices
NOUN **1.** a range of different things that are available to choose from: *a wider choice of treatments* **2.** something that you choose: *You've made a good choice.* **3.** Choice is the power or right to choose: *I had no choice.*

choir choirs
NOUN a group of singers, for example in a church

choke chokes choking choked
VERB **1.** If you choke, you stop being able to breathe properly, usually because something is blocking your windpipe: *the diner choked on a fish bone* **2.** If things choke a place, they fill it so much that it is blocked or clogged up: *The creek was choked with old tires.*

cholera
NOUN Cholera is a serious disease causing severe diarrhea and vomiting. It is caused by eating or drinking infected food or water.

cholesterol
NOUN Cholesterol is a substance found in all animal fats, tissues, and blood.

KNOWING WORDS: WORD HISTORY

BE WORD SHARP!

Words are like living things. They grow and change.

Chocolate comes from two Central American words, **xococ** (bitter) and **atl** (water). Chocolate comes from the cacao bean. By itself, the bean tastes bitter, and was originally mixed with water and spices as a drink. Spanish sailors first brought chocolate drinks back to Europe in the 1500s. These drinks were sweetened and thickened to make the chocolate we most often see today.

NEL

Cc

choose chooses choosing chose chosen
VERB To choose something is to decide to have it or do it: *He chose to live in Kenya.*

choosy choosier choosiest
ADJECTIVE fussy and difficult to satisfy: *a choosy customer*

⚠️ **HEADS UP**

Don't confuse **choose** and **chose**. **Choose** is the present tense of the verb, and **chose** is the past tense.

chop chops chopping chopped
VERB **1.** To chop something is to cut it with quick, heavy strokes using an axe or a knife. NOUN **2.** a small piece of meat containing a bone, usually cut from the ribs

chopper choppers
NOUN *an informal word* a helicopter

choppy choppier choppiest
ADJECTIVE Choppy water has a lot of waves because it is windy.

chopstick chopsticks
NOUN Chopsticks are a pair of thin sticks for eating food.

choral
ADJECTIVE relating to singing by a choir: *choral music*

chord chords
NOUN a group of two or more musical notes played together

chore chores
NOUN an uninteresting job that has to be done: *the chore of cleaning*

choreography
NOUN Choreography is the art of composing dance steps and movements.
choreographer NOUN

chortle chortles chortling chortled
VERB To chortle is to laugh with amusement.

chorus choruses chorusing chorused
NOUN **1.** a large group of singers **2.** a part of a song, which is repeated after each verse VERB **3.** If people chorus something, they all say or sing it at the same time.

Christ
NOUN Christ is the name for Jesus. Christians believe that Jesus is the son of God.

christen christens christening christened
VERB When a baby is christened, he or she is named by a member of the clergy in a religious ceremony called baptism.

Christian Christians
NOUN **1.** a person who believes in Jesus Christ and his teachings
ADJECTIVE **2.** relating to Christ and his teachings: *the Christian faith* **3.** good, kind, and considerate
Christianity NOUN

Christmas Christmases
NOUN the Christian festival celebrating the birth of Christ, falling on December 25

chromatic
ADJECTIVE A chromatic scale is one that is based on an octave of 12 halftones.

chrome
NOUN Chrome is metal plated with chromium, a hard grey metal.

chromosome chromosomes
NOUN In biology, a chromosome is a part of a cell that contains genes that determine the characteristics of an animal or plant.

chronic
ADJECTIVE lasting a very long time or never stopping: *a chronic illness*
chronically ADVERB

chronicle chronicles chronicling chronicled
NOUN **1.** a record of a series of events described in the order in which they happened VERB **2.** To chronicle a series of events is to record or describe them in the order in which they happened.

chronological
ADJECTIVE arranged in the order in which things happened: *Tell me the whole story in chronological order.*
chronologically ADVERB

chronology
NOUN The chronology of events is the order in which they happened.

chrysalis chrysalises
NOUN a butterfly or moth when it is developing from being a caterpillar to being a fully grown adult

chrysanthemum chrysanthemums
NOUN a plant with large, brightly coloured flowers

chubby chubbier chubbiest
ADJECTIVE plump and round: *his chubby cheeks*

chuck chucks chucking chucked
VERB *an informal word* To chuck something is to throw it casually.

chuckle chuckles chuckling chuckled
VERB When you chuckle, you laugh quietly.

Cc

chug chugs chugging chugged
VERB When a machine or engine chugs, it makes a continuous dull thudding sound.

> **⚠ HEADS UP**
>
> There are many words that imitate a sound: *chug, clank, bang, buzz, zip*. Look up **onomatopoeia**.

chum chums
NOUN *an informal word* a friend

chunk chunks
NOUN a thick piece of something

chunky chunkier chunkiest
ADJECTIVE Someone who is chunky is broad and heavy but usually short.

church churches
NOUN **1.** a building where Christians go for religious services and worship **2.** In the Christian religion, a church is one of the groups with its own particular beliefs, customs, and clergy: *the Catholic Church*

churn churns
NOUN a container used for making milk or cream into butter

chute chutes
NOUN a steep slope or channel used to slide things down: *a garbage chute*

chutney
NOUN Chutney is a strong-tasting thick sauce made from fruit, vinegar, and spices.

cider
NOUN Cider is a drink made from apples.

cigar cigars
NOUN a roll of dried tobacco leaves, which people smoke

cigarette cigarettes
NOUN a thin roll of tobacco covered in thin paper, which people smoke

cinder cinders
NOUN Cinders are small pieces of burnt material left after something such as wood or coal has burned.

cinema cinemas
NOUN **1.** a place where people go to watch movies **2.** Cinema is the business or art of making movies: *She studied cinema at university.*

cinnamon
NOUN Cinnamon is a sweet spice that comes from the bark of an Asian tree.

cipher ciphers
NOUN a secret code or system of writing used to send secret messages

circa
PREPOSITION *a formal word* about or approximately; used especially before dates: *The picture was painted circa 1840.*

circle circles circling circled
NOUN **1.** a completely regular round shape. Every point on its edge is the same distance from the centre. **2.** a group of people with the same interests: *a circle of friends* **3.** a number of people or things arranged to form a circle: *We sat in a circle around the campfire.*
VERB **4.** To circle is to move around and around as though going around the edge of a circle: *A police helicopter circled above.*

circuit circuits
NOUN **1.** any closed line or path, often circular, for example a racetrack; also the distance around this path: *three circuits of the 26-lap race* **2.** An electrical circuit is a complete route around which an electric current can flow.

circular circulars
ADJECTIVE **1.** in the shape of a circle **2.** A circular argument or theory is not valid because it uses a statement to prove a conclusion and the conclusion to prove the statement. *Exercising is good because exercise is good for you* is an example of a circular argument.
NOUN **3.** a letter or advertisement sent to a lot of people at the same time
circularity NOUN

circulate circulates circulating circulated
VERB **1.** When something circulates or when you circulate it, it moves easily around an area: *an open place where the air can circulate freely* **2.** When you circulate something among people, you pass it around or tell it to all the people: *We circulate a regular newsletter.*

circulation circulations
NOUN **1.** The circulation of something is the act of circulating it or the action of it circulating: *traffic circulation* **2.** The circulation of a newspaper or magazine is the number of copies that are sold of each issue. **3.** Your circulation is the movement of blood through your body.

circumcise circumcises circumcising circumcised
VERB If a boy or man is circumcised, the foreskin at the end of his penis is removed.
circumcision NOUN

circumference circumferences
NOUN The circumference of a circle is its outer line or edge; also the length of this line.

Cc

circumstance circumstances
NOUN **1.** The circumstances of a situation or event are the conditions that affect what happens: *He did well under the circumstances.* **2.** Someone's circumstances are that person's position and conditions in life: *Her circumstances had changed.*

circus circuses
NOUN a show given by a travelling group of entertainers such as clowns, acrobats, and specially trained animals

cistern cisterns
NOUN a tank in which water is stored

citadel citadels
NOUN a fortress in or near a city

cite cites citing cited
VERB **1.** *a formal word* If you cite something, you quote it or refer to it: *He cited a line from his last poem.* **2.** If someone is cited in a legal action, that person is officially called to appear in court.

citizen citizens
NOUN The citizens of a country or city are the people who live in it or belong to it: *Canadian citizens*

citizenship
NOUN the status of being a citizen, with all the rights and duties that go with it: *She's applying for Canadian citizenship.*

citrus fruit citrus fruits
NOUN Citrus fruits are juicy, tropical fruits such as oranges, lemons, and grapefruit.

city cities
NOUN a large community or municipality where many people live and work

civic
ADJECTIVE relating to a city or citizens: *the civic centre*

civil
ADJECTIVE **1.** relating to the citizens of a country: *civil rights* **2.** relating to people or things that are not connected with the armed forces or the church: *a civil court, a civil marriage* **3.** polite
civilly ADVERB
civility NOUN

civil engineering
NOUN Civil engineering is the design and construction of roads, bridges, and public buildings.

civilian civilians
NOUN a person who is not in the armed forces

civilization civilizations
NOUN **1.** a society that has a highly developed social organization, scientific development, and technology: *the tale of a lost civilization*

2. Civilization is an advanced state of social organization, scientific development, and technology.

civilized
ADJECTIVE **1.** A civilized society is one with a developed social organization. **2.** A civilized person is polite and reasonable.

civil servant civil servants
NOUN a person who works in the civil service

civil service
NOUN The civil service is the government departments responsible for the administration of a country.

civil war civil wars
NOUN a war between groups of people who live in the same country

cL an abbreviation for *centilitres*

clad
ADJECTIVE *a literary or poetic word* Someone who is clad in particular clothes is wearing them.

claim claims claiming claimed
VERB **1.** If you claim that something is the case, you say that it is the case: *He claims to have lived in the same house all his life.* **2.** If you claim something, you ask for it because it belongs to you or you have a right to it: *She claimed her suitcase at the baggage counter.*
NOUN **3.** a statement that something is the case, or that you have a right to something: *They will make a claim for damages.*

claimant claimants
NOUN someone who is making a claim, especially for money

clairvoyant clairvoyants
ADJECTIVE **1.** able to know about things that will happen in the future
NOUN **2.** a person who is, or claims to be, clairvoyant

clam clams
NOUN a kind of shellfish

clamber clambers clambering clambered

Instead of **CLAMMY** try...

VERB If you clamber somewhere, you climb there with difficulty.

soggy boots
a sweaty T-shirt
muggy weather
a dank dungeon
a moist handshake

clammy
clammier clammiest
ADJECTIVE unpleasantly damp and sticky: *clammy hands*

Cc

clamour clamours clamouring clamoured
VERB **1.** If people clamour for something, they demand it noisily or angrily: *We clamoured for an explanation.*
NOUN **2.** Clamour is noisy or angry shouts or demands by a lot of people.

clamp clamps clamping clamped
NOUN **1.** an object with movable parts that is used to hold two things firmly together
VERB **2.** To clamp things together is to fasten them or hold them firmly with a clamp.
clamp down on
VERB **3.** To clamp down on something is to become stricter in controlling it: *The prime minister has clamped down on all expenditures.*

clan clans
NOUN a group of families related to one another by being descended from the same ancestor

clandestine
ADJECTIVE secret and hidden: *a clandestine meeting with friends*

clang clangs clanging clanged
VERB When something metal clangs or when you clang it, it makes a loud, deep sound.

clank clanks clanking clanked
VERB If something metal clanks, it makes a loud noise.

clap claps clapping clapped
VERB **1.** When you clap, you hit your hands together loudly to show your appreciation. **2.** If you clap someone on the back or shoulder, you hit that person in a friendly way. **3.** If you clap something somewhere, you put it there quickly and firmly: *I clapped a hand over my mouth.*
NOUN **4.** a sound made by clapping your hands **5.** A clap of thunder is a sudden loud noise of thunder.

clapper clappers
NOUN A clapper is a small piece of metal that hangs inside a bell and strikes the side to make the bell sound.

claret clarets
NOUN a type of red wine

clarify clarifies clarifying clarified
VERB To clarify something is to make it clear and easier to understand: *Discussion will clarify your thoughts.*
clarification NOUN

clarinet clarinets
NOUN a woodwind musical instrument with a straight tube and a single reed

clarity
NOUN The clarity of something is its clearness.

clash clashes clashing clashed
VERB **1.** If people clash with each other, they fight or argue. **2.** Ideas or styles that clash are so different that they do not go together. **3.** If two events clash, they happen at the same time so you cannot go to both. **4.** When metal objects clash, they hit each other with a loud noise.
NOUN **5.** a fight or argument **6.** A clash of ideas, styles, or events is a situation in which they do not go together. **7.** a loud noise made by metal objects when they hit each other

clasp clasps clasping clasped
VERB **1.** To clasp something means to hold it tightly or fasten it: *He clasped his hands.*
NOUN **2.** a fastening such as a hook or catch

class classes classing classed
NOUN **1.** A class of people or things is a group of them of a particular type or quality: *The oboe belongs to a class of musical instruments known as woodwinds.* **2.** students who are taught together in a group, or a lesson that they have together **3.** Someone who has class is elegant in appearance or behaviour.
VERB **4.** To class something means to arrange it in a particular group or to consider it as belonging to a particular group: *They are officially classed as visitors.*

classic classics
ADJECTIVE **1.** typical and therefore a good model or example of something: *a classic case of misuse* **2.** of very high quality: *one of the classic movies of all time* **3.** simple in style and form: *a classic suit*
NOUN **4.** something of the highest quality: *one of the great classics of rock music* **5.** Classics is the study of Latin and Greek, and the literature of ancient Greece and Rome.

classical
ADJECTIVE **1.** traditional in style, form, and content: *classical ballet* **2.** Classical music is serious music considered to be of lasting value. **3.** characteristic of the style of ancient Greece and Rome: *Classical friezes decorate the walls.*
classically ADVERB

classified
ADJECTIVE officially declared secret by the government: *access to classified information*

classify classifies classifying classified
VERB To classify things is to arrange them into groups with similar characteristics: *We can classify the differences into three groups.*
classification NOUN

Cc

classroom classrooms
NOUN a room in a school where students have lessons

classy classier classiest
ADJECTIVE *an informal word* stylish and elegant

clatter clatters clattering clattered
VERB **1.** When things clatter, they hit each other with a loud rattling noise.
NOUN **2.** a loud rattling noise made by hard things hitting each other

clause clauses
NOUN **1.** a section of a legal document **2.** In grammar, a clause is a group of words with a subject and a verb. An independent clause can stand alone as a complete sentence: *I put on my coat.* A dependent clause is not a complete sentence and can only modify an independent clause: *Before I went outside, I put on my coat.*

claustrophobia
NOUN Claustrophobia is a fear of being in enclosed spaces.
claustrophobic ADJECTIVE

claw claws clawing clawed
NOUN **1.** An animal's claws are hard, curved nails at the end of its feet. **2.** The claws of a crab or lobster are the two jointed parts, used for grasping things.
VERB **3.** If an animal claws something, it digs its claws into it.

clay
NOUN Clay is a type of earth that is soft and sticky when wet and hard when baked dry. It is used to make pottery and bricks.

clean cleaner cleanest; cleans cleaning cleaned
ADJECTIVE **1.** free from dirt or marks **2.** free from germs or infection **3.** If humour is clean it is not obscene and does not involve bad language. **4.** A clean movement is skilful and accurate. **5.** Clean also means free from fault or error: *a clean driving record* VERB **6.** To clean something is to remove dirt from it.
cleanly ADVERB
cleaner NOUN

Instead of **CLEAN** try...

freshly **laundered** sheets
an **immaculate** kitchen
spotless dishes
a **tidy** desk
a **flawless** record
sparkling white teeth
a **well-kept** apartment
a **sanitary** hospital room

cleanliness
NOUN Cleanliness is the practice of keeping yourself and your surroundings clean.

cleanse cleanses cleansing cleansed
VERB To cleanse something is to make it completely free from dirt.

clear clearer clearest; clears clearing cleared
ADJECTIVE **1.** easy to understand, see, or hear: *He made it clear he did not want to talk.* **2.** easy to see through: *a clear liquid* **3.** free from obstructions or unwanted things: *The sidewalk is clear of snow.*
VERB **4.** To clear an area is to remove unwanted things from it. **5.** If you clear a fence or other obstacle, you jump over it without touching it. **6.** When fog or mist clears, it disappears. **7.** If someone is cleared of a crime, that person is proved to be not guilty.
clearly ADVERB
clear up
VERB **8.** If you clear up, you tidy a place and put things away. **9.** When a problem or misunderstanding is cleared up, it is solved or settled.

clearance
NOUN If someone is given clearance to do something, that person gets official permission to do it.

clearing clearings
NOUN an area of bare ground in a forest

cleavage cleavages
NOUN the space between a woman's breasts

cleaver cleavers
NOUN a knife with a large, square blade, used especially by butchers

cleft clefts
NOUN a narrow opening made by splitting

clementine clementines
NOUN a type of small citrus fruit that is a cross between an orange and a tangerine

clench clenches clenching clenched
VERB **1.** When you clench your fist, you curl your fingers up tightly. **2.** When you clench your teeth, you squeeze them together tightly.

clergy
PLURAL NOUN The clergy are specially trained and ordained ministers who perform religious services in the Christian Church.

clerical
ADJECTIVE **1.** relating to work done in an office: *clerical jobs with the city council* **2.** relating to the clergy

Cc

clerk clerks
NOUN **1.** a salesperson or cashier in a store **2.** a person who keeps records or accounts in an office, bank, or law court

clever cleverer cleverest
ADJECTIVE **1.** intelligent and quick to understand things **2.** very effective or skilful: *a clever plan*
cleverly ADVERB
cleverness NOUN

cliché clichés
NOUN an idea or phrase that is no longer effective because it has been used so much

click clicks clicking clicked
VERB **1.** When something clicks or when you click it, it makes a short snapping sound. **2.** When you click on an area of a computer screen, you point the cursor at it and press one of the buttons on the mouse in order to make something happen.
NOUN **3.** a sound of something clicking: *I heard the click of a bolt.*

client clients
NOUN someone who pays a professional person or company to receive a service

clientele
NOUN The clientele of a place is its customers.

cliff cliffs
NOUN a steep, high rock face by the sea

climate climates
NOUN **1.** The climate of a place is the typical weather conditions there: *The climate was dry in the summer.* **2.** the general attitude and opinion of people at a particular time: *the Canadian political climate*
climatic ADJECTIVE

climax climaxes
NOUN The climax of a process, story, or piece of music is the most exciting moment in it, usually near the end.

climb climbs climbing climbed
VERB **1.** To climb is to move upward. **2.** If you climb somewhere, you move there with difficulty: *She climbed out of the back seat.*
NOUN **3.** a movement upward: *this long climb up the slope, the rapid climb in crime*
climber NOUN

clinch clinches clinching clinched
VERB If you clinch an agreement or an argument, you settle it in a definite way: *He clinched a deal.*

cling clings clinging clung
VERB To cling to something is to hold onto it or stay closely attached to it: *still clinging to old-fashioned values*

clinic clinics
NOUN a building where people go for medical treatment

clinical
ADJECTIVE **1.** relating to the medical treatment of patients: *clinical tests* **2.** Clinical behaviour or thought is logical and unemotional: *the cold, clinical attitudes of his colleagues*
clinically ADVERB

clip clips clipping clipped
NOUN **1.** a small metal or plastic object used for holding things together **2.** a short piece of a film shown by itself
VERB **3.** If you clip things together, you fasten them with clips. **4.** If you clip something, you cut bits from it to shape it: *clipped hedges*

clippers
PLURAL NOUN Clippers are tools used for cutting.

clipping clippings
NOUN an article cut from a newspaper or magazine

clique cliques
NOUN a small group of people who stick together and do not mix with other people

clitoris clitorises
NOUN a small, highly sensitive piece of flesh near the opening of a woman's vagina

cloak cloaks cloaking cloaked
NOUN **1.** a wide, loose coat, usually without sleeves
VERB **2.** To cloak something is to cover or hide it: *The valley was cloaked in mist.*

cloakroom cloakrooms
NOUN a room in a public building, such as a theatre, for coats

clock clocks
NOUN **1.** a device that measures and shows the time
PHRASE **2.** If you work **around the clock**, you work all day and night.

clockwise
ADJECTIVE OR ADVERB in the same direction as the hands on a clock

clockwork
NOUN **1.** Toys that work by clockwork move when they are wound up with a key.
PHRASE **2.** If something happens **like clockwork**, it happens with no problems or delays.

clog clogs clogging clogged
VERB **1.** To clog something is to block it: *pavements clogged with people*
NOUN **2.** Clogs are heavy wooden shoes.

clone clones cloning cloned
NOUN **1.** In biology, a clone is an animal or

Cc

plant that has been produced artificially from the cells of another animal or plant and is therefore identical to it.
VERB **2.** To clone an animal or plant is to produce it as a clone.

close closes closing closed; closer closest
VERB **1.** To close something is to shut it. **2.** To close a road or entrance is to block it so that no one can go in or out. **3.** If a store closes at a certain time, then it does not do business after that time.
ADJECTIVE OR ADVERB **4.** near to something: *a restaurant close to their home*
ADJECTIVE **5.** People who are close to each other are very friendly and know each other well. **6.** You say the weather is close when it is uncomfortably warm and there is not enough air.
closely ADVERB
closeness NOUN
closed ADJECTIVE
close down
VERB **7.** If a business closes down, all work stops there permanently.

Instead of **CLOSE** try…

an **intimate** relationship
a **neighbouring** building
keep a pencil **handy**
a **dear** friend
a **loving** family
a **nearby** market
a storm is **at hand**
an **approaching** birthday

closet closets closeting closeted
NOUN **1.** a cupboard
VERB **2.** If you are closeted somewhere, you shut yourself away alone or in private with another person.
ADJECTIVE **3.** Closet beliefs or habits are kept private and secret: *a closet romantic*

close-up close-ups
NOUN a detailed close view of something, especially a photograph taken close to the subject

closure closures
NOUN **1.** The closure of a business is the permanent shutting of it. **2.** The closure of a road is the blocking of it so it cannot be used.

clot clots clotting clotted
NOUN **1.** a lump, especially one that forms when blood thickens
VERB **2.** When a substance such as blood clots, it thickens and forms a lump.

cloth cloths
NOUN **1.** Cloth is fabric made by a process such as weaving. **2.** a piece of material used for wiping or protecting things

clothe clothes clothing clothed
VERB To clothe someone is to give that person clothes to wear.

clothes
PLURAL NOUN the things people wear on their bodies

clothing
NOUN the clothes people wear

cloud clouds clouding clouded
NOUN **1.** a mass of water vapour, smoke, or dust that forms in the air and is seen floating in the sky
VERB **2.** If something clouds or is clouded, it becomes cloudy or difficult to see through: *The sky clouded over.* **3.** Something that clouds an issue makes it more confusing.

cloudy cloudier cloudiest
ADJECTIVE **1.** full of clouds: *the cloudy sky* **2.** difficult to see through: *a glass of cloudy liquid*

clout
NOUN *an informal word* Someone who has clout has influence.

clove cloves
NOUN **1.** Cloves are small, strong-smelling, dried flower buds from a tropical tree, used as a spice in cooking. **2.** A clove of garlic is one of the separate sections of the bulb.

clover
NOUN Clover is a small plant with leaves made up of three similar parts.

clown clowns clowning clowned
NOUN **1.** an entertainer who wears funny clothes and makeup and does silly things to make people laugh
VERB **2.** If you clown, you do silly things to make people laugh.

cloying
ADJECTIVE unpleasantly sickly sweet, or sentimental: *something less cloying than whipped cream*

club clubs clubbing clubbed
NOUN **1.** an organization of people with a particular interest, who meet regularly; also the place where they meet **2.** a thick, heavy stick used as a weapon **3.** a stick with a shaped head that a golf player uses to hit the ball **4.** Clubs is one of the four suits in a pack of playing cards. It is marked by a black symbol in the shape of a clover leaf.
VERB **5.** To club someone is to hit that person hard with a heavy object.

⚠ **HEADS UP** Cloth is a noun, pronounced CLAWTH. **Clothe** is a verb, pronounced CLOHTH.

Cc

cluck clucks clucking clucked
VERB When a hen clucks, it makes a short, repeated, high-pitched sound.

clue clues
NOUN something that helps to solve a problem or mystery

clump clumps clumping clumped
NOUN **1.** a small group of things close together
VERB **2.** If you clump around, you walk with heavy footsteps.

clumsiness
NOUN awkwardness in the way someone or something moves

clumsy clumsier clumsiest
ADJECTIVE **1.** moving awkwardly and carelessly **2.** said or done without thought or tact: *He made a clumsy attempt at an apology.*
clumsily ADVERB

cluster clusters clustering clustered
NOUN **1.** A cluster of things is a group of them together: *a cluster of huts at the foot of the mountain*
VERB **2.** If people cluster together, they stay together in a close group.

clutch clutches clutching clutched
VERB **1.** If you clutch something, you hold it tightly or seize it.
PLURAL NOUN **2.** If you are in someone's clutches, that person has power or control over you.

clutter clutters cluttering cluttered
NOUN **1.** Clutter is an untidy mess.
VERB **2.** Things that clutter a place fill it and make it untidy.

cm the abbreviation for *centimetres*

co-
PREFIX The prefix *co-* means *together*: *She is now co-writing a book with her colleague.*

coach coaches coaching coached
NOUN **1.** a person who coaches a sport or a subject **2.** a bus, especially a tour bus, used for taking passengers on long journeys **3.** a section of a train that carries passengers **4.** a four-wheeled vehicle with a roof, pulled by horses, which people used to travel in
VERB **5.** If someone coaches you, that person teaches you and helps you to get better at something, such as a sport or a subject.

coal coals
NOUN **1.** Coal is a hard, black rock obtained from under the earth and burned as fuel.
2. A coal is a piece of burning coal or wood.

coalition coalitions
NOUN a temporary alliance, especially between different political parties forming a government

coarse coarser coarsest
ADJECTIVE **1.** Something that is coarse is rough in texture, often consisting of large particles: *a coarse blanket* **2.** Someone who is coarse talks or behaves in a crude or rather offensive way.
coarsely ADVERB
coarseness NOUN

coast coasts coasting coasted
NOUN **1.** the edge of the land where it meets the sea
VERB **2.** A vehicle that is coasting is moving without engine power.
coastal ADJECTIVE

coast guard coast guards
NOUN an official who watches the sea near a coast to get help for sailors when they need it, and to prevent smuggling

coastline coastlines
NOUN the outline of a coast, especially its appearance as seen from the sea or air

coat coats coating coated
NOUN **1.** a piece of clothing with sleeves, which you wear outside over your other clothes **2.** An animal's coat is the fur or hair on its body. **3.** A coat of paint or varnish is a layer of it.
VERB **4.** To coat something means to cover it with a thin layer of something: *walnuts coated with chocolate*

SPELL-CHECK THIS!

A computer's spell-check won't catch wrong **homophones** (words that are spelled differently but sound the same).

▼✕

| 1 | 2 | 3 | 4 | 5 |

The movie had a warning about course language.

In this sentence, **course** should be **coarse**. **Coarse** means *rough*. **Course** means *a series of classes*.

NEL

Cc

coat hanger coat hangers
NOUN a curved piece of wood, metal, or plastic that you hang clothes on

coating coatings
NOUN a layer of something

coax coaxes coaxing coaxed
VERB If you coax someone to do something, you gently persuade that person to do it.

cobalt
NOUN Cobalt is a hard, silvery white metal that is used for producing a blue dye.

cobble cobbles
NOUN Cobbles or cobblestones are stones with a rounded surface that were used in the past for making roads.

cobbler cobblers
NOUN a person who makes or mends shoes

cobra cobras
NOUN a type of large poisonous snake from Africa and Asia

cobweb cobwebs
NOUN the very thin net that a spider spins for catching insects, especially one that has gathered dust

cocaine
NOUN Cocaine is an addictive drug.

cock cocks
NOUN an adult male chicken; also used for any male bird

cockatoo cockatoos
NOUN a type of parrot with a crest on the head, found in Australia and Southeast Asia

cockerel cockerels
NOUN a young cock, usually less than one year old

cockpit cockpits
NOUN The place in a plane where the pilot sits.

cockroach cockroaches
NOUN An insect with long feelers and a long, flat, shiny body. It scavenges for food.

cocktail cocktails
NOUN an alcoholic drink made from several ingredients

cocky cockier cockiest *an informal word*
ADJECTIVE conceited or too self-confident
cockiness NOUN

cocoa
NOUN Cocoa is a brown powder made from the seeds of a tropical tree and used for making chocolate. It is also a hot drink made from this powder.

coconut coconuts
NOUN a very large nut with white flesh, milky juice, and a hard, hairy shell

cocoon cocoons
NOUN a silky covering over the larvae of moths and some other insects

cod
NOUN Cod, or codfish, is a large, edible fish found in the North Atlantic

code codes
NOUN a system of replacing the letters or words in a message with other letters or words, so that people cannot understand the message unless they know the system
coded ADJECTIVE

coffee
NOUN Coffee is a substance made by roasting and grinding the beans of a tropical shrub; it is also a hot drink made from the beans.

coffin coffins
NOUN a box in which a dead body is buried or cremated

cog cogs
NOUN a wheel with teeth, which turns another wheel or part of a machine

cognac
NOUN Cognac is a kind of brandy.

coherent
ADJECTIVE **1.** If something such as a paragraph or story is coherent, its parts fit together well and do not contradict one another.
2. If someone is coherent, what that person is saying makes sense and is not jumbled or confused.
coherence NOUN

cohesive
ADJECTIVE If something is cohesive, its parts fit together well: *The team must work as a cohesive unit.*
cohesion NOUN

coil coils coiling coiled
NOUN **1.** a length of rope or wire wound into a series of loops; also one of the loops
VERB **2.** If something coils, it turns into a series of loops.

coin coins coining coined
NOUN **1.** a small metal disc that is used as money
VERB **2.** If you coin a word or a phrase, you invent it.

coinage
NOUN The coinage of a country is the coins that are used there.

coincide coincides coinciding coincided
VERB **1.** If two events coincide, they happen at about the same time. **2.** When two people's ideas or opinions coincide, they agree: *What she said coincided exactly with his own thinking.*

Cc

coincidence coincidences

NOUN **1.** what happens when two similar things occur at the same time by chance: *I had moved to a new city, and by coincidence, my best friend's family was planning to move there, too.* **2.** the fact that two things are surprisingly the same
coincidental ADJECTIVE
coincidentally ADVERB

coke

NOUN Coke is a grey fuel produced from coal.

colander colanders

NOUN a bowl-shaped container with holes in it, used for washing or draining food

cold colder coldest; colds

ADJECTIVE **1.** having a low temperature
2. Someone who is cold does not show much affection.
NOUN **3.** You can refer to cold weather as the cold: *She was complaining about the cold.*
4. a minor illness in which you sneeze and may have a sore throat
coldly ADVERB
coldness NOUN

Instead of **COLD** try…

a stinging frost
a biting wind
a wintry day
frigid water
crisp fall air
bleak weather
my hands were raw
unusually chilly for June

cold-blooded

ADJECTIVE **1.** Someone who is cold-blooded does not show any pity: *a cold-blooded killer* **2.** A cold-blooded animal has a body temperature that changes according to the surrounding temperature.

cold war

NOUN Cold war is a state of extreme unfriendliness between countries not actually at war.

coleslaw

NOUN Coleslaw is a salad of chopped cabbage and other vegetables.

colic

NOUN Colic is pain in a baby's stomach.

collaborate collaborates collaborating collaborated

VERB When people collaborate, they work together to produce something: *The two bands have collaborated in the past.*
collaboration NOUN
collaborator NOUN

collage collages

NOUN a piece of art, writing, music, or a movie that combines different parts and forms

collapse collapses collapsing collapsed

VERB **1.** If something such as a building collapses, it falls down suddenly. If a person collapses, that person falls down suddenly because he or she is ill. **2.** If something such as a system or a business collapses, it suddenly stops working: *Many small businesses collapsed last year.*
NOUN **3.** The collapse of something is what happens when it stops working: *the collapse of his marriage*

collapsible

ADJECTIVE A collapsible object can be folded flat when it is not in use: *a collapsible ironing board*

collar collars

NOUN **1.** The collar of a shirt or coat is the part around the neck, which is usually folded over. **2.** a leather band around the neck of a dog or cat

collateral

NOUN Collateral is money or property that is used as a guarantee that someone will repay a loan, and which the lender can take if the loan is not repaid.

colleague colleagues

NOUN A person's colleagues are the people he or she works with.

collect collects collecting collected

VERB **1.** To collect things is to gather them together for a special purpose or as a hobby: *She collects coins and stamps.* **2.** If you collect someone or something from a place, you call there and take that person or thing away: *We had to collect my sister from school.* **3.** When things collect in a place, they gather there over a period of time: *Dust collects under the bed.*
collector NOUN

collected

ADJECTIVE calm and self-controlled

collection collections

NOUN **1.** a group of things acquired over a period of time: *a collection of paintings* **2.** Collection is the collecting of something: *tax collection* **3.** the organized collecting of money, for example for charity, or the sum of money collected

collective collectives

ADJECTIVE **1.** involving every member of a group of people: *The apple growers made a collective decision to stop spraying with chemical fertilizers.*

NOUN **2.** a group of people who share the responsibility both for running something and for doing the work
collectively ADVERB

collective noun collective nouns
NOUN a noun that refers to a single unit made up of a number of things, for example *flock* and *swarm*

college colleges
NOUN **1.** a place that offers training in one or more occupations, where students study after they have left high school **2.** one of the institutions into which some universities are divided

collide collides colliding collided
VERB If a moving object collides with something, it hits it.

collie collies
NOUN a dog that is used for rounding up sheep

colliery collieries
NOUN a coal mine

collision collisions
NOUN A collision occurs when a moving object hits something.

colloquial
ADJECTIVE Colloquial words and phrases are informal and used especially in conversation.
colloquially ADVERB
colloquialism NOUN

cologne
NOUN Cologne is a kind of weak perfume.

colon colons
NOUN **1.** the punctuation mark (:) **2.** part of your intestine

colonel colonels
NOUN an army officer with a fairly high rank

colonial
ADJECTIVE relating to a colony

colonize colonizes colonizing colonized
VERB **1.** When people colonize a place, they go to live there and take control of it: *the Europeans who colonized North America* **2.** When a lot of animals colonize a place, they go there and make it their home: *Toads are colonizing the whole park.*
colonization NOUN
colonist NOUN

colony colonies
NOUN **1.** a country controlled by a more powerful country **2.** a group of people who settle in a country controlled by their homeland

colossal
ADJECTIVE very large

colour colours colouring coloured
NOUN **1.** the appearance something has as a result of reflecting light **2.** a substance used to give colour **3.** A person's colour is the normal colour of his or her skin. **4.** A person **of colour** has non-European ancestry. **5.** Colour is also a quality that makes something interesting or exciting: *bringing more culture and colour to the city*
VERB **6.** If you colour something, you give it a colour. **7.** If something colours your opinion, it affects the way that you think about something.
coloured ADJECTIVE
colourless ADJECTIVE
colouring NOUN

colour-blind
ADJECTIVE Someone who is colour-blind cannot distinguish between certain colours.

colourful
ADJECTIVE **1.** full of colour **2.** interesting or exciting
colourfully ADVERB

colt colts
NOUN a young male horse, usually under four or five years old

column columns
NOUN **1.** a tall, solid, upright cylinder, especially one supporting a part of a building **2.** a group of people moving in a long line

columnist columnists
NOUN a journalist who writes a regular article in a newspaper or magazine

coma comas
NOUN Someone who is in a coma is in a state of deep unconsciousness.

comb combs combing combed
NOUN **1.** a flat object with pointed teeth used for tidying your hair
VERB **2.** When you comb your hair, you tidy it with a comb. **3.** If you comb a place, you search it thoroughly to try to find someone or something.

combat combats combatting combatted
NOUN **1.** Combat is fighting: *his first experience of combat*
VERB **2.** To combat something means to try to stop it happening or developing: *a way to combat crime*

combination combinations
NOUN **1.** a mixture of things: *a combination of charm and skill* **2.** a series of letters or numbers that are used to open a combination lock

! HEADS UP Coloured, meaning *of non-European ancestry*, is offensive and should be avoided.

Cc

combine combines combining combined
VERB **1.** To combine things is to cause them to exist together: *to combine a career with being a mother* **2.** To combine things also means to join them together to make a single thing: *Combine all the ingredients.* **3.** If something combines two qualities or features, it has them both: *a movie that combines great charm and sparkling performances*

combustion
NOUN Combustion is the act of burning something or the process of burning.

come comes coming came come
VERB **1.** To come to a place is to move there or arrive there. **2.** To come to a place also means to reach as far as that place: *The water came up to his waist.* **3.** *Come* is used to say that someone or something reaches a particular state: *They came to power in 1997. We had come to a decision.* **4.** When a particular time or event comes, it happens: *The peak of his career came early in 1990.* **5.** If you come from a place, you were born there or it is your home.
PHRASE **6.** A time or event **to come** is a future time or event: *The public will thank them in years to come.*

come about
VERB **7.** The way something comes about is the way it happens: *The discussion came about because of the proposed changes.*

come across
VERB **8.** If you come across something, you find it by chance.

come along
VERB **9.** If something is coming along, it is making progress: *Let's go and see how dinner is coming along.*

come between
VERB **10.** If something comes between two people, it causes unfriendly feelings between them.

come up
VERB **11.** If something comes up in a conversation or meeting, it is mentioned or discussed.

come up with
VERB **12.** If you come up with a plan or idea, you suggest it.

comeback comebacks
NOUN To make a comeback means to be popular or successful again.

comedian comedians
NOUN an entertainer whose job is to make people laugh

comedienne comediennes
NOUN a female comedian

comedy comedies
NOUN a light-hearted play or movie with a happy ending

comet comets
NOUN an object that travels around the sun leaving a bright trail behind it

comfort comforts comforting comforted
NOUN **1.** Comfort is the state of being physically relaxed: *He settled back in comfort.* **2.** Comfort is also a feeling of relief from worries or unhappiness: *The thought is a great comfort to me.*
PLURAL NOUN **3.** Comforts are things that make your life easier and more pleasant: *all the comforts of home*
VERB **4.** To comfort someone is to make that person less worried or unhappy.

comfortable
ADJECTIVE **1.** If you are comfortable, you are physically relaxed. **2.** Something that is comfortable makes you feel relaxed: *a comfortable bed* **3.** If you feel comfortable in a particular situation, you are not afraid or embarrassed.

comfortably ADVERB

comic comics
ADJECTIVE **1.** funny: *a comic monologue*
NOUN **2.** someone who tells jokes **3.** a magazine or book that contains stories told in pictures

comical
ADJECTIVE funny: *a comical sight*

comma commas
NOUN the punctuation mark (,)

command commands commanding commanded
VERB **1.** To command someone to do something is to order that person to do it. **2.** If you command something such as respect, you receive it because of your personal qualities. **3.** To command something, such as an army, means to have authority or control of it: *to command a ship*
NOUN **4.** an order to do something **5.** Your command of something is your knowledge of it and your ability to use this knowledge: *a good command of English*

commandant commandants
NOUN a military officer in charge of a place or group of people

commander commanders
NOUN an officer in charge of a military operation or organization

commandment commandments
NOUN an order or law, especially a religious one

commando commandos
NOUN Commandos are soldiers who have been specially trained to carry out raids.

comma splice
NOUN Joining two independent clauses with a comma is a mistake called a comma splice.

commemorate commemorates commemorating commemorated
VERB **1.** An object that commemorates a person or an event is intended to remind people of that person or event. **2.** If you commemorate an event, you do something special to show that you remember it.
commemorative ADJECTIVE
commemoration NOUN

commence commences commencing commenced
VERB *a formal word* To commence is to begin.
commencement NOUN

commend commends commending commended
VERB To commend someone or something is to praise that person: *He has been commended for his work.*
commendation NOUN
commendable ADJECTIVE

comment comments commenting commented
VERB **1.** If you comment on something, you make a remark about it.
NOUN **2.** a remark about something: *She received many comments about her work.*

commentary commentaries
NOUN a description of an event, which is broadcast on radio or television while the event is happening

commentator commentators
NOUN someone who gives a radio or television commentary

commerce
NOUN Commerce is the buying and selling of goods.

commercial commercials
ADJECTIVE **1.** relating to commerce
2. Commercial activities involve producing goods on a large scale in order to make money: *the commercial fishing business*
NOUN **3.** an advertisement on television, radio, or on a movie screen
commercially ADVERB

commission commissions commissioning commissioned
VERB **1.** If someone commissions a piece of work, that person formally asks someone to do it: *a study commissioned by the government*
NOUN **2.** a piece of work that has been commissioned **3.** Commission is money paid to a salesperson each time a sale is made. **4.** an official body appointed to investigate or control something

commit commits committing committed
VERB **1.** To commit a crime or sin is to do it. **2.** If you commit yourself, you state an opinion or state that you will do something. **3.** If someone is committed to a hospital or prison, that person is officially sent there.
committal NOUN

commitment commitments
NOUN **1.** Commitment is a strong belief in an idea or system. **2.** something that regularly takes up some of your time: *family commitments*

committed
ADJECTIVE A committed person is dedicated to something for a long period of time: *a committed vegetarian*

committee committees
NOUN a group of people who make decisions on behalf of a larger group

commodity commodities
NOUN *a formal word* Commodities are things that are bought, sold, or traded.

common commoner commonest
ADJECTIVE **1.** Something that is common exists in large numbers or happens often: *a common complaint* **2.** If something is common to two or more people, they all have it or use it: *I realized we had a common interest.* **3.** Common is used to indicate that something is of the ordinary kind and not special: *common salt*
PHRASE **4.** If two things or people have something **in common**, they both have it.
commonly ADVERB

commoner commoners
NOUN someone who is not a member of the nobility

commonplace
ADJECTIVE Something that is commonplace is not unusual: *Ten years ago, cellphones were a novelty; today they are commonplace.*

common sense
NOUN Your common sense is your natural ability to behave sensibly and make good judgments.

commotion
NOUN A commotion is a lot of noise and excitement.

communal
ADJECTIVE shared by a group of people: *a communal garden*

Cc

⚠ **HEADS UP** Business done over the Internet is called **e-commerce**.

commune communes
NOUN a group of people who live together and share everything

communicate communicates communicating communicated
VERB **1.** If you communicate with someone, you keep in touch with that person. **2.** If you communicate information or a feeling to someone, you make that person aware of it.

communication communications
NOUN **1.** Communication is the process by which people or animals exchange information.
PLURAL NOUN **2.** Communications are the systems by which people communicate or broadcast information, especially using electricity or radio waves.
NOUN **3.** *a formal use* a message: *Your communication came too late for me to change my plans.*

communicative
ADJECTIVE Someone who is communicative is willing to talk to people.

communion
NOUN Communion is the sharing of thoughts and feelings.

communism
NOUN Communism is the doctrine that the state should control the means of production and that there should be no private property.
communist ADJECTIVE OR NOUN

community communities
NOUN all the people living in a particular area; also used to refer to particular groups within a society: *the heart of the local community, the Asian community*

commute commutes commuting commuted
VERB People who commute travel a long distance to work every day.
commuter NOUN

compact
ADJECTIVE taking up very little space: *a compact microwave*

compact disc the full name for CD

companion companions
NOUN someone you travel or spend time with
companionship NOUN

company companies
NOUN **1.** a business that sells goods or provides a service: *the record company* **2.** a group of actors, opera singers, or dancers: *an opera company* **3.** If you have company, you have a friend or visitor with you: *I enjoyed her company.*

comparable
ADJECTIVE If two things are comparable, they are similar in size or quality: *Playing the drums is not comparable to playing the violin.*
comparably ADVERB

comparative comparatives
ADJECTIVE **1.** You add *comparative* to indicate that something is true only when compared with what is normal: *eight years of comparative calm*
NOUN **2.** In grammar, the comparative is the form of an adjective that indicates that the person or thing described has more of a particular quality than someone or something else. For example, *quicker*, *better*, and *easier* are all comparatives.
comparatively ADVERB

⚠ HEADS UP

Comparatives are in the middle: *older*, *younger*. **Superlatives** are at the extremes: *oldest*, *youngest*.

compare compares comparing compared
VERB **1.** When you compare things, you look at them together and see in what ways they are different or similar. **2.** If you compare one thing to another, you say that it is like the other thing: *He compared life to a journey that we all take.*

comparison comparisons
NOUN When you make a comparison, you consider two things together and see in what ways they are different or similar.

compartment compartments
NOUN **1.** a section of a railway car **2.** one of the separate parts of an object: *a special compartment inside your vehicle*

compass compasses
NOUN **1.** an instrument with a magnetic needle for finding directions **2.** a hinged instrument for drawing circles and curved lines and for measuring distances

compassion
NOUN pity and sympathy for someone who is suffering

compassionate
ADJECTIVE feeling or showing sympathy and pity for others
compassionately ADVERB

compatible
ADJECTIVE If people or things are compatible, they can live or work together successfully.
compatibility NOUN

compatriot compatriots
NOUN Your compatriots are people from your own country.

compel compels compelling compelled
VERB To compel someone to do something is to force that person to do it.

compelling
ADJECTIVE **1.** If a story or event is compelling, it is extremely interesting: *a compelling novel* **2.** A compelling argument or reason makes you believe that something is true or should be done: *compelling new evidence*

compensate compensates compensating compensated
VERB **1.** To compensate someone is to give that person money to replace something lost or damaged. **2.** If one thing compensates for another, it cancels out its bad effects: *The trip more than compensated for the hardship.*
compensatory ADJECTIVE

compensation compensations
NOUN something that makes up for loss or damage

compete competes competing competed
VERB **1.** When people or companies compete, they try to prove that they or their products are the best. **2.** If you compete in a contest or game, you take part in it.

competent
ADJECTIVE Someone who is competent at something can do it satisfactorily: *a very competent engineer*
competently ADVERB
competence NOUN

competition competitions
NOUN **1.** When there is competition between people or groups, they are all trying to get something that not everyone can have: *There's a lot of competition for places on the team.* **2.** an event in which people take part to find who is best at something **3.** When there is competition between companies, each company is trying to get people to buy its goods or services.

competitive
ADJECTIVE **1.** A competitive situation is one in which people or companies are competing with each other: *a crowded and competitive market* **2.** A competitive person is eager to be more successful than others. **3.** Goods sold at competitive prices are often cheaper than other goods of the same kind.
competitively ADVERB

competitor competitors
NOUN a person or company that is competing to become the most successful

compilation compilations
NOUN A compilation is a book, record, or program consisting of several items that were originally produced separately: *a compilation of his short stories*

compile compiles compiling compiled
VERB When someone compiles a book or report, that person makes it by putting together several items.

complacent
ADJECTIVE If someone is complacent, that person is unconcerned about a serious situation and does nothing about it.
complacency NOUN

complain complains complaining complained
VERB **1.** If you complain, you say that you are not satisfied with something. **2.** If you complain of pain or illness, you say that you have it.

complaint complaints
NOUN If you make a complaint, you complain about something.

complement complements complementing complemented
VERB **1.** If one thing complements another, the two things go well together: *The tiled floor complements the pine furniture.*
NOUN **2.** If one thing is a complement to another, it goes well with it. **3.** In grammar, a complement is a word or phrase, used after a verb, that gives information about the subject or object of a sentence. For example, in the sentence *Rover is a big dog*, *a big dog* is the complement.
complementary ADJECTIVE

complete completes completing completed
ADJECTIVE **1.** to the greatest degree possible: *a complete mess* **2.** If something is complete, none of it is missing: *a complete set of tools* **3.** When a task is complete, it is finished: *The planning stage is now complete.*
VERB **4.** If you complete something, you finish it. **5.** If you complete a form, you fill it in.
completely ADVERB
completion NOUN

complex complexes
ADJECTIVE **1.** Something that is complex has many different parts: *a very complex problem*
NOUN **2.** A complex is a group of buildings, roads, or other things connected with one another in some way: *a hotel and restaurant complex* **3.** If someone has a complex, that person has an emotional problem because of a past experience: *an inferiority complex*
complexity NOUN

Cc

complexion complexions
NOUN the quality of the skin on your face: *a healthy, glowing complexion*

complicate complicates complicating complicated
VERB To complicate something is to make it more difficult to understand or deal with.

complicated
ADJECTIVE Something that is complicated has so many parts or aspects that it is difficult to understand or deal with.

complication complications
NOUN something that makes a situation more difficult to deal with: *One possible complication was that it was late in the year.*

compliment compliments complimenting complimented
NOUN **1.** If you pay someone a compliment, you tell that person that you admire something about him or her.
VERB **2.** If you compliment someone, you pay that person a compliment.

complimentary
ADJECTIVE **1.** If you are complimentary about something, you express admiration for it.
2. A complimentary seat, ticket, or publication is given to you free.

comply complies complying complied
VERB If you comply with an order or rule, you obey it.
compliance NOUN

component components
NOUN The components of something are the parts it is made of.

compose composes composing composed
VERB **1.** If something is composed of particular things or people, it is made up of them. **2.** To compose a piece of music, letter, or speech means to write it. **3.** If you compose yourself, you become calm after being excited or upset.

composed
ADJECTIVE calm and in control of your feelings

composer composers
NOUN someone who writes music

composition compositions
NOUN **1.** The composition of something is the things it consists of: *the composition of the ozone layer* **2.** The composition of a poem or piece of music is the writing of it. **3.** a piece of music or writing

compost
NOUN Compost is a mixture of decaying plants added to soil to help plants grow.

composure
NOUN Someone's composure is that person's ability to stay calm: *He was able to recover his composure.*

compound compounds compounding compounded
NOUN **1.** an enclosed area of land with buildings used for a particular purpose: *the military compound* **2.** In chemistry, a compound is a substance consisting of two or more different substances or chemical elements.
VERB **3.** To compound something is to put together different parts to make a whole.
4. To compound a problem is to make it worse by adding to it: *Water shortages were compounded by taps left running.*

compound word
NOUN a word that is made by joining two or more separate words. For example, the word *highway* is made by joining the words *high* and *way.*

comprehend comprehends comprehending comprehended
VERB *a formal word* To comprehend something is to understand or appreciate it: *He did not fully comprehend what was puzzling me.*
comprehension NOUN

comprehensible
ADJECTIVE able to be understood

comprehensive
ADJECTIVE Something that is comprehensive

SPELL-CHECK THIS!

A computer's spell-check won't catch wrong **homophones** (words that are spelled differently but sound the same).

The shoes **complimented** the rest of the outfit.

In this sentence, **complimented** should be **complemented**. Complement means *make complete*. Compliment means *praise*.

NEL

Cc

includes everything necessary or relevant: *a comprehensive guide to wilderness hiking*
comprehensively ADVERB

compress compresses compressing compressed
VERB To compress something is to squeeze it or shorten it so that it takes up less space: *compressed air*
compression NOUN

comprise comprises comprising comprised
VERB *a formal word* What something comprises is what it consists of: *Central Canada comprises two provinces: Ontario and Québec.*

compromise compromises compromising compromised
NOUN **1.** an agreement in which people accept less than they originally wanted: *In the end they reached a compromise.*
VERB **2.** When people compromise, they agree to accept less than they originally wanted.
compromising ADJECTIVE

compulsion compulsions
NOUN a very strong desire to do something

compulsive
ADJECTIVE You use *compulsive* to describe someone who cannot stop doing something: *a compulsive liar*

compulsory
ADJECTIVE If something is compulsory, you have to do it: *School attendance is compulsory.*

computer computers
NOUN an electronic machine that can quickly make calculations, store and find information, or run other machines

computer-aided design
NOUN Computer-aided design, or computer-assisted design is the use of computers and computer graphics to help design things. It is usually shortened to CAD.

computerize computerizes computerizing computerized
VERB When a system or process is computerized, the work is done by computers.

computing
NOUN Computing is the use of computers and the writing of programs for them.

comrade comrades
NOUN Your comrades are your companions, friends, or fellow workers.
comradeship NOUN

con cons conning conned *an informal word*
VERB **1.** If someone cons you, that person

tricks you into doing or believing something.
NOUN **2.** a trick in which someone deceives you into doing or believing something

concave
ADJECTIVE A concave surface curves inward, rather than being level or bulging outward.

conceal conceals concealing concealed
VERB To conceal something is to hide it: *She concealed her diary under her bed.*
concealment NOUN

concede concedes conceding conceded
VERB **1.** If you concede something, you admit that it is true: *I conceded that he was entitled to his views.* **2.** When someone concedes defeat, that person accepts that he or she has lost something, such as a contest or an election.

conceit
NOUN Conceit is someone's excessive pride in his or her appearance or abilities.

conceited
ADJECTIVE Someone who is conceited is too proud of his or her appearance or abilities.

conceivable
ADJECTIVE If something is conceivable, you can believe that it could exist or be true: *It's conceivable that you also met her.*
conceivably ADVERB

conceive conceives conceiving conceived
VERB **1.** If you can conceive of something, you can imagine it or believe it: *Could you conceive of doing such a thing yourself?*
2. If you conceive something such as a plan, you think of it and work out how it could be done. **3.** When a woman conceives, she becomes pregnant.

concentrate concentrates concentrating concentrated
VERB **1.** If you concentrate on something, you give it all your attention. **2.** When something is concentrated in one place, it is all there rather than in several places: *The population of Canada is mostly concentrated in the cities.*
concentration NOUN

concentrated
ADJECTIVE A concentrated liquid has been made stronger by having water removed from it: *concentrated orange juice*

concentration camp concentration camps
NOUN a prison camp, especially one set up by the Nazis during World War Two

concept concepts
NOUN an abstract or general idea: *the concept of tolerance*
conceptual ADJECTIVE
conceptually ADVERB

Cc

conception conceptions
NOUN **1.** Your conception of something is the idea you have of it. **2.** Conception is the process by which a woman becomes pregnant.

concern concerns concerning concerned
NOUN **1.** Concern is a feeling of worry about something or someone: *public concern about violence* **2.** If something is your concern, it is your responsibility. **3.** a business: *a large manufacturing concern*
VERB **4.** If something concerns you or if you are concerned about it, it worries you. **5.** You say that something concerns you if it affects or involves you: *It concerns you and me.*
PHRASE **6.** If something is **of concern** to you, it is important to you.
concerned ADJECTIVE

concerning
PREPOSITION You use *concerning* to show what something is about: *The principal had questions concerning our behaviour during lunch hour.*

concert concerts
NOUN a public performance by musicians

concerted
ADJECTIVE A concerted action is done by several people together: *My brothers and I made a concerted effort to get the house clean before Dad got home.*

concerto concertos
NOUN a piece of music for a solo instrument and an orchestra

concession concessions
NOUN If you make a concession, you agree to let someone have or do something: *Her one concession was to let me bring the dog into the building.*

conch conches
NOUN a shellfish with a large, brightly coloured shell; also the shell itself

concise
ADJECTIVE giving all the necessary information using as few words as necessary: *a concise guide to the city*

conclude concludes concluding concluded
VERB **1.** If you conclude something, you decide that it is so because of the other things that you know: *An inquiry concluded that her story was untrue.* **2.** When you conclude something, you finish it: *I concluded my book report with a quotation from the book.*
concluding ADJECTIVE

conclusion conclusions
NOUN **1.** a decision made after thinking carefully about something **2.** the finish or ending of something

conclusive
ADJECTIVE Facts that are conclusive show that something is certainly true.
conclusively ADVERB

concoct concocts concocting concocted
VERB **1.** If you concoct an excuse or explanation, you invent one. **2.** If you concoct something, you make it by mixing several things together.
concoction NOUN

concourse concourses
NOUN a wide hall in a building where people walk about or gather together

concrete
NOUN **1.** Concrete is a solid building material made by mixing cement, sand, and water.
ADJECTIVE **2.** definite, rather than general or vague: *I don't really have any concrete plans.* **3.** real and physical, rather than abstract: *concrete evidence*

concur concurs concurring concurred
VERB *a formal word* To concur is to agree: *She concurred with me.*

concurrent
ADJECTIVE If things are concurrent, they are happening at the same time.
concurrently ADVERB

concussed
ADJECTIVE confused or unconscious because of a blow to the head
concussion NOUN

condemn condemns condemning condemned
VERB **1.** If you condemn something, you say that it is bad and unacceptable: *Teachers condemned the new plans.* **2.** If someone is condemned to a punishment, that person is given it: *He was condemned to a life sentence for his crimes.* **3.** If you are condemned to something unpleasant, you must suffer it: *Many third world populations are condemned to poverty.* **4.** When a building is condemned, it is going to be pulled down because it is unsafe.
condemnation NOUN

condensation
NOUN Condensation is a coating of tiny drops formed on a surface by steam or vapour.

> ⚠ **HEADS UP**
>
> **Condensation** happens when steam cools into water. **Evaporation** is the opposite, when water boils into steam.

Cc

condense condenses condensing condensed
VERB **1.** If you condense a piece of writing or a speech, you shorten it. **2.** When a gas or vapour condenses, it changes into a liquid.

condescending
ADJECTIVE If you are condescending, you behave in a way that shows you think you are superior to other people.

condition conditions conditioning conditioned
NOUN **1.** the state someone or something is in
PLURAL NOUN **2.** The conditions in which something is done are the location and other factors likely to affect it: *The very difficult conditions continued to affect our performance.* **3.** a requirement that must be met for something else to be possible: *A perfect driving record was a condition of the job as a truck driver.* **4.** You can refer to an illness or other medical problem as a condition: *a heart condition*
PHRASE **5.** If you are **out of condition**, you are unfit.
VERB **6.** If someone is conditioned to behave or think in a certain way, that person does it as a result of his or her upbringing or training.

conditional
ADJECTIVE If one thing is conditional on another, it can only happen if the other thing happens: *Our going to the game is conditional on finishing our chores.*

condolence condolences
NOUN Condolence is sympathy expressed to a bereaved person.

condominium condominiums
NOUN an individually owned apartment or townhouse on land that is jointly owned by all. It is usually shortened to *condo*.

condone condones condoning condoned
VERB If you condone someone's bad behaviour, you accept it and do not try to stop it: *We cannot condone violence.*

conducive
ADJECTIVE If something is conducive to something else, it makes it likely to happen: *a situation that is conducive to relaxation*

conduct conducts conducting conducted
VERB **1.** To conduct an activity or task is to carry it out: *He seemed to be conducting a conversation with that man.* **2.** The way you conduct yourself is the way you behave. **3.** When someone conducts an orchestra or choir, that person stands in front of it and directs it. **4.** If something conducts heat or electricity, heat or electricity can pass through it.

NOUN **5.** If you take part in the conduct of an activity or task, you help to carry it out. **6.** Your conduct is your behaviour.

conductor conductors
NOUN **1.** someone who conducts an orchestra or choir **2.** a substance that conducts heat or electricity

cone cones
NOUN **1.** a regular three-dimensional shape with a circular base and a point at the top **2.** A fir cone or pine cone is the fruit of a fir or pine tree.

confectionery
NOUN Confectionery is candy.

confederation confederations
NOUN **1.** a group of countries or states joined together for a special purpose **2.** In Canada, Confederation is the name given to the agreement and the event that joined Ontario, Québec, Nova Scotia, and New Brunswick as a nation in 1867. Confederation later included the present provinces and territories. **3.** Confederation is also the name given to the political union of Newfoundland and Labrador with Canada in 1949.

confer confers conferring conferred
VERB When people confer, they discuss something in order to make a decision.

conference conferences
NOUN a meeting at which formal discussions take place

confess confesses confessing confessed
VERB If you confess to something, you admit it: *The man has confessed to his crimes and will be arrested.*

confession confessions
NOUN If you make a confession, you admit you have done something wrong.

confetti
NOUN Confetti is small pieces of coloured paper thrown over the bride and groom at a wedding.

confidant confidants
NOUN *a formal word* a person you discuss your private problems with

confide confides confiding confided
VERB If you confide in or to someone, you tell that person a secret: *She confided in me that she was very worried.*

confidence confidences
NOUN **1.** If you have confidence in someone, you feel you can trust that person. **2.** Someone who has confidence is sure of his or her own abilities or qualities. **3.** a secret you tell someone

Cc

confident
ADJECTIVE **1.** If you are confident about something, you are sure it will happen the way you want it to. **2.** People who are confident are sure of their own abilities or qualities.
confidently ADVERB

confidential
ADJECTIVE Confidential information is meant to be kept secret.
confidentially ADVERB
confidentiality NOUN

confine confines confining confined
VERB **1.** If something is confined to one place, person, or thing, it exists only in that place or affects only that person or thing. **2.** If you confine yourself to doing or saying something, it is the only thing you do or say: *They confined themselves to discussing the weather.* **3.** If you are confined to a place, you cannot leave it: *She was confined to bed for two days.*
PLURAL NOUN **4.** The confines of a place are its boundaries: *They have never travelled outside the confines of their own province.*
confinement NOUN

confined
ADJECTIVE A confined space is small and enclosed by walls.

confirm confirms confirming confirmed
VERB **1.** To confirm something is to say or show that it is true: *Police confirmed that they had received a call.* **2.** If you confirm an arrangement or appointment, you say it is definite.
confirmation NOUN

confirmed
ADJECTIVE You use *confirmed* to describe someone who has a belief or way of life that is unlikely to change: *a confirmed bachelor*

confiscate confiscates confiscating confiscated
VERB To confiscate something is to take it away from someone as a punishment.

conflict conflicts conflicting conflicted
NOUN **1.** Conflict is disagreement and argument: *conflict between workers and management* **2.** a war or battle **3.** When there is a conflict of ideas or interests, people have different ideas or interests that cannot all be satisfied.
VERB **4.** When ideas or interests conflict, they are different and cannot all be satisfied.

conform conforms conforming conformed
VERB **1.** If you conform, you behave the way people expect you to. **2.** If something conforms to a law or to someone's wishes, it is what is required or wanted.
conformist NOUN OR ADJECTIVE

confront confronts confronting confronted
VERB **1.** If you are confronted with a problem or task, you have to deal with it. **2.** If you confront someone, you meet that person face to face. **3.** If you confront someone with evidence or a fact, you present it to that person in order to accuse him or her of something.

confrontation confrontations
NOUN a serious dispute or fight: *a confrontation between police and fans*

confuse confuses confusing confused
VERB **1.** If you confuse two things, you mix them up and think one of them is the other: *You are confusing facts with opinion.* **2.** To confuse someone means to make that person uncertain about what is happening or what to do. **3.** To confuse a situation means to make it more complicated.

confused
ADJECTIVE **1.** uncertain about what is happening or what to do **2.** in an

Instead of CONFUSED try...

untidy
mess

a bewildered look

the police are baffled

muddled thinking

the message mystified us

perplexed by a problem

confusing
ADJECTIVE puzzling or bewildering

confusion
NOUN a bewildering state or untidy mess

congeal congeals congealing congealed
VERB When a liquid congeals, it becomes very thick and sticky.

congenial
ADJECTIVE If something is congenial, it is pleasant and suits you: *We wanted to talk in congenial surroundings.*

congenital
ADJECTIVE If someone has a congenital disease or disability, that person has it from birth but did not inherit it.

congested
ADJECTIVE **1.** When a road is congested, it is so full of traffic that normal movement is impossible. **2.** If your nose is congested, it is blocked and you cannot breathe properly.
congestion NOUN

Cc

conglomerate conglomerates
NOUN a large business organization consisting of several companies

congratulate congratulates congratulating congratulated
VERB If you congratulate someone, you express pleasure at something good that has happened to that person, or praise him or her for some achievement.
congratulation NOUN
congratulatory ADJECTIVE

congregate congregates congregating congregated
VERB When people congregate, they gather together somewhere.
congregation NOUN

congress congresses
NOUN a large meeting held to discuss ideas or policies: *a medical congress*

conical
ADJECTIVE shaped like a cone

conifer conifers
NOUN any type of evergreen tree that produces cones
coniferous ADJECTIVE

conjecture
NOUN Conjecture is guesswork about something: *There was no evidence, only conjecture.*

conjugate conjugates conjugating conjugated
VERB When you conjugate a verb, you list the different forms of it you use with the pronouns *I*, *you* (singular), *he*, *she*, *it*, *you* (plural), and *they*.

conjunction conjunctions
NOUN **1.** In grammar, a conjunction is a word that links two other words or two clauses, for example *and*, *but*, *while*, and *that*.
PHRASE **2.** If two or more things are done in conjunction, they are done together.

conjure conjures
VERB If you conjure something, you cause it to appear as if by magic: *The magician conjured a bouquet of roses from his hat.*

connect connects connecting connected
VERB **1.** To connect two things is to join them together. **2.** If you connect something with something else, you think of the two things as being linked: *High blood pressure is closely connected to heart disease.*

connection connections
NOUN **1.** a link or relationship between things **2.** the point where two wires or pipes are joined together: *a loose connection*
PLURAL NOUN **3.** Someone's connections are the people that person knows: *He had powerful connections in the government.*

connective connectives
NOUN a word or short phrase that connects clauses, phrases, or words

connoisseur connoisseurs
NOUN someone who knows a lot about the arts, or about food or drink: *a great connoisseur of opera*

> ⚠ **HEADS UP**
>
> The word **connoisseur** is taken from French, and so is its pronunciation: kon-uh-SUR.

connotation connotations
NOUN The connotations of a word or name are what it makes you think of. For example, the word *fat* has a connotation of unpleasantness, while *chubby* has a connotation of cuteness.

conquer conquers conquering conquered
VERB **1.** To conquer people is to take control of their country by force. **2.** If you conquer something difficult or dangerous, you succeed in controlling it: *Conquer your fear!*
conqueror NOUN

conquest conquests
NOUN **1.** Conquest is the conquering of a country or group of people. **2.** Conquests are lands captured by conquest.

conscience consciences
NOUN the part of your mind that tells you what is right and wrong

conscientious
ADJECTIVE Someone who is conscientious is very careful to do his or her work properly.
conscientiously ADVERB

conscious
ADJECTIVE **1.** If you are conscious of something, you are aware of it: *She was not conscious of the time.* **2.** A conscious action or effort is done deliberately: *I made a conscious decision not to hide.* **3.** Someone who is conscious is awake, rather than asleep or unconscious: *She was still conscious when she was taken to hospital.*
consciously ADVERB
consciousness NOUN

consecrated
ADJECTIVE A consecrated building or place is one that has been officially declared to be holy.

consecutive
ADJECTIVE Consecutive events or periods of time happen one after the other: *We won eight consecutive games.*

115

Cc

consensus
NOUN Consensus is general agreement among a group of people: *The consensus was that it could be done.*

consent consents consenting consented
NOUN **1.** Consent is permission to do something: *He reluctantly gave his consent to having his picture taken.* **2.** Consent is also agreement between two or more people: *By common consent it was the best game of these championships.*
VERB **3.** If you consent to something, you agree to it or allow it.

consequence consequences
NOUN **1.** The consequences of something are its results or effects: *the dire consequences of a major hurricane.* **2.** *a formal use* If something is of consequence, it is important.

consequent
ADJECTIVE Consequent describes something as being the result of something else: *an earthquake in 1980 and its consequent damage*
consequently ADVERB

conservation
NOUN Conservation is the preservation of the environment.
conservationist NOUN OR ADJECTIVE

conservative conservatives
NOUN **1.** Someone who is conservative is not willing to accept changes or new ideas. **2.** A conservative estimate or guess is a cautious or moderate one.
conservatively ADVERB
conservatism NOUN

conservatory conservatories
NOUN a school for instruction in music.

conserve conserves conserving conserved
VERB If you conserve a supply of something, you make it last: *the only way to conserve energy*

consider considers considering considered
VERB **1.** If you consider something to be the case, you think or judge it to be so: *The coach does not consider him an ideal team member.* **2.** To consider something is to think about it carefully: *If an offer were made, we would consider it.* **3.** If you consider someone's needs or feelings, you pay attention to them.

considerable
ADJECTIVE A considerable amount of something is a lot of it: *a considerable sum of money*
considerably ADVERB

considerate
ADJECTIVE Someone who is considerate pays attention to other people's needs and feelings.

consideration considerations
NOUN **1.** Consideration is careful thought about something: *a decision demanding careful consideration* **2.** If you show consideration for someone, you pay attention to that person's needs and feelings.
3. something that has to be thought about: *Money was also a consideration.*

considered
ADJECTIVE A considered opinion or judgment is arrived at by careful thought.

considering
CONJUNCTION OR PREPOSITION You say considering to indicate that you are taking something into account: *I know that must sound callous, considering that we have been best friends for years.*

consign consigns consigning consigned
VERB *a formal word* To consign something to a particular place is to send or put it there.

consignment consignments
NOUN A consignment of goods is a load of them being delivered somewhere.

consist consists consisting consisted
VERB What something consists of is its different parts or members: *The brain consists of millions of nerve cells.*

consistency consistencies
NOUN **1.** Consistency is the quality of being consistent. **2.** The consistency of a substance is how thick or smooth it is: *the consistency of cream*

consistent
ADJECTIVE **1.** If you are consistent, you keep doing something the same way: *one of our most consistent performers* **2.** If something such as a statement or argument is consistent, there are no contradictions in it.
consistently ADVERB

console consoles consoling consoled
VERB **1.** To console someone who is unhappy is to make that person more cheerful.
NOUN **2.** a panel with switches or knobs for operating a machine
consolation NOUN

consolidate consolidates consolidating consolidated
VERB **1.** To consolidate debts or companies, for example, is to combine them. **2.** To consolidate something you have gained or achieved is to make it more secure.
consolidation NOUN

Cc

consonant consonants
NOUN a sound such as *p* or *m* that you make by stopping the air flowing freely through your mouth

consort consorts consorting consorted
VERB **1.** *a formal word* If you consort with someone, you spend a lot of time with that person.
NOUN **2.** the wife or husband of a king or queen

consortium consortia
NOUN a group of businesses working together for a length of time or for a certain purpose

conspicuous
ADJECTIVE If something is conspicuous, people can see or notice it very easily.
conspicuously ADVERB

conspiracy conspiracies
NOUN When there is a conspiracy, a group of people secretly plan to do something wrong.

conspirator conspirators
NOUN someone involved in a conspiracy

conspire conspires conspiring conspired
VERB **1.** When people conspire, they secretly plan to do something wrong. **2.** When events conspire toward a particular result, they seem to work together to cause it: *Circumstances conspired to doom the business.*

constable constables
NOUN a police officer of the lowest rank

constant
ADJECTIVE **1.** Something that is constant happens all the time or is always there: *a city under constant attack* **2.** If an amount or level is constant, it stays the same. **3.** People who are constant stay loyal to a person or idea.
constantly ADVERB
constancy NOUN

constellation constellations
NOUN a group of stars

consternation
NOUN Consternation is anxiety or dismay: *There was some consternation when it began raining.*

constipated
ADJECTIVE Someone who is constipated is unable to pass solid waste from his or her bowels.
constipation NOUN

constituency constituencies
NOUN the area represented by an elected member of a government

constituent constituents
NOUN **1.** Constituents are the voters who live in a constituency. **2.** The constituents of something are its parts: *the major constituents of bone*

constitute constitutes constituting constituted
VERB If groups of things constitute something, they are what it consists of: *Jewellery constitutes 80 percent of the store's stock.*

constitution constitutions
NOUN **1.** The constitution of a country is the system of laws that formally states people's rights and duties. **2.** Your constitution is your health: *a very strong constitution*
constitutional ADJECTIVE
constitutionally ADVERB

constrained
ADJECTIVE If someone feels constrained to do something, that person feels that he or she should do that thing.

constraint constraints
NOUN something that limits someone's freedom of action: *constraints on spending*

constrict constricts constricting constricted
VERB To constrict something is to squeeze it tightly.
constriction NOUN

construct constructs constructing constructed
VERB To construct something is to build or make it.

construction constructions
NOUN **1.** The construction of something is the building or making of it: *the construction of the harbour* **2.** something built or made: *The bookcase was a solid construction built of wood.*

constructive
ADJECTIVE Constructive criticism and comments are helpful.
constructively ADVERB

consul consuls
NOUN an official who lives in a foreign city and who looks after people there who are citizens of his or her own country
consular ADJECTIVE

consulate consulates
NOUN the place where a consul works

consult consults consulting consulted
VERB **1.** If you consult someone, you ask for that person's opinion or advice. **2.** When people consult each other, they exchange ideas and opinions. **3.** If you consult a book or map, you look at it for information.

consultant consultants
NOUN someone who gives expert advice: *a management consultant*

 **HEADS UP** The word **consortium** is pronounced cun-SOAR-shum.

Cc

consultation consultations
NOUN **1.** a meeting held to discuss something **2.** Consultation is discussion or the seeking of advice: *There has to be much better consultation with the public.*
consultative ADJECTIVE

consume consumes consuming consumed
VERB **1.** *a formal word* If you consume something, you eat or drink it. **2.** To consume fuel or energy is to use it up.

consumer consumers
NOUN someone who buys things or uses services: *two new magazines for teenage consumers*

consumerism
NOUN Consumerism is the belief that a country will have a strong economy if its people buy a lot of goods and spend a lot of money.

consuming
ADJECTIVE A consuming passion or interest is more important to you than anything else.

consummate
ADJECTIVE You use *consummate* to describe someone who is very good at something: *a consummate politician*

consumption
NOUN The consumption of fuel or food is the using of it, or the amount used.

contact contacts contacting contacted
NOUN **1.** If you are in contact with someone, you regularly talk to or write to that person. **2.** When things are in contact, they are touching each other. **3.** someone you know in a place or organization from whom you can get help or information
VERB **4.** If you contact someone, you telephone, e-mail, or write to that person.

contact lens contact lenses
NOUN Contact lenses are small plastic lenses that you put in your eyes instead of wearing glasses, to help you see better.

contagious
ADJECTIVE A contagious disease can be caught by touching people or things infected with it.

contain contains containing contained
VERB **1.** If a substance contains something, that thing is a part of it: *Chocolate bars contain sugar.* **2.** The things a box or room contains are the things inside it. **3.** *a formal use* To contain something also means to stop it increasing or spreading: *efforts to contain the disease*
containment NOUN

container containers
NOUN **1.** something such as a box or a bottle that you keep things in **2.** a large sealed metal box for transporting things

contaminate contaminates contaminating contaminated
VERB If something is contaminated by dirt, chemicals, or radiation, it is made impure and harmful: *foods contaminated with lead*
contamination NOUN

contemplate contemplates contemplating contemplated
VERB **1.** To contemplate is to think carefully about something for a long time. **2.** If you contemplate doing something, you consider doing it: *I contemplated taking a job after school.* **3.** If you contemplate something, you look at it for a long time: *He contemplated her drawings.*
contemplation NOUN
contemplative ADJECTIVE

contemporary contemporaries
ADJECTIVE **1.** produced or happening now: *contemporary literature*
NOUN **2.** Someone's contemporaries are other people living or active at the same time as that person: *Shakespeare and his contemporaries*

contempt
NOUN If you treat someone or something with contempt, you show no respect for that person or thing at all.

contemptible
ADJECTIVE not worthy of any respect: *this contemptible piece of nonsense*

contemptuous
ADJECTIVE showing contempt
contemptuously ADVERB

contend contends contending contended
VERB **1.** To contend with a difficulty is to deal with it: *They had to contend with injuries.* **2.** *a formal use* If you contend that something is true, you say firmly that it is true. **3.** When people contend for something, they compete for it.
contender NOUN

content contents contenting contented
PLURAL NOUN **1.** The contents of something are the things inside it.
NOUN **2.** The content of an article or speech is what is expressed in it. **3.** Content is the proportion of something that a substance contains: *White bread is inferior to whole wheat bread in fibre content.*
ADJECTIVE **4.** happy and satisfied with your life **5.** willing to do or have something: *He would be content to telephone her.*

⚠ **HEADS UP** The noun **content** is pronounced CAWN-tent; the verb and adjective, cun-TENT.

Cc

VERB **6.** If you content yourself with something, you are satisfied with it: *She contented herself with second place in the competition.*

contented
ADJECTIVE happy and satisfied with your life
contentedly ADVERB
contentment NOUN

contention contentions
NOUN *a formal word* Someone's contention is the idea or opinion that person is expressing: *It is their contention that students should be assigned homework daily.*

contest contests contesting contested
NOUN **1.** a competition or game: *a story-writing contest*
VERB **2.** If you contest a statement or decision, you object to it formally.

contestant contestants
NOUN someone taking part in a competition

context contexts
NOUN **1.** The context of something consists of matters related to it that help to explain it: *What is the historical context of the event?* **2.** The context of a word or sentence consists of the words or sentences before and after it.

continent continents
NOUN a very large area of land, such as Africa or Asia
continental ADJECTIVE

contingency contingencies
NOUN something that might happen in the future: *I need to examine all possible contingencies.*

contingent contingents
NOUN a group of people representing a country or organization: *a strong Canadian contingent at the Winter Olympics*

continual
ADJECTIVE **1.** happening all the time without stopping: *a continual headache* **2.** happening again and again: *the continual snide remarks*
continually ADVERB

> ⚠ **HEADS UP**
>
> Don't confuse **continual** and **continuous**. A phone ringing is **continual**. A dial tone is **continuous**.

continuation continuations
NOUN **1.** The continuation of something is the continuing of it: *the continuation of the human race* **2.** Something that is a

continuation of an event follows it and seems like a part of it: *a meeting, which was a continuation of the conference*

continue continues continuing continued
VERB **1.** If you continue to do something, you keep doing it. **2.** If something continues, it does not stop. **3.** You also say something continues when it starts again after stopping: *She continued after a pause.*

continuous
ADJECTIVE **1.** Continuous means happening or existing without stopping. **2.** A continuous line or surface has no gaps or holes in it.
continuously ADVERB
continuity NOUN

contorted
ADJECTIVE twisted into an unnatural, unattractive shape

contour contours
NOUN **1.** The contours of something are its general shape. **2.** On a map, a contour is a line joining points of equal height.

contract contracts contracting contracted
NOUN **1.** a written legal agreement about the sale of something or work done for money
VERB **2.** When something contracts, it gets smaller or shorter. **3.** *a formal use* If you contract an illness, you get it: *Her husband contracted a virus.*
contractual ADJECTIVE

contraction contractions
NOUN Shortening a combination of two words makes a contraction, like *don't* for *do not*. An apostrophe shows where one or two letters have been left out.

> ⚠ **HEADS UP**
>
> A **contraction** shows missing letters: *can't, she's*. An **abbreviation** just shortens a word or phrase: *Dr., MP.*

contractor contractors
NOUN a person or company who does work for other people or companies: *a building contractor*

contradict contradicts contradicting contradicted
VERB If you contradict someone, you say that what that person has just said is not true, and that something else is.
contradiction NOUN
contradictory ADJECTIVE

contraption contraptions
NOUN a strange-looking machine or piece of equipment

Cc

contrary

ADJECTIVE **1.** Contrary ideas or opinions are opposed to each other and cannot be held by the same person.
PHRASE **2.** You say **on the contrary** when you are contradicting what someone has just said.

contrast contrasts

NOUN **1.** a great difference between things: *the contrast between good and evil* **2.** If one thing is a contrast to another, it is very different from it: *The bride's white dress is a sharp contrast to the groom's dark suit.*

contrast contrasts contrasting contrasted

VERB **1.** If you contrast things, you describe or emphasize the differences between them. **2.** If one thing contrasts with another, it is very different from it: *The interview contrasted completely with the one she gave in Edmonton.*

contravene contravenes contravening contravened

VERB *a formal word* If you contravene a law or rule, you do something that it forbids.

contribute contributes contributing contributed

VERB **1.** If you contribute to something, you do things to help it succeed: *The elderly have much to contribute to the community.* **2.** If you contribute money, you give it to help to pay for something. **3.** If something contributes to an event or situation, it is one of its causes: *The dry summer has contributed to perfect conditions.*
contribution NOUN
contributor NOUN
contributory ADJECTIVE

contrive contrives contriving contrived

VERB *a formal word* If you contrive to do something difficult, you scheme or plot to make it happen: *He contrived to escape from his kidnappers.*

contrived

ADJECTIVE Something that is contrived is unnatural: *a contrived compliment*

control controls controlling controlled

NOUN **1.** Control of a country or organization is the power to make the important decisions about how it is run. **2.** Your control over something is your ability to make it work the way you want it to. **3.** The controls on a machine are knobs or other devices used to work it.
VERB **4.** To control a country or organization means to have the power to make decisions about how it is run. **5.** To control something such as a machine or system means to make it work the way you want it to. **6.** If you

control yourself, you make yourself behave calmly when you are angry or upset.
PHRASE **7.** If something is **out of control**, nobody has any power over it.
controller NOUN

controversial

ADJECTIVE Something that is controversial causes a lot of discussion and argument, because many people disapprove of it.

controversy controversies

NOUN discussion and argument because many people disapprove of something

conundrum conundrums

NOUN *a formal word* a puzzling problem

convalesce convalesces convalescing convalesced

VERB When people convalesce, they rest and regain their health after an illness or operation.

convection

NOUN Convection is the process by which heat travels through gases and liquids.

convene convenes convening convened *a formal word*

VERB **1.** To convene a meeting is to arrange for it to take place. **2.** When people convene, they come together for a meeting.

convenience conveniences

NOUN **1.** The convenience of something is the fact that it is easy to use or that it makes something easy to do. **2.** something useful

convenient

ADJECTIVE If something is convenient, it is easy to use or it makes something easy to do.
conveniently ADVERB

convention conventions

NOUN **1.** an accepted way of behaving or doing something: *Punctuation is a language convention.* **2.** a large meeting of an organization or political group: *the Liberal convention*

conventional

ADJECTIVE **1.** You say that people are conventional when there is nothing unusual about their way of life. **2.** Conventional methods are the ones that are usually used.
conventionally ADVERB

converge converges converging converged

VERB To converge is to meet or join at a particular place.

conversation conversations

NOUN If you have a conversation with someone, you spend time talking to that person.
conversational ADJECTIVE
conversationalist NOUN

⚠ **HEADS UP** The noun **contrast** is pronounced CAWN-trast; the verb is cun-TRAST.

Cc

converse converses conversing conversed
VERB **1.** *a formal use* When people converse, they talk to each other.
NOUN **2.** The converse of something is its opposite: *Don't you think that the converse might also be possible?*
conversely ADVERB

convert converts converting converted
VERB **1.** To convert one thing into another is to change it so that it becomes the other thing. **2.** If someone converts you, that person persuades you to change your religious or political beliefs.
NOUN **3.** someone who has changed his or her religious or political beliefs
conversion NOUN
convertible ADJECTIVE

convex
ADJECTIVE A convex surface bulges outward, rather than being level or curving inward.

convey conveys conveying conveyed
VERB **1.** To convey information or ideas is to cause them to be known or understood.
2. *a formal use* To convey people or things to a place is to transport them there.

conveyor belt conveyor belts
NOUN a moving strip used in factories and some retail stores for moving objects along

convict convicts convicting convicted
VERB **1.** To convict someone of a crime is to find that person guilty.
NOUN **2.** someone serving a prison sentence

conviction convictions
NOUN **1.** a strong belief or opinion **2.** The conviction of someone is what happens when that person is found guilty in a court of law.

convince convinces convincing convinced
VERB To convince someone of something is to persuade that person that it is true.

convincing
ADJECTIVE *Convincing* is used to describe things or people that can make you believe something is true: *a convincing argument*
convincingly ADVERB

convoluted
ADJECTIVE Something that is convoluted has many twists and bends: *the convoluted patterns of these designs*

convoy convoys
NOUN a group of vehicles or ships travelling together

convulsion convulsions
NOUN If someone has convulsions, that person's muscles move violently and uncontrollably.

coo coos cooing cooed
VERB When pigeons and doves coo, they make a soft flutelike sound.

cook cooks cooking cooked
VERB **1.** To cook food is to prepare it for eating by heating it.
NOUN **2.** someone who prepares and cooks food

cooker cookers
NOUN a device for cooking food

cookery
NOUN Cookery is the activity of preparing and cooking food.

cookie cookies
NOUN **1.** a sweet biscuit **2.** a small file placed on a user's computer by a website, containing information about the user's preferences that will be used on any future visits he or she may make to the site

cool cooler coolest; cools cooling cooled
ADJECTIVE **1.** Something cool has a low temperature but is not cold. **2.** If you are cool in a difficult situation, you stay calm and unemotional.
VERB **3.** When something cools or when you cool it, it becomes less warm.
coolly ADVERB
coolness NOUN

coop coops
NOUN a cage for chickens or rabbits

KNOWING WORDS: WORD BUILDING

BE WORD SHARP!

To build a compound word, put two or more base words together.

cook heating food to eat

cookbook a book of recipes

cook-off a cooking competition

cookout a picnic outdoors with a barbecue

cookstove a stove used for cooking

cookware pots, pans, and cooking utensils

Cc

co-operate co-operates co-operating co-operated
VERB **1.** When people co-operate, they work or act together. **2.** To co-operate also means to do what someone asks.
co-operation NOUN

co-operative co-operatives
NOUN **1.** a business or organization run by the people who work for it, and who share its benefits or profits
ADJECTIVE **2.** A co-operative activity is done by people working together. **3.** Someone who is co-operative does what you ask that person to do.

coordinate coordinates coordinating coordinated
VERB **1.** To coordinate an activity is to organize the people or things involved in it: *to coordinate the campaign*
PLURAL NOUN **2.** Coordinates are a pair of numbers or letters that tell you how far along and up or down a point is on a grid.
coordination NOUN
coordinator NOUN

cop cops
NOUN *an informal word* a police officer

cope copes coping coped
VERB If you cope with a problem or task, you deal with it successfully.

copious
ADJECTIVE *a formal word* existing or produced in large quantities: *I wrote copious notes during class.*

copper
NOUN Copper is a soft, reddish brown metal.

copse copses
NOUN a small group of trees growing close together

copy copies copying copied
NOUN **1.** something made to look like something else **2.** A copy of a book, newspaper, or recording is one of many identical ones produced at the same time.
VERB **3.** If you copy what someone does, you do the same thing. **4.** If you copy something, you make a copy of it.
copier NOUN

copyright copyrights
NOUN If someone has the copyright on a piece of writing or music, it cannot be copied or performed without that person's permission.

coral corals
NOUN Coral is a hard substance that forms in the sea from the skeletons of tiny animals called corals.

cord cords
NOUN **1.** Cord is strong, thick string. **2.** Electrical wire covered in rubber or plastic is also called cord.

cordial cordials
ADJECTIVE **1.** warm and friendly: *a cordial greeting*
NOUN **2.** a sweet drink made from fruit juice

cordon cordons cordoning cordoned
NOUN **1.** a line or ring of police or soldiers preventing people entering or leaving a place
VERB **2.** If police or soldiers cordon off an area, they stop people entering or leaving by forming themselves into a line or ring.

corduroy
NOUN Corduroy is a thick cloth with parallel raised lines on the outside.

core cores
NOUN **1.** the hard central part of a fruit such as an apple **2.** the most central part of an object or place: *the earth's core* **3.** the most important part of something: *the core of the government's problems*

cork corks
NOUN **1.** Cork is the very light, spongelike bark of a Mediterranean tree. **2.** a piece of cork pushed into the end of a bottle to close it

corkscrew corkscrews
NOUN a device for pulling corks out of bottles

cormorant cormorants
NOUN a dark-coloured bird with a long neck

corn corns
NOUN **1.** Corn is a tall plant whose seeds grow in rows on a core. **2.** a small painful area of hard skin on your foot

cornea corneas
NOUN the transparent skin that covers the outside of your eyeball

corner corners cornering cornered
NOUN **1.** a place where two sides or edges of something meet: *a small corner of one shelf, a street corner*
VERB **2.** To corner people or animals is to get them into a place from which escape is impossible.

cornet cornets
NOUN a small brass instrument used in brass and military bands

cornflower cornflowers
NOUN a small plant with bright flowers, usually blue

cornice cornices
NOUN a decorative strip of plaster, wood, or stone along the top edge of a wall

Cc

cornstarch
NOUN Cornstarch is a fine white flour made from corn and used in cooking to thicken sauces.

corny cornier corniest
ADJECTIVE very obvious or sentimental and not at all original: *corny old love songs*

coronary coronaries
NOUN If someone has a coronary, blood cannot reach his or her heart because of a blood clot.

coronation coronations
NOUN the ceremony at which a king or queen is crowned

coroner coroners
NOUN an official who investigates the deaths of people who have died in a violent or unusual way

coronet coronets
NOUN a small crown

corporal corporals
NOUN an officer of low rank in the army or air force

corporal punishment
NOUN Corporal punishment is the punishing of people by beating them.

corporate
ADJECTIVE *a formal word* belonging to or done by all members of a group together: *a corporate decision*

corporation corporations
NOUN a large business

corps
NOUN **1.** a part of the armed forces with special duties: *the Engineering Corps* **2.** a small group of people who do a special job: *a dedicated corps of volunteers*

corpse corpses
NOUN a dead body

corpuscle corpuscles
NOUN a red or white blood cell

correct corrects correcting corrected
ADJECTIVE **1.** If something is correct, there are no mistakes in it. **2.** The correct thing in a particular situation is the right one: *Each has the correct number of coins.* **3.** Correct behaviour is considered to be socially acceptable.
VERB **4.** If you correct something that is wrong, you make it right.
correctly ADVERB
corrective ADJECTIVE OR NOUN

correction corrections
NOUN the act of making something right

correlate correlates correlating correlated
VERB If two things correlate or are correlated, they are closely connected or strongly influence each other: *Obesity correlates with increased risk of stroke and diabetes.*
correlation NOUN

correspond corresponds corresponding corresponded
VERB **1.** If one thing corresponds to another, it has a similar purpose, function, or status. **2.** If numbers or amounts correspond, they are the same. **3.** When people correspond, they write or e-mail to each other.

correspondence
NOUN **1.** Correspondence is the writing of letters or e-mails; also the letters or e-mails written. **2.** If there is a correspondence between two things, those things are closely related or very similar.

correspondent correspondents
NOUN a newspaper, television, or radio reporter

corresponding
ADJECTIVE **1.** You use *corresponding* to describe a change that results from a change in something else: *the rise in interest rates and corresponding fall in house prices* **2.** You also use *corresponding* to describe something that has a similar purpose or status to something else: *Bull is the name for the adult male elephant, and the corresponding female name is cow.*
correspondingly ADVERB

corridor corridors
NOUN a passage in a building

corrode corrodes corroding corroded
VERB When metal corrodes, it is gradually destroyed by a chemical or rust.
corrosion NOUN
corrosive ADJECTIVE

corrugated
ADJECTIVE Corrugated metal or cardboard is made in wavelike folds to make it stronger.

corrupt corrupts corrupting corrupted
ADJECTIVE **1.** Corrupt people act dishonestly or illegally in return for money or power: *corrupt government officials*
VERB **2.** To corrupt someone means to make that person dishonest or immoral.
corruptible ADJECTIVE

corruption
NOUN Corruption is dishonesty and illegal behaviour by people in positions of power.

corset corsets
NOUN Corsets are stiff underwear worn, especially in former times, by some women around their hips and waist to make them look slimmer.

⚠ **HEADS UP** The *p* in **corps** is silent. It is pronounced CORE.

Cc

cosmetic cosmetics
NOUN **1.** Cosmetics are substances such as lipstick and face powder that improve a person's appearance.
ADJECTIVE **2.** Cosmetic changes improve the appearance of something without changing its basic form.

cosmic
ADJECTIVE belonging or relating to the universe

cosmopolitan
ADJECTIVE A cosmopolitan place is full of people from many countries.

cosmos
NOUN The cosmos is the universe.

cosset cossets cosseting cosseted
VERB If you cosset someone, you spoil that person and protect him or her too much.

cost costs costing cost
NOUN **1.** The cost of something is the amount of money needed to buy it, do it, or make it. **2.** The cost of achieving something is the loss or injury in achieving it: *the total cost in human misery*
VERB **3.** You use *cost* to talk about the amount of money you have to pay for things: *The air fares were going to cost a lot.* **4.** If a mistake costs you something, you lose that thing because of the mistake: *reckless behaviour that could cost him his job*

costly costlier costliest
ADJECTIVE expensive: *a costly piece of jewellery*

costume costumes
NOUN **1.** a set of clothes worn by an actor **2.** Costume is the clothing worn in a particular place or during a particular period: *eighteenth-century costume*

cot cots
NOUN a narrow camp bed, usually made of canvas. It folds up when it is not in use.

cottage cottages
NOUN a small house in the country

cottage cheese
NOUN Cottage cheese is a type of soft, white, lumpy cheese.

cotton cottons
NOUN Cotton is cloth made from the soft fibres of the cotton plant; also the fibres themselves.

cotton batting
NOUN Cotton batting is soft, fluffy cotton, often used for dressing wounds or applying cosmetics.

couch couches couching couched
NOUN **1.** a long, soft piece of furniture that more than one person can sit on
VERB **2.** If a statement is couched in a particular type of language, it is expressed in that language: *a comment couched in impertinent terms*

cough coughs coughing coughed
VERB **1.** When you cough, you force air out of your throat with a sudden harsh noise.
NOUN **2.** an illness that makes you cough a lot; also the noise you make when you cough

could
VERB **1.** You use *could* to say that you were able or allowed to do something: *He could hear voices. She could come and go as she wanted.* **2.** You also use *could* to say that something might happen or might be the case: *It could rain.* **3.** You use *could* when you are asking for something politely: *Could you tell me the name of that movie?*

coulomb coulombs
NOUN a metric unit used to measure electric charge

council councils
NOUN a group of people elected to look after the affairs of a city, town, district, or county

! HEADS UP

Don't confuse **council** and **counsel**. **Council** means *a group of leaders.* **Counsel** means *give advice.*

councillor councillors
NOUN an elected member of a local council

counsel counsels counselling counselled
NOUN **1.** *a formal use* To give someone counsel is to give that person advice.
VERB **2.** To counsel people is to give them advice about their problems.
counselling NOUN
counsellor NOUN

count counts counting counted
VERB **1.** To count is to say all the numbers in order up to a particular number. **2.** If you count all the things in a group, you add them up to see how many there are. **3.** What counts in a situation is whatever is most important. **4.** To count as something means to be regarded as that thing: *I'm not sure whether this counts as harassment.* **5.** If you can count on someone or something, you can rely on that person or thing.
NOUN **6.** a number reached by counting **7.** *a formal use* If something is wrong on a particular count, it is wrong in that respect: *Your conclusion is wrong on two counts.* **8.** a European nobleman

Cc

countdown countdowns
NOUN the counting aloud of numbers in reverse order before something happens, especially before a spacecraft is launched

countenance countenances
NOUN *a formal word* Someone's countenance is his or her face.

counter counters countering countered
NOUN **1.** a long, flat surface over which goods are sold in a store **2.** a small, flat, round object used in board games
VERB **3.** If you counter something that is being done, you take action to make it less effective: *I countered her accusation with one of my own.*

counteract counteracts counteracting counteracted
VERB To counteract something is to reduce its effect by producing an opposite effect.

counterfeit counterfeits counterfeiting counterfeited
ADJECTIVE **1.** Something counterfeit is not genuine but has been made to look genuine to deceive people: *counterfeit money*
VERB **2.** To counterfeit something is to make a counterfeit version of it.

counterpart counterparts
NOUN The counterpart of a person or thing is another person or thing with a similar function in a different place: *Unlike his Canadian counterpart, an American senator is elected by the people.*

countess countesses
NOUN the wife of a count or earl, or a woman with the same rank as a count or earl

counting
PREPOSITION You say *counting* when including something in a calculation: *There are five in our family, not counting the dog.*

countless
ADJECTIVE too many to count: *There had been countless demonstrations.*

country countries
NOUN **1.** one of the political areas the world is divided into **2.** The country is land away from towns and cities. **3.** *Country* is used to refer to an area with particular features or associations: *the heart of apple country*

countryman countrymen
NOUN Your countrymen are people from your own country.

countryside
NOUN The countryside is land away from towns and cities.

county counties
NOUN a geographical region into which some countries, provinces, and states are divided for local government

coup coups
NOUN When there is a coup, a group of people seize power in a country.

> ⚠ **HEADS UP**
> **Coup** is a French word from the phrase *coup d'état*. We use the French pronunciation: KOO.

couple couples coupling coupled
NOUN **1.** two people who are married or having a sexual or romantic relationship **2.** A couple of things or people means two of them: *a couple of weeks ago*
VERB **3.** If one thing is coupled with another, the two things are done or dealt with together: *Its stores offer high quality coupled with low prices.*

couplet couplets
NOUN two lines of poetry together, especially two that rhyme

coupon coupons
NOUN a piece of printed paper that, when you hand it in, entitles you to pay less than usual for something

courage
NOUN Courage is the quality shown by people who do things knowing they are dangerous or difficult.
courageous ADJECTIVE
courageously ADVERB

coureur de bois coureurs de bois
NOUN In the past, a coureur de bois was a French or Métis fur trader or woodsman.

courier couriers
NOUN someone employed to deliver letters or packages quickly

course courses
NOUN **1.** a series of lessons or lectures **2.** a series of medical treatments: *a course of injections* **3.** one of the parts of a meal **4.** A course or a course of action is one of the things you can do in a situation. **5.** a piece of land where a sport such as golf is played **6.** the route a ship or aircraft takes **7.** If something happens in the course of a period of time, it happens during that period: *Ten people died in the course of the day.*
PHRASE **8.** If you say **of course**, you are showing that something is totally expected or that you are sure about something: *Of course she wouldn't do that.*

Cc

court courts courting courted
NOUN **1.** a place where legal matters are decided by a judge and jury. The judge and jury can also be referred to as the court. **2.** a place where a game such as tennis or badminton is played **3.** the place where a king or queen lives and carries out ceremonial duties
VERB **4.** *an old-fashioned use* If a man and woman are courting, they are spending a lot of time together because they intend to get married.

courteous
ADJECTIVE Courteous behaviour is polite and considerate.

courtesy
NOUN Courtesy is polite, considerate behaviour.

courtier courtiers
NOUN Courtiers were noblemen and noblewomen at the court of a king or queen.

court-martial courts-martial court-martialling court-martialled
NOUN **1.** a military trial
VERB **2.** If a member of the armed forces is court-martialled, that person is tried by a court-martial.

courtship
NOUN Courtship is the activity of courting or the period of time during which a man and a woman are courting.

courtyard courtyards
NOUN a flat area of ground surrounded by buildings or walls

cousin cousins
NOUN Your cousin is the child of your uncle or aunt.

cove coves
NOUN a small bay

covenant covenants
NOUN a formal written agreement or promise

cover covers covering covered
VERB **1.** If you cover something, you put something else over it to protect it or hide it. **2.** If something covers something else, it forms a layer over it: *Tears covered his face.* **3.** If you cover a particular distance, you travel that distance: *He covered 52 kilometres in 210 laps.* **4.** If a possession is covered, it is insured against damage or loss.
NOUN **5.** something put over an object to protect it or keep it warm **6.** The cover of a book or magazine is its outside. **7.** In the open, cover consists of trees, rocks, or other places where you can shelter or hide.

cover up
VERB **8.** If you cover up something you do not want people to know about, you hide it from them: *He lied to cover up his crime.*
cover-up NOUN

coverage
NOUN **1.** The coverage of something in the news is the reporting of it. **2.** Insurance coverage is a guarantee that money will be paid if something is lost or harmed.

covering coverings
NOUN a layer of something that protects or conceals something else: *A morning blizzard left a covering of snow.*

covert
ADJECTIVE *a formal word* Covert activities are secret, rather than open.
covertly ADVERB

covet covets coveting coveted
VERB *a formal word* If you covet something, you want it very much.

cow cows
NOUN a large animal kept on farms for its milk

coward cowards
NOUN someone who is easily frightened and who avoids dangerous or difficult situations
cowardice NOUN

cowardly
ADJECTIVE easily scared

cowboy cowboys
NOUN a man employed to look after cattle, especially in Western Canada and the US

cower cowers cowering cowered
VERB When someone cowers, that person crouches or moves backwards because he or she is afraid.

coy coyer coyest
ADJECTIVE If someone is coy, that person pretends to be shy and modest.
coyly ADVERB

coyote coyotes
NOUN a North American animal like a small wolf

cozy cozier coziest; cozies
ADJECTIVE **1.** warm and comfortable: *her cozy new apartment* **2.** Cozy activities are pleasant and friendly: *a cozy chat*
NOUN **3.** a soft cover put over a teapot to keep the tea warm
cozily ADVERB
coziness NOUN

crab crabs
NOUN a sea creature with four pairs of legs, two pincers, and a flat, round body covered by a shell

crack cracks cracking cracked
VERB **1.** If something cracks, it becomes

Cc

damaged, with lines appearing on its surface. **2.** If you crack a joke, you tell it. **3.** If you crack a problem or code, you solve it.
NOUN **4.** one of the lines appearing on something when it cracks **5.** a narrow gap

cracker crackers
NOUN **1.** a thin, crisp biscuit that is often eaten with cheese **2.** a small paper-covered tube that pulls apart with a bang and usually has a toy and paper hat inside

crackle crackles crackling crackled
VERB **1.** If something crackles, it makes a rapid series of short, harsh noises.
NOUN **2.** a short, harsh noise

cradle cradles cradling cradled
NOUN **1.** a bed for a baby
VERB **2.** If you cradle something in your arms or hands, you hold it there carefully.

craft crafts
NOUN **1.** an activity such as weaving, carving, or pottery **2.** a skilful occupation: *the writer's craft* **3.** a boat, plane, or spacecraft

craftsman craftsmen
NOUN a man who makes things skilfully with his hands
craftsmanship NOUN
craftsperson NOUN
craftswoman NOUN

crafty craftier craftiest
ADJECTIVE Someone who is crafty gets what he or she wants by tricking people in a clever way.

crag crags
NOUN a steep rugged rock or peak

craggy craggier craggiest
ADJECTIVE A craggy mountain or cliff is steep and rocky.

cram crams cramming crammed
VERB If you cram people or things into a place, you put more in than there is room for.

cramp cramps
NOUN Cramp or cramps is a pain caused by a muscle contracting.

cramped
ADJECTIVE If a room or building is cramped, it is not big enough for the people or things in it.

cranberry cranberries
NOUN Cranberries are sour-tasting red berries, often made into a sauce.

crane cranes craning craned
NOUN **1.** a machine that moves heavy things by lifting them in the air **2.** a large bird with a long neck and long legs
VERB **3.** If you crane your neck, you extend your head in a particular direction to see or hear something better.

crank cranks cranking cranked
NOUN **1.** *an informal use* someone with strange ideas who behaves in an odd way **2.** a device you turn to make something move: *The adjustment is made by turning the crank.*
VERB **3.** If you crank something, you make it move by turning a handle.

cranny crannies
NOUN a very narrow opening in a wall or rock: *nooks and crannies*

crash crashes crashing crashed
NOUN **1.** an accident in which a moving vehicle hits something violently **2.** the failure of a computer system **3.** a sudden loud noise: *the crash of the waves on the rocks* **4.** the sudden failure of a business or financial institution
VERB **5.** When a vehicle crashes, it hits something and is badly damaged. **6.** When a computer crashes, it suddenly stops working.

crate crates
NOUN a large box used for transporting or storing things

crater craters
NOUN a wide hole in the ground caused by something hitting it or by an explosion

cravat cravats
NOUN In former times, a piece of cloth a man wore around his neck tucked into his shirt collar.

crave craves craving craved
VERB If you crave something, you want it very much: *I crave her approval.*
craving NOUN

crawl crawls crawling crawled
VERB **1.** When you crawl, you move forward on your hands and knees. **2.** When a vehicle crawls, it moves very slowly. **3.** *an informal use* If a place is crawling with people or things, it is full of them: *The ground is crawling with ants.*
crawler NOUN

crayfish crayfishes crayfish
NOUN a small shellfish like a lobster

crayon crayons
NOUN a pencil-shaped stick of coloured wax for drawing with

craze crazes
NOUN something that is very popular for a short time

Cc

crazy crazier craziest
ADJECTIVE *an informal word* **1.** very strange or foolish: *a crazy idea, That guy is crazy.* **2.** If you are crazy about something, you are very enthusiastic about it: *I was crazy about dancing.*
crazily ADVERB
craziness NOUN

creak creaks creaking creaked
VERB **1.** If something creaks, it makes a harsh sound when it moves or when you stand on it.
NOUN **2.** a harsh squeaking noise
creaky ADJECTIVE

cream creams
NOUN **1.** Cream is a thick, yellowish white liquid taken from the top of milk. **2.** Cream is also a substance people can rub on their skin to make it soft.
ADJECTIVE **3.** yellowish white
creamy ADJECTIVE

crease creases creasing creased
NOUN **1.** an irregular line that appears on cloth or paper when it is crumpled **2.** a straight line on something that has been pressed or folded neatly
VERB **3.** To crease something is to make lines appear on it.
creased ADJECTIVE

create creates creating created
VERB **1.** To create something is to cause it to happen or exist: *He created a beautiful sculpture out of the modelling clay.* **2.** When someone creates a new product or process, that person invents it.
creator NOUN
creation NOUN

creative
ADJECTIVE **1.** Creative people are able to invent and develop original ideas. **2.** Creative activities involve the inventing and developing of original ideas: *creative writing*
creatively ADVERB
creativity NOUN

creature creatures
NOUN any living thing that moves about

credence
NOUN *a formal word* If something gives credence to a theory or story, it makes it easier to believe.

credentials
PLURAL NOUN Your credentials are your past achievements or other things in your background that make you qualified for something.

credible
ADJECTIVE If someone or something is credible, you can believe or trust that person or thing.
credibility NOUN

credit credits crediting credited
NOUN **1.** If you are allowed credit, you can take something and pay for it later: *to buy goods on credit* **2.** If you get the credit for something, people praise you for it. **3.** If you say someone is a credit to his or her family or school, you mean that that person's family or school should be proud of him or her.
PLURAL NOUN **4.** The list of people who helped make a movie, recording, video, or television program is called the credits.
VERB **5.** If you are credited with an achievement, people believe that you were responsible for it.

creditable
ADJECTIVE satisfactory or fairly good: *a creditable performance*

credit card credit cards
NOUN a plastic card that allows someone to buy goods on credit

creditor creditors
NOUN Your creditors are the people you owe money to.

credulous
ADJECTIVE If someone is credulous, he or she is too ready to believe anything.

creed creeds
NOUN **1.** a religion **2.** any set of beliefs, principles, or opinions: *Her creed is family comes before work.*

creek creeks
NOUN a small freshwater stream

creep creeps creeping crept
VERB To creep is to move quietly and slowly.

creepy creepier creepiest
ADJECTIVE *an informal word* strange and frightening: *a creepy feeling*

cremate cremates cremating cremated
VERB When someone is cremated, that person's dead body is burned.
cremation NOUN

crematorium crematoriums
NOUN a building in which the bodies of dead people are burned

crepe
NOUN **1.** Crepe is a crinkled material made from cotton, silk, or wool. **2.** Crepe is also a type of rubber with a rough surface. **3.** A crêpe is a large, very thin pancake, usually served rolled up with a filling.

⚠ HEADS UP Crepe and **crêpe** are pronounced in the same way: CRAYP.

Cc

crescendo crescendos
NOUN When there is a crescendo in a piece of music, the music gets louder.

crescent crescents
NOUN a curved shape that is wider in its middle than at the ends, which are pointed

cress
NOUN a plant with small, strong-tasting leaves. It is used in salads.

crest crests
NOUN **1.** The crest of a hill or wave is its highest part. **2.** a tuft of feathers on top of a bird's head **3.** a small picture or design that is the emblem of a noble family, a city or town, or an organization
crested ADJECTIVE

crevice crevices
NOUN a narrow crack or gap in rock

crew crews
NOUN **1.** The crew of a ship, airplane, or spacecraft are the people who operate it. **2.** people with special technical skills who work together: *the camera crew*

crib cribs cribbing cribbed
VERB **1.** *an informal use* If you crib, you copy what someone else has written and pretend it is your own work.
NOUN **2.** a baby's bed

crick cricks
NOUN a pain in your neck or back caused by muscles becoming stiff

cricket crickets
NOUN **1.** Cricket is an outdoor game played by two teams who take turns at scoring runs by hitting a ball with a bat. **2.** a small jumping insect that produces sounds by rubbing its wings together
cricketer NOUN

crime crimes
NOUN an illegal action for which you can be punished by law: *a serious crime*

criminal criminals
NOUN **1.** someone who has committed a crime
ADJECTIVE **2.** involving or related to crime: *criminal activities*
criminally ADVERB

criminology
NOUN the scientific study of crime and criminals
criminologist NOUN

crimson
NOUN OR ADJECTIVE dark purplish red

cringe cringes cringing cringed
VERB If you cringe, you back away from someone or something because you are afraid or embarrassed.

crinkle crinkles crinkling crinkled
VERB **1.** If something crinkles, it becomes slightly creased.
NOUN **2.** Crinkles are small creases.

cripple cripples crippling crippled
VERB To cripple something is to damage it severely: *The severe storm crippled the ship.*
crippled ADJECTIVE
crippling ADJECTIVE

crisis crises
NOUN a serious or dangerous situation

crisp crisper crispest
ADJECTIVE **1.** Something that is crisp is fresh and firm: *crisp lettuce leaves* **2.** If the air or the weather is crisp, it is pleasantly fresh, cold, and dry: *crisp wintry days*

crispy crispier crispiest
ADJECTIVE Crispy food is pleasantly hard and crunchy: *I like my toast crispy.*

criterion criteria
NOUN a standard by which you judge or decide something

critic critics
NOUN **1.** someone who writes reviews of books, movies, plays, or musical performances **2.** A critic of a person or system is someone who criticizes the person or system publicly: *the government's critics*

critical
ADJECTIVE **1.** A critical time is one that is very important in determining what happens in the future: *critical months in the history of the world* **2.** A critical situation is a very serious one: *An oil spill can cause critical damage to marine life.* **3.** If an ill or injured person is critical, that person is in danger of dying. **4.** If you are critical of something or someone, you express severe judgments or opinions about that thing or person. **5.** If you are critical, you examine and judge something carefully: *a critical look at the way he led his life*
critically ADVERB

critical literacy
NOUN the process of analyzing a text to understand its underlying values and beliefs

criticism criticisms
NOUN **1.** When there is criticism of someone or something, people express disapproval of that person or thing. **2.** If you make a criticism, you point out a fault you think someone or something has.

criticize criticizes criticizing criticized
VERB If you criticize someone or something, you say what you think is wrong with that person or thing.

croak croaks croaking croaked
VERB **1.** When animals and birds croak, they make harsh, low sounds.
NOUN **2.** a harsh, low sound

crochet
NOUN Crochet is a way of making clothes and other things out of thread or yarn, using a needle with a small hook at the end.

crockery
NOUN Crockery is plates, cups, and saucers.

crocodile crocodiles
NOUN a large, scaly, meat-eating reptile that lives in tropical rivers

crocus crocuses
NOUN a plant with yellow, purple, or white flowers, which grows in early spring

croissant croissants
NOUN a light, crescent-shaped roll, often eaten at breakfast

crony cronies
NOUN *an old-fashioned word* Your cronies are the friends you spend a lot of time with.

crook crooks
NOUN **1.** *an informal use* a criminal **2.** The crook of your arm or leg is the soft inside part where you bend your elbow or knee.

crooked
ADJECTIVE **1.** bent or twisted **2.** Someone who is crooked is dishonest.

croon croons crooning crooned
VERB To croon is to sing or hum quietly and gently: *He crooned a love song.*

crop crops cropping cropped
NOUN **1.** Crops are plants such as wheat and potatoes that are grown for food. **2.** the plants collected at harvest time: *There should be a healthy crop this year.*
VERB **3.** To crop someone's hair is to cut it very short.

croquet
NOUN Croquet is a game in which the players use long-handled mallets to hit balls through metal arches pushed into a lawn.

cross crosses crossing crossed; crosser crossest
VERB **1.** If you cross something such as a room or a road, you go to the other side of it.
2. Lines or roads that cross meet and go across each other. **3.** If a thought crosses your mind, you think of it. **4.** If you cross your arms, legs, or fingers, you put one on top of the other.
NOUN **5.** a vertical bar or line crossed by a shorter horizontal bar or line; also used to describe any object shaped like this
6. a written mark shaped like an X: *I drew a small bicycle and put a cross by it.*
7. Something that is a cross between two things is neither one thing nor the other, but a mixture of both.
ADJECTIVE **8.** Someone who is cross is angry.
crossly ADVERB

cross-country
NOUN **1.** Cross-country is the sport of running across open countryside, rather than on roads or on a track. **2.** Cross-country is also the sport of skiing across open countryside.
ADVERB OR ADJECTIVE **3.** across a country

crossing crossings
NOUN **1.** a place where you can cross a road safely **2.** a journey by ship to a place on the other side of the sea

cross-legged
ADJECTIVE If you are sitting cross-legged, you are sitting on the floor with knees pointing outward and your feet tucked under.

cross-section cross-sections
NOUN A cross-section of a group of people is a representative sample of them.

crotch crotches
NOUN the part of your body between the tops of your legs

crouch crouches crouching crouched
VERB If you are crouching, you are leaning forward with your legs bent under you.

KNOWING WORDS: WORD BUILDING

BE WORD SHARP!

To build a compound word, put two or more base words together.

cross intersect

crossbow a weapon with a bow set across a shaft

cross-eyed with eyes that look toward each other

crossfire attacks coming from different directions

crossroad an intersection

crossword a puzzle with words crossing each other

NEL

Cc

crow crows crowing crowed
NOUN **1.** a large black bird
VERB **2.** When a rooster crows, it utters a loud squawking sound.

crowbar crowbars
NOUN a heavy, iron bar used as a lever or for forcing things open

crowd crowds crowding crowded
NOUN **1.** a large group of people
VERB **2.** When people crowd somewhere, they gather there close together.

crowded
ADJECTIVE A crowded place is full of people.

crown crowns crowning crowned
NOUN **1.** a circular ornament worn on a royal person's head **2.** The crown of something, such as your head, is the top part of it.
VERB **3.** When a king or queen is crowned, a crown is put on his or her head during the coronation ceremony. **4.** When something crowns an event, it is the final part of it: *The news crowned a dreadful week.*

crucial
ADJECTIVE If something is crucial, it is very important in determining how something else will be in the future.

crucify crucifies crucifying crucified
VERB To crucify someone is to tie or nail them to a large wooden cross and leave them there to die.
crucifixion NOUN

crude cruder crudest
ADJECTIVE **1.** rough and simple: *a crude weapon, a crude method of entry* **2.** A crude person speaks or behaves in a rude and offensive way: *You can be quite crude at times.*
crudely ADVERB
crudity NOUN

cruel crueller cruellest
ADJECTIVE Cruel people deliberately cause pain or distress to other people or to animals.
cruelly ADVERB

cruelty
NOUN cruel behaviour

cruise cruises cruising cruised
NOUN **1.** a holiday in which you travel on a ship and visit places
VERB **2.** When a vehicle cruises, it moves at a constant moderate speed.

cruiser cruisers
NOUN **1.** a police car used for patrolling streets and highways **2.** a large, fast warship

crumb crumbs
NOUN Crumbs are very small pieces of bread or cake.

crumble crumbles crumbling crumbled
VERB When something crumbles, it breaks into small pieces.

crumbly
ADJECTIVE Something crumbly easily breaks into small pieces.

crumpet crumpets
NOUN a round, flat, breadlike cake, which you eat toasted

crumple crumples crumpling crumpled
VERB To crumple paper or cloth is to squash it so that it is full of creases.

crunch crunches crunching crunched
VERB If you crunch something, you crush it noisily, for example between your teeth or under your feet.

crunchy crunchier crunchiest
ADJECTIVE Crunchy food is hard or crisp and makes a noise when you eat it.

crusade crusades
NOUN a long and determined attempt to achieve something: *the crusade for human rights*
crusader NOUN

crush crushes crushing crushed
VERB **1.** To crush something is to destroy its shape by squeezing it. **2.** To crush a substance is to turn it into liquid or powder by squeezing or grinding it. **3.** To crush an army or political organization is to defeat it completely.
NOUN **4.** a dense crowd of people

crust crusts
NOUN **1.** the hard outside part of a loaf of bread **2.** a hard layer on top of something: *The snow had a fine crust on it.*

crusty crustier crustiest
ADJECTIVE **1.** Something that is crusty has a hard outside layer. **2.** Crusty people are impatient and irritable.

crutch crutches
NOUN a support like a long stick that you lean on to help you walk when you have an injured foot or leg

crux
NOUN the most important or difficult part of a problem or argument

cry cries crying cried
VERB **1.** When you cry, tears appear in your eyes. **2.** To cry something is to shout it or say it loudly: *See you soon! they cried.*
NOUN **3.** If you have a cry, you cry for a period of time. **4.** a shout or other loud sound made with your voice **5.** a loud sound made by some birds: *the cry of a seagull*

Cc

crypt crypts
NOUN an underground room beneath a church, usually used as a burial place

cryptic
ADJECTIVE A cryptic remark or message has a hidden meaning.

crystal crystals
NOUN **1.** a piece of a mineral that has formed naturally into a regular shape **2.** Crystal is a type of transparent rock, used in jewellery. **3.** Crystal is also a kind of very high-quality glass.
crystalline ADJECTIVE

crystallize crystallizes crystallizing crystallized
VERB **1.** If a substance crystallizes, it turns into crystals. **2.** If an idea crystallizes, it becomes clear in your mind.

cub cubs
NOUN Some young wild animals are called cubs: *a lion cub*

cube cubes cubing cubed
NOUN **1.** a three-dimensional shape with six equally sized square surfaces **2.** If you multiply a number by itself twice, you get its cube.
VERB **3.** To cube a number is to multiply it by itself twice.

cubic
ADJECTIVE used in measurements of volume: *cubic centimetres*

cubicle cubicles
NOUN a small enclosed area in a place such as a public washroom or office workspace

cuckoo cuckoos
NOUN a grey bird with a two-note call that lays its eggs in other birds' nests

cucumber cucumbers
NOUN a long, thin, green-skinned fruit eaten raw in salads

cuddle cuddles cuddling cuddled
VERB **1.** If you cuddle someone, you hold that person affectionately in your arms.
NOUN **2.** If you give someone a cuddle, you hold that person affectionately in your arms.

cuddly cuddlier cuddliest
ADJECTIVE Cuddly people, animals, or toys are soft or pleasing in some way so that you want to cuddle them.

cue cues
NOUN **1.** something said or done by a performer that is a signal for another performer to begin: *That actor never misses a cue.* **2.** a long stick used to hit the balls in snooker and billiards

cuff cuffs
NOUN the end part of a sleeve

cuff link cuff links
NOUN Cuff links are small objects for holding shirt cuffs together.

cuisine
NOUN The cuisine of a region is the style of cooking that is typical of it.

cul-de-sac cul-de-sacs
NOUN a road that does not lead to any other roads because one end is blocked off

culinary
ADJECTIVE *a formal word* connected with the kitchen or cooking

cull culls culling culled
VERB **1.** If you cull things, you gather them from different places or sources: *information culled from movies*
NOUN **2.** When there is a cull, weaker animals are killed to reduce the numbers in a group.

culminate culminates culminating culminated
VERB To culminate in something is to finally develop into it: *a campaign that culminated in a stunning success*
culmination NOUN

culprit culprits
NOUN someone who has done something harmful or wrong

cult cults
NOUN A cult is a religious group with special rituals, usually connected with the worship of a particular person.

cultivate cultivates cultivating cultivated
VERB **1.** To cultivate land is to grow crops on it. **2.** If you cultivate a feeling or attitude, you try to develop it in yourself or other people.
cultivation NOUN

culture cultures
NOUN **1.** Culture refers to the arts and to people's appreciation of them: *He was a man of culture.* **2.** The culture of a particular society is its ideas, customs, and art: *Japanese culture* **3.** In science, a culture is a group of bacteria or cells grown in a laboratory.
cultured ADJECTIVE
cultural ADJECTIVE

cumulative
ADJECTIVE Something that is cumulative keeps being added to.

cunning
ADJECTIVE **1.** Someone who is cunning uses clever and deceitful methods to get what he or she wants.
NOUN **2.** Cunning is the ability to get what you want using clever and deceitful methods.
cunningly ADVERB

⚠ **HEADS UP** The word **cuisine** is pronounced kwi-ZEEN.

Cc

cup cups cupping cupped

NOUN **1.** a small, round container with a handle, which you drink out of **2.** a large metal container with two handles, given as a prize

VERB **3.** If you cup your hands, you put them together to make a shape like a cup.

cupboard cupboards

NOUN a piece of furniture or a closet with a door and shelves

curable

ADJECTIVE If a disease or illness is curable, it can be cured.

curator curators

NOUN the person in a museum or art gallery in charge of its contents

curb curbs curbing curbed

VERB **1.** To curb something is to keep it within limits: *policies designed to curb absences from work*

NOUN **2.** A curb is a raised concrete border along the edge of a street or driveway. **3.** If a curb is placed on something, it is kept within limits: *the curb on spending*

curdle curdles curdling curdled

VERB When milk curdles, it turns sour.

curd

NOUN Curds are the thick white substance formed when milk turns sour.

cure cures curing cured

VERB **1.** To cure an illness is to end it. **2.** To cure a sick or injured person is to make that person well. **3.** If something cures you of a habit or attitude, it stops you having it. **4.** To cure food, tobacco, or an animal skin is to treat it in order to preserve it.

NOUN **5.** A cure for an illness is something that ends it.

curfew curfews

NOUN If there is a curfew, people must stay indoors between particular times at night.

curiosity curiosities

NOUN **1.** Curiosity is the desire to know about something or about many things. **2.** something unusual and interesting

curious

ADJECTIVE **1.** Someone who is curious wants to know more about something. **2.** Something that is curious is unusual and hard to explain.

curiously ADVERB

curl curls curling curled

NOUN **1.** Curls are lengths of hair shaped in tight curves and circles. **2.** a curved or spiral shape: *the curls of smoke from the campfire*

VERB **3.** If something curls, it moves in a curve

or spiral. **4.** If you curl, you play the game of curling.

curly ADJECTIVE

curler curlers

NOUN Curlers are plastic or metal tubes that women roll their hair around to make it curly.

curlew curlews

NOUN a large, brown bird with a long, curved beak and a loud cry

curling

NOUN Curling is a game played on ice in which players slide heavy, round, polished stones toward a marked circle at the end of the rink.

currant currants

NOUN **1.** Currants are small, dried grapes, often put in cakes and cookies. **2.** Currants are also blackcurrants or redcurrants.

currency currencies

NOUN **1.** A country's currency is its coins and banknotes, or its monetary system generally: *foreign currency, a strong economy and a weak currency* **2.** If something such as an idea has currency, it is used a lot at a particular time.

current currents

NOUN **1.** a strong continuous movement of the water in a river or in the sea **2.** An air current is a flowing movement of air. **3.** An electric current is a flow of electricity through a wire or circuit.

ADJECTIVE **4.** Something that is current is happening, being done, or being used now.

currently ADVERB

current events

PLURAL NOUN Current events are political and social events discussed in newspapers and on television and radio.

curriculum curriculums

NOUN the different courses taught at a school or university

curriculum vitae curricula vitae

NOUN A curriculum vitae is a written account of personal details, education, and work experience, which a person sends when he or she applies for a job.

curried

ADJECTIVE Curried food has been flavoured with hot spices: *curried lamb*

curry curries currying curried

NOUN **1.** Curry is a dish made with a mixture of hot spices; also the spice itself

PHRASE **2.** To **curry favour** with someone means to try to please that person by flattery or by doing things to help him or her.

curse curses cursing cursed
VERB **1.** To curse is to swear because you are angry. **2.** If you curse someone or something, you say angry things about that person using swear words.
NOUN **3.** what you say when you curse **4.** something supernatural that is supposed to cause unpleasant things to happen to someone **5.** a thing or person that causes a lot of distress: *the curse of poverty*
cursed ADJECTIVE

cursor cursors
NOUN an arrow or box on a computer monitor that indicates where the next letter or symbol is

cursory
ADJECTIVE When you give something a cursory glance or examination, you look at it briefly without paying attention to detail.

curt curter curtest
ADJECTIVE If someone is curt, that person speaks in a brief and rather rude way.
curtly ADVERB

curtail curtails curtailing curtailed
VERB *a formal word* To curtail something is to reduce or restrict it: *Injury curtailed his career.*

curtain curtains
NOUN **1.** a hanging piece of material that can be pulled across a window for privacy or to keep out the light **2.** a large piece of material that hangs in front of the stage in a theatre until a performance begins

curtsy curtsies curtsying curtsied
VERB **1.** When a woman curtsies, she lowers her body briefly, bending her knees, to show respect.
NOUN **2.** the movement a woman makes when she curtsies: *She gave a mock curtsy.*

curve curves curving curved
NOUN **1.** a smooth, gradually bending line
VERB **2.** When something curves, it moves in a curve or has the shape of a curve: *The track curved away below him. Her mouth curved slightly.*
curved ADJECTIVE

cushion cushions cushioning cushioned
NOUN **1.** a soft object put on a seat to make it more comfortable
VERB **2.** To cushion something is to reduce its effect: *Our support helped to cushion the shock for them.*

custard
NOUN Custard is a sweet, yellow sauce or dessert made from milk and eggs or milk and a powder.

custodian custodians
NOUN the person in charge of looking after a building

custody
NOUN **1.** To have custody of children means to have the legal right to keep them and look after them: *She won custody of her younger son.*
PHRASE **2.** Someone who is **in custody** is being kept in prison until he or she can be tried in a court.
custodial ADJECTIVE

custom customs
NOUN **1.** a traditional activity: *an ancient Chinese custom* **2.** something usually done at a particular time or in particular circumstances by a person or by the people in a society: *It was the school's custom to have a talent show every spring.* **3.** Customs is the place at a border, airport, or harbour where you have to declare any goods you are bringing into a country. **4.** *a formal use* If a store or business has your custom, you buy things or go there regularly: *Banks are desperate to get your custom.*

customary
ADJECTIVE usual: *his customary modesty, her customary greeting*
customarily ADVERB

custom-built
ADJECTIVE Something that is custom-built (or custom-made) is made to someone's special requirements.

customer customers
NOUN **1.** A store's or business's customers are the people who buy its goods or services. **2.** *an informal use* You can use customer to refer to someone when describing what that person is like to deal with: *a tough customer*

cut cuts cutting cut
VERB **1.** If you cut something, you use a knife, scissors, or some other sharp tool to divide it or remove parts of it. **2.** If you cut yourself, you injure yourself on a sharp object. **3.** If you cut the amount of something, you reduce it: *Some costs could be cut.* **4.** When writing is cut, parts of it are not printed or broadcast. **5.** To cut from one scene or shot to another in a movie is to go instantly to the other scene or shot.
NOUN **6.** a division or injury made with a knife or other sharp tool **7.** a reduction: *I need to make a five-minute cut in my presentation.* **8.** a large piece of meat ready for cooking
ADJECTIVE **9.** Well-cut clothes have been well designed and made: *this beautifully cut coat*

Cc

cut back
VERB **10.** To cut back or cut back on spending means to reduce it.
cutback NOUN

cut down
VERB **11.** If you cut down on an activity, you do it less often: *cutting down on watching TV*

cut off
VERB **12.** To cut someone off means to separate that person from things that he or she is normally connected with: *The president had cut himself off from the people.* **13.** If a supply of something is cut off, you no longer get it: *The water had been cut off.* **14.** If your telephone or telephone call is cut off, it is disconnected.

cut out
VERB **15.** If you cut out something you are doing, you stop doing it: *Cut out eating sweets.* **16.** If an engine cuts out, it suddenly stops working.

cute cuter cutest
ADJECTIVE pretty or attractive

cuticle cuticles
NOUN Cuticles are the pieces of skin that cover the base of your fingernails and toenails.

cutlass cutlasses
NOUN a curved sword that was used by sailors

cutlery
NOUN Cutlery is knives, forks, and spoons.

cutlet cutlets
NOUN a small piece of meat that you fry or grill

cutting cuttings
NOUN **1.** something cut from a newspaper or magazine **2.** a part cut from a plant and used to grow a new plant
ADJECTIVE **3.** A cutting remark is unkind and likely to hurt someone.

c.v. an abbreviation for CURRICULUM VITAE

cyanide
NOUN Cyanide is an extremely poisonous chemical.

cyber-
PREFIX Words that begin with *cyber-* have something to do with computers in their meaning. For example, a *cybercafé* is a place where computers are provided for customers to use.

cyberpet cyberpets
NOUN an electronic toy that imitates the activities of a pet, and that needs to be fed and entertained

cyberspace
NOUN Cyberspace is the Internet.

cycle cycles cycling cycled
VERB **1.** When you cycle, you ride a bicycle. NOUN **2.** a bicycle or a motorcycle **3.** a series of events that are repeated again and again in the same order: *the cycle of births and deaths* **4.** a single complete series of movements or events in an electrical, electronic, mechanical, or organic process **5.** a series of songs or poems intended to be performed or read together

cyclical
ADJECTIVE happening over and over again in cycles: *a clear cyclical pattern*

cyclist cyclists
NOUN someone who rides a bicycle

cyclone cyclones
NOUN a violent tropical storm

cygnet cygnets
NOUN a young swan

cylinder cylinders
NOUN **1.** a regular, three-dimensional shape with two equally sized, flat, circular ends joined by a curved surface **2.** the part in an engine in which the piston moves backward and forward
cylindrical ADJECTIVE

cymbal cymbals
NOUN a circular brass plate used as a percussion instrument. Cymbals are clashed together or hit with a stick.

cynic cynics
NOUN a cynical person

cynical
ADJECTIVE believing that people always behave selfishly or dishonestly
cynically ADVERB
cynicism NOUN

cypress cypresses
NOUN a type of evergreen tree with small, dark green leaves and round cones

cyst cysts
NOUN a growth containing liquid that can form under your skin or inside your body

czar czars
NOUN the title of the former emperors of Russia

czarina czarinas
NOUN a female czar or wife of a czar

Dd

dab dabs dabbing dabbed
VERB **1.** If you dab something, you touch it with quick, light strokes: *She dabbed some lotion onto the burn.*
NOUN **2.** a small amount of something that is put on a surface: *a dab of perfume*

dabble dabbles dabbling dabbled
VERB If you dabble in something, you work or play at it without being seriously involved in it: *All his life he dabbled in poetry.*

dachshund dachshunds
NOUN a small dog with a long body and very short legs

dad dads
NOUN *an informal word* Your dad is your father.

⚠ HEADS UP

Words like **dad** and **mom** are only capitalized when they're used as names: *my mom, Are we there yet, Dad?*

daddy-longlegs
NOUN an insect related to the spider with very long legs

daffodil daffodils
NOUN a plant with a yellow, trumpet-shaped flower

daft dafter daftest
ADJECTIVE silly and not sensible

dagger daggers
NOUN a weapon with a short, pointed blade

dahlia dahlias
NOUN a type of brightly coloured garden flower

daily
ADJECTIVE **1.** occurring every day: *our daily visit to the gym* **2.** of or relating to a single day or to one day at a time: *the average daily rainfall*

dainty daintier daintiest
ADJECTIVE very delicate and pretty
daintily ADVERB

dairy dairies
NOUN **1.** a store or business that supplies milk and milk products
ADJECTIVE **2.** Dairy products are foods made from milk, such as butter, cheese, cream, and yogurt. **3.** A dairy farm is one that keeps cattle to produce milk.

dais
NOUN a raised platform, normally at one end of a hall and used by a speaker

daisy daisies
NOUN a plant with a tall, leafy stem and a flower with a yellow centre surrounded by white petals

dale dales
NOUN a valley

Dalmation Dalmatians
NOUN a large dog with short, white hair and black or brown spots

dam dams
NOUN a barrier built across a river to hold back water

damage damages damaging damaged
VERB **1.** To damage something means to harm or spoil it.
NOUN **2.** Damage to something is injury or harm done to it. **3.** Damages is the money awarded by a court to compensate someone for loss or harm.
damaging ADJECTIVE

dame dames
NOUN the title given to a woman who has been awarded knighthood

damn damns damning damned
VERB **1.** To damn something or someone means to curse or condemn that thing or person.
INTERJECTION **2.** *Damn* is a swearword.
damned ADJECTIVE

damnation
NOUN Damnation is eternal punishment.

damp damper dampest
ADJECTIVE **1.** slightly wet
NOUN **2.** Damp is slight wetness, especially in the air or in the walls of a building.
dampness NOUN

dampen dampens dampening dampened
VERB **1.** If you dampen something, you make it slightly wet. **2.** To dampen something also means to reduce its liveliness or strength: *Don't let their poor sportsmanship dampen your enthusiasm for the game.*

damper
PHRASE To **put a damper on** something means to stop it from being enjoyable: *The snowstorm put a damper on our plans to go tobogganing.*

dance dances dancing danced
VERB **1.** To dance means to move your feet and body rhythmically in time to music.
NOUN **2.** a series of rhythmic movements or

Dd

steps in time to music **3.** a social event where people dance with each other
dancer NOUN
dancing NOUN

dandelion dandelions
NOUN a wild plant with a yellow flower that forms a ball of fluffy seeds when the flower matures

dandruff
NOUN Dandruff is small, loose scales of dead skin off someone's scalp.

dandy dandies
NOUN *an old-fashioned use* a man who always dresses in very smart clothes

danger dangers
NOUN **1.** Danger is the possibility that someone may be harmed or killed.
2. something or someone that can hurt or harm you

dangerous
ADJECTIVE able to or likely to cause hurt or harm
dangerously ADVERB

dangle dangles dangling dangled
VERB When something dangles or when you dangle it, it swings or hangs loosely.

dank danker dankest
ADJECTIVE A dank place is unpleasantly damp and chilly.

dapper
ADJECTIVE neatly dressed

dappled
ADJECTIVE marked with patches of a different or darker shade

dare dares daring dared
VERB **1.** To dare someone means to challenge that person to do something in order to prove his or her courage. **2.** To dare to do something means to have the courage to do it.
NOUN **3.** a challenge to do something dangerous

daredevil daredevils
NOUN a person who enjoys doing dangerous things

daring
ADJECTIVE **1.** bold and willing to take risks
NOUN **2.** the courage required to do things that are dangerous

dark darker darkest
ADJECTIVE **1.** If it is dark, there is not enough light to see properly. **2.** Dark colours or surfaces reflect little light and so look deep-coloured or dull. **3.** *Dark* is also used to describe thoughts or ideas that are sinister or unpleasant.

NOUN **4.** The dark is the lack of light in a place.
darkly ADVERB
darkness NOUN

darken darkens darkening darkened
VERB If something darkens, or if you darken it, it becomes darker than it was.

darkroom darkrooms
NOUN a room from which daylight is shut out so that photographic film can be developed

darling darlings
NOUN **1.** Someone who is lovable or a favourite may be called a darling.
ADJECTIVE **2.** much admired or loved: *his darling daughter*

darn darns darning darned
VERB **1.** To darn a hole in a garment means to mend it by weaving thread or yarn across the hole.
NOUN **2.** a part of a garment that has been darned

dart darts darting darted
NOUN **1.** a small pointed arrow **2.** Darts is a game in which the players throw darts at a round board divided into numbered sections.
VERB **3.** To dart about means to move quickly and suddenly from one place to another.

dash dashes dashing dashed
VERB **1.** To dash somewhere means to rush there. **2.** If something is dashed against something else, it strikes the thing or is thrown violently against it. **3.** If hopes or ambitions are dashed, they are ruined or frustrated.
NOUN **4.** a sudden movement or rush
5. a small quantity of something **6.** the punctuation mark (—) that shows a change of subject, or that may be used instead of brackets

dashboard dashboards
NOUN the instrument panel in a motor vehicle

dashing
ADJECTIVE A dashing man is stylish and confident: *He was a dashing figure in his younger days.*

data
NOUN **1.** information, usually in the form of facts or statistics **2.** any information put into a computer and that the computer works on or processes

⚠️ **HEADS UP**

The singular form of **data** is **datum**, but it's hardly ever used. Can you think of why it isn't?

Dd

database databases
NOUN a collection of information stored in a computer

date dates dating dated
NOUN **1.** a particular day or year that can be named **2.** If you have a date, you have an appointment to meet someone; also used to refer to the person you are meeting. **3.** a small, dark-brown, sticky fruit with a stone inside, which grows on palm trees
VERB **4.** If you are dating someone, you have a romantic relationship with that person. **5.** If you date something, you find out the time when it began or was made. **6.** If something dates from a particular time, that is when it happened or was made.
PHRASE **7.** If something is **out of date**, it is old-fashioned or no longer valid.

 HEADS UP

There are many ways to write a date: Friday, April 3, 2009; Apr. 3/09; 09-04-03.

dated
ADJECTIVE no longer fashionable

datum the singular form of DATA

daub daubs daubing daubed
VERB If you daub something such as mud or paint on a surface, you smear it there.

daughter daughters
NOUN Someone's daughter is that person's female child.

daughter-in-law daughters-in-law
NOUN Someone's daughter-in-law is the wife of that person's son.

daunt daunts daunting daunted
VERB If something daunts you, you feel worried about whether you can succeed in doing it: *She was not the type of woman to be daunted by failure.*
daunting ADJECTIVE

dawn dawns dawning dawned
NOUN **1.** the time in the morning when light first appears in the sky **2.** the beginning of something: *the dawn of the information age*
VERB **3.** If day is dawning, morning light is beginning to appear.
PHRASE **4.** If an idea or fact **dawns on you**, you realize it.

day days
NOUN **1.** one of the seven 24-hour periods of time in a week, measured from one midnight to the next **2.** Day is the period of light between sunrise and sunset. **3.** You can refer to a particular day or days meaning a particular period in history: *in Laurier's day*

daybreak
NOUN Daybreak is the time in the morning when light first appears in the sky.

daydream daydreams daydreaming daydreamed
NOUN **1.** a series of pleasant thoughts about things that you would like to happen
VERB **2.** When you daydream, you drift off into a daydream.

daylight
NOUN **1.** Daylight is the period during the day when it is light. **2.** Daylight is also the light from the sun.

day-to-day
ADJECTIVE happening every day as part of a person's ordinary routine

day trip day trips
NOUN a journey for pleasure to a place and back again on the same day

daze
PHRASE If you are **in a daze**, you are confused and bewildered.

dazed
ADJECTIVE If you are dazed, you are stunned and unable to think clearly.

dazzle dazzles dazzling dazzled
VERB **1.** If someone or something dazzles you, you are very impressed by that person's or thing's brilliance. **2.** If a bright light dazzles you, it blinds you for a moment.
dazzling ADJECTIVE

de-
PREFIX When the prefix *de-* is added to a noun or verb, it changes the meaning to its opposite: *decode*

HEADS UP

De- usually means *do the opposite*: *de-ice, deforest.*
Un- means *not*: **unable, unfriendly.**

dead
ADJECTIVE **1.** no longer living or supporting life **2.** no longer used or no longer functioning: *a dead language*
NOUN **3.** the middle part of night or winter, when it is quietest and at its darkest or coldest

dead end dead ends
NOUN a street that is closed off at one end

Dd

deadline deadlines
NOUN a time or date before which something must be completed: *May 1 is the deadline for applying to hockey camp.*

deadlock deadlocks
NOUN a situation in which neither side in a dispute is willing to give in

deadly deadlier deadliest
ADJECTIVE **1.** likely or able to cause death
ADVERB OR ADJECTIVE **2.** *Deadly* is used to emphasize how serious or unpleasant a situation is: *He is deadly serious about his comeback.*

deadpan
ADJECTIVE OR ADVERB showing no emotion or expression

deaf deafer deafest
ADJECTIVE **1.** partially or totally unable to hear **2.** refusing to listen or pay attention to something: *They were deaf to all pleas for financial help.*
deafness NOUN

deafening
ADJECTIVE If a noise is deafening, it is so loud that you cannot hear anything else.

deal deals dealing dealt
NOUN **1.** an agreement or arrangement, especially in business
VERB **2.** If you deal with something, you do what is necessary to sort it out: *You must learn to deal with stress.* **3.** If you deal in a particular type of goods, you buy and sell those goods. **4.** If you deal someone or something a blow, you hurt or harm that person or thing: *The team was dealt a heavy blow when it lost its star player.*

dealer dealers
NOUN a person or company whose business involves buying or selling things: *a car dealer*

dealings
PLURAL NOUN Your dealings with people are the relations you have with them or the business you do with them.

dean deans
NOUN In a university or college, a dean is a person responsible for administration or for the welfare of students.

dear dears; dearer dearest
NOUN **1.** *Dear* is used as a sign of affection: *You're such a dear!*
ADJECTIVE **2.** much loved: *my dear son*
3. Something that is dear is very expensive.
4. You use *dear* at the beginning of a letter before the name of the person you are writing to.
dearly ADVERB

dearth
NOUN a shortage of something

death deaths
NOUN Death is the end of the life of a person or animal.

debacle debacles
NOUN *a formal word* a sudden, disastrous failure

debase debases debasing debased
VERB To debase something means to reduce its value or quality.

debatable
ADJECTIVE not absolutely certain: *The justness of the punishment is debatable.*

debate debates debating debated
NOUN **1.** Debate is argument or discussion: *There is much debate as to the benefit of taking vitamins.* **2.** a formal discussion in which opposing views are expressed
VERB **3.** When people debate something, they discuss it in a fairly formal manner. **4.** If you are debating whether or not to do something, you are considering it: *He was debating whether or not he should tell her.*

debilitating
ADJECTIVE *a formal word* If something is debilitating, it makes you very weak: *a debilitating illness*

debit debits debiting debited
VERB **1.** to take money from a bank account
NOUN **2.** a record of the money that has been taken out of a bank account

debrief debriefs debriefing debriefed
VERB When someone is debriefed, that person is asked to give a report on a task that he or she has just completed.
debriefing NOUN

debris
NOUN Debris is fragments or rubble left after something has been destroyed.

debt debts
NOUN **1.** a sum of money that is owed to one person by another **2.** Debt is the state of owing money.

debtor debtors
NOUN a person who owes money

debut debuts
NOUN a performer's first public appearance

deca-
PREFIX Words beginning with *deca-* often have *ten* in their meaning: *decathlon*

decade decades
NOUN a period of ten years

decadence

NOUN Decadence is a decline in standards of morality and behaviour.
decadent ADJECTIVE

decaffeinated

ADJECTIVE Decaffeinated coffee or tea has had most of the caffeine removed.

decanter decanters

NOUN a glass bottle with a stopper, from which wine and other drinks are served

decapitate decapitates decapitating decapitated

VERB To decapitate someone means to cut off that person's head.

decathlon decathlons

NOUN a sports contest in which athletes compete in ten different events

⚠ HEADS UP

If there are ten events in a **decathlon**, how many do you think are in a **biathlon**? a **triathlon**?

decay decays decaying decayed

VERB **1.** When things decay, they rot or go bad.
NOUN **2.** Decay is the process of decaying.

deceased *a formal word*

ADJECTIVE **1.** A deceased person is someone who has recently died.
NOUN **2.** The deceased is someone who has recently died.

deceit

NOUN Deceit is behaviour that is intended to mislead people into believing something that is not true.
deceitful ADJECTIVE

deceive deceives deceiving deceived

VERB If you deceive someone, you make that person believe something that is not true.

decelerate decelerates decelerating decelerated

VERB If something decelerates, it slows down.
deceleration NOUN

December

NOUN December is the twelfth and last month of the year. It has 31 days.

decency

NOUN **1.** Decency is behaviour that is respectable and follows accepted moral standards. **2.** Decency is also behaviour that shows kindness and respect toward people: *No one had the decency to tell me to my face.*

decent

ADJECTIVE **1.** of an acceptable standard or quality: *My grandfather gets a decent pension.* **2.** Decent people are honest and respectable.
decently ADVERB

decentralize decentralizes decentralizing decentralized

VERB To decentralize an organization means to reorganize it so that power is transferred from one main administrative centre to smaller local units.
decentralization NOUN

deception deceptions

NOUN **1.** something that is intended to trick or deceive someone: *Pretending to be ill was not a very clever deception.* **2.** Deception is the act of deceiving someone.

deceptive

ADJECTIVE likely to make people believe something that is not true
deceptively ADVERB

decibel decibels

NOUN a unit for measuring the intensity of sound

decide decides deciding decided

VERB If you decide to do something, you choose to do it.

deciduous

ADJECTIVE Deciduous trees lose their leaves in the autumn every year.

decimal decimals

ADJECTIVE **1.** The decimal system expresses numbers using all the digits from 0 to 9.
NOUN **2.** a fraction in which a dot called a decimal point is followed by numbers representing tenths, hundredths, and thousandths. For example, 0.5 represents $\frac{5}{10}$ (or $\frac{1}{2}$); 0.05 represents $\frac{5}{100}$ (or $\frac{1}{20}$).

decimate decimates decimating decimated

VERB To decimate a group of people or animals means to kill or destroy a large number of them.

decipher deciphers deciphering deciphered

VERB If you decipher a piece of writing or a message, you work out its meaning.

decision decisions

NOUN a choice or judgment that is made about something: *The editor's decision is final.*

decisive

ADJECTIVE **1.** having great influence on the result of something: *It was the decisive moment of the race.* **2.** A decisive person is one who is able to make decisions firmly.

decisively ADVERB
decisiveness NOUN

deck decks
NOUN **1.** a floor or platform built into a ship
2. a set of playing cards

declaration declarations
NOUN a firm, forceful statement, often an official announcement: *a declaration of peace*

declare declares declaring declared
VERB **1.** If you declare something, you state it forcefully or officially: *O Canada was declared our national anthem in 1980.*
2. If you declare goods or earnings, you state what you have bought or earned, in order to pay tax or duty.

decline declines declining declined
VERB **1.** If something declines, it becomes smaller or weaker: *The polar bear population has declined quite dramatically recently.* **2.** If you decline something, you politely refuse to accept it or do it: *I declined his invitation to the movies.*
NOUN **3.** a gradual weakening or decrease: *a decline in the birth rate*

decode decodes decoding decoded
VERB If you decode a coded message, you convert it into ordinary language.
decoder NOUN

decommission decommissions decommissioning decommissioned
VERB When something such as a nuclear reactor or large machine is decommissioned, it is taken to pieces or removed from service because it is no longer going to be used.

decompose decomposes decomposing decomposed
VERB If something decomposes, it decays through chemical or bacterial action.

décor
NOUN The décor of a room or house is the style in which it is decorated and furnished.

Instead of DECORATE try...

ice a cake
paper the walls
adorn with jewellery
garnish a plate of food
brighten a room with paint

decorate decorates decorating decorated
VERB **1.** If you decorate something, you make it more attractive by adding some ornament or colour to it. **2.** If you decorate a room or building, you paint or wallpaper it.

decoration decorations
NOUN Decorations are features added to something to make it more attractive.

decorative
ADJECTIVE intended to look attractive

decorator decorators
NOUN a person whose job is planning colour schemes and the style and arrangement of furniture in rooms and buildings

decorum
NOUN *a formal word* Decorum is polite and correct behaviour.

decoy decoys
NOUN a person or object that is used to lead someone or something into danger

decrease decreases decreasing decreased
VERB **1.** If something decreases or if you decrease it, it becomes less in quantity or size.
NOUN **2.** a lessening in the amount of something; also the amount by which something becomes less
decreasing ADJECTIVE

decree decrees decreeing decreed
VERB **1.** If someone decrees something, that person states formally that it will happen.
NOUN **2.** an official decision or order, usually by governments or rulers: *The dictator decreed that a 10:00 p.m. curfew would be in effect for all citizens.*

dedicate dedicates dedicating dedicated
VERB If you dedicate yourself to something, you devote your time and energy to it.
dedication NOUN

deduce deduces deducing deduced
VERB If you deduce something, you work it out from other facts that you know are true.

deduct deducts deducting deducted
VERB To deduct an amount from a total amount means to subtract it from the total.

deduction deductions
NOUN **1.** an amount that is taken away from a total **2.** a conclusion that you have reached because of other things that you know are true

deed deeds
NOUN **1.** something that is done that is remarkable or significant: *Volunteering at the retirement home is a good deed.* **2.** a legal document, especially concerning the ownership of land or buildings

deem deems deeming deemed
VERB *a formal use* If you deem something to be true, you judge or consider it to be true: *His ideas were deemed unacceptable.*

Dd

deep deeper deepest
ADJECTIVE **1.** situated or extending a long way
down from the top surface of something,
or a long way inward: *a deep hole* **2.** great
or intense: *deep suspicion* **3.** low in pitch:
a deep voice **4.** strong and fairly dark in
colour: *The cranberry juice was deep ruby in
colour.*
deeply ADVERB

deepen deepens deepening deepened
VERB If something deepens or is deepened, it
becomes deeper or more intense.

deer
NOUN a large, hoofed mammal with long
slender legs and small, split hooves

deface defaces defacing defaced
VERB If you deface a wall or notice, you
spoil it by writing or drawing on it: *She
deliberately defaced her sister's poster.*

default defaults defaulting defaulted
VERB **1.** If someone defaults on something that
the person has legally agreed to do, he or she
fails to do it: *He defaulted on the loan.*
PHRASE **2.** If something happens **by default**, it
happens because something else that might
have prevented it has failed to happen.

defeat defeats defeating defeated
VERB **1.** If you defeat someone or something,
you win a victory, or cause that person or
thing to fail.
NOUN **2.** the state of being beaten or of
failing or an occasion on which someone is
beaten or fails to achieve something: *It was a
crushing defeat for the junior lacrosse team.*

defecate defecates defecating defecated
VERB To defecate means to get rid of waste
matter from the bowels through the anus.

defect defects defecting defected
NOUN **1.** a fault or flaw in something
VERB **2.** If someone defects, that person leaves
his or her own country or organization and
joins an opposing one.
defection NOUN

defective
ADJECTIVE imperfect or faulty: *defective
eyesight*

defence defences
NOUN **1.** Defence is action that is taken
to protect someone or something from
attack. **2.** any arguments used in support
of something that has been criticized or
questioned **3.** the case presented in a court of
law by a lawyer for the person on trial; also
the person on trial and his or her lawyers
4. A country's defences are its military
resources, such as its armed forces and
weapons.

defend defends defending defended
VERB **1.** To defend someone or something
means to protect that person or thing from
harm or danger. **2.** If you defend a person
or his or her ideas and beliefs, you argue in
support of them. **3.** To defend someone in
court means to represent that person and
argue the case for him or her. **4.** In a game
such as soccer or hockey, to defend means
to try to prevent being scored upon by your
opponents.

defendant defendants
NOUN a person who has been accused of a
crime in a court of law

defender defenders
NOUN **1.** a person who protects someone or
something from harm or danger **2.** a person
who argues in support of something

defensible
ADJECTIVE able to be defended against criticism
or attack

defensive
ADJECTIVE **1.** intended or designed for
protection: *defensive equipment* **2.** Someone
who is defensive feels unsure and threatened
by other people's opinions and attitudes:
*Don't get defensive; I was only joking about
your singing.*
defensively ADVERB
defensiveness NOUN

SPELL-CHECK THIS!

A computer's
spell-check won't
catch wrong
homophones (words
that are spelled
differently but
sound the same).

We almost hit the dear on the highway.

In this sentence, **dear** should be **deer**. A deer
is an animal. **Dear** means *much loved.*

NEL

Dd

defer defers deferring deferred
VERB **1.** If you defer something, you delay or postpone it until a future time. **2.** If you defer to someone, you agree with that person or do what he or she wants.

deference
NOUN Deference is polite and respectful behaviour.
deferential ADJECTIVE

defiance
NOUN Defiance is behaviour that shows that you are not willing to obey or behave in the expected way: *a gesture of defiance*
defiant ADJECTIVE
defiantly ADVERB

deficiency deficiencies
NOUN a lack of something: *vitamin deficiency*

deficient
ADJECTIVE lacking in something

deficit deficits
NOUN the amount by which money an organization receives is less than money spent

define defines defining defined
VERB If you define something, you say clearly what it is or what it means: *She defined the word before using it in a sentence.*

definite
ADJECTIVE **1.** firm and unlikely to be changed: *The answer is a definite yes.* **2.** certain or true rather than guessed or imagined: *definite proof*
definitely ADVERB

definition definitions
NOUN a statement explaining the meaning of a word or idea

definitive
ADJECTIVE **1.** final and unable to be questioned or altered: *a definitive answer* **2.** most complete, or the best of its kind: *a definitive history of science fiction*
definitively ADVERB

deflate deflates deflating deflated
VERB **1.** If you deflate something such as a tire or balloon, you let out all the air or gas in it. **2.** If you deflate someone, you reduce that person's excitement or eagerness about something.

deflect deflects deflecting deflected
VERB To deflect something means to turn it aside or make it change direction.
deflection NOUN

deforestation
NOUN Deforestation is the cutting down of all the trees in an area.

deformed
ADJECTIVE disfigured or abnormally shaped

defraud defrauds defrauding defrauded
VERB If someone defrauds you, that person cheats you out of something that should be yours.

defrost defrosts defrosting defrosted
VERB **1.** If you defrost a freezer or refrigerator, you remove the ice from it. **2.** If you defrost frozen food, you let it thaw out.

deft defter deftest
ADJECTIVE Someone who is deft is quick and skilful in his or her movements.
deftly ADVERB

defunct
ADJECTIVE no longer existing or functioning

defuse defuses defusing defused
VERB **1.** To defuse a dangerous or tense situation means to make it less dangerous or tense. **2.** To defuse a bomb means to remove its fuse or detonator so that it cannot explode.

defy defies defying defied
VERB **1.** If you defy a person or a law, you openly refuse to obey. **2.** *a formal use* If you defy someone to do something that you think is impossible, you challenge that person to do it: *I defy you to stop me.*

degenerate degenerates degenerating degenerated
VERB **1.** If something degenerates, it becomes worse: *The election campaign degenerated into farce.*
ADJECTIVE **2.** having low standards of morality
NOUN **3.** someone whose standards of morality are so low that people find that person's behaviour shocking or disgusting
degeneration NOUN

degrade degrades degrading degraded
VERB If something degrades people, it humiliates them and makes them feel that they are not respected.
degradation NOUN
degrading ADJECTIVE

degree degrees
NOUN **1.** an amount of a feeling or quality: *a degree of pain* **2.** a unit of measurement of temperature; often written as ° after a number: *20°C* **3.** a unit of measurement of angles in mathematics, and of latitude and longitude: *The ship was 20° off course.* **4.** the qualification awarded by a college or university after a student fulfills certain academic requirements

dehydrated
ADJECTIVE If someone is dehydrated, that person is weak or ill due to a loss of too much water from his or her body.

Dd

deity deities
NOUN a god or goddess

déjà vu
NOUN Déjà vu is the feeling that you have already experienced in the past exactly the same sequence of events as is happening now.

dejected
ADJECTIVE miserable and unhappy
dejection NOUN

deke dekes deking deked
NOUN **1.** in hockey, a movement, such as a fake shot, intended to draw a defensive player out of position.
VERB **2.** If you deke an opponent in a hockey game, you attempt to draw that player out of position.

delay delays delaying delayed
VERB **1.** If you delay doing something, you put it off until a later time. **2.** If something delays you, it hinders you or slows you down.
NOUN **3.** Delay is time during which something is delayed.

delectable
ADJECTIVE very pleasing or delightful

delegate delegates delegating delegated
NOUN **1.** a person appointed to take over a task on behalf of a group of people
VERB **2.** If you delegate duties, you give them to someone who can then act on your behalf.

delegation delegations
NOUN **1.** a group of people chosen to represent a larger group of people
2. Delegation is the giving of duties, responsibilities, or power to someone who can then act on your behalf.

delete deletes deleting deleted
VERB To delete something means to cross it out or remove it: *He had deleted the computer file by mistake.*
deletion NOUN

deliberate deliberates deliberating deliberated
ADJECTIVE **1.** done on purpose or planned in advance: *It was a deliberate insult.* **2.** careful and not hurried in speech and action: *She was very deliberate in her movements.*
VERB **3.** If you deliberate about something, you think about it seriously and carefully.
deliberately ADVERB

deliberation deliberations
NOUN Deliberation is careful consideration of a subject.

delicacy delicacies
NOUN **1.** Delicacy is finely fashioned or textured: *the delicacy of handmade lace*
2. Something said or done with delicacy is said or done tactfully so that nobody is

offended. **3.** Delicacies are rare or expensive foods that are considered especially nice to eat.

delicate
ADJECTIVE **1.** fine, graceful, or subtle in character: *a delicate fragrance* **2.** fragile and needing to be handled carefully: *delicate antique quilts* **3.** precise or sensitive, and able to notice very small changes: *a delicate instrument*
delicately ADVERB

delicatessen delicatessens
NOUN a store that sells unusual or imported foods, cooked meats, smoked fish, and salads

delicious
ADJECTIVE very pleasing, especially to taste
deliciously ADVERB

delight delights delighting delighted
NOUN **1.** Delight is great pleasure or joy.
VERB **2.** If something delights you, or if you are delighted by it, it gives you a lot of pleasure.
delighted ADJECTIVE

delightful
ADJECTIVE very pleasant and attractive

delinquent delinquents
NOUN a person who commits minor crimes
delinquency NOUN

delirious
ADJECTIVE **1.** unable to speak or act in a rational way because of illness or fever
2. wildly excited and happy
deliriously ADVERB

deliver delivers delivering delivered
VERB **1.** If you deliver something to someone, you take it and give it to that person. **2.** To deliver a lecture or speech means to give it.

delivery deliveries
NOUN **1.** Delivery, or a delivery, is the bringing of mail or goods to a person or business.
2. Someone's delivery is the way in which he or she gives a speech.

dell dells
NOUN *a literary or poetic word* a small wooded valley

delta deltas
NOUN a low, flat area at the mouth of a river where the river has split into several branches to enter the sea

delude deludes deluding deluded
VERB To delude people means to deceive them into believing something that is not true.

deluge deluges deluging deluged
NOUN **1.** a sudden, heavy downpour of rain
VERB **2.** To be deluged with things means to be overwhelmed by a great number of them.

Dd

delusion delusions
NOUN a mistaken or misleading belief or idea

deluxe
ADJECTIVE rich, luxurious, or of superior quality

delve delves delving delved
VERB If you delve into something, you seek out more information about it.

demand demands demanding demanded
VERB **1.** If you demand something, you ask for it forcefully and urgently. **2.** If a job or situation demands a particular quality, it needs it: *This situation demands hard work.* NOUN **3.** a forceful request for something: *My mom kept rejecting my demands for a later curfew.* **4.** If there is a demand for something, a lot of people want to buy it or have it: *The demand for the final book in the series exceeded all expectations.*

demean demeans demeaning demeaned
VERB If you demean yourself, you do something that makes people have less respect for you.
demeaning ADJECTIVE

demeanour
NOUN Your demeanour is the way you behave and the impression that this creates.

demented
ADJECTIVE Someone who is demented behaves in a wild or violent way.

dementia
NOUN *a medical word* Dementia is a partial or total loss of mental powers such as memory or the ability to distinguish reality from unreality.

demi-
PREFIX The prefix *demi-* means half.

demise
NOUN *a formal word* Someone's demise is his or her death.

demo demos
NOUN *an informal word* a demonstration of a product and how it is used: *We watched him give a demo of his newest invention.*

democracy democracies
NOUN Democracy is a system of government in which the people choose their leaders by voting for them in elections.

democrat democrats
NOUN a person who believes in democracy, personal freedom, and equality

democratic
ADJECTIVE having representatives elected by the people
democratically ADVERB

demography
NOUN Demography is the study of the changes in the size and structure of populations.
demographic ADJECTIVE

demolish demolishes demolishing demolished
VERB To demolish a building means to pull it down or break it up.
demolition NOUN

demon demons
NOUN **1.** an evil spirit or devil
ADJECTIVE **2.** skilful, keen, and energetic: *a demon tennis player*
demonic ADJECTIVE

demonstrate demonstrates demonstrating demonstrated
VERB **1.** To demonstrate a fact or theory means to prove or show it to be true. **2.** If you demonstrate something to somebody, you show and explain it by using or doing the thing yourself: *She demonstrated how to use the software.* **3.** If people demonstrate, they take part in a march or rally to show their opposition or support for something.

demonstration demonstrations
NOUN **1.** a talk or explanation to show how to do or use something **2.** Demonstration is proof that something exists or is true. **3.** a public march or rally in support of or opposition to something
demonstrator NOUN

KNOWING WORDS: WORD HISTORY

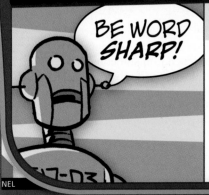

BE WORD SHARP!

Words are like living things. They grow and change.

Democracy comes from the Greek words **demos** (people) and **kratos** (rule). In Ancient Greece, people were picked to become leaders through a lottery. In modern democracies, leaders are picked, or *elected*, by the votes of the people. There are a few other English words that use **demo-** as a prefix to mean *people*. Can you find one on this page?

Dd

demote demotes demoting demoted
VERB A person who is demoted is put
in a lower rank or position, often as a
punishment.
demotion NOUN

demure

Instead of **DEMURE** try…

ADJECTIVE
Someone who is
demure is quiet,
shy, and behaves
very modestly.
demurely ADVERB

a **shy** child

a **coy** admirer

a **reserved** smile

an **unassuming** attitude

a **modest** young woman

den dens
NOUN **1.** the home of
some wild animals such as
bears or foxes **2.** a secret
place where people meet

denial denials
NOUN **1.** A denial of something is a statement
that it is untrue: *He published a firm denial
of the report.* **2.** The denial of a request for
something to which you have a right is the
refusal of it: *the denial of human rights*

denigrate denigrates denigrating denigrated
VERB *a formal word* To denigrate someone
means to criticize that person in order to
damage his or her reputation.

denim
NOUN Denim is strong cotton cloth, used for
making clothes.

denomination denominations
NOUN **1.** a particular group that has slightly
different religious beliefs from other groups
within the same faith **2.** a unit in a system of
weights, values, or measures: *The gift cards
come in denominations of 25, 50, and 100
dollars.*

denominator denominators
NOUN In mathematics, the denominator is the
bottom part of a fraction.

denote denotes denoting denoted
VERB If one thing denotes another, it is a sign
of it or it represents it: *A yellow traffic signal
denotes caution.*

denounce denounces denouncing denounced
VERB **1.** If you denounce someone or
something, you express very strong
disapproval of that person or thing:
*He publicly denounced government
environmental policy.* **2.** If you denounce
someone, you give information against that
person: *He denounced his former partner as
a thief.*

dense denser densest
ADJECTIVE **1.** thickly crowded or packed
together: *the dense crowd* **2.** difficult to see
through: *dense black smoke*
densely ADVERB

density densities
NOUN the degree to which something is filled
or occupied: *a very high population density*

dent dents denting dented
VERB **1.** To dent something means to damage
it by hitting it and making a hollow in its
surface.
NOUN **2.** a hollow in the surface of something

dental
ADJECTIVE relating to the teeth: *a dental
appointment*

dentist dentists
NOUN a person who is qualified to treat
people's teeth

dentistry
NOUN Dentistry is the branch of medicine
concerned with disorders of the teeth.

denture
NOUN a full or partial set of artificial teeth

denunciation denunciations
NOUN A denunciation of someone or
something is severe public criticism of that
person or thing.

deny denies denying denied
VERB **1.** If you deny something that has been
said, you state that it is untrue. **2.** If you
deny that something is the case, you refuse
to believe it: *He denied the existence of life
on other planets.* **3.** If you deny someone
something, you refuse to give it to that
person: *They were denied permission to
attend the movie.*

deodorant deodorants
NOUN a substance or spray used to hide
unpleasant smells

depart departs departing departed
VERB When you depart, you leave.
departure NOUN

department departments
NOUN one of the sections into which an
organization or store is divided: *the
marketing department, the footwear
department*
departmental ADJECTIVE

depend depends depending depended
VERB **1.** If you depend on someone or
something, you trust and rely on that person
or thing. **2.** If one thing depends on another,
it is influenced by it: *Your result on the exam
depends mainly on how well you prepared
for it.*

Dd

dependable
ADJECTIVE reliable and trustworthy

dependant dependants
NOUN someone who relies on another person for financial support

dependence
NOUN Dependence is a constant need that someone has for something or someone in order to survive or operate properly.

dependency dependencies
NOUN **1.** Dependency is the reliance on someone or something to give you what you need: *drug dependency* **2.** a country or area controlled by another country

dependent
ADJECTIVE reliant on someone or something

depict depicts depicting depicted
VERB To depict someone or something means to represent that person or thing in painting or sculpture.

deplete depletes depleting depleted
VERB To deplete something means to reduce greatly the amount of it that is available for use.
depletion NOUN

deplorable
ADJECTIVE shocking or regrettable: *deplorable conditions*

deplore deplores deploring deplored
VERB If you deplore something, you condemn it because you feel it is wrong.

deploy deploys deploying deployed
VERB To deploy troops or resources means to organize or position them so that they can be used effectively.
deployment NOUN

deport deports deporting deported
VERB If a government deports people, it sends them out of the country because they have committed a crime or because they do not have the right to be there.
deportation NOUN

depose deposes deposing deposed
VERB If someone is deposed, that person is removed from a position of power.

deposit deposits depositing deposited
VERB **1.** If you deposit something, you put it down or leave it somewhere. **2.** If you deposit money or valuables, you put them somewhere for safekeeping.
NOUN **3.** a sum of money given in partial payment for goods or services

depot depots
NOUN a place where large supplies of materials or equipment may be stored

depraved
ADJECTIVE morally bad

depress depresses depressing depressed
VERB **1.** If something depresses you, it makes you feel sad and gloomy. **2.** If wages or prices are depressed, their value falls.
depressive ADJECTIVE

depressant depressants
NOUN a drug that reduces nervous activity and so has a calming effect

depressed
ADJECTIVE **1.** unhappy and gloomy **2.** A place that is depressed has little economic activity and therefore low incomes and high unemployment: *depressed industrial areas*

depression depressions
NOUN **1.** a state of mind in which someone feels unhappy and has no energy or enthusiasm **2.** a time of industrial and economic decline

deprive deprives depriving deprived
VERB If you deprive someone of something, you take it away or prevent that person from having it.
deprived ADJECTIVE
deprivation NOUN

depth depths
NOUN **1.** The depth of something is the measurement or distance between its top and bottom, or between its front and back.
2. The depth of something such as emotion is its intensity: *the depth of her hostility*

deputation deputations
NOUN a small group of people sent to speak or act on behalf of others

deputy deputies
NOUN Someone's deputy is a person appointed to act in his or her place.

deranged
ADJECTIVE disturbed, insane, or behaving in a wild and uncontrolled way

derby derbies
NOUN A derby is a contest or race: *We went to the fishing derby on Saturday.*

derelict
ADJECTIVE abandoned and falling into ruins

deride derides deriding derided
VERB To deride someone or something means to mock that person or thing with contempt.

derision
NOUN Derision is an attitude of contempt or scorn toward something or someone.

derivation derivations
NOUN The derivation of something is its origin or source.

Dd

derivative derivatives
NOUN **1.** something that has developed from an earlier source
ADJECTIVE **2.** not original, but based on or copied from something else: *The novel was not deliberately derivative.*

derive derives deriving derived
VERB **1.** *a formal use* If you derive something from someone or something, you get it from that person or thing: *She derived so much joy from music.* **2.** If something derives from something else, it develops from it.

derogatory
ADJECTIVE critical and scornful: *He made derogatory remarks about them.*

descant descants
NOUN The descant to a tune is another tune played at the same time and at a higher pitch.

descend descends descending descended
VERB **1.** To descend means to move downward. **2.** If you descend on people or on a place, you arrive unexpectedly.

descendant descendants
NOUN A person's descendants are the people in later generations who are related to that person.

descended
ADJECTIVE If you are descended from certain people who lived in the past, your family originally derived from them.

descent descents
NOUN **1.** a movement or slope from a higher to a lower position or level **2.** Your descent is your family's origins.

describe describes describing described
VERB To describe someone or something means to give an account of that person or thing in words.

description descriptions
NOUN an account of something in words
descriptive ADJECTIVE

desert deserts
NOUN a region of land with very little plant life, usually because of low rainfall

desert deserts deserting deserted
VERB To desert a person means to leave or abandon that person: *His friends had deserted him.*
desertion NOUN

deserter deserters
NOUN someone who leaves the armed forces without permission

deserve deserves deserving deserved
VERB If you deserve something, you are entitled to it or earn it because of your qualities, achievements, or actions: *She deserved a rest.*

deserving
ADJECTIVE worthy of being helped, rewarded, or praised: *a deserving charity*

design designs designing designed
VERB **1.** To design something means to plan it, especially by preparing a detailed sketch or drawings from which it can be built or made.
NOUN **2.** a drawing or plan from which something can be built or made **3.** The design of something is its shape and style.
designer NOUN

designate designates designating designated
VERB **1.** To designate someone or something means to formally label or name that person or thing: *The building was designated a non-smoking area.* **2.** If you designate someone to do something, you appoint that person to do it: *He designated his daughter as his successor in the family business.*

designation designations
NOUN a name or title

desirable
ADJECTIVE **1.** worth having or doing: *a desirable job* **2.** sexually attractive
desirability NOUN

desire desires desiring desired
VERB **1.** If you desire something, you want it very much.
NOUN **2.** a strong feeling of wanting something **3.** Desire for someone is a strong sexual attraction to that person.

desist desists desisting desisted
VERB *a formal word* To desist from doing something means to stop doing it.

desk desks
NOUN a piece of furniture designed for working at or writing on

desktop desktops
NOUN **1.** the top of a desk
ADJECTIVE **2.** of a convenient size to be used on a desk or table: *a desktop computer*

desolate
ADJECTIVE **1.** deserted and bleak: *a desolate mountainous region* **2.** lonely, very sad, and without hope: *He was desolate without her.*
desolation NOUN

despair despairs despairing despaired
NOUN **1.** Despair is a total loss of hope.
VERB **2.** If you despair, you lose hope: *He despaired of finishing the book report before class.*
despairing ADJECTIVE

Dd

desperate

ADJECTIVE **1.** If you are desperate, you are so worried or frightened that you will try anything to improve your situation: *a desperate attempt to save their*

Instead of DESPERATE try...

friendship
2. A desperate person is violent and dangerous. **3.** A desperate situation is extremely dangerous or serious.

a dire situation
drastic measures
frantic behaviour
an urgent request
a panicked look

desperately ADVERB
desperation NOUN

despicable

ADJECTIVE deserving contempt

despise despises despising despised

VERB If you despise someone or something, you dislike that person or thing very much.

despite

PREPOSITION in spite of: *She watered the garden, despite the forecast for rain.*

despondent

ADJECTIVE discouraged and unhappy
despondency NOUN

dessert desserts

NOUN a sweet food served after the main course of a meal

destination destinations

NOUN a place to which someone or something is going or is being sent

destined

ADJECTIVE meant or intended to happen: *I was destined for fame and fortune.*

destiny destinies

NOUN **1.** Your destiny is all the things that happen to you in your life, especially when they are considered to be outside human control. **2.** Destiny is the force that some people believe controls everyone's life.

destitute

ADJECTIVE without money, shelter, or possessions, and therefore in great need
destitution NOUN

destroy destroys destroying destroyed

VERB **1.** To destroy something means to damage it so much that it is completely ruined. **2.** To destroy something means to put an end to it: *Three weeks of camping in wet weather destroyed their friendship.*

destruction

NOUN Destruction is the act of destroying something or the state of being destroyed.

destructive

ADJECTIVE causing or able to cause great harm, damage, or injury
destructiveness NOUN

desultory

ADJECTIVE passing from one thing to another in a fitful or random way: *A desultory, embarrassed chatter began again.*

detach detaches detaching detached

VERB To detach something means to remove it: *The hood can be detached.*
detachable ADJECTIVE

detached

ADJECTIVE **1.** separate or standing apart: *a detached house* **2.** having no real interest or emotional involvement in something: *He observed me with a detached curiosity.*

detachment detachments

NOUN **1.** Detachment is the feeling of not being personally involved with something: *A stranger can view your problems with detachment.* **2.** a small group of soldiers sent to do a special job

detail details

NOUN **1.** an individual fact or feature of something: *We discussed every detail of the performance.* **2.** Detail is all the small features that make up the whole of something: *Look at the detail.*
detailed ADJECTIVE

detain detains detaining detained

VERB **1.** To detain someone means to force that person to stay: *She was being detained for interrogation.* **2.** If you detain someone, you delay that person: *I won't detain you any longer.*

detect detects detecting detected

VERB **1.** If you detect something, you notice it: *I detected a glimmer of interest in his eyes.* **2.** To detect something means to find it: *Cancer can be detected by X-rays.*
detectable ADJECTIVE

detection

NOUN **1.** Detection is the act of noticing, discovering, or sensing something. **2.** Detection is also the work of investigating crime.

detective detectives

NOUN a person, usually a police officer, whose job is to investigate crimes

detector detectors

NOUN an instrument that is used to detect the presence of something: *a metal detector*

Dd

detention
NOUN The detention of someone is that person's arrest or imprisonment.

deter deters deterring deterred
VERB To deter someone means to discourage or prevent that person from doing something by creating a feeling of fear or doubt: *Are criminals deterred by the threat of punishment?*

detergent detergents
NOUN a chemical substance used for washing or cleaning things

deteriorate deteriorates deteriorating deteriorated
VERB If something deteriorates, it gets worse: *My father's health has deteriorated lately.*
deterioration NOUN

determination
NOUN Determination is great firmness in carrying out a purpose, after you have made up your mind to do something: *They shared a determination to win the contest.*

determine determines determining determined
VERB **1.** If something determines a situation or result, it causes it or controls it: *The track surface determines her tactics in a race.*
2. To determine something means to decide or settle it firmly: *The date has still to be determined.* **3.** To determine something means to find out or calculate the facts about it: *The collector examined the coin to determine whether it was genuine.*

determined
ADJECTIVE firmly decided: *She was determined not to repeat her error.*
determinedly ADVERB

determiner determiners
NOUN a word that can go before a noun or noun phrase to show, for instance, which thing you are referring to: *my* house, *this* book

deterrent deterrents
NOUN something that prevents you from doing something by making you worried or afraid of what will happen if you do it: *Prison was not an appropriate deterrent for the delinquent.*
deterrence NOUN

detest detests detesting detested
VERB If you detest someone or something, you strongly dislike that person or thing.

detonate detonates detonating detonated
VERB To detonate a bomb or mine means to cause it to explode.
detonator NOUN

detour detours
NOUN an alternative, less direct route

detract detracts detracting detracted
VERB To detract from something means to make it seem less good or less valuable.

detriment
NOUN Detriment is disadvantage or harm: *Poor diet is a detriment to a person's health.*
detrimental ADJECTIVE

deuce deuces
NOUN In tennis, deuce is the score of 40 each.

devalue devalues devaluing devalued
VERB To devalue something means to lower its status, importance, or worth.
devaluation NOUN

devastate devastates devastating devastated
VERB To devastate an area or place means to damage it severely or destroy it.
devastation NOUN

devastated
ADJECTIVE very shocked or upset: *The children were devastated by the news.*

develop develops developing developed
VERB **1.** When something develops or is developed, it grows or becomes more advanced: *The sneezing developed into a full-blown cold.* **2.** To develop an area of land means to build on it. **3.** To develop an illness or a fault means to become affected by it.

developer developers
NOUN a person or company that builds on land

development developments
NOUN **1.** Development is gradual growth or progress. **2.** The development of land or water is the process of making it more useful or profitable by the expansion of industry or housing: *the development of abandoned industrial property* **3.** a new stage in a series of events: *developments in technology*
developmental ADJECTIVE

deviant deviants
ADJECTIVE **1.** Deviant behaviour is unacceptable or different from what society considers normal.
NOUN **2.** someone whose behaviour or beliefs are different from what people consider to be acceptable
deviance NOUN

deviate deviates deviating deviated
VERB To deviate means to differ or depart from what is usual or acceptable.
deviation NOUN

device devices
NOUN **1.** a machine or tool that is used for a particular purpose: *a device to help you open jars* **2.** a plan or scheme: *a device to pressure him into selling*

Dd

devil devils
NOUN **1.** In Christianity and Judaism, the Devil is the spirit of evil and enemy of God. **2.** an evil spirit

devious
ADJECTIVE insincere and dishonest
deviousness NOUN

devise devises devising devised
VERB To devise something means to work it out: *Besides diets, he devised strenuous exercise routines.*

> ⚠ **HEADS UP**
>
> **Device** with a *c* is a noun that means *tool*. **Devise** with an *s* is a verb that means *plan*.

devoid
ADJECTIVE lacking in a particular quality: *Her glance was devoid of expression.*

devote devotes devoting devoted
VERB If you devote yourself to something, you give all your time, energy, or money to it: *She has devoted herself to women's causes.*

devoted
ADJECTIVE very loving and loyal

devotee devotees
NOUN a fanatical or enthusiastic follower of something

devotion
NOUN Devotion to someone or something is great love or affection for that person or thing.
devotional ADJECTIVE

devour devours devouring devoured
VERB If you devour something, you eat it hungrily or greedily.

devout
ADJECTIVE deeply and sincerely religious: *a devout Buddhist*
devoutly ADVERB

dew
NOUN Dew is drops of moisture that form on the ground and other cool surfaces at night.

dexterity
NOUN Dexterity is skill or agility in using your hands or mind: *You need mental dexterity to solve those puzzles.*
dexterous ADJECTIVE

diabetes
NOUN Diabetes is a disease in which certain people have too much sugar in their blood, because they do not produce enough insulin to absorb it.
diabetic NOUN OR ADJECTIVE

diabolical
ADJECTIVE extremely wicked and cruel: *He has a diabolical sense of humour.*

diagnose diagnoses diagnosing diagnosed
VERB To diagnose an illness or problem means to identify exactly what is wrong.

diagnosis diagnoses
NOUN the identification of what is wrong with someone who is ill
diagnostic ADJECTIVE

diagonal
ADJECTIVE in a slanting direction
diagonally ADVERB

diagram diagrams
NOUN a drawing that shows or explains the important parts of something

dial dials dialling dialled
NOUN **1.** the face of a clock or meter, with divisions marked on it so that a time or measurement can be recorded and read **2.** a part of a device, such as a radio, used to control or tune it
VERB **3.** To dial a telephone number means to press the number keys to select the required number.

dialect dialects
NOUN a form of a language spoken in a particular geographical area

dialogue dialogues
NOUN **1.** In a novel, play, or movie, dialogue is conversation. **2.** Dialogue is communication or discussion between people or groups of people: *The prime minister sought dialogue with the American president.*

dialysis
NOUN Dialysis is a treatment used for some kidney diseases, in which blood is filtered by a special machine to remove waste products.

diameter diameters
NOUN The diameter of a circle is the length of a straight line drawn across it through its centre.

diamond diamonds
NOUN **1.** a precious stone made of pure carbon **2.** a shape with four straight sides of equal length forming two opposite angles less than 90° and two opposite angles greater than 90° **3.** Diamonds is one of the four suits in a pack of playing cards. It is marked by a red diamond-shaped symbol.
ADJECTIVE **4.** A diamond anniversary is the sixtieth anniversary of an event.

Dd

diaphragm diaphragms
NOUN In mammals, the diaphragm is the muscular wall that separates the lungs from the stomach.

diarrhea
NOUN Diarrhea is a condition in which the feces are more liquid and frequent than usual.

diary diaries
NOUN a book that has a separate space or page for each day of the year on which to keep a record of experiences during each day
diarist NOUN

dice dices dicing diced
VERB To dice food means to cut it into small cubes.
diced ADJECTIVE

dictate dictates dictating dictated
VERB **1.** If you dictate something, you say or read it aloud for someone else to write down. **2.** To dictate something means to command or state what must happen: *What we wear is largely dictated by our daily routine.*
dictation NOUN

dictator dictators
NOUN a ruler who has complete power in a country, especially one who has taken power by force
dictatorial ADJECTIVE

diction
NOUN Someone's diction is the clarity with which that person speaks or sings.

dictionary dictionaries
NOUN a book in which words are listed alphabetically and explained, or equivalent words are given in another language

die dies dying died
VERB **1.** When people, animals, or plants die, they stop living. **2.** When something dies, dies away, or dies down, it gradually fades away: *The sound of her footsteps died away.*

die off, die out
VERB **3.** When something dies off or dies out, it ceases to exist.

diesel
NOUN **1.** a heavy fuel used in trains, buses, and trucks **2.** a vehicle with a diesel engine

diet diets
NOUN **1.** Someone's diet is the usual food that person eats: *a vegetarian diet* **2.** a special restricted selection of foods that people eat to improve their health or regulate their weight
dietary ADJECTIVE
dieter NOUN

dietician dieticians
NOUN a person trained to advise people about healthy eating

differ differs differing differed
VERB **1.** If two or more things differ, they are unlike each other. **2.** If people differ, they have opposing views or disagree about something.

difference differences
NOUN **1.** The difference between things is the way in which they are unlike each other: *What is the difference between these two stories?* **2.** The difference between two numbers is the amount by which one is less than another. **3.** A difference in someone or something is a significant change in that person or thing: *You wouldn't believe the difference in her.*

different
ADJECTIVE **1.** unlike something else **2.** unusual and out of the ordinary **3.** distinct and separate: *The team supports a different charity each year.*
differently ADVERB

differentiate differentiates differentiating differentiated
VERB **1.** To differentiate between things means to recognize or show how one is unlike the other. **2.** Something that differentiates one

KNOWING WORDS: IDIOMS

BE WORD SHARP!

Idioms add colour to language by playing with the meanings of words.

die stop functioning
cross my heart and hope to die promise
do or die risk everything to avoid failure
never say die never accept failure
to die for very good
want to curl up and die be very embarrassed

thing from another makes it distinct and unlike the other.

differentiation NOUN

difficult

ADJECTIVE **1.** not easy to do, understand, or solve: *a very difficult decision to make* **2.** hard to deal with, especially because of being unreasonable or unpredictable: *a difficult child*

difficulty difficulties

NOUN **1.** a problem: *The bus driver had some difficulty driving in poor weather conditions.* **2.** Difficulty is the fact or quality of being difficult.

diffident

ADJECTIVE timid and lacking in self-confidence

diffidently ADVERB

diffidence NOUN

diffract diffracts diffracting diffracted

VERB When rays of light or sound waves diffract, they break up after hitting an obstacle.

diffraction NOUN

diffuse diffuses diffusing diffused

VERB **1.** If something diffuses, it spreads out or scatters in all directions.

ADJECTIVE **2.** spread out over a wide area

diffusion NOUN

dig digs digging dug

VERB **1.** If you dig, you break up soil or sand, especially with a spade or garden fork. **2.** To dig something into an object means to push, thrust, or poke it in.

NOUN **3.** a prod or jab, especially in the ribs **4.** *an informal use* A dig at someone is a spiteful or unpleasant remark intended to hurt or embarrass that person.

digest digests digesting digested

VERB **1.** To digest food means to break it down in the stomach so that it can be easily absorbed and used by the body. **2.** If you digest information or a fact, you understand it and take it in.

digestible ADJECTIVE

digestion digestions

NOUN **1.** Digestion is the process of digesting food. **2.** Your digestion is your ability to digest food: *Camomile tea aids poor digestion.*

digestive ADJECTIVE

digit digits

NOUN **1.** *a formal use* Your digits are your fingers or toes. **2.** a written symbol for any of the numbers from 0 to 9

digital

ADJECTIVE **1.** displaying information, especially time, by numbers, rather than by a pointer

moving around a dial: *a digital watch*

ADJECTIVE **2.** using information processed electronically as binary digits: *a digital camera, a digital recording*

digitally ADVERB

dignified

ADJECTIVE full of dignity

dignitary dignitaries

NOUN a person who holds a high official position

dignity

NOUN Dignity is behaviour that is serious, calm, and controlled: *She conducted herself with dignity at the meeting.*

digression digressions

NOUN A digression in speech or writing is leaving the main subject for a while.

dike dikes

NOUN a thick wall that prevents water from flooding onto land from a river or from the sea

dilapidated

ADJECTIVE falling to pieces and generally in a bad condition: *a dilapidated barn*

dilate dilates dilating dilated

VERB To dilate means to become wider and larger: *The pupil of the eye dilates in the dark.*

dilated ADJECTIVE

dilation NOUN

dilemma dilemmas

NOUN a situation in which a difficult choice has to be made among alternatives

diligent

ADJECTIVE hard-working, and showing care and perseverance

diligently ADVERB

diligence NOUN

dill

NOUN a herb with yellow flowers and flavourful seeds and leaves

dilute dilutes diluting diluted

VERB To dilute a liquid means to add water or another liquid to it to make it less concentrated.

dilution NOUN

dim dimmer dimmest; dims dimming dimmed

ADJECTIVE **1.** badly lit and lacking in brightness **2.** very vague and unclear in your mind: *dim recollections of childhood* **3.** *an informal use* stupid: *He is rather dim.*

VERB **4.** If lights dim or are dimmed, they become less bright.

dimly ADVERB

dimness NOUN

Dd

dimension dimensions
NOUN **1.** A dimension of a situation is an aspect or factor that influences the way you understand it: *Knowing the background of the author gives her novel an added dimension.* **2.** You can talk about the size or extent of something as its dimensions: *It was an explosion of major dimensions.*
3. The dimensions of something are also its measurements, for example the length, width, and height of a box.

diminish diminishes diminishing diminished
VERB If something diminishes or if you diminish it, it becomes reduced in size or importance.

diminutive
ADJECTIVE very small

dimmer dimmers
NOUN A dimmer, or dimmer switch, allows you to adjust the brightness of an electric light.

dimple dimples
NOUN a small hollow in someone's cheek or chin

din dins
NOUN a loud and unpleasant noise

dine dines dining dined
VERB *a formal use* To dine means to eat dinner in the evening: *We dined together in the hotel.*

diner diners
NOUN **1.** a person who is having dinner in a restaurant **2.** a small, inexpensive restaurant

dinghy dinghies
NOUN a small boat that can be rowed, sailed, or powered by an outboard motor

dingy dingier dingiest
ADJECTIVE dirty, dark, and rather depressing: *a dingy hallway*

dinner dinners
NOUN **1.** the main meal of the day, eaten either in the evening or at midday **2.** a formal social occasion in the evening, at which a meal is served

dinosaur dinosaurs
NOUN a large reptile that lived in prehistoric times

dint
PHRASE **By dint of** means by means of: *He succeeds by dint of hard work.*

dip dips dipping dipped
VERB **1.** If you dip something into a liquid, you lower it or plunge it quickly into the liquid. **2.** If something dips, it slopes downward or goes below a certain level: *The sun dipped below the horizon.* **3.** To dip also

means to make a quick, slight downward movement: *She dipped her fingers into the cool water.*
NOUN **4.** a rich creamy mixture that you scoop up with crackers or raw vegetables and eat: *an avocado dip* **5.** *an informal use* a swim

diploma diplomas
NOUN a certificate awarded to a student who has successfully completed a course of study

diplomacy
NOUN **1.** Diplomacy is the managing of relationships between countries. **2.** Diplomacy is also skill in dealing with people without offending or upsetting them.
diplomatic ADJECTIVE
diplomatically ADVERB

diplomat diplomats
NOUN an official who negotiates and deals with another country on behalf of his or her own country

dire direr direst
ADJECTIVE disastrous, urgent, or terrible: *people in dire need of help*

direct directs directing directed
ADJECTIVE **1.** moving or aimed in a straight line or by the shortest route: *the direct route home* **2.** straightforward, and without delay or evasion: *Please give a direct answer.*
3. without anyone or anything intervening: *The organization has direct control of its own funding.* **4.** exact: *the direct opposite*
VERB **5.** To direct something means to guide and control it. **6.** To direct people or things means to send them, tell them, or show them the way. **7.** To direct a movie, a play, or a television program means to organize the way it is made and performed.

direct current
NOUN Direct current is a term used in physics to refer to an electric current that always flows in the same direction.

direction directions
NOUN **1.** the general line that someone or something is moving or pointing in: *If you walk in that direction for about five minutes, you will come to a park.* **2.** Direction is the controlling and guiding of something: *He was chopping vegetables under the chef's direction.*
PLURAL NOUN **3.** Directions are instructions that tell you how to do something or how to get somewhere.

directive directives
NOUN an instruction that must be obeyed: *a directive banning pesticide use*

Dd

directly

ADVERB in a straight line or immediately: *He looked directly at his friend.*

director directors

NOUN **1.** a member of the board of a company or institution **2.** the person responsible for the planning, guiding, and rehearsing of a television program, play, or movie

directorial ADJECTIVE

directorate directorates

NOUN a board of directors of a company or organization

directory directories

NOUN **1.** a book that gives lists of facts, such as names and addresses, and is usually arranged in alphabetical order

2. in computing, a list of the folders and files stored on a disk or drive

direct speech

NOUN the reporting of what someone has said by quoting the exact words

dirge dirges

NOUN a slow, sad piece of music, sometimes played or sung at funerals

dirt

NOUN **1.** Dirt is any unclean substance, such as dust, mud, or stains. **2.** Dirt is also earth or soil.

dirty dirtier dirtiest

ADJECTIVE **1.** marked or covered with dirt **2.** unfair or dishonest: *a dirty fight* **3.** about sex in a way that many people find offensive: *dirty jokes*

dis-

PREFIX The prefix *dis-* is added to the beginning of a word to form a word that means the opposite: *discontented, dishonest*

disability disabilities

NOUN a physical or mental condition or illness that restricts someone's way of life

disable disables disabling disabled

VERB If something disables someone, it injures or harms that person physically or mentally and severely affects his or her life.

disablement NOUN

disabled

ADJECTIVE lacking one or more physical powers, such as the ability to walk or to coordinate one's movements

disadvantage disadvantages

NOUN an unfavourable or harmful circumstance

disadvantaged ADJECTIVE

disaffected

ADJECTIVE If someone is disaffected with an idea or organization, that person no longer believes in it or supports it: *disaffected voters*

disagree disagrees disagreeing disagreed

VERB **1.** If you disagree with someone, you have a different view or opinion. **2.** If you disagree with an action or proposal, you disapprove of it or believe it is wrong: *He disagreed with the choices she made.* **3.** If food or drink disagrees with you, it makes you feel unwell.

disagreeable

ADJECTIVE unpleasant or unhelpful and unfriendly: *a disagreeable odour*

disagreement disagreements

NOUN **1.** a dispute about something **2.** an objection to something

disappear disappears disappearing disappeared

VERB **1.** If something or someone disappears, that person or thing goes out of sight or becomes lost. **2.** To disappear also means to stop existing or happening: *The pain has disappeared.*

disappearance NOUN

disappoint disappoints disappointing disappointed

VERB If someone or something disappoints you, that person or thing fails to live up to what you expected.

KNOWING WORDS: WORD BUILDING

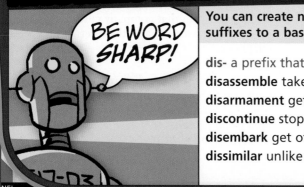

BE WORD SHARP!

You can create new words by adding prefixes and suffixes to a base word.

dis- a prefix that gives a base word the opposite meaning

disassemble take apart

disarmament getting rid of military forces and weapons

discontinue stop doing something

disembark get off a vehicle

dissimilar unlike

Dd

disappointed
ADJECTIVE sad because something has not happened

disappointment disappointments
NOUN **1.** a feeling of being disappointed
2. something that disappoints you

disapproval
NOUN the belief that something is wrong or inappropriate

disapprove disapproves disapproving disapproved
VERB To disapprove of something or someone means to believe that thing or person is wrong or bad: *Everyone disapproved of their marrying so young.*
disapproving ADJECTIVE

disarm disarms disarming disarmed
VERB **1.** To disarm means to get rid of weapons. **2.** If someone disarms you, that person overcomes your anger or doubt by charming or soothing you: *I was almost disarmed by his friendly manner.*
disarming ADJECTIVE

disarray
NOUN Disarray is a state of disorder and confusion: *The room was in disarray.*

disaster disasters
NOUN **1.** an event or accident that causes great distress or destruction **2.** a complete failure
disastrous ADJECTIVE
disastrously ADVERB

disband disbands disbanding disbanded
VERB When a group or an organization disbands, it officially ceases to exist.

disc discs
NOUN **1.** a flat round object: *a compact disc*
2. one of the thin circular pieces of cartilage that separate the bones in your spine

⚠ HEADS UP

When you're talking about computers, use the spelling **disk**. For a CD, use **disc**.

discard discards discarding discarded
VERB To discard something means to get rid of it, because you no longer want it or find it useful.

discern discerns discerning discerned
VERB *a formal word* To discern something means to notice or understand it clearly: *The movie had no plot that I could discern.*

discernible
ADJECTIVE able to be seen or recognized: *no discernible talent*

discerning
ADJECTIVE having good taste and judgment
discernment NOUN

discharge discharges discharging discharged
VERB **1.** If something discharges or is discharged, it is given or sent out: *Oil discharged from the torn hull of the ship into the ocean.* **2.** To discharge someone from a hospital means to allow that person to leave.
3. If someone is discharged from a job, that person is dismissed from it.
NOUN **4.** a substance that is released from the inside of something: *a thick nasal discharge*
5. a dismissal or release from a job or an institution

discipline disciplines disciplining disciplined
NOUN **1.** Discipline is making people obey rules and punishing them when they break them. **2.** Discipline is the ability to behave and work in a controlled way.
VERB **3.** If you discipline yourself, you train yourself to behave and work in an ordered way. **4.** To discipline someone means to punish that person.
disciplinary ADJECTIVE
disciplined ADJECTIVE

disc jockey disc jockeys
NOUN someone who plays recorded music on the radio, at a party, or at a night club. Disc jockey is often shortened to deejay.

disclose discloses disclosing disclosed
VERB To disclose something means to make it known or allow it to be seen.
disclosure NOUN

discomfort discomforts
NOUN **1.** Discomfort is distress or slight pain.
2. Discomfort is also a feeling of worry or embarrassment. **3.** Discomforts are things that make you uncomfortable.

disconcert disconcerts disconcerting disconcerted
VERB If something disconcerts you, it makes you feel uneasy or embarrassed.
disconcerting ADJECTIVE

disconnect disconnects disconnecting disconnected
VERB **1.** To disconnect something means to detach it from something else. **2.** If a business disconnects you, that company cuts you off from a service, such as the Internet or telephone.

discontent
NOUN Discontent is a feeling of dissatisfaction with conditions or with life in general: *The principal was aware of the discontent this policy had caused.*
discontented ADJECTIVE

Dd

discord
NOUN Discord is unpleasantness or quarrelling between people.

discount discounts discounting discounted
NOUN **1.** a reduction in the price of something
VERB **2.** If you discount something, you reject it or ignore it: *I haven't discounted her connection with the kidnapping case.*

discourage discourages discouraging discouraged
VERB To discourage someone means to take away that person's enthusiasm to do something.
discouraging ADJECTIVE
discouragement NOUN

discourse discourses *a formal word*
NOUN **1.** a formal talk or piece of writing intended to teach or explain something
2. Discourse is serious conversation between people on a particular subject.

discover discovers discovering discovered
VERB When you discover something, you find it or find out about it.
discovery NOUN
discoverer NOUN

discredit discredits discrediting discredited
VERB **1.** To discredit someone means to damage that person's reputation. **2.** To discredit an idea means to cause it to be doubted or not believed.

discreet
ADJECTIVE If you are discreet, you avoid causing embarrassment when dealing with secret or private matters.
discreetly ADVERB

discrepancy discrepancies
NOUN a difference between two things that ought to be the same: *There was a discrepancy between the descriptions given by the two witnesses.*

discrete
ADJECTIVE *a formal word* separate and distinct: *two discrete sets of nerves*

discretion
NOUN **1.** Discretion is the quality of behaving with care and tact so as to avoid embarrassment or distress to other people: *Count on my discretion.* **2.** Discretion is also freedom and authority to make decisions and take action according to your own judgment: *Teachers have very limited discretion in decision making.*
discretionary ADJECTIVE

discriminate discriminates discriminating discriminated
VERB **1.** To discriminate between things means to recognize and understand the differences

between them. **2.** To discriminate against a person or group means to treat that person or group unfairly, usually because of race, colour, or sex.
discrimination NOUN
discriminatory ADJECTIVE

discus discuses
NOUN a heavy, circular stone or metal plate, thrown by athletes

discuss discusses discussing discussed
VERB **1.** When people discuss something, they talk about it in detail. **2.** To discuss a question is to look at the points or arguments of both sides and try to reach your own opinion.

discussion discussions
NOUN a conversation or piece of writing in which a subject is considered in detail

disdain
NOUN Disdain is a feeling of superiority over or contempt for someone or something: *The candidates shared an equal disdain for the press.*
disdainful ADJECTIVE

disease diseases
NOUN an unhealthy condition in people, animals, or plants
diseased ADJECTIVE

disembodied
ADJECTIVE **1.** separate from or existing without a body: *The archaeologist found a disembodied skull in the pit she was excavating.* **2.** seeming not to be attached or to come from anyone: *disembodied voices*

disenchanted
ADJECTIVE disappointed with something, and no longer believing that it is good or worthwhile: *He became very disenchanted with politics.*
disenchantment NOUN

disfigure disfigures disfiguring disfigured
VERB To disfigure something means to spoil its appearance: *Graffiti or posters disfigured every wall.*

disgrace disgraces disgracing disgraced
NOUN **1.** Disgrace is a loss of approval or respect. **2.** If something is a disgrace, it is unacceptable: *The overcrowded prisons were a disgrace.* **3.** If someone is a disgrace to a group of people, that person's behaviour makes the group feel ashamed: *Your behaviour is a disgrace to your friends and your family.*
VERB **4.** If you disgrace yourself, your behaviour causes other people to disapprove of you strongly.

Dd

disgraceful

ADJECTIVE If something is disgraceful, people disapprove of it strongly and think that those who are responsible for it should be ashamed.

disgracefully ADVERB

disgruntled

ADJECTIVE discontented or in a bad mood: *They were disgruntled by the bad weather and the delay of their flight.*

disguise disguises disguising disguised

VERB **1.** To disguise something means to change its appearance so that people do not recognize it. **2.** To disguise a feeling means to hide it: *I tried to disguise my relief.*

NOUN **3.** something you wear or something you do to alter your appearance so that you cannot be recognized by other people

disgust disgusts disgusting disgusted

NOUN **1.** Disgust is a strong feeling of dislike or disapproval.

VERB **2.** To disgust someone means to make that person feel a strong sense of dislike or disapproval.

disgusted ADJECTIVE

disgusting

ADJECTIVE very unpleasant and offensive

dish dishes

NOUN **1.** a shallow container for cooking or serving food **2.** food of a particular kind or food cooked in a particular way: *two fish dishes to choose from*

disheartened

ADJECTIVE If you are disheartened, you feel disappointed.

dishevelled

ADJECTIVE If someone looks dishevelled, that person's appearance is untidy.

dishonest

ADJECTIVE not truthful or able to be trusted

dishonestly ADVERB

dishonesty

NOUN Dishonesty is behaviour that is meant to deceive people, either by not telling the truth or by cheating.

dishwasher dishwashers

NOUN **1.** a machine for washing and drying dishes **2.** a person whose job is washing dishes

disillusioned

ADJECTIVE If you are disillusioned with something, you are disappointed because it is not as good as you had expected.

disinfectant disinfectants

NOUN a chemical substance that kills germs

disintegrate disintegrates disintegrating disintegrated

VERB **1.** If something disintegrates, it becomes weakened and is not effective: *My confidence disintegrated.* **2.** If an object disintegrates, it breaks into many pieces and so is destroyed.

disintegration NOUN

disinterest

NOUN **1.** Disinterest is a lack of interest. **2.** Disinterest is also a lack of personal involvement in a situation.

disinterested

ADJECTIVE If someone is disinterested, that person is not going to gain or lose from the situation he or she is involved in, and so can act in a way that is fair to both sides: *a disinterested judge*

⚠ **HEADS UP**

A **disinterested** person is fair and unbiased. An **uninterested** person doesn't care at all.

disjointed

ADJECTIVE If thought or speech is disjointed, it jumps from subject to subject and so is difficult to follow.

disk disks

NOUN **1.** In a computer, the disk is the part where information is stored: *The program takes up 2.5 megabytes of disk space.* **2.** another spelling of DISC

dislike dislikes disliking disliked

VERB **1.** If you dislike something or someone, you do not like that thing or person.

NOUN **2.** Dislike is a feeling that you have when you do not like someone or something.

dislocate dislocates dislocating dislocated

VERB To dislocate your bone or joint means to put it out of place.

dislodge dislodges dislodging dislodged

VERB To dislodge something means to move it or force it out of place.

dismal

ADJECTIVE rather gloomy and depressing: *dismal weather*

dismally ADVERB

dismantle dismantles dismantling dismantled

VERB To dismantle something means to take it apart.

dismay dismays dismaying dismayed

NOUN **1.** Dismay is a feeling of fear and worry.

Dd

VERB **2.** If someone or something dismays you, that person or thing fills you with alarm and worry.

dismember dismembers dismembering dismembered

VERB *a formal word* To dismember a person or animal means to cut or tear that person's or animal's body into pieces.

dismiss dismisses dismissing dismissed

VERB **1.** If you dismiss something, you decide to ignore it because it is not important enough for you to think about. **2.** To dismiss an employee means to ask that person to leave his or her job. **3.** If someone in authority dismisses you, that person tells you to leave.

dismissal NOUN

dismissive

ADJECTIVE If you are dismissive of something or someone, you show that you think that thing or person is of little importance or value: *a dismissive gesture*

disobey disobeys disobeying disobeyed

VERB To disobey a person or an order means to deliberately refuse to do what you are told.

disorder disorders

NOUN **1.** Disorder is a state of untidiness. **2.** Disorder is also a lack of organization: *The men fled in disorder.* **3.** a disease: *a stomach disorder*

disorganized

ADJECTIVE If something is disorganized, it is confused and badly prepared or badly arranged.

disorganization NOUN

disown disowns disowning disowned

VERB To disown someone or something means to refuse to admit any connection with that person or thing.

disparaging

ADJECTIVE critical and scornful: *disparaging remarks*

disparate

ADJECTIVE *a formal word* Things that are disparate are utterly different from one another.

disparity NOUN

dispatch dispatches dispatching dispatched

VERB **1.** To dispatch someone to a particular place means to send that person there for a special reason: *The prime minister dispatched the minister of defence on a fact-finding visit.*

NOUN **2.** an official written message, often sent to an army or government headquarters

dispel dispels dispelling dispelled

VERB To dispel fears or beliefs means to drive them away or to destroy them: *The myths are being dispelled.*

dispensary dispensaries

NOUN a place where medicines are prepared and given out, especially in a hospital or clinic

dispense dispenses dispensing dispensed

VERB **1.** *a formal use* To dispense something means to give it out: *Guidance counsellors dispense advice.* **2.** To dispense medicines means to prepare them and give them out. **3.** To dispense with something means to do without it or do away with it: *We'll dispense with formalities.*

dispenser dispensers

NOUN a machine or container from which you can get things: *a soap dispenser*

disperse disperses dispersing dispersed

VERB **1.** When something disperses, it scatters over a wide area. **2.** When people disperse or when someone disperses them, they move apart and go in different directions.

dispersion NOUN

dispirited

ADJECTIVE depressed and having no enthusiasm for anything

dispiriting

ADJECTIVE Something dispiriting makes you depressed: *a dispiriting defeat*

displace displaces displacing displaced

VERB **1.** If one thing displaces another, it forces the thing out of its usual place and occupies that place itself. **2.** If people are displaced, they are forced to leave their home or country.

displacement

NOUN Displacement is the removal of something from its usual or correct place or position.

display displays displaying displayed

VERB **1.** If you display something, you show it or make it visible to people. **2.** If you display something such as an emotion, you behave in a way that shows you feel it.

NOUN **3.** an arrangement of things designed to attract people's attention

displease displeases displeasing displeased

VERB If someone or something displeases you, that person or thing makes you annoyed, dissatisfied, or offended.

displeasure NOUN

disposable

ADJECTIVE designed to be thrown away after use: *disposable diapers*

Dd

disposal

NOUN Disposal is the act of getting rid of something that is no longer wanted or needed.

dispose disposes disposing disposed

VERB **1.** To dispose of something means to get rid of it. **2.** If you are disposed to do something, you are willing to do it.

disprove disproves disproving disproved

VERB If someone disproves an idea, belief, or theory, that person shows that it is not true.

dispute disputes disputing disputed

NOUN **1.** an argument

VERB **2.** To dispute a fact or theory means to question the truth of it.

disqualify disqualifies disqualifying disqualified

VERB If someone is disqualified from a competition or activity, that person is officially stopped from taking part in it: *She was disqualified from the contest because she was over the age limit.*

disqualification NOUN

disquiet

NOUN Disquiet is worry or anxiety.

disquieting ADJECTIVE

disregard disregards disregarding disregarded

VERB **1.** To disregard something means to pay little or no attention to it.

NOUN **2.** Disregard is a lack of attention or respect for something: *They exhibited a flagrant disregard of the law.*

disrepair

PHRASE If something is **in disrepair** or **in a state of disrepair**, it is broken or in poor condition.

disrespect

NOUN Disrespect is contempt or lack of respect: *his disrespect for authority*

disrespectful ADJECTIVE

⚠ **HEADS UP**

In slang, **disrespect** is also used as a verb, and often shortened to **dis**: *He was dissing my style.*

disrupt disrupts disrupting disrupted

VERB To disrupt something such as an event or system means to break it up or throw it into confusion: *Strikes disrupted public transit in the city. Her rude behaviour disrupted the class.*

disruption NOUN

disruptive ADJECTIVE

dissatisfied

ADJECTIVE not pleased or not contented

dissatisfaction NOUN

dissect dissects dissecting dissected

VERB To dissect a plant or a dead body means to cut it up so that it can be scientifically examined.

dissection NOUN

dissent dissents dissenting dissented

NOUN **1.** Dissent is strong difference of opinion: *political dissent*

VERB **2.** When people dissent, they express a difference of opinion about something.

dissenting ADJECTIVE

dissertation dissertations

NOUN a long essay, especially as a requirement for a university degree

disservice

NOUN To do someone a disservice means to do something that harms that person.

dissident dissidents

NOUN someone who disagrees with and criticizes the strict and unjust government of his or her country

dissipate dissipates dissipating dissipated

VERB **1.** *a formal word* When something dissipates or is dissipated, it completely disappears: *The storm clouds dissipated, revealing a sunny, blue sky.* **2.** If someone dissipates time, money, or effort, that person wastes it.

dissolve dissolves dissolving dissolved

VERB **1.** If you dissolve something or if it dissolves in a liquid, it becomes mixed with and absorbed in the liquid. **2.** To dissolve an organization or institution means to officially end it.

dissuade dissuades dissuading dissuaded

VERB To dissuade someone from doing something or from believing something means to persuade that person not to do it or not to believe it.

distance distances distancing distanced

NOUN **1.** The distance between two points is how far it is between them. **2.** Distance is the fact of being far away in space or time.

VERB **3.** If you distance yourself from people or things or are distanced from them, you become less involved with them.

distant

ADJECTIVE **1.** far away in space or time **2.** A distant relative is one who is not closely related to you. **3.** Someone who is distant is cold and unfriendly.

distantly ADVERB

Dd

distaste

NOUN Distaste is a dislike of something that you find offensive.

distasteful

ADJECTIVE If you find something distasteful, you think it is unpleasant or offensive.

distil distils distilling distilled

VERB When a liquid is distilled, it is heated until it evaporates and then cooled to enable purified liquid to be collected.

distillation NOUN

distillery distilleries

NOUN a place where whisky or other strong alcoholic drink is made, using a process of distillation

distinct

ADJECTIVE **1.** If one thing is distinct from another, it is recognizably different from it: *The word bear has two distinct meanings.* **2.** If something is distinct, you can hear, smell, or see it clearly and plainly: *There was a distinct buzzing noise.* **3.** If something such as a fact, idea, or intention is distinct, it is clear and definite: *She had a distinct feeling someone was watching them.*

distinctly ADVERB

distinction distinctions

NOUN **1.** a difference between two things: *a distinction between the body and the soul* **2.** Distinction is a quality of excellence and superiority: *a man of distinction* **3.** a special honour or claim: *It had the distinction of being the tallest building in the world.*

distinctive

ADJECTIVE Something that is distinctive has a special quality that makes it recognizable: *a distinctive voice*

distinctively ADVERB

distinguish distinguishes distinguishing distinguished

VERB **1.** To distinguish between things means to recognize the difference between them: *I've learned to distinguish between business and friendship.* **2.** To distinguish something means to make it out by seeing, hearing, or tasting it: *I heard shouting but was unable to distinguish the words.* **3.** If you distinguish yourself, you do something that makes people think highly of you.

distinguishable ADJECTIVE
distinguishing ADJECTIVE

distort distorts distorting distorted

VERB **1.** If you distort a statement or an argument, you represent it in an untrue or misleading way. **2.** If something is distorted, it is changed so that it seems strange or unclear: *His voice was distorted.* **3.** If an object is distorted, it is twisted or pulled out of shape.

distorted ADJECTIVE
distortion NOUN

distract distracts distracting distracted

VERB If something distracts you, your attention is taken away from what you are doing.

distracted ADJECTIVE
distractedly ADVERB
distracting ADJECTIVE

distraction distractions

NOUN **1.** something that takes people's attention away from something **2.** an activity that is intended to amuse or relax someone

distraught

ADJECTIVE so upset and worried that you cannot think clearly: *He was distraught over the death of his mother.*

distress distresses distressing distressed

NOUN **1.** Distress is great suffering caused by pain or sorrow. **2.** Distress is also the state of needing help because of difficulties or danger. VERB **3.** To distress someone means to make that person feel alarmed or unhappy: *Her death had profoundly distressed me.*

distressing

ADJECTIVE very worrying or upsetting

distribute distributes distributing distributed

VERB **1.** To distribute things, such as leaflets, means to hand them out or deliver them: *They publish and distribute brochures.* **2.** If things are distributed, they are spread throughout an area or space: *Distribute the cheese evenly on top of the quiche.* **3.** To distribute something means to divide it and share it out among a number of people.

distribution distributions

NOUN **1.** Distribution is the delivering of something to various people or organizations: *the distribution of store catalogues* **2.** Distribution is the sharing out of something to various people: *distribution of power*

distributor distributors

NOUN a company that supplies goods to other businesses that then sell them to the public

district districts

NOUN an area of a city, town, or country: *a residential district*

distrust distrusts distrusting distrusted

VERB **1.** If you distrust someone, you are suspicious because you are not sure whether that person is honest. NOUN **2.** Distrust is suspicion.

distrustful ADJECTIVE

Dd

disturb disturbs disturbing disturbed
VERB **1.** If you disturb someone, you break into his or her peace or privacy. **2.** If something disturbs you, it makes you feel upset or worried. **3.** If something is disturbed, it is moved out of position or meddled with.
disturbing ADJECTIVE

disturbance disturbances
NOUN **1.** Disturbance is the state of being disturbed. **2.** a violent or unruly incident in public

disuse
NOUN Something that has fallen into disuse is neglected or no longer used.
disused ADJECTIVE

ditch ditches
NOUN a trench, usually at the side of a road, to drain away excess water

dither dithers dithering dithered
VERB To dither means to be unsure and hesitant.

ditto Ditto means *the same*. In written lists, ditto is represented by a mark (") to avoid repetition.

ditty ditties
NOUN *an old-fashioned word* a short, simple song or poem

diva divas
NOUN a great or leading female singer, especially in opera

dive dives diving dived
VERB **1.** To dive means to jump headfirst into water with your arms above your head. **2.** If you go diving, you go down under the surface of the sea or a lake using special breathing equipment. **3.** If an aircraft or bird dives, it flies in a steep downward path, or drops sharply.
diver NOUN
diving NOUN

diverge diverges diverging diverged
VERB **1.** If opinions or facts diverge, they differ: *Theory and practice sometimes diverged.* **2.** If two things such as roads or paths that have been going in the same direction diverge, they separate and go off in different directions.
divergence NOUN
divergent ADJECTIVE

diverse
ADJECTIVE **1.** If a group of things is diverse, it is made up of different kinds of things: *a diverse range of goods and services* **2.** People, ideas, or objects that are diverse are very different from one another.
diversity NOUN

diversify diversifies diversifying diversified
VERB To diversify means to increase the variety of something: *The music store has diversified and also sells DVDs and video games.*
diversification NOUN

diversion diversions
NOUN **1.** something that takes your attention away from what you should be concentrating on: *A snack break created a welcome diversion.* **2.** a pleasant or amusing activity

divert diverts diverting diverted
VERB To divert something means to change the course or direction it is following.
diverting ADJECTIVE

divide divides dividing divided
VERB **1.** When something divides or is divided, it is split up and separated into two or more parts. **2.** If something divides two areas, it forms a barrier between them. **3.** If people divide over something or if something divides them, it causes strong disagreement between them. **4.** In mathematics, when you divide, you calculate how many times one number contains another.
NOUN **5.** a separation: *the class divide*

dividend dividends
NOUN **1.** a portion of a company's profits that is paid to shareholders **2.** In mathematics, a dividend is a number or quantity to be divided by another. For example, in *16 ÷ 2*, the dividend is *16*.

divine divines divining divined
ADJECTIVE **1.** having the qualities of a god or goddess
VERB **2.** To divine something means to discover it by guessing.
divinely ADVERB

divinity divinities
NOUN **1.** Divinity is the study of religion. **2.** Divinity is the state of being a god. **3.** a god or goddess

division divisions
NOUN **1.** Division is the separation of something into two or more distinct parts. **2.** Division is also the process of dividing one number by another. **3.** a difference of opinion that causes separation between ideas or groups of people: *There were divisions in the Conservative Party on economic policy.* **4.** any one of the parts into which something is split: *the Research Division*
divisional ADJECTIVE

divisor divisors
NOUN a number by which another number is divided

Dd

divorce divorces divorcing divorced
NOUN **1.** Divorce is the formal and legal ending of a marriage.
VERB **2.** When a married couple divorces, the marriage is legally ended.
divorced ADJECTIVE
divorcee NOUN

divulge divulges divulging divulged
VERB To divulge information means to reveal it.

Diwali
NOUN a Hindu religious festival in honour of the goddess of wealth. It is celebrated by feasting, exchanging gifts, and lighting lamps.

DIY
NOUN DIY is the activity of making or repairing things yourself. DIY is an abbreviation for *do-it-yourself*.

dizzy dizzier dizziest
ADJECTIVE having or causing a whirling sensation
dizziness NOUN

DNA
NOUN DNA is deoxyribonucleic acid, which is found in the cells of all living things. It is responsible for passing on characteristics from parents to their children.

do does doing did done
VERB **1.** Do is an auxiliary verb that is used to form questions, negatives, and to give emphasis to the main verb of a sentence.
2. If someone does a

Instead of **DO** try…

accomplish a good deed
attempt a stunt
perform a role
act properly
commit a crime
execute a command
practise a dance routine
calculate a math problem

task or activity, that person performs it and finishes it: *He just didn't want to do any work.* **3.** If you ask what people do, you want to know what their job is: *What will you do when you leave school?* **4.** If you do well at something, you are successful. If you do badly, you are unsuccessful. **5.** If something will do, it is adequate but not the most suitable option: *The sketch isn't perfect, but it will do.*
NOUN **6.** *an informal use* a party or other social event

do up
VERB **7.** To do something up means to fasten it.

docile
ADJECTIVE quiet, calm, and easily controlled

dock docks docking docked
NOUN **1.** an enclosed area in a harbour where ships go to be loaded, unloaded, or repaired **2.** In a court of law, the dock is the place where the accused person stands or sits.
VERB **3.** When a ship docks, it is brought into dock at the end of its voyage. **4.** To dock someone's wages means to deduct an amount from the sum that person would normally receive. **5.** To dock an animal's tail means to cut part of it off.

doctor doctors doctoring doctored
NOUN **1.** a person who is qualified in medicine and treats people who are ill **2.** A doctor of an academic subject is someone who has been awarded the highest academic degree: *She is a Doctor of Philosophy.*
VERB **3.** To doctor something means to alter it in order to deceive people: *The map was doctored and sold as an antique.*

doctorate doctorates
NOUN the highest university degree
doctoral ADJECTIVE

doctrine doctrines
NOUN a set of beliefs or principles held by a group
doctrinal ADJECTIVE

document documents documenting documented
NOUN **1.** a piece of paper that provides an official record of something **2.** a piece of text or graphics stored in a computer as a file that can be amended or altered by document processing software
VERB **3.** If you document something, you make a detailed record of it.
documentation NOUN

documentary documentaries
NOUN **1.** a radio or television program, or a movie that gives information on real events
ADJECTIVE **2.** Documentary evidence is made up of written or official records.

dodge dodges dodging dodged
VERB **1.** If you dodge someone or something, you move suddenly to avoid being seen, hit, or caught. **2.** If you dodge something such as an issue or accusation, you avoid dealing with it.

dodgy
ADJECTIVE *an informal word* dangerous, risky, or unreliable: *He has a dodgy heart.*

Dd

dodo dodos
NOUN a large, flightless bird that is now extinct

doe does
NOUN a female deer, rabbit, or hare

does the third person singular of the present tense of DO

dog dogs dogging dogged
NOUN **1.** a four-legged, meat-eating animal, kept as a pet, or to guard property, or for hunting
VERB **2.** If you dog someone, you follow that person very closely.

dog-eared
ADJECTIVE A book that is dog-eared has been used so much that the corners of the pages are turned down or worn.

dogged
ADJECTIVE showing determination to continue with something, even if it is very difficult: *dogged persistence*
doggedly ADVERB

dogma dogmas
NOUN a belief or system of beliefs held by a religious or political group

dogmatic
ADJECTIVE Someone who is dogmatic about something is convinced that he or she is right about it.
dogmatism NOUN

doldrums
AN INFORMAL PHRASE If you are **in the doldrums**, you are depressed or bored.

dole doles doling doled
VERB If you dole something out, you give a certain amount of it to each individual in a group.

doll dolls
NOUN a child's toy that looks like a baby or person

dollar dollars
NOUN the main unit of currency in Canada, the US, and some other countries. A dollar is worth 100 cents.

dollop dollops
NOUN an amount of food, served casually in a lump: *a dollop of mashed potatoes*

dolphin dolphins
NOUN a mammal that lives in the sea and looks like a large fish with a long snout

domain domains
NOUN **1.** a particular area of activity or interest: *the domain of science* **2.** an area over which someone has control or influence: *He claims the kitchen as his domain.*

dome domes
NOUN a round roof
domed ADJECTIVE

domestic
ADJECTIVE **1.** happening or existing within one particular country: *domestic and foreign politics* **2.** involving or concerned with the home and family: *routine domestic chores*

domesticated
ADJECTIVE If a wild animal or plant has been domesticated, it has been controlled or cultivated.

dominance
NOUN **1.** Dominance is power or control. **2.** If something has dominance over other similar things, it is more powerful or important than they are: *the dominance of the United States in the movie business*
dominant ADJECTIVE

dominate dominates dominating dominated
VERB **1.** If something or someone dominates a situation or event, that person or thing is the most powerful or important thing in it and has control over it: *The civil service dominated public affairs.* **2.** If a person or country dominates other people or places, that person or country has power or control over them. **3.** If something dominates an area, it towers over it: *The valley was dominated by high surrounding cliffs.*
dominating ADJECTIVE
domination NOUN

domineering
ADJECTIVE Someone who is domineering tries to control other people: *a domineering parent*

dominion
NOUN Dominion is control or authority that a person or a country has over other people.

domino dominoes
NOUN Dominoes are small rectangular blocks marked with two groups of spots on one side, used for playing the game called dominoes.

don dons donning donned
NOUN **1.** In some Canadian universities or colleges, a don is a person who is in charge of a student residence.
VERB **2.** *a literary or poetic use* If you don clothing, you put it on.

donate donates donating donated
VERB To donate something to a charity or organization means to give it as a gift.
donation NOUN

done the past participle of DO

donkey donkeys
NOUN an animal like a horse, but smaller and with longer ears

donor donors
NOUN **1.** someone who gives blood while he or she is alive or an organ after death to help someone who is ill: *a kidney donor* **2.** someone who gives something such as money to a charity or other organization

doodle doodles doodling doodled
NOUN **1.** a drawing done when you are thinking about something else or when you are bored
VERB **2.** To doodle means to draw doodles.

doom
NOUN Doom is a terrible fate or event in the future that you can do nothing to prevent.

doomed
ADJECTIVE If someone or something is doomed to an unpleasant or unhappy experience, that person is certain to suffer it: *doomed to failure*

doomsday
NOUN Doomsday is the end of the world.

door doors
NOUN a swinging or sliding panel for opening or closing the entrance to something; also the entrance itself

doorway doorways
NOUN an opening in a wall for a door

dope dopes doping doped
NOUN **1.** Dope is an illegal drug.
VERB **2.** If someone dopes you, that person puts a drug into your food or drink.

dormant
ADJECTIVE Something that is dormant is not active, growing, or being used: *The buds will remain dormant until spring.*

dormitory dormitories
NOUN a large bedroom where several people sleep

dormouse dormice
NOUN an animal, like a large mouse, with a furry tail

dosage dosages
NOUN the amount of a medicine or a drug that should be taken

dose doses
NOUN a measured amount of a medicine or drug

dossier dossiers
NOUN a collection of papers with information on a particular subject or person

dot dots dotting dotted
NOUN **1.** a very small, round mark
VERB **2.** If things dot an area, they are scattered all over it: *Fishing villages dot the coastline.*
PHRASE **3.** If you arrive somewhere **on the dot**, you arrive there at exactly the right time.

dotcom dotcoms
NOUN a company that does most of its business on the Internet

dote dotes doting doted
VERB If you dote on someone, you love that person very much.
doting ADJECTIVE

double doubles doubling doubled
ADJECTIVE **1.** twice the usual size: *a double scoop of ice cream* **2.** consisting of two parts: *double doors*
VERB **3.** If something doubles, it becomes twice as large. **4.** To double for someone means you will take that person's place: *I'll double for you at the meeting.*
NOUN **5.** Your double is someone who looks exactly like you. **6.** Doubles is a game of tennis or badminton that two people play against two other people.
doubly ADVERB

double bass double basses
NOUN a musical instrument like a large violin, which you play standing up

double-cross double-crosses double-crossing double-crossed
VERB If someone double-crosses you, that person cheats you by pretending to do what you both planned, but in fact the person does the opposite.

double-decker double-deckers
ADJECTIVE **1.** having two tiers or layers: *a double-decker sandwich*
NOUN **2.** a bus, train, or airplane with two floors

doubt doubts doubting doubted
NOUN **1.** Doubt is a feeling of uncertainty about whether something is true or possible.
VERB **2.** If you doubt something, you think that it is probably not true or possible.

doubtful
ADJECTIVE unlikely or uncertain

dough
NOUN **1.** Dough is a mixture of flour and water and sometimes other ingredients, used to make things such as bread, pastry, and biscuits. **2.** *an informal use* Dough is money.

doughnut doughnuts
NOUN a ring of sweet dough cooked in hot fat

dour
ADJECTIVE severe and unfriendly: *The dour neighbour frightened many children.*

douse douses dousing doused
VERB If you douse a fire, you stop it from burning by throwing water over it.

Dd

dove doves
NOUN a bird like a small pigeon

dovetail dovetails dovetailing dovetailed
VERB If two things dovetail together, they fit together closely or neatly.

dowager dowagers
NOUN a woman who has inherited property or a title from her dead husband

dowdy dowdier dowdiest
ADJECTIVE wearing dull and unfashionable clothes

down downs downing downed
PREPOSITION OR ADVERB **1.** Down means toward the ground, toward a lower level, or in a lower place. **2.** If you go down a road or river, you go along it.
ADVERB **3.** If you put something down, you place it on a surface. **4.** If an amount of something goes down, it decreases.
ADJECTIVE **5.** If you feel down, you feel depressed.
VERB **6.** If you down a drink, you drink it quickly.
NOUN **7.** Down is the small, soft feathers on young birds.

downcast
ADJECTIVE **1.** feeling sad and dejected **2.** If your eyes are downcast, they are looking toward the ground.

downfall
NOUN **1.** The downfall of a successful or powerful person or institution is that person's or institution's failure. **2.** Something that is someone's downfall is the thing that causes that person's failure: *His pride may be his downfall.*

downgrade downgrades downgrading downgraded
VERB If you downgrade something, you give it less importance or make it less valuable.

downhill
ADVERB **1.** moving down a slope **2.** becoming worse: *The business has gone downhill in the last ten years.*

download downloads downloading downloaded
VERB **1.** If you download data you transfer it from the memory of one computer to that of another, especially over the Internet.
NOUN **2.** a piece of data transferred in this way

downpour downpours
NOUN a heavy fall of rain

downright
ADJECTIVE OR ADVERB You use *downright* to emphasize something: *Staff are often discourteous and sometimes downright rude. You were downright brilliant in the math competition.*

downstairs
ADVERB **1.** going down a staircase toward the ground floor
ADJECTIVE OR ADVERB **2.** on a lower floor or on the ground floor

downstream
ADJECTIVE OR ADVERB Something that is downstream or moving downstream is nearer or moving nearer to the mouth of a river from a point further up.

down-to-earth
ADJECTIVE sensible and practical: *a down-to-earth approach*

downtrodden
ADJECTIVE People who are downtrodden are treated badly by those with power, and do not have the ability to fight back.

downturn downturns
NOUN a decline in the economy or in the success of a company or industry

downward
ADVERB OR ADJECTIVE If you move or look downward, you move or look toward the ground or toward a lower level: *His eyes travelled downward. She slipped on the downward slope.*

downwind
ADVERB If something moves downwind, it moves in the same direction as the wind: *Sparks from the bonfire drifted downwind.*

dowry dowries
NOUN In some cultures, a woman's dowry is money or property that her father gives to the man she marries.

doze dozes dozing dozed
VERB **1.** When you doze, you sleep lightly for a short period.
NOUN **2.** a short, light sleep

dozen dozens
NOUN A dozen things are 12 of them.

Dr. *Dr.* is short for *Doctor* and is used before the name of someone with the highest form of academic degree or who practises medicine.

drab drabber drabbest
ADJECTIVE dull and unattractive
drabness NOUN

draft drafts drafting drafted
NOUN **1.** an early rough version of a document or speech
VERB **2.** When you draft a document or speech, you write the first rough version of

⚠ **HEADS UP** After a number, the singular **dozen** is used: *I'd like three dozen apples.*

Dd

it. **3.** To draft people means to select them for military service: *He was drafted into the army when he turned 18.*

drafty draftier draftiest
ADJECTIVE A place that is drafty has currents of cold air blowing through it.

drag drags dragging dragged
VERB **1.** If you drag a heavy object somewhere, you pull it slowly and with difficulty. **2.** If you drag someone somewhere, you make that person go although he or she may be unwilling. **3.** If things drag behind you, they trail along the ground as you move along. **4.** If an event or a period of time drags, it is boring and seems to last a long time.
NOUN **5.** Drag is the resistance to the motion of a body passing through air or a fluid.

dragon dragons
NOUN In stories and legends, a dragon is a fierce animal like a large lizard with wings and claws that breathes fire.

dragonfly dragonflies
NOUN a colourful insect, which is often found near water

dragoon dragoons dragooning dragooned
NOUN **1.** In former times, dragoons were mounted infantry soldiers.
VERB **2.** If you dragoon someone into something, you force that person to do it.

drain drains draining drained
VERB **1.** If you drain something, you cause liquid to flow out of it. **2.** If you drain a glass, you drink all its contents. **3.** If liquid drains somewhere, it flows there. **4.** If something drains strength or resources, it gradually uses them up: *I was drained of energy after working all weekend on my report.*
NOUN **5.** a pipe or channel that carries water or sewage away from a place **6.** a metal grid in a road, through which rainwater or melted snow flows

drainage
NOUN **1.** Drainage is the system of pipes, drains, or ditches used to drain water or other liquid away from a place. **2.** Drainage is also the process of draining water away, or the way in which a place drains: *To grow these vegetables well, you need good drainage.*

drake drakes
NOUN a male duck

drama dramas
NOUN **1.** a serious play for the theatre, television, or radio **2.** Drama is plays and the theatre in general. **3.** You can refer to the exciting events or aspects of a situation as drama: *the drama of real life*

dramatic
ADJECTIVE A dramatic change or event happens suddenly and is very noticeable: *a dramatic departure from tradition*
dramatically ADVERB

dramatist dramatists
NOUN a person who writes plays

drape drapes draping draped
VERB If you drape a piece of cloth, you arrange it so that it hangs down or covers something in loose folds.

drastic
ADJECTIVE A drastic course of action is very severe and is usually taken urgently: *It's time for drastic action.*
drastically ADVERB

draught another spelling of DRAFT

draw draws drawing drew drawn
VERB **1.** When you draw, you use a pencil, pen, or crayon to make a picture or diagram. **2.** To draw near means to move closer. To draw away or draw back means to move away. **3.** If you draw something in a particular direction, you pull it there smoothly and gently: *He drew his feet under the chair.* **4.** If you draw a deep breath, you breathe in deeply. **5.** If you draw the curtains, you pull them so that they cover or uncover the window. **6.** If something such as water or energy is drawn from a source, it is taken from it: *He drew a pail of water from the well.* **7.** If you draw a conclusion, you arrive at it from the facts you know. **8.** If you draw a distinction or a comparison between two things, you point out that it exists.
NOUN **9.** the result of a game or competition in which nobody wins

draw up
VERB **10.** To draw up a plan, document, or list means to prepare it and write it out.

drawback drawbacks
NOUN a problem that makes something less acceptable or desirable: *Shortcuts usually have a drawback.*

drawbridge drawbridges
NOUN a bridge that can be pulled up or lowered

drawer drawers
NOUN a sliding, box-shaped part of a piece of furniture used for storing things

drawing drawings
NOUN **1.** a picture made with a pencil, pen, or crayon **2.** Drawing is the skill or work of making drawings.

drawing room drawing rooms
NOUN *an old-fashioned word* a room in a house where people relax or entertain guests

Dd

drawl drawls drawling drawled
VERB If someone drawls, that person speaks slowly with long vowel sounds.

drawn Drawn is the past participle of DRAW.

dread dreads dreading dreaded
VERB **1.** If you dread something, you feel very worried and frightened about it: *He was dreading the journey.*
NOUN **2.** Dread is a feeling of great fear or anxiety.
dreaded ADJECTIVE

dreadful
ADJECTIVE very bad or unpleasant
dreadfully ADVERB

dream dreams dreaming dreamed
NOUN **1.** a series of events that you experience in your mind while asleep **2.** a situation or event that you often think about because you would very much like it to happen: *his dream of winning the lottery*
VERB **3.** When you dream, you see events in your mind while you are asleep. **4.** When you dream about something happening, you often think about it because you would very much like it to happen. **5.** If someone dreams up a plan or idea, that person invents it. **6.** If you say you would not dream of doing something, you are emphasizing that you would not do it: *I wouldn't dream of giving the plot away.*
ADJECTIVE **7.** too good to be true: *a dream holiday*
dreamer NOUN

dreamy dreamier dreamiest
ADJECTIVE Someone with a dreamy expression looks as if he or she is thinking about something very pleasant.

dreary drearier dreariest
ADJECTIVE dull or boring

dregs
PLURAL NOUN The dregs of a liquid are the last drops left at the bottom of a container, and any sediment left with it.

drenched
ADJECTIVE soaking wet

dress dresses dressing dressed
NOUN **1.** a piece of clothing for women or girls made up of a skirt and top attached **2.** Dress is any clothing worn by men or women.
VERB **3.** When you dress, you put clothes on. **4.** If you dress for a special occasion, you put on formal clothes. **5.** To dress a wound means to clean it up and treat it.

dresser dressers
NOUN a piece of furniture with drawers for clothes

dressing gown dressing gowns
NOUN an item of clothing that is put on over nightwear

dressing room dressing rooms
NOUN a room used for getting changed and putting on makeup, especially a backstage room at a theatre

dress rehearsal dress rehearsals
NOUN the last rehearsal of a show or play, using costumes, scenery, and lighting

dribble dribbles dribbling dribbled
VERB **1.** When liquid dribbles down a surface, it trickles down it in drops or a thin stream. **2.** If a person or animal dribbles, saliva trickles from the mouth. **3.** In sport, to dribble a ball means to move it along by repeatedly tapping it with your foot, your hand, or a stick.
NOUN **4.** a small quantity of liquid flowing in a thin stream or drops

drift drifts drifting drifted
VERB **1.** When something drifts, it is carried along by the wind or by water. **2.** When people drift, they move aimlessly from one place or activity to another. **3.** If you drift off to sleep, you gradually fall asleep.
NOUN **4.** A snow drift is a pile of snow heaped up by the wind. **5.** The drift of an argument or a speech is its main point.
drifter NOUN

KNOWING WORDS: IDIOMS

BE WORD SHARP!

Idioms add colour to language by playing with the meanings of words.

dream an imagined situation
a dream come true a goal achieved after a long time
a pipe dream an impossible hope
beyond your wildest dreams more than you ever hoped for
like a dream working very well
living in a dream world not in touch with reality

Dd

drill drills drilling drilled
NOUN **1.** a tool for making holes: *an electric drill* **2.** Drill is a routine exercise or routine training: *a fire drill*
VERB **3.** To drill into something means to make a hole in it using a drill. **4.** If you drill people, you teach them to do something by repetition.

drink drinks drinking drank drunk
VERB **1.** When you drink, you take liquid into your mouth and swallow it. **2.** To drink also means to drink alcohol: *He drinks little and eats carefully.*
NOUN **3.** an amount of liquid suitable for drinking **4.** an alcoholic drink
drinker NOUN

drip drips dripping dripped
VERB **1.** When liquid drips, it falls in small drops. **2.** When an object drips, drops of liquid fall from it.
NOUN **3.** a drop of liquid falling from something **4.** a device for allowing liquid food to enter the bloodstream of a person who cannot eat properly because of illness

drive drives driving drove driven
VERB **1.** To drive a vehicle means to operate it and control its movements. **2.** If something or someone drives you to do something, that thing or person forces you to do it: *The excessive noise from the neighbours drove her to complain.* **3.** If you drive a post or nail into something, you force it in by hitting it with a hammer. **4.** If something drives a machine, it supplies the power that makes it work.
NOUN **5.** a journey in a vehicle **6.** a driveway **7.** Drive is energy and determination.
driver NOUN
driving NOUN

drivel
NOUN Drivel is nonsense: *She is still writing mindless drivel.*

drive-through
NOUN a restaurant or other business that is specially designed for customers to use while staying in their cars

driveway
NOUN a private road that leads from a public road to a person's house

drizzle
NOUN Drizzle is light rain.

dromedary dromedaries
NOUN a camel that has one hump

drone drones droning droned
VERB **1.** If something drones, it makes a low, continuous humming noise. **2.** If someone

drones on, that person keeps talking or reading aloud in a boring way.
NOUN **3.** a continuous low dull sound

drool drools drooling drooled
VERB If someone drools, saliva dribbles from the mouth without that person being able to stop it.

droop droops drooping drooped
VERB If something droops, it hangs or sags downward with no strength or firmness.

drop drops dropping dropped
VERB **1.** If you drop something, you let it fall. **2.** If something drops, it falls straight down. **3.** If a level or amount drops, it becomes less. **4.** If your voice drops, or if you drop your voice, you speak more quietly. **5.** If you drop something that you are doing or dealing with, you stop doing it or dealing with it: *She dropped the subject and never mentioned it again.* **6.** If you drop a hint, you give someone a hint in a casual way. **7.** If you drop something or someone somewhere, you deposit or leave that thing or person there.
NOUN **8.** A drop of liquid is a very small quantity of it that forms or falls in a round shape. **9.** a decrease: *a huge drop in income* **10.** the distance between the top and bottom of something tall, such as a cliff or building: *It is a sheer drop to the foot of the cliff.*

droplet droplets
NOUN a small drop

droppings
PLURAL NOUN Droppings are the feces of birds and small animals.

drought droughts
NOUN a long period during which there is no rain

> ⚠ **HEADS UP**
>
> Unlike most other words that end in **-ought** (like **bought** and **fought**), **drought** is pronounced DROWT.

drove Drove is the past tense of DRIVE

drown drowns drowning drowned
VERB **1.** When someone drowns or is drowned, that person dies because he or she has gone underwater and cannot breathe. **2.** If a noise drowns out a sound, it is louder than the sound and makes it impossible to hear it.

drowsy drowsier drowsiest
ADJECTIVE feeling sleepy

Dd

drudgery

NOUN Drudgery is hard, boring work.

drug drugs drugging drugged

NOUN **1.** a chemical given to people to treat disease **2.** Drugs are chemical substances that some people smoke, swallow, smell, or inject because of their stimulating effects.

VERB **3.** To drug a person or animal means to give a drug to make that person or animal unconscious. **4.** To drug food or drink means to add a drug to it in order to make someone unconscious.

drugged ADJECTIVE

drum drums drumming drummed

NOUN **1.** a musical instrument consisting of a skin stretched tightly over a round frame **2.** an object or container shaped like a drum: *an oil drum*

VERB **3.** If something is drumming on a surface, it is hitting it regularly, making a continuous beating sound. **4.** If you drum something into someone, you keep saying it to that person until he or she understands it or remembers it.

drummer NOUN

drumstick drumsticks

NOUN **1.** a stick used for beating a drum **2.** A chicken drumstick is the lower part of the leg of a chicken that is cooked and eaten.

drunk drunks **1.** Drunk is the past participle of DRINK.

ADJECTIVE **2.** If someone is drunk, that person has drunk so much alcohol that he or she cannot speak clearly or behave sensibly.

NOUN **3.** a person who is drunk, or who often gets drunk

drunken ADJECTIVE

drunkenly ADVERB

drunkenness NOUN

dry drier driest; dries drying dried

ADJECTIVE **1.** Something that is dry contains or uses no water or liquid. **2.** Dry bread or toast is eaten without a topping. **3.** Dry sherry or wine does not taste sweet. **4.** Dry also means plain and sometimes boring: *the dry facts* **5.** Dry humour is subtle and sarcastic.

VERB **6.** When you dry something, or when it dries, liquid is removed from it.

dry up

VERB **7.** If something dries up, it becomes completely dry. **8.** *an informal use* If you dry up, you forget what you were going to say, or find that you have nothing left to say.

dryness NOUN

dryly ADVERB

dry-clean dry-cleans dry-cleaning dry-cleaned

VERB When clothes are dry-cleaned, they are cleaned with a liquid chemical rather than with water.

dryer dryers

NOUN a device for removing moisture from something by heating or by hot air: *a hair dryer*

dual

ADJECTIVE having two parts, functions, or aspects: *Many airplanes have dual controls.*

dub dubs dubbing dubbed

VERB **1.** If something is dubbed a particular name, it is given that name: *She was dubbed Ginger because of her red hair.* **2.** If a film is dubbed, the voices on the soundtrack are not those of the actors, but those of other actors speaking in a different language.

dubious

ADJECTIVE **1.** not entirely honest, safe, or reliable: *dubious sales techniques* **2.** doubtful: *I felt dubious about the entire proposition.*

dubiously ADVERB

duchess duchesses

NOUN a woman who has the same rank as a duke, or who is a duke's wife or widow

duchy duchies

NOUN the land owned and ruled by a duke or duchess

duck ducks ducking ducked

NOUN **1.** a bird that lives in water and has webbed feet and a large flat bill

VERB **2.** If you duck, you move your head quickly downward in order to avoid being hit by something. **3.** If you duck a duty or responsibility, you avoid it. **4.** To duck someone means to push that person briefly under water.

duckling ducklings

NOUN a young duck

duct ducts

NOUN **1.** a pipe or channel through which liquid or gas is sent **2.** a bodily passage through which liquid such as tears can pass

dud duds

NOUN something that does not function properly

due dues

ADJECTIVE **1.** expected to happen or arrive: *The baby is due in December.* **2.** If you give something due consideration, you give it the consideration it needs.

PHRASE **3.** **Due to** means because of: *Headaches can be due to stress.*

ADVERB **4.** Due means exactly in a particular direction: *About a kilometre due west lay the ocean.*

Dd

PLURAL NOUN **5.** Dues are sums of money that you pay regularly to an organization you belong to.

duel duels
NOUN **1.** in former times, a fight arranged between two people using deadly weapons, to settle a quarrel **2.** Any contest or conflict between two people can be referred to as a duel.

duet duets
NOUN a piece of music sung or played by two people

dug Dug is the past tense and past participle of DIG.

dugout dugouts
NOUN **1.** a canoe made by hollowing out a log **2.** a shelter dug in the ground for protection

duke dukes
NOUN a nobleman with a rank just below that of a prince

dull duller dullest; dulls dulling dulled
ADJECTIVE **1.** not interesting in any way **2.** slow to learn or understand **3.** not bright, sharp, or clear **4.** A dull day or dull sky is very cloudy. **5.** Dull feelings are weak and not intense: *He should have been angry but felt only dull resentment.*
VERB **6.** If something dulls or is dulled, it becomes less bright, sharp, or clear.
dully ADVERB
dullness NOUN

duly
ADVERB **1.** *a formal use* If something is duly done, it is done in the correct way: *I wish to record my support for the duly elected student council.* **2.** If something duly happens, it is something that you expected to happen: *Two chicks duly emerged from their eggs.*

dumb dumber dumbest
ADJECTIVE **1.** unable to speak by nature: *dumb animals* **2.** *an informal use* slow to understand or stupid

dumbfounded
ADJECTIVE speechless with amazement: *She was too dumbfounded to answer.*

dummy dummies
NOUN **1.** an imitation or model of something that is used for display
ADJECTIVE **2.** imitation or substitute: *Stage actors use dummy weapons during battle scenes.*

dump dumps dumping dumped
VERB **1.** When unwanted waste is dumped, it is left somewhere. **2.** If you dump something, you throw it down or put it down somewhere in a careless way.

NOUN **3.** a place where garbage is left **4.** a storage place, especially used by the military for storing supplies: *an ammunition dump* **5.** *an informal use* You refer to a place as a dump when it is unattractive and unpleasant to live in.

dumpling dumplings
NOUN a small lump of dough that is cooked and eaten with meat and vegetables

dunce dunces
NOUN a person who cannot learn something that someone is trying to teach

dune dunes
NOUN A dune or sand dune is a hill of sand heaped up by the wind.

dung
NOUN Dung is the feces from large animals, sometimes called manure.

dungarees
PLURAL NOUN Dungarees are trousers that have a bib covering the chest and straps over the shoulders.

dungeon dungeons
NOUN an underground prison

dunk dunks dunking dunked
VERB **1.** To dunk something means to dip it briefly into a liquid: *He dunked the cookie in a glass of milk.*
NOUN **2.** a shot in basketball when the player jumps up high and scores by pushing the ball down through the basket. If the player pushes the ball down very hard, that's called a slam dunk.

duo duos
NOUN **1.** a pair of musical performers; also a piece of music written for two players **2.** Any two people doing something together can be referred to as a duo.

dupe dupes duping duped
VERB **1.** If someone dupes you, that person tricks you.
NOUN **2.** someone who has been tricked

duplicate duplicates duplicating duplicated
VERB **1.** To duplicate something means to make an exact copy of it.
NOUN **2.** something that is identical to something else
ADJECTIVE **3.** identical to or an exact copy of: *a duplicate key*
duplication NOUN

durable
ADJECTIVE strong and lasting for a long time
durability NOUN

duration
NOUN The duration of something is the length of time during which it happens or exists.

duress

NOUN If you do something under duress, you are forced to do it, and you do it very unwillingly.

during

PREPOSITION happening throughout a particular time or at a particular point in time: *I plan to work in the library during my afternoon break.*

dusk

NOUN Dusk is the time just before nightfall when it is not completely dark.

dust dusts dusting dusted

NOUN **1.** Dust is dry, fine, powdery material such as particles of earth, dirt, or pollen. VERB **2.** When you dust furniture or other objects, you remove dust from them using a duster. **3.** If you dust a surface with powder, you cover it lightly with the powder.

duster dusters

NOUN a cloth used for removing dust from furniture and other objects

dusty dustier dustiest

ADJECTIVE covered with dust

dutiful

ADJECTIVE doing everything you are expected to do

dutifully ADVERB

duty duties

NOUN **1.** something you ought to do or feel you should do, because it is your responsibility: *Teachers have a duty to listen to students.* **2.** a task that you do as part of your job

NOUN **3.** Duty is tax paid to the government on some goods, especially imports.

duty-free

ADJECTIVE Duty-free goods are sold at airports, border crossings, or on planes or ships at a cheaper price than usual because they are not taxed: *duty-free perfume*

duvet duvets

NOUN a comforter with a removable cover, filled with feathers or other material, used on a bed in place of a top sheet and blankets

DVD DVDs

NOUN an abbreviation for *digital video disc.* A DVD is a type of compact disc that can store large amounts of video and sound information. Its full name is **DVD-ROM**, which stands for *Digital Video Disc Read-Only Memory. Read-only* means the information on the disc may be displayed or used but not altered.

dwarf dwarfs dwarfing dwarfed

VERB **1.** If one thing dwarfs another, it is so much bigger that it makes the other look very small.

ADJECTIVE **2.** smaller than average

NOUN **3.** a person who is much smaller than average size

dwell dwells dwelling dwelt

VERB **1.** *a literary or poetic use* To dwell somewhere means to live there. **2.** If you **dwell on** something or dwell upon it, you think or write about it a lot.

dwelling dwellings

NOUN *a formal word* Someone's dwelling is the place where that person lives.

dwindle dwindles dwindling dwindled

VERB If something dwindles, it becomes smaller or weaker.

dye dyes dyeing dyed

VERB **1.** To dye something means to change its colour by applying coloured liquid to it. NOUN **2.** a colouring substance that is used to change the colour of something such as cloth or hair

dying

ADJECTIVE **1.** likely to die soon **2.** *an informal use* If you are **dying for something**, you want it very much.

dyke another spelling of DIKE

dynamic dynamics

ADJECTIVE **1.** A dynamic person is full of energy, ambition, and new ideas. **2.** relating to energy or forces that produce motion PLURAL NOUN **3.** In physics, dynamics is the study of the forces that change or produce the motion of bodies or particles. **4.** The dynamics of a society or a situation are the forces that cause it to change. **5.** Dynamics is the various degrees of loudness needed in the performance of a piece of music, or the symbols used to indicate this in written music.

dynamite

NOUN Dynamite is a kind of explosive.

dynasty dynasties

NOUN a series of rulers of a country all belonging to the same family

dysentery

NOUN an infection of the bowel that causes fever, stomach pain, and severe diarrhea

dyslexia

NOUN Dyslexia is difficulty with reading caused by a slight disorder of the brain. **dyslexic** ADJECTIVE OR NOUN

Ee

each

ADJECTIVE OR PRONOUN **1.** every one of something considered separately: *Each time he went out, he would buy a plant.*
PHRASE **2.** If people do something to **each other**, each person does it to the other or others: *She and I smiled at each other.*

eager

ADJECTIVE wanting very much to do or have something
eagerly ADVERB
eagerness NOUN

eagle eagles
NOUN a large bird of prey

ear ears
NOUN **1.** the parts of your body on either side of your head with which you hear sounds
2. An ear of corn or wheat is the top part of the stalk that contains seeds.

eardrum eardrums
NOUN Your eardrums are thin pieces of tightly stretched skin inside your ears that vibrate so that you can hear sounds.

early earlier earliest
ADJECTIVE **1.** before the arranged or expected time: *He wasn't late for our meeting; I was early.* **2.** near the beginning of a day, evening, or other period of time: *the early 1970s*
ADVERB **3.** before the arranged or expected time: *We arrived early.*

earmark earmarks earmarking earmarked
VERB If you earmark something for a special purpose, you keep it for that purpose.

earn earns earning earned
VERB **1.** If you earn money, you get it in return for work that you do. **2.** If you earn something such as praise, you receive it because you deserve it.
earner NOUN

earnest

ADJECTIVE **1.** sincere in what you say or do: *I answered with an earnest smile.*
PHRASE **2.** If something begins in **earnest**, it happens to a greater or more serious extent than before: *The snow began to fall in earnest.*
earnestly ADVERB

earnings

PLURAL NOUN Your earnings are money that you earn in return for work that you do.

earphones

PLURAL NOUN small speakers that you wear on your ears to listen to music or other programming

earring earrings
NOUN Earrings are pieces of jewellery that you wear on your ears.

earshot

PHRASE If you are **within earshot** of something, you can hear it.

earth earths
NOUN **1.** Earth is the planet on which we live. **2.** The earth is also the dry land on the surface of the planet, especially the soil in which things grow. **3.** a hole in the ground where a fox or other animal lives

> ⚠ **HEADS UP**
>
> You should capitalize **earth** when you're using it as a name: *The third planet from the sun is called Earth.*

earthenware

NOUN pottery made of baked clay

earthly

ADJECTIVE concerned with life on earth rather than a spiritual world

earthquake earthquakes
NOUN a shaking of the ground caused by movement of the earth's crust

earthworm earthworms
NOUN a reddish brown worm that lives under the ground

earthy earthier earthiest
ADJECTIVE **1.** looking or smelling like earth
2. Someone who is earthy is open and direct, often in a crude way: *Her earthy language surprised us.*

earwig earwigs
NOUN a small, thin, brown insect that has a pair of pincers at the end of its body

ease eases easing eased
NOUN **1.** lack of difficulty, worry, or hardship: *He had sailed through life with relative ease.*
VERB **2.** When something eases, or when you ease something, it becomes less severe or less intense: *to ease the pain* **3.** If you ease something somewhere, you move it there slowly and carefully: *My dad eased himself into his chair.*

easel easels
NOUN an upright frame that supports a picture that someone is painting

Ee

easily

ADVERB **1.** without difficulty **2.** without a doubt: *The song is easily one of their finest.*

east

NOUN **1.** East is the direction in which you look to see the sun rise. **2.** The east of a place is the part that is toward the east when you are in the centre: *the east of Africa* **3.** The East is the part of any country, especially Canada, toward the east. **4.** The East is also the countries in the south and east of Asia

ADJECTIVE OR ADVERB **5.** East means in or toward the east: *The entrance faces east.*

ADJECTIVE **6.** An east wind blows from the east.

Easter

NOUN a Christian religious festival celebrating the resurrection of Christ

easterly

ADJECTIVE **1.** Easterly means to or toward the east. **2.** An easterly wind blows from the east.

eastern

ADJECTIVE in or from the east: *a remote, eastern corner of the country*

eastward

ADVERB **1.** Eastward means toward the east: *The eastward expansion of the city threatened wildlife and farmland.*

ADJECTIVE **2.** The eastward part of something is the east part.

easy easier easiest

ADJECTIVE **1.** able to be done without difficulty: *It's easy to break a twig.*
2. comfortable and without any worries: *an easy life*

eat eats eating ate eaten

VERB **1.** To eat means to chew and swallow food. **2.** When you eat, you have a meal: *We like to eat early.*

Instead of **EAT** try...

eat away
VERB **3.** If something is eaten away, it is slowly destroyed: *The sea had eaten away at the headland.*

gobble junk food

devour apple pie

lions feed at night

dine at a restaurant

consume 2000 calories a day

eaves

PLURAL NOUN The eaves of a roof are the lower edges that jut out over the walls.

eavesdrop eavesdrops eavesdropping eavesdropped

VERB If you eavesdrop, you listen secretly to what other people are saying.

ebb ebbs ebbing ebbed

VERB **1.** When the sea or the tide ebbs, it flows back. **2.** If a person's feeling or strength ebbs, it gets weaker: *The strength ebbed from his body.*

ebony

NOUN **1.** a hard, dark-coloured wood, used for making furniture

NOUN OR ADJECTIVE **2.** very deep black

ebullient

ADJECTIVE *a formal word* lively and full of enthusiasm

ebullience NOUN

eccentric eccentrics

ADJECTIVE **1.** having habits or opinions that other people think are odd or peculiar

NOUN **2.** someone who is eccentric

eccentricity NOUN

eccentrically ADVERB

echelon echelons

NOUN a level of power or responsibility in an organization

echo echoes echoing echoed

NOUN **1.** a sound that is caused by sound waves reflecting off a surface **2.** a repetition, imitation, or reminder of something: *Echoes of the past are everywhere.*

VERB **3.** If a sound echoes, it is reflected off a surface so that you can hear it again after the original sound has stopped.

eclipse eclipses

NOUN An eclipse occurs when a celestial body such as a planet or moon passes in front of another and hides it from view for a short time.

eco-

PREFIX Words beginning with *eco-* have something to do with ecology or the environment: *ecosystem*

⚠ **HEADS UP**

Many new words have been created by adding **eco-** to base words: *eco-friendly*, *eco*tourism, *eco*terrorism.

ecology

NOUN the science that studies the relationship between living things and their environment

ecological ADJECTIVE

ecologically ADVERB

ecologist NOUN

Ee

economic
ADJECTIVE concerning the management of the money, industry, and trade of a country

economical
ADJECTIVE **1.** concerning making a profit: *economical to produce* **2.** Something that is economical is cheap to use or operate. **3.** Someone who is economical spends money carefully.
economically ADVERB

economics
NOUN Economics is the study of the production and distribution of goods, services, and wealth in a society and the organization of its money, industry, and trade.

economist economists
NOUN a person who studies or writes about economics

economy economies
NOUN **1.** The economy of a country is the system it uses to organize and manage its money, industry, and trade; also used of the wealth that a country gets from business and industry. **2.** Economy is the careful use of things to save money, time, or energy: *He completed the task with an economy of movement.*

ecosystem ecosystems
NOUN the relationship between plants and animals and their environment

ecstasy ecstasies
NOUN Ecstasy is a feeling of extreme happiness.
ecstatic ADJECTIVE
ecstatically ADVERB

eczema
NOUN a skin disease that causes the surface of the skin to become rough and itchy

-ed
SUFFIX The suffix *-ed* is used to form the past tense of most English verbs: *jumped, tried*

eddy eddies
NOUN a circular movement in water or air

edge edges edging edged
NOUN **1.** The edge of something is a border or line where it ends or meets something else. **2.** The edge of a blade is its thin, sharp side. **3.** If you have the edge over someone, you have an advantage over that person.
VERB **4.** If you edge something, you make a border for it: *The veil was edged with matching lace.* **5.** If you edge somewhere, you move there very gradually: *The ferry edged its way out into the river.*

edgy edgier edgiest
ADJECTIVE anxious and irritable

edible
ADJECTIVE safe and pleasant to eat

edifice edifices
NOUN *a formal word* a large and impressive building

edit edits editing edited
VERB **1.** If you edit a piece of writing, you correct it so that it is fit for publishing. **2.** To edit a film or television program means to select different parts of it and arrange them in a particular order. **3.** Someone who edits a publication, such as a newspaper or magazine, is in charge of it and decides what will be printed in it.

edition editions
NOUN An edition of a book or magazine is a particular version of it printed at one time.

editor editors
NOUN **1.** a person who is responsible for the content of a publication such as a newspaper or magazine **2.** a person who checks books and makes corrections to them before they are published **3.** a person who selects different parts of a television program or a film and arranges them in a particular order
editorship NOUN

editorial editorials
ADJECTIVE **1.** involved in preparing a newspaper, book, or magazine for publication: *the editorial department* **2.** involving the contents and the opinions of a newspaper or magazine: *an editorial comment*
NOUN **3.** an article in a newspaper or magazine that gives the opinions of the editor or publisher on a particular topic
editorially ADVERB

educate educates educating educated
VERB To educate someone means to teach that person so he or she gains knowledge about something.

educated
ADJECTIVE having a high standard of learning and culture

education
NOUN the process of gaining knowledge and understanding through learning or the system of teaching people
educational ADJECTIVE
educationally ADVERB

eel eels
NOUN a long, thin, snakelike fish

eerie eerier eeriest
ADJECTIVE strange and frightening: *an eerie silence*
eerily ADVERB

Ee

effect effects

NOUN **1.** a direct result of someone or something on another person or thing: *the effect of divorce on children* **2.** An effect that someone or something has is the overall impression or result that person or thing has: *The effect of the décor was cozy and warm.* PHRASE **3.** If something **takes effect** at a particular time, it starts to happen or starts to produce results at that time: *The law will take effect next year.*

effective

ADJECTIVE **1.** working well and producing the intended results **2.** coming into operation or beginning officially: *The agreement has become effective immediately.*
effectively ADVERB

effeminate

ADJECTIVE A man who is effeminate behaves, looks, or sounds like a woman.

efficient

ADJECTIVE capable of doing something well without wasting time or energy
efficiently ADVERB
efficiency NOUN

effigy effigies

NOUN a statue or model of a person

effluent effluents

NOUN Effluent is liquid waste that comes out of factories or sewage systems.

effluvium effluvia

NOUN Effluvium is an unpleasant smell or gas that is given off by something, especially something that is decaying.

effort efforts

NOUN **1.** Effort is the physical or mental energy needed to do something. **2.** an attempt or struggle to do something: *I go to the gym in an effort to keep fit.*

effortless

ADJECTIVE done easily
effortlessly ADVERB

e.g. The abbreviation e.g. means *for example*, and is abbreviated from the Latin expression *exempli gratia*.

egalitarian

ADJECTIVE favouring equality for all people: *an egalitarian country*

egg eggs

NOUN **1.** an oval or rounded object laid by female birds, reptiles, fishes, and insects. A baby creature develops inside the egg until it is ready to hatch. **2.** a hen's egg used as food **3.** In a female animal, an egg is a cell produced in the body that can develop into a baby if it is fertilized.

eggplant eggplants

NOUN a dark-purple, pear-shaped fruit eaten as a vegetable

ego egos

NOUN Your ego is your opinion of what you are worth: *It'll do her good and boost her ego.*

egocentric

ADJECTIVE only thinking of yourself

egotism

NOUN Egotism is behaviour and attitudes that show that you believe you are more important than other people.
egotist NOUN
egotistical ADJECTIVE

Eid-ul-Adha

NOUN an annual Muslim festival marking the end of the pilgrimage to Mecca known as the hajj. Animals are sacrificed and their meat is shared among the poor.

eight eights

NOUN the number 8
eighth ADJECTIVE, ADVERB

eighteen

NOUN the number 18
eighteenth ADJECTIVE, ADVERB

eighty eighties

NOUN the number 80
eightieth ADJECTIVE, ADVERB

either

ADJECTIVE, PRONOUN, OR CONJUNCTION **1.** one or the other of two possible alternatives: *You can spell it either way. Either of these schemes would cost billions of dollars. Either*

SPELL-CHECK THIS!

A computer's spell-check won't catch wrong **homophones** (words that are spelled differently but sound the same).

▼× | 1 2 3 4 5

These new rules won't effect me.

In this sentence, **effect** should be **affect**.
Affect is a verb that means *influence*.
Effect is a noun that means *result*.

NEL

take it or leave it.
ADJECTIVE **2.** both one and the other: *on either side of the head*

ejaculate ejaculates ejaculating ejaculated
VERB **1.** When a man ejaculates, he discharges semen from his penis. **2.** If you ejaculate, you suddenly say something.
ejaculation NOUN

eject ejects ejecting ejected
VERB If you eject someone or something, you forcefully push or send that person or thing out: *He was ejected from the club.*
ejection NOUN

elaborate elaborates elaborating elaborated
ADJECTIVE **1.** having many different parts: *an elaborate system of drains* **2.** carefully planned, detailed, and exact: *elaborate plans* **3.** highly decorated and complicated: *elaborate designs*
VERB **4.** If you elaborate on something, you add more information or detail about it.
elaborately ADVERB
elaboration NOUN

eland elands
NOUN a large African antelope with twisted horns

elapse elapses elapsing elapsed
VERB When time elapses, it passes by: *Five years elapsed before we saw our cousins again.*

elastic
ADJECTIVE **1.** able to stretch easily
NOUN **2.** Elastic is rubber material that stretches and returns to its original shape.
elasticity NOUN

elation
NOUN Elation is a feeling of great happiness.
elated ADJECTIVE

elbow elbows elbowing elbowed
NOUN **1.** Your elbow is the joint between the upper part of your arm and your forearm.
VERB **2.** If you elbow someone aside, you push that person away with your elbow.

elder eldest; elders
ADJECTIVE **1.** Your elder brother or sister is older than you.
NOUN **2.** a senior member of a group who has influence or authority

> ⚠ **HEADS UP**
> Use **eldest** within a family: *the eldest child.* Otherwise, use **oldest**: *his oldest friend, the oldest statue.*

elderly
ADJECTIVE **1.** Elderly is a polite way to describe an old person.
NOUN **2.** The elderly are old people: *Priority is given to services for the elderly.*

elect elects electing elected
VERB **1.** If you elect someone, you choose that person to fill a position, by voting: *He's just been elected president.* **2.** *a formal use* If you elect to do something, you choose to do it: *She has elected to stay on the team.*
ADJECTIVE **3.** *a formal use* voted into a position, but not yet carrying out the duties of the position: *the vice-president elect*

election elections
NOUN the selection of one or more people for an official position by voting
electoral ADJECTIVE

electorate electorates
NOUN all the people who have the right to vote in an election

electric
ADJECTIVE **1.** powered or produced by electricity **2.** very tense or exciting: *The atmosphere is electric.*

electrical
ADJECTIVE using or producing electricity: *electrical equipment*
electrically ADVERB

electrician electricians
NOUN a person whose job is to install and repair electrical equipment

electricity
NOUN Electricity is a form of energy used for heating and lighting, and to provide power for machines.

electrified
ADJECTIVE connected to a supply of electricity

electrifying
ADJECTIVE Something that is electrifying makes you feel very excited.

electro-
PREFIX The prefix *electro-* means *electric* or involving electricity.

electrocute electrocutes electrocuting electrocuted
VERB If someone is electrocuted, that person is killed by touching something that is connected to electricity.
electrocution NOUN

electrode electrodes
NOUN a small piece of metal that allows an electric current to pass between a source of power and a piece of equipment

Ee

electron electrons
NOUN In physics, an electron is a tiny particle of matter, smaller than an atom.

electronic
ADJECTIVE If something is electronic, it has transistors or silicon chips that control an electric current.
electronically ADVERB

electronics
NOUN Electronics is the technology of electronic devices such as televisions and computers; also the study of how these devices work.

elegant
ADJECTIVE attractive and graceful or stylish: *an elegant and beautiful gown*
elegantly ADVERB
elegance NOUN

elegy elegies
NOUN a sad poem or song about someone who has died

element elements
NOUN **1.** a part of something that combines with other parts to make a whole **2.** In chemistry, an element is a substance that is made up of only one type of atom. **3.** a metal coil in a heating device, such as a stove, that reddens with heat **4.** An element of a quality is a certain amount of it: *the element of surprise* **5.** The elements of a subject are the basic and most important points. **6.** The elements are the weather conditions: *Our open boat is exposed to the elements.*

elemental
ADJECTIVE *a formal word* simple and basic, but powerful: *elemental emotions*

elementary
ADJECTIVE simple, basic, and straightforward: *an elementary course in woodwork*

elementary school elementary schools
NOUN a school of five to eight grades for children aged six and over.

elephant elephants
NOUN a very large four-legged mammal with a long trunk, large ears, and ivory tusks

elevate elevates elevating elevated
VERB **1.** To elevate someone to a higher status or position means to give that person greater status or importance: *He was elevated to the rank of major in the army.* **2.** To elevate something means to raise it up.

elevation elevations
NOUN **1.** The elevation of someone or something is the raising of that person or thing to a higher level or position. **2.** The elevation of a place is its height above sea level or above the ground.

eleven
NOUN Eleven is the number 11.
eleventh ADJECTIVE, ADVERB

elf elves
NOUN In folklore, an elf is a small, mischievous fairy.

elicit elicits eliciting elicited
VERB **1.** *a formal use* If you elicit information, you find it out by asking careful questions. **2.** If you elicit a response or reaction, you make it happen: *He elicited sympathy from the audience.*

eligible
ADJECTIVE suitable or having the right qualifications for something: *You will be eligible for a scholarship if you improve your grades.*
eligibility NOUN

eliminate eliminates eliminating eliminated
VERB **1.** If you eliminate something or someone, you get rid of that person or thing: *They eliminated him from their list of suspects.* **2.** If a team or a person is eliminated from a competition, that team or person can no longer take part.
elimination NOUN

elite elites
NOUN a group of the most powerful, rich, or talented people in a society

Elizabethan
ADJECTIVE relating to the period of time during which England's Queen Elizabeth I reigned (1533–1603): *an Elizabethan dress*

elk elks
NOUN a large kind of deer

ellipse ellipses
NOUN an oval shape, like a circle seen from an angle

ellipsis ellipses
NOUN An ellipsis is a series of dots [...] that is used to show where words have been left out in a piece of writing.

elm elms
NOUN a tall tree with broad leaves

elocution
NOUN the art or study of speaking clearly or well in public

elongated
ADJECTIVE long and thin

elope elopes eloping eloped
VERB If two people elope, they run away secretly to get married.

eloquent
ADJECTIVE able to speak or write skilfully and

Ee

with ease: *an eloquent politician*
eloquently ADVERB
eloquence NOUN

else
ADVERB **1.** other than something or more than something: *Can you think of anything else?*
PHRASE **2.** You say **or else** to introduce a possibility or an alternative: *You have to hurry or else you will miss the bus.*

elsewhere
ADVERB in or to another place: *He would rather be elsewhere.*

elude eludes eluding eluded
VERB **1.** If a fact or idea eludes you, you cannot understand it or remember it. **2.** If you elude someone or something, you escape from or avoid that person or thing: *The hacker eluded the authorities.*

elusive
ADJECTIVE difficult to find, achieve, describe, or remember: *an elusive idea, an elusive odour*

elves the plural of ELF

em-
PREFIX The prefix *em-* is another form of the prefix *en-*.

emaciated
ADJECTIVE extremely thin and weak, because of illness or lack of food

e-mail e-mails e-mailing e-mailed
NOUN **1.** the sending of messages from one computer to another **2.** a message sent in this way
VERB **3.** If you e-mail someone, you send an e-mail to that person.

⚠ HEADS UP

The prefix **e-**, meaning *electronic*, is now used with many words and short forms: *e-business*, *e-card*, *e-zine*.

emancipation
NOUN The emancipation of a person means the act of freeing him or her from harmful or unpleasant restrictions.

embargo embargoes
NOUN an order made by a government to stop trade with another country

embark embarks embarking embarked
VERB **1.** If you embark, you go onto a ship or plane at the start of a journey. **2.** If you embark on something, you start it: *She embarked on a career in law.*

embarrass embarrasses embarrassing embarrassed
VERB If you embarrass someone, you make that person feel ashamed or awkward: *I won't embarrass you by asking for details.*
embarrassing ADJECTIVE

embarrassed
ADJECTIVE ashamed or awkward

embarrassment embarrassments
NOUN shame and awkwardness

embassy embassies
NOUN the building in which an ambassador and his or her staff work

embedded
ADJECTIVE Something that is embedded is fixed firmly and deeply: *glass decorated with embedded threads*

ember embers
NOUN Embers are glowing pieces of coal or wood from a dying fire.

embittered
ADJECTIVE If you are embittered, you are angry and resentful about things that have happened to you.

emblazoned
ADJECTIVE If something is emblazoned with designs, it is decorated with them: *vases emblazoned with bold and colourful images*

emblem emblems
NOUN an object or a design used as a symbol to represent an organization, a nation, or an idea: *The beaver is an emblem of Canada.*

embody embodies embodying embodied
VERB **1.** To embody a quality or idea means to contain it or express it: *A young dancer embodies the spirit of fun.* **2.** If a number of things are embodied in one thing, they are contained in it: *the principles embodied in his report*
embodiment NOUN

embossed
ADJECTIVE decorated with designs that are raised slightly from the surface: *an embossed birthday card*

embrace embraces embracing embraced
VERB **1.** If you embrace someone, you hug that person to show affection or as a greeting.
2. If you embrace a belief or cause, you accept it and believe in it.
NOUN **3.** a hug

embroider embroiders embroidering embroidered
VERB If you embroider fabric, you sew a decorative design onto it.

embroidery
NOUN Embroidery is decorative designs sewn onto fabric.

Ee

embroiled
ADJECTIVE If someone is embroiled in an argument or conflict, that person is deeply involved in it and cannot get out of it: *The two companies are now embroiled in the courts.*

embryo embryos
NOUN **1.** the unborn young of a human or animal from the time the egg is fertilized **2.** an undeveloped plant inside a seed
embryonic ADJECTIVE

emerald emeralds
NOUN **1.** a bright-green precious stone
NOUN OR ADJECTIVE **2.** bright green

emerge emerges emerging emerged
VERB **1.** If someone emerges from a place, that person comes out of it in order to be seen. **2.** If something emerges, it becomes known or begins to be recognized as existing: *It later emerged that he planned the surprise.*
emergence NOUN
emergent ADJECTIVE

emergency emergencies
NOUN an unexpected and serious event that needs immediate action to deal with it

emigrant emigrants
NOUN a person who leaves his or her native country and goes to live permanently in another one

emigrate emigrates emigrating emigrated
VERB If you emigrate, you leave your native country and go to live permanently in another one.

 HEADS UP

Don't confuse **emigrate** and **immigrate**. *He emigrated from Greece to Canada. He immigrated to Canada from Greece.*

emigration
NOUN Emigration is the process of emigrating, especially by large numbers of people at various periods of history.

eminence
NOUN Eminence is the quality of being well-known and respected for what you do: *an environmentalist of eminence*

eminent
ADJECTIVE well-known and respected for what you do: *an eminent scientist*

eminently
ADVERB *a formal word* very: *eminently reasonable*

emission emissions
NOUN *a formal word* The emission of something such as gas or radiation is the release of it into the atmosphere.

emit emits emitting emitted
VERB To emit something means to give it out or release it: *She emitted a long, low whistle.*

emoticon emoticons
NOUN a symbol used in e-mail that represents a particular emotion and is made up of normal keyboard characters that are viewed sideways. For example, the symbol (:+(means *frightened* or *scared.*

emotion emotions
NOUN a strong feeling, such as love or fear

emotional
ADJECTIVE **1.** causing strong feelings: *an emotional appeal for help* **2.** to do with feelings rather than your physical condition: *emotional support* **3.** showing your feelings openly: *The child is in a very emotional state.*
emotionally ADVERB

emotive
ADJECTIVE concerning emotions, or stirring up strong emotions: *emotive language*

empathize empathizes empathizing empathized
VERB If you empathize with someone, you understand how that person is feeling.
empathy NOUN

emperor emperors
NOUN a male ruler of an empire

emphasis emphases
NOUN Emphasis is special importance or extra stress given to something.

emphasize emphasizes emphasizing emphasized
VERB If you emphasize something, you make it known that it is very important: *It was emphasized that the matter was of immediate concern.*

emphatic
ADJECTIVE expressed strongly and with force to show how important something is: *I answered both questions with an emphatic Yes.*
emphatically ADVERB

empire empires
NOUN **1.** a group of countries controlled by one country **2.** a powerful group of companies controlled by one person or group

employ employs employing employed
VERB **1.** If you employ someone, you pay that person to work for you. **2.** If you employ

Ee

something for a particular purpose, you make use of it: *the techniques employed in turning grapes into wine*

employee employees
NOUN a person who is paid to work for another person or for an organization

employer employers
NOUN An employer is the person or organization that someone works for.

employment
NOUN Employment is the state of having a paid job.

empower empowers empowering empowered
VERB If you are empowered to do something, you have the authority or power to do it.

empress empresses
NOUN a woman who rules an empire, or the wife of an emperor

empty emptier emptiest; empties emptying emptied
ADJECTIVE **1.** having nothing or nobody inside **2.** without purpose, value, or meaning: *empty promises*
VERB **3.** If you empty something,

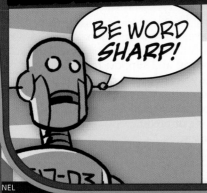

Instead of **EMPTY** try…

barren tundra
a **vacant** room
a **deserted** town
a **blank** notebook
an **abandoned** building

or empty its contents, you remove the contents.
emptiness NOUN

emu emus
NOUN a large Australian bird that can run fast but cannot fly

emulate emulates emulating emulated
VERB If you emulate someone or something, you imitate that person or thing.
emulation NOUN

emulsion emulsions
NOUN a mixture of liquids that do not dissolve in each other

en-
PREFIX **1.** The prefix *en-* means *to surround* or *cover*: *enclose, encrusted* **2.** The prefix *en-* also means *to cause to be in a certain state or condition*: *enamoured, endanger*

-en
SUFFIX The suffix *-en* means to *develop, create, or intensify something*: *deepen, loosen*

enable enables enabling enabled
VERB To enable something to happen means to make it possible.

enact enacts enacting enacted
VERB **1.** If a government enacts a law or bill, it officially passes it so that it becomes law. **2.** If you enact a story or play, you act it out.
enactment NOUN

enamel enamels enamelling enamelled
NOUN **1.** a substance like glass, used to decorate or protect metal or china **2.** The enamel on your teeth is the hard, white substance that forms the outer part.
VERB **3.** If you enamel something, you decorate or cover it with enamel.
enamelled ADJECTIVE

enamoured
ADJECTIVE If you are enamoured with someone or something, you like that person or thing very much.

encapsulate encapsulates encapsulating encapsulated
VERB If something encapsulates facts or ideas, it contains or represents them in brief form.

encased
ADJECTIVE Something that is encased is surrounded or covered with a substance: *encased in plaster*

-ence
SUFFIX The suffix *-ence* is used to form nouns that mean *a state, condition, or quality*: *residence, patience*

KNOWING WORDS: WORD BUILDING

BE WORD SHARP!

You can create new words by adding prefixes and suffixes to a base word.

-ence a noun suffix that refers to a state or quality

absence being absent

violence being violent

negligence being negligent

patience being patient

silence being silent

Ee

enchanted
ADJECTIVE If you are enchanted by someone or something, you are fascinated or charmed by that person or thing.

enchanting
ADJECTIVE attractive, delightful, or charming: *an enchanting baby*

encircle encircles encircling encircled
VERB To encircle someone or something means to completely surround that person or thing.

enclave enclaves
NOUN a place that is surrounded by areas that are different from it in some important way, for example because the people there are from a different culture: *a Canadian enclave in Bosnia*

enclose encloses enclosing enclosed
VERB To enclose an object or area means to surround it with something solid.
enclosed ADJECTIVE

enclosure enclosures
NOUN an area of land surrounded by a wall or fence and used for a particular purpose

encompass encompasses encompassing encompassed
VERB To encompass a number of things means to include all of those things: *The book encompassed all aspects of mathematics.*

encore encores
NOUN a short, extra performance given by an entertainer because the audience asks for it

encounter encounters encountering encountered
VERB 1. If you encounter someone or something, you meet or are faced with that person or thing: *She was the most gifted musician he ever encountered.*
NOUN 2. a meeting, especially when it is difficult or unexpected

encourage encourages encouraging encouraged
VERB 1. If you encourage someone, you give that person courage and confidence to do something. 2. If someone or something encourages a particular activity, that person or thing supports it: *The government will encourage the creation of additional daycare centres.*
encouraging ADJECTIVE
encouragement NOUN

encroach encroaches encroaching encroached
VERB If something encroaches on a place or on your time or attention, it gradually takes up or takes away more and more of it.
encroachment NOUN

encrusted
ADJECTIVE covered with a crust or layer of something: *a necklace encrusted with gold*

encyclopedia encyclopedias
NOUN a book or set of books giving information about many different subjects

encyclopedic
ADJECTIVE knowing or giving information about many different things

end ends ending ended
NOUN 1. The end of a period of time or an event is the last part. 2. The end of something is the farthest point of it: *the room at the end of the hallway* 3. the purpose for which something is done: *This exercise serves no useful end.*
VERB 4. If something ends or if you end it, it comes to a finish.

Instead of **END** try...

the year came to a **close**
the **climax** of the novel
the **foot** of the bed
the city's **limits**
a happy **ending**
the **edge** of a cliff
the essay's **conclusion**
a **finale** with fireworks

endanger endangers endangering endangered
VERB To endanger something means to cause it to be in a dangerous and harmful situation: *a driver who endangers the safety of others*

endear endears endearing endeared
VERB When you endear someone to you, you make that person very fond of you.
endearing ADJECTIVE
endearingly ADVERB

endeavour endeavours endeavouring endeavoured
VERB 1. *a formal word* If you endeavour to do something, you try very hard to do it.
NOUN 2. an effort to do or achieve something

endless
ADJECTIVE having or seeming to have no end
endlessly ADVERB

endorse endorses endorsing endorsed
VERB 1. If you endorse someone or something, you give approval and support to that person or thing. 2. If you endorse a cheque or other document, you write your signature on it to show that you are entitled to receive a stated amount of cash or credit.
endorsement NOUN

endowed
ADJECTIVE If someone is endowed with a quality or ability, that person has it or is given it: *He was endowed with great willpower.*

endurance
NOUN Endurance is the ability to put up with a difficult situation for a period of time.

endure endures enduring endured
VERB **1.** If you endure a difficult situation, you put up with it calmly and patiently.
2. If something endures, it lasts or continues to exist: *The old alliance still endures.*
enduring ADJECTIVE

enemy enemies
NOUN a person or group that is hostile or opposed to another person or group

energetic
ADJECTIVE having energy or enthusiasm
energetically ADVERB

energy energies
NOUN **1.** the physical strength to do active things **2.** the power that drives machinery **3.** power from natural resources such as oil, coal, or water, which makes machinery work

enforce enforces enforcing enforced
VERB If you enforce a law or a rule, you make sure that it is obeyed.
enforceable ADJECTIVE
enforcement NOUN

engage engages engaging engaged
VERB **1.** If you engage in an activity, you take part in it: *She tried to engage her brother in a debate.* **2.** To engage someone means to make or keep someone interested in something: *He engaged the bus driver in conversation.*

engaged
ADJECTIVE **1.** When two people are engaged, they have agreed to marry each other.
2. If someone or something is engaged, that person or thing is occupied or busy: *The principal was engaged in her work when I entered her office.*

engagement engagements
NOUN **1.** an agreement that two people have made with each other to get married; also, the time period during which two people are engaged **2.** an appointment that you have with someone

engine engines
NOUN **1.** a machine designed to convert heat or other kinds of energy into mechanical movement **2.** a railway locomotive

engineer engineers engineering engineered
NOUN **1.** a person trained in designing and building machinery and electrical devices, or roads and bridges **2.** a person who drives a train locomotive
VERB **3.** If you engineer an event or situation, you arrange it cleverly, usually for your own advantage.

engineering
NOUN Engineering is the profession of designing and constructing machinery and electrical devices, or roads and bridges.

English
NOUN English is the language first spoken in England. It is now spoken throughout the world.

engrave engraves engraving engraved
VERB To engrave means to cut letters or designs into a hard surface with a tool.

engraving engravings
NOUN a picture or design that has been cut into a hard surface
engraver NOUN

engrossed
ADJECTIVE If you are engrossed in something, it holds all your attention: *She was engrossed in a video game.*

engulf engulfs engulfing engulfed
VERB To engulf something means to completely cover or surround it: *Fog engulfed the boat as it sailed out to sea.*

KNOWING WORDS: WORD HISTORY

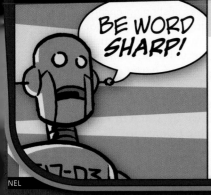

BE WORD SHARP!

Words are like living things. They grow and change.

Engine started off as the Latin word **ingenium**, meaning a *talent you are born with*. When it came into French as **engin**, it meant *skill* or *cleverness*, and that's what it meant when English borrowed it. It then began to mean *a clever invention*, and later wound up with the meaning it has today. Can you think of other English words that might be related to the Latin word **ingenium**?

Ee

enhance enhances enhancing enhanced
VERB To enhance something means to make it more valuable or attractive: *Fresh paint and new furniture enhanced the beauty of the house.*
enhancement NOUN

enigma enigmas
NOUN anything that is puzzling or difficult to understand

enigmatic
ADJECTIVE mysterious, puzzling, or difficult to understand: *an enigmatic stranger*
enigmatically ADVERB

enjoy enjoys enjoying enjoyed
VERB **1.** If you enjoy something, you find pleasure and satisfaction in it. **2.** If you enjoy something, you are lucky to have it or experience it: *My grandmother has enjoyed a long life.*

enjoyable
ADJECTIVE giving pleasure or satisfaction

enjoyment
NOUN Enjoyment is the feeling of pleasure or satisfaction you get from something you enjoy.

enlarge enlarges enlarging enlarged
VERB **1.** When you enlarge something, it gets bigger.
PHRASE **2.** If you **enlarge on** a subject, you give more details about it.

enlargement enlargements
NOUN **1.** An enlargement of something is the action of making it bigger. **2.** something, especially a photograph, that has been made bigger

enlighten enlightens enlightening enlightened
VERB To enlighten someone means to give that person more knowledge or understanding of something.
enlightening ADJECTIVE
enlightenment NOUN

enlightened
ADJECTIVE well-informed and willing to consider different opinions: *an enlightened government*

enlist enlists enlisting enlisted
VERB **1.** If someone enlists, that person joins the armed forces. **2.** If you enlist someone's help, you persuade that person to help you in something that you are doing.

enliven enlivens enlivening enlivened
VERB To enliven something means to make it livelier or more cheerful.

en masse
ADVERB If people do something en masse, they do it together and at the same time.

enormity enormities
NOUN **1.** The enormity of a problem or difficulty is its great size and seriousness. **2.** something that is thought to be a terrible crime or offence

enormous
ADJECTIVE very large in size or amount
enormously ADVERB

enough
ADJECTIVE OR ADVERB **1.** as much or as many as required: *He did not have enough money for a slice of pizza.*
NOUN **2.** Enough is the quantity necessary for something: *There's not enough cake to go around.*
ADVERB **3.** very or fairly: *She could manage well enough without me.*

enquire another spelling of INQUIRE

enquiry another spelling of INQUIRY

enrage enrages enraging enraged
VERB If something enrages you, it makes you very angry.
enraged ADJECTIVE

enrich enriches enriching enriched
VERB To enrich something means to improve the quality or value of it: *More parks will enrich our neighbourhood.*
enriched ADJECTIVE
enrichment NOUN

enrol enrols enrolling enrolled
VERB If you enrol in something such as a course or a college, you register to join or become a member of it.
enrolment NOUN

en route
ADVERB If something happens en route to a place, it happens on the way there.

ensconced
ADJECTIVE If you are ensconced in a particular place, you are settled there firmly and comfortably.

ensemble ensembles
NOUN **1.** a group of things or people considered as a whole rather than separately **2.** a small group of musicians who play or sing together

enshrine enshrines enshrining enshrined
VERB If something such as an idea or a right is enshrined in a society, constitution, or a law, it is protected by it: *Human rights are enshrined in the Charter of Rights and Freedoms.*

ensign ensigns
NOUN a flag flown by a ship to show what country that ship belongs to

Ee

ensue ensues ensuing ensued
VERB If something ensues, it happens after another event, usually as a result of it: *He refused to help me clean and an argument ensued.*
ensuing ADJECTIVE

ensure ensures ensuring ensured
VERB To ensure that something happens means to make certain that it happens: *We make every effort to ensure the information given is correct.*

> ⚠ **HEADS UP**
>
> Ensure means *make sure*.
> Insure means *arrange payment in case of loss or damage.*

entangled
ADJECTIVE If you are entangled in problems or difficulties, you are involved in them.

enter enters entering entered
VERB **1.** To enter a place means to go into it. **2.** If you enter an organization or institution, you join and become a member of it: *She entered politics in 2002.* **3.** If you enter a competition, you take part in it. **4.** If you enter something in a diary or on a list, you write it down.

enterprise enterprises
NOUN **1.** a business or company **2.** a project or task, especially one that is challenging

enterprising
ADJECTIVE If you are enterprising, you are bold and full of initiative when you take on new projects: *an enterprising group of students*

entertain entertains entertaining entertained
VERB **1.** If you entertain people, you keep them amused or interested. **2.** If you entertain guests, you receive them into your house and give them food and hospitality.

entertainer entertainers
NOUN someone whose job is to amuse and please audiences, for example a comedian or singer

entertainment entertainments
NOUN anything people watch or do for pleasure

enthral enthrals enthralling enthralled
VERB If you enthral someone, you hold that person's attention and interest completely.
enthralling ADJECTIVE

enthuse enthuses enthusing enthused
VERB If you enthuse about something, you talk about it with enthusiasm and excitement.

enthusiasm enthusiasms
NOUN Enthusiasm is interest, eagerness, or delight in something that you enjoy.

enthusiastic
ADJECTIVE showing great excitement, eagerness, or approval for something: *She was enthusiastic about graphic design.*
enthusiastically ADVERB

entice entices enticing enticed
VERB If you entice someone to do something, you tempt that person to do it: *We tried to entice the mouse out of the hole with a piece of cheese.*

enticing
ADJECTIVE extremely attractive and tempting

entire
ADJECTIVE all of something: *the entire month of July*

entirely
ADVERB wholly and completely: *He and I were entirely different.*

entirety
PHRASE If something happens to something **in its entirety**, it happens to all of it: *This message will now be repeated in its entirety.*

entitle entitles entitling entitled
VERB If something entitles you to have or do something, it gives you the right to have or do it.
entitlement NOUN

entity entities
NOUN any complete thing that is not divided and not part of anything else

entourage entourages
NOUN a group of people who follow or travel with a famous or important person

entrails
PLURAL NOUN Entrails are the inner parts, especially the intestines, of people or animals.

entrance entrances
NOUN **1.** The entrance of a building or area is its doorway or gate. **2.** A person's entrance is his or her arrival in a place, or the way in which that person arrives: *Each creation is designed for the model to make a dramatic entrance.* **3.** In the theatre, an actor makes his or her entrance when he or she comes onto the stage. **4.** Entrance is the right to enter a place: *He had gained entrance to the building by pretending to be a janitor.*

entrance entrances entrancing entranced
VERB If something entrances you, it gives you a feeling of wonder and joy.
entrancing ADJECTIVE

Ee

entrant entrants
NOUN a person who officially enters a competition

entrenched
ADJECTIVE If a belief, custom, or power is entrenched, it is firmly established.

entrepreneur entrepreneurs
NOUN a person who sets up and runs a business, especially one in which risks are involved, in order to make a profit
entrepreneurial ADJECTIVE

entrust entrusts entrusting entrusted
VERB If you entrust something to someone, you give that person the care and protection of it: *He was entrusted with the children's education.*

entry entries
NOUN **1.** Entry is the act of entering a place. **2.** a place through which you enter somewhere **3.** anything that is entered or recorded: *Send your entry to the address below.*

enumerate enumerates enumerating enumerated
VERB **1.** name one by one: *She enumerated the capitals of each province and territory.* **2.** count **3.** In Canada, to enumerate means to include people in a list of eligible voters in an area.

envelop envelops enveloping enveloped
VERB To envelop something means to cover or surround it completely: *A dense fog enveloped the field.*

envelope envelopes
NOUN a flat covering of paper with a flap that can be folded over to seal it, which is used to hold a letter

enviable
ADJECTIVE If you describe something as enviable, you mean that you wish you had it yourself.

envious
ADJECTIVE full of envy
enviously ADVERB

environment environments
NOUN **1.** Your environment is the circumstances and conditions in which you live: *a good environment to grow up in* **2.** The environment is the natural world around us: *the waste that is dumped in the environment*
environmental ADJECTIVE
environmentally ADVERB

environmentalist environmentalists
NOUN a person who is concerned with the problems of the natural environment, such as pollution

envisage envisages envisaging envisaged
VERB If you envisage a situation or state of affairs, you can picture it in your mind as being true or likely to happen.

envoy envoys
NOUN a messenger, sent especially from one government to another

envy envies envying envied
NOUN **1.** Envy is a feeling of resentment you have when you wish you could have what someone else has.
VERB **2.** If you envy someone, you want what that person has.

enzyme enzymes
NOUN a chemical substance, usually a protein, produced by cells in the body

ephemeral
ADJECTIVE lasting only a short time

epic epics
NOUN **1.** a long story of heroic events and actions
ADJECTIVE **2.** very impressive or ambitious: *epic adventures*

epidemic epidemics
NOUN **1.** an occurrence of a disease in one area, spreading quickly and affecting many people **2.** a rapid development or spread of something: *the country's crime epidemic*

epigram epigrams
NOUN a short saying that expresses an idea in a clever and amusing way, for example *I can resist everything but temptation.*

epigraph
NOUN **1.** a quotation at the beginning of a book **2.** an inscription on a monument or building

epilepsy
NOUN is a condition of the brain that causes convulsions and periods of unconsciousness
epileptic NOUN OR ADJECTIVE

episode episodes
NOUN **1.** an event or experience that stands out from others: *After this episode, she found it impossible to trust him.* **2.** one of several parts of a novel, story, or television show: *I never miss an episode of my favourite show.*

epistle epistles
NOUN *a formal word* a letter, especially a long, formal, or instructive one

epitaph epitaphs
NOUN some words on a tomb about the person who has died

epithet epithets
NOUN a word or short phrase used to describe some characteristic of a person

Ee

epitome
NOUN *a formal word* The epitome of something is the most typical example of its sort: *She was the epitome of the successful woman.*

epoch epochs
NOUN a long period of time

eponymous
ADJECTIVE *a formal word* The eponymous hero or heroine of a play or book is the person whose name forms its title: *the eponymous hero of Eric the Viking*

equal equals equalling equalled
ADJECTIVE **1.** having the same size, amount, value, or standard **2.** If you are equal to a task, you have the necessary ability to deal with it.
NOUN **3.** Your equals are people who have the same ability, status, or rights as you.
VERB **4.** If one thing equals another, it is as good or remarkable as the other: *He equalled the team captain's scoring record.*
equally ADVERB
equality NOUN

equate equates equating equated
VERB If you equate a particular thing with something else, you believe that it is similar or equal: *You can't equate lives with money.*

equation equations
NOUN a mathematical formula stating that two amounts or values are the same

equator
NOUN an imaginary line drawn around the middle of the earth, lying halfway between the North Pole and the South Pole
equatorial ADJECTIVE

equestrian
ADJECTIVE relating to or involving horses

equine
ADJECTIVE relating to horses

equip equips equipping equipped
VERB If a person or thing is equipped with something, that person or thing has it or is provided with it: *All boats are equipped with oars and life jackets.*

equipment
NOUN Equipment is all the things that are needed or used for a particular job or activity.

equitable
ADJECTIVE fair and reasonable

equity
NOUN Equity is the quality of being fair and reasonable: *It is important to distribute resources with some sense of equity.*

equivalent equivalents
ADJECTIVE **1.** equal in use, size, value, or effect
NOUN **2.** something that has the same use, value, or effect as something else: *The French equivalent of yes is oui.*
equivalence NOUN

-er
SUFFIX **1.** When the suffix -er is used to form some nouns it means *for* or *belonging to*: *fastener, Northerner* **2.** The suffix -er is also used to form nouns that mean *someone or something that does something*: *climber, teacher, baker* **3.** The suffix -er is used to make adjectives and adverbs that have the meaning *more*: *lighter, funnier*

era eras
NOUN a period of time distinguished by a particular feature: *the technological era*

eradicate eradicates eradicating eradicated
VERB To eradicate something means to get rid of it or destroy it completely.
eradication NOUN

erase erases erasing erased
VERB To erase something means to remove it.

erect erects erecting erected
VERB **1.** To erect something means to put it up or construct it: *The building was erected in 1900.*
ADJECTIVE **2.** in a straight and upright position: *She held herself erect and looked directly at him.*

KNOWING WORDS: WORD BUILDING

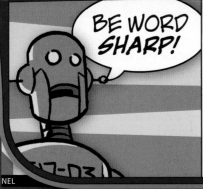

BE WORD SHARP!

You can create new words by adding prefixes and suffixes to a base word.

equi- a prefix that means *equal*

equidistant equally far from two points

equilateral with sides of equal length

equilibrium an equal balance

equinox a date when night and day are equally long

equivalent having an equal value

Ee

erection erections
NOUN **1.** the process of erecting something **2.** anything that has been erected **3.** the firm and enlarged condition of the penis or clitoris

ermine
NOUN Ermine is expensive white fur.

erode erodes eroding eroded
VERB If something erodes or is eroded, it is gradually worn or eaten away and destroyed.

erosion
NOUN the gradual wearing away and destruction of something: *soil erosion*

erotic
ADJECTIVE involving or arousing sexual desire
erotically ADVERB
eroticism NOUN

err errs erring erred
VERB If you err, you make a mistake.

errand errands
NOUN a short trip you make in order to do a small job for someone

erratic
ADJECTIVE not following a regular pattern or a fixed course: *Police officers noticed his erratic driving.*
erratically ADVERB

erroneous
ADJECTIVE Ideas or methods that are erroneous are incorrect or only partly correct.
erroneously ADVERB

Instead of **ERROR** try...

error errors
NOUN a mistake or something that you have done wrong

a silly mistake

a slip of the tongue

a lapse in judgment

an oversight in the plan

an embarrassing blunder

erudite
ADJECTIVE having great academic knowledge

erupt erupts erupting erupted
VERB **1.** When a volcano erupts, it violently throws out a lot of hot lava and ash. **2.** When a situation erupts, it starts up suddenly and violently: *An argument erupted.*
eruption NOUN

escalate escalates escalating escalated
VERB If a situation escalates, it becomes greater in size, seriousness, or intensity.

escalator escalators
NOUN a mechanical moving staircase

escapade escapades
NOUN an adventurous or daring incident that causes trouble

escape escapes escaping escaped
VERB **1.** To escape means to get free from someone or something. **2.** If you escape something unpleasant or difficult, you manage to avoid it: *He escaped additional punishment for his crimes.* **3.** If something escapes you, you cannot remember it: *It was an actor whose name escapes me for the moment.*
NOUN **4.** an act of escaping from a particular place or situation: *her escape from the icy water* **5.** a situation or activity that distracts you from something unpleasant: *Online games provide an escape.*

escapee escapees
NOUN someone who has escaped, especially an escaped prisoner

escapism
NOUN avoiding the real and unpleasant things in life by thinking about pleasant or fantastic things: *Most horror movies are simple escapism.*
escapist ADJECTIVE

eschew eschews eschewing eschewed
VERB *a formal word* If you eschew something, you deliberately avoid or keep away from it.

escort escorts escorting escorted
NOUN **1.** a person or vehicle that travels with another in order to protect or guide that person **2.** a person who accompanies another person of the opposite sex to a social event
VERB **3.** If you escort someone, you go with that person somewhere, especially in order to protect or guide him or her.

-ese
SUFFIX The suffix *-ese* forms adjectives and nouns that show where a person or thing comes from: *Japanese*

especially
ADVERB You say especially to show that something applies more to one thing, person, or situation than to any other: *Regular eye tests are important, especially for the elderly.*

espionage
NOUN Espionage is the act of spying to get secret information, especially to find out military or political secrets.

espouse espouses espousing espoused
VERB *a formal word* If you espouse a policy, cause, or plan, you give your support to it: *They espoused human rights.*

espresso
NOUN Espresso is strong coffee made by forcing steam through ground coffee.

Ee

-ess
SUFFIX The suffix *-ess* added at the end of a noun indicates a female: *lioness*

essay essays
NOUN a piece of writing on a particular subject

essence essences
NOUN **1.** The essence of something is its most basic and most important part, which gives it its identity: *the very essence of being a child* **2.** a concentrated liquid used for flavouring food: *vanilla essence*

essential essentials
ADJECTIVE **1.** vitally important and absolutely necessary: *Good ventilation is essential in a greenhouse.* **2.** very basic, important, and typical: *the essential aspects of law*
PLURAL NOUN **3.** things that are very important or necessary: *the bare essentials of furnishings*
essentially ADVERB

-est
SUFFIX The suffix *-est* is used to form adjectives and adverbs that have the meaning *most*: *greatest, furthest*

establish establishes establishing established
VERB **1.** To establish something means to set it up in a permanent way. **2.** If you establish yourself or become established as something, you achieve a strong reputation for a particular activity: *He had just established himself as a movie star.* **3.** If you establish a fact or establish the truth of something, you discover it and can prove it: *The officer's first priority is to establish the cause of the accident.*
established ADJECTIVE

establishment establishments
NOUN **1.** The establishment of an organization or system is the act of setting it up. **2.** a store, business, or some other sort of organization or institution **3.** The Establishment is the group of people in a country who have power and influence: *lawyers, businesspeople, and other pillars of the Establishment*

estate estates
NOUN **1.** a large area of privately owned land in the country, together with all the property on it **2.** An estate consists of all the possessions a person leaves behind when he or she dies.

esteem
NOUN admiration and respect that you feel for another person
esteemed ADJECTIVE

estimate estimates estimating estimated
VERB **1.** If you estimate an amount or quantity, you calculate it approximately. **2.** If you estimate something, you make a guess about it based on the evidence you have available: *He estimated that it would take about two hours to clean the house.*
NOUN **3.** a guess at an amount, quantity, or outcome, based on the evidence you have available **4.** a formal statement from a company who may do some work for you, telling you how much it is likely to cost

estimation estimations
NOUN **1.** an approximate calculation of something that can be measured **2.** the opinion or impression you form about a person or situation

estranged
ADJECTIVE **1.** If a husband and wife are estranged, they no longer live together. **2.** If someone is estranged from his or her family or friends, that person has quarrelled with them and no longer keeps in touch with them.

estrogen
NOUN a female sex hormone that regulates the reproductive cycle

estuary estuaries
NOUN the wide part of a river near where it joins the sea and where fresh water mixes with salt water

etc. a written abbreviation for ET CETERA

et cetera *Et cetera* is used at the end of a list to indicate that other items of the same type you have mentioned could have been mentioned if there had been time or space.

> **⚠ HEADS UP**
> Note: e.g. comes at the beginning of an example, and etc. comes at the end: *e.g., bread, milk, eggs, etc.*

etch etches etching etched
VERB **1.** If you etch a design or pattern on a surface, you cut into the surface by using acid or a sharp tool. **2.** If something is etched on your mind or memory, it has made such a strong impression on you that you feel you will never forget it.
etched ADJECTIVE

etching etchings
NOUN a picture printed from a metal plate that has had a design cut into it

Ee

eternal
ADJECTIVE lasting forever, or seeming to last forever: *eternal flame*
eternally ADVERB

eternity eternities
NOUN **1.** Eternity is time without end, or a state of existing outside time. **2.** a period of time that seems to go on forever: *We arrived there after an eternity.*

ether
NOUN a colourless liquid that burns easily. It is used in industry as a solvent and in medicine as an anesthetic.

ethereal
ADJECTIVE light and delicate: *misty, ethereal landscapes*
ethereally ADVERB

ethical
ADJECTIVE in agreement with accepted principles of behaviour that are thought to be right: *There are ethical issues involved in cloning animals.*
ethically ADVERB

ethics
PLURAL NOUN Ethics are moral beliefs about right and wrong: *The medical profession has a code of ethics.*

ethnic
ADJECTIVE **1.** involving different racial groups of people: *ethnic minorities* **2.** relating to a particular racial or cultural group within a society: *ethnic food*
ethnically ADVERB

ethos
NOUN a set of ideas and attitudes that is associated with a particular group of people: *the ethos of journalism*

etiquette
NOUN a set of rules for behaviour in a particular social situation

-ette
SUFFIX The suffix -ette is used to form nouns that have *small* as part of their meaning: *dinette, diskette*

etymology
NOUN Etymology is the study of the origin and changes of form in words.

eucalyptus eucalyptuses
NOUN an evergreen tree, grown mostly in Australia; also the wood and oil from this tree

euphemism euphemisms
NOUN a polite word or expression that you can use instead of one that might offend or upset people. For example, *pass away* is a euphemism for *die.*
euphemistic ADJECTIVE
euphemistically ADVERB

euphoria
NOUN a powerful feeling of great happiness
euphoric ADJECTIVE

Europe
NOUN Europe is the second smallest continent. It has Asia on its eastern side, with the Arctic to the north, the Atlantic to the west, and the Mediterranean and Africa to the south.

European Europeans
ADJECTIVE **1.** belonging or relating to Europe
NOUN **2.** someone who comes from Europe

euthanasia
NOUN Euthanasia is the act of painlessly killing a dying person in order to stop his or her suffering.

evacuate evacuates evacuating evacuated
VERB If people are evacuated, they are removed from a place of danger to a place of safety: *The town had to be evacuated due to flooding from the hurricane.*
evacuation NOUN
evacuee NOUN

evade evades evading evaded
VERB **1.** If you evade someone or something, you keep moving in order to keep out of that person's or thing's way: *For two months he evaded police.* **2.** If you evade a problem or question, you avoid dealing with it.

evaluate evaluates evaluating evaluated
VERB If you evaluate something, you assess its strengths and weaknesses.

evaluation evaluations
NOUN **1.** Evaluation is assessing something's strengths and weaknesses. **2.** To carry out an evaluation of a design, product, or system is to do an assessment to find out how well it works or will work.

evaporate evaporates evaporating evaporated
VERB **1.** When a liquid evaporates, it gradually becomes less and less because it has changed from a liquid into a gas. **2.** If a substance has been evaporated, some or all the liquid has been taken out so that it is concentrated or dry.
evaporation NOUN

evasion evasions
NOUN deliberately avoiding doing something: *tax evasion*

evasive
ADJECTIVE deliberately trying to avoid talking about or doing something: *She was evasive about her past.*

Ee

eve eves
NOUN the evening or day before an event or occasion: *on the eve of his graduation*

even evens evening evened
ADJECTIVE **1.** flat and level: *an even layer of chocolate* **2.** regular and without variation: *an even temperature* **3.** In mathematics, numbers that are even can be divided exactly by two: *14 is an even number.* **4.** Scores that are even are exactly the same.
ADVERB **5.** *Even* is used to suggest that something is unexpected or surprising: *I haven't even got a bank account.* **6.** *Even* is also used to say that something is greater in degree than something else: *This was an opportunity to obtain even more money.*
PHRASE **7. Even if** or **even though** is used to introduce something that is surprising in relation to the main part of the sentence: *She was too kind to say anything, even though she was upset.*
evenly ADVERB

evening evenings
NOUN the part of the day between late afternoon and the time you go to bed

event events
NOUN **1.** something that happens, especially when it is unusual or important **2.** one of the competitions that are part of an organized occasion, especially in sports
PHRASE **3.** If you say **in any event**, you mean whatever happens: *In any event, we must get on with our own lives.*

eventful
ADJECTIVE full of interesting and important events

eventual
ADJECTIVE happening or being achieved in the end: *He remained confident of eventual victory.*

eventuality eventualities
NOUN a possible future event or result: *equipment to cope with most eventualities*

eventually
ADVERB in the end: *Eventually I got to the train station, but my train had already left.*

ever
ADVERB **1.** at any time: *Have you ever seen anything like it?* **2.** at all times: *The president will come under ever more pressure to resign.*

evergreen evergreens
NOUN a tree or bush which has green leaves all year

everlasting
ADJECTIVE never coming to an end

every
ADJECTIVE **1.** *Every* is used to refer to all the members of a particular group, separately and one by one: *Every classroom has a computer.* **2.** *Every* is used to mean the greatest or the best possible degree of something: *He has every reason to avoid the subject.* **3.** *Every* is also used to indicate that something happens at regular intervals: *renewable every five years*
PHRASE **4. Every other** means each alternate: *I see my aunt at least every other week.*

everybody
PRONOUN **1.** all the people in a group: *She obviously thinks everybody in the place knows her.* **2.** all the people in the world: *Everybody needs to eat.*

everyday
ADJECTIVE usual or ordinary: *the everyday drudgery of work*

everyone
PRONOUN **1.** all the people in a group **2.** all the people in the world

everything
PRONOUN **1.** all or the whole of something **2.** the most important thing: *When I was younger, my toys were everything to me.*

everywhere
ADVERB in or to all places

evict evicts evicting evicted
VERB To evict someone means to officially force that person to leave a building or piece of land.
eviction NOUN

SPELL-CHECK THIS!

A computer's spell-check won't catch a word that is spelled correctly but used in the wrong way.

▼✕

I practise at the skate park almost everyday.

In this sentence, **everyday** should be **every day**. **Every day** means *daily*. **Everyday** means *ordinary*.

Ee

evidence
NOUN **1.** Evidence is anything you see, read, or are told that gives you reason to believe something. **2.** Evidence is the information used in court to attempt to prove or disprove something.

evident
ADJECTIVE easily noticed or understood: *His love of nature is evident in his paintings.*
evidently ADVERB

evil evils
NOUN **1.** Evil is a force or power that is believed to cause wicked or bad things to happen. **2.** a very unpleasant or harmful situation or activity: *the evils of war*
ADJECTIVE **3.** Someone or something that is evil is morally wrong or bad: *evil influences*

evoke evokes evoking evoked
VERB To evoke an emotion, memory, or reaction means to cause it: *Enthusiasm was evoked by the appearance of the prince.*

evolution
NOUN **1.** Evolution is a process of gradual change taking place over many generations during which living things slowly change as they adapt to different environments.
2. Evolution is also any process of gradual change and development over a period of time: *the evolution of her latest theory*
evolutionary ADJECTIVE

evolve evolves evolving evolved
VERB **1.** If something evolves or if you evolve it, it develops gradually over a period of time: *They were given a brief time to evolve a system of training.* **2.** When living things evolve, they gradually change and develop into different forms over a period of time.

ewe ewes
NOUN a female sheep

ex-
PREFIX The prefix *ex-* means *former*: *ex-husband*

exacerbate exacerbates exacerbating exacerbated
VERB To exacerbate something means to make it worse.

exact exacts exacting exacted
ADJECTIVE **1.** correct and complete in every detail: *an exact replica of the original trading post* **2.** accurate and precise, as opposed to approximate: *Mystery surrounds the exact circumstances of his death.*
VERB **3.** *a formal word* If somebody or something exacts something from you, that person or thing demands or obtains it from you, especially through force: *The officer exacted a confession from the culprit.*

exactly
ADVERB **1.** with complete accuracy and precision: *That's exactly what happened.*
2. You can use *exactly* to emphasize the truth of a statement, or a similarity or close relationship between one thing and another: *It's exactly the same colour.*
INTERJECTION **3.** an expression implying total agreement

exaggerate exaggerates exaggerating exaggerated
VERB **1.** If you exaggerate, you make the thing you are describing seem better, worse, bigger, or more important than it really is.
2. To exaggerate something means to make it more noticeable than usual: *Actors often exaggerate movements for the benefit of those sitting in the back row.*

exaggeration exaggerations
NOUN a statement that goes beyond the truth. For example, it is an exaggeration to say that you are so hungry you could eat a horse.

exalted
ADJECTIVE *a formal word* Someone who is exalted is very important.

exam exams
NOUN an examination

examination examinations
NOUN **1.** an official test, set to find out your knowledge or skill in a subject **2.** If you make an examination of something, you inspect it very carefully: *She carried out a careful examination of the hull.* **3.** A medical examination is a check by a doctor to find out the state of your health.

examine examines examining examined
VERB **1.** If you examine something, you inspect it very carefully. **2.** To examine a subject is to look closely at the issues involved and form your own opinion. **3.** To examine someone means to find out that person's knowledge or skill in a particular subject by testing him or her. **4.** If a doctor examines you, he or she checks your body to find out the state of your health.

examiner examiners
NOUN a person who sets or marks an exam

example examples
NOUN **1.** something that represents or is typical of a group or set: *some examples of early Canadian painting* **2.** If you say someone or something is an example to people, you mean that people can imitate and learn from that person or thing.
PHRASE **3.** You use **for example** to give an example of something you are talking about.

EXAGGERATION ▼✕

a statement that goes beyond the truth

"... the wind was so strong it blew Salina right off her feet!!!"

Here is an exaggeration. Salina wasn't *really* blown off her feet. The boy is just saying this for emphasis.

Ee

exasperate exasperates exasperating exasperated
VERB If someone or something exasperates you, that person or thing irritates you and makes you angry.
exasperating ADJECTIVE
exasperation NOUN

excavate excavates excavating excavated
VERB To excavate means to remove earth from the ground by digging.
excavation NOUN

exceed exceeds exceeding exceeded
VERB To exceed something such as a limit means to go beyond it or to become greater than it: *the first aircraft to exceed the speed of sound*

exceedingly
ADVERB extremely or very much

excel excels excelling excelled
VERB If someone excels in something, that person is very good at doing it.

Excellency Excellencies
NOUN a title used to address an official of very high rank, such as an ambassador or the Governor General

excellent
ADJECTIVE very good
excellence NOUN

except
PREPOSITION Except means other than or apart from: *All my family were musicians except my father.*

⚠ **HEADS UP**

Except means *other than*: *Everyone except me got a gift.* **Accept** means *receive: I can't accept this gift.*

exception exceptions
NOUN somebody or something that is not included in a general statement or rule: *English, like every language, has exceptions to its rules.*

exceptional
ADJECTIVE **1.** unusually talented or clever **2.** unusual and likely to happen very rarely
exceptionally ADVERB

excerpt excerpts
NOUN a short piece of writing or music that is taken from a larger piece

excess excesses
NOUN **1.** Excess is behaviour that goes beyond normally acceptable limits: *a life of excess* **2.** a larger amount of something than is needed, usual, or healthy: *an excess of energy*

ADJECTIVE **3.** more than is needed, allowed, or healthy: *excess weight*
PHRASE **4.** In **excess of** a particular amount means more than that amount: *a fortune in excess of ten million dollars* **5.** If you do something to **excess**, you do it too much: *He ate to excess.*

excessive
ADJECTIVE too great in amount or degree: *using excessive force*
excessively ADVERB

exchange exchanges exchanging exchanged
VERB **1.** To exchange things means to give or receive one thing in return for another: *They exchange letters during the summer.*
NOUN **2.** the act of giving or receiving something in return for something else: *an exchange of gifts* **3.** a place where people trade and do business: *the stock exchange*

excise
NOUN Excise is a tax put on goods produced for sale in the country that produces them.

excitable
ADJECTIVE easily excited

excite excites exciting excited
VERB **1.** If somebody or something excites you, that person or thing makes you feel very happy and nervous or very interested and enthusiastic. **2.** If something excites a particular feeling, it causes somebody to have that feeling: *Their behaviour excited my suspicion.*

excited
ADJECTIVE happy and unable to relax
excitedly ADVERB

Instead of **EXCITED** try...

an enthusiastic crowd
too charged to sleep
anxious to get going
thrilled to be there
wild with desire
ecstatic with joy
a passionate speech
feverish anticipation

excitement
NOUN interest and enthusiasm

exciting
ADJECTIVE making you feel happy and enthusiastic

exclaim exclaims exclaiming exclaimed
VERB When you exclaim, you cry out suddenly or loudly because you are excited or shocked.

Ee

exclamation exclamations
NOUN a word or phrase spoken suddenly to express a strong feeling

exclamation mark exclamation marks
NOUN a punctuation mark (!) used in writing to express a strong feeling

exclude excludes excluding excluded
VERB **1.** If you exclude something, you deliberately do not include it or do not consider it. **2.** If you exclude somebody from a place or an activity, you prevent that person from entering the place or taking part in the activity.
exclusion NOUN

exclusive exclusives
ADJECTIVE **1.** available to or for the use of a small group of rich or privileged people: *an exclusive club* **2.** belonging to a particular person or group only: *exclusive rights to coverage of the Olympic Games*
NOUN **3.** a story or interview that appears in only one newspaper or on only one television program
exclusively ADVERB

excrement
NOUN Excrement is the solid waste matter that is passed out of a person's or animal's body through the bowels.

excrete excretes excreting excreted
VERB When you excrete waste matter from your body, you get rid of it, for example by going to the toilet or by sweating.
excretion NOUN
excretory ADJECTIVE

excruciating
ADJECTIVE unbearably painful
excruciatingly ADVERB

excursion excursions
NOUN a short journey or outing

excuse excuses excusing excused
NOUN **1.** a reason that you give to explain why something has been done, has not been done, or will not be done
VERB **2.** If you excuse yourself or something that you have done, you give reasons defending your actions. **3.** If you excuse somebody for something wrong he or she has done, you forgive that person for it. **4.** If you excuse somebody from a duty or responsibility, you free that person from it: *He was excused from standing trial because of ill health.*
PHRASE **5.** You say **excuse me** to try to catch somebody's attention or to apologize for an interruption or for rude behaviour.

execute executes executing executed
VERB **1.** To execute somebody means to kill that person as a punishment for a crime. **2.** If you execute something such as a plan or an action, you carry it out or perform it: *The crime had been planned and executed in Montréal.*
execution NOUN

executioner executioners
NOUN a person whose job is to execute criminals

executive executives
NOUN **1.** a person who is employed by a company at a senior level **2.** The executive of an organization is a committee that has the authority to make decisions and ensure that they are carried out.
ADJECTIVE **3.** concerned with making important decisions and ensuring that they are carried out: *the company's executive director*

executor executors
NOUN a person you appoint to carry out the instructions in your will

exemplary
ADJECTIVE **1.** being a good example and worthy of imitation: *an exemplary performance* **2.** serving as a warning: *an exemplary tale*

exemplify exemplifies exemplifying exemplified
VERB To exemplify something means to be a typical example of it: *This aircraft exemplifies the advantages of technological co-operation between countries.*

exempt exempts exempting exempted
ADJECTIVE **1.** excused from a rule or duty: *exempt from final exams*
VERB **2.** To exempt someone from a rule, duty, or obligation means to excuse that person from it.
exemption NOUN

exercise exercises exercising exercised
NOUN **1.** Exercise is any activity that you do to get fit or remain healthy. **2.** Exercises are also activities that you do to practise and train for a particular skill: *piano exercises, a mathematical exercise*
VERB **3.** When you exercise, you do activities that help you to get fit and remain healthy. **4.** If you exercise your rights or responsibilities, you use them.

exert exerts exerting exerted
VERB **1.** To exert pressure means to apply it. **2.** If you exert yourself, you make a physical or mental effort to do something.

exertion exertions
NOUN Exertion is vigorous physical effort or exercise.

Ee

exhale exhales exhaling exhaled
VERB When you exhale, you breathe out.

exhaust exhausts exhausting exhausted
VERB **1.** To exhaust somebody means to make that person very tired: *Swimming several lengths of the pool left her exhausted.* **2.** If you exhaust a supply of something such as money or food, you use it up completely. **3.** If you exhaust a subject, you talk about it so much that there is nothing else to say about it.
NOUN **4.** waste gases or steam that comes out of an engine
exhaustion NOUN

exhaustive
ADJECTIVE thorough and complete: *an exhaustive series of tests*
exhaustively ADVERB

exhibit exhibits exhibiting exhibited
VERB **1.** To exhibit things means to show them in a public place for people to see. **2.** If you exhibit your feelings or abilities, you display them so that other people can see them.
NOUN **3.** anything that is put on show for the public to see

exhibition exhibitions
NOUN a public display of works of art, products, or skills

exhibitor exhibitors
NOUN a person whose work is being shown in an exhibition

exhilarating
ADJECTIVE Something that is exhilarating makes you feel very happy and excited.

exile exiles exiling exiled
NOUN **1.** A person who lives in exile has been banished from his or her own country, usually for political reasons. **2.** a person who lives in exile
VERB **3.** If somebody is exiled, that person is sent away from his or her own country and not allowed to return.

exist exists existing existed
VERB If something exists, it is present in the world as a real or living thing.

existence
NOUN **1.** Existence is the state of being or existing. **2.** a way of living or being: *an idyllic existence*

exit exits exiting exited
NOUN **1.** a way out of a place **2.** If you make an exit, you leave a place.
VERB **3.** To exit means to go out. **4.** An actor exits when he or she leaves the stage.

exodus
NOUN An exodus is the departure of a large number of people from a place.

exotic
ADJECTIVE **1.** attractive or interesting through being unusual: *exotic fabrics* **2.** coming from a foreign country: *exotic plants*

expand expands expanding expanded
VERB **1.** If something expands or you expand it, it becomes larger in number or size. **2.** If you expand on something, you give more details about it: *I plan to expand on that theme in my essay.*
expansion NOUN

expanse expanses
NOUN a very large or widespread area: *a vast expanse of pine forests*

expansive
ADJECTIVE **1.** Something that is expansive is very wide or extends over a very large area: *the expansive countryside* **2.** Someone who is expansive is friendly, open, or talkative.

expatriate expatriates
NOUN someone who is living in a country that is not his or her own

expect expects expecting expected
VERB **1.** If you expect something to happen, you believe that it will happen: *The snow is expected to end today.* **2.** If you are expecting somebody or something, you believe that person or thing is going to arrive or to happen: *I was expecting my cousin to come through the door.* **3.** If you expect something, you believe that it is your right to get it or have it: *He seemed to expect a reply.*

expectancy
NOUN Expectancy is the feeling that something is about to happen, especially something exciting.

expectant
ADJECTIVE **1.** If you are expectant, you believe that something is about to happen, especially something exciting. **2.** An expectant mother or father is someone whose baby is going to be born soon.
expectantly ADVERB

expectation expectations
NOUN Expectation or an expectation is a strong belief or hope that something will happen.

expedient expedients
NOUN **1.** an action or plan that achieves a particular purpose but that may not be morally acceptable: *Many businesses have improved their profitability by the simple expedient of cutting staff.*
ADJECTIVE **2.** Something that is expedient is useful or convenient in a particular situation.
expediency NOUN

Ee

expedition expeditions
NOUN **1.** an organized journey made for a special purpose, such as to explore; also the party of people who make such a journey **2.** a short journey or outing: *shopping expeditions*
expeditionary ADJECTIVE

expel expels expelling expelled
VERB **1.** If someone is expelled from a school or club, that person is officially told to leave because he or she has behaved badly. **2.** If a gas or liquid is expelled from a place, it is forced out of it.

expend expends expending expended
VERB To expend energy, time, or money means to use it up or spend it.

expendable
ADJECTIVE no longer useful or necessary, and therefore able to be got rid of

expenditure
NOUN Expenditure is the total amount of money spent on something.

expense expenses
NOUN **1.** Expense is the money that something costs: *the expense of installing an alarm system*
PLURAL NOUN **2.** Expenses are the money somebody spends while doing something connected with his or her work. Expenses are paid back to the person by his or her employer.

expensive
ADJECTIVE costing a lot of money
expensively ADVERB

experience experiences experiencing experienced
NOUN **1.** Experience consists of all the things that you have done or that have happened to you. **2.** the knowledge or skill you have in a particular activity **3.** something that you do or something that happens to you, especially something new or unusual
VERB **4.** If you experience a situation or feeling, it happens to you or you are affected by it.

experienced
ADJECTIVE skilled or knowledgeable through doing something for a long time

experiment experiments experimenting experimented
NOUN **1.** the testing of something, either to find out its effect or to prove something
VERB **2.** If you experiment with something, you do a scientific test on it to prove or discover something.

experimentation NOUN
experimental ADJECTIVE
experimentally ADVERB

expert experts
NOUN **1.** a person who is very skilled at doing something or very knowledgeable about a particular subject
ADJECTIVE **2.** having or requiring special skill or knowledge: *expert advice*
expertly ADVERB

expertise
NOUN Expertise is special skill or knowledge.

expire expires expiring expired
VERB When something expires, it reaches the end of the period of time for which it is valid: *My bus pass expires in the summer.*
expiry NOUN

explain explains explaining explained
VERB If you explain something, you give details about it or reasons for it so that it can be understood.

explanation explanations
NOUN a helpful or clear description
explanatory ADJECTIVE

explicit
ADJECTIVE shown or expressed clearly and openly: *an explicit threat, explicit orders*
explicitly ADVERB

explode explodes exploding exploded
VERB **1.** If something such as a bomb explodes, it bursts loudly and with great force, often causing damage. **2.** If somebody explodes, that person expresses strong feelings suddenly or violently: *I half expected him to explode in anger.* **3.** When something increases suddenly and rapidly, it can be said to explode: *Sales of men's toiletries have exploded.*

exploit exploits exploiting exploited
VERB **1.** If you exploit a person or a situation, you take advantage of that person for your own ends: *Critics claim he exploited the actors in his movie.* **2.** If you exploit something, you make the best use of it, often for profit: *exploiting the power of computers*
NOUN **3.** something daring or interesting that somebody has done: *Her courage and exploits were legendary.*
exploitation NOUN

explore explores exploring explored
VERB **1.** If you explore a place, you travel in it to find out what it is like. **2.** If you explore an idea, you think about it carefully.
exploration NOUN
exploratory ADJECTIVE
explorer NOUN

 **HEADS UP** Explore is pronounced with a long o, but **exploratory** has short o's.

Ee

explosion explosions
NOUN a sudden violent burst of energy, for example one caused by a bomb

explosive explosives
ADJECTIVE **1.** capable of exploding or likely to explode **2.** happening suddenly and making a loud noise **3.** An explosive situation is one that is likely to have serious or dangerous effects.
NOUN **4.** a substance or device that can explode

exponent exponents
NOUN **1.** An exponent of an idea or plan is someone who puts it forward. **2.** An exponent of a skill or activity is someone who is good at it.

export exports exporting exported
VERB **1.** To export goods means to send them to another country and sell them there.
NOUN **2.** Exports are goods that are sent to another country and sold.
exporter NOUN

expose exposes exposing exposed
VERB **1.** To expose something means to uncover it and make it visible. **2.** To expose a person to something dangerous means to put that person in a situation that might be harmful: *exposed to toxins* **3.** To expose a person or situation means to reveal the truth about that person or thing.

exposition expositions
NOUN a detailed explanation of a particular subject
expository ADJECTIVE

exposure exposures
NOUN **1.** Exposure is the exposing of something. **2.** Exposure is the harmful effect on the body caused by very cold weather.

express expresses expressing expressed
VERB **1.** When you express an idea or feeling, you show what you think or feel by saying or doing something. **2.** If you express a quantity in a particular form, you write it down in that form: *The result of the equation is usually expressed as a percentage.*
ADJECTIVE **3.** very fast: *express delivery service*
NOUN **4.** a fast train or bus that stops at only a few places

expression expressions
NOUN **1.** Your expression is the look on your face that shows what you are thinking or feeling. **2.** The expression of ideas or feelings is the showing of them through words, actions, or art. **3.** a word or phrase used in communicating: *the expression Cool it!*

expressive
ADJECTIVE **1.** showing feelings clearly **2.** full of expression

expressway expressways
NOUN a divided highway designed for fast-moving traffic, using ramps to enter and exit and overpasses for roads that cross the highway

expulsion expulsions
NOUN The expulsion of someone from a place or institution is the act of officially banning that person from that place or institution: *the high number of school expulsions*

exquisite
ADJECTIVE extremely beautiful and pleasing

extend extends extending extended
VERB **1.** If something extends for a distance, it continues and stretches into the distance. **2.** If something extends from a surface or an object, it sticks out from it. **3.** If you extend something, you make it larger or longer: *The table had been extended to seat 20.*

extension extensions
NOUN **1.** a room or building that is added to an existing building **2.** an extra period of time for which something continues to exist or be valid: *an extension to his visa* **3.** a telephone connected to the same line as another telephone

extensive
ADJECTIVE **1.** covering a large area **2.** very great in effect: *extensive repairs*
extensively ADVERB

extent extents
NOUN The extent of something is its length, area, or size.

exterior exteriors
NOUN **1.** The exterior of something is its outside. **2.** Your exterior is your outward appearance.

exterminate exterminates exterminating exterminated
VERB When animals or people are exterminated, they are deliberately killed.
extermination NOUN

external
ADJECTIVE existing or happening on the outside or outer part of something
externally ADVERB

extinct
ADJECTIVE **1.** An extinct species of animal or plant is no longer in existence. **2.** An extinct volcano is no longer likely to erupt.
extinction NOUN

Ee

extinguish extinguishes extinguishing extinguished
VERB To extinguish a light or fire means to put it out.

extra extras
ADJECTIVE **1.** more than is usual, necessary, or expected
NOUN **2.** anything that is additional **3.** a person who is hired to play a very small and unimportant part in a movie

extra-
PREFIX The prefix *extra-* means *outside* or *beyond*: *extraordinary*

extract extracts extracting extracted
VERB **1.** To extract something from a place means to take it out or get it out, often by force. **2.** If you extract information from someone, you get it from that person with difficulty.
NOUN **3.** a small section taken from a book or piece of music

extraction
NOUN **1.** Your extraction is the country or people that your family originally comes from: *a Canadian citizen of Malaysian extraction* **2.** Extraction is the process of taking or getting something out of a place.

extraordinary
ADJECTIVE unusual or surprising
extraordinarily ADVERB

extravagant
ADJECTIVE **1.** spending or costing more money than is reasonable or affordable **2.** going beyond reasonable limits
extravagantly ADVERB
extravagance NOUN

extravaganza extravaganzas
NOUN a spectacular and expensive public show

extreme extremes
ADJECTIVE **1.** very great in degree or intensity: *extreme caution* **2.** going beyond what is usual or reasonable: *extreme weather*

conditions **3.** at the furthest point or edge of something: *the extreme northern corner of Labrador*
NOUN **4.** the highest or furthest degree of something
extremely ADVERB

extremist extremists
NOUN a person who uses unreasonable or violent methods to bring about political change
extremism NOUN

extremity extremities
NOUN The extremities of something are its furthest ends or edges.

extricate extricates extricating extricated
VERB To extricate someone from a place or a situation means to free that person from it.

extrovert extroverts
NOUN a person who is more interested in other people and the world than his or her own thoughts and feelings

exuberant
ADJECTIVE full of energy and cheerfulness
exuberantly ADVERB
exuberance NOUN

exude exudes exuding exuded
VERB If someone exudes a quality or feeling, that person seems to have it to a great degree.

eye eyes eyeing eying eyed
NOUN **1.** the organ in the body by which people or animals see **2.** the small hole at the end of a needle through which you pass the thread
VERB **3.** To eye something means to look at it carefully or suspiciously.

eyesore eyesores
NOUN Something that is an eyesore is unpleasant to look at.

eyrie eyries
NOUN the nest of an eagle or other bird of prey

KNOWING WORDS: WORD BUILDING

BE WORD SHARP!

To build a compound word, put two or more base words together.

eye the organ of sight

eyebrows the lines of hair above your eyes

eyelashes the hairs that grow from your eyelids

eyelid the skin that covers each of your eyes

eyesight the ability to see

eyewitness someone who has seen an event

Ff

fable fables
NOUN a story intended to teach a moral lesson

fabled
ADJECTIVE well-known because many stories have been told about it: *the fabled city of Troy*

fabric fabrics
NOUN **1.** cloth: *tough fabric for tents* **2.** The fabric of a building is its walls, roof, and other parts. **3.** The fabric of a society or system is its structure, laws, and customs: *the fabric of Canadian society*

fabricate fabricates fabricating fabricated
VERB **1.** If you fabricate a story or an explanation, you invent it in order to deceive people. **2.** To fabricate something is to make or manufacture it.
fabrication NOUN

fabulous
ADJECTIVE **1.** wonderful or very impressive: *a fabulous dinner* **2.** not real, but happening in stories and legends: *The dragon is a fabulous creature.*

façade façades
NOUN **1.** the front outside wall of a building **2.** a false outward appearance: *the façade of honesty*

face faces facing faced
NOUN **1.** the front part of your head from your chin to your forehead **2.** the expression someone has or is making: *a grim face*

Instead of FACE try...

- a startled **look**
- an air of **disgust**
- a puzzled **expression**
- a disapproving **glare**
- a friendly **demeanour**

3. a surface or side of something, especially the most important side: *the north face of Mount Logan* **4.** the main aspect or general appearance of something: *Computer graphics has changed the face of animation.*
VERB **5.** To face something or someone is to be opposite the thing or to look toward it: *a room that faces onto the street* **6.** If you face something difficult or unpleasant, you have

to deal with it: *She faced a terrible dilemma.*
PHRASE **7. On the face of it** means judging by the appearance of something or your initial reaction to it: *On the face of it the hill looks very steep.*

faceless
ADJECTIVE without character or individuality: *faceless bureaucrats*

facelift facelifts
NOUN **1.** an operation to tighten the skin on someone's face to make that person look younger **2.** If you give something a facelift, you clean it or improve its appearance.

facet facets
NOUN **1.** a single part or aspect of something: *the many facets of his talent* **2.** one of the flat, cut surfaces of a precious stone

facetious
ADJECTIVE amusing but in a silly or inappropriate way: *He didn't appreciate my facetious suggestion.*

facial
ADJECTIVE appearing on or being part of the face: *facial expressions*

facilitate facilitates facilitating facilitated
VERB To facilitate something is to make it easier for it to happen: *appliances that facilitate housework*

facility facilities
NOUN **1.** a building or centre that is specially equipped to serve a certain purpose: *shopping facilities, a sports facility* **2.** A facility for something is an ability to do it easily or well: *a facility for writing*

fact facts
NOUN **1.** a piece of knowledge or information that is true or something that has actually happened
PHRASE **2. In fact, as a matter of fact**, and **in point of fact** mean *actually* or *really* and are used for emphasis or when making an additional comment: *Very few people, in fact, have this ability.*
factual ADJECTIVE
factually ADVERB

faction factions
NOUN a small group of people belonging to a larger group, but differing from the larger group in some aims or ideas: *a conservative faction of the government*

fact of life facts of life
NOUN **1.** The facts of life are basic information about sex. **2.** If you say that something is a fact of life, you mean that it is something that people expect to happen,

even though they might find it shocking or unpleasant: *Poverty is a fact of life for many people.*

factor factors

NOUN **1.** something that helps to cause a result: *Air pollution is a major factor in asthma.* **2.** The factors of a number are the whole numbers that will divide exactly into it. For example, 2 and 5 are factors of 10. **3.** If something increases by a particular factor, it is multiplied that number of times: *The amount of energy used has increased by a factor of 8.*

factory factories

NOUN a building or group of buildings where goods are made in large quantities

faculty faculties

NOUN **1.** Your faculties are your physical and mental abilities: *My grandfather's mental faculties are as sharp as ever.* **2.** In some universities, a faculty is a group of related departments; also the teaching staff of a college or university: *the science faculty*

fad fads

NOUN a temporary fashion or craze: *the latest exercise fad*

fade fades fading faded

VERB If something fades, the intensity of its colour, brightness, or sound is gradually reduced.

Fahrenheit

NOUN a scale of temperature in which the freezing point of water is 32° and the boiling point is 212°

fail fails failing failed

VERB **1.** If someone fails to achieve something, that person is not successful. **2.** If you fail an exam, your marks are too low and you do not pass. **3.** If you fail to do something that you should have done, you do not do it: *I failed to let her know about the meeting.* **4.** If something fails, it becomes less effective or stops working properly: *The power failed. His grandmother's eyesight began to fail.* PHRASE **5. Without fail** means definitely or regularly: *Every Sunday her mom would call without fail.*

failing failings

NOUN **1.** a fault in something or someone PREPOSITION **2.** used to introduce an alternative: *Failing a decent snowfall, we will postpone the sleigh ride.*

failure failures

NOUN **1.** lack of success: *Not all conservation programs ended in failure.* **2.** an unsuccessful person, thing, or action: *The venture was a complete failure* **3.** Your failure to do

something is not doing something that you were expected to do: *a statement explaining his failure to turn up as a speaker* **4.** a weakness in something

faint fainter faintest; faints fainting fainted

ADJECTIVE **1.** A sound, colour, or feeling that is faint is not very strong or intense. **2.** If you feel faint, you feel weak, dizzy, and unsteady. VERB **3.** If you faint, you lose consciousness for a short time.

faintly ADVERB

fair fairer fairest; fairs

ADJECTIVE **1.** reasonable and just: *a fair grade* **2.** quite large: *a fair-sized envelope* **3.** moderately good or likely to be correct: *He had a fair idea of what to expect.* **4.** having light-coloured hair or pale skin **5.** with pleasant and dry weather: *We hope to have fair weather for our hike.* NOUN **6.** a gathering for showing livestock, crafts, and manufactured goods, often with games, rides, shows, and refreshments **7.** an exhibition of goods produced by a particular industry: *a book fair*

fairly ADVERB

fairness NOUN

fairground fairgrounds

NOUN an outdoor area where a fair is set up

fairway fairways

NOUN the area of trimmed grass between a tee and a green on a golf course

fairy fairies

NOUN In folklore and myth, fairies are small, imaginary creatures with magical powers.

fairy tale fairy tales

NOUN a story involving fairies, elves, or other imaginary creatures with magical powers

faith faiths

NOUN **1.** Faith is a feeling of confidence, trust, or optimism about something. **2.** Someone's faith is that person's religion.

faithful

ADJECTIVE **1.** loyal to someone or something and remaining firm in support of that person or thing **2.** accurate and truthful: *a faithful copy of an original*

faithfully ADVERB

faithfulness NOUN

fake fakes faking faked

NOUN **1.** an imitation of something made to trick people into thinking that it is genuine ADJECTIVE **2.** imitation and not genuine: *fake fur* VERB **3.** If you fake a feeling, you pretend that you are experiencing it.

Ff

falcon falcons
NOUN a bird of prey that can be trained to hunt other birds or small animals

fall falls falling fell fallen
VERB **1.** If someone or something falls or falls over, that person or thing drops toward the ground. **2.** If something falls somewhere, it lands there: *The spotlight fell on her.*
3. If something falls in amount or strength, it becomes less: *My grades fell slightly last month but they should be back up by the end of the school year.* **4.** If a person or group in a position of power falls, that person or group loses that position and someone else or another group takes control. **5.** Someone who falls in battle is killed. **6.** If, for example, you fall asleep, fall ill, or fall in love, you change quite quickly to that new state. **7.** Something that falls on a particular date occurs on that date.
NOUN **8.** If you have a fall, you accidentally fall over. **9.** A fall of snow, or other substance is a quantity of it that has fallen to the ground. **10.** A fall in something is a reduction in its amount or strength. **11.** In Canada, autumn is also called the fall.

fall down
VERB **12.** An argument or idea that falls down on a particular point is weak on that point and as a result will be unsuccessful.

fall for
VERB **13.** If you fall for someone, you become strongly attracted to that person and fall in love. **14.** If you fall for a trick or lie, you are deceived by it.

fall out
VERB **15.** If people fall out, they disagree and quarrel.

fall through
VERB **16.** If an arrangement or plan falls through, it fails or is abandoned.

fallacy fallacies
NOUN something false that is generally believed to be true

Fallopian tubes
PLURAL NOUN In a female mammal's body, the Fallopian tubes are the slender tubes along which the eggs pass from the ovaries to the uterus.

fallout
NOUN radioactive particles that fall to the earth after a nuclear explosion

fallow
ADJECTIVE Land that is fallow is not being used for crop growing so that it has the chance to rest and improve.

false
ADJECTIVE **1.** untrue or incorrect: *I think that's a false statement.* **2.** not real or genuine but intended to seem real: *false hair* **3.** unfaithful or deceitful
falsely ADVERB

falsehood falsehoods
NOUN **1.** the quality or fact of being untrue: *the difference between truth and falsehood*
2. a lie

falsify falsifies falsifying falsified
VERB If you falsify something, you change it in order to deceive people.
falsification NOUN

falter falters faltering faltered
VERB If someone or something falters, that person or thing hesitates or become unsure or unsteady: *Her voice faltered.*

fame
NOUN the state of being very well known

famed
ADJECTIVE very well known: *an area famed for its beauty*

familiar
ADJECTIVE **1.** well known or easy to recognize: *familiar faces* **2.** knowing or understanding something well: *I am not familiar with that story.*
familiarity NOUN
familiarize VERB

KNOWING WORDS: WORD HISTORY

BE WORD SHARP!

Words are like living things. They grow and change.

In Roman mythology, Fama was the goddess of celebrities and rumours. The Romans used the word **fama** to mean *talk*. By the time the word was borrowed from Latin into English, there were lots of words for *talk*, so **fame** came to mean *a quality that makes people talk about you.*

Ff

family families
NOUN **1.** a group of people who are related, especially a parent, his or her partner if there is one, and children if there are any; also all the people who are related to each other, including aunts and uncles, cousins, and grandparents **2.** a group of related species of animals or plants
familial ADJECTIVE

family planning
NOUN the practice of controlling the number of children a person has, usually by contraception

family room family rooms
NOUN a room in a house where people sit and relax

famine famines
NOUN a serious shortage of food that may cause many deaths

famished
ADJECTIVE *an informal word* very hungry

famous
ADJECTIVE very well known

famously
ADVERB *an old-fashioned word* If people get on famously, they enjoy each other's company very much.

fan fans fanning fanned
NOUN **1.** If you are a fan of someone or something, you like that person or thing very much. **2.** a handheld or mechanical object that creates a draft of cool air when it moves
VERB **3.** To fan people or things is to create a draft in their direction: *The gentle wind fanned her from all sides.*
fan out
VERB **4.** If people or things fan out, they move outward in different directions.

fanatic fanatics
NOUN a person who is very extreme in supporting a cause or in his or her enthusiasm for a particular activity
fanaticism NOUN

fanatical
ADJECTIVE If you are fanatical about something, you are very extreme in your enthusiasm or support for it.
fanatically ADVERB

fancy fancies fancying fancied; fancier fanciest
VERB **1.** If you fancy something, you want to have it or do it: *Do you fancy some ice cream?*
ADJECTIVE **2.** special and elaborate: *dressed up in fancy clothes*
fanciful ADJECTIVE

fanfare fanfares
NOUN a short, loud, musical introduction to a special event, usually played on trumpets

fang fangs
NOUN Fangs are long, pointed teeth.

fantasize fantasizes fantasizing fantasized
VERB If you fantasize, you imagine pleasant but unlikely events or situations.

fantastic
ADJECTIVE **1.** wonderful and very pleasing: *a fantastic view of the sea* **2.** strange and difficult to believe: *fantastic animals found nowhere else on earth*
fantastically ADVERB

fantasy fantasies
NOUN **1.** a story or situation that exists only in the imagination **2.** Fantasy is the activity of imagining things; also the things that you imagine: *She can't distinguish between fantasy and reality.* **3.** Fantasy is the people or situations in books or films that are created in the writer's imagination and do not reflect reality.

far farther farthest; further furthest
ADVERB **1.** If something is far away from other things, it is a long distance away. **2.** Far also means very much or to a great extent or degree: *far more important*
ADJECTIVE **3.** Far means very distant: *in the far north of Nunavut* **4.** Far also describes the more distant of two things rather than the nearer one: *the far corner of the classroom*
PHRASE **5.** By **far** and **far and away** are used to say that something is the best: *Walking is by far the best way to get around.* **6.** So **far** means up to the present moment: *So far, it's been good news.* **7.** As **far as**, so **far as**, and **in so far as** mean to the degree or extent that something is true: *As far as I know he is progressing well.*

farce farces
NOUN **1.** a humorous play in which ridiculous and unlikely situations occur **2.** a disorganized and ridiculous situation
farcical ADJECTIVE

fare fares faring fared
NOUN **1.** the amount charged for a journey in a vehicle or airplane
VERB **2.** How someone fares in a particular situation is how that person does in that situation: *The team has not fared well in this tournament.*

Far East
NOUN The Far East consists of the countries of eastern Asia, including China, Japan, and Malaysia.
Far Eastern ADJECTIVE

Ff

farewell
INTERJECTION **1.** Farewell means goodbye.
ADJECTIVE **2.** saying goodbye: *a farewell speech, a farewell wave*

far-fetched
ADJECTIVE unlikely to be true

farm farms farming farmed
NOUN **1.** an area of land together with buildings, used for growing crops and raising animals
VERB **2.** Someone who farms uses land to grow crops and raise animals.
farmer NOUN
farming NOUN

farmhouse farmhouses
NOUN the main house on a farm

farmyard farmyards
NOUN an area surrounded by farm buildings

far-sighted
ADJECTIVE **1.** a condition of the eyes in which nearby objects are out of focus **2.** If you make a far-sighted decision, you are planning wisely for the future.

fascinate fascinates fascinating fascinated
VERB If something fascinates you, it interests you so much that you think about it and nothing else.
fascinating ADJECTIVE

fascism
NOUN an extreme right-wing political ideology or system of government with a powerful dictator and state control of most activities. Nationalism is encouraged and political opposition is not allowed.
fascist NOUN OR ADJECTIVE

fashion fashions fashioning fashioned
NOUN **1.** a style of dress or way of behaving that is popular at a particular time **2.** The fashion in which someone does something is the way in which that person does it.
VERB **3.** If you fashion something, you make or shape it.

fashionable
ADJECTIVE Something that is fashionable is very popular with a lot of people at the same time.
fashionably ADVERB

fast faster fastest; fasts fasting fasted
ADJECTIVE **1.** moving or done at great speed **2.** If a clock is fast, it shows a time that is later than the real time.
ADVERB **3.** quickly and without delay
4. Something that is held fast is firmly fixed.
PHRASE **5.** If you are **fast asleep**, you are in a deep sleep.
VERB **6.** If you fast, you eat no food at all for a period of time, sometimes for religious reasons.
NOUN **7.** a period of time during which someone does not eat food

fasten fastens fastening fastened
VERB **1.** To fasten something is to close it or attach it firmly to something else. **2.** If you fasten your hands around or onto something, you hold it tightly with your hands.
fastener NOUN
fastening NOUN

fast food
NOUN food that is prepared and served quickly after you have ordered it

fastidious
ADJECTIVE extremely choosy and concerned about neatness and cleanliness

fast-track fast-tracks fast-tracking fast-tracked
VERB To fast-track something is to make it happen or put it into effect as quickly as possible, usually giving it priority over other things.

fat fatter fattest; fats
ADJECTIVE **1.** Someone who is fat has too much weight on his or her body. **2.** large or lengthy: *a fat pile of letters*
NOUN **3.** Fat is the greasy, cream-coloured substance that animals and humans have under their skin, which is used to store energy and to help keep them warm. **4.** Fat is also the greasy solid or liquid substance found in fruits, seeds, nuts, and some plants.
fatness NOUN
fatty ADJECTIVE

fatal
ADJECTIVE **1.** causing death: *fatal injuries*
2. very important or significant and likely to have an undesirable effect: *The mistake was fatal to my plans.*

Instead of **FATAL** try...

a lethal poison

terminal cancer

a mortal wound

a deadly accident

an incurable disease

fatally
ADVERB

fatality fatalities
NOUN a death caused by accident or violence

fate fates
NOUN **1.** Fate is a power that is believed to control events.
2. Someone's fate is what happens to that person: *She was resigned to her fate.*

fateful
ADJECTIVE having an important, often disastrous, effect: *a fateful decision*

Ff

father fathers fathering fathered
NOUN **1.** A person's father is his or her male parent. **2.** The father of something is the man who invented or started it: *Alexander Graham Bell was the father of the telephone.*
VERB **3.** *a literary or poetic use* When a man fathers a child, he has children or he has the responsibilities of a parent.
fatherly ADJECTIVE
fatherhood NOUN

father-in-law fathers-in-law
NOUN A person's father-in-law is the father of his or her husband or wife.

fathom fathoms fathoming fathomed
NOUN **1.** a nonmetric unit for measuring the depth of water. It is equal to about 1.83 metres.
VERB **2.** If you fathom something, you understand it after careful thought: *He tried to fathom what it meant.*

fatigue fatigues fatiguing fatigued
NOUN **1.** Fatigue is extreme tiredness.
VERB **2.** If you are fatigued by something, it makes you extremely tired.

fault faults faulting faulted
NOUN **1.** If something bad is your fault, you are to blame for it. **2.** a weakness or imperfection in someone or something **3.** a large crack in rock caused by movement of the earth's crust
PHRASE **4.** If you are **at fault**, you are mistaken or are to blame for something: *I was at fault and accepted responsibility for my actions.*
VERB **5.** If you fault someone, you criticize what that person is doing because he or she is not doing it well.
faultless ADJECTIVE

faulty faultier faultiest
ADJECTIVE containing flaws or errors

favour favours favouring favoured
NOUN **1.** If you regard someone or something with favour, you like or support that person or thing. **2.** If you do someone a favour, you do something helpful for that person.
PHRASE **3.** Something that is **in someone's favour** is a help or advantage to that person: *The arguments seemed to be in our favour.* **4.** If you are **in favour of** something, you agree with it and think it should happen.
VERB **5.** If you favour something or someone, you prefer that person or thing.

favourable
ADJECTIVE **1.** of advantage or benefit to someone **2.** positive and expressing approval
favourably ADVERB

favourite favourites
ADJECTIVE **1.** Your favourite person or thing is the one you like best.
NOUN **2.** Someone's favourite is the person or thing he or she likes best. **3.** the animal or person expected to win in a race or contest

favouritism
NOUN Favouritism is behaviour in which you are unfairly more helpful or more generous to one person than to other people.

fawn fawns fawning fawned
NOUN **1.** a very young deer
NOUN OR ADJECTIVE **2.** pale yellowish brown
VERB **3.** To fawn on someone is to seek that person's approval by flattering him or her.

fax faxes
NOUN an exact copy of a document sent electronically along a telephone line

fear fears fearing feared
NOUN **1.** Fear is an unpleasant feeling of danger. **2.** a thought that something undesirable or unpleasant might happen: *I have a fear of failure.*
VERB **3.** If you fear someone or something, you are frightened of that person or thing. **4.** If you fear something unpleasant, you are worried that it is likely to happen: *The artist feared that his paintings would be forgotten.*

Instead of **FEAR** try...
jump from **fright**
scream in **terror**
a look of **dismay**
a **phobia** of sharks
dread of tomorrow's exam

fearful
ADJECTIVE **1.** afraid and full of fear **2.** extremely unpleasant or worrying: *The world's in such a fearful mess.*
fearfully ADVERB

fearless
ADJECTIVE afraid of nothing
fearlessly ADVERB

fearsome
ADJECTIVE terrible or frightening: *a powerful, fearsome weapon*

feasible
ADJECTIVE possible and likely to happen: *Your plan is just not feasible.*
feasibility NOUN

feast feasts
NOUN a large and special meal for many people

feat feats
NOUN an impressive and difficult achievement: *It was an astonishing feat to cross the falls on a tightrope.*

Ff

feather feathers
NOUN one of the light, fluffy things covering a bird's body
feathery ADJECTIVE

feature features featuring featured
NOUN **1.** an interesting or important part or characteristic of something **2.** Someone's features are the various parts of his or her face. **3.** a special article or program dealing with a particular subject **4.** a full-length movie or other show
VERB **5.** To feature something is to emphasize it as an important part or subject.
featureless ADJECTIVE

February
NOUN February is the second month of the year. It has 28 days, except in a leap year, when it has 29 days.

feces
PLURAL NOUN the solid waste substances discharged from a person's or animal's body

fed the past tense and past participle of FEED

federal
ADJECTIVE relating to the central or national government of any country that is a federation: *a federal court*

federation federations
NOUN an organization uniting a number of groups that have joined together for a common purpose

fed up
ADJECTIVE *an informal expression* unhappy or bored

fee fees
NOUN a charge or payment for a job, service, or activity

feeble feebler feeblest
ADJECTIVE weak or lacking in power or influence: *feeble and stupid arguments*

feed feeds feeding fed
VERB **1.** To feed people or animals is to give them food. **2.** When an animal or baby feeds, it eats. **3.** To feed something is to supply what is needed for it to operate or exist: *The information was fed into a computer database.*
NOUN **4.** Feed is food for animals.

feedback
NOUN **1.** Feedback is comments and information about the quality or success of something. **2.** Feedback is also a condition in which some of the power, sound, or information produced by electronic equipment goes back into it.

feel feels feeling felt
VERB **1.** If you feel an emotion or sensation, you experience it: *I felt a bit ashamed.* **2.** If you feel that something is the case, you believe it to be so: *She feels that she is in control of her life.* **3.** If you feel something, you touch it. **4.** If something feels warm or cold, for example, you experience its warmth or coldness through the sense of touch: *Real marble feels cold to the touch.* **5.** To feel the effect of something is to be affected by it: *The shock waves of this disaster will be felt by people from all over the world.*
NOUN **6.** The feel of something is how it feels to you when you touch it: *the feel of this fabric*
PHRASE **7.** If you **feel like** doing something, you want to do it.

feeler feelers
NOUN An insect's feelers are the two thin antennae on its head with which it senses things around it.

feeling feelings
NOUN **1.** an emotion or reaction: *feelings of envy* **2.** a physical sensation: *a feeling of pain* **3.** Feeling is the ability to experience the sense of touch in your body: *He had no feeling in his hands.* **4.** Your feelings about something are your general attitudes or thoughts about it: *He has strong feelings about our national sport.*

feet the plural of FOOT

KNOWING WORDS: IDIOMS

BE WORD SHARP!

Idioms add colour to language by playing with the meanings of words

feet the bottom parts of your legs
drag your feet be very slow
get your feet wet try something new
have cold feet lose courage, often before a big event
have your feet on the ground be practical
on your feet capable, independent

NEL

Ff

feign feigns feigning feigned
VERB If you feign an emotion or state, you pretend to experience it: *to feign a headache.*

feline
ADJECTIVE relating to the cat family

fell fells felling felled
1. the past tense of FALL
VERB **2.** To fell a tree is to cut it down.

fellow fellows
NOUN **1.** *an informal use* a man: *I knew a fellow by that name.* **2.** a senior member of an academic society or a university college **3.** Your fellows are the people who share work or an activity with you.
ADJECTIVE **4.** You use *fellow* to describe people who have something in common with you: *his fellow editors*

fellowship fellowships
NOUN **1.** a feeling of friendliness that a group of people have when they are doing things together **2.** a group of people who join together because they have interests in common: *I belong to a gamers' fellowship.* **3.** an academic post at a university that involves research work

felt
1. the past tense and past participle of FEEL
NOUN **2.** Felt is a thick cloth made by pressing short threads together.

female females
NOUN **1.** a person or animal that belongs to the sex that gives birth to young or produces eggs
ADJECTIVE **2.** concerning or relating to females

feminine
ADJECTIVE **1.** relating to women or considered to be typical of women **2.** belonging to a particular class of nouns in some languages, such as French
femininity NOUN

feminism
NOUN Feminism is the belief that women should have the same rights and opportunities as men.
feminist NOUN OR ADJECTIVE

fence fences fencing fenced
NOUN **1.** a wooden or wire barrier between two areas of land **2.** a temporary barrier used to stop snow from drifting, or rocks or soil from sliding
VERB **3.** To fence an area of land is to surround it with a fence. **4.** When two people fence, they use special swords to fight each other as a sport.

fend fends fending fended
PHRASE **1.** If you have to **fend for yourself**, you have to look after yourself.

VERB **2.** If you fend off an attack or unwelcome attention, you defend and protect yourself.

ferment ferments fermenting fermented
VERB When wine, beer, or fruit ferments, a chemical change takes place in it, often producing alcohol.
fermentation NOUN

fern ferns
NOUN a plant with long, feathery leaves and no flowers

ferocious
ADJECTIVE violent and fierce: *ferocious dogs, ferocious storms*
ferociously ADVERB
ferocity NOUN

ferret ferrets
NOUN a small, fierce animal related to the weasel and kept for hunting rats and rabbits

ferry ferries ferrying ferried
NOUN **1.** a boat that carries people and vehicles across short stretches of water
VERB **2.** To ferry people or goods somewhere is to transport them there, usually on a short, regular journey.

fertile
ADJECTIVE **1.** capable of producing offspring or plants **2.** creative: *fertile minds*
fertility NOUN

fertilize fertilizes fertilizing fertilized
VERB **1.** When an egg, plant, or female is fertilized, the process of reproduction begins by sperm joining with the egg, or by pollen coming into contact with the reproductive part of a plant. **2.** To fertilize land is to put manure or chemicals onto it to feed plants.

fertilizer fertilizers
NOUN a substance put onto soil to improve plant growth

fervent
ADJECTIVE showing strong, sincere, and enthusiastic feeling: *a fervent nationalist*
fervently ADVERB

fervour
NOUN a very strong feeling for or belief in something: *a wave of political fervour*

fester festers festering festered
VERB If a wound festers it becomes infected and produces pus.

festival festivals
NOUN **1.** an organized series of events and performances, sometimes involving competitions: *the tulip festival, a drama festival* **2.** a day or period of time set aside for celebrating, often in memory of some person or event

Ff

festive
ADJECTIVE full of happiness and celebration: *a festive time of singing and dancing*

festivity festivities
NOUN celebration and happiness: *the wedding festivities*

festooned
ADJECTIVE If something is festooned with objects, the objects are hanging across it in large numbers.

fetch fetches fetching fetched
VERB **1.** If you fetch something, you go to where it is and bring it back. **2.** If something fetches a particular sum of money, it is sold for that amount: *Portraits fetch the highest prices.*

fetching
ADJECTIVE attractive in appearance: *a fetching purple dress*

fete fetes feting feted
NOUN **1.** an entertainment, party, or celebration
VERB **2.** Someone who is feted receives a public welcome or entertainment as an honour.

fetus fetuses
NOUN an unborn child or animal in the womb
fetal ADJECTIVE

feud feuds feuding feuded
NOUN **1.** a long-term and very bitter quarrel, especially between families
VERB **2.** When people feud, they take part in a feud.

feudalism
NOUN Feudalism is a social and political system that was common in the Middle Ages in Europe. Under this system, ordinary people were given land and protection by a lord, and in return they worked and fought for him.
feudal ADJECTIVE

fever fevers
NOUN **1.** Fever is a condition occurring during illness, in which the patient has a very high body temperature. **2.** A fever is extreme excitement or agitation: *spring fever, cabin fever*

feverish
ADJECTIVE **1.** in a state of extreme excitement or agitation: *increasingly feverish activity* **2.** suffering from a high body temperature
feverishly ADVERB

few fewer fewest
ADJECTIVE OR NOUN **1.** used to refer to a small number of things: *The gallery owns one of only a few paintings by that artist. I saw him a few moments ago.*
PHRASE **2. Quite a few** means quite a large number of things.

> **! HEADS UP**
> Use **fewer** when you can count things: *fewer players*. When you can't count, use **less**: *less team spirit*.

fiancé fiancés
NOUN A woman's fiancé is the man to whom she is engaged.

fiancée fiancées
NOUN A man's fiancée is the woman to whom he is engaged.

> **! HEADS UP**
> **Fiancé** and **fiancée** are spelled differently, but both can be pronounced either fee-ON-say or fee-on-SAY.

fiasco fiascos
NOUN an event or attempt that fails completely, especially in a ridiculous or disorganized way: *The game ended in a complete fiasco.*

fib fibs fibbing fibbed
NOUN **1.** a small, unimportant lie
VERB **2.** If you fib, you tell a small lie.

fibre fibres
NOUN **1.** a thin thread of a substance used to make cloth **2.** Fibre is also a part of plants that can be eaten but not digested; it helps food pass quickly through the body.
fibrous ADJECTIVE

fickle
ADJECTIVE Fickle people keep changing their mind about what they like or want.

fiction fictions
NOUN **1.** Fiction is stories about people and events that have been invented by the author. **2.** something that is not true
fictional ADJECTIVE
fictitious ADJECTIVE

fiddle fiddles fiddling fiddled
VERB **1.** If you fiddle with something, you keep moving it or touching it restlessly. **2.** *an informal use* If someone fiddles with something, that person makes minor adjustments to that thing: *I fiddled with the*

dial until the radio station came in clearly.
NOUN **3.** a violin
fiddler NOUN

fidelity

NOUN Fidelity is remaining firm in your beliefs, friendships, or loyalty to another person.

fidget fidgets fidgeting fidgeted

VERB **1.** If you fidget, you keep changing your position because of nervousness or boredom.
NOUN **2.** someone who fidgets
fidgety ADJECTIVE

field fields fielding fielded

NOUN **1.** an area of land where crops are grown or animals are kept **2.** an area of land where sports are played: *a football field* **3.** A coal field, oil field, or gold field is an area where coal, oil, or gold is found. **4.** a particular subject or area of interest: *He runs a business in the field of advertising.*
ADJECTIVE **5.** A **field trip** or a **field study** involves research or activity in the natural environment rather than theoretical or laboratory work. **6.** In an athletic competition, the **field events** are the events such as the high jump and the javelin, which do not take place on a running track.
VERB **7.** In baseball and cricket, when you field the ball, you stop it after the ball has been hit. **8.** To field questions is to answer or deal with them skilfully.

fielder fielders

NOUN In baseball and cricket, the fielders are the team members who stand at various parts of the playing area and try to prevent runs from being scored by stopping a hit ball.

field marshal field marshals

NOUN an officer of the highest rank in the armies of some countries

fieldwork

NOUN Fieldwork is the study of something in the environment where it naturally lives or occurs, rather than in a class or laboratory.

fiend fiends

NOUN **1.** a devil or evil spirit **2.** a very wicked or cruel person **3.** *an informal use* someone who is very keen on a particular thing: *a fitness fiend*

fierce fiercer fiercest

ADJECTIVE **1.** very aggressive or angry **2.** extremely strong or intense: *a sudden fierce pain, a fierce storm*
fiercely ADVERB

fiery fierier fieriest

ADJECTIVE **1.** involving fire or seeming like fire: *a huge, fiery sun* **2.** showing great anger, energy, or passion: *a fiery debate*

fifteen

NOUN the number 15
fifteenth ADJECTIVE, ADVERB

fifth fifths

ADJECTIVE **1.** The fifth item in a series is the one counted as number five.
NOUN **2.** one of five equal parts

fifty fifties

NOUN the number 50
fiftieth ADJECTIVE, ADVERB

fifty-fifty

ADVERB **1.** divided equally into two portions
ADJECTIVE **2.** just as likely not to happen as to happen: *You've got a fifty-fifty chance of being right.*

fig figs

NOUN a soft, sweet fruit full of tiny seeds. It grows in hot countries and is often eaten dried.

fight fights fighting fought

VERB **1.** When people fight, they take part in a battle, a war, a boxing match, or in some other struggle or conflict. **2.** To fight for something is to try in a very determined way to achieve it: *I must fight for respect.*
NOUN **3.** a situation in which people hit or try to hurt each other **4.** a determined attempt to prevent or achieve something: *the fight for independence* **5.** an angry disagreement

fighter fighters

NOUN someone who physically fights another person

figurative

ADJECTIVE If you use a word or expression in a figurative sense, you use it with a more abstract or imaginative meaning than its ordinary one.
figuratively ADVERB

figure figures figuring figured

NOUN **1.** a written number or the amount a number stands for **2.** a geometrical shape **3.** a diagram or table in a written text **4.** the shape of a human body, sometimes one that you cannot see properly: *A human figure leaped at him.* **5.** a person or character: *He was a major figure in the trial.*
VERB **6.** To figure in something is to appear or be included in it: *the many people who have figured in his life* **7.** *an informal use* If you figure that something is the case, you guess or conclude this: *We figure the fire broke out around four in the morning.*

Ff

figurehead figureheads
NOUN the leader of a movement or organization who has no real power

figure of speech figures of speech
NOUN A figure of speech is an expression such as a simile or idiom in which the words are not used in their literal sense.

file files filing filed
NOUN **1.** a folder in which a group of papers or records is kept; also used of the information kept in the file **2.** In computing, a file is a stored set of related data with its own name. **3.** a line of people one behind the other **4.** a long steel tool with a rough surface, used for smoothing and shaping hard materials
VERB **5.** When someone files a document, that person puts it in its correct place with similar documents. **6.** When a group of people file somewhere, they walk one behind the other in a line. **7.** If you file something, you smooth or shape it with a file.

fill fills filling filled
VERB **1.** If you fill something or if it fills up, it becomes full. **2.** If something fills a need, it satisfies the need: *A new kitten had in some small way filled the gap left by the loss of her first cat.* **3.** To fill a job vacancy is to appoint someone to do that job.
NOUN **4.** If you have had your fill of something, you do not want any more.
fill in
VERB **5.** If you fill someone in, you give that person information to bring him or her up to date.
fill out
VERB **6.** If you fill out a form, you write information in the appropriate spaces.

fillet fillets filleting filleted
NOUN **1.** a piece of fish or meat with the bones and fat removed
VERB **2.** To fillet fish or meat is to prepare it by cutting out the bones.

filling fillings
NOUN **1.** the food mixture inside a sandwich, cake, or pie **2.** a small amount of metal or plastic put into a hole in a tooth by a dentist

filly fillies
NOUN a female horse or pony under the age of four

film films filming filmed
NOUN **1.** a series of moving pictures projected onto a screen and shown at a theatre or on television; a movie **2.** a thin flexible strip of plastic used in a camera to record images when exposed to light **3.** a very thin layer of powder or liquid on a surface

VERB **4.** If you film someone, you use a camera to record his or her movements on film.

filter filters filtering filtered
NOUN **1.** a device that allows some substances, lights, or sounds to pass through it, but not others: *a filter against the harmful rays of the sun*
VERB **2.** To filter a substance is to pass it through a filter. **3.** If something filters somewhere, it gets there slowly or faintly: *Traffic filtered into the city.*
filtration NOUN

filth
NOUN **1.** Filth is disgusting dirt and muck. **2.** People often use the word *filth* to refer to very bad language or to sexual material that is thought to be crude and offensive.
filthy ADJECTIVE

fin fins
NOUN a thin, flat structure on the body of a fish, used to help guide it through the water

final finals
ADJECTIVE **1.** last in a series, or happening at the end of something **2.** A decision that is final cannot be changed or questioned.
NOUN **3.** the last and most important examination or set of examinations of a school term
PLURAL NOUN **4.** the last game or contest in a series that decides the overall winner

finale finales
NOUN the last section of a piece of music or a show

finalist finalists
NOUN a person taking part in the final of a competition

finalize finalizes finalizing finalized
VERB If you finalize something, you complete all the arrangements for it.

finally
ADVERB If something finally happens, it happens after a long wait.

finance finances financing financed
VERB **1.** To finance a project or a large purchase is to provide the money for it.
NOUN **2.** Finance is the management of money, loans, and investments.
PLURAL NOUN **3.** Finances are the money or loans used to pay for something.

financial
ADJECTIVE relating to or involving money
financially ADVERB

financier financiers
NOUN a person who deals with the finances of large businesses

! HEADS UP The word **finale** is pronounced fuh-NAL-ee.

Ff

finch finches
NOUN a small bird with a short, strong beak

find finds finding found
VERB **1.** If you find someone or something, you discover that person or thing, either as a result of searching or by chance. **2.** If you find that something is the case, you become aware of it or realize it: *I found my fists were clenched.* **3.** Something that is found in a particular place typically lives or exists there: *The polar bear is found only in arctic regions.* **4.** When a court or jury finds a person guilty or not guilty, the court or jury decides that the person is guilty or innocent: *He was found guilty and sentenced to life imprisonment.*
NOUN **5.** If you describe something as a find, you mean that you have recently discovered it and it is valuable and useful.
finder NOUN

find out
VERB **6.** If you find out something, you learn or discover something that you did not know. **7.** If you find someone out, you discover that that person has been doing something he or she should not have been doing.

findings
PLURAL NOUN Someone's findings are the conclusions that person reaches as a result of investigation.

fine finer finest; fines fining fined
ADJECTIVE **1.** very good or very beautiful: *a fine school, fine clothes* **2.** satisfactory or suitable: *This coat is perfectly fine for cold weather.* **3.** very narrow or thin **4.** A fine detail, adjustment, or distinction is very delicate, exact, or subtle: *There is a very fine line between fibbing and lying.* **5.** When the weather is fine, it is not raining and is bright or sunny.
NOUN **6.** a sum of money paid as a punishment
VERB **7.** Someone who is fined has to pay a sum of money as a punishment.

finery
NOUN Finery is very beautiful clothing and jewellery.

finesse
NOUN If you do something with finesse, you do it with skill and subtlety.

finger fingers fingering fingered
NOUN **1.** Your fingers are the four long, jointed parts of your hands, sometimes including the thumbs.
VERB **2.** If you finger something you feel it with your fingers.

fingernail fingernails
NOUN Your fingernails are the hard coverings at the ends of your fingers.

fingerprint fingerprints
NOUN a mark made showing the pattern on the skin at the tip of a person's finger

finish finishes finishing finished
VERB **1.** When you finish something, you reach the end of it and complete it. **2.** When something finishes, it ends or stops.
NOUN **3.** The finish of something is the end or last part of it. **4.** The finish that something has is the texture or appearance of its surface: *a healthy, glossy finish*

finite
ADJECTIVE having a particular size or limit that cannot be increased: *There's only a finite amount of money to spend.*

fir firs
NOUN a tall, pointed evergreen tree that has thin, needlelike leaves and produces cones

fire fires firing fired
NOUN **1.** Fire is the flame produced when something burns. **2.** a pile or mass of burning material **3.** the shooting of weapons: *enemy fire*
VERB **4.** If you fire a weapon or fire a bullet, you operate the weapon so that the bullet or missile is released. **5.** If you fire questions at someone, you ask that person a lot of questions very quickly. **6.** *an informal use* If an employer fires someone, he or she dismisses that person from a job.
PHRASE **7.** If someone **opens fire**, that person starts shooting.

firearm firearms
NOUN a gun

fire department fire departments
NOUN the organization that has the job of putting out fires

fire engine fire engines
NOUN a large vehicle that carries equipment for putting out fires

fire escape fire escapes
NOUN an emergency exit or staircase for use if there is a fire

fire extinguisher fire extinguishers
NOUN a metal cylinder containing water or foam for spraying onto a fire

firefighter firefighters
NOUN a person whose job is to put out fires and rescue trapped people

firefly fireflies
NOUN an insect that glows in the dark

Ff

fire hall fire halls
NOUN A fire hall is a building where fire engines are kept and where firefighters wait to be called out.

fireplace fireplaces
NOUN the opening beneath a chimney where a fire can be lit

fireproof
ADJECTIVE resistant to fire

fire station
NOUN a fire hall

firework fireworks
NOUN a small container of gunpowder and other chemicals that explodes and produces coloured sparks or smoke when lit

firing squad firing squads
NOUN a group of soldiers ordered to shoot a person condemned to death

firm firmer firmest; firms
ADJECTIVE **1.** Something that is firm does not move easily when pressed or pushed, or when weight is put on it. **2.** A firm grasp or push is one with controlled force or pressure. **3.** A firm decision is definite. **4.** If you are firm, you behave with authority that shows you will not change your mind.
NOUN **5.** a business selling or producing something
firmly ADVERB
firmness NOUN

first
ADJECTIVE **1.** done or in existence before anything else **2.** more important than anything else: *Her experiment won first prize.*
ADVERB **3.** done or occurring before anything else
NOUN **4.** a person or thing that is first: *I was the first to arrive at school.*
firstly ADVERB

first aid
NOUN First aid is medical treatment given to an ill or injured person.

first class
ADJECTIVE **1.** Something that is first class is of the highest quality or standard. **2.** First-class accommodation on a train, airplane, or ship is the best and most expensive type of accommodation.

first-hand
ADJECTIVE First-hand knowledge or experience is gained directly rather than from books or other people.

First Nation First Nations
NOUN **1.** in Canada, a group of Aboriginal people that make up a community sharing the same culture and heritage

ADJECTIVE **2.** *First Nations* is used when describing things that have to do with any of these groups: *a First Nations school*

First Peoples
PLURAL NOUN the Aboriginal peoples living in Canada, including the First Nations, Inuit, and Métis

> **⚠ HEADS UP**
>
> **First Peoples** and **Aboriginal** are general terms. Use specific names like *Cree*, *Inuit*, or *Métis*, if possible.

first-rate
ADJECTIVE excellent

fiscal
ADJECTIVE involving money

fish fish *or* fishes fishing fished
NOUN **1.** a cold-blooded creature living in water. A fish has a spine, gills, fins, and a scaly skin **2.** Fish is the flesh of fish eaten as food.
VERB **3.** To fish is to try to catch fish for food or sport. **4.** If you fish for information, you try to get it in an indirect way.
fishing NOUN
fisherman NOUN

fishery fisheries
NOUN the business or industry of catching fish

fishy fishier fishiest
ADJECTIVE **1.** smelling or tasting of fish **2.** *an informal use* suspicious or doubtful: *He spotted something fishy going on.*

fission
NOUN **1.** Fission is the splitting of something into parts. **2.** Fission is the splitting that occurs when the nucleus of an atom absorbs a neutron. Fission releases an enormous amount of energy.

fissure fissures
NOUN a deep crack in rock

fist fists
NOUN a hand with the fingers curled tightly toward the palm

fit fits fitting fitted; fitter fittest
VERB **1.** Something that fits is the right shape or size for a particular person or position. **2.** If you fit something somewhere, you put it there carefully or securely: *Very carefully, he fitted the files inside the compartment.* **3.** If something fits a particular situation, person, or thing, it is suitable or appropriate: *a punishment that fitted the crime*
NOUN **4.** The fit of something is how it fits: *This coat is a good fit.* **5.** If someone has

⚠ HEADS UP The plural of **fish** is usually **fish**, but **fishes** is used to refer to different kinds of fish.

NEL

Ff

a fit, that person's muscles suddenly start contracting violently and he or she may lose consciousness. **6.** A fit of laughter, coughing, anger, or panic is a sudden, uncontrolled outburst.
ADJECTIVE **7.** good enough or suitable: *This housing is not fit for habitation.* **8.** Someone who is fit is healthy and has strong muscles as a result of regular exercise.
fitness NOUN

fitful
ADJECTIVE happening at irregular intervals and not continuous: *a fitful sleep*
fitfully ADVERB

fitter fitters
NOUN a person who assembles or installs machinery

fitting fittings
ADJECTIVE **1.** right or suitable: *a fitting reward for his efforts*
NOUN **2.** If you have a fitting, you try on a garment that is being made to see if it fits properly.
PLURAL NOUN **3.** fittings are the small parts that are fixed to a piece of equipment or furniture

five fives
NOUN the number 5

fix fixes fixing fixed
VERB **1.** If you fix something broken, you mend it. **2.** If you fix something somewhere, you attach it or put it there securely. **3.** If you fix your attention on something, you concentrate on it. **4.** If you fix something, you make arrangements for it: *The party is fixed for September 24.* **5.** To fix something is to arrange the outcome unfairly or dishonestly.
NOUN **6.** *an informal use* If you are in a fix, you are in a difficult situation.
fixed ADJECTIVE
fixedly ADVERB

fixation fixations
NOUN an extreme and obsessive interest in something

fixture fixtures
NOUN a piece of furniture or equipment that is fixed into position in a house

fizz fizzes fizzing fizzed
VERB Something that fizzes makes a hissing sound.

fizzle fizzles fizzling fizzled
VERB Something that fizzles makes a weak hissing or spitting sound.

fizzy fizzier fizziest
ADJECTIVE Fizzy drinks have carbon dioxide in them to make them bubbly.

fjord fjords
NOUN a long, narrow inlet of the sea between very high cliffs, especially in Norway

flab
NOUN Flab is large amounts of surplus fat on someone's body.

flabbergasted
ADJECTIVE extremely surprised

flabby flabbier flabbiest
ADJECTIVE Someone who is flabby is fat and unfit, with loose flesh on his or her body.

flag flags flagging flagged
NOUN **1.** a rectangular or square cloth that has a particular colour and design, and is used as the symbol of a nation or as a signal
VERB **2.** If you or your spirits flag, you start to lose energy or enthusiasm.

flagrant
ADJECTIVE very shocking and bad in an obvious way: *a flagrant defiance of the rules*

flagship flagships
NOUN **1.** a ship carrying the commander of the fleet **2.** the most outstanding product or asset of an organization

flail flails flailing flailed
VERB If someone's arms or legs flail about, they move in a wild, uncontrolled way.

flair
NOUN Flair is a natural ability to do something well or stylishly.

flak
NOUN **1.** Flak is gunfire from the ground against airplanes. **2.** If you get flak for doing something, you get a lot of severe criticism.

flake flakes flaking flaked
NOUN **1.** a small, thin piece of something
VERB **2.** When something such as paint flakes, small, thin pieces of it come off.
flaky ADJECTIVE
flaked ADJECTIVE

flamboyant
ADJECTIVE behaving in a very showy and confident way
flamboyance NOUN

flame flames
NOUN **1.** a flickering tongue or blaze of fire **2.** A flame of passion, desire, or anger is a sudden strong feeling.

flamenco
NOUN Flamenco is a type of very lively, fast Spanish dancing, accompanied by guitar music.

flamingo flamingos
NOUN a wading bird with pink feathers, long legs, and a long neck

 **HEADS UP** The word **fjord** is pronounced FYOURD.

NEL

213

Ff

flammable
ADJECTIVE easy to set on fire

flan flans
NOUN an open pie with a custard or fruit filling

flank flanks flanking flanked
NOUN **1.** the side of an animal between the ribs and the hip
VERB **2.** If you are flanked by a particular thing or person, you have that thing or person at your side: *The actor was flanked by four bodyguards.*

flannel flannels
NOUN Flannel is a lightweight, woollen fabric.

flap flaps flapping flapped
VERB **1.** Something that flaps moves up and down or from side to side with a snapping sound.
NOUN **2.** a loose piece of something, such as paper or skin, that is attached at one edge

flare flares flaring flared
NOUN **1.** a device that produces a brightly coloured flame, used especially as an emergency signal
VERB **2.** If a fire flares or flares up, it suddenly burns much more vigorously. **3.** If violence or a conflict flares or flares up, it suddenly starts or becomes more serious.

flash flashes flashing flashed
NOUN **1.** a sudden, short burst of light
VERB **2.** If a light flashes, it shines for a very short period, often repeatedly. **3.** Something that flashes past moves or happens so fast that you almost miss it. **4.** If you flash something, you show it briefly: *The reclusive singer flashed his face at the crowd.*
PHRASE **5.** Something that happens **in a flash** happens suddenly and lasts a very short time.

flashback flashbacks
NOUN a scene in a movie, play, or story that returns to events in the past

flashlight flashlights
NOUN a portable electric light operated by batteries

flashy flashier flashiest
ADJECTIVE expensive and fashionable in appearance, in a vulgar or showy way: *flashy clothes*

flat flats flatter flattest
NOUN **1.** In music, a flat is a note or key a semitone lower than that described by the same letter. It is represented by the symbol (♭).
ADJECTIVE **2.** Something that is flat is level and smooth. **3.** A flat object is not very tall or deep: *a low, flat building* **4.** A flat tire or ball does not have enough air in it. **5.** A flat refusal or denial is complete and firm. **6.** Something that is flat is without emotion or interest. **7.** A flat rate or price is fixed and the same for everyone: *The company charges a flat fee for its advice.* **8.** A musical instrument or note that is flat is slightly too low in pitch.
ADVERB **9.** Something that is done in a particular time flat, takes exactly that time: *They found them in two minutes flat.*
flatly ADVERB
flatness NOUN

flatfish
NOUN a sea fish with a wide, flat body, such as a plaice or sole

flatten flattens flattening flattened
VERB If you flatten something or if it flattens, it becomes flat or flatter.

flatter flatters flattering flattered
VERB **1.** If you flatter someone, you praise him or her in an exaggerated way, either to please that person or to persuade him or her to do something. **2.** If you are flattered by something, it makes you feel pleased and important: *He was very flattered by the applause.* **3.** If you flatter yourself that something is the case, you believe, perhaps mistakenly, something good about yourself or your abilities. **4.** Something that flatters you makes you appear more attractive.
flattering ADJECTIVE

flattery
NOUN Flattery is flattering words or behaviour.

flatulence
NOUN Flatulence is the uncomfortable state of having too much gas in your stomach or intestine.

flaunt flaunts flaunting flaunted
VERB If you flaunt your possessions or talents, you display them too obviously or proudly.

flautist another spelling of FLUTIST

flavour flavours flavouring flavoured
NOUN **1.** The flavour of food is its taste.
2. The flavour of something is its distinctive characteristic or quality.
VERB **3.** If you flavour food with a spice or herb, you add it to the food to give it a particular taste.
flavouring NOUN

flaw flaws
NOUN **1.** a fault or mark, for example in a piece of fabric or glass **2.** a weak point or undesirable quality in a theory, plan, or person's character
flawed ADJECTIVE
flawless ADJECTIVE

FLASHBACK

a scene in a movie, play, or story that returns to events in the past

"It all started three days ago…"

Here is an example of a flashback. A flashback tells the reader about an event that happened earlier in the story.

RAMON PEREZ

Ff

flax
NOUN a plant with small, narrow leaves and blue or yellow flowers, which is used for making linseed oil and linen

flay flays flaying flayed
VERB **1.** To flay someone or something is to strip the skin off that person or thing by whipping. **2.** To flay someone is to criticize that person severely.

flea fleas
NOUN a small, wingless, jumping insect that feeds on blood

fleck flecks
NOUN a small, coloured mark or particle
flecked ADJECTIVE

fled the past tense and past participle of FLEE

fledgling fledglings
NOUN **1.** a young bird that is learning to fly
ADJECTIVE **2.** Fledgling means new, or young and inexperienced: *the fledgling Minister of the Environment*

flee flees fleeing fled
VERB To flee from someone or something is to run away from that person or thing.

fleece fleeces fleecing fleeced
NOUN **1.** A sheep's fleece is its coat of wool.
VERB **2.** To fleece someone is to cheat that person out of money or belongings.

fleet fleets
NOUN **1.** a group of ships travelling together under one command **2.** a group of motor vehicles or aircraft owned by the same organization

fleeting
ADJECTIVE lasting for a very short time

flesh
NOUN **1.** Flesh is the soft part of the body. **2.** The flesh of a fruit or vegetable is the soft inner part that you eat.
fleshy ADJECTIVE

flew the past tense of FLY

flex flexes flexing flexed
VERB If you flex your muscles, you bend and stretch them.

flexible
ADJECTIVE **1.** able to be bent easily without breaking **2.** able to adapt to changing circumstances
flexibility NOUN

flick flicks flicking flicked
VERB **1.** If you flick something, you move it sharply with your finger. **2.** If something flicks somewhere, it moves with a short, sudden movement: *The frog flicked its tongue and caught a fly.*

NOUN **3.** a sudden, quick movement, or a sharp touch with the finger: *a sideways flick of the head*

flicker flickers flickering flickered
VERB **1.** If a light or a flame flickers, it shines and moves unsteadily.
NOUN **2.** a short, unsteady light or movement of light: *the flicker of candlelight* **3.** A flicker of a feeling is a very brief experience of it: *a flicker of interest*

flight flights
NOUN **1.** a journey made by airplane **2.** Flight is the action of flying or the ability to fly. **3.** Flight is also the act of running away. **4.** A flight of stairs or steps is a set between landings or storeys.

flight attendant flight attendants
NOUN a person who looks after passengers on an aircraft

flightless
ADJECTIVE Flightless birds, such as penguins and ostriches, are birds that cannot fly.

flimsy flimsier flimsiest
ADJECTIVE **1.** made of something very thin or weak and not providing much protection **2.** not very convincing: *flimsy evidence*

flinch flinches flinching flinched
VERB If you flinch, you make a sudden, small movement in fear or pain.

fling flings flinging flung
VERB **1.** If you fling something, you throw it with a lot of force.
NOUN **2.** a short period devoted to pleasure and free from any restrictions or rules

flint flints
NOUN Flint is a hard, greyish black form of quartz. It produces a spark when struck with steel.

flip flips flipping flipped
VERB If you flip something, you turn or move it quickly and sharply: *He flipped over the first page.*

flippant
ADJECTIVE showing an inappropriate lack of seriousness: *a flippant attitude to money*
flippancy NOUN

flipper flippers
NOUN **1.** one of the broad, flat limbs of sea animals, for example seals or penguins, used for swimming **2.** Flippers are broad, flat pieces of rubber that you can attach to your feet to help you swim.

flirt flirts flirting flirted
VERB **1.** If you flirt with someone, you behave as if you are sexually attracted to that person but without serious intentions. **2.** If you

Ff

flirt with an idea, you consider it without seriously intending to do anything about it.
NOUN **3.** someone who often flirts with people
flirtation NOUN
flirtatious ADJECTIVE

flit flits flitting flitted
VERB To flit somewhere is to fly or move there with quick, light movements.

float floats floating floated
VERB **1.** Something that floats is supported by water. **2.** Something that floats through the air moves along gently, supported by the air.
NOUN **3.** a light object that floats and either supports something or someone or regulates the level of liquid in a tank

flock flocks flocking flocked
NOUN **1.** a group of birds, sheep, or goats
VERB **2.** If people flock somewhere, they go there in large numbers.

flog flogs flogging flogged
VERB **1.** an informal use If you flog something, you sell it. **2.** To flog someone is to beat that person with a whip or stick.
flogging NOUN

flood floods flooding flooded
NOUN **1.** a large amount of water covering an area that is usually dry **2.** A flood of something is a large amount of it suddenly occurring: a flood of words
VERB **3.** If liquid floods an area, or if a river floods, the water or liquid overflows, covering the surrounding area. **4.** If people or things flood into a place, they come there in large numbers: Fans flooded into the arena to watch the last game of the season.

floodgates
PHRASE To **open the floodgates** is suddenly to give a lot of people the opportunity to do something they could not do before.

floodlight floodlights
NOUN a very powerful outdoor lamp used to light up areas such as public buildings and sports grounds
floodlit ADJECTIVE

floor floors flooring floored
NOUN **1.** the part of a room you walk on **2.** one of the levels in a building: the top floor of an apartment **3.** the ground at the bottom of a valley, forest, or the sea
VERB **4.** If a remark or question floors you, you are completely unable to deal with it or answer it.

floorboard floorboards
NOUN one of the long planks of wood from which a floor is made

flop flops flopping flopped
VERB **1.** If someone or something flops, that person or thing falls loosely and heavily. **2.** an informal use Something that flops fails.
NOUN **3.** an informal use something that is completely unsuccessful

floppy floppier floppiest
ADJECTIVE tending to hang downward in a rather loose way: a floppy, oversize jacket

floral
ADJECTIVE patterned with flowers or made from flowers: floral, cotton dresses

florid
ADJECTIVE **1.** highly elaborate and extravagant: florid language **2.** having a red face

florist florists
NOUN a person or store selling flowers

floss
NOUN Dental floss is soft, silky threads or fibre that you use to clean between your teeth.

flotation flotations
NOUN Flotation is the act of floating.

flotilla flotillas
NOUN a small fleet or a group of small ships

flotsam
NOUN Flotsam is garbage or wreckage floating at sea or washed up on the shore.

flounce flounces flouncing flounced
VERB **1.** If you flounce somewhere, you walk there with exaggerated movements suggesting that you are feeling angry or impatient about something: She flounced out of the classroom.
NOUN **2.** a big frill around the bottom of a dress or skirt

flounder flounders floundering floundered
VERB **1.** To flounder is to struggle to move or stay upright, for example in water or mud. **2.** If you flounder in a conversation or situation, you find it difficult to decide what to say or do.
NOUN **3.** a type of edible flatfish

flour
NOUN Flour is a powder made from finely ground grain, usually wheat, and used for baking and cooking.
floured ADJECTIVE
floury ADJECTIVE

flourish flourishes flourishing flourished
VERB **1.** Something that flourishes develops or functions successfully or healthily. **2.** If you flourish something, you wave or display it so that people notice it.
NOUN **3.** a bold sweeping or waving movement

Ff

flout flouts flouting flouted
VERB If you flout a convention or law, you deliberately disobey it.

flow flows flowing flowed
VERB **1.** If something flows, it moves or happens in a steady, continuous stream. NOUN **2.** A flow of something is a steady, continuous movement of it; also the rate at which it flows: *a steady flow of complaints, the flow of the river*

flow chart flow charts
NOUN a diagram showing the sequence of steps that lead to various results

flower flowers flowering flowered
NOUN **1.** the part of a plant containing the reproductive organs from which the fruit or seeds develop
VERB **2.** When a plant flowers, it produces flowers.

flowery
ADJECTIVE Flowery language is full of elaborate expressions.

flown the past participle of FLY

flu
NOUN Flu is an illness similar to a very bad cold, which causes headaches, sore throat, weakness, and aching muscles. Flu is short for influenza.

fluctuate fluctuates fluctuating fluctuated
VERB Something that fluctuates is irregular and changeable: *fluctuating between feeling well and not so well*

flue flues
NOUN a pipe that takes fumes and smoke away from a fireplace, stove, or boiler

fluent
ADJECTIVE **1.** able to speak a foreign language correctly and without hesitation **2.** able to express yourself clearly and without hesitation
fluently ADVERB

fluff fluffs fluffing fluffed
NOUN **1.** Fluff is soft, light, woolly threads or fibres bunched together.
VERB **2.** If you fluff something up or out, you brush or shake it to make it seem larger and lighter: *Fluff the rice up with a fork before serving.*
fluffy ADJECTIVE

fluid fluids
NOUN **1.** a liquid
ADJECTIVE **2.** Fluid movement is smooth and flowing. **3.** A fluid arrangement or plan is flexible and without a fixed structure.
fluidity NOUN

fluke flukes
NOUN an accidental success or piece of good luck

flung the past tense of FLING

fluorescent
ADJECTIVE **1.** having a very bright appearance when light is shone on it, as if it is shining itself: *fluorescent yellow dye* **2.** A fluorescent light is in the form of a tube and shines with a hard, bright light.

fluoride
NOUN Fluoride is a mixture of chemicals that is meant to prevent tooth decay.

flurry flurries
NOUN a short rush of activity or movement

flush flushes flushing flushed
NOUN **1.** A flush is a rosy red colour: *The flowers are cream with a pink flush.* **2.** In cards, a flush is a hand all of one suit.
VERB **3.** If you flush, your face goes red. **4.** If you flush a toilet or something such as a pipe, you force water through it to clean it.
ADJECTIVE **5.** Something that is flush with a surface is level with it or flat against it.

flustered
ADJECTIVE If you are flustered, you feel confused, nervous, and rushed.

flute flutes
NOUN a musical wind instrument consisting of a long, metal tube with holes and keys. It is held sideways to the mouth and played by blowing across a hole in its side.

fluted
ADJECTIVE decorated with long grooves

flutist flutists
NOUN someone who plays the flute

flutter flutters fluttering fluttered
VERB **1.** If something flutters, it flaps or waves with small, quick movements.
NOUN **2.** If you are in a flutter, you are excited and nervous.

flux
NOUN Flux is a state of constant change: *stability in a world of flux*

fly flies flying flew flown
NOUN **1.** an insect with two pairs of wings **2.** The front opening on a pair of trousers is the fly. **3.** The fly of a tent is either a flap at the entrance or an outer layer providing protection from rain.
VERB **4.** When a bird, insect, or aircraft flies, it moves through the air. **5.** If someone or something flies, that person or thing moves or goes very quickly. **6.** If you fly at someone or let fly at that person, you attack or criticize him or her suddenly

and aggressively.
flying ADJECTIVE OR NOUN
flyer NOUN

fly-fishing
NOUN Fly-fishing is a method of fishing using imitation flies as bait.

flying fox flying foxes
NOUN a large bat that eats fruit, found in Australia, Africa, and Asia

flying saucer flying saucers
NOUN a large, disc-shaped spacecraft that some people claim to have seen

foal foals foaling foaled
NOUN **1.** a young horse
VERB **2.** When a female horse foals, she gives birth.

foam foams foaming foamed
NOUN **1.** Foam is a mass of tiny bubbles.
2. Foam is light, spongy material used, for example, in furniture or packaging.
VERB **3.** When something foams, it forms a mass of small bubbles.

fob off fobs off fobbing off fobbed off
VERB an informal use If you fob someone off, you provide that person with something that is not very good or not adequate.

focus focuses focusing focused; focuses
VERB **1.** If you focus an instrument or your eyes on an object, you adjust it or them so that the image is clear.
NOUN **2.** The focus of something is its centre of attention: The focus of the conversation had moved around during the meal.
focal ADJECTIVE

fodder
NOUN Fodder is food for farm animals or horses.

foe foes
NOUN an enemy

fog fogs fogging fogged
NOUN **1.** Fog is a thick mist of water droplets suspended in the air.
VERB **2.** If glass fogs up, it becomes clouded with steam or condensation.
foggy ADJECTIVE

foil foils foiling foiled
VERB **1.** If you foil someone's attempt at something, you prevent that person from succeeding.
NOUN **2.** Foil is thin, paper-like sheets of metal used to wrap food. **3.** Something that is a good foil for something else contrasts with it and makes its good qualities more noticeable. **4.** a thin, light sword with a button on the tip, used in fencing

foist foists foisting foisted
VERB If you foist something on someone, you force or impose it on that person or thing.

fold folds folding folded
VERB **1.** If you fold something, you bend it so that one part lies over another. **2.** an informal use If a business folds, it fails and closes down. **3.** In cooking, if you fold one ingredient into another, you mix it in gently.
NOUN **4.** a crease or bend in paper or cloth **5.** a small enclosed area for sheep

folder folders
NOUN **1.** a thin piece of folded cardboard for keeping loose papers together **2.** In computing, a folder is a named area of a computer disk where you can group together files and subdirectories.

foliage
NOUN Foliage is leaves and plants.

folk folks
NOUN **1.** Folk or folks are people.
ADJECTIVE **2.** Folk music, dance, or art is traditional or representative of the ordinary people of an area.

folklore
NOUN Folklore is the traditional stories and beliefs of a community.

follicle follicles
NOUN a small sac or cavity in the body: hair follicles

follow follows following followed
VERB **1.** If you follow someone, you move along behind that person. If you follow a path or a sign, you move along in that direction. **2.** Something that follows a particular thing happens after it.
3. Something that follows is true or logical as a result of something else being the case: Just because her mother is a good athlete, it doesn't follow that she will also be athletic.
4. If you follow instructions or advice, you do what you are told. **5.** If you follow an explanation or the plot of a story, you understand each stage of it.

follower followers
NOUN The followers of a person or belief are the people who support that person or belief.

folly follies
NOUN Folly is a foolish act or foolish behaviour.

fond fonder fondest
ADJECTIVE If you are fond of someone or something, you like that person or thing.
fondly ADVERB
fondness NOUN

fondle fondles fondling fondled
VERB To fondle something is to stroke it affectionately.

font fonts
NOUN In printing and computers, a font is a complete set of type or characters of one size and style.

food foods
NOUN Food is any substance consumed by an animal or plant to provide energy.

food chain food chains
NOUN a series of living things that are linked because each one feeds on the next one in the series. For example, a plant may be eaten by a rabbit, which may be eaten by a fox.

foodstuff foodstuffs
NOUN anything used for food

fool fools fooling fooled
NOUN **1.** someone who behaves in a silly or stupid way
VERB **2.** If you fool someone, you deceive or trick that person.

foolhardy
ADJECTIVE foolish and involving too great a risk

foolish
ADJECTIVE very silly or unwise

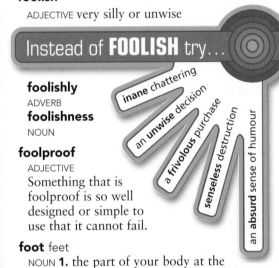

Instead of **FOOLISH** try...

foolishly
ADVERB
foolishness
NOUN

inane chattering
an unwise decision
a frivolous purchase
senseless destruction
an absurd sense of humour

foolproof
ADJECTIVE
Something that is foolproof is so well designed or simple to use that it cannot fail.

foot feet
NOUN **1.** the part of your body at the end of your leg **2.** the bottom, base, or lower end of something: *the foot of the mountain, the foot of a page* **3.** a nonmetric unit of length equal to about 30.5 centimetres **4.** In poetry, a foot is the basic unit of rhythm containing two or three syllables.

footage
NOUN Footage is a length of film: *My father sent his footage of the tornado to the local television station.*

football footballs
NOUN **1.** In North America, football is a game in which an inflated oval ball can be kicked, passed, or carried toward a goal. In the United Kingdom and many other countries, football is soccer. **2.** a ball used in either of these games

footing
NOUN **1.** Footing is a secure grip by or for your feet: *He missed his footing and fell flat.* **2.** a footing is the basis or nature of a relationship or situation: *Steps to put the nation on friendly footing.*

footstep footsteps
NOUN the sound or mark made by someone walking

for
PREPOSITION **1.** meant to be given to or used by a particular person, or done in order to help or benefit that person: *The private beaches are for their exclusive use. I can edit this essay for you.* **2.** *For* is used when explaining the reason, cause, or purpose of something: *This is my excuse for being late for class.* **3.** You use *for* to express a quantity, time, or distance: *Ours was the only house for many kilometres. I can read for hours at a time.* **4.** If you are for something, you support it or approve of it: *votes for or against independence*

forage forages foraging foraged
VERB When a person or animal forages, that person or animal searches for food.

KNOWING WORDS: WORD BUILDING

BE WORD SHARP!

To build a compound word, put two or more base words together.

foot the bottom part (of a leg)
foothill a hill at the bottom of a mountain
foothold a place from which to climb
footnote a note at the bottom of a page
footpath a path for people to walk on
footprint a mark left by a foot

Ff

foray forays
NOUN **1.** a brief attempt to do or get something: *her first foray into acting* **2.** an attack or raid by soldiers

forbid forbids forbidding forbade forbidden
VERB If you forbid someone to do something, you order that person not to do it.
forbidden ADJECTIVE

force forces forcing forced
VERB **1.** To force someone to do something is to make that person do it. **2.** To force something is to use violence or great strength to move or open it.
NOUN **3.** a pressure to do something, sometimes with violence or great strength **4.** The force of something is its strength or power: *The force of the explosion shook buildings.* **5.** a person or thing that has a lot of influence or effect: *She became the dominant force in tennis.* **6.** an organized group of people working or acting together: *a police force* **7.** In physics, force is a pushing or pulling influence that changes a body from a state of rest to one of motion, or changes its rate of motion.
PHRASE **8.** A law or rule that is **in force** is currently valid and must be obeyed.

forceful
ADJECTIVE powerful and convincing: *a forceful, highly political lawyer*
forcefully ADVERB

forceps
PLURAL NOUN Forceps are a pair of tongs or pincers used by a doctor or surgeon.

forcible
ADJECTIVE **1.** involving physical force or violence **2.** convincing and making a strong impression: *a forcible reminder*
forcibly ADVERB

ford fords fording forded
NOUN **1.** a shallow place in a river where it is possible to cross on foot or in a vehicle
VERB **2.** To ford a river is to cross it.

forearm forearms
NOUN the part of your arm between your elbow and your wrist

forebear forebears
NOUN Your forebears are your ancestors.

foreboding forebodings
NOUN a strong feeling of approaching disaster

forecast forecasts forecasting forecast
NOUN **1.** a prediction of what will happen, especially a statement about what the weather will be like
VERB **2.** To forecast an event is to predict what will happen.

forefather forefathers
NOUN Your forefathers are your ancestors.

forefinger forefingers
NOUN the finger next to your thumb

forefront
NOUN The forefront of something is the most important and progressive part of it.

forego another spelling of FORGO

foregoing
A FORMAL PHRASE You can say **the foregoing** when talking about something that has just been said: *The foregoing discussion has highlighted the difficulties.*

foregone conclusion foregone conclusions
NOUN A foregone conclusion is a result or conclusion that is bound to happen.

foreground
NOUN In a picture, the foreground is the part that seems nearest to you.

forehand forehands
NOUN OR ADJECTIVE a stroke in tennis, squash, or badminton made with the palm of your hand facing in the direction that you hit the ball

forehead foreheads
NOUN the area at the front of your head, above your eyebrows and below your hairline

foreign
ADJECTIVE **1.** belonging to or involving countries other than your own: *foreign coins, foreign travel* **2.** unfamiliar or uncharacteristic: *Such enthusiasm was foreign to him.* **3.** A foreign object has got into something, usually by accident, and should not be there: *a foreign object in my eye*
foreigner NOUN

foreman foremen
NOUN **1.** a person in charge of a group of workers, for example on a building site **2.** The foreman of a jury is the spokesperson.

foremost
ADJECTIVE The foremost of a group of things is the most important or the best.

forensic
ADJECTIVE relating to or involving the scientific examination of objects involved in a crime

forerunner forerunners
NOUN The forerunner of something is the person who first introduced or achieved it, or the first example of it.

foresee foresees foreseeing foresaw foreseen
VERB If you foresee something, you predict or expect that it will happen.
foreseeable ADJECTIVE

foreshadowing foreshadowings
NOUN a hint or symbol of future events: *Dark clouds gathered, like a foreshadowing of the end of peace in the kingdom.*
foreshadow VERB

foresight
NOUN Foresight is the ability to know what is likely to happen ahead of time.

foreskin foreskins
NOUN A man's foreskin is the fold of skin covering the end of his penis.

forest forests
NOUN a large area of trees growing close together

forestry
NOUN Forestry is the study and work of growing and maintaining forests.

foretaste foretastes
NOUN a slight taste or experience of something in advance

foretell foretells foretelling foretold
VERB If you foretell something, you predict that it will happen.

forever
ADVERB permanently or continually

forewarn forewarns forewarning forewarned
VERB If you forewarn someone, you warn that person in advance about something.

foreword forewords
NOUN an introduction in a book

forfeit forfeits forfeiting forfeited
VERB **1.** If you forfeit something, you have to give it up as a penalty.
NOUN **2.** something that you have to give up or do as a penalty

forge forges forging forged
NOUN **1.** a place where a blacksmith works making metal goods by hand
VERB **2.** To forge metal is to hammer and bend it into shape while hot. **3.** To forge a relationship is to create a strong and lasting relationship. **4.** Someone who forges money, documents, or paintings makes illegal copies of them. **5.** To forge ahead is to progress quickly.

forgery forgeries
NOUN Forgery is the crime of forging money, documents, or paintings; also something that has been forged.
forger NOUN

forget forgets forgetting forgot forgotten
VERB **1.** If you forget something, you fail to remember or think about it. **2.** If you forget yourself, you behave in an unacceptable, uncontrolled way.
forgetful ADJECTIVE

forget-me-not forget-me-nots
NOUN a small plant with tiny blue flowers

forgive forgives forgiving forgave forgiven
VERB If you forgive someone for doing something bad, you stop feeling angry and resentful toward that person.
forgiving ADJECTIVE

forgiveness
NOUN the act of forgiving

forgo forgoes forgoing forwent forgone
VERB If you forgo something pleasant, you give it up or do not insist on having it.

fork forks forking forked
NOUN **1.** a pronged instrument used for eating food **2.** a tool with three or four prongs: *a garden fork, a tuning fork* **3.** a y-shaped junction or division in a road or river
VERB **4.** To fork something is to move or turn it with a fork.
fork out
VERB **5.** *an informal use* If you fork out for something, you pay for it, often unwillingly.

forlorn
ADJECTIVE **1.** lonely, unhappy, and pitiful **2.** desperate and without any expectation of success: *a forlorn attempt at friendship*
forlornly ADVERB

form forms forming formed
NOUN **1.** A particular form of something is a type or kind of it: *Water in the form of snow is still water.* **2.** The form of something is the shape or pattern of something: *a brooch in the form of a bright green lizard* **3.** a sheet of paper with questions and spaces for you to fill in the answers
VERB **4.** The things that form something are the things it consists of: *events that were to form the basis of her novel* **5.** When someone forms something or when it forms, it is created, organized, or started.

formal
ADJECTIVE **1.** correct, serious, and conforming to accepted conventions: *a very formal letter of apology* **2.** official and publicly recognized: *a formal agreement*
formally ADVERB

formaldehyde
NOUN a poisonous, strong-smelling gas, used for preserving specimens in biology.

formality formalities
NOUN an action or process that is carried out as part of an official procedure

format formats
NOUN the way in which something is arranged or presented

NEL

THE WRITER'S EDGE

FORESHADOWING ▼×

a hint or symbol of future events

"Oh no! Our friendship award ... it's broken!"

Here's an example of foreshadowing. Foreshadowing gives the reader clues about what might happen later in the story. What do you think will happen later between the two friends?

AGNES GARBOWSKA

Ff

formation formations
NOUN **1.** The formation of something is the process of developing and creating it. **2.** the pattern or shape of something

formative
ADJECTIVE having an important and lasting influence on character and development: *Friends are a formative influence in a child's life.*

former
ADJECTIVE **1.** happening or existing before now or in the past: *a former tennis champion* NOUN **2.** You use *the former* to refer to the first of two things just mentioned: *If I had to choose between happiness and money, I would have the former.*
formerly ADVERB

formidable
ADJECTIVE very difficult to deal with or overcome, and therefore frightening or impressive: *formidable opponents*

formula formulas
NOUN **1.** a group of letters, numbers, and symbols that stand for a mathematical or scientific rule **2.** a list of quantities of substances that when mixed make another substance, for example in chemistry **3.** a plan or set of rules for dealing with a particular problem: *my secret formula for staying healthy and fit*

formulate formulates formulating formulated
VERB If you formulate a plan or thought, you create it and express it in a clear and precise way.

forsake forsakes forsaking forsook forsaken
VERB To forsake someone or something is to give up or abandon that person or thing.

fort forts
NOUN **1.** a strong building built for defence PHRASE **2.** If you **hold the fort** for someone, you manage that person's affairs while he or she is away.

forte fortes
ADJECTIVE AND ADVERB **1.** In music, forte is an instruction to play or sing something loudly. NOUN **2.** If something is your forte, you are particularly good at doing it.

forth
ADVERB **1.** out and forward from a starting place: *Champlain set forth on his epic voyage of discovery.* **2.** into view: *He brought forth a slim volume of his newly published verse.*

forthcoming
ADJECTIVE **1.** planned to happen soon: *their forthcoming holiday* **2.** given or made

available: *Medical aid might be forthcoming.* **3.** willing to give information: *She was not too forthcoming about her background.*

forthright
ADJECTIVE Someone who is forthright is direct and honest about his or her opinions and feelings.

fortification fortifications
NOUN Fortifications are buildings, walls, and ditches used to protect a place.

fortitude
NOUN Fortitude is calm and patient courage.

fortress fortresses
NOUN a castle or well-protected town built for defence

fortuitous
ADJECTIVE happening by chance or good luck: *a fortuitous winning goal*

fortunate
ADJECTIVE **1.** Someone who is fortunate is lucky. **2.** Something that is fortunate brings success or advantage: *a fortunate turn of events*
fortunately ADVERB

fortune fortunes
NOUN **1.** Fortune is good luck. **2.** A fortune is a large amount of money. PHRASE **3.** If someone **tells your fortune**, that person predicts your future.

forty forties
NOUN the number 40
fortieth ADJECTIVE, ADVERB

forum forums
NOUN **1.** a place or meeting in which people can exchange ideas and discuss public issues **2.** a square in ancient Roman towns where people met to discuss business and politics

forward forwards forwarding forwarded
ADVERB OR ADJECTIVE **1.** Forward means in the front or toward the front: *A photographer moved forward to capture the moment.* **2.** Forward means in or toward a future time: *an atmosphere of looking forward and making fresh starts* **3.** Forward also means developing or progressing: *The new committee will push forward the plans.* ADVERB **4.** If someone or something is put forward, that person or thing is suggested as being suitable for something. VERB **5.** If you forward a letter that you have received, you send it on to the person to whom it is addressed at his or her new address. NOUN **6.** In a game such as soccer or hockey, a forward is a player in an attacking position.

fossil fossils
NOUN the remains or impression of an animal

Ff

or plant from a previous age, preserved in rock

fossilize VERB

fossil fuel fossil fuels

NOUN Fossil fuels are fuels such as coal, oil, and natural gas, which have been formed by rotting animals and plants from millions of years ago.

foster fosters fostering fostered

VERB **1.** If someone fosters a child, that person is paid to look after the child for a period of time, but does not become his or her legal parent. **2.** If you foster something such as an activity or an idea, you help its development and growth by encouraging people to do or think it: *to foster and maintain this goodwill*

foster child NOUN

foster home NOUN

foster parent NOUN

fought the past tense and past participle of FIGHT

foul fouler foulest; fouls fouling fouled

ADJECTIVE **1.** Something that is foul is very unpleasant to smell, taste, or see, or is offensive.

Instead of **FOUL** try...

polluted air

a rank odour

rancid garbage

filthy gym clothes

contaminated water

VERB **2.** To foul something is to make it dirty: *Dogs must not be allowed to foul the pavement. Emissions from the factory fouled the air.*

NOUN **3.** In sport, a foul is an act of breaking the rules.

found founds founding founded

1. Found is the past tense and past participle of FIND.

VERB **2.** If someone founds an organization or institution, that person sets it up.

foundation foundations

NOUN **1.** The foundation of a belief or way of life is the basic ideas or attitudes on which it is built. **2.** a solid layer of concrete or bricks in the ground, on which a building is built to give it a firm base **3.** an organization set up by money left in someone's will for research or charity

founder founders foundering foundered

NOUN **1.** The founder of an institution or organization is the person who sets it up.

VERB **2.** If something founders, it fails.

foundry foundries

NOUN a factory where metal is melted and made into objects

fountain fountains

NOUN an ornamental structure consisting of a jet of water forced into the air by a pump

fountain pen fountain pens

NOUN a pen that supplies ink to a nib from a container inside the pen

four fours

NOUN **1.** the number 4

PHRASE **2.** If you are on all fours, you are on your hands and knees.

fourteen

NOUN the number 14

fourteenth ADJECTIVE, ADVERB

fourth

ADJECTIVE **1.** The fourth item in a series is the one counted as number four.

NOUN **2.** one of four equal parts

fowl fowls

NOUN a bird such as chicken or duck that is kept or hunted for its meat or eggs

fox foxes foxing foxed

NOUN **1.** a doglike wild animal with reddish brown fur, a pointed face and ears, and a thick tail

VERB **2.** *an informal use* If someone foxes you, that person outwits you by being crafty.

foxglove foxgloves

NOUN a plant with a tall spike of purple or white, trumpet-shaped flowers

foxhound foxhounds

NOUN a dog trained for hunting foxes

foyer foyers

NOUN a large area just inside the main doors of a movie theatre, hotel, or public building where people wait or gather

fracas

NOUN a rough, noisy quarrel or fight

fraction fractions

NOUN **1.** In arithmetic, a fraction is a part of a whole number. **2.** a tiny proportion or amount of something: *an area a fraction of the size of Toronto*

fractional ADJECTIVE

fractionally ADVERB

fractious

ADJECTIVE When small children are fractious, they become upset or angry very easily, often because they are tired.

fracture fractures fracturing fractured

NOUN **1.** a crack or break in something, especially a bone

VERB **2.** If something fractures, it breaks.

fragile
ADJECTIVE easily broken or damaged: *fragile glass, a fragile relationship*
fragility NOUN

fragment fragments fragmenting fragmented
NOUN **1.** a small piece or part of something
VERB **2.** If something fragments, it breaks into small pieces or different parts.
fragmentation NOUN
fragmented ADJECTIVE

fragmentary
ADJECTIVE made up of small pieces, or parts that are not connected: *fragmentary notes in a journal*

fragrance fragrances
NOUN a sweet or pleasant smell

fragrant
ADJECTIVE Something that is fragrant smells sweet or pleasant.

frail frailer frailest
ADJECTIVE **1.** Someone who is frail is not strong or healthy. **2.** Something that is frail is easily broken or damaged.
frailty NOUN

frame frames framing framed
NOUN **1.** the structure surrounding a door, window, or picture **2.** a structure over which something is built **3.** The frames of a pair of glasses are the wire or plastic parts that hold the lenses. **4.** Your frame is your body: *his large frame* **5.** one of the many separate photographs of which a movie is made up
VERB **6.** To frame a picture is to put it into a frame: *I've framed pictures that I've pulled out of magazines.* **7.** The language something is framed in is the language used to express it.

framework frameworks
NOUN **1.** a structure acting as a support or frame **2.** a set of rules, beliefs, or ideas that you use to decide what to do

franchise franchises
NOUN **1.** the right given by a company to someone to allow that person to sell its goods or services **2.** The franchise is the right to vote in an election: *a franchise that gave the vote to less than two percent of the population*

francophone francophones
NOUN **1.** In Canada, a francophone is a person whose native language is French.
ADJECTIVE **2.** in Canada, a person who speaks French as his or her native language **3.** made up of francophones: *a francophone school, francophone Canada*

frank franker frankest
ADJECTIVE If you are frank, you say things in an open and honest way.
frankly ADVERB
frankness NOUN

frantic
ADJECTIVE If you are frantic, you behave in a wild, desperate way because you are anxious or frightened.
frantically ADVERB

fraternal
ADJECTIVE *Fraternal* is used to describe friendly actions and feelings between groups of people: *an affectionate, fraternal greeting*

fraternity fraternities
NOUN **1.** Fraternity is friendship between groups of people. **2.** a group of people with something in common: *the golfing fraternity*

fraud frauds
NOUN **1.** Fraud is the crime of getting money by deceit or trickery. **2.** something that deceives people in an illegal or immoral way **3.** someone who is not what he or she pretends to be

fraudulent
ADJECTIVE dishonest or deceitful: *fraudulent cheques*

fraught
ADJECTIVE If something is fraught with problems or difficulties, it is full of them: *Modern life is fraught with hazards.*

fray frays fraying frayed
VERB **1.** If cloth or rope frays, its threads or strands become worn and it is likely to tear or break.
NOUN **2.** a fight or argument

freak freaks
NOUN **1.** someone whose appearance or behaviour is very unusual
ADJECTIVE OR NOUN **2.** A freak event is very unusual and unlikely to happen: *a freak blizzard in June*

freckle freckles
NOUN Freckles are small, light brown spots on someone's skin, especially on the face.
freckled ADJECTIVE

free freer freest; frees freeing freed
ADJECTIVE **1.** not controlled or limited: *the free flow of aid, free trade* **2.** Someone who is free is no longer a prisoner. **3.** To be free of something unpleasant is not to have it: *She wanted her aunt's life to be free of worry.* **4.** If someone is free, that person is not busy or occupied: *Are you free for dinner?* **5.** If a place, seat, or machine is free, it is not occupied or not being used. **6.** If something is free, you can have it without paying for it.

Ff

VERB **7.** If you free someone or something that is imprisoned, fastened, or trapped, you release that person or thing.

freedom

NOUN **1.** If you have the freedom to do something, you have the scope or are allowed to do it: *We have the freedom to decide our own futures.* **2.** When prisoners gain their freedom, they escape or are released. **3.** When there is freedom from something unpleasant, people are not affected by it: *freedom from guilt*

freehold freeholds

NOUN the right to own a house or piece of land for life without conditions

freelance

ADJECTIVE OR ADVERB A freelance worker is not employed by one organization, but is paid for each job he or she does.

freely

ADVERB Freely means without restriction: *the pleasure of being able to walk around freely*

free-range

ADJECTIVE Free-range eggs are laid by hens that can move and feed freely on an area of open ground.

freestyle

NOUN Freestyle refers to sports competitions, especially swimming, in which competitors can use any style or method.

freeway freeways

NOUN A road designed for fast-moving traffic.

free will

PHRASE If you do something **of your own free will**, you do it by choice and not because you are forced to.

freeze freezes freezing froze frozen

VERB **1.** When a liquid freezes, it becomes solid because it is very cold. **2.** If you freeze, you suddenly become very still and quiet. **3.** When the temperature freezes, it reaches zero degrees or colder. **4.** When a part of the body is frozen, it is injected with anesthetic. **5.** When wages or prices are frozen, they are officially prevented from rising. NOUN **6.** a period of freezing weather

freezer freezers

NOUN a large refrigerator that freezes and stores food for a long time

freezing

ADJECTIVE extremely cold

freight

NOUN Freight is the load of goods moved by trucks, ships, or other transport; also the moving of these goods.

French

NOUN **1.** French is the main language spoken in France, and is also spoken by many people in Canada and some European countries. ADJECTIVE **2.** belonging or relating to France **3.** belonging or relating to French Canada

French horn French horns

NOUN a brass musical wind instrument consisting of a tube wound in a circle

frenetic

ADJECTIVE Frenetic behaviour is wild and excited.

frenzy frenzies

NOUN If someone is in a frenzy, his or her behaviour is wild and uncontrolled.
frenzied ADJECTIVE

frequency frequencies

NOUN **1.** The frequency of an event is how often it happens: *He was not known to call anyone with great frequency.* **2.** The frequency of a sound or radio wave is the rate at which it vibrates.

frequent frequents frequenting frequented

ADJECTIVE **1.** often happening: *Her visits were frequent. They move at frequent intervals.* VERB **2.** If you frequent a place, you go there often.
frequently ADVERB

fresco frescoes

NOUN a picture painted on a plastered wall while the plaster is still wet

fresh fresher freshest

ADJECTIVE **1.** A fresh thing replaces a previous one, or is added to it: *footprints filled in by fresh snow, fresh evidence* **2.** Fresh food is newly made or obtained, and not canned or frozen. **3.** Fresh water is not salty, for example the water in a stream. **4.** If the weather is fresh, it is fairly cool and windy. **5.** If you are fresh from something, you have experienced it recently: *fresh from teacher's college*
freshly ADVERB
freshness NOUN

freshwater

ADJECTIVE **1.** A freshwater lake or pool contains water that is not salty. **2.** A freshwater creature lives in a river, lake, or pool that is not salty.

fret frets fretting fretted

VERB **1.** If you fret about something, you worry about it. NOUN **2.** The frets on a stringed instrument, such as a guitar, are the metal ridges across its neck.
fretful ADJECTIVE

Ff

Freudian slip Freudian slips
NOUN something that you say or do that reveals your unconscious thoughts

friction
NOUN **1.** the force that stops things from moving freely when they rub against each other **2.** Friction between people is disagreement and quarrels.

Friday Fridays
NOUN the day between Thursday and Saturday

fridge fridges
NOUN the same as a REFRIGERATOR

friend friends
NOUN Your friends are people you know well and like to spend time with.

friendly friendlier friendliest
ADJECTIVE **1.** If you are friendly to someone, you behave in a kind and pleasant way to that person. **2.** People who are friendly with each other like each other and enjoy spending time together.

friendliness
NOUN

friendship friendships
NOUN **1.** Your friendships are the special relationships that you have with your friends. **2.** Friendship is the state of being friends with someone.

frieze friezes
NOUN a strip of decoration or carving along the top of a wall or column

frigate frigates
NOUN a small, fast warship

fright
NOUN Fright is a sudden feeling of fear.

frighten frightens frightening frightened
VERB If something frightens you, it makes you afraid.

frightened
ADJECTIVE having feelings of fear about something

frightening
ADJECTIVE causing someone to feel fear

frightful
ADJECTIVE very bad or unpleasant: *frightful news*

Instead of **FRIENDLY** try...

a **kind** word
a **welcoming** host
a **sympathetic** ear
an **affectionate** cat
a **close** relationship

frigid
ADJECTIVE **1.** very cold: *frigid weather* **2.** Frigid behaviour is cold and unfriendly: *frigid stares*

frill frills
NOUN a strip of cloth with many folds, attached to something as a decoration
frilly ADJECTIVE

fringe fringes
NOUN **1.** a decoration on clothes and other objects, consisting of a row of hanging strips or threads **2.** The fringes of a place are the parts farthest from its centre: *the western fringe of the Amazon basin*
fringed ADJECTIVE

frisk frisks frisking frisked
VERB *an informal use* If someone frisks you, that person searches you quickly with his or her hands to see if you are hiding a weapon in your clothes.

frisky friskier friskiest
ADJECTIVE A frisky animal is energetic and wants to play.

fritter fritters frittering frittered
NOUN **1.** Fritters consist of food dipped in batter and fried: *apple fritters*
VERB **2.** If you fritter away your time or money, you waste it on unimportant things.

frivolous
ADJECTIVE Someone who is frivolous behaves in a silly or light-hearted way, especially when he or she should be serious or sensible.
frivolity NOUN

frizzy frizzier frizziest
ADJECTIVE Frizzy hair has stiff, wiry curls.

frog frogs
NOUN a small, amphibious creature with smooth skin, prominent eyes, and long back legs that it uses for jumping

frolic frolics frolicking frolicked
VERB When animals or children frolic, they run around and play in a lively way.

from
PREPOSITION **1.** You use *from* to describe the source of a material: *Bricks are made from clay.* **2.** You use *from* to say what the source, origin, or starting point of something is: *a call from a public telephone, people from a city 100 kilometres away* **3.** If you take something from an amount, you reduce the amount by that much: *A sum of money was wrongly taken from his account.* **4.** You also use *from* when stating the range of something: *a score from one to five*

frond fronds
NOUN Fronds are long leaves from a fern or palm.

Ff

front fronts fronting fronted
NOUN **1.** The front of something is the part that faces forward. **2.** In a war, the front is the place where two armies are fighting. **3.** In meteorology, a front is the line where a mass of cold air meets a mass of warm air. **4.** A front is an outward appearance, often one that is false: *I put up a brave front.* PHRASE **5. In front** means ahead or further forward. **6.** If you do something **in front** of someone, you do it when that person is present.
frontal ADJECTIVE

frontage frontages
NOUN The frontage of a building is the wall that faces a street.

frontier frontiers
NOUN **1.** the part of a settled country where the wilderness begins **2.** a border between two countries

frost frosts
NOUN When there is a frost, the temperature outside falls below freezing.

frostbite
NOUN Frostbite is damage to your fingers, toes, or ears caused by extreme cold.

frosty frostier frostiest
ADJECTIVE **1.** If it is frosty, the temperature outside is below the freezing point. **2.** If someone is frosty, that person is unfriendly or disapproving.

froth froths frothing frothed
NOUN **1.** Froth is a mass of small bubbles on the surface of a liquid.
VERB **2.** If a liquid froths, small bubbles appear on its surface.
frothy ADJECTIVE

frown frowns frowning frowned
VERB **1.** If you frown, you move your eyebrows closer together, because you are annoyed, worried, or concentrating.
NOUN **2.** a disapproving expression on someone's face

froze the past tense of FREEZE

frozen
1. Frozen is the past participle of FREEZE. ADJECTIVE **2.** If you say you are frozen, you mean you are extremely cold.

fructose
NOUN Fructose is a type of sugar found in many fruits and in honey.

frugal
ADJECTIVE **1.** Someone who is frugal spends very little money. **2.** A frugal meal is small and cheap.
frugality NOUN

fruit fruits
NOUN **1.** the part of a plant that develops after the flower and contains the seeds. Many fruits are edible.
PLURAL NOUN **2.** The fruits of something are its good results: *the fruits of her labours*

fruitful
ADJECTIVE Something that is fruitful has good and useful results: *a fruitful experience*

fruitless
ADJECTIVE Something that is fruitless does not achieve anything: *a fruitless effort*

fruity fruitier fruitiest
ADJECTIVE Something that is fruity smells or tastes of fruit.

frustrate frustrates frustrating frustrated
VERB **1.** If something frustrates you, it prevents you doing what you want and makes you upset and angry: *Everyone gets frustrated now and then.* **2.** To frustrate something such as a plan is to prevent it from succeeding: *She hopes to frustrate his evil plan.*
frustrated ADJECTIVE
frustrating ADJECTIVE
frustration NOUN

fry fries frying fried
VERB When you fry food, you cook it in a pan containing hot fat or oil.

fuchsia fuchsias
NOUN a plant or small bush with pink, purple, or white flowers that hang downward

fudge fudges fudging fudged
NOUN **1.** Fudge is a soft, brown candy made from butter, milk, and sugar.
VERB **2.** If you fudge something, you avoid making clear or definite decisions or statements about it: *He was carefully fudging his message.*

fuel fuels fuelling fuelled
NOUN **1.** Fuel is a substance such as coal or gasoline that is burned to provide heat or power.
VERB **2.** A machine or vehicle that is fuelled by a substance works by burning the substance as a fuel: *power stations fuelled by coal*

fugitive fugitives
NOUN someone who is running away or hiding, especially from the police

fulcrum fulcrums
NOUN the point on which something is balancing or pivoting

-ful
SUFFIX **1.** The suffix *-ful* is used to form adjectives with the meaning *full of*: *careful* **2.** The suffix *-ful* is used to form nouns that mean *the amount needed to fill*: *spoonful*

⚠ **HEADS UP** The word **fuchsia** is pronounced FEW-shuh.

Ff

fulfill fulfills fulfilling fulfilled
VERB **1.** If you fulfill a promise, hope, or duty, you carry it out or achieve it. **2.** If something fulfills you, it gives you satisfaction.
fulfilling ADJECTIVE
fulfillment NOUN

full fuller fullest
ADJECTIVE **1.** containing or having as much as it is possible to hold: *His room is full of posters.* **2.** complete or whole: *to eat a full meal, a full 20 years later* **3.** loose and made from a lot of fabric: *full sleeves* **4.** rich and strong in sound: *a full alto voice*
ADVERB **5.** completely and directly: *Turn the taps on full.*
PHRASE **6.** Something that has been done or described **in full** has been dealt with completely.
fullness NOUN
fully ADVERB

full-blooded
ADJECTIVE having great commitment and enthusiasm: *a full-blooded sprint for third place*

full-blown
ADJECTIVE complete and fully developed: *a full-blown love of music*

full-fledged
ADJECTIVE completely developed: *She is a full-fledged and mature human being.*

full moon full moons
NOUN the moon when it appears as a complete circle

full-time
ADJECTIVE involving work for the whole of each normal workweek

fulsome
ADJECTIVE exaggerated and elaborate, and often sounding insincere: *His most fulsome praise was reserved for his boss.*

fumble fumbles fumbling fumbled
VERB If you fumble, you feel or handle something clumsily.

fume fumes fuming fumed
NOUN **1.** Fumes are unpleasant-smelling gases and smoke, often toxic, that are produced by burning, and by some chemicals.
VERB **2.** If you are fuming, you are very angry.

fun
NOUN **1.** Fun is pleasant, enjoyable, and light-hearted activity.
PHRASE **2.** If you **make fun** of someone, you tease that person or make jokes about him or her.

function functions functioning functioned
NOUN **1.** The function of something is the purpose or job of that thing. **2.** a large

formal dinner, reception, or party
VERB **3.** When something functions, it operates or works.

functional
ADJECTIVE **1.** relating to the way something works **2.** designed for practical use rather than for decoration or attractiveness: *Those work boots are designed to be functional.* **3.** working properly: *fully functional smoke alarms*

fund funds funding funded
NOUN **1.** an amount of available money, usually for a particular purpose: *a pension fund* **2.** A fund of something is a lot of it: *He had a fund of hilarious tales on the subject.*
VERB **3.** Someone who funds something provides money for it: *research funded by pharmaceutical companies*

fundamental fundamentals
ADJECTIVE **1.** basic and central: *the fundamental right of freedom of choice, fundamental changes*
PLURAL NOUN **2.** The fundamentals of something are its most basic and important parts: *teaching small children the fundamentals of road safety*

funeral funerals
NOUN a ceremony or religious service for the burial or cremation of a dead person

funereal
ADJECTIVE depressing and gloomy

fungicide fungicides
NOUN a chemical used to kill or prevent fungus

fungus fungi
NOUN a plant such as a mushroom or mould that does not have leaves and grows on other living things
fungal ADJECTIVE

funk
NOUN **1.** a depressed mood **2.** Funk is a style of music with a strong rhythm based on jazz and blues.

funnel funnels funnelling funnelled
NOUN **1.** an open cone narrowing to a tube, used for pouring substances into containers **2.** a metal chimney on a ship or steam engine
VERB **3.** If something is funnelled somewhere, it is directed through a narrow space into that place.

funny funnier funniest
ADJECTIVE **1.** causing amusement or laughter: *a funny old movie* **2.** strange or puzzling: *That's funny; I thought I locked the door when I left.*
funnily ADVERB

Ff

fur furs
NOUN **1.** Fur is the soft, thick body hair of many animals. **2.** a coat made from an animal's fur
furry ADJECTIVE

furious
ADJECTIVE **1.** extremely angry **2.** involving great energy, effort, or speed: *the furious speed of technological development*
furiously ADVERB

furlong furlongs
NOUN a nonmetric unit of distance equal to about 201.2 metres, used mostly in horse races

furnace furnaces
NOUN an enclosed structure for heating water or air, which then circulates throughout a building

furnish furnishes furnishing furnished
VERB **1.** If you furnish a room, you put furniture into it. **2.** *a formal use* If you furnish someone with something, you supply or provide it for that person.

furnishings
PLURAL NOUN The furnishings of a room or house are the furniture and fittings in it.

furniture
NOUN Furniture is movable objects such as tables and chairs.

furor
NOUN an angry and excited reaction or protest

furrow furrows furrowing furrowed
NOUN **1.** a long, shallow trench made by a plough
VERB **2.** When someone furrows his or her brow, that person frowns.

further furthers furthering furthered
1. a comparative form of FAR
ADJECTIVE **2.** additional or more: *There was no further rain.*
VERB **3.** If you further something, you help it to progress: *He wants to further his acting career.*

furthermore
ADVERB *a formal use* used to introduce additional information: *There is no record of such a letter. Furthermore, it is company policy never to send such letters.*

furthest a superlative form of FAR

furtive
ADJECTIVE secretive, sly, and cautious: *a furtive smile*
furtively ADVERB

fury
NOUN Fury is violent or extreme anger.

fuse fuses fusing fused
NOUN **1.** a safety device in a plug or electrical appliance consisting of a piece of wire that melts to stop the electric current if a fault occurs **2.** a long cord attached to some types of simple bombs that is lit to detonate
VERB **3.** If two things fuse, they join or become combined: *to fuse two styles of music*

fuselage fuselages
NOUN the main part of an aircraft

fusion
NOUN **1.** Fusion is what happens when two substances join by melting together. **2.** Fusion is also nuclear fusion.
ADJECTIVE **3.** Fusion is used to refer to food or a style of cooking that brings together ingredients or cooking techniques from several different countries.

fuss fusses fussing fussed
NOUN **1.** Fuss is unnecessarily anxious or excited behaviour.
VERB **2.** If someone fusses, that person behaves with unnecessary anxiety and concern for unimportant things.

fussy fussier fussiest
ADJECTIVE **1.** likely to fuss a lot: *He was unusually fussy about keeping things perfect.* **2.** with too much elaborate detail or decoration: *a fussy gown*

futile
ADJECTIVE having no chance of success: *a futile attempt to calm him down*
futility NOUN

future futures
NOUN **1.** The future is the period of time after the present. **2.** Something that has a future is likely to succeed: *She sees no future in an acting career.*
ADJECTIVE **3.** relating to or occurring at a time after the present: *to predict future events*
4. The future tense of a verb is the form used to express something that will happen in the future.

futuristic
ADJECTIVE very modern and strange, as if belonging to a time in the future: *futuristic cars*

fuzz
NOUN **1.** short fluffy hairs
PLURAL NOUN **2.** *an informal use* The fuzz are the police.

⚠ HEADS UP The word **fuselage** is pronounced FEW-zuh-lawj.

Gg

g an abbreviation for *grams*

gabble gabbles gabbling gabbled
VERB If you gabble, you talk so fast that it is difficult for people to understand you.

gable gables
NOUN Gables are the triangular parts at the top of the outside walls at each end of a house.

gadget gadgets
NOUN a small machine or tool
gadgetry NOUN

gaffe gaffes
NOUN a social blunder or mistake

gag gags gagging gagged
NOUN **1.** a strip of cloth that is tied around someone's mouth to stop that person from speaking
VERB **2.** To gag someone means to put a gag around that person's mouth. **3.** If you gag, you choke and nearly vomit.

gaggle gaggles
NOUN **1.** a group of geese **2.** *an informal use* a noisy group: *a gaggle of children*

gaiety
NOUN liveliness and fun

gaily
ADVERB in a happy and cheerful way

gain gains gaining gained
VERB **1.** If you gain something, you get it gradually: *My father spent years at night school trying to gain a degree.* **2.** If you gain from a situation, you get some advantage from it. **3.** If you gain on someone, you gradually catch up to that person.
NOUN **4.** an increase: *a gain in speed* **5.** an advantage that you get for yourself: *Some people use whatever influence they have for personal gain.*

gait gaits
NOUN Someone's gait is his or her way of walking: *an awkward gait*

gala galas
NOUN a special public celebration or performance: *the museum's opening gala*

galaxy galaxies
NOUN **1.** an enormous group of stars that extends over many millions of kilometres **2. The Galaxy** is the Milky Way. It contains the solar system and appears as a pale band in the sky.
galactic ADJECTIVE

gale gales
NOUN an extremely strong wind

gall galls galling galled
NOUN **1.** If someone has the gall to do something, that person has enough courage or impudence to do it: *He even has the gall to interrupt the teacher.*
VERB **2.** If something galls you, it makes you extremely annoyed.

gallant
ADJECTIVE **1.** brave and honourable: *They have put up a gallant fight for pensioners' rights.* **2.** polite and considerate toward women
gallantly ADVERB
gallantry NOUN

gall bladder gall bladders
NOUN an organ in your body that stores bile and that is next to your liver

galleon galleons
NOUN a large sailing ship used in the sixteenth and seventeenth centuries

gallery galleries
NOUN **1.** a building or room where works of art are shown **2.** In a theatre or large hall, the gallery is a raised area at the back or sides: *the public gallery in Parliament*

galley galleys
NOUN **1.** a kitchen in a ship or aircraft, or any very compact kitchen **2.** a ship, driven by oars, used in ancient and medieval times

gallon gallons
NOUN a nonmetric unit of liquid volume equal to about 4.55 litres

gallop gallops galloping galloped
VERB **1.** When a horse gallops, it runs very fast, so that during each stride all four feet are off the ground at the same time.
NOUN **2.** a very fast run

gallows
NOUN A gallows is a framework on which criminals used to be hanged.

gallstone gallstones
NOUN a small, painful lump that can develop in your gall bladder

galore
ADJECTIVE in very large numbers: *chocolates galore*

galoshes
PLURAL NOUN Galoshes are waterproof rubber shoes that you wear over your ordinary shoes to stop them from getting wet.

galvanized
ADJECTIVE Galvanized metal has been coated with zinc by an electrical process to protect it from rust.

gambit gambits

NOUN something that someone does to gain an advantage in a situation: *Commentators are calling the plan a clever political gambit.*

gamble gambles gambling gambled

VERB **1.** When people gamble, they bet money on the result of a game or race. **2.** If you gamble something, you risk losing it in the hope of gaining an advantage: *The company gambled everything on the new factory.*
NOUN **3.** If you take a gamble, you take a risk in the hope of gaining an advantage.

gambler NOUN

gambling NOUN

game games

NOUN **1.** an enjoyable activity with a set of rules, which is played by individuals or teams against each other **2.** an enjoyable activity played by small children: *a game of marbles* **3.** You might describe something as a game when it is designed to gain advantage: *the political game* **4.** Game is wild animals or birds that are hunted for sport or for food.
PLURAL NOUN **5.** Games are sports played at school or in a competition.
ADJECTIVE **6.** *an informal use* Someone who is game is willing to try something unusual or difficult.

gamely ADVERB

gamekeeper gamekeepers

NOUN a person employed to look after game animals and birds on a country estate

gamut

NOUN *a formal word* The gamut of something is the whole range of things that can be included in it: *the whole gamut of human emotions*

gander ganders

NOUN an adult male goose

gang gangs ganging ganged

NOUN **1.** a group of people who join together for some purpose, for example to commit a crime

VERB **2.** *an informal use* If people gang up on you, they join together to oppose you.

gangplank gangplanks

NOUN a plank used for boarding and leaving a ship or boat

gangrene

NOUN Gangrene is decay in the tissues of part of the body, caused by an inadequate blood supply.

gangrenous ADJECTIVE

gangster gangsters

NOUN a violent criminal who is a member of a gang

gannet gannets

NOUN a large sea bird that dives to catch fish

gap gaps

NOUN **1.** a space between two things or a hole in something solid **2.** a place where something is missing: *There is a gap in this data set.* **3.** A gap between things, people, or ideas is a great difference between them: *the gap between fantasy and reality*

gape gapes gaping gaped

VERB **1.** If you gape at someone or something, you stare at that person or thing with your mouth open in surprise. **2.** Something that gapes is wide open: *gaping holes in the wall*

garage garages

NOUN **1.** a building where a vehicle can be kept **2.** a place where motor vehicles are repaired and where gasoline is sold

garb

NOUN Someone's garb is his or her clothes: *dressed in the garb of a painter*

garbage

NOUN **1.** Garbage is waste material, especially from a household. **2.** If you say something is garbage, you mean it is nonsense.

garbled

ADJECTIVE Garbled messages are jumbled and the details may be wrong.

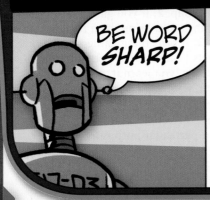

KNOWING WORDS: IDIOMS

BE WORD SHARP!

Idioms add colour to language by playing with the meanings of words.

game a fun activity

ahead of the game have an advantage

fair game open to criticism

he's/she's got game he/she is highly skilled

not all fun and games occasionally unpleasant

off your game not playing well

Gg

garden gardens
NOUN **1.** an area of land where flowers, fruit, or vegetables are grown **2.** a park with many beds of plants that are arranged in an attractive manner: *a botanical garden*
gardening NOUN

gardener gardeners
NOUN a person who looks after a garden as a job or as a hobby

gargle gargles gargling gargled
VERB When you gargle, you rinse the back of your throat by putting some liquid in your mouth and making a bubbling sound without swallowing.

gargoyle gargoyles
NOUN a stone carving below the roof of an old building, in the shape of an imaginary creature or animal and often having a waterspout at the mouth

garish
ADJECTIVE bright and harsh to look at: *garish, bright red boots*

garland garlands
NOUN a circle of flowers and leaves that is worn around the neck or head

garlic
NOUN Garlic is the small, white bulb of an onionlike plant that is made up of small sections called cloves. Garlic has a strong taste and smell and is used in cooking.

garment garments
NOUN a piece of clothing

garnet garnets
NOUN a type of gemstone, usually red in colour

garnish garnishes garnishing garnished
NOUN **1.** something such as a sprig of parsley that is used in cooking for decoration
VERB **2.** To garnish food means to decorate it with a garnish.

garret garrets
NOUN an attic

garrison garrisons
NOUN a group of soldiers stationed in a fort or town in order to guard it; also used of the buildings in which these soldiers live

garrote garrotes garroting garroted
VERB To garrote someone means to strangle that person with a piece of wire, cord, or some other material.

garter garters
NOUN a piece of elastic worn around the top of a stocking to hold it up

gas gases; gasses gassing gassed
NOUN **1.** any airlike substance that is not liquid or solid, such as oxygen **2.** a mixture of gases that are used as fuel, which are obtained from coal or other substances **3.** gasoline
VERB **4.** To gas people or animals means to kill them with poisonous gas.

gas chamber gas chambers
NOUN a room in which people or animals are killed with poisonous gas

gash gashes gashing gashed
NOUN **1.** a long, deep cut
VERB **2.** If you gash something, you make a long, deep cut in it.

gas mask gas masks
NOUN a large mask with special filters attached, which people wear over their face to protect them from poisonous gas

gasoline
NOUN a motor fuel distilled from petroleum

gasp gasps gasping gasped
VERB **1.** If you gasp, you quickly draw in your breath through your mouth because you are surprised or in pain.
NOUN **2.** a sharp intake of breath through the mouth

gastric
ADJECTIVE occurring in the stomach or involving the stomach: *gastric pain*

gate gates
NOUN **1.** a barrier that can open and shut and is used to close the entrance to a garden or field **2.** a barrier, such as one stopping traffic at a railway crossing

gate-crash gate-crashes gate-crashing gate-crashed
VERB If you gate-crash a party, you go to it when you have not been invited.

gateway gateways
NOUN **1.** an entrance through a wall or fence where there is a gate **2.** Something that is considered to be the entrance to a larger or more important thing can be described as the gateway to the larger thing: *Winnipeg is the gateway to West.*

gather gathers gathering gathered
VERB **1.** When people gather, they come together in a group. **2.** If you gather a number of things, you bring them together in one place. **3.** If something gathers speed or strength, it gets faster or stronger. **4.** If you gather something, you learn it, often from what someone says.

gathering gatherings
NOUN a meeting of people who have come together for a particular purpose

gauche
ADJECTIVE socially awkward

⚠ **HEADS UP** The word **garrote** is pronounced guh-ROT.

Gg

gaudy gaudier gaudiest
ADJECTIVE very colourful in a cheap and tasteless way

gauge gauges gauging gauged
VERB **1.** If you gauge something, you estimate it or calculate it: *The captain gauged the wind at over 30 knots.*
NOUN **2.** a piece of equipment that measures the amount of something: *a rain gauge*
3. something that is used as a standard by which you judge a situation: *Some people see high grades as a gauge of intelligence.* **4.** On railways, the gauge is the distance between the two rails on a railway line.

gaunt
ADJECTIVE A person who looks gaunt is thin and bony.

gauntlet gauntlets
NOUN **1.** Gauntlets are long, thick gloves worn for protection, for example by motorcyclists.
PHRASE **2.** If you **throw down the gauntlet**, you challenge someone.

gave the past tense of GIVE

gay gayer gayest; gays
ADJECTIVE **1.** Someone who is gay is homosexual. **2.** *an old-fashioned use* Gay people or places are lively and full of fun.
NOUN **3.** a homosexual person

gaze gazes gazing gazed
VERB If you gaze at something, you look steadily at it for a long time.

gazelle gazelles
NOUN a small antelope found in Africa and Asia

gazette gazettes
NOUN a newspaper or journal

gear gears gearing geared
NOUN **1.** a piece of machinery that controls the rate at which energy is converted into movement. Gears in vehicles control the speed and power of the vehicle. **2.** The gear for an activity is the clothes and equipment that you need for it.
VERB **3.** If someone or something is geared to a particular event or purpose, that person or thing is prepared for it.

geek geeks *informal*
NOUN a person who is obsessive about an interest or hobby: *a computer geek*

geese the plural of GOOSE

gel gels gelling gelled
NOUN **1.** a smooth, soft, jellylike substance: *shower gel, hair gel*
VERB **2.** If a liquid gels, it turns into a gel.
3. If a vague thought or plan gels, it becomes more definite.

gelatin
NOUN a clear, tasteless substance, obtained from meat and bones, used to make liquids firm and jellylike

gelding geldings
NOUN a horse that has been castrated

gem gems
NOUN **1.** a jewel or precious stone **2.** You can describe someone or something that is extremely good or beautiful as a gem: *A gem of a novel.*

gender genders
NOUN **1.** Gender is the sex of a person or animal: *the female gender* **2.** the classification of nouns as masculine, feminine, and neuter in certain languages

gene genes
NOUN one of the parts of a living cell that controls the physical characteristics of an organism. Genes are passed on from one generation to the next.

general generals
ADJECTIVE **1.** relating to the whole of something or to most things in a group: *your general health* **2.** true, suitable, or relevant in most situations: *a general scientific truth* **3.** including or involving a wide range of different things: *a general hospital* **4.** having complete responsibility over a wide area of work or a large number of people: *the general secretary*
NOUN **5.** the highest-ranking officer in the Canadian army or air force
PHRASE **6. In general** means usually.
generally ADVERB

general election general elections
NOUN an election for a new government, which all the people of a country may vote in

generalize generalizes generalizing generalized
VERB To generalize means to say that something is true in most cases, ignoring minor details.
generalization NOUN

general practitioner general practitioners
NOUN a GP

generate generates generating generated
VERB To generate something means to create or produce it: *We use wind power to generate electricity on our farm.*

generation generations
NOUN all the people of about the same age; also the period of time between one generation and the next, usually considered to be about 25 to 30 years

Gg

generator generators
NOUN a machine that produces electricity from another form of energy such as wind or water power

generic
ADJECTIVE A generic term is a name that applies to all the members of a group of similar things.

generosity
NOUN the willingness to give money, time, or help

generous
ADJECTIVE **1.** A generous person is very willing to give money or time. **2.** Something that is generous is very large: *a generous serving of cake*
generously ADVERB
generosity NOUN

genesis
NOUN *a formal word* The genesis of something is its beginning.

genetics
NOUN Genetics is the science of the way that characteristics are passed on from generation to generation by means of genes.
genetic ADJECTIVE
genetically ADVERB

genial
ADJECTIVE cheerful, friendly, and kind
genially ADVERB

genie genies
NOUN a magical being from folklore that obeys the wishes of the person who controls it

genitals
PLURAL NOUN The genitals are the reproductive organs. The technical name is genitalia.
genital ADJECTIVE

genius geniuses
NOUN **1.** a highly intelligent, creative, or talented person **2.** Genius is great intelligence, creativity, or talent: *a poet of genius*

genocide
NOUN *a formal word* Genocide is the systematic murder of all members of a particular race or group.

genome genomes
NOUN all of the genes contained in a single cell of an organism

genre genres
NOUN *a formal word* a particular style in literature or art

genteel
ADJECTIVE very polite and refined

gentility
NOUN Gentility is excessive politeness and refinement.

gentle gentler gentlest
ADJECTIVE mild and calm; not violent or rough: *a gentle man*
gently ADVERB
gentleness NOUN

gentleman gentlemen
NOUN a man who is polite and considerate of others; also a polite way of referring to any man
gentlemanly ADJECTIVE

gentry
PLURAL NOUN The gentry are people from the upper classes, especially in Britain.

genuine
ADJECTIVE **1.** real and not false or pretend: *a genuine smile, genuine silver* **2.** A genuine person is sincere and honest.
genuinely ADVERB
genuineness NOUN

genus genera
NOUN In biology, a genus is a class of animals or closely related plants.

geo-
PREFIX Words beginning with *geo-* have something to do with the earth: *geography, geologist*

KNOWING WORDS: WORD BUILDING

BE WORD SHARP!

You can create new words by adding prefixes and suffixes to a base word.

geo- means *involving the earth*

geocentric seeing Earth as the centre of the universe

geophysics the study of the earth's physics

geopolitics international politics across the world

geosciences any of the earth sciences

geothermal involving heat from the earth

Gg

geography

NOUN the study of the physical features of the earth, together with the climate, natural resources, and population in different parts of the world

geographical ADJECTIVE

geographically ADVERB

geology

NOUN the study of the earth's structure, especially the layers of rock and soil that make up the surface of the earth

geological ADJECTIVE

geologist NOUN

geometric

ADJECTIVE **1.** consisting of regular lines and shapes, such as squares, triangles, and circles: *bold geometric designs* **2.** involving geometry

geometry

NOUN Geometry is the branch of mathematics dealing with lines, angles, curves, and spaces.

geranium geraniums

NOUN a garden plant with red, pink, or white flowers

gerbil gerbils

NOUN a small rodent with long back legs, often kept as a pet

geriatric

ADJECTIVE **1.** relating to the medical care of old people: *a geriatric nurse* **2.** Someone or something that is geriatric is very old: *a geriatric patient*

NOUN **3.** an old person, especially as a patient

geriatrics NOUN

germ germs

NOUN **1.** a very small organism that causes disease **2.** *a formal use* The germ of an idea or plan is the beginning of it.

German measles another name for RUBELLA

germinate germinates germinating germinated

VERB **1.** When a seed germinates, it starts to grow. **2.** When an idea or plan germinates, it starts to develop.

germination NOUN

gerrymander gerrymanders gerrymandering gerrymandered

VERB To gerrymander is to change political boundaries in an area so that a particular party or politician gets a bigger share of votes in an election.

gestation

NOUN Gestation is the time during which a fetus is growing inside its mother's womb.

gesticulate gesticulates gesticulating gesticulated

VERB If you gesticulate, you move your hands and arms around while you are talking.

gesticulation NOUN

gesture gestures gesturing gestured

NOUN **1.** a movement of your hands or head that conveys a message or feeling **2.** an action symbolizing something: *a gesture of support*

VERB **3.** If you gesture, you move your hands or head in order to communicate a message or feeling.

get gets getting got

VERB **1.** *Get* often means the same as *become*: *I always draw the curtains once it gets dark.* **2.** If you get something, you come to have that thing: *I got new boots on the weekend.* **3.** If you get something done, you do it or you persuade someone to do it: *You can get your homework done in time.* **4.** If you get somewhere, you go there: *I must get home.* **5.** If you get something, you fetch it or are given it: *I'll get us all some hot chocolate. I got your message.* **6.** If you get a joke or get the point of something, you understand it.

get across

VERB **7.** If you get an idea across, you make people understand it.

get at

VERB **8.** If you can get at something, you are able to access that thing. **9.** If you ask someone what he or she is getting at, you are asking that person to explain what he or she means.

get away with

VERB **10.** If you get away with something dishonest, you are not found out or punished for doing it.

get by

VERB **11.** If you get by, you have just enough money to live on.

get over with

VERB **12.** If you want to get something unpleasant over with, you want it to be finished quickly.

get through

VERB **13.** If you get through to someone, you make that person understand what you are saying. **14.** If you get through to someone on the telephone, you succeed in talking to that person.

getaway getaways

NOUN a place to go for a rest or vacation

get-together get-togethers

NOUN *an informal word* an informal meeting or party

geyser geysers

NOUN a spring through which hot water and steam gush up in spurts

Gg

ghastly ghastlier ghastliest
ADJECTIVE extremely horrible and unpleasant:
a ghastly crime, ghastly food

gherkin gherkins
NOUN a small, pickled cucumber

ghetto ghettoes
NOUN a part of a city where many poor
people of a particular race live

ghost ghosts
NOUN the spirit of a dead person, believed to
haunt people or places

ghoulish
ADJECTIVE very interested in unpleasant things
such as death and murder: *ghoulish curiosity*

giant giants
NOUN **1.** a huge person in a myth or legend
ADJECTIVE **2.** much larger than other similar
things: *giant prawns, a giant wave*

gibberish
NOUN Gibberish is speech that makes no sense
at all.

gibbon gibbons
NOUN an ape with very long arms

gibe gibes
NOUN an insulting remark

giddy giddier giddiest
ADJECTIVE If you feel giddy, you feel unsteady
on your feet, usually because you are ill or
dizzy.
giddily ADVERB

gift gifts
NOUN **1.** a present **2.** a natural skill or ability:
a gift for comedy

gifted
ADJECTIVE having a special ability: *gifted tennis
players*

gig gigs
NOUN a performance by a band, singer, or
other performer

gigantic
ADJECTIVE extremely large

giggle giggles giggling giggled
VERB **1.** To giggle means to laugh in a nervous
or embarrassed way.
NOUN **2.** a short, nervous laugh
giggly ADJECTIVE

gilded
ADJECTIVE Something that is gilded is covered
with a thin layer of gold.

gill gills
NOUN The gills of a fish are the organs on its
sides, which it uses for breathing.

gilt gilts
NOUN **1.** a thin layer of gold
ADJECTIVE **2.** covered with a thin layer of gold:
a book with gilt edges

gimmick gimmicks
NOUN a device that is not really necessary
but is used to attract interest: *All performers
need a good gimmick.*
gimmicky ADJECTIVE

gin
NOUN Gin is a strong, colourless, alcoholic
drink made from grain and juniper berries.

ginger
NOUN **1.** Ginger is a plant root with a hot,
spicy flavour, used in cooking.
ADJECTIVE **2.** bright orange or red: *a cat with
ginger fur*

gingerbread
NOUN Gingerbread is a sweet,
ginger-flavoured cookie or cake.

gingerly
ADVERB If you move gingerly, you move
cautiously: *They walked gingerly down the
stairs.*

gingham
NOUN Gingham is checked cotton cloth.

giraffe giraffes
NOUN a tall, four-legged African mammal
with a very long neck

girder girders
NOUN a large metal beam used in the
construction of a bridge or a building

girdle girdles
NOUN an garment worn under clothing and
around the hips or waist, usually by women,
to give the body a slenderer appearance

girl girls
NOUN a female child
girlish ADJECTIVE
girlhood NOUN

girlfriend girlfriends
NOUN Someone's girlfriend is a female
companion, especially the female with whom
a person is having a romantic relationship.

girth
NOUN The girth of something is the
measurement around it.

gist
NOUN the general meaning or most important
points in a piece of writing or speech

give gives giving gave given
VERB **1.** If you give someone something, you
hand it to that person or provide it for him
or her: *I gave her a book. A family friend
gave me my job.* **2.** *Give* is also used to
express physical actions and speech: *He*

gave a friendly smile. She gave a lovely performance **3.** If you give a party or a meal, you are the host at it. **4.** If something gives, it collapses under pressure.

NOUN **5.** If a material has give, it will bend or stretch when pulled or put under pressure.

PHRASE **6.** You use **give or take** to indicate that an amount you are mentioning is not exact: *About two years, give or take a month or so.* **7.** If something **gives way** to something else, it is replaced by it. **8.** If something **gives way,** it collapses.

give in
VERB **9.** If you give in, you admit that you are defeated.

give out
VERB **10.** If something gives out, it stops working: *the motor gave out*

give up
VERB **11.** If you give something up, you stop doing it: *I can't give up my hobby.* **12.** If you give up, you admit that you cannot do something. **13.** If you give someone up, you let the police know where that person is hiding.

given
1. the past participle of GIVE
ADJECTIVE **2.** fixed or specified: *My style can change at any given moment.*

glaciation
NOUN In geography, glaciation is the condition of being covered with sheet ice.

glacier glaciers
NOUN a huge, frozen mass of slow-moving ice

glad gladder gladdest
ADJECTIVE happy and pleased: *They'll be glad to get away from it all.*
gladly ADVERB
gladness NOUN

glade glades
NOUN a grassy space in a forest

gladiator gladiators
NOUN In ancient Rome, gladiators were slaves trained to fight in arenas to provide entertainment.

gladiolus gladioli
NOUN a garden plant with spikes of brightly coloured flowers on a long stem

glamour
NOUN The glamour of a fashionable or attractive person or place is the charm and excitement that that person or place has: *the glamour of Paris*
glamorous ADJECTIVE

glance glances glancing glanced
VERB **1.** If you glance at something, you look

at it quickly. **2.** If one object glances off another, it hits it at an angle and bounces away in another direction.
NOUN **3.** a quick look

gland glands
NOUN organs in your body, such as the thyroid gland and the sweat glands, that either produce chemical substances for your body to use, or that help to get rid of waste products from your body
glandular ADJECTIVE

glare glares glaring glared
VERB **1.** If you glare at someone, you look at that person angrily.
NOUN **2.** a hard, angry look **3.** Glare is extremely bright light.

glass glasses
NOUN **1.** Glass is a hard, transparent substance that is easily broken, used to make windows and bottles. **2.** a container for drinking out of, made from glass

glasses
PLURAL NOUN Glasses are two lenses in a frame, which some people wear over their eyes to improve their eyesight.

glassy
ADJECTIVE **1.** smooth and shiny like glass: *glassy water* **2.** A glassy look shows no feeling or expression.

glaze glazes glazing glazed
NOUN **1.** A glaze on pottery or on food is a smooth, shiny surface.
VERB **2.** To glaze pottery or food means to cover it with a glaze. **3.** To glaze a window means to fit a sheet of glass into a window frame.

glaze over
VERB **4.** If your eyes glaze over, they lose all expression, usually because you are bored.

glazed
ADJECTIVE Someone who has a glazed expression looks bored.

gleam gleams gleaming gleamed
VERB **1.** If something gleams, it shines and reflects light.
NOUN **2.** a pale, shining light

> **⚠ HEADS UP**
>
> **Gleam** is one of many **gl-** words that relate to light, like *glimmer, glint, glisten, glitter,* and *glow.*

glean gleans gleaning gleaned
VERB To glean information means to collect it from various sources.

Gg

glee
NOUN *an old-fashioned word* Glee is joy and delight.
gleeful ADJECTIVE
gleefully ADVERB

glen glens
NOUN a deep, narrow valley, especially in Scotland or Ireland

glide glides gliding glided
VERB **1.** To glide means to move smoothly: *I saw three cygnets gliding up the stream.*
2. When birds or airplanes glide, they float on air currents.

glider gliders
NOUN an airplane without an engine, which flies by floating on air currents

glimmer glimmers glimmering glimmered
NOUN **1.** a faint, unsteady light **2.** A glimmer of a feeling or quality is a faint sign of it: *a glimmer of intelligence*

glimpse glimpses glimpsing glimpsed
NOUN **1.** a brief sight of something: *They caught a glimpse of their hero.*
VERB **2.** If you glimpse something, you see it very briefly.

glint glints glinting glinted
VERB **1.** If something glints, it reflects quick flashes of light.
NOUN **2.** a quick flash of light **3.** A glint in someone's eye is a brightness expressing some emotion: *a glint of mischief in her eyes*

glisten glistens glistening glistened
VERB If something glistens, it shines or sparkles.

glitter glitters glittering glittered
VERB **1.** If something glitters, it shines in a sparkling way: *a glittering crown*
NOUN **2.** Glitter is sparkling light.

gloat gloats gloating gloated
VERB If you gloat, you cruelly show your pleasure about your own success or someone else's failure: *Their rivals were gloating over their triumph.*

global
ADJECTIVE concerning the whole world: *a global tour, global warming*

globalization
NOUN **1.** the process by which a company expands so that it can do business internationally **2.** the process by which cultures throughout the world become more and more similar for a variety of reasons, including increased global business and better international communications

global warming
NOUN an increase in the world's overall temperature believed to be caused by the greenhouse effect

globe globes
NOUN **1.** a ball-shaped object, especially one with a map of the earth on it **2.** You can refer to the world as the globe.

gloom
NOUN **1.** Gloom is darkness or dimness.
2. Gloom is also a feeling of unhappiness or despair.

gloomy gloomier gloomiest
ADJECTIVE **1.** dark and depressing **2.** feeling very sad
gloomily ADVERB

glorify glorifies glorifying glorified
VERB If you glorify something, you make that thing seem better than it really is: *Some movies glorify violence.*
glorification NOUN

glorious
ADJECTIVE **1.** beautiful and impressive to look at: *glorious beaches* **2.** very pleasant and giving a feeling of happiness: *glorious sunshine* **3.** involving great fame and success: *a glorious career*
gloriously ADVERB

glory glories glorying gloried
NOUN **1.** Glory is fame and admiration for an achievement. **2.** something considered splendid or admirable: *the true glory of the ocean at sunset*
VERB **3.** If you are in your glory when doing something, you take great delight in that activity: *She is in her glory when skating on a frozen pond.*

gloss glosses glossing glossed
NOUN **1.** Gloss is a bright shine on a surface.
2. Gloss is also an attractive appearance that may hide less attractive qualities: *to put a positive gloss on the events* **3.** If you gloss over a problem or fault, you try to ignore it or deal with it very quickly.

glossary glossaries
NOUN a list of explanations of specialist words, usually found at the back of a book

glossy glossier glossiest
ADJECTIVE smooth and shiny: *glossy lipstick, glossy paper*

glove gloves
NOUN Gloves are coverings that you wear over your hands for warmth or protection.

glow glows glowing glowed
NOUN **1.** a dull, steady light **2.** a strong feeling of pleasure or happiness
VERB **3.** If something glows, it shines with a

⚠ **HEADS UP** A **glossary** lets a writer explain new words without interrupting the flow of a piece of writing.

dull, steady light: *A light glowed behind the curtains.* **4.** If you are glowing, you look very happy or healthy.

glower glowers glowering glowered
VERB If you glower, you stare angrily.

glowing
ADJECTIVE A glowing description praises someone or something very highly: *a glowing character reference*

glucose
NOUN Glucose is a type of sugar found in plants and that animals and people make in their bodies from food to provide energy.

glue glues gluing glued
NOUN **1.** a substance used for sticking things together
VERB **2.** If you glue one object to another, you stick them together using glue.

glum glummer glummest
ADJECTIVE miserable and depressed
glumly ADVERB

glut gluts
NOUN a greater quantity of things than is needed

gluten
NOUN a sticky protein found in cereal grains

glutton gluttons
NOUN **1.** a person who eats too much **2.** If you are a glutton for something, such as punishment or hard work, you seem very eager for it.
gluttony NOUN

gnarled
ADJECTIVE old, twisted, and rough: *gnarled fingers*

gnat gnats
NOUN a tiny, flying insect that bites

gnaw gnaws gnawing gnawed
VERB **1.** To gnaw something means to bite at it repeatedly. **2.** If a feeling gnaws at you, it keeps worrying you: *The question gnawed at him for days.*

gnome gnomes
NOUN in folklore, a tiny, old man that lives in the earth and guards treasures

gnu gnus
NOUN a large African antelope

go goes going went gone
VERB **1.** If you go somewhere, you move or travel there. **2.** You can use go to mean *become*: *She felt she was going crazy.* **3.** You can use go to describe the state that someone or something is in: *Our arrival went unnoticed.* **4.** If something goes well, it is successful. If it goes badly, it is unsuccessful. **5.** If a machine or clock goes, it works and is

not broken. **6.** You use go before giving the sound something makes or before quoting a song or saying: *The bell goes ding-dong. The cow went moo.*
NOUN **7.** an attempt at doing something
PHRASE **8.** If someone is always **on the go**, that person is always busy and active. **9. To go** means remaining: *I've got one more year of school to go.*

go back on
VERB **10.** If you go back on a promise or agreement, you do not do what you promised or agreed.

go down
VERB **11.** If something goes down well, people like it. If it goes down badly, they don't.

go for
VERB **12.** If someone goes for you, that person attacks you.

go in for
VERB **13.** If you go in for something, you decide to take part in it.

go into
VERB **14.** If one number goes into another, it can be divided into it.

go off
VERB **15.** If you go off someone or something, you stop liking that person or thing. **16.** If a bomb goes off, it explodes.

go on
VERB **17.** If you go on doing something, you continue to do it. **18.** If you go on about something, you keep talking about it in a boring way. **19.** Something that is going on is happening.

go out with
VERB **20.** If you go out with someone, you have a romantic relationship with that person.

go over
VERB **21.** If you go over something, you think about it or discuss it carefully.

go through
VERB **22.** If you go through an unpleasant event, you experience it. **23.** If a law or agreement goes through, it is approved and becomes official. **24.** If you go through with something, you do it even though it is unpleasant.

go with
VERB **25.** If one thing goes with another, they are appropriate together.

goad goads goading goaded
VERB If you goad someone, you encourage that person to do something by making him or her angry or excited: *Her friends goaded her into jumping off the highest diving platform.*

Gg

go-ahead
NOUN If someone gives you the go-ahead for something, that person gives you permission to do it.

goal goals
NOUN **1.** in games like hockey or football, the space into which the players try to get the ball or puck in order to score a point **2.** an instance of this **3.** Your goal is something that you hope to achieve.

goalie goalies
NOUN in games like soccer or hockey, the player who stands in the goal and tries to stop the other team from scoring

goat goats
NOUN an animal, like a sheep, with coarse hair, a beard, and horns

gob gobs
NOUN *an informal use* a lump or mass of something: *He put a gob of butter on his pancakes.*

gobble gobbles gobbling gobbled
VERB **1.** If you gobble food, you eat it very quickly. **2.** When a turkey gobbles, it makes a loud, gurgling sound.

gobbledygook
NOUN Gobbledygook is language that is impossible to understand because it is so formal or complicated.

goblet goblets
NOUN a glass with a long stem

goblin goblins
NOUN in folklore, an ugly, mischievous creature

god gods
NOUN **1.** The name **God** is given to the being who is worshipped by Christians, Jews, and Muslims as the creator and ruler of the world. **2.** any of the beings that are believed in many religions to have power over an aspect of life or a part of the world: *Dionysus, the Greek god of wine.* **3.** If someone is your god, you admire and respect that person very much.

godchild godchildren
NOUN If you are someone's godchild, that person agreed to be responsible for your religious upbringing when you were baptized in a Christian church.
goddaughter NOUN
godson NOUN

goddess goddesses
NOUN a female god

godparent godparents
NOUN A person's godparent is someone who agrees to be responsible for his or her religious upbringing when that person is baptized in a Christian church.
godfather NOUN
godmother NOUN

godsend godsends
NOUN something that comes unexpectedly and helps you very much

goggles
PLURAL NOUN Goggles are special glasses that fit closely around your eyes to protect them.

gold
NOUN **1.** Gold is a valuable, yellow-coloured metal. It is used for making jewellery and as an international currency. **2.** *Gold* is also used to mean things that are made of gold.
ADJECTIVE **3.** bright yellow

golden
ADJECTIVE **1.** gold in colour: *golden syrup* **2.** made of gold: *a golden chain* **3.** excellent or ideal: *a golden hero, a golden opportunity*

golden rule golden rules
NOUN the rule that people should behave toward others as they would want others to behave toward them

golden wedding golden weddings
NOUN a fiftieth wedding anniversary

goldfish goldfish
NOUN a small, orange-coloured fish, often kept in a pond or a bowl

goldsmith goldsmiths
NOUN a person whose job is making jewellery out of gold

golf
NOUN Golf is a game in which players use special clubs to hit a small ball into holes that are spread out over a large area of grassy land.
golfer NOUN

golf course golf courses
NOUN an area of grassy land where people play golf

gondola gondolas
NOUN **1.** a long, narrow boat, used on the canals in Venice, that is propelled with a long pole **2.** a broadcasting booth built high up in a hockey arena, near the roof

gone the past participle of GO

gong gongs
NOUN a flat, circular piece of metal that is hit with a hammer to make a loud sound, often as a signal for something

good better best; goods

ADJECTIVE **1.** pleasant, acceptable, or satisfactory: *good news, a good movie*
2. skilful or successful: *good at art*

Instead of **GOOD** try...

a positive attitude
humane treatment
a wise decision
a skilled artist
helpful advice
a generous offer
an apt description
favourable conditions

3. kind, thoughtful, and loving: *She was grateful to him for being so good to her.*
4. well-behaved: *Have the children been good?*
5. enjoyable: *a good time*
NOUN **6.** Good is moral and spiritual justice and virtue: *the forces of good and evil*
7. Good also refers to anything that is desirable or beneficial as opposed to harmful: *The break has done me good.*
PLURAL NOUN **8.** Goods are objects that people own or that are sold in stores: *leather goods*
PHRASE **9. For good** means forever. **10. As good as** means almost: *The election is as good as decided.*

⚠ HEADS UP

Good is an adjective. **Well** is an adverb. Remembering this is ... *a good way to write well!*

goodbye
INTERJECTION You say *goodbye* when you are leaving someone or ending a telephone conversation.

Good Friday
NOUN Good Friday is the Friday before Easter, when Christians remember the crucifixion of Christ.

good-natured
ADJECTIVE friendly, pleasant, and cheerful

goodness
NOUN **1.** Goodness is the quality of being kind.
INTERJECTION **2.** People say *Goodness!* or *My goodness!* when they are surprised.

goodwill
NOUN Goodwill is kindness and helpfulness: *Messages of goodwill were exchanged.*

goody goodies
NOUN *an informal word* Goodies are enjoyable things, often food.

goose geese
NOUN a fairly large bird with webbed feet and a long neck

gooseberry gooseberries
NOUN a round, green berry that grows on a bush and has a sharp taste

gore gores goring gored
VERB If an animal gores someone, it wounds that person badly with its horns or tusks.

gorge gorges gorging gorged
NOUN **1.** a deep, narrow valley
VERB **2.** If you gorge yourself, you eat a lot of food greedily.

gorgeous
ADJECTIVE extremely pleasant or attractive: *a gorgeous sunset*

gorilla gorillas
NOUN a large, strong ape with very dark fur

gorse
NOUN a dark-green, wild shrub that has sharp prickles and small yellow flowers

gory gorier goriest
ADJECTIVE very bloody

gosling goslings
NOUN a young goose

gospel gospels
NOUN **1.** a set of ideas that someone strongly believes in: *the so-called gospel of work*
ADJECTIVE **2.** Gospel music is a style of religious music that originated in African-American churches in the southern United States.

gossip gossips gossiping gossiped
NOUN **1.** Gossip is informal conversation, often concerning people's private affairs.
2. Someone who is a gossip enjoys talking about other people's private affairs.
VERB **3.** If you gossip, you talk informally with someone, especially about other people.

got
1. Got is the past tense and past participle of GET. **2.** You can use *have got* instead of the more formal *have* when talking about possessing things: *I have got more books that I can carry.* **3.** You can use *have got to* instead of the more formal *have to* when talking about something that must be done: *He has got to win.*

gouge gouges gouging gouged
VERB **1.** If you gouge a hole in something, you make a hole in it with a pointed object. **2.** If you gouge something out, you force it out of position with your fingers or a sharp tool.

Gg

goulash
NOUN Goulash is a type of meat stew that is highly seasoned.

gourd gourds
NOUN a large fruit with a hard outside

gourmet gourmets
NOUN a person who enjoys good food and drink and knows a lot about it

gout
NOUN a disease that causes someone's joints to swell painfully, especially in his or her toes

govern governs governing governed
VERB **1.** To govern a country means to control it. **2.** Something that governs a situation influences it: *Her actions are governed by a strong sense of what is morally right.*

governess governesses
NOUN a woman who was employed to teach the children in a family and who lived with the family, especially in the past

government governments
NOUN **1.** The government is the group of people who govern a country. **2.** Government is the control and organization of a country.
governmental ADJECTIVE

governor governors
NOUN **1.** the ruler of a colony or the representative of a king or queen in a colony; also the head of a state government in the United States **2.** a person who controls and organizes an institution

Governor General Governors General
NOUN in Canada, the chief representative of the King or Queen, appointed for a term of five years

gown gowns
NOUN **1.** a long, formal dress **2.** a long, dark cloak worn by people such as judges and graduating students

GP *GP* is an abbreviation for general practitioner, a doctor who works in the community rather than in a hospital.

grab grabs grabbing grabbed
VERB **1.** If you grab something, you take it or pick it up roughly. **2.** If you grab an opportunity, you take advantage of it eagerly. **3.** *an informal use* If an idea grabs you, it excites you.
NOUN **4.** A grab at an object is an attempt to grab it.

grace graces gracing graced
NOUN **1.** Grace is an elegant way of moving. **2.** Grace is also a pleasant, kind way of behaving.
VERB **3.** Something that graces a place makes it more attractive. **4.** If someone important

graces an event, that person kindly agrees to be present at it.
graceful ADJECTIVE
gracefully ADVERB

gracious
ADJECTIVE kind, polite, and pleasant
graciously ADVERB

grade grades grading graded
VERB **1.** To grade things means to arrange them according to quality.
NOUN **2.** the level that students are divided into at a school, corresponding to one year of study **3.** The grade of something is its quality. **4.** the mark that you get for an exam or piece of written work

gradient gradients
NOUN a slope or the steepness of a slope

gradual
ADJECTIVE happening or changing slowly over a long period of time

gradually
ADVERB happening or changing slowly over a long period of time

graduate graduates graduating graduated
NOUN **1.** a person who has completed a course of study at a school, university, or college
VERB **2.** When students graduate, they complete a course of study at a school, university, or college. **3.** To graduate from one thing to another means to progress gradually toward the second thing.
graduation NOUN

graffiti
NOUN Graffiti is slogans or drawings scribbled on walls.

graft grafts grafting grafted
NOUN **1.** a piece of living tissue that is used to replace by surgery a damaged or unhealthy part of a person's body
VERB **2.** To graft one thing to another means to attach it.

grain grains
NOUN **1.** a cereal plant, such as wheat, that is grown as a crop and used for food **2.** Grains are seeds of a cereal plant. **3.** A grain of sand or salt is a tiny particle of it. **4.** Grain is the pattern of lines in a piece of wood made by the fibres in it.
PHRASE **5.** If something **goes against the grain**, you find it difficult to accept because it is against your principles.

gram grams
NOUN a unit of weight equal to one-thousandth of a kilogram

Gg

grammar

NOUN Grammar is the rules of a language relating to the ways you can combine words to form sentences.

grammatical

ADJECTIVE **1.** relating to grammar: *grammatical knowledge* **2.** following the rules of grammar correctly: *grammatical sentences*

grammatically ADVERB

granary granaries

NOUN a building for storing grain

grand grander grandest

ADJECTIVE **1.** magnificent in appearance and size: *a grand house* **2.** very important: *the grand scheme of your life* **3.** *an informal use* very pleasant or enjoyable: *It was a grand day.* **4.** A grand total is the final complete amount.

NOUN **5.** *an informal use* a thousand dollars

grandly ADVERB

grandchild grandchildren

NOUN Someone's grandchildren are the children of his or her son or daughter.

granddaughter granddaughters

NOUN Someone's granddaughter is the daughter of his or her son or daughter.

grandeur

NOUN Grandeur is great beauty and magnificence.

grandfather grandfathers

NOUN Your grandfather is your father's father or your mother's father.

grandfather clock grandfather clocks

NOUN a clock in a tall wooden case that stands on the floor

grandiose

ADJECTIVE intended to be very impressive, but seeming ridiculous: *a grandiose gesture of love*

grandma grandmas

NOUN *an informal word* Your grandma is your grandmother.

grandmother grandmothers

NOUN Your grandmother is your father's mother or your mother's mother.

grandpa grandpas

NOUN *an informal word* Your grandpa is your grandfather.

grandparent grandparents

NOUN Your grandparents are your parents' parents.

grand piano grand pianos

NOUN a large, flat piano with horizontal strings

grandson grandsons

NOUN Someone's grandson is the son of his or her son or daughter.

grandstand grandstands

NOUN a structure with seats and usually a roof for spectators at an event such as a parade or race

granite

NOUN Granite is a very hard rock used in building.

granny grannies

NOUN *an informal word* Your granny is your grandmother.

grant grants granting granted

NOUN **1.** an amount of money that an official body gives to someone for a particular purpose: *a grant for research*

VERB **2.** If you grant something to someone, you allow that person to have it. **3.** If you grant that something is true, you admit that it is true.

PHRASES **4.** If you **take something for granted**, you believe it without thinking about it. If you **take someone for granted**, you benefit from that person without showing that you are grateful.

granule granules

NOUN a very small piece of something: *granules of salt*

grape grapes

NOUN a small green, red, or purple fruit, eaten raw or used to make wine

grapefruit grapefruits

NOUN a large, round, yellow citrus fruit

grapevine grapevines

NOUN **1.** a climbing plant that grapes grow on **2.** If you hear some news **through the grapevine**, that news has been passed on from person to person, usually unofficially or secretly.

graph graphs

NOUN a diagram in which a line shows how two sets of numbers or measurements are related

-graph

SUFFIX The suffix *-graph* means *written or recorded* or *something made by writing, drawing, or recording: telegraph, autograph*

graphic graphics

ADJECTIVE **1.** A graphic description is very detailed and lifelike. **2.** relating to drawing or painting

PLURAL NOUN **3.** Graphics are drawings and pictures composed of simple lines and strong colours: *computerized graphics*

graphically ADVERB

 ⚠ **HEADS UP** The word **grandiose** is pronounced gran-dee-OSE.

Gg

graphic organizer
NOUN a chart or diagram used to arrange or sort information in a visual way

graphite
NOUN a black form of carbon that is used in pencil leads

grapple grapples grappling grappled
VERB **1.** If you grapple with someone, you struggle with that person while fighting. **2.** If you grapple with a problem, you try hard to solve it.

grasp grasps grasping grasped
VERB **1.** If you grasp something, you hold it firmly. **2.** If you grasp an idea, you understand it.
NOUN **3.** a firm hold **4.** Your grasp of something is your understanding of it.

grass grasses
NOUN Grass is the common, green plant that grows on lawns and in parks.
grassy ADJECTIVE

grasshopper grasshoppers
NOUN an insect with long back legs that it uses for jumping and making a high-pitched sound

grate grates grating grated
NOUN **1.** a framework of metal bars in a fireplace
VERB **2.** To grate food means to shred it into small pieces by rubbing it against a grater. **3.** When something grates on something else, it rubs against it making a harsh sound. **4.** If something grates on you, it irritates you.

grateful
ADJECTIVE If you are grateful for something, you are glad you have it and want to thank the person who gave it to you.
gratefully ADVERB

grater graters
NOUN a small, metal tool used for grating food

gratify gratifies gratifying gratified
VERB **1.** If you are gratified by something, you are pleased by it. **2.** If you gratify a wish or feeling, you satisfy it.

grating gratings
NOUN **1.** a metal frame with bars across it fastened over a window or in the ground
ADJECTIVE **2.** A grating sound is harsh and unpleasant: *grating melodies*

gratis
ADVERB OR ADJECTIVE free: *food and drink supplied gratis*

gratitude
NOUN Gratitude is the feeling of being grateful.

gratuitous
ADJECTIVE unnecessary: *a gratuitous attack*
gratuitously ADVERB

grave graves; graver gravest
NOUN **1.** a place where a dead body is buried
ADJECTIVE **2.** very serious: *grave danger*

grave
ADJECTIVE In French and some other languages, a grave accent is a line sloping downward from left to right placed over a vowel to indicate a change in pronunciation, as in the word *poème* (poem).

gravel
NOUN Gravel is small stones used for making roads and paths.

gravestone gravestones
NOUN a large stone placed over someone's grave, with his or her name on it

graveyard graveyards
NOUN an area of land where dead bodies are buried

gravitate gravitates gravitating gravitated
VERB When people gravitate toward something, they go toward it because they are attracted by it.

gravitation
NOUN Gravitation is the force that causes objects to be attracted to each other.
gravitational ADJECTIVE

gravity
NOUN **1.** Gravity is the force that makes things fall when you drop them. **2.** The gravity of a situation is its seriousness.

SPELL-CHECK THIS!

A computer's spell-check won't catch wrong **homophones** (words that are spelled differently but sound the same).

The movie's special effects were grate.

In this sentence, **grate** should be **great**. **Great** means *excellent*. **Grate** means *affect harshly*.

Gg

gravy
NOUN Gravy is a brown sauce made from meat juices.

graze grazes grazing grazed
VERB **1.** When animals graze, they eat grass. **2.** If something grazes a part of your body, it scrapes against it, injuring you slightly.
NOUN **3.** a slight injury caused by something scraping against your skin

grease greases greasing greased
NOUN **1.** Grease is an oily substance used for lubricating machines. **2.** Grease is also melted animal fat, used in cooking.
VERB **3.** If you grease something, you lubricate it with grease.
greasy ADJECTIVE

great greater greatest
ADJECTIVE **1.** very large: *a great sea, great efforts* **2.** very important: *a great artist* **3.** *an informal use* very good: *We had a great time.*

Instead of **GREAT** try…

a **celebrated** musician
an **important** question
first-rate service
a **rave** review
an **admirable** effort
exceptional intelligence
a **superb** action scene
an **outstanding** achievement

greatly ADVERB
greatness NOUN

Great Dane Great Danes
NOUN a very large dog with short hair

great-grandfather great-grandfathers
NOUN Your great-grandfather is your father's or mother's grandfather.

great-grandmother great-grandmothers
NOUN Your great-grandmother is your father's or mother's grandmother.

greed
NOUN Greed is a desire for more of something than you really need.

greedy greedier greediest
ADJECTIVE wanting more of something than you really need
greedily ADVERB
greediness NOUN

green greener greenest; greens
ADJECTIVE OR NOUN **1.** Green is a colour between yellow and blue on the spectrum.
NOUN **2.** an area of smooth, short grass around each hole on a golf course
PLURAL NOUN **3.** Greens are green vegetables.

ADJECTIVE **4.** *Green* is used to describe things that are concerned with environmental issues: *green products* **6.** *an informal use* Someone who is green is young and inexperienced.

greenery
NOUN Greenery is a lot of trees, bushes, or other green plants together in one place.

greenhouse greenhouses
NOUN a glass building in which people grow plants that need to be kept warm

greenhouse effect
NOUN the gradual rise in temperature in the earth's atmosphere due to heat being absorbed from the sun and being trapped by gases such as carbon dioxide in the air around the earth

greet greets greeting greeted
VERB **1.** If you greet someone, you say something friendly like *hello* to that person when you meet him or her. **2.** If you greet something in a particular way, you react to it in that way: *He was greeted with deep suspicion.*

greeting greetings
NOUN something friendly that you say to someone when you meet: *Her greeting was warm.*

gregarious
ADJECTIVE Someone who is gregarious enjoys being with other people.

grenade grenades
NOUN a small bomb, containing explosives or tear gas, which can be thrown

grew the past tense of GROW

grey greyer greyest; greys greying greyed
ADJECTIVE OR NOUN **1.** Grey is a colour between black and white.
ADJECTIVE **2.** with grey hair: *He went grey when he was quite young.*
VERB **3.** If someone is greying, that person's hair is going grey.
greyness NOUN

greyhound greyhounds
NOUN a thin dog with long legs that can run very fast

grid grids
NOUN **1.** a pattern of lines crossing each other to form squares **2.** The grid is the network of wires and cables by which electricity is distributed throughout a country.

grief
NOUN **1.** Grief is extreme sadness.
PHRASE **2.** If someone or something **comes to grief**, that person or thing fails or is injured.

grievance grievances
NOUN a reason for complaining

grieve grieves grieving grieved
VERB **1.** If you grieve, you are extremely sad, especially because someone has died. **2.** If something grieves you, it makes you feel sad.

grievous
ADJECTIVE *a formal word* extremely serious: *grievous damage*
grievously ADVERB

grill grills grilling grilled
NOUN **1.** a metal frame on which you cook food over direct heat
VERB **2.** If you grill food, you cook it on a grill. **3.** *an informal use* If you grill someone, you ask that person a lot of questions in a very intense way.

grille grilles
NOUN a metal framework over a window or piece of machinery, used for protection

grim grimmer grimmest
ADJECTIVE **1.** If a situation or piece of news is grim, it is very unpleasant and worrying: *There are grim times ahead.* **2.** Grim places are unattractive and depressing. **3.** If someone is grim, that person is very serious or stern.
grimly ADVERB

grimace grimaces grimacing grimaced
NOUN **1.** a twisted facial expression indicating disgust or pain
VERB **2.** When someone grimaces, that person makes a grimace.

grime
NOUN Grime is thick dirt that gathers on the surface of something.
grimy ADJECTIVE

grin grins grinning grinned
VERB **1.** If you grin, you smile broadly.
NOUN **2.** a broad smile
PHRASE **3.** If you **grin and bear it**, you accept a difficult situation without complaining.

grind grinds grinding ground
VERB **1.** If you grind something such as pepper, you crush it into a fine powder.
2. If you grind your teeth, you rub your upper and lower teeth together.
PHRASE **3.** If something **grinds to a halt**, it stops: *Progress ground to a halt.*

grip grips gripping gripped
NOUN **1.** a firm hold **2.** a handle **3.** Your grip on a situation is your control over it.
VERB **4.** If you grip something, you hold it firmly.
PHRASE **5.** If you **come to grips with** a situation or problem, you start to deal with it effectively.

grisly grislier grisliest
ADJECTIVE very nasty and horrible: *a grisly murder scene*

grit grits gritting gritted
NOUN **1.** Grit consists of very small stones or sand.
PHRASE **2.** To **grit your teeth** means to decide to carry on in a difficult situation.
gritty ADJECTIVE

grizzled
ADJECTIVE Grizzled hair is grey. A grizzled person has grey hair.

grizzly grizzlies
NOUN a large, greyish brown bear found in North America

groan groans groaning groaned
VERB **1.** If you groan, you make a long, low sound of pain, unhappiness, or disapproval.
NOUN **2.** the sound you make when you groan

grocer grocers
NOUN a shopkeeper who sells many kinds of food and other household goods

grocery groceries
NOUN **1.** A grocery, or **grocery store**, is a place where you can buy food and other household items.
PLURAL NOUN **2.** Groceries are the goods that you buy in a grocer's store.

groin groins
NOUN the area where your legs join the main part of your body at the front

groom grooms grooming groomed
NOUN **1.** At a wedding, the groom is the bridegroom. **2.** someone who looks after horses in a stable
VERB **3.** To groom an animal means to clean its fur. **4.** If you groom someone for a job, you prepare that person for it by teaching him or her the required skills.

groove grooves
NOUN a deep line cut into a surface
grooved ADJECTIVE

grope gropes groping groped
VERB **1.** If you grope for something you cannot see, you search for it with your hands. **2.** If you grope for something such as the solution to a problem, you try to think of it.

gross grosser grossest
ADJECTIVE **1.** extremely bad: *a gross betrayal*
2. Gross speech or behaviour is very vulgar.
3. Someone's gross income is his or her total income before any deductions are made.
4. The gross weight of something is its total weight including the weight of its container.
grossly ADVERB

⚠ **HEADS UP** Grisly, meaning *horrible*, and **grizzly**, meaning *the bear*, are pronounced the same: GRIZZ-lee.

NEL

Gg

grotesque
ADJECTIVE **1.** exaggerated and absurd: *It was the most grotesque thing she had ever heard.* **2.** very strange and ugly: *The book had pictures of grotesque creatures.*
grotesquely ADVERB

grotto grottoes
NOUN a small cave that people visit because it is attractive

ground grounds grounding grounded
NOUN **1.** The ground is the surface of the earth. **2.** a piece of land that is used for a particular purpose: *a training ground, a camping ground*
PLURAL NOUN **3.** The grounds of a house or building are the land belonging to it and surrounding it. **4.** *a formal use* The grounds for something are the reasons for it: *genuine grounds for caution*
VERB **5.** *a formal use* If something is grounded in something else, it is based on it. **6.** If an aircraft is grounded, it has to remain on the ground. **7.** Ground is the past tense and past participle of GRIND.

ground floor ground floors
NOUN The ground floor of a building is the floor that is level with the ground.

grounding
NOUN If you have a grounding in a skill or subject, you have had basic instruction in it.

groundless
ADJECTIVE not based on reason or evidence: *groundless accusations*

group groups grouping grouped
NOUN **1.** A group of things or people is a number of them that are linked together in some way. **2.** a number of people or things of a certain kind: *Milk and cheese belong to the dairy group.*
VERB **3.** When things or people are grouped together, they are linked together in some way.

grouping groupings
NOUN a number of things or people that are linked together in some way

grouse grouse
NOUN a fat, brown or grey bird, often hunted for sport

grove groves
NOUN *a literary or poetic word* a group of trees growing close together

grovel grovels grovelling grovelled
VERB If you grovel, you behave in an unpleasantly humble way toward someone you regard as important.

grow grows growing grew grown
VERB **1.** To grow means to increase in size or amount. **2.** If a tree or plant grows somewhere, it is alive there. **3.** To grow also means to pass gradually into a particular state. **4.** If one thing grows from another, it develops from it. **5.** *an informal use* If something grows on you, you gradually get to like it.

grow up
VERB **6.** When a child grows up, he or she becomes an adult.

growl growls growling growled
VERB **1.** When an animal growls, it makes a low, rumbling sound, usually because it is angry. **2.** If you growl, you say something in a low, rough, angry voice.
NOUN **3.** the sound an animal makes when it growls

grown-up grown-ups
NOUN **1.** *an informal use* an adult
ADJECTIVE **2.** A grown-up person is an adult, or someone who behaves like an adult.

growth growths
NOUN **1.** When there is a growth in something, it gets bigger: *the growth of the fishing industry* **2.** Growth is the process by which something develops to its full size. **3.** an abnormal lump that grows inside or on a person, animal, or plant

grub grubs
NOUN **1.** a wormlike insect that has just hatched from its egg **2.** *an informal use* Grub is food.

grubby grubbier grubbiest
ADJECTIVE dirty

grudge grudges grudging grudged
NOUN **1.** If you have a grudge against someone, you resent that person because he or she has harmed you in the past.
VERB **2.** If you grudge someone something, you give it to that person unwillingly, or are displeased that he or she has it.

grudging
ADJECTIVE done or felt unwillingly: *grudging admiration*
grudgingly ADVERB

gruel
NOUN Gruel is oatmeal boiled in water or milk.

gruelling
ADJECTIVE difficult and tiring: *a gruelling race*

gruesome
ADJECTIVE shocking and horrible: *gruesome pictures*

gruff gruffer gruffest
ADJECTIVE If someone's voice is gruff, it sounds rough and unfriendly.

Gg

grumble grumbles grumbling grumbled
VERB **1.** If you grumble, you complain in a bad-tempered way.
NOUN **2.** a bad-tempered complaint

grumpy grumpier grumpiest
ADJECTIVE bad-tempered

grunt grunts grunting grunted
VERB **1.** If a person or a pig grunts, that person or pig makes a short, low, gruff sound.
NOUN **2.** the sound a person or a pig makes when grunting

guarantee guarantees guaranteeing guaranteed
NOUN **1.** If something is a guarantee of something else, it makes it certain that it will happen. **2.** a written promise that if a product develops a fault it will be replaced or repaired free
VERB **3.** If someone or something guarantees something, that person or thing makes certain that it will happen: *Money may not guarantee success.*
guarantor NOUN

guard guards guarding guarded
VERB **1.** If you guard an object, you stay near that object to protect it. **2.** If you guard a person, you stop that person from making trouble or escaping. **3.** If you guard against something, you are careful to avoid that thing from happening.
NOUN **4.** a person or group of people who guard a person, object, or place **5.** Any object that covers something to prevent it from causing harm can be called a guard: *a skate guard, shin guards*

guardian guardians
NOUN **1.** someone who has been legally appointed to look after a child **2.** A guardian of something is someone who protects that thing: *a guardian of the law*
guardianship NOUN

Instead of **GUESS** try...

infer the meaning
I can only suppose
predict the weather
estimate your weight
speculate what will happen

guerrilla guerrillas
NOUN a member of a small, unofficial army fighting an official army

guess guesses guessing guessed
VERB **1.** If you guess something, you form or express an opinion that it is the case, without having much information.
NOUN **2.** an attempt to give the correct answer to something without having much information, or without working it out properly

guest guests
NOUN **1.** someone who stays at your home or who attends an event because he or she has been invited **2.** The guests in a hotel are the people staying there.

guffaw
NOUN a loud, coarse laugh

guidance
NOUN Guidance is help and advice.

guide guides guiding guided
NOUN **1.** a person or thing that shows the way around places **2.** a book that gives you information or instructions: *a Vancouver street guide*
VERB **3.** If you guide someone in a particular direction, you lead that person in that direction. **4.** If you are guided by something, it influences your actions or decisions.

guidebook guidebooks
NOUN a book that gives information about a place

guide dog guide dogs
NOUN a dog that has been trained to lead a blind person

guideline guidelines
NOUN a piece of advice about how something should be done

guild guilds
NOUN a society of people: *the Literacy Guild*

guile
NOUN Guile is cunning and deceit.
guileless ADJECTIVE

guillotine guillotines
NOUN a machine used for beheading people, especially in the past

guilt
NOUN **1.** Guilt is an unhappy feeling of having done something wrong. **2.** Someone's guilt is the fact that he or she has done something wrong: *The law will decide their guilt.*

guilty guiltier guiltiest
ADJECTIVE **1.** If you are guilty of doing something wrong, you did it: *He was guilty of theft.* **2.** If you feel guilty, you are unhappy because you have done something wrong.
guiltily ADVERB

guinea pig guinea pigs
NOUN **1.** a small, furry animal without a tail, often kept as a pet **2.** a person used to try something out on: *a guinea pig for a new drug*

Gg

guise guises
NOUN a misleading appearance: *He hid his intentions under the guise of friendship.*

guitar guitars
NOUN a musical instrument with six strings that are strummed or plucked
guitarist NOUN

gulf gulfs
NOUN **1.** a very large bay **2.** a wide gap or difference between two things or people

gull gulls
NOUN a sea bird with long wings, white and grey or black feathers, and webbed feet

gullet gullets
NOUN the passage that goes from your mouth to your stomach

gullible
ADJECTIVE easily tricked
gullibility NOUN

gully gullies
NOUN a long, narrow valley

gulp gulps gulping gulped
VERB **1.** If you gulp food or drink, you swallow large quantities of it. **2.** If you gulp, you swallow air, because you are nervous.
NOUN **3.** A gulp of food or drink is a large quantity of it swallowed at one time.

gum gums
NOUN **1.** Gum is a soft, flavoured substance that people chew but do not swallow.
2. A sticky juice secreted by some trees that hardens in air and dissolves in water. **3.** Your gums are the firm flesh in which your teeth are set.

gun guns
NOUN a weapon that fires bullets or shells

gunfire
NOUN Gunfire is the repeated firing of guns.

gunpowder
NOUN Gunpowder is an explosive powder made from a mixture of potassium nitrate and other substances.

gunshot gunshots
NOUN the sound of a gun being fired

guppy guppies
NOUN a small, brightly coloured tropical fish

gurdwara
NOUN a Sikh place of worship

gurgle gurgles gurgling gurgled
VERB **1.** To gurgle means to make a bubbling sound.
NOUN **2.** a bubbling sound

guru gurus
NOUN in Hinduism, a spiritual leader and teacher

gush gushes gushing gushed
VERB **1.** When liquid gushes from something, it flows out of it in large quantities. **2.** When people gush, they express admiration or pleasure in an exaggerated way.
gushing ADJECTIVE

gust gusts
NOUN a sudden rush of wind
gusty ADJECTIVE

gusto
NOUN Gusto is energy and enthusiasm: *Her gusto for life was amazing.*

gut guts gutting gutted
PLURAL NOUN **1.** Your guts are your internal organs, especially your intestines. **2.** *an informal use* courage
VERB **3.** To gut a dead fish means to remove its internal organs. **4.** If a building is gutted, the inside of it is destroyed, especially by fire.

gutter gutters
NOUN **1.** the edge of a road next to the pavement, where rain collects and flows away **2.** a channel fixed to the edge of a roof, where rain collects and flows away

guttural
ADJECTIVE Guttural sounds are produced at the back of a person's throat.

guy guys
NOUN *an informal use* a man or boy

guzzle guzzles guzzling guzzled
VERB To guzzle something means to drink or eat it quickly and greedily.

gym gyms
NOUN **1.** a gymnasium **2.** a school subject involving exercise, sports, and games

gymnasium gymnasiums
NOUN a room with special equipment for physical exercises

gymnast gymnasts
NOUN someone who is trained in gymnastics
gymnastic ADJECTIVE

gymnastics
NOUN Gymnastics is physical exercises, especially ones that develop or display physical ability and coordination.

gynecology
NOUN Gynecology is the branch of medical science concerned with the female reproductive system.
gynecologist NOUN
gynecological ADJECTIVE

gypsy gypsies
NOUN a wandering person

gyrate gyrates gyrating gyrated
VERB To gyrate means to move around in a circle.

 **HEADS UP** The word **guise** is pronounced GUYZ.

Hh

habit habits

NOUN **1.** something that you do often: *He got into the habit of eating out.* **2.** something that you keep doing and find it difficult to stop doing: *a caffeine habit* **3.** a distinctive garment worn by members of some religious orders

habitual ADJECTIVE

habitually ADVERB

habitant habitants

NOUN **1.** a French-Canadian farmer

ADJECTIVE **2.** to do with rural French Canada, especially in the past

habitat habitats

NOUN the natural home of a plant or animal

hack hacks hacking hacked

VERB **1.** If you hack at something, you cut it using rough strokes.

NOUN **2.** a writer or journalist who produces work fast without worrying about quality

hacker hackers

NOUN *an informal word* someone who uses a computer to break into the computer system of a company or government

hackles

PLURAL NOUN **1.** A dog's hackles are the hairs on the back of its neck that rise when it is angry.

PHRASE **2.** Something that **makes your hackles rise** makes you angry.

hackneyed

ADJECTIVE A hackneyed phrase is meaningless because it has been used too often.

hacksaw hacksaws

NOUN a small saw with a narrow blade set in a frame, used for cutting metal

haddock

NOUN an edible fish of the North Atlantic

hag hags

NOUN *an offensive word* an ugly, old woman

haggard

ADJECTIVE A person who is haggard looks very tired and ill.

haggis

NOUN Haggis is a Scottish dish made of the internal organs of a sheep, boiled together with oatmeal and spices in a skin.

haggle haggles haggling haggled

VERB If you haggle with someone, you argue with that person, usually about the cost of something.

hail hails hailing hailed

NOUN **1.** Hail is frozen rain. **2.** A hail of things is a lot of them falling together: *a hail of insults, a hail of protest*

VERB **3.** When it is hailing, frozen rain is falling. **4.** If someone hails you, that person calls you to attract your attention or greet you: *She hailed a taxi.*

hair hairs

Instead of **HAIR** try…

NOUN Hair consists of the long, threadlike strands that grow from the skin of animals and humans.

curly locks

a dog's coat

silky tresses

a wild mane

a hamster's fur

haircut haircuts

NOUN the cutting of someone's hair; also the style in which it is cut

hairdo hairdos

NOUN a hairstyle

hairdresser hairdressers

NOUN someone who is trained to cut and style people's hair; also a store where this is done

hairdressing NOUN OR ADJECTIVE

hairline hairlines

NOUN **1.** the edge of the area on your forehead where hair growth ends

ADJECTIVE **2.** A line so fine that you can hardly see it: *a hairline fracture*

hairpin hairpins

NOUN **1.** a U-shaped wire used to hold hair in position

ADJECTIVE **2.** A hairpin bend is a U-shaped bend in the road.

hair-raising

ADJECTIVE very frightening or exciting

hairstyle hairstyles

NOUN Someone's hairstyle is the way in which that person's hair is arranged or cut.

hairy hairier hairiest

ADJECTIVE **1.** covered in a lot of hair

2. *an informal use* difficult, exciting, and frightening: *He had lived through many hairy adventures.*

hajj

NOUN The hajj is the pilgrimage to Mecca that all Muslims are expected to make at least once in their life.

halcyon

ADJECTIVE **1.** *a literary or poetic word* peaceful, gentle, and calm: *halcyon colours of yellow and turquoise*

PHRASE **2. Halcyon days** are a happy and carefree time in the past: *the halcyon days of childhood*

half halves
NOUN, ADJECTIVE, OR ADVERB **1.** Half refers to one of two equal parts that make up a whole: *the two halves of the brain. They chatted for another half hour. The bottle was only half full.*
ADVERB **2.** You can use *half* to say that something is only partly true: *I half expected him to explode in anger.*

half-baked
ADJECTIVE *an informal word* Half-baked ideas or plans have not been properly thought out.

half-brother half-brothers
NOUN Your half-brother is the son of either your mother or your father but not of your other parent.

half-hearted
ADJECTIVE showing no real effort or enthusiasm

half-sister half-sisters
NOUN Your half-sister is the daughter of either your mother or your father but not of your other parent.

half-time
NOUN Half-time is a short break between two parts of a game when the players have a rest.

halfway
ADVERB at the middle of the distance between two points in place or time: *We are halfway through the semester. He stopped halfway down the ladder.*

halibut halibuts
NOUN a large, edible flatfish of the Atlantic and Pacific

hall halls
NOUN **1.** a passageway through a building with rooms leading off it **2.** the room just inside the front entrance of a house that leads into other rooms **3.** a large room or building used for public events: *a concert hall*

hallmark hallmarks
NOUN **1.** A hallmark is the most typical quality of a person or group: *Loyalty is the hallmark of a friend.* **2.** an official mark on gold or silver indicating the quality of the metal

hallowed
ADJECTIVE respected as being holy: *hallowed ground*

Halloween
NOUN Halloween is the evening of October 31, and is celebrated by people dressing up in costume.

hallucinate hallucinates hallucinating hallucinated
VERB If you hallucinate, you see strange things in your mind because of illness or drugs.
hallucination NOUN
hallucinatory ADJECTIVE

halo halos
NOUN a circle of light around the head of a holy figure that represents holiness

halt halts halting halted
VERB **1.** To halt when moving means to stop. **2.** To halt development or action means to stop it.
NOUN **3.** a short standstill

halter halters
NOUN a strap fastened around a horse's head so that it can be led easily

halve halves halving halved
VERB **1.** If you halve something, you divide it into two equal parts. **2.** To halve something also means to reduce its size or amount by half.

ham hams
NOUN **1.** meat from the hind leg of a pig, salted and cured **2.** *an informal use* a bad actor who exaggerates emotions and gestures **3.** *an informal use* someone who is interested in amateur radio

hamburger hamburgers
NOUN a flat disc of ground beef, seasoned and fried, eaten in a split bun or bread roll; also the meat itself

hammer hammers hammering hammered
NOUN **1.** a tool consisting of a heavy piece of metal at the end of a handle, used for hitting nails into things
VERB **2.** If you hammer something, you hit it repeatedly, with a hammer or with your fist. **3.** If you hammer an idea into someone, you keep repeating it and telling that person about it.

hammock hammocks
NOUN a piece of net or canvas hung between two supports and used as a bed

hamper hampers hampering hampered
NOUN **1.** a large, rectangular basket with a lid: *a laundry hamper, a picnic hamper*
VERB **2.** If you hamper someone, you make it difficult for that person to move or progress.

hamster hamsters
NOUN a small, furry rodent that is often kept as a pet

hamstring hamstrings
NOUN Your hamstring is a tendon behind your knee joining your thigh muscles to the bones of your lower leg.

hand hands handing handed
NOUN **1.** Your hand is the part of your body beyond the wrist, with four fingers and a thumb. **2.** Your hand is also your writing style. **3.** The hand of someone in a situation is that person's influence or the part that person plays in it: *He had a hand in the game's design.* **4.** If you give someone a hand, you help that person to do something. **5.** When an audience gives someone a big hand, they applaud. **6.** The hands of a clock or watch are the pointers that point to the numbers. **7.** In cards, a hand is one round of a card game or the cards a person is holding in a round.
VERB **8.** If you hand something to someone, you give it to that person.
PHRASE **9.** Something that is **at hand** is near in time or space: *Winter is at hand.*
10. Something that is **on hand** is available and ready for use. **11.** You use **on the one hand** to introduce the first part of an argument or discussion with two different points of view. **12.** You use **on the other hand** to introduce the second part of an argument or discussion with two different points of view. **13.** If you do something **by hand**, you do it using your hands rather than a machine.

hand down
VERB **14.** Something that is handed down is passed from one generation to another.

handbag handbags
NOUN a small bag used mainly by women to carry money and personal items

handbook handbooks
NOUN a book giving information and instructions about something

handcuff handcuffs
NOUN Handcuffs are two metal rings linked by a chain that are locked around a prisoner's wrists.

handful handfuls
NOUN **1.** A handful of something is the amount of it you can hold in your hand: *I picked up a handful of seeds.* **2.** a small quantity: *Only a handful of people knew.* **3.** Someone or something that is a handful is difficult to control: *My new puppy is quite a handful.*

handicap handicaps handicapping handicapped
NOUN **1.** something that makes it difficult for a person to achieve something **2.** In sport, a handicap is a disadvantage or an advantage given to competitors according to their skill, in order to give them an equal chance of winning.
VERB **3.** If something handicaps someone, it makes it difficult for that person to achieve something.

> ⚠ **HEADS UP**
>
> Don't use **handicapped** as a noun. Put people first: *a person with a disability, a woman who is blind.*

handicraft handicrafts
NOUN Handicrafts are activities such as embroidery or pottery that involve making things with your hands; also the items produced.

handiwork
NOUN Your handiwork is something that you have done or made yourself.

handkerchief handkerchiefs
NOUN a small square of fabric used for blowing your nose

handle handles handling handled
NOUN **1.** The handle of an object is the part by which it is held or controlled. **2.** a small

KNOWING WORDS: IDIOMS

BE WORD SHARP!

Idioms add colour to language by playing with the meanings of words.

hand the part of an arm below the wrist

give someone a hand help that person

hands are tied unable to do anything

have your hands full be as busy as possible

in/on your hands in your care

off your hands no longer in your care

Hh

lever used to open and close a door or window

VERB **3.** If you handle an object, you hold it in your hands to examine it. **4.** If you handle something, you deal with it or control it: *I have learned how to handle pressure.*

handlebars
PLURAL NOUN Handlebars are the bar and handles at the front of a bicycle, used for steering.

handout handouts
NOUN **1.** a piece of paper giving information about something **2.** a gift of food, clothing, or money given to a poor person

hand-picked
ADJECTIVE carefully chosen: *a hand-picked team of assistants*

handset handsets
NOUN The handset of a telephone is the part that you speak into and listen with.

handshake handshakes
NOUN the grasping and shaking of a person's hand by another person

handsome
ADJECTIVE **1.** very attractive in appearance **2.** large and generous: *a handsome profit*
handsomely ADVERB

handwriting
NOUN Someone's handwriting is his or her style of writing as it looks on the page.

handy handier handiest
ADJECTIVE **1.** conveniently near **2.** easy to handle or use **3.** skilful

hang hangs hanging hung
VERB **1.** If you hang something somewhere, you attach it to a high point: *She hung heavy, red velvet curtains in the living room.* **2.** If something, such as a jacket, is hanging on another thing, such as a hook, that thing is dangling by its top from the hook. **3.** When you hang wallpaper, you stick it onto a wall. **4.** To hang someone means to kill that person by suspending him or her by a rope around the neck.
PHRASE **5.** When you **get the hang of something**, you understand it and are able to do it.
hang around
VERB **6.** *an informal use* To hang around means to wait somewhere. **7.** To hang around with someone means to spend a lot of time with that person.
hang on
VERB **8.** If you hang on to something, you hold it tightly or keep it. **9.** *an informal use* To hang on means to wait.
hang over
VERB **10.** If a future event or possibility is hanging over you, it worries or frightens

you: *They have an eviction notice hanging over them.*
hang up
VERB **11.** When you hang up, you disconnect to end a telephone call.

hangar hangars
NOUN a large building where aircraft are kept

hanger hangers
NOUN a coat hanger

hanger-on hangers-on
NOUN a person who follows or depends upon another person, especially for personal gain

hang-glider hang-gliders
NOUN an aircraft without an engine and consisting of a large frame covered in fabric, from which the pilot hangs in a harness

hangover hangovers
NOUN a feeling of sickness and headache after drinking too much alcohol

hangup hangups
NOUN A hangup about something is a continual feeling of embarrassment or fear about it.

hanker hankers hankering hankered
VERB If you hanker after something, you continually want it.
hankering NOUN

hanky hankies
NOUN *an informal word* a handkerchief

Hanukkah
NOUN In Judaism, Hanukkah is an eight-day festival that celebrates the rededication of the Temple in Israel.

haphazard
ADJECTIVE not organized or planned
haphazardly ADVERB

hapless
ADJECTIVE *a literary or poetic word* unlucky

happen happens happening happened
VERB **1.** When something happens, it occurs or takes place. **2.** If you happen to do something, you do it by chance.
happening NOUN

happiness
NOUN a feeling of great contentment or pleasure

happy happier happiest
ADJECTIVE **1.** feeling, showing, or producing contentment or pleasure: *a happy smile, a happy atmosphere* **2.** satisfied that something is right: *I wasn't very happy about the decision he made.* **3.** willing: *I would be happy to help.* **4.** fortunate or lucky: *a happy coincidence*
happily ADVERB

happy-go-lucky
ADJECTIVE carefree and unconcerned

Hh

harangue harangues haranguing harangued
NOUN **1.** a long, forceful, passionate speech
VERB **2.** To harangue someone means to talk to that person at length passionately and forcefully about something.

harass harasses harassing harassed
VERB If someone harasses you, that person troubles or annoys you continually.
harassed ADJECTIVE
harassment NOUN

harbinger harbingers
NOUN a person or thing that announces or indicates the approach of a future event: *The robin is a harbinger of spring.*

harbour harbours harbouring harboured
NOUN **1.** a protected area of deep water where boats can be moored
VERB **2.** To harbour someone means to hide that person secretly in your house. **3.** If you harbour a feeling, you have it for a long time: *She's still harbouring great bitterness toward me.*

hard harder hardest

ADJECTIVE **1.** Something that is hard is firm, solid, or stiff: *a hard piece of cheese*
2. requiring a lot of

Instead of **HARD** try...

a complex puzzle
a demanding job
a firm mattress
tiring work
solid concrete
a forceful push
a piercing stare
a difficult problem

effort: *hard work*
3. difficult: *These are hard times.*
4. Someone who is hard has no kindness or pity: *Don't be hard on him.* **5.** Hard evidence or facts can be proved to be true.
6. Hard water contains a lot of lime. Soap does not easily produce lather in hard water. **7.** Hard drugs are very strong illegal drugs. **8.** Hard drink is strong alcohol.
ADVERB **9.** earnestly or intently: *They tried hard to attract tourists* **10.** An event that follows hard upon something takes place immediately afterwards.
PHRASE **11.** Something that is **hard and fast** is fixed and not able to be changed: *hard and fast rules* **12.** If someone is **hard of hearing**, that person is somewhat deaf. **13.** *an informal expression* If someone is **hard up** that person has hardly any money.
hardness NOUN

hard-core
ADJECTIVE If someone is hard-core, that person is the most committed or established in a group: *a hard-core fan of science fiction*

hardcover hardcovers
NOUN a book with a stiff cover

harden hardens hardening hardened
VERB To harden means to become hard or get harder.
hardening NOUN
hardened ADJECTIVE

hard labour
NOUN physical work that is difficult and tiring, used in some countries as a punishment for a crime

hardly
ADVERB **1.** almost not or not quite: *I could hardly believe it.* **2.** certainly not: *It's hardly a secret.*

hard-nosed
ADJECTIVE tough, practical, and realistic

hardship hardships
NOUN Hardship is a time or situation of suffering and difficulty.

hardware
NOUN **1.** Hardware is tools and equipment for use in the home and garden. **2.** Hardware is also computer machinery rather than computer programs.

hardwood hardwoods
NOUN strong, hard wood from a tree such as an oak; also the tree itself

hardy hardier hardiest
ADJECTIVE tough and able to endure very difficult or cold conditions: *a hardy race of pioneers*

hare hares haring hared
NOUN **1.** an animal like a large rabbit, but with longer ears and legs
VERB **2.** To hare off means to run very fast: *He hared off down the corridor.*

hark harks harking harked
VERB **1.** *a literary or poetic use* To hark means to listen.
PHRASE **2.** To **hark back to** something in the past means to refer back to it or recall it.

harm harms harming harmed
VERB **1.** To harm someone or something means to injure or damage that person or thing.
NOUN **2.** Harm is injury or damage.

harmful
ADJECTIVE having a bad effect on something: *While most stress is harmful, some is beneficial.*

harmless
ADJECTIVE **1.** safe to use or be near **2.** unlikely to cause problems or annoyance: *The dog is harmless and really quite friendly.*
harmlessly ADVERB

harmonic
ADJECTIVE using musical harmony

harmonica harmonicas
NOUN a small musical instrument that you play by blowing and sucking while moving it across your lips

harmonious
ADJECTIVE **1.** showing agreement, peacefulness, and friendship: *a harmonious relationship* **2.** consisting of parts that blend well together making an attractive whole: *harmonious interior décor*
harmoniously ADVERB

harmony harmonies
NOUN **1.** Harmony is a state of peaceful agreement and co-operation: *the promotion of racial harmony* **2.** Harmony is the structure and relationship of chords in a piece of music. **3.** Harmony is the pleasant combination of two or more notes played at the same time.

harness harnesses harnessing harnessed
NOUN **1.** a set of straps and fittings fastened around a horse so that it can pull a vehicle, or fastened around someone's body to attach something: *a safety harness*
VERB **2.** If you harness something, you bring it under control to use it: *harnessing public opinion*

harp harps harping harped
NOUN **1.** a musical instrument consisting of a triangular frame with vertical strings that you pluck with your fingers
VERB **2.** If someone harps on something, that person keeps talking about it, especially in a boring way.

harpoon harpoons
NOUN a barbed spear attached to a rope, thrown or fired from a gun and used for catching whales or large fish

harpsichord harpsichords
NOUN a musical instrument like a small piano, with strings that are plucked when the keys are pressed

harrowing
ADJECTIVE very upsetting or disturbing: *a harrowing experience*

harsh harsher harshest
ADJECTIVE severe, difficult, and unpleasant: *harsh weather conditions, harsh criticism*
harshly ADVERB
harshness NOUN

harvest harvests harvesting harvested
NOUN **1.** the cutting and gathering of a crop; also the ripe crop when it is gathered, and the time of gathering
VERB **2.** To harvest food means to gather it when it is ripe.
harvester NOUN

has-been has-beens
NOUN *an informal expression* a person who is no longer important or successful

hash hashes
NOUN **1.** Hash is a dish made of small pieces of meat and vegetables cooked together.
PHRASE **2.** If you **make a hash of** a job, you do it badly.

hassle hassles hassling hassled
NOUN **1.** *an informal word* Something that is a hassle is difficult or causes trouble.
VERB **2.** If you hassle someone, you annoy that person by repeatedly asking him or her to do something.

haste
NOUN Haste is doing something quickly, especially too quickly.

hasten hastens hastening hastened
VERB To hasten means to move quickly or do something quickly.

hasty hastier hastiest
ADJECTIVE done suddenly and quickly, often without enough care or thought
hastily ADVERB

hat hats
NOUN a covering for the head

hatch hatches hatching hatched
VERB **1.** When an egg hatches, or when a bird or reptile hatches, the egg breaks open and the young bird or reptile emerges. **2.** To hatch a plot means to plan it.
NOUN **3.** a covered opening in a floor or wall

hatchback hatchbacks
NOUN a car with a door at the back that opens upward

hatchet hatchets
NOUN **1.** a small axe
PHRASE **2.** To **bury the hatchet** means to resolve a disagreement and become friends again.

hate hates hating hated
VERB **1.** If you hate someone or something, you have a strong dislike for that person or thing.
NOUN **2.** Hate is a strong dislike.

hateful
ADJECTIVE extremely unpleasant

Hh

hatred
NOUN Hatred is an extremely strong feeling of dislike.

hat trick hat tricks
NOUN In sports, a hat trick is three goals scored in a single game by the same player: *He completed his hat trick in the second period.*

haughty haughtier haughtiest
ADJECTIVE showing excessive pride: *He behaved in a haughty manner.*
haughtily ADVERB

haul hauls hauling hauled
VERB **1.** To haul something somewhere means to pull it with great effort.
NOUN **2.** a quantity of something obtained: *a good haul of fish*
PHRASE **3.** Something that you describe as **a long haul** takes a lot of time and effort to achieve: *Rebuilding the town after the tornado is going to be a long haul.*

haunches
PLURAL NOUN Your haunches are your buttocks and the tops of your legs: *He squatted on his haunches.*

haunt haunts haunting haunted
VERB **1.** If someone or something haunts a place, that person or thing is seen or heard there regularly: *I heard that a ghost haunts this house.* **2.** If a memory or a fear haunts you, it continually worries you.
NOUN **3.** A person's favourite haunt is a place he or she likes to visit often.

haunted
ADJECTIVE **1.** If a place is haunted, it is thought to be regularly visited by a ghost: *a haunted house* **2.** very worried or troubled: *a haunted expression*

haunting
ADJECTIVE extremely beautiful or sad so that it makes a lasting impression on you: *haunting landscapes, a haunting melody*

have has having had
VERB **1.** Have is an auxiliary verb, used to form the past tense or to express completed actions: *They have never met. I have lost your book.* **2.** If you have something, you own or possess it: *We have two tickets for the concert.* **3.** If you have something, you experience it, it happens to you, or you are affected by it: *I have an idea! He had a marvellous time.* **4.** To have a child or baby animal means to give birth to it: *When is she having the baby?*
PHRASE **5.** If you **have to** do something, you must do it.

haven havens
NOUN a safe place

havoc
NOUN **1.** Havoc is disorder and confusion.
PHRASE **2.** To **play havoc** with something means to cause great disorder and confusion: *Food allergies often play havoc with the immune system.*

hawk hawks hawking hawked
NOUN **1.** a bird of prey with short, rounded wings and a long tail
VERB **2.** To hawk goods means to sell them by taking them around from place to place.

hawthorn hawthorns
NOUN a small, thorny tree producing white blossom and red berries

hay
NOUN Hay is grass that has been cut and dried and is used as animal feed.

hay fever
NOUN Hay fever is an allergy to pollen and grass, causing sneezing and watering eyes.

haystack haystacks
NOUN a large, firmly built pile of hay, usually covered and left out in the open

hazard hazards hazarding hazarded
NOUN **1.** a substance, object, or action that could be dangerous to you
VERB **2.** If you hazard something, you put it at

KNOWING WORDS: WORD HISTORY

BE WORD SHARP!

Words are like living things. They grow and change.

The phrase **hat trick** comes from the game of cricket. A **bowler** (like a pitcher in baseball) who took three wickets in a row (a bit like pitching three consecutive strikes) would be given a hat as a prize. Now **hat trick** is used in other sports, especially hockey, where fans will throw their hats onto the ice if a player scores three goals in a game.

NEL

Hh

risk: *hazarding the health of his crew*

PHRASE **3.** If you **hazard a guess**, you make a guess.

hazardous ADJECTIVE

haze

NOUN If there is a haze, you cannot see clearly because there is moisture or smoke in the air.

hazel hazels

NOUN **1.** a small tree producing edible nuts

ADJECTIVE **2.** greenish brown in colour

hazy hazier haziest

ADJECTIVE dim or vague: *hazy sunshine, a hazy memory*

he

PRONOUN *He* is used to refer to a man or boy whose identity is clear.

head heads heading headed

NOUN **1.** Your head is the part of your body that has your eyes, brain, and mouth in it. **2.** Your head is also your mind and mental abilities: *She has a head for figures.* **3.** The head of something is the top, start, or most important end: *at the head of the table* **4.** The head of a group or organization is the person in charge. **5.** A head is also anything rounded that is shaped like a head: *a head of lettuce, the head of a pin* **6.** When you toss a coin, the side called heads is the one with the head on it.

VERB **7.** To head a group or organization means to be in charge: *My mother heads the organization.* **8.** To head in a particular direction means to move in that direction: *He is heading for a breakdown.* **9.** To head a ball means to hit it with your head.

PHRASE **10.** If you **lose your head**, you panic. **11.** If you can't **make head nor tail of something**, you cannot understand it. **12.** If something is **over someone's head**, it is too difficult for that person to understand.

head off

VERB **13.** If you head off someone or something, you make that person or thing change direction or prevent something from happening: *to head off a stampeding herd of cattle*

headache headaches

NOUN **1.** a pain in your head **2.** Something that is a headache is causing a lot of difficulty or worry: *Delays in receiving money owed is a major headache for small businesses.*

heading headings

NOUN a piece of writing that is written or printed at the top of a page

headland headlands

NOUN a narrow piece of land jutting out into the sea

headlight headlights

NOUN The headlights on a motor vehicle are the large powerful lights at the front.

headline headlines

NOUN A newspaper headline is the title of a newspaper article printed in large, bold type.

headphones

PLURAL NOUN Headphones are a pair of small speakers that you wear over your ears to listen to music or other programming without other people hearing.

headquarters

NOUN The headquarters of an organization is the main place from which it is run.

headroom

NOUN Headroom is the amount of space below a roof or surface under which an object must pass or fit.

headstone headstones

NOUN a large stone standing at one end of a grave and showing the name of the person buried there

headstrong

ADJECTIVE determined to do something in your own way and ignoring other people's advice

headway

NOUN Headway is progress with work or some other activity: *We raked leaves all morning but seemed to make little headway.*

KNOWING WORDS: IDIOMS

BE WORD SHARP!

Idioms add colour to language by playing with the meanings of words.

head the top part (of a body)

get your head around understand

go to your head make you conceited

head over heels completely and foolishly

keep your head stay calm

over your head beyond your understanding

headwind headwinds
NOUN a wind blowing in the opposite direction to the way you are travelling

heady
ADJECTIVE extremely exciting: *the heady days when flight was new*

heal heals healing healed
VERB If something heals or if you heal it, it becomes healthy or normal again: *He had a nasty wound that had not healed properly.*
healer NOUN

health
NOUN **1.** Your health is the condition of your body: *My grandfather's health is not good.*
2. Health is also the state of being free from disease and feeling well.

health food health foods
NOUN food that is free from added chemicals and is considered to be good for your health

healthy healthier healthiest
ADJECTIVE **1.** Someone who is healthy is fit and strong and does not have any diseases.
2. Something that is healthy is good for you: *a healthy diet* **3.** An organization or system that is healthy is successful: *a healthy economy*
healthily ADVERB

heap heaps heaping heaped
NOUN **1.** a pile of things
VERB **2.** If you heap things, you pile them up. **3.** To heap something such as praise on someone means to give that person a lot of it.

hear hears hearing heard
VERB **1.** When you hear sounds, you are aware of them because they reach your ears.
2. When you hear about something, you are informed about it. **3.** When a judge hears a case, he or she listens to it in court in order to make a decision on it.
PHRASE **4.** When you **hear from** someone, that person writes to you or phones you. **5.** If you say that you **won't hear of** something, you mean you refuse to allow it.

hear out
VERB **6.** If you hear someone out, you listen to that person without interrupting.

hearing hearings
NOUN **1.** Hearing is the sense that makes it possible for you to be aware of sounds: *My hearing is poor.* **2.** a court trial or official meeting to hear facts about an incident
3. If someone gives you a hearing, that person lets you give your point of view and listens to you.

hearsay
NOUN Hearsay is information that you have heard from other people rather than something that you know personally to be true.

hearse hearses
NOUN a large car that carries the coffin at a funeral

heart hearts
NOUN **1.** the organ in your chest that pumps the blood around your body **2.** Your heart is also thought of as the centre of your emotions. **3.** Heart is courage, determination, or enthusiasm: *The team was losing heart after eight straight losses.* **4.** The heart of something is the most central and important part of it. **5.** a shape similar to a heart, used especially as a symbol of love **6.** Hearts is one of the four suits in a pack of playing cards. It is marked by a red, heart-shaped symbol.

heartache heartaches
NOUN Heartache is very great sadness and emotional suffering.

heart attack heart attacks
NOUN a serious medical condition in which the heart suddenly beats irregularly or stops completely

heartbreak heartbreaks
NOUN Heartbreak is great sadness and emotional suffering.
heartbreaking ADJECTIVE

heartbroken
ADJECTIVE very sad and emotionally upset: *She was heartbroken at his death.*

SPELL-CHECK THIS!

A computer's spell-check won't catch wrong **homophones** (words that are spelled differently but sound the same).

"Where were you? I've been hear for an hour!"

In this sentence, **hear** should be **here**.
Here means *at this place.*
Hear means *listen to.*

heartburn

NOUN Heartburn is a painful burning sensation in your chest, caused by indigestion.

heartening

ADJECTIVE encouraging or uplifting: *heartening news*

heart failure

NOUN Heart failure is a serious condition in which someone's heart does not work as well as it should, sometimes stopping completely.

heartfelt

ADJECTIVE sincerely and deeply felt: *Our heartfelt sympathy goes out to you.*

hearth hearths

NOUN the part of the floor directly in front of a fireplace

heartless

ADJECTIVE cruel and unkind

heart-rending

ADJECTIVE causing great sadness and pity: *a heart-rending story*

heartthrob heartthrobs

NOUN someone who is attractive to a lot of people

heart-to-heart heart-to-hearts

NOUN a discussion in which two people talk about their deepest feelings

hearty heartier heartiest

ADJECTIVE **1.** cheerful and enthusiastic: *hearty congratulations* **2.** strongly felt: *a hearty dislike for her teacher* **3.** A hearty meal is large and satisfying.

heartily ADVERB

heat heats heating heated

NOUN **1.** Heat is warmth or the quality of being hot; also the temperature of something that is warm or hot. **2.** Heat is strength of feeling, especially of anger or excitement. **3.** a contest or race in a competition held to decide who will play in the final VERB **4.** To heat something means to raise its temperature.

heater NOUN

heathen heathens

NOUN *an old-fashioned word* someone who is thought to have no religion as regarded by those who follow an established religion

heather

NOUN a plant with small, purple or white flowers that grows wild on hills, especially in northern regions of Europe

heating

NOUN Heating is the equipment used to heat a building; also the process and cost of running the equipment to provide heat.

heat wave heat waves

NOUN a period of time during which the weather is much hotter than usual

heave heaves heaving heaved

VERB **1.** To heave something means to move or throw it with a lot of effort. **2.** If your stomach heaves, you vomit or suddenly feel sick. **3.** If you heave a sigh, you sigh loudly. NOUN **4.** If you give something a heave, you move or throw it with a lot of effort.

heaven heavens

NOUN **1.** In some religions, heaven is a place of happiness where God is believed to live and where good people are believed to go when they die. **2.** If you describe a situation or place as heaven, you mean that it is wonderful: *The cake was pure heaven.* PHRASE **3.** You say **for heaven's sake** or **good heavens!** to express surprise.

heavenly

ADJECTIVE **1.** relating to heaven: *a heavenly choir* **2.** *an informal use* wonderful: *his heavenly blue eyes*

heavy heavier heaviest; heavies

ADJECTIVE **1.** great in weight or force: *He received a heavy blow to the head in the accident. How heavy are you?* **2.** great in degree or amount: *heavy casualties* **3.** solid and thick in appearance: *heavy shoes* **4.** using a lot of something quickly: *The van is heavy on gas.* **5.** serious and difficult to deal with or understand: *That was a heavy speech. It all got a bit heavy when the police arrived.* **6.** Food that is heavy is solid and difficult to digest: *a heavy meal* **7.** When it is heavy, the weather is hot, humid, and still. **8.** Someone with a heavy heart is very sad. NOUN **9.** *an informal use* the villain in a play

heavily ADVERB

heaviness NOUN

heavy-duty

ADJECTIVE Heavy-duty equipment is strong and can withstand hard use.

heavy-handed

ADJECTIVE showing a lack of care or thought or using too much authority: *heavy-handed police tactics*

heavyweight heavyweights

NOUN **1.** a boxer in the heaviest weight group **2.** an important person with a lot of influence

heckle heckles heckling heckled

VERB If members of an audience heckle a speaker or entertainer, they interrupt and shout rude remarks.

heckler NOUN

Hh

hectare hectares
NOUN a unit for measuring areas of land, equal to 10 000 square metres

hectic
ADJECTIVE involving a lot of rushed activity: *a hectic schedule*

hedge hedges hedging hedged
NOUN **1.** a row of bushes forming a barrier or boundary
VERB **2.** If you hedge against something unpleasant happening, you protect yourself.
3. If you hedge, you avoid answering a question or dealing with a problem.
PHRASE **4.** If you **hedge your bets**, you support two or more people or courses of action to avoid the risk of error.

hedgehog hedgehogs
NOUN a small, brown animal with sharp spikes covering its back

hedonism
NOUN Hedonism is the belief that gaining pleasure is the most important thing in life.
hedonistic ADJECTIVE

heed heeds heeding heeded
VERB **1.** If you heed someone's advice, you pay attention to it.
NOUN **2.** If you take or pay heed to something, you give it careful attention.

heel heels heeling heeled
NOUN **1.** the back part of your foot **2.** The heel of a shoe or sock is the part that fits over your heel.
VERB **3.** To heel means to follow closely behind someone: *She's teaching her dog to heel.*
PHRASE **4.** A person or place that looks **down at the heel** looks untidy and in poor condition.

hefty heftier heftiest
ADJECTIVE of great size, force, or weight: *a hefty fine, hefty books*

height heights
NOUN **1.** The height of an object is its measurement from the bottom to the top.
2. a high position or place: *They stood on a height overlooking the river.* **3.** The height of something is its peak, or the time when it is most successful or intense: *the height of the tourist season, at the height of his career*

heighten heightens heightening heightened
VERB If something heightens a feeling or experience, it increases its intensity.

heinous
ADJECTIVE evil and terrible: *heinous crimes*

heir heirs
NOUN the person who is entitled to inherit property or a title after the owner's death

heiress heiresses
NOUN a female with the right to inherit property or a title after the owner's death

heirloom heirlooms
NOUN something belonging to a family that has been passed from one generation to another

helicopter helicopters
NOUN an aircraft with rotating blades above it that enable it to take off vertically, hover, and fly

helium
NOUN Helium is a gas that is lighter than air and that is used to fill balloons.

hell
NOUN **1.** In some religions, hell is the place where souls of evil people are believed to go to be punished after death. **2.** *an informal use* If you say that something is hell, you mean it is very unpleasant.
INTERJECTION **3.** *Hell* is also an exclamation of annoyance or dismay.

hellbent
ADJECTIVE determined to do something whatever the consequences

hellish
ADJECTIVE *an informal word* very unpleasant

hello
INTERJECTION You say *Hello* as a greeting or when you answer the phone.

helm helms
NOUN **1.** The helm on a boat is the position from which it is steered, and the wheel or tiller.
PHRASE **2. At the helm** means in a position of leadership or control.

helmet helmets
NOUN a hard hat worn to protect the head

help helps helping helped
VERB **1.** To help someone means to make something easier or better for that person.
NOUN **2.** If you need or give help, you need or give assistance. **3.** someone or something that helps you: *He really is a good help.*
PHRASE **4.** If you **help yourself** to something, you take it. **5.** If you **can't help** something, you cannot control it or change it: *I can't help feeling sorry for her.*

Instead of **HELP** try...

support a charity
serve a customer
benefit the poor
assist on a project
comfort a sad friend

⚠ HEADS UP The word **heinous** is pronounced HEY-nus.

Hh

helper helpers
NOUN a person who gives assistance

helpful
ADJECTIVE **1.** If someone is helpful, that person helps you by doing something for you.
2. Something that is helpful makes a situation more pleasant or easier to tolerate.
helpfully ADVERB

helping helpings
NOUN an amount of food that you get in a single serving

helpless
ADJECTIVE unable to cope on your own: *a helpless child*
helplessly ADVERB
helplessness NOUN

hem hems hemming hemmed
NOUN **1.** The hem of a garment is an edge that has been turned over and sewn in place.
VERB **2.** To hem something means to make a hem on it.
hem in
VERB **3.** If someone is hemmed in, that person is surrounded and prevented from moving.

hemisphere hemispheres
NOUN one half of the earth, the brain, or a sphere

hemoglobin
NOUN Hemoglobin is a substance in red blood cells that carries oxygen around the body.

hemorrhage
NOUN A hemorrhage is serious bleeding, especially inside a person's body.

hemorrhoids
PLURAL NOUN Hemorrhoids are painful lumps around the anus that are caused by swollen veins.

hemp
NOUN a tall plant, some varieties of which are used to make rope, and others to produce the drug marijuana

hen hens
NOUN an adult female chicken

hence
ADVERB **1.** *a formal word* for this reason: *It sells more papers, and hence more money is made.* **2.** from now or from the time mentioned: *The play is due to open two weeks hence.*

henceforth
ADVERB *a formal word* from this time onward: *His life henceforth revolved around her.*

henchman henchmen
NOUN The henchmen of a powerful person are the people employed to do violent or dishonest work for that person.

hepatitis
NOUN Hepatitis is a serious infectious disease causing inflammation of the liver.

her
PRONOUN OR ADJECTIVE *Her* is used to refer to a woman or girl.

herald heralds heralding heralded
NOUN **1.** In the past, especially in the Middle Ages, a herald was a messenger.
VERB **2.** Something that heralds a future event is a sign of that event.

herb herbs
NOUN a plant whose leaves are used in medicine or to flavour food
herbal ADJECTIVE
herbalist NOUN

herbivore herbivores
NOUN an animal that eats only plants

herd herds herding herded
NOUN **1.** a large group of animals
VERB **2.** To herd animals or people means to make them move together as a group.

here
ADVERB **1.** in the place where you are, or the place mentioned or indicated
PHRASE **2. Here and there** means in various unspecified places: *dense forests broken here and there by small towns*

hereafter
ADVERB *a formal word* after this time or point: *the Assembly of First Nations (referred to hereafter as AFN)*

hereby
ADVERB *a formal word* used in documents and statements to indicate that a declaration is official: *All vacation is hereby cancelled.*

hereditary
ADJECTIVE passed on to a child from a parent: *a hereditary disease*

heredity
NOUN Heredity is the process by which characteristics are passed from parents to their children through the genes.

herein
ADVERB *a formal word* in this place or document

heresy heresies
NOUN Heresy is belief or behaviour considered to be wrong because it disagrees with what is generally accepted, especially with regard to religion.
heretic NOUN
heretical ADJECTIVE

herewith
ADVERB *a formal word* with this letter or document: *I herewith return your cheque.*

Hh

heritage
NOUN the possessions or traditions that have been passed from one generation to another

hermit hermits
NOUN a person who lives alone, with a simple way of life, especially for religious reasons

hernia hernias
NOUN a medical condition in which part of the intestine sticks through a weak point in the surrounding tissue

hero heroes
NOUN **1.** the main male character in a book, movie, or play **2.** a person who has done something brave or good

heroic
ADJECTIVE brave, courageous, and determined
heroically ADVERB

heroine heroines
NOUN **1.** the main female character in a book, movie, or play **2.** a woman who has done something brave or good

⚠ **HEADS UP**

Unlike most other words that end in –ine (like **line** and **mine**), **heroine** is pronounced HAIR-oh-in.

heroism
NOUN Heroism is great courage and bravery.

heron herons
NOUN a wading bird with very long legs and a long beak and neck

herpes
NOUN Herpes is a virus that causes painful red spots on the skin.

herring herrings
NOUN a silvery fish that lives in large shoals in northern seas

hers
PRONOUN *Hers* refers to something that belongs to or relates to a woman or girl.

herself
PRONOUN **1.** *Herself* is used when the same woman or girl does an action and is affected by it: *She pulled herself out of the water.*
2. *Herself* is used to emphasize *she*.

hertz
NOUN A hertz is a unit of frequency equal to one cycle per second.

hesitant
ADJECTIVE If you are hesitant, you do not do something immediately because you are uncertain or worried.
hesitantly ADVERB

hesitate hesitates hesitating hesitated
VERB To hesitate means to pause or show uncertainty.
hesitation NOUN

heterosexual heterosexuals
ADJECTIVE **1.** involving a sexual relationship between a man and a woman: *heterosexual couples*
NOUN **2.** a person who is sexually attracted to people of the opposite sex

hewn
ADJECTIVE carved from a substance: *a cave, hewn out of the hillside*

hexagon hexagons
NOUN a shape with six straight sides
hexagonal ADJECTIVE

heyday
NOUN The heyday of a person or thing is the period when that person or thing is most successful or popular: *In his heyday, he was the best player in the division.*

hi
INTERJECTION *Hi!* is an informal greeting.

hiatus hiatuses
NOUN *a formal word* a pause or gap

hibernate hibernates hibernating hibernated
VERB Animals that hibernate spend the winter in a state like deep sleep.
hibernation NOUN

hibiscus hibiscuses
NOUN a type of tropical shrub with brightly coloured flowers

hiccup hiccups hiccupping hiccupped
NOUN **1.** Hiccups are short, uncontrolled choking sounds in your throat that you sometimes get if you have been eating or drinking too quickly. **2.** *an informal use* a minor problem
VERB **3.** When you hiccup, you make little choking sounds.

hide hides hiding hid hidden
VERB **1.** To hide something means to put it where it cannot be seen, or to prevent it from being discovered: *He was unable to hide his disappointment.*
NOUN **2.** the skin of a large animal

hideous
ADJECTIVE extremely ugly or unpleasant
hideously ADVERB

hideout hideouts
NOUN a hiding place

hierarchy hierarchies
NOUN a system in which people or things are ranked according to how important they are
hierarchical ADJECTIVE

high higher highest; highs

ADJECTIVE **1.** a long way above the ground
2. great in degree, quantity, or intensity: *This bank has high interest rates. There is a high risk of heart disease* **3.** toward

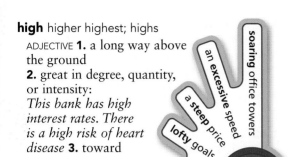

Instead of **HIGH** try…

soaring office towers
an excessive speed
a steep price
lofty goals
a shrill voice
an acute fever
a leading priority
an elevated platform

the top of a scale of importance or quality: *high fashion*
4. close to the top of a range of sound or notes: *The human voice can reach a very high pitch.* **5.** *an informal use* Someone who is high on a drug or alcohol is affected by having taken it.
ADVERB **6.** at or to a height
NOUN **7.** a high point or level: *Morale reached a new high.* **8.** *an informal use* Someone who is on a high is an excited and optimistic mood.

highbrow
ADJECTIVE concerned with serious, intellectual subjects

higher education
NOUN Higher education is education at universities and colleges.

high jump
NOUN The high jump is an athletic event involving jumping over a high bar.

highland highlands
NOUN an area that is higher and hillier than the surrounding region

highlight highlights highlighting highlighted
VERB **1.** If you highlight a point or problem, you emphasize and draw attention to it.

NOUN **2.** The highlight of something is the most interesting part of it: *His show was the highlight of the festival.* **3.** a lighter area of a painting, showing where light shines on things **4.** Highlights are also light-coloured streaks in someone's hair.

highly
ADVERB **1.** extremely: *It is highly unlikely I'll be able to replace it.* **2.** toward the top of a scale of importance, admiration, or respect: *They hired highly qualified personnel. She thought highly of him.*

high-minded
ADJECTIVE Someone who is high-minded has strong moral principles.

Highness *Highness* is used in titles and forms of address for members of a royal family other than a king or queen: *Her Royal Highness, Princess Alexandra*

high-pitched
ADJECTIVE A high-pitched sound is high and often shrill.

high-rise
ADJECTIVE High-rise buildings are very tall.

high school high schools
NOUN school that follows elementary school. It is also called secondary school.

high tech
NOUN High tech, or high technology, is the development and use of advanced electronics and computers.

high tide
NOUN On a coast, high tide is the time, usually twice a day, when the sea is at its highest level.

highway highways
NOUN a main road connecting towns or cities

highwayman highwaymen
NOUN In the past, highwaymen were robbers on horseback who used to rob travellers on public roads.

KNOWING WORDS: IDIOMS

BE WORD SHARP!

Idioms add colour to language by playing with the meanings of words.

high toward the top

high and dry alone and without help

high roller someone who spends money freely

high spirits happy excitement

high time almost too late

search high and low look everywhere

hijack hijacks hijacking hijacked
VERB If someone hijacks a plane or vehicle, that person illegally takes control of it during a journey.
hijacking NOUN

hike hikes hiking hiked
NOUN **1.** a long walk, usually in the country
VERB **2.** To hike means to walk long distances, usually in the country.
hiker NOUN

hilarious
ADJECTIVE very funny
hilariously ADVERB

hilarity
NOUN Hilarity is great amusement and laughter: *His antics caused great hilarity in the classroom.*

hill hills
NOUN a rounded area of land higher than the land surrounding it
hilly ADJECTIVE

hilt hilts
NOUN The hilt of a sword or knife is its handle.

him
PRONOUN You use *him* to refer to a man or boy.

himself
PRONOUN **1.** *Himself* is used when the same man or boy does an action and is affected by it: *My little brother dressed himself without any difficulty.* **2.** *Himself* is used to emphasize *he.*

hind hinds
ADJECTIVE **1.** used to refer to the back part of an animal: *the hind legs*
NOUN **2.** a female deer

hinder hinders hindering hindered
VERB If you hinder someone or something, you get in the way and make something difficult for that person or thing.

hindrance hindrances
NOUN **1.** Someone or something that is a hindrance causes difficulties or is an obstruction. **2.** Hindrance is the act of hindering someone or something.

hindsight
NOUN Hindsight is the ability to understand an event after it has actually taken place: *With hindsight, I realized how odd the situation was.*

Hinduism
NOUN an Indian religion that has many gods and believes that people have another life on earth after death
Hindu NOUN

hinge hinges hinging hinged
NOUN **1.** the movable joint that attaches a door or window to its frame
VERB **2.** Something that hinges on a situation or event depends entirely on that situation or event: *Victory or defeat hinged on her final putt.*

hint hints hinting hinted
NOUN **1.** an indirect suggestion **2.** a helpful piece of advice
VERB **3.** If you hint at something, you suggest it indirectly.

hinterland hinterlands
NOUN The hinterland is an area that is far from major cities.

hip hips
NOUN Your hips are the two parts at the sides of your body between your waist and your upper legs.

hippie hippies
NOUN In the 1960s and 1970s, hippies were people who rejected conventional society and tried to live a life based on peace and love.

hippo hippos
NOUN *an informal word* a hippopotamus

hippopotamus hippopotamuses
NOUN a large African animal, with thick wrinkled skin and short legs, that lives near rivers

hire hires hiring hired
VERB If you hire someone, you pay that person to do a job for you.

hirsute
ADJECTIVE *a formal word* hairy

his
ADJECTIVE OR PRONOUN *His* refers to something that belongs or relates to a man or boy.

hiss hisses hissing hissed
VERB **1.** To hiss means to make a long *s* sound, especially to show disapproval or aggression.
NOUN **2.** a long *s* sound

histogram histograms
NOUN a graph, consisting of rectangles of varying sizes, that shows the frequency of values of a quantity

historian historians
NOUN a person who studies and writes about history

historic
ADJECTIVE important in the past or likely to be seen as important in the future

historical
ADJECTIVE **1.** occurring in the past, or relating to the study of the past: *historical events*

2. describing or representing the past: *historical novels*

historically ADVERB

history histories

NOUN History is the study of the past. A history is a record of the past: *The town is steeped in history. I asked my father about our family history.*

histrionic histrionics

ADJECTIVE **1.** Histrionic behaviour is very dramatic and full of exaggerated emotion. PLURAL NOUN **2.** Histrionics are histrionic behaviour.

hit hits hitting hit

VERB **1.** If you hit someone, you strike that person forcefully, usually causing hurt or damage. **2.** If you hit an

Instead of **HIT** try…

- swat a fly
- strike a chord
- slap on the back
- whack a golf ball
- bump another car

object, you collide with it. **3.** To hit a ball or other object means to make it move by hitting it with something. **4.** If something hits you, it affects you badly and suddenly: *The recession has hit the tourist industry hard.* **5.** If something hits a particular point or place, it reaches it: *The book hit Canada just at the right time.* **6.** If you hit on an idea or solution, you suddenly think of it. NOUN **7.** a person or thing that is popular and successful **8.** the action of hitting something: *Give it a good hard hit with the hammer.* PHRASE **9.** *an informal use* If you **hit it off** with someone, you become friendly with that person the first time you meet him or her.

hit-and-miss

ADJECTIVE happening in an unpredictable way or without being properly organized

hit-and-run

ADJECTIVE A hit-and-run car accident is one in which the person who has caused the damage drives away without stopping.

hitch hitches hitching hitched

NOUN **1.** a slight problem or difficulty: *The process was completed without a hitch.* VERB **2.** *an informal use* If you hitch, you travel by getting lifts from passing vehicles: *It is not safe to hitch a ride, alone or in groups.*

hitchhiking

NOUN Hitchhiking is travelling by getting free lifts from passing vehicles.

hi tech

ADJECTIVE another spelling of HIGH TECH

hither *an old-fashioned word*

ADVERB **1.** used to refer to movement toward the place where you are PHRASE **2.** If you travel **hither and yon** you go to all sorts of places far and near.

hitherto

ADVERB *a formal word* until now: *What he was aiming at had not hitherto been attempted.*

HIV

NOUN HIV is a virus that reduces people's resistance to illness and can cause AIDS. HIV is an abbreviation for *human immunodeficiency virus.*

hive hives hiving hived

NOUN **1.** a place in which bees live; a beehive **2.** A place that is a hive of activity is very busy with a lot of people working hard. PHRASE **3.** If part of something such as a group or business is **hived off**, it is separated from a larger group or business: *The children were hived off into groups based on age.*

hoard hoards hoarding hoarded

VERB **1.** To hoard things means to save them even though they may no longer be useful. NOUN **2.** a store of things that has been saved or hidden

hoarse hoarser hoarsest

ADJECTIVE A hoarse voice sounds rough and unclear.

hoarsely ADVERB

hoax hoaxes hoaxing hoaxed

NOUN **1.** a trick or an attempt to deceive someone VERB **2.** To hoax someone means to trick or deceive that person.

hobble hobbles hobbling hobbled

VERB **1.** If you hobble, you walk awkwardly because of pain or injury. **2.** If you hobble an animal, you tie its legs together to restrict its movement.

hobby hobbies

NOUN something that you do for enjoyment in your spare time

hock hocks

NOUN The hock of a horse or other animal is the angled joint in its back leg.

hockey

NOUN Hockey is a game played on ice in which two teams of six players use long sticks with curved ends to try to hit a black rubber disc, called a puck, into the other team's net.

Hh

hoe hoes hoeing hoed
NOUN **1.** a long-handled gardening tool, used to remove weeds and break up the soil
VERB **2.** To hoe the ground means to use a hoe on it.

hog hogs hogging hogged
NOUN **1.** a castrated male pig raised for meat
VERB **2.** *an informal use* If you hog something, you take more than your share of it, or keep it for too long.
PHRASE **3.** *an informal use* If you **go whole hog**, you do something completely or thoroughly in a bold or extravagant way.

hoist hoists hoisting hoisted
VERB **1.** To hoist something means to lift it, especially using a crane or other machinery.
NOUN **2.** a machine for lifting heavy things

hold holds holding held
VERB **1.** To hold something means to carry or keep it in place, usually with your hand or arms. **2.** Someone who holds power, office, or an opinion has it or possesses it. **3.** If you hold something such as a meeting or an election, you arrange it and cause it to happen. **4.** If something holds, it is still available or valid: *The offer still holds*. **5.** If you hold someone responsible for something, you consider that person responsible for it. **6.** If something holds a certain amount, it can contain that amount: *The theatre holds 150 people*. **7.** If you hold something such as theatre tickets, you keep or reserve it for a period of time: *Can you hold these tickets for me until tomorrow?* **8.** To hold something down means to keep it or to keep it under control: *to hold down a job* **9.** If you hold on to something, you continue it or keep it even though it might be difficult: *They are keen to hold on to their culture*. **10.** To hold something back means to prevent it, keep it under control, or not reveal it: *He failed to hold back the tears*.
NOUN **11.** If someone or something has a hold over you, that person or thing has power, control, or influence over you: *The party has a considerable hold over its own leader*.

12. a way of holding something or the act of holding it: *He reached for the rope and finally got a hold of it*. **13.** the place where cargo or luggage is stored in a ship or a plane

holder NOUN

hole holes holing holed
NOUN **1.** an opening or hollow in something **2.** *an informal use* If you are in a hole, you are in a difficult situation. **3.** *an informal use* A hole in a theory or argument is a weakness or error in it. **4.** In golf, a hole is one of the small holes into which you have to hit the ball.
VERB **5.** To hole something means to make a hole or holes in that thing.

holiday holidays holidaying holidayed
NOUN **1.** a period of time spent away from home for enjoyment **2.** a time when you are not working or not at school

holiness
NOUN **1.** Holiness is the state or quality of being holy. **2.** *Your Holiness* and *His Holiness* are titles used to address the Pope or to refer to leaders of some religions.

hollow hollows hollowing hollowed
ADJECTIVE **1.** Something that is hollow has space inside it rather than being solid. **2.** An opinion or situation that is hollow has no real value or worth: *a hollow gesture* **3.** A hollow sound is dull and has a slight echo: *the hollow sound of his footsteps on the stairs*
NOUN **4.** a hole in something or a part of a surface that is lower than the rest: *a pleasant village in a lush hollow*
VERB **5.** To hollow means to make a hollow: *They hollowed out crude dwellings from the soft rock*.

holly
NOUN an evergreen tree or shrub with spiky leaves. It often has red berries in winter.

holocaust holocausts
NOUN **1.** a large-scale destruction or loss of

SPELL-CHECK THIS!

A computer's spell-check won't catch wrong **homophones** (words that are spelled differently but sound the same).

It took us the hole afternoon to dig that whole.

In this sentence, **hole** and **whole** are mixed up. **Hole** means *empty space*. **Whole** means *entire*.

life, especially the result of war or fire **2. The Holocaust** was the mass murder of Jews in Europe by the Nazis during World War II.

holster holsters
NOUN a holder for a handgun, worn at the side of the body or under the arm

holy holier holiest
ADJECTIVE **1.** relating to something sacred in a particular religion: *the holy city* **2.** Someone who is holy is religious and leads a pure and good life.

homage
NOUN Homage is an act of respect and admiration: *The thronging crowds paid homage to the great hero.*

home homes
NOUN **1.** Your home is the building or place in which you live or feel you belong. **2.** a building in which elderly or ill people live and are looked after: *He has been confined to a nursing home since his stroke.*
ADJECTIVE **3.** connected with or involving your home: *He gave them his home phone number.*

homeland homelands
NOUN Your homeland is your native country.

homeless
ADJECTIVE **1.** having no home
PLURAL NOUN **2.** The homeless are people who have no home.
homelessness NOUN

homely
ADJECTIVE plain or unattractive

homeopathy
NOUN Homeopathy is a way of treating illness by giving the patient tiny amounts of a substance that would normally cause illness in a healthy person.
homeopathic ADJECTIVE

homeowner homeowners
NOUN a person who owns the home in which he or she lives

homesick
ADJECTIVE unhappy because of being away from home and missing family and friends

homespun
ADJECTIVE not sophisticated or complicated: *The book is simple homespun philosophy.*

homestead homesteads
NOUN a house and its land and other buildings, especially a farm

homeward
ADJECTIVE OR ADVERB toward home: *the homeward journey*

homework
NOUN **1.** Homework is schoolwork given

to students to be done in the evening at home. **2.** Homework is also research and preparation: *You certainly need to do your homework before buying a car.*

homicide homicides
NOUN Homicide is the crime of murder.
homicidal ADJECTIVE

homing
ADJECTIVE A homing device is able to guide itself to a target. An animal with a homing instinct is able to find its way home.

homograph homographs
NOUN Homographs are words with different meanings that are spelled in the same way but may be pronounced differently. For example, *tear* meaning *to rip* and *tear* meaning *a drop of salt water from the eye* are homographs.

homophone homophones
NOUN Homophones are words with different meanings that are pronounced in the same way but are spelled differently. For example, *write* and *right* are homophones.

Homo sapiens
NOUN *a formal expression* Homo sapiens is the scientific name for human beings.

homosexual homosexuals
NOUN **1.** a person who is sexually attracted to someone of the same sex
ADJECTIVE **2.** sexually attracted to someone of the same sex
homosexuality NOUN

hone hones honing honed
VERB **1.** If you hone a tool, you sharpen it. **2.** If you hone a quality or ability, you develop and improve it: *He had a sharply honed sense of justice.*

honest
ADJECTIVE truthful and trustworthy
honestly ADVERB

honesty
NOUN Honesty is the quality of being truthful and trustworthy.

honey
NOUN Honey is a sweet, edible, sticky substance produced by bees.

honeycomb honeycombs
NOUN a wax structure consisting of rows of six-sided cells made by bees for the storage of honey and their eggs

honeymoon honeymoons
NOUN a holiday taken by a couple who have just gotten married

honeysuckle
NOUN a climbing plant with fragrant pink or cream flowers

Hh

honk honks honking honked
NOUN **1.** a short, loud sound like that made by a car horn or a goose
VERB **2.** When something honks, it makes a short, loud sound.

honorary
ADJECTIVE An honorary title or job is given as a mark of respect, and does not involve the usual qualifications or work: *She was awarded an honorary degree.*

honour honours honouring honoured
NOUN **1.** Your honour is your good reputation and the respect that other people have for you: *This is a war fought by people totally without honour.* **2.** an award or privilege given as a mark of respect **3.** Honours is an advanced course or program of study.
PHRASE **4.** If something is done **in honour of** someone, it is done out of respect for that person: *Some cultures hold minor festivals in honour of the dead.*
VERB **5.** If you honour someone, you give that person special praise or attention, or an award. **6.** If you honour an agreement or promise, you do what was agreed or promised.

honourable
ADJECTIVE worthy of respect or admiration: *He should do the honourable thing and resign.*

hood hoods
NOUN **1.** a loose covering for the head, usually part of a coat or jacket **2.** a cover on a piece of equipment or vehicle, usually curved and movable: *The mechanic had the hood up to work on the engine.*
hooded ADJECTIVE

-hood
SUFFIX The suffix *-hood* is added at the end of words to form nouns that indicate a state or show the people of a group: *childhood*

hoof hoofs
NOUN the hard, bony part of certain animals' feet

hook hooks hooking hooked
NOUN **1.** a curved piece of metal or plastic that is used for catching, holding, or hanging things: *picture hooks* **2.** a curving movement, for example of the fist in boxing, or of a golf ball
VERB **3.** If you hook one thing onto another, you attach it there using a hook.
PHRASE **4.** If you are **let off the hook**, something happens so that you avoid punishment or a difficult situation.

hooked
ADJECTIVE addicted to something; also obsessed by something: *She is hooked on caffeine. I'm hooked on exercise.*

hooligan hooligans
NOUN a destructive and violent young person
hooliganism NOUN

hoop hoops
NOUN a large ring, often used as a toy

hoot hoots hooting hooted
VERB **1.** To hoot means to make a long *oo* sound like an owl: *hooting with laughter* **2.** If a car horn hoots, it makes a loud honking noise.
NOUN **3.** a sound like that made by an owl or a car horn

hooves a plural of HOOF

hop hops hopping hopped
VERB **1.** If you hop, you jump on one foot. **2.** When animals or birds hop, they jump with two feet together. **3.** *an informal use* If you hop into or out of something, you move there quickly and easily: *You only have to hop on the bus to get there.*
NOUN **4.** a jump on one leg **5.** Hops are flowers of the hop plant, which are dried and used for making beer.

hope hopes hoping hoped
VERB **1.** If you hope that something will happen or hope that it is true, you want it to happen or be true.
NOUN **2.** Hope is a wish or feeling of desire

KNOWING WORDS: WORD BUILDING

BE WORD SHARP!

You can create new words by adding prefixes and suffixes to a base word.

-hood a noun suffix that indicates a state

adulthood being an adult

likelihood being likely

nationhood being a nation

parenthood being a parent

sainthood being a saint

and expectation: *There was little hope of recovery.*
hopeful ADJECTIVE
hopefully ADVERB

hopeless
ADJECTIVE **1.** having no hope: *She shook her head in hopeless bewilderment.* **2.** certain to fail or be unsuccessful **3.** bad or inadequate: *I'm hopeless at remembering birthdays.*
hopelessly ADVERB
hopelessness NOUN

hopper hoppers
NOUN a large, funnel-shaped container into which grain, sand, or other material is poured into a grinder

horde hordes
NOUN a large group or number of people or animals: *hordes of tourists*

horizon horizons
NOUN **1.** the distant line where the sky seems to touch the land or sea **2.** Your horizons are the limits of what you want to do or are interested in: *Travel broadens your horizons.* PHRASE **3.** If something is **on the horizon**, it is almost certainly going to happen or be done in the future: *Political change was on the horizon.*

horizontal
ADJECTIVE flat and parallel with the horizon or with a line considered as a base: *The design was a series of vertical and horizontal black lines.*
horizontally ADVERB

hormone hormones
NOUN a chemical made by one part of your body that stimulates or has a specific effect on another part of your body
hormonal ADJECTIVE

horn horns
NOUN **1.** one of the hard, pointed growths on the heads of animals such as goats **2.** a musical instrument made of brass that is narrow at one end and wide at the other **3.** On vehicles, a horn is a warning device that makes a loud noise.

hornet hornets
NOUN a type of very large wasp

horoscope horoscopes
NOUN a prediction about what is going to happen to someone, based on the position of the stars when that person was born

horrendous
ADJECTIVE very unpleasant and shocking: *horrendous injuries*

horrible
ADJECTIVE **1.** disagreeable and unpleasant: *A*

horrible nausea rose within him.* **2.** causing shock, fear, or disgust: *horrible crimes*
horribly ADVERB

horrid
ADJECTIVE very unpleasant indeed: *We were all so horrid to her.*

horrific
ADJECTIVE so bad or unpleasant that people are horrified: *a horrific attack*

horrify horrifies horrifying horrified
VERB If something horrifies you, it makes you feel dismay or disgust: *a crime trend that will horrify people*
horrifying ADJECTIVE

horror horrors
NOUN **1.** a strong feeling of alarm, dismay, and disgust: *He gazed in horror at the spider.* **2.** If you have a horror of something, you fear it very much: *She had a horror of fire.*

horse horses
NOUN **1.** a large animal with a mane and long tail, on which people can ride **2.** a piece of gymnastics equipment with four legs, used for jumping over

horseback
NOUN OR ADJECTIVE You refer to someone who is riding a horse as someone **on horseback**.

horsepower
NOUN Horsepower is a nonmetric unit of power used for measuring how powerful an engine is, equal to about 746 watts.

horseradish
NOUN the white root of a plant made into a hot-tasting sauce, often served cold with beef

horseshoe horseshoes
NOUN a U-shaped piece of metal, nailed to the hard surface of a horse's hoof to protect it; also anything of this shape, often regarded as a good-luck symbol

horsy
ADJECTIVE very keen on horses and riding

horticulture
NOUN Horticulture is the study and practice of growing flowers, fruit, and vegetables.
horticultural ADJECTIVE

hose hoses hosing hosed
NOUN **1.** a long, flexible tube through which liquid or gas can be passed: *Be sure you don't leave the garden hose on.*
VERB **2.** If you hose something, you wash or water it using a hose: *The patio is dirty and should be hosed down before the furniture is set out.*

hosiery
NOUN Hosiery consists of tights, socks, and similar items, especially in stores.

hospice hospices
NOUN a hospital that provides care for people who are dying

hospitable
ADJECTIVE friendly, generous, and welcoming to guests or strangers
hospitality NOUN

hospital hospitals
NOUN a place where sick and injured people are treated and cared for

host hosts hosting hosted
NOUN **1.** The host of an event is the person who entertains guests: *He is a most generous host who takes his guests to the best restaurants in town.* **2.** a plant or animal with smaller plants or animals living on or in it **3.** A host of things is a large number of them: *a host of close friends*
VERB **4.** To host an event means to organize it or act as host at it.

hostage hostages
NOUN a person who is illegally held prisoner and threatened with injury or death unless certain demands are met by other people

hostel hostels
NOUN a large building in which people can stay or live: *a hostel for battered women*

hostess hostesses
NOUN The hostess of an event is a woman who entertains guests or visitors and provides food or accommodation for them.

hostile
ADJECTIVE **1.** unfriendly, aggressive, and unpleasant: *a hostile audience* **2.** relating to or involving the enemies of a country: *hostile territory*

hostility hostilities
NOUN aggression or unfriendly behaviour toward a person or thing

hot hotter hottest
ADJECTIVE **1.** having a high temperature: *a hot climate* **2.** very spicy and causing a burning sensation in your mouth: *a hot curry* **3.** new, recent, and exciting: *hot news and gossip* **4.** dangerous or difficult to deal with: *The testing of drugs and other substances on animals is a hot issue.*
hotly ADVERB

hotbed hotbeds
NOUN A hotbed of some type of activity is a place that seems to encourage it: *The city was a hotbed of crime.*

hot dog hot dogs
NOUN a sausage served in a long bun split lengthwise

hotel hotels
NOUN a building where people stay, paying for their room and meals

hothouse hothouses
NOUN **1.** a large, heated greenhouse **2.** a place or situation of intense intellectual activity: *a hothouse of technological innovation*

hot seat
NOUN *an informal expression* Someone who is in the hot seat has to make difficult decisions for which he or she will be held responsible.

hound hounds hounding hounded
NOUN **1.** a dog, especially one used for hunting or racing
VERB **2.** If someone hounds you, that person constantly pursues or troubles you.

hour hours
NOUN **1.** a unit of time equal to 60 minutes, of which there are 24 in a day **2.** The hour for something is the time when it happens: *The hour for launching the rocket approached.* **3.** The hour is also the time of day: *What are you doing up at this hour?* **4.** an important or difficult time: *The hour has come. He is the hero of the hour.*
PLURAL NOUN **5.** The hours that you keep are the times that you usually go to bed and get up.
hourly ADJECTIVE OR ADVERB

house houses housing housed
NOUN **1.** a building where a person or family lives **2.** a building used for a particular purpose: *an auction house, the opera house* **3.** In a theatre, the house is the part where the audience sits; also the audience itself: *The show had a packed house calling for more.*
VERB **4.** To house something means to keep it or contain it: *The basement housed a store of valuable antiques.*

houseboat houseboats
NOUN a small boat that people can live on or use for vacationing on

household households
NOUN **1.** all the people who live as a group in a house or apartment
PHRASE **2.** Someone who is **a household name** is very well known.
householder NOUN

housekeeper housekeepers
NOUN a person who is employed to do the cooking and cleaning in a house

House of Commons
NOUN The House of Commons is the part of the federal Parliament made up of elected representatives; also the place where they meet.

Hh

housewife housewives
NOUN a married woman who does the chores in her home, and does not have a paid job

housing
NOUN Housing is the buildings in which people live: *the serious housing shortage*

hovel hovels
NOUN a small house that is dirty or badly in need of repair

hover hovers hovering hovered
VERB **1.** When a bird, insect, or aircraft hovers, it stays in the same position in the air. **2.** If someone is hovering, that person is hesitating because he or she cannot decide what to do: *He was hovering nervously around the sick animal.*

hovercraft hovercraft
NOUN a vehicle that can travel over water or land supported by a cushion of air

how
ADVERB **1.** *How* is used to ask about, explain, or refer to the way in which something is done, known, or experienced: *How did this happen? He knew how quickly rumours could spread.* **2.** *How* is used to ask about or refer to a measurement or quantity: *How much is it for the skis? I wonder how old he is.* **3.** *How* is used to emphasize a word or statement that follows it: *How odd!*

however
ADVERB **1.** You use *however* when you are adding a comment that seems to contradict or contrast with what has just been said: *For all his compassion, he is, however, surprisingly restrained.* **2.** You use *however* to say that something makes no difference to a situation: *However hard she tried, nothing seemed to work.*

howl howls howling howled
VERB **1.** To howl means to make a long, loud, wailing noise, such as that made by a dog when it is upset: *A distant coyote howled at the moon. The wind howled through the trees.*
NOUN **2.** a long, loud, wailing noise

hub hubs
NOUN **1.** the centre part of a wheel **2.** the most important or active part of a place or organization: *The kitchen is the hub of most households.*

hubbub
NOUN Hubbub is great noise or confusion: *the general hubbub of conversation*

huddle huddles huddling huddled
VERB **1.** If you huddle up or are huddled, you are curled up with your arms and legs close to your body. **2.** When people or animals huddle together, they sit or stand close to each other, often for warmth.
NOUN **3.** A huddle of people or things is a small group of them.

hue hues
NOUN **1.** *a literary or poetic use* a colour or a particular shade of a colour
PHRASE **2.** If people raise a **hue and cry**, they are very angry about something and protest.

huff
PHRASE If you are **in a huff**, you are sulking or offended about something.
huffy ADJECTIVE

hug hugs hugging hugged
VERB **1.** If you hug someone, you put your arms around that person and hold him or her close to you. **2.** To hug the ground or a stretch of water or land means to keep very close to it: *The road hugs the coast for hundreds of kilometres.*
NOUN **3.** If you give someone a hug, you hold that person close to you.

huge huger hugest
ADJECTIVE extremely large in amount, size, or degree
hugely ADVERB

Instead of **HUGE** try...
a **vast** distance
a **monster** truck
a **weighty** burden
an **extensive** collection
a **bulky** piece of luggage

hulk hulks
NOUN **1.** a large, heavy person or thing **2.** the body of a ship that has been wrecked or abandoned
hulking ADJECTIVE

hull hulls
NOUN The hull of a ship is the main part of its body that sits in the water.

hum hums humming hummed
VERB **1.** To hum means to make a continuous low noise: *The generator hummed faintly.* **2.** If you hum, you sing with your lips closed.
NOUN **3.** a continuous low noise: *the hum of the fridge*

human humans
ADJECTIVE **1.** to do with the typical character of most people: *Intolerance appears deeply ingrained in human nature.*
NOUN **2.** a person
humanly ADVERB

human being human beings
NOUN a person

Hh

humane
ADJECTIVE showing kindness and sympathy toward others: *Medicine is regarded as the most humane of professions.*
humanely ADVERB

humanism
NOUN Humanism is the belief in people's ability to achieve happiness and fulfillment without the need for religion.

humanitarian humanitarians
NOUN **1.** a person who works for the welfare of all people
ADJECTIVE **2.** concerned with the welfare of all people: *humanitarian aid*
humanitarianism NOUN

humanity
NOUN **1.** Humanity is people in general: *I have faith in humanity.* **2.** Humanity is also the condition of being human: *He denies his humanity.* **3.** Someone who has humanity is kind and sympathetic.

human rights
PLURAL NOUN Human rights are the rights of individuals to freedom and justice.

humble humbler humblest; humbles humbling humbled
ADJECTIVE **1.** A humble person is modest and thinks that he or she has very little value.
2. Something that is humble is small or not very important: *Just a dash of spice will transform a humble casserole.*
VERB **3.** To humble someone means to make that person feel humiliated.
humbly ADVERB
humbled ADJECTIVE

humbug humbugs
NOUN nonsense or foolishness

humdrum
ADJECTIVE ordinary, dull, and boring: *humdrum domestic tasks*

humid
ADJECTIVE If it is humid, the air feels damp, heavy, and warm.

humidex
NOUN The humidex is a measurement used to indicate the level of discomfort that results from a combination of humidity and heat.

humidity
NOUN Humidity is the amount of moisture in the air, or the state of being humid.

humiliate humiliates humiliating humiliated
VERB To humiliate someone means to make that person feel ashamed or appear stupid to other people.
humiliation NOUN

humility
NOUN Humility is the quality of being modest and humble.

hummingbird hummingbirds
NOUN a small bird with powerful wings that make a humming noise as they beat

humour humours humouring humoured
NOUN **1.** Humour is the quality of being funny: *They discussed it with tact and humour.* **2.** Humour is also the ability to be amused by certain things: *She's got a peculiar sense of humour.* **3.** Someone's humour is the mood he or she is in: *He hasn't been in a good humour lately.*
VERB **4.** If you humour someone, you are especially kind to that person and do whatever he or she wants.
humorous ADJECTIVE

hump humps
NOUN a small, rounded lump or mound: *a camel's hump*

hunch hunches hunching hunched
NOUN **1.** a feeling or suspicion about something, not based on facts or evidence
VERB **2.** If you hunch your shoulders, you raise your shoulders and lean forward.

hunchback hunchbacks
NOUN *an old-fashioned word* someone who has a large hump on his or her back

hundred hundreds
NOUN the number 100
hundredth ADJECTIVE, ADVERB

hunger hungers hungering hungered
NOUN **1.** Hunger is the need to eat or the desire to eat. **2.** A hunger for something is a strong desire for it: *a hunger for winning*
VERB **3.** If you hunger for something, you want it very much.

hunger strike hunger strikes
NOUN a refusal to eat anything at all, especially by prisoners, as a form of protest

hungry hungrier hungriest
ADJECTIVE needing or wanting to eat: *Many people are going hungry in that country.*
hungrily ADVERB

hunk hunks
NOUN A hunk of something is a large piece of it.

hunt hunts hunting hunted
VERB **1.** To hunt means to chase wild animals to kill them for food or for sport. **2.** If you hunt for something, you search for it.
NOUN **3.** the act of hunting: *Police launched a hunt for an abandoned car.*
hunter NOUN
hunting ADJECTIVE OR NOUN

hurdle hurdles
NOUN **1.** one of the frames or barriers that

you jump over in a race called hurdles: *She won the 400 metre hurdles.* **2.** a problem or difficulty: *Those who leave school early often face many hurdles when seeking employment.*

hurl hurls hurling hurled
VERB **1.** To hurl something means to throw it with great force. **2.** If you hurl insults at someone, you insult that person aggressively and repeatedly.

hurrah
INTERJECTION an exclamation of excitement or approval

hurricane hurricanes
NOUN a violent, tropical storm with winds of more than 120 kilometres per hour

hurry hurries hurrying hurried
VERB **1.** To hurry means to move or do something as quickly as possible: *She hurried through the empty*

Instead of **HURRY** try...

dash out the door

rush to the doctor

scramble to get ready

barrel through a crowd

hustle to make it on time

streets.
2. To hurry something means to make it happen more quickly: *You can't hurry nature.*
NOUN **3.** Hurry is the speed with which you do something: *He was in a hurry to leave.*
hurried ADJECTIVE
hurriedly ADVERB

hurt hurts hurting hurt
VERB **1.** To hurt someone means to cause that person physical pain. **2.** If a part of your body hurts, you feel pain there. **3.** If you hurt yourself, you injure yourself. **4.** To hurt someone also means to make that person unhappy by being unkind or thoughtless toward him or her: *I didn't want to hurt his feelings.*
ADJECTIVE **5.** If someone feels hurt, that person feels unhappy because of someone's unkindness toward him or her: *He felt hurt by all the lies.*
hurtful ADJECTIVE

hurtle hurtles hurtling hurtled
VERB To hurtle means to move or travel very fast, especially in an uncontrolled way.

husband husbands
NOUN A husband is a married man considered in relation to his spouse.

husbandry
NOUN **1.** Husbandry is the art or skill of farming. **2.** Husbandry is also the art or skill of managing something carefully and economically.

hush hushes hushing hushed
VERB **1.** If you tell someone to hush, you are telling that person to be quiet. **2.** To hush something up means to keep it secret, especially something dishonest involving important people: *The government has hushed up a series of scandals.*
NOUN **3.** If there is a hush, it is quiet and still: *A hush fell over the audience as the curtain rose.*
hushed ADJECTIVE

husk husks
NOUN Husks are the dry outer coverings of grain or seeds.

husky huskier huskiest; huskies
ADJECTIVE **1.** A husky voice is rough or hoarse. NOUN **2.** a large, strong dog with a thick coat, often used to pull sleds across snow

hustle hustles hustling hustled
VERB To hustle someone means to make that person move by pushing and jostling him or her: *The guards hustled him out of the car.*

hut huts
NOUN a small, simple building, with one or two rooms

hutch hutches
NOUN a wooden box with wire mesh at one side, in which small pets such as rabbits can be kept

hyacinth hyacinths
NOUN a spring flower with many small, bell-shaped flowers

hybrid hybrids
NOUN **1.** a plant or animal that has been bred from two different types of plant or animal **2.** anything that is a mixture of two other things

hydra hydras
NOUN a microscopic, freshwater creature that has a slender tubular body and tentacles around the mouth

hydrangea hydrangeas
NOUN a garden shrub with large clusters of pink or blue flowers

hydraulic
ADJECTIVE operated by water or other fluid that is under pressure

hydro
NOUN **1.** electricity produced by using the energy of falling water **2.** electricity as a utility, distributed by a power company

Hh

hydro-

PREFIX Words beginning with *hydro-* have something to do with water. For example, *hydroelectricity* is made using water power.

hydrogen

NOUN Hydrogen is the lightest gas and the simplest chemical element.

hyena hyenas

NOUN a wild, doglike animal of Africa and Asia that hunts in packs

hygiene

NOUN Hygiene is the practice of keeping yourself and your surroundings clean, especially to stop the spread of disease.

hygienic ADJECTIVE

hymn hymns

NOUN in Christianity, a song of praise

hyper-

PREFIX The prefix *hyper-* means *very much*

hyperbole

NOUN Hyperbole is a style of speech or writing that uses exaggeration: *I could play this game forever.*

hyperlink hyperlinks

NOUN a word, phrase, or picture in a computer document that a user may click to move to another part of the document, or to another document

hypertext hypertexts

NOUN computer software that allows users to create, store, and view text and move between related items easily

hyphen hyphens

NOUN a punctuation mark used to join together words or parts of words, as, for example, in the word *left-handed*

hyphenate VERB

hyphenation NOUN

hypnosis

NOUN Hypnosis is an artificially produced state of relaxation in which the mind is very receptive to suggestion.

hypnotize hypnotizes hypnotizing hypnotized

VERB To hypnotize someone means to put that person into a state in which he or she seems to be asleep but can respond to questions and suggestions.

hypnotic ADJECTIVE

hypnotism NOUN

hypnotist NOUN

hypochondriac hypochondriacs

NOUN people who are hypochondriacs worry about their health all the time, being convinced that they are ill when there is actually nothing wrong with them

hypocrisy hypocrisies

NOUN Hypocrisy is pretending to have beliefs or qualities that you do not really have, so that you seem a better person than you are.

hypocritical ADJECTIVE

hypocrite NOUN

hypodermic hypodermics

NOUN a medical instrument with a hollow needle, used for giving people injections, or for taking blood samples

hypothermia

NOUN Hypothermia is a condition in which a person is very ill because his or her body temperature has been unusually low for a long time.

hypothesis hypotheses

NOUN an explanation or theory that has not yet been proved to be correct

hypothetical

ADJECTIVE based on assumption rather than on fact or reality

hysterectomy hysterectomies

NOUN an operation to remove a woman's womb

hysteria

NOUN Hysteria is a state of uncontrolled excitement or panic.

hysterical

ADJECTIVE **1.** Someone who is hysterical is in a state of uncontrolled excitement or panic. **2.** *an informal use* Something that is hysterical is extremely funny.

hysterically ADVERB

hysterics NOUN

KNOWING WORDS: WORD BUILDING

BE WORD SHARP!

You can create new words by adding prefixes and suffixes to a base word.

hyper- a prefix that means *very much* or *excessively*

hyperactive excessively active

hypercritical excessively critical

hypersensitive excessively sensitive

hypertension excessively high blood pressure

hyperventilate breathe excessively, causing dizziness

NEL

Ii

I

PRONOUN A speaker or writer uses *I* to refer to himself or herself: *I like that colour.*

ibis ibises

NOUN a large wading bird with a long, thin, curved bill that lives in warm countries

-ible

SUFFIX Words that end in *-ible* form adjectives with the meaning *able to* or *causing*: *visible, horrible*

-ic, -ical

SUFFIX Words that end in *-ic* and *-ical* form adjectives from nouns. For example, *historic* or *historical* are formed from *history*.

ice ices icing iced

NOUN **1.** water that has frozen solid **2.** a frozen surface for sports and recreation such as hockey or skating
VERB **3.** If you ice a cake, you cover it with icing.
PHRASE **4.** If you do something to **break the ice**, you make people feel relaxed and comfortable.

ice up

VERB **5.** If something ices up, it becomes covered with a layer of ice.

ice age ice ages

NOUN a period of time lasting thousands of years when much of the earth's surface was covered with ice

iceberg icebergs

NOUN a large mass of ice floating in the sea

icecap icecaps

NOUN a layer of ice and snow that permanently covers the North or South Pole

ice cream ice creams

NOUN a frozen, sweet food made from cream

ice cube ice cubes

NOUN Ice cubes are small cubes of ice put in drinks to make them cold.

ice hockey

NOUN hockey

ice skate ice skates ice skating ice skated
1. the full name for SKATE
VERB **2.** If you ice skate, you move around on ice wearing ice skates.

icicle icicles

NOUN a piece of ice shaped like a pointed stick that hangs down from a surface

icing

NOUN a mixture of powdered sugar and other ingredients, used to decorate cakes

icon icons

NOUN **1.** a picture on a computer screen representing a program that can be activated by moving the cursor over it and clicking on it **2.** a well-known person or thing that is considered a symbol of something important in a particular culture: *The maple leaf is one of Canada's most famous icons.*

ICT an abbreviation for *information and communications technology*

icy icier iciest

ADJECTIVE **1.** Something that is icy is very cold: *an icy wind* **2.** Something that is icy has ice on it: *The icy highway was the cause of many traffic accidents today.*
icily ADVERB

id

NOUN In psychology, your id is your basic instincts and unconscious thoughts.

idea ideas

NOUN **1.** a plan, suggestion, or thought that you have after thinking about a problem **2.** an opinion or belief: *old-fashioned ideas about technology* **3.** An idea of something is what you know about it: *They had no idea of where they were, so they asked for directions.*

ideal ideals

NOUN **1.** a principle or idea that you try to achieve because it seems perfect to you
ADJECTIVE **2.** An ideal condition is exactly as you would wish: *ideal weather* **3.** The ideal person or thing is the best possible person or thing for the situation.

idealism

NOUN behaviour that is based on a person's ideals
idealist NOUN
idealistic ADJECTIVE

idealize idealizes idealizing idealized

VERB If you idealize someone or something, you regard that person or thing as being perfect.
idealization NOUN

ideally

ADVERB **1.** If you say that ideally something should happen, you mean that you would like it to happen, but you know that it is not possible. **2.** Ideally means perfectly: *The hotel is ideally placed for business travellers.*

identical

ADJECTIVE exactly the same: *identical twins*
identically ADVERB

Ii

identification

NOUN **1.** The identification of someone or something is the act of identifying that person or thing. **2.** Identification is a document, such as a driver's licence or passport, that proves who you are.

identify identifies identifying identified

VERB **1.** To identify someone or something is to recognize or name that person or thing. **2.** If you identify with someone, you understand his or her feelings and ideas.

identifiable ADJECTIVE

identity identities

NOUN the characteristics that make you who you are

ideology ideologies

NOUN a set of political beliefs

ideological ADJECTIVE

ideologically ADVERB

idiom idioms

NOUN a colourful expression that is used and easily understood by people speaking the same language, even though its meaning isn't obvious from the individual words, for example *catch a cold, pain in the neck*

idiosyncrasy idiosyncrasies

NOUN Someone's idiosyncrasies are his or her own habits and likes or dislikes.

idiosyncratic ADJECTIVE

idiot idiots

NOUN someone who is stupid or foolish

idiotic

ADJECTIVE extremely foolish or silly

idle idles idling idled

ADJECTIVE If you are idle, you are doing nothing.

idleness NOUN

idly ADVERB

idol idols

NOUN **1.** a famous person who is loved and admired by fans **2.** a picture or statue that is worshipped as if it were a god

idyll idylls

NOUN a situation that is peaceful and beautiful

idyllic ADJECTIVE

i.e. The abbreviation i.e. means *that is*, and is used before giving more information. It is an abbreviation for the Latin expression *id est*.

if

CONJUNCTION **1.** on the condition that: *I will stay if I can.* **2.** whether: *I asked her if she wanted to go.*

igloo igloos

NOUN a traditional Inuit dome-shaped house built out of blocks of snow

igneous

ADJECTIVE *a technical word* Igneous rocks are formed by hot liquid rock cooling and becoming hard.

ignite ignites igniting ignited

VERB If you ignite something or if it ignites, it starts burning.

ignition ignitions

NOUN In a motor vehicle, the ignition is the part of the engine where the fuel is ignited.

ignominious

ADJECTIVE shameful or considered wrong: *It was an ignominious end to a brilliant career.*

ignominiously ADVERB

ignominy NOUN

ignoramus ignoramuses

NOUN an ignorant person

ignorant

ADJECTIVE **1.** If you are ignorant of something, you do not know about it: *He was completely ignorant of the rules.* **2.** Someone who is ignorant does not know about things in general: *I thought of asking, but didn't want to seem ignorant.*

ignorantly ADVERB

ignorance NOUN

ignore ignores ignoring ignored

VERB If you ignore someone or something, you deliberately do not take any notice of that person or thing.

iguana iguanas

NOUN a large tropical lizard

il-

PREFIX The prefix *il-* means *not* or *the opposite of*, and is the form of *in-* that is used before the letter *l*: *illegible*

ill ills

ADJECTIVE **1.** unhealthy or sick **2.** harmful or unkind: *ill deeds*

NOUN **3.** a difficulty or problem: *Poverty is a terrible social ill.*

PHRASE **4.** If you feel **ill at ease**, you feel unable to relax.

illegal

ADJECTIVE forbidden by the law

illegally ADVERB

illegality NOUN

illegible

ADJECTIVE Writing that is illegible is unclear and very difficult to read.

illegitimate

ADJECTIVE *an old-fashioned word* A person who is illegitimate was born to parents who were not married to each other at the time.

illegitimacy NOUN

IDIOM

▼×

a colourful expression that is used and easily understood by people speaking the same language, even though its meaning isn't obvious from the individual words

"Tell him to hit the road!"

Here is one example of an idiom. *Tell him to hit the road* doesn't have anything to do with hitting. In this case, it means *have nothing more to do with him.*

ill-fated
ADJECTIVE doomed to end unhappily: *her ill-fated attempt to break the world record*

illicit
ADJECTIVE not allowed by law or not approved of by society: *illicit drugs*

illiterate
ADJECTIVE unable to read or write
illiteracy NOUN

illness illnesses
NOUN **1.** Illness is the experience of being ill. **2.** a particular disease: *the treatment of common illnesses*

illogical
ADJECTIVE An illogical feeling or action is not reasonable or sensible.
illogically ADVERB

ill-treat ill-treats ill-treating ill-treated
VERB If you ill-treat people or things you hurt or damage them or treat them cruelly.
ill-treatment NOUN

illuminate illuminates illuminating illuminated
VERB To illuminate something is to shine light on it to make it easier to see.

illumination illuminations
NOUN Illumination is lighting.

illusion illusions
NOUN **1.** a false belief that you think is true: *Their hopes proved to be an illusion.* **2.** a false appearance of reality that deceives the eye: *Painters create the illusion of space.*

illusory
ADJECTIVE seeming to be true, but actually false: *an illusory truce*

illustrate illustrates illustrating illustrated
VERB **1.** If you illustrate a point, you explain it or make it clearer, often by using examples. **2.** If you illustrate a book, you put pictures in it.
illustrator NOUN
illustrative ADJECTIVE

illustration illustrations
NOUN **1.** an example or a story that is used to make a point clear **2.** a picture in a book

illustrious
ADJECTIVE An illustrious person is famous and respected.

ill will
NOUN Ill will is a feeling of hostility.

im-
PREFIX The prefix *im-* means *not* or *the opposite of*, and is the form of *in-* that is used before the letters *b*, *m*, and *p*: *imbalance, immature, impatient*

image images
NOUN **1.** a mental picture of someone or something **2.** the appearance that a person, group, or organization presents to the public

imagery
NOUN Imagery is detailed descriptive language that creates a mental picture or other sensory impression in the mind of the reader: *The description of the calm lake is an example of the water imagery used throughout the story.*

imaginary
ADJECTIVE Something that is imaginary exists only in your mind, not in real life.

imagination imaginations
NOUN the ability to form new and exciting ideas

imaginative
ADJECTIVE Someone who is imaginative can easily form new or exciting ideas in his or her mind.
imaginatively ADVERB

imagine imagines imagining imagined
VERB **1.** If you imagine something, you form an idea of it in your mind, or you think you have seen or heard it but you have not really. **2.** If you imagine that something is the case, you believe it is the case: *I imagine that's what you plan to do.*
imaginable ADJECTIVE

imam
NOUN a person who leads a group in prayer in a mosque

imbalance imbalances
NOUN If there is an imbalance between things, they are unequal: *The imbalance between rich and poor is becoming more obvious over time.*

imbecile imbeciles
NOUN a stupid person

imitate imitates imitating imitated
VERB To imitate someone or something is to copy that person or thing.
imitator NOUN
imitative ADJECTIVE

imitation imitations
NOUN a copy of something else

immaculate
ADJECTIVE **1.** completely clean and tidy: *The apartment was immaculate.* **2.** without any mistakes at all: *his usual immaculate guitar accompaniment*
immaculately ADVERB

immaterial
ADJECTIVE Something that is immaterial is not important.

THE WRITER'S EDGE

I STOOD AT THE EDGE OF THE RIVER.

IT WAS A PERFECT MORNING. MIST WAS RISING OFF THE RIVER. A GENTLE BREEZE BROUGHT THE SMELL OF CEDAR AND PINE.

PLOP!

THE SNOWY MOUNTAIN PEAKS STOOD TALL AGAINST THE BLUE SKY. A LONE HAWK DRIFTED ABOVE THE TREES. I CAST MY LINE AND HEARD THE PLOP OF THE LURE HITTING THE WATER. I KNEW THE FISH WOULD BE THERE...

IMAGERY

▼×

detailed descriptive language that creates a mental picture or other sensory impression in the mind of the reader

"A gentle breeze brought the smell of cedar and pine."

Here is an example of imagery. The words help the reader feel, smell, and see what is being described.

SCOTT CHANTLER

281

immature

ADJECTIVE **1.** Something that is immature has not finished growing or developing. **2.** A person who is immature does not behave in a sensible, adult way.
immaturity NOUN

immediate

ADJECTIVE **1.** Something that is immediate happens or is done without delay. **2.** Your immediate relatives and friends are the ones most closely connected or related to you.

immediately

ADVERB **1.** If something happens immediately it happens right away. **2.** Immediately means very near in time or position: *immediately behind the house*

immemorial

ADJECTIVE If something has been happening from time immemorial, it has been happening longer than anyone can remember.

immense

ADJECTIVE very large
immensely ADVERB
immensity NOUN

immerse immerses immersing immersed
VERB **1.** If you are immersed in an activity, you are completely involved in it. **2.** If you immerse something in a liquid, you put it into the liquid so that it is completely covered.

immersion immersions
NOUN a method of teaching a second language by using only that language, especially at a school or in a classroom

immigrant immigrants
NOUN someone who has come to live permanently in a new country
immigrate VERB
immigration NOUN

> ⚠ **HEADS UP**
>
> *We came to Canada from Peru. We are Peruvian **emigrants**, and Canadian **immigrants**.*

imminent

ADJECTIVE If something is imminent, it is going to happen very soon.
imminently ADVERB
imminence NOUN

immobile

ADJECTIVE not moving
immobility NOUN

immoral

ADJECTIVE If you describe someone or his or her behaviour as immoral, you mean that that person's behaviour does not fit in with most people's idea of what is right and proper.
immorality NOUN

immortal

ADJECTIVE **1.** Something that is immortal is famous and will be remembered for a long time: *Shakespeare's immortal love story.* **2.** In stories, someone who is immortal will never die.

immortality

NOUN Immortality is never dying. In many religions, people believe that the soul or some other essential part of a person lives forever or continues to exist in some form.

immovable

ADJECTIVE Something that is immovable is fixed and cannot be moved.
immovably ADVERB

immune

ADJECTIVE **1.** If you are immune to a particular disease, you cannot catch it. **2.** If someone or something is immune to something, that person or thing is able to avoid it or is not affected by it: *He seems immune to criticism.*
immunity NOUN

immune system

NOUN Your body's immune system consists of your white blood cells, which fight disease by producing antibodies to kill germs that come into your body.

imp imps
NOUN a mischievous child
impish ADJECTIVE

impact impacts
NOUN **1.** The impact that someone or something has is the impression that person or thing makes or the effect that person or thing has. **2.** Impact is the action of one object hitting another, usually with a lot of force: *The aircraft crashed into a ditch, exploding on impact.*

impair impairs impairing impaired
VERB To impair something is to damage it so that it stops working properly: *Travel had made him weary and impaired his judgment.*

impale impales impaling impaled
VERB If you impale something, you pierce it with a sharp object.

impart imparts imparting imparted
VERB To impart information to someone is to pass it on to that person.

impartial

ADJECTIVE Someone who is impartial has a

view of something that is fair or not biased.

impartially ADVERB
impartiality NOUN

impasse

NOUN a difficult situation in which it is impossible to find a solution

impassioned

ADJECTIVE full of emotion: *an impassioned plea*

impassive

ADJECTIVE showing no emotion
impassively ADVERB

impatient

ADJECTIVE **1.** Someone who is impatient becomes annoyed easily or is quick to lose his or her temper when things go

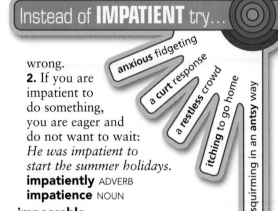

Instead of **IMPATIENT** try...

anxious fidgeting
a **curt** response
a **restless** crowd
itching to go home
squirming in an **antsy** way

wrong.
2. If you are impatient to do something, you are eager and do not want to wait: *He was impatient to start the summer holidays.*
impatiently ADVERB
impatience NOUN

impeccable

ADJECTIVE excellent, without any faults
impeccably ADVERB

impede impedes impeding impeded
VERB If you impede someone, you make that person's progress difficult.

impediment impediments
NOUN something that makes it difficult to move, develop, or do something properly: *a speech impediment*

impelled

ADJECTIVE If you feel impelled to do something, you feel strongly that you must do it.

impending

ADJECTIVE Something that is impending is going to happen very soon: *a sense of impending doom*

impenetrable

ADJECTIVE impossible to get through

imperative

ADJECTIVE **1.** Something that is imperative is extremely urgent or important.
NOUN **2.** In grammar, an imperative is the form of a verb that is used for giving orders.

imperfect

ADJECTIVE **1.** Something that is imperfect has faults or problems.
NOUN **2.** In grammar, the imperfect is a tense used to describe continuous or repeated actions that happened in the past.
imperfectly ADVERB
imperfection NOUN

imperial

ADJECTIVE **1.** Imperial means relating to an empire or an emperor or empress: *an imperial palace* **2.** The imperial system of measurement is the traditional British measuring system that uses inches, feet, and yards; ounces and pounds; and pints, quarts, and gallons.

imperialism

NOUN a system of rule in which a rich and powerful nation controls other nations
imperialist ADJECTIVE OR NOUN

imperious

ADJECTIVE proud and domineering: *an imperious manner*
imperiously ADVERB

impersonal

ADJECTIVE Something that is impersonal makes you feel that individuals and their feelings do not matter: *impersonal rooms, impersonal service*
impersonally ADVERB

impersonate impersonates impersonating impersonated
VERB If you impersonate someone, you pretend to be that person.
impersonation NOUN
impersonator NOUN

impertinent

ADJECTIVE disrespectful and rude: *impertinent questions*
impertinently ADVERB
impertinence NOUN

impetuous

ADJECTIVE If you are impetuous, you act quickly without thinking: *an impetuous gamble*
impetuously ADVERB
impetuosity NOUN

impetus

NOUN **1.** An impetus is the stimulating effect that something has on a situation, which causes it to develop more quickly. **2.** In physics, impetus is the force that starts an object moving and resists changes in speed or direction.

impinge impinges impinging impinged
VERB If something impinges on your life, it has an effect on you and influences you: *He says his private life doesn't impinge on his professional life.*

implacable
ADJECTIVE Someone who is implacable is being harsh and refuses to change his or her mind.
implacably ADVERB

implant implants implanting implanted
VERB **1.** To implant something into a person's body is to put it there, usually by means of an operation.
NOUN **2.** something that has been implanted into someone's body

implausible
ADJECTIVE very unlikely: *implausible stories*
implausibly ADVERB

implement implements implementing implemented
VERB **1.** If you implement something such as a plan, you carry it out: *The organization will implement the changes in the new year.*
NOUN **2.** An implement is a tool.
implementation NOUN

implicate implicates implicating implicated
VERB If you are implicated in a crime, you are shown to be involved in it.

implication implications
NOUN something that is suggested or implied, but not stated directly

implicit
ADJECTIVE **1.** meant, but not clearly stated: *implicit criticism* **2.** If you have an implicit belief in something, you have no doubts about it: *He had implicit faith in the noble intentions of his friend.*
implicitly ADVERB

implore implores imploring implored
VERB If you implore someone to do something, you beg that person to do it.

imply implies implying implied
VERB If you imply that something is the case, you suggest it in an indirect way.

import imports importing imported
VERB **1.** If you import something from another country, you bring it into your country or have it sent there.
NOUN **2.** a product that is made in another country and sent to your own country for use there
importation NOUN
importer NOUN

important
ADJECTIVE **1.** Something that is important is worth taking seriously. **2.** An important person has great influence or power.
importantly ADVERB
importance NOUN

impose imposes imposing imposed
VERB **1.** If you impose something on people, you force it on them: *My dad imposed an early curfew on us.* **2.** If someone imposes on you, that person unreasonably expects you to do something for him or her.
imposition NOUN

imposing
ADJECTIVE having an impressive appearance or manner: *an imposing building*

impossible
ADJECTIVE Something that is impossible cannot happen, be done, or be believed.
impossibly ADVERB
impossibility NOUN

impostor impostors
NOUN a person who pretends to be someone else in order to get things he or she wants

impotent
ADJECTIVE **1.** Someone who is impotent has no power to influence people or events.

Instead of **IMPORTANT** try...

a significant difference
an influential politician
serious matters
a critical point
a decisive victory
a momentous event
an essential ingredient
a meaningful discussion

SPELL-CHECK THIS!

A computer's spell-check won't catch a word that is spelled correctly but used in the wrong way.

Her smile inferred that she knew the answer.

In this sentence, **inferred** should be **implied**.
Imply means *indicate without saying*.
Infer means *suppose*.

2. A man who is impotent is unable to have or maintain an erection during sexual intercourse.
impotently ADVERB
impotence NOUN

impound impounds impounding impounded
VERB If something you own is impounded, the police or other officials take it.

impoverished
ADJECTIVE Someone who is impoverished is poor.

impractical
ADJECTIVE not practical, sensible, or realistic

impregnable
ADJECTIVE A building or other structure that is impregnable is so strong that it cannot be broken into or captured.

impregnated
ADJECTIVE If something is impregnated with a substance, it has absorbed the substance so that it spreads right through it: *sponges impregnated with soap and water*

impresario impresarios
NOUN a person who manages theatrical or musical events or companies

impress impresses impressing impressed
VERB **1.** If you impress someone, you make that person admire or respect you. **2.** If you impress something on someone, you make that person understand the importance of it.

impression impressions
NOUN **1.** An impression of someone or something is the way that person or thing looks or seems to you. **2.** If you **make an impression**, you have a strong effect on people you meet.

impressionable
ADJECTIVE easy to influence: *impressionable teenagers*

Impressionism
NOUN a style of painting that is concerned with the impressions created by light and shapes, rather than with exact details
Impressionist NOUN

impressive
ADJECTIVE If something is impressive, it impresses you: *an impressive display of old-fashioned cars*

imprint imprints imprinting imprinted
NOUN **1.** If something leaves an imprint on your mind, it has a strong and lasting effect.
2. the mark left by the pressure of one object on another
VERB **3.** If something is imprinted on your memory, it is firmly fixed there.

imprison imprisons imprisoning imprisoned
VERB If you are imprisoned, you are locked up, usually in a prison.
imprisonment NOUN

improbable
ADJECTIVE not probable or likely to happen
improbably ADVERB

impromptu
ADJECTIVE An impromptu action is one done without planning or organization.

improper
ADJECTIVE **1.** rude or shocking: *improper behaviour* **2.** illegal or dishonest: *improper dealings* **3.** not suitable or correct: *an improper diet*
improperly ADVERB

improve improves improving improved
VERB If something improves or if you improve it, it gets better or becomes more valuable.

improvement improvements
NOUN the fact or process of getting better

improvise improvises improvising improvised
VERB **1.** If you improvise something, you make or do something without planning in advance, and with whatever materials are available. **2.** When musicians or actors improvise, they make up the music or words as they go along.
improvised ADJECTIVE
improvisation NOUN

impudence
NOUN disrespectful talk or behaviour toward someone

impudent
ADJECTIVE If someone is impudent, something that person says or does is lacking in respect.
impudently ADVERB

impulse impulses
NOUN a strong urge to do something: *She felt a sudden impulse to confide in him.*

impulsive
ADJECTIVE If you are impulsive, you do things suddenly, without thinking carefully.
impulsively ADVERB

impure
ADJECTIVE Something that is impure contains small amounts of other things, such as dirt.

impurity impurities
NOUN **1.** Impurity is the quality of being impure: *the impurity of the water* **2.** If something contains impurities, it contains small amounts of dirt or other substances that should not be there.

Ii

in

PREPOSITION OR ADVERB *In* is used to indicate position, direction, time, and manner: *in Canada, in the past few years*

in-

PREFIX **1.** The prefix *in-* is added to the beginning of some words to form a word with the opposite meaning: *insincere* **2.** The prefix *in-* also means *in, into,* or *in the course of: infiltrate*

inability

NOUN a lack of ability to do something

inaccessible

ADJECTIVE impossible or very difficult to reach

inaccurate

ADJECTIVE not accurate or correct

inadequate

ADJECTIVE **1.** If something is inadequate, there is not enough of it. **2.** not good enough in quality for a particular purpose **3.** If someone feels inadequate, that person feels he or she does not possess the skills necessary to do a particular job or to cope with life in general.
inadequately ADVERB
inadequacy NOUN

inadvertent

ADJECTIVE not intentional: *Forgetting to send you an invitation was inadvertent.*
inadvertently ADVERB

inane

ADJECTIVE silly or stupid
inanely ADVERB
inanity NOUN

inanimate

ADJECTIVE An inanimate object is not alive.

inappropriate

ADJECTIVE not suitable for a particular purpose or occasion: *It was quite inappropriate to ask such questions.*
inappropriately ADVERB

inarticulate

ADJECTIVE If you are inarticulate, you are unable to express yourself well or easily in speech.

inasmuch

CONJUNCTION *Inasmuch as* means *to the extent that*: *She's giving herself a hard time inasmuch as she feels guilty.*

inaudible

ADJECTIVE not loud enough to be heard
inaudibly ADVERB

inaugurate inaugurates inaugurating inaugurated

VERB **1.** To inaugurate a new leader is to officially establish that person in his or her new position in a special ceremony: *The prime minister will be inaugurated next Monday.* **2.** To inaugurate something is to open it for use, often with a ceremony: *The Trans-Canada Trail was inaugurated in 2000.*
inauguration NOUN
inaugural ADJECTIVE

inborn

ADJECTIVE An inborn quality is one that you were born with.

incandescent

ADJECTIVE Something that is incandescent gives out light when it is heated.
incandescence NOUN

incapable

ADJECTIVE **1.** Someone who is incapable of doing something is not able to do it: *He is incapable of changing a light bulb.* **2.** An incapable person is weak and helpless.

incarcerate incarcerates incarcerating incarcerated

VERB To incarcerate someone is to lock that person up.
incarceration NOUN

incendiary

ADJECTIVE An incendiary weapon is one that sets fire to things: *incendiary bombs*

incense

NOUN Incense is a spicy substance that is burned to create a sweet smell.

incensed

ADJECTIVE If you are incensed by something, it makes you extremely angry.

KNOWING WORDS: WORD BUILDING

BE WORD SHARP!

You can create new words by adding prefixes and suffixes to a base word.

in-, il-, im-, ir- prefixes that make an opposite meaning

inappropriate not appropriate

inexpensive not expensive

illegal not legal

impossible not possible

irregular not regular

incentive incentives
NOUN something that encourages you to do something

inception
NOUN *a formal word* The inception of a project is the start of it.

incessant
ADJECTIVE continuing without stopping: *incessant talking*
incessantly ADVERB

incest
NOUN Incest is the crime of two people who are closely related having sex with each other.
incestuous ADJECTIVE

inch inches inching inched
NOUN **1.** a nonmetric unit of length equal to about 2.54 centimetres
VERB **2.** To inch forward is to move forward slowly.

incident incidents
NOUN an event: *a driving incident*

incidental
ADJECTIVE occurring as a minor part of something: *incidental fees*
incidentally ADVERB

incinerate incinerates incinerating incinerated
VERB If you incinerate something, you burn it.
incineration NOUN

incinerator incinerators
NOUN a furnace for burning garbage

incipient
ADJECTIVE beginning to happen or appear: *incipient panic*

incision incisions
NOUN a sharp cut, usually made by a surgeon operating on a patient

incisive
ADJECTIVE Incisive language is clear and forceful.

incite incites inciting incited
VERB If you incite someone to do something, you encourage that person to do it by making him or her angry or excited.
incitement NOUN

inclination inclinations
NOUN If you have an inclination to do something, you want to do it.

incline inclines inclining inclined
VERB **1.** If you are inclined to behave in a certain way, you often behave that way or you want to behave that way.
NOUN **2.** a slope

include includes including included
VERB If one thing includes another, it has the second thing as one of its parts.
including PREPOSITION

inclusion
NOUN The inclusion of one thing in another is the act of making it part of the other thing.

inclusive
ADJECTIVE Something that is inclusive avoids bias and respects all communities. For example, inclusive language is free of stereotypes and avoids racist and sexist words and expressions.

incognito
ADVERB If you are travelling incognito, you are travelling in disguise.

incoherent
ADJECTIVE If someone is incoherent, that person is talking in an unclear or rambling way.
incoherently ADVERB
incoherence NOUN

income incomes
NOUN the money a person earns

income tax
NOUN Income tax is a part of someone's earnings that he or she has to pay regularly to the government.

incoming
ADJECTIVE coming in: *incoming trains, an incoming phone call*

incomparable
ADJECTIVE Something that is incomparable is so good that it cannot be compared with anything else.
incomparably ADVERB

incompatible
ADJECTIVE Two things or people are incompatible if they are unable to live or exist together because they are completely different.
incompatibility NOUN

incompetent
ADJECTIVE Someone who is incompetent does not have the ability to do something properly.
incompetently ADVERB
incompetence NOUN

incomplete
ADJECTIVE Something that is incomplete is not finished, or is missing some part.
incompletely ADVERB

incomprehensible
ADJECTIVE not able to be understood

inconceivable
ADJECTIVE impossible to believe

Ii

inconclusive
ADJECTIVE not leading to a decision or to a definite result

incongruous
ADJECTIVE Something that is incongruous seems strange because it does not fit into a place or situation.
incongruously ADVERB

inconsequential
ADJECTIVE Something that is inconsequential is not very important.

inconsistent
ADJECTIVE Someone or something that is inconsistent is unpredictable and behaves differently in similar situations.
inconsistently ADVERB
inconsistency NOUN

inconspicuous
ADJECTIVE not easily seen or obvious
inconspicuously ADVERB

incontinent
ADJECTIVE Someone who is incontinent is unable to control his or her bladder or bowels.

inconvenience inconveniences inconveniencing inconvenienced
NOUN **1.** If something causes inconvenience, it causes difficulty or problems.
VERB **2.** To inconvenience someone is to cause that person trouble, difficulty, or problems.
inconvenient ADJECTIVE
inconveniently ADVERB

incorporate incorporates incorporating incorporated
VERB If something is incorporated into another thing, it becomes part of that thing.
incorporation NOUN

Instead of **INCREASE** try...

heighten the chances
raise the volume
expand a list
hike taxes
multiply the amount
extend vacation time
boost your performance
deepen your understanding

incorrect
ADJECTIVE wrong or untrue
incorrectly ADVERB

increase increases increasing increased
VERB **1.** If something increases, it becomes larger in amount.

NOUN **2.** a rise in the number, level, or amount of something
increasingly ADVERB

incredible
ADJECTIVE **1.** totally amazing **2.** impossible to believe
incredibly ADVERB

incredulous
ADJECTIVE If you are incredulous, you are unable to believe something because it is very surprising or shocking.
incredulously ADVERB
incredulity NOUN

increment increments
NOUN the amount by which something increases
incremental ADJECTIVE

incriminate incriminates incriminating incriminated
VERB If something incriminates you, it suggests that you are involved in a crime.

incubate incubates incubating incubated
VERB When eggs incubate, they are kept warm until they are ready to hatch.
incubation NOUN

incubator incubators
NOUN a piece of hospital equipment in which sick or weak newborn babies are kept warm

incumbent incumbents *a formal word*
ADJECTIVE **1.** If it is incumbent on you to do something, it is your duty to do it.
NOUN **2.** the person in a particular official position

incur incurs incurring incurred
VERB If you incur something unpleasant, you cause it to happen.

incurable
ADJECTIVE **1.** An incurable disease is one that cannot be cured. **2.** An incurable habit is one that cannot be changed: *an incurable romantic*
incurably ADVERB

indebted
ADJECTIVE If you are indebted to someone, you are grateful to that person.

indecent
ADJECTIVE Something that is indecent is shocking or vulgar, usually because it concerns nakedness or sex.
indecently ADVERB
indecency NOUN

indeed
ADVERB You use *indeed* to strengthen a point that you are making: *The desserts are very good indeed.*

indefatigable
ADJECTIVE People who never get tired of doing something are indefatigable.

indefinite
ADJECTIVE **1.** If something is indefinite, the finish time has not been decided: *indefinite plans* **2.** Indefinite also means vague or not exact: *indefinite words and pictures*
indefinitely ADVERB

indefinite article indefinite articles
NOUN the grammatical term for *a* and *an*

indelible
ADJECTIVE unable to be removed: *indelible ink*
indelibly ADVERB

indemnity
NOUN *a formal word* Indemnity is protection against damage or loss.

indentation indentations
NOUN a dent or a groove in a surface or on the edge of something

independence
NOUN **1.** Independence is not relying on anyone else. **2.** A nation or state gains its independence when it stops being ruled or governed by another country and has its own government and laws.

independent
ADJECTIVE **1.** Something that is independent happens or exists separately from other people or things: *Results are assessed by an independent panel.* **2.** Someone who is independent does not need other people's help: *a fiercely independent person* **3.** An independent nation is one that is not ruled or governed by another country.
independently ADVERB

indeterminate
ADJECTIVE not certain or definite: *some indeterminate point in the future*

index indexes
NOUN **1.** an alphabetical list at the back of a book, referring to items in the book **2.** an alphabetical list, such as all the books in a library, arranged by title, author, or subject

index finger index fingers
NOUN your first finger, next to your thumb

Indian Ocean
NOUN the ocean separating Africa and Australasia

indicate indicates indicating indicated
VERB **1.** If something indicates something, it shows that it is true: *a gesture that clearly indicates his relief* **2.** If you indicate something to someone, you point to it. **3.** If you indicate a fact, you mention it.

indication indications
NOUN a sign of what someone feels or what is likely to happen

indicative
ADJECTIVE **1.** If something is indicative of something else, it is a sign of that thing: *A headache is often indicative of eyestrain.*
NOUN **2.** If a verb is used in the indicative, it is in the form used for making statements.

indicator indicators
NOUN **1.** something that tells you what something is like or what is happening **2.** A car's indicators are the lights at the front and back, which are used to show when it is turning left or right. **3.** a substance used in chemistry that shows if another substance is an acid or alkali by changing colour when it comes into contact with it

indict indicts indicting indicted
VERB *a formal word* To indict someone is to charge that person officially with a crime.
indictment NOUN
indictable ADJECTIVE

indifferent
ADJECTIVE **1.** If you are indifferent to something, you have no interest in it. **2.** If something is indifferent, it is of poor quality or low standard: *a pair of indifferent paintings*
indifferently ADVERB
indifference NOUN

indigenous
ADJECTIVE If something is indigenous to a place, it comes from that place: *a plant indigenous to Asia*

indigestion
NOUN Indigestion is a pain you get when you find it difficult to digest food.

indignant
ADJECTIVE If you are indignant, you feel angry about something that you think is unfair.
indignantly ADVERB

indignation
NOUN Indignation is anger about something that you think is unfair.

indignity indignities
NOUN something that makes you feel embarrassed or humiliated: *the indignity suffered at the hands of bullies*

indigo
NOUN OR ADJECTIVE dark, violet blue

indirect
ADJECTIVE Something that is indirect is not done or caused directly by a particular person or thing, but by someone or something else.
indirectly ADVERB

Ii

⚠ **HEADS UP** The word **indict** is pronounced in-DITE.

indirect speech
ADJECTIVE a report of what someone said that gives the context of the speech without repeating the exact words. For example, *She said that she would walk* is the indirect form of *I will walk*.

indiscriminate
ADJECTIVE not involving careful thought or choice: *an indiscriminate bombing campaign*
indiscriminately ADVERB

indispensable
ADJECTIVE If something is indispensable, you cannot do without it: *A warm winter coat is indispensable.*

indistinct
ADJECTIVE not clear: *indistinct voices*
indistinctly ADVERB

individual individuals
ADJECTIVE **1.** relating to one particular person or thing: *Each student needs individual attention.* **2.** Someone who is individual behaves quite differently from the way other people behave.
NOUN **3.** a person, different from any other person: *wealthy individuals*
individually ADVERB

individualist individualists
NOUN someone who likes to do things in his or her own way
individualistic ADJECTIVE

individuality
NOUN If something has individuality, it is different from all other things, and therefore is very interesting and noticeable.

indomitable
ADJECTIVE *a formal word* impossible to overcome: *an indomitable spirit*

indoor
ADJECTIVE situated or happening inside a building

indoors
ADVERB If something happens indoors, it takes place inside a building.

induce induces inducing induced
VERB **1.** To induce a state is to cause it: *His manner was rough and suspicious but he did not induce fear.* **2.** If you induce someone to do something, you persuade that person to do it.

inducement inducements
NOUN something offered to encourage someone to do something

indulge indulges indulging indulged
VERB **1.** If you indulge in something, you allow yourself to do something that you enjoy. **2.** If you indulge someone, you let that person have or do what he or she wants, often in a way that is not good for that person.

indulgence indulgences
NOUN **1.** something you allow yourself to have because it gives you pleasure
2. Indulgence is the act of indulging yourself or another person.

indulgent
ADJECTIVE If you are indulgent, you treat someone with special kindness: *an indulgent father*
indulgently ADJECTIVE

industrial
ADJECTIVE relating to industry

industrialist industrialists
NOUN a person who owns or controls a lot of factories

Industrial Revolution
NOUN The Industrial Revolution took place in Britain in the late eighteenth and early nineteenth century, when machines began to be used more in factories and more goods were produced as a result.

industrious
ADJECTIVE An industrious person works very hard.

industry industries
NOUN **1.** Industry is the work and processes involved in any branch of business, trade, or manufacture. **2.** all the people and processes involved in manufacturing a particular thing

inedible
ADJECTIVE not fit to eat

inefficient
ADJECTIVE badly organized, wasteful, and slow: *Using a shovel is an inefficient way to clear the parking lot of snow.*
inefficiently ADVERB
inefficiency NOUN

inept
ADJECTIVE without skill: *an inept lawyer*
ineptitude NOUN

inequality inequalities
NOUN a difference in size, status, wealth, or position between different things, groups, or people

inert
ADJECTIVE Something that is inert does not move and appears lifeless: *an inert body lying on the floor*

inertia
NOUN If you have a feeling of inertia, you feel very lazy and unwilling to do anything.

inevitable
ADJECTIVE certain to happen
inevitably ADVERB
inevitability NOUN

inexhaustible
ADJECTIVE Something that is inexhaustible will never be used up: *an inexhaustible supply of ideas*

inexorable
ADJECTIVE *a formal word* Something that is inexorable cannot be prevented from continuing: *the inexorable increase in the number of cars*
inexorably ADVERB

inexpensive
ADJECTIVE not costing much

inexperienced
ADJECTIVE lacking experience of a situation or activity: *inexperienced drivers*
inexperience NOUN

inexplicable
ADJECTIVE If something is inexplicable, you cannot explain it: *For some inexplicable reason, I still felt uneasy.*
inexplicably ADVERB

inextricably
ADVERB If two or more things are inextricably linked, they cannot be separated.

infallible
ADJECTIVE never wrong: *No computer is infallible.*
infallibility NOUN

infamous
ADJECTIVE well known because of something bad or evil: *a book about the country's most infamous murder cases*

infant infants
NOUN **1.** a baby
ADJECTIVE **2.** designed for babies: *infant toys*
infancy NOUN
infantile ADJECTIVE

infantry
NOUN In an army, the infantry are soldiers who fight on foot rather than in tanks or on horses.

infatuated
ADJECTIVE If you are infatuated with someone, you have such strong feelings of love or passion that you cannot think sensibly about that person.
infatuation NOUN

infect infects infecting infected
VERB To infect someone or something is to cause disease in that person.

infection infections
NOUN **1.** a disease caused by germs: *a chest infection* **2.** Infection is the state of being infected: *If you wash your hands often, there is a very small risk of infection.*

infectious
ADJECTIVE spreading from one person to another: *an infectious disease*

infer infers inferring inferred
VERB If you infer something, you work out that it is true on the basis of information that you already have.
inference NOUN

⚠ **HEADS UP**

Don't confuse **infer** and **imply**. Check out the spell-check feature on page 284 to see an example.

inferior inferiors
ADJECTIVE **1.** having a lower position than something or someone else **2.** of low quality: *inferior chocolate*
NOUN **3.** Your inferiors are people in a lower position than you.
inferiority NOUN

infernal
ADJECTIVE very unpleasant: *infernal noise*

inferno infernos
NOUN a very large, dangerous fire

infertile
ADJECTIVE **1.** Infertile soil is of poor quality and plants cannot grow well in it.
2. Someone who is infertile cannot have children.

infested
ADJECTIVE Something that is infested has a large number of animals or insects living on it and causing damage: *The apartments are damp and infested with rats.*
infestation NOUN

infidelity infidelities
NOUN Infidelity is being unfaithful to a spouse or sexual partner.

infighting
NOUN Infighting is quarrelling or rivalry between members, or groups of members, of the same organization.

infiltrate infiltrates infiltrating infiltrated
VERB If people infiltrate an organization, they gradually enter it in secret to spy on its activities.
infiltration NOUN

infinite
ADJECTIVE without any limit or end: *an infinite number of possibilities*
infinitely ADVERB

infinitive infinitives
NOUN In grammar, the infinitive is the base form of the verb. It often has *to* in front of it, for example *to go* or *to see*.

infinity
NOUN **1.** Infinity is a number that is larger than any other number and can never be given an exact value. **2.** Infinity is also a point that can never be reached, further away than any other point: *skies stretching on into infinity*

infirmary infirmaries
NOUN a place for the care of sick or injured people, especially in an institution such as a school or summer camp

inflamed
ADJECTIVE If part of your body is inflamed, it is red and swollen, usually because of infection.

inflammable
ADJECTIVE An inflammable material burns easily.

⚠️ **HEADS UP**

Don't be deceived—**inflammable** and **flammable** both mean *easily set on fire*. The opposite is **nonflammable**.

inflammation
NOUN Inflammation is painful redness or swelling of part of the body.

inflammatory
ADJECTIVE Inflammatory actions are likely to make people very angry.

inflate inflates inflating inflated
VERB When you inflate something, you fill it with air or gas to make it swell.
inflatable ADJECTIVE

inflation
NOUN Inflation is an increase in the price of goods and services in a country.
inflationary ADJECTIVE

inflection inflections
NOUN **1.** a change in the tone or pitch of a voice. **2.** a change in the form of a word that shows its grammatical function, for example a change that makes a noun plural

inflexible
ADJECTIVE fixed and unable to be altered: *an inflexible routine*

inflict inflicts inflicting inflicted
VERB If you inflict something unpleasant on someone, you make that person suffer it.

influence influences influencing influenced
NOUN **1.** Influence is power that a person has over other people. **2.** An influence is also the power to cause an effect or change: *the influence of the moon on the tides*
VERB **3.** To influence someone or something means to have an effect on that person or thing.

influential
ADJECTIVE Someone who is influential has a lot of influence over people.

influenza
NOUN *a formal word* Influenza is the full name for flu.

influx
NOUN a steady arrival of people or things: *a large influx of tourists*

inform informs informing informed
VERB **1.** If you inform someone of something, you tell that person about it. **2.** If you inform on a person, you tell the police about a crime that person has committed.
informant NOUN

informal
ADJECTIVE relaxed and casual: *an informal meeting*
informally ADVERB
informality NOUN

⚠️ **HEADS UP**

Informal language is used in everyday speech and writing. **Formal language** is used in speeches, documents, etc.

information
NOUN If you have information on or about something, you know something about it.

informative
ADJECTIVE Something that is informative gives you useful information.

informer informers
NOUN someone who tells the police that another person has committed a crime

infrastructure infrastructures
NOUN the basic physical structures or features necessary for a system or organization to work

infringe infringes infringing infringed
VERB **1.** If you infringe a law, you break it.
2. To infringe on people's rights is to not

allow them the rights to which they are entitled.
infringement NOUN

infuriate infuriates infuriating infuriated
VERB If someone infuriates you, that person makes you very angry.
infuriating ADJECTIVE

infuse infuses infusing infused
VERB **1.** If you infuse someone with a feeling such as enthusiasm or joy, you fill that person with it. **2.** If you infuse a substance such as a herb or medicine, you pour hot water onto it and leave it for the water to absorb the flavour.
infusion NOUN

ingenious
ADJECTIVE very clever and using new ideas: *an ingenious invention*
ingeniously ADVERB

ingenuity
NOUN Ingenuity is cleverness and skill at inventing things or working out plans.

ingot ingots
NOUN a brick-shaped lump of metal, especially gold

ingrained
ADJECTIVE If habits and beliefs are ingrained, they are difficult to change or destroy.

ingredient ingredients
NOUN Ingredients are the things that something is made from, especially in cooking and baking.

inhabit inhabits inhabiting inhabited
VERB If you inhabit a place, you live there.

inhabitant inhabitants
NOUN The inhabitants of a place are the people who live there.

inhale inhales inhaling inhaled
VERB When you inhale, you breathe in.
inhalation NOUN

inherent
ADJECTIVE Inherent qualities or characteristics of something are natural parts of it: *his inherent common sense*
inherently ADVERB

inherit inherits inheriting inherited
VERB **1.** If you inherit money or property, you receive it from someone who has died. **2.** If you inherit a quality or characteristic from a parent or ancestor, it is passed on to you at birth.
inheritor NOUN

inheritance inheritances
NOUN something that is passed on from another person

inhibit inhibits inhibiting inhibited
VERB If you inhibit someone from doing something, you prevent that person from doing it.

inhibited
ADJECTIVE People who are inhibited find it difficult to relax and to show their emotions.

inhibition inhibitions
NOUN Inhibitions are feelings of fear or embarrassment that make it difficult for someone to relax and to show his or her emotions.

inhospitable
ADJECTIVE **1.** An inhospitable place is unpleasant or difficult to live in. **2.** If someone is inhospitable, that person does not make people who visit him or her feel welcome.

inhuman
ADJECTIVE not human, or without human kindness or decency: *inhuman treatment of animals*

inhumane
ADJECTIVE extremely cruel
inhumanity NOUN

inimitable
ADJECTIVE If you have an inimitable characteristic, no one else can imitate it: *her inimitable sense of style*

initial initials
ADJECTIVE **1.** first, or at the beginning: *Shock and dismay were my initial reactions to what he said.*
NOUN **2.** the first letter of a word
initially ADVERB

initiate initiates initiating initiated
VERB **1.** If you initiate something, you make it start or happen. **2.** If you initiate someone into a group or club, you allow that person to become a member of it, usually by means of a special ceremony.
initiation NOUN

initiative initiatives
NOUN **1.** an attempt to get something done **2.** If you have initiative, you decide what to do and then do it, without needing the advice of other people.

inject injects injecting injected
VERB **1.** If a substance is injected into someone or something, that substance is forced into a passage, cavity, or tissue: *to inject a flu vaccine, to inject fuel into an engine* **2.** If you inject something new into a situation, you add it.
injection NOUN

li

⚠ **HEADS UP** The word **inimitable** is pronounced in-NIM-uh-tuh-bull.

Ii

injunction injunctions
NOUN an order issued by a court of law to stop someone from doing something

injure injures injuring injured
VERB To injure someone is to damage part of his or her body.

injury injuries
NOUN hurt or damage, especially to part of a person's body or to his or her feelings: *She suffered acute injury to her pride. The knee injury forced him to retire from the professional game.*

injustice injustices
NOUN **1.** Injustice is lack of justice and fairness. **2.** If you do someone an injustice, you judge that person too harshly.

ink
NOUN Ink is the coloured liquid used for writing or printing.

inkling inklings
NOUN a vague idea about something

inlaid
ADJECTIVE decorated with small pieces of wood, metal, or stone: *decorative plates inlaid with brass*
inlay NOUN

inland
ADVERB OR ADJECTIVE toward or near the middle of a country, away from the sea

in-law in-laws
NOUN Your in-laws are your relatives by marriage.

inlet inlets
NOUN a narrow bay

inline skate inline skates
NOUN a roller skate that has four wheels set in one straight line on the bottom of the boot

inmate inmates
NOUN someone who lives in a prison or an institution

inn inns
NOUN a small country hotel

innards
PLURAL NOUN The innards of something are its inside parts.

innate
ADJECTIVE An innate quality is one that you were born with: *an innate sense of fairness*
innately ADVERB

inner
ADJECTIVE contained inside a place or object: *an inner room*

innermost
ADJECTIVE deepest and most secret: *our innermost feelings*

inning
NOUN In baseball and cricket, an inning is a period when a particular team is batting.

innocence
NOUN inexperience of evil or unpleasant things

innocent
ADJECTIVE **1.** not guilty of a crime **2.** without experience of evil or unpleasant things: *an innocent child*

Instead of **INNOCENT** try...

a naive attitude
pure intentions
a clear conscience
a blameless victim
a harmless question

innocently
ADVERB

innocuous
ADJECTIVE not harmful

innovation innovations
NOUN a completely new idea, product, or system of doing things

innuendo innuendos
NOUN an indirect reference to something, especially something suggestive or unpleasant

innumerable
ADJECTIVE too many to be counted: *innumerable cups of coffee*

input inputs
NOUN **1.** Input consists of all the money, information, and other resources that are put into a job, project, or company to make it work. **2.** In computing, input is information that is fed into a computer.

inquest inquests
NOUN an official inquiry to find out what caused a person's death

inquire inquires inquiring inquired
VERB If you inquire about something, you ask for information about it.
inquiring ADJECTIVE
inquiry NOUN

inquisition inquisitions
NOUN an official investigation, especially one that is very thorough and uses harsh methods of questioning

inquisitive
ADJECTIVE Someone who is inquisitive is very curious and eager to find out about things.
inquisitively ADVERB

inroad inroads
NOUN If something makes an inroad on or into something, it starts affecting it.

insane
ADJECTIVE Someone who is insane has a severe mental illness.
insanely ADVERB
insanity NOUN

insatiable
ADJECTIVE A desire or urge that is insatiable is very great: *an insatiable curiosity*
insatiably ADVERB

inscribe inscribes inscribing inscribed
VERB If you inscribe words on an object, you write or carve them on it.

inscription inscriptions
NOUN the words that are written or carved on something

inscrutable
ADJECTIVE Someone who is inscrutable does not show what he or she is really thinking.

insect insects
NOUN a small creature with six legs and usually wings, whose body is divided into three parts

insecticide insecticides
NOUN a poisonous chemical used to kill insects

insecure
ADJECTIVE **1.** If you are insecure, you feel unsure of yourself and doubt whether other people like you. **2.** Something that is insecure is not safe or well protected: *Many people feel their jobs are insecure.*
insecurity NOUN

insensitive
ADJECTIVE If you are insensitive, you do not notice when you are upsetting people.
insensitivity NOUN

insert inserts inserting inserted
VERB If you insert an object into something, you put it inside.
insertion NOUN

inshore
ADJECTIVE at sea, but close to the shore: *an inshore fishery*

inside insides
NOUN **1.** the part of something that is surrounded by the main part and often hidden: *The inside of the box was lined with newspaper.*
ADJECTIVE **2.** surrounded by the main part and often hidden: *an inside pocket*
PREPOSITION **3.** in or to the interior of: *inside the house*
PLURAL NOUN **4.** Your insides are the parts inside your body.
PHRASE **5. Inside out** means with the inside part facing outward.

insider insiders
NOUN a person who is involved in a situation and so knows more about it than other people

insidious
ADJECTIVE Something that is insidious is unpleasant and develops slowly without being noticed: *the insidious progress of the disease*
insidiously ADVERB

insight insights
NOUN If you gain insight into a problem, you gradually get a deep and accurate understanding of it.

insignia
NOUN the badge or symbol of a particular organization, military order, or team

insignificant
ADJECTIVE small and unimportant
insignificance NOUN

insincere
ADJECTIVE Someone who is insincere pretends to have feelings that he or she does not really have.

insinuate insinuates insinuating insinuated
VERB If you insinuate something unpleasant, you hint about it.
insinuation NOUN

insipid
ADJECTIVE **1.** An insipid person or activity is dull and boring. **2.** Food that is insipid has very little taste.

insist insists insisting insisted
VERB If you insist on something, you demand it forcefully.
insistent ADJECTIVE
insistence NOUN

insolent
ADJECTIVE very rude and disrespectful
insolently ADVERB
insolence NOUN

insoluble
ADJECTIVE **1.** impossible to solve: *an insoluble problem* **2.** unable to dissolve: *substances that are insoluble in water*

insolvent
ADJECTIVE unable to pay your debts
insolvency NOUN

insomnia
NOUN Insomnia is difficulty in sleeping.
insomniac NOUN

inspect inspects inspecting inspected
VERB To inspect something is to examine it carefully to check that everything is all right.
inspection NOUN

li

inspector inspectors
NOUN **1.** someone who inspects things **2.** a high-ranking police officer

inspire inspires inspiring inspired
VERB **1.** If something inspires you, it gives you new ideas and enthusiasm to do something. **2.** To inspire an

Instead of **INSPIRE** try…

incite a crowd
instil confidence
spark a movement
stir the imagination
motivate to take action

emotion in someone is to make that person feel this emotion.
inspired ADJECTIVE
inspiring ADJECTIVE
inspiration NOUN

instability
NOUN Instability is a lack of stability: *political instability*

install installs installing installed
VERB **1.** If you install a piece of equipment in a place, you put it there so it is ready to be used. **2.** To install someone in an important job is to officially give that person that position. **3.** If you install yourself in a place, you settle there and make yourself comfortable.
installation NOUN

instalment instalments
NOUN **1.** If you pay for something in instalments, you pay small amounts of money regularly over a period of time. **2.** one of the parts of something issued at different times in a series: *The story was printed in five instalments.*

instance instances
NOUN **1.** a particular example or occurrence of an event or situation: *Handing in his homework early was another instance of his keen behaviour.*
PHRASE **2.** You use **for instance** to give an example of something you are talking about.

instant instants
NOUN **1.** a moment or short period of time: *In an instant they were gone.*
ADJECTIVE **2.** immediate and without delay: *The movie was an instant success.*
instantly ADVERB

instantaneous
ADJECTIVE happening immediately and without delay: *The applause was instantaneous.*
instantaneously ADVERB

instead
ADVERB in place of something: *Take the stairs instead of the elevator.*

instigate instigates instigating instigated
VERB Someone who instigates a situation makes it happen.
instigation NOUN
instigator NOUN

instil instils instilling instilled
VERB If you instil an idea or feeling into someone, you make that person think or feel it.

instinct instincts
NOUN a natural tendency to do something: *My first instinct was to protect myself.*
instinctive ADJECTIVE
instinctively ADVERB

institute institutes instituting instituted
NOUN **1.** an organization for teaching or research
VERB **2.** *a formal use* If you institute a rule or system, you introduce it.

institution institutions
NOUN **1.** a custom or system regarded as an important tradition within a society: *The family is an institution to be cherished.* **2.** a large, important organization, for example a university or bank
institutional ADJECTIVE

instruct instructs instructing instructed
VERB **1.** If you instruct someone to do something, you tell that person to do it. **2.** If someone instructs you in a subject or skill, that person teaches you about it.
instructor NOUN
instructive ADJECTIVE
instruction NOUN

instrument instruments
NOUN **1.** a tool or device used for a particular job: *a special instrument that cuts through metal* **2.** A musical instrument is an object, such as a piano or flute, played to make music.

instrumental
ADJECTIVE **1.** If you are instrumental in doing something, you help to make it happen. **2.** Instrumental music is performed using only musical instruments, and not voices.

insufficient
ADJECTIVE not enough for a particular purpose
insufficiently ADVERB

insular
ADJECTIVE Someone who is insular is unwilling to meet new people or to consider new ideas.
insularity NOUN

insulate insulates insulating insulated
VERB If you insulate something, you cover

Ii

it with a layer to keep it warm or to stop electricity passing through it.

insulation NOUN

insulator NOUN

insulin

NOUN Insulin is a substance that controls the level of sugar in the blood. People who have diabetes do not produce insulin naturally and have to take regular doses of it.

insult insults insulting insulted

VERB **1.** If you insult someone, you offend that person by being rude to him or her.

NOUN **2.** a rude remark that offends you

insulting ADJECTIVE

insure insures insuring insured

VERB **1.** If you insure something or yourself, you pay money regularly to a company so that if there is an accident or damage, the company will pay for medical treatment or repairs. **2.** If you do something to insure against something unpleasant happening, you do it to prevent the unpleasant thing from happening or to protect yourself if it does happen.

insurance NOUN

insurrection insurrections

NOUN a violent action taken against the rulers of a country

intact

ADJECTIVE complete, and not changed or damaged in any way: *The rear of the aircraft remained intact when it crashed.*

intake intakes

NOUN A person's intake of food, drink, or air is the amount that he or she takes in.

integral

ADJECTIVE If something is an integral part of a whole thing, it is an essential part.

integrate integrates integrating integrated

VERB **1.** If a person integrates into a group, he or she becomes part of it. **2.** To integrate things is to combine them so that they become closely linked or form one thing: *a plan to integrate the coal and steel industries*

integration NOUN

integrity

NOUN **1.** Integrity is the quality of being honest and following your principles. **2.** The integrity of a group of people is their being united as one whole.

intellect intellects

NOUN Intellect is the ability to understand ideas and information.

intellectual intellectuals

ADJECTIVE **1.** involving thought, ideas, and understanding: *an intellectual exercise*

NOUN **2.** someone who enjoys thinking about complicated ideas

intellectually ADVERB

intelligence

NOUN A person's intelligence is his or her ability to understand and learn things quickly and well.

intelligent

ADJECTIVE able to understand and learn things quickly and well

intelligently ADVERB

intelligentsia

NOUN The intelligentsia are intellectual people, considered as a group.

intelligible

ADJECTIVE able to be understood: *I heard very few intelligible remarks.*

intend intends intending intended

VERB **1.** If you intend to do something, you have decided or planned to do it: *She intended to move back to Newfoundland.* **2.** If something is intended for a particular use, you have planned that it should have this use: *The booklet is intended to be kept handy.*

intense

ADJECTIVE **1.** very great in strength or amount: *intense heat* **2.** If a person is intense, he or she takes things very seriously and has very strong feelings.

intensely ADVERB

intensity NOUN

intensify intensifies intensifying intensified

VERB To intensify something is to make it greater or stronger.

intensive

ADJECTIVE involving a lot of energy or effort over a very short period of time: *an intensive training course*

intent intents

NOUN **1.** A person's intent is his or her purpose or intention.

ADJECTIVE **2.** If you are intent on doing something, you are determined to do it.

intently ADVERB

intention intentions

NOUN If you have an intention to do something, you have a plan of what you are going to do.

intentional

ADJECTIVE If something is intentional, it is done on purpose.

intentionally ADVERB

inter-

PREFIX The prefix *inter-* means *between*: *inter-school competitions*

 **HEADS UP** Inter-school means *between schools*. Intra-school means *inside the school*.

Ii

interact interacts interacting interacted
VERB The way two people or things interact is the way they work together, communicate, or react with each other.
interaction NOUN

interactive
ADJECTIVE Interactive television, computers, and games react to decisions made by the viewer, user, or player.

intercept intercepts intercepting intercepted
VERB If you intercept someone or something that is going from one place to another, you stop that person or thing.

interchange interchanges
NOUN An interchange is the act or process of exchanging things or ideas.
interchangeable ADJECTIVE

intercom intercoms
NOUN a device consisting of a microphone and a loudspeaker, which you use to speak to people in another room

intercourse
NOUN **1.** Intercourse or sexual intercourse is the act of having sex. **2.** communications or dealings between people: *Intercourse between cultures has enriched our society.*

interest interests interesting interested
NOUN **1.** If you have an interest in something or if something is of interest, you want to learn or hear more about it. **2.** Your interests are your hobbies. **3.** If you have an interest in something being done, you want it to be done because it will benefit you. **4.** Interest is an extra payment made by someone who has borrowed money. It is also a payment by a bank or company to someone who has invested money in that bank or company. Interest is worked out as a percentage of the sum of money borrowed or invested.
VERB **5.** Something that interests you attracts your attention so that you want to learn or hear more about it.
interested ADJECTIVE

> ⚠ **HEADS UP**
>
> A **disinterested** person is fair and unbiased. An **uninterested** person doesn't care.

interesting
ADJECTIVE making you want to learn more
interestingly ADVERB

interface interfaces
NOUN **1.** The interface between two subjects or systems is the area in which they affect each other or are linked. **2.** The user interface of a computer program is how it is presented on the computer screen and how easy it is to operate.

interfere interferes interfering interfered
VERB **1.** If you interfere in a situation, you try to influence it, although it does not really concern you. **2.** Something that interferes with a situation has a damaging effect on it.
interference NOUN
interfering ADJECTIVE

interim
ADJECTIVE intended for use only until something permanent is arranged: *an interim government, an interim report*

interior interiors
NOUN **1.** the inside part of something
ADJECTIVE **2.** Interior means inside: *They painted the interior walls white.*

interjection interjections
NOUN a word or phrase spoken suddenly to express surprise, pain, or anger

interlude interludes
NOUN a short break from an activity

intermediary intermediaries
NOUN someone who tries to get two groups of people to come to an agreement

intermediate
ADJECTIVE An intermediate level occurs in the middle, between two other stages: *The language school offers beginner, intermediate, and advanced classes.*

interminable
ADJECTIVE If something is interminable, it goes on for a very long time: *an interminable wait for the bus*
interminably ADVERB

intermission intermissions
NOUN an interval between two parts of a musical performance or play

intermittent
ADJECTIVE happening only occasionally
intermittently ADVERB

internal
ADJECTIVE happening inside a person, place, or object
internally ADVERB

international
ADJECTIVE involving different countries
internationally ADVERB

Internet
NOUN The Internet is a worldwide communication system that people use through computers.

Ii

interplay

NOUN The interplay between two things is the way they react with one another.

interpret interprets interpreting interpreted

VERB **1.** If you interpret what someone says or does, you decide what it means. **2.** If you interpret a foreign language that someone is speaking, you translate it.

interpretation NOUN
interpreter NOUN

interrogate interrogates interrogating interrogated

VERB If you interrogate someone, you question that person thoroughly to get information from him or her.

interrogation NOUN
interrogator NOUN

interrogative

ADJECTIVE **1.** in the form of a question
NOUN **2.** an interrogative word, especially a pronoun

⚠ HEADS UP

The interrogatives that make a good news article are called the five W's: **Who, What, When, Where,** and **Why.**

interrupt interrupts interrupting interrupted

VERB **1.** If you interrupt someone, you start talking while that person is talking. **2.** If you interrupt a process or activity, you stop it from continuing for a time.

interruption NOUN

intersect intersects intersecting intersected

VERB When two roads intersect, they cross each other.

intersection NOUN

interspersed

ADJECTIVE If something is interspersed with things, these things occur at various points in it.

interval intervals

NOUN the period of time between two moments or dates

intervene intervenes intervening intervened

VERB If you intervene in a situation, you step in to prevent conflict between people.

intervention NOUN

intervening

ADJECTIVE An intervening period of time is one that separates two events.

interview interviews interviewing interviewed

NOUN **1.** a meeting at which someone asks you questions about yourself to see if you are suitable for a particular job **2.** a conversation in which a journalist asks a famous person questions

VERB **3.** If you interview someone, you ask that person questions to obtain information about him or her.

intestine intestines

NOUN An intestine is either one of the two long tubes that carry food from your stomach through to your bowels, and in which the food is digested.

intestinal ADJECTIVE

intimate intimates intimating intimated

ADJECTIVE **1.** If two people are intimate, there is a close relationship between them. **2.** An intimate matter is very private and personal. **3.** An intimate knowledge of something is very deep and detailed.

VERB **4.** If you intimate something, you hint at it: *He did intimate that he is planning to quit the team.*

intimately ADVERB
intimacy NOUN
intimation NOUN

intimidate intimidates intimidating intimidated

VERB If you intimidate someone, you frighten that person in a threatening way.

intimidated ADJECTIVE
intimidating ADJECTIVE
intimidation NOUN

into

PREPOSITION **1.** If something goes into something else, it goes inside it. **2.** If you bump or crash into something, you hit it. **3.** *an informal use* If you are into something, you like it very much: *Nowadays, I'm really into healthy food.*

intolerable

ADJECTIVE If something is intolerable, it is so bad that it is difficult to put up with it.

intolerably ADVERB

intonation

NOUN Your intonation is the way that your voice rises and falls as you speak.

intoxicated

ADJECTIVE If someone is intoxicated, that person is drunk.

intoxicating ADJECTIVE
intoxication NOUN

intra-

PREFIX The prefix *intra-* means *within* or *inside*: *intravenous*

intractable

ADJECTIVE *a formal word* stubborn and difficult to deal with or control

Ii

intransitive

ADJECTIVE An intransitive verb is one that does not have a direct object. For example, *sings* is intransitive in *She sings*, but not in *She sings a song*.

intravenous

ADJECTIVE Intravenous foods or drugs are given to sick people through their veins.
intravenously ADVERB

intrepid

ADJECTIVE not worried by danger: *an intrepid explorer*
intrepidly ADVERB

intricate

ADJECTIVE Something that is intricate has many fine details: *walls and ceilings covered with intricate patterns*
intricately ADVERB
intricacy NOUN

intrigue intrigues intriguing intrigued

NOUN **1.** Intrigue is the making of secret plans, often with the intention of harming other people: *political intrigue*
VERB **2.** If something intrigues you, you are fascinated by it and curious about it.
intriguing ADJECTIVE

intrinsic

ADJECTIVE *a formal word* The intrinsic qualities of something are its basic qualities.
intrinsically ADVERB

introduce introduces introducing introduced

VERB **1.** If you introduce one person to another, you tell them each other's name so that they can get to know each other. **2.** When someone introduces a person or thing, that person says a few words at the beginning to tell you about that person or thing. **3.** If you introduce someone to something, that person learns about it for the first time.
introductory ADJECTIVE

introduction introductions

NOUN **1.** The introduction of someone or something is the act of presenting that person or thing for the first time. **2.** An introduction is something that introduces something, especially a piece of writing at the beginning of a book, which usually tells you what the book is about.

introvert introverts

NOUN someone who spends more time thinking about private feelings than about the world around him or her, and who often finds it difficult to talk to others
introverted ADJECTIVE

intrude intrudes intruding intruded

VERB To intrude on someone or something is to disturb that person or thing: *I don't want to intrude on my brother while he's reading.*
intruder NOUN
intrusion NOUN
intrusive ADJECTIVE

intuition intuitions

NOUN Your intuition is a feeling you have about something that you cannot explain: *My intuition is right about him.*
intuitive ADJECTIVE
intuitively ADVERB

Inuit

PLURAL NOUN an Aboriginal people living mainly in the Canadian Arctic and along the northwest coast of Alaska. The singular of Inuit is Inuk.

> ⚠ **HEADS UP**
>
> **Inuit**, which means *the people*, should be used instead of the term **Eskimo**, which is considered insulting.

inundated

ADJECTIVE If you are inundated by letters or requests, you receive so many that you cannot deal with them all.

invade invades invading invaded

VERB **1.** If an army invades a country, it enters it by force. **2.** If someone invades your privacy, that person disturbs you when you want to be alone.
invader NOUN

invalid invalids

NOUN someone who is so ill that he or she needs to be looked after by someone else

invalid

ADJECTIVE **1.** If an argument or result is invalid, it is not acceptable because it is based on a mistake or poor reasoning. **2.** If a law, marriage, or election is invalid, it is illegal because it has not been carried out properly.
invalidate VERB

invaluable

ADJECTIVE extremely useful: *This book contains invaluable tips.*

invariably

ADVERB If something invariably happens, it almost always happens.

invasion invasions

NOUN **1.** The invasion of a country or territory is the act of entering it by force. **2.** an unwanted disturbance or intrusion: *an invasion of her privacy*

Ii

invent invents inventing invented
VERB **1.** If you invent a device or process, you are the first person to think of it or to use it. **2.** If you invent a story or an excuse, you make it up.
inventor NOUN
invention NOUN
inventive ADJECTIVE
inventiveness NOUN

inventory inventories
NOUN a written list of all the objects in a place

inverse
ADJECTIVE *a formal word* If there is an inverse relationship between two things, one decreases as the other increases.

invertebrate invertebrates
NOUN *a technical word* a creature that does not have a spine

inverted
ADJECTIVE upside down or back to front

invest invests investing invested
VERB **1.** If you invest money, you pay it into a bank or buy shares so that you will receive a profit. **2.** If you invest in something useful, you buy it because it will help you do something better. **3.** If you invest money, time, or energy in something, you try to make it a success.
investor NOUN
investment NOUN

investigate investigates investigating investigated
VERB To investigate something is to try to find out all the facts about it.
investigator NOUN
investigation NOUN

inveterate
ADJECTIVE having lasted for a long time and not likely to stop: *an inveterate gambler*

invincible
ADJECTIVE unable to be defeated
invincibility NOUN

invisible
ADJECTIVE If something is invisible, you cannot see it because it is hidden, very small, or imaginary.
invisibly ADVERB
invisibility NOUN

invite invites inviting invited
VERB **1.** If you invite someone to an event, you ask that person to come to it. **2.** If you invite someone to do something, you ask that person to do it: *My mother has been invited to speak at the conference.*
inviting ADJECTIVE
invitation NOUN

invoice invoices
NOUN a bill for services or goods

invoke invokes invoking invoked
VERB *a formal word* If you invoke a law, you use it to justify what you are doing.

involuntary
ADJECTIVE sudden and uncontrollable
involuntarily ADVERB

involve involves involving involved
VERB If a situation involves someone or something, it includes that person or thing.
involvement NOUN

inward
ADJECTIVE **1.** Your inward thoughts and feelings are private.
ADJECTIVE OR ADVERB **2.** If something moves inward, it moves toward the inside or centre of something.
inwardly ADVERB

iodine
NOUN Iodine is a bluish-black substance used in medicine and photography.

ion ions
NOUN Ions are electrically charged atoms.

iota
NOUN an extremely small amount: *He did not have an iota of proof.*

IQ IQs
NOUN Your IQ is your level of intelligence shown by the results of a special test. IQ is an abbreviation for *intelligence quotient.*

ir-
PREFIX The prefix *ir-* means *not* or *the opposite of*, and is the form of *in-* that is used before the letter *r*: *irrational*

irate
ADJECTIVE very angry

iris irises
NOUN **1.** the round, coloured part of your eye **2.** a tall plant with long leaves and large blue, yellow, or white flowers

irk irks irking irked
VERB If something irks you, it annoys you.
irksome ADJECTIVE

iron irons ironing ironed
NOUN **1.** Iron is a hard, dark metal used to make steel, and things like gates and fences. Small amounts of iron are found in blood. **2.** a device that heats up and that you rub over clothes to remove creases
VERB **3.** If you iron clothes, you use a hot iron to remove creases from them.
ironing NOUN

iron out
VERB **4.** If you iron out difficulties, you solve them.

Ii

Iron Age

NOUN The Iron Age was a time about 3000 years ago when people first started to make tools out of iron.

irony

NOUN **1.** Irony is a form of humour in which you say the opposite of what you really mean: *"Lovely day!" she said, as she struggled through the snowstorm.* **2.** There is irony in a situation when there is an unexpected or unusual connection between things or events: *The house that burned down belonged to the fire chief, and we all saw the irony in that.*
ironic ADJECTIVE
ironically ADVERB

irrational

ADJECTIVE Irrational feelings are not based on logical reasons: *irrational fears*
irrationally ADVERB
irrationality NOUN

irregular

ADJECTIVE **1.** not smooth or even **2.** not forming a regular pattern: *irregular walls* **3.** Irregular things are uneven or unequal, or are not symmetrical.
irregularly ADVERB
irregularity NOUN

irrelevant

ADJECTIVE not directly connected with a subject: *He either ignored questions or gave irrelevant answers.*
irrelevance NOUN

irrepressible

ADJECTIVE Someone who is irrepressible is lively and cheerful.

irresistible

ADJECTIVE **1.** unable to be controlled: *an irresistible urge to yawn* **2.** extremely attractive: *Kittens are irresistible.*
irresistibly ADVERB

irrespective

ADJECTIVE If you say something will be done irrespective of certain things, you mean it will be done without taking those things into account.

irresponsible

ADJECTIVE An irresponsible person does things without considering the consequences: *an irresponsible driver*
irresponsibly ADVERB
irresponsibility NOUN

irrigate irrigates irrigating irrigated
VERB To irrigate land is to supply it with water brought through pipes or ditches.
irrigated ADJECTIVE
irrigation NOUN

irritable

ADJECTIVE easily annoyed

irritate irritates irritating irritated
VERB **1.** If something irritates you, it annoys you. **2.** If something irritates part of your body, it makes it tender, sore, or itchy.
irritant NOUN
irritation NOUN

is the third person, present tense of BE

-ish

SUFFIX The suffix -ish forms adjectives that mean *fairly* or *rather*: *smallish, greenish*

Islam

NOUN Islam is the Muslim religion, which teaches that there is only one God, Allah, and Mohammed is his prophet. The holy book of Islam is the Qur'an.
Islamic ADJECTIVE

island islands
NOUN a piece of land surrounded on all sides by water
islander NOUN

isle isles
NOUN *a literary or poetic word* an island, especially a small one

-ism

SUFFIX **1.** The suffix -ism forms nouns that refer to an action or condition: *criticism, heroism* **2.** The suffix -ism also forms nouns that refer to a political or economic system or a system of beliefs: *Marxism, socialism* **3.** The suffix -ism also forms nouns that refer to a type of prejudice: *racism, sexism*

isolate isolates isolating isolated
VERB **1.** If something isolates you or if you isolate yourself, you are set apart from other people. **2.** If you isolate something, you separate it from everything else.
isolated ADJECTIVE
isolation NOUN

isosceles

ADJECTIVE An isosceles triangle has two sides of the same length.

ISP an abbreviation for *Internet Service Provider*

issue issues issuing issued
NOUN **1.** an important subject that people are talking about **2.** a particular edition of a newspaper or magazine
VERB **3.** If you issue a statement or a warning, you say it formally and publicly. **4.** If someone issues something, that person officially gives it: *The company issued plastic cards to its staff.*

IRONY

a form of humour in which you say the opposite of what you really mean

"I really hope I also get your awesome haircut and mustache!"

Here is an example of irony. The robot doesn't really want the scientist's ridiculous hair and mustache.

J. BONE

-ist

SUFFIX **1.** The suffix *-ist* forms nouns and adjectives that refer to someone who is involved in a certain activity, or who believes in a certain system or religion: *chemist, motorist, Buddhist* **2.** The suffux *-ist* also forms nouns and adjectives that refer to someone who has a certain prejudice: *racist*

isthmus isthmuses

NOUN a narrow strip of land connecting two larger areas

it

PRONOUN **1.** *It* is used to refer to something that has already been mentioned, or to a situation or fact: *It was a difficult decision.* **2.** *It* is used as the subject of an impersonal verb: *It is snowing.* **3.** You use *it* to make statements about the weather, time, or date: *It's noon.*

> ⚠ **HEADS UP**
>
> **It's** is short for *it is.*
> **Its** is a pronoun, like *his* or *her.*

italics

PLURAL NOUN Italics are letters printed in a special sloping way, and are often used to emphasize something. All the examples in this dictionary are in italics.
italic ADJECTIVE

itch itches itching itched

VERB **1.** When your skin itches, it has an unpleasant feeling and you want to scratch it. **2.** If you are itching to do something, you are impatient to do it.
NOUN **3.** an unpleasant feeling on your skin that you want to scratch
itchy ADJECTIVE

item items

NOUN **1.** one of a collection or list of objects **2.** a newspaper or magazine article

itinerary itineraries

NOUN a plan of a journey, showing a route to follow and places to visit

-itis

SUFFIX The suffix *-itis* is added to the name of a part of the body to refer to disease or inflammation in that part: *appendicitis, tonsillitis*

its

ADJECTIVE OR PRONOUN *Its* refers to something belonging to or relating to a thing or animal that has already been mentioned: *The lion lifted its head.*

itself

PRONOUN **1.** *Itself* is used when the same thing, child, or animal does an action and is affected by it: *Canada prides itself on its multiculturalism.* **2.** *Itself* is used to emphasize *it.*

-ity

SUFFIX The suffix *-ity* forms nouns that refer to a state or condition: *continuity, technicality*

-ive

SUFFIX The suffix *-ive* forms adjectives and some nouns: *massive, detective*

ivory

NOUN **1.** the valuable, creamy-white bone that forms the tusk of an elephant
ADJECTIVE **2.** creamy white

ivy

NOUN a plant that creeps along the ground and up walls

-ize

SUFFIX The suffix *-ize* forms verbs: *legalize, analyze, apologize*

KNOWING WORDS: WORD BUILDING

BE WORD SHARP!

You can create new words by adding prefixes and suffixes to a base word.

-ity a noun suffix that refers to a quality or state

agility the quality of being agile

diversity the quality of being diverse

flexibility the quality of being flexible

immaturity the quality of being immature

possibility the quality of being possible

Jj

jab jabs jabbing jabbed
VERB **1.** To jab something means to poke at it roughly.
NOUN **2.** a sharp or sudden poke

jack jacks jacking jacked
NOUN **1.** a piece of equipment for lifting heavy objects, especially for lifting a car when changing a wheel **2.** an electrical device to receive a plug: *a telephone jack*
VERB **3.** To jack up an object means to raise it, especially by using a jack.

jackal jackals
NOUN a wild animal related to the dog

jacket jackets
NOUN **1.** a short coat reaching to

Instead of **JACKET** try…

a warm **parka**
a formal **blazer**
a leather **jerkin**
a heavy **overcoat**
a light **windbreaker**

the waist or hips **2.** an outer covering for something: *a book jacket*

jackpot jackpots
NOUN In a gambling game, the jackpot is the top prize.

jade
NOUN a hard green stone used for making jewellery and ornaments

jagged
ADJECTIVE sharp and spiky

jaguar jaguars
NOUN a large member of the cat family with spots on its back

jail jails jailing jailed
NOUN **1.** a building where people convicted of a crime or awaiting trial are locked up
VERB **2.** To jail someone means to lock that person up in a jail.

jailer jailers
NOUN a person who is in charge of the prisoners in a jail

jam jams jamming jammed
NOUN **1.** a food, made by boiling fruit and sugar together until it sets **2.** a situation in which it is impossible to move: *a traffic jam*
AN INFORMAL PHRASE **3.** If someone is **in a jam**, that person is in a difficult

Instead of **JAM** try…

block a drain
squeeze people in
force through a tube
cram information in
stuff an envelope full

situation.
VERB **4.** If people or things are jammed into a place, they are squeezed together so closely that they can hardly move.
5. To jam something somewhere means to push it there roughly: *He jammed his foot on the brake*. **6.** If something is jammed, it is stuck or unable to work properly. **7.** To jam a radio signal means to interfere with it and prevent it from being received clearly.

jamboree jamborees
NOUN a gathering of large numbers of people enjoying themselves

jangle jangles jangling jangled
VERB **1.** If something jangles, it makes a harsh, metallic ringing noise.
NOUN **2.** the sound made by metal objects striking against each other

janitor janitors
NOUN the person hired to take care of a building

KNOWING WORDS: IDIOMS

BE WORD SHARP!

Idioms add colour to language by playing with the meanings of words.

jack a lifting tool, or an average person

every man jack everyone

jack of all trades a person skilled in many kinds of work

jacked up on something jumpy, due to caffeine or drugs

all work and no play makes Jack a dull boy get out more

jack up raise significantly, as in a price

January
NOUN January is the first month of the year. It has 31 days.

jar jars jarring jarred
NOUN **1.** a glass container with a wide top used for storing food
VERB **2.** If something jars on you, you find it unpleasant or annoying.

jargon
NOUN Jargon consists of words that are used in special or technical ways by particular groups of people, often making the language difficult to understand.

jasmine
NOUN a climbing plant with small, sweet-scented white flowers

jaundice
NOUN Jaundice is an illness affecting the liver, in which the skin and the whites of the eyes become yellow.

jaundiced
ADJECTIVE pessimistic and lacking enthusiasm: *He takes a jaundiced view of politicians.*

jaunt jaunts
NOUN a journey or trip you go on for pleasure

jaunty jauntier jauntiest
ADJECTIVE expressing cheerfulness and self-confidence: *a jaunty tune, to walk with jaunty steps*
jauntily ADVERB

javelin javelins
NOUN a long spear that is thrown in sports competitions

jaw jaws
NOUN **1.** A person's or animal's jaw is the bone in which the teeth are set. **2.** A person's or animal's mouth and teeth are that person's or animal's jaws.

jay jays
NOUN a kind of noisy chattering bird. The **Canada jay** and the **blue jay** are Canadian species of this bird.

jazz jazzes jazzing jazzed
NOUN **1.** Jazz is a style of popular music with a strong rhythm and improvisation of a basic melody.
VERB **2.** *an informal use* To jazz something up means to make it more colourful or exciting.

jazzy jazzier jazziest
ADJECTIVE *an informal word* bright and showy

jealous
ADJECTIVE **1.** If you are jealous, you feel worried that a person you love may love or prefer someone else. **2.** If you are jealous, you feel bitterness toward someone who has something that you would like to have.
3. If you are jealous of something you have, you feel you must try to keep it from other people.
jealously ADVERB
jealousy NOUN

jeans
PLURAL NOUN Jeans are casual denim pants.

jeep jeeps
NOUN *a trademark* a small road vehicle with four-wheel drive

jeer jeers jeering jeered
VERB **1.** If you jeer at someone, you insult that person in a loud, unpleasant way.
NOUN **2.** Jeers are rude and insulting remarks.
jeering ADJECTIVE

jelly jellies
NOUN **1.** a food that is liquid when hot but firm when cold **2.** a jellylike substance: *petroleum jelly*

jellyfish jellyfishes
NOUN a sea animal with a clear, soft body and tentacles that may sting

jeopardize jeopardizes jeopardizing jeopardized
VERB To jeopardize something means to do something that puts it at risk: *She jeopardized her health.*

jeopardy
NOUN If someone or something is in jeopardy, that person or thing is at risk of failing or of being destroyed.

jerk jerks jerking jerked
VERB **1.** To jerk something means to give it a sudden, sharp pull. **2.** If something jerks, it moves suddenly and sharply.
NOUN **3.** a sudden, sharp movement
jerky ADJECTIVE
jerkily ADVERB

jerkin jerkins
NOUN a short, sleeveless jacket

jersey jerseys
NOUN **1.** a knitted garment for the upper half of the body: *The captain of the hockey team has a large C embroidered on his jersey.*
2. Jersey is a type of knitted woollen or cotton fabric used to make clothing.

jest jests jesting jested
NOUN **1.** a joke
VERB **2.** To jest means to speak jokingly.

jester jesters
NOUN In the past, a jester was a man who was kept to amuse a king or queen.

Jesus
NOUN Jesus, or Jesus Christ, was a teacher and prophet who founded the Christian religion. Christians believe that Jesus is the son of God and the saviour of the world.

SHE SHOOTS...

...SHE SCORES!

A *SHORT-HANDED GOAL!* I CAN'T BELIEVE IT!

SHE NAILED ONE FROM *THE SLOT* AND IT WENT STRAIGHT THROUGH *THE FIVE-HOLE!*

JARGON ▼×

words that are used in special or technical ways by particular groups of people, often making the language difficult to understand

"short-handed goal" "from the slot" "through the five-hole"

Here are some examples of hockey jargon. **Short-handed** means *having fewer players,* **slot** means the *part of the rink right in front of the goalie,* and **five-hole** means *between the goalie's legs.*

SCOTT CHANTLER

307

jet jets jetting jetted

NOUN **1.** a plane that is able to fly very fast **2.** a stream of liquid, gas, or flame forced out under pressure **3.** Jet is a hard, black stone, usually highly polished and used in jewellery and ornaments.

VERB **4.** To jet somewhere means to fly there in a plane, especially a jet.

jet lag

NOUN Jet lag is a feeling of tiredness or confusion that people have after a long flight across different time zones.

jettison jettisons jettisoning jettisoned

VERB If you jettison something, you throw it away because you no longer want it.

jetty jetties

NOUN a wide, stone wall or wooden platform at the edge of the sea or a river, where boats can be moored

jewel jewels

NOUN a precious stone used to decorate valuable ornaments or jewellery

jewelled ADJECTIVE

jeweller jewellers

NOUN a person who makes jewellery or who sells and repairs jewellery and watches

jewellery

NOUN Jewellery consists of ornaments that people wear, such as rings or necklaces, made of plastics or metals and sometimes decorated with precious stones.

jib jibs

NOUN a small sail toward the front of a sailing boat

jibe another spelling of GIBE

jig jigs jigging jigged

NOUN **1.** a type of lively folk dance

VERB **2.** If you jig, you dance around in a lively, bouncy manner.

jiggle jiggles jiggling jiggled

VERB If you jiggle something, you move it around with quick, jerky movements.

jigsaw puzzle jigsaw puzzles

NOUN a picture on cardboard that has been cut up into small pieces, which have to be put together again

jihad jihads

NOUN a holy war waged to defend or further the ideals of Islam

jilt jilts jilting jilted

VERB If you jilt someone, you suddenly break off your relationship with that person.

jilted ADJECTIVE

jingle jingles jingling jingled

NOUN **1.** a short, catchy phrase or rhyme set to music and used to advertise something on radio or television **2.** the sound of something jingling

VERB **3.** When something jingles, it makes a tinkling sound like small bells.

jinx jinxes

NOUN someone or something that is thought to bring bad luck: *He was beginning to think he was a jinx because the team lost every game he attended.*

jinxed

ADJECTIVE If something is jinxed it is considered to be unlucky: *I think this house is jinxed.*

jitters

PLURAL NOUN *an informal word* If you have got the jitters, you are feeling very nervous.

jittery ADJECTIVE

job jobs

NOUN **1.** the work that someone does to earn money **2.** a duty or responsibility: *It is my job to shovel the sidewalk.*

jobless

ADJECTIVE without any work

jockey jockeys jockeying jockeyed

NOUN **1.** someone who rides a horse in a race

VERB **2.** To jockey for position means to manoeuvre in order to gain an advantage over other people.

jocular

ADJECTIVE A jocular comment is intended to make people laugh.

jodhpurs

PLURAL NOUN Jodhpurs are pants worn when riding a horse. They are loose above the knees and close-fitting below the knees.

jog jogs jogging jogged

VERB **1.** To jog means to run slowly and rhythmically, often as a form of exercise. **2.** If you jog something, you knock it slightly so that it shakes or moves. **3.** If someone or something jogs your memory, that person or thing reminds you of something.

NOUN **4.** a slow run

jogger NOUN

jogging NOUN

join joins joining joined

VERB **1.** When two things join, or when one thing joins another, they come together. **2.** If you join a club or organization, you become a member of it or start taking part in it. **3.** To join two things means to fasten them.

NOUN **4.** a place where two things are fastened together

join up

VERB **5.** If someone joins up, that person becomes a member of the armed forces.

⚠ **HEADS UP** The word **jodhpurs** is pronounced JAWD-purrs.

Jj

joiner joiners
NOUN a person who makes wooden window frames, doors, and furniture

joint joints jointing jointed
ADJECTIVE **1.** shared by or belonging to two or more people: *a joint bank account*
NOUN **2.** a part of the body where two bones meet and are joined together so that they can move, for example a knee or hip **3.** a place where two things are fixed together
VERB **4.** To joint meat means to cut it into large pieces according to where the bones are.
jointly ADVERB
jointed ADJECTIVE

joist joists
NOUN a large beam used to support floors or ceilings

joke jokes joking joked
NOUN **1.** something that you say or do to make people laugh, such as tell

Instead of **JOKE** try…

a funny story
2. anything that you think is ridiculous and not worthy of respect: *The plan was a joke.*
VERB **3.** If you are joking, you are teasing someone.
jokingly ADVERB

a **gag** gift
only a **jest**
a **witty quip**
a sly **wisecrack**
an April Fools' Day **prank**

joker jokers
NOUN In a pack of cards, a joker is an extra card that does not belong to any of the four suits, but is used in some games.

jolly jollier jolliest
ADJECTIVE happy, cheerful, and pleasant

jolt jolts jolting jolted
VERB **1.** To jolt means to move or shake roughly and violently. **2.** If you are jolted by something, it gives you an unpleasant surprise.
NOUN **3.** a sudden, jerky movement **4.** an unpleasant shock or surprise

jostle jostles jostling jostled
VERB To jostle means to push roughly against people in a crowd.

jot jots jotting jotted
VERB If you jot something down, you write it quickly in the form of a short, informal note.
jotting NOUN

joule joules
NOUN a unit of energy or work

journal journals
NOUN **1.** a magazine that deals with a particular subject, trade, or profession **2.** a diary that someone keeps regularly

journalism
NOUN Journalism is the work of collecting, writing, and publishing news in newspapers, magazines, and on television and radio.
journalist NOUN
journalistic ADJECTIVE

journey journeys journeying journeyed
NOUN **1.** the act of travelling from one place to another
VERB **2.** *a formal use* To journey somewhere means to travel there: *He intended to journey up the Hayes River to York Factory.*

joust jousts
NOUN In medieval times, a joust was a competition between knights fighting on horseback, using lances.

jovial
ADJECTIVE cheerful and friendly
jovially ADVERB
joviality NOUN

joy joys
NOUN **1.** Joy is a feeling of great happiness. **2.** something that makes you happy or gives you pleasure: *It was a joy to hear them sing.*

joyful
ADJECTIVE **1.** causing pleasure and happiness **2.** Someone who is joyful is extremely happy.
joyfully ADVERB

joyous
ADJECTIVE *a formal word* joyful
joyously ADVERB

joyride joyrides
NOUN a drive in a stolen car for pleasure
joyriding NOUN
joyrider NOUN

joystick joysticks
NOUN a small handle used as a control for some computer and video games

jubilant
ADJECTIVE feeling or expressing great happiness or triumph
jubilantly ADVERB

jubilation
NOUN Jubilation is a feeling of great happiness and triumph.

jubilee jubilees
NOUN a special anniversary of an event such as a coronation: *Queen Elizabeth celebrated her Golden Jubilee in 2002.*

Jj

Judaism

NOUN Judaism is the religion of the Jewish people. It is based on a belief in one God, and draws its laws and authority from the Old Testament.

Judaic ADJECTIVE

judge judges judging judged

NOUN **1.** the person in a law court who decides how the law should be applied to people who appear in the court **2.** someone who decides the winner in a contest or competition

VERB **3.** If you judge someone or something, you form an opinion about that person or thing based on the evidence that you have. **4.** To judge a contest or competition means to decide on the winner.

judgment judgments

NOUN an opinion or decision based on evidence

judicial

ADJECTIVE relating to judgment or to justice: *a judicial review*

judiciary

NOUN The judiciary is the branch of government concerned with justice and the legal system.

judicious

ADJECTIVE sensible and showing good judgment

judiciously ADVERB

judo

NOUN Judo is a sport in which two people try to force each other to the ground using special throwing techniques.

jug jugs

NOUN a container with a lip or spout used for holding or serving liquids

juggle juggles juggling juggled

VERB To juggle means to throw objects into the air, catching them in sequence, and tossing them up again so there are several in the air at one time.

juggler NOUN

jugular jugulars

NOUN The jugular or jugular vein is one of the veins in the neck that carry blood from the head back to the heart.

juice juices

NOUN **1.** Juice is the liquid that can be squeezed or extracted from fruit or other food. **2.** Juices in the body are fluids: *gastric juices*

juicy juicier juiciest

ADJECTIVE **1.** Juicy food has a lot of juice in it. **2.** Something that is juicy is interesting, exciting, or scandalous: *a juicy bit of gossip*

jukebox jukeboxes

NOUN a large record player found in cafés and pubs that automatically plays a selected record when coins are inserted

July

NOUN July is the seventh month of the year. It has 31 days.

jumble jumbles jumbling jumbled

NOUN **1.** an untidy mixture of things

VERB **2.** To jumble things means to mix them up untidily.

jumbo

ADJECTIVE very large: *jumbo packs of elastic bands*

jump jumps jumping jumped

VERB **1.** To jump means to spring off the ground using your leg muscles. **2.** To jump something means to spring off the ground and move over or across it. **3.** If someone jumps, that person makes a sudden sharp movement of surprise. **4.** If an amount or level jumps, it suddenly increases.

NOUN **5.** a spring into the air, sometimes over an object

jumpy jumpier jumpiest

ADJECTIVE nervous and worried

KNOWING WORDS: IDIOMS

BE WORD SHARP!

Idioms add colour to language by playing with the meanings of words.

jump leap in the air

jump on the bandwagon do what is currently popular

jump out of your skin be very startled

jump the gun start doing something too soon

jump through hoops endure many tests to achieve a goal

jump to conclusions make unfair assumptions

Jj

junction junctions
NOUN a place where roads or railway lines meet or cross

June
NOUN June is the sixth month of the year. It has 30 days.

jungle jungles
NOUN **1.** a dense tropical forest **2.** a tangled mass of plants or other objects

junior juniors
ADJECTIVE **1.** Someone who is junior to other people has a lower position in an organization. **2.** Junior also means younger. **3.** relating to childhood: *a junior school*
NOUN **4.** someone who holds an unimportant position in an organization

junior high school
NOUN a school consisting of Grades 7, 8, and 9

juniper junipers
NOUN an evergreen shrub with small blue cones

junk junks
NOUN **1.** old items that are thrown away **2.** a Chinese sailing boat

Instead of **JUNK** try...

clutter all over the room

a garbage heap

kitchen waste

rock debris

scrap metal

cheap rubbish

scattered trash

litter on the streets

with a flat bottom and square sails

junk food
NOUN Junk food is food low in nutritional value, which is eaten as well as or instead of proper meals.

junkie junkies
NOUN **1.** *an informal word* a drug addict **2.** an addict of any kind: *a movie junkie*

Jupiter
NOUN Jupiter is the largest planet in the solar system and the fifth from the sun.

jurisdiction
NOUN **1.** *a formal word* Jurisdiction is the power or right of the courts to apply laws and make legal judgments: *The court held that it did not have the jurisdiction to examine the merits of the case.* **2.** Jurisdiction is power or authority: *The airport was under French jurisdiction.*

juror jurors
NOUN a member of a jury

jury juries
NOUN a group of people in a court of law who have been selected to listen to the facts of a case on trial, and to decide whether the accused person is guilty or not

just
ADJECTIVE **1.** fair and impartial: *She arrived at a just decision.* **2.** morally right or proper: *a just reward*
ADVERB **3.** If something has just happened, it happened a very short time ago. **4.** If you just do something, you do it by a very small amount: *They only just won.* **5.** simply or only: *It was just an excuse not to mow the lawn.* **6.** exactly: *A holiday is just what she needed.*
justly ADVERB

justice justices
NOUN **1.** Justice is fairness and reasonableness. **2.** The system of justice in a country is the way in which laws are maintained by the courts. **3.** a judge

justify justifies justifying justified
VERB **1.** If you justify an action or idea, you prove or explain why it is reasonable or necessary. **2.** To justify text that you have typed or keyed into a computer is to adjust the spaces between the words so each full line in a paragraph fills the space between the left- and right-hand margins of the page.
justification NOUN
justifiable ADJECTIVE

jut juts jutting jutted
VERB If something juts out, it sticks out beyond or above a surface or edge.

jute
NOUN Jute is a strong fibre made from the bark of a plant, used to make rope and sacks.

juvenile juveniles
ADJECTIVE **1.** suitable for young people **2.** childish and silly: *a juvenile game*
NOUN **3.** a young person not old enough to be considered an adult

juxtapose juxtaposes juxtaposing juxtaposed
VERB If you juxtapose things or ideas, you put them close together, often to emphasize the difference between them.
juxtaposition NOUN

Kk

kaleidoscope kaleidoscopes
NOUN a toy consisting of a tube with a hole at one end. When you look through the hole and twist the other end of the tube, you can see a changing pattern of colours.

kamikaze
NOUN In World War II, a kamikaze was a Japanese pilot who flew an aircraft loaded with explosives directly into an enemy target knowing he would be killed doing so.

kangaroo kangaroos
NOUN a large Australian animal with very strong back legs that it uses for jumping

karate
NOUN Karate is a sport in which people fight each other using only their hands, elbows, feet, and legs.

karma
NOUN In Buddhism and Hinduism, karma is actions you take that affect you in your present and future lives.

kayak kayaks
NOUN a covered canoe with a small opening for the person sitting in it, originally used by the Inuit

kea kea
NOUN a large, greenish parrot found in New Zealand

kebab kebabs
NOUN pieces of meat or vegetable stuck on a stick and grilled

keel keels keeling keeled
NOUN **1.** the specially shaped bottom of a ship that supports the sides and sits in the water VERB **2.** If someone or something keels over, that person or thing falls down sideways.

keen keener keenest
ADJECTIVE **1.** Someone who is keen shows great eagerness and enthusiasm. **2.** If you are keen on someone or something, you are attracted to or fond of that person or thing. **3.** quick to notice or understand things **4.** Keen senses let you see, hear, smell, and taste things very clearly or strongly.
keenly ADVERB
keenness NOUN

keep keeps keeping kept
VERB **1.** To keep someone or something in a particular condition means to make that person or thing stay in that condition: *We'll walk to keep warm.* **2.** If you keep something, you have it and look after it.

3. To keep something also means to store it in the usual place: *I keep my diary in my desk drawer.* **4.** If you keep doing something, you do it repeatedly or continuously: *He kept looking out the window.* **5.** If you keep a promise, you do what you promised to do. **6.** If you keep a secret, you do not tell anyone else. **7.** If you keep a diary, you write something in it every day. **8.** If you keep someone from going somewhere, you delay that person so that he or she is late. **9.** To keep someone means to provide that person with money, food, and clothing.
NOUN **10.** Your keep is the cost of the food you eat, your housing, and your clothing: *She does not contribute toward her keep.* **11.** the main tower inside the walls of a castle

keep up
VERB **12.** If you keep up with other people, you move or work at the same speed as they do.

keeper keepers
NOUN a person whose job is to look after the animals in a zoo

keeping
NOUN **1.** If something is in your keeping, it has been given to you to look after for a while.
PHRASE **2.** If one thing is in keeping with another, the two things are suitable or appropriate together.

keepsake keepsakes
NOUN something that someone gives you to remind you of a particular person or event

keg kegs
NOUN a small barrel

kennel kennels
NOUN **1.** a shelter for a dog **2.** A kennel is a place where dogs can be kept for a short period of time, or where they are bred.

kernel kernels
NOUN the part of a nut that is inside the shell

kerosene
NOUN Kerosene is a thin oil that is used as fuel.

kestrel kestrels
NOUN a small falcon

ketchup
NOUN Ketchup is a sauce made from tomatoes, vinegar, and spices.

kettle kettles
NOUN a metal container with a spout, in which you boil water

key keys keying keyed
NOUN **1.** a shaped piece of metal that fits into a hole so that you can undo a lock **2.** The

⚠ **HEADS UP** The word **kaleidoscope** is pronounced cuh-LIE-duh-scope.

NEL

Kk

keys on something such as a keyboard, piano, or cash register are the buttons that you press to use it. **3.** an explanation of the symbols used in a map or diagram **4.** In music, a key is a scale of notes. **5.** In basketball, the key is the space in front of the basket.
VERB **6.** If you key in information on a computer keyboard, you type it.

keyboard keyboards
NOUN a row of levers or buttons on a piano, computer, or calculator

kg an abbreviation for *kilograms*

khaki
NOUN **1.** Khaki is a strong, yellowish brown material, used especially for military uniforms.
NOUN OR ADJECTIVE **2.** yellowish brown

kick kicks kicking kicked
VERB **1.** If you kick something, you hit it with your foot.
NOUN **2.** If you give something a kick, you hit it with your foot. **3.** *an informal use* If you get a kick out of doing something, you enjoy doing it very much.
kick off
VERB **4.** When players kick off, they start a football game.
kick-off NOUN

kid kids kidding kidded
NOUN **1.** *an informal use* a child **2.** a young goat
VERB **3.** If you kid people, you tease them by deceiving them in fun.

kidnap kidnaps kidnapping kidnapped
VERB To kidnap someone is to take that person away by force and demand a ransom in exchange for returning him or her.
kidnapper NOUN
kidnapping NOUN

kidney kidneys
NOUN Your kidneys are two organs in your body that remove waste products from your blood.

kill kills killing killed
VERB **1.** To kill a person, animal, or plant is to make that person, animal, or plant die. **2.** If something is killing you, it is causing you severe pain or discomfort: *My arms are killing me.*
NOUN **3.** The kill is an animal that is killed.
killer NOUN

kiln kilns
NOUN an oven for baking china or pottery until it becomes hard and dry

kilo kilos
NOUN a kilogram

kilogram kilograms
NOUN a unit of weight equal to 1000 grams

kilohertz
NOUN a unit of measurement of radio waves equal to 1000 hertz

kilometre kilometres
NOUN a unit of distance equal to 1000 metres

kilowatt kilowatts
NOUN a unit of power equal to 1000 watts

kilt kilts
NOUN a tartan skirt worn by men as part of Scottish Highland dress

kimono kimonos
NOUN a long, loose garment with wide sleeves and a sash, worn in Japan

kin
PLURAL NOUN Your kin are your relatives.

kind kinds; kinder kindest
NOUN **1.** A particular kind of thing is something of the same type or sort as other things: *that kind of movie*
ADJECTIVE **2.** Someone who is kind is considerate and generous toward other people.
kindly ADVERB

kindergarten kindergartens
NOUN a class for children that prepares them for Grade 1

KNOWING WORDS: IDIOMS

BE WORD SHARP!

Idioms add colour to language by playing with the meanings of words.

kick hit with your foot

just for kicks just for fun

kick around be present, but casually or with no purpose

kick back relax

kick in begin having an effect

kick yourself be mad at yourself because of a silly error

Kk

kindle kindles kindling kindled
VERB **1.** If you kindle a fire, you light it. **2.** If something kindles a feeling in you, it causes you to have that feeling.

kindling
NOUN Kindling is bits of dry wood or paper that you use to start a fire.

kindness
NOUN the quality of being considerate toward other people

kindred
ADJECTIVE If you say that someone is a kindred spirit, you mean that that person has the same interests or opinions as you.

kinetic energy
NOUN Kinetic energy is the energy that is produced when something moves.

king kings
NOUN **1.** a man who is the head of state in a country **2.** a chess piece that can only move one square at a time **3.** In a pack of playing cards, a king is a card with a picture of a king on it.

kingdom kingdoms
NOUN **1.** a country that is governed by a king or queen **2.** The divisions of the natural world are called kingdoms: *the animal kingdom*

kingfisher kingfishers
NOUN a brightly coloured bird that lives near water and feeds on fish

king-size
ADJECTIVE larger than the normal size: *a king-size bed*

kink kinks
NOUN a dent or curve in something that is normally straight

kinship
NOUN Kinship is a family relationship to other people.

kiosk kiosks
NOUN an information booth

kipper kippers
NOUN a smoked herring

kiss kisses kissing kissed
VERB **1.** When you kiss someone, you touch that person with your lips as a sign of love or affection.
NOUN **2.** When you give someone a kiss, you kiss that person.

kit kits
NOUN **1.** a collection of things that you use for a job or other activity **2.** a set of parts that you put together to make something

kitchen kitchens
NOUN a room used for cooking and preparing food

kite kites
NOUN **1.** a frame covered with paper or cloth that is attached to a piece of string, and that you fly in the air **2.** a large bird of prey with a long tail and long wings

kitten kittens
NOUN a young cat

kitty kitties
NOUN a fund of money that has been given by a group of people who will use it to pay for or do things together

kiwi kiwi
NOUN a type of bird found in New Zealand. Kiwis cannot fly.

kiwi fruit kiwi fruits
NOUN a fruit with a brown, hairy skin and green flesh

km an abbreviation for *kilometres*

knack
NOUN an ability to do something difficult while making it look easy: *the knack of making friends*

knead kneads kneading kneaded
VERB If you knead dough, you press it and squeeze it with your hands before baking it.

knee knees
NOUN the joint in your leg between your ankle and your hip

kneecap kneecaps
NOUN the flat bone at the front of the knee

kneel kneels kneeling knelt
VERB When you kneel, you bend your legs and lower your body until your knees are touching the ground.

knell knells
NOUN *a literary or poetic word* the sound of a bell rung to announce a death or at a funeral

knick-knack
NOUN A knick-knack is a small ornament.

knife knives; knifes knifing knifed
NOUN **1.** a sharp, metal tool that you use to cut things
VERB **2.** To knife someone or something is to stab that person or thing with a knife.

knight knights knighting knighted
NOUN **1.** a man who has been given the title *Sir* by a king or queen **2.** In medieval Europe, a knight was a man who served a monarch or lord as a mounted soldier. **3.** a chess piece that is usually in the shape of a horse's head

Kk

VERB **4.** To knight a man is to give him the title *Sir*.

knighthood NOUN

knit knits knitting knitted
VERB If you knit a piece of clothing, you make it by working lengths of wool together, either using needles held in the hands, or with a machine.

knitting NOUN

knob knobs
NOUN **1.** a round handle **2.** a round switch on a machine: *the knobs of a radio*

knock knocks knocking knocked
VERB **1.** If you knock on something, you strike it with your hand or fist. **2.** If you knock a part of your body against something, you bump into it forcefully. **3.** *an informal use* To knock someone is to criticize that person.
NOUN **4.** a firm blow on something solid: *There was a knock at the door.*

knock out
VERB **5.** To knock someone out is to hit that person so hard that he or she becomes unconscious.

knocker knockers
NOUN a metal lever attached to a door, which you use to knock on the door

knockout knockouts
NOUN a punch in boxing that knocks a boxer unconscious

knoll knolls
NOUN *a literary or poetic word* a gently sloping hill with a rounded top

knot knots knotting knotted
NOUN **1.** a fastening made by looping a piece of string around itself and pulling the ends tight **2.** a small lump visible on the surface of a piece of wood **3.** A knot of people is a small group of them. **4.** a unit of speed used for ships and aircraft
VERB **5.** If you knot a piece of string, you tie a knot in it.

know knows knowing knew known
VERB **1.** If you know a fact, you have it in your mind and you do not need to learn it.
2. People you know are not strangers because you have met them and spoken to them.

know-how
NOUN Know-how is the ability to do something that is quite difficult or technical.

knowing
ADJECTIVE A knowing look is one that shows that you know or understand something that other people do not.
knowingly ADVERB

knowledge
NOUN Your knowledge is all the information and facts that you know.

knowledgeable
ADJECTIVE Someone who is knowledgeable knows a lot about a subject: *She was very knowledgeable about Canadian history.*

knuckle knuckles
NOUN Your knuckles are the joints at the end of your fingers where they join your hand.

koala koalas
NOUN an Australian animal with grey fur and small, tufted ears. Koalas live in trees and eat eucalyptus leaves.

Koran another spelling of QUR'AN

kosher
ADJECTIVE Kosher food has been specially prepared to be eaten according to Jewish law.

kumquat kumquats
NOUN a very small round or oval citrus fruit

kung fu
NOUN Kung fu is a Chinese martial art that involves using your hands and feet.

KNOWING WORDS: IDIOMS

BE WORD SHARP!

Idioms add colour to language by playing with the meanings of words.

know be aware

before you know it surprisingly quickly

be in the know have privileged information

not know what hit you be surprised by something bad

knowing no bounds unlimited

know what's what be well informed

Ll

L an abbreviation for *litres*

lab labs
NOUN *an informal word* a laboratory

label labels labelling labelled
NOUN **1.** a piece of paper or other material attached to something as an identification
VERB **2.** If you label something, you put a label on it.

laboratory laboratories
NOUN a place where scientific experiments are carried out

laborious
ADJECTIVE needing a lot of effort or time
laboriously ADVERB

labour labours labouring laboured
NOUN **1.** Labour is hard work. **2.** The workforce of a country or industry is sometimes called its labour: *unskilled labour* **3.** Labour is also the last stage of pregnancy when a woman gives birth to a baby.
VERB **4.** To labour means to work hard.
labourer NOUN

Labrador retriever Labrador retrievers
NOUN a large dog with short black or golden hair

labyrinth labyrinths
NOUN a complicated series of paths or passages

lace laces lacing laced
NOUN **1.** Lace is a very fine, decorated cloth made with a lot of holes in it. **2.** Laces are cords with which you fasten your shoes.
VERB **3.** When you lace up your shoes, you tie a bow in the laces. **4.** To lace someone's food or drink means to put a small amount of alcohol, a drug, or poison in it: *black coffee laced with arsenic*
lacy ADJECTIVE

lack lacks lacking lacked
NOUN **1.** If there is a lack of something, it is not present when or where it is needed.
VERB **2.** If something is lacking, it is not present when or where it is needed. **3.** If someone or something lacks something, that person or thing does not have it or does not have enough of it: *She was lacking in stamina.*

lacklustre
ADJECTIVE not interesting or exciting

laconic
ADJECTIVE using very few words

lacquer lacquers
NOUN Lacquer is thin, clear paint that you put on wood to protect it and make it shiny.

lacrosse
NOUN Lacrosse is a ball game in which two teams try to score goals using long sticks with nets on the end of them.

lad lads
NOUN a boy or young man

ladder ladders laddering laddered
NOUN a wooden or metal frame used for climbing that consists of horizontal steps fixed to two vertical poles

laden
ADJECTIVE To be laden with something means to be carrying or holding a lot of it: *bushes laden with ripe fruit*

ladle ladles ladling ladled
NOUN **1.** a long-handled spoon with a deep, round bowl, which you use to serve soup
VERB **2.** If you ladle out food, you serve it with a ladle.

lady ladies
NOUN **1.** a woman, especially one who is considered to be well-mannered **2.** In Britain, Lady is a title used in front of the name of a woman from the nobility, such as a lord's wife.

ladybug ladybugs
NOUN a small flying beetle with a round red body patterned with black spots

lady-in-waiting ladies-in-waiting
NOUN a woman who acts as companion to a queen or princess

ladylike
ADJECTIVE behaving in a polite and socially correct way

lag lags lagging lagged
VERB To lag behind is to make slower progress than other people.

lagoon lagoons
NOUN an area of water separated from the sea by reefs or sand

laid the past tense and past participle of LAY

lain the past participle of some meanings of LIE

lair lairs
NOUN a place where a wild animal lives

lake lakes
NOUN an area of fresh water surrounded by land

lama lamas
NOUN a Buddhist priest or monk

lamb lambs
NOUN **1.** a young sheep **2.** Lamb is the meat from a lamb.

lame
ADJECTIVE **1.** Someone who is lame has an injured leg and cannot walk easily. **2.** A lame excuse is not very convincing.
lamely ADVERB
lameness NOUN

lament laments lamenting lamented
VERB **1.** To lament something means to express sorrow or regret about it.
NOUN **2.** an expression of sorrow or regret **3.** a song or poem expressing grief at someone's death

lamentable
ADJECTIVE disappointing and regrettable

laminated
ADJECTIVE consisting of several thin sheets or layers stuck together: *laminated wood*

lamp lamps
NOUN a device that produces light

lamppost lampposts
NOUN a tall column in a street, with a lamp at the top

lampshade lampshades
NOUN a decorative covering over an electric light bulb that prevents the bulb from giving out too harsh a light

lance lances lancing lanced
VERB **1.** To lance a boil or abscess means to stick a sharp instrument into it in order to release the fluid.
NOUN **2.** a long, wooden spear with a sharp iron or steel tip

land lands landing landed
NOUN **1.** Land is an area of ground. **2.** Land is also the part of the earth that is not covered by water. **3.** a country: *our native land*
VERB **4.** When a plane lands, it arrives back on the ground after a flight. **5.** *an informal use* If you land something you have been trying to get, you succeed in getting it: *to land a job, to land a fish*

landing landings
NOUN **1.** a flat area in a building at the top of a flight of stairs **2.** The landing of an airplane is its arrival back on the ground after a flight: *a smooth landing*

landlady landladies
NOUN a woman who owns a house or small hotel and who rents rooms to people

landlord landlords
NOUN a man who owns a house or small hotel and who rents rooms to people

landmark landmarks
NOUN **1.** a noticeable feature in a landscape, which you can use to check your position **2.** an important stage in the development of something: *The play is a landmark in Canadian theatre.*

landowner landowners
NOUN someone who owns land, especially a large area of the countryside

landscape landscapes
NOUN **1.** The landscape is the view over an area of open land. **2.** a painting of the countryside

landslide landslides
NOUN **1.** a large amount of loose earth and rocks falling down a mountainside **2.** a victory in an election won by a large number of votes

lane lanes
NOUN **1.** a narrow road, especially in the country **2.** one of the strips on a road marked with lines to guide drivers

language languages
NOUN **1.** human speech, spoken or written **2.** the system of words that a people, nation, or group of peoples use to communicate with each other **3.** Your language is the style in which you express yourself: *His language is often obscure.*

languid
ADJECTIVE slow and lacking energy
languidly ADVERB

languish languishes languishing languished
VERB If you languish, you endure an unpleasant situation for a long time: *Many languished in poverty.*

lanky lankier lankiest
ADJECTIVE Someone who is lanky is tall and thin and moves rather awkwardly.

lantern lanterns
NOUN a lamp in a metal frame with glass sides

lap laps lapping lapped
NOUN **1.** Your lap is the flat area formed by your thighs when you are sitting down. **2.** one circuit of a racetrack
VERB **3.** When an animal laps up liquid, it drinks using its tongue to get the liquid into its mouth. **4.** If you lap someone in a race, you overtake that person when he or she is still on the previous lap. **5.** When water laps against something, it gently moves against it in little waves.

lapel lapels
NOUN a flap that is joined on to the collar of a jacket or coat

⚠ HEADS UP The word **lamb** is pronounced lam—the b is silent.

LI

lapse lapses lapsing lapsed
NOUN **1.** a moment of bad behaviour by someone who usually behaves well **2.** a slight mistake **3.** a period of time between two events
VERB **4.** If you lapse into a different way of behaving, you start behaving that way: *The offenders lapsed into a sullen silence.* **5.** If a legal document or contract lapses, it is not renewed on the date when it expires.

lard
NOUN Lard is fat from a pig, used in cooking.

larder larders
NOUN a place, such as a pantry, in which you store food

large larger largest
ADJECTIVE **1.** Someone or something that is large is much bigger than average.
PHRASE **2.** If a prisoner is **at large**, that prisoner has escaped from prison.

largely
ADVERB to a great extent: *The public is largely unaware of this.*

lark larks
NOUN **1.** a small brown bird with a distinctive song **2.** If you do something for a lark, you do it in a high-spirited or mischievous way for fun.

larva larvae
NOUN an insect, which looks like a short, fat worm, at the stage before it becomes an adult

laryngitis
NOUN Laryngitis is an infection of the throat that causes you to lose your voice.

larynx larynxes
NOUN the part of your throat containing the vocal cords, through which air passes between your nose and lungs

lasagna
NOUN Lasagna is an Italian dish made with wide, flat sheets of pasta, meat or vegetables, cheese, and tomato sauce.

laser lasers
NOUN a machine that produces a powerful concentrated beam of light that is used to cut very hard materials and to perform some kinds of surgery

lash lashes lashing lashed
NOUN **1.** the hair growing on the edge of your eyelids **2.** a strip of leather at the end of a whip **3.** Lashes are blows struck with a whip.
lash out
VERB **4.** To lash out at someone means to criticize that person severely.

lass lasses
NOUN a girl or young woman

lasso lassos lassoing lassoed
NOUN **1.** a length of rope with a noose at one end, used by cowboys to catch cattle and horses
VERB **2.** To lasso an animal means to catch it by throwing the noose of a lasso around its neck.

last lasts lasting lasted
ADJECTIVE **1.** The last thing or event is the most recent one: *last year* **2.** The last thing that remains is the only one left after all the others have gone: *The last family left the village in 1950.*
ADVERB **3.** If you last did something on a particular occasion, you have not done it since then: *They last met in Kenora.* **4.** The thing that happens last in a sequence of events is the final one: *He added the milk last.*
VERB **5.** If something lasts, it continues to exist or happen: *The speech lasted 50 minutes.* **6.** To last also means to remain in good condition: *The mixture will last for up to two weeks in the fridge.*
PHRASE **7.** At last means after a long time.
lastly ADVERB

last-ditch
ADJECTIVE A last-ditch attempt to do something is a final attempt to succeed when everything else has failed.

latch latches latching latched
NOUN **1.** a simple fastening for a door, gate, or window **2.** a type of door lock that locks automatically when you close the door and that has to be opened with a key
VERB **3.** *an informal use* If you latch onto someone or something, you become attached to that person or thing.

late later latest
ADJECTIVE OR ADVERB **1.** Something that happens late happens toward the end of a period of time: *the late evening, late in the morning* **2.** If you arrive late, or do something late, you arrive or do it after the time you were expected to.
ADJECTIVE **3.** A late event happens after the time when it usually takes place: *a late breakfast* **4.** *a formal use* Late means dead: *my late grandmother*

lately
ADVERB Events that happened lately happened recently.

LI

latent
ADJECTIVE A latent quality is hidden at the moment, but may emerge in the future: *a latent talent for art*

lateral
ADJECTIVE relating to the sides of something, or moving in a sideways direction

lathe lathes
NOUN a machine that holds and turns a piece of wood or metal against a tool to cut and shape it

lather lathers
NOUN Lather is the foam that you get when you rub soap in water.

latitude latitudes
NOUN The latitude of a place is its distance north or south of the equator, measured in degrees.

latrine latrines
NOUN a hole or trench in the ground used as a toilet at a camp

latter
ADJECTIVE OR NOUN **1.** You use *latter* to refer to the second of two things that are mentioned: *They were eating sandwiches and cakes, the latter bought from a bakery.*
ADJECTIVE **2.** *Latter* also describes the second or end part of something: *The latter part of his career.*

latterly
ADVERB *a formal word Latterly* means recently: *It's only latterly that this has become an issue.*

lattice lattices
NOUN a structure made of strips that cross over each other diagonally leaving holes in between

laudable
ADJECTIVE *a formal word* deserving praise: *his laudable*

Instead of **LAUGH** try...

volunteer activities

laugh laughs laughing laughed
VERB **1.** When you laugh, you make a noise that shows that you are amused or happy.
NOUN **2.** the noise you make when you laugh
laughter NOUN

snicker behind your back
giggle embarrassedly
howl with glee
chuckle heartily
bray loudly
cackle evilly
wildly guffaw
titter behind your hands

laughable
ADJECTIVE absurd

laughingstock
NOUN someone who has been made to seem ridiculous

launch launches launching launched
VERB **1.** To launch a ship means to send it into the water for the first time. **2.** To launch a rocket means to send it into space. **3.** When a company launches a new product, it has an advertising campaign to promote the product.
NOUN **4.** a motorboat used for short trips

launch pad launch pads
NOUN A launch pad, or a launching pad, is the place from which space rockets take off.

launder launders laundering laundered
VERB To launder clothes, sheets, or towels means to wash and iron them.

laundry laundries
NOUN **1.** a business that washes and irons clothes and sheets **2.** Laundry is also the dirty clothes and sheets that are being washed, or are about to be washed.

lava
NOUN Lava is the very hot, liquid rock that comes shooting out of an erupting volcano, and becomes solid as it cools.

lavatory lavatories
NOUN a toilet

lavender
NOUN **1.** a small bush with bluish pink flowers that have a strong, pleasant scent
ADJECTIVE **2.** bluish pink

lavish lavishes lavishing lavished
ADJECTIVE **1.** If you are lavish, you are very generous with your time, money, or gifts. **2.** A lavish amount is a large amount.
VERB **3.** If you lavish money or affection on someone, you give that person a lot of it.
lavishly ADVERB

law laws
NOUN **1.** The law is the system of rules developed by the government of a country, which regulates what people may and may not do and deals with people who break these rules. **2.** The law is also the profession of people such as lawyers, whose job involves the application of the laws of a country. **3.** one of the rules established by a government or a religion, which tells people what they may and may not do **4.** a scientific fact that allows you to explain how things work in the physical world
lawful ADJECTIVE
lawfully ADVERB

NEL

law-abiding
ADJECTIVE obeying the law and not causing any trouble

lawless
ADJECTIVE having no regard for the law

lawn lawns
NOUN an area of cultivated grass

lawn mower lawn mowers
NOUN a machine for cutting grass

lawsuit lawsuits
NOUN a civil court case between two people, as opposed to the police prosecuting someone for a criminal offence

lawyer lawyers
NOUN a person who is qualified in law, and whose job is to advise people about the law and represent them in court

lax
ADJECTIVE careless and not strict enough: *a lax attitude toward homework*

laxative laxatives
NOUN something that you eat or drink to stop you from being constipated

lay lays laying laid
VERB **1.** When you lay something somewhere, you put it down so that it lies there. **2.** If you lay something, you arrange it or set it out. **3.** If you lay the table, you put cutlery on the table for a meal. **4.** When a bird lays an egg, it produces the egg out of its body. **5.** If you lay a trap for someone, you create a situation in which you will be able to catch that person. **6.** Lay is the past tense of some senses of LIE.

lay off
VERB **7.** When workers are laid off, their employers tell them not to come to work for a while because there is a shortage of work. **8.** *an informal use* If you tell someone to lay off, you want that person to stop doing something annoying.

lay on
VERB **9.** If you lay on a meal or entertainment, you provide it.

layer layers
NOUN a single thickness of something: *layers of clothing*

layman laymen
NOUN someone who does not have specialized knowledge of a subject: *a layman's guide to computers*

layout layouts
NOUN The layout of something is the pattern in which it is arranged.

laze lazes lazing lazed
VERB If you laze, you relax and do no work: *We spent a few days lazing around by the pool.*

lazy lazier laziest
ADJECTIVE idle and unwilling to work
lazily ADVERB
laziness NOUN

leach leaches leaching leached
VERB When minerals are leached from rocks, they are dissolved by water that filters through the rock.

lead leads leading led
VERB **1.** If you lead someone somewhere, you go in front of that person in order to show him or her the way. **2.** If one thing leads to another, it causes the second thing to happen. **3.** a person who leads a group of people is in charge of them
NOUN **4.** If the police have a lead, they have a clue that might help them to solve a crime.

lead
NOUN Lead is a soft, grey, heavy metal.

leaden
ADJECTIVE **1.** dark grey: *a leaden sky* **2.** heavy and slow-moving

leader leaders
NOUN **1.** someone who is in charge of a country, an organization, or a group of people **2.** the person who is winning in a competition or race **3.** a newspaper article that expresses the newspaper's opinions

KNOWING WORDS: IDIOMS

BE WORD SHARP!

Idioms add colour to language by playing with the meanings of words.

lay put down

lay down the law impose the rules

lay of the land the way a situation is arranged

lay it on thick exaggerate

lay it on someone tell someone something

lay waste to something destroy something

LI

leadership
NOUN **1.** the group of people in charge of an organization **2.** Leadership is the ability to be a good leader.

leading
ADJECTIVE particularly important, respected, or advanced

leaf leaves; leafs leafing leafed
NOUN **1.** the flat, green growth on the end of a twig or branch of a tree or other plant
VERB **2.** If you leaf through a book, magazine, or newspaper, you turn pages over quickly.
leafy ADJECTIVE

leaflet leaflets
NOUN a piece of paper with information or advertising printed on it

league leagues
NOUN **1.** a group of countries, clubs, or people who have joined together for a particular purpose or because they share a common interest: *a bowling league, a league of nations* **2.** a unit of distance used in former times, equal to about five kilometres

leak leaks leaking leaked
VERB **1.** If a pipe or container leaks, it has a hole that lets gas or liquid escape. **2.** If liquid or gas leaks, it escapes from a pipe or container. **3.** If someone in an organization leaks information, that person gives the information to someone who is not supposed to have it: *The letter was leaked to the press.*
NOUN **4.** If a pipe or container has a leak, it has a hole that lets gas or liquid escape. **5.** If there is a leak in an organization, someone inside the organization is giving information to people who are not supposed to have it.
leaky ADJECTIVE

leakage leakages
NOUN an escape of gas or liquid from a pipe or container

lean leans leaning leaned; leaner leanest
VERB **1.** When you lean in a particular direction, you bend your body in that direction. **2.** When you lean on something, you rest your body against it for support. **3.** If you lean on someone, you depend on that person. **4.** If you lean toward particular ideas, you approve of them and follow them: *parents who lean toward strictness*
ADJECTIVE **5.** having little or no fat: *lean cuts of meat* **6.** A lean period is a time when food or money is in short supply.

leap leaps leaping leaped
VERB **1.** If you leap somewhere, you jump over a long distance or high in the air.
NOUN **2.** a jump over a long distance or high in the air

leap year leap years
NOUN a year, occurring every four years, in which there are 366 days. The extra day is February 29.

learn learns learning learned
VERB **1.** When you learn something, you gain knowledge or a skill through studying or training. **2.** If you learn of something, you find out about it: *She had first learned of his illness that morning.*
learner NOUN

learned
ADJECTIVE A learned person has a lot of knowledge gained from years of study.

learning
NOUN Learning is knowledge that has been acquired through serious study.

lease leases leasing leased
NOUN **1.** an agreement that allows someone to use a house or apartment in return for rent
VERB **2.** To lease property means to allow someone to use it in return for rent.

leash leashes
NOUN a length of leather or chain attached to a dog's collar so that the dog can be controlled

least
NOUN **1.** The least is the smallest possible amount of something.
ADJECTIVE **2.** as small or as few as possible
ADVERB **3.** Least is a superlative form of LITTLE.
PHRASE **4.** You use **at least** to show that you are referring to the minimum amount of something, and that you think the true amount is greater: *At least 200 people were injured.*

leather
NOUN Leather is the tanned skin of some animals, used to make shoes and clothes.
leathery ADJECTIVE

leave leaves leaving left
VERB **1.** When you leave a place, you go away from it. **2.** If you leave someone somewhere, that person stays behind after you go away. **3.** If you leave a job or organization, you stop being part of it: *He left his job shortly after the summer holidays ended.* **4.** If money or possessions are left to someone, an arrangement has been made for those possessions to be given to that person after the owner has died. **5.** In subtraction, when you take one number from another, it leaves a third number.
NOUN **6.** a period of holiday or absence from a job

⚠ **HEADS UP** The adjective **learned** is pronounced LEARN-id.

LI

lecherous
ADJECTIVE constantly thinking about sex

lectern lecterns
NOUN a sloping stand that people use to rest books or notes on from which they can read while giving a talk

lecture lectures lecturing lectured
NOUN **1.** a formal talk intended to teach people about a particular subject **2.** a talk intended to tell someone off
VERB **3.** Someone who lectures teaches in a college or university.

lecturer lecturers
NOUN a teacher in a college or university

led the past tense and past participle of LEAD

ledge ledges
NOUN a narrow shelf on the side of a cliff or rock face, or on the outside of a building, directly under a window

ledger ledgers
NOUN a book in which accounts are kept

lee
NOUN **1.** the sheltered side of a place: *the lee of the mountain*
ADJECTIVE **2.** the side of a ship away from the wind

leech leeches
NOUN a small worm that lives in water and feeds by sucking the blood from other animals

leek leeks
NOUN a long vegetable of the onion family, which is white at one end and has green leaves at the other

leer leers leering leered
VERB **1.** To leer at someone means to smile at that person in an unpleasant or sexually suggestive way.
NOUN **2.** an unpleasant or sexually suggestive smile

leeway
NOUN If something gives you some leeway, it allows you more flexibility in your plans, for example by giving you time to finish an activity.

left
NOUN **1.** The left is one of two sides of something. For example, on a page, English writing begins on the left. **2.** People and political groups who hold socialist or communist views are referred to as the Left. **3.** Left is the past tense and past participle of LEAVE.
ADJECTIVE OR ADVERB **4.** Left means on or toward the left side of something: *Turn left at the next intersection.*

left-handed
ADJECTIVE OR ADVERB Someone who is left-handed does things, such as writing, with his or her left hand.

leftist leftists
NOUN OR ADJECTIVE someone who holds left-wing political views

leftover
NOUN the bits of food that have not been eaten at the end of the meal

left-wing
ADJECTIVE believing more strongly in socialism, or less strongly in capitalism or conservatism, than other members of the same party or group
left winger NOUN

leg legs
NOUN **1.** Your legs are the two limbs that stretch from your hips to your feet. **2.** The legs of a pair of pants are the parts that cover your legs. **3.** The legs of an object such as a table are the parts that rest on the floor and support the object's weight. **4.** A leg of a journey is one part of it.

legacy legacies
NOUN **1.** property or money that someone gets in the will of a person who has died **2.** something that exists as a result of a previous event or time: *the legacy of a strict upbringing*

SPELL-CHECK THIS!

A computer's spell-check won't catch wrong **homophones** (words that are spelled differently but sound the same).

She lead the team to victory.

In this sentence, **lead** should be **led**. **Led** is the past tense of **lead** (meaning *direct*), pronounced LEED. **Lead**, pronounced LED, is a heavy metal.

NEL

LI

legal

ADJECTIVE **1.** relating to the law: *the Canadian legal system* **2.** allowed by the law: *The strike was perfectly legal.*
legally ADVERB

legal aid

NOUN Legal aid is a system that provides the services of a lawyer free, or very cheaply, to people who cannot afford the full fees.

legality

NOUN The legality of an action means whether or not it is allowed by the law: *They challenged the legality of the scheme.*

legalize legalizes legalizing legalized
VERB To legalize something that is illegal means to change the law so that it becomes legal.
legalization NOUN

legend legends
NOUN **1.** an old story that was once believed to be true, but which is probably untrue
2. If you refer to someone or something as a legend, you mean that person or thing is very famous: *His career has become a legend.*
legendary ADJECTIVE

⚠️ **HEADS UP**

Legends glorify a great person or event that may have been real. **Myths** usually explain religious beliefs.

leggings

PLURAL NOUN Leggings are a very close-fitting garment made of stretch material, worn on the legs mainly by young women.

legible

ADJECTIVE Writing that is legible is clear enough to be read.

legion legions
NOUN **1.** In ancient Rome, a legion was a military unit of between 3000 and 6000 soldiers. **2.** a large military force: *the French Foreign Legion* **3.** Legions of people are large numbers of them.

legislate legislates legislating legislated
VERB *a formal word* When a government legislates, it creates new laws.

legislation

NOUN Legislation is a law or set of laws created by a government.

legislative

ADJECTIVE relating to the making of new laws: *a legislative council*

legislator legislators
NOUN *a formal word* a person involved in making or passing laws

legislature

NOUN *a formal word* the parliament in a country, which is responsible for making new laws

legitimate

ADJECTIVE Something that is legitimate is reasonable or acceptable according to existing laws or standards: *a legitimate charge for parking the car*
legitimacy NOUN
legitimately ADVERB

leisure

NOUN **1.** Leisure is time during which you do not have to work, and can do what you enjoy doing.
PHRASES **2.** If you do something **at leisure**, or **at your leisure**, you do it at a convenient time.

leisurely

ADJECTIVE OR ADVERB A leisurely action is done in an unhurried and calm way.

lemming lemmings
NOUN a small rodent that lives in cold, northern countries

lemon lemons
NOUN **1.** a yellow citrus fruit with a sour taste
ADJECTIVE **2.** pale yellow

lemonade

NOUN a sweet drink made from lemons, water, and sugar

lend lends lending lent
VERB **1.** If you lend someone something, you give it to that person for a period of time and then he or she gives it back to you.
2. If a bank lends money, it gives the money to someone and the money has to be repaid in the future, usually with interest.
PHRASE **3.** If you **lend someone a hand**, you help that person.
lender NOUN

length lengths
NOUN **1.** The length of something is the horizontal distance from one end to the other. **2.** The length of an event or activity is the amount of time it lasts for. **3.** The length of something is also the fact that it is long rather than short: *Despite its length, this book is a rewarding read.* **4.** a long piece of something

lengthen lengthens lengthening lengthened
VERB To lengthen something means to make it longer.

lengthwise

ADVERB If you measure something lengthwise, you measure the horizontal distance from one end to the other.

lengthy lengthier lengthiest

ADJECTIVE Something that is lengthy lasts for a long time.

lenient

ADJECTIVE If someone in authority is lenient, that person is less severe than expected.

leniently ADVERB

leniency NOUN

lens lenses

NOUN **1.** a curved piece of glass designed to focus light in a certain way, for example in a camera, telescope, or pair of glasses **2.** The lens in your eye is the part behind the iris that focuses light.

lent the past tense and past participle of LEND

lentil lentils

NOUN Lentils are small, dried, red or brown seeds that are cooked and eaten, for example in soups.

leopard leopards

NOUN a wild Asian or African big cat, with yellow fur and black or brown spots

leotard leotards

NOUN a tight-fitting costume covering the body and legs, which is worn for dancing or exercise

leper lepers

NOUN someone who has leprosy

leprosy

NOUN Leprosy is an infectious disease that attacks the skin and nerves.

lesbian lesbians

NOUN a homosexual woman

lesbianism NOUN

lesion lesions

NOUN a wound or injury

less

ADJECTIVE OR ADVERB **1.** Less means a smaller amount, or not as much in quality: *They left less than three weeks ago. She has become less frightened of the dark now.* **2.** Less is a comparative form of LITTLE.

PREPOSITION **3.** You use *less* to show that you are subtracting one number from another: *Eight less two leaves six. He's been gone a year less two days.*

-less

SUFFIX The suffix *-less* means *without*: *hopeless, fearless*

lessen lessens lessening lessened

VERB If something lessens, it is reduced in amount, size, or quality.

lesser

ADJECTIVE smaller in importance or amount than something else

lesson lessons

NOUN **1.** a fixed period of time during which a class of students is taught by a teacher **2.** an experience that makes you understand something important that you had not realized before

lest

CONJUNCTION *an old-fashioned word* as a precaution in case something unpleasant or unwanted happens: *I was afraid to open the door lest the stranger should follow me.*

let lets letting let

VERB **1.** If you let someone do something, you allow that person to do it. **2.** If someone lets a house or apartment that he or she owns, that person rents it out. **3.** You can say *let's* or *let us* when you want to suggest doing something with someone else: *Let's go to a movie.*

PHRASE **4.** If you **let yourself in for** something, you agree to do it although you do not really want to.

let off

VERB **5.** If someone in authority lets you off, that person does not punish you for something you have done wrong. **6.** If you let off a firework or explosive, you light it or detonate it.

KNOWING WORDS: WORD BUILDING

BE WORD SHARP!

You can create new words by adding prefixes and suffixes to a base word.

-less an adjectival suffix that means *without*

breathless without breath

careless without any care or thought

featureless without any features

homeless without a home

meaningless without any meaning

lethal
ADJECTIVE able to kill someone: *a lethal weapon*

lethargic
ADJECTIVE If you feel lethargic, you have no energy or enthusiasm.

lethargy
NOUN Lethargy is a lack of energy and enthusiasm.

letter letters
NOUN **1.** Letters are written symbols that go together to make words. **2.** a piece of writing addressed to someone, and usually sent through the mail

lettering
NOUN Lettering is writing, especially when you are describing the type of letters used: *bold lettering*

lettuce lettuces
NOUN a vegetable with green leaves eaten raw in salad

leukemia
NOUN Leukemia is a serious illness that affects the blood.

level levels levelling levelled
ADJECTIVE **1.** A surface that is level is smooth, flat, and parallel to the ground.
VERB **2.** To level a piece of land means to make it flat. **3.** If you level a criticism at someone, you say or write something critical about that person.
ADVERB **4.** If you draw level with someone, you get closer to that person so that you are moving next to him or her.
NOUN **5.** a point on a scale that measures the amount, importance, or difficulty of something **6.** The level of a liquid is the height it comes up to in a container.
level off, level out
VERB **7.** If something levels off or levels out, it stops increasing or decreasing: *Profits are beginning to level off.*

level crossing level crossings
NOUN a place where road traffic is allowed to drive across a railway track

level-headed
ADJECTIVE Someone who is level-headed is sensible and calm in emergencies.

lever levers
NOUN **1.** a handle on a machine that you pull in order to make the machine work **2.** a long bar that you wedge underneath a heavy object and press down on to make the object move

leverage
NOUN Leverage is knowledge or influence that you can use to make someone do something that you want them to do.

levy levies levying levied
NOUN **1.** *a formal word* an amount of money that you pay in tax
VERB **2.** When a government levies a tax, it makes people pay the tax and organizes the collection of the money.

lewd
ADJECTIVE sexually coarse and crude

lexicography
NOUN the profession of writing dictionaries
lexicographer NOUN

liability liabilities
NOUN **1.** Someone's liability is that person's responsibility for something. **2.** In business, a company's liabilities are its debts. **3.** *an informal use* If you describe someone as a liability, you mean that that person causes a lot of problems or embarrassment.

liable
ADJECTIVE **1.** If you say that something is liable to happen, you mean that you think it will probably happen. **2.** If you are liable for something you have done, you are legally responsible for it.

liaise liaises liaising liaised
VERB To liaise with someone or an organization means to keep that person or organization informed.

liaison liaisons
NOUN Liaison is communication between two organizations or two sections of an organization.

liar liars
NOUN a person who tells lies

libel libels libelling libelled
NOUN **1.** Libel is something written about someone that is not true, and for which the writer can be made to pay damages in court.
VERB **2.** To libel someone means to write or say something untrue about that person.
libellous ADJECTIVE

liberal liberals
NOUN **1.** someone who believes in political progress, social welfare, and individual freedom
ADJECTIVE **2.** Someone who is liberal is tolerant of a wide range of behaviour, standards, or opinions. **3.** To be liberal with something means to be generous with it. **4.** A liberal quantity of something is a large amount of it.
liberally ADVERB
liberalism NOUN

LI

liberate liberates liberating liberated
VERB To liberate people means to free them from prison or from an unpleasant situation.
liberation NOUN
liberator NOUN

liberty
NOUN Liberty is the freedom to choose how you want to live, without government restrictions.

libido libidos
NOUN Someone's libido is his or her sexual drive.

librarian librarians
NOUN a person who works in, or is in charge of, a library

library libraries
NOUN **1.** a building in which books are kept for people to come and read or borrow **2.** a collection of books, records, or videos

lice the plural of LOUSE

licence licences
NOUN **1.** an official document that entitles you to carry out a particular activity, for example to drive a car **2.** Licence is the freedom to do what you want, especially when other people consider that it is being used irresponsibly.

license licenses licensing licensed
VERB To license an activity means to give official permission for it to be carried out.

lichen lichens
NOUN Lichen is a green, mosslike growth on rocks or tree trunks.

lick licks licking licked
VERB **1.** If you lick something, you move your tongue over it.
NOUN **2.** the action of licking

licorice
NOUN Licorice is a root used to flavour candy; also the candy itself.

lid lids
NOUN the top of a container, which you open in order to reach what is inside

lie lies lying lay lain
VERB **1.** To lie somewhere means to rest there horizontally. **2.** If you say where something lies, you are describing where it is: *The farm lies between two valleys.*

lie lies lying lied
VERB **1.** To lie means to say something that is not true.
NOUN **2.** something you say that is not true

lieu
PHRASE If one thing happens **in lieu** of another, it happens instead of it.

lieutenant lieutenants
NOUN a junior officer in the army or navy

life lives
NOUN **1.** Life is the quality of being able to grow and develop, which is present in people, plants, and animals. **2.** Your life is your existence from the time you are born until the time you die. **3.** The life of a machine is the period of time for which it is likely to work. **4.** If you refer to the life in a place, you are talking about the amount of activity there: *The town was full of life.* **5.** If criminals are sentenced to life, they are sent to prison for the rest of their lives, or until they are granted parole.

lifeblood
NOUN The lifeblood of something is the most essential part of it.

lifeboat lifeboats
NOUN **1.** a boat kept on shore, which is sent out to rescue people who are in danger at sea **2.** a small boat kept on a ship, which is used if the ship starts to sink

life expectancy life expectancies
NOUN Your life expectancy is the number of years you can expect to live.

lifeguard lifeguards
NOUN a person whose job is to rescue people who are in difficulty in the sea or in a swimming pool

life jacket life jackets
NOUN a jacket that keeps you afloat in water

KNOWING WORDS: IDIOMS

BE WORD SHARP!

Idioms add colour to language by playing with the meanings of words.

life existence

for dear life with all your might

for the life of you in any way

life and limb safety and survival

large as life in person

larger than life beyond the ordinary, extreme

NEL

LI

lifeless
ADJECTIVE **1.** Someone who is lifeless is dead.
2. If you describe a person or place as lifeless, you mean that that person or place is dull.

lifelike
ADJECTIVE A picture or sculpture that is lifelike looks very real or alive.

lifeline lifelines
NOUN **1.** something that helps you to survive or helps an activity to continue **2.** a rope thrown to someone who is in danger of drowning

lifelong
ADJECTIVE existing throughout someone's life: *He had a lifelong interest in music.*

lifespan lifespans
NOUN **1.** Someone's lifespan is the length of time during which he or she is alive **2.** The lifespan of a product or organization is the length of time it exists or is useful.

lifetime lifetimes
NOUN Your lifetime is the period of time during which you are alive.

lift lifts lifting lifted
VERB **1.** To lift something means to move it to a higher position. **2.** When fog or mist lifts, it clears away. **3.** To lift a ban on something means to remove it. **4.** *an informal use* To lift things means to steal them.
NOUN **5.** the act of lifting: *The skaters performed a difficult lift during their routine.*
6. If you give someone a lift, you drive that person somewhere in a car or on a motorcycle.

ligament ligaments
NOUN a piece of tough tissue in your body that connects your bones

light lights lighting lighted; lighter lightest
NOUN **1.** Light is brightness from the sun, fire, or lamps, which enables you to see things.
2. a lamp or other device that gives out brightness **3.** If you give someone a light, you give that person a match or lighter to light something, like tobacco or wood.
ADJECTIVE **4.** A place that is light is bright because of the sun or the use of lamps. **5.** A light colour is pale. **6.** A light object does not weigh much. **7.** A light task is fairly easy.
8. Light books or music are entertaining and are not intended to be serious.
VERB **9.** To light a place means to cause it to be filled with light. **10.** To light a fire means to make it start burning. **11.** To light upon something means to find it by accident.
lightly ADVERB
lightness NOUN

lighten lightens lightening lightened
VERB **1.** When something lightens, it becomes less dark. **2.** To lighten a load means to make it less heavy.

lighter lighters
NOUN a device for lighting things such as candles, pipes, or fires

light-headed
ADJECTIVE If you feel light-headed, you feel slightly dizzy.

light-hearted
ADJECTIVE Someone who is light-hearted is cheerful and has no worries.

lighthouse lighthouses
NOUN a tower by the sea, or other large body of water, that sends out a powerful light to guide ships and warn them of danger

lighting
NOUN **1.** The lighting in a room or building is the way that it is lit. **2.** Lighting in the theatre or for a movie is the special lights that are directed on the performers or scene.

lightning
NOUN Lightning is the bright flashes of light in the sky that are produced by natural electricity during a thunderstorm.

lightweight lightweights
NOUN **1.** a boxer in one of the lighter weight groups
ADJECTIVE **2.** Something that is lightweight does not weigh very much: *a lightweight jacket*

light-year light-years
NOUN a unit of distance equal to the distance that light travels in a year

like likes liking liked
PREPOSITION **1.** If one thing is like another, it is similar to it.
NOUN **2.** *The like* means other similar things of the sort just mentioned: *cups, plates, pots, and the like*
PHRASE **3.** If you **feel like** something, you want to do it or have it: *I feel like a walk.*
VERB **4.** If you like something or someone, you find that person or thing pleasant.

> **! HEADS UP**
>
> In slang speech, **like** is used with the verb **be** to mean *say*: *So I'm like "no way," and she's like "uh-huh."*

-like

SUFFIX The suffix *-like* means *resembling* or *similar to*: *a balloonlike object*

likeable

ADJECTIVE Someone who is likeable is very pleasant and friendly.

likelihood

NOUN If there is a likelihood that something will happen, it will probably happen.

likely likelier likeliest

ADJECTIVE Something that is likely will probably happen or is probably true.

liken likens likening likened

VERB If you liken one thing to another, you say that those things are similar.

likeness likenesses

NOUN If two things have a likeness to each other, they are similar in appearance.

likewise

ADVERB Likewise means similarly: *She sat down and he did likewise.*

liking

NOUN If you have a liking for someone or something, you like that person or thing.

lilac

NOUN **1.** a shrub with large clusters of pink, white, or mauve flowers
ADJECTIVE **2.** pale purple

lilt lilts

NOUN A lilt in someone's voice is a pleasant rising and falling sound in it.
lilting ADJECTIVE

lily lilies

NOUN a plant with trumpet-shaped flowers of various colours

limb limbs

NOUN **1.** Your limbs are your arms and legs. **2.** The limbs of a tree are its branches. PHRASE **3.** If you have gone **out on a limb**, you have done something risky.

limber up limbers up limbering up limbered up

VERB If you limber up, you stretch your muscles before doing a sport.

limbo

NOUN **1.** If you are in limbo, you are in an uncertain situation over which you feel you have no control. **2.** The limbo is a Caribbean dance in which the dancer has to pass under a low bar while leaning backwards.

lime limes

NOUN **1.** a small green citrus fruit similar to a lemon **2.** A lime tree is a large tree with pale green leaves. **3.** Lime is a chemical substance that is used in cement.

limelight

NOUN If someone is in the limelight, that person is getting a lot of attention.

limerick limericks

NOUN an amusing nonsense poem of five lines

limestone

NOUN Limestone is a white rock that is used for building and making cement.

limit limits limiting limited

NOUN **1.** a boundary or an extreme beyond which something cannot go: *the speed limit* VERB **2.** To limit something means to prevent it from becoming bigger, spreading, or making progress: *He did all he could to limit the damage.*

limitation limitations

NOUN **1.** The limitation of something is the reducing or controlling of it. **2.** If you talk about the limitations of a person or thing, you are talking about the limits of that person's or thing's abilities.

limited

ADJECTIVE Something that is limited is rather small in amount or extent: *a limited number of passes to the concert*

limousine limousines

NOUN a large, luxurious car, usually driven by a chauffeur

limp limps limping limped; limper limpest

VERB **1.** If you limp, you walk unevenly because you have hurt your leg or foot.

KNOWING WORDS: WORD BUILDING

BE WORD SHARP!

You can create new words by adding prefixes and suffixes to a base word.

-like an adjectival suffix that means *similar to*

childlike innocent, like a child

dreamlike unreal, like a dream

lifelike realistic, like a living thing

springlike warm, like springtime

viselike tight, like a vise

LI

NOUN **2.** an uneven way of walking
ADJECTIVE **3.** Something that is limp is soft and floppy, and not stiff or firm: *limp lettuce*

limpet limpets
NOUN a shellfish with a pointed shell, which attaches itself very firmly to rocks

line lines lining lined
NOUN **1.** a long, thin mark **2.** a number of people or things positioned one behind the other **3.** a route along which someone or something moves: *a railway line* **4.** In a piece of writing, a line is a number of words together: *I rarely forgot my lines as an actor.* **5.** Someone's line of work is the kind of work he or she does. **6.** The line someone takes is the attitude that person has toward something: *He took a hard line with lying.* **7.** In a store or business, a line is a type of product: *That line has been discontinued.* VERB **8.** To line something means to cover its inside surface or edge with something: *Cottages lined the edge of the harbour.*

line up
VERB **9.** When people line up, they stand in a line. **10.** When you line something up, you arrange it for a special occasion: *A tour is being lined up for July.*

lineage lineages
NOUN Someone's lineage is all the people from whom he or she is directly descended.

linear
ADJECTIVE arranged in a line or in a strict sequence, or happening at a constant rate

line dancing
NOUN a type of dancing performed by rows of people to country music

linen
NOUN **1.** Linen is a type of cloth made from a plant called flax. **2.** Linen is also household goods made of cloth, such as sheets and tablecloths.

liner liners
NOUN something that serves as a lining for something else: *a boot liner*

linesman linesmen
NOUN in sports, an official who watches the field, rink, or court, and indicates when the ball or puck goes outside the lines

-ling
SUFFIX The suffix *-ling* means *small*: *duckling*

linger lingers lingering lingered
VERB To linger means to remain for a long time: *Economic problems lingered in the background.*

lingerie
NOUN Lingerie is women's nightclothes and underclothes.

lingo lingoes
NOUN *an informal word* a language, especially a dialect or jargon regarded as incomprehensible to the general public: *the lingo of programmers*

linguist linguists
NOUN someone who studies foreign languages or the way in which language works

lining linings
NOUN any material used to line the inside of something

link links linking linked
NOUN **1.** a relationship or connection between two things: *the link between sunbathing and skin cancer* **2.** a physical connection between two things or places: *a high-speed rail link between the cities* **3.** one of the rings in a chain
VERB **4.** To link people, places, or things means to join them together.
linkage NOUN

linoleum
NOUN a floor covering with a shiny surface

lint
NOUN fuzz or fluff consisting of tiny bits of fibre from yarn or cloth

KNOWING WORDS: IDIOMS

BE WORD SHARP!

Idioms add colour to language by playing with the meanings of words.

line a long, thin mark

cross the line do something unacceptable

draw the line set a limit

in the line of fire/duty while at war/work

read between the lines find a hidden meaning

out of line not acceptable

lion lions
NOUN a large member of the cat family that comes from Africa. Lions have light brown fur, and the male has a long mane. A female lion is called a lioness.

lip lips
NOUN **1.** Your lips are the edges of your mouth. **2.** The lip of a jug is the slightly pointed part through which liquids are poured.

lip-read lip-reads lip-reading lip-read
VERB To lip-read means to watch someone's lips when that person is talking in order to understand what he or she is saying.

lipstick lipsticks
NOUN a coloured substance that women wear on their lips

liqueur liqueurs
NOUN a strong, sweet, alcoholic drink, usually drunk after a meal

liquid liquids
NOUN **1.** any substance that is not a solid or a gas, and that can be poured
ADJECTIVE **2.** Something that is liquid is in the form of a liquid: *liquid nitrogen, liquid soap* **3.** In commerce and finance, a person's or company's liquid assets are the things that can be sold quickly to raise cash.

liquidate liquidates liquidating liquidated
VERB **1.** To liquidate a company means to close it down and to use its assets to pay off its debts. **2.** *an informal use* To liquidate a person means to murder that person.
liquidation NOUN
liquidator NOUN

liquor
NOUN Liquor is any strong alcoholic drink.

lisp lisps lisping lisped
NOUN **1.** Someone who has a lisp pronounces the sounds *s* and *z* like *th*.
VERB **2.** To lisp means to speak with a lisp.

list lists listing listed
NOUN **1.** a set of words or items written one below the other
VERB **2.** If you list a number of things, you make a list of them.

listen listens listening listened
VERB If you listen to something, you hear it and pay attention to it.
listener NOUN

listless
ADJECTIVE lacking energy and enthusiasm
listlessly ADVERB

lit a past tense and past participle of LIGHT

litany litanies
NOUN something, especially a list of things, that is repeated often or in a boring or insincere way: *a tedious litany of complaints*

literacy
NOUN Literacy is the ability to read and write.
literate ADJECTIVE

literal
ADJECTIVE **1.** The literal meaning of a word is its most basic meaning. **2.** A literal translation from a foreign language is one that has been translated exactly word for word.
literally ADVERB

literary
ADJECTIVE connected with literature: *literary critics*

literary device literary devices
NOUN A literary device is a writing technique used to create an effect on the reader. Some examples of literary devices are *analogy, irony, metaphor, mood, symbolism,* and *tone.*

literature
NOUN **1.** Literature consists of novels, plays, and poetry. **2.** The literature on a subject is everything that has been written about it.

lithe
ADJECTIVE supple and graceful

litmus
NOUN In chemistry, litmus is a substance that turns red under acid and blue under alkali conditions.

litmus test litmus tests
NOUN something that is regarded as a simple and accurate test of a particular thing, such as a person's attitude to an issue: *The referendum was seen as a litmus test of Canadian unity.*

litre litres
NOUN a unit of liquid volume. One litre of water has a mass of one kilogram.

litter litters littering littered
NOUN **1.** Litter is garbage in the street and other public places. **2.** Cat litter is a gravelly substance you put in a container where you want your cat to urinate and defecate. **3.** a number of baby animals born at the same time to the same mother
VERB **4.** If things litter a place, they are scattered all over it.

little less lesser least
ADJECTIVE **1.** small in size or amount
NOUN **2.** A little is a small amount or degree:

LI

Would you like a little fruit juice? **3.** Little also means not much: *He has little to say.*
ADVERB **4.** to a small amount or degree: *We were a little afraid. She ate little.*

live lives living lived
VERB **1.** If you live in a place, that is where your home is. **2.** To live means to be alive. **3.** If something lives up to your expectations, it is as good as you thought it would be.
ADJECTIVE OR ADVERB **4.** Live television or radio is broadcast while the event is taking place: *a live concert*
ADJECTIVE **5.** Live animals or plants are alive, rather than dead or artificial: *a live spider* **6.** Something is live if it is directly connected to an electrical supply: *Those wires are live.* **7.** Live ammunition or bullets have not yet been exploded.
live down
VERB **8.** If you cannot live down a mistake or failure, you cannot make people forget it.

livelihood livelihoods
NOUN Someone's livelihood is his or her job or the source of his or her income.

lively
ADJECTIVE full of life and enthusiasm: *lively conversation*
liveliness NOUN

liven livens livening livened
VERB To liven things up means to make them more lively or interesting.

liver livers
NOUN **1.** Your liver is a large organ in your body that cleans your blood and helps digestion. **2.** Liver is also the liver of some animals, which may be cooked and eaten.

livestock
PLURAL NOUN Livestock are farm animals.

livid
ADJECTIVE **1.** extremely angry **2.** dark purple or bluish: *livid bruises*

living
ADJECTIVE **1.** If someone is living, that person

is alive: *her only living relative*
NOUN **2.** The work you do for a living is the work you do in order to earn money to live.

living room living rooms
NOUN the room where people relax and entertain in their homes

lizard lizards
NOUN a long, thin, dry-skinned reptile found in hot, dry countries

llama llamas
NOUN a South American animal related to the camel

load loads loading loaded
NOUN **1.** something being carried **2.** *an informal use* Loads means a lot: *loads of work, loads of food*
VERB **3.** To load a vehicle or animal means to put a large number of things into it or onto it.

loaf loaves; loafs loafing loafed
NOUN **1.** a large piece of bread baked in a shape that can be cut into slices
VERB **2.** To loaf around means to be lazy and not do any work.

loan loans loaning loaned
NOUN **1.** a sum of money that you borrow **2.** the act of borrowing or lending something: *I am grateful to her for the loan of that book.*
VERB **3.** If you loan something to someone, you lend it to that person.

loath
ADJECTIVE If you are loath to do something, you are very unwilling to do it.

loathe loathes loathing loathed
VERB To loathe someone or something means to feel strong dislike for that person or thing.
loathing NOUN
loathsome ADJECTIVE

lob lobs lobbing lobbed
VERB **1.** If you lob something, you throw it high in the air.
NOUN **2.** In tennis, a lob is a stroke in which the player hits the ball high in the air.

KNOWING WORDS: IDIOMS

BE WORD SHARP!

Idioms add colour to language by playing with the meanings of words.

live exist

know where you live know enough about you to harm you

live and breathe something be absorbed in something

live and let live not interfere with other people's lives

live it up have a good time

live on the edge do exciting or dangerous things

LI

lobby lobbies lobbying lobbied

NOUN **1.** The lobby in a building is the main entrance area with corridors and doors leading off it. **2.** a group of people trying to persuade an organization that something should be done: *the environmental lobby*

VERB **3.** To lobby an MP or an organization means to try to persuade that person or organization to do something, for example by writing lots of letters.

lobe lobes

NOUN **1.** The lobe of your ear is the rounded soft part at the bottom. **2.** any rounded part of something: *the frontal lobe of the brain*

lobster lobsters

NOUN an edible shellfish with two front claws and eight legs

local locals

ADJECTIVE **1.** Local means in, near, or belonging to the area in which you live: *the local newspaper* **2.** A local anesthetic numbs only one part of your body and does not send you to sleep.

NOUN **3.** The locals are the people who live in a particular area.

locally ADVERB

locality localities

NOUN an area of a country or city: *a large map of the locality*

localized

ADJECTIVE existing or happening in only one place: *localized pain*

locate locates locating located

VERB **1.** To locate someone or something means to find out where that person or thing is. **2.** If something is located in a place, it is in that place.

location locations

NOUN **1.** a place, or the position of something PHRASE **2.** If a movie is made **on location**, it is made away from a studio.

lock locks locking locked

VERB **1.** If you lock something, you close it and fasten it with a key. **2.** If something locks into place, it moves into place and becomes firmly fixed there.

NOUN **3.** a device on something that fastens it and prevents it from being opened except with a key **4.** A lock on a canal is a place where the water level can be raised or lowered to allow boats to go between two parts of the canal that have different water levels. **5.** A lock of hair is a small bunch of hair.

locker lockers

NOUN a small cupboard for your personal belongings, for example at school

locket lockets

NOUN a piece of jewellery consisting of a small case that you can keep a photograph in, and that you wear on a chain around your neck

locksmith locksmiths

NOUN a person who makes or fixes locks

locomotive locomotives

NOUN a railway engine

locust locusts

NOUN an insect like a large grasshopper, which travels in huge swarms and eats crops

lodge lodges lodging lodged

NOUN **1.** an inn, hotel, or motel

VERB **2.** If you lodge in someone else's house, you live there and pay that person rent. **3.** If something lodges somewhere, it gets stuck there: *My kite is lodged in the top of that tree.* **4.** If you lodge a complaint, you formally make it.

lodger lodgers

NOUN a person who lives in someone's house and pays rent

lodgings

PLURAL NOUN If you live in lodgings, you live in someone else's house and pay that person rent.

loft lofts

NOUN an upper floor of a business building such as a factory or warehouse, especially when used as a living space

lofty loftier loftiest

ADJECTIVE **1.** very high: *a lofty hall* **2.** very noble and important: *lofty ideals* **3.** proud and superior: *her lofty manner*

log logs logging logged

NOUN **1.** a thick branch or piece of tree trunk that has fallen or been cut down **2.** the captain's official record of everything that happens on board a ship

VERB **3.** If you log something, you officially make a record of it, for example in a ship's log. **4.** To log in or on to a computer system means to gain access to it, usually by giving your name and password. To log off or out means to finish using the system.

logic

NOUN Logic is a way of reasoning involving a series of statements, each of which must be true if the statement before it is true.

logical

ADJECTIVE **1.** A logical argument uses logic. **2.** A logical course of action or decision is sensible or reasonable in the circumstances: *the logical conclusion*

logically ADVERB

LI

logistics
NOUN *a formal word* The logistics of a complicated undertaking is the skilful organization of it.

logo logos
NOUN The logo of an organization is a special design that is put on all its products.

-logy
SUFFIX The suffix *-logy* is used to form words that refer to the study of something: *biology, geology*

loin loins
NOUN **1.** *an old-fashioned use* Your loins are the front part of your body between your waist and your thighs. **2.** Loin is a piece of meat from the back or sides of an animal: *loin of pork*

loiter loiters loitering loitered
VERB To loiter means to stand around idly with no real purpose.

loll lolls lolling lolled
VERB **1.** If you loll somewhere, you sit or lie there in an idle, relaxed way. **2.** If your head or tongue lolls, it hangs loosely.

lollipop lollipops
NOUN a hard candy on the end of a stick

lone
ADJECTIVE A lone person or thing is the only one in a particular place: *a lone climber on the mountainside*

lonely lonelier loneliest
ADJECTIVE **1.** If you are lonely, you are unhappy because you are alone. **2.** A lonely place is an isolated one that very few people visit: *a lonely hillside*
loneliness NOUN

loner loners
NOUN a person who likes to be alone

lonesome
ADJECTIVE lonely and sad

long longer longest; longs longing longed
ADJECTIVE **1.** continuing for a great amount of time: *There had been no rain for a long time.*

ADJECTIVE **2.** great in length or distance: *a long dress, a long road*
ADVERB **3.** for a certain period of time: *How long will it last?* **4.** for an extensive period of time: *long into the following year*
PHRASE **5.** If something **no longer** happens, it does not happen any more. **6. Before long** means soon. **7.** If one thing is true **as long as** another thing is true, it is true only if the other thing is true.
VERB **8.** If you long for something, you want it very much.

longevity
NOUN *a formal word* Longevity is long life.

longhand
NOUN If you write something in longhand, you do it in your own handwriting rather than using shorthand or a keyboard.

longing longings
NOUN a strong wish for something

longitude longitudes
NOUN The longitude of a place is its distance east or west of a line passing through Greenwich, England, measured in degrees.

⚠ **HEADS UP**

Remember this: lines of **longitude** run **along** the time zones. Lines of **latitude** run **flat** like the equator.

long jump
NOUN The long jump is an athletic event in which you jump as far as possible after taking a long run.

long-range
ADJECTIVE **1.** able to be used over a great distance: *long-range missiles* **2.** extending a long way into the future: *a long-range weather forecast*

long-sighted
ADJECTIVE another name for FAR-SIGHTED

long-standing
ADJECTIVE having existed for a long time: *a long-standing tradition*

long-suffering
ADJECTIVE very patient: *her long-suffering sister*

long-term
ADJECTIVE extending a long way into the future: *long-term plans*

long-winded
ADJECTIVE long and boring: *a long-winded letter*

Instead of **LONG** try...

a **prolonged** explanation
a **lasting** friendship
a **sustained** effort
a **lengthy** delay
an **extensive** list
an **endless** saga
a **protracted** argument
an **extended** period of time

LI

look looks looking looked

VERB **1.** If you look at something, you turn your eyes toward it so that you can see it. **2.** If you look at a subject or situation, you study it or judge it. **3.** If you describe the way that someone or something looks, you are describing the appearance of that person or thing.

NOUN **4.** If you have a look at something, you look at it. **5.** the way someone or

Instead of LOOK try...

glance briefly

review carefully

thoughtfully gaze

peer through a hole

peek before it's ready

something appears, especially the expression on a person's face **6.** If you talk about someone's looks, you are talking about how attractive that person is.

INTERJECTION **7.** You say *look out* to warn someone of danger.

look after

VERB **8.** If you look after someone or something, you take care of that person.

look down

VERB **9.** If you look down on someone, you think that that person is inferior to you.

look for

VERB **10.** If you look for someone or something, you try to find that person or thing.

look forward

VERB **11.** If you are looking forward to something, you want it to happen because you think you will enjoy it.

look up

VERB **12.** To look up information means to find it out in a book or online. **13.** If you look someone up, you go to see that person after not having seen him or her for a long time. **14.** If a situation is looking up, it is improving.

look up to

VERB **15.** If you look up to someone, you admire and respect that person.

look-alike look-alikes

NOUN a person who looks very like someone else: *an Elvis look-alike*

lookout lookouts

NOUN **1.** someone who is watching for danger, or a place where that person watches for danger

PHRASE **2.** If you are **on the lookout** for something, you are watching for it or waiting expectantly for it.

loom looms looming loomed

NOUN **1.** a machine for weaving cloth

VERB **2.** If something looms in front of you, it suddenly appears as a tall, unclear, and sometimes frightening shape. **3.** If a situation or event is looming, it is likely to happen soon and is important or of concern.

loon loons

NOUN a large diving bird with webbed feet that has a loud, wild cry

loonie loonies

NOUN the Canadian one-dollar coin. It takes its name from the image of a loon on one side of the coin.

loony loonies *an informal word*

ADJECTIVE **1.** Behaviour or people can be described as loony if they are crazy or eccentric.

NOUN **2.** a crazy or eccentric person

loop loops looping looped

NOUN **1.** a curved or circular shape in something long, such as a piece of string

VERB **2.** If you loop rope or string around an object, you place a loop around the object.

loophole loopholes

NOUN a small mistake or omission in the law that allows you to do something that the law really intends that you should not do

loose looser loosest

ADJECTIVE **1.** If something is loose, it is not firmly held, fixed, or attached. **2.** Loose clothes are rather large and do not fit closely.

ADVERB **3.** To set animals loose means to set them free after they have been tied up or kept in a cage.

loosely ADVERB

⚠ HEADS UP

Don't confuse **loose** (LOOS) and **lose** (LOOZ): *That collar is too **loose**. We don't want to **lose** the dog!*

loosen loosens loosening loosened

VERB To loosen something means to make it looser.

loot loots looting looted

VERB **1.** To loot stores and houses means to steal goods from them during a battle or riot.

NOUN **2.** Loot is stolen money or goods.

lop lops lopping lopped

VERB If you lop something off, you cut it off with one quick stroke.

lopsided

ADJECTIVE Something that is lopsided is uneven because its two sides are different sizes or shapes.

lord lords

NOUN **1.** a ruler, master, or chief **2.** In the United Kingdom, lord is a title used in front of the names of some noblemen of certain ranks: *Lord Beaverbrook was born in Ontario.* **3.** In Christianity, Lord is a name given to God and Jesus Christ.

lore

NOUN The lore of a place, people, or subject is all the traditional knowledge and stories about it.

lose loses losing lost

VERB **1.** If you lose something, you cannot find it, or you no longer have it because it has been taken away from you: *I lost my science notebook.* **2.** If you lose a relative or friend, that person dies: *She lost her brother last year.* **3.** If you lose a fight or an argument, you are beaten. **4.** If a business loses money, it is spending more money than it is earning.
loser NOUN

loss losses

NOUN **1.** The loss of something is the losing of it.
PHRASE **2.** If you are **at a loss**, you do not know what to do.

lost

ADJECTIVE **1.** If you are lost, you do not know where you are. **2.** If something is lost, you cannot find it. **3.** Lost is the past tense and past participle of LOSE.

lot lots

NOUN **1.** A lot of something, or lots of something, is a large amount of it. **2.** A lot means very much or very often: *I love her a lot.* **3.** a number of things considered as a group: *This lot of tickets will go on sale at midnight.* **4.** In an auction, a lot is one of the things being sold.

lotion lotions

NOUN a liquid that you put on your skin to protect or soften it: *suntan lotion*

lottery lotteries

NOUN a method of raising money by selling tickets from which a winner is selected at random

lotus lotuses

NOUN a large water lily, found in Africa and Asia

loud louder loudest

ADJECTIVE OR ADVERB **1.** A loud noise has a high volume of sound: *a loud explosion* **2.** If you describe clothing as loud, you mean that it is too bright: *a loud tie*
loudly ADVERB

loudspeaker loudspeakers

NOUN a piece of equipment that makes your voice louder when you speak into a microphone connected to it

lounge lounges lounging lounged

NOUN **1.** a room with comfortable chairs where people can relax: *a theatre lounge, a hotel lounge*
VERB **2.** If you lounge around, you lean against something or sit or lie around in a lazy and comfortable way.

louse lice

NOUN a small insect that lives on people's bodies: *head lice*

lousy lousier lousiest

ADJECTIVE *an informal word* **1.** of bad quality or very unpleasant: *The weather is lousy.* **2.** ill or unhappy: *I feel lousy.*

lout louts

NOUN a young man who behaves in an aggressive and rude way

lovable

ADJECTIVE having very attractive qualities and therefore easy to love: *a lovable puppy*

love loves loving loved

VERB **1.** If you love someone, you have strong emotional feelings of affection for that person. **2.** If you love something, you like it very much: *We both love fishing.* **3.** If you would love to do something, you want very much to do it: *I would love to live in Prince Edward Island.*
NOUN **4.** Love is a strong emotional feeling of affection for someone or something. **5.** a strong liking for something **6.** In tennis, love is a score of zero.
PHRASE **7.** If you are **in love** with someone, you feel strongly attracted to that person romantically or sexually. **8.** When two people **make love**, they have sex.

love affair love affairs

NOUN a romantic and often sexual relationship between two people who are not married to each other

lovely lovelier loveliest

ADJECTIVE very beautiful, attractive, and pleasant
loveliness NOUN

lover lovers

NOUN **1.** A person's lover is someone that he or she has a sexual relationship with but is not married to. **2.** Someone who is a lover of something, for example art or music, is very fond of it.

LI

loving
ADJECTIVE feeling or showing love
lovingly ADVERB

low lower lowest
ADJECTIVE **1.** Something that is low is close to the ground, or measures a short distance from the ground to the top: *a low stool*
2. *Low* means small in value or amount.
3. *Low* is used to describe people who are considered not respectable: *mixing with low company*
ADVERB **4.** in a low position, level, or degree
NOUN **5.** a level or amount that is less than before: *Sales hit a new low.*

lower lowers lowering lowered
VERB **1.** To lower something means to move it downward. **2.** To lower something also means to make it less in value or amount.

lowland lowlands
NOUN an area of flat, low land
lowland ADJECTIVE

lowly lowlier lowliest
ADJECTIVE low in importance, rank, or status

low tide
NOUN On a coast, low tide is the time, usually twice a day, when the sea is at its lowest level.

loyal
ADJECTIVE firm in your friendship or support for someone or something
loyally ADVERB
loyalty NOUN

loyalist loyalists
NOUN a person who remains firm in his or her support for a government or ruler

lozenge lozenges
NOUN **1.** a type of candy with medicine in it, which you suck to relieve a sore throat or cough **2.** a diamond or rhombus shape

lubricate lubricates lubricating lubricated
VERB To lubricate something such as a machine means to put oil or an oily substance onto it, so that it moves smoothly and friction is reduced.
lubrication NOUN
lubricant NOUN

lucid
ADJECTIVE **1.** Lucid writing or speech is clear and easy to understand. **2.** Someone who is lucid after having been ill or delirious is able to think clearly again.

luck
NOUN Luck is anything that seems to happen by chance and not through your own efforts.

luckless
ADJECTIVE unsuccessful or unfortunate: *We reduced our luckless opponents to shattered wrecks.*

lucky luckier luckiest
ADJECTIVE **1.** Someone who is lucky has a lot of good luck. **2.** Something that is lucky happens by chance and has good effects or consequences.
luckily ADVERB

lucrative
ADJECTIVE Something that is lucrative earns you a lot of money: *a lucrative business*

ludicrous
ADJECTIVE completely foolish, unsuitable, or ridiculous

lug lugs lugging lugged
VERB If you lug a heavy object around, you carry it with difficulty.

luggage
NOUN Your luggage is the bags and suitcases that you take with you when you travel.

lukewarm
ADJECTIVE **1.** slightly warm: *a mug of lukewarm coffee* **2.** not very enthusiastic or interested: *The report was given a polite but lukewarm response.*

lull lulls lulling lulled
NOUN **1.** a pause in something, or a short time when it is quiet and nothing much happens: *There was a temporary lull in the fighting.*
VERB **2.** If you are lulled into feeling safe, someone or something causes you to feel safe at a time when you are not safe: *We had been lulled into a false sense of security.*

lullaby lullabies
NOUN a song used for sending a baby or child to sleep

lumber lumbers lumbering lumbered
NOUN **1.** Lumber is wood that has been cut up and prepared for use.
VERB **2.** If you lumber around, you move heavily and clumsily.

luminary luminaries
NOUN *a literary or poetic word* a person who is famous or an expert in a particular subject

luminous
ADJECTIVE Something that is luminous glows in the dark, usually because it has been treated with a special substance: *The luminous dial on the clock.*
luminosity NOUN

lump lumps lumping lumped
NOUN **1.** A lump of something is a solid piece of it, of any shape or size: *a big lump of dough* **2.** a bump on the surface of

LI

something
VERB **3.** If you lump people or things together, you combine them into one group or consider them as being similar in some way.
PHRASE **4.** A **lump sum** is a large sum of money given or received all at once.
lumpy ADJECTIVE

lunacy
NOUN **1.** Lunacy is extremely foolish or eccentric behaviour. **2.** *an old-fashioned use* Lunacy is also severe mental illness.

lunar
ADJECTIVE relating to the moon

lunatic lunatics
NOUN **1.** If you call someone a lunatic, you mean that that person is very foolish: *He drives like a lunatic!* **2.** an insane person
ADJECTIVE **3.** Lunatic behaviour is very stupid, foolish, or dangerous.

lunch lunches lunching lunched
NOUN **1.** a meal eaten in the middle of the day, between breakfast and dinner
VERB **2.** When you lunch, you eat lunch.

luncheon luncheons
NOUN *a formal word* Luncheon is lunch.

lung lungs
NOUN Your lungs are the two organs inside your ribcage with which you breathe.

lunge lunges lunging lunged
NOUN **1.** a sudden forward movement: *He made a lunge for the ball.*
VERB **2.** To lunge means to make a sudden movement in a particular direction.

lurch lurches lurching lurched
VERB **1.** To lurch means to make a sudden, jerky movement.
NOUN **2.** a sudden, jerky movement

lure lures luring lured
VERB **1.** To lure someone means to entice that person into going somewhere or doing something.
NOUN **2.** something that you find very attractive

lurid
ADJECTIVE **1.** involving a lot of sensational detail: *lurid stories in the press* **2.** very brightly coloured or patterned

lurk lurks lurking lurked
VERB To lurk somewhere means to remain there hidden from the person you are waiting for.

luscious
ADJECTIVE very tasty: *luscious fruit*

lush lusher lushest
ADJECTIVE In a lush field or garden, the grass or plants are healthy and growing thickly.

lust lusts lusting lusted
NOUN **1.** Lust is a very strong feeling of sexual desire for someone. **2.** A lust for something is a strong desire to have it: *a lust for money*
VERB **3.** To lust for or after someone means to desire that person sexually. **4.** If you lust for or after something, you have a very strong desire to possess it: *She lusted after fame.*

lustful
ADJECTIVE feeling or expressing strong sexual desire

lustre
NOUN Lustre is soft, shining light reflected from the surface of something: *the lustre of silk*

lute lutes
NOUN an old-fashioned stringed musical instrument that is plucked like a guitar

luxuriant
ADJECTIVE Luxuriant plants, trees, and gardens are large, healthy, and growing strongly.

luxurious
ADJECTIVE very expensive and full of luxury
luxuriously ADVERB

luxury luxuries
NOUN **1.** Luxury is great comfort in expensive and beautiful surroundings: *a life of luxury* **2.** something that you enjoy very much but do not have very often, usually because it is expensive

-ly
SUFFIX **1.** The suffix *-ly* forms adjectives that describe a quality: *friendly* **2.** The suffix *-ly* also forms adjectives that refer to how often something happens or is done: *yearly* **3.** The suffix *-ly* also forms adverbs that refer to how or in what way something is done: *quickly, nicely*

lying
NOUN **1.** Lying is telling lies.
ADJECTIVE **2.** A lying person often tells lies. **3.** Lying is also the present participle of LIE.

lynch lynches lynching lynched
VERB If a crowd lynches someone, it kills that person in a violent way without first holding a legal trial.

lynx lynxes
NOUN a wildcat with a short tail and tufted ears

lyric lyrics
NOUN **1.** The lyrics of a song are the words.
ADJECTIVE **2.** Lyric poetry is written in a simple and direct style, and is usually about love.

lyrical
ADJECTIVE poetic and romantic

! HEADS UP The word **lustre** is pronounced LUS-tur.

Mm

m an abbreviation for *metres*

macabre
ADJECTIVE A macabre event is gruesome and horrible: *a macabre horror story*

macadamia macadamias
NOUN an Australian tree that produces edible nuts

macaroni
NOUN Macaroni is short hollow tubes of pasta.

macaroon macaroons
NOUN a sweet, chewy cookie flavoured with almonds or coconut

mace maces
NOUN a war club used in the Middle Ages

machete machetes
NOUN a large, heavy knife with a big blade

machine machines machining machined
NOUN **1.** a piece of equipment that uses energy to make it work
VERB **2.** If you machine something, you make it or work on it using a machine.

machine gun machine guns
NOUN a gun that works automatically, firing bullets one after the other

machinery
NOUN Machinery is machines in general.

machismo
NOUN Machismo is exaggerated or aggressive male behaviour.

macho
ADJECTIVE A man who is described as macho behaves in an aggressively masculine way.

mackerel mackerels
NOUN a saltwater fish with blue and silver stripes

mad madder maddest
ADJECTIVE **1.** Someone who is mad has a mental illness that often causes that person to behave in strange ways. **2.** *an informal use* Someone who is mad is very angry. **3.** If you describe someone as mad, you mean that that person is very foolish: *He said we were mad to spend so much money on DVDs and video games.* **4.** If you are mad about someone or something, you like that person or thing very much: *My sister is mad about golf.*
madness NOUN
madman NOUN
madwoman NOUN

madam
NOUN *Madam* is a polite or formal way of addressing a woman.

maddening
ADJECTIVE irritating *a maddening habit*

madly
ADVERB If you do something madly, you do it in a fast, excited way.

madrigal madrigals
NOUN a song sung by several people without instruments

magazine magazines
NOUN **1.** a weekly or monthly publication with articles and photographs **2.** a place for storing goods and supplies, such as a military supply depot

magenta
NOUN OR ADJECTIVE dark reddish purple

maggot maggots
NOUN a creature that looks like a small worm and lives on decaying things. Maggots turn into flies.

magic
NOUN **1.** In fairy tales, magic is a special power that can make impossible things happen. **2.** Magic is the art of performing tricks to entertain people.

magical
ADJECTIVE wonderful and romantic
magically ADVERB

magician magicians
NOUN **1.** a person who performs tricks as entertainment **2.** a person who is thought to have magical powers

magistrate magistrates
NOUN an official who acts as a judge in a court that deals with less serious crimes

magnanimous
ADJECTIVE generous and forgiving

magnate magnates
NOUN someone who is very rich and powerful in business

magnet magnets
NOUN a piece of iron that attracts iron or steel toward it, and that points toward north if allowed to swing freely
magnetic ADJECTIVE
magnetism NOUN

magnificent
ADJECTIVE extremely beautiful or impressive
magnificently ADVERB
magnificence NOUN

magnify magnifies magnifying magnified
VERB When a microscope or lens magnifies

⚠ HEADS UP Mad, meaning *mentally ill*, may be perceived as insulting and is best avoided.

something, it makes that thing appear bigger than it actually is.

magnification NOUN

magnifying glass magnifying glasses
NOUN a lens that makes things appear bigger than they really are

magnitude
NOUN The magnitude of something is its great size or importance.

magnolia magnolias
NOUN a tree that has large white or pink flowers in spring

magpie magpies
NOUN a large, black and white bird with a long tail

mahogany
NOUN Mahogany is a hard, reddish brown wood from a tropical evergreen tree.

maid maids
NOUN a female servant

maiden maidens
NOUN **1.** *a literary or poetic use* a young unmarried woman
ADJECTIVE **2.** a first attempt of its kind: *a maiden voyage*

maiden name maiden names
NOUN the surname a woman has before she marries

mail mails mailing mailed
NOUN **1.** Your mail is the letters and parcels or messages delivered to you by the post office or by electronic means.
VERB **2.** If you mail a letter, you send it by mail.

mail order
NOUN Mail order is a system of buying goods by mail.

maim maims maiming maimed
VERB To maim someone is to injure that person very badly for life.

main mains
ADJECTIVE **1.** most important: *the main event*
NOUN **2.** a large pipe that carries gas or water to buildings and sewage from them

mainframe mainframes
NOUN a large computer that can be used by many people at the same time

mainland
NOUN The mainland is the main part of a continent or country in contrast to islands around its coast.

mainly
ADVERB true in most cases

mainstay
NOUN The mainstay of something is the main support of that thing.

mainstream
NOUN The mainstream is the most ordinary and conventional group of people or ideas in a society.

maintain maintains maintaining maintained
VERB **1.** If you maintain something, you keep it going or keep it at a particular rate or level: *I wanted to maintain our friendship.*
2. If you maintain someone, you provide that person regularly with money for what he or she needs. **3.** To maintain a machine or a building is to keep it in good condition.
4. If you maintain that something is true, you believe it is true and say so.

maintenance
NOUN **1.** Maintenance is the process of keeping something in good condition.
2. Maintenance is also money that a person sends regularly to someone to provide for the things he or she needs.

maize another name for CORN

majesty majesties
NOUN **1.** Majesty is great dignity and impressiveness. **2.** You say *His Majesty* when you are talking about a king, and *Her Majesty* when you are talking about a queen.
majestic ADJECTIVE
majestically ADVERB

major majors
ADJECTIVE **1.** more important or more significant than other things: *There were over 50 major injuries as a result of the accident.* **2.** A major scale in music has a standard sequence of full and half steps between notes. A major key is one of the keys in which most Western music is written.
NOUN **3.** an officer in the armed forces of the rank immediately above captain

majority majorities
NOUN **1.** The majority of people or things in a group is more than half of the group.
2. In an election, the majority is the number of votes cast for the winner when that number is more than half of the total number of votes for all candidates.

make makes making made
VERB **1.** To make something is to produce or construct it, or to cause it to happen. **2.** To make something is to do it: *He was about to make a speech.* **3.** To make something is to prepare it: *I'll make some salad dressing.*
4. If someone makes you do something, that person forces you to do it: *Mom made me clean the bathroom.*
NOUN **5.** The make of a product is the name of the company that manufactured it: *What make of car do you drive?*

Mm

make up
VERB **6.** If a number of things make up something, they form that thing. **7.** If you make up a story, you invent it. **8.** If you make yourself up, you put makeup on. **9.** If two people make up, they become friends again after a quarrel.

makeup
NOUN **1.** Makeup is cosmetics such as coloured creams and powders that are put on the face to improve a person's appearance. **2.** A person's makeup is his or her character or personality.

making
NOUN **1.** The making of something is the act or process of creating or producing it.
PHRASE **2.** When you describe someone as something **in the making**, you mean that that person is gradually becoming that thing: *a captain in the making*

maladjusted
ADJECTIVE A maladjusted person is not able to cope with the demands of daily living.

malaise
NOUN Malaise is a feeling of dissatisfaction or unhappiness.

malaria
NOUN Malaria is a tropical disease, caught from mosquitoes, that causes fever and shivering.

male males
NOUN **1.** a person or animal belonging to the sex that cannot give birth or lay eggs
ADJECTIVE **2.** concerning or relating to men

male chauvinist male chauvinists
NOUN a man who thinks that men are better than women

malevolent
ADJECTIVE wanting or intending to cause harm
malevolence NOUN

malfunction malfunctions malfunctioning malfunctioned
VERB **1.** If a machine malfunctions, it fails to work properly.
NOUN **2.** the failure of a machine to work properly

malice
NOUN Malice is a desire to cause harm to people.

malicious
ADJECTIVE Malicious talk or behaviour is intended to harm someone.

malign maligns maligning maligned
VERB To malign someone is to say unpleasant and untrue things about that person.

malignant
ADJECTIVE **1.** A malignant disease or tumour could cause death if it is allowed to continue. **2.** harmful and cruel

mallard mallards
NOUN a wild duck. The male has a green head.

mallet mallets
NOUN a wooden hammer with a square head

malnutrition
NOUN Malnutrition is poor nutrition, caused by not eating enough healthy food.

malodorous
ADJECTIVE If you describe something as malodorous, you mean it smells bad.

malpractice
NOUN If someone such as a doctor or lawyer breaks the rules of his or her profession, that doctor's or lawyer's behaviour is called malpractice.

malt
NOUN Malt is roasted grain, usually barley, which is used in making beer, whisky, and vinegar.

mammal mammals
NOUN Animals that give birth to live young and who feed them with milk from the mother's body are called mammals. Human beings, dogs, and whales are all mammals.

mammoth mammoths
ADJECTIVE **1.** very large: *a mammoth outdoor concert*
NOUN **2.** a huge animal that looked like a hairy elephant with long, curved tusks. Mammoths became extinct a long time ago.

man men; mans manning manned
NOUN **1.** an adult male human being
2. Human beings, or an individual human being: *the history of man. All men are equal.*
VERB **3.** To man something is to be in charge of it or operate it: *Two officers were manning the radar screens.*

⚠ HEADS UP

Man and **mankind** are out-of-date words meaning *all humans*. Use non-sexist words like **people**.

manacle manacles
NOUN Manacles are metal rings or clamps attached to a prisoner's wrists or ankles.

manage manages managing managed
VERB **1.** If you manage to do something, you succeed in doing it: *We managed to*

Mm

find somewhere to sit. **2.** If you manage an organization or business, you are responsible for controlling it.

manageable
ADJECTIVE able to be managed

management
NOUN **1.** The management of a business is the controlling and organizing of it. **2.** The people who control an organization are called the management.

manager managers
NOUN a person responsible for running a business or organization: *a bank manager*

mandarin mandarins
NOUN a type of small orange that is easy to peel

mandate mandates
NOUN A government's mandate is the authority it has to carry out particular policies as a result of winning an election.

mandatory
ADJECTIVE If something is mandatory, there is a law or rule stating that it must be done: *There is a mandatory life sentence for that type of crime.*

mandolin mandolins
NOUN a musical instrument like a small guitar with a pear-shaped or deep, rounded body

mane manes
NOUN the long hair growing from the neck of a lion or horse

manger mangers
NOUN a feeding box in a barn or stable

mangle mangles mangling mangled
VERB **1.** If something is mangled, it is crushed and twisted. **2.** do very badly: *I mangled my lines during our first rehearsal.*

mango mangoes
NOUN a sweet, yellowish fruit that grows in tropical countries

manhole manholes
NOUN a covered hole in the ground leading to a drain, tunnel, or sewer

manhood
NOUN Manhood is the state of being a man rather than a boy.

mania manias
NOUN **1.** a strong liking for something: *my uncle's mania for plant collecting* **2.** a mental illness

maniac maniacs
NOUN a person who is violent and dangerous

manic
ADJECTIVE energetic and excited: *My brother's manic behaviour concerned me, as he is usually so calm.*

manicure manicures
NOUN a special treatment for the hands and fingernails
manicurist NOUN

manifest manifests manifesting manifested
a formal word
ADJECTIVE **1.** obvious or easily seen: *her manifest enthusiasm*
VERB **2.** To manifest something is to make people aware of it: *Fear can manifest itself in many ways.*

manifestation manifestations
NOUN *a formal word* A manifestation of something is a sign that it is happening or exists: *The illness may be a manifestation of stress.*

manifesto manifestoes
NOUN a published statement of the aims and policies of a political party

manipulate manipulates manipulating manipulated
VERB **1.** To manipulate people or events is to control or influence them to produce a particular result. **2.** If you manipulate a piece of equipment, you control it in a skilful way.
manipulation NOUN
manipulator NOUN
manipulative ADJECTIVE

mankind
NOUN *Mankind* is used to refer to all human beings: *a threat to mankind*

manly manlier manliest
ADJECTIVE having qualities that are typically masculine: *He laughed a deep, manly laugh.*

manna
NOUN If something appears like manna from heaven, it appears suddenly as if by a miracle and helps you in a difficult situation.

manner manners
NOUN **1.** The manner in which you do something is the way you do it. **2.** Your manner is the way in which you behave and talk: *his kind manner*
PLURAL NOUN **3.** If you have good manners, you behave very politely.

mannerism mannerisms
NOUN a gesture or a way of speaking that is characteristic of a person

manoeuvre manoeuvres manoeuvring manoeuvred
VERB **1.** If you manoeuvre something into a place, you skilfully move it there: *It took expertise to manoeuvre the boat so close to the shore.*
NOUN **2.** a clever move you make in order to change a situation to your advantage

 **HEADS UP** The word **manoeuvre** is pronounced muh-NEW-ver.

NEL

Mm

manor manors
NOUN a large country house with land

manpower
NOUN Workers can be referred to as manpower.

mansion mansions
NOUN a very large house

manslaughter
NOUN Manslaughter is the accidental killing of a person.

mantelpiece mantelpieces
NOUN a shelf over a fireplace

mantle mantles
NOUN *a literary or poetic word* To take on the mantle of something is to take on responsibility for it: *She has taken on the mantle as Canada's greatest living author.*

mantra mantras
NOUN a word or short phrase continually repeated to help concentration

manual manuals
ADJECTIVE **1.** Manual work involves physical strength. **2.** operated by hand rather than by electricity or by a motor: *a manual gearshift*
NOUN **3.** an instruction book that tells you how to use a machine
manually ADVERB

manufacture manufactures manufacturing manufactured
VERB **1.** To manufacture goods is to make them by hand or by machine.
NOUN **2.** The manufacture of goods is the making of them in a factory: *the manufacture of automobiles*
manufacturer NOUN

manure
NOUN Manure is animal feces used to fertilize the soil.

many
ADJECTIVE **1.** If there are many people or things, there are a large number of them. **2.** You also use *many* to ask how great a quantity is or to give information about it:

How many tickets do you require?
PRONOUN **3.** a large number of people or things: *Many of us went to the park.*

map maps mapping mapped
NOUN **1.** a detailed drawing of an area as it would appear if you saw it from above
VERB **2.** If you map out a plan, you work out in detail what you will do.

maple maples
NOUN a tree that has large leaves with a number of points

mar mars marring marred
VERB To mar something is to spoil it: *The game was marred by violence.*

marathon marathons
NOUN **1.** a race in which people run 42.195 kilometres along roads
ADJECTIVE **2.** A marathon task is a large one that takes a long time.

marble marbles
NOUN **1.** Marble is a very hard, cold stone that is often polished to show the coloured patterns in it. **2.** a small, coloured ball of clay, glass, or stone used in games

march marches marching marched
NOUN **1.** March is the third month of the year. It has 31 days. **2.** an organized protest in which a large group of people walk somewhere together
VERB **3.** When soldiers march, they walk with quick, regular steps in time with each other. **4.** To march somewhere is to walk quickly in a determined way: *He marched out of the room.*

mare mares
NOUN an adult female horse

margarine margarines
NOUN a substance that is similar to butter but made from vegetable oil

margin margins
NOUN **1.** If you win a contest by a large or small margin, you win it by a large or small amount. **2.** an extra amount that allows you

KNOWING WORDS: WORD BUILDING

BE WORD SHARP!

You can create new words by adding prefixes and suffixes to a base word.

man- a prefix meaning *using the hands*

manipulate handle in a skilful way

manoeuvre move in a skilful way

manual done using your hands

manufacture make by hand or machine

manuscript a piece of writing not yet published

Mm

more freedom in doing something: *a small margin of error* **3.** the blank space at each side on a written or printed page

marginal
ADJECTIVE **1.** small and not very important: *a marginal increase in pay* **2.** written or printed in a margin: *marginal notes*
marginally ADVERB

marigold marigolds
NOUN a type of yellow or orange garden flower

marijuana
NOUN Marijuana is a drug that is smoked.

marina marinas
NOUN a harbour for pleasure boats and yachts

marinate marinates marinating marinated
VERB To marinate food is to soak it in a mixture of oil and vinegar to flavour it before cooking.

marine marines
ADJECTIVE **1.** relating to or involving the sea: *marine animals*
NOUN **2.** a soldier who serves with the navy

marital
ADJECTIVE relating to or involving marriage: *marital problems*

maritime
ADJECTIVE relating to the sea and ships: *maritime trade*

marjoram
NOUN a herb with small, rounded leaves and tiny, pink flowers

mark marks marking marked
NOUN **1.** a small stain or damaged area on a surface: *I can't get this mark off my jeans.* **2.** a written or printed symbol: *He made a few marks with his pen.* **3.** a letter or number showing how well you have done in homework or in an exam
VERB **4.** If something marks a surface, it damages it in some way. **5.** If you mark something, you write a symbol on it

or identify it in some other way. **6.** When a teacher marks your work, he or she decides how good it is and gives it a mark. **7.** To mark something is to be a sign of it: *The accident marked a tragic end to the day.* **8.** In some sports, if you mark your opposing player, you stay close to that person, trying to prevent him or her from getting the ball or puck.

marked
ADJECTIVE very obvious: *a marked improvement*
markedly ADVERB

market markets marketing marketed
NOUN **1.** a place where goods or animals are bought and sold **2.** The market for a product is the number of people who want to buy it: *the market for cars*
VERB **3.** To market a product is to sell it in an organized way.

marketing
NOUN Marketing is the part of a business concerned with the way a product is sold.

market research
NOUN Market research is research into what people want and buy.

marksman marksmen
NOUN someone who can shoot a weapon very accurately

marlin marlins
NOUN a large fish found in tropical seas that has a very long upper jaw

marmalade
NOUN a jam made from citrus fruit

maroon
NOUN OR ADJECTIVE dark brownish red

marooned
ADJECTIVE If you are marooned in a place, you are stranded there and cannot leave it.

marquee marquees
NOUN a very large tent used at a fair or other outdoor entertainment

marriage marriages
NOUN **1.** the relationship between two spouses **2.** Marriage is the act of marrying someone.

marrow marrows
NOUN the soft, fatty substance that fills the cavities of most bones

marry marries marrying married
VERB When two people marry, they become each other's spouse.
married ADJECTIVE

Mars
NOUN Mars is a planet in the solar system and the fourth from the sun.

Instead of **MARK** try...

a stain on the carpet
a nick from shaving
a crayon smudge
an ink blot
a marker streak
a scratch on the desk
a red blotch on your skin
a notch for keeping score

Mm

marsh marshes
NOUN an area of land that is permanently wet

marshal marshals marshalling marshalled
VERB **1.** If you marshal things or people, you gather them together and organize them: *We were marshalled into the auditorium for the presentation.*
NOUN **2.** an officer of the highest rank in some armed forces

marshmallow marshmallows
NOUN a soft, spongy candy made using corn syrup, sugar, gelatine, and flavouring

marsupial marsupials
NOUN an animal that carries its young in a pouch. Koala bears and kangaroos are marsupials

martial
ADJECTIVE relating to or involving war or soldiers: *martial music*

martial arts
PLURAL NOUN The martial arts are the techniques of self-defence that come from East Asia, for example karate or judo.

Martian Martians
NOUN **1.** an imaginary creature from the planet Mars
ADJECTIVE **2.** to do with the planet Mars

martyr martyrs martyring martyred
NOUN **1.** someone who suffers or chooses to die rather than change his or her beliefs
VERB **2.** If someone is martyred, that person is killed because of his or her beliefs.
martyrdom NOUN

marvel marvels marvelling marvelled
VERB **1.** If you marvel at something, it fills you with surprise or wonder: *We marvelled at the majestic mountains.*
NOUN **2.** something that makes you feel great surprise or admiration: *a marvel of high technology*

marvellous
ADJECTIVE wonderful or excellent
marvellously ADVERB

marzipan
NOUN Marzipan is a paste made of almonds, sugar, and egg. It is put on top of cakes or used to make small candies.

mascara
NOUN Mascara is a substance that can be used to colour eyelashes and make them look longer.

mascot mascots
NOUN a person, animal, or toy that is thought to bring good luck: *The team mascot is a moose.*

masculine
ADJECTIVE **1.** typical of men, rather than women: *a masculine voice, masculine features* **2.** belonging to a particular class of nouns in some languages, such as French, German, and Latin
masculinity NOUN

mash mashes mashing mashed
VERB If you mash vegetables, you crush them after they have been cooked.

mask masks masking masked
NOUN **1.** something you wear over your face for protection or disguise: *a surgical mask*
VERB **2.** If you mask something, you cover it so that it is protected or so that it cannot be seen.

masochist masochists
NOUN someone who gets pleasure from his or her own suffering
masochism NOUN

mason masons
NOUN a person who is skilled at making things with stone or brick

masonry
NOUN Masonry is pieces of stone that form part of a wall or building.

masquerade masquerades masquerading masqueraded
VERB If you masquerade as something, you pretend to be it: *He masqueraded as a doctor.*

mass masses massing massed
NOUN **1.** a large amount of something **2.** The masses are the ordinary people in society considered as a group: *opera for the masses* **3.** In physics, the mass of an object is the amount of physical matter that it has.
ADJECTIVE **4.** involving a large number of people: *mass unemployment*
VERB **5.** When people mass, they gather together in a large group.

massacre massacres massacring massacred
NOUN **1.** the killing of a very large number of people in a violent and cruel way
VERB **2.** To massacre people is to kill large numbers of them in a violent and cruel way.

massage massages massaging massaged
VERB **1.** To massage someone is to rub his or her body in order to help that person relax or to relieve pain.
NOUN **2.** A massage is treatment that involves rubbing the body.

massive
ADJECTIVE extremely large: *a massive iceberg*
massively ADVERB

⚠ **HEADS UP** The word **masquerade** is pronounced mass-kuh-RAID.

Mm

mass-produce mass-produces mass-producing mass-produced
VERB To mass-produce something is to make it in large quantities: *They began mass-producing cameras after the war.*

mast masts
NOUN the tall, upright pole that supports the sails of a boat

master masters mastering mastered
NOUN **1.** a person who has authority over others, such as the employer of servants, or the owner of slaves or animals **2.** If you are master of a situation, you have control over it: *She was master of her own destiny.* **3.** a great artist, or a picture by a great artist
VERB **4.** If you master a difficult situation, you succeed in controlling it. **5.** If you master something, you learn how to do it properly: *She found it easy to master the program.*

masterful
ADJECTIVE showing control and authority

masterly
ADJECTIVE extremely clever or well done: *a masterly exhibition of skating skills*

mastermind masterminds masterminding masterminded
VERB **1.** If you mastermind a complicated activity, you plan and organize it.
NOUN **2.** The mastermind behind something is the person responsible for planning it.

masterpiece masterpieces
NOUN a thing that is done or made with wonderful skill: *This model ship is a masterpiece.*

masturbate masturbates masturbating masturbated
VERB If someone masturbates, that person touches his or her own genitals in order to get sexual pleasure.
masturbation NOUN

mat mats
NOUN **1.** a small piece of carpet or other thick material that is placed on the floor to protect it from damage **2.** a small piece of cloth, card, or plastic that is placed under a dish to protect a surface such as a table from damage **3.** a dull, flat colour, paint, or surface
ADJECTIVE **4.** A mat surface is dull rather than shiny: *mat black plastic*

matador matadors
NOUN a person who fights and tries to kill bulls as part of a public entertainment

match matches matching matched
NOUN **1.** a small, thin stick of wood that produces a flame when you strike it against a rough surface **2.** a game or contest

VERB **3.** If one thing matches another, the two things look the same or have similar qualities.

mate mates mating mated
NOUN **1.** one of a pair of things **2.** The first mate on a ship is the officer who is next in importance to the captain. **3.** An animal's mate is its sexual partner.
VERB **4.** When a male and female animal mate, they come together sexually in order to breed.

material materials
NOUN **1.** Material is cloth. **2.** a substance from which something is made: *the materials to make red dye* **3.** The equipment for a particular activity can be referred to as materials: *building materials* **4.** Material for a book, play, or film is the information or ideas on which it is based.
ADJECTIVE **5.** involving possessions and money: *concerned with material comforts*
materially ADVERB

materialism
NOUN Materialism is thinking that money and possessions are the most important things in life.
materialistic ADJECTIVE

materialize materializes materializing materialized
VERB If something materializes, it actually happens or appears: *Unfortunately, our plan for the party did not materialize.*

maternal
ADJECTIVE relating to or involving a mother: *her maternal instincts*

maternity
ADJECTIVE relating to or involving pregnant women and birth: *a maternity ward in a hospital*

mathematics
NOUN Mathematics is the study of numbers, quantities, and shapes.
mathematical ADJECTIVE
mathematically ADVERB
mathematician NOUN

matinée matinées
NOUN an afternoon performance of a play or movie

matrimony
NOUN *a formal word* Matrimony is marriage.
matrimonial ADJECTIVE

matrix matrices
NOUN **1.** *a formal use* the framework in which something grows and develops **2.** In mathematics, a matrix is a set of numbers or elements set out in rows and columns.

Mm

matron matrons
NOUN an older married woman or widow

matted
ADJECTIVE Hair that is matted is tangled, with the strands sticking together.

matter matters mattering mattered
NOUN **1.** something that you have to deal with **2.** Matter is any substance: *There is a small bit of matter clinging to your sweater.* **3.** Books and magazines are reading matter.
VERB **4.** If something matters to you, it is important.
PHRASE **5.** If you ask **What's the matter?** you are asking what is wrong.

matter-of-fact
ADJECTIVE showing no emotion

matting
NOUN Matting is thick, woven material such as rope or straw, used as a floor covering.

mattress mattresses
NOUN a large, thick pad filled with springs or feathers that is put on a bed to make it comfortable

mature matures maturing matured
VERB **1.** When a child or young animal matures, that child or animal becomes an adult. **2.** When something matures, it reaches complete development.
ADJECTIVE **3.** Mature means fully developed and emotionally balanced.
maturely ADVERB
maturity NOUN

maudlin
ADJECTIVE Someone who is maudlin is sad and sentimental, often because he or she is drunk.

maul mauls mauling mauled
VERB If someone is mauled by an animal, that person is savagely attacked and badly injured by it.

mausoleum mausoleums
NOUN a large, stately tomb

mauve
NOUN OR ADJECTIVE pale purple

maxim maxims
NOUN a short saying that gives a rule for good or sensible behaviour: *Instant action: that's my maxim.*

maximize maximizes maximizing maximized
VERB To maximize something is to make it as great or effective as possible: *Studying hard will maximize my chances of getting a good grade.*

maximum
ADJECTIVE **1.** The maximum amount is the most that is possible: *the maximum recommended dosage*

NOUN **2.** The maximum is the most that is possible: *A maximum of 50 people are allowed on the bus.*

may
VERB **1.** If something may happen, it is possible that it will happen: *It may arrive quite soon.* **2.** If someone may do something, that person is allowed to do that thing: *Please may I be excused?* **3.** You can use *may* when saying that, although something is true, something else is also true: *This may be true, but it is only part of the story.* **4.** a formal use You also use *may* to express a wish that something will happen: *May you live to be 100.*
NOUN **5.** May is the fifth month of the year. It has 31 days.

 HEADS UP

In formal language, **may** means *be allowed to*. **Can** means *be able to*. Informally, **can** is used for both.

maybe
ADVERB You use *maybe* when you are stating a possibility that you are not certain about: *Maybe I should bring an umbrella.*

mayhem
NOUN You can refer to a confused and chaotic situation as mayhem: *There was complete mayhem in the classroom.*

mayonnaise
NOUN a thick salad dressing made with egg yolks and oil

mayor mayors
NOUN a person who has been elected to lead and represent the people of a city, town, or village

maze mazes
NOUN a system of complicated passages through which it is difficult to find your way: *a maze of dark tunnels*

MD an abbreviation for *Doctor of Medicine*

me
PRONOUN A speaker or writer uses *me* to refer to himself or herself.

meadow meadows
NOUN a field of grass

meagre
ADJECTIVE very small and poor: *his meagre pension*

meal meals
NOUN an occasion when people eat, or the food they eat at that time

Mm

mean means meaning meant; meaner meanest
VERB **1.** If you ask what something means, you want to know what it refers to or what its message is. **2.** If you mean what you say, you are serious: *My teacher always means what he says.* **3.** If something means a lot to you, it is important to you. **4.** If one thing means another, it shows that the second thing is true or will happen: *Major fog will mean long delays at the airport.* **5.** If you mean to do something, you intend to do it: *I meant to phone you, but didn't have time.* **6.** If something is meant to be true, it is supposed to be true: *I found a road that wasn't meant to be there according to the map.*
ADJECTIVE **7.** Someone who is mean is unwilling to spend much money. **8.** Someone who is mean is unkind or cruel: *He apologized for being so mean to her.*
PLURAL NOUN **9.** A means of doing something is a method or object that makes it possible: *The tests were marked by means of a computer.* **10.** Someone's means are that person's money and income: *a person of means*
NOUN **11.** In mathematics, the mean is the average of a set of numbers.
meanness NOUN

meander meanders meandering meandered
VERB If a road or river meanders, it has a lot of bends or curves in it.

meaning meanings
NOUN **1.** The meaning of a word is what it refers to or expresses. **2.** The meaning of what someone says, or of a book or a movie, is the thoughts or ideas that it is intended to express. **3.** If something has meaning, it seems to be worthwhile and to have real purpose.
meaningful ADJECTIVE
meaningfully ADVERB
meaningless ADJECTIVE

means test means tests
NOUN a check of a person's money and income to see whether he or she needs money or benefits from the government

meantime
PHRASE **In the meantime** means in the period of time between two events: *My next exam isn't until next week; in the meantime, I plan to study and rest.*

meanwhile
ADVERB **1.** Meanwhile means while something else is happening.
NOUN **2.** Meanwhile also means the time between two events.

measles
NOUN Measles is an infectious illness in which you have red spots on your skin.

measly
ADJECTIVE *an informal word* very small or inadequate: *a measly portion of food*

measure measures measuring measured
VERB **1.** When you measure something, you find out how big it is. **2.** If something measures a particular distance, its length or depth is that distance: *slivers of glass measuring a few millimetres across*
NOUN **3.** a unit in which size, speed, or depth is expressed **4.** A measure of something is a certain amount of it: *There has been a measure of agreement between both groups.* **5.** Measures are actions carried out to achieve a particular result: *Tough measures are needed to maintain order.*
measurement NOUN

measured
ADJECTIVE careful and deliberate: *walking at the same measured pace*

measurement measurements
NOUN **1.** the result that you obtain when you measure something **2.** Measurement is the activity of measuring something. **3.** Your measurements are the sizes of your chest, waist, and hips that you use to buy the correct size of clothes.

meat meats
NOUN Meat is the flesh of animals that is cooked and eaten.
meaty ADJECTIVE

SPELL-CHECK THIS!

A computer's spell-check won't catch wrong **homophones** (words that are spelled differently but sound the same).

We usually <u>meat</u> first thing in the morning.

In this sentence, **meat** should be **meet**.
Meet means *get together*.
Meat means *animal flesh used as food*.

mecca

NOUN **1.** If a place is a mecca for people of a particular kind, many of them go there because it is of special interest to them: *The island is a mecca for bird lovers.* **2.** Mecca is the holiest city of Islam, to which many Muslims make pilgrimages.

mechanic mechanics

NOUN **1.** a person who repairs and maintains engines and machines
PLURAL NOUN **2.** The mechanics of something is the way in which something works or is done: *the mechanics of accounting*
NOUN **3.** Mechanics is also the scientific study of movement and the forces that affect objects.

mechanical

ADJECTIVE **1.** A mechanical device has moving parts and is used to do a physical task.
2. A mechanical action is done automatically without thinking about it: *He gave a mechanical smile.*
mechanically ADVERB

mechanism mechanisms

NOUN **1.** a part of a machine that does a particular task: *a locking mechanism* **2.** part of your behaviour that is automatic: *the body's defence mechanisms*

medal medals

NOUN a small disc of metal given as an award for bravery or as a prize in some competitions

medallion medallions

NOUN a round piece of metal worn as an ornament on a chain around the neck

medallist medallists

NOUN a person who has won a medal in an athletic competition: *a gold medallist at the Olympics*

meddle meddles meddling meddled

VERB To meddle is to interfere and try to change things without being asked.

media

PLURAL NOUN You can refer to forms of communication such as television, radio, newspapers, movies, and the Internet as media.

> ⚠ **HEADS UP**
>
> **Media** is the plural of **medium**, so use it with a plural verb: *The media are all reporting the same thing.*

mediaeval another spelling of MEDIEVAL

media literacy

NOUN the process of analyzing a media text to understand its purpose and how it tries to influence its audience.

median medians

ADJECTIVE **1.** The median value of a set is the middle value when the set is arranged in order.
NOUN **2.** In statistics, the middle number or point of a series. The median of 1, 3, 4, 8, 9 is 4.

mediate mediates mediating mediated

VERB If you mediate between two groups, you try to settle a dispute between them.
mediation NOUN
mediator NOUN

medical medicals

ADJECTIVE **1.** relating to the prevention and treatment of illness and injuries
NOUN **2.** a thorough examination of your body by a doctor
medically ADVERB

medication medications

NOUN Medication is a substance that is used to treat illness.

medicinal

ADJECTIVE relating to the treatment of illness: *a valuable medicinal herb*

medicine medicines

NOUN **1.** Medicine is the treatment of illness and injuries by doctors and nurses. **2.** a substance that you drink or swallow to help cure an illness

medieval

ADJECTIVE relating to the Middle Ages, a period between about 1100 CE and 1500 CE, especially in Europe

mediocre

ADJECTIVE of poor quality: *a mediocre student, a mediocre meal*
mediocrity NOUN

meditate meditates meditating meditated

VERB **1.** If you meditate, you remain in a calm, silent state for a period of time, often as a religious act. **2.** If you meditate on something, you think about it very deeply.
meditation NOUN

medium media *or* mediums

ADJECTIVE **1.** If something is of medium size or degree, it is neither large nor small: *a medium sweater*
NOUN **2.** a means that you use to communicate something. The plural is *media*: *the medium of television* **3.** a person who

claims to be able to speak to the dead and to receive messages from them. The plural is *mediums*.

medley medleys
NOUN **1.** a mixture of different things, creating an interesting effect **2.** a number of different songs or tunes sung or played one after the other

meek meeker meekest
ADJECTIVE A meek person is timid and does what other people say.
meekly ADVERB

meet meets meeting met
VERB **1.** If you meet someone, you happen to be in the same place as that person. **2.** If you meet a visitor you go to be with that person when he or she arrives. **3.** When a group of people meet, they gather together for a purpose. **4.** If something meets a need, it can fulfill that need: *services intended to meet the needs of the elderly* **5.** If something meets with a particular reaction, it gets that reaction from people: *My speech was met with silence.*

meeting meetings
NOUN **1.** an event in which people discuss proposals and make decisions together **2.** a junction or place where two or more things meet

megabyte megabytes
NOUN a unit of storage in a computer, equal to one million bytes

⚠ **HEADS UP**
In measurements, the prefix mega- means *million*: *megawatt*. In everyday language, it just means *big*: *megastar*.

melancholy
ADJECTIVE OR NOUN If you feel melancholy, you feel sad.

melee melees
NOUN a situation where there are a lot of people rushing around

mellow mellower mellowest; mellows mellowing mellowed
ADJECTIVE **1.** Mellow light is soft and golden. **2.** A mellow sound is smooth and pleasant to listen to: *the mellow clarinet* VERB **3.** If someone mellows, that person becomes more pleasant or relaxed: *He certainly hasn't mellowed with age.*

melodic
ADJECTIVE relating to melody

melodious
ADJECTIVE pleasant to hear: *a melodious voice*

melodrama melodramas
NOUN a story or play in which people's emotions are exaggerated

melodramatic
ADJECTIVE behaving in an exaggerated, emotional way

melody melodies
NOUN a tune

melon melons
NOUN a large, juicy fruit with a green or yellow skin and many seeds inside

melt melts melting melted
VERB **1.** When something melts or when you melt it, it changes from a solid to a liquid because it has been heated. **2.** If something melts, it disappears: *The crowd melted away. My inhibitions melted.*

member members
NOUN **1.** A member of a group is one of the people or things belonging to the group: *members of the family* **2.** A member of an organization is a person who has joined the organization.

Member of Parliament Members of Parliament
NOUN in Canada, a person who has been elected to represent people in Parliament in Ottawa

membership
NOUN **1.** Membership in an organization is the state of being a member of it. **2.** The people who belong to an organization are its membership.

membrane membranes
NOUN a very thin piece of skin or tissue that connects or covers plant or animal organs or cells: *the nasal membrane*

memento mementos
NOUN an object that you keep because it reminds you of a person or a special occasion: *a memento of our trip to Iqaluit*

memo memos
NOUN a note from one person to another within the same organization. Memo is short for *memorandum*.

memoirs
PLURAL NOUN If someone writes memoirs, that person writes a record of his or her life and experiences.

memorable
ADJECTIVE If something is memorable, it is likely to be remembered because it is special or unusual: *a memorable victory*
memorably ADVERB

Mm

memorandum memorandums
NOUN a memo

memorial memorials
NOUN **1.** a structure built to remind people of a famous person or event: *a war memorial made of black marble*
ADJECTIVE **2.** A memorial event or prize is in honour of someone who has died, so that he or she will be remembered.

memory memories
NOUN **1.** Your memory is your ability to remember things. **2.** something you remember about the past: *My grandparents shared memories of their school days with me.* **3.** the part in which information is stored in a computer

men the plural of MAN

menace menaces menacing menaced
NOUN **1.** someone or something that is likely to cause serious harm: *In dry weather, forest fires are a great menace.* **2.** Menace is the quality of being threatening: *an atmosphere of menace*
VERB **3.** If someone or something menaces you, that person or thing threatens to harm you.
menacingly ADVERB

menagerie menageries
NOUN a collection of different wild animals

mend mends mending mended
VERB If you mend something that is broken, you repair it.

menial
ADJECTIVE Menial work is boring and tiring and lacks prestige.

meningitis
NOUN Meningitis is a serious infectious illness that affects the brain and spinal cord.

menopause
NOUN the time during which a female gradually stops menstruating. This usually happens when she is between the ages of 45 and 55.

menstruate menstruates menstruating menstruated
VERB When a female menstruates, blood comes from her womb. This normally happens once a month.
menstruation NOUN
menstrual ADJECTIVE

-ment
SUFFIX The suffix *-ment* forms nouns that refer to a state or a feeling: *contentment*

mental
ADJECTIVE **1.** relating to the process of thinking or intelligence: *mental arithmetic* **2.** relating to the health of the mind: *mental health*
mentally ADVERB

mentality mentalities
NOUN an attitude or way of thinking: *the teen mentality*

mention mentions mentioning mentioned
VERB **1.** If you mention something, you talk about it briefly.
NOUN **2.** a brief comment about someone or something: *He made no mention of his past.*

mentor mentors mentoring mentored
NOUN **1.** A mentor is an experienced adviser.
VERB **2.** If you mentor someone, you teach that person and give that person advice.

menu menus
NOUN **1.** a list of the foods you can eat in a restaurant **2.** a list of different options shown on a computer screen

mercenary mercenaries
NOUN **1.** a soldier who is paid to fight for a foreign country
ADJECTIVE **2.** Someone who is mercenary is mainly interested in getting money.

merchandise
NOUN Merchandise is goods that are sold: *There is merchandise in the warehouse.*

merchant merchants
NOUN a retail storekeeper

KNOWING WORDS: WORD BUILDING

BE WORD SHARP!

You can create new words by adding prefixes and suffixes to a base word.

-ment a noun suffix that refers to a state or a feeling

amazement a state of being amazed

agreement a state of having agreed on something

embarrassment a feeling of being embarrassed

excitement a feeling of being excited

fulfillment a state of being fulfilled

merchant marine
NOUN The merchant marine is the boats and sailors involved in carrying goods for trade.

merciful
ADJECTIVE **1.** showing kindness or forgiveness **2.** considered to be fortunate as a relief from suffering: *Death came as a merciful release.*
mercifully ADVERB

merciless
ADJECTIVE showing no kindness or forgiveness
mercilessly ADVERB

mercury
NOUN **1.** a silver-coloured metallic element that is liquid at room temperature. It is used in thermometers. **2.** Mercury is also the planet in the solar system that is nearest to the sun.

mercy mercies
NOUN If you show mercy, you show kindness or forgiveness and do not punish someone as severely as you could.

mere merest
ADJECTIVE used to emphasize how unimportant or small something is: *It's a mere seven-minute journey by boat.*
merely ADVERB

merge merges merging merged
VERB When two things merge, they combine together to make one thing: *The companies merged in 2001.*
merger NOUN

meringue meringues
NOUN a type of crisp, sweet cookie made with egg whites and sugar

merino merinos
NOUN a breed of sheep with long, fine wool

merit merits meriting merited
NOUN **1.** If something has merit, it is good or worthwhile. **2.** The merits of something are its advantages or good qualities.
VERB **3.** If something merits a particular treatment, it deserves that treatment: *She merits a place on the debating team.*

mermaid mermaids
NOUN In stories, a mermaid is a woman with a fish's tail instead of legs, who lives in the sea.

merry merrier merriest
ADJECTIVE happy and cheerful: *He was, for all his shyness, a merry man.*
merrily ADVERB

merry-go-round merry-go-rounds
NOUN a large, rotating platform with models of animals or vehicles on it, on which people, usually children, ride at a fair

mesh
NOUN Mesh is threads of wire or plastic twisted together like a net: *a fence made of wire mesh*

mess messes messing messed
NOUN **1.** something untidy **2.** a situation that is full of problems and trouble **3.** a room or building in which members of the armed forces eat: *the officers' mess*
VERB **4.** If you mess something up, you spoil it or do it wrong.
mess about, mess around
VERB **5.** If you mess about or mess around, you do things without any real purpose.
messy ADJECTIVE

message messages
NOUN **1.** a piece of information or a request that you send someone or leave for that person **2.** an idea that someone tries to communicate to people, for example in a play or a speech: *the story's anti-drug message*

messaging
NOUN Messaging or text messaging is the sending and receiving of short pieces of information between cellphones, using both letters and numbers to produce shortened forms of words.

messenger messengers
NOUN someone who takes a message to someone for someone else

Messiah
NOUN **1.** in Judaism, the Messiah is the king of the Jewish people who will be sent by God. **2.** For Christians, the Messiah is Jesus Christ.

Messrs.
Messrs. is the plural of **Mr.** It is often used in the names of businesses: *Messrs. Brown and Levine, Solicitors.*

met the past tense and past participle of MEET

metabolism metabolisms
NOUN Your metabolism is the chemical processes in your body that use food for growth and energy.
metabolic ADJECTIVE

metacognition
NOUN the process of thinking about your own thought processes and changing them so that you become a better learner

metal metals
NOUN Metal is a chemical element such as iron, steel, copper, or lead. Metals are good conductors of heat and electricity.
metallic ADJECTIVE

Mm

metamorphic

ADJECTIVE Metamorphic rock is rock that has been altered from its original state by heat or pressure.

metamorphosis metamorphoses

NOUN When a metamorphosis occurs, a person or thing changes into something completely different: *the metamorphosis of a larva into an insect*

metaphor metaphors

NOUN an imaginative way of describing something as another thing, to suggest that it has the typical qualities of that other thing: *My friend is shy—he's a mouse when you first meet him.*
metaphorical ADJECTIVE
metaphorically ADVERB

meteor meteors

NOUN a piece of rock or metal that burns very brightly when it enters Earth's atmosphere from space

meteoric

ADJECTIVE A meteoric rise to power, success, or fame happens very quickly.

meteorite meteorites

NOUN a piece of rock from space that has landed on Earth

meteorological

ADJECTIVE relating to or involving the weather or weather forecasting
meteorology NOUN

meter meters

NOUN a device that measures and records something: *a gas meter, a parking meter*

methane

NOUN Methane is a colourless gas with no smell that is found in coal gas and produced by decaying vegetable matter. It burns easily and can be used as a fuel.

method methods

NOUN **1.** a particular way of doing something: *the traditional method of making bread* **2.** a way that an experiment or test is carried out: *Describe the method as well as the result obtained.*

methodical

ADJECTIVE Someone who is methodical does things carefully and in an organized way.
methodically ADVERB

meticulous

ADJECTIVE A meticulous person does things very carefully and with great attention to detail.
meticulously ADVERB

Métis Métis

NOUN **1.** a person descended from mixed European and First Nations people who lived in Western Canada during the early 1800s
ADJECTIVE **2.** to do with the Métis

metre metres

NOUN **1.** a unit of length equal to 100 centimetres **2.** In poetry, metre is the rhythmic arrangement of words and syllables.

metric

ADJECTIVE relating to the system of measurement that uses metres, grams, and litres

metropolis metropolises

NOUN a very large city

metropolitan

ADJECTIVE relating or belonging to a large, busy city: *metropolitan districts*

mettle

NOUN If you are on your mettle, you are ready to do something as well as you can because you know you are being tested or challenged.

mew mews mewing mewed

VERB **1.** When a cat mews, it makes a short, high-pitched noise.
NOUN **2.** the short, high-pitched sound that a cat makes

mg an abbreviation for *milligram*

miasma miasmas

NOUN an unhealthy or unpleasant atmosphere, especially one caused by decaying things

mice the plural of MOUSE

micro-

PREFIX The prefix *micro-* means *very small*.

microchip microchips

NOUN a small piece of silicon on which electronic circuits for a computer are printed

microphone microphones

NOUN a device that is used to record, transmit, or increase the volume of sounds

microprocessor microprocessors

NOUN a microchip that can be programmed to do a large number of tasks or calculations

microscope microscopes

NOUN a piece of equipment that magnifies very small objects so that you can study them

microscopic

ADJECTIVE very small: *microscopic parasites*

microwave microwaves

NOUN A microwave or microwave oven is a type of oven that cooks food very quickly by radiation.

METAPHOR ▼✕

an imaginative way of describing something as another thing, to suggest that it has the typical qualities of that other thing

"He's not a man, he's a mountain!"

Here's the metaphor. It describes the villain in a way that gives the reader the impression that the man is huge and unbreakable.

KANAKO DAMERUM

353

mid-

PREFIX The prefix *mid-* is used to form words that refer to the middle part of a place or period of time: *mid-Atlantic, the mid-70s, midsentence*

midday

NOUN Midday is 12 o'clock in the middle of the day.

middle middles

NOUN **1.** The middle of something is the part furthest from each edge, end, or outside surface of something.

ADJECTIVE **2.** The middle one in a series or a row is the one that has an equal number of people or things on each side of it: *the middle house*

middle age

NOUN Middle age is the period of your life when you are between about 40 and 60 years old.

middle-aged ADJECTIVE

Middle Ages

PLURAL NOUN In European history, the Middle Ages were the period between about 1100 CE and 1500 CE.

middle class middle classes

NOUN The middle classes are the people in a society who are neither wealthy nor poor.

Middle English

NOUN Middle English was the English language from about 1100 CE until about 1450 CE.

middle-of-the-road

ADJECTIVE Middle-of-the-road means moderate and avoiding extremes: *middle-of-the-road tastes in fashion*

middle school middle schools

NOUN a school between elementary and high school

middling

ADJECTIVE of average quality or ability

midge midges

NOUN a small flying insect that can bite people

midget midgets

NOUN a thing that is smaller than usual in size for its kind

midnight

NOUN Midnight is 12 o'clock at night.

midriff midriffs

NOUN the middle of your body between your waist and your chest

midst

NOUN If you are in the midst of a crowd or an event, you are in the middle of it.

midsummer

ADJECTIVE relating to the period in the middle of summer: *a lovely midsummer morning in July*

midway

ADVERB in the middle of a distance or period of time: *They scored midway through the second half.*

midwife midwives

NOUN a person who is trained to help women at the birth of a baby

midwifery NOUN

might

VERB **1.** If you say something might happen, you mean that it is possible that it will happen: *I might stay awhile.* **2.** If you say that someone might do something, you are suggesting that that person do that thing: *You might like to go and see it.* **3.** Might is also the past tense of MAY.

NOUN **4.** *a literary or poetic use* Might is strength or power: *the full might of the Navy, to study with all your might*

mightily

ADVERB *a literary or poetic word* to a great degree or extent: *I was mightily relieved by the decision.*

mighty mightier mightiest

ADJECTIVE *a literary or poetic word* very powerful or strong: *a mighty army on the march*

migraine migraines

NOUN a severe headache that makes you feel very ill

migrate migrates migrating migrated

VERB **1.** If people migrate, they move from one place to another, especially to find work. **2.** When birds or animals migrate, they move at a particular season to a different place, usually to breed or to find new feeding grounds: *The birds migrate each year to warmer climates.*

migration NOUN
migratory ADJECTIVE
migrant NOUN OR ADJECTIVE

mike mikes

NOUN *an informal word* a microphone

mild milder mildest

ADJECTIVE **1.** Something that is mild is not strong and does not have any powerful or damaging effects: *a mild shampoo* **2.** Someone who is mild is gentle and kind. **3.** Mild weather is warmer than usual: *The region has mild winters and hot summers.* **4.** Mild emotions or attitudes are not very great or extreme: *mild surprise*

mildly ADVERB

mildew

NOUN Mildew is a soft white fungus that grows on things when they are warm and damp.

mile miles

NOUN a nonmetric unit of distance equal to about 1.6 kilometres

⚠ **HEADS UP**

Kilometres are standard in Canada, but we still use some old words like mileage.

mileage mileages

NOUN **1.** Your mileage is the total distance that you have travelled. **2.** The amount of mileage that you get out of something is how useful that thing is to you.

militant militants

ADJECTIVE **1.** A militant person is very active in trying to bring about extreme political or social change: *a militant environmentalist*
NOUN **2.** a person who tries to bring about extreme political or social change
militancy NOUN

military

ADJECTIVE **1.** related to or involving the armed forces of a country: *military bases*
NOUN **2.** The military are the armed forces of a country.
militarily ADVERB

militia militias

NOUN an organization that operates like an army but whose members are not professional soldiers

milk milks milking milked

NOUN **1.** Milk is the white liquid produced by female cows, goats, and some other animals to feed their young. Some people drink milk and use it to make butter, cheese, and yogurt. **2.** Milk is also the white liquid that a baby drinks from its mother's breasts.
VERB **3.** When someone milks a cow or a goat, that person gets milk from it by pulling the teats of its udder. **4.** If you milk something such as a business or charity, you drain it of its contents, information, or wealth: *They milked money from a hospital charity.*

milky milkier milkiest

ADJECTIVE **1.** pale creamy white: *milky white skin* **2.** like milk or containing a lot of milk: *milky tea*

Milky Way

NOUN The Milky Way is a strip of stars appearing as a pale band in the sky.

mill mills milling milled

NOUN **1.** a building where grain is ground to make flour **2.** a factory for making materials such as steel, wool, or cotton **3.** a small device for grinding coffee or spices into powder: *a pepper mill*
VERB **4.** grind or crush something in a mill

millennium millenniums

NOUN *a formal word* a period of 1000 years

millennium bug

NOUN a computer software problem caused by the change of date at the start of the year 2000

miller millers

NOUN the person who operates a mill, especially a flour mill

milligram milligrams

NOUN a unit of mass equal to one-thousandth of a gram

millilitre millilitres

NOUN a unit of liquid volume equal to one-thousandth of a litre

millimetre millimetres

NOUN a unit of length equal to a tenth of a centimetre or one-thousandth of a metre

million millions

NOUN the number 1 000 000
millionth ADJECTIVE, ADVERB

millionaire millionaires

NOUN a rich person who has a million or more dollars or property worth that amount

millstone millstones

PHRASE If something is **a millstone around your neck**, it is an unpleasant problem or responsibility from which you feel you cannot escape.

mime mimes miming mimed

NOUN **1.** Mime is the use of movements and gestures to express something or to tell a story without using speech.
VERB **2.** If you mime something, you describe or express it using mime.

mimic mimics mimicking mimicked

VERB **1.** If you mimic someone's actions or voice, you imitate that person in an amusing way.
NOUN **2.** a person who can imitate others
mimicry NOUN

minaret minarets

NOUN a tall, thin tower on a mosque

mince minces mincing minced

VERB **1.** If you mince meat, you chop it into very small pieces. **2.** To mince about is to walk with small quick steps in an affected, effeminate way.

Mm

mind minds minding minded

NOUN **1.** Your mind is your ability to think, together with all the thoughts you have and your memory.

PHRASE **2.** If you **change your mind**, you change a decision that you have made or an opinion that you have.

VERB **3.** If you do not mind something, you are not annoyed by it or bothered about it. **4.** If you say that you wouldn't mind something, you mean that you would like that thing: *I wouldn't mind a glass of water.* **5.** If you mind a child or mind something for someone, you look after it for a while: *My mother is minding the office.*

mindful

ADJECTIVE *a formal word* If you are mindful of something, you think about it carefully before taking action: *mindful of their needs*

mindless

ADJECTIVE **1.** Mindless actions are regarded as stupid and destructive: *mindless violence* **2.** A mindless job or activity is simple and repetitive.

mine mines mining mined

PRONOUN **1.** *Mine* refers to something belonging or relating to the person who is speaking or writing: *a friend of mine*

NOUN **2.** a series of holes or tunnels in the ground from which diamonds, coal, or other minerals are dug out: *a diamond mine, a coal mine* **3.** a bomb hidden in the ground or underwater, which explodes when people or things touch it

VERB **4.** To mine diamonds, coal, or other minerals is to obtain these substances from underneath the ground.

miner NOUN

mining NOUN

minefield minefields

NOUN an area of land or water where mines have been hidden

mineral minerals

NOUN a substance such as tin, salt, or coal that is formed naturally in rocks and in the earth: *rich mineral deposits*

mineral water

NOUN Mineral water is water that comes from a natural spring and contains mineral salts or gases. It is sometimes drunk as a beverage.

minestrone

NOUN Minestrone is soup containing small pieces of vegetables and pasta.

minesweeper minesweepers

NOUN a ship for clearing away underwater mines

mingle mingles mingling mingled

VERB If things mingle, they become mixed together: *His cries of joy mingled with theirs.*

mini-

PREFIX The prefix *mini-* is used to form nouns referring to something smaller or less important than similar things: *a TV miniseries, miniskirt*

miniature miniatures

ADJECTIVE **1.** a tiny copy of something much larger

NOUN **2.** a very small, detailed painting, often of a person

minibus minibuses

NOUN a van with seats in the back, which is used as a small bus

minimal

ADJECTIVE very small in quality, quantity, or degree: *He has minimal work experience.*

minimally ADVERB

minimize minimizes minimizing minimized

VERB If you minimize something, you reduce it to the smallest amount possible: *We wore an extra layer of clothing to minimize the cold.*

minimum

ADJECTIVE **1.** The minimum amount is the smallest amount that is possible: *a minimum wage*

NOUN **2.** The minimum is the smallest amount that is possible: *a minimum of three weeks*

minister ministers

NOUN **1.** A minister is a person who is in charge of a particular government department: *the Minister of Education* **2.** A minister in a Protestant church is a member of the clergy.

ministerial

ADJECTIVE relating to a government minister or ministry: *ministerial duties*

ministry ministries

NOUN **1.** a government department that deals with a particular area of work: *the Ministry of Finance* **2.** Members of the clergy can be referred to as the ministry: *Her son is in the ministry.*

mink minks

NOUN Mink is an expensive fur used to make coats or hats.

minnow minnows

NOUN a very small freshwater fish

minor minors

ADJECTIVE **1.** not as important or serious as other things: *a minor injury* **2.** A minor scale in music has a standard sequence of full and half steps between notes that is different from a major scale. A minor key is one of the

⚠ HEADS UP The word **ministerial** is pronounced min-ni-STEER-ee-uhl.

Mm

keys in which most Western music is written.
NOUN **3.** *a formal use* a young person who is not considered to be legally responsible for an action: *laws concerning the employment of minors*

minority minorities
NOUN **1.** The minority of people or things in a group is a number of them forming less than half of the whole: *Only a minority of people want this.* **2.** A minority is a group of people of a particular race or religion living in a place where most people are of a different race or religion.

minstrel minstrels
NOUN a singer in medieval times

mint mints minting minted
NOUN **1.** Mint is a herb used for flavouring in cooking. **2.** a peppermint-flavoured candy **3.** The mint is the place where the official coins of a country are made.
VERB **4.** When coins or medals are minted, they are made.
ADJECTIVE **5.** If something is in mint condition, it is in very good condition, like new.

minus
PREPOSITION **1.** You use *minus* to show that one number is being subtracted from another: *Ten minus six equals four.*
ADJECTIVE **2.** *Minus* is used when talking about temperatures below 0°C or 0°F.

minuscule
ADJECTIVE very small

minute minutes minuting minuted
NOUN **1.** a unit of time equal to 60 seconds **2.** The minutes of a meeting are the written records of what was said and decided.

minute
ADJECTIVE extremely small: *a minute amount of pesticide*
minutely ADVERB

minutiae
PLURAL NOUN *a formal word* Minutiae are small, unimportant details.

miracle miracles
NOUN **1.** a wonderful and surprising event that goes against the laws of nature **2.** any very surprising and fortunate event: *It was a miracle that I finally got a job.*
miraculous ADJECTIVE
miraculously ADVERB

mirage mirages
NOUN an image that you can see in the distance in very hot weather, but that does not actually exist

mire
NOUN *a literary or poetic word* Mire is swampy ground or mud.

mirror mirrors mirroring mirrored
NOUN **1.** a piece of glass that reflects light and in which you can see your reflection
VERB **2.** To mirror something is to have similar features to that thing: *His own shock was mirrored on her face.*

mirth
NOUN *a literary or poetic word* Mirth is great amusement and laughter.

mis-
PREFIX The prefix *mis-* means *wrong* or *false*: *misbehaviour, misconception*

misbehave misbehaves misbehaving misbehaved
VERB If a child misbehaves, he or she behaves badly.
misbehaviour NOUN

miscarriage miscarriages
NOUN **1.** If a woman has a miscarriage, she gives birth to a baby before it is properly formed and it dies. **2.** A miscarriage of justice is a wrong decision made by a court, which causes an innocent person to be punished.

miscellaneous
ADJECTIVE A miscellaneous group is made up of people or things that are different from each other.

mischief
NOUN action or behaviour that causes trouble or harm, often not intentionally
mischievous ADJECTIVE

misconception misconceptions
NOUN a wrong idea about something: *Another misconception is that cancer is infectious.*

misconduct
NOUN Misconduct is bad or unacceptable behaviour: *The athlete was found guilty of misconduct.*

misdemeanour misdemeanours
NOUN *a formal word* a minor wrongdoing

miser misers
NOUN a person who enjoys saving money but hates spending it
miserly ADJECTIVE

miserable
ADJECTIVE **1.** If you are miserable, you are very unhappy. **2.** If a place or a situation is miserable, it makes you feel depressed: *a miserable little apartment*
miserably ADVERB

misery miseries
NOUN Misery is great unhappiness.

misfire misfires misfiring misfired
VERB If a plan misfires, it goes wrong.

HEADS UP Minute meaning *small* is pronounced my-NYOOT.

Mm

misfit misfits
NOUN a person who is not accepted by other people because he or she is thought to be strange or eccentric

misfortune misfortunes
NOUN an unpleasant occurrence that is regarded as bad luck: *I had the misfortune to fall off my bike.*

misgiving misgivings
NOUN If you have misgivings, you are worried or unhappy about something: *I had misgivings about his teaching methods.*

misguided
ADJECTIVE A misguided opinion or action is wrong because it is based on a misunderstanding or bad information.

misinform misinforms misinforming misinformed
VERB If you are misinformed, you are given wrong or inaccurate information.
misinformation NOUN

misinterpret misinterprets misinterpreting misinterpreted
VERB To misinterpret something is to understand it wrongly: *You completely misinterpreted what I wrote.*

misjudge misjudges misjudging misjudged
VERB If you misjudge someone or something, you form an incorrect idea or opinion about that person or thing.

mislay mislays mislaying mislaid
VERB If you mislay something, you lose it because you have forgotten where you put it.

mislead misleads misleading misled
VERB To mislead someone is to make that person believe something that is not true.

misplaced
ADJECTIVE A misplaced feeling is inappropriate or directed at the wrong thing or person: *misplaced loyalty*

misprint misprints
NOUN a mistake, such as a spelling mistake, in something that has been printed

misrepresent misrepresents misrepresenting misrepresented
VERB To misrepresent someone is to give an inaccurate or misleading account of what that person has said or done.
misrepresentation NOUN

miss misses missing missed
VERB **1.** If you miss something, you fail to hit it when you aim at it: *His shot missed the target and landed on the ground.* **2.** If you miss something, you do not notice it: *You can't miss her in her bright yellow jacket.* **3.** If you miss someone or something, you

feel sad that that person or thing is no longer with you: *We miss our father.* **4.** If you miss a chance or opportunity, you fail to take advantage of it. **5.** If you miss a passenger vehicle, you arrive too late to catch it.
NOUN **6.** an act of missing something that you were aiming at **7.** *Miss* is used before the name of a woman or girl who is not married as a form of address: *Did you know Miss Smith?*

missile missiles
NOUN a weapon that moves long distances through the air and explodes when it reaches its target; also used of any object thrown as a weapon

mission missions
NOUN **1.** an important task that you have to do **2.** a group of people who have been sent to a foreign country to carry out an official task: *He became head of the peacekeeping mission.* **3.** a journey made by a military airplane or space rocket to carry out a task **4.** If you have a mission, there is something that you believe it is your duty to try to achieve. **5.** the workplace of a religious group that is working for a Christian church

missionary missionaries
NOUN a Christian who has been sent to a foreign country to work for his or her church

missive missives
NOUN *an old-fashioned word* a letter or message

mist mists misting misted
NOUN **1.** Mist consists of a large number of tiny drops of water in the air, which makes it hard to see clearly.
VERB **2.** If your eyes mist, you cannot see very far because there are tears in your eyes. **3.** If glass mists over or mists up, it becomes covered with condensation so that you cannot see through it.

mistake mistakes mistaking mistook mistaken
NOUN **1.** an action or opinion that

Instead of MISTAKE try...

is wrong or is not what you intended
VERB **2.** If you mistake someone or something for another person or thing, you wrongly think that that person or thing is the other person or thing: *I mistook him for the owner of the house.*

a social **gaffe**
a silly **blunder**
a **subtraction error**
a slight **inaccuracy**
a **typo** in the newspaper

mistaken
ADJECTIVE **1.** If you are mistaken about something, you are wrong about it. **2.** If you have a mistaken belief or opinion, you believe something that is not true.
mistakenly ADVERB

mister A man is sometimes addressed in a very informal way as *mister*: *Where do you live, mister?*

mistletoe
NOUN a plant that grows on trees and has white berries on it

mistook the past tense of MISTAKE

mistreat mistreats mistreating mistreated
VERB To mistreat people or animals is to treat them badly and make them suffer.

mistress mistresses
NOUN **1.** A married man's mistress is a woman who is not his wife and who he is having a sexual relationship with. **2.** A dog's mistress is the woman or girl who is the dog's owner.

mistrust mistrusts mistrusting mistrusted
VERB **1.** If you mistrust someone, you do not feel that you can trust that person.
NOUN **2.** Mistrust is a feeling that you cannot trust someone.

misty mistier mistiest
ADJECTIVE full of or covered with mist

misunderstand misunderstands misunderstanding misunderstood
VERB If you misunderstand something or someone, you do not properly understand that thing or what that person says or does: *He misunderstood the math problem.*

misunderstanding misunderstandings
NOUN If two people have a misunderstanding, they have a slight quarrel or disagreement.

misuse misuses misusing misused
NOUN **1.** The misuse of something is the incorrect or dishonest use of it: *the misuse of public money*
VERB **2.** To misuse something is to use it incorrectly or dishonestly.

mite mites
NOUN a very tiny creature that lives in the fur of animals

mitigating
ADJECTIVE *a formal word* Mitigating circumstances make a crime easier to understand and perhaps justify.

mitten mittens
NOUN Mittens are gloves that have one section that covers your thumb and another section for the rest of your fingers together.

mix mixes mixing mixed
VERB **1.** If you mix things, you combine them or shake or stir them together.
PHRASE **2.** If you are **mixed up in** a crime or a scandal, you are involved in it.
mix up
VERB **3.** If you mix up two things or people, you confuse them: *People often mix us up and greet us by each other's name.*

mixed
ADJECTIVE **1.** consisting of several things of the same general kind: *a mixed salad* **2.** for both males and females: *a mixed choir*

mixed-up
ADJECTIVE If you are mixed-up, you are confused, often emotionally: *I'm mixed-up about what I should do after high school.*

mixer mixers
NOUN a machine used for mixing things together: *a cement mixer*

mixture mixtures
NOUN several different things mixed together

mix-up mix-ups
NOUN a mistake in something that was planned: *a mix-up with the bookings*

mL an abbreviation for *millilitres*

mm an abbreviation for *millimetres*

mnemonic mnemonics
NOUN a word, phrase, or rhyme that helps you remember information: *The rhyme "i before e except after c" is a mnemonic.*

moan moans moaning moaned
VERB **1.** If you moan, you make a low, sad sound because you are in pain. **2.** *an informal use* If you moan about something, you complain about it.
NOUN **3.** a low cry of pain or misery

moat moats
NOUN a wide, water-filled ditch around a building such as a castle

mob mobs mobbing mobbed
NOUN **1.** a large, disorganized crowd of people: *A violent mob attacked the team bus.*
VERB **2.** If a lot of people mob someone, they crowd around the person in a disorderly way: *The band was mobbed by fans.*

mobile mobiles
ADJECTIVE **1.** able to move or be moved freely and easily: *a mobile phone* **2.** If you are mobile, you are able to travel or move about from one place to another.
NOUN **3.** a decoration consisting of several small objects that hang from threads and move when a breeze blows **4.** a cellphone
mobility NOUN

Mm

moccasin moccasins

NOUN Moccasins are flat, soft leather shoes with a raised seam above the toe.

mock mocks mocking mocked

VERB **1.** If you mock someone, you say something scornful or imitate that person's behaviour.

ADJECTIVE **2.** not genuine: *mock surprise, a mock trial, a mock examination*

mockery

NOUN Mockery is the expression of scorn or ridicule of someone.

mode modes

NOUN **1.** A mode of life or behaviour is a particular way of living or behaving. **2.** In mathematics, the mode is the biggest in a set of groups.

model models modelling modelled

NOUN OR ADJECTIVE **1.** a copy of something that shows what it looks like or how it works: *a model aircraft*

NOUN **2.** Something that is described as, for example, a model of perfection is absolutely perfect. **3.** a type or version of a machine: *Which model of cellphone did you choose?* **4.** a person who poses for a painter or a photographer **5.** a person who wears the clothes that are being displayed at a fashion show

ADJECTIVE **6.** Someone who is described as, for example, a model student, is an excellent student.

VERB **7.** If you model yourself on someone, you copy that person's behaviour because you admire him or her. **8.** To model clothes is to display them by wearing them. **9.** To model shapes or figures is to make them out of clay or wood.

modem modems

NOUN a piece of equipment that links a computer to the telephone system so that data can be transferred from one machine to another via the telephone line

moderate moderates moderating moderated

ADJECTIVE **1.** Moderate views are not extreme, and usually favour gradual changes rather than major ones. **2.** A moderate amount of something is neither large nor small.

NOUN **3.** a person whose political views are not extreme

VERB **4.** If you moderate something or if that thing moderates, it becomes less extreme or violent: *The weather moderated.*

moderately ADVERB

moderation

NOUN Moderation is control of your behaviour that stops you from acting in an extreme way: *eat in moderation*

modern

ADJECTIVE **1.** relating to the present time: *modern society* **2.** new and involving the latest ideas and equipment: *modern technology*

modernity NOUN

modernize modernizes modernizing modernized

VERB To modernize something is to introduce new methods or equipment to it.

modest

ADJECTIVE **1.** quite small in size or amount **2.** Someone who is modest does not boast about his or her abilities or possessions. **3.** shy and easily embarrassed

modestly ADVERB

modesty NOUN

modification modifications

NOUN a small change made to improve something: *I made some modifications to my bicycle.*

modify modifies modifying modified

VERB If you modify something, you change it slightly in order to improve it.

module modules

NOUN **1.** one of the parts that when put together form a whole unit or object: *There are four modules in this online training course.* **2.** a part of a machine or system that does a particular task **3.** a part of a spacecraft that can do certain things away from the main body: *the lunar module*

modular ADJECTIVE

mohair

NOUN a very soft, fluffy wool obtained from Angora goats

moist moister moistest

ADJECTIVE slightly wet

moisten moistens moistening moistened

VERB If you moisten something, you make it slightly wet.

moisture

NOUN Moisture is tiny drops of water in the air or on the ground.

molar molars

NOUN Your molars are the large teeth at the back of your mouth.

mole moles

NOUN **1.** a dark, slightly raised spot on your skin **2.** a small animal with black fur. Moles

⚠ **HEADS UP** The *t* in **moisten** is silent. It is pronounced MOY-sun.

live in tunnels underground. **3.** *an informal use* a member of an organization who is working as a spy for a rival organization

molecule molecules
NOUN the smallest amount of a substance that can exist
molecular ADJECTIVE

molest molests molesting molested
VERB To molest someone is to touch that person, especially a woman or child, in a sexual way. This is illegal.
molester NOUN

mollify mollifies mollifying mollified
VERB To mollify someone is to do something to make that person less upset or angry.

mollusc molluscs
NOUN an animal with a soft body and no backbone. Snails, slugs, clams, and mussels are all molluscs.

molten
ADJECTIVE Molten rock or metal has been heated to a very high temperature and has become a thick liquid.

moment moments
NOUN **1.** a very short period of time: *I paused for a moment.* **2.** The moment at which something happens is the point in time at which it happens: *At that moment, the doorbell rang.*
PHRASE **3.** If something is happening **at the moment**, it is happening now.

momentary
ADJECTIVE Something that is momentary lasts for only a few seconds: *a momentary lapse of concentration*
momentarily ADVERB

momentous
ADJECTIVE very important, often because of its future effect: *a momentous occasion*

momentum
NOUN **1.** Momentum is the ability that something has to keep developing: *The runner gained momentum toward the end of the race.* **2.** Momentum is also the ability that an object has to continue moving as a result of the speed it already has.

monarch monarchs
NOUN a queen, king, or other royal person who reigns over a country

monarchy monarchies
NOUN a system in which a queen or king reigns in a country

monastery monasteries
NOUN a building in which monks live
monastic ADJECTIVE

Monday Mondays
NOUN Monday is the day between Sunday and Tuesday.

money
NOUN Money is the coins or banknotes that you use to buy something.

mongrel mongrels
NOUN a dog with parents of different breeds

monitor monitors monitoring monitored
VERB **1.** If you monitor something, you regularly check its condition and progress: *Her health will be monitored daily.*
NOUN **2.** a person or thing used to check or record things **3.** the visual display unit of a computer **4.** a school student chosen to do special duties by the teacher

monk monks
NOUN a member of a male religious community

monkey monkeys
NOUN an animal that has a long tail and climbs trees

mono-
PREFIX The prefix *mono-* is used at the beginning of nouns and adjectives that have *one* as part of their meaning: *monopoly, monogamy*

monocle monocles
NOUN a glass lens worn in front of one eye only and held in place by the curve of the eye socket

monogamy
NOUN Monogamy is the custom of being married to only one person at a time.
monogamous ADJECTIVE

monologue monologues
NOUN a long speech by one person during a play or a conversation

monopoly monopolies
NOUN control of most of an industry by one or a few large companies

monotone monotones
NOUN a tone that does not vary: *He droned on in a boring monotone.*

monotonous
ADJECTIVE having a regular pattern that is very dull and boring: *monotonous work*
monotony NOUN

monsoon monsoons
NOUN the season of very heavy rain in southeast Asia

monster monsters
NOUN **1.** a large, imaginary creature that looks very frightening **2.** a cruel or frightening person
ADJECTIVE **3.** extremely large: *a monster truck*

Mm

monstrosity monstrosities
NOUN something that is large and extremely ugly: *a concrete monstrosity in the middle of the city*

monstrous
ADJECTIVE extremely shocking or unfair: *a monstrous crime*
monstrously ADVERB

montage montages
NOUN a picture or movie consisting of a combination of several different items, usually arranged to produce an emotional effect

month months
NOUN one of the 12 periods that a year is divided into

monthly monthlies
ADJECTIVE Monthly describes something that happens or appears once a month: *monthly student council meetings*

monument monuments
NOUN a large stone structure built to remind people of a famous person or event: *a monument to the hero*

monumental
ADJECTIVE **1.** A monumental building or sculpture is very large and important. **2.** very large or extreme: *We face a monumental task.*

moo moos mooing mooed
VERB When a cow moos, it makes a long, deep sound.

mood moods
NOUN **1.** the way you are feeling at a particular time: *She was in a really cheerful mood.* **2.** the feeling or attitude that a story expresses through features like word choice, character description, and setting.

moody moodier moodiest
ADJECTIVE **1.** Someone who is moody is depressed or unhappy: *My brother, despite his charm, could sulk and be moody.* **2.** Someone who is moody often changes his or her mood for no apparent reason.

moon moons
NOUN The moon is an object moving around Earth, which you see as a shining circle or crescent in the sky at night. Some other planets also have moons.

moonlight moonlights moonlighting moonlighted
NOUN **1.** Moonlight is the light that comes from the moon at night.
VERB **2.** *an informal use* If someone is moonlighting, that person has a second job

in order to supplement the wages earned at a regular job.
moonlit ADJECTIVE

moor moors mooring moored
NOUN **1.** a high area of open land
VERB **2.** If a boat is moored, it is attached to the land with a rope.

mooring moorings
NOUN a place where a ship or boat can be tied

moose
NOUN a large North American deer with flat antlers

moot moots mooting mooted
VERB *a formal word* When something is mooted, it is suggested for discussion: *The project was first mooted in 1988.*

mop mops mopping mopped
NOUN **1.** a tool for cleaning floors, consisting of a sponge or string head attached to a long handle **2.** a large amount of loose or untidy hair
VERB **3.** To mop a floor is to clean it with a mop. **4.** To mop a surface is to wipe it with a dry cloth to remove liquid.

mope mopes moping moped
VERB If you mope, you feel miserable and not interested in anything.

moped mopeds
NOUN a type of small motorcycle

moral morals
PLURAL NOUN **1.** Morals are values based on beliefs about the correct and acceptable way to behave.
ADJECTIVE **2.** concerned with whether behaviour is right or acceptable: *moral values*
morality NOUN
morally ADVERB

morale
NOUN Morale is the amount of confidence and optimism that you have: *The morale of the team was high after its last win.*

morbid
ADJECTIVE having a great interest in unpleasant things, especially death

more
ADJECTIVE **1.** *More* means a greater number or extent than something else: *He's got more chips than me.* **2.** used to refer to an additional thing or amount of something: *The detective found some more clues.*
NOUN **3.** a greater number or extent
ADVERB **4.** to a greater degree or extent: *more amused than concerned* **5.** You can use *more* in front of adjectives and adverbs to form comparatives: *You look more beautiful than ever.*

THE CITY WAS WRAPPED IN SILENCE.

THE STREETS WERE DESERTED...

A GHOST TOWN.

IT WAS AS IF EVERYONE WAS HOLED UP INSIDE, FEARING THE LIGHT OF DAY.

MOOD

▼✕

the feeling or attitude that a story expresses through features like word choice, character description, and setting

"The city was wrapped in silence."

Here is an example of words that help to set a mood. They create a feeling of being all alone. What other words could develop this mood further?

ANDY BELANGER

Mm

moreover
ADVERB used to introduce a piece of information that supports or expands the previous statement: *They have accused the government of corruption. Moreover, they have named names.*

morgue morgues
NOUN a building where unclaimed dead bodies are kept until they are identified and removed

moribund
ADJECTIVE no longer having a useful function and about to come to an end: *a moribund industry*

morning mornings
NOUN **1.** the early part of the day, ending at noon **2.** the part of the day between midnight and noon: *He was born at three in the morning.*

moron morons
NOUN *an informal word* a very stupid person
moronic ADJECTIVE

morose
ADJECTIVE miserable and badtempered

morphine
NOUN Morphine is a drug that is used to relieve pain.

Morse code
NOUN a code used for sending messages in which each letter is represented by a series of dots and dashes

morsel morsels
NOUN a small piece of food

mortal mortals
ADJECTIVE **1.** unable to live forever: *Remember that you are mortal.* **2.** A mortal wound is one that causes death.
NOUN **3.** an ordinary person

mortality
NOUN **1.** Mortality is the fact that all people must die. **2.** Mortality also refers to the number of people who die at any particular time: *a low infant mortality rate*

mortar mortars
NOUN **1.** a mixture of sand, water, and cement used to hold bricks firmly together **2.** a short cannon that fires missiles high into the air for a short distance

mortgage mortgages mortgaging mortgaged
NOUN **1.** a loan that you get, usually from a bank, in order to buy a house
VERB **2.** If you mortgage your house, you use it as a guarantee to a bank or company in order to borrow money. The bank or company can take the house from you if you do not pay back the money you have borrowed.

mortifying
ADJECTIVE embarrassing or humiliating: *My friend's rude behaviour was mortifying.*

mortuary mortuaries
NOUN a special room or building where dead bodies are kept before being buried or cremated

mosaic mosaics
NOUN a design made of small coloured stones or pieces of coloured glass set into concrete or plaster

Moslem another spelling of MUSLIM

mosque mosques
NOUN a building where Muslims go to worship

mosquito mosquitoes
NOUN Mosquitoes are small insects that bite people in order to suck their blood.

moss mosses
NOUN Moss is a soft, green or brown plant that grows on damp soil or stone.
mossy ADJECTIVE

most
ADJECTIVE OR PRONOUN **1.** Most of a group of people or things means nearly all of them: *Most people don't share your views.* **2.** The most means a larger amount than anyone or anything else: *She has the most talent in the group.*
ADVERB **3.** You can use *most* in front of adjectives or adverbs to form superlatives: *the most beautiful sunset I've ever seen*

mostly
ADVERB *Mostly* is used to show that a statement is generally true: *My friends are mostly artists.*

motel motels
NOUN a hotel providing overnight accommodation for people in the middle of a car journey

moth moths
NOUN an insect like a butterfly that usually flies at night

mother mothers mothering mothered
NOUN **1.** Your mother is the woman who gave birth to you. **2.** Your mother could also be the woman who has looked after you and brought you up.
VERB **3.** To mother someone is to look after that person and bring him or her up.

motherhood
NOUN Motherhood is the state of being a mother.

⚠ **HEADS UP** The *t* in **mortgage** is silent. It is pronounced MORE-gidj.

Mm

mother-in-law mothers-in-law
NOUN Someone's mother-in-law is the mother of that person's husband or wife.

motif motifs
NOUN a design that is used as a decoration

motion motions motioning motioned
NOUN **1.** Motion is the process of continually moving or changing position: *the motion of the ship* **2.** an action or gesture: *Apply with a brush using circular motions.* **3.** a proposal that people discuss and vote on at a meeting
VERB **4.** If you motion to someone, you make a movement with your hand in order to show that person what he or she should do: *I motioned him to proceed.*

motionless
ADJECTIVE not moving at all: *He sat motionless.*

motivate motivates motivating motivated
VERB **1.** If you are motivated by something, it makes you behave in a particular way: *She is motivated by learning rather than high grades.* **2.** If you motivate someone, you make that person feel determined to do something.
motivated ADJECTIVE
motivation NOUN

motive motives
NOUN a reason or purpose for doing something: *There was no motive for the attack.*

motley
ADJECTIVE A motley collection is made up of people or things of very different types.

motor motors
NOUN **1.** a part of a vehicle or a machine that uses electricity or fuel to produce movement so that the machine can work
ADJECTIVE **2.** concerned with or relating to vehicles with a gasoline or diesel engine: *a motor vehicle*

motorboat motorboats
NOUN a boat with an engine

motorcycle motorcycles
NOUN a two-wheeled vehicle with an engine that is ridden like a bicycle
motorcyclist NOUN

motorist motorists
NOUN a person who drives an automobile

mottled
ADJECTIVE covered with patches of different colours: *mottled leaves*

motto mottoes
NOUN a short sentence or phrase that is a rule for good or sensible behaviour

mould moulds moulding moulded
VERB **1.** To mould someone or something is to influence and change that person so he or she develops in a particular way: *Early experiences mould our behaviour for life.*
2. To mould a substance is to make it into a particular shape: *Mould the mixture into flat round cakes.*
NOUN **3.** a container used to make something into a particular shape: *a jelly mould*
4. Mould is a soft, grey or green substance that can form on old food or damp walls.
mouldy ADJECTIVE

moult moults moulting moulted
VERB When an animal or bird moults, it loses its hair or feathers so new ones can grow.

mound mounds
NOUN **1.** a small hill that is artificially made, usually with a heap of earth or stones **2.** a large, untidy pile: *a mound of blankets*

mount mounts mounting mounted
VERB **1.** To mount a campaign or event is to organize it and carry it out. **2.** If something is mounting, it is increasing: *Economic problems are mounting.* **3.** *a formal use* To mount something is to go to the top of it: *He mounted the steps.* **4.** If you mount a horse, you climb on its back. **5.** If you mount an object in a particular place, you fix it there to display it.
NOUN **6.** *Mount* is also used as part of the name of a mountain: *Mount Logan*

mountain mountains
NOUN **1.** a very high piece of land with steep sides **2.** a large amount of something: *mountains of paperwork*

mountaineer mountaineers
NOUN a person who climbs mountains

mountainous
ADJECTIVE A mountainous area has a lot of mountains.

mourn mourns mourning mourned
VERB **1.** If you mourn for someone who has died, you are very sad and think about that person a lot. **2.** If you mourn something, you are sad because you no longer have it: *He mourned the loss of his dog.*

mourner mourners
NOUN a person who attends a funeral

mournful
ADJECTIVE very sad

mourning
NOUN If someone is in mourning, that person may wear special clothes or behave in a quiet and restrained way because a member of his or her family has died.

mouse mice

NOUN **1.** a small rodent with a long tail **2.** a small device moved by hand to control the position of the cursor on a computer screen

mousse mousses

NOUN a light, fluffy food made from whipped eggs and cream

moustache another spelling of MUSTACHE

mouth mouths mouthing mouthed

NOUN **1.** your lips, or the space behind them where your tongue and teeth are **2.** The mouth of a cave or a hole is the entrance to it. **3.** The mouth of a river is the place where it flows into another body of water.
VERB **4.** If you mouth something, you form words with your lips without making any sound: *He mouthed a thank-you to the jurors.*

mouthful NOUN

mouthpiece mouthpieces

NOUN **1.** the part you speak into on a telephone **2.** the part of a musical instrument you put to your mouth **3.** The mouthpiece of an organization is the person who publicly states its opinions and policies.

movable

ADJECTIVE Something that is movable can be moved from one place to another.

move moves moving moved

VERB **1.** To move means to go to a different place or position. To move something means to change its place or position. **2.** If you move, you go to live in a different place. **3.** If something moves you, it causes you to feel a deep emotion: *Her story moved us to tears.*
NOUN **4.** a change from one place or position to another: *We were watching his every move.* **5.** the act of moving house **6.** the act of putting a piece or counter in a game in a different position: *It's your move next.*

movement movements

NOUN **1.** Movement involves changing position or going from one place to another.
PLURAL NOUN **2.** Your movements are everything you do during a period of time: *The police asked him for an account of his movements during the previous morning.*
NOUN **3.** a group of people who share the same beliefs or aims: *the peace movement* **4.** one of the major sections of a piece of classical music

moving

ADJECTIVE Something that is moving makes you feel deep sadness or emotion.

movingly ADVERB

mow mows mowing mowed mown

VERB **1.** To mow grass is to cut it with a lawnmower. **2.** To mow down a large number of people is to kill them all violently.

mower mowers

NOUN a machine for cutting grass

MP MPs

NOUN a person who has been elected to represent people in a country's parliament. MP is an abbreviation for *Member of Parliament.*

MP3 player MP3 players

NOUN a device that plays audio or video files, often used for listening to music downloaded from the Internet

Mr. *Mr.* is used before a man's name when you are speaking or referring to him.

Mrs. *Mrs.* is used before the name of a married woman when you are speaking or referring to her.

Ms. *Ms.* is used before a woman's name when you are speaking or referring to her. Ms. does not specify whether a woman is married or not.

much

ADVERB **1.** You use *much* to emphasize that something is true to a great extent: *I feel much better now.* **2.** If something does not happen much, it does not happen very often.
ADJECTIVE OR PRONOUN **3.** You use *much* to ask questions or give information about the size or amount of something: *How much money do you need?*

muck mucks mucking mucked

NOUN **1.** *an informal use* Muck is dirt or some other unpleasant substance. **2.** Muck is also manure.
VERB **3.** *an informal use* If you muck about, you behave stupidly and waste time.

mucky ADJECTIVE

mucus

NOUN Mucus is a liquid produced in parts of your body, for example in your nose.

mud

NOUN Mud is wet, sticky earth.

muddle muddles muddling muddled

NOUN **1.** A muddle is a state of disorder or untidiness: *Their finances are in a muddle.*
VERB **2.** If you muddle things, you mix them up.

muddy muddier muddiest

ADJECTIVE **1.** covered in mud **2.** A muddy colour is dull and not clear: *a mottled, muddy brown*

⚠ **HEADS UP** The word **mucus** is pronounced MYOO-cuss.

Mm

muesli

NOUN Muesli is a mixture of chopped nuts, cereal flakes, and dried fruit that you can eat for breakfast with milk.

muffin muffins

NOUN a small, round cake, often eaten with butter: *a bran muffin, a blueberry muffin*

muffled

ADJECTIVE A muffled sound is quiet or difficult to hear: *a muffled explosion*

mug mugs mugging mugged

NOUN **1.** a large, deep cup with a handle **2.** *an informal use* a person's face

VERB **3.** *an informal use* If someone mugs you, that person attacks you in order to steal your money.

mugging NOUN

mugger NOUN

muggy muggier muggiest

ADJECTIVE Muggy weather is unpleasantly warm and humid.

mule mules

NOUN the offspring of a female horse and a male donkey

mull mulls mulling mulled

VERB If you mull something over, you think about it for a long time before making a decision.

multi-

PREFIX The prefix *multi-* is used to form words that refer to something that has many parts or aspects: *a multistorey parking garage*

multicultural

ADJECTIVE If a society is multicultural, that society contains several distinct cultures.

multiculturalism

NOUN **1.** the fact or condition of being multicultural **2.** a policy supporting or promoting the independent identities of several distinct cultural groups that exist side by side within a society

multimedia

NOUN **1.** in computing, you use *multimedia* to refer to products that use sound, pictures, film, and ordinary text to convey information **2.** in the classroom, all the things like TV, computers, and books that are used as teaching aids are called multimedia

multinational multinationals

NOUN a very large company with branches in many countries

multiple multiples

ADJECTIVE **1.** having or involving many different functions or things: *He suffered from multiple injuries in the crash.*

NOUN **2.** The multiples of a number are other numbers that it will divide into exactly. For example, 6, 9, and 12 are multiples of 3.

multiple sclerosis

NOUN Multiple sclerosis is a serious disease that attacks the nervous system, affecting a person's ability to move.

multiplication

NOUN **1.** Multiplication is the process of multiplying one number by another. **2.** The multiplication of things is a large increase in their number: *the multiplication of universities*

multiplicity

NOUN If there is a multiplicity of things, there is a large number or variety of them.

multiply multiplies multiplying multiplied

VERB **1.** When something multiplies, it increases greatly in number: *As we climbed higher, the hazards multiplied.* **2.** When you multiply one number by another, you calculate the total you would get if you added the first number to itself a particular number of times. For example, two multiplied by three is equal to two plus two plus two, which equals six.

multitude multitudes

NOUN *a formal word* a very large number of people or things

mom moms

NOUN *an informal word* Your mom is your mother.

mumble mumbles mumbling mumbled

VERB If you mumble, you speak very quietly and indistinctly.

mummy mummies

NOUN a dead body that was preserved long ago by being rubbed with special oils and wrapped in cloth

mumps

NOUN Mumps is an infectious illness that causes painful swelling in the neck glands.

munch munches munching munched

VERB If you munch something, you chew it steadily and thoroughly.

mundane

ADJECTIVE very ordinary and not interesting or unusual: *a mundane job*

municipal

ADJECTIVE belonging to a city or town that has its own local government: *a municipal swimming pool*

munitions

PLURAL NOUN Munitions are bombs, guns, and other military supplies.

Mm

mural murals
NOUN a picture painted on a wall

murder murders murdering murdered
NOUN **1.** Murder is the deliberate killing of a person.
VERB **2.** To murder someone is to kill that person deliberately.
murderer NOUN

murderous
ADJECTIVE **1.** likely to murder someone: *murderous gangsters* **2.** A murderous attack or other action results in the death of many people: *murderous acts of terrorism*

murky murkier murkiest
ADJECTIVE dark or dirty and unpleasant: *a murky pool*

murmur murmurs murmuring murmured
VERB **1.** If you murmur, you say something very softly.
NOUN **2.** something that someone says that can hardly be heard

muscle muscles muscling muscled
NOUN **1.** Your muscles are pieces of flesh that you can expand or contract in order to move parts of your body.
VERB **2.** *an informal use* If you muscle in on something, you force your way into a situation in which you are not welcome.

muscular
ADJECTIVE **1.** involving or affecting your muscles: *muscular strength* **2.** Someone who is muscular has strong, firm muscles.

muse muses musing mused
VERB *a literary or poetic use* To muse is to think about something for a long time.

museum museums
NOUN a building where many interesting or valuable objects are kept and displayed

mush
NOUN A mush is a thick, soft substance.

mushroom mushrooms mushrooming mushroomed
NOUN **1.** a fungus with a short stem and a round top. Some types of mushroom are edible.
VERB **2.** If something mushrooms, it appears and grows very quickly: *Small farming communities mushroomed into cities.*

mushy mushier mushiest
ADJECTIVE **1.** Mushy fruits or vegetables are too soft: *mushy tomatoes* **2.** *an informal use* Mushy stories are too sentimental.

music
NOUN **1.** Music is a pattern of sounds performed by people singing or playing instruments. **2.** Music is also the written symbols that represent musical sounds: *I taught myself to read music.*

musical musicals
ADJECTIVE **1.** relating to playing or studying music: *a musical instrument*
NOUN **2.** a play or movie that uses songs and dance to tell the story
musically ADVERB

musician musicians
NOUN a person who plays a musical instrument as his or her job or hobby

musk
NOUN Musk is a substance with a strong, sweet smell. It is used to make perfume.
musky ADJECTIVE

musket muskets
NOUN an old-fashioned gun with a long barrel

Muslim Muslims
NOUN **1.** a person who believes in Islam and lives according to its rules
ADJECTIVE **2.** relating to Islam

muslin
NOUN Muslin is a very thin cotton material.

mussel mussels
NOUN a kind of shellfish with a black shell

must
VERB **1.** If something must happen, it is very important or necessary that it happens: *You must be 16 before you can get a driver's licence.* **2.** If you tell someone that he or she must do something, you are suggesting that that person does this thing: *You must try this cake: it's delicious.*
NOUN **3.** something that is absolutely necessary: *Visiting the museum is a must for all visitors.*

mustache mustaches
NOUN A man's mustache is hair growing on his upper lip.

mustard
NOUN Mustard is a spicy-tasting yellow or brown paste made from seeds.

muster musters mustering mustered
VERB If you muster something such as energy or support, you gather it together: *as much calm as he could muster*

musty mustier mustiest
ADJECTIVE smelling stale and damp: *musty old books*

mutate mutates mutating mutated
VERB If something mutates, its structure or appearance alters in some way: *Viruses react to change and can mutate fast.*
mutation NOUN
mutant NOUN OR ADJECTIVE

Mm

mute
ADJECTIVE *a formal word* not giving out sound or speech: *mute amazement*

muted
ADJECTIVE **1.** Muted colours or sounds are soft and gentle. **2.** A muted reaction is not very strong.

mutilate mutilates mutilating mutilated
VERB **1.** If someone is mutilated, that person's body is badly injured: *Her leg was badly mutilated.* **2.** If you mutilate something, you deliberately damage or spoil it: *Almost every book had been mutilated.*
mutilation NOUN

mutiny mutinies
NOUN A mutiny is a rebellion against someone in authority.

mutter mutters muttering muttered
VERB To mutter is to speak in a very low and perhaps angry voice: *My sister muttered something under her breath.*

mutton
NOUN Mutton is the meat of an adult sheep.

mutual
ADJECTIVE used to describe something that two or more people share: *They had a mutual interest in rugby.*

mutually
ADVERB Mutually describes a situation in which two or more people feel the same way about each other: *a mutually supportive relationship*

muzzle muzzles muzzling muzzled
NOUN **1.** the nose and mouth of an animal **2.** a cover or a strap for a dog's nose and mouth to prevent it from biting **3.** the open end of a gun through which the bullets come out
VERB **4.** To muzzle a dog is to put a muzzle on it.

my
ADJECTIVE *My* refers to something belonging or relating to the person speaking or writing: *I held my breath.*

> ⚠ **HEADS UP**
>
> **My** always comes before a noun: *That's my money.* **Mine** almost always comes after the noun: *That money is mine!*

myna mynas
NOUN a tropical bird that can mimic speech and sounds

myriad myriads
NOUN OR ADJECTIVE *a literary or poetic word* a very large number of people or things

myrrh
NOUN Myrrh is a fragrant substance used in perfume and incense.

myself
PRONOUN **1.** *Myself* is used when the person speaking or writing does an action and is affected by it: *I was ashamed of myself.* **2.** *Myself* is also used to emphasize I: *I find it a bit odd myself.*

mysterious
ADJECTIVE **1.** strange and not well understood **2.** secretive about something: *Stop being so mysterious.*
mysteriously ADVERB

mystery mysteries
NOUN something that is not understood or known about

mystic mystics
NOUN **1.** a religious person who spends long hours meditating
ADJECTIVE **2.** Mystic means the same as mystical.

mystical
ADJECTIVE involving spiritual powers and influences: *a mystical experience*
mysticism NOUN

mystify mystifies mystifying mystified
VERB If something mystifies you, you find it impossible to understand.

mystique
NOUN Mystique is an atmosphere of mystery and importance associated with a particular person or thing.

myth myths
NOUN **1.** an untrue belief or explanation **2.** a story that was made up long ago to explain natural events and religious beliefs: *Viking myths*

mythical
ADJECTIVE imaginary, untrue, or existing only in myths: *a mythical beast*

mythology
NOUN Mythology refers to stories that have been made up in the past to explain natural events or justify religious beliefs.
mythological ADJECTIVE

Nn

nag nags nagging nagged
VERB **1.** If you nag someone, you keep complaining to that person about something. **2.** If something nags at you, it keeps worrying you.

nail nails nailing nailed
NOUN **1.** a small piece of metal with a sharp point at one end that you hammer into objects to hold them together **2.** Your nails are the thin, hard areas covering the ends of your fingers and toes.
VERB **3.** If you nail something somewhere, you fit it there using a nail.

naive
ADJECTIVE foolishly believing that things are easier or less complicated than they really are
naively ADVERB
naivete NOUN

naked
ADJECTIVE **1.** not wearing any clothes or not covered by anything **2.** shown openly and without the addition of anything else: *naked aggression, the naked truth*
nakedness NOUN

name names naming named
NOUN **1.** a word that you use to identify a person, place, or thing **2.** Someone's name is also his or her reputation: *My only wish now is to clear my name.*
VERB **3.** If you name someone or something, you give that person or thing a name or you say that person's or thing's name. **4.** If you name a price or a date, you say what you want it to be.

nameless
ADJECTIVE You describe someone or something as nameless when you do not know that person's or thing's name, or when a name has not yet been given to that person or thing.

namely
ADVERB Namely means *that is*. It is used to introduce more detailed information about what you have just said: *My grandparents own some land, namely a farm and a 20-hectare maple bush.*

namesake namesakes
NOUN Your namesake is someone with the same name as you: *I also share a birthday with my namesake.*

nanny nannies
NOUN a woman whose job is to look after young children

nap naps napping napped
NOUN **1.** a short sleep
VERB **2.** When you nap, you have a short sleep.

nape napes
NOUN The nape of your neck is the back of it.

napkin napkins
NOUN a small piece of cloth or paper used to wipe your hands and mouth after eating

narcotic narcotics
NOUN a drug, especially an illegal one, that affects mood or behaviour

narrate narrates narrating narrated
VERB If you narrate a story, you tell it.
narration NOUN

narrative narratives
NOUN a story or an account of events

narrator narrators
NOUN **1.** a person who is reading or telling a story out loud **2.** a character in a novel who tells the story

narrow narrower narrowest; narrows narrowing narrowed
ADJECTIVE **1.** having a small distance from one side to the other: *a narrow stream* **2.** concerned only with a few aspects of something and ignoring the important

KNOWING WORDS: IDIOMS

BE WORD SHARP!

Idioms add colour to language by playing with the meanings of words.

name a word to identify a person, place, or thing

call someone names insult someone by using bad names

clear your name prove you are not guilty

in name only supposed to be, but isn't

in the name of on the authority of

name of the game the main point

Nn

points: *people with a narrow point of view*
3. A narrow escape or victory is one that you only just achieve.
VERB **4.** To narrow means to become less wide: *The road narrowed.*
narrowly ADVERB

narrow-minded
ADJECTIVE unwilling to consider new ideas

nasal
ADJECTIVE **1.** relating to the nose: *the nasal passages* **2.** Nasal sounds are made by breathing out through your nose as you speak.

nasty nastier nastiest
ADJECTIVE very unpleasant: *a nasty shock*
nastily ADVERB
nastiness NOUN

nation nations
NOUN a community of people occupying and possessing a defined territory, united under one government: *the Canadian nation*

HEADS UP
In Canada, **nation** can also mean *a people with a shared history*: the Québécois nation, First Nations.

national nationals
ADJECTIVE **1.** relating to the whole of a country: *a national newspaper, national laws* **2.** typical of a particular country: *national dress, a national trait*
NOUN **3.** A national of a country is a citizen of that country: *Many Canadian nationals travel to warmer climates during the winter.*
nationally ADVERB

national anthem national anthems
NOUN a country's official patriotic song

nationalism
NOUN **1.** Nationalism is love of your own country. **2.** Nationalism is also a desire for the independence of a country; also a political movement aiming to achieve such independence.
nationalist NOUN
nationalistic ADJECTIVE

nationality nationalities
NOUN Nationality is the fact of belonging to a particular country.

nationalize nationalizes nationalizing nationalized
VERB To nationalize an industry means to

bring it under the control and ownership of a national government.
nationalization NOUN

nationwide
ADJECTIVE OR ADVERB happening all over a country: *a nationwide search, a nationwide election*

native natives
ADJECTIVE **1.** Your native country is the country where you were born. **2.** *Native* also refers to a member of a people who are descended from the original inhabitants of a region or country. In Canada, this name may be offensive to a First Nations, Métis, or Inuit person, and should be replaced by the name *Aboriginal*. **3.** Your native language is the language that you first learned to speak. **4.** Animals or plants that are native to a place live or grow there naturally and have not been brought there by people.
NOUN **5.** A native of a place is someone who was born there.

natter natters nattering nattered
VERB *an informal word* If you natter, you talk for a long period of time about unimportant things.

natural naturals
ADJECTIVE **1.** normal and to be expected: *It was only natural that he was tempted.* **2.** not trying to pretend or hide anything: *The doctor's natural manner reassured her.* **3.** existing or happening in nature: *natural disasters* **4.** A natural ability is one you were born with. **5.** Your natural mother or father is your mother or father by birth and not someone who has adopted you.
NOUN **6.** someone who is born with a particular ability: *My sister is a natural at sports.* **7.** In music, a natural is a note that is not a sharp or a flat. It is represented by the symbol (♮).
naturally ADVERB

nature natures
NOUN **1.** Nature is animals, plants, and all the other things in the world not made by people. **2.** The nature of a person or thing is the basic character of that person or thing: *I liked his warm, generous nature.*

naughty naughtier naughtiest
ADJECTIVE **1.** behaving badly **2.** rude or indecent: *naughty language*
naughtiness NOUN

nausea
NOUN Nausea is a feeling in your stomach that you are going to be sick.
nauseous ADJECTIVE

Nn

nautical
ADJECTIVE relating to ships or navigation

naval
ADJECTIVE relating to or having a navy: *naval officers, naval bases*

navel navels
NOUN the small hollow on the front of your body just below your waist

navigate navigates navigating navigated
VERB **1.** When someone navigates, that person works out the direction in which a ship, plane, or car should go, using maps and sometimes instruments. **2.** To navigate a stretch of water means to travel safely across it: *It was the first time I had navigated the rapids.*
navigation NOUN
navigator NOUN

navy navies
NOUN **1.** the part of a country's armed forces that fights at sea
ADJECTIVE **2.** dark blue

N.B. You write N.B. to draw attention to what you are going to write next. N.B. is an abbreviation for the Latin *nota bene*, which means *note well*.

near nearer nearest; nears nearing neared
PREPOSITION **1.** not far from
ADJECTIVE **2.** not far away in distance **3.** not far away in time **4.** You can also use *near* to mean almost: *a night of near disaster*
VERB **5.** When you are nearing something, you are approaching it and will soon reach it: *The dog began to bark as the letter carrier neared the porch.*

Instead of **NEAR** try...

nearby
ADJECTIVE
OR ADVERB
only a short distance away

nearly
ADVERB not completely but almost

near-sighted
ADJECTIVE If you are near-sighted, you cannot see things clearly when they are far away.

neat neater neatest
ADJECTIVE **1.** tidy and in order **2.** able and willing to keep things in order: *He is a very neat person.*
neatly ADVERB
neatness NOUN

close by the school

keep a pencil handy

beside the other books

a storm is approaching

verging on a breakthrough

necessarily
ADVERB Something that is not necessarily the case is not always or inevitably the case.

necessary
ADJECTIVE **1.** Something that is necessary is needed or must be done. **2.** *a formal use* Necessary also means certain or inevitable:
a necessary consequence of war

Instead of **NECESSARY** try...

our **vital** organs

essential nutrients

required for graduation

attendance is **mandatory**

fundamental human rights

necessity
necessities
NOUN **1.** Necessity is the need to do something: *There is no necessity for any of this.* **2.** A necessity is a basic requirement.

neck necks
NOUN **1.** the part of your body that joins your head to the rest of your body **2.** the long narrow part at the top of a bottle

necklace necklaces
NOUN a piece of jewellery that is worn around the neck

nectar
NOUN Nectar is a sweet liquid produced by flowers and attractive to insects.

nectarine nectarines
NOUN a kind of peach with a smooth skin

née
ADJECTIVE *Née* is used to indicate what a female's surname was before she got married: *Sara Black, née Wells*

need needs needing needed
VERB **1.** If you need something, you believe that you must have it or do it.
NOUN **2.** Your needs are the things that you need to have. **3.** a strong feeling that you must have or do something: *I just felt the need to write about it.*

needle needles needling needled
NOUN **1.** a small, thin piece of metal used for sewing that is pointed at one end and has a hole at the other **2.** Needles are also long, thin pieces of steel or plastic, used for knitting. **3.** the part of a syringe that a doctor or nurse sticks into your body **4.** the thin piece of metal or plastic on a dial that moves to show a measurement **5.** The needles of a pine tree are its leaves.
VERB **6.** *an informal use* If someone needles you, that person annoys or provokes you.

needless
ADJECTIVE unnecessary
needlessly ADVERB

needy needier neediest
ADJECTIVE very poor

negative negatives
ADJECTIVE **1.** A negative answer means *no*.
2. Someone who is negative sees only problems and disadvantages: *Why are you so negative about everything?* **3.** If a medical or scientific test is negative, it shows that something has not happened or is not present: *The blood test came back negative.*
4. A negative number is less than zero.
NOUN **5.** the image that is first produced when you take a photograph using film
negatively ADVERB

> ⚠ **HEADS UP**
>
> Don't use two negatives in the same sentence: *I don't know **nothing*** should be *I don't know **anything***.

neglect neglects neglecting neglected
VERB **1.** If you neglect something, you do not look after it properly. **2.** *a formal use* If you neglect to do something, you fail to do it: *He had neglected to give her his address.*
NOUN **3.** Neglect is failure to look after something or someone properly: *Most of the plants died from neglect.*
neglectful ADJECTIVE

negligent
ADJECTIVE not taking enough care: *Her negligent driving resulted in an accident.*
negligence NOUN

negligible
ADJECTIVE very small and unimportant: *a negligible amount of fat*

negotiable
ADJECTIVE able to be changed or agreed by discussion: *All prices are negotiable.*

negotiate negotiates negotiating negotiated
VERB **1.** When people negotiate, they have formal discussions in order to reach an agreement about something. **2.** If you negotiate an obstacle, you manage to get over it or around it.
negotiation NOUN
negotiator NOUN

neigh neighs neighing neighed
VERB **1.** When a horse neighs, it makes a loud, high-pitched sound.
NOUN **2.** a loud sound made by a horse

neighbour neighbours
NOUN **1.** Your neighbour is someone who lives next door to you or near you. **2.** Your neighbour is also someone standing or sitting next to you: *I got chatting with my neighbour in the studio.*

neighbourhood neighbourhoods
NOUN a district where people live: *a safe neighbourhood*

neighbouring
ADJECTIVE situated nearby: *schools in neighbouring areas*

neither
ADJECTIVE OR PRONOUN used to indicate that a negative statement refers to two or more things or people: *It's neither a play nor a musical. Neither of them spoke.*

neo-
PREFIX The prefix *neo-* means *new* or *modern*: *neolithic, neoclassical*

nephew nephews
NOUN Someone's nephew is the son of that person's sister or brother.

Neptune
NOUN Neptune is the planet in the solar system that is eighth from the sun.

nerve nerves
NOUN **1.** a long, thin fibre that sends messages between your brain and other parts of your body **2.** If you talk about someone's nerves, you are referring to how able that person is to remain calm in a difficult situation: *It needs confidence and strong nerves.* **3.** Nerve is courage: *The golfer held his nerve to sink the putt.* **4.** *an informal use* Nerve is boldness or rudeness: *He had the nerve to swear at me.*
INFORMAL PHRASE **5.** If someone **gets on your nerves**, that person irritates you.

nerve-racking
ADJECTIVE making you feel very worried and tense: *a nerve-racking experience*

nervous
ADJECTIVE **1.** worried and frightened **2.** a state of anticipation or anxiety that affects your emotions or mental health
nervously ADVERB
nervousness NOUN

nervous breakdown nervous breakdowns
NOUN an illness in which someone suffers from deep depression, stress, or anxiety

nervous system nervous systems
NOUN Your nervous system is the nerves in your body together with your brain and spinal cord.

-ness

SUFFIX The suffix *-ness* forms nouns from adjectives: *tenderness, happiness*

nest nests nesting nested

NOUN **1.** a place that a bird makes to lay its eggs in; also a place that some insects and other animals make to rear their young in
VERB **2.** When birds nest, they build a nest and lay eggs in it.

nestle nestles nestling nestled

VERB If you nestle somewhere, you settle there comfortably, often pressing up against someone else: *A new puppy nestled in her lap.*

nestling nestlings

NOUN a young bird that has not yet learned to fly, and so has not left the nest

net nets

NOUN **1.** a piece of material made of threads woven together with small spaces in between **2.** The Net is the same as the INTERNET. ADJECTIVE **3.** A net result or amount is final, after everything has been considered: *a net profit of 171 million dollars* **4.** The net weight of something is its weight without its wrapping.

netball

NOUN Netball is a game similar to basketball, played by two teams of seven players, in which each team tries to score goals by throwing a ball through a net at the top of a pole.

netting

NOUN Netting is material made of threads or metal wires woven together with small spaces in between.

nettle nettles

NOUN a wild plant covered with little hairs that sting

network networks

NOUN **1.** a large number of lines or roads that cross each other at many points: *a small network of side roads* **2.** A network of people or organizations is a large number of them that work together as a system: *the public telephone network* **3.** A television or radio network is a group of broadcasting stations that transmit many of the same programs at the same time. **4.** a group of computers connected to each other

neuron neurons

NOUN a cell that is part of the nervous system and conducts messages to and from the brain

neurosis neuroses

NOUN Neurosis is mental illness that causes people to have strong and unreasonable fears and worries.

neurotic

ADJECTIVE having strong and unreasonable fears and worries: *He was almost neurotic about being followed.*

neuter neuters neutering neutered

VERB **1.** When an animal is neutered, its reproductive organs are removed.
ADJECTIVE **2.** In some languages, a neuter noun or pronoun is one that is not masculine or feminine.

neutral neutrals

ADJECTIVE **1.** People who are neutral do not support either side in a disagreement or war. **2.** The neutral wire in an electric plug is the one that is neither positive nor negative. **3.** A neutral colour is not definite or striking, for example pale grey. **4.** In chemistry, a neutral substance is neither acid nor alkaline.
NOUN **5.** a person or country that does not support either side in a disagreement or war **6.** Neutral is the position between the gears of a vehicle in which the engine is not connected to the gears and so cannot move the vehicle.
neutrality NOUN

neutron neutrons

NOUN an atomic particle that has no electrical charge

never

ADVERB at no time in the past, present, or future

KNOWING WORDS: WORD BUILDING

BE WORD SHARP!

You can create new words by adding prefixes and suffixes to a base word.

-ness a suffix that turns an adjective into a noun

alertness the quality of being alert

darkness the condition of being dark

laziness the quality of being lazy

nosiness the quality of being nosy

illness the condition of being ill

nevertheless
ADVERB in spite of what has just been said: *They dress plainly but nevertheless look quite smart.*

new newer newest
ADJECTIVE **1.** recently made, created, or discovered: *a new house, a new plan, a new virus* **2.** not used or owned before: *We've got a new car.* **3.** different or unfamiliar: *a name*

Instead of **NEW** try…

cutting edge research

the **latest** fashion

a **rookie** player

a **fresh** start

a **novel** idea

recent developments

an **original** screenplay

an **up-to-date** computer

that was new to me

newborn
ADJECTIVE born recently

newcomer newcomers
NOUN someone who has recently arrived in a place

newly
ADVERB recently: *the newly born baby*

new moon new moons
NOUN The moon is a new moon when it is a thin crescent shape at the start of its four-week cycle.

news
NOUN News is information about things that have happened.

newspaper newspapers
NOUN a publication, on large sheets of paper, that is produced regularly and contains news and articles

newt newts
NOUN a small amphibious creature with moist skin, short legs, and a long tail

New Year
NOUN New Year is the time when people celebrate the start of a year.

next
ADJECTIVE **1.** coming immediately after something else: *Their next child was a girl.* **2.** in a position nearest to something: *in the next room*
ADVERB **3.** coming immediately after something else: *My cousin arrived next.*
PHRASE **4.** If one thing is **next to** another, it is at the side of it.

next-door
ADJECTIVE OR ADVERB in the house next to yours

nib nibs
NOUN the pointed end of a pen

nibble nibbles nibbling nibbled
VERB **1.** When you nibble something, you take small bites of it.
NOUN **2.** a small bite of something

nice nicer nicest

a **relaxing** atmosphere

a **stylish** outfit

a **kind** gesture

fine work

Instead of **NICE** try…

ADJECTIVE **1.** pleasant or attractive **2.** thoughtful and kind
nicely ADVERB

bright weather

a **winning** smile

a **welcome** change

a **good-natured** person

nicety niceties
NOUN a small detail: *the social niceties*

niche niches
NOUN **1.** a hollow area in a wall **2.** If you say that you have found your niche, you mean that you have found a job or way of life that is exactly right for you.

nick nicks nicking nicked
VERB **1.** If you nick something, you make a small cut in its surface: *He nicked his chin.*
NOUN **2.** a small cut in the surface of something

nickel
NOUN Nickel is a silver-coloured metal that is used in making steel.

nickname nicknames nicknaming nicknamed
NOUN **1.** an informal name given to someone
VERB **2.** If you nickname someone, you give that person a nickname.

nicotine
NOUN Nicotine is an addictive substance found in tobacco.

niece nieces
NOUN Someone's niece is the daughter of that person's sister or brother.

nifty
ADJECTIVE pleasing or cleverly done

night nights
NOUN Night is the time between sunset and sunrise, when it is dark.

nightclub nightclubs
NOUN a place where people go late in the evening to drink and dance

Nn

nightgown nightgowns
NOUN a loose dress that a female wears to sleep in

nightfall
NOUN Nightfall is the time of day when it starts to get dark.

nightingale nightingales
NOUN a small, brown European bird, the male of which sings very beautifully, especially at night

nightly
ADJECTIVE OR ADVERB happening every night: *the nightly news*

nightmare nightmares
NOUN a very frightening dream; also used of any very unpleasant or frightening situation: *The ice storm was a nightmare.*
nightmarish ADJECTIVE

nil
NOUN Nil means zero or nothing. It is used especially in sports scores.

nimble nimbler nimblest
ADJECTIVE **1.** able to move quickly and easily **2.** able to think quickly and cleverly
nimbly ADVERB

nine nines
NOUN the number 9
ninth ADJECTIVE, ADVERB

nineteen
NOUN the number 19
nineteenth ADJECTIVE, ADVERB

ninety nineties
NOUN the number 90
ninetieth ADJECTIVE, ADVERB

nip nips nipping nipped
VERB **1.** *an informal use* If you nip somewhere, you go there quickly. **2.** To nip someone or something means to pinch that person or thing slightly.
NOUN **3.** a light pinch

nipple nipples
NOUN Your nipples are the two small pieces of projecting flesh on your chest. Babies suck milk through the nipples on their mothers' breasts.

nirvana
NOUN Nirvana is the ultimate state of spiritual enlightenment that can be achieved in the Hindu and Buddhist religions.

nit nits
NOUN Nits are the eggs of a kind of louse that sometimes lives in people's hair.

nitrogen
NOUN Nitrogen is a chemical element usually found as a gas. It forms about 78 percent of Earth's atmosphere.

no
INTERJECTION **1.** used to say that something is not true or to refuse something
ADJECTIVE **2.** none at all or not at all: *She gave no reason. You're no friend of mine.*
ADVERB **3.** used with a comparative to mean *not*: *no later than July 24*

No. a written abbreviation for NUMBER

nobility
NOUN **1.** Nobility is the quality of being noble: *the unmistakable nobility of his character* **2.** The nobility of a society are all the people who have titles and high social rank.

noble nobler noblest; nobles
ADJECTIVE **1.** honest and brave, and deserving admiration **2.** very impressive: *the noble Rocky Mountains*
NOUN **3.** a member of the nobility
nobly ADVERB

nobleman noblemen
NOUN a man who is a member of the nobility
noblewoman NOUN

nobody nobodies
PRONOUN **1.** not a single person
NOUN **2.** Someone who is a nobody is not at all important.

nocturnal
ADJECTIVE **1.** happening at night: *a nocturnal journey through the city* **2.** active at night: *a nocturnal animal*

nod nods nodding nodded
VERB **1.** When you nod, you move your head up and down, usually to show agreement.
NOUN **2.** a movement of your head up and down
nod off
VERB **3.** If you nod off, you fall asleep.

noise noises
NOUN a sound, especially one that is loud or unpleasant

noisy noisier noisiest
ADJECTIVE making a lot of noise or full of noise: *a noisy crowd*
noisily ADVERB
noisiness NOUN

nomad nomads
NOUN a member of a people who travel from place to place rather than living in just one place
nomadic ADJECTIVE

nominal
ADJECTIVE **1.** Something that is nominal is supposed to have a particular identity or status, but in reality does not have it: *the nominal leader of his party* **2.** A nominal amount of money is very small compared to

the value of something: *I am prepared to sell my shares at a nominal price.*
nominally ADVERB

nominate nominates nominating nominated
VERB If you nominate someone for a job or position, you formally suggest that that person get it.
nomination NOUN

non-
PREFIX The prefix *non-* means *not*: *non-smoking*

nonchalant
ADJECTIVE seeming calm and not worried
nonchalance NOUN
nonchalantly ADVERB

non-commissioned non-commissioned
NOUN an officer such as a sergeant or corporal who has been promoted from the lower ranks

nondescript
ADJECTIVE Someone or something nondescript has no special or interesting qualities or details: *a nondescript coat*

none
PRONOUN not a single thing or person, or not even a small amount of something

nonfiction
NOUN Nonfiction is writing that gives facts and information rather than telling a story.

nonplussed
ADJECTIVE confused and unsure about how to react

nonsense
NOUN Nonsense is foolish and meaningless words or behaviour.
nonsensical ADJECTIVE

non-stop
ADJECTIVE OR ADVERB continuing without any pauses or breaks: *non-stop excitement*

noodle noodles
NOUN Noodles are a kind of pasta shaped into long, thin pieces.

nook nooks
NOUN *a literary or poetic word* a small, sheltered place

noon
NOUN Noon is midday.

no one
PRONOUN not a single person

noose nooses
NOUN a loop at the end of a piece of rope, with a knot that tightens when the rope is pulled

nor
CONJUNCTION used after *neither* or after a negative statement, to add something else that the negative statement applies to: *They had neither the time nor the money for the sport.*

norm
NOUN If something is the norm, it is the usual and expected thing: *cultures where large families are the norm*

normal
ADJECTIVE usual and ordinary: *I try to lead a normal life.*
normality NOUN

normally
ADVERB **1.** usually: *I don't normally like dancing.* **2.** in a way that is normal: *The fetus is developing normally.*

north
NOUN **1.** The north is the direction to your left when you are looking toward the place where the sun rises. **2.** The north of a place or country is the part that is toward the north when you are in the centre of that place or country.
ADVERB OR ADJECTIVE **3.** North means toward the north: *The helicopter took off and headed north.*
ADJECTIVE **4.** A north wind blows from the north.

Nn

KNOWING WORDS: WORD BUILDING

BE WORD SHARP!

You can create new words by adding prefixes and suffixes to a base word.

non- a prefix that means *not*

nonflammable not flammable

non-issue something that's not a relevant issue

non-profit not done for profit

non-renewable not able to be replaced

non-stick designed not to stick, like some frying pans

Nn

North America

NOUN North America is the third-largest continent, consisting of Canada, the United States, and Mexico.

North American North Americans

ADJECTIVE **1.** belonging or relating to North America

NOUN **2.** someone who comes from North America

northeast

NOUN, ADVERB, OR ADJECTIVE Northeast is halfway between north and east.

northeasterly

ADJECTIVE **1.** Northeasterly means to or toward the northeast. **2.** A northeasterly wind blows from the northeast.

northeastern

ADJECTIVE in or from the northeast

northerly

ADJECTIVE **1.** Northerly means to or toward the north: *travelling in a northerly direction* **2.** A northerly wind blows from the north.

northern

ADJECTIVE in or from the north: *the rivers of northern Canada*

North Pole

NOUN The North Pole is the most northerly point of the earth's surface.

northward

ADVERB **1.** Northward means toward the north: *We continued northward.* ADJECTIVE **2.** The northward part of something is the north part.

northwest

NOUN, ADVERB, OR ADJECTIVE Northwest is halfway between north and west.

northwesterly

ADJECTIVE **1.** Northwesterly means to or toward the northwest. **2.** A northwesterly wind blows from the northwest.

northwestern

ADJECTIVE in or from the northwest

nose noses

NOUN **1.** the part of your face above your mouth that you use for smelling and breathing **2.** the front part of a ship or aircraft

nostalgia

NOUN Nostalgia is a feeling of affection for the past, and sadness that things have changed.

nostalgic ADJECTIVE

nostril nostrils

NOUN Your nostrils are the two openings in your nose that you breathe through.

nosy nosier nosiest

ADJECTIVE trying to find out about things that do not concern you

not

ADVERB used to make a sentence negative, to refuse something, or to deny something

notable

ADJECTIVE important or interesting: *The production is notable for some outstanding performances.*

notably ADVERB

notch notches

NOUN a small V-shaped cut in a surface

note notes noting noted

NOUN **1.** a short letter or e-mail **2.** a written piece of information that helps you to remember something: *You should make a note of that.* **3.** In music, a note is a musical sound of a particular pitch, or a written symbol that represents it. **4.** an atmosphere, feeling, or quality: *There was a note of regret in his voice. The presentation ended on an optimistic note.*

VERB **5.** If you note a fact, you become aware of it or you mention it: *I noted that the rain had stopped.*

PHRASE **6.** If you **make a note of** something, you write it down so that you will remember it. **7.** If you **take note of** something, you pay attention to it: *The world hardly took note of this crisis.*

notebook notebooks

NOUN a small book for writing notes in

noted

ADJECTIVE well known and admired: *a noted Canadian history scholar*

nothing

PRONOUN not anything: *There was nothing to do.*

notice notices noticing noticed

VERB **1.** If you notice something, you become aware of it.

NOUN **2.** Notice is attention or awareness: *I'm glad he brought it to my notice.* **3.** a written announcement **4.** Notice is also advance warning about something: *We were lucky to get this guest speaker at such short notice.*

PHRASE **5.** If you **hand in your notice**, you tell your employer that you intend to leave your job after a fixed period of time.

noticeable

ADJECTIVE obvious and easy to see: *a noticeable improvement*

noticeably ADVERB

notify notifies notifying notified

VERB To notify someone of something means

to officially inform that person of it: *You must notify them of any change of address.*

notification NOUN

notion notions
NOUN an idea or belief

notorious
ADJECTIVE well known for something bad: *The area has become notorious for overpriced restaurants.*
notoriously ADVERB
notoriety NOUN

notwithstanding
PREPOSITION *a formal word* in spite of: *Notwithstanding his age, the recent graduate had an important job.*

nougat
NOUN Nougat is a kind of chewy candy containing nuts and sometimes fruit.

noun nouns
NOUN a word that refers to a person, thing, or idea. Examples of nouns are *president*, *table*, *sun*, and *beauty*.

nourish nourishes nourishing nourished
VERB To nourish people or animals means to provide them with food.

nourishing
ADJECTIVE Food that is nourishing makes you strong and healthy.

nourishment
NOUN Nourishment is food that your body needs in order to remain healthy: *Vegetables provide nourishment.*

novel novels
NOUN **1.** a book that tells an invented story
ADJECTIVE **2.** new and interesting: *a very novel experience*

novelist novelists
NOUN a person who writes novels

novelty novelties
NOUN **1.** Novelty is the quality of being new and interesting: *The novelty had worn off.*
2. something new and interesting: *The Internet has been around for so many years that it is no longer a novelty.* **3.** a small, unusual object sold as a gift or souvenir

November
NOUN November is the eleventh month of the year. It has 30 days.

novice novices
NOUN **1.** someone who is not yet experienced at something **2.** someone who is preparing to become a monk or nun

now
ADVERB **1.** at the present time or moment
CONJUNCTION **2.** as a result or consequence of a particular fact: *Things have got better now there is a new leader.*
PHRASE **3.** **Just now** means very recently: *My father drove me back to the camp just now.*
4. If something happens **now and then**, it happens sometimes but not regularly.

nowadays
ADVERB at the present time: *Nowadays, e-mail is more common than handwritten letters.*

nowhere
ADVERB not anywhere

noxious
ADJECTIVE harmful or poisonous: *a noxious gas*

nozzle nozzles
NOUN a spout fitted onto the end of a pipe or hose to control the flow of a liquid

nuance nuances
NOUN a small difference in sound, colour, or meaning: *the nuances of his music*

nuclear
ADJECTIVE **1.** relating to the energy produced when the nuclei of atoms are split: *nuclear power, the nuclear industry* **2.** relating to weapons that explode, using the energy released by atoms: *nuclear war* **3.** relating to the structure and behaviour of the nuclei of atoms: *nuclear physics*

nuclear reactor nuclear reactors
NOUN A nuclear reactor is a device that is used to obtain nuclear energy.

nucleus nuclei
NOUN **1.** the central part of an atom or cell
2. The nucleus of something is the basic central part of it to which other things are added: *They have retained the nucleus of the team that won the World Cup.*

nude nudes
ADJECTIVE **1.** naked
NOUN **2.** a picture or statue of a naked person
nudity NOUN

nudge nudges nudging nudged
VERB **1.** If you nudge someone, you push that person gently, usually with your elbow.
NOUN **2.** a gentle push

nudist nudists
NOUN a person who believes in wearing no clothes

nugget nuggets
NOUN a small, rough lump of something, especially gold

nuisance nuisances
NOUN someone or something that is annoying or inconvenient

⚠ **HEADS UP** The word **nougat** is pronounced NEW-guht.

null

PHRASE **Null and void** means not legally valid: *Other documents were declared to be null and void.*

numb numbs numbing numbed

ADJECTIVE **1.** unable to feel anything: *My legs felt numb. He was numb with grief.*

VERB **2.** If something numbs you, it makes you unable to feel anything: *The cold numbed my fingers.*

number numbers numbering numbered

NOUN **1.** a word or a symbol used for counting or calculating **2.** Someone's number is the series of numbers that you use to telephone that person. **3.** A number of things is a quantity of them: *My cousin has introduced me to a large number of people.* **4.** a song or piece of music

VERB **5.** If things number a particular amount, there are that many of them: *At that time, the city's population numbered about 460 000.* **6.** If you number something, you give it a number: *The picture is signed and numbered by the artist.* **7.** To be numbered among a particular group means to belong to it: *Only the best are numbered among their champions.*

numeral numerals

NOUN a symbol that represents a number: *a wristwatch with Roman numerals*

numerical

ADJECTIVE expressed in numbers or relating to numbers: *a numerical value*

numerous

ADJECTIVE existing or happening in large numbers

nurse nurses nursing nursed

NOUN **1.** a person whose job is to look after people who are ill

VERB **2.** If you nurse someone, you look after that person when he or she is ill. **3.** If you nurse a feeling, you feel it strongly for a long time: *He nursed a grudge against the rival team.*

nursery nurseries

NOUN **1.** a room in which young children sleep and play **2.** a place where plants are grown and sold

nursery school nursery schools

NOUN a school for children from three to five years old

nursing home nursing homes

NOUN a residence providing personal or nursing care for people who are elderly

nurture nurtures nurturing nurtured

VERB *a formal word* If you nurture a young child or a plant, you look after it carefully.

nut nuts

NOUN **1.** a fruit with a hard shell and an edible centre that grows on certain trees **2.** a piece of metal with a hole in the middle that a bolt screws into

nutmeg

NOUN a spice used for flavouring in cooking

nutrient nutrients

NOUN Nutrients are substances that help plants or animals to grow: *the nutrients in the soil*

nutrition

NOUN Nutrition is the food that you eat, considered from the point of view of how it helps you to grow and remain healthy: *The effects of poor nutrition are evident.*

nutritional ADJECTIVE

nutritionist NOUN

nutritious

ADJECTIVE containing substances that help you to grow and remain healthy

nutty nuttier nuttiest

ADJECTIVE **1.** tasting of nuts **2.** *an informal use* crazy or very foolish

nylon nylons

NOUN Nylon is a type of strong artificial material: *nylon rope*

KNOWING WORDS: IDIOMS

BE WORD SHARP!

Idioms add colour to language by playing with the meanings of words.

number a word or symbol used for counting

without number too many to be counted

do a number on someone do something bad to someone

have someone's number know someone's character

number crunching working with numbers

your days are numbered you don't have long to live

Oo

oaf oafs
NOUN a clumsy or stupid person

oak oaks
NOUN a large tree that produces acorns. It has a hard wood that is often used to make furniture.

oar oars
NOUN a wooden pole with a wide, flat end, used for rowing a boat

⚠ HEADS UP

The word **oasis** is pronounced oh-AY-sis. The plural, **oases**, is pronounced oh-AY-sees.

oasis oases
NOUN a small area in a desert where water and plants are found

oat oats
NOUN Oats are a type of grain.

oath oaths
NOUN a formal promise, especially a promise to tell the truth in a court of law

oatmeal
NOUN oats that are ground or rolled, or porridge made from oats

obedient
ADJECTIVE If you are obedient, you do what you are told to do.
obediently ADVERB
obedience NOUN

obelisk obelisks
NOUN a stone pillar built in honour of a person or an event

obese
ADJECTIVE extremely fat
obesity NOUN

obey obeys obeying obeyed
VERB If you obey a person or an order, you do what you are told to do.

obituary obituaries
NOUN a piece of writing about the life and achievements of someone who has just died

object objects objecting objected
NOUN **1.** anything solid that you can touch or see, and that is not alive **2.** an aim or purpose **3.** The object of your feelings or actions is the person that they are directed toward. **4.** In grammar, the object of a verb or preposition is the word or phrase that follows it and describes the person or thing affected.
VERB **5.** If you object to something, you dislike it or disapprove of it.

⚠ HEADS UP

In a sentence, a **subject** does the action. An **object** has the action done to it.

objection objections
NOUN If you have an objection to something, you dislike it or disapprove of it.

objectionable
ADJECTIVE unpleasant and offensive

objective objectives
NOUN **1.** an aim: *The protection of the countryside is their main objective.*
ADJECTIVE **2.** If you are objective, you are not influenced by personal feelings or prejudices: *an objective approach*
objectively ADVERB
objectivity NOUN

obligation obligations
NOUN something that you must do because it is your duty

obligatory
ADJECTIVE required by a rule or law: *Attendance in class is obligatory.*

oblige obliges obliging obliged
VERB **1.** If you are obliged to do something, you have to do it. **2.** If you oblige someone, you help that person.
obliging ADJECTIVE

oblique
ADJECTIVE **1.** An oblique remark is not direct, and is therefore difficult to understand. **2.** An oblique line slopes at an angle.

obliterate obliterates obliterating obliterated
VERB To obliterate something is to destroy it completely.
obliteration NOUN

oblivion
NOUN Oblivion is unconsciousness or complete lack of awareness of your surroundings.
oblivious ADJECTIVE
obliviously ADVERB

oblong oblongs
NOUN **1.** a four-sided shape with two parallel short sides, two parallel long sides, and four right angles
ADJECTIVE **2.** shaped like an oblong

obnoxious
ADJECTIVE extremely unpleasant

Oo

Oo

oboe oboes
NOUN a woodwind musical instrument with a double reed
oboist NOUN

obscene
ADJECTIVE indecent and likely to upset people: *obscene language*
obscenely ADVERB
obscenity NOUN

obscure obscures obscuring obscured
ADJECTIVE **1.** Something that is obscure is known by only a few people: *an obscure language, an obscure novel* **2.** Something obscure is difficult to see or to understand: *The news was shrouded in obscure language.*
VERB **3.** To obscure something is to make it difficult to see or understand: *His view was obscured by trees.*
obscurity NOUN

observance
NOUN The observance of a law or custom is the practice of obeying or following it.

observant
ADJECTIVE Someone who is observant notices things that are not easy to see.

observation observations
NOUN **1.** Observation is the act of watching something carefully or noticing something: *Her keen observation helped her to spot the flaw in the design.* **2.** something that you have seen or noticed **3.** a remark **4.** Observation is the ability to notice things that are not easy to see.

observatory observatories
NOUN a room or building containing telescopes and other equipment for studying the sun, moon, and stars

observe observes observing observed
VERB **1.** To observe something is to watch it carefully. **2.** To observe something is to notice it. **3.** If you observe that something is the case, you make a comment about it. **4.** To observe a law or custom is to obey or follow it.
observer NOUN
observable ADJECTIVE

obsession obsessions
NOUN If someone has an obsession about something, that person cannot stop thinking about that thing.
obsessed ADJECTIVE
obsessive ADJECTIVE

obsolete
ADJECTIVE out of date and no longer used

obstacle obstacles
NOUN something that is in your way that makes it difficult to do something

obstetrics
NOUN Obstetrics is the branch of medicine concerned with pregnancy and childbirth.
obstetrician NOUN

obstinate
ADJECTIVE Someone who is obstinate is stubborn and unwilling to change his or her mind.
obstinately ADVERB
obstinacy NOUN

obstruct obstructs obstructing obstructed
VERB If something obstructs a road or path, it blocks it.
obstruction NOUN
obstructive ADJECTIVE

obtain obtains obtaining obtained
VERB If you obtain something, you get it.
obtainable ADJECTIVE

obtrusive
ADJECTIVE noticeable in an unpleasant way: *a remarkably obtrusive lawn ornament*

obtuse
ADJECTIVE **1.** Someone who is obtuse is stupid or slow to understand things. **2.** An obtuse angle is an angle between 90° and 180°.

obvious
ADJECTIVE easy to see or understand
obviously ADVERB

occasion occasions occasioning occasioned
NOUN **1.** a time when something happens **2.** an important event **3.** An occasion for doing something is an opportunity for doing it.
VERB **4.** *a formal use* To occasion something is to cause it: *damage occasioned by fire*

occasional
ADJECTIVE happening sometimes but not often: *an occasional outing*
occasionally ADVERB

occult
NOUN The occult is the knowledge and study of supernatural and magical forces or powers.

occupancy
NOUN The occupancy of a building is the act of living or working in it.

occupant occupants
NOUN The occupants of a building are the people who live or work in it.

occupation occupations
NOUN **1.** a job or profession **2.** a hobby or something you do for pleasure **3.** The occupation of a country is the act of invading it and taking control of it.
occupational ADJECTIVE

Oo

occupy occupies occupying occupied
VERB **1.** The people who occupy a building are the people who live or work there. **2.** When people occupy a place, they move into it and take control of it: *Demonstrators occupied the building.* **3.** To occupy a position in a system or plan is to have that position: *His phone-in show occupies a daytime slot.* **4.** If something occupies you, you spend your time doing it: *That problem occupies me night and day.*
occupier NOUN

occur occurs occurring occurred
VERB **1.** If something occurs, it happens or exists: *The discussion occurred at my house.* **2.** If something occurs to you, you suddenly think of it.

occurrence occurrences
NOUN **1.** an event **2.** The occurrence of something is the fact that it happens or exists: *the occurrence of diseases*

ocean oceans
NOUN **1.** the sea **2.** The ocean is a large expanse of salt water that covers much of the earth and is divided into five main areas; the Pacific Ocean, the Atlantic Ocean, the Indian Ocean, the Antarctic Ocean, and the Arctic Ocean.
oceanic ADJECTIVE

o'clock
ADVERB You use *o'clock* after the number of the hour to say what the time is.

octagon octagons
NOUN a shape with eight straight sides
octagonal ADJECTIVE

octave octaves
NOUN the difference in pitch between the first note and the eighth note of a musical scale

October
NOUN October is the tenth month of the year. It has 31 days.

octopus octopuses
NOUN a sea creature with eight long tentacles, which it uses to catch food

odd odder oddest; odds
ADJECTIVE **1.** Something odd is strange or unusual. **2.** Odd things do not match each other: *odd socks* **3.** Odd numbers are numbers that cannot be divided exactly by two.
ADVERB **4.** You use *odd* after a number to say that it is approximate: *I've read 20-odd plays.*
PLURAL NOUN **5.** The probability of something happening is called the odds: *The odds are*

against the record being beaten.
oddly ADVERB
oddness NOUN

oddity oddities
NOUN something very strange

oddment
NOUN Oddments are things that are left over after other things have been used.

odds and ends
PLURAL NOUN You can refer to a collection of small, unimportant things as odds and ends.

ode odes
NOUN a poem written in praise of someone or something

odious
ADJECTIVE extremely unpleasant

odour odours
NOUN *a formal word* a strong smell
odorous ADJECTIVE

odyssey odysseys
NOUN a long and eventful journey

of
PREPOSITION **1.** consisting of or containing: *a collection of short stories, a cup of coffee* **2.** used when naming something or describing a characteristic of something: *the city of North Bay, a person of great power and influence* **3.** belonging to or connected with: *a friend of mine, the cover of the book*

off
PREPOSITION OR ADVERB **1.** indicating movement away from or out of a place: *They had just stepped off the plane. She got up and marched off.* **2.** indicating separation or distance from a place: *They vacationed on some islands off the coast of Australia. The whole park has been fenced off.* **3.** not working: *It was my brother's night off.*
ADVERB OR ADJECTIVE **4.** not switched on: *He turned the radio off. The off switch is the red button.*
ADJECTIVE **5.** cancelled or postponed: *The concert was off.* **6.** Food that is off has gone sour or bad.
PREPOSITION **7.** not liking or not using something: *He went right off sweet food.*

⚠ **HEADS UP**

In everyday speech, some people say **off of** when they mean **off**. Just use **off** in writing: *Step off the bus.*

Oo

offal

NOUN Offal is liver, kidneys, and other parts of animals that can be eaten.

offence offences

NOUN **1.** a crime: *a driving offence*
PHRASE **2.** If something **gives offence**, it upsets people. If you **take offence**, you are upset by someone or something.

offend offends offending offended

VERB **1.** If you offend someone, you upset that person. **2.** *a formal use* To offend or to offend a law is to commit a crime.
offender NOUN

offensive offensives

ADJECTIVE **1.** Something offensive is vulgar and upsetting: *offensive behaviour, offensive language* **2.** Offensive actions or weapons are used in attacking someone.
NOUN **3.** an attack: *a full-scale offensive against the rebels*
offensively ADVERB

offer offers offering offered

VERB **1.** If you offer something to someone, you ask that person if he or she would like it.
NOUN **2.** something that someone says he or she will give you or do for you: *He refused the offer of food and water.* **3.** a special low price for a product in a store: *You will need a coupon to qualify for the special offer.*

offering offerings

NOUN something that is offered or given to someone

offhand

ADJECTIVE **1.** Something that is offhand is done or made without previous thought or planning.
ADVERB **2.** If you know something offhand, you know it without having to think very hard: *I couldn't tell you offhand how long he's been here.*

office offices

NOUN **1.** a room where people work at desks **2.** a government department: *Privy Council Office, the Office for Disability Issues* **3.** Someone who holds office has an important job or position in government or in an organization.

officer officers

NOUN a person with a position of authority in the armed forces, the police, or a government organization

official officials

ADJECTIVE **1.** approved by the government or by someone in authority: *the official figures* **2.** done or used by someone in authority as part of that person's job: *an official uniform*

NOUN **3.** a person who holds a position of authority in an organization
officially ADVERB

officialdom

NOUN You can refer to officials in government or other organizations as officialdom.

officiate officiates officiating officiated

VERB To officiate at a ceremony is to be in charge and perform the official part of the ceremony.

offing

PHRASE If something is **in the offing**, it is likely to happen soon: *A change is in the offing.*

offline

ADJECTIVE **1.** If a computer is offline, it is switched off or not connected to the Internet.
ADVERB **2.** If you do something offline, you do it while not connected to the Internet.

offset offsets offsetting offset

VERB If one thing is offset by another thing, its effect is reduced or cancelled out by that thing: *This tedium can be offset by reading a book.*

offshoot offshoots

NOUN something that has developed from another thing: *The technology we use is an offshoot of the automobile industry.*

offshore

ADJECTIVE OR ADVERB in or from the part of the sea near the shore: *an offshore wind, a wreck 15 kilometres offshore*

offside

ADJECTIVE In some sports, if a player is offside, that player has broken a rule by moving too far forward.

offspring

NOUN Offspring are the children of a person or animal.

often

ADVERB happening many times or a lot of the time

ogle ogles ogling ogled

VERB To ogle someone is to stare at that person in a way that indicates sexual interest.

ogre ogres

NOUN a cruel, frightening giant in a fairy tale

ohm ohms

NOUN In physics, an ohm is a unit used to measure electrical resistance.

oil oils oiling oiled

NOUN **1.** Oil is a thick, sticky liquid used as a fuel and for lubrication. **2.** Oil is also a thick, greasy liquid made from plants or animals: *cooking oil, bath oil*
VERB **3.** If you oil something, you put oil in it or on it.

Oo

oil painting oil paintings
NOUN a picture that has been painted with thick paints made from coloured powder and a kind of oil

oilskin oilskins
NOUN a piece of clothing made from a thick, waterproof material, worn especially by sailors

oily
ADJECTIVE Something that is oily is covered with or contains oil: *an oily rag, oily skin*

ointment ointments
NOUN a smooth, thick substance that you put on sore skin to heal it

OK
ADJECTIVE *an informal word* OK means all right: *Tell me if this sounds OK.*

old older oldest
ADJECTIVE **1.** having lived or existed for a long time: *an old woman, old clothes*
2. Old is used to give the age of someone or something: *This photo is five years old.*
3. Old also means former: *my old art teacher*

olden
PHRASE **In the olden days** means long ago.

Old English
NOUN Old English was the English language from the fifth century CE until about 1100 CE. Old English is also known as Anglo-Saxon.

old-fashioned
ADJECTIVE **1.** Something that is old-fashioned is no longer fashionable: *old-fashioned shoes*
2. Someone who is old-fashioned believes in the values and standards of the past.

oleander oleanders
NOUN an evergreen shrub with fragrant white, pink, or purple flowers

olive olives
NOUN **1.** a small, green or black fruit containing a stone. Olives are usually pickled and eaten as a snack or crushed to produce oil.
ADJECTIVE OR NOUN **2.** dark, yellowish green

-ology
SUFFIX The suffix *-ology* is used to form words that refer to the study of something: *biology, geology*

Olympic Games
PLURAL NOUN The Olympic Games are a set of sporting contests held in a different city every four years.

ombudsman ombudsmen
NOUN The ombudsman is a person who investigates complaints against the government or a public organization.

omelette omelettes
NOUN a dish made by beating eggs together and cooking them in a flat pan

omen omens
NOUN something that is thought to be a sign of what will happen in the future: *He saw this success as a good omen for his trip.*

ominous
ADJECTIVE suggesting that something unpleasant is going to happen: *an ominous sign*
ominously ADVERB

omission omissions
NOUN **1.** something that has not been included or done: *There are some striking omissions in the survey.* **2.** Omission is the act of not including or not doing something: *controversy over the omission of several well-known novelists*

omit omits omitting omitted
VERB **1.** If you omit something, you do not include it. **2.** *a formal use* If you omit to do something, you do not do it.

omnibus omnibuses
NOUN **1.** a book containing a collection of stories or articles by the same author or about the same subject
ADJECTIVE **2.** comprising several items: *an omnibus edition*

KNOWING WORDS: WORD BUILDING

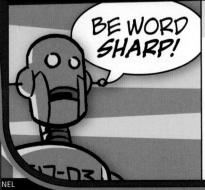

BE WORD SHARP!

You can create new words by adding prefixes and suffixes together.

-ology a suffix that means *the study of*

biology the study of living things (bio = life)

ecology the study of environments (eco = environmental)

geology the study of the earth's materials (geo = earth)

sociology the study of social patterns (socio = social)

toxicology the study of poisons (toxi = poisonous)

Oo

omnipotent

ADJECTIVE having very great or unlimited power: *omnipotent emperors*

omnipotence NOUN

omnivore

NOUN An omnivore is an animal that eats all kinds of food, including meat and plants.

omnivorous ADJECTIVE

on

PREPOSITION **1.** touching or attached to something: *The woman was sitting on the sofa.* **2.** If you are on a bus, plane, or train, you are inside it. **3.** If something happens on a particular day, that is when it happens: *It is his birthday on Monday.* **4.** If something is done on an instrument or machine, it is done using that instrument or machine: *He preferred to play on his computer.* **5.** A book or talk on a particular subject is about that subject.

ADVERB **6.** If you have a piece of clothing on, you are wearing it.

ADJECTIVE **7.** A machine or switch that is on is working. **8.** If an event is on, it is happening or taking place: *The race is definitely on.*

once

ADVERB **1.** If something happens once, it happens one time only. **2.** If something was once true, it was true in the past, but is no longer true.

CONJUNCTION **3.** If something happens once another thing has happened, it happens immediately afterward: *Once I finish my math homework, I have to start working on my history essay.*

PHRASE **4.** If you do something at once, you do it immediately. If several things happen at once, they all happen at the same time.

one ones

NOUN **1.** One is the number 1.

ADJECTIVE **2.** If you refer to the one person or thing of a particular kind, you mean the only person or thing of that kind: *My one aim is to look after the horses well.* **3.** One also means *a*; used when emphasizing something: *They got one incredible shock.*

PRONOUN **4.** One refers to a particular thing or person: *My uncle's business was a good one.* **5.** One also means people in general: *One likes to have the opportunity to chat.*

one-off one-offs

NOUN something that happens or is made only once

onerous

ADJECTIVE *a formal word* difficult or unpleasant: *an onerous task*

oneself

PRONOUN *Oneself* is used when you are talking about people in general: *One could hardly hear oneself talk.*

one-sided

ADJECTIVE **1.** If an activity or relationship is one-sided, one of the people has a lot more success or involvement than the other: *a one-sided contest* **2.** A one-sided argument or report considers the facts or a situation from only one point of view.

one-way

ADJECTIVE **1.** One-way streets are streets along which vehicles can drive in only one direction. **2.** A one-way ticket is one that you can use to travel to a place, but not to travel back again.

ongoing

ADJECTIVE continuing to happen: *an ongoing process of learning*

onion onions

NOUN a small, round vegetable with a brown skin like paper and a very strong taste

online

ADJECTIVE **1.** If a computer is online, it is switched on or connected to the Internet.

ADVERB **2.** If you do something online, you do it while connected to the Internet.

onlooker onlookers

NOUN someone who is watching an event

only

ADVERB **1.** You use *only* to indicate the one thing or person involved: *Only your sister knows whether she will continue.* **2.** You use *only* to emphasize that something is unimportant or small: *He's only a little boy.* **3.** You can use *only* to introduce something that happens immediately after something else: *We had come up with one plan, only to discard it for another.*

ADJECTIVE **4.** If you talk about the only thing or person, you mean that there are no others: *that band's only hit single* **5.** If you are an only child, you have no brothers or sisters.

CONJUNCTION **6.** *Only* also means *but* or *except*: *He was like you, only blond.*

PHRASE **7. Only too** means extremely: *I would be only too happy to swap places with you.*

onomatopoeia

NOUN the use of words that sound like the thing that they represent. *Hiss* and *buzz* are examples of onomatopoeia.

onomatopoeic ADJECTIVE

onset

NOUN The onset of something unpleasant is the beginning of it: *the onset of winter storms*

ONOMATOPOEIA

▼✕

the use of words that sound like the thing that they represent

"Clump"

Here is one example of onomatopoeia. The word *clump* sounds like the noise of someone walking with heavy steps. Can you find other examples on this page?

Oo

onslaught onslaughts
NOUN a violent attack

onto
PREPOSITION If you put something onto an object, you put it on it.

onus
NOUN a formal word If the onus is on you to do something, it is your duty to do it.

onward
ADVERB **1.** continuing to happen from a particular time: *He could not speak a word from that moment onward.* **2.** travelling forward: *After visiting our display, the judges moved onward to the exhibit.*

onyx
NOUN a semiprecious stone used for making ornaments and jewellery

ooze oozes oozing oozed
VERB When a thick liquid oozes, it flows slowly: *The cold mud oozed over her new shoes.*

opal opals
NOUN a pale or whitish semiprecious stone used for making jewellery

opaque
ADJECTIVE If something is opaque, you cannot see through it: *opaque glass windows*

open opens opening opened
VERB **1.** When you open something, or when it opens, you move it so that it is no longer closed: *She opened the door.*
2. When a store or office opens, people are able to go in. **3.** To open something also means to start it: *He tried to open a bank account.*
ADJECTIVE **4.** Something that is open is not closed or fastened: *an open box of chocolates* **5.** If you have an open mind, you are willing to consider new ideas or suggestions. **6.** Someone

who is open is honest and frank. **7.** When a store or office is open, people are able to go in. **8.** An open area of water or land is a large, empty area: *open country* **9.** If something is open to you, it is possible for you to do it: *There is no other course open to us but to wait out the storm.*
10. If a situation is still open, it is still being considered: *Even if the case remains open, the full facts may never be revealed.*
PHRASE **11. In the open** means outside.
12. In the open also means not secret.
openly ADVERB

opening openings
ADJECTIVE **1.** Opening means coming first: *opening day of the hunting season*
NOUN **2.** The opening of a book or movie is the first part of it. **3.** a hole or space **4.** a chance or opportunity: *I decided to wait for an opening before asking to stay out past curfew.*

open-minded
ADJECTIVE willing to consider new ideas and suggestions

opera operas
NOUN a play in which the words are sung rather than spoken
operatic ADJECTIVE

operate operates operating operated
VERB **1.** To operate is to work: *We are shocked at the way that business operates.*
2. When you operate a machine, you make it work. **3.** When surgeons operate, they cut open a patient's body to remove or repair a damaged part.

operation operations
NOUN **1.** a complex, planned event: *a full-scale military operation* **2.** a form of medical treatment in which a surgeon cuts open a patient's body to remove or repair a damaged part
PHRASE **3.** If something is **in operation**, it is working or being used: *The theme park is in operation from April to the end of September.*

operational
ADJECTIVE working or able to be used: *an operational aircraft*

Instead of **OPEN** try...

his mouth was **agape**
a **spacious** foyer
the door is **ajar**
a **vacant** lot
an **unlocked** gate
a **receptive** mind
a **candid** conversation
willing to try new things

Oo

operative

ADJECTIVE Something that is operative is working or having an effect.

operator operators

NOUN **1.** someone who operates a machine: *a computer operator* **2.** someone who runs a business: *a tour operator*

opinion opinions

NOUN a belief or view

opinionated

ADJECTIVE Someone who is opinionated has strong views and refuses to accept that he or she might be wrong.

opinion piece

NOUN a piece of writing that expresses the writer's point of view on an issue

opium

NOUN Opium is a drug made from the seeds of a poppy. It is used in medicine to relieve pain.

opponent opponents

NOUN someone who is against you in an argument or a contest

opportune

ADJECTIVE *a formal word* happening at a convenient time: *The king's death was opportune for the prince.*

opportunism

NOUN Opportunism is taking advantage of any opportunity to gain money or power for oneself.

opportunist NOUN

opportunity opportunities

NOUN a chance to do something

oppose opposes opposing opposed

VERB If you oppose something, you disagree with it and try to prevent it.

opposed

ADJECTIVE **1.** If you are opposed to something, you disagree with it: *He was totally opposed to cellphones in schools.* **2.** Opposed also means opposite or very different: *two opposed schools of thought*

PHRASE **3.** If you refer to one thing **as opposed** to another, you are emphasizing that it is the first thing rather than the second that concerns you: *We discussed the merits of walking for exercise as opposed to jogging.*

opposite opposites

PREPOSITION OR ADVERB **1.** If one thing is opposite another, it is facing it: *the store opposite the station, the house opposite ours* ADJECTIVE **2.** The opposite part of something is the part farthest away from you: *the opposite side of town* **3.** If things are opposite, they are completely different: *I take the opposite view to yours.*

NOUN **4.** If two things are completely different, they are opposites.

opposition

NOUN **1.** If there is opposition to something, people disagree with it and try to prevent it. **2.** The political parties who are not in power are referred to as the opposition. **3.** In a game or sports event, the opposition is the person or team that you are competing against.

oppressed

ADJECTIVE People who are oppressed are treated cruelly or unfairly.

oppress VERB

oppressor NOUN

oppression

NOUN cruel and unfair treatment of people

oppressive

ADJECTIVE **1.** If the weather is oppressive, it is hot and humid. **2.** An oppressive situation makes you feel depressed or concerned: *The silence became oppressive.* **3.** An oppressive system treats people cruelly or unfairly: *oppressive laws*

oppressively ADVERB

opt opts opting opted

VERB If you opt for something, you choose it. If you opt out of something, you choose not to be involved in it.

optical

ADJECTIVE **1.** concerned with vision, light, or images: *an optical scanner* **2.** relating to the appearance of things: *an optical illusion*

optic ADJECTIVE

optician opticians

NOUN someone who tests people's eyes, and makes and sells glasses and contact lenses

optimism

NOUN Optimism is a feeling of hopefulness about the future.

optimist NOUN

optimistic

ADJECTIVE hopeful about the future

optimistically ADVERB

optimum

ADJECTIVE the best that is possible: *Six is the optimum number of participants for a good meeting.*

option options

NOUN a choice between two or more things

optional ADJECTIVE

opulent

ADJECTIVE grand and expensive-looking: *an opulent waterfront estate*

Oo

opus opera
NOUN an artistic work, especially a piece of music

or
CONJUNCTION **1.** used to link two different things: *I didn't know whether to laugh or cry.* **2.** used to introduce a warning: *Clean your room or else you can't go to a movie tonight.*

-or
SUFFIX The suffix *-or* is used to form nouns from verbs: *actor, conductor*

oracle oracles
NOUN **1.** In ancient times, an oracle was a priest or priestess through whom a prediction about the future was given by a god. **2.** a prophecy made by a priest or other person with great authority or wisdom

oral orals
ADJECTIVE **1.** spoken rather than written: *oral history* **2.** Oral describes things that are used in your mouth or done with your mouth: *an oral vaccine*
NOUN **3.** an examination that is spoken rather than written
orally ADVERB

orange oranges
NOUN **1.** a round citrus fruit that is juicy and sweet and has a thick reddish yellow skin
ADJECTIVE OR NOUN **2.** reddish yellow

orangutan orangutans
NOUN a large ape with reddish brown hair

orator orators
NOUN someone who is good at making speeches

oratory
NOUN Oratory is the art and skill of making formal public speeches.

orbit orbits orbiting orbited
NOUN **1.** the curved path followed by an object going around a planet or the sun
VERB **2.** If something orbits a planet or the sun, it goes round and round it.

orchard orchards
NOUN a piece of land where fruit trees are grown

orchestra orchestras
NOUN a large group of musicians who play musical instruments together
orchestral ADJECTIVE

orchestrate orchestrates orchestrating orchestrated
VERB **1.** To orchestrate something is to organize it very carefully in order to produce a particular result. **2.** To orchestrate a piece of music is to rewrite it so that it can be played by an orchestra.
orchestration NOUN

orchid orchids
NOUN a plant with beautiful and unusual flowers

ordain ordains ordaining ordained
VERB When someone is ordained, that person is made a member of the clergy in the Christian church.

ordeal ordeals
NOUN a difficult and extremely unpleasant experience: *Exams are always an ordeal for my brother.*

order orders ordering ordered
NOUN **1.** a command given by someone in authority **2.** If things are arranged or done in a particular order, they are arranged or done in that sequence: *in alphabetical order* **3.** Order is a situation in which everything is in the correct place or done at the correct time. **4.** something that you ask to be brought to you or sent to you
VERB **5.** To order someone to do something is to tell that person firmly to do it. **6.** When you order something, you ask for it to be brought or sent to you.
PHRASE **7.** If you do something **in order to** achieve a particular thing, you do it because you want to achieve that thing.

KNOWING WORDS: WORD BUILDING

BE WORD SHARP!

You can create new words by adding prefixes and suffixes to a base word.

-or a suffix used to form nouns from verbs

calculator a thing that calculates equations

collector a person who collects something

investor a person who invests money in something

projector a thing that projects images onto a screen

survivor a person who survived something

Oo

orderly

ADJECTIVE Something that is orderly is organized or arranged well.

ordinarily

ADVERB If something ordinarily happens, it usually happens.

ordinary

ADJECTIVE Ordinary means not special or different in any way.

ordination

NOUN When someone's ordination takes place, that person is made a member of the Christian clergy.

ordnance

NOUN Weapons and other military supplies are referred to as ordnance.

ore ores

NOUN Ore is rock or earth from which metal can be obtained.

oregano

NOUN a herb used for flavouring in cooking

organ organs

NOUN **1.** Your organs are parts of your body that have a particular function, for example your heart or lungs. **2.** a large musical instrument with pipes of different lengths through which air is forced. It has various keyboards, which are played like a piano.

organic

ADJECTIVE **1.** Something that is organic is produced by or found in plants or animals: *decaying organic matter* **2.** Organic food is produced without the use of artificial fertilizers or pesticides.

organically ADVERB

organism organisms

NOUN any living animal or plant

organist organists

NOUN someone who plays the organ

organization organizations

NOUN **1.** any group or business **2.** The organization of something is the act of planning and arranging it.

organizational ADJECTIVE

organize organizes organizing organized

VERB **1.** If you organize an event, you plan and arrange it. **2.** If you organize things, you arrange them in a sensible order.

organized ADJECTIVE

organizer NOUN

orgasm orgasms

NOUN the moment of greatest pleasure and excitement during sexual activity

orgy orgies

NOUN **1.** a wild, uncontrolled party involving a lot of drinking and sexual activity **2.** You can refer to a period of intense activity as an orgy of that activity: *an orgy of violence*

orient orients orienting oriented

VERB **1.** If you orient yourself, you establish your position in relation to the other things around you: *It takes a while to orient yourself in a strange city.*

NOUN **2.** *a literary or poetic use* The Orient is east Asia or Eastern civilizations.

oriental

ADJECTIVE relating to east Asia or Eastern civilizations

orientation orientations

NOUN a meeting or event during which information or training in a subject is provided

oriented

ADJECTIVE If someone is interested in a particular thing, you can say that that person is oriented toward it: *She is oriented toward a career in the theatre.*

orienteering

NOUN Orienteering is a sport in which people run from one place to another in the countryside, using a map and compass to guide them.

origin origins

NOUN **1.** You can refer to the beginning or cause of something as its origin or origins. **2.** You can refer to someone's family background as that person's origin or origins: *She was of French origin.*

original originals

ADJECTIVE **1.** Original describes things that existed at the beginning, rather than being added later, or things that were the first of their kind to exist: *the original owner of the cottage* **2.** Original means imaginative and clever: *a stunningly original idea*

NOUN **3.** a work of art or a document that is the one that was first produced, and not a copy

originally ADVERB

originality NOUN

originate originates originating originated

VERB When something originates, or you originate it, it begins to happen or exist.

originator NOUN

ornament ornaments

NOUN a small, attractive object that you display in your home or that you wear in order to look attractive

ornamental

ADJECTIVE designed to be attractive rather than useful: *an ornamental pond*

Oo

ornamentation
NOUN Ornamentation is decoration on a building, a piece of furniture, or a work of art.

ornate
ADJECTIVE Something that is ornate has a lot of decoration on it.

ornithology
NOUN Ornithology is the study of birds.
ornithologist NOUN

orphan orphans orphaning orphaned
NOUN **1.** a child whose parents are dead
VERB **2.** If a child is orphaned, his or her parents die.

orphanage orphanages
NOUN a place where orphans are looked after

orthodox
ADJECTIVE **1.** Orthodox beliefs or methods are the ones that most people have or use and that are considered standard. **2.** People who are orthodox believe in the older, more traditional ideas of their religion or political party.
orthodoxy NOUN

osmosis
NOUN *a technical use* Osmosis is the process by which a liquid moves through a membrane from a weaker solution to a more concentrated one.

osprey ospreys
NOUN a large bird of prey that catches fish with its feet

ostensibly
ADVERB If something is done ostensibly for a reason, that seems to be the reason for it: *He submitted his resignation, ostensibly on medical grounds.*

ostentatious
ADJECTIVE **1.** Something that is ostentatious is intended to impress people, for example by looking expensive: *ostentatious sculptures* **2.** People who are ostentatious try to impress other people with their wealth or importance.
ostentatiously ADVERB
ostentation NOUN

ostrich ostriches
NOUN The ostrich is the largest bird in the world. Ostriches cannot fly.

other others
ADJECTIVE OR PRONOUN **1.** Other people or things are different people or things: *All the other children had gone home. One of the cabinets came from the palace; the other is a copy.*

PHRASE **2.** The other day or the other week means recently: *She bought four pairs of shoes the other day.*

otherwise
ADVERB **1.** You use *otherwise* to say a different situation would exist if a particular fact or occurrence was not the case: *You had to learn to swim pretty quickly, otherwise you sank.* **2.** *Otherwise* means apart from the thing mentioned: *She had written to her daughter, but otherwise refused to take sides.* **3.** *Otherwise* also means in a different way: *The majority voted otherwise.*

otter otters
NOUN a small, furry animal with a long tail. Otters swim well and eat fish.

ouch
INTERJECTION You say ouch when you suddenly feel pain.

⚠ HEADS UP
Words like *Ouch*, *Eek*, and *Yow* can be used in comics and graphic texts to show a startled reaction.

ought
VERB If you say that someone ought to do something, you mean that that person should do it: *He ought to see a doctor.*

ounce ounces
NOUN a nonmetric unit of weight equal to about 28.35 grams

our
ADJECTIVE *Our* refers to something belonging or relating to the speaker or writer and one or more other people: *We recently sold our house.*

ours
PRONOUN *Ours* refers to something belonging or relating to the speaker or writer and one or more other people: *a friend of ours from Saskatoon*

ourselves
PRONOUN **1.** *Ourselves* is used when the same speaker or writer and one or more other people do an action and are affected by it: *We didn't injure ourselves too badly in the accident.* **2.** *Ourselves* is used to emphasize *we.*

oust ousts ousting ousted
VERB If you oust someone, you force that person out of a job or a place: *He was ousted from the board.*

Oo

out

ADVERB **1.** toward the outside of a place: *Two dogs rushed out of the house.* **2.** not at home: *She was out when I called last night.* **3.** in the open air: *They are playing out in bright sunshine.* **4.** no longer shining or burning: *The lights went out.*

ADJECTIVE **5.** unacceptable or unfashionable: *That style of shoe is out.* **6.** incorrect: *Your timing was out in your solo.*

out-

PREFIX **1.** The prefix *out-* means *exceeding* or *going beyond*: *outdo, outclass* **2.** The prefix *out-* also means *on the outside* or *away from the centre*: *outback, outpost*

out-and-out

ADJECTIVE entire or complete: *an out-and-out lie*

outboard motor outboard motors

NOUN a motor that can be fixed to the back of a small boat

outbreak outbreaks

NOUN If there is an outbreak of something unpleasant, such as war, it suddenly occurs.

outburst outbursts

NOUN **1.** a sudden, strong expression of an emotion, especially anger: *She broke into an angry outburst about how unfairly the work was divided.* **2.** a sudden occurrence of violent activity: *an outburst of gunfire*

outcast outcasts

NOUN someone who is rejected by other people

outclassed

ADJECTIVE If you are outclassed, you are much worse than your opponent at a particular activity.

outcome outcomes

NOUN a result: *the outcome of the election*

outcrop outcrops

NOUN a large piece of rock that sticks out of the ground

outcry outcries

NOUN If there is an outcry about something, a lot of people are angry about it: *a public outcry over alleged fraud*

outdated

ADJECTIVE no longer in fashion

outdo outdoes outdoing outdid outdone

VERB If you outdo someone, you do a particular thing better than that person does.

outdoor

ADJECTIVE happening or used outside: *outdoor activities*

outdoors

ADVERB outside: *It was too chilly to sit outdoors.*

outer

ADJECTIVE The outer parts of something are the parts furthest from the centre: *the outer door of the office*

outer space

NOUN Outer space is everything beyond Earth's atmosphere.

outfit outfits

NOUN **1.** a set of clothes **2.** *an informal use* an organization

outgoing

ADJECTIVE **1.** Outgoing describes someone who is leaving a job or place: *the outgoing president* **2.** Someone who is outgoing is friendly and not shy.

outgrow outgrows outgrowing outgrew outgrown

VERB **1.** If you outgrow a piece of clothing, you grow too big for it. **2.** If you outgrow a way of behaving, you stop it because you have grown older and more mature.

outhouse outhouses

NOUN an enclosed outdoor toilet separate from the main building

outing outings

NOUN a trip made for pleasure

outlandish

ADJECTIVE very unusual or odd: *outlandish clothes*

KNOWING WORDS: IDIOMS

BE WORD SHARP!

Idioms add colour to language by playing with the meanings of words.

out toward the outside

on the outs fighting or not speaking to each other

out and about outside and going to different places

out of it in a daze

out of sorts confused and upset

out of the blue unexpectedly

outlaw outlaws outlawing outlawed
VERB **1.** If something is outlawed, it is made illegal.
NOUN **2.** In the past, an outlaw was a criminal.

outlay outlays
NOUN an amount of money spent on something: *a cash outlay of 300 dollars*

outlet outlets
NOUN **1.** An outlet for your feelings or ideas is a way of expressing them. **2.** a hole or pipe through which water or air can flow away **3.** a store that sells goods made by a particular manufacturer

outline outlines outlining outlined
VERB **1.** If you outline a plan or idea, you explain it in a general way. **2.** You say that something is outlined when you can see its shape because there is a light behind it.
NOUN **3.** a general explanation or description of something **4.** The outline of something is its shape.

outlive outlives outliving outlived
VERB To outlive someone is to live longer than that person does.

outlook
NOUN **1.** Your outlook is your general attitude toward life. **2.** The outlook of a situation is the way it is likely to develop: *The Canadian economy's outlook is uncertain.*

outlying
ADJECTIVE Outlying places are far from cities.

outmoded
ADJECTIVE old-fashioned and no longer useful: *an outmoded form of transport*

outnumber outnumbers outnumbering outnumbered
VERB If there are more items in one group than in another, the first group outnumbers the second.

out of
PREPOSITION **1.** If you do something out of a particular feeling, you are motivated by that feeling: *Out of curiosity, she went along.* **2.** *Out of* also means *from*: *old instruments made out of wood* **3.** If you are out of something, you no longer have any of it: *I do hope we're not out of fuel again.* **4.** If you are out of the rain, sun, or wind, you are sheltered from it. **5.** You also use *out of* to indicate proportion. For example, one out of five means one in every five.

out of date
ADJECTIVE old-fashioned and no longer in style

out of doors
ADVERB outside: *Sometimes we eat out of doors.*

outpatient outpatients
NOUN Outpatients are people who receive treatment in a hospital without staying overnight.

outpost outposts
NOUN a small collection of buildings a long way from a main centre: *a remote mountain outpost*

output outputs
NOUN **1.** Output is the amount of something produced by a person or organization. **2.** The output of a computer is the information that it produces.

outrage outrages outraging outraged
VERB **1.** If something outrages you, it angers and shocks you: *I was outraged at what had happened to her.*
NOUN **2.** Outrage is a feeling of anger and shock. **3.** something very shocking or violent
outrageous ADJECTIVE
outrageously ADVERB

outright
ADJECTIVE **1.** absolute: *an outright rejection*
ADVERB **2.** in an open and direct way: *Have you asked him outright?* **3.** completely and totally: *My aunt owns the company outright.*

outset
NOUN The outset of something is the beginning of it: *the outset of his journey*

outshine outshines outshining outshone
VERB If you outshine someone, you perform better than that person does.

outside
NOUN **1.** The outside of something is the part that surrounds or encloses the rest of it.
PREPOSITION **2.** on or to the exterior of: *outside the house* **3.** *Outside* also means *not included in something*: *outside school hours*
ADJECTIVE **4.** *Outside* means *not inside*: *an outside pool*
ADVERB **5.** out of doors

outsider outsiders
NOUN **1.** someone who does not belong to a particular group **2.** a competitor considered unlikely to win in a race

outsize
ADJECTIVE much larger than usual: *outsize feet*

outskirts
PLURAL NOUN The outskirts of a city or town are the parts around the edge of it.

outspoken
ADJECTIVE Outspoken people give their opinions openly, even if they shock other people.

outstanding
ADJECTIVE **1.** extremely good: *The collection*

Oo

contains hundreds of outstanding works of art. **2.** Money that is outstanding is still owed: *an outstanding debt of 500 dollars*

outstretched
ADJECTIVE If your arms are outstretched, they are stretched out as far as possible.

outstrip outstrips outstripping outstripped
VERB If one thing outstrips another thing, it becomes bigger or more successful, or moves faster than the other thing.

outward
ADJECTIVE OR ADVERB **1.** Outward means away from a place or toward the outside: *the outward journey from the interior of British Columbia, the door opened outward*
ADJECTIVE **2.** The outward features of someone are the ones that person appears to have, rather than the ones he or she actually has: *He never showed any outward signs of emotion.*
outwardly ADVERB

outweigh outweighs outweighing outweighed
VERB If you say that the advantages of something outweigh its disadvantages, you mean that the advantages are more important than the disadvantages.

outwit outwits outwitting outwitted
VERB If you outwit someone, you use your intelligence to defeat that person.

oval ovals
NOUN **1.** a round shape, similar to a circle but wider in one direction than the other
ADJECTIVE **2.** shaped like an oval: *an oval table*

ovary ovaries
NOUN A female's ovaries are the two organs in her body that produce eggs.

ovation ovations
NOUN a long burst of applause

oven ovens
NOUN the part of a stove that you use for baking or roasting food

over
PREPOSITION **1.** Over something means directly above it or covering it: *Hang the picture over the fireplace. He put his hands over his eyes.* **2.** A view over an area is a view across that area: *The pool and terrace look out over the ocean.* **3.** If something is over a road or river it is on the opposite side of the road or river: *Drive over the bridge, then turn left.* **4.** Something that is over a particular amount is more than that amount. **5.** *Over* indicates a topic that is causing concern: *A customer was arguing over the bill.* **6.** If something happens over a period of time, it happens during that period: *I went to Newfoundland over the holidays.*
ADVERB OR PREPOSITION **7.** If you lean over, you bend your body in a particular direction: *He bent over and rummaged in a drawer. She was hunched over her keyboard.*
ADVERB **8.** *Over* is used to indicate a position: *Stand over by the window. Come over here.* **9.** If something rolls or turns over, it is moved so that its other side is facing upward: *He flipped over the envelope.*
ADJECTIVE **10.** Something that is over is completely finished.
PHRASE **11. All over** a place means everywhere in that place: *wildflowers all over the field*

over-
PREFIX The prefix *over-* means *to too great an extent* or *too much*: *overprotective, overindulge, overact*

overall overalls
ADJECTIVE OR ADVERB **1.** Overall means taking into account all the parts or aspects of something: *The overall quality of students' work had shown a marked improvement. Overall, things are not really too bad.*
PLURAL NOUN **2.** Overalls are a piece of clothing that looks like trousers and a part that covers the chest. You wear overalls to protect your other clothes when you are working.

overawed
ADJECTIVE If you are overawed by something, you are very impressed by it and a little afraid of it.

KNOWING WORDS: IDIOMS

BE WORD SHARP!

Idioms add colour to language by playing with the meanings of words.

over on top of

all over the place disorganized

over and over repeatedly

over and above besides

over the top excessive or unnecessary

over with finished

Oo

overbearing

ADJECTIVE trying to dominate other people: *He is so overbearing that people find it difficult to get along with him.*

overboard

ADVERB If you fall overboard, you fall over the side of a ship or boat into the water.

overcast

ADJECTIVE If it is overcast, the sky is covered by cloud.

overcoat overcoats

NOUN a thick, warm coat

overcome overcomes overcoming overcame overcome

VERB **1.** If you overcome a problem or a feeling, you manage to deal with it or control it.
ADJECTIVE **2.** If you are overcome by a feeling, you feel it very strongly.

overcrowded

ADJECTIVE If a place is overcrowded, there are too many things or people in it.

overdo overdoes overdoing overdid overdone

VERB If you overdo something, you do it too much or in an exaggerated way: *It is important never to overdo new exercises.*

overdose overdoses

NOUN a larger dose of a drug than is safe

overdraft overdrafts

NOUN an agreement with a bank that allows someone to spend more money than that person has in his or her account

overdrawn

ADJECTIVE If someone is overdrawn, that person has taken more money from his or her bank account than the account has in it.

overdrive

NOUN Overdrive is an extra, higher gear in a vehicle, which is used at high speeds to reduce engine wear and save gas.

overdue

ADJECTIVE If someone or something is overdue, that person or thing is late: *The payments are overdue.*

overestimate overestimates overestimating overestimated

VERB If you overestimate something, you think that it is bigger, more important, or better than it really is: *We had overestimated his popularity.*

overflow overflows overflowing overflowed overflown

VERB If a liquid overflows, it spills over the edges of its container. If a river overflows, it flows over its banks.

overgrown

ADJECTIVE A place that is overgrown is covered with weeds because it has not been looked after: *an overgrown path*

overhang overhangs overhanging overhung

VERB If one thing overhangs another, it sticks out sideways above it: *old trees whose branches overhang a path*

overhaul overhauls overhauling overhauled

VERB **1.** If you overhaul something, you examine it thoroughly and repair any faults.
NOUN **2.** If you give something an overhaul, you examine it and repair or improve it.

overhead overheads

ADVERB OR ADJECTIVE **1.** Overhead means above you: *seagulls flying overhead*
PLURAL NOUN **2.** The overheads of a business are the costs of running it.

overhear overhears overhearing overheard

VERB If you overhear someone's conversation, you hear what that person is saying to someone else.

overjoyed

ADJECTIVE extremely pleased: *My cousin was overjoyed to see me.*

overlaid

ADJECTIVE If something is overlaid by something else, it is covered by it.

overland

ADJECTIVE OR ADVERB travelling across land rather than going by sea or air: *My aunt and uncle are on an overland trek to India.*

overlap overlaps overlapping overlapped

VERB If one thing overlaps another, one part of it covers part of the other thing.

overleaf

ADVERB on the next page: *Write to us at the address shown overleaf.*

overload overloads overloading overloaded

VERB If you overload someone or something, you give that person or thing too much to do or to carry.

overlook overlooks overlooking overlooked

VERB **1.** If a building or window overlooks a place, it has a view over that place. **2.** If you overlook something, you ignore it or do not notice it.

overly

ADVERB excessively: *I'm not overly fond of jazz.*

overnight

ADJECTIVE OR ADVERB **1.** during the night: *Further rain was forecast overnight.*
2. sudden or suddenly: *The song was an overnight success. Good players don't*

Oo

become bad ones overnight.
ADJECTIVE **3.** for use when you go away for one or two nights: *an overnight bag*

overpower overpowers overpowering overpowered
VERB **1.** If you overpower someone, you seize that person despite his or her struggles because you are stronger than him or her. **2.** If a feeling overpowers you, it affects you very strongly.
overpowering ADJECTIVE

overrate overrates overrating overrated
VERB If you overrate something, you think that it is better or more important than it really is.
overrated ADJECTIVE

overreact overreacts overreacting overreacted
VERB If you overreact, you react in an extreme way.

overriding
ADJECTIVE more important than anything else: *an overriding duty*

overrule overrules overruling overruled
VERB To overrule a person or his or her decisions is to decide that that person's decisions are incorrect.

overrun overruns overrunning overran overrun
VERB **1.** If an army overruns a country, it occupies it very quickly. **2.** If animals or plants overrun a place, they spread quickly over it. **3.** If an event overruns, it continues for longer than it was meant to.

overseas
ADJECTIVE OR ADVERB **1.** abroad: *an overseas tour, travelling overseas*
ADJECTIVE **2.** from abroad: *overseas students*

oversee oversees overseeing oversaw overseen
VERB To oversee a job is to make sure it is done properly.
overseer NOUN

overshadow overshadows overshadowing overshadowed
VERB If something is overshadowed, it is made unimportant by something else that is better or more important.

oversight oversights
NOUN something that you forget to do or fail to notice

overstate overstates overstating overstated
VERB If you overstate something, you exaggerate its importance.

overstep oversteps overstepping overstepped
PHRASE If you overstep something, you go beyond a limit: *She overstepped the bounds of politeness when she invited herself over for dinner.*

overt
ADJECTIVE open and obvious: *overt signs of stress*
overtly ADVERB

overtake overtakes overtaking overtook overtaken
VERB If you overtake someone, you pass that person because you are moving faster than him or her.

overthrow overthrows overthrowing overthrew overthrown
VERB If a government is overthrown, it is removed from power by force.

overtime
NOUN **1.** Overtime is time that someone works in addition to his or her normal working hours. **2.** In some sports, overtime is a period of play that goes beyond the normal game time.
ADVERB **3.** If someone works overtime, that person does work in addition to his or her normal working hours.

overtone
NOUN If something has an overtone of an emotion or attitude, it suggests it without showing it openly: *the political overtone of the trial*

overture overtures
NOUN **1.** a piece of music that is the introduction to an opera or play **2.** If you make overtures to someone, you approach that person because you want to start a friendly or business relationship with him or her.

overturn overturns overturning overturned
VERB **1.** To overturn something is to turn it upside down or onto its side. **2.** If someone overturns a legal decision, that person changes it by using his or her higher authority.

overview overviews
NOUN a general understanding or description of a situation

overweight
ADJECTIVE too fat, and therefore unhealthy: *overweight businessmen*

Instead of **OVERWEIGHT** try…

a **stout** build

a **plump** poodle

a **rounded** figure

a **buxom** brunette

a **portly** gentleman

Oo

overwhelm overwhelms overwhelming overwhelmed
VERB **1.** If you are overwhelmed by something, it affects you very strongly: *My friend appeared overwhelmed by the news.* **2.** If one group of people overwhelms another group, it gains complete control or victory over the other one.
overwhelming ADJECTIVE
overwhelmingly ADVERB

overwork overworks overworking overworked
VERB If you overwork, you work too hard.

overwrought
ADJECTIVE extremely upset: *He didn't get angry or overwrought.*

ovulate ovulates ovulating ovulated
VERB When a woman or female animal ovulates, she produces ova or eggs from an ovary.

ovum ova
NOUN a reproductive cell of a woman or female animal. The ovum is fertilized by a male sperm to produce young.

owe owes owing owed
VERB **1.** If you owe someone money, that person has lent it to you and you have not yet paid it back. **2.** If you owe a quality or skill to someone, that person is responsible for giving it to you: *He owes his success to his mother.* **3.** If you say that you owe someone gratitude or loyalty, you mean that that person deserves it from you.

owl owls
NOUN a bird of prey that hunts at night, with large eyes and a short, hooked beak

own owns owning owned
ADJECTIVE **1.** If something is your own, it belongs to you or is associated with you: *She stayed in her own house.*
VERB **2.** If you own something, it belongs to you.
PHRASE **3. On your own** means alone.

owner owners
NOUN The owner of something is the person it belongs to.

ownership
NOUN If you have ownership of something, you own it: *He shared the ownership of a sailboat.*

ox oxen
NOUN Oxen are cattle that are used for carrying or pulling things.

oxide oxides
NOUN a compound of oxygen and another chemical element

oxidize oxidizes oxidizing oxidized
VERB When a substance oxidizes, it changes chemically by reacting with oxygen.
oxidation NOUN

oxygen
NOUN a colourless and odourless gas in the air. It makes up about 21 percent of Earth's atmosphere. With an extremely small number of exceptions, living things need oxygen to survive, and things cannot burn without it.

oxymoron oxymorons
NOUN two words that contradict each other placed beside each other, for example *deafening silence*

oyster oysters
NOUN a large, flat shellfish. Some oysters can be eaten, and others produce pearls.

ozone
NOUN Ozone is a form of oxygen that is poisonous and has a strong smell. There is a layer of ozone high above Earth's surface.

ozone layer
NOUN The ozone layer is that part of Earth's atmosphere that protects living things from the harmful radiation of the sun.

KNOWING WORDS: IDIOMS

BE WORD SHARP!

Idioms add colour to language by playing with the meanings of words.

own belonging to or associated with you

come into your own achieve the success you deserve

each to his/her own everyone has different preferences

hold your own keep your position in a conflict

own up confess

blow your own horn boast about your achievements

NEL

Pp

Pp

p p is the written abbreviation for *page*. The plural is pp.

pace paces pacing paced
NOUN **1.** The pace of something is the speed at which it moves or happens. **2.** the length of a step in walking, used as a measurement of distance
VERB **3.** If you pace up and down, you continually walk around because you are anxious or impatient.

pacemaker pacemakers
NOUN a small electronic device put into someone's heart to control that person's heartbeat

Pacific Ocean
NOUN the ocean separating North and South America from Asia and Australia

pacifist pacifists
NOUN someone who is opposed to all violence and war
pacifism NOUN

pacify pacifies pacifying pacified
VERB If you pacify someone who is angry, you calm that person.

pack packs packing packed
VERB **1.** If you pack, you put things neatly into a suitcase, bag, or box. **2.** If people pack into a place, that place becomes crowded with them.
NOUN **3.** a group or set of similar people or things: *a pack of thieves, a pack of lies* **4.** a packet or collection of something: *a pack of gum* **5.** A pack of playing cards is a complete set. **6.** A pack of dogs or wolves is a group of them.
pack it in
VERB **7.** *an informal use* If you pack it in, you quit what you are doing.

package packages
NOUN **1.** a group of items packed or wrapped together: *I received a package of gifts from my aunt in Corner Brook.* **2.** a box or other container in which items are packed: *a package of paper*
packaged ADJECTIVE

packaging
NOUN Packaging is the container or wrapping in which an item is sold or sent.

packed
ADJECTIVE very full: *The auditorium was packed with people.*

packet packets
NOUN a small package or parcel

pact pacts
NOUN a formal agreement or treaty between individuals, groups, or countries

pad pads padding padded
NOUN **1.** a thick, soft piece of material **2.** a number of pieces of paper fixed together at one end **3.** The pads of an animal such as a cat or dog are the soft, fleshy parts on the bottom of its paws. **4.** a flat surface from which helicopters take off or rockets are launched
VERB **5.** If you pad something, you put a pad inside it or over it to protect it or change its shape. **6.** If you pad around, you walk softly.
padding NOUN

paddle paddles paddling paddled
NOUN **1.** a short pole with a broad blade at one or both ends, used to move a small boat or a canoe
VERB **2.** If someone paddles a boat, that person moves it using a paddle. **3.** If you paddle, you walk in shallow water.

paddock paddocks
NOUN a small field where horses are kept

paddy paddies
NOUN A paddy is an area in which rice is grown.

padlock padlocks padlocking padlocked
NOUN **1.** a lock made up of a metal case with a U-shaped bar attached to it, which can be put through a metal loop and then closed. It is unlocked by turning a key in the lock on the case.
VERB **2.** If you padlock something, you lock it with a padlock.

pagan pagans
ADJECTIVE **1.** involving beliefs and worship outside the main religions of the world: *pagan customs*
NOUN **2.** someone who believes in a pagan religion
paganism NOUN

page pages paging paged
NOUN **1.** one side of one of the pieces of paper in a book or magazine; also the sheet of paper itself **2.** In medieval times, a page was a young boy servant who was learning to be a knight.
VERB **3.** To page someone is to send a signal or message to a small electronic device that that person is carrying.

pageant pageants
NOUN a grand, colourful show or parade or a performance of a historical scene

Pp

pagoda pagodas
NOUN a tall, elaborately decorated Buddhist or Hindu temple

pail pails
NOUN a bucket

pain pains paining pained
NOUN **1.** Pain is an unpleasant feeling of physical hurt. **2.** Pain is also an unpleasant feeling of deep unhappiness.
VERB **3.** If something pains you, it makes you very unhappy.
painless ADJECTIVE
painlessly ADVERB

painful
ADJECTIVE **1.** causing emotional pain **2.** causing physical pain
painfully ADVERB

painkiller painkillers
NOUN a medicine that reduces or stops pain

painstaking
ADJECTIVE very careful and thorough: *years of painstaking research*

paint paints painting painted
NOUN **1.** Paint is a coloured liquid used to decorate buildings, or to make a picture.
VERB **2.** If you paint a picture of something, you make a picture of it using paint.
3. When you paint something such as a wall, you cover it with paint.
painter NOUN
painting NOUN

pair pairs pairing paired
NOUN **1.** two things of the same type or that do the same thing: *a pair of socks* **2.** You use *pair* when referring to certain objects that have two main matching parts that cannot be used separately: *a pair of scissors, a pair of jeans*
pair off
VERB **3.** When people pair off, they become grouped in pairs.
pair up
VERB **4.** If you pair up with someone, you agree to do something together.

pal pals
NOUN *an informal word* a friend

palace palaces
NOUN a large, grand house, especially the official home of a king or queen

palatable
ADJECTIVE Palatable food tastes pleasant.

palate palates
NOUN **1.** the top of the inside of your mouth **2.** Someone's palate is that person's sense of taste: *dishes to tempt every palate*

pale paler palest
ADJECTIVE white and without much colour or brightness

palette palettes
NOUN a flat piece of wood or other material on which an artist mixes colours

pall palls palling palled
VERB **1.** If something palls, it becomes less interesting or less enjoyable: *Even the tastiest food palls if it is served day after day.*
NOUN **2.** a thick cloud of smoke **3.** a cloth covering a coffin

palm palms
NOUN **1.** a tropical tree with no branches and a crown of long leaves **2.** the flat surface of your hand that your fingers bend toward

palpable
ADJECTIVE obvious and easily sensed: *Happiness was palpable in the air.*
palpably ADVERB

paltry
ADJECTIVE a very small amount of something: *a paltry sum of money*

pamper pampers pampering pampered
VERB If you pamper someone, you give that person kindness and comfort.

pamphlet pamphlets
NOUN a short printed document giving information about something

pan pans panning panned
NOUN **1.** a round metal container with a long handle, in which things are cooked on top of a stove

SPELL-CHECK THIS!

A computer's spell-check won't catch wrong **homophones** (words that are spelled differently but sound the same).

▼×

The **pail** blue paint is in the **pale** over there.

In this sentence, **pail** and **pale** are mixed up. A **pail** is a bucket. **Pale** means *light in colour*.

NEL

VERB **2.** When a film, TV, or video camera pans, it moves in a wide sweep to take in a whole scene or to follow a subject. **3.** *an informal use* To pan something is to criticize it strongly.

panacea panaceas
NOUN something that is supposed to cure everything

panache
NOUN Something that is done with panache is done confidently and stylishly.

pancake pancakes
NOUN a thin, flat piece of fried batter, cooked in a pan

pancreas pancreases
NOUN an organ in the body situated behind the stomach. It helps the body to digest food.

panda pandas
NOUN A panda or giant panda is a large animal like a bear that lives in China. It has black fur with large patches of white.

pandemonium
NOUN Pandemonium is a state of noisy confusion: *There was pandemonium in the halls after the fire alarm rang.*

pander panders pandering pandered
VERB If you pander to someone, you do everything that person wants.

pane panes
NOUN a sheet of glass in a window or door

panel panels
NOUN **1.** a small group of people who are chosen to do something: *a panel of judges* **2.** a flat piece of wood that is part of a larger object: *door panels* **3.** A control panel is a surface containing switches and instruments to operate a machine.
panelled ADJECTIVE

panelling
NOUN Panelling is rectangular pieces of wood covering an inside wall.

pang pangs
NOUN a sudden, strong feeling of sadness or pain

panic panics panicking panicked
NOUN **1.** Panic is a sudden, overwhelming feeling of fear or anxiety.
VERB **2.** If you panic, you become so afraid or anxious that you cannot act sensibly.

panorama panoramas
NOUN an extensive view over a wide area of land: *a fine panorama over the hills*
panoramic ADJECTIVE

pansy pansies
NOUN a small garden flower with large, round petals

pant pants panting panted
VERB If you pant, you breathe quickly and loudly through your mouth.

panther panthers
NOUN a large wild animal belonging to the cat family, especially the black leopard

pantomime pantomimes
NOUN a play without words, in which the actors express themselves by gestures

pantry pantries
NOUN a small room where food is kept

pants
PLURAL NOUN Pants are also trousers.

papaya papayas
NOUN a fruit with sweet, yellow flesh

paper papers papering papered
NOUN **1.** Paper is a material made from wood pulp or other fibrous substance and used for writing on or wrapping things. **2.** a newspaper **3.** an article or an essay, especially one to be read publicly
PLURAL NOUN **4.** Papers are official documents, for example a passport for identification.
VERB **5.** If you paper a wall, you put wallpaper on it.

paperback paperbacks
NOUN a book with a thin cardboard cover

paperwork
NOUN Paperwork is the part of a job that involves dealing with letters and records.

SPELL-CHECK THIS!

A computer's spell-check won't catch wrong **homophones** (words that are spelled differently but sound the same).

The gymnast was curled on the floor, wincing in pane.

In this sentence, **pane** should be **pain**.
Pain means an *unpleasant feeling of hurt*.
A **pane** is a sheet of glass.

Pp

papier-mâché

NOUN Papier-mâché is a hard substance made from mashed wet paper mixed with glue and moulded when moist to make things such as bowls and ornaments.

paprika

NOUN Paprika is a red powder made from a kind of pepper.

par

PHRASE **1.** Something that is **on a par** with something else is similar in quality or amount: *This regular season game was on a par with last year's Stanley Cup Final in level of excitement.* **2.** Something that is **below par** or **under par** is below its normal standard.

NOUN **3.** In golf, par is the number of strokes that it is thought a good player should take for a hole or all the holes on a particular golf course.

parable parables

NOUN a short story used to teach a moral lesson

parachute parachutes

NOUN a circular piece of fabric attached by lines to a person or package so that that person or thing can fall safely to the ground from an aircraft

parade parades parading paraded

NOUN **1.** a line of people or vehicles standing or moving together as a display

VERB **2.** When people parade, they walk together in a group as a display.

paradise

NOUN According to some religions, paradise is a wonderful place where good people go when they die.

paradox paradoxes

NOUN something that contains two ideas that seem to contradict each other: *More haste, less speed.*

paradoxical ADJECTIVE

paraffin

NOUN Paraffin is a flammable, white, waxy substance that is used for making candles, cosmetics, or for coating or sealing.

paragon paragons

NOUN someone whose behaviour is perfect in some way: *a paragon of elegance*

paragraph paragraphs

NOUN A paragraph is a group of sentences relating to the same idea or topic, which form a section of a piece of writing. Paragraphs begin on a new line.

parallel parallels

NOUN **1.** Something that is a parallel to something else has similar qualities or

features to it.

ADJECTIVE **2.** If two lines are parallel, they are the same distance apart along the whole of their length.

parallelogram parallelograms

NOUN a four-sided shape in which each side is parallel to the opposite side

paralysis

NOUN Paralysis is loss of the power to move.

paralyze paralyzes paralyzing paralyzed

VERB If something paralyzes you, it causes loss of feeling and movement in your body.

paramedic paramedics

NOUN a person who does some types of medical work, such as emergency first aid and who usually works in an ambulance

parameter parameters

NOUN a limit that affects the way something is done: *the general parameters set by the head of our club*

paramilitary

ADJECTIVE A paramilitary organization has a military structure but is not the official army of a country.

paramount

ADJECTIVE more important than anything else: *Safety is paramount when driving a car.*

paranoia

NOUN Paranoia is a mental illness in which someone believes that other people are trying to harm him or her.

paranoid

ADJECTIVE Someone who is paranoid believes wrongly that other people are trying to harm him or her.

parapet parapets

NOUN a low wall along the edge of a bridge or roof

paraphernalia

NOUN miscellaneous items, especially the equipment needed for a particular activity

paraphrase paraphrases paraphrasing paraphrased

NOUN **1.** A paraphrase of a piece of writing or speech is the same thing said in a different way: *a paraphrase of the popular song*

VERB **2.** If you paraphrase what someone has said, you express it in a different way.

parasite parasites

NOUN a small animal or plant that lives on or inside a larger animal or plant

parasitic ADJECTIVE

parasol parasols

NOUN an object like an umbrella that provides shelter from the sun

⚠ **HEADS UP** The word **papier-mâché** is pronounced PAY-per-ma-SHAY.

Pp

paratrooper paratroopers
NOUN Paratroopers are soldiers trained to be dropped by parachute.

parcel parcels parcelling parcelled
NOUN **1.** something that is wrapped up
VERB **2.** If you parcel something up, you make it into a parcel.

parched
ADJECTIVE **1.** If the ground is parched, it is very dry and in need of water. **2.** If you are parched, you are very thirsty.

parchment
NOUN Parchment is thick, yellowish paper of very good quality.

pardon pardons pardoning pardoned
NOUN **1.** You say **pardon** or **beg your pardon** to express surprise or an apology, or when you have not heard what someone has said.
VERB **2.** If you pardon someone, you forgive that person for doing something wrong.

pare pares paring pared
VERB When you pare fruit or vegetables, you cut off the skin.

parent parents
NOUN A parent is a father or mother.
parental ADJECTIVE

parentage
NOUN A person's parentage is his or her parents and ancestors.

parentheses
PLURAL NOUN a pair of punctuation marks ( ) placed around a word or phrase that adds detail but is not essential

parish parishes
NOUN an area with its own church and minister or priest

parishioner parishioners
NOUN a person who lives in a parish and attends its church

parity
NOUN *a formal word* If there is parity between things, they are equal: *Canadian currency reached parity with US currency in 2007.*

park parks parking parked
NOUN **1.** a public area with grass and trees **2.** an area of land kept in a natural state as a place for outdoor recreation and as a refuge for wildlife: *Grasslands National Park is in Saskatchewan.*
VERB **3.** When someone parks a vehicle, that person drives it into a position where it can be left.
parked ADJECTIVE
parking NOUN

parliament parliaments
NOUN the group of elected representatives who make the laws of a country
parliamentary ADJECTIVE

parlour parlours
NOUN *an old-fashioned word* a room for receiving or entertaining guests in a house

parochial
ADJECTIVE concerned only with local matters: *narrow parochial interests*

parody parodies parodying parodied
NOUN **1.** an amusing imitation of the style of an author or a work of art
VERB **2.** If you parody something, you make fun of that thing by imitating it.

parole
NOUN When prisoners are given parole, they are released early on condition that they behave well.

parrot parrots
NOUN a brightly coloured tropical bird with a curved beak

parry parries parrying parried
VERB **1.** If you parry a question, you cleverly avoid answering it: *I parried her questions by asking her one.* **2.** If you parry a blow, you push aside your attacker's arm to defend yourself.

parsley
NOUN a herb with curly leaves used for flavouring in cooking

parsnip parsnips
NOUN a long, pointed, cream-coloured root vegetable

part parts parting parted
NOUN **1.** one of the pieces or aspects of something **2.** one of the roles in a play or movie, played by an actor or actress
3. Someone's part in something is that person's involvement in it: *He was punished for his part in the plot.*
PHRASE **4.** If you **take part** in an activity, you do it together with other people.
VERB **5.** If things that are next to each other part, they move away from each other. **6.** If two people part, they leave each other.

partake partakes partaking partook partaken
VERB *a formal word* If you partake of food, you eat it: *She partook of the refreshments.*

partial
ADJECTIVE **1.** not complete or whole: *a partial explanation, partial success* **2.** liking something very much: *I'm very partial to winter sports.* **3.** supporting one side in a dispute, rather than being fair and without bias
partially ADVERB

⚠️ **HEADS UP** The word **parentheses** is pronounced puh-REN-thuh-sees.

Pp

participate participates participating participated
VERB If you participate in an activity, you take part in it.
participant NOUN
participation NOUN

participle participles
NOUN In grammar, a participle is a form of a verb used with an auxiliary verb in compound tenses and often as an adjective. English has two participles: the past participle, which describes a completed action, and the present participle, which describes a continuing action. For example, in *He has gone*, *gone* is a past participle and in *She is winning*, *winning* is a present participle.

particle particles
NOUN **1.** a basic unit of matter, such as an atom, molecule, or electron **2.** a very small piece of something

particular particulars
ADJECTIVE **1.** relating or belonging to only one person or thing: *That particular place is dangerous.* **2.** especially great or intense: *Pay particular attention to the next speaker.* **3.** Someone who is particular has high standards and is not easily satisfied.
PLURAL NOUN **4.** Particulars are facts or details.
particularly ADVERB

parting partings
NOUN an occasion when one person leaves another

partisan partisans
ADJECTIVE **1.** favouring or supporting one person or group: *a partisan crowd*
NOUN **2.** a member of an unofficial armed force fighting to free his or her country from enemy occupation

partition partitions partitioning partitioned
NOUN **1.** something that separates one part of a room from another **2.** Partition is the division of a country into independent areas.
VERB **3.** To partition something is to divide it into separate parts.

partly
ADVERB to some extent but not completely

partner partners partnering partnered
NOUN **1.** Someone's partner is the person he or she is married to or is living with.
2. Your partner is the person you are doing something with, for example in a dance or a game. **3.** Business partners are joint owners of their business.
VERB **4.** If you partner someone, you are

that person's partner for a game or social occasion.
partnership NOUN

part of speech parts of speech
NOUN a particular grammatical class of word, such as *noun* or *adjective*

partook the past tense of PARTAKE

partridge partridges
NOUN a brown game bird with a round body and a short tail

part-time
ADJECTIVE involving work for only a part of the working day or week

party parties
NOUN **1.** a social event held for people to enjoy themselves **2.** an organization whose members share the same political beliefs and campaign for election to government **3.** a group that is doing something together **4.** *a formal use* one of the people involved in a legal agreement or dispute

pass passes passing passed
VERB **1.** To pass something is to move past it. **2.** To pass in a particular direction is to move in that direction: *We passed through the gate.* **3.** If you pass something to someone, you hand it to that person or transfer it to him or her. **4.** If you pass a period of time doing something, you spend it that way: *He hoped to pass the long night with a good book.* **5.** When a period of time passes, it happens and finishes. **6.** If you pass a test, you are considered to be of an acceptable standard. **7.** When a new law or proposal is passed, it is formally approved. **8.** When a judge passes sentence on someone, the judge states what the punishment will be. **9.** If you pass the ball or puck in a game, you get it to another player on your team.
NOUN **10.** the transfer of the ball or puck in a game to another player on the same team **11.** an official document that allows you to go somewhere **12.** a narrow route between mountains

pass away, pass on
VERB **13.** Someone who has passed away has died.

pass out
VERB **14.** If someone passes out, he or she faints.

passable
ADJECTIVE of an acceptable standard: *a passable imitation of his dad*

passage passages
NOUN **1.** a space that connects two places **2.** a long, narrow corridor **3.** a section of a book or piece of music

Pp

passé
ADJECTIVE no longer fashionable

passenger passengers
NOUN a person travelling in a motor vehicle, aircraft, or ship

passerby passersby
NOUN someone who is walking past someone or something

passing
ADJECTIVE lasting only for a short time: *a passing phase, a passing idea*

passion passions
NOUN **1.** Passion is a very strong feeling of physical attraction. **2.** Passion is also any strong emotion.

passionate
ADJECTIVE expressing very strong feelings about something
passionately ADVERB

passive
ADJECTIVE **1.** remaining calm and showing no feeling when provoked
NOUN **2.** In grammar, the passive or passive voice is the form of the verb in which the person or thing to which an action is being done is the grammatical subject of the sentence, and is given more emphasis as a result. For example, the passive of *The committee rejected your application* is *Your application was rejected by the committee.*
passively ADVERB
passivity NOUN

Passover
NOUN an eight-day Jewish festival held in spring

passport passports
NOUN an official identification document that you need to show when you travel abroad

password passwords
NOUN **1.** a secret word known to only a few people. It allows people on the same side to recognize a friend. **2.** a word, number, or set of characters you need to know to get into some computers or computer files

past
NOUN **1.** The past is the period of time before the present.
ADJECTIVE **2.** Past things are things that happened or existed before the present: *the past 30 years*
PREPOSITION OR ADVERB **3.** You use *past* when you are telling the time: *It was ten past eleven.* **4.** If you go past something, you move toward it and continue until you are on the other side: *They drove rapidly past their cottage.*
PREPOSITION **5.** Something that is past a place is situated on the other side of it: *It's just past the mall.*

pasta
NOUN Pasta is a dried mixture of flour, eggs, and water, formed into different shapes.

paste pastes pasting pasted
NOUN **1.** Paste is a soft, sticky mixture that can be easily spread: *tomato paste*
VERB **2.** If you paste something onto a surface, you stick it to that surface with glue.

pastel
ADJECTIVE Pastel colours are pale and soft.

pasteurized
ADJECTIVE If a liquid such as milk has been pasteurized, it has been treated with a special heating process to kill bacteria.

pastime pastimes
NOUN a hobby or something you do just for pleasure

pastoral
ADJECTIVE characteristic of peaceful country life and landscape: *pastoral scenes*

past participle past participles
NOUN In grammar, the past participle of a verb is the form, usually ending in *ed* or *en*, which is used to make some past tenses and

SPELL-CHECK THIS!

A computer's spell-check won't catch wrong **homophones** (words that are spelled differently but sound the same).

Three days had past since I'd last seen my wallet.

In this sentence, past should be **passed**.
Passed means *went by*.
Past means *time before*.

Pp

the passive. For example *walked* in *She has walked the dog* and *broken* in *My leg was broken* are past participles.

pastry pastries
NOUN **1.** Pastry is a mixture of flour, fat, and water, rolled flat and used for making pies and other baked foods. **2.** a piece of pastry, such as a tart

past tense
NOUN In grammar, the past tense is the tense of a verb that you use mainly to refer to things that happened or existed before the time of writing or speaking.

pasture pastures
NOUN Pasture is an area of grass on which farm animals graze.

pasty pastier pastiest
ADJECTIVE Someone who is pasty looks pale and unhealthy.

pat pats patting patted
VERB **1.** If you pat something, you tap it lightly with your hand held flat.
NOUN **2.** a light tap with the hand

patch patches patching patched
NOUN **1.** a piece of material used to cover a hole in something **2.** an area of a surface that is different in appearance from the rest: *a bald patch*
VERB **3.** If you patch something, you mend it by fixing a patch over the hole.
patch up
VERB **4.** If you patch something up, you mend it hurriedly or temporarily.

patchwork
ADJECTIVE **1.** A patchwork quilt is made from many small pieces of material sewn together.
NOUN **2.** Something that is a patchwork is made up of many parts.

patchy patchier patchiest
ADJECTIVE Something that is patchy is unevenly spread or incomplete in parts: *patchy fog on the hills*

pâté
NOUN Pâté is a mixture of meat, fish, or vegetables blended into a paste.

patent patents patenting patented
NOUN **1.** an official right given to an inventor to be the only person or company allowed to make or sell a new product
VERB **2.** If you patent something, you obtain a patent for it.
ADJECTIVE **3.** obvious: *This was patent nonsense.*
patently ADVERB

paternal
ADJECTIVE relating to a father: *paternal pride*

paternity
NOUN Paternity is the state or fact of being a father.

path paths
NOUN **1.** a strip of ground for people to walk on **2.** Your path is the area ahead of you and the direction in which you are moving.

pathetic
ADJECTIVE **1.** If something is pathetic, it makes you feel pity. **2.** Pathetic also means very poor or unsuccessful: *a pathetic attempt to be funny*
pathetically ADVERB

pathological
ADJECTIVE extreme and uncontrollable: *a pathological fear of snakes*
pathologically ADVERB

pathology
NOUN Pathology is the study of diseases and the way they develop.
pathologist NOUN

pathos
NOUN Pathos is a quality in literature or art that causes great sadness or pity.

pathway pathways
NOUN a path

patience
NOUN Patience is the ability to stay calm in a difficult or irritating situation.

patient patients
ADJECTIVE **1.** If you are patient, you stay calm in a difficult or irritating situation.
NOUN **2.** a person receiving medical treatment from a doctor or in a hospital
patiently ADVERB

patio patios
NOUN a paved area close to a house

patriarch patriarchs
NOUN the male head of a family or tribe
patriarchal ADJECTIVE

patriot patriots
NOUN someone who loves his or her country and feels very loyal toward it
patriotic ADJECTIVE
patriotism NOUN

patrol patrols patrolling patrolled
VERB **1.** When soldiers, police, or guards patrol an area, they walk or drive around to make sure there is no trouble.
NOUN **2.** a group of people patrolling an area

patron patrons
NOUN **1.** a person who supports or gives money to artists, writers, or musicians **2.** The patrons of a restaurant, store, or other place of business are the people who use it.
patronage NOUN

patronize patronizes patronizing patronized
VERB **1.** If someone patronizes you, that person treats you kindly, but in a way that suggests that you are less intelligent or inferior to him or her. **2.** If you patronize a restaurant, store, or other place of business, you are a customer there.
patronizing ADJECTIVE

patron saint patron saints
NOUN The patron saint of a place or group of people is a saint who is believed to look after them.

patter patters pattering pattered
VERB **1.** If something patters on a surface, it makes quick, light tapping sounds.
NOUN **2.** a series of light tapping sounds: *a patter of light rain*

pattern patterns
NOUN **1.** a decorative design of repeated shapes **2.** The pattern of something is the way it is usually done or happens: *a perfectly normal pattern of behaviour* **3.** a diagram or shape used as a guide for making something, for example clothes
patterned ADJECTIVE

paunch paunches
NOUN If a person has a paunch, he or she has a fat stomach.

pauper paupers
NOUN *an old-fashioned word* a very poor person

pause pauses pausing paused
VERB **1.** If you pause, you stop what you are doing for a short time.
NOUN **2.** a short period when you stop what you are doing **3.** a short period of silence

pave paves paving paved
VERB When an area of ground is paved, it is covered with flat blocks of stone, asphalt, or concrete.

pavement pavements
NOUN a covering or surface for streets, sidewalks, and highways made of stones, gravel, concrete, or asphalt

pavilion pavilions
NOUN a building, usually open-sided, used for a special purpose: *a park pavilion*

paw paws pawing pawed
NOUN **1.** The paws of an animal such as a cat or bear are its feet with claws and soft pads.
VERB **2.** If an animal paws something, it hits it or scrapes at it with its paws.

pawn pawns pawning pawned
VERB **1.** If you pawn something, you leave it with a pawnbroker in exchange for money.
NOUN **2.** the smallest and least valuable playing piece in chess

pawnbroker pawnbrokers
NOUN a dealer who lends money in return for personal property left with him or her, which may be sold if the loan is not repaid on time

pay pays paying paid
VERB **1.** When you pay money to someone, you give it to that person because you are buying something or owe it to him or her. **2.** If it pays to do something, it is to your advantage to do it: *They say it pays to advertise.* **3.** If you pay for something that you have done, you suffer as a result. **4.** If you pay attention to something, you give it your attention. **5.** If you pay a visit to someone, you visit that person.
NOUN **6.** Someone's pay is that person's salary or wages.

Instead of **PAY** try...
foot the bill
settle a debt
grant an expense
chip in for a present
compensate for work

payable
ADJECTIVE **1.** An amount of money that is payable has to be paid or can be paid: *All fees are payable in advance.* **2.** If a cheque is made payable to you, you are the person who should receive the money.

payment payments
NOUN **1.** Payment is the act of paying money. **2.** a sum of money paid

payroll payrolls
NOUN Someone who is on an organization's payroll is employed and paid by that organization.

PC PCs
NOUN **1.** a personal computer
ADJECTIVE **2.** short for POLITICALLY CORRECT

PE
NOUN PE is an abbreviation for *physical education.*

pea peas
NOUN Peas are small, round, green seeds that grow in pods and are eaten as a vegetable.

peace
NOUN **1.** a state of calm and quiet when there is no disturbance of any kind **2.** When a country is at peace, it is not at war.
peaceable ADJECTIVE

peaceful
ADJECTIVE quiet and calm
peacefully ADVERB

Pp

peach peaches
NOUN **1.** a soft, round fruit with yellow flesh and a yellow and red skin
ADJECTIVE **2.** pale pink with a hint of orange

peacock peacocks
NOUN a large bird with green and blue feathers. The male has a long tail that it can spread out in a fan.

peak peaks peaking peaked
NOUN **1.** The peak of an activity or process is the point at which it is strongest or most successful. **2.** the pointed top of a mountain
VERB **3.** When something peaks, it reaches its highest value or its greatest level of success.
peaked ADJECTIVE

peal peals pealing pealed
NOUN **1.** A peal of bells is the musical sound made by bells ringing one after another.
VERB **2.** When bells peal, they ring one after the other.

peanut peanuts
NOUN Peanuts are small, oval nuts that grow under the ground.

pear pears
NOUN a fruit that is narrow at the top and wide and rounded at the bottom

pearl pearls
NOUN a hard, round, creamy-white object used in jewellery. Pearls grow inside the shell of an oyster.

peasant peasants
NOUN a person who works on the land, especially in a poor country

peat
NOUN Peat is dark brown, decaying plant material found in cool, wet regions. Dried peat can be used as fuel.

pebble pebbles
NOUN a smooth, round stone

peck pecks pecking pecked
VERB **1.** If a bird pecks something, it bites at it quickly with its beak. **2.** If you peck someone on the cheek, you give that person a quick kiss.
NOUN **3.** a quick bite by a bird **4.** a quick kiss on the cheek

peculiar
ADJECTIVE **1.** strange, odd, or unusual
2. relating or belonging only to a particular person or thing: *a gesture peculiar to her*
peculiarly ADVERB
peculiarity NOUN

pedal pedals pedalling pedalled
NOUN **1.** a control lever on a machine or vehicle that you press with your foot

VERB **2.** When you pedal a bicycle, you push the pedals around with your feet to move along.

pedantic
ADJECTIVE If a person is pedantic, he or she is too concerned with unimportant details and traditional rules.

peddle peddles peddling peddled
VERB Someone who peddles something sells it.

pedestal pedestals
NOUN a base on which a statue, vase, or lamp stands

pedestrian pedestrians
NOUN **1.** someone who is walking
ADJECTIVE **2.** Pedestrian means ordinary and dull: *a pedestrian performance*

pediatrician pediatricians
NOUN a doctor who specializes in treating children

pediatrics
NOUN Pediatrics is the area of medicine that deals with children's diseases.
pediatric ADJECTIVE

pedigree pedigrees
NOUN **1.** the list of ancestors of an animal that is descended from a single breed
2. Someone's pedigree is that person's background or ancestry.

peek peeks peeking peeked
VERB **1.** If you peek at something, you have a quick look at it: *I peeked around the corner.*
NOUN **2.** a quick look at something

peel peels peeling peeled
NOUN **1.** The peel of a fruit is the skin.
VERB **2.** When you peel fruit or vegetables, you remove the skin. **3.** If a surface is peeling, it is coming off in thin layers.
peeling NOUN

peep peeps peeping peeped
VERB **1.** If you peep at something, you have a quick look at it. **2.** If something peeps out from behind something else, a small part of it becomes visible: *a handkerchief peeping out of his pocket*
NOUN **3.** a quick look at something

peer peers peering peered
VERB **1.** If you peer at something, you look at it very hard.
NOUN **2.** Your peers are the people who are of the same age and social status as yourself.

peer group peer groups
NOUN Your peer group is the people who are of the same age and social status as yourself.

peerless
ADJECTIVE so magnificent or perfect that nothing can equal it: *a peerless leader*

Pp

peg pegs pegging pegged
NOUN **1.** a plastic or wooden clip used for hanging wet clothes on a line **2.** a hook on a wall where you can hang things
VERB **3.** If you peg clothes on a line, you fix them there with pegs. **4.** If a price is pegged at a certain level, it is fixed at that level.

pejorative
ADJECTIVE A pejorative word expresses criticism.

Pekingese Pekingese
NOUN a small, long-haired dog with a flat nose

pelican pelicans
NOUN a large water bird with a pouch beneath its beak in which it stores fish

pellet pellets
NOUN a small ball of paper, lead, or other material

pelt pelts pelting pelted
VERB **1.** If you pelt someone you throw things with force at that person. **2.** fall quickly and heavily as snow, rain, or hail
NOUN **3.** the skin and fur of an animal

pelvis pelvises
NOUN the wide, curved group of bones at hip level at the base of your spine
pelvic ADJECTIVE

pen pens penning penned
NOUN **1.** a long, thin instrument used for writing with ink **2.** a small fenced area in which farm animals are kept for a short time
VERB **3.** a literary or poetic use If someone pens a letter or an article, that person writes it. **4.** If you are penned in or penned up, you are confined in an uncomfortably small area.

penal
ADJECTIVE relating to the punishment of criminals

penalize penalizes penalizing penalized
VERB If you are penalized, you are made to suffer some disadvantage as a punishment for something.

penalty penalties
NOUN **1.** a punishment or disadvantage that someone is made to suffer **2.** In some sports, a penalty is a disadvantage to a team or player for breaking the rules.

penance
NOUN If you do penance, you do something unpleasant to show that you are sorry for something wrong that you have done.

penchant
NOUN a formal word If you have a penchant for something, you have a particular liking for it: a penchant for long hikes in the woods

pencil pencils
NOUN a long, thin stick of wood with graphite in the centre, used for drawing or writing

pendant pendants
NOUN a piece of jewellery attached to a chain and worn around the neck

pending a formal word
ADJECTIVE **1.** Something that is pending is waiting to be dealt with or will happen soon.
PREPOSITION **2.** Something that is done pending a future event is done until the event happens: Pending her return, let's prepare dinner.

pendulum pendulums
NOUN a rod with a weight at one end in a clock that swings regularly from side to side to control the clock

penetrate penetrates penetrating penetrated
VERB To penetrate an area that is difficult to get into is to succeed in getting into it.
penetration NOUN

penetrating
ADJECTIVE **1.** loud and high-pitched: a penetrating voice **2.** having or showing deep understanding: penetrating questions

penguin penguins
NOUN a black-and-white bird with webbed feet and small wings like flippers

penicillin
NOUN Penicillin is a powerful antibiotic obtained from fungus and used to treat infections.

peninsula peninsulas
NOUN an area of land almost surrounded by water

penis penises
NOUN A man's penis is the part of his body that he uses when urinating and having sexual intercourse.

penitent
ADJECTIVE Someone who is penitent is deeply sorry for having done something wrong.
penitence NOUN

penknife penknives
NOUN a small knife with a blade that folds back into the handle

pennant pennants
NOUN a triangular flag identifying a sports team or club, or used by ships for signalling

penniless
ADJECTIVE Someone who is penniless has no money.

pen pal pen pals
NOUN someone living in a different place or country whom you write to regularly, although you may never have met each other

---

⚠ **HEADS UP** The word **Pekingese** is pronounced pee-ki-NEEZ.

pension pensions
NOUN a regular sum of money paid to a retired person or as compensation

pensioner pensioners
NOUN someone who gets a pension, especially a retired person

pensive
ADJECTIVE deep in thought

pentagon pentagons
NOUN a shape with five straight sides

pentathlon pentathlons
NOUN a sports contest in which athletes compete in five different events

penthouse penthouses
NOUN a luxurious apartment at the top of a building

pent-up
ADJECTIVE Pent-up emotions have been held back for a long time without release.

penultimate
ADJECTIVE The penultimate thing in a series is the one before the last.

peony peonies
NOUN a garden plant with large pink, white, or red flowers

people peoples peopling peopled
PLURAL NOUN **1.** People are men, women, and children.
NOUN **2.** all the men, women, and children of a particular country or race
VERB **3.** If an area is peopled by a group, that group of people lives there.

pepper peppers
NOUN **1.** a hot-tasting, powdered spice used for flavouring in cooking **2.** a hollow green, red, or yellow fruit eaten as a vegetable, with sweet-flavoured flesh

peppermint peppermints
NOUN a plant with a strong taste. It is used for making candies and in medicine.

per
PREPOSITION *Per* is used to mean *each*: *The class meets two evenings per week.*

perceive perceives perceiving perceived
VERB If you perceive something that is not obvious, you see it or realize it.

percent percents
NOUN You use **percent** to talk about amounts as a proportion of a hundred. An amount that is ten percent (10%) of a larger amount is equal to ten hundredths of the larger amount: *Nine percent of the class failed the exam.*

percentage percentages
NOUN a fraction expressed as a number of hundredths: *A high percentage of homes have more than one television.*

perceptible
ADJECTIVE Something that is perceptible can be seen: *a barely perceptible nod*

perception perceptions
NOUN **1.** Perception is the recognition of things using the senses, especially the sense of sight. **2.** Someone who has perception realizes or notices things that are not obvious. **3.** Your perception of someone or something is your understanding of that person or thing.

perceptive
ADJECTIVE Someone who is perceptive realizes or notices things that are not obvious.
perceptively ADVERB

perch perches perching perched
VERB **1.** If you perch on something, you sit on the edge of it. **2.** When a bird perches on something, it rests on it.
NOUN **3.** a short rod for a bird to rest on **4.** an edible freshwater fish

percolator percolators
NOUN a special pot for making and serving coffee

percussion
NOUN Percussion instruments are musical instruments that you hit to produce sounds.
percussionist NOUN

perennial
ADJECTIVE continually occurring or never ending: *The damp cellar was a perennial problem.*

perfect perfects perfecting perfected
ADJECTIVE **1.** of the highest standard and without fault: *His French was perfect.*
2. complete or absolute: *They have a perfect right to say so.* **3.** In English grammar, the perfect tense of a verb is formed with the present tense of *have* and the past participle of the main verb: *I have lost my homework.*
VERB **4.** If you perfect something, you make it as good as it can possibly be.
perfectly ADVERB
perfection NOUN

Instead of **PERFECT** try...

an **ideal** scenario

a **polished** speech

a **foolproof** system

a **flawless** performance

impeccable taste in clothes

Pp

perfectionist perfectionists
NOUN someone who always tries to do everything perfectly

perforated
ADJECTIVE Something that is perforated has had small holes made in it.
perforation NOUN

perform performs performing performed
VERB **1.** To perform a task or action is to do it. **2.** To perform is to act, dance, or play music in front of an audience.
performer NOUN

performance performances
NOUN **1.** an entertainment provided for an audience **2.** The performance of a task or action is the doing of it. **3.** Someone's or something's performance is how successful that person or thing is: *your poor performance on the history exam*

perfume perfumes
NOUN **1.** Perfume is a pleasant-smelling liquid that people put on their bodies. **2.** The perfume of something is its pleasant smell.
perfumed ADJECTIVE

perfunctory
ADJECTIVE done quickly without interest or care: *a perfunctory kiss*

perhaps
ADVERB You use *perhaps* when you are not sure whether something is true or possible.

peril perils
NOUN *a formal word* Peril is great danger.
perilous ADJECTIVE
perilously ADVERB

perimeter perimeters
NOUN The perimeter of an area or figure is the whole of its outer edge.

period periods
NOUN **1.** a particular length of time **2.** one of the parts the day is divided into at school **3.** A female's period is the monthly bleeding from her womb.
ADJECTIVE **4.** relating to a historical period of time: *period furniture*
periodic ADJECTIVE
periodically ADVERB

periodical periodicals
NOUN a magazine

peripheral
ADJECTIVE **1.** of little importance in comparison with other things: *a peripheral activity* **2.** on or relating to the edge of an area

periphery peripheries
NOUN The periphery of an area is its outside edge.

perish perishes perishing perished
VERB *a formal use* If someone or something perishes, that person or thing is killed or destroyed.
perishable ADJECTIVE

perjury
NOUN *a formal or legal word* If someone commits perjury, that person tells a lie in court while under oath.
perjure VERB

perk perks perking perked
NOUN **1.** an extra, such as a company car, offered by an employer in addition to a salary. Perk is an abbreviation of *perquisite*.
VERB **2.** *an informal expression* When someone perks up, that person becomes more cheerful.
perky ADJECTIVE

permanent
ADJECTIVE lasting forever, or present all the time
permanently ADVERB
permanence NOUN

permeable
ADJECTIVE *a formal word* If something is permeable, liquids are able to pass through it: *permeable rock*

permeate permeates permeating permeated
VERB To permeate something is to spread through it and affect every part of it: *The feeling of failure permeates everything I do.*

permissible
ADJECTIVE allowed by the rules

permission
NOUN If you have permission to do something, you are allowed to do it.

permissive
ADJECTIVE allowing a great deal of freedom: *a permissive society, permissive parents*
permissiveness NOUN

permit permits permitting permitted
VERB **1.** To permit something is to allow it or make it possible.
NOUN **2.** an official document that says that you are allowed to do something

permutation permutations
NOUN one possible arrangement of a number of things

pernicious
ADJECTIVE *a formal word* very harmful: *pernicious habits*

peroxide
NOUN Peroxide is a chemical used for bleaching hair or as an antiseptic.

perpendicular
ADJECTIVE upright, or at right angles to a horizontal line

 **HEADS UP** The word **pernicious** is pronounced per-NISH-us.

Pp

perpetrate perpetrates perpetrating perpetrated
VERB *a formal word* To perpetrate a crime is to commit it.
perpetrator NOUN

perpetual
ADJECTIVE never ending: *a perpetual toothache*
perpetually ADVERB
perpetuity NOUN

perpetuate perpetuates perpetuating perpetuated
VERB To perpetuate a situation or belief is to cause it to continue: *The television series will perpetuate the myths.*

perplexed
ADJECTIVE If you are perplexed, you are puzzled and do not know what to do.

persecute persecutes persecuting persecuted
VERB To persecute someone is to treat that person cruelly and unfairly over a long period of time.
persecution NOUN
persecutor NOUN

persevere perseveres persevering persevered
VERB If you persevere, you keep trying to do something and do not give up.
perseverance NOUN

persimmon persimmons
NOUN a sweet, red tropical fruit

persist persists persisting persisted
VERB **1.** If something undesirable persists, it continues to exist. **2.** If you persist in doing something, you continue in spite of opposition or difficulty.
persistence NOUN
persistent ADJECTIVE

person people
NOUN **1.** a man, woman, or child **2.** In grammar, the first person is the speaker (I), the second person is the person being spoken to (you), and the third person is anyone else being referred to (he, she, they).

personal
ADJECTIVE **1.** Personal means belonging or relating to a particular person rather than to people in general: *my personal feeling* **2.** Personal matters relate to your feelings, relationships, and health, which you may not wish to discuss with other people.
personally ADVERB

personality personalities
NOUN **1.** Your personality is your character and nature. **2.** a famous person in entertainment or sport

personal response
NOUN a written or spoken description of the reader's feelings and thoughts about a text

personification
NOUN **1.** Personification is a form of imagery in which something that isn't human is described as if it were: *The trees sighed and whispered as the impatient breeze stirred their branches.* **2.** Someone who is the personification of some quality is a living example of that quality: *He was the personification of evil.*

personify personifies personifying personified
VERB **1.** Someone who personifies a particular quality seems to be an example of it. **2.** If you personify a thing, you write or speak of it as if it has human qualities, for example *The sun is trying to come out.*

personnel
NOUN The personnel of an organization are the people who work for it.

perspective perspectives
NOUN **1.** A particular perspective is one way of thinking about something. **2.** Perspective is a method artists use to make some people and things seem further away than others.

perspiration
NOUN Perspiration is the moisture that appears on your skin when you are hot or frightened.

perspire perspires perspiring perspired
VERB If someone perspires, that person sweats.

persuade persuades persuading persuaded
VERB If someone persuades you, that person makes you do something or believe something by giving you very good reasons.
persuasion NOUN
persuasive ADJECTIVE

pertaining
ADJECTIVE *a formal word* If information or questions are pertaining to a place or thing, they are about that place or thing: *issues pertaining to teenagers*

pertinent
ADJECTIVE especially relevant to the subject being discussed: *He asks pertinent questions.*

perturbed
ADJECTIVE Someone who is perturbed is worried.

pervade pervades pervading pervaded
VERB Something that pervades a place is present and noticeable throughout it: *a fear that pervades the community*
pervasive ADJECTIVE

perverse
ADJECTIVE Someone who is perverse deliberately does things that are unreasonable or harmful.
perversely ADVERB
perversity NOUN

THE WRITER'S EDGE

50x

She paused
to shyly smile before
admitting, "Finlay, you are the
only boy who could warm me from
the inside out. Please don't leave me."
I laid the flowers near the Sea of
Tranquility and sheepishly said, "Moon,
thank you for being my friend."
And as I hugged the moon I
whispered, "I love you."

I often contemplate, while I explore space, if you could see a slight blush spill over the moon's face the first night she was hugged.

PERSONIFICATION ▾✕

a form of imagery in which something that isn't human is described as if it were human

"...see a slight blush spill over the moon's face the first night she was hugged."

Here is an example of personification. The moon is being talked about as if it were a woman.

413

pervert perverts perverting perverted
VERB **1.** *a formal use* To pervert something is to interfere with it so that it is no longer what it should be: *a conspiracy to pervert the course of justice*
NOUN **2.** a person whose sexual behaviour is considered abnormal or harmful
perversion NOUN

perverted
ADJECTIVE **1.** Someone who is perverted has disgusting or unacceptable behaviour or ideas, especially sexual behaviour or ideas. **2.** Something that is perverted is completely wrong: *a perverted sense of value*

pessimism
NOUN Pessimism is the tendency to believe that bad things will happen.
pessimist NOUN

pessimistic
ADJECTIVE believing that bad things will happen
pessimistically ADVERB

pest pests
NOUN **1.** an insect or small animal that damages plants or food supplies **2.** someone who keeps bothering or annoying you

pester pesters pestering pestered
VERB If you pester someone, you keep bothering that person or asking him or her to do something.

pesticide pesticides
NOUN Pesticides are chemicals sprayed onto plants to kill insects and grubs.

pet pets petting petted
NOUN **1.** a tame animal kept at home
ADJECTIVE **2.** Someone's pet theory or pet project is something that he or she particularly supports or feels strongly about.
VERB **3.** If you pet a person or animal, you stroke that person or animal affectionately.

petal petals
NOUN The petals of a flower are the coloured outer parts.

peter out peters out petering out petered out
VERB If something peters out, it gradually comes to an end.

petite
ADJECTIVE A woman or girl who is petite is small and slim.

petition petitions petitioning petitioned
NOUN **1.** a document demanding official action that is signed by a lot of people **2.** a formal request to a court for legal action to be taken
VERB **3.** If you petition someone in authority, you make a formal request to that person: *They petitioned the city council to increase funding for public parks and pools.*

petrified
ADJECTIVE If you are petrified, you are very frightened.

petroleum
NOUN Petroleum is thick, dark oil found under the earth or under the seabed.

petticoat petticoats
NOUN a piece of women's or girl's underwear like a very thin skirt

petty pettier pettiest
ADJECTIVE **1.** Petty things are small and unimportant. **2.** Petty behaviour consists of doing small things that are selfish and unkind.

petulant
ADJECTIVE showing unreasonable and childish impatience or anger
petulantly ADVERB
petulance NOUN

petunia petunias
NOUN a garden plant with large trumpet-shaped flowers

pew pews
NOUN a long, wooden seat with a back, which people sit on in church

pewter
NOUN Pewter is a silvery-grey metal made from a mixture of tin and lead.

pH
NOUN The pH of a solution or of the soil is a measurement of how acid or alkaline it is. Acid solutions have a pH of less than 7 and alkaline solutions have a pH greater than 7. The abbreviation pH stands for *potential hydrogen.*

phallus phalluses
NOUN a penis or a symbolic model of a penis
phallic ADJECTIVE

phantom phantoms
NOUN **1.** a ghost
ADJECTIVE **2.** imagined or unreal: *a phantom ship*

Pharaoh Pharaohs
NOUN Pharaoh is the title given to the kings of ancient Egypt.

pharmaceutical
ADJECTIVE connected with the industrial production of medicines

pharmacist pharmacists
NOUN a person who is qualified to prepare and sell medicines

pharmacy pharmacies
NOUN a store where medicines are sold

Pp

phase phases phasing phased
NOUN **1.** a particular stage in the development of something
phase in, phase out
VERB **2.** To phase something in or out is to cause it to happen gradually in stages.

PhD PhDs
NOUN a degree awarded to someone who has done advanced research in a subject. PhD is an abbreviation for *Doctor of Philosophy*.

pheasant pheasants
NOUN a large, long-tailed game bird

phenomenal
ADJECTIVE extraordinarily great or good
phenomenally ADVERB

phenomenon phenomena
NOUN something that happens or exists, especially something remarkable or something being considered in a scientific way: *a well-known geographical phenomenon*

philanthropist philanthropists
NOUN someone who freely gives help or money to people in need
philanthropic ADJECTIVE
philanthropy NOUN

philistine philistines
NOUN If you call someone a philistine, you mean that that person does not like art, literature, or music.

philosophical
ADJECTIVE Someone who is philosophical does not get upset when disappointing things happen.

philosophy philosophies
NOUN **1.** Philosophy is the study or creation of ideas about existence, knowledge, or beliefs. **2.** a set of beliefs that a person has
philosopher NOUN

phlegm
NOUN Phlegm is a thick mucus that you get in your throat when you have a cold.

phobia phobias
NOUN a great fear or hatred of something: *The man had a phobia about flying.*
phobic ADJECTIVE

-phobia
SUFFIX The suffix *-phobia* means *fear of*: *claustrophobia*

phoenix phoenixes
NOUN an imaginary bird which, according to myth, burns itself to ashes every 500 years and rises from the fire again

phone phones phoning phoned
NOUN **1.** a piece of electronic equipment that allows you to speak to someone in another place by keying in or dialling that person's number
VERB **2.** If you phone someone, you key in or dial that person's number and speak to him or her using a phone.

-phone
SUFFIX **1.** The suffix *-phone* means *giving off sound*: *telephone, xylophone* **2.** The suffix *-phone* is also used to refer to a speaker of a language: *Francophone, Anglophone*

phony phonier phoniest
ADJECTIVE *an informal word* false and intended to deceive

photo photos
NOUN *an informal word* a photograph

photo-
PREFIX The prefix *photo-* means *light* or *using light*: *photography, photocopy*

photocopier photocopiers
NOUN a machine that makes instant copies of documents by photographing them

photocopy photocopies photocopying photocopied
NOUN **1.** a copy of a document produced by a photocopier
VERB **2.** If you photocopy a document, you make a copy of it using a photocopier.

photo essay
NOUN a series of photographs arranged to tell a story or create an emotional response

KNOWING WORDS: WORD BUILDING

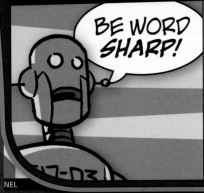

BE WORD SHARP!

You can create new words by adding prefixes and suffixes to a base word.

-phobia a suffix that means *fear of*

agoraphobia fear of open spaces (agora = open space)

acrophobia fear of heights (acro = high)

claustrophobia fear of tight spaces (claustro = shut)

necrophobia fear of death (necro = death)

xenophobia fear of strangers (xeno = foreign, strange)

photogenic
ADJECTIVE Someone who is photogenic always looks nice in photographs.

photograph photographs photographing photographed
NOUN **1.** a picture made using a camera
VERB **2.** When you photograph someone, you take a picture of that person by using a camera.
photographer NOUN
photography NOUN

photographic
ADJECTIVE connected with photography

photosynthesis
NOUN Photosynthesis is the process by which the action of sunlight on the chlorophyll in plants produces the substances that keep the plants alive.

phrasal verb phrasal verbs
NOUN a verb such as *take over* or *break in*, which is made up of a verb and an adverb or preposition

phrase phrases phrasing phrased
NOUN **1.** a group of words considered as a unit
VERB **2.** If you phrase something in a particular way, you choose those words to express it: *I should have phrased that better.*

physical
ADJECTIVE **1.** concerning the body rather than the mind **2.** relating to things that can be touched or seen, especially with regard to their size or shape: *the physical characteristics of the machinery, the physical world*
physically ADVERB

physical education
NOUN Physical education is instruction in sports, exercise, and taking care of the body.

physician physicians
NOUN a doctor

physics
NOUN Physics is the scientific study of matter, energy, gravity, electricity, heat, and sound.
physicist NOUN

physio-
PREFIX The prefix *physio-* means to do with the body or natural functions: *physiotherapy*

physiology
NOUN Physiology is the scientific study of the way the bodies of living things work.

physiotherapy
NOUN Physiotherapy is medical treatment that involves exercise and massage.
physiotherapist NOUN

physique physiques
NOUN A person's physique is the shape and size of his or her body.

pi
NOUN Pi is a number, approximately 3.142 and symbolized by the Greek letter π. Pi is the ratio of the circumference of a circle to its diameter.

piano pianos
NOUN a large musical instrument with a row of black and white keys. When the keys are pressed, little hammers hit wires to produce the different notes.
pianist NOUN

piccolo piccolos
NOUN a high-pitched wind instrument like a small flute

pick picks picking picked
VERB **1.** To pick something is to choose it. **2.** If you pick a flower or fruit, or pick something from a place, you remove it with your fingers. **3.** If someone picks a lock, that person opens it with a piece of wire instead of a key.
NOUN **4.** The pick of a group of people or things are the best ones in it. **5.** a choice, or the act of making that choice: *The strawberry ice cream is my pick.*

pick on
VERB **6.** If you pick on someone, you criticize that person unfairly or treat him or her unkindly.

pick up
VERB **7.** If you pick someone up, you collect that person from the place where he or she is waiting.

pickaxe pickaxes
NOUN a tool consisting of a curved, pointed iron bar attached in the middle to a long handle

picket pickets picketing picketed
VERB **1.** When a group of people picket a place of work, they stand outside to persuade other workers to join a strike.
NOUN **2.** a pointed stake or peg driven into the ground, used to form part of a fence

pickings
PLURAL NOUN leftovers or remaining scraps of something

pickle pickles pickling pickled
NOUN **1.** Pickles are vegetables or fruit

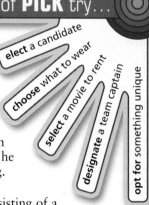

Instead of **PICK** try...
elect a candidate
choose what to wear
select a movie to rent
designate a team captain
opt for something unique

Pp

preserved in vinegar or salt water.
VERB **2.** To pickle food is to preserve it in vinegar or salt water.

pickpocket pickpockets
NOUN a thief who steals from people's pockets or handbags

picnic picnics picnicking picnicked
NOUN **1.** a meal eaten out of doors
VERB **2.** People who are picnicking are having a picnic.

pictorial
ADJECTIVE relating to or using pictures: *a pictorial record of the railway*

picture pictures picturing pictured
NOUN **1.** a drawing, painting, or photograph of someone or something **2.** If you have a picture of something in your mind, you have an idea or impression of it.
VERB **3.** If someone is pictured in a newspaper or magazine, a photograph of that person is printed in it. **4.** If you picture

Instead of **PICTURESQUE** try...

an **idyllic** valley
a **scenic** lookout
spectacular scenery
a **striking** landscape
a **breathtaking** view

something, you think of it and imagine it clearly: *That is how I always picture him.*

picturesque
ADJECTIVE A place that is picturesque is very attractive and unspoiled.

pie pies
NOUN a dish of meat, vegetables, or fruit covered with pastry

piece pieces piecing pieced
NOUN **1.** one of the parts into which a thing is divided or broken: *The cup broke into pieces. We each had a piece of pie.* **2.** a

limited or small quantity of something: *a piece of land, a piece of bread*
VERB **3.** If you piece together a number of things, you gradually put them together to make something complete.

piecemeal
ADVERB OR ADJECTIVE done gradually and at irregular intervals: *a piecemeal approach to rebuilding an engine*

pier piers
NOUN a large structure that sticks out into the water, which people can walk along and where ships can land

pierce pierces piercing pierced
VERB If a sharp object pierces something, it goes through it, making a hole.

piercing
ADJECTIVE **1.** A piercing sound is high-pitched and unpleasant. **2.** Someone with piercing eyes seems to look at you very intensely.

piety
NOUN Piety is strong and devout religious belief or behaviour.

pig pigs
NOUN a farm animal kept for its meat. It has pinkish skin, short legs, and a snout.

pigeon pigeons
NOUN a largish bird with grey feathers, often seen in towns and cities

pigeonhole pigeonholes
NOUN one of the sections in a frame on a wall where letters can be left

piggyback piggybacks
NOUN If you give someone a piggyback, you carry that person on your back, supporting him or her under the knees.

piglet piglets
NOUN a young pig

pigment pigments
NOUN a substance that gives something a particular colour
pigmentation NOUN

KNOWING WORDS: IDIOMS

BE WORD SHARP!

Idioms add colour to language by playing with the meanings of words.

piece a part of something

a piece of cake a very easy task

a piece of your mind a scolding

a piece of work a difficult or annoying person

go/fall to pieces break down and fall apart

speak/say your piece express your opinion

Pp

pigpen pigpens
NOUN a small, enclosed area where pigs are kept

pigtail pigtails
NOUN a length of braided hair hanging from the back of the head

pike pikes
NOUN **1.** a large freshwater fish of northern countries, with strong teeth **2.** a medieval weapon consisting of a pointed metal blade attached to a long pole

pile piles piling piled
NOUN **1.** a quantity of things lying one on top of another **2.** the soft surface of certain fabrics consisting of many threads standing on end
VERB **3.** If you pile things somewhere, you put them one on top of the other.

pile-up pile-ups
NOUN *an informal word* an accident involving several vehicles

pilfer pilfers pilfering pilfered
VERB Someone who pilfers steals small things over a period of time.

pilgrim pilgrims
NOUN a person who travels to a holy place for religious reasons
pilgrimage NOUN

pill pills
NOUN a small tablet or capsule of medicine that you swallow

pillage pillages pillaging pillaged
VERB If a group of people pillage a place, they steal from it using violence.

pillar pillars
NOUN **1.** a tall, narrow, solid structure, usually supporting part of a building **2.** Someone who is described as a pillar of a particular group is an active and important member of it: *a pillar of the community*

pillory pillories pillorying pilloried
VERB If someone is pilloried, he or she is criticized severely by a lot of people.

pillow pillows
NOUN a rectangular cushion that you rest your head on when you are in bed

pillowcase pillowcases
NOUN a cover for a pillow that can be removed and washed

pilot pilots piloting piloted
NOUN **1.** a person who is trained to fly an aircraft **2.** a person who goes on board to guide ships through local waters to a port
VERB **3.** To pilot something is to control its movement or to guide it.
ADJECTIVE **4.** a small test of a plan or product, done to see if it would be successful

pimple pimples
NOUN a small spot on the skin
pimply ADJECTIVE

PIN PINs
NOUN an abbreviation for *personal identification number*: a number used by the holder of a bank card or credit card

pin pins pinning pinned
NOUN **1.** a thin, pointed piece of metal used to fasten together things such as pieces of fabric or paper
VERB **2.** If you pin something somewhere, you fasten it there with a pin. **3.** If someone pins you in a particular position, that person holds you there so that you cannot move.
4. If you try to pin something down, you try to get or give a clear and exact description of it or statement about it.

pinafore pinafores
NOUN an apronlike garment with no sleeves, worn over a dress, especially by young girls

pincers
PLURAL NOUN **1.** Pincers are a tool used for gripping and pulling things. They consist of two pieces of metal hinged in the middle.
2. The pincers of a crab or lobster are its front claws.

pinch pinches pinching pinched
VERB **1.** If you pinch something, you squeeze it between your thumb and first finger.
NOUN **2.** A pinch of something is the amount that you can hold between your thumb and first finger: *a pinch of salt*

pinched
ADJECTIVE If someone's face is pinched, it looks thin and pale.

pine pines pining pined
NOUN **1.** an evergreen tree with very thin, needlelike leaves
VERB **2.** If you pine for someone or something, you are sad because you cannot be with that person or have that thing.

pineapple pineapples
NOUN a large, oval fruit with sweet, yellow flesh and a thick, lumpy brown skin

Ping-Pong
NOUN another name for TABLE TENNIS

pink pinker pinkest
ADJECTIVE pale reddish white

pinnacle pinnacles
NOUN **1.** a tall, pointed piece of stone or rock **2.** The pinnacle of something is its best or highest level: *the pinnacle of her career*

pinpoint pinpoints pinpointing pinpointed
VERB If you pinpoint something, you explain or discover exactly what or where it is.

pinstripe
ADJECTIVE Pinstripe cloth has very narrow vertical stripes.

pint pints
NOUN a nonmetric unit of liquid volume equal to about 0.568 litres

pioneer pioneers pioneering pioneered
NOUN **1.** A pioneer is a person who settles in a region that has not been settled before.
2. Someone who is a pioneer in a particular activity is one of the first people to develop it.
VERB **3.** Someone who pioneers a new process or invention is the first person to develop it.

pious
ADJECTIVE very religious and moral

pip pips
NOUN Pips are the hard seeds in a fruit.

pipe pipes piping piped
NOUN **1.** a long, hollow tube through which liquid or gas can flow **2.** an object used for smoking tobacco. It consists of a small, hollow bowl attached to a tube.
VERB **3.** To pipe a liquid or gas somewhere is to transfer it through a pipe.

pipeline pipelines
NOUN a large underground pipe that carries oil or gas over a long distance

piper pipers
NOUN a person who plays the bagpipes

piping
NOUN Piping consists of pipes and tubes.

piranha piranhas
NOUN a small, fierce fish with sharp teeth

pirate pirates
NOUN Pirates are sailors who attack and rob other ships at sea.

pirouette pirouettes
NOUN In ballet, a pirouette is a fast, spinning step done on the toes.

pistil pistils
NOUN In a flower, the pistil is the female reproductive part made up of the carpel or two or more carpels fused together.

pistol pistols
NOUN a small gun held in the hand

piston pistons
NOUN a cylinder or disc that slides up and down inside a tube. Pistons make parts of engines move.

pit pits
NOUN **1.** a large hole in the ground **2.** a large hole in the ground containing a certain material: *a tar pit, a gravel pit* **3.** a small hollow in the surface of something

pitch pitches pitching pitched
NOUN **1.** The pitch of a sound is how high or low it is. **2.** In baseball, a pitch is the throwing of a ball toward a batter.
VERB **3.** If you pitch something somewhere, you throw it with a lot of force. **4.** If you pitch something at a particular level of difficulty, you set it at that level: *Any movie must be pitched at a level to suit its intended audience.* **5.** When you pitch a tent, you fix it in an upright position.

pitcher pitchers
NOUN a large jug

pitfall pitfalls
NOUN The pitfalls of a situation are its difficulties or dangers.

pith
NOUN the white substance between the outer skin and the flesh of an orange or lemon

pitiful
ADJECTIVE Someone or something that is pitiful is in such a sad or weak situation that you feel pity for that person or thing.

pittance
NOUN a very small amount of money

KNOWING WORDS: WORD HISTORY

BE WORD SHARP!

Words are like living things. They grow and change.

Pioneer started out as the French word **pionnier**, which meant *a soldier who goes ahead of an army to prepare the route.* It came into English as **pionner**, but was later changed to **pioneer** to match words like **engineer** and **volunteer**. The first European settlers in North America were known as pioneers. Today, a pioneer is still someone who goes someplace first.

NEL

pitted
ADJECTIVE covered in small hollows: *Sidewalks often become pitted from salt.*

pity pities pitying pitied
VERB **1.** If you pity someone, you feel very sorry for that person.
NOUN **2.** Pity is a feeling of being sorry for someone. **3.** If you say that it is a pity about something, you are expressing your disappointment about it.

pivot pivots pivoting pivoted
VERB **1.** If something pivots, it balances or turns on a central point: *to pivot on your heel*
NOUN **2.** the central point on which something balances or turns
pivotal ADJECTIVE

pixie pixies
NOUN an imaginary little creature in fairy tales

pizza pizzas
NOUN a flat piece of dough covered with cheese, vegetables, and other toppings

placard placards
NOUN a large notice carried at a demonstration or displayed in a public place

placate placates placating placated
VERB If you placate someone, you stop that person from feeling angry by doing something to please him or her.

place places placing placed
NOUN **1.** any point, building, or area **2.** the position where something belongs: *She set the book in its place on the shelf.* **3.** a space at a table set with cutlery where one person can eat **4.** a position in time or space: *I lost my place in the book.* **5.** a particular point or stage in a sequence of things: *second place in the race*
VERB **6.** If you place something somewhere, you put it there. **7.** If you place an order, you order something.
PHRASE **8.** When something **takes place**, it happens.

placebo placebos
NOUN a substance given to a patient in place of a drug and from which, though it has no active ingredients, the patient may imagine he or she gets some benefit

placenta placentas
NOUN The placenta is the mass of veins and tissues in the womb of a pregnant woman or animal. It gives the fetus food and oxygen.

placid
ADJECTIVE calm and not easily excited or upset
placidly ADVERB

plagiarism
NOUN Plagiarism is copying someone else's work or idea and pretending that it is your own.
plagiarist NOUN
plagiarize VERB

plague plagues plaguing plagued
NOUN **1.** a very infectious disease that spreads rapidly and kills large numbers of people **2.** A plague of unpleasant things is a large number of them occurring at the same time: *a plague of rats*
VERB **3.** If problems plague you, they keep causing you trouble.

plaice
NOUN an edible European flatfish

plaid plaids
NOUN Plaid is woven material with a tartan design.

plain plainer plainest; plains
ADJECTIVE **1.** very simple in style, with no pattern or decoration: *plain walls* **2.** obvious and easy to recognize or understand: *plain language* **3.** A person who is plain is not considered attractive.
ADVERB **4.** You can use *plain* before a noun or adjective to emphasize it: *You were just plain funny.*
NOUN **5.** a large, flat area of land with very few trees
plainly ADVERB

KNOWING WORDS: IDIOMS

BE WORD SHARP!

Idioms add colour to language by playing with the meanings of words.

place a particular location

all over the place disorganized

go places achieve success

know your place accept your role in a group

out of place not appropriate

be put in your place be told that you're too arrogant

NEL

Pp

plaintiff plaintiffs
NOUN a person who has brought a court case against another person

plait plaits plaiting plaited
VERB **1.** If you plait three lengths of hair or rope together, you twist them over each other in turn to make one thick length.
NOUN **2.** a braid

plan plans planning planned
NOUN **1.** a method of achieving something that has been worked out beforehand **2.** a detailed diagram or drawing of something that is to be made
VERB **3.** If you plan something, you decide in detail what it is to be and how to do it.
4. If you are planning to do something, you intend to do it: *They plan to marry in the summer.*

plane planes planing planed
NOUN **1.** a vehicle with wings and engines that enable it to fly; an airplane **2.** a flat surface **3.** You can refer to a particular level of something as a particular plane: *He took his dancing skills to a higher plane.* **4.** a tool with a flat bottom with a sharp blade in it. You move it over a piece of wood to remove thin pieces from the surface.
VERB **5.** If you plane a piece of wood, you smooth its surface with a plane.

planet planets
NOUN a round object in space that moves around a star and is lit by light from that star
planetary ADJECTIVE

plank planks
NOUN a long, rectangular piece of wood

plankton
NOUN Plankton is a layer of tiny plants and animals that live just below the surface of a sea or lake.

plant plants planting planted
NOUN **1.** a living thing that grows in the earth and has stems, leaves, and roots **2.** a factory or power station: *a bottling plant*
VERB **3.** When you plant a seed or plant, you put it into the ground. **4.** If you plant something somewhere, you put it there firmly or secretly.

plantation plantations
NOUN **1.** a large area of land where crops such as tea, cotton, or sugar are grown **2.** a large number of trees planted together

plaque plaques
NOUN **1.** a flat piece of metal that is fixed to a wall and has an inscription in memory of a famous person or event **2.** Plaque is a substance that forms around your teeth and consists of bacteria, saliva, and food.

plasma
NOUN Plasma is the clear fluid part of blood.

plaster plasters plastering plastered
NOUN **1.** Plaster is a paste made of sand, lime, and water, which is used to form a smooth surface for interior walls and ceilings.
VERB **2.** To plaster a wall is to cover it with a layer of plaster.
plasterer NOUN

plastered
ADJECTIVE **1.** If something is plastered to a surface, it is stuck there. **2.** If something is plastered with things, those things are all over its surface.

plastic plastics
NOUN **1.** Plastic is a substance made by a chemical process, which can be moulded when soft to make a wide range of objects.
ADJECTIVE **2.** made of plastic

plastic surgery
NOUN Plastic surgery is surgery to replace or repair damaged skin or to improve a person's appearance by changing the shape of his or her features.

plate plates
NOUN **1.** a flat dish used to hold food **2.** a flat piece of metal or other hard material used for various purposes in machinery or building: *heavy steel plates used in shipbuilding*

plateau plateaus
NOUN a large area of high and fairly flat land

plated
ADJECTIVE Metal that is plated is covered with a thin layer of silver or gold.

platform platforms
NOUN **1.** a raised structure on which someone or something can stand **2.** the raised area in a railway station where passengers get on and off trains

platinum
NOUN Platinum is a valuable silver-coloured metal.

platitude platitudes
NOUN a statement made as if it were significant but that has become meaningless or boring because it has been used so many times before

platonic
ADJECTIVE A platonic relationship is simply one of friendship and does not involve sexual attraction.

Pp

platoon platoons
NOUN a small group of soldiers, commanded by a lieutenant

platter platters
NOUN a large serving plate

platypus platypuses
NOUN A platypus or duck-billed platypus is an Australian mammal that lives in rivers. It has brown fur, webbed feet, and a snout like a duck.

plaudit plaudits
NOUN *a formal word* A plaudit is an expression of admiration.

plausible
ADJECTIVE An explanation that is plausible seems likely to be true.
plausibility NOUN

play plays playing played
VERB **1.** When children play, they take part in games or use toys. **2.** When you play a sport or game, you take part in it. **3.** If an actor plays a character in a play or movie, he or she performs that role. **4.** If you play a musical instrument, you produce music from it. **5.** If you play music, you listen to it.
NOUN **6.** a piece of drama performed in the theatre or on television
player NOUN

playful
ADJECTIVE **1.** friendly and light-hearted: *a playful pat on the head* **2.** lively: *a playful puppy*
playfully ADVERB

playground playgrounds
NOUN a special area for children to play in

playing card playing cards
NOUN Playing cards are cards printed with numbers or pictures that are used to play various games.

playing field playing fields
NOUN an area of grass where people play sports

playwright playwrights
NOUN a person who writes plays

plaza plazas
NOUN a shopping centre

plea pleas
NOUN **1.** an emotional request: *a plea for help* **2.** In a court of law, someone's plea is the statement that he or she is guilty or not guilty.

plead pleads pleading pleaded
VERB **1.** If you plead with someone, you ask that person in an intense emotional way to do something. **2.** When someone pleads guilty or not guilty, that person states in court that he or she is guilty or not guilty of a crime.

pleasant
ADJECTIVE **1.** enjoyable or attractive
2. friendly or charming

Instead of **PLEASANT** try…

fine weather

a lovely meal

agreeable company

a likeable character

a well-mannered child

pleasantly
ADVERB

please pleases pleasing pleased
1. You say please when you are asking someone politely to do something.
VERB **2.** If something pleases you, it makes you feel happy and satisfied.

pleased
ADJECTIVE happy or satisfied

pleasing
ADJECTIVE attractive, satisfying, or enjoyable: *a pleasing appearance*

pleasure pleasures
NOUN **1.** Pleasure is a feeling of happiness, satisfaction, or enjoyment. **2.** an activity that you enjoy
pleasurable ADJECTIVE

pleat pleats
NOUN a permanent fold in fabric made by folding one part over another

plebiscite plebiscites
NOUN *a formal word* a vote on a matter of national importance in which all the voters in a country can take part

pledge pledges pledging pledged
NOUN **1.** a solemn promise
VERB **2.** If you pledge something, you promise that you will do it or give it.

plentiful
ADJECTIVE existing in large numbers or amounts and readily available: *Fruit and vegetables were plentiful.*
plentifully ADVERB

plenty
NOUN If there is plenty of something, there is a lot of it.

plethora
NOUN A plethora of something is an amount that is greater than you need.

pleurisy
NOUN Pleurisy is a serious illness in which a person's lungs become inflamed and breathing is difficult.

pliable
ADJECTIVE **1.** If something is pliable, you can bend it without breaking it. **2.** Someone who is pliable can be easily influenced.

pliers
PLURAL NOUN Pliers are a tool with metal jaws for holding small objects and bending wire.

plight
NOUN Someone's plight is the very difficult or dangerous situation that he or she is in: *the plight of the refugees*

plinth plinths
NOUN a block of stone on which a statue or pillar stands

plod plods plodding plodded
VERB If you plod somewhere, you walk there slowly and heavily.

plonk plonks plonking plonked
VERB If you plonk something down, you put it down heavily and carelessly.

plop plops plopping plopped
NOUN **1.** a gentle sound made by something light dropping into a liquid
VERB **2.** If something plops into a liquid, it drops into it with a gentle sound.

plot plots plotting plotted
NOUN **1.** a secret plan made by a group of people **2.** The plot of a novel or play is the story. **3.** a small piece of land
VERB **4.** If people plot to do something, they plan it secretly: *His family is plotting to disinherit him.* **5.** If someone plots the course of a plane or ship on a map, or plots a graph, that person marks the points in the correct places.

plough ploughs ploughing ploughed
NOUN **1.** a large farming tool that turns the soil over before seeds are planted
VERB **2.** When someone ploughs land, that person uses a plough to turn over the soil.

ploy ploys
NOUN a clever plan or way of behaving in order to get something that you want

pluck plucks plucking plucked
VERB **1.** To pluck a fruit or flower is to remove it with a sharp pull. **2.** To pluck a chicken or other dead bird means to pull its feathers out before cooking it. **3.** When you pluck a stringed instrument, you pick or pull the strings and let them go.
NOUN **4.** Pluck is courage
plucky ADJECTIVE

plug plugs plugging plugged
NOUN **1.** a plastic object with metal prongs that can be pushed into a socket to connect an appliance to an electricity supply **2.** a disc of rubber or metal with which you block up the hole in a sink or bathtub
VERB **3.** If you plug a hole, you block it with something.

plum plums
NOUN a small fruit with a smooth, red or yellow skin and a large stone in the middle

plumage
NOUN A bird's plumage is its feathers.

plumber plumbers
NOUN a person who connects and repairs water pipes

plumbing
NOUN The plumbing in a building is the system of water pipes, sinks, and toilets.

plume plumes
NOUN a large, brightly coloured feather

plummet plummets plummeting plummeted
VERB If something plummets, it falls very quickly: *Sales have plummeted.*

plump plumper plumpest
ADJECTIVE fat: *a small, plump baby*

plunder plunders plundering plundered
VERB If someone plunders a place, that person steals things from it.

plunge plunges plunging plunged
VERB **1.** If something plunges, it falls suddenly. **2.** If you plunge an object into something, especially a liquid, you push it in quickly. **3.** If you plunge into an activity or state, you suddenly become involved in it or affected by it: *She plunged into her homework.*
NOUN **4.** a sudden fall

plural plurals
NOUN the form of a word that is used to refer to two or more people or things, for example the plural of *chair* is *chairs*, and the plural of *mouse* is *mice*

pluralism
NOUN Pluralism is the belief that it is possible for different social and religious groups to live together peacefully while keeping their own beliefs and traditions.
pluralist ADJECTIVE OR NOUN

plural noun plural nouns
NOUN In this dictionary, *plural noun* is the name given to a noun that is used only in the plural, for example *scissors* or *police.*

plus
PREPOSITION **1.** You use *plus* to show that one number is being added to another: *Two plus two equals four.* **2.** You can use *plus* when you mention an additional item: *He wrote a history of Ontario plus a history of Canadian literature.*
ADJECTIVE **3.** slightly more than the number mentioned: *a career of 25 years plus*

Pp

plush
ADJECTIVE expensive and smart: *a plush hotel*

Pluto
NOUN Pluto is the second-largest known dwarf planet in the solar system. Pluto was originally classified as a planet.

ply plies plying plied
VERB **1.** If you ply someone with things or questions, you keep giving that person things or asking him or her questions. **2.** To ply a trade is to do a particular job as your work. NOUN **3.** Ply is the thickness of a material such as wool or wood, measured by the number of strands or layers it is made from.

plywood
NOUN Plywood is wooden board made from several thin sheets of wood glued together under pressure.

p.m. used to specify times between 12 noon and 12 midnight, for example *He went to bed at 9 p.m.* It is an abbreviation for the Latin *post meridiem*, meaning *after noon*.

pneumatic
ADJECTIVE operated by or filled with compressed air: *a pneumatic drill*

pneumonia
NOUN Pneumonia is a serious disease that affects a person's lungs and makes breathing difficult.

poach poaches poaching poached
VERB **1.** If someone poaches animals from someone else's land, that person illegally catches the animals for food. **2.** When you poach food, you cook it gently in hot liquid.
poacher NOUN

pocket pockets
NOUN **1.** a small pouch that forms part of a piece of clothing **2.** A pocket of something is a small area of it: *There are still pockets of gold in the mine.*

pod pods
NOUN a long, narrow seed container that grows on plants such as peas or beans

podium podiums
NOUN a small platform, often one on which someone stands to make a speech

poem poems
NOUN a piece of writing in which the words are arranged in short, rhythmic lines, often with a rhyme

poet poets
NOUN a person who writes poems

poetic
ADJECTIVE **1.** very beautiful and expressive: *a pure and poetic love* **2.** relating to poetry
poetically ADVERB

poetry
NOUN Poetry is poems, considered as a form of literature.

poignant
ADJECTIVE Something that is poignant has a strong emotional effect on you, often making you feel sad: *a moving and poignant moment*
poignancy NOUN

point points pointing pointed
NOUN **1.** an opinion or fact expressed by someone: *You've made a good point.* **2.** a quality: *Tact was never her strong point.* **3.** the purpose or meaning something has: *He completely missed the point in most of his argument.* **4.** a position or time: *At some point during the party, my friend started telling jokes.* **5.** a single mark in a competition **6.** the thin, sharp end of something such as a needle or knife **7.** The points of a compass are the 32 directions indicated on it. **8.** The decimal point in a number is the dot separating the whole number from the fraction. **9.** a particular aim or purpose: *What is the point of seeing a movie more than once?*
VERB **10.** If you point at something, you stick out your finger to show where it is. **11.** If something points in a particular direction, it faces that way.

point-blank
ADJECTIVE **1.** Something that is shot at point-blank range is shot with a gun held very close to it.
ADVERB **2.** If you say something point-blank, you say it directly without explanation or apology.

pointed
ADJECTIVE **1.** A pointed object has a thin, sharp end. **2.** Pointed comments express criticism.
pointedly ADVERB

pointer pointers
NOUN a piece of information that helps you to understand something: *Here are a few pointers to help you make a choice.*

pointless
ADJECTIVE Something that is pointless has no purpose.
pointlessly ADVERB

point of view points of view
NOUN **1.** Your point of view is your opinion about something or your attitude toward it. **2.** The point of view in a story is the perspective from which it is told.

poise
NOUN Someone who has poise is calm and dignified.

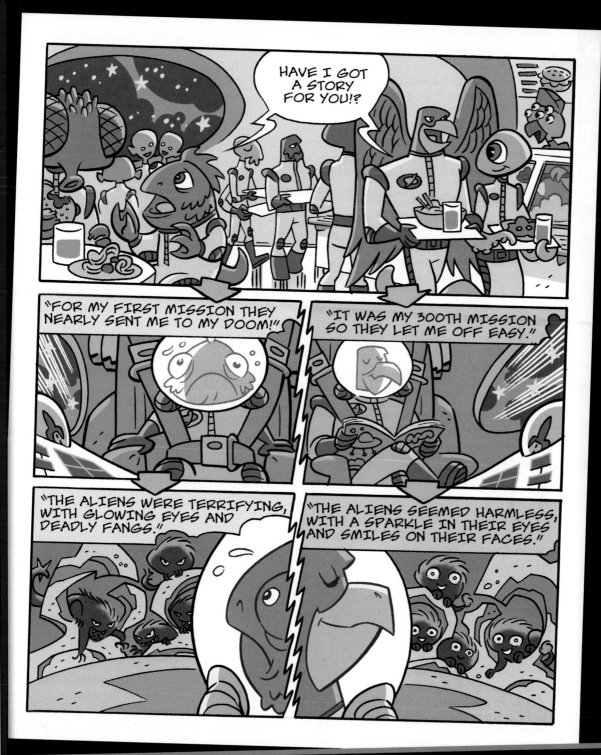

POINT OF VIEW

the perspective from which a story is told

"Have I got a story for you!"

Here, the same events are told from two different points of view. The two narrators see things quite differently!

J. BONE

Pp

poised
ADJECTIVE If you are poised to do something, you are ready to do it at any moment.

poison poisons poisoning poisoned
NOUN **1.** Poison is a substance that can kill people or animals if they swallow it or absorb it.
VERB **2.** To poison someone is to try to kill that person with poison.

poisonous
ADJECTIVE containing something that causes death or illness

poke pokes poking poked
VERB **1.** If you poke someone or something, you push at that person quickly with your finger or a sharp object. **2.** Something that pokes out of another thing appears from underneath or behind it: *roots poking out of the earth*
NOUN **3.** a sharp jab or prod

poker pokers
NOUN **1.** Poker is a card game in which the players make bets on the cards dealt to them. **2.** a long, metal rod used for stirring an open fire

polar
ADJECTIVE relating to the area around the North and South Pole

polar bear polar bears
NOUN a large, white bear that lives in the area around the North Pole

pole poles
NOUN **1.** a long, rounded piece of wood or metal **2.** The earth's poles are the two opposite ends of its axis: *the North Pole, the South Pole*

pole vault
NOUN The pole vault is an athletic event in which contestants jump over a high bar using a long, flexible pole to lift themselves into the air.

police polices policing policed
PLURAL NOUN **1.** The police are the people who are officially responsible for making sure that people obey the law.
VERB **2.** To police an area is to keep law and order there by means of the police or an armed force.

policeman policemen
NOUN a man who is a member of a police force
policewoman NOUN

policy policies
NOUN **1.** a set of plans, especially in politics or business: *the new economic policy* **2.** An insurance policy is a document that shows an agreement made with an insurance company.

polio
NOUN Polio is an infectious disease that is caused by a virus and often results in paralysis. Polio is short for *poliomyelitis*.

polish polishes polishing polished
VERB **1.** If you polish something, you put polish on it or rub it with a cloth to make it shine. **2.** If you polish a skill or technique you have, you work on it in order to improve it.
NOUN **3.** Polish is a substance that you put on an object to clean it and make it shine: *shoe polish* **4.** Something that has polish is elegant and of good quality.
polished ADJECTIVE

polite
ADJECTIVE **1.** Someone who is polite has good manners and behaves considerately toward other people. **2.** Polite society is cultivated and refined.
politely ADVERB

politeness
NOUN the quality of having good manners and behaving considerately

political
ADJECTIVE **1.** relating to the state, government, or public administration **2.** relating to or interested in politics
politically ADVERB

politically correct
ADJECTIVE careful not to offend or designed not to offend minority or disadvantaged groups

politician politicians
NOUN a person involved in the government of a country

politics
NOUN Politics is the activity and planning concerned with achieving power and control in a country or organization.

polka polkas
NOUN a fast dance in which couples dance together in circles around the room

poll polls polling polled
NOUN **1.** a survey in which people are asked their opinions about something **2.** the place where votes are cast or counted
VERB **3.** If you are polled on something, you are asked your opinion about it as part of a survey.

pollen
NOUN Pollen is a fine yellow powder produced by flowers in order to fertilize other flowers of the same species.

⚠ HEADS UP Use the gender-free term **police officer** rather than **policeman** or **policewoman**.

NEL

Pp

pollinate pollinates pollinating pollinated
VERB To pollinate a plant is to fertilize it with pollen.
pollination NOUN

pollutant pollutants
NOUN a substance that causes pollution

pollute pollutes polluting polluted
VERB To pollute water or air is to make it dirty and dangerous to use or live in.
polluted ADJECTIVE

pollution
NOUN Pollution of the environment happens when dirty or dangerous substances get into the air, water, or soil.

polo
NOUN Polo is a game played between two teams of players on horseback. The players use wooden hammers with long handles to hit a ball.

polyester
NOUN a artificial fibre, used especially to make clothes

polygamy
NOUN Polygamy is having more than one spouse at the same time.
polygamous ADJECTIVE

polygon polygons
NOUN any two-dimensional shape whose sides are all straight

polystyrene
NOUN Polystyrene is a very light plastic, used especially as insulating material or to make containers.

polyethylene
NOUN Polyethylene is a type of plastic that is used to make thin sheets or bags.

polyunsaturated
ADJECTIVE Polyunsaturated oils and margarines are made mainly from vegetable fats and are considered to be healthier than saturated oils.
polyunsaturate NOUN

pomegranate pomegranates
NOUN a round fruit with a thick, reddish skin. It contains a lot of small seeds.

pomp
NOUN Pomp is the use of ceremony, fine clothes, and decorations on special occasions: *The knight was buried with much pomp.*

pompous
ADJECTIVE behaving in a way that is too serious and self-important
pomposity NOUN

pond ponds
NOUN a small, usually artificial, area of water

ponder ponders pondering pondered
VERB If you ponder, you think about something deeply: *He was pondering the problem when I stopped by.*

ponderous
ADJECTIVE dull, slow, and serious: *the ponderous commentary*

pony ponies
NOUN a small horse

ponytail ponytails
NOUN a hairstyle in which long hair is tied at the back of the head and hangs down like a tail

poodle poodles
NOUN a type of dog with curly hair

pool pools pooling pooled
NOUN **1.** a small area of still water **2.** Pool is a game in which players try to hit coloured balls into pockets around a special table using long sticks called cues. **3.** A pool of people, money, or things is a group or collection used or shared by several people.
VERB **4.** If people pool their resources, they gather together the things they have so that they can be shared or used by all of them.

poor poorer poorest
ADJECTIVE **1.** Poor people have very little money and few possessions. **2.** You use *poor* to show sympathy: *Poor you!* **3.** *Poor* also means of a low quality or standard: *a poor performance*

poorly
ADJECTIVE **1.** feeling unwell or ill
ADVERB **2.** badly: *a poorly planned event*

pop pops popping popped
NOUN **1.** Pop is modern music played and enjoyed especially by young people. **2.** You can refer to carbonated, non-alcoholic drinks as pop. **3.** a short, sharp sound
VERB **4.** If something pops, it makes a sudden sharp sound. **5.** If you pop something somewhere, you put it there quickly: *I'd just popped the pie into the oven.* **6.** If you pop somewhere, you go there quickly: *His father popped out to buy some milk.*

popcorn
NOUN Popcorn is a snack consisting of kernels of corn heated until they puff up and burst into a white mass.

Pope Popes
NOUN The Pope is the head of the Roman Catholic Church.

poplar poplars
NOUN a type of tall, thin tree

Pp

poppy poppies
NOUN a plant with a large red flower on a hairy stem

populace
NOUN *a formal word* The populace of a country is its people.

popular
ADJECTIVE **1.** liked or approved of by a lot of people **2.** involving or intended for ordinary people: *popular music, popular science*
popularly ADVERB
popularity NOUN
popularize VERB

Instead of **POPULAR** try...

a **trendy** style
a **standard** reply
a **beloved** celebrity
a **sought-after** album
a **widespread** demand

populate
populates
populating
populated
VERB The people or animals that populate an area live there.

population populations
NOUN The population of a place is the people who live there, or the number of people living there.

porcelain
NOUN Porcelain is a delicate, hard material used to make dishes and ornaments.

porch porches
NOUN a covered area at the entrance to a building

porcupine porcupines
NOUN a large rodent with long spines covering its body

pore pores poring pored
NOUN **1.** The pores in your skin or on the surface of a plant are very small holes that allow moisture to pass through.
VERB **2.** If you pore over a piece of writing or a diagram, you study it carefully.

pork
NOUN the meat from a pig used for food

pornography
NOUN Pornography refers to magazines and films that are designed to cause sexual excitement by showing naked people and sexual acts.
pornographic ADJECTIVE

porpoise porpoises
NOUN a sea mammal related to the dolphin

porridge
NOUN Porridge is a thick, sticky food made from oats cooked in water or milk.

port ports
NOUN **1.** a town or area that has a harbour or docks
ADJECTIVE **2.** The port side of a ship is the left side when you are facing the front.

-port
SUFFIX The suffix *-port* comes at the end of words that have something to do with *carrying* in their meaning: *transport*

portable
ADJECTIVE designed to be easily carried: *a portable television*

porter porters
NOUN **1.** A porter in a railway station, hotel, or airport is a person whose job is to carry or move things. **2.** a person whose job is to be in charge of the entrance of a building, greeting and directing visitors

portfolio portfolios
NOUN a thin, flat case for carrying papers

porthole portholes
NOUN a small window in the side of a ship or aircraft

portion portions
NOUN a part or amount of something: *a portion of fresh fruit*

portrait portraits
NOUN a picture or photograph of someone

portray portrays portraying portrayed
VERB When an actor, artist, or writer portrays someone or something, he or she represents or describes that person or thing.
portrayal NOUN

pose poses posing posed
VERB **1.** If something poses a problem, it is the cause of the problem. **2.** If you pose a question, you ask it. **3.** If you pose as someone else, you pretend to be that person in order to deceive people.
NOUN **4.** a way of standing, sitting, or lying: *The model assumed a pose for the photographer.*

poser posers
NOUN a difficult problem

poseur poseurs
NOUN someone who behaves or dresses in an exaggerated way in order to impress people

posh posher poshest
ADJECTIVE *an informal word* smart, fashionable, and expensive: *a posh restaurant*

position positions positioning positioned
NOUN **1.** The position of someone or something is the place where that person or thing is or ought to be: *Would the cast members take their positions, please.*
2. When someone or something is in a

particular position, that person or thing is sitting or lying in that way: *I raised myself to a sitting position.* **3.** a job in an organization **4.** The position that you are in at a particular time is the situation that you are in: *Your poor behaviour has put me in a difficult position.*
VERB **5.** To position something somewhere is to put it there: *The nurse positioned a cushion behind the patient's head.*

positive
ADJECTIVE **1.** completely sure about something: *I was positive he knew about that money.* **2.** confident and hopeful: *I felt very positive about everything.* **3.** showing approval or encouragement: *I anticipate a positive response.* **4.** providing definite proof of the truth or identity of something: *positive evidence* **5.** A positive number is greater than zero.
positively ADVERB

possess possesses possessing possessed
VERB **1.** If you possess a particular quality, you have it. **2.** If you possess something, you own it. **3.** If a feeling or belief possesses you, it strongly influences you: *Absolute terror possessed her.*
possessor NOUN

possession possessions
NOUN **1.** If something is in your possession or if you are in possession of it, you have it. **2.** Your possessions are the things that you own or that you have with you.

possessive
ADJECTIVE **1.** A person who is possessive about someone or something wants to keep that person or thing to himself or herself. NOUN **2.** In grammar, the possessive is the form of a noun or pronoun used to show possession. For example, *my* is the possessive form of *I* in *my bedroom* and *dog's* is the possessive form of *dog* in *dog's tail.*

possibility possibilities
NOUN something that might be true or might happen: *the possibility of snow*

possible
ADJECTIVE **1.** likely to happen or able to be done **2.** likely or capable of being true or correct
possibly ADVERB

post posts posting posted
NOUN **1.** a strong, upright pole fixed into the ground: *The horse is tied to a post.* **2.** a job or official position in an organization
VERB **3.** If you are posted somewhere, you are sent by your employers to work there.

post-
PREFIX The prefix *post-* means after a particular time or event: *his postwar career*

postage
NOUN Postage is the money that you pay to send letters and parcels by mail.

postal
ADJECTIVE to do with mail or the post office

postal code postal codes
NOUN a short sequence of letters and numbers at the end of an address that helps the post office to sort the mail

postcard postcards
NOUN a card, often with a picture on one side, which you write on and send without an envelope

poster posters
NOUN a large notice or picture that is stuck on a wall as an advertisement or for decoration

posterior posteriors
NOUN *an informal word* A person's posterior is his or her bottom.

posterity
NOUN *a formal word* You can refer to the future and the people who will be alive then as posterity: *to record the voyage for posterity*

posthumous
ADJECTIVE happening or awarded after a person's death: *a posthumous medal*
posthumously ADVERB

post-mortem post-mortems
NOUN a medical examination of a dead body to find out how the person died

post office post offices
NOUN a place where mail is received and sorted for delivery, and where other postal services are provided

postpone postpones postponing postponed
VERB If you postpone an event, you arrange for it to take place at a later time than was originally planned.
postponement NOUN

posture postures
NOUN Your posture is the position or manner in which you hold your body.

posy posies
NOUN a small bunch of flowers

pot pots
NOUN a deep, round container

potassium nitrate
NOUN a white chemical compound used to make gunpowder, fireworks, and fertilizers. Potassium nitrate is also called saltpetre.

⚠ **HEADS UP** The word **posthumous** is pronounced PAWS-chuh-muhs.

Pp

potato potatoes
NOUN a white vegetable that has a brown or red skin and grows underground

potent
ADJECTIVE effective or powerful: *a potent cocktail*
potency NOUN

potential
ADJECTIVE **1.** capable of becoming the thing mentioned: *potential customers, potential danger*
NOUN **2.** Your potential is your ability to achieve success in the future.
potentially ADVERB

potential energy
NOUN Potential energy is the energy stored in something.

pothole potholes
NOUN **1.** a hole in the surface of a road caused by bad weather or traffic **2.** an underground cavern

potion potions
NOUN a drink containing medicine, poison, or supposed magical powers

potter potters pottering pottered
NOUN a person who makes pottery

pottery
NOUN **1.** Pottery is pots, dishes, and other items made from clay and fired in a kiln.
2. Pottery is also the craft of making pottery.

potty potties
NOUN a bowl that a small child can sit on and use as a toilet while being toilet trained

pouch pouches
NOUN **1.** a small, soft container with a fold-over top: *a letter carrier's pouch*
2. Animals like kangaroos have a pouch, which is a pocket of skin in which they carry their young.

poultry
NOUN Chickens, turkeys, and other birds kept for their meat or eggs are referred to as poultry.

pounce pounces pouncing pounced
VERB If an animal or person pounces on something, that animal or person leaps and grabs that thing.

pound pounds pounding pounded
NOUN **1.** a nonmetric unit of weight equal to about 0.454 kilograms
VERB **2.** If you pound something, you hit it repeatedly with your fist: *Someone was pounding on the door.* **3.** If you pound a substance, you crush it into a powder or paste: *He pounded some walnuts for the cake.* **4.** If your heart is pounding, it is beating very strongly and quickly. **5.** If you pound somewhere, you run there with heavy noisy steps.

pour pours pouring poured
VERB **1.** If you pour a liquid out of a container, you make it flow out by tipping the container. **2.** If something pours somewhere, it flows there quickly and in large quantities: *Sweat poured down his face.* **3.** When it is raining heavily, you can say that it is pouring.

pout pouts pouting pouted
VERB If you pout, you stick out your lips or bottom lip.

poverty
NOUN the state of being very poor

powder powders powdering powdered
NOUN **1.** Powder consists of many tiny particles of a solid substance.
VERB **2.** If you powder a surface, you cover it with powder.
powdery ADJECTIVE

power powers powering powered
NOUN **1.** Someone who has power has a lot of control over people and activities.
2. Someone who has the power to do something has the ability to do it: *the power of speech* **3.** Power is also the authority to do something: *the power of arrest* **4.** The power of something is the physical strength that it has to move things. **5.** Power is energy obtained, for example, by burning fuel or using the wind or water. **6.** In physics, power is the energy transferred from one thing to another in one second. It is measured in watts.
VERB **7.** Something that powers a machine provides the energy for it to work.

powerful
ADJECTIVE **1.** able to control people and events **2.** having great physical strength **3.** having a strong effect
powerfully ADVERB

powerless
ADJECTIVE unable to control or influence events: *I was powerless to save her.*

powerhouse powerhouses
NOUN a place where electricity is generated

power play power plays
NOUN In the game of hockey, a power play is a special combination of players put on the ice when the opposition has fewer than six players on the ice, usually because one or more players is serving a penalty.

430

Pp

practicable
ADJECTIVE If a task or plan is practicable, it can be carried out successfully: *a practicable option*

practical
ADJECTIVE **1.** The practical aspects of something are those that involve experience and real situations rather than ideas or theories: *the practical difficulties of teaching science* **2.** sensible and likely to be effective: *practical, low-heeled shoes* **3.** Someone who is practical is able to deal effectively and sensibly with problems.
practicality NOUN

practically
ADVERB **1.** almost but not completely or exactly: *The house was practically a wreck.* **2.** in a practical way: *practically minded*

practice practices
NOUN **1.** You can refer to something that people do regularly as a practice: *the practice of shaking hands* **2.** Practice is regular training or exercise: *I need more practice.* **3.** A doctor's, dentist's, or lawyer's practice is his or her business.

practise practises practising practised
VERB **1.** If you practise something, you do it regularly in order to improve. **2.** People who practise a religion, custom, or craft regularly take part in the activities associated with it: *a practising Buddhist* **3.** Someone who practises medicine or law works as a doctor or lawyer.

⚠ **HEADS UP**

Practice and **practise** sound the same, but **practice** is a noun and **practise** is a verb. Check out **advice/advise**.

practised
ADJECTIVE Someone who is practised at doing something is very skilful at it: *a practised performer*

practitioner practitioners
NOUN You can refer to someone who works in a particular profession as a practitioner: *a medical practitioner*

pragmatic
ADJECTIVE A pragmatic way of considering or doing something is a practical rather than theoretical way of considering or doing that thing: *He is pragmatic about the risks involved.*
pragmatically ADVERB
pragmatism NOUN

prairie prairies
NOUN a large area of flat, grassy land in North America

praise praises praising praised
VERB **1.** If you praise someone or something, you express strong approval of that person's or thing's qualities or achievements.
NOUN **2.** Praise is what is said or written in approval of someone's qualities or achievements.

prance prances prancing pranced
VERB Someone who is prancing around is walking with exaggerated movements.

prank pranks
NOUN a childish trick

prattle prattles prattling prattled
VERB If someone prattles on, that person talks a lot without saying anything important.

prawn prawns
NOUN an edible shellfish resembling a shrimp

pray prays praying prayed
VERB When someone prays, that person speaks to God or a god to give thanks or to ask for help.

prayer prayers
NOUN **1.** Prayer is the activity of praying. **2.** the words said when someone prays

pre-
PREFIX The prefix *pre-* means *before a particular time or event*: *preheat, prewash*

KNOWING WORDS: WORD BUILDING

BE WORD SHARP!

You can create new words by adding prefixes and suffixes to a base word.

pre- a prefix that means *before*

preheat warm an oven before cooking

prejudge judge something before you experience it

pre-order order something before it is available to buy

pre-pay pay before receiving something in return

preschool classes before kindergarten

Pp

preach preaches preaching preached
VERB When someone preaches, that person
gives a short talk on a religious or moral
subject as part of a church service.
preacher NOUN

precarious
ADJECTIVE **1.** If your situation is precarious,
you may fail in what you are doing at any
time. **2.** Something that is precarious is likely
to fall because it is not well balanced or
secured.
precariously ADVERB

precaution precautions
NOUN an action that is intended to prevent
something from happening: *It's always worth
taking precautions against accidents.*
precautionary ADJECTIVE

precede precedes preceding preceded
VERB **1.** Something that precedes another thing
happens or occurs before it. **2.** If you precede
someone somewhere, you go in front of that
person.
preceding ADJECTIVE

precedence
NOUN If something takes precedence over
other things, it is the most important thing
and should be dealt with first.

precedent precedents
NOUN An action or decision that is regarded
as a precedent is used as a guide in taking
similar action or decisions later.

precinct precincts
NOUN The precincts of a place are its
buildings and land: *the school precinct*

precious
ADJECTIVE Something that is precious is
valuable or very important and

Instead of **PRECIOUS** try...

should be
looked
after or used
carefully.

an **adored** pet

cherished moments

treasured memories

a **priceless** piece of art

wasting **invaluable** time

precipice
precipices
NOUN a very
steep rock face

precipitate precipitates
precipitating precipitated
VERB *a formal use* If something
precipitates an event or situation, it
causes it to happen suddenly.

precipitation
NOUN *a formal word* Precipitation is rain,
snow, or hail; used especially when stating

the amount that falls during a particular
period.

precise
ADJECTIVE exact and accurate in every detail:
precise measurements
precisely ADVERB
precision NOUN

preclude precludes precluding precluded
VERB *a formal word* If something precludes
an event or situation, it prevents it from
happening: *The meal precluded serious
conversation.*

precocious
ADJECTIVE Precocious children behave in a way
that seems too advanced for their age.

preconceived
ADJECTIVE Preconceived ideas about something
have been formed without any real
experience or information.
preconception NOUN

precondition preconditions
NOUN If something is a precondition for
another thing, it must happen before the
second thing can take place.

precursor precursors
NOUN A precursor of something that exists
now is a similar thing that existed at an
earlier time: *Real tennis is an ancient
precursor of the modern game.*

predator predators
NOUN an animal that kills and eats other
animals
predatory ADJECTIVE

predecessor predecessors
NOUN Someone's predecessor is a person who
used to do his or her job before.

predetermined
ADJECTIVE decided in advance or controlled by
previous events rather than left to chance

predicament predicaments
NOUN a difficult situation

predict predicts predicting predicted
VERB If someone predicts an event, that person
says that it will happen in the future.

prediction predictions
NOUN something that is forecast in advance

predominant
ADJECTIVE more important or more noticeable
than anything else in a particular set of
people or things: *Yellow is the predominant
colour in the house.*
predominantly ADVERB

predominate predominates predominating
predominated
VERB If one type of person or thing

predominates, it is the most common, frequent, or noticeable person or thing: *Pink flowers predominate in the bouquet.*
predominance NOUN

pre-eminent
ADJECTIVE recognized as being the most important in a particular group: *the pre-eminent experts in the area*
pre-eminence NOUN

pre-empt pre-empts pre-empting pre-empted
VERB *a formal word* If you pre-empt something, you prevent it by doing something else that makes it pointless or impossible: *a wish to pre-empt any further publicity*

preen preens preening preened
VERB When a bird preens its feathers, it cleans them using its beak.

preface prefaces
NOUN an introduction at the beginning of a book explaining what the book is about or why it was written

prefer prefers preferring preferred
VERB If you prefer one thing to another, you like it better than the other thing.
preferable ADJECTIVE
preferably ADVERB

preference preferences
NOUN **1.** If you have a preference for something, you like it more than other things: *a preference for white* **2.** When making a choice, if you give preference to one type of person or thing, you try to choose that type.

preferential
ADJECTIVE A person who gets preferential treatment is treated better than others.

prefix prefixes
NOUN a letter or group of letters added to the beginning of a word to make a new word, for example *semi-*, *pre-*, and *un-*

⚠ **HEADS UP**
Knowing a prefix can help you decipher new words. Look for prefixes like **dis-** (*not*), **mis-** (*false*), and **re-** (*again*).

pregnant
ADJECTIVE A female who is pregnant has a baby developing in her womb.
pregnancy NOUN

prehistoric
ADJECTIVE existing at a time in the past before anything was written down

prejudice prejudices
NOUN **1.** Prejudice is an unreasonable and unfair judgment or opinion. **2.** Prejudice is also an intolerance toward certain people or groups: *racial prejudice*
prejudiced ADJECTIVE
prejudicial ADJECTIVE

preliminary
ADJECTIVE Preliminary activities take place before something starts, in preparation for it: *the preliminary rounds of the competition*

prelude preludes
NOUN Something that is an introduction to a more important event can be described as a prelude to that event.

premature
ADJECTIVE happening too early, or earlier than expected: *premature baldness*
prematurely ADVERB

premeditated
ADJECTIVE planned in advance: *a premeditated attack*

premier premiers
NOUN **1.** The leader of the cabinet of a provincial government in Canada is referred to as the premier.
ADJECTIVE **2.** considered to be the best or most important: *the premier lacrosse player in the league*

premiere premieres
NOUN the first public performance of a new play or movie

premise premises
PLURAL NOUN **1.** The premises of an organization are all the buildings it occupies on one site.
NOUN **2.** a statement that you suppose is true and use as the basis for an idea or argument

premium premiums
NOUN an extra sum of money that has to be paid: *Paying a premium for a better space is worthwhile.*

premonition premonitions
NOUN a feeling that something unpleasant is going to happen

preoccupation preoccupations
NOUN If you have a preoccupation with something, it is very important to you and you keep thinking about it.

preoccupied
ADJECTIVE Someone who is preoccupied is deep in thought or totally involved with something.

Pp

preparatory

ADJECTIVE Preparatory activities are done before doing something else in order to prepare for it.

prepare prepares preparing prepared

VERB If you prepare something, you make it ready for a particular purpose or event: *He was preparing the meal.*

preparation NOUN

prepared

ADJECTIVE If you are prepared to do something, you are willing to do it.

preposition prepositions

NOUN a word such as *by*, *for*, *into*, or *with*, which usually has a noun as its object

preposterous

ADJECTIVE extremely unreasonable and ridiculous: *a preposterous statement*

prerequisite prerequisites

NOUN *a formal word* Something that is a prerequisite for another thing must happen or exist before the other thing is possible: *Self-esteem is a prerequisite for a happy life.*

prerogative prerogatives

NOUN *a formal word* Something that is the prerogative of a person is that person's special privilege or right.

prescribe prescribes prescribing prescribed

VERB When a doctor prescribes treatment, he or she states what treatment a patient should have.

prescription prescriptions

NOUN a piece of paper on which the doctor has written the name of a medicine needed by a patient

presence

NOUN **1.** Someone's presence in a place is the fact of that person's being there: *His presence made me happy.* **2.** If you are in someone's presence, you are in the same place as that person is. **3.** Someone who has presence has an impressive appearance or manner.

present presents presenting presented

ADJECTIVE **1.** If someone is present somewhere, that person is there: *He had been present at the birth of his son.* **2.** A present situation is one that exists now rather than in the past or the future.

NOUN **3.** The present is the period of time that is taking place now. **4.** something that you give to someone for that person to keep

VERB **5.** If you present someone with something, you give it to that person: *She presented a bravery award to the girl.*

6. Something that presents a difficulty or a challenge causes it or provides it. **7.** The person who presents a radio or television show introduces each part or each guest.

presenter NOUN

presentable

ADJECTIVE neat or attractive and suitable for people to see

presentation presentations

NOUN **1.** the act of presenting or a way of presenting something **2.** The presentation of a piece of work is the way it looks or the impression it gives. **3.** To give a presentation is to give a talk or demonstration to an audience of something you have been studying or working on.

present-day

ADJECTIVE existing or happening now: *present-day farming practices*

presently

ADVERB **1.** If something will happen presently, it will happen soon: *I'll finish the job presently.* **2.** Something that is presently happening is happening now: *Some progress is presently being made.*

present participle present participles

NOUN In grammar, the present participle of an English verb is the form that ends in *-ing*. It is used to form some tenses, and can be used to form adjectives and nouns from a verb.

present tense

NOUN In grammar, the present tense is the tense of a verb that you use mainly to talk about things that happen or exist at the time of writing or speaking.

preservative preservatives

NOUN a substance or chemical that stops things from decaying

preserve preserves preserving preserved

VERB **1.** If you preserve something, you take action so that it remains as it is. **2.** If you preserve food, you treat it to prevent it from decaying.

NOUN **3.** Preserves are foods such as jam or chutney that have been made with a lot of sugar or vinegar.

preservation NOUN

preside presides presiding presided

VERB A person who presides over a formal event is in charge of it.

president presidents

NOUN **1.** A president is the elected leader of a republic: *the president of the United States of America* **2.** The president of an organization is the person who has the highest position.

presidency NOUN

presidential ADJECTIVE

Pp

press presses pressing pressed
VERB **1.** If you press something, you push it or hold it firmly against something else: *Press the blue button.* **2.** If you press clothes, you iron them. **3.** If you press for something, you try hard to persuade someone to agree to it: *She was pressing for improvements to the education system.* **4.** If you press charges, you make an accusation against someone, which has to be decided in a court of law. NOUN **5.** Newspapers and the journalists who work for them are called the press.

press conference press conferences
NOUN When someone gives a press conference, that person has a meeting to answer questions put by reporters.

pressing
ADJECTIVE Something that is pressing needs to be dealt with immediately: *pressing needs*

pressure pressures pressuring pressured
NOUN **1.** Pressure is the force that is produced by pushing on something. **2.** If you are under pressure, you have too much to do and not enough time, or someone is trying hard to persuade you to do something. VERB **3.** If you pressure someone, you try hard to persuade that person to do something.

prestige
NOUN If you have prestige, people admire you because of your position.
prestigious ADJECTIVE

presumably
ADVERB If you say that something is presumably the case, you mean you assume that it is: *Presumably you have studied for today's exam.*

presume presumes presuming presumed
VERB If you presume something, you think that it is the case, although you have no proof.
presumption NOUN

presumptuous
ADJECTIVE Someone who behaves in a presumptuous way does things that he or she has no right to do.

pretence pretences
NOUN a way of behaving that is false and intended to deceive people

pretend pretends pretending pretended
VERB If you pretend that something is the case, you try to make people believe that it is, although in fact it is not: *I pretended to enjoy the meal.*

pretender pretenders
NOUN A pretender to a throne or title is someone who claims it but whose claim is being questioned.

pretension pretensions
NOUN Someone with pretensions claims to be more important than he or she really is.

pretentious
ADJECTIVE Someone or something is pretentious if that person or thing seems to be important when in fact, that is not the case.

pretext pretexts
NOUN a false reason given to hide the real reason for doing something

pretty prettier prettiest
ADJECTIVE **1.** attractive in a delicate way
ADVERB **2.** *an informal use* fairly or rather: *He spoke pretty good English.*
prettily ADVERB
prettiness NOUN

prevail prevails prevailing prevailed
VERB **1.** If a custom or belief prevails in a particular place, it is normal or most common there: *This attitude has prevailed in our city for many years.* **2.** If someone or something prevails, that person or thing succeeds in being stronger or more powerful than an opposing force: *In recent years peace has prevailed.*
prevailing ADJECTIVE

prevalent
ADJECTIVE very common or widespread: *Colds are prevalent in the winter.*
prevalence NOUN

prevent prevents preventing prevented
VERB If you prevent something, you stop it from happening or being done.
preventable ADJECTIVE
prevention NOUN

preventive
ADJECTIVE intended to help prevent things such as disease or crime: *preventive health care*

Instead of **PREVENT** try...
foil a robbery
inhibit growth
avert a disaster
hinder progress
thwart an attack

preview previews
NOUN **1.** an opportunity to see something, such as a movie or exhibition, before it is shown to the public **2.** a part of a computer program that allows you to look at what you have input or added to a document or spreadsheet as it will appear when it is printed

previous
ADJECTIVE happening or existing before something else in time or position: *previous reports, the previous year*
previously ADVERB

Instead of **PREVIOUSLY** try...
- one-time partners
- known beforehand
- had been seen already
- once owned by a king
- we'd formerly been friends

prey preys preying preyed
NOUN **1.** The creatures that an animal hunts and eats are called its prey.
VERB **2.** An animal that preys on another kind of animal lives by hunting and eating it.

price prices pricing priced
NOUN **1.** The price of something is the amount of money you have to pay to buy it.
VERB **2.** To price something at a particular amount is to fix its price at that amount.

priceless
ADJECTIVE Something that is priceless is so valuable that it is difficult to work out how much it is worth.

pricey pricier priciest
ADJECTIVE *an informal word* expensive

prick pricks pricking pricked
VERB **1.** If you prick something, you stick a sharp pointed object into it.
NOUN **2.** a small, sharp pain caused when something pricks you

prickle prickles prickling prickled
NOUN **1.** Prickles are small, sharp points or thorns on plants.
VERB **2.** If your skin prickles, it feels as if a lot of sharp points are being stuck into it.
prickly ADJECTIVE

pride prides priding prided
NOUN **1.** Pride is a feeling of satisfaction you have when you have done something well. **2.** Pride is also a feeling of being better than other people. **3.** A pride of lions is a group of them.
VERB **4.** If you pride yourself on a quality or skill, you are proud of it: *She prides herself on punctuality.*

priest priests
NOUN **1.** a member of the clergy in some Christian churches **2.** In many non-Christian religions, a priest is a man who has special duties in the place where people worship.
priestly ADJECTIVE

priestess priestesses
NOUN a female priest in a non-Christian religion

priesthood
NOUN The priesthood is the position of being a priest.

prim primmer primmest
ADJECTIVE Someone who is prim always behaves very correctly.

primarily
ADVERB You use *primarily* to indicate the main or most important feature of something: *I went to the museum primarily to see the dinosaur exhibit.*

primary
ADJECTIVE *Primary* is used to describe something that is extremely important for someone or something: *the primary aim of his research*

primary colour primary colours
NOUN The primary colours are red, yellow, and blue, from which other colours can be obtained by mixing.

primary school primary schools
NOUN the first three or four grades of elementary school

primate primates
NOUN a member of the group of animals that includes humans, monkeys, and apes

prime primes priming primed
ADJECTIVE **1.** main or most important: *a prime cause of brain damage* **2.** of the best quality: *in prime condition*
NOUN **3.** Someone's prime is the stage when that person is at his or her strongest, most active, or most successful.
VERB **4.** If you prime someone, you give that person information about something in advance to prepare him or her: *We are primed for every lesson.*

prime minister prime ministers
NOUN The prime minister is the leader of the federal government in Canada.

primeval
ADJECTIVE belonging to a very early period in the history of the world

primitive
ADJECTIVE **1.** connected with a society that lives very simply without industries or a writing system: *the primitive peoples of the world* **2.** very simple, basic, or old-fashioned: *a very small, primitive cottage*

primrose primroses
NOUN a small plant that has pale yellow flowers in spring

Pp

prince princes
NOUN a male member of a royal family, especially the son of a king or queen
princely ADJECTIVE

princess princesses
NOUN a female member of a royal family, usually the daughter of a king or queen, or the wife of a prince

principal principals
ADJECTIVE **1.** main or most important: *the principal source of food*
NOUN **2.** the person in charge of a school or college
principally ADVERB

⚠ **HEADS UP**

Don't confuse **principal** and **principle**: The *principal* lesson from my parents was to uphold moral *principles*.

principality principalities
NOUN a small state or country ruled by a prince

principle principles
NOUN **1.** a belief you have about the way you should behave: *a person of principle* **2.** a general rule or scientific law that explains how something happens or works: *the principle of evolution in nature*

print prints printing printed
VERB **1.** To print a newspaper or book is to reproduce it in large quantities using a mechanical or electronic copying process.
2. If you print when you are writing, you do not join the letters together.
NOUN **3.** The letters and numbers on the pages of a book or newspaper are referred to as the print. **4.** a photograph, or a printed copy of a painting **5.** Footprints and fingerprints can be referred to as prints.
printer NOUN

printing
NOUN the process of producing printed material such as books and newspapers

printout printouts
NOUN a printed copy of information from a computer

prior
ADJECTIVE **1.** planned or done at an earlier time: *I have a prior engagement.*
PHRASE **2.** Something that happens **prior to** a particular time or event happens before it.

priority priorities
NOUN something that needs to be dealt with first: *My priority is finishing this assignment.*

prioritize prioritizes prioritizing prioritized
VERB To prioritize things is to decide which is the most important and deal with it first.

prism prisms
NOUN **1.** an object made of clear glass with many flat sides. It separates light passing through it into the colours of the rainbow.
2. In mathematics, a prism is any polyhedron with two identical parallel ends and sides which are parallelograms.

prison prisons
NOUN a building where criminals are confined

prisoner prisoners
NOUN someone who is kept in prison or held somewhere against his or her will

pristine
ADJECTIVE *a formal word* very clean or new and in perfect condition

private privates
ADJECTIVE **1.** for the use of one person rather than people in general: *a private bathroom*
2. taking place between a small number of people and kept secret from others: *a private conversation* **3.** owned or run by individuals or companies rather than by the government: *a private company*
NOUN **4.** a soldier of the lowest rank
privacy NOUN
privately ADVERB

private school private schools
NOUN a school that does not receive money from the government, and parents pay for their children to attend

privatize privatizes privatizing privatized
VERB If the government privatizes a state-owned industry or organization, it allows it to be bought and owned by a private individual or group.

privilege privileges
NOUN a special right or advantage given to a person or group: *the privileges of being a member of this club*
privileged ADJECTIVE

privy
ADJECTIVE *a formal use* If you are privy to something secret, you have been told about it.

prize prizes prizing prized
NOUN **1.** a reward given to the winner of a competition or game
ADJECTIVE **2.** of the highest quality or standard: *his prize dahlia*
VERB **3.** Something that is prized is wanted and admired for its value or quality.

pro pros
NOUN **1.** *an informal use* a professional
PHRASE **2.** The **pros and cons** of a situation are its advantages and disadvantages.

pro-
PREFIX The prefix *pro-* means supporting or in favour of: *pro-democracy protests*

probability probabilities
NOUN **1.** The probability of something happening is how likely it is to happen: *the probability of success* **2.** If something is a probability, it is likely to happen: *The probability is that you will be feeling better.*

probable
ADJECTIVE Something that is probable is likely to be true or correct, or likely to happen: *the most probable outcome*

probably
ADVERB Something that is probably the case is likely but not certain.

Instead of **PROBABLY** try...

possibly true
that will **likely** work
perhaps the best way
we will **no doubt** succeed
presumably how it will go

probation
NOUN
Probation is a period of time during which a person convicted of a crime is supervised by a probation officer instead of being sent to prison.
probationary ADJECTIVE

probe probes probing probed
VERB **1.** If you probe, you ask a lot of questions to discover the facts about something.
NOUN **2.** a long, thin instrument used by doctors and dentists when examining a patient

problem problems
NOUN **1.** an unsatisfactory situation that causes difficulties **2.** a puzzle or question that you solve using logical thought or mathematics
problematic ADJECTIVE

procedural text
NOUN a set of instructions that tells you how to do or make something

procedure procedures
NOUN a way of doing something, especially the correct or usual way: *It's standard procedure.*
procedural ADJECTIVE

proceed proceeds proceeding proceeded
VERB **1.** If you proceed to do something, you start doing it, or continue doing it: *She proceeded to tell them the story.* **2.** *a formal use* If you proceed in a particular direction, you move in that direction: *The taxi proceeded along the lonely road.*
PLURAL NOUN **3.** The proceeds from a fundraising event are the money obtained from it.

proceedings
PLURAL NOUN **1.** You can refer to an organized and related series of events as the proceedings: *He was determined to see the proceedings from start to finish.* **2.** Legal proceedings are legal action taken against someone.

process processes processing processed
NOUN **1.** a series of actions intended to achieve a particular result or change
PHRASE **2.** If you are **in the process** of doing something, you have started doing it but have not yet finished.
VERB **3.** When something such as food or information is processed, it is treated or dealt with.

procession processions
NOUN a group of people or vehicles moving in a line, often as part of a ceremony

processor processors
NOUN In computing, a processor is the central chip in a computer that controls its operations.

proclaim proclaims proclaiming proclaimed
VERB If someone proclaims something, that person announces it or makes it known: *The prisoner proclaimed her innocence before the judge.*
proclamation NOUN

procure procures procuring procured
VERB *a formal word* If you procure something, you obtain it.

prod prods prodding prodded
VERB If you prod something, you give it a push with your finger or with something pointed.

prodigy prodigies
NOUN someone who shows an extraordinary natural ability at an early age

produce produces producing produced
VERB **1.** To produce something is to make it or cause it: *This tree doesn't produce many apples.* **2.** If you produce something from somewhere, you bring it out so it can be seen.
NOUN **3.** Produce is food that is grown to be sold: *fresh produce*

Pp

producer producers

NOUN The producer of a CD, movie, or play is the person in charge of making it or putting it on.

product products

NOUN **1.** something that is made to be sold: *high-quality products* **2.** In mathematics, the product of two or more numbers or quantities is the result of multiplying them together.

production productions

NOUN **1.** Production is the process of manufacturing or growing something in large quantities: *modern methods of production* **2.** Production is also the amount of goods manufactured or food grown by a country or company: *Production has fallen by five percent.* **3.** A production of a play, opera, or other show is a series of performances of it.

productive

ADJECTIVE **1.** To be productive means to produce a large number of things: *Farms were more productive in these areas.* **2.** If something such as a meeting is productive, good or useful things happen as a result of it.

productivity

NOUN Productivity is the rate at which things are produced or dealt with.

profane

ADJECTIVE *a formal word* showing disrespect for a religion or religious things: *profane language*

profess professes professing professed

VERB **1.** *a formal word* If you profess to do or have something, you claim to do or have that thing. **2.** If you profess a feeling or opinion, you express it: *He professes a lasting affection for Newfoundland.*

profession professions

NOUN **1.** a type of job that requires advanced education or training **2.** You can use *profession* to refer to all the people who have a particular profession: *the medical profession*

professional professionals

ADJECTIVE **1.** Professional means relating to the work of someone who is qualified in a particular profession: *I think you need professional advice.* **2.** Professional also describes activities when they are done to earn money rather than as a hobby: *professional hockey* **3.** A professional piece of work is of a very high standard.

NOUN **4.** a person who has been trained in a profession **5.** someone who plays a sport to earn money rather than as a hobby

professor professors

NOUN a teacher of the highest rank in a college or university

professorial ADJECTIVE

proficient

ADJECTIVE If you are proficient at something, you can do it well.

proficiency NOUN

profile profiles

NOUN **1.** Your profile is the outline of your face seen from the side. **2.** A profile of someone is a short description of that person's life and character.

profit profits profiting profited

NOUN **1.** When someone sells something, the profit is the amount that person gains by selling it for more than it cost him or her to buy or make.

VERB **2.** If you profit from something, you gain or benefit from it.

profitable ADJECTIVE

profound

ADJECTIVE **1.** great in degree or intensity: *a profound need to please* **2.** showing great and deep intellectual understanding: *a profound question*

profoundly ADVERB

KNOWING WORDS: WORD HISTORY

BE WORD SHARP!

Words are like living things. They grow and change.

Profile started out as the Latin words **pro**, meaning *forth*, and **filum**, meaning *thread*. It came into Italian as **profilare**, meaning *draw in outline*, as someone would do with a piece of thread, following the lines of a shadow. A profile still means an outline of a person's face, but now also means an outline of a person's life. More recently, it has also come to mean *judge a person based on appearance*, as in **racial profiling**.

Pp

profuse
ADJECTIVE very large in quantity or number: *There were profuse apologies for his absence.*
profusely ADVERB

program programs programming programmed
NOUN **1.** a set of instructions that a computer follows to perform a particular task **2.** a planned series of events: *a program of official engagements* **3.** a particular piece presented as a unit on television or radio, such as a play, show, or discussion **4.** a booklet giving information about a play, concert, or show that you are attending
VERB **5.** When someone programs a computer, that person writes a program and puts it into the computer.
programmer NOUN

progress progresses progressing progressed
NOUN **1.** Progress is the process of gradually improving or getting near to achieving something: *I am now making some real progress toward finding a solution to this problem.* **2.** The progress of something is the way in which it develops or continues: *news on the progress of the cleanup effort*
VERB **3.** If you progress, you become more advanced or skilful. **4.** To progress is to continue: *As the evening progressed, sadness turned to rage.*
PHRASE **5.** Something that is **in progress** is happening: *A basketball game was in progress.*
progression NOUN

progressive
ADJECTIVE **1.** having modern ideas about how things should be done **2.** happening gradually: *a progressive illness*

prohibit prohibits prohibiting prohibited
VERB If someone prohibits something, that person forbids it or makes it illegal.
prohibition NOUN

prohibitive
ADJECTIVE If the cost of something is prohibitive, it is so high that people cannot afford it.

project projects projecting projected
NOUN **1.** a carefully planned attempt to achieve something or to study something over a period of time
VERB **2.** Something that is projected is planned or expected to happen in the future: *The population aged 65 or over is projected to increase.* **3.** To project an image onto a screen is to make it appear there using equipment such as a projector. **4.** Something

that projects sticks out beyond a surface or edge.
projection NOUN

projector projectors
NOUN a piece of equipment that produces a large image on a screen by shining light through a photographic slide or film strip

proliferate proliferates proliferating proliferated
VERB If things proliferate, they quickly increase in number.
proliferation NOUN

prolific
ADJECTIVE producing a lot of something: *this prolific artist*

prologue prologues
NOUN a speech or section that introduces a play or book

prolong prolongs prolonging prolonged
VERB If you prolong something, you make it last longer.
prolonged ADJECTIVE

prom proms
NOUN *an informal word* a formal dance for a high school or college class, usually toward the end of the school year

promenade promenades
NOUN a leisurely walk in a public place, usually to meet other people

prominent
ADJECTIVE **1.** Prominent people are important. **2.** Something that is prominent is very noticeable: *a prominent tall building*
prominence NOUN
prominently ADVERB

promiscuous
ADJECTIVE Someone who is promiscuous has sex with many different people.
promiscuity NOUN

promise promises promising promised
VERB **1.** If you promise to do something, you

Instead of **PROMISE** try...

say that you will definitely do it.
2. Something that promises to have a particular quality shows signs that it will have that quality: *This promised to be a very long night.*

an **oath** of secrecy
a written **guarantee**
my word is my **bond**
a **vow** to return home
a **pledge** to our customers

Pp

NOUN **3.** a statement made by someone that he or she will definitely do something: *He made a promise to me.* **4.** Someone or something that shows promise seems likely to be very successful.

promising ADJECTIVE

promontory promontories
NOUN an area of high land sticking out into a body of water

promote promotes promoting promoted
VERB **1.** If someone promotes something, that person tries to make that thing happen. **2.** If someone promotes a product such as a movie or a book, that person tries to make it popular by advertising. **3.** If someone is promoted, that person is given a more important job at work.

promoter NOUN

promotion NOUN

prompt prompts prompting prompted
VERB **1.** If something prompts someone to do something, it makes that person decide to do it: *Curiosity prompted him to push at the door.* **2.** If you prompt someone when he or she stops speaking, you tell that person what to say next or encourage him or her to continue.
ADJECTIVE **3.** A prompt action is done without any delay: *a prompt reply*

promptly ADVERB

prone
ADJECTIVE **1.** If you are prone to something, you have a tendency to be affected by it or to do it: *She is prone to depression.* **2.** If you are prone, you are lying flat and face downward: *lying prone on the grass*

prong prongs
NOUN The prongs of a fork are the long, narrow, pointed parts.

pronoun pronouns
NOUN In grammar, a pronoun is a word that is used to replace a noun. *He*, *she*, and *them* are all pronouns.

pronounce pronounces pronouncing pronounced
VERB When you pronounce a word, you say it.

pronounced
ADJECTIVE very noticeable: *He talks with a pronounced Newfoundland accent.*

pronouncement pronouncements
NOUN a formal statement

pronunciation pronunciations
NOUN the way a word is usually said

proof
NOUN If you have proof of something, you have evidence that shows that it is true or exists.

proofread
VERB If you proofread a piece of writing, you read it and mark corrections in grammar, usage, spelling, and punctuation.

prop props propping propped
VERB **1.** If you prop an object somewhere, you support it or rest it against something: *I propped my book against the sugar bowl and read while I ate breakfast.*
NOUN **2.** a stick or other object used to support something **3.** all the objects and furniture used by the actors in a play

propaganda
NOUN Propaganda is exaggerated or false information that is published or broadcast in order to influence people.

propagate propagates propagating propagated
VERB **1.** If people propagate an idea, they spread it to try to influence many other people. **2.** If you propagate plants, you grow more of them from an original one.

propagation NOUN

propel propels propelling propelled
VERB To propel something is to cause it to move in a particular direction.

propeller propellers
NOUN a device on a boat or aircraft with rotating blades that make the boat or aircraft move

propensity propensities
NOUN *a formal word* a tendency to behave in a particular way

proper
ADJECTIVE **1.** correct or suitable: *Put things in their proper place.* **2.** accepted or conventional: *proper behaviour* **3.** identifying a particular person, place, or organization: *It is customary to capitalize a proper name.*

properly ADVERB

proper noun proper nouns
NOUN the name of a person, place, or organization

⚠ **HEADS UP**

Proper nouns name a specific person, place, or thing, and are always capitalized: *Lara, Calgary, Labour Day.*

property properties
NOUN **1.** A person's property is the things that belong to that person. **2.** a building and the land belonging to it **3.** a characteristic or quality: *Nickel and iron have different chemical properties.*

Pp

prophecy prophecies
NOUN a statement about what someone believes will happen in the future

prophesy prophesies prophesying prophesied
VERB If someone prophesies something, that person says it will happen.

prophet prophets
NOUN a person who predicts what will happen in the future

prophetic
ADJECTIVE correctly predicting what will happen: *It was a prophetic warning.*

proportion proportions
NOUN **1.** A proportion of an amount or group is a part of it: *a tiny proportion of the population* **2.** The proportion of one amount to another is its size in comparison with the other amount: *There is a high proportion of girls to boys in our class.*
PLURAL NOUN **3.** You can refer to the size of something as its proportions: *a red umbrella of vast proportions*

proportional
ADJECTIVE If one thing is proportional to another, it remains the same size in comparison with the other: *proportional increases in profit*
proportionally ADVERB
proportionately ADVERB

proportional representation
NOUN Proportional representation is a system of voting in elections in which the number of representatives of each party is in proportion to the number of people who voted for it.

proposal proposals
NOUN a plan that has been suggested: *business proposals*

propose proposes proposing proposed
VERB **1.** If you propose a plan or idea, you suggest it. **2.** If you propose to do something, you intend to do it: *And how do you propose to do that?* **3.** When someone proposes a toast to a particular person, he or she asks people to drink a toast to that person. **4.** If someone proposes to another person, he or she asks that person to marry him or her.

proposition propositions
NOUN **1.** a statement expressing a theory or opinion **2.** an offer or suggestion: *an attractive proposition*

proprietor proprietors
NOUN The proprietor of a business is the owner.

propriety
NOUN *a formal word* Propriety is what is socially or morally acceptable: *a model of propriety*

propulsion
NOUN Propulsion is the power that moves something.

prose
NOUN Prose is written language in contrast to poetry.

prosecute prosecutes prosecuting prosecuted
VERB If someone is prosecuted, that person is charged with a crime and has to stand trial.
prosecutor NOUN

prosecution
NOUN The lawyers who try to prove that a person on trial is guilty are called the prosecution.

prospect prospects prospecting prospected
NOUN **1.** If there is a prospect of something happening, there is a possibility that it will happen: *There was little prospect of going home before dinner.* **2.** Someone's prospects are that person's chances of being successful in the future.
VERB **3.** If someone prospects for gold or oil, that person looks for it.
prospector NOUN

prospective
ADJECTIVE *Prospective* is used to say that someone wants to be or is likely to be something. For example, the prospective owner of something is the person who wants to own it.

prospectus prospectuses
NOUN a booklet giving details about an educational institution or a company

prosper prospers prospering prospered
VERB When people or businesses prosper, they are successful and make a lot of money.
prosperous ADJECTIVE
prosperity NOUN

prostitute prostitutes
NOUN a person who has sex in exchange for money
prostitution NOUN

prostrate
ADJECTIVE lying face downward on the ground

protagonist protagonists
NOUN *a formal word* **1.** Someone who is a protagonist of an idea or movement is a leading supporter of it. **2.** a main character in a play or story

protect protects protecting protected
VERB To protect someone or something is to prevent that person or thing from being

⚠ HEADS UP Prophecy is pronounced PRAWF-uh-see. Prophesy is pronounced PRAWF-uh-sigh.

harmed or damaged.
protection NOUN
protective ADJECTIVE
protector NOUN

protection protections
NOUN **1.** the act of preventing harm or damage **2.** something that keeps a person or thing safe

protégé protégés
NOUN Someone who is the protégé of an older, more experienced person is helped and guided by that person.

HEADS UP

Protégé comes from the French word for *protected*. We still used the French pronunciation, PRO-tuh-zhay.

protein proteins
NOUN Protein is a substance that is found in food such as meat and eggs, and is needed by bodies for growth.

protest protests protesting protested
VERB **1.** If you protest something, you say or demonstrate publicly that you disagree with it: *They protested the destruction of the forest.*
NOUN **2.** a demonstration or statement showing that you disagree with something

Protestant Protestants
NOUN OR ADJECTIVE a member of one of the Christian churches that separated from the Catholic Church in the sixteenth century

protestation protestations
NOUN a strong declaration that something is true or not true: *his protestations of love*

protocol
NOUN Protocol is the system of rules about the correct way to behave in formal situations.

proton protons
NOUN a particle that forms part of the nucleus of an atom and has a positive electrical charge

prototype prototypes
NOUN a first model of something that is made so that the design can be tested and improved

protracted
ADJECTIVE lasting longer than usual: *a protracted dispute*

protractor protractors
NOUN a flat, semicircular instrument used for measuring angles

protrude protrudes protruding protruded
VERB *a formal word* If something is protruding from a surface or edge, it is sticking out.
protrusion NOUN

Instead of **PROUD** try…

a superior manner
a vain self-image
a pleased smile
a noble history
a smug grin
a satisfied sigh
a dignified life
honoured to be Canadian

proud prouder proudest
ADJECTIVE
1. feeling pleasure and satisfaction at something you own or have achieved: *I was proud of our players today.* **2.** having great dignity and self-respect: *too proud to ask for money*
proudly ADVERB

prove proves proving proved
VERB **1.** To prove that something is true is to provide evidence that it is definitely true: *A letter from his mother proved that he lived there.* **2.** If something proves to be the case, it becomes clear that it is so: *My first impressions of her proved wrong.*

proverb proverbs
NOUN a short sentence that gives advice or makes a comment about life
proverbial ADJECTIVE

provide provides providing provided
VERB **1.** If you provide something for someone, you give it to that person or make it available for him or her. **2.** If you provide for someone, you give that person the things he or she needs.

provided
CONJUNCTION If you say that something will happen provided something else happens, you mean that the first thing will happen only if the second thing does.

providence
NOUN Providence is God or a force that is believed to arrange the things that happen to us.

province provinces
NOUN **1.** one of the ten main political and administrative divisions in Canada **2.** one of the areas into which some large countries are divided, each province having its own administration

Pp

provincial
ADJECTIVE to do with a province: *provincial sales tax*

provision provisions
NOUN **1.** The provision of something is the act of making it available to people: *the provision of health care*
PLURAL NOUN **2.** Provisions are supplies of food.

provisional
ADJECTIVE A provisional arrangement has not yet been made definite and so might be changed.

proviso provisos
NOUN a condition in an agreement

provocation provocations
NOUN an act done deliberately to annoy someone

provocative
ADJECTIVE intended to annoy people or make them react: *a provocative speech*

provoke provokes provoking provoked
VERB **1.** If you provoke someone, you deliberately try to make that person angry.
2. If something provokes an unpleasant reaction, it causes it: *illness provoked by tension or worry*

prow prows
NOUN the front part of a boat

prowess
NOUN Prowess is outstanding ability: *his prowess at tennis*

prowl prowls prowling prowled
VERB If a person or animal prowls around, that person or animal moves around quietly and secretly, as if hunting.

proximity
NOUN *a formal word* Proximity is nearness to someone or something.

proxy
PHRASE If you do something **by proxy**, someone else does it on your behalf: *voting by proxy*

prude prudes
NOUN someone who is too easily shocked by sex or nudity
prudish ADJECTIVE

prudent
ADJECTIVE behaving in a sensible and cautious way: *It is prudent to plan ahead.*
prudence NOUN
prudently ADVERB

prune prunes pruning pruned
NOUN **1.** a dried plum

VERB **2.** When someone prunes a tree or shrub, that person cuts back some of the branches.

pry pries prying pried
VERB If someone is prying, that person is trying to find out about something secret or private.

PS PS is written before an additional message at the end of a letter. PS is an abbreviation for *postscript*.

pseudo-
PREFIX The prefix *pseudo-* is used to form adjectives and nouns indicating that something is not what it is claimed to be: *pseudo-scientific theories*

pseudonym pseudonyms
NOUN a name an author uses rather than his or her real name

psyche psyches
NOUN your mind and your deepest feelings

psychiatry
NOUN Psychiatry is the branch of medicine concerned with mental illness.
psychiatrist NOUN
psychiatric ADJECTIVE

psychic
ADJECTIVE supposedly having unusual mental powers such as the ability to read people's minds or predict the future

psychoanalysis
NOUN Psychoanalysis is the examination and treatment of someone who is mentally ill by encouraging that person to talk about his or her feelings and past events in order to discover the cause of the illness.
psychoanalyst NOUN
psychoanalyze VERB

psychology
NOUN Psychology is the scientific study of the mind and of the reasons for people's behaviour.
psychological ADJECTIVE
psychologist NOUN

psychopath psychopaths
NOUN a mentally ill person who behaves violently without feeling guilt
psychopathic ADJECTIVE

psychosis psychoses
NOUN a severe mental illness
psychotic ADJECTIVE

pterodactyl pterodactyls
NOUN Pterodactyls were flying reptiles in prehistoric times.

⚠ HEADS UP The *p* is silent in words that begin with *ps* (**psychic**) and *pt* (**pterodactyl**).

Pp

PTO PTO is an abbreviation for *please turn over*. It is written at the bottom of a page to indicate that the writing continues on the other side.

puberty
NOUN Puberty is the stage when a person's body changes from that of a child into that of an adult.

pubic
ADJECTIVE relating to the area around and above a person's genitals

public
NOUN **1.** You can refer to people in general as the public.
ADJECTIVE **2.** relating to people in general: *There was some public support for the idea.*
3. provided for everyone to use, or open to anyone: *public transport*
publicly ADVERB

publication publications
NOUN **1.** The publication of a book is the act of printing it and making it available. **2.** a book or magazine: *medical publications*

publicity
NOUN Publicity is information or advertisements about an item or event.

publicize publicizes publicizing publicized
VERB When someone publicizes a fact or event, that person advertises it and makes it widely known.

public school public schools
NOUN In Canada and the United States, a public school is a school that is maintained by the taxes paid by the public.

public servant public servants
NOUN a person who works in a department or branch of the government

public service
NOUN a service done for the benefit of a community

publish publishes publishing published
VERB **1.** When a company publishes a book, newspaper, or magazine, that company prints copies of it and distributes it. **2.** When you publish a piece of your writing, you create a final copy that is ready to be shared with the intended audience.
publishing NOUN

publisher publishers
NOUN The publisher of a book, newspaper, or magazine is the person or company that prints copies of it and distributes it.

puck pucks
NOUN a hard, black, rubber disc used in the game of hockey

pudding puddings
NOUN **1.** a soft, cooked food, usually sweet: *rice pudding, chocolate pudding* **2.** a sweet, cakelike dessert, usually steamed or baked

puddle puddles
NOUN a small, shallow pool of liquid

puerile
ADJECTIVE Puerile behaviour is silly and childish.

puff puffs puffing puffed
VERB **1.** If you are puffing, you are breathing loudly and quickly with your mouth open.
2. If something puffs out or puffs up, it swells and becomes larger and rounder.
NOUN **3.** a small amount of air or smoke that is released

puffin puffins
NOUN a black and white seabird with a large, brightly coloured beak

pug pugs
NOUN a small, short-haired dog with a flat nose

puke pukes puking puked
VERB *an informal word* If someone pukes, that person vomits.

pull pulls pulling pulled
VERB **1.** When you pull something, you hold it and move it toward you. **2.** When something is pulled by a vehicle or animal, it is attached to it and moves along behind it: *Four oxen can pull a single plough.* **3.** When you pull a curtain or blind, you move it so that it covers or uncovers the window. **4.** If you pull a muscle, you injure it by stretching it too far or too quickly. **5.** When a vehicle pulls away, pulls out, or pulls in, it moves in that direction.
NOUN **6.** The pull of something is its attraction or influence: *the pull of the past*
pull out
VERB **7.** If you pull out of something, you leave it or decide not to continue with it: *The coach pulled our team out of the tournament.*
pull through
VERB **8.** When someone pulls through, that person recovers from a serious illness.
pull together
VERB **9.** work in harmony

pulley pulleys
NOUN a device for lifting heavy weights. The weight is attached to a rope that passes over a wheel or series of wheels.

pullover pullovers
NOUN a sweater put on by pulling it over the top of the head

pulmonary
ADJECTIVE *a formal word* relating to the lungs or to the veins and arteries carrying blood between the lungs and the heart

pulp
NOUN If something is turned into a pulp, it is crushed until it is soft and moist.

pulpit pulpits
NOUN the small raised platform in a church where a member of the clergy stands to preach

pulse pulses pulsing pulsed
NOUN **1.** Your pulse is the regular beating of blood through your body, the rate of which you can feel at your wrists and elsewhere.
VERB **2.** If something is pulsing, it is moving or vibrating with rhythmic, regular movements: *She could feel the blood pulsing in her eardrums.*

puma pumas
NOUN a wild animal belonging to the cat family

pumice
NOUN Pumice stone is very lightweight, grey stone that can be used to soften areas of hard skin.

pummel pummels pummelling pummelled
VERB If you pummel something, you beat it with your fists.

pump pumps pumping pumped
NOUN **1.** a machine that is used to force a liquid or gas to move in a particular direction **2.** a low-cut shoe with no laces, straps, or other fastenings
VERB **3.** To pump a liquid or gas somewhere is to force it to flow in that direction, using a pump. **4.** If you pump money into something, you put a lot of money into it.

pumpkin pumpkins
NOUN a very large, round, orange fruit eaten as a vegetable

pun puns
NOUN a clever and amusing use of words so that what you say has two different meanings, for example: *When a clock is hungry, it goes back four seconds.*

punch punches punching punched
VERB **1.** If you punch someone, you hit that person hard with your fist.
NOUN **2.** a hard blow with the fist **3.** a tool used for making holes **4.** Punch is a drink made from a mixture of different types of fruit juices and often contains alcohol.

punctual
ADJECTIVE arriving at the correct time
punctually ADVERB
punctuality NOUN

punctuate punctuates punctuating punctuated
VERB **1.** Something that is punctuated by a particular thing is interrupted by it at intervals: *a grey day punctuated by periods of rain* **2.** When you punctuate a piece of writing, you put punctuation into it.

punctuation
NOUN The marks in writing such as periods, question marks, and commas are called punctuation or punctuation marks.

puncture punctures puncturing punctured
NOUN **1.** If a tire has a puncture, a small hole has been made in it and it has become flat.
VERB **2.** To puncture something is to make a small hole in it.

pungent
ADJECTIVE having a strong smell or taste
pungency NOUN

punish punishes punishing punished
VERB To punish someone who has done something wrong is to make that person suffer because of it.

punishment punishments
NOUN something unpleasant done to someone because he or she has done something wrong

punitive
ADJECTIVE harsh and intended as a punishment: *punitive military action*

punk
NOUN Punk or punk rock is an aggressive style of rock music.

punt punts
NOUN a long, flat-bottomed boat. You move it along by pushing a pole against the bottom of a body of water.

puny punier puniest
ADJECTIVE very small and weak

pup pups
NOUN a young dog. Some other young animals such as seals are also called pups.

pupil pupils
NOUN **1.** The pupils at a school are the students who go there. **2.** Your pupils are the small, round, black holes in the centre of your eyes.

puppet puppets
NOUN a doll or toy animal that is moved by pulling strings or by putting your hand inside its body

puppy puppies
NOUN a young dog

purchase purchases purchasing purchased
VERB **1.** When you purchase something, you buy it.
NOUN **2.** something you have bought
purchaser NOUN

PUN

a clever and amusing use of words so that what you say has two different meanings

"I thought you liked rock music!"

Here is an example of a pun. It uses two meanings of **rock**: *stone* and *rock and roll*.

Pp

pure purer purest
ADJECTIVE **1.** Something that is pure is not mixed with anything else: *pure wool, pure white* **2.** Pure also means clean and free from harmful substances: *The water is pure enough to drink.* **3.** People who are pure have not done anything considered to be sinful. **4.** Pure also means complete and total: *a matter of pure luck*
purity NOUN

purée purées
NOUN a food that has been mashed or blended to a thick, smooth consistency

purely
ADVERB involving only one feature and not including anything else: *purely professional*

purge purges purging purged
VERB To purge something is to remove undesirable things from it: *to purge the country of criminals*

purify purifies purifying purified
VERB To purify something is to remove all dirty or harmful substances from it.
purification NOUN

purist purists
NOUN someone who believes that something should be done in a particular, correct way: *a language purist*

puritan puritans
NOUN someone who believes in strict moral principles and avoids physical pleasures
puritanical ADJECTIVE

purple
NOUN **1.** a colour midway between red and blue
ADJECTIVE **2.** reddish blue

purport purports purporting purported
VERB *a formal word* Something that purports to be or have a particular thing is claimed to be or have it: *a government that purports to disapprove of smoking*

purpose purposes
NOUN **1.** The purpose of something is the reason for it: *the purpose of the meeting* **2.** If you have a particular purpose, this is what you want to achieve: *The purpose of my speech is to convince my classmates that global warming is a reality.*
PHRASE **3.** If you do something **on purpose**, you do it deliberately.
purposely ADVERB
purposeful ADJECTIVE

purr purrs purring purred
VERB When a cat purrs, it makes a low, vibrating sound because it is contented.

purse purses pursing pursed
NOUN **1.** a bag or case for carrying money and other personal items
VERB **2.** If you purse your lips, you move them into a tight, rounded shape.

purser pursers
NOUN the officer responsible for the paperwork and the welfare of passengers on a ship

pursue pursues pursuing pursued
VERB **1.** If you pursue an activity or plan, you do it or make efforts to achieve it: *I decided to pursue a career in photography.* **2.** If you pursue someone, you follow that person to try to catch him or her.
pursuer NOUN
pursuit NOUN

purveyor purveyors
NOUN *a formal word* A purveyor of goods or services is a person who sells them or provides them.

pus
NOUN Pus is a thick, yellowish liquid that forms in an infected wound.

push pushes pushing pushed
VERB **1.** When you push something, you press it using force in order to move it. **2.** If you push someone into doing something, you force or persuade that person to do it: *His mother pushed him into auditioning for a part.* **3.** *an informal use* Someone who pushes drugs sells them illegally.

KNOWING WORDS: IDIOMS

BE WORD SHARP!

Idioms add colour to language by playing with the meanings of words.

push press forward

push around treat roughly

push for advocate strongly

push it/push your luck take an unwise risk

push on keep going despite difficulty

if push comes to shove if a problem must be faced

NEL

pushing

PREPOSITION Someone who is pushing a particular age is nearly that age: *pushing 60*

pushover

NOUN *an informal word* **1.** something that is easy **2.** someone who is easily persuaded or defeated

pushy pushier pushiest

ADJECTIVE *an informal word* behaving in a forceful and determined way

put puts putting put

VERB **1.** When you put something somewhere, you move it into that place or position. **2.** If you put an idea or remark in a particular way, you express it that way: *I think you've put that very well.* **3.** To put someone or something in a particular state or situation means to cause that person to be in it: *It puts us both in an awkward position.* **4.** You can use *put* to express an estimate of the size or importance of something: *Her wealth is now put at 290 million dollars.*

put down

VERB **5.** To put someone down is to criticize that person and make him or her appear foolish. **6.** If an animal is put down, it is killed because it is very ill or dangerous.

put off

VERB **7.** If you put something off, you delay doing it. **8.** To put someone off is to discourage that person.

put out

VERB **9.** If you put a fire out or put the light out, you make it stop burning or shining. **10.** If you are put out, you are annoyed or upset.

put up

VERB **11.** If you put up resistance to something, you argue or fight against it: *She put up a tremendous struggle.*

put up with

VERB **12.** If you put up with something, you tolerate it even though you disagree with it or dislike it.

putt putts

NOUN In golf, a putt is a gentle stroke made in an effort to roll the ball into the hole.

putty

NOUN Putty is a paste used to fix panes of glass into frames.

puzzle puzzles puzzling puzzled

VERB **1.** If something puzzles you, it confuses you and you do not understand it: *There was something about her that puzzled me.* NOUN **2.** A puzzle is a game or question that requires a lot of thought to complete or solve.

puzzled ADJECTIVE

puzzlement NOUN

Instead of **PUZZLED** try…

a **bewildered** stare

the riddle **stumped** us

police are still **baffled**

the crowd was **mystified**

perplexed by the problem

PVC

NOUN PVC is a plastic used for making clothing, pipes, and many other things. PVC is an abbreviation for *polyvinyl chloride*.

pygmy pygmies

NOUN a very small person, especially one who belongs to a racial group in which all the people are small

pyjamas

PLURAL NOUN Pyjamas are loose pants and a top that you wear in bed.

pylon pylons

NOUN an orange plastic cone used on roads to mark an area to be avoided

pyramid pyramids

NOUN **1.** a three-dimensional shape with a flat base and flat, triangular sides sloping upward to a point **2.** The Pyramids are ancient stone structures built as tombs for Egyptian kings and queens.

pyre pyres

NOUN a high pile of wood on which a dead body or religious offering is burned

python pythons

NOUN a large snake that kills animals by squeezing them with its body

Qq

quack quacks quacking quacked
VERB When a duck quacks, it makes a loud, harsh sound.

quad quads
NOUN Quad is an abbreviation of *quadriceps*.

quadr-
PREFIX The prefix *quadr-* means *four*.

quadriceps
NOUN a large muscle in four parts at the front of your thigh, often called *quad* for short

quagmire quagmires
NOUN a soft, wet area of land that you sink into if you walk on it

quail quails quailing quailed
NOUN **1.** a type of small game bird with a round body and short tail
VERB **2.** If you quail, you feel or look afraid.

quaint quainter quaintest
ADJECTIVE attractively old-fashioned or unusual: *quaint customs*
quaintly ADVERB

quake quakes quaking quaked
VERB If you quake, you shake and tremble because you are very frightened.

qualification qualifications
NOUN **1.** Your qualifications are your skills and achievements, especially as officially recognized at the end of a course of training or study. **2.** something you add to a statement to make it less strong: *It is a good novel and yet cannot be recommended without qualification.*

qualify qualifies qualifying qualified
VERB **1.** When you qualify, you pass the examinations or tests that you need to pass to do a particular job or to take part in a sporting event. **2.** If you qualify a statement, you add a detail or explanation to make it less strong: *I would qualify that by putting it into context.* **3.** If you qualify for something, you become entitled to have it: *You qualify for a discount.*
qualified ADJECTIVE

quality qualities
NOUN **1.** The quality of something is how good it is: *The quality of food at this restaurant is very poor.* **2.** a characteristic: *These qualities are essential for success.*

qualm qualms
NOUN If you have qualms about what you are doing, you worry that it might not be right.

quandary quandaries
NOUN If you are in a quandary, you cannot decide what to do.

quantity quantities
NOUN **1.** an amount you can measure or count: *a small quantity of salt* **2.** Quantity is the amount of something that there is: *emphasis on quantity rather than quality*

quarantine
NOUN If people or animals are in quarantine, they are kept away from others for a time because they might have an infectious disease.

quarrel quarrels quarrelling quarrelled
NOUN **1.** an angry argument
VERB **2.** If people quarrel, they have an angry argument.

quarry quarries quarrying quarried
NOUN **1.** a place where stone is removed from the ground by digging or blasting **2.** A person's or animal's quarry is an animal that is being hunted
VERB **3.** To quarry stone means to remove it from a quarry by digging or blasting.

quart quarts
NOUN a nonmetric unit of liquid volume equal to about 1.136 litres

quarter quarters
NOUN **1.** one of four equal parts **2.** You can refer to a particular area in a city as a quarter: *the French quarter* **3.** You can

KNOWING WORDS: WORD BUILDING

BE WORD SHARP!

You can create new words by adding prefixes and suffixes to a base word.

quad- a prefix that means *four*

quadrangle a courtyard with buildings on four sides

quadrilateral a shape with four straight sides

quadruped an animal with four legs

quadruple four times an amount

quadruplets four siblings born at the same time

NEL

Qq

use *quarter* to refer vaguely to a particular person or group of people: *You are very popular in certain quarters.*
PLURAL NOUN **4.** A soldier's or a servant's quarters are the rooms that that soldier or servant lives in.

quarterly quarterlies
ADJECTIVE OR ADVERB **1.** Quarterly means happening regularly every three months: *my quarterly report*
NOUN **2.** a magazine or journal published every three months

quartet quartets
NOUN a group of four musicians who sing or play together; also a piece of music written for four instruments or singers

quartz
NOUN Quartz is a kind of hard, shiny crystal used in making very accurate watches and clocks.

quash quashes quashing quashed
VERB To quash something is to reject it officially: *The judge quashed the appeal.*

quasi-
PREFIX The prefix *quasi-* means *resembling something*, but not actually being that thing: *a quasi-official document*

quaver quavers quavering quavered
VERB If your voice quavers, it sounds unsteady, usually because you are nervous.

quay quays
NOUN a place where boats are tied up and loaded or unloaded

⚠ **HEADS UP**
Quay is an alternate spelling of **key**, as in *the Florida Keys*. Both words are pronounced the same: KEE.

queasy queasier queasiest
ADJECTIVE feeling slightly sick

queen queens
NOUN **1.** a female monarch or a woman married to a king **2.** a female bee or ant that lays eggs **3.** In chess, the queen is the most powerful piece, which can move in any direction. **4.** In a pack of cards, a queen is a card with a picture of a queen on it.

queen mother queen mothers
NOUN the widow of a king and the mother of the reigning monarch

queer queerer queerest
ADJECTIVE Queer means very strange.

quell quells quelling quelled
VERB **1.** To quell a rebellion or riot means to put an end to it by using force. **2.** If you quell a feeling such as fear or grief, you stop yourself from feeling it: *trying to quell the loneliness*

quench quenches quenching quenched
VERB If you quench your thirst, you have a drink so that you are no longer thirsty.

query queries querying queried
NOUN **1.** a question
VERB **2.** If you query something, you ask about it because you think it might not be right: *No one queried my decision.*

quest quests
NOUN a long search for something

question questions questioning questioned
NOUN **1.** a sentence that asks for information **2.** If there is some question about something, there is doubt about it. **3.** a problem that needs to be discussed: *Can we get back to the question of my curfew?*
VERB **4.** If you question someone, you ask that person questions. **5.** If you question something, you express doubts about it: *He never stopped questioning his own beliefs.*
PHRASE **6.** If something is **out of the question**, it is impossible.

questionable
ADJECTIVE possibly not true or not honest

question mark question marks
NOUN the punctuation mark (?) that is used at the end of a question

questionnaire questionnaires
NOUN a list of questions that asks for information

queue queues queuing queued
NOUN **1.** a line of people or vehicles waiting for something
VERB **2.** When people queue, they stand in a line waiting for something.

quibble quibbles quibbling quibbled
VERB **1.** If you quibble, you argue about something unimportant.
NOUN **2.** a minor objection

quiche quiches
NOUN a pie served as a main dish. It contains a filling usually of eggs, cheese, and cream mixed with other ingredients.

quick quicker quickest
ADJECTIVE **1.** moving with great speed **2.** lasting only a short time: *a quick chat* **3.** happening without any delay: *a quick response* **4.** intelligent and able to understand things easily

Qq

quickly
ADVERB with great speed

quicksand quicksands
NOUN an area of deep, wet sand that you sink into if you walk on it

quiet quieter quietest
ADJECTIVE **1.** Someone or something that is quiet makes very little noise or no noise at all. **2.** Quiet also means peaceful: *a quiet evening at home* **3.** A quiet event happens with very little fuss or publicity: *a quiet wedding* NOUN **4.** Quiet is silence

Instead of **QUIET** try...

a hushed remark
a soft melody
a serene lake
a still night
a gentle voice
a low murmur
a subdued reply
an inaudible squeak

quietly ADVERB

quieten quietens quietening quietened
VERB To quieten someone means to make that person become quiet.

quill quills
NOUN **1.** a pen made from a feather **2.** A bird's quills are the large feathers on its wings and tail. **3.** A porcupine's quills are its spines.

quilt quilts
NOUN A quilt for a bed is a cover, especially a cover that is padded.

quilted
ADJECTIVE Quilted clothes or coverings are made of layers of material sewn together.

quint quints
NOUN Quint is the same as QUINTUPLET.

quince quinces
NOUN an acid-tasting fruit used for making jam and marmalade

quintessential
ADJECTIVE *a formal word* A person or thing that is quintessential seems to represent the basic nature of something in a pure, concentrated form: *a quintessential athlete*

quintet quintets
NOUN a group of five musicians who sing or play together; also a piece of music written for five instruments or singers

quintuplet quintuplets
NOUN Quintuplets are five children born at the same time to the same mother.

quip quips quipping quipped
NOUN **1.** an amusing or clever remark VERB **2.** To quip means to make an amusing or clever remark.

quirk quirks
NOUN **1.** an odd habit or characteristic: *an interesting quirk of human nature* **2.** an unexpected event or development: *a quirk of fate*
quirky ADJECTIVE

quit quits quitting quit
VERB If you quit something, you leave it or stop doing it: *My father quit his job as a salesman.*

quite
ADVERB **1.** fairly, but not very: *quite old* **2.** completely: *She lay quite still.* PHRASE **3.** You use **quite a** to emphasize that something is large or impressive: *It was quite a party.*

quiver quivers quivering quivered
VERB **1.** If something quivers, it trembles. NOUN **2.** a trembling movement: *a quiver of panic*

quiz quizzes quizzing quizzed
NOUN **1.** a short or informal test VERB **2.** If you quiz someone, you question that person closely about something.

quizzical
ADJECTIVE amused and questioning: *a quizzical smile*

quota quotas
NOUN a number or quantity of something that is officially allowed: *A quota of three boxes of cookies must be sold by each club member.*

quotation quotations
NOUN an extract from a book or speech that is quoted

quotation marks
PLURAL NOUN the pair of punctuation marks (" ") used to indicate dialogue, or a quotation. Quotation marks are also used around the titles of short stories, newspaper articles, magazine articles, and episodes of TV shows.

quote quotes quoting quoted
VERB **1.** If you quote something that someone has written or said, you repeat that person's exact words. **2.** If you quote a fact, you state it because it supports what you are saying. NOUN **3.** an extract from a book or speech **4.** an estimate of how much a job or a service will cost

Qur'an
NOUN The Qur'an is the holy book of Islam.

Rr

rabbi rabbis
NOUN a Jewish religious leader

rabbit rabbits
NOUN a small animal with long ears

rabble
NOUN a noisy, disorderly crowd

rabid
ADJECTIVE **1.** used to describe someone who is extreme in a belief: *a rabid idealist, a rabid socialist* **2.** A rabid dog or other animal has rabies.

rabies
NOUN an infectious disease that causes people and animals, especially dogs, to go mad and die

raccoon raccoons
NOUN a small, greyish animal with a long, striped tail and a dark patch around each eye

race races racing raced
NOUN **1.** a competition to see who is fastest, for example in running or driving **2.** one of the major groups that human beings can be divided into according to their physical features
VERB **3.** If you race someone, you compete with that person in a race. **4.** If you race something or if it races, it goes at its greatest rate: *Her heart raced uncontrollably.* **5.** If you race somewhere, you go there as quickly as possible: *The horses raced away out of sight.*
racing NOUN

racehorse racehorses
NOUN a horse trained to run in races

racetrack racetracks
NOUN a track, usually oval in shape, on which horses, dogs, or cars can race

racial
ADJECTIVE relating to the different races that people belong to: *racial harmony*
racially ADVERB

racism
NOUN Racism is the treatment of some people as inferior because of their race.
racist NOUN OR ADJECTIVE

rack racks racking racked
NOUN **1.** a piece of equipment for holding things or hanging things on
VERB **2.** If you are racked by something, you suffer because of it: *She was racked by guilt.*
AN INFORMAL PHRASE **3.** If you **rack your brains**, you try hard to think of or remember something.

racket rackets
NOUN **1.** If someone is making a racket, that person is making a lot of noise. **2.** an illegal way of making money: *a drugs racket*
3. Racket is another spelling of RACQUET.

racquet racquets
NOUN a wide bat with strings across it used in tennis and similar games

radar
NOUN Radar is equipment used to track ships or aircraft that are out of sight by using radio signals that are reflected back from the object and shown on a screen.

radiant
ADJECTIVE **1.** Someone who is radiant is so happy that it shows in his or her face.
2. glowing brightly
radiance NOUN

radiate radiates radiating radiated
VERB **1.** If things radiate from a place, they form a pattern like lines spreading out from the centre of a circle. **2.** If you radiate a quality or emotion, it shows clearly in your face and behaviour: *He radiated health.*

radiation
NOUN the stream of particles given out by a radioactive substance

KNOWING WORDS: WORD HISTORY

BE WORD SHARP!

Words are like living things. They grow and change.

Radar is an acronym, which means its letters are taken from the first letter (or letters) of the words that make up its meaning. In radar's case, the letters are taken from *radio detecting and ranging*. **Sonar** is a similar word that comes from *sound navigation ranging*. Another commonly used acronym is **laser** (*light amplification by stimulated emission of radiation*). New acronyms pop into language all the time. Can you think of any others?

Rr

radiator radiators
NOUN **1.** a hollow, metal device for heating a room, usually connected to a central heating system **2.** the part of a car that is filled with water to cool the engine

radical radicals
NOUN **1.** Radicals are people who think there should be great changes in society, and try to make them happen.
ADJECTIVE **2.** very significant, important, or basic: *a radical change in the law*
radically ADVERB
radicalism NOUN

radii the plural of RADIUS

radio radios radioing radioed
NOUN **1.** Radio is a system of sending sound over a distance by transmitting electrical signals. **2.** Radio is also the broadcasting of programs to the public by radio. **3.** a piece of equipment for listening to radio programs
VERB **4.** To radio someone means to send that person a message by radio: *The pilot radioed that a fire had started.*

radioactive
ADJECTIVE giving off powerful and harmful rays
radioactivity NOUN

radiotherapy
NOUN the treatment of diseases such as cancer using radiation
radiotherapist NOUN

radish radishes
NOUN a small salad vegetable with a red skin, white flesh, and a hot taste

radium
NOUN a radioactive element that is used in the treatment of cancer

radius radii
NOUN The radius of a circle is the length of a straight line drawn from its centre to its circumference.

raffia
NOUN a material made from palm leaves and used for making mats and baskets

raffle raffles
NOUN a competition in which people buy numbered tickets and win a prize if they have the ticket that is chosen

raft rafts
NOUN a structure used as a boat or floating platform, usually made from pieces of wood fastened together

rafter rafters
NOUN Rafters are the sloping pieces of wood that support a roof.

rag rags
NOUN **1.** a piece of old cloth used to clean or wipe things **2.** If someone is dressed in rags, that person is wearing old, torn clothes.

rage rages raging raged
NOUN **1.** Rage is great anger.
VERB **2.** To rage about something means to speak angrily about it. **3.** If something such as a storm or battle is raging, it is continuing with great force or violence: *The fire still raged out of control.*

ragged
ADJECTIVE Ragged clothes are old and torn.

raid raids raiding raided
VERB **1.** To raid a place means to enter it by force to attack it or steal something.
NOUN **2.** the raiding of a building or a place: *We made a raid on the refrigerator for snacks before starting the movie.*

rail rails
NOUN **1.** a fixed, horizontal bar used as a support or for hanging things on **2.** Rails are the steel bars that trains run along.
3. Rail is the railway considered as a means of transport: *I plan to go by rail.*

railing railings
NOUN A railing is a fence made from metal bars.

railway railways
NOUN a route along which trains travel on steel rails

rain rains raining rained
NOUN **1.** water falling from the clouds in small drops
VERB **2.** When it is raining, rain is falling.
rainy ADJECTIVE

rainbow rainbows
NOUN an arch of different colours that sometimes appears in the sky

after it has been raining

raincoat raincoats
NOUN a waterproof coat

rainfall
NOUN the amount of rain that falls in a place during a particular period

Instead of **RAIN** try...

a sudden cloudburst
a heavy torrent
a steady drizzle
a gentle mist
a light patter
intermittent showers
a thunderous downpour
washed away by a deluge

rainforest rainforests

NOUN a dense forest of tall trees, usually in a tropical area where there is a lot of rain

rainwater

NOUN rain that has been collected

raise raises raising raised

VERB **1.** If you raise something, you make it higher: *She went to the window and raised the blinds. There is a public campaign to raise standards of literacy among schoolchildren.* **2.** If you raise your voice, you speak more loudly. **3.** To raise money for a cause means to get people to donate money toward it. **4.** To raise children means to look after them until they are grown up. **5.** If you raise a subject, you mention it.

raisin raisins

NOUN a sweet, partially dried grape

rake rakes raking raked

NOUN **1.** a garden tool with a row of metal teeth and a long handle
VERB **2.** If you rake leaves off the grass, you move them with a rake.

rake up

VERB **3.** If you rake up something embarrassing from the past, you remind someone about it.

rally rallies rallying rallied

NOUN **1.** a large public meeting held to show support for something **2.** a competition in which vehicles are raced over public roads **3.** In tennis or squash, a rally is a continuous series of shots exchanged by the players.
VERB **4.** When people rally to something, they gather together to continue a struggle or to support something.

ram rams ramming rammed

VERB **1.** If one vehicle rams another, it crashes into it. **2.** To ram something somewhere means to push it there firmly: *He rammed his key into the lock.*
NOUN **3.** an adult, male sheep

RAM

NOUN In computing, RAM is a storage space that can be filled with data but which loses its contents when the machine is switched off. RAM stands for *random access memory.*

Ramadan

NOUN the ninth month of the Muslim year, during which Muslims eat and drink nothing during daylight

ramble rambles rambling rambled

NOUN **1.** a long walk for pleasure
VERB **2.** To ramble means to go for a ramble.
3. To ramble also means to talk in a confused way: *He then started rambling and repeating himself.*

rambler NOUN

ramification ramifications

NOUN The ramifications of a decision or plan are all its consequences and effects.

ramp ramps

NOUN a sloping surface connecting two different levels

rampage rampages rampaging rampaged

VERB **1.** To rampage means to rush about wildly causing damage.
PHRASE **2.** To go **on the rampage** means to rush about in a wild or violent way.

rampant

ADJECTIVE If something such as crime or disease is rampant, it is growing or spreading uncontrollably.

rampart ramparts

NOUN Ramparts are earth banks, often with a wall on top, built to protect a castle, fort, or city.

ramshackle

ADJECTIVE If something, such as a building, is ramshackle, it is in very poor condition.

ranch ranches

NOUN a large farm where cattle or horses are reared

rancid

ADJECTIVE Rancid food has gone bad.

rancour

NOUN *a formal word* Rancour is bitter hatred.
rancorous ADJECTIVE

random

ADJECTIVE **1.** A random choice or arrangement is not based on any definite plan.
PHRASE **2.** If you do something **at random**, you do it without any definite plan: *He chose a few books at random.*
randomly ADVERB

range ranges ranging ranged

NOUN **1.** The range of something is the maximum distance over which it can reach things or detect things: *This mortar has a range of 15 000 metres.* **2.** a number of different things of the same kind: *A wide range of colours is available.* **3.** a set of values on a scale: *The average age range is between 35 and 55.* **4.** A range of mountains is a line of them. **5.** A rifle range or firing range is a place where people practise shooting at targets.
VERB **6.** When a set of things ranges between two points, those things vary within these points on a scale: *temperatures ranging between 5 and 12 degrees Celsius*

Rr

ranger rangers
NOUN someone whose job is to look after a forest or park

rank ranks ranking ranked
NOUN **1.** Someone's rank is that person's official level in a job or profession. **2.** The ranks are the ordinary members of the armed forces, rather than the officers. **3.** The ranks of a group are its members: *We welcomed five new members to our ranks.* **4.** a row of people or things
VERB **5.** To rank someone or something means to give that person or thing a place on a graded scale: *I was asked to rank the provinces in order of population.*
ADJECTIVE **6.** complete and absolute: *rank stupidity* **7.** having a strong, unpleasant smell: *the rank smell of unwashed clothes*

ransack ransacks ransacking ransacked
VERB To ransack a place means to disturb everything and leave it in a mess, in order to search for or steal something.

ransom ransoms
NOUN money that is demanded to free someone who has been kidnapped

rant rants ranting ranted
VERB To rant means to talk loudly in an excited or angry way.

rap raps rapping rapped
VERB **1.** If you rap something, you hit it with a series of quick blows.
NOUN **2.** a quick knock or blow on something: *A rap on the door signalled his arrival.* **3.** Rap is a style of poetry spoken to music with a strong rhythmic beat.

rape rapes raping raped
VERB **1.** When a someone is raped, that person is forced to have sexual contact without his or her consent.
NOUN **2.** Rape is the act or crime of raping a person: *victims of rape* **3.** a plant with yellow flowers that is grown as a crop for oil and fodder
rapist NOUN

rapid rapids
ADJECTIVE **1.** happening or moving very quickly: *There has been rapid industrial expansion in this area. He took a few rapid steps.*
PLURAL NOUN **2.** An area of a river where the water moves extremely fast over rocks is referred to as rapids.
rapidly ADVERB
rapidity NOUN

rapier rapiers
NOUN a long, thin sword with a sharp point

rapport
NOUN *a formal word* If there is a rapport between two people, they find it easy to understand each other's feelings and attitudes.

rapt
ADJECTIVE If you are rapt, you are so interested in something that you are not aware of other things: *sitting with rapt attention in front of the movie screen*

rapture
NOUN Rapture is a feeling of extreme delight.
rapturous ADJECTIVE
rapturously ADVERB

rare rarer rarest
ADJECTIVE **1.** Something that is rare is not common or does not happen often: *He spotted the rare bird with his binoculars. Such major disruptions are rare.* **2.** Rare meat has been lightly cooked.
rarely ADVERB

rarefied
ADJECTIVE seeming to have little connection with ordinary life: *He grew up in a rarefied literary atmosphere.*

raring
ADJECTIVE If you are raring to do something, you are very eager to do it.

rarity rarities
NOUN **1.** something that is interesting or valuable because it is unusual **2.** The rarity of something is the fact that it is not common.

SPELL-CHECK THIS!

A computer's spell-check won't catch wrong **homophones** (words that are spelled differently but sound the same).

They found the diamond rapped in old newspaper.

In this sentence, **rapped** should be **wrapped**. **Wrap** means *fold around*. **Rap** means either *knock quickly* or *recite hip hop lyrics*.

NEL

Rr

rascal rascals

NOUN If you refer to someone as a rascal, you mean that that person does bad or mischievous things.

Instead of **RASH** try...

- a hasty move
- thoughtless acts
- impulsive purchases
- foolhardy behaviour
- an irrational decision

rash rashes

ADJECTIVE **1.** If you are rash, you do something hasty and foolish. NOUN **2.** an area of red spots that appears on your skin when you are ill or have an allergy **3.** A rash of events is a lot of them happening in a short time: *a rash of strikes* **rashly** ADVERB

rasher rashers

NOUN a thin slice of bacon

rasp rasps rasping rasped

VERB **1.** To rasp means to make a harsh, unpleasant sound. NOUN **2.** a coarse file with rows of raised teeth, used for smoothing wood or metal

raspberry raspberries

NOUN a small, soft, red fruit that grows on a bush

rat rats

NOUN a long-tailed animal that looks like a large mouse

rate rates rating rated

NOUN **1.** The rate of something is the speed or frequency with which it happens: *Your heart rate speeds up when you exercise.* **2.** a comparison of two quantities measured in different units: *I walk at a rate of about three kilometres per hour.* **3.** the cost or charge for something **4.** Rates are a local tax, often paid on property. VERB **5.** The way you rate someone or something is your opinion of that person or thing: *He was rated as one of Canada's top young players.* PHRASE **6.** If you say **at this rate** something will happen, you mean it will happen if things continue in the same way: *At this rate, we'll be lucky to get home before six.* **7.** You say **at any rate** when you want to add to or amend what you have just said: *He is the least appealing character, to me at any rate.*

rather

ADVERB **1.** Rather means to a certain extent: *We got along rather well. The reality is rather more complex.* PHRASE **2.** If you **would rather** do a particular thing, you would prefer to do it. **3.** If you do one thing **rather than** another, you choose to do the first thing instead of the second.

ratify ratifies ratifying ratified

VERB *a formal word* To ratify a written agreement means to approve it formally, usually by signing it. **ratification** NOUN

rating ratings

NOUN **1.** a score based on the quality or status of something **2.** Ratings are statistics showing how popular each television program is.

ratio ratios

NOUN a relationship that shows how many times one thing is bigger than another: *The adult to child ratio is 1 to 6.*

⚠ **HEADS UP**

Something to remember: a **ratio** shows the *relationship* between two separate amounts.

ration rations rationing rationed

NOUN **1.** Your ration of something is the amount you are allowed to have. PLURAL NOUN **2.** Rations are the food given each day to a soldier or member of an expedition. VERB **3.** When something is rationed, you are only allowed a limited amount of it, because there is a shortage.

rational

ADJECTIVE When people are rational, their judgments are based on reason rather than emotion. **rationally** ADVERB **rationality** NOUN

rationale

NOUN The rationale for a course of action or for a belief is the set of reasons on which it is based.

rattle rattles rattling rattled

VERB **1.** When something rattles, it makes short, regular, knocking sounds. **2.** If something rattles you, it upsets you: *He was obviously rattled by events.* NOUN **3.** the noise something makes when it rattles **4.** a baby's toy that makes a noise when it is shaken

rattlesnake rattlesnakes

NOUN a poisonous snake that has a triangular head and makes a rattling noise with its tail

Rr

raucous
ADJECTIVE A raucous voice is loud and rough.

ravage ravages ravaging ravaged *a formal word*
VERB **1.** To ravage something means to seriously harm or damage it: *a country ravaged by floods*
NOUN **2.** The ravages of something are its damaging effects: *the ravages of fire, the ravages of war*

rave raves raving raved
VERB **1.** If someone raves, that person talks in an angry, uncontrolled way: *He started raving about being treated badly.* **2.** *an informal use* If you rave about something, you talk about it very enthusiastically.
ADJECTIVE **3.** *an informal use* If something gets a rave review, it is praised enthusiastically.

raven ravens
NOUN **1.** a large, black bird with a deep, harsh call
ADJECTIVE **2.** Raven hair is black and shiny.

ravenous
ADJECTIVE very hungry

ravine ravines
NOUN a deep, narrow valley with steep sides

raving ravings
ADJECTIVE **1.** If someone is raving, that person is delirious or frenzied: *a raving lunatic*
NOUN **2.** Someone's ravings are crazy things he or she writes or says.

ravioli
NOUN Ravioli consists of small squares of pasta filled with meat, cheese, or vegetables and served with a sauce.

ravishing
ADJECTIVE Someone or something that is ravishing is very beautiful: *a ravishing landscape*

raw
ADJECTIVE **1.** Raw food has not been cooked. **2.** A raw substance is in its natural state: *raw sugar* **3.** If part of your body is raw, the skin has come off or been rubbed away. **4.** Someone who is raw is too young or too new in a job or situation to know how to behave.

raw material raw materials
NOUN Raw materials are the various substances used to make something.

ray rays
NOUN **1.** a beam of light or radiation **2.** A ray of hope is a small amount that makes an unpleasant situation seem slightly better. **3.** a large sea fish with eyes on the top of its body, and a long tail

raze razes razing razed
VERB To raze a building, town, or forest means to completely destroy it: *The town was razed to the ground during the occupation.*

razor razors
NOUN a tool that people use for shaving

razor blade razor blades
NOUN a small, sharp, flat piece of metal fitted into a razor for shaving

re-
PREFIX **1.** The prefix *re-* is used to form nouns and verbs that refer to the repetition of an action or process: *reread, remarry* **2.** The prefix *re-* is also used to form verbs that refer to going back to a previous condition: *refresh, renew*

reach reaches reaching reached
VERB **1.** When you reach a place, you arrive there. **2.** When you reach for something, you stretch out your arm to it. **3.** If something reaches a place or point, it extends as far as that place or point: *She has a cloak that reaches to the ground.* **4.** If someone or something reaches a stage or level, that person or thing gets to it: *Attendance at the fair reached record levels this year.* **5.** To reach an agreement or decision means to succeed in achieving it.
PHRASE **6.** If a place is **within reach**, it is near enough to be reached or seen: *Is the park*

KNOWING WORDS: WORD BUILDING

BE WORD SHARP!

You can create new words by adding prefixes and suffixes to a base word.

re- a prefix that means *again*

redirect direct again, in a different direction

re-examine examine again more closely

reinvent invent again, in a new way

reshape shape again, in a new way

retouch touch again, as with a paintbrush

NEL

Rr

within reach or will I have to take a bus there? **7.** If something is **out of reach**, you cannot get to it by stretching out your arm: *The top shelf is out of my reach.*

react reacts reacting reacted
VERB **1.** When you react to something, you behave in a particular way because of it: *He reacted badly to the news.* **2.** If one substance reacts with another, a chemical change takes place when they are put together.

reaction reactions
NOUN **1.** Your reaction to something is what you feel, say, or do because of it: *Reaction to the visit is mixed.* **2.** Your reaction is your ability to move quickly in response to something that happens: *Tennis requires fast reactions.* **3.** a negative physical response to something that is breathed, eaten, or touched: *an allergic reaction* **4.** In a chemical reaction, a chemical change takes place when two substances are put together.

reactionary reactionaries
ADJECTIVE **1.** Someone who is reactionary tries to prevent political or social change.
NOUN **2.** Reactionaries are reactionary people.

reactor reactors
NOUN a device that is used to produce nuclear energy

read reads reading read
VERB **1.** When you read, you look at something written and follow it or say it aloud. **2.** If you can read someone's moods or mind, you can judge what he or she is feeling or thinking. **3.** When you read a meter or gauge, you look at it and record the figure on it.

reader readers
NOUN a person who reads

readership
NOUN The readership of a newspaper or magazine consists of the people who read it regularly.

readily
ADVERB **1.** willingly and eagerly: *She readily agreed to go to the movie with me.* **2.** easily done or quickly obtainable: *Help is readily available.*

reading readings
NOUN **1.** Reading is the activity of reading books. **2.** The reading on a meter or gauge is the figure or measurement it shows.

readjust readjusts readjusting readjusted
VERB **1.** If you readjust, you adapt to a new situation. **2.** If you readjust something, you alter it to a different position.

ready
ADJECTIVE **1.** having reached the required stage, or prepared for action or use: *I'm ready for bed. In a few days' time, the plums will be ready to eat.* **2.** willing or eager to do something: *He says he's ready for college.* **3.** easily produced or obtained: *ready money*
readiness NOUN

ready-made
ADJECTIVE already made and therefore able to be used immediately

reaffirm reaffirms reaffirming reaffirmed
VERB To reaffirm something means to state it again: *They reaffirmed their support for the campaign.*

real
ADJECTIVE **1.** actually existing and not imagined or invented **2.** genuine and not imitation: *Who's to know if they're real guns?* **3.** true or actual and not mistaken: *This was the real reason for her call.*

> ⚠️ **HEADS UP**
>
> In everyday speech, people often say **real** when they mean **really**: *That's real good.* Don't do this in formal writing.

real estate
NOUN Real estate is property in the form of land and buildings rather than personal possessions.

realism
NOUN Realism is the recognition of the true nature of a situation: *I prefer realism and common sense to fantasy and foolishness.*
realist NOUN

realistic
ADJECTIVE **1.** recognizing and accepting the true nature of a situation **2.** representing things in a way that is true to life: *His novels are more realistic than his short stories.*
realistically ADVERB

reality
NOUN **1.** Reality is the real nature of things, rather than the way someone imagines it: *Fiction and reality were increasingly blurred.* **2.** If something has become reality, it actually exists or is actually happening.

realize realizes realizing realized
VERB **1.** If you realize something, you become aware of it. **2.** If your hopes or fears are realized, what you hoped for or feared actually happens: *Our worst fears were realized.* **3.** To realize a sum of money means to receive it as a result of selling goods or shares.
realization NOUN

Rr

really

ADVERB **1.** used to add emphasis to what is being said: *I'm not really surprised.* **2.** used to indicate that you are talking about the true facts about something: *What was really going on?*

realm realms

NOUN *a formal word* **1.** You can refer to any area of thought or activity as a realm: *the realm of politics* **2.** a country with a king or queen: *defence of the realm*

reap reaps reaping reaped

VERB **1.** To reap a crop such as corn means to cut and gather it. **2.** When people reap benefits or rewards, they get them as a result of hard work or careful planning.
reaper NOUN

reappear reappears reappearing reappeared

VERB When people or things reappear, you can see them again, because they have come back: *The stolen ring reappeared three years later in a pawn shop.*
reappearance NOUN

reappraisal reappraisals

NOUN *a formal word* If there is a reappraisal, people think about something again and decide whether they want to change it: *a reappraisal of the plan to cut library funding*

rear rears rearing reared

NOUN **1.** The rear of something is the part at the back.
VERB **2.** To rear children or young animals means to bring them up until they are able to look after themselves. **3.** When a horse rears, it raises the front part of its body, so that its front legs are in the air.

rear admiral rear admirals

NOUN a senior officer in the navy

rearrange rearranges rearranging rearranged

VERB To rearrange something means to organize or arrange it in a different way.

reason reasons reasoning reasoned

NOUN **1.** The reason for something is the fact or situation that explains why it happens or that causes it to happen. **2.** If you have reason to believe or feel something, there are definite reasons why you believe it or feel it: *He had every reason to be upset by the loss of his pet.* **3.** Reason is the ability to think and make judgments.
VERB **4.** If you reason that something is true, you decide it is true after considering all the facts. **5.** If you reason with someone, you persuade that person to accept sensible arguments.

reasonable

ADJECTIVE **1.** Reasonable behaviour is fair and sensible. **2.** If an explanation is reasonable, there are good reasons for thinking it is correct. **3.** A reasonable amount is a fairly large amount. **4.** A reasonable price is fair and not too high.
reasonably ADVERB

reasoning

NOUN Reasoning is the process by which you reach a conclusion after considering all the facts.

reassess reassesses reassessing reassessed

VERB If you reassess something, you consider whether it still has the same value or importance.
reassessment NOUN

reassure reassures reassuring reassured

VERB If you reassure someone, you say or do things that make that person less worried.
reassurance NOUN

rebate rebates

NOUN money paid back to someone who has paid too much for something

rebel rebels rebelling rebelled

NOUN **1.** Rebels are people who are fighting their own country's army to change the political system. **2.** Someone who is a rebel rejects society's values and behaves differently from other people.
VERB **3.** To rebel means to fight against authority and reject accepted values.

rebellion rebellions

NOUN A rebellion is organized and often violent opposition to authority.

rebellious

ADJECTIVE unwilling to obey and likely to rebel against authority

rebuff rebuffs rebuffing rebuffed

VERB **1.** If you rebuff someone, you reject what that person offers: *She rebuffed their offers of help.*
NOUN **2.** a rejection of an offer

rebuild rebuilds rebuilding rebuilt

VERB When something such as a town or building is rebuilt, it is built again after being damaged or destroyed.

rebuke rebukes rebuking rebuked

VERB To rebuke someone means to speak severely to that person about something he or she has done.

recall recalls recalling recalled

VERB **1.** To recall something means to remember it. **2.** If you are recalled to a place, you are ordered to return there. **3.** If a company recalls products, it asks people to return them because they are faulty.

Rr

recap recaps recapping recapped
VERB To recap means to repeat and summarize the main points of an explanation or discussion.

recapture recaptures recapturing recaptured
VERB **1.** When you recapture a pleasant feeling, you experience it again: *She may never recapture that past confidence.* **2.** When soldiers recapture a place, they capture it from the people who took it from them. **3.** When animals or prisoners are recaptured, they are caught after they have escaped.

recede recedes receding receded
VERB **1.** When something recedes, it moves away into the distance. **2.** If a person's hair is receding, that person is starting to go bald at the front.

receipt receipts
NOUN **1.** a piece of paper confirming that money or goods have been received **2.** In a store or theatre, the money received is often called the receipts: *Box-office receipts were down last month.* **3.** *a formal use* The receipt of something is the receiving of it: *You have to sign here and acknowledge receipt.*

receive receives receiving received
VERB **1.** When you receive something, someone gives it to you, or you get it after it has been sent to you. **2.** To receive something also means to have it happen to you: *injuries he received in a car crash* **3.** When you receive visitors or guests, you welcome them. **4.** If something is received in a particular way, that is how people react to it: *The decision has been received with great disappointment.*

receiver receivers
NOUN the part of a telephone you hold near to your ear and mouth

recent
ADJECTIVE Something recent

reception
receptions
NOUN
1. In a hotel or office, reception is the place near the entrance where appointments or inquiries are dealt with. **2.** a formal party

3. The reception someone or something gets is the way people react to that person or thing: *The astronaut's return to her hometown met with a rapturous reception.* **4.** If your radio or television gets good reception, the sound or picture is clear.

receptionist receptionists
NOUN The receptionist in a hotel or office deals with people when they arrive, answers the telephone, and arranges appointments.

receptive
ADJECTIVE Someone who is receptive to ideas or suggestions is willing to consider them.

recess recesses
NOUN **1.** a period when work, study, or a proceeding is stopped: *We will take a short recess before the next meeting. We have a brief recess after English class.* **2.** a place where part of a wall has been built further back than the rest

recession recessions
NOUN a period when a country's economy is less successful and more people become unemployed

recharge recharges recharging recharged
VERB To recharge a battery means to charge it with electricity again after it has been used.

recipe recipes
NOUN **1.** a list of ingredients and instructions for cooking something **2.** If something is a recipe for disaster or for success, it is likely to result in disaster or success.

recipient recipients
NOUN The recipient of something is the person receiving it.

reciprocal
ADJECTIVE A reciprocal agreement involves two people, groups, or countries helping each other in a similar way: *a reciprocal agreement on trade*

reciprocate reciprocates reciprocating reciprocated
VERB If you reciprocate someone's feelings or behaviour, you feel or behave in the same way toward that person.

recital recitals
NOUN a performance of music, song, or dance by one person or several performers

recite recites reciting recited
VERB If you recite a poem or something you have learned, you say it aloud.
recitation NOUN

reckless
ADJECTIVE showing a complete lack of care about danger or damage: *a reckless dive into shallow water*
recklessly ADVERB
recklessness NOUN

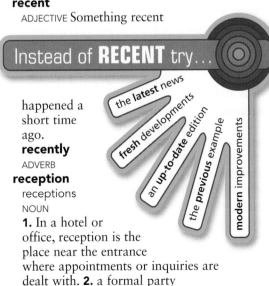

Instead of **RECENT** try...

the **latest** news

fresh developments

an **up-to-date** edition

the **previous** example

modern improvements

happened a short time ago.
recently
ADVERB

NEL

reckon reckons reckoning reckoned
VERB **1.** *an informal use* If you reckon that something is true, you think it is true: *I reckoned he was still fond of her.* **2.** To reckon an amount means to calculate it.
PHRASE **3.** If you **reckon on** something, you rely on it happening when making your plans: *He reckons on being world champion.*
PHRASE **4.** If you **reckon with** something, you expect that thing to happen: *He had not reckoned with the strength of her feelings.*

reckoning reckonings
NOUN a calculation: *There were a thousand or so, by my reckoning.*

reclaim reclaims reclaiming reclaimed
VERB **1.** When you reclaim something, you collect it after leaving it somewhere or losing it. **2.** To reclaim land means to make it suitable for use, for example by draining it.
reclamation NOUN

recline reclines reclining reclined
VERB To recline means to lie or lean back at an angle: *a photo of him reclining on his bed*

recluse recluses
NOUN Someone who is a recluse lives alone and avoids other people.
reclusive ADJECTIVE

recognize recognizes recognizing recognized
VERB **1.** If you recognize someone or something, you realize that you know who or what that person or thing is: *The receptionist recognized me at once.* **2.** To recognize something also means to accept and acknowledge it: *The school board recognized him as an outstanding teacher.*
recognition NOUN
recognizable ADJECTIVE
recognizably ADVERB

recommend recommends recommending recommended
VERB If you recommend something to someone, you praise that thing and suggest that that person try it.
recommendation NOUN

reconcile reconciles reconciling reconciled
VERB **1.** To reconcile two things that seem to oppose one another means to make them work or exist together successfully: *The designs reconciled style with comfort.* **2.** When people are reconciled, they become friendly again after a quarrel. **3.** If you reconcile yourself to an unpleasant situation, you accept it.
reconciliation NOUN

reconnaissance
NOUN Reconnaissance is the gathering of military information.

> ⚠ **HEADS UP**
>
> **Reconnaissance** is pronounced re-KON-uh-sens. It's often shortened to **recce** (REH-ki) or **recon** (RE-kon).

reconsider reconsiders reconsidering reconsidered
VERB To reconsider something means to think about it again to decide whether to change it.
reconsideration NOUN

reconstruct reconstructs reconstructing reconstructed
VERB **1.** To reconstruct something that has been damaged means to build it again.
2. To reconstruct a past event means to get a complete description of it from small pieces of information.
reconstruction NOUN

record records recording recorded
NOUN **1.** If you keep a record of something, you keep a written account or store information in a computer: *medical records* **2.** a round, flat piece of plastic on which music has been recorded **3.** an achievement that is the best of its type **4.** Your record is what is known about your achievements or past activities: *She had a distinguished teaching record.*
VERB **5.** If you record information, you write it down or put it into a computer. **6.** To record sound means to put it on tape, record, or compact disc.
ADJECTIVE **7.** higher, lower, better, or worse than ever before: *Profits are at a record high.*

recorder recorders
NOUN a small woodwind instrument

recording recordings
NOUN A recording of something is a record, CD, audiotape, DVD, or video of it.

recount recounts recounting recounted
VERB **1.** If you recount a story, you tell it.
NOUN **2.** a second count of votes in an election when the result is very close

recoup recoups recouping recouped
VERB If you recoup money that you have spent or lost, you get it back.

recourse
NOUN *a formal word* If you have recourse to something, you use it to help you: *The countries settled their differences without recourse to war.*

Rr

recover recovers recovering recovered
VERB **1.** To recover from an illness or unhappy experience means to get well again or get over it. **2.** If you recover a lost object or your ability to do something, you get it back.

recovery
NOUN **1.** the act of getting better again **2.** the act of getting something back

recreate recreates recreating recreated
VERB To recreate something means to succeed in making it happen or exist again: *a museum that faithfully recreates old buildings*

recreation recreations
NOUN Recreation is all the things that you do for enjoyment in your spare time.
recreational ADJECTIVE

recrimination recriminations
NOUN Recriminations are accusations made by people about each other.

recruit recruits recruiting recruited
VERB **1.** To recruit people means to get them to join a group or help with something.
NOUN **2.** someone who has joined the armed forces or some other organization
recruitment NOUN

rectangle rectangles
NOUN a four-sided shape with four right angles
rectangular ADJECTIVE

rectify rectifies rectifying rectified
VERB *a formal word* If you rectify something that is wrong, you put it right.

rectum rectums
NOUN the bottom end of the tube down which waste food passes out of your body
rectal ADJECTIVE

recuperate recuperates recuperating recuperated
VERB When you recuperate, you gradually recover after being ill or injured.
recuperation NOUN

recur recurs recurring recurred
VERB If something recurs, it happens or occurs again: *His hamstring injury recurred after the first game.*
recurrence NOUN
recurrent ADJECTIVE

recurring
ADJECTIVE happening or occurring many times: *a recurring dream*

recycle recycles recycling recycled
VERB To recycle used products means to process them so that they can be used again: *recycled glass*

red redder reddest; reds
NOUN OR ADJECTIVE **1.** Red is the colour of blood or of a ripe tomato.
ADJECTIVE **2.** Red hair is between orange and brown in colour.

redcurrant redcurrants
NOUN a very small, bright red fruit that grows in bunches on a bush

redeem redeems redeeming redeemed
VERB **1.** If a feature redeems an unpleasant thing or situation, it makes it seem less bad. **2.** If you redeem yourself, you do something that gives people a good opinion of you again. **3.** If you redeem something, you get it back by paying for it.

redemption
NOUN Redemption is the state of being redeemed.

red-handed
PHRASE To **catch someone red-handed** means to catch that person doing something wrong.

red-hot
ADJECTIVE Red-hot metal has been heated to such a high temperature that it has turned red.

redress redresses redressing redressed *a formal word*
VERB **1.** To redress a wrong means to put it right.
NOUN **2.** If you get redress for harm done to you, you are compensated for it.

SPELL-CHECK THIS!

A computer's spell-check won't catch wrong **homophones** (words that are spelled differently but sound the same).

If only they had red the warning signs!

In this sentence, **red** should be **read**.
Read (pronounced RED) is the past tense of **read** (pronounced REED). **Red** is a colour.

red tape

NOUN Red tape is official rules and procedures that seem unnecessary and cause delay.

reduce reduces reducing reduced

VERB **1.** To reduce something means to make it smaller in size or amount. **2.** You can use *reduce* to say that someone or something is changed to a weaker or inferior state: *She reduced them to tears. The village was reduced to rubble.*

reduction reductions

NOUN When there is a reduction in something, it is made smaller.

redundancy redundancies

NOUN **1.** Redundancy is the state of being redundant. **2.** The number of redundancies is the number of people made redundant.

redundant

ADJECTIVE **1.** When people are made redundant, they lose their jobs because there is no more work for them or no money to pay them. **2.** When something becomes redundant, it is no longer needed.

reed reeds

NOUN **1.** Reeds are hollow-stemmed plants that grow in shallow water or wet ground. **2.** a thin piece of cane or metal inside some wind instruments that vibrates when air is blown over it

reef reefs

NOUN a long line of rocks, coral, or sand close to the surface of the sea

reek reeks reeking reeked

VERB **1.** To reek of something means to smell strongly and unpleasantly of it.

NOUN **2.** If there is a reek of something, there is a strong unpleasant smell of it.

reel reels reeling reeled

NOUN **1.** a cylindrical object around which you wrap something, often part of a device that you turn as a control

VERB **2.** When someone reels, that person moves unsteadily as if he or she is going to fall. **3.** If your mind is reeling, you are confused because you have too much to think about.

reel off

VERB **4.** If you reel off information, you repeat it from memory quickly and easily.

re-elect re-elects re-electing re-elected

VERB When someone is re-elected, that person wins an election again and is able to stay in power.

refer refers referring referred

VERB **1.** If you refer to something, you mention it. **2.** If you refer to a book or other resource, you look at it to find something out. **3.** When a problem or issue is referred to someone, that person is formally asked to deal with it: *The doctor referred his patient to a specialist.*

referee referees

NOUN in some sports, such as hockey and soccer, the official who controls or judges the play

reference references

NOUN **1.** A reference to someone or something is a mention of that person or thing. **2.** Reference is the act of referring to something or someone for information or advice: *He made that decision without reference to her.* **3.** a number or name that tells you where to find information or identifies a document **4.** If someone gives you a reference when you apply for a job, that person provides information about your abilities.

referendum referendums

NOUN a vote in which all the people eligible to vote are officially asked whether they agree with a policy or proposal

refine refines refining refined

VERB To refine a raw material such as oil means to process it to remove impurities.

refined

ADJECTIVE **1.** very polite and well-mannered **2.** processed to remove impurities

SPELL-CHECK THIS!

A computer's spell-check won't catch wrong **homophones** (words that are spelled differently but sound the same).

Have you ever had a dream you were sure was reel?

In this sentence, **reel** should be **real**. **Real** means *true*. **Reel** means *wind around*.

Rr

refinement refinements

NOUN **1.** Refinements are minor improvements. **2.** Refinement is politeness and good manners.

refinery refineries

NOUN a factory where substances such as oil or sugar are refined

reflect reflects reflecting reflected

VERB **1.** If something reflects an attitude or situation, it shows what it is like: *His off-duty hobbies reflected his maritime interests.* **2.** If something reflects light or heat, the light or heat bounces off it. **3.** When something is reflected in a mirror or water, you can see its image in it. **4.** When you reflect, you think about something.
reflective ADJECTIVE
reflectively ADVERB

reflection reflections

NOUN **1.** If something is a reflection of something else, it shows what it is like: *This is a terrible reflection of the times.* **2.** an image in a mirror or water **3.** Reflection is the process by which light and heat are bounced off a surface. **4.** Reflection is also thought: *After days of reflection, she decided to leave.*

reflex reflexes

NOUN **1.** A reflex or reflex action is a sudden uncontrollable movement that you make as a result of pressure or a blow. **2.** If you have good reflexes, you respond very quickly when something unexpected happens.
ADJECTIVE **3.** A reflex angle is between 180° and 360°.

reflexive reflexives

ADJECTIVE OR NOUN In grammar, a reflexive verb or pronoun is one that refers back to the subject of the sentence: *She washed herself.*

reform reforms reforming reformed

NOUN **1.** Reforms are major changes to laws or institutions: *a program of economic reform*
VERB **2.** When laws or institutions are reformed, major changes are made to them. **3.** When people reform, they stop committing crimes or doing other unacceptable things.
reformer NOUN

refraction

NOUN Refraction is the bending of a ray of light, for example when it enters water or glass.

refrain refrains refraining refrained

VERB **1.** *a formal use* If you refrain from doing something, you do not do it: *Please refrain from running in the hall.*
NOUN **2.** The refrain of a song is a short, simple part, repeated many times.

refresh refreshes refreshing refreshed

VERB **1.** If something refreshes you when you are hot or tired, it makes you feel cooler or more energetic: *A glass of fruit juice will refresh you.*
PHRASE **2.** To **refresh someone's memory** means to remind that person of something he or she had forgotten.

refreshing

ADJECTIVE You say that something is refreshing when it is pleasantly different from what you are used to: *The countryside is a refreshing contrast to the city.*

refreshment refreshments

NOUN Refreshments are drinks and small amounts of food provided at an event.

refrigerator refrigerators

NOUN a container in which you store food to keep it cold and fresh

refuel refuels refuelling refuelled

VERB When an aircraft or vehicle is refuelled, it is filled with more fuel.

refuge refuges

NOUN **1.** a place where you go for safety
PHRASE **2.** If you **take refuge**, you go somewhere for safety or behave in a way that will protect you: *They took refuge in a bomb shelter. My sister took refuge in silence.*

refugee refugees

NOUN Refugees are people who have been forced to leave their country and live elsewhere.

refund refunds refunding refunded

NOUN **1.** money returned to you because you have paid too much for something or because you have returned goods
VERB **2.** To refund someone's money means to return it to that person after he or she has paid for something with it.

refurbish refurbishes refurbishing refurbished

VERB *a formal word* To refurbish a building means to redecorate it and repair damage.
refurbishment NOUN

refusal refusals

NOUN A refusal is when someone says firmly that he or she will not do, allow, or accept something.

refuse refuses refusing refused

VERB **1.** If you refuse to do something, you say or decide firmly that you will not do it. **2.** If someone refuses something, that person does not allow it or does not accept it: *The United States has refused her a visa. He offered me a second helping of cake, which I refused.*

⚠ HEADS UP **Refuse** meaning *decide not to do* is pronounced ri-FYUZE.

Rr

refuse
NOUN Refuse is garbage or waste.

refute refutes refuting refuted
VERB *a formal word* To refute a theory or argument means to prove that it is wrong.

regain regains regaining regained
VERB To regain something means to get it back.

regal
ADJECTIVE very grand and suitable for a king or queen: *regal splendour*
regally ADVERB

regard regards regarding regarded
VERB **1.** To regard someone or something in a particular way means to think of that person in that way or have that opinion of him or her: *We all regard him as a friend. Many disapprove of the tax, regarding it as unfair.* **2.** *a literary or poetic use* To regard someone in a particular way also means to look at that person in that way: *She regarded him curiously for a moment.*
NOUN **3.** If you have a high regard for someone, you have a very good opinion of that person.
PHRASE **4. Regarding, as regards, with regard to,** and **in regard to** are all used to indicate what you are talking or writing about: *There was always some question regarding education. With regard to your grades, they would be higher if you put more effort into studying.* **5.** *Regards* is used in various expressions to express friendly feelings: *Give my regards to your husband.*

regardless
PREPOSITION OR ADVERB done or happening in spite of something else: *He led from the front, regardless of the danger.*

regatta regattas
NOUN a series of races for boats held as a special event

regency regencies
NOUN a period when a country is ruled by a regent

regenerate regenerates regenerating regenerated
VERB *a formal word* To regenerate something means to develop and improve it after it has been declining: *a scheme to regenerate the docks area of the city*
regeneration NOUN

regent regents
NOUN someone who rules in place of a king or queen who is ill or too young to rule

reggae
NOUN a type of music, originally from Jamaica, with a strong beat and lyrics

regime regimes
NOUN a system of government, and the people who are ruling a country: *a communist regime*

regiment regiments
NOUN a large group of soldiers commanded by a colonel
regimental ADJECTIVE

regimented
ADJECTIVE very strictly controlled: *the regimented life of the orphanage*
regimentation NOUN

region regions
NOUN **1.** a large area of land **2.** You can refer to any area or part as a region: *the pelvic region*
PHRASE **3. In the region of** means approximately: *The scheme will cost in the region of six million dollars.*
regional ADJECTIVE
regionally ADVERB

register registers registering registered
NOUN **1.** an official list or record of things: *the electoral register* **2.** *a technical use* a style of speaking or writing used in particular circumstances or social occasions
VERB **3.** When something is registered, it is recorded on an official list: *The car was registered in my mother's name.* **4.** If an instrument registers a measurement, it shows it. **5.** If your face registers a feeling, it expresses it.
registration NOUN

registrar registrars
NOUN **1.** a person who keeps official records of births, marriages, and deaths **2.** At a college or university, the registrar is a senior administrative official.

registry registries
NOUN a place where official records are kept

regret regrets regretting regretted
VERB **1.** If you regret something, you are sorry that it happened. **2.** You can say that you regret something as a way of apologizing: *We regret any inconvenience to passengers.*
NOUN **3.** If you have regrets, you are sad or sorry about something.
regretful ADJECTIVE
regretfully ADVERB

⚠ HEADS UP

Regrettable means *unfortunate*: *a regrettable situation.* **Regretful** means *sorry*: *I was regretful after the accident.*

Rr

regrettable
ADJECTIVE unfortunate and undesirable: *a regrettable accident*
regrettably ADVERB

regular regulars
ADJECTIVE **1.** even and equally spaced: *soft music with a regular beat* **2.** A regular shape has equal angles and equal sides: *a regular polygon* **3.** Regular events or activities happen often and according to a pattern, for example each day or each week: *The trains to Montréal are fairly regular.* **4.** If you are a regular customer or visitor somewhere, you go there often. **5.** usual or normal: *I had my regular breakfast of oatmeal and orange juice.* **6.** having a well-balanced appearance: *a regular geometrical shape*
NOUN **7.** People who go to a place often are known as its regulars.
regularly ADVERB
regularity NOUN

regulate regulates regulating regulated
VERB To regulate something means to control the way it operates: *Sweating helps to regulate the body's temperature.*
regulator NOUN

regulation regulations
NOUN **1.** Regulations are official rules.
2. Regulation is the control of something: *regulation of provincial parks*

regurgitate regurgitates regurgitating regurgitated
VERB To regurgitate food means to bring it back from the stomach before it is digested.

rehabilitate rehabilitates rehabilitating rehabilitated
VERB To rehabilitate someone who has been ill or in prison means to help that person lead a normal life.
rehabilitation NOUN

rehearsal rehearsals
NOUN a practice of a performance in preparation for the actual event

rehearse rehearses rehearsing rehearsed
VERB To rehearse a performance means to practise it in preparation for the actual event.

reign reigns reigning reigned
VERB **1.** When a king or queen reigns, he or she rules a country. **2.** You can say that something reigns when it is a noticeable feature of a situation or period of time: *Panic reigned after his assassination.*
NOUN **3.** The reign of a king or queen is the period during which he or she reigns.

rein reins
NOUN **1.** Reins are the thin leather straps that you hold when you are riding a horse.

PHRASE **2.** To keep a tight rein on someone or something means to control that person firmly.

reincarnation
NOUN People who believe in reincarnation believe that when you die, you are born again as another creature.

reindeer
NOUN Reindeer are deer with large antlers. They live in northern regions.

reinforce reinforces reinforcing reinforced
VERB **1.** To reinforce something means to strengthen it: *a reinforced steel barrier*
2. If something reinforces an idea or claim, it provides evidence to support it.

reinforcement reinforcements
NOUN **1.** Reinforcements are additional soldiers sent to join an army in battle.
2. Reinforcement is the reinforcing of something.

reinstate reinstates reinstating reinstated
VERB **1.** To reinstate someone means to give that person back a position that he or she has lost. **2.** To reinstate something means to bring it back: *Parliament voted against reinstating capital punishment.*
reinstatement NOUN

reiterate reiterates reiterating reiterated
VERB *a formal word* If you reiterate something, you say it again.
reiteration NOUN

reject rejects rejecting rejected
VERB **1.** If you reject someone or something, you dismiss or ignore that person or thing because that person or thing is inadequate, unwelcome, or undesired. **2.** If a body rejects a transplanted organ or tissue, that organ or tissue does not survive.
NOUN **3.** a person or thing put aside because that person or thing is inadequate, unwelcome, or undesired
rejection NOUN

rejoice rejoices rejoicing rejoiced
VERB To rejoice means to be very pleased about something: *The whole country rejoiced after his downfall.*

rejoin rejoins rejoining rejoined
VERB If you rejoin someone, you go back to that person soon after leaving him or her: *She rejoined her friends in the cafeteria.*

rejuvenate rejuvenates rejuvenating rejuvenated
VERB To rejuvenate someone means to make that person feel young again.
rejuvenation NOUN

⚠️ **HEADS UP** Don't confuse **reign** and **rein**. **Reign** means *rule* and **rein** means *leather straps*.

Rr

relapse relapses

NOUN If a sick person has a relapse, his or her health suddenly gets worse after improving.

relate relates relating related

VERB **1.** If something relates to something else, it is connected or concerned with it: *The statistics relate only to northern Ontario.* **2.** If you can relate to someone, you can understand that person's thoughts and feelings. **3.** To relate a story means to tell it.

Instead of **RELATE** try...

recount a story

describe an event

chronicle a history

impart knowledge

relay important news

relation relations

NOUN **1.** If there is a relation between two things, they are similar or connected in some way: *This theory bears no relation to reality.* **2.** Your relations are the members of your family. **3.** Relations between people are their feelings and behaviour toward each other: *Relations between the friends had not improved.*

relationship relationships

NOUN **1.** The relationship between two people or groups is the way they feel and behave toward each other. **2.** a close friendship, especially one involving romantic feelings **3.** The relationship between two things is the way in which they are connected: *the relationship between studying and high grades*

relative relatives

ADJECTIVE **1.** compared to other things or people of the same kind: *The fighting resumed after a period of relative calm. He is a relative novice.* **2.** You use *relative* when comparing the size or quality of two things: *the relative benefits of eating more fruit and vegetables and taking vitamins* NOUN **3.** Your relatives are the members of your family.

relative pronoun relative pronouns

NOUN a pronoun that links two parts of a sentence

relax relaxes relaxing relaxed

VERB **1.** If you relax, you become calm and your muscles lose their tension. **2.** If you relax your hold, you hold something less tightly. **3.** To relax something also means to make it less strict or controlled: *The rules governing student conduct were relaxed.*
relaxation NOUN

relaxed

ADJECTIVE **1.** calm and not worried or tense **2.** If a place or situation is relaxed, it is calm and peaceful.

relay relays relaying relayed

NOUN **1.** A relay race or relay is a race between teams, with each team member running one part of the race. VERB **2.** To relay a television or radio signal means to send it on. **3.** If you relay information, you tell it to someone else.

release releases releasing released

VERB **1.** To release someone or something means to set that person free or remove restraints from him or her. **2.** To release something also means to issue it or make it available: *He is releasing a CD of love songs.* NOUN **3.** When the release of someone or something takes place, that person or thing is set free. **4.** A press release or publicity release is an official written statement given to reporters. **5.** A new release is a new recording, movie, or other product that has just become available.

relegate relegates relegating relegated

VERB To relegate something or someone means to give that person or thing a less important position or status.
relegation NOUN

relent relents relenting relented

VERB If someone relents, that person agrees to something he or she had previously not allowed.

relentless

ADJECTIVE never stopping and never becoming less intense: *Her questions were relentless.*
relentlessly ADVERB

relevant

ADJECTIVE If something is relevant, it is connected with and is appropriate to what is being discussed: *We have passed all relevant information on to the police.*
relevance NOUN

reliable

ADJECTIVE **1.** Reliable people and things can be trusted to do what you want. **2.** If information is reliable, you can assume that it is correct.
reliably ADVERB
reliability NOUN

reliant

ADJECTIVE If you are reliant on someone or something, you depend on that person or thing: *They are not wholly reliant on charity.*
reliance NOUN

relic relics

NOUN **1.** Relics are objects or customs that

have survived from an earlier time. **2.** an object regarded as holy because it is thought to be connected with a saint

relief
NOUN **1.** If you feel relief, you are glad and thankful because a bad situation is over or has been avoided. **2.** Relief is also money, food, or clothing provided for poor or hungry people.

relief map relief maps
NOUN a map showing the shape of mountains and hills by shading

relieve relieves relieving relieved
VERB **1.** If something relieves an unpleasant feeling, it makes it less unpleasant: *This pill will relieve much of the pain.* **2.** *a formal use* If you relieve someone, you do that person's job or duty for a period of time. **3.** If someone is relieved of his or her duties, that person is dismissed from his or her job. **4.** If you relieve yourself, you urinate.

religion religions
NOUN **1.** Religion is the belief in a god or gods and all the activities connected with such beliefs. **2.** a system of religious belief

religious
ADJECTIVE **1.** connected with religion: *religious worship* **2.** Someone who is religious has a strong belief in a god or gods.

religiously
ADVERB If you do something religiously, you do it regularly as a duty: *He stuck religiously to the rules.*

relinquish relinquishes relinquishing relinquished
VERB *a formal word* If you relinquish something, you give it up.

relish relishes relishing relished
VERB **1.** If you relish something, you enjoy it: *He relished the idea of making some money.* NOUN **2.** Relish is enjoyment: *She told me with relish of the wonderful times she had.* **3.** Relish is also a condiment such as chopped pickled vegetables or fruit.

relive relives reliving relived
VERB If you relive a past experience, you remember it and imagine it happening again.

relocate relocates relocating relocated
VERB If people or businesses are relocated, they are moved to a different place.
relocation NOUN

reluctant
ADJECTIVE If you are reluctant to do something, you are unwilling to do it.
reluctance NOUN

reluctantly
ADVERB If you do something reluctantly, you do it although you do not want to.

rely relies relying relied
VERB **1.** If you rely on someone, you need that person and depend on him or her: *She relies on her father for emotional support.* **2.** If you can rely on someone to do something, you can trust that person to do it: *They can always be relied on to turn up.*

remain remains remaining remained
VERB **1.** If you remain in a particular place, you stay there. **2.** If you remain in a particular state, you stay the same and do not change: *The two men remained silent.* **3.** Something that remains still exists or is left over: *Huge amounts of garbage remain to be collected.*
PLURAL NOUN **4.** The remains of something are the parts that are left after most of it has been destroyed: *the remains of an ancient mosque* **5.** You can refer to a dead body as remains: *More human remains have been unearthed today.*

remainder
NOUN The remainder of something is the part that is left: *He gulped down the remainder of his milk.*

remand remands remanding remanded
VERB **1.** If a judge remands someone who is accused of a crime, the trial is postponed and the person is ordered to come back at a later date.
PHRASE **2.** If someone is **on remand**, that person is in prison waiting for his or her trial to begin.

remark remarks remarking remarked

Instead of **REMARK** try...

VERB **1.** If you remark on something, you mention it or comment on it: *She had remarked on the boy's improvement.*
NOUN **2.** something you say, often in a casual way

wisely **observe**
quickly **mention**
confidently **declare**
reflect **thoughtfully**
comment as an aside

remarkable
ADJECTIVE impressive and unexpected: *It was a remarkable achievement.*
remarkably ADVERB

remarry remarries remarrying remarried
VERB If someone remarries, that person gets married again.

remedial

ADJECTIVE **1.** Remedial activities are to help someone improve his or her health after being ill. **2.** Remedial exercises are designed to improve someone's ability in something: *the remedial reading class*

remedy remedies remedying remedied

NOUN **1.** a way of dealing with a problem: *a remedy for colic*

VERB **2.** If you remedy something that is wrong, you correct it: *We have to remedy the situation immediately.*

remember remembers remembering remembered

VERB **1.** If you can remember someone or something from the past, you can bring that person into your mind or think about him or her. **2.** If you remember to do something, you do it when you intended to: *I remembered to book reservations.*

remembrance

NOUN If you do something in remembrance of a dead person, you are showing that he or she is remembered with respect and affection.

remind reminds reminding reminded

VERB **1.** If someone reminds you of a fact, that person says something to make you think about it: *Remind me to buy bread, will you?* **2.** If someone reminds you of another person, that person looks similar and makes you think of him or her.

reminder reminders

NOUN **1.** If one thing is a reminder of another, the first thing makes you think of the second: *a reminder of better times* **2.** a note sent to tell someone not to forget to do something

reminiscent

ADJECTIVE Something that is reminiscent of something else reminds you of it.

remission

NOUN When an illness or disease is in remission, the seriousness or intensity of that illness or disease has decreased.

remittance remittances

NOUN *a formal word* payment for something sent through the mail

remnant remnants

NOUN a small part of something left after the rest has been used or destroyed

remorse

NOUN *a formal word* Remorse is a strong feeling of guilt.

remorseful ADJECTIVE

remote remoter remotest

ADJECTIVE **1.** Remote areas are far away from places where most people live. **2.** far away in time: *the remote past* **3.** If you say a person is remote, you mean that person does not want to be friendly: *She is severe, solemn, and remote.* **4.** If there is only a remote possibility of something happening, it is unlikely to happen.

remoteness NOUN

remote control

NOUN Remote control is a system of controlling a machine or vehicle from a distance using radio or electronic signals; also the device used for operating a remote control system.

remotely

ADVERB used to emphasize a negative statement: *He isn't remotely keen.*

removal

NOUN The removal of something is the act of taking it away.

remove removes removing removed

VERB **1.** If you remove something from a place, you take it off or away. **2.** If you are removed from a position of authority, you are not allowed to continue your job. **3.** If you remove an undesirable feeling or attitude, you get rid of it: *Most of her fears had been removed.*

removable ADJECTIVE

Renaissance

NOUN The Renaissance was a period from the fourteenth to sixteenth centuries in Europe when there was a great revival in the arts and learning.

renal

ADJECTIVE *a technical word* concerning the kidneys: *renal failure*

rename renames renaming renamed

VERB If you rename something, you give it a new name.

render renders rendering rendered

VERB You can use *render* to say that something is changed into a different state: *The bomb was quickly rendered harmless.*

rendezvous

NOUN **1.** a meeting: *The colleagues arranged a six o'clock rendezvous.* **2.** a place where you have arranged to meet someone: *The new mall became a popular rendezvous.*

rendition renditions

NOUN *a formal word* a performance of a dramatic role, poem, or piece of music

renew renews renewing renewed

VERB **1.** To renew an activity or relationship means to begin it again. **2.** To renew a licence or contract means to extend the period of time for which it is valid.

renewal NOUN

Rr

renewable renewables
ADJECTIVE **1.** able to be renewed **2.** a form of energy such as wind power or solar power that is not depleted when it is used

renounce renounces renouncing renounced
VERB *a formal word* If you renounce something, you reject it or give it up.
renunciation NOUN

renovate renovates renovating renovated
VERB If you renovate an old building or machine, you repair it and restore it to good condition.
renovation NOUN

renowned
ADJECTIVE well-known for something good: *He is not renowned for his patience.*
renown NOUN

rent rents renting rented
VERB **1.** If you rent something, you pay the owner a regular sum of money in return for being able to use it.
NOUN **2.** Rent is the amount of money you pay regularly to rent land or accommodation.

rental
ADJECTIVE **1.** concerned with the renting out of goods and services: *the region's largest movie-rental company*
NOUN **2.** the amount of money you pay when you rent something

reorganize reorganizes reorganizing reorganized
VERB To reorganize something means to organize it in a new way in order to make it more efficient or acceptable.
reorganization NOUN

rep reps
NOUN *an informal word* Rep is an abbreviation for *representative*.

repair repairs repairing repaired
NOUN **1.** something you do to fix something that is damaged or broken
VERB **2.** If you repair something, you fix it.

repay repays repaying repaid
VERB **1.** To repay money means to give it back to the person who lent it. **2.** If you repay a favour, you do something to help the person who helped you.
repayment NOUN

repeal repeals repealing repealed
VERB If the government repeals a law, it cancels it so that it is no longer valid.

repeat repeats repeating repeated
VERB **1.** If you repeat something, you say, write, or do it again. **2.** If you repeat what someone has said, you tell someone else about it: *Don't repeat that to anyone.*

NOUN **3.** something that is done or happens again: *a repeat of last year's success*
repeated ADJECTIVE
repeatedly ADVERB

repel repels repelling repelled
VERB **1.** If something repels you, you find it horrible and disgusting. **2.** When soldiers repel an attacking force, they successfully defend themselves against it. **3.** When a magnetic pole repels an opposite pole, it forces the opposite pole away.

repellent repellents
ADJECTIVE **1.** able to repel something: *a water-repellent coat* **2.** *a formal use* horrible and disgusting: *I found him repellent.*
NOUN **3.** Repellents are things, especially a chemical, that can keep other things away: *insect repellent*

repent repents repenting repented
VERB *a formal word* If you repent, you are sorry for something bad you have done.
repentance NOUN
repentant ADJECTIVE

repercussion repercussions
NOUN The repercussions of an event are the effects it has at a later time.

repertoire repertoires
NOUN A performer's repertoire is all the pieces of music or dramatic parts he or she has learned and can perform.

repertory repertories
NOUN Repertory is the practice of performing a number of plays in a theatre for a short time, using the same actors in each play.

repetition repetitions
NOUN If there is a repetition of something, it happens again: *We don't want a repetition of last week's fiasco.*

⚠ HEADS UP

Repetition makes writing boring. To avoid overusing a word, find synonyms, like those for **reply** on the next page.

repetitive
ADJECTIVE A repetitive activity involves a lot of repetition and is boring: *dull and repetitive work*

replace replaces replacing replaced
VERB **1.** When one thing replaces another, the first thing takes the place of the second. **2.** If you replace something that is damaged or lost, you get a new one. **3.** If you replace something, you put it back where it was before: *She replaced the book on the shelf.*

replacement replacements

NOUN **1.** The replacement for someone or something is the person or thing that takes the place of the other person or thing. **2.** The replacement of a person or thing happens when that person or thing is replaced by another person or thing.

replay replays replaying replayed

VERB **1.** If a game is replayed, the teams play it again. **2.** If you replay a recording or movie, you play it again: *Replay the first few seconds of the song, please.*

NOUN **3.** the playing again of a section of a recording or a transmission, for example from a news item or a game

replenish replenishes replenishing replenished

VERB If you replenish something, you make it full or complete again.

replica replicas

NOUN an accurate copy of something: *a replica of the historic fort*

replicate VERB

reply replies replying replied

VERB **1.** If you reply to something, you say or write an answer.

Instead of **REPLY** try...

NOUN
2. what you say or write when you answer someone

retort jokingly
happily answer
counter angrily
respond to an e-mail
acknowledge by nodding

report reports reporting reported

VERB **1.** If you report that something has happened, you tell someone about it or give an official account of it: *He reported the theft to the police.* **2.** To report someone to an authority means to make an official complaint about that person. **3.** If you report to a person or place, you go there and say you have arrived.

NOUN **4.** an account of an event or situation

reported speech another name for INDIRECT SPEECH

reporter reporters

NOUN someone who writes news articles or broadcasts news reports

repossess repossesses repossessing repossessed

VERB If a store or company repossesses goods that have not been paid for, that store or company takes them back.

represent represents representing represented

VERB **1.** If you represent someone, you act on

that person's behalf: *lawyers representing relatives of the victims* **2.** If a sign or symbol represents something, it stands for it. **3.** To represent something in a particular way means to describe it in that way: *The press tends to represent him as a hero.*

representation representations

NOUN **1.** Representation is the state of being represented by someone: *Was there any student representation?* **2.** You can describe a picture or statue of someone as a representation of that person.

representative representatives

NOUN **1.** a person chosen to act on behalf of another person or a group

ADJECTIVE **2.** A representative selection is typical of the group it belongs to: *The photos chosen are not representative of his work.*

repress represses repressing repressed

VERB **1.** If you repress a feeling, you succeed in not showing or feeling it: *I couldn't repress my anger any longer.* **2.** To repress people means to restrict their freedom and control them by force.

repression NOUN

repressive

ADJECTIVE Repressive governments use force and unjust laws to restrict and control people.

reprieve reprieves reprieving reprieved

VERB **1.** If someone who has been sentenced to death is reprieved, that person's sentence is changed and he or she is not executed.

NOUN **2.** a delay before something unpleasant happens: *The zoo won a reprieve from closure.*

reprimand reprimands reprimanding reprimanded

VERB **1.** If you reprimand someone, you officially tell that person that he or she should not have done something.

NOUN **2.** something said or written by a person in authority when that person in authority is reprimanding someone

reprisal reprisals

NOUN Reprisals are violent actions taken by one group of people against another group that has harmed them.

reproach reproaches reproaching reproached
a formal word

NOUN **1.** If you express reproach, you show that you feel sad and angry about what someone has done: *a long letter of reproach*

VERB **2.** If you reproach someone, you tell that person, rather sadly, that he or she has done something wrong.

reproachful ADJECTIVE

reproduce reproduces reproducing reproduced
VERB **1.** To reproduce something means to make a copy of it. **2.** When living things reproduce, they produce more of their own kind: *Bacteria reproduce by splitting into two.*

reproduction reproductions
NOUN **1.** a modern copy of a painting or piece of furniture **2.** Reproduction is the process by which a living thing produces more of its kind: *the study of animal reproduction*

reproductive
ADJECTIVE relating to the reproduction of living things: *the female reproductive system*

reptile reptiles
NOUN a cold-blooded animal, such as a snake or a lizard, which has scaly skin and lays eggs
reptilian ADJECTIVE

republic republics
NOUN a country that has a president rather than a king or queen or prime minister
republican NOUN OR ADJECTIVE
republicanism NOUN

repulse repulses repulsing repulsed
VERB **1.** If you repulse someone who is being friendly, you put that person off by behaving coldly toward him or her: *He repulses friendly advances.* **2.** To repulse an attacking force means to fight it and cause it to retreat. **3.** If something repulses you, you find it horrible and disgusting and you want to avoid it.

repulsion
NOUN **1.** Repulsion is a strong feeling of disgust. **2.** Repulsion is a force separating two objects, such as the force between two like electrical charges.

repulsive
ADJECTIVE horrible and disgusting

reputable
ADJECTIVE known to be good and reliable: *a well-established and reputable firm*

reputation reputations
NOUN The reputation of something or someone is the opinion that people have of that person or thing: *The college had a good reputation.*

reputed
ADJECTIVE If something is reputed to be true, some people say that it is true: *the reputed author of that poem*
reputedly ADVERB

request requests requesting requested
VERB **1.** If you request something, you ask for it politely or formally.
NOUN **2.** If you make a request for something, you request it.

Requiem Requiems
NOUN **1.** A Requiem or requiem mass is a mass celebrated for someone who has recently died, especially in the Catholic Church. **2.** a piece of music for singers and an orchestra, originally written for a requiem mass

require requires requiring required
VERB **1.** If you require something, you need it. **2.** If you are required to do something, you have to do it because someone says you must: *The rules require employers to provide safety training.*

requirement requirements
NOUN something that you must have or must do: *A college diploma is the minimum requirement for this position.*

requisite requisites *a formal word*
ADJECTIVE **1.** necessary for a particular purpose: *She filled in the requisite paperwork.*
NOUN **2.** something that is necessary for a particular purpose

rescue rescues rescuing rescued
VERB **1.** If you rescue someone, you save that person from a dangerous or unpleasant situation.
NOUN **2.** Rescue is help that saves someone from a dangerous or unpleasant situation.
rescuer NOUN

research researches researching researched
NOUN **1.** Research is work that involves studying something and trying to find out facts about it.
VERB **2.** If you research something, you try to discover facts about it.
researcher NOUN

resemblance
NOUN If there is a resemblance between two things, they are similar to each other: *There was a remarkable resemblance between the cousins.*

resemble resembles resembling resembled
VERB To resemble something means to be similar to it.

resent resents resenting resented
VERB If you resent something, you feel bitter and angry about it.

resentful
ADJECTIVE bitter and angry: *He felt very resentful about losing his job.*
resentfully ADVERB

resentment resentments
NOUN a feeling of anger or bitterness

reservation reservations

NOUN **1.** If you have reservations about something, you are not sure that it is right. **2.** If you make a reservation, you book a place in advance. **3.** an area of land set aside for Native Americans in the US: *a Sioux reservation*

reserve reserves reserving reserved

VERB **1.** If something is reserved for a particular person or purpose, it is kept specially for that person or thing.
NOUN **2.** a supply of something for future use **3.** a tract of land set aside by the Federal Government for the exclusive use of a First Nations band **4.** In sports, a reserve is someone who is available to play in case a member of the team is unable to play. **5.** A nature reserve is an area of land where animals, birds, or plants are officially protected. **6.** If someone shows reserve, that person keeps his or her feelings hidden.
reserved ADJECTIVE

reservoir reservoirs

NOUN a lake used for storing water before it is supplied to people

reshuffle reshuffles

NOUN a reorganization of people or things

reside resides residing resided

VERB *a formal word* If a quality resides in something, the quality is in that thing.

residence residence

NOUN *a formal word* a house

resident residents

NOUN **1.** A resident of a house or area is someone who lives there.
ADJECTIVE **2.** If someone is resident in a house or area, that person lives there.

residential

ADJECTIVE **1.** A residential area contains mainly houses rather than offices or factories. **2.** providing accommodation: *residential care for the elderly*

residue residues

NOUN a small amount of something that remains after most of it has gone: *an increase in toxic residues found in drinking water*
residual ADJECTIVE

resign resigns resigning resigned

VERB **1.** If you resign from a job, you formally announce that you are leaving it. **2.** If you resign yourself to an unpleasant situation, you realize that you have to accept it.
resigned ADJECTIVE

resignation resignations

NOUN **1.** Someone's resignation is a formal statement of his or her intention to leave a job. **2.** Resignation is the reluctant acceptance of an unpleasant situation or fact.

resilient

ADJECTIVE able to recover quickly from unpleasant or damaging events
resilience NOUN

resin resins

NOUN **1.** Resin is a sticky substance produced by some trees. **2.** Resin is also a substance produced chemically and used to make plastics.

resist resists resisting resisted

VERB **1.** If you resist something, you refuse to accept it and try to prevent it: *The banning of books will be fiercely resisted by the school board.* **2.** If you resist someone, you fight back against that person.

resistance resistances

NOUN **1.** Resistance to something such as change is a refusal to accept it. **2.** Resistance to an attack consists of fighting back: *The demonstrators offered no resistance.* **3.** Your body's resistance to germs or disease is its power to not be harmed by them. **4.** Resistance is also the power of a substance to resist the flow of an electrical current through it.

resistant

ADJECTIVE **1.** opposed to something and wanting to prevent it: *Some people are very resistant to change.* **2.** If something is resistant to a particular thing, it is not harmed or affected by it: *Certain insects are resistant to this spray.*

resolute

ADJECTIVE *a formal word* Someone who is resolute is determined not to change his or her mind.
resolutely ADVERB

resolution resolutions

NOUN **1.** Resolution is determination. **2.** If you make a resolution, you promise yourself to do something. **3.** a formal decision taken at a meeting **4.** *a formal use* The resolution of a problem is the solving of it.

resolve resolves resolving resolved

VERB **1.** If you resolve to do something, you firmly decide to do it. **2.** If you resolve a problem, you find a solution to it.
NOUN **3.** Resolve is absolute determination.

resonance resonances

NOUN **1.** Resonance is sound produced by an object vibrating as a result of another sound nearby. **2.** Resonance is also a deep, clear, and echoing quality of sound.

resonate resonates resonating resonated
VERB If something resonates, it vibrates and produces a deep, strong sound.

resort resorts resorting resorted
VERB **1.** If you resort to a course of action, you do it because you have no alternative.
NOUN **2.** a place where people spend their holidays
PHRASE **3.** If you do something **as a last resort**, you do it because you can find no other way of solving a problem.

resounding
ADJECTIVE **1.** loud and echoing: *a resounding round of applause* **2.** A resounding success is a great success.

resource resources
NOUN The resources of a country, organization, or person are the materials, money, or skills that country, organization, or person has.

resourceful
ADJECTIVE A resourceful person is good at finding ways of dealing with problems.
resourcefulness NOUN

respect respects respecting respected
VERB **1.** If you respect someone, you have a good opinion of that person's character or ideas. **2.** If you respect someone's rights or wishes, you do not do things that he or she would not like, or would consider wrong: *It is about time they started respecting the law.*
NOUN **3.** If you have respect for someone, you have a good opinion of that person.
PHRASE **4.** You can say **in this respect** to refer to a particular feature: *At least in this respect we are equals.*

respectable
ADJECTIVE **1.** considered to be acceptable and morally correct: *respectable behaviour*
2. adequate or reasonable: *respectable grades*
respectability NOUN
respectably ADVERB

respectful
ADJECTIVE showing respect for someone: *We were taught to be respectful to our elders.*
respectfully ADVERB

respective
ADJECTIVE belonging or relating individually to the people or things just mentioned: *They went into their respective rooms to pack.*

respectively
ADVERB in the same order as the items just mentioned: *The Canadian and Australian teams finished first and second, respectively.*

respiration
NOUN *a technical word* Your respiration is your breathing.

respiratory
ADJECTIVE *a technical word* relating to breathing: *respiratory diseases*

respire respires respiring respired
VERB To respire is to breathe.

respite
NOUN *a formal word* a short rest from something unpleasant

respond responds responding responded
VERB When you respond to something, you react to it by doing or saying something.

respondent respondents
NOUN **1.** a person who answers a questionnaire or a request for information
2. In a court case, the respondent is the defendant.

response responses
NOUN Your response to an event is your reaction or reply to it: *There has been no response to his remarks yet.*

responsibility responsibilities
NOUN **1.** If you have responsibility for something, it is your duty to deal with it or look after it: *The garden was to have been his responsibility.* **2.** If you accept responsibility for something that has happened, you agree that you caused it or were to blame: *We must all accept responsibility for our own mistakes.*

responsible
ADJECTIVE **1.** If you are responsible for something, it is your job to deal with it. **2.** If you are responsible for something bad that has happened, you are to blame for it.
3. A responsible person behaves properly and sensibly without needing to be supervised.
4. A responsible job involves making careful judgments about important matters.
responsibly ADVERB

responsive
ADJECTIVE **1.** quick to show interest and pleasure **2.** taking notice of events and reacting in an appropriate way: *The course is responsive to students' needs.*

rest rests resting rested
NOUN **1.** The rest of something is all the remaining parts of it. **2.** If you have a rest, you sit or lie quietly and relax.
VERB **3.** If you rest, you relax and do not do anything active for a while.

restaurant restaurants
NOUN a place where you can buy and eat a meal

restaurateur restaurateurs
NOUN someone who owns or manages a restaurant

 **HEADS UP** The word **respite** is pronounced RESS-pit.

restful
ADJECTIVE Something that is restful helps you feel calm and relaxed.

restless
ADJECTIVE finding it hard to remain still or relaxed because of boredom or

Instead of **RESTLESS** try...

impatience
restlessness
NOUN
restlessly ADVERB

jumpy nerves
a fitful sleep
agitated moaning
fretful hand-wringing
pacing in an antsy way

restore restores restoring restored
VERB **1.** To restore something means to cause it to exist again or to return to its previous state: *He was anxious to restore his reputation.* **2.** To restore an old building or work of art means to clean and repair it.
restoration NOUN

restrain restrains restraining restrained
VERB To restrain someone or something means to hold that person or thing back in order to prevent that person or thing from doing an action.

restrained
ADJECTIVE behaving in a controlled way

restraint restraints
NOUN **1.** Restraints are rules or conditions that limit something: *wage restraints* **2.** Restraint is calm, controlled behaviour.

restrict restricts restricting restricted
VERB **1.** If you restrict something, you prevent it from becoming too large or varied. **2.** To restrict people or animals means to limit their movement or actions.
restrictive ADJECTIVE

restriction restrictions
NOUN a rule or situation that limits what you can do: *financial restrictions*

result results resulting resulted
NOUN **1.** The result of an action or situation is the situation that is caused by it: *As a result of the incident, he got a three-game suspension.* **2.** The result is also the final marks, figures, or situation at the end of an exam, calculation, or contest: *Have they announced the election results? The result was calculated to three decimal places.*
VERB **3.** If something results in a particular event, it causes that event to happen. **4.** If something results from a particular event, it

is caused by that event: *The fire had resulted from carelessness.*
resultant ADJECTIVE

resume resumes resuming resumed
VERB If you resume an activity or position, you return to it after a break.
resumption NOUN

resurgence
NOUN If there is a resurgence of an attitude or activity, it reappears and grows stronger.
resurgent ADJECTIVE

resurrect resurrects resurrecting resurrected
VERB If you resurrect something, you make it exist again after it has disappeared or ended.
resurrection NOUN

resuscitate resuscitates resuscitating resuscitated
VERB If you resuscitate someone, you make that person conscious again after he or she has lost consciousness.
resuscitation NOUN

retail
NOUN The retail price is the price at which something is sold in the stores.
retailer NOUN

retain retains retaining retained
VERB To retain something means to keep it.
retention NOUN

retaliate retaliates retaliating retaliated
VERB If you retaliate, you do something to harm or upset someone because that person has already acted in a similar way toward you.
retaliation NOUN

retard retarding retarded
VERB delay or hinder: *Deep snow retarded the arrival of the rescue team.*

rethink rethinks rethinking rethought
VERB If you rethink something, you think about how it should be changed: *We have to rethink our strategy.*

reticent
ADJECTIVE Someone who is reticent is unwilling to tell people about things.
reticence NOUN

retina retinas
NOUN the light-sensitive part at the back of your eyeball that receives an image and sends it to your brain

retinue retinues
NOUN a group of helpers or friends travelling with an important person

retire retires retiring retired
VERB **1.** When older people retire, they give up work. **2.** *a formal use* If you retire, you

Rr

leave to go into another room, or to bed: *She retired early with a good book.*
retired ADJECTIVE
retirement NOUN

retort retorts retorting retorted
VERB **1.** To retort means to reply angrily.
NOUN **2.** a short, angry reply

retract retracts retracting retracted
VERB **1.** If you retract something you have said, you say that you did not mean it.
2. When something is retracted, it moves inward or backwards: *The wheels were retracted shortly after takeoff.*
retraction NOUN
retractable ADJECTIVE

retreat retreats retreating retreated
VERB **1.** To retreat means to move backwards away from something or someone. **2.** If you retreat from something difficult or unpleasant, you avoid doing it.
NOUN **3.** If an army moves away from the enemy, this is referred to as a retreat. **4.** a quiet place that you can go to rest or do things in private

retribution
NOUN *a formal word* Retribution is punishment: *the threat of retribution*

retrieve retrieves retrieving retrieved
VERB If you retrieve something, you get it back.
retrieval NOUN

retriever retrievers
NOUN a large dog often used by hunters to bring back birds and animals that have been shot

retro-
PREFIX The prefix *retro-* means *back* or *backwards*: *retrospective*

retrospect
NOUN When you consider something in retrospect, you think about it afterward and often have a different opinion from the one you had at the time: *In retrospect, I probably shouldn't have resigned.*

retrospective
ADJECTIVE concerning things that happened in the past
retrospectively ADVERB

return returns returning returned
VERB **1.** When you return to a place, you go back after you have been away. **2.** If you return something to someone, you give it back to that person. **3.** When you return a ball during a game, you hit it back to your opponent. **4.** When a judge or jury returns a verdict, the judge or jury announces it.
NOUN **5.** Your return is your arrival back at a place. **6.** The return on an investment is the profit or interest you get from it.
ADJECTIVE **7.** to do with going to or coming back from a place: *a return ticket*
PHRASE **8.** If you do something **in return** for a favour, you do it to repay the favour.

reunion reunions
NOUN a party or meeting for people who have not seen each other for a long time

reunite reunites reuniting reunited
VERB If people are reunited, they meet again after they have been separated for some time.

rev revs revving revved *an informal word*
VERB **1.** When you rev the engine of a vehicle, you press the accelerator to increase the engine speed.
NOUN **2.** The speed of an engine is measured in revolutions per minute, referred to as revs: *I noticed that the engine revs had dropped.*

revamp revamps revamping revamped
VERB To revamp something means to improve or repair it.

reveal reveals revealing revealed
VERB **1.** To reveal something means to tell people about it: *They were not ready to reveal any of the details.* **2.** If you reveal something that has been hidden, you uncover it.

revel revels revelling revelled
VERB If you revel in a situation, you enjoy it very much.
revelry NOUN

revelation revelations
NOUN **1.** a surprising or interesting fact made known to people **2.** If an experience is a revelation, it makes you realize or learn something.

revenge revenges revenging revenged
NOUN **1.** Revenge involves hurting someone who has hurt you.
VERB **2.** If you revenge yourself on someone who has hurt you, you hurt that person in return.

revenue revenues
NOUN Revenue is money that a government, company, or organization receives: *government tax revenues*

revered
ADJECTIVE If someone is revered, that person is respected and admired: *He is still revered as the father of the nation.*

reverence
NOUN Reverence is a feeling of great respect.

reversal reversals

NOUN If there is a reversal of a process or policy, it is changed to the opposite process or policy.

reverse reverses reversing reversed

VERB **1.** When someone reverses a process, that person changes it to the opposite process: *They won't reverse the decision to close all outdoor pools.* **2.** If you reverse the order of things, you arrange them in the opposite order. **3.** When you reverse a car, you drive it backwards.

NOUN **4.** The reverse is the opposite of what has just been said or done.

ADJECTIVE **5.** Reverse means opposite to what is usual or to what has just been described.

reversible

ADJECTIVE Reversible clothing can be worn with either side on the outside.

revert reverts reverting reverted

VERB *a formal word* To revert to a former state or type of behaviour means to go back to it.

review reviews reviewing reviewed

NOUN **1.** a written article, or an item on television or radio, giving an opinion, especially of a new book or movie **2.** When there is a review of a situation or system, it is examined to decide whether changes are needed.

VERB **3.** To review something such as a movie or a book means to give an account expressing an opinion of it. **4.** To review something means to examine it to decide whether changes are needed.

reviewer NOUN

revise revises revising revised

VERB If you revise a piece of writing, you make major changes to its content, structure, or wording.

revision NOUN

revive revives reviving revived

VERB **1.** When a feeling or practice is revived, it becomes active or popular again. **2.** When you revive someone who has fainted, that person becomes conscious again.

revival NOUN

revolt revolts revolting revolted

NOUN **1.** a violent attempt by a group of people to change their country's political system

VERB **2.** When people revolt, they fight against the authority that governs them. **3.** If something revolts you, it is so horrible that you feel disgust.

revolting

ADJECTIVE horrible and disgusting: *The smell in the cell was revolting.*

revolution revolutions

NOUN **1.** a violent attempt by a large group of people to change the political system of their country **2.** an important change in an area of human activity: *the Industrial Revolution* **3.** one complete turn in a circle

revolutionary revolutionaries

ADJECTIVE **1.** involving great changes: *a revolutionary new cooling system*

NOUN **2.** a person who takes part in a revolution

revolve revolves revolving revolved

VERB **1.** If something revolves around something else, it centres on that as the most important thing: *My job revolves around the telephone.* **2.** When something revolves, it turns in a circle around a central point: *The Moon revolves around Earth.*

revolver revolvers

NOUN a small gun held in the hand

revulsion

NOUN Revulsion is a strong feeling of disgust or disapproval.

reward rewards rewarding rewarded

NOUN **1.** something you are given because you have done something good

VERB **2.** If you reward someone, you give that person a reward.

rewarding

ADJECTIVE Something that is rewarding gives you a lot of satisfaction.

rewind rewinds rewinding rewound

VERB If you rewind a tape on a tape recorder or video, you make the tape go backwards.

rhapsody rhapsodies

NOUN a short piece of music that is very passionate and flowing

rhetoric

NOUN Rhetoric is speech or writing that is intended to persuade people.

rhetorical

ADJECTIVE **1.** A rhetorical question is one that is asked in order to make a statement rather than to get an answer. **2.** Rhetorical language is intended to be grand and impressive.

rheumatism

NOUN Rheumatism is an illness that makes your joints and muscles stiff and painful.

rheumatic ADJECTIVE

rhino rhinos

NOUN *an informal word* a rhinoceros

rhinoceros rhinoceroses
NOUN a large African or South Asian animal with one or two horns on its nose

rhododendron rhododendrons
NOUN an evergreen bush with large coloured flowers

rhombus rhombuses
NOUN a shape with four equal sides and no right angles

rhubarb
NOUN a plant with long red stems that can be cooked with sugar and eaten

rhyme rhymes rhyming rhymed
VERB **1.** If two words rhyme, they have a similar sound: *Mill rhymes with hill.*
NOUN **2.** a word that rhymes with another **3.** a short poem with rhyming lines

rhythm rhythms
NOUN **1.** Rhythm is a regular movement or beat. **2.** a regular pattern of changes, for example, in the seasons
rhythmic ADJECTIVE
rhythmically ADVERB

rib ribs
NOUN Your ribs are the curved bones that go from your backbone to your chest.
ribbed ADJECTIVE

ribbon ribbons
NOUN a long, narrow piece of cloth used for decoration

rib cage rib cages
NOUN Your rib cage is the framework of bones made up of your ribs, which protects your internal organs like your heart and lungs.

rice
NOUN a tall grass that produces edible grains. Rice is grown in warm countries on wet ground.

rich richer richest; riches
ADJECTIVE **1.** Someone who is rich has a lot of money and possessions. **2.** Something that is rich in something contains a large amount of it: *Liver is particularly rich in vitamin A.* **3.** Rich food contains a large amount of fat, oil, or sugar. **4.** Rich colours, smells, and sounds are strong and pleasant.
PLURAL NOUN **5.** Riches are valuable possessions or large amounts of money: *the oil riches of Alberta*
richness NOUN

richly
ADVERB **1.** If someone is richly rewarded, that person is rewarded well with something valuable. **2.** If you feel strongly that someone deserves something, you can say it is richly deserved.

rickets
NOUN Rickets is a disease that causes soft bones in children if they do not get enough vitamin D.

rickety
ADJECTIVE likely to collapse or break: *a rickety wooden dock*

rickshaw rickshaws
NOUN a hand-pulled cart for carrying passengers, used especially in Asia

ricochet ricochets ricochetting ricochetted
VERB When an object ricochets, it hits a surface and bounces away from it.

rid rids ridding rid
VERB **1.** *a formal use* To rid a place of something unpleasant means to succeed in removing it.
PHRASE **2.** When you **get rid** of something you do not want, you remove or destroy it.

riddle riddles
NOUN **1.** a puzzle that seems to be nonsense, but that has an entertaining solution **2.** Something that is a riddle puzzles you.

riddled
ADJECTIVE full of something undesirable: *The report was riddled with errors.*

ride rides riding rode ridden
VERB **1.** When you ride a horse or a bike, you sit on it and control it as it moves along. **2.** When you ride in a car, you travel in it.
NOUN **3.** a journey on a horse, bike, or in a motor vehicle

rider riders
NOUN **1.** a person riding on a horse, bicycle, or motor vehicle **2.** an additional statement that changes or puts a condition on what has already been said

ridge ridges
NOUN **1.** a long, narrow piece of high land **2.** a raised line on a flat surface

ridicule ridicules ridiculing ridiculed
VERB **1.** To ridicule someone means to make fun of that person in an unkind way.
NOUN **2.** Ridicule is unkind laughter and mockery.

ridiculous
ADJECTIVE very foolish
ridiculously ADVERB

rife
ADJECTIVE *a formal word* very common: *Unemployment was rife.*

rifle rifles rifling rifled
NOUN **1.** a gun with a long barrel
VERB **2.** When someone rifles something, that person makes a quick search through it to steal things.

Rr

rift rifts
NOUN **1.** a serious quarrel between friends that damages their friendship **2.** a split in something solid, especially in the ground

rig rigs rigging rigged
VERB **1.** If someone rigs an election or contest, that person dishonestly arranges for a particular person to win.
NOUN **2.** a large structure used for extracting oil or gas from the ground or sea bed
rig up
VERB **3.** If you rig up a device or structure, you make it quickly and fix it in place: *They had even rigged up a makeshift aerial.*

right rights righting righted
ADJECTIVE OR ADVERB **1.** correct and in accordance with the facts: *That clock never tells the right time. That's absolutely right.*
2. on or toward

Instead of **RIGHT** try…

the appropriate reaction
the **proper** approach
the **correct** answer
the **exact** amount
suitable clothes
the **desirable** outcome
that account is accurate
that doesn't seem fitting

the right side of something
ADJECTIVE **3.** The right choice or decision is the best or most suitable one. **4.** The right people or places are those that have influence or are socially admired: *He was always to be seen in the right places.* **5.** The right side of something is the side intended to be seen and to face outward.
NOUN **6.** *Right* is used to refer to principles of morally correct behaviour: *At least he knew right from wrong.* **7.** If you have a right to do something, you are morally or legally entitled to do it. **8.** The right is one of the two sides of something. For example, when you look at the word *to*, the *o* is to the right of the *t*. **9.** The Right refers to people who support the political ideas of capitalism and conservatism rather than socialism.
ADVERB **10.** *Right* is used to emphasize a precise place: *I'm right here.* **11.** *Right* means immediately: *I had to decide right then.*
VERB **12.** If you right something, you correct it or put it back in an upright position.
rightly ADVERB

right angle right angles
NOUN an angle of 90°

righteous
ADJECTIVE Righteous people behave in a way that is morally good.

rightful
ADJECTIVE Someone's rightful possession is one that he or she has a moral or legal right to.
rightfully ADVERB

right-handed
ADJECTIVE OR ADVERB Someone who is right-handed does things such as writing and painting with his or her right hand.

right-wing
ADJECTIVE believing more strongly in capitalism or conservatism, or less strongly in socialism, than other members of the same party or group
right winger NOUN

rigid
ADJECTIVE **1.** Rigid laws or systems cannot be changed and are considered severe. **2.** A rigid object is stiff and does not bend easily.
rigidly ADVERB
rigidity NOUN

rigorous
ADJECTIVE very careful and thorough
rigorously ADVERB

rigour rigours
NOUN *a formal word* The rigours of a situation are the things that make it hard or unpleasant: *the rigours of hard labour*

rim rims
NOUN the outside or top edge of an object such as a wheel or a cup

rind rinds
NOUN Rind is the thick outer skin of some fruit or the hard outer edge of cheese.

ring rings ringing rang rung
VERB **1.** When a bell rings, it makes a clear, loud sound. **2.** To ring something means to draw a circle around it. **3.** If something is ringed with something else, it has that thing all the way around it: *The courthouse was ringed with police.*
NOUN **4.** the sound made by a bell **5.** a small circle of metal or other material worn on your finger **6.** an object or group of things in the shape of a circle **7.** At a boxing match or circus, the ring is the place where the fight or performance takes place. **8.** an organized group of people who are involved in an illegal activity: *an international spy ring*

ringer ringers
NOUN *an informal word* a person or thing that is almost identical to another

ringleader ringleaders

NOUN the leader of a group of people who get involved in mischief or crime

rink rinks

NOUN a large, smooth area of ice or floor for people to skate on; also the building that contains a rink

rinse rinses rinsing rinsed

VERB **1.** When you rinse something, you wash it in clean water.

NOUN **2.** the act of washing something in clean water

riot riots rioting rioted

NOUN **1.** When there is a riot, a crowd of people behave noisily and violently.

VERB **2.** To riot means to behave noisily and violently.

PHRASE **3.** To **run riot** means to behave in a wild and uncontrolled way.

rip rips ripping ripped

VERB **1.** When you rip something, you tear it violently. **2.** If you rip something away, you remove it quickly and violently.

NOUN **3.** a long split in cloth or paper

rip off

VERB **4.** *an informal expression* If someone rips you off, that person cheats you by charging you too much money.

R.I.P. R.I.P. is an abbreviation often written on gravestones, meaning *rest in peace.*

ripe riper ripest

ADJECTIVE **1.** When fruit or grain is ripe, it is fully developed and ready to be eaten. **2.** If a situation is ripe for something to happen, it is ready for it.

ripeness NOUN

ripen ripens ripening ripened

VERB When crops ripen, they become ripe.

ripple ripples rippling rippled

NOUN **1.** Ripples are little waves on the surface of calm water. **2.** If there is a ripple of laughter or applause, people laugh or applaud gently for a short time.

VERB **3.** When the surface of water ripples, little waves appear on it.

rise rises rising rose risen

VERB **1.** If something rises, it moves upward. **2.** *a formal use* When you rise, you stand up. **3.** To rise also means to get out of bed. **4.** When the sun rises, it first appears. **5.** The place where a river rises is where it begins. **6.** If land rises, it slopes upward. **7.** If a sound or wind rises, it becomes higher or stronger. **8.** If an amount rises, it increases. **9.** If you rise to a challenge or a remark, you respond to it rather than ignoring it: *He rose to the challenge with enthusiasm.* **10.** When people rise up, they start fighting against

people in authority.

NOUN **11.** an increase **12.** Someone's rise is the process by which he or she becomes more powerful or successful: *his rise to fame*

riser risers

NOUN An early riser is someone who likes to get up early in the morning.

risk risks risking risked

NOUN **1.** a chance that something unpleasant or dangerous might happen

VERB **2.** If you risk something unpleasant, you do something knowing that the unpleasant thing might happen as a result: *If he doesn't play, he risks losing his place on the team.* **3.** If you risk someone's life, you put that person in a dangerous situation in which he or she might be killed.

risky ADJECTIVE

rite rites

NOUN a religious ceremony

ritual rituals

NOUN **1.** a series of actions carried out according to the custom of a particular society or group: *This is the most ancient of the Buddhist rituals.*

ADJECTIVE **2.** Ritual activities happen as part of a tradition or ritual: *fasting and ritual dancing*

ritualistic ADJECTIVE

rival rivals rivalling rivalled

NOUN **1.** Your rival is the person you are competing with.

VERB **2.** If something rivals something else, it is of the same high standard or quality: *As a holiday destination, the Yukon rivals British Columbia for beauty.*

rivalry rivalries

NOUN Rivalry is active competition between people.

river rivers

NOUN a natural feature consisting of water flowing for a long distance between two banks

rivet rivets

NOUN a short, round pin with a flat head that is used to fasten sheets of metal together

riveting

ADJECTIVE If you find something riveting, you find it fascinating and it holds your attention: *I find tennis riveting.*

road roads

NOUN a long piece of hard ground specially surfaced so that people and vehicles can travel along it easily

road map road maps

NOUN **1.** a map intended for drivers **2.** a plan or guide for future actions: *a road map for peace*

road rage

NOUN Road rage is aggressive behaviour by a driver as a reaction to the behaviour of another driver.

roam roams roaming roamed

VERB If you roam around, you wander around without any particular purpose: *Hens were roaming around the yard.*

roar roars roaring roared

VERB **1.** If something roars, it makes a very loud noise. **2.** To roar with laughter or anger means to laugh or shout very noisily. **3.** When a lion roars, it makes a loud, angry sound.
NOUN **4.** a very loud noise

roast roasts roasting roasted

VERB **1.** When you roast meat or other food, you cook it using dry heat in an oven or over a fire.
ADJECTIVE **2.** Roast meat has been roasted.
NOUN **3.** a piece of meat that has been roasted

rob robs robbing robbed

VERB **1.** If someone robs you, that person steals your possessions. **2.** If you rob someone of something that person needs or deserves, you deprive him or her of it: *The former child star said acting robbed him of his childhood.*

robber robbers

NOUN Robbers are people who steal money or property using force or threats: *bank robbers*
robbery NOUN

robe robes

NOUN a long, loose piece of clothing that covers the body: *She put on her robe and went to the kitchen for breakfast.*

robin robins

NOUN a small bird with a red breast

robot robots

NOUN a machine that is programmed to move and perform tasks automatically

robust

ADJECTIVE very strong and healthy
robustly ADVERB

rock rocks rocking rocked

NOUN **1.** Rock is the hard mineral substance that forms the surface of the earth. **2.** a large piece of rock: *She picked up a rock and threw it into the lake.* **3.** Rock or rock music is music with simple tunes and a very strong beat.
VERB **4.** When something rocks or when you rock it, it moves regularly backwards and forward or from side to side: *She rocked the baby.* **5.** If something rocks people, it shocks and upsets them: *The quiet northern*

community was rocked by a crime wave. **6.** If someone's marriage or relationship is **on the rocks**, it is unsuccessful and about to end.

rocket rockets rocketing rocketed

NOUN **1.** a space vehicle, usually shaped like a long, pointed tube **2.** an explosive missile: *They fired rockets into a number of government buildings.* **3.** a firework that explodes when it is high in the air
VERB **4.** If prices rocket, they increase very quickly.

rocking chair rocking chairs

NOUN a chair on two curved pieces of wood that rocks back and forth when you sit in it

rock'n'roll

NOUN Rock'n'roll is a style of music with a strong beat that was especially popular in the 1950s.

rocky

ADJECTIVE covered with rocks

rod rods

NOUN a long, thin pole or bar, usually made of wood or metal: *a fishing rod*

rodent rodents

NOUN a small mammal with sharp front teeth that it uses for gnawing

rodeo rodeos

NOUN a public entertainment in which cowboys show different skills such as riding horses

roe

NOUN Roe is the eggs of a fish.

rogue rogues

NOUN **1.** You can refer to a man who behaves dishonestly as a rogue.
ADJECTIVE **2.** a vicious animal that lives apart from its herd or pack

role roles

NOUN **1.** Someone's role is that person's position and function in a situation or society. **2.** An actor's role is the character that he or she plays: *her first leading role*

roll rolls rolling rolled

VERB **1.** When something rolls or when you roll it, it moves along a surface, turning over and over. **2.** When vehicles roll along, they move: *Tanks rolled into the village.* **3.** If you roll your eyes, you make them turn up or go from side to side. **4.** If you roll something flexible into a cylinder or ball, you wrap it several times around itself: *He rolled up the twine and put it away.*
NOUN **5.** A roll of paper or cloth is a long piece of it that has been rolled into a tube: *a roll of wrapping paper* **6.** a small, rounded, individually baked piece of bread **7.** an

⚠ **HEADS UP** The word **rogue** is pronounced ROHG.

NEL

official list of people's names: *the electoral roll* **8.** A roll on a drum is a long, rumbling sound made on it.

roll call roll calls
NOUN If you take a roll call, you call a list of names to see who is present.

roller rollers
NOUN **1.** a cylinder that turns around in a machine or piece of equipment **2.** Rollers are tubes that you can wind your hair around to make it curly.

Rollerblade Rollerblades
NOUN *a trademark* a brand of inline skates

roller coaster roller coasters
NOUN a pleasure ride at an amusement park, consisting of a small railway that goes up and down very steep slopes

roller skate roller skates roller skating roller skated
NOUN **1.** Roller skates are shoes with four small wheels underneath.
VERB **2.** If you roller skate, you move along wearing roller skates.

rolling pin rolling pins
NOUN a wooden cylinder used for rolling pastry dough to make it flat

ROM
NOUN In computing, ROM is a storage device that holds data permanently and cannot be altered by the programmer. ROM stands for *read only memory*.

Roman Catholic the same as CATHOLIC

romance romances
NOUN **1.** a relationship between two people who are in love with each other **2.** Romance is the pleasure and excitement of doing something new and unusual: *the romance of foreign travel* **3.** a novel about a love affair

romantic romantics
ADJECTIVE OR NOUN **1.** A romantic person has ideas that are not realistic, for example about love or about ways of changing society: *a romantic idealist*
ADJECTIVE **2.** connected with love: *a romantic relationship* **3.** Something that is romantic is beautiful in a way that strongly affects your feelings: *It is one of the most romantic places to visit.* **4.** Romantic describes a style of music, literature, and art popular in Europe in the late eighteenth and early nineteenth centuries, which emphasized feeling and imagination rather than order and form.
romantically ADVERB
romanticism NOUN

roof roofs
NOUN **1.** The roof of a building is the covering on top of it. **2.** The roof of your mouth or of a cave is the highest part.

roofing
NOUN Roofing is material used for covering roofs.

rooftop rooftops
NOUN the outside part of the roof of a building

rook rooks
NOUN a chess piece that can move any number of squares in a straight but not diagonal line

room rooms
NOUN **1.** a separate section in a building, divided from other rooms by walls **2.** If there is plenty of room, there is a lot of space: *There wasn't enough room for her hockey gear.*

roost roosts roosting roosted
NOUN **1.** a place where birds rest or build their nests
VERB **2.** When birds roost, they settle somewhere for the night.

root roots rooting rooted
NOUN **1.** The roots of a plant are the parts that grow under the ground. **2.** The root of a hair is the part beneath the skin. **3.** You can refer to the place or culture that you grew up in as your roots. **4.** The root of something is its original cause or basis: *We got to the root of the problem.* **5.** a word or part word to which prefixes and/or suffixes have been added: *The root of* disrespectful *is* respect.
VERB **6.** To root through things means to search through them, pushing them aside: *She rooted through his bag.*
root out
VERB **7.** If you root people or things out, you find them and force them out: *a major drive to root out corruption*

rooted
ADJECTIVE developed from or strongly influenced by something: *songs rooted in traditional Inuit music*

rope ropes roping roped
NOUN **1.** a thick, strong length of twisted cord
VERB **2.** If you rope one thing to another, you tie them together with rope.

rose roses
NOUN **1.** a large garden flower that has a pleasant smell and grows on a bush with thorns
NOUN OR ADJECTIVE **2.** reddish pink

Rr

rosemary
NOUN a herb with fragrant, spiky leaves, used for flavouring in cooking

rosette rosettes
NOUN a large badge of coloured ribbons gathered into a circle, which is worn as a prize in a competition or to support a political party

roster rosters
NOUN a list of people who take it in turn to do a particular job: *He put himself first on the new roster for domestic chores.*

rostrum rostrums
NOUN a raised platform on which someone stands to speak to an audience or conduct an orchestra

rosy rosier rosiest
ADJECTIVE **1.** reddish pink **2.** If a situation seems rosy, it is likely to be good or successful. **3.** If a person looks rosy, that person has pink cheeks and looks healthy.

rot rots rotting rotted
VERB **1.** When food or wood rots, it decays and can no longer be used. **2.** When something rots another substance, it causes it to decay: *Sugary drinks rot your teeth.*
NOUN **3.** Rot is the condition that affects things when they rot: *The timber frame was not protected against rot.*

rotate rotates rotating rotated
VERB When something rotates, it turns with a circular movement: *He rotated the camera 180°.*
   rotation NOUN

rotor rotors
NOUN **1.** The rotor is the part of a machine that turns. **2.** The rotors or rotor blades of a helicopter are the four long, flat pieces of metal on top of it that rotate and lift it off the ground.

rotten
ADJECTIVE **1.** decayed and no longer of use: *The front bay window frame is rotten.* **2.** *an informal use* of very poor quality: *I think it's a rotten idea.* **3.** *an informal use* very unfair, unkind, or unpleasant:

Instead of ROUGH try...

That's a rotten thing to say!

rough rougher roughest; roughs
ADJECTIVE **1.** uneven and not smooth **2.** not using enough care or

coarse skin
choppy seas
a bumpy ride
a jagged edge
rugged terrain

gentleness: *Don't be so rough or you'll break it.* **3.** difficult or unpleasant: *Teachers have been given a rough time.* **4.** approximately correct: *At a rough guess, it is five times more profitable.* **5.** If the sea is rough, there are large waves because of bad weather. **6.** A rough town or area has a lot of crime or violence.
NOUN OR ADJECTIVE **7.** A rough or a rough sketch is a drawing or description that shows the main features but does not show the details. **8.** On a golf course, the rough is the part of the course next to a fairway where the grass has not been cut.
roughly ADVERB
roughness NOUN

round rounder roundest; rounds rounding rounded
ADJECTIVE **1.** Something round is shaped like a ball or a circle. **2.** complete or whole: *round numbers*
NOUN **3.** one of a series of events: *After round three, two Canadians shared the lead.* **4.** a sequence of regularly recurring actions or events: *a round of drinks*
round up
VERB **5.** If you round up people or animals, you gather them together.

⚠ **HEADS UP**

In Canada, **around** is preferred, but **round** is sometimes used in its place for a more literary flavour.

roundabout
ADJECTIVE indirect: *I heard about it in a roundabout way.*

rounded
ADJECTIVE curved in shape, without any points or sharp edges

round-the-clock
ADJECTIVE happening continuously

rouse rouses rousing roused
VERB **1.** If someone rouses you, that person wakes you up. **2.** If you rouse yourself to do something, you make yourself get up and do it. **3.** If something rouses you, it makes you feel very emotional and excited.

rout routs routing routed
VERB To rout your opponents means to defeat them completely and easily.

route routes
NOUN a way from one place to another

routine routines
ADJECTIVE **1.** Routine activities are done regularly.
NOUN **2.** the usual way or order in which you do things **3.** a boring repetition of tasks
routinely ADVERB

roving
ADJECTIVE **1.** wandering or roaming: *roving cattle* **2.** not restricted to any particular location or area: *a roving reporter*

row rows rowing rowed
NOUN **1.** A row of people or things is several of them arranged in a line.
VERB **2.** When you row a boat, you use oars to make it move through the water.

rowdy rowdier rowdiest
ADJECTIVE rough and noisy

royal royals
ADJECTIVE **1.** belonging to or involving a queen, a king, or a member of his or her family **2.** suitable for a king or queen: *a royal welcome*
NOUN **3.** *an informal use* Members of the royal family are sometimes referred to as the royals.

royalist royalists
NOUN someone who supports a king or queen or a royal government

royalty royalties
NOUN **1.** The members of a royal family are sometimes referred to as royalty. **2.** Royalties are payments made to authors and musicians from the sales of their books or recordings.

rub rubs rubbing rubbed
VERB **1.** If you rub something, you move your hand or a cloth back and forth over it.
rub out
VERB **2.** To rub out something written means to remove it by rubbing it with an eraser or a cloth.

rubber rubbers
NOUN **1.** Rubber is a strong, elastic substance used for making tires, boots, and other products. **2.** a small piece of rubber used to rub out pencil mistakes

rubbish
NOUN **1.** Rubbish is unwanted things or waste material. **2.** You can refer to nonsense or something of very poor quality as rubbish.

rubble
NOUN Bits of old brick and stone are referred to as rubble.

rubella
NOUN a contagious disease that gives you a sore throat and red spots. German measles is another name for rubella.

rubric rubrics
NOUN *a formal word* a set of instructions at the beginning of an official document

ruby rubies
NOUN a type of red jewel

rudder rudders
NOUN a piece of wood or metal at the back of a boat or plane that is moved to make the boat or plane turn

rude ruder rudest
ADJECTIVE **1.** not polite **2.** unexpected and unpleasant: *a rude awakening*
rudely ADVERB
rudeness NOUN

rudimentary
ADJECTIVE *a formal word* very basic or not developed: *He had only a rudimentary knowledge of French.*

rudiments
PLURAL NOUN When you learn the rudiments of something, you learn only the simplest and most basic things about it.

ruff ruffs
NOUN **1.** a stiff, circular collar with many pleats in it, worn especially in the sixteenth century **2.** a thick band of fur or feathers around the neck of a bird or animal

ruffle ruffles ruffling ruffled
VERB **1.** If you ruffle someone's hair, you move your hand quickly back and forth over that person's head. **2.** If something ruffles you, it makes you annoyed or upset.
NOUN **3.** Ruffles are small folds made in a piece of material for decoration.

rug rugs
NOUN **1.** a small carpet **2.** a blanket that you can use to cover your knees or for sitting on outdoors

rugby
NOUN Rugby is a game played by two teams, who try to kick and throw an oval ball to their opponents' end of the field.

rugged
ADJECTIVE **1.** rocky and wild: *the rugged east coast of Canada* **2.** having strong features: *his rugged good looks*

ruin ruins ruining ruined
VERB **1.** If you ruin something, you destroy or spoil it completely. **2.** If someone is ruined, that person has lost all his or her money.
NOUN **3.** Ruin is the state of being destroyed or completely spoiled. **4.** A ruin or the ruins of something refers to the parts that are left after it has been severely damaged: *the ruins of a nineteenth-century farmhouse*

Rr

rule rules ruling ruled

NOUN **1.** Rules are statements that tell you what you are allowed to do.
VERB **2.** To rule a country or group of people means to have power over that country or those people. **3.** *a formal use* When someone in authority rules on a particular matter, that person gives an official decision about it.
PHRASE **4. As a rule** means *usually* or *generally*: *As a rule, I eat my meals in front of the TV.*

rule out

VERB **5.** If you rule out an idea or course of action, you reject it. **6.** If one thing rules out another, it prevents it from happening or being possible: *The accident ruled out a future for him in football.*

ruler rulers

NOUN **1.** a person who rules a country
2. a long, flat piece of wood or plastic with straight edges marked in units such as centimetres, used for measuring or drawing straight lines

rum

NOUN Rum is a strong alcoholic drink made from sugar cane juice.

rumble rumbles rumbling rumbled

VERB **1.** If something rumbles, it makes a continuous low noise: *Another train rumbled past the house.*
NOUN **2.** a continuous low noise: *the distant rumble of traffic*

rummage rummages rummaging rummaged

VERB If you rummage somewhere, you search for something, moving things about carelessly.

rumour rumours rumoured

NOUN **1.** a story that people are talking about that may or may not be true
VERB **2.** If something is rumoured, people are suggesting that it has happened.

rump rumps

NOUN **1.** An animal's rump is its rear end.
2. the buttocks

run runs running ran

VERB **1.** When you run, you move quickly, leaving the ground during each stride.
2. If you say that a road or river runs in a particular direction, you are describing its course. **3.** If you run your hand or an object over something, you move it over it. **4.** If someone runs in an election, that person stands as a candidate: *He announced he would run for student council president.*
5. If you run a business or an activity, you are in charge of it. **6.** If you run an experiment, a computer program, or a tape, you start it and let it continue: *He ran a series of computer checks.* **7.** If you run someone somewhere in a car, you drive that person there: *Could you run me to the library?* **8.** If you run water, you turn on a tap to make it flow: *We heard him running the kitchen tap.* **9.** If your nose is running, it is producing a lot of mucus. **10.** If the dye in something runs, the colour comes out when it is washed. **11.** If a feeling runs through your body, it affects you quickly and strongly. **12.** If an amount is running at a particular level, it is at that level: *Inflation is currently running at 2.6 percent.* **13.** If someone or something is running late, that person or thing has taken more time than was planned. **14.** If an event or contract runs for a particular time, it lasts for that time.
NOUN **15.** If you go for a run, you run for pleasure or exercise. **16.** If a play or show has a run of a particular length of time, it is on for that time. **17.** A run of success or failure is a series of successes or failures.
18. In cricket or baseball, a player scores one run by running between marked places on the field after hitting the ball.

runaway runaways

NOUN a person who has escaped from a place or left it secretly and hurriedly

KNOWING WORDS: IDIOMS

BE WORD SHARP!

Idioms add colour to language by playing with the meanings of words.

run move quickly

on the run in retreat

run away leave suddenly and secretly

run into meet by chance

run over hit with a moving vehicle

run out of have no more

Rr

rundown
ADJECTIVE **1.** tired and not well **2.** neglected and in poor condition
NOUN **3.** *an informal use* If you give someone the rundown on a situation, you tell that person the basic, important facts about it.

rung rungs
NOUN The rungs on a ladder are the bars that form the steps.

runner runners
NOUN **1.** a person who runs, especially as a sport **2.** a person who takes messages or runs errands **3.** A runner on a plant such as a strawberry is a long shoot from which a new plant develops. **4.** The runners on drawers are the thin strips on which they move.

runner-up runners-up
NOUN a person or team that comes second in a race or competition

running
ADJECTIVE **1.** continuing without stopping over a period of time: *a running commentary* **2.** Running water is flowing rather than standing still.

runny runnier runniest
ADJECTIVE **1.** more liquid than usual: *Warm the honey until it becomes runny.* **2.** If someone's nose or eyes are runny, liquid is coming out of them.

run-on sentence
NOUN Joining two sentences without the proper punctuation or connecting words is a mistake called a run-on sentence.

runt runts
NOUN The runt of a litter of animals is the smallest and weakest.

runway runways
NOUN a long strip of ground used by airplanes for taking off or landing

rupture ruptures rupturing ruptured
NOUN **1.** a breakage or bursting open of something, especially a pipe, vessel, or body part
VERB **2.** To rupture something means to cause it to tear or burst: *a ruptured spleen*

rural
ADJECTIVE relating to or involving the countryside

ruse ruses
NOUN *a formal word* an action that is intended to trick someone

rush rushes rushing rushed
VERB **1.** To rush means to move fast or do something quickly. **2.** If you rush someone into doing something, you make that person do it without allowing him or her enough time to think.
NOUN **3.** If you are in a rush, you are busy and do not have enough time to do things. **4.** If there is a rush for something, there is a sudden increase in demand for it: *There was a rush for tickets.* **5.** a plant with long, thin stems that grows near water

rush hour rush hours
NOUN The rush hour is one of the busy parts of the day when most people are travelling to or from work.

rusk rusks
NOUN a hard, dry biscuit

rust rusts rusting rusted
NOUN **1.** Rust is a reddish brown substance that forms on iron or steel that has been in contact with water and that is decaying gradually.
NOUN OR ADJECTIVE **2.** reddish brown
VERB **3.** When a metal object rusts, it becomes covered in rust.

rustic
ADJECTIVE simple in a way considered to be typical of the countryside: *a rustic old log cabin*

rustle rustles rustling rustled
VERB When something rustles, it makes soft sounds as it moves.
rustling ADJECTIVE OR NOUN

rusty rustier rustiest
ADJECTIVE **1.** affected by rust: *a rusty iron gate* **2.** If someone's knowledge is rusty, it is not as good as it used to be because that person has not used it for a long time: *My German is a bit rusty these days.*

rut ruts
NOUN **1.** a deep, narrow groove in the ground made by the wheels of a vehicle
PHRASE **2.** If someone is **in a rut**, that person has become fixed in his or her way of doing things.

ruthless
ADJECTIVE very harsh or cruel: *a ruthless leader*
ruthlessness NOUN
ruthlessly ADVERB

rye
NOUN a type of cereal grass that produces light brown grain

Ss

sable sables

NOUN a very expensive fur used for making coats and hats; also the wild animal from which this fur is obtained

sabotage sabotages sabotaging sabotaged

NOUN **1.** the deliberate damaging of things such as machinery to gain military advantage or for political reasons

VERB **2.** If something is sabotaged, it is deliberately damaged.

saboteur NOUN

sabre sabres

NOUN **1.** a heavy, curved sword **2.** a light sword used in fencing

saccharin

NOUN a chemical used instead of sugar to sweeten things

sachet sachets

NOUN a small, closed packet, containing a small amount of something such as perfumed powder, used especially for scenting linens and clothes

sack sacks sacking sacked

NOUN **1.** a large bag made of rough material used for carrying or storing goods

VERB **2.** If a city or village is sacked, it is invaded and robbed.

sacred

ADJECTIVE holy, or connected with religion or religious ceremonies: *sacred ground*

sacrifice sacrifices sacrificing sacrificed

VERB **1.** If you sacrifice something valuable or important, you give it up. **2.** To sacrifice an animal means to kill it as an offering to a god.

NOUN **3.** the killing of an animal as an offering to a god or gods **4.** the action of giving something up

sacrificial ADJECTIVE

sacrilege

NOUN Sacrilege is behaviour that shows great disrespect for something holy.

sacrilegious ADJECTIVE

sacrosanct

ADJECTIVE regarded as too important to be criticized or changed: *Freedom of the press is sacrosanct.*

sad sadder saddest

ADJECTIVE **1.** If you are sad, you feel unhappy. **2.** Something sad makes you feel unhappy: *a sad story*

sadly ADVERB

sadden saddens saddening saddened

VERB If something saddens you, it makes you feel sad.

saddle saddles saddling saddled

NOUN **1.** a leather seat that you sit on when you are riding a horse **2.** The saddle on a bicycle is the seat.

VERB **3.** If you saddle a horse, you put a saddle on it.

sadism

NOUN Sadism is the obtaining of pleasure from making people suffer pain or humiliation.

sadist NOUN

sadistic ADJECTIVE

sadness

NOUN the feeling of being unhappy

safari safaris

NOUN an expedition for hunting or observing wild animals

safe safer safest; safes

ADJECTIVE **1.** Something that is safe does not cause harm or danger. **2.** If you are safe, you are not in any danger. **3.** If it is safe to say something, you can say it with little risk of being wrong.

NOUN **4.** a strong metal box with a special lock, in which you can keep valuable things

safely ADVERB

safeguard safeguards safeguarding safeguarded

VERB **1.** To safeguard something means to protect it.

NOUN **2.** something designed to protect people or things

safekeeping

NOUN If something is given to you for safekeeping, it is given to you to look after.

safety

NOUN the state of being safe from harm or danger

sag sags sagging sagged

VERB When something sags, it hangs down loosely or sinks downward in the middle.

sagging ADJECTIVE

saga sagas

NOUN a very long story, usually with many different adventures: *a saga of rivalry, honour, and love*

sage sages

NOUN **1.** *a literary or poetic use* a very wise person **2.** a herb used for flavouring in cooking

sail sails sailing sailed

NOUN **1.** Sails are large pieces of material attached to a ship's mast. The wind blows

⚠ **HEADS UP** The word **sachet** is pronounced sa-SHAY.

against the sail and moves the ship.
VERB **2.** When a ship or other vessel sails, it moves across water. **3.** If you sail somewhere, you go there by ship.

sailor sailors
NOUN a person who works or does tasks on a sailboat or other vessel as a job or for recreation

saint saints
NOUN a person who, after death, is formally recognized by a Christian Church as deserving special honour because of having lived a very holy life

saintly
ADJECTIVE behaving in a very good or holy way

sake sakes
PHRASE **1.** If you do something **for someone's sake**, you do it to help or please that person. **2.** You use **for the sake of** to say why you are doing something: *reading for the sake of interest*

salad salads
NOUN a mixture of raw vegetables

salami
NOUN a kind of spicy sausage

salary salaries
NOUN a regular, fixed payment to an employee

sale sales
NOUN **1.** The sale of goods is the selling of them. **2.** an occasion when a store sells things at reduced prices
PLURAL NOUN **3.** The sales of a product are the numbers that are sold.

salesperson salespeople
NOUN someone who sells products for a company
salesman NOUN
saleswoman NOUN

salient
ADJECTIVE *a formal word* The salient points or facts are the important ones.

saliva
NOUN Saliva is the watery liquid in your mouth that helps you chew and digest food.

sallow
ADJECTIVE Sallow skin looks pale and unhealthy.

salmon salmons salmon
NOUN a large, edible, silver-coloured fish with pink flesh

salmonella
NOUN Salmonella is a kind of bacteria that can cause severe food poisoning.

salon salons
NOUN a place where hairdressers work

salt salts
NOUN **1.** Salt is a white substance found naturally in sea water. It is used to flavour and preserve food. **2.** a chemical compound formed from an acid base

salty saltier saltiest
ADJECTIVE containing salt or tasting of salt

salute salutes saluting saluted
NOUN **1.** a formal sign of respect. Soldiers give a salute by raising their right hand to their forehead.
VERB **2.** If you salute someone, you give that person a salute.

salvage salvages salvaging salvaged
VERB **1.** If you salvage things, you save them, for example from a wrecked ship or a destroyed building.
NOUN **2.** You refer to things saved from a wrecked ship or destroyed building as salvage.

salvation
NOUN **1.** When someone's salvation takes place, that person is saved from harm or evil. **2.** To be someone's salvation means to save that person from harm or evil.

salvo salvos *or* salvoes
NOUN the firing of several guns or missiles at the same time

same
ADJECTIVE **1.** If two things are the same, they are like one another. **2.** Same means just one thing and not two different ones: *They were born in the same town.*

sample samples sampling sampled
NOUN **1.** A sample of something is a small amount of it that you can try or test: *a sample of a new product*
VERB **2.** If you sample something, you try it: *I sampled his cooking.*

samurai
NOUN A samurai was a member of an ancient Japanese warrior class.

sanctimonious
ADJECTIVE pretending to be very religious and virtuous

sanction sanctions sanctioning sanctioned
VERB **1.** To sanction something means to officially approve of it or allow it.
NOUN **2.** Sanction is official approval of something. **3.** a severe punishment or penalty intended to make people obey the law **4.** Sanctions are sometimes taken by countries against a country that has broken international law.

Ss

sanctity
NOUN If you talk about the sanctity of something, you are saying that it should be respected because it is very important: *the sanctity of human life*

sanctuary sanctuaries
NOUN **1.** a place where you are safe from harm or danger **2.** a place where wildlife is protected: *a bird sanctuary*

sand sands sanding sanded
NOUN **1.** Sand consists of tiny pieces of stone. Beaches are made of sand.
VERB **2.** If you sand something, you rub sandpaper over it to make it smooth.

sandal sandals
NOUN Sandals are light shoes with straps, worn in warm weather.

sandpaper
NOUN Sandpaper is strong paper with a coating of sand on it, used for rubbing surfaces to make them smooth.

sandstone
NOUN Sandstone is a type of rock formed from sand, often used for building.

sandwich sandwiches sandwiching sandwiched
NOUN **1.** two slices of bread with a filling between them
VERB **2.** If one thing is sandwiched between two others, it is in a narrow space between them: *a small store sandwiched between a bar and an office*

sandy sandier sandiest
ADJECTIVE **1.** A sandy area is covered with sand. **2.** Sandy hair is light orange-brown.

sane saner sanest
ADJECTIVE **1.** If someone is sane, that person has a normal and healthy mind. **2.** A sane action is sensible and reasonable.

sanguine
ADJECTIVE *a formal word* cheerful and confident

sanitary
ADJECTIVE Sanitary means concerned with keeping things clean and hygienic: *improving the sanitary conditions*

sanitary napkin sanitary napkins
NOUN A sanitary napkin is pad of thick, soft material that women wear during their periods.

sanitation
NOUN Sanitation is the process of keeping places clean and hygienic, especially by providing a sewage system and clean water supply.

sanity
NOUN Your sanity is your ability to think and act normally and reasonably.

sap saps sapping sapped
VERB **1.** If something saps your strength or confidence, it gradually weakens and destroys it.
NOUN **2.** Sap is the watery liquid in plants.

sapling saplings
NOUN a young tree

sapphire sapphires
NOUN a blue precious stone

sarcastic
ADJECTIVE saying or doing the opposite of what you really mean in order to mock or insult someone: *a sarcastic remark*
sarcasm NOUN
sarcastically ADVERB

sarcophagus sarcophaguses
NOUN a stone coffin used in ancient times

sardine sardines
NOUN a small edible sea fish

sardonic
ADJECTIVE mocking or scornful: *a sardonic grin*
sardonically ADVERB

sari saris
NOUN a piece of clothing worn especially by Indian women, consisting of a long piece of material folded around the body

sartorial
ADJECTIVE *a formal word* relating to clothes: *sartorial elegance*

sash sashes
NOUN a long piece of cloth worn as an ornament around the waist or over one shoulder

Satan
NOUN Satan is the Devil.

satanic
ADJECTIVE caused by or influenced by Satan: *satanic forces*

satchel satchels
NOUN a small bag, often with a long shoulder strap, used for carrying books or other items

satellite satellites
NOUN **1.** a spacecraft sent into orbit around the earth to collect information or as part of a communications system **2.** a natural object in space that moves around a planet or star

satin satins
NOUN Satin is a kind of smooth, shiny silk.

satire satires
NOUN Satire is the use of mocking or ironical

⚠ HEADS UP The word **sanguine** is pronounced SANG-gwin.

humour, especially in literature, to show how foolish or wicked some people are.
satirical ADJECTIVE

satisfaction
NOUN Satisfaction is the feeling of pleasure you get when you do something you wanted or needed to do.

satisfactory
ADJECTIVE acceptable or adequate: *a satisfactory explanation*
satisfactorily ADVERB

satisfied
ADJECTIVE happy because you have got what you want

satisfy satisfies satisfying satisfied
VERB **1.** To satisfy someone means to give that person enough of something to make him or her pleased or contented. **2.** To satisfy someone that something is the case means to convince that person of it. **3.** To satisfy the requirements for something means to fulfill them.

satisfying
ADJECTIVE Something that is satisfying gives you a feeling of pleasure and fulfillment.

saturated
ADJECTIVE **1.** very wet **2.** If a place is saturated with things, it is completely full of them.
saturation NOUN

Saturday Saturdays
NOUN the day between Friday and Sunday

Saturn
NOUN Saturn is the planet in the solar system that is sixth from the sun.

sauce sauces
NOUN a liquid eaten with food to give it more flavour

saucepan saucepans
NOUN a deep, metal cooking pot with a handle and a lid

saucer saucers
NOUN a small, curved plate for a cup

saucy saucier sauciest
ADJECTIVE A person who is saucy shows a lack of respect for someone.

sauna saunas
NOUN If you have a sauna, you go into a very hot room in order to sweat.

saunter saunters sauntering sauntered
VERB To saunter somewhere means to walk there slowly and casually.

sausage sausages
NOUN a mixture of ground meat and herbs formed into a tubular shape and served cooked

sauté sautés sautéeing sautéed
VERB To sauté food means to fry it quickly in a small amount of oil or butter.

savage savages savaging savaged
ADJECTIVE **1.** cruel and violent: *savage fighting*
NOUN **2.** If you call someone a savage, you mean that that person is violent and uncivilized.
VERB **3.** If an animal savages you, it attacks you and bites you.
savagely ADVERB

savagery
NOUN Savagery is cruel and violent behaviour.

save saves saving saved
VERB **1.** If you save someone, you rescue that person: *He saved my life.* **2.** If you save someone or something, you keep that person or thing safe. **3.** If you save something, you keep it so that you can use it later: *He'd saved up enough money to buy a computer.* **4.** To save time, money, or effort means to prevent it from being wasted: *You could have saved us the trouble.*
PREPOSITION **5.** Save means except: *I was alone in the store save for the salesperson.*

saving savings
NOUN **1.** a reduction in the amount of time or money used
2. Your savings are the money you have saved.

saviour saviours
NOUN **1.** If someone saves you from danger, you can refer to that person as your saviour.
2. In Christianity, the Saviour is Jesus Christ.

savour savours savouring savoured
VERB If you savour something, you take your time with it and enjoy it fully: *He savoured the piece of chocolate.*

savoury
ADJECTIVE **1.** Savoury is salty or spicy.
2. Something that is not very savoury is not very respectable: *the less savoury places*

saw saws sawing sawed
1. Saw is the past tense of SEE.
NOUN **2.** a tool, with a blade with sharp teeth along one edge, for cutting wood
VERB **3.** If you saw something, you cut it with a saw.

⚠ HEADS UP

Saw can stand on its own: *I saw you there.* Seen needs a helping verb: *I have seen you there.*

sawdust
NOUN Sawdust is the fine powder produced when you saw wood.

saxophone saxophones
NOUN a curved metal wind instrument often played in jazz bands

say says saying said
VERB **1.** When you say something, you speak words. **2.** *Say* is used to give an example: *a maximum fee of, say, a million dollars* NOUN **3.** If you have a say in something, you can give your opinion and influence decisions.

Instead of **SAY** try...

don't **breathe** a word

explain carefully

state your name

angrily hiss

announce loudly

assert confidently

mutter to yourself

manage to **wheeze**

saying sayings
NOUN a well-known sentence or phrase that usually offers advice or wisdom

scab scabs
NOUN a hard, dry covering that forms over a wound
scabby ADJECTIVE

scaffolding
NOUN Scaffolding is a framework of poles and boards that is used by workers to stand on while they are working on the outside structure of a building.

scald scalds scalding scalded
VERB **1.** If you scald yourself, you burn yourself with very hot liquid or steam. NOUN **2.** a burn caused by scalding

scale scales scaling scaled
NOUN **1.** The scale of something is its size or extent: *the sheer scale of the disaster* **2.** a set of levels or numbers used for measuring things **3.** The scale of a map, plan, or model is the relationship between the size of something on the map, plan, or model and its size in the real world: *a scale of 1:10 000* **4.** an upward or downward sequence of musical notes **5.** The scales of a fish or reptile are the small pieces of hard skin covering its body. PLURAL NOUN **6.** Scales are a piece of equipment used for weighing things. VERB **7.** If you scale something, you climb it.

scalene
ADJECTIVE A scalene triangle has sides that are all of different lengths.

scallop scallops
NOUN Scallops are edible shellfish with two flat, fan-shaped shells.

scalp scalps scalping scalped
NOUN **1.** Your scalp is the skin under the hair on your head. **2.** the piece of skin and hair removed when someone is scalped VERB **3.** To scalp someone means to remove the skin and hair from that person's head in one piece.

scalpel scalpels
NOUN a knife with a thin, sharp blade, used by surgeons

scaly
ADJECTIVE covered with scales

scamper scampers scampering scampered
VERB To scamper means to move quickly and lightly.

scampi
PLURAL NOUN large shrimp or prawns, especially when used in Italian dishes

scan scans scanning scanned
VERB **1.** If you scan something, you look at all of it carefully: *I scanned the horizon to the northeast.* **2.** If a machine scans something, it examines it by means of a beam of light or X-rays. NOUN **3.** an examination or search by a scanner: *a brain scan*

scandal scandals
NOUN a situation or event that people think is shocking and immoral
scandalous ADJECTIVE

scanner scanners
NOUN **1.** a machine that is used to examine, identify, or record things by means of a beam of light or X-rays **2.** a machine that converts text or images into a form that can be stored on a computer

scant scanter scantest
ADJECTIVE If something receives scant attention, it does not receive enough attention.

scapegoat scapegoats
NOUN If someone is made a scapegoat, that person is blamed for something, although it may not be his or her fault.

scar scars scarring scarred
NOUN **1.** a mark left on your skin after a wound has healed **2.** a permanent effect on someone's mind that results from a very unpleasant experience: *the scars of war* VERB **3.** If an injury scars you, it leaves a

Ss

permanent mark on your skin. **4.** If an unpleasant experience scars you, it has a permanent effect on you.

scarce scarcer scarcest
ADJECTIVE If something is scarce, there is not very much of it.
scarcity NOUN

scarcely
ADVERB Scarcely means hardly: *I can scarcely hear her.*

scare scares scaring scared
VERB **1.** If something scares you, it frightens you.
NOUN **2.** If something gives you a scare, it scares you. **3.** If there is a scare about something, a lot of people are worried about it: *a food-contamination scare*
scared ADJECTIVE

scarecrow scarecrows
NOUN an object shaped like a person put in a field to scare birds away

scarf scarves
NOUN a piece of cloth worn around your neck or head to keep you warm

scarlet
NOUN OR ADJECTIVE bright red

scary scarier scariest
ADJECTIVE *an informal word* frightening

scathing
ADJECTIVE harsh and scornful: *scathing comments*

scatter scatters scattering scattered
VERB **1.** To scatter things means to throw or drop them all over an area. **2.** If people scatter, they suddenly move away in different directions.

scattering
NOUN A scattering of things is a small number of them spread over a large area: *a scattering of islands*

scavenge scavenges scavenging scavenged
VERB If you scavenge for things, you search for them among waste and garbage.
scavenger NOUN

scenario scenarios
NOUN **1.** The scenario of a movie or play is a summary of its plot. **2.** the way a situation could possibly develop in the future: *the worst possible scenario*

scene scenes
NOUN **1.** part of a play or movie in which a series of events happens in one place **2.** Pictures and views are sometimes called scenes: *a village scene* **3.** The scene of an event is the place where it happened. **4.** an area of activity: *the music scene*

scenery
NOUN **1.** You can refer to all the natural features of a place, for example mountains and lakes, as the scenery. **2.** In a theatre, the scenery is the painted background that represents where the action is happening.

scenic
ADJECTIVE A scenic place or route has nice views.

scent scents scenting scented
NOUN **1.** a smell, especially a pleasant one **2.** Scent is perfume.
VERB **3.** When an animal scents something, it becomes aware of it by smelling it.

sceptic another spelling of SKEPTIC

sceptre sceptres
NOUN an ornamental rod carried by a king or queen as a symbol of power

schedule schedules scheduling scheduled
NOUN **1.** a plan that gives a list of events or tasks, together with the times at which each thing should be done
VERB **2.** If something is scheduled to happen, it has been planned and arranged: *Their journey was scheduled for the end of May.*

schema schemata
NOUN **1.** *a technical word* an outline of a plan or theory **2.** a mental model that the mind uses to understand new experiences or to view the world

scheme schemes scheming schemed
NOUN **1.** a plan or arrangement: *a five-year development scheme*
VERB **2.** When people scheme, they make secret plans.

schism schisms
NOUN a split or division within a group or organization

schizophrenia
NOUN Schizophrenia is a serious mental illness that prevents someone from relating his or her thoughts and feelings to what is happening around him or her.
schizophrenic NOUN OR ADJECTIVE

scholar scholars
NOUN a person who studies an academic subject and knows a lot about it

scholarly
ADJECTIVE having or showing a lot of knowledge

scholarship scholarships
NOUN **1.** If you get a scholarship to a school or university, your studies are paid for by the school or university or by some other organization. **2.** Scholarship is academic study and knowledge.

 **! HEADS UP** The word **sceptre** is pronounced SEP-ter.

school schools schooling schooled
NOUN **1.** a place where children are educated **2.** University departments and colleges are sometimes called schools: *My oldest son is in medical school.* **3.** You can refer to a large group of dolphins or fish as a school.
VERB **4.** When someone is schooled in something, that person is taught it: *They were schooled in the modern techniques of dance.*

schoolchild schoolchildren
NOUN Schoolchildren are children who go to school.
schoolboy NOUN
schoolgirl NOUN

schooling
NOUN Your schooling is the education you get at school.

schooner schooners
NOUN a sailing ship

science sciences
NOUN **1.** Science is the study of the nature and behaviour of natural things and the knowledge obtained about them. **2.** a branch of science, for example physics or biology

science fiction
NOUN Stories about events happening in the future or in other parts of the universe are called science fiction.

scientific
ADJECTIVE **1.** relating to science or to a particular science: *scientific knowledge* **2.** done in a systematic way, using experiments or tests: *this scientific method*
scientifically ADVERB

scientist scientists
NOUN an expert in one of the sciences who does work connected with it

scintillating
ADJECTIVE lively and witty: *scintillating conversation*

scissors
PLURAL NOUN Scissors are a cutting tool with two sharp blades.

scoff scoffs scoffing scoffed
VERB **1.** If you scoff, you speak in a scornful, mocking way about something. **2.** *an informal use* If you scoff food, you eat it quickly and greedily.

scold scolds scolding scolded
VERB If you scold someone, you tell that person off.

scone scones
NOUN Scones are small cakes made from flour and fat and usually eaten with butter.

scoop scoops scooping scooped
VERB **1.** If you scoop something up, you pick it up using a spoon or the palm of your hand.
NOUN **2.** an object like a large spoon that is used for picking up food such as ice cream

scooter scooters
NOUN **1.** a small, light motorcycle **2.** a simple cycle that a child rides by standing on it and pushing the ground with one foot

scope
NOUN **1.** If there is scope for doing something, the opportunity to do it exists. **2.** The scope of something is the whole subject area that it deals with or includes.

-scope
SUFFIX The suffix *-scope* is used to form nouns that refer to an instrument used for observing or detecting: *microscope, telescope*

scorching
ADJECTIVE extremely hot: *another scorching summer*

score scores scoring scored
VERB **1.** If you score in a game, you get a goal, a run, a point, or points. **2.** To score in a game also means to record the score obtained by the players. **3.** If you score a success or victory, you achieve it. **4.** To score a surface means to cut a line into it.
NOUN **5.** The score in a game is the number of goals, runs, or points obtained by the two teams. **6.** Scores of things means very many of them: *Scores of people are coming to the party.* **7.** *an old-fashioned use* A score is 20 of something. **8.** The score of a piece of music is the written version of it.
scorer NOUN

scorn scorns scorning scorned
NOUN **1.** Scorn is great contempt: *a look of scorn*
VERB **2.** If you scorn someone, you treat that person with great contempt. **3.** *a formal use* If you scorn something, you refuse to accept it.

scornful
ADJECTIVE showing contempt: *his scornful comment*
scornfully ADVERB

scorpion scorpions
NOUN an animal that looks like a small lobster, with a long tail that has a poisonous sting on the end

scotch scotches
NOUN Scotch is a type of whisky.

scoundrel scoundrels
NOUN *an old-fashioned word* a man who cheats and deceives people

⚠ **HEADS UP** The c in **scintillating** is silent. It is pronounced SIN-tuh-late-ing.

Ss

scour scours scouring scoured
VERB **1.** If you scour a place, you look all over it in order to find something: *The police scoured the area for evidence.* **2.** If you scour something such as a pan, you clean it by rubbing it with something rough.

scourge scourges
NOUN something that causes a lot of suffering: *hay fever is the scourge of summer for many people*

scout scouts scouting scouted
NOUN **1.** someone who is sent to an area to find out the position of an enemy
VERB **2.** If you scout around for something, you look around for it.

scowl scowls scowling scowled
VERB **1.** If you scowl, you frown because you are angry: *They were scowling at me.*
NOUN **2.** an angry expression

scrabble scrabbles scrabbling scrabbled
VERB If you scrabble at something, you scrape at it with your hands or feet.

scramble scrambles scrambling scrambled
VERB **1.** If you scramble over something, you climb over it using your hands to help you.
NOUN **2.** a difficult climb over or up something

scrap scraps scrapping scrapped
NOUN **1.** A scrap of something is a very small piece of it: *a scrap of cloth*
PLURAL NOUN **2.** Scraps are pieces of leftover food.
ADJECTIVE OR NOUN **3.** Scrap metal or scrap is metal from old machinery or cars that can be reused.
VERB **4.** If you scrap something, you get rid of it: *They considered scrapping the skating program.*

scrapbook scrapbooks
NOUN a book in which you stick things such as pictures or newspaper articles

scrape scrapes scraping scraped
VERB **1.** If you scrape a surface, you rub a rough or sharp object against it. **2.** If something scrapes, it makes a harsh noise by rubbing against something: *the sound of nails scraping across a blackboard*

scratch scratches scratching scratched
VERB **1.** To scratch something means to make a small cut on it accidentally: *They were always getting scratched by cats.* **2.** If you scratch, you rub your skin with your nails because it is itching.
NOUN **3.** a small cut

scrawl scrawls scrawling scrawled
VERB **1.** If you scrawl something, you write it in a careless and untidy way.
NOUN **2.** You can refer to careless and untidy writing as a scrawl.

scrawny scrawnier scrawniest
ADJECTIVE thin and bony: *a small, scrawny dog*

scream screams screaming screamed
VERB **1.** If you scream, you shout or cry in a loud, high-pitched voice.
NOUN **2.** a loud, high-pitched cry

screech screeches screeching screeched
VERB **1.** To screech means to make an unpleasant, high-pitched noise: *The wheels screeched as the car turned the corner.*
NOUN **2.** an unpleasant, high-pitched noise

screen screens screening screened
NOUN **1.** a flat, vertical surface on which a picture is shown: *a television screen* **2.** a vertical panel used to separate different parts of a room or to protect something
VERB **3.** To screen a movie or television program means to show it. **4.** If you screen someone, you put something in front of that person to protect him or her.

screenplay screenplays
NOUN The screenplay of a movie is the script.

screw screws screwing screwed
NOUN **1.** a small, sharp piece of metal used for fixing things together or for fixing something to a wall
VERB **2.** If you screw things together, you fix them together using screws. **3.** If you screw something onto something else, you fix it there by twisting it around and around: *He screwed the top onto the juice bottle.*
screw up
VERB **4.** If you screw something up, you make a serious error: *She tried to draw the intricate pattern but screwed it up.*

screwdriver screwdrivers
NOUN a tool for turning screws

scribble scribbles scribbling scribbled
VERB **1.** If you scribble something, you write it quickly and roughly. **2.** To scribble also means to make meaningless marks: *When my sister was two she scribbled on a wall.*
NOUN **3.** You can refer to something written or drawn quickly and roughly as a scribble.

scrimp scrimps scrimping scrimped
VERB If you scrimp, you live cheaply and spend as little money as you can.

script scripts
NOUN the written version of a play or movie

scripture scriptures
NOUN Scripture refers to sacred writings, especially the Bible.
scriptural ADJECTIVE

Ss

scroll scrolls
NOUN a long roll of paper or parchment with writing on it

scrounge scrounges scrounging scrounged
VERB *an informal word* If you scrounge something, you get it by asking for it rather than by earning or buying it.
scrounger NOUN

scrub scrubs scrubbing scrubbed
VERB **1.** If you scrub something, you clean it with a stiff brush and water.
NOUN **2.** If you give something a scrub, you scrub it. **3.** Scrub consists of low trees and bushes.

scruff
NOUN The scruff of your neck is the back of your neck or collar.

scruffy scruffier scruffiest
ADJECTIVE dirty and untidy: *two scruffy youths*

scrum scrums
NOUN When rugby players form a scrum, they form a group and push against each other with their heads down in an attempt to get the ball.

scrunchie scrunchies
NOUN a loop of elastic loosely covered with material that is used to hold hair in a ponytail

scruple scruples
NOUN a moral principle that makes you unwilling to do something that seems wrong: *She had no scruples about keeping the money she found on the street.*

scrupulous
ADJECTIVE **1.** always doing what is honest or morally right **2.** paying very careful attention to detail: *a long and scrupulous search*
scrupulously ADVERB

scrutinize scrutinizes scrutinizing scrutinized
VERB If you scrutinize something, you examine it very carefully.

scrutiny
NOUN If something is under scrutiny, it is being observed very carefully.

scuba diving
NOUN Scuba diving is the sport of swimming underwater with tanks of compressed air on your back.

> ⚠ **HEADS UP**
>
> **Scuba** is an acronym for *self-contained underwater breathing apparatus.*
> Check out **radar** for more acronyms.

scuff scuffs scuffing scuffed
VERB **1.** If you scuff your feet, you drag them along the ground when you are walking. **2.** If you scuff your shoes, you mark them by scraping or rubbing them.

scuffle scuffles scuffling scuffled
NOUN **1.** a short, rough fight
VERB **2.** When people scuffle, they fight roughly.

sculpt sculpts sculpting sculpted
VERB When something is sculpted, it is carved or shaped in stone, wood, or clay.

sculptor sculptors
NOUN someone who makes sculptures

sculpture sculptures
NOUN **1.** a work of art produced by carving or shaping stone or clay **2.** Sculpture is the art of making sculptures.

scum
NOUN Scum is a layer of a dirty substance on the surface of a liquid.

scurrilous
ADJECTIVE abusive and damaging to someone's good name: *scurrilous stories*

scurry scurries scurrying scurried
VERB To scurry means to run quickly with short steps.

scurvy
NOUN Scurvy is a disease caused by a lack of vitamin C.

scuttle scuttles scuttling scuttled
VERB **1.** To scuttle means to run quickly. **2.** To scuttle a ship means to sink it deliberately by making holes in the bottom.
NOUN **3.** a container for coal

scythe scythes
NOUN a tool with a long handle and a curved blade used for cutting grass or grain

sea seas
NOUN **1.** The sea is the salty water that covers much of the earth's surface. **2.** A sea of people or things is a very large number of them: *a sea of Canadian flags*

seagull seagulls
NOUN a common white, grey, or black bird that usually lives near the water

seahorse seahorses
NOUN a small fish that swims upright, with a head that resembles a horse's head

seal seals sealing sealed
NOUN **1.** an official mark on a document which shows that it is genuine **2.** a device or substance that is used to fasten or close something tightly so that nothing can pass through it **3.** a large mammal with flippers, that lives partly on land and partly in the sea

VERB **4.** If you seal an envelope, you stick down the flap. **5.** If you seal an opening, you cover it securely so that air, gas, or liquid cannot get through.

sea lion sea lions
NOUN a type of large seal

seam seams
NOUN **1.** a line of stitches joining two pieces of cloth **2.** A seam of a mineral such as coal is a long, narrow layer of it beneath the ground.

seaman seamen
NOUN a sailor

séance séances
NOUN a meeting in which people try to communicate with the spirits of dead people

search searches searching searched
VERB **1.** If you search for something, you look for it in several places. **2.** If a person is searched, his or her body and clothing is examined to see if he or she is hiding anything.
NOUN **3.** an attempt to find something

search engine search engines
NOUN a service on the Internet that enables users to search for items of interest

searching
ADJECTIVE intended to discover the truth about something: *searching questions*

searchlight searchlights
NOUN a powerful light whose beam can be turned in different directions

searing
ADJECTIVE A searing pain is very sharp.

seashore
NOUN The seashore is the land along the edge of the sea.

seasick
ADJECTIVE feeling sick because of the movement of a boat
seasickness NOUN

seaside
NOUN The seaside is an area next to the sea.

season seasons seasoning seasoned
NOUN **1.** The seasons are the periods into which a year is divided and which have their own typical weather conditions. The seasons are spring, summer, autumn, and winter.
2. a period of the year when something usually happens: *the football season, the hunting season*
VERB **3.** If you season food, you add salt, pepper, or spices to it.

seasonal
ADJECTIVE happening during one season or one time of the year: *seasonal work*

seasoned
ADJECTIVE very experienced: *a seasoned professional*

seasoning
NOUN Seasoning is flavouring such as salt and pepper.

season ticket season tickets
NOUN a ticket that gives a person the right to attend a series of games or entertainments for a stated period of time

seat seats seating seated
NOUN **1.** something you can sit on **2.** The seat of a piece of clothing is the part that covers your bottom. **3.** If someone wins a seat in parliament, that person is elected.
VERB **4.** If you seat yourself somewhere, you sit down. **5.** If a place seats a particular number of people, it has enough seats for that number: *The new theatre can seat 570 people.*

seat belt seat belts
NOUN a strap that you fasten across your body for safety when travelling in a car or an aircraft

seating
NOUN The seating in a place is the number or arrangement of seats there.

seaweed
NOUN Plants that grow in the sea are called seaweed.

secluded
ADJECTIVE quiet and hidden from view: *a secluded beach*
seclusion NOUN

second seconds seconding seconded
ADJECTIVE **1.** The second item in a series is the one counted as number two.
NOUN **2.** one of the 60 parts that a minute is divided into
PLURAL NOUN **3.** Seconds are goods that are sold cheaply because they are slightly faulty.
VERB **4.** If you second a proposal, you formally agree with it so that it can be discussed or voted on. **5.** If you are seconded somewhere, you are sent there temporarily to work.
secondly ADVERB

secondary
ADJECTIVE **1.** Something that is secondary is less important than something else.
2. Secondary education is education for students after elementary school or junior high school.

secondary school secondary schools
NOUN a school that students attend after elementary school or junior high school

Ss

second-class
ADJECTIVE **1.** Second-class things are regarded as less important than other things of the same kind: *He has been treated as a second-class citizen.*
ADJECTIVE OR ADVERB **2.** Second-class services are cheaper and therefore slower or less comfortable than first-class ones.

second cousin second cousins
NOUN Your second cousins are the children of your parents' cousins.

second-hand
ADJECTIVE OR ADVERB **1.** Something that is second-hand has already been owned by someone else: *a second-hand car* **2.** If you hear a story second-hand, you hear it indirectly, rather than from the people involved.

second-rate
ADJECTIVE of poor quality: *a second-rate movie*

secret secrets
ADJECTIVE **1.** Something that is

Instead of **SECRET** try...

a **covert** attack
a **concealed** door
a **hidden** camera
a **confidential** file
a **closet** soap opera fan

secret is told to only a small number of people and hidden from everyone else: *a secret meeting*
NOUN **2.** a fact told to only a small number of people and hidden from everyone else
secretly ADVERB
secrecy NOUN

secret agent secret agents
NOUN a spy

secretary secretaries
NOUN **1.** a person employed by an organization to keep records, write letters, and do office work **2.** In some countries, ministers in charge of some government departments are also called secretaries: *the Secretary of State for Multiculturalism*
secretarial ADJECTIVE

secrete secretes secreting secreted
VERB **1.** When part of a plant or animal secretes a liquid, it produces it. **2.** *a formal use* If you secrete something somewhere, you hide it.
secretion NOUN

secretive
ADJECTIVE Secretive people tend to hide their feelings and intentions.

secret service
NOUN A country's secret service is the government department in charge of espionage.

sect sects
NOUN a religious or political group that has broken away from a larger group

sectarian
ADJECTIVE strongly supporting a particular sect: *sectarian rituals*

section sections
NOUN A section of something is one of the parts it is divided into: *this section of the highway*

sector sectors
NOUN **1.** A sector of something, especially a country's economy, is one part of it: *the private sector* **2.** A sector of a circle is one of the two parts formed when you draw two straight lines from the centre to the circumference.

secular
ADJECTIVE having no connection with religion: *secular education*

secure secures securing secured
VERB **1.** *a formal use* If you secure something, you manage to get it: *They secured the rights to her story.* **2.** If you secure a place, you make it safe from harm or attack.
3. To secure something also means to fasten it firmly: *One end of the boat was secured to the pier.*
ADJECTIVE **4.** If a place is secure, it is tightly locked or well protected. **5.** If an object is secure, it is firmly fixed in place. **6.** If you feel secure, you feel safe and confident.
securely ADVERB

security
NOUN OR ADJECTIVE **1.** Security means all the precautions taken to protect a place: *Security forces arrested one member of the gang.*
NOUN **2.** A feeling of security is a feeling of being safe.

sedate sedates sedating sedated
ADJECTIVE **1.** quiet and dignified
VERB **2.** To sedate someone means to give a drug to calm that person down or make him or her sleep.
sedately ADVERB

sedative sedatives
NOUN **1.** a drug that calms you down or makes you sleep
ADJECTIVE **2.** having a calming or soothing effect: *antihistamines that have a sedative effect*
sedation NOUN

Ss

sedentary

ADJECTIVE A sedentary occupation is one in which you spend most of your time sitting down.

sediment

NOUN **1.** Sediment is solid material that settles at the bottom of a liquid: *It is common for sediment to settle in the bottom of a jug of apple cider.* **2.** Sediment is also small particles of rock that have been worn down and deposited together by water, ice, and wind.

sedimentary

ADJECTIVE Sedimentary rocks are formed from fragments of shells or rocks that have become compressed. Sandstone and limestone are sedimentary rocks.

seduce seduces seducing seduced

VERB If you are seduced into doing something, you are persuaded to do it because it seems very attractive.

seductive

ADJECTIVE **1.** A seductive person is sexually attractive. **2.** Something seductive is very attractive and tempting.

seductively ADVERB

see sees seeing saw seen

VERB **1.** If you see something, you are looking at it or you notice it. **2.** If you see someone, you visit that person or meet him or her: *I went to see my dentist.* **3.** If you see someone to a place, you accompany that person there. **4.** To see something also means to realize or understand it: *I see what you mean.* **5.** If you say you will see what is happening, you mean you will find out. **6.** If you say you will see if you can do something, you mean you will try to do it. **7.** If you see that something is done, you make sure that it is done. **8.** If you see to something, you deal with it. **9.** *See* is used to say that an event takes place during a particular period of time: *The next couple of years saw two momentous developments.*

PHRASE **10.** *an informal use* **Seeing that** or **seeing as** means because: *I took my brother out for lunch, seeing as it was his birthday.*

seed seeds

NOUN **1.** The seeds of a plant are the small, hard parts from which new plants can grow. **2.** The seeds of a feeling or process are its beginning or origins: *the seeds of mistrust*

seedling seedlings

NOUN a young plant grown from a seed

seedy seedier seediest

ADJECTIVE untidy and shabby: *a seedy hotel*

seek seeks seeking sought

VERB *a formal word* **1.** To seek something means to try to find it, obtain it, or achieve it: *The police were still seeking information about the crime.* **2.** If you seek to do something, you try to do it: *The new prime minister sought to reunite the country.*

seem seems seeming seemed

VERB If something seems to be the case, it appears to be the case or you think it is the case: *He seemed such a quiet young man.*

seeming

ADJECTIVE appearing to be real or genuine: *this seeming disregard for human life*

seemingly ADVERB

seep seeps seeping seeped

VERB If a liquid or gas seeps through something, it flows through very slowly.

seesaw seesaws

NOUN a long plank, supported in the middle, on which two people sit, one on each end, and move up and down in turn

seething

ADJECTIVE If you are seething about something, you are very angry but it does not show.

segment segments

NOUN **1.** A segment of something is one part of it. **2.** The segments of something such as an orange are the sections that you can divide it into. **3.** A segment of a circle is one of the two parts formed when you draw a straight line across it.

KNOWING WORDS: IDIOMS

BE WORD SHARP!

Idioms add colour to language by playing with the meanings of words.

see view

as far as I can see in the way that I understand

see fit consider to be reasonable

see out/through finish

see to it ensure something happens

wait and see be patient until a later time

segregate segregates segregating segregated
VERB To segregate two groups of people means to keep them apart from each other.
segregated ADJECTIVE
segregation NOUN

seize seizes seizing seized
VERB **1.** If you seize something, you grab it firmly: *He seized the railing when he lost his balance.* **2.** To seize a place or to seize control of it means to take control of it quickly and suddenly. **3.** If you seize an opportunity, you take advantage of it. **4.** If you seize on something, you immediately show great interest in it: *MPs have seized on a new report.*

seizure seizures
NOUN **1.** a sudden, violent attack of an illness, especially a heart attack or an epileptic fit **2.** If there is a seizure of power, a group of people suddenly take control using force.

seldom

Instead of **SELDOM** try...

ADVERB
not very often:
They seldom speak to each other.

we rarely have time

not often talked about

I exercise sporadically

you hardly ever say so

they use it infrequently

select selects selecting selected
VERB **1.** If you select something, you choose it.
ADJECTIVE **2.** of good quality: *That store carries a select line of merchandise.*
selector NOUN

selection selections
NOUN **1.** Selection is the choosing of people or things: *the selection of student council candidates* **2.** A selection of people or things is a set of them chosen from a larger group. **3.** The selection of goods in a store is the range of goods available: *a good selection of jeans*

selective
ADJECTIVE choosing things carefully: *I am selective about what I eat.*
selectively ADVERB

self selves
NOUN Your self is your basic personality or nature: *My best friend is her normal, dependable self.*

self-
PREFIX **1.** The prefix *self-* means *done to*

yourself or *by yourself*: *self-help, self-control*
2. The prefix *self-* also means doing something automatically: *self-rising flour*

self-assured
ADJECTIVE behaving in a way that shows confidence in yourself

self-centred
ADJECTIVE thinking only about yourself and not about other people

self-confessed
ADJECTIVE admitting to having certain characteristics: *a self-confessed liar, a self-confessed chocolate addict*

self-confident
ADJECTIVE confident of your own abilities or worth
self-confidence NOUN

self-conscious
ADJECTIVE nervous and easily embarrassed, and worried about what other people think of you
self-consciously ADVERB

self-control
NOUN Self-control is the ability to restrain yourself and not show your feelings.

self-defence
NOUN Self-defence is the use of special physical techniques to protect yourself when someone attacks you.

self-employed
ADJECTIVE working for yourself and organizing your own finances, rather than working for an employer

self-esteem
NOUN Your self-esteem is your good opinion of yourself.

self-evident
ADJECTIVE Self-evident facts are completely obvious and need no proof or explanation.

self-indulgent
ADJECTIVE allowing yourself to do or have things you enjoy, especially as a treat

self-interest
NOUN If you do something out of self-interest, you do it for your own benefit rather than to help other people.

selfish
ADJECTIVE caring only about yourself, and not about other people
selfishly ADVERB
selfishness NOUN

selfless
ADJECTIVE putting other people's interests before your own

self-made
ADJECTIVE rich and successful through your own efforts: *a self-made millionaire*

self-respect

NOUN Self-respect is a feeling of confidence and pride in your own abilities and worth.

self-righteous

ADJECTIVE convinced that you are better or more virtuous than other people

self-righteousness NOUN

self-rising flour

ADJECTIVE Self-rising flour contains baking powder to make it rise.

self-serve

ADJECTIVE A self-serve business is one where you serve yourself: *a self-serve gas station*

self-sufficient

ADJECTIVE **1.** producing or making everything you need, and so not needing to buy things **2.** able to live such a way that you do not need other people

sell sells selling sold

VERB **1.** If you sell something, you let someone have it in return for money. **2.** If a store sells something, it has it available for people to buy: *This store sells several varieties of grapes.* **3.** If something sells, people buy it: *This book will sell.*

sell out

VERB **4.** If a store has sold out of something, it has sold it all.

seller NOUN

semblance

NOUN If there is a semblance of something, it seems to exist, although it might not really exist: *an effort to restore a semblance of normality*

semen

NOUN Semen is the liquid containing sperm produced by a man's or male animal's sex organs.

semi-

PREFIX The prefix *semi-* means *half* or *partly*: *semicircle, a semi-private room in a hospital*

semicircle semicircles

NOUN a half of a circle, or something with this shape

semicircular ADJECTIVE

semicolon semicolons

NOUN the punctuation mark (;), used to separate different parts of a sentence or to indicate a pause

semi-detached

ADJECTIVE A semi-detached house is joined to another house on one side.

semifinal semifinals

NOUN A semifinal is a match in a competition played to decide who plays in the final.

semifinalist NOUN

seminar seminars

NOUN a meeting of a small number of university students or teachers to discuss a particular topic

semipermeable

ADJECTIVE A semipermeable material is one that certain substances with small enough molecules can pass through but that others with larger molecules cannot.

semiprecious

ADJECTIVE Semiprecious stones are stones such as opals or turquoises that are used in jewellery. They are less valuable than precious stones.

semitone semitones

NOUN an interval representing the difference in pitch between a note and its sharpened or flattened equivalent. Two semitones are equal to one tone.

senate senates

NOUN A senate is a governing or lawmaking assembly. In Canada, the **Senate** is the upper branch of Parliament that consists of appointed senators.

senator senators

NOUN a member of a senate

send sends sending sent

VERB **1.** If you send something to someone, you arrange for it to be delivered to that person. **2.** To send a radio signal or message means to transmit it. **3.** If you send someone somewhere, you tell that person to go there or arrange for him or her to go. **4.** If you send for someone, you send a message asking that person to come and see you. **5.** If you send off for something, you write and ask for it to be sent to you. **6.** To send people or things in a particular direction means to make them move in that direction: *The bucking horse sent him tumbling from the saddle.*

senile

ADJECTIVE If elderly people become senile, they become confused and cannot look after themselves.

senility NOUN

senior seniors

ADJECTIVE **1.** The senior people in an organization or profession have the highest and most important jobs.

NOUN **2.** Someone who is your senior is older than you.

seniority NOUN

senior citizen senior citizens

NOUN a person who is 65 years of age or older

Ss

sensation sensations

NOUN **1.** a feeling, especially a physical feeling **2.** If something is a sensation, it causes great excitement and interest.

sensational

ADJECTIVE **1.** causing great excitement and interest **2.** extremely good: *a sensational party*

sensationally ADVERB

sense senses sensing sensed

NOUN **1.** Your senses are the physical abilities of sight, hearing, smell, touch, and taste. **2.** a feeling: *a sense of guilt* **3.** A sense of a word is one of its meanings. **4.** Sense is the ability to think and behave sensibly.

VERB **5.** If you sense something, you become aware of it.

PHRASE **6.** If something **makes sense**, you can understand it or it seems sensible: *It makes sense to find out as much as you can.*

senseless

ADJECTIVE **1.** A senseless action has no meaning or purpose: *senseless destruction* **2.** If someone is senseless, that person is unconscious.

sensibility sensibilities

NOUN Your sensibility is your ability to experience deep feelings: *a man of sensibility rather than reason*

sensible

ADJECTIVE showing good sense and judgment

sensibly ADVERB

sensitive

ADJECTIVE **1.** If you are sensitive to other people's feelings, you understand them. **2.** If you are sensitive about something, you are worried or easily upset about it: *He was sensitive about his height.* **3.** A sensitive subject or issue needs to be dealt with carefully because it can make people angry or upset. **4.** Someone who is sensitive to a particular thing is easily affected or harmed by it: *sensitive to perfume*

sensitively ADVERB

sensitivity NOUN

sensor sensors

NOUN an instrument that reacts to physical conditions such as light or heat

sensual

ADJECTIVE giving pleasure to your physical senses rather than to your mind: *the sensual pleasure of a massage*

sensuality NOUN

sensuous

ADJECTIVE giving pleasure through the senses

sensuously ADVERB

sentence sentences sentencing sentenced

NOUN **1.** a group of words that makes a statement, question, or command. When written down, a sentence begins with a capital letter and ends with a period, exclamation mark, or question mark. **2.** In a law court, a sentence is a punishment given to someone who has been found guilty of a crime.

VERB **3.** When a guilty person is sentenced, that person is told officially what his or her punishment will be.

sentiment sentiments

NOUN **1.** a feeling, attitude, or opinion: *I doubt my parents share my sentiments.* **2.** Sentiment consists of feelings or emotions: *The sympathy card expressed a very kind sentiment.*

sentimental

ADJECTIVE **1.** feeling or expressing tenderness or sadness to an exaggerated extent: *sentimental love stories* **2.** relating to a person's emotions: *things of sentimental value*

sentimentality NOUN

sentinel sentinels

NOUN *an old-fashioned word* a sentry

sentry sentries

NOUN a soldier who keeps watch and guards a camp or building

separate separates separating separated

ADJECTIVE **1.** If something is separate from something else, the two things are not connected.

VERB **2.** To separate people or things means to cause them to be apart from each other. **3.** If people or things separate, they move away from each other. **4.** If a married couple separate, they decide to live apart.

separately ADVERB

separation NOUN

sepia

ADJECTIVE OR NOUN deep brown, like the colour of old photographs

September

NOUN September is the ninth month of the year. It has 30 days.

septic

ADJECTIVE If a wound becomes septic, it becomes infected with harmful bacteria.

sepulchre sepulchres

NOUN *a literary or poetic word* a large tomb

sequel sequels

NOUN **1.** A sequel to a book or movie is another book or movie that continues the story. **2.** The sequel to an event is a result or consequence of it: *The sequel to the tsunami was widespread homelessness.*

⚠ **HEADS UP** The word **sepulchre** is pronounced SEP-uhl-kur.

sequence sequences

NOUN **1.** A sequence of events is a number of them coming one after the other: *the whole sequence of events that had brought me to this place* **2.** The sequence in which things are arranged is the order in which they are arranged: *Do things in the right sequence.*

sequin sequins

NOUN Sequins are small, shiny, coloured discs sewn on clothes to decorate them.

serenade serenades serenading serenaded

VERB **1.** If you serenade someone you love, you sing or play music to that person outside his or her window.

NOUN **2.** a song sung outside a person's window by someone who loves him or her

serene

ADJECTIVE peaceful and calm: *She had a serene air.*

serenely ADVERB

serenity NOUN

serf serfs

NOUN Serfs were servants in medieval Europe who had to work on their master's land and could not leave without his permission.

sergeant sergeants

NOUN **1.** in the Canadian armed forces, a non-commissioned officer of middle rank **2.** a police officer just above a constable in rank

sergeant major sergeant majors

NOUN a non-commissioned army officer of the highest rank

serial serials

NOUN a story that is broadcast or published in a number of parts over a period of time: *a television serial*

serial number serial numbers

NOUN An object's serial number is a number you can see on it, which identifies it and distinguishes it from other objects of the same kind.

series

NOUN **1.** A series of things is a number of them coming one after the other: *a series of loud explosions* **2.** A radio or television series is a set of programs with the same title.

serious

ADJECTIVE **1.** A serious problem or situation is very bad and worrying. **2.** Serious matters are important and should be thought about carefully. **3.** If you are serious about something, you are sincere about it: *She is really serious about learning to play the drums.* **4.** People who are serious are thoughtful and quiet.

seriousness NOUN

seriously

ADVERB **1.** You say *seriously* to emphasize that you mean what you say: *Seriously, though, something must be done.*

PHRASE **2.** If you **take something seriously**, you regard it as important.

sermon sermons

NOUN a talk on a religious or moral subject given as part of a church service

serpent serpents

NOUN a snake

serrated

ADJECTIVE having a row of V-shaped points along the edge, like a saw: *green, serrated leaves*

servant servants

NOUN someone who is employed to work in another person's house

serve serves serving served

VERB **1.** If you serve countries, organizations, or people, you do useful work for them. **2.** To serve as something means to act or be used as that thing: *the room that served as their office* **3.** If something serves people in a particular place, it provides them with something they need: *a recycling plant that serves the entire northern region of the province* **4.** If you serve food or drink to people, you give it to them. **5.** To serve customers in a store means to help them and provide them with what they want. **6.** To serve a prison sentence, an apprenticeship, or as a soldier means to spend time doing it. **7.** When you serve in some sports such as tennis or badminton, you throw the ball or shuttlecock into the air and hit it over the net to start playing.

NOUN **8.** the act of serving a ball or shuttlecock

server servers

NOUN a computer or computer program that supplies information or resources to a number of computers on a network

service services servicing serviced

NOUN **1.** a system organized to provide something for the public: *the bus service* **2.** If you give your services to an organization or to people, you work for them or help them in some way: *services to the community* **3.** In a store or restaurant, service is the process of being served. **4.** a religious ceremony **5.** When it is your service in a game such as tennis or badminton, it is your turn to serve.

VERB **6.** When a machine or vehicle is serviced, it is examined and adjusted so that it will continue working efficiently.

Ss

serviceman servicemen
NOUN a man in the army, navy, or air force
servicewoman NOUN

service station service stations
NOUN a place that sells gasoline, oil, spare parts, and snacks

servile
ADJECTIVE too eager to obey people
servility NOUN

serving servings
NOUN **1.** a helping of food
ADJECTIVE **2.** A serving spoon or dish is used for serving food.

session sessions
NOUN **1.** a meeting of an official group: *an emergency session of the Supreme Court* **2.** a period during which meetings are held regularly: *the end of the parliamentary session* **3.** The period during which an activity takes place can also be called a session: *a training session*

set sets setting set
NOUN **1.** Several things make a set when they belong together or form a group: *a set of weights* **2.** In mathematics a set is a collection of numbers or other things, that are treated as a group. **3.** a television set **4.** The set for a play or movie is the scenery or furniture on the stage or in the studio. **5.** In some sports such as tennis, a set is a group of six or more games. There are usually several sets in a match.
VERB **6.** If something is set somewhere, that is where it is: *The house was set back from the beach.* **7.** When the sun sets, it goes below the horizon. **8.** When you set the table, you prepare it for a meal by putting plates and cutlery on it. **9.** When you set a clock or a control, you adjust it to a particular point or position. **10.** If you set someone a piece of work or a target, you give it to that person to do or to achieve. **11.** When something such as jam or cement sets, it becomes firm or hard.
ADJECTIVE **12.** Something that is set is fixed and not varying: *a set fee* **13.** If you are set to do something, you are ready or likely to do it. **14.** If you are set on doing something, you are determined to do it. **15.** If a play or story is set at a particular time or in a particular place, the events in it take place at that time or in that place

set about
VERB **16.** If you set about doing something, you start doing it.

set back
VERB **17.** If something sets back a project or scheme, it delays it.

set off
VERB **18.** When you set off, you start a journey. **19.** To set something off means to cause it to detonate.

set out
VERB **20.** When you set out, you start a journey. **21.** If you set out to do something, you start trying to do it.

set up
VERB **22.** If you set something up, you make all the necessary preparations for it: *We have done all we can to set up a system of communication.*

setback setbacks
NOUN something that delays or hinders you

settee settees
NOUN a long, comfortable seat for two or three people to sit on

setter setters
NOUN a long-haired breed of dog originally used in hunting

setting settings
NOUN **1.** The setting of something is its surroundings or circumstances: *The setting of the novel in a dark castle made the story very scary.* **2.** The settings on a machine are the different positions to which the controls can be adjusted.

settle settles settling settled
VERB **1.** To settle an argument means to put an end to it: *The dispute was settled.* **2.** If something is settled, it has all been decided and arranged. **3.** If you settle on something or settle for it, you choose it: *We settled for orange juice and pancakes.* **4.** When you settle a bill, you pay it. **5.** If you settle in a place, you make it your permanent home. **6.** If you settle yourself somewhere, you sit down and make yourself comfortable. **7.** If something settles, it sinks slowly down and comes to rest: *A black dust settled on the desk.*

settle down
VERB **8.** When someone settles down, that person starts living a quiet life in one place, especially when he or she gets married. **9.** To settle down means to become quiet or calm.

settlement settlements
NOUN **1.** an official agreement between people who have been involved in a conflict: *the last chance for a peaceful settlement* **2.** a place where people have settled and built homes

settler settlers
NOUN someone who settles in a new country: *the first settlers in Québec*

seven sevens
NOUN the number 7

seventeen
NOUN the number 17
seventeenth ADJECTIVE, ADVERB

seventh sevenths
ADJECTIVE, ADVERB **1.** The seventh item in a series is the one counted as number seven. NOUN **2.** one of seven equal parts

seventy seventies
NOUN the number 70
seventieth ADJECTIVE, ADVERB

sever severs severing severed
VERB **1.** To sever something means to cut it off or cut right through it. **2.** If you sever a connection with someone or something, you end it completely: *She severed her ties with her childhood friends.*

several
ADJECTIVE Several people or things means a small number of them.

severe

Instead of **SEVERE** try...

dire consequences
a **critical** injury
a **violent** storm
an **acute** fever
a **grave** illness
pitiless weather
morbid obesity
grim depression

ADJECTIVE
1. extremely bad or unpleasant: *severe stomach pains* **2.** stern and harsh: *I think she was too severe with that young man.*
severely ADVERB
severity NOUN

sew sews sewing sewed sewn
VERB When you sew things together, you join them using a needle and thread.
sewing NOUN

sewage
NOUN Sewage is dirty water and waste that is carried away in sewers.

sewer sewers
NOUN an underground channel that carries off sewage

sex sexes
NOUN **1.** The sexes are the two groups, male and female, into which people and animals are divided. **2.** The sex of a person or animal is the characteristic of being either male or female. **3.** Sex is the physical activity by which people and animals produce young.

sexism
NOUN Sexism is discrimination against the members of one sex, usually women.
sexist ADJECTIVE OR NOUN

sextet sextets
NOUN a group of six musicians who sing or play together; also a piece of music written for six instruments or singers

sextuplet sextuplets
NOUN Sextuplets are six children born at the same time to the same mother.

sexual
ADJECTIVE **1.** connected with the act of sex or with people's desire for sex: *sexual attraction* **2.** relating to the difference between males and females: *sexual equality* **3.** relating to the biological process by which people and animals produce young: *sexual reproduction*
sexually ADVERB

sexual intercourse
NOUN Sexual intercourse is the physical act of sex between two people.

sexuality
NOUN A person's sexuality is his or her ability to experience sexual feelings.

sexy sexier sexiest
ADJECTIVE sexually attractive or exciting: *a sexy dress, a sexy sports car*

shabby shabbier shabbiest
ADJECTIVE **1.** old and worn in appearance: *a shabby overcoat* **2.** dressed in old, worn-out clothes: *a shabby figure crouching in a doorway* **3.** behaving in a mean or unfair way: *shabby treatment*
shabbily ADVERB

shack shacks
NOUN a roughly built or poorly maintained hut, cabin, or house

shackle shackles shackling shackled
PLURAL NOUN **1.** Shackles are two metal rings joined by a chain fastened around a prisoner's wrists or ankles.
VERB **2.** To shackle someone means to put shackles on that person. **3.** *a literary or poetic use* If you are shackled by something, it restricts or hampers you.

shade shades shading shaded
NOUN **1.** Shade is an area of darkness and coolness that the sun does not reach: *The table was in the shade.* **2.** a lampshade **3.** The shades of a colour are its different forms. For example, olive green is a shade of green.
VERB **4.** If a place is shaded by trees or buildings, they prevent the sun from shining on it. **5.** If you shade your eyes, you put your hand in front of them to protect them from a bright light.

Ss

shadow shadows shadowing shadowed
NOUN **1.** the dark shape made when an object prevents light from reaching a surface
2. Shadow is darkness caused by light not reaching a place.
VERB **3.** To shadow someone means to follow that person and watch him or her closely.

shadow cabinet
NOUN The shadow cabinet consists of the leaders of the main opposition party, each of whom is concerned with a particular ministry.

shadowy
ADJECTIVE **1.** A shadowy place is dark and full of shadows. **2.** A shadowy figure or shape is difficult to see because it is dark or misty.

shady shadier shadiest
ADJECTIVE A shady place is sheltered from sunlight by trees or buildings.

shaft shafts
NOUN **1.** a vertical passage, for example one for an elevator or one in a mine **2.** A shaft of light is a beam of light. **3.** A shaft in a machine is a rod that revolves and transfers movement in the machine: *the drive shaft*

shaggy shaggier shaggiest
ADJECTIVE Shaggy hair or fur is long and untidy.

shake shakes shaking shook shaken
VERB **1.** To shake something means to move it quickly from side to side or up and down.
2. If something shakes, it moves from side to side or up and down with small, quick movements. **3.** If your voice shakes, it trembles because you are nervous or angry.
4. If something shakes you, it shocks and upsets you. **5.** When you shake your head, you move it from side to side in order to say *no.*
NOUN **6.** If you give something a shake, you shake it.
PHRASE **7.** When you **shake hands** with someone, you grasp that person's hand as a way of greeting him or her.

shaky shakier shakiest
ADJECTIVE weak and unsteady: *Confidence in the economy is still shaky.*
shakily ADVERB

shall
VERB **1.** If I say I shall do something, I mean that I intend to do it. **2.** If I say something shall happen, I am emphasizing that it will definitely happen, or I am ordering it to happen: *You shall listen to my instructions.*
3. *Shall* is also used in questions when you are asking what to do, or making a suggestion: *Shall we sit down? Shall I go and check for you?*

shallow shallower shallowest; shallows
ADJECTIVE **1.** Shallow means not deep.
2. Shallow also means not involving serious thought or sincere feelings: *a shallow mind*
PLURAL NOUN **3.** The shallows are the shallow part of a river or lake.

sham shams

Instead of **SHAM** try…

imitation jewellery
a phony wedding
a bogus excuse
a mock test
a dummy copy
feigned curiosity
a forged document
an artificial account

NOUN **1.** Something that is a sham is not real or genuine.
ADJECTIVE **2.** not real or genuine: *a sham display of affection*

shambles
NOUN If an event is a shambles, it is confused and badly organized.

shame shames shaming shamed
NOUN **1.** Shame is the feeling of guilt or embarrassment you get when you know you have done something foolish or wrong.
2. Shame is also something that makes people lose respect for you: *Their violent behaviour on ice brought shame to the team.*
3. If you say something is a shame, you mean you are sorry about it: *It's a shame you can't come to visit.*
VERB **4.** If something shames you, it makes you feel ashamed. **5.** If you shame someone into doing something, you force that person to do it by making him or her feel ashamed not to: *The two children shamed their parents into giving up smoking.*

shameful
ADJECTIVE If someone's behaviour is shameful, that person ought to be ashamed of his or her behaviour.
shamefully ADVERB

shameless
ADJECTIVE behaving in an indecent or unacceptable way, but showing no shame: *shameless dishonesty*
shamelessly ADVERB

shampoo shampoos shampooing shampooed
NOUN **1.** Shampoo is a soapy liquid used for

washing your hair.
VERB **2.** When you shampoo your hair, you wash it with shampoo.

shamrock shamrocks
NOUN a plant with three round leaves on each stem, which is the national emblem of Ireland

shanghai shanghais shanghaiing shanghaied
an informal word
VERB **1.** If someone is shanghaied, that person is kidnapped and forced to work on a ship. **2.** If you shanghai someone, you trick or force that person into doing something.

shanty shanties
NOUN **1.** a small, roughly built hut or cabin **2.** A sea shanty is a song sailors used to sing.

shape shapes shaping shaped
NOUN **1.** The shape of something is the form or pattern of its outline, for example whether it is round or square. **2.** something with a definite form, for example a circle or triangle **3.** The shape of something such as an organization is its structure and size.
VERB **4.** If you shape an object, you form it into a particular shape: *Shape the clay into balls.* **5.** To shape something means to cause it to develop in a particular way: *events that shaped his life*

shapeless
ADJECTIVE not having a definite shape

shapely shapelier shapeliest
ADJECTIVE If someone or something is shapely, that person or thing has a pleasing shape.

shard shards
NOUN a small fragment of pottery, glass, or metal

share shares sharing shared
VERB **1.** If two people share something, they both use it, do it, or have it: *We shared a textbook in math class.* **2.** If you share an idea or a piece of news with someone, you tell it to that person.
NOUN **3.** A share of something is a portion of it. **4.** The shares of a company are the equal parts into which its ownership is divided. People can buy shares as an investment.

shareholder shareholders
NOUN a person who owns shares in a company

shark sharks
NOUN **1.** Sharks are large, powerful fish with sharp teeth. **2.** a person who cheats people out of money

sharp sharper sharpest; sharps
ADJECTIVE **1.** A sharp object has a fine edge or point that is good for cutting or piercing things. **2.** A sharp outline or distinction is easy to see. **3.** A sharp person is quick to notice or understand things. **4.** A sharp change is sudden and significant: *a sharp rise in prices* **5.** If you say something in a sharp way, you say it firmly and rather angrily. **6.** A sharp sound is short, sudden, and quite loud. **7.** A sharp pain is sudden and painful. **8.** A sharp taste is slightly sour. **9.** A musical instrument or note that is sharp is slightly too high in pitch.
ADVERB **10.** If something happens at a certain time sharp, it happens at that time precisely: *You'll begin at eight o'clock sharp.*
NOUN **11.** In music, a sharp is a note or key a semitone higher than that described by the same letter. It is represented by the symbol (♯).
sharply ADVERB
sharpness NOUN

sharpen sharpens sharpening sharpened
VERB **1.** To sharpen an object means to make its edge or point sharper. **2.** If your senses or abilities sharpen, you become quicker at noticing or understanding things.
sharpener NOUN

shatter shatters shattering shattered
VERB **1.** If something shatters, it breaks into a lot of small pieces. **2.** If something shatters your hopes or beliefs, it destroys them completely. **3.** If you are shattered by an event or piece of news, you are shocked and upset by it.

shattering
ADJECTIVE making you feel shocked and upset: *a shattering event*

shave shaves shaving shaved
VERB **1.** When someone shaves, that person removes hair from the face or another part of the body with a razor. **2.** If you shave off part of a piece of wood, you cut thin pieces from it
NOUN **3.** When someone has a shave, that person shaves hair from the face or another part of the body.

shaven
ADJECTIVE If part of someone's body is shaven, it has been shaved: *a shaven head*

shaver shavers
NOUN an electric razor

shaving
NOUN A shaving is a small, very thin piece of wood that has been cut from a larger piece.

shawl shawls
NOUN a large piece of cloth worn around the head or shoulders

she
PRONOUN *She* is used to refer to a woman or girl whose identity is clear.

sheaf sheaves
NOUN **1.** A sheaf is a bundle of cut grain that is tied in the middle for drying, loading, and stacking. **2.** A sheaf is a bundle of things that are alike: *a sheaf of papers*

shear shears shearing sheared shorn
VERB **1.** To shear a sheep means to cut the wool off it.
PLURAL NOUN **2.** Shears are a tool like a large pair of scissors: *kitchen shears, grass shears*

shearer shearers
NOUN someone whose job is to shear sheep

sheath sheaths
NOUN a covering for the blade of a knife

shed sheds shedding shed
NOUN **1.** a small building used for storing things
VERB **2.** When an animal sheds hair or skin, some of its hair or skin drops off. When a tree sheds its leaves, its leaves fall off. **3.** If you shed tears, you cry.

sheen
NOUN a gentle brightness on the surface of something

sheep
NOUN A sheep is a farm animal with a thick, woolly coat. Sheep are kept for meat and wool.

sheep dip sheep dips
NOUN a liquid disinfectant used to keep sheep clean and free of pests

sheepdog sheepdogs
NOUN a breed of dog often used for controlling sheep

sheepish
ADJECTIVE If you look sheepish, you look embarrassed because you feel shy or foolish.
sheepishly ADVERB

sheepskin
NOUN Sheepskin is the skin and wool of a sheep, used for making rugs and coats.

sheer sheerer sheerest
ADJECTIVE **1.** Sheer means complete and total: *sheer exhaustion* **2.** A sheer cliff or drop is vertical. **3.** Sheer fabrics are very light and delicate.

sheet sheets
NOUN **1.** a large, rectangular piece of cloth used to cover a bed **2.** A sheet of paper is a rectangular piece of it. **3.** A sheet of glass or metal is a large, flat piece of it.

shelf shelves
NOUN a flat piece of wood, metal, or glass fixed to a wall and used for putting things on

shell shells shelling shelled
NOUN **1.** The shell of an egg or nut is its hard covering. **2.** The shell of an animal such as a tortoise, snail, or crab is the hard, protective covering on its back. **3.** The shell of a building or other structure is its frame: *The room was just an empty shell.* **4.** a container filled with explosives that can be fired from a gun
VERB **5.** If you shell peas or nuts, you remove their natural covering. **6.** To shell a place means to fire large explosive shells at it.

shellfish shellfish
NOUN a small sea creature with a shell

shelter shelters sheltering sheltered
NOUN **1.** a small building made to protect people from bad weather or danger **2.** If a place provides shelter, it provides protection from bad weather or danger.
VERB **3.** If you shelter in a place, you stay there and are safe. **4.** If you shelter someone, you provide that person with a place to stay when he or she is in danger.

sheltered
ADJECTIVE **1.** A sheltered place is protected from wind and rain. **2.** If you lead a sheltered life, you do not experience unpleasant or upsetting things.

shelve shelves shelving shelved
VERB If you shelve a plan, you decide to postpone it for a while.

shepherd shepherds shepherding shepherded
NOUN **1.** a person who looks after sheep
VERB **2.** If you shepherd someone somewhere, you accompany that person there.

sheriff sheriffs
NOUN In the US, a sheriff is a person elected to enforce the law in a county.

sherry sherries
NOUN Sherry is a kind of strong wine.

shield shields shielding shielded
NOUN **1.** a large piece of a strong material like metal or plastic that soldiers or police carry to protect themselves **2.** If something is a shield against something, it gives protection from it.
VERB **3.** To shield someone means to protect that person from something.

shift shifts shifting shifted
VERB **1.** If you shift something, you move it. If something shifts, it moves: *to shift the rubble* **2.** If an opinion or situation shifts, it changes slightly.

NOUN **3.** A shift in an opinion or situation is a slight change. **4.** a set period during which people work: *the night shift*

shimmer shimmers shimmering shimmered
VERB **1.** If something shimmers, it shines with a faint, flickering light.
NOUN **2.** a faint, flickering light

shin shins
NOUN Your shin is the front part of your leg between your knee and your ankle.

shine shines shining shone

Instead of **SHINING** try…

VERB **1.** When something shines, it gives out or reflects a bright light: *The stars shone brilliantly.* **2.** If you shine a flashlight or light somewhere, you point it there.

glittering eyes
a *glowing* lantern
sparkling sunlight
gleaming headlights
the *shimmering* lake

shingle shingles
NOUN **1.** Shingles are thin pieces of asphalt, wood, or clay used to cover roofs. **2.** Shingle consists of small pebbles on the seashore. **3.** Shingles is a disease that causes a painful red rash, especially around the waist.

shining
ADJECTIVE **1.** Shining things are very bright, usually because they are reflecting light: *shining stainless steel tables* **2.** A shining example of something is a very good or typical example of that thing: *a shining example of courage*

shinny shinnies
NOUN a simple kind of hockey played on the ice with skates, or without skates on the street or in a field, sometimes with a ball instead of a puck

shiny shinier shiniest
ADJECTIVE Shiny things are bright and look as if they have been polished: *a shiny brass plate*

ship ships shipping shipped
NOUN **1.** a large boat that carries passengers or cargo
VERB **2.** If people or things are shipped somewhere, they are transported there.

-ship
SUFFIX The suffix *-ship* is used to form nouns that refer to a condition or position: *fellowship, partnership*

shipment shipments
NOUN **1.** a quantity of goods that are transported somewhere: *a shipment of olive oil* **2.** The shipment of goods is the transporting of them.

shipping
NOUN **1.** Shipping is the transport of cargo on ships. **2.** You can also refer to ships generally as shipping: *There is a lot of shipping in the harbour.*

shipwreck shipwrecks
NOUN When there is a shipwreck, a ship is destroyed in an accident at sea: *He was drowned in a shipwreck.*

shipyard shipyards
NOUN a place where ships are built and repaired

shirk shirks shirking shirked
VERB To shirk a task means to avoid doing it.

shirt shirts
NOUN a piece of clothing worn on the upper part of the body, having a collar, sleeves, and buttons down the front

shiver shivers shivering shivered
VERB **1.** When you shiver, you tremble slightly because you are cold or scared.
NOUN **2.** a slight trembling caused by cold or fear

shoal shoals
NOUN **1.** A shoal is a place in a body of water where the water is shallow. **2.** A shoal of fish is a large group of them swimming together.

shock shocks shocking shocked
NOUN **1.** If you have a shock, you have a sudden, upsetting experience. **2.** Shock is a person's emotional and physical condition when something very unpleasant or upsetting has happened to him or her. **3.** In medicine, shock is a serious physical condition in which the blood cannot circulate properly because of an injury. **4.** a slight movement in something when it is hit by something else: *The straps help to absorb shocks.* **5.** A shock of hair is a thick mass of it.
VERB **6.** If something shocks you, it upsets you because it is unpleasant and unexpected: *I was shocked by his appearance.* **7.** You can say that something shocks you when it offends you because it is disgusting or immoral.
shocked ADJECTIVE

shock absorber shock absorbers
NOUN Shock absorbers are devices fitted near the wheels of a motor vehicle. They help to prevent the vehicle from bouncing up and down.

shocking
ADJECTIVE **1.** very bad: *It's been a shocking year.* **2.** disgusting or immoral: *a shocking event*

shoddy shoddier shoddiest
ADJECTIVE badly made or done: *a shoddy piece of work*

shoe shoes shoeing shod
NOUN **1.** Shoes are strong coverings for your feet. They cover most of your foot, but not your ankle.
VERB **2.** To shoe a horse means to fix horseshoes onto its hoofs.

shoestring
NOUN *an informal word* If you do something on a shoestring, you do it using very little money.

shoot shoots shooting shot
VERB **1.** To shoot people or animals means to kill or injure them by firing a gun at them. **2.** To shoot an arrow means to fire it from a bow. **3.** If something shoots in a particular direction, it moves there quickly and suddenly: *They shot back into the yard.* **4.** When a movie is shot, it is filmed: *The whole movie was shot in Vancouver.* **5.** In some sports, to shoot means to kick or hit the ball or puck toward the goal.
NOUN **6.** an occasion when people hunt animals or birds with guns **7.** a plant that is beginning to grow, or a new part growing from a plant

shooting shootings
NOUN an incident in which someone is shot

shooting star shooting stars
NOUN a meteor

shop shops shopping shopped
NOUN **1.** a place where things are sold **2.** a place where a particular type of work is done: *a bicycle repair shop*
VERB **3.** When you shop, you go to a store or stores to buy things.
shopper NOUN

shopkeeper shopkeepers
NOUN someone who manages a small store

shoplifting
NOUN Shoplifting is stealing goods from stores.
shoplifter NOUN

shopping
NOUN the action of buying goods from a store

shop steward shop stewards
NOUN a trade union member elected to represent fellow workers, usually in a factory or office

shore shores shoring shored
NOUN **1.** The shore of a body of water is the land along the edge of it.
VERB **2.** If you shore something up, you reinforce it or strengthen it: *a post to shore up the ceiling during the renovation*

shoreline shorelines
NOUN the edge of a body of water, where land and water meet

shorn
1. Shorn is the past participle of SHEAR.
ADJECTIVE **2.** Grass or hair that is shorn is cut very short.

short shorter shortest; shorts
ADJECTIVE **1.** not lasting very long **2.** small in length, distance, or height: *a short climb, the short road* **3.** not using many words: *a short speech* **4.** If you are short with someone, you speak to that person in an abrupt way. **5.** If you have a short temper, you get angry very quickly. **6.** If you are short of something, you do not have enough of it. **7.** If a name is short for another name, it is a short version of it.
PLURAL NOUN **8.** Shorts are pants with short legs.
ADVERB **9.** If you stop short of a place, you do not quite reach it.
PHRASE **10. Short of** is used to say that a level or amount has not quite been reached: *a few votes short of a majority*

KNOWING WORDS: IDIOMS

BE WORD SHARP!

Idioms add colour to language by playing with the meanings of words.

short not long

caught short be unexpectedly unprepared

cut short stop suddenly

fall short fail to reach an expected goal

make short work of deal with quickly

sell yourself short not give yourself due credit

Ss

shortage shortages

NOUN If there is a shortage of something, there is not enough of it.

shortbread

NOUN Shortbread is a rich cookie made from flour, butter, and sugar.

short-circuit short-circuits

NOUN a fault in an electrical system when two points accidentally become connected and the electricity travels directly between them rather than through the complete circuit

shortcoming shortcomings

NOUN Shortcomings are faults or weaknesses.

shortcut shortcuts

NOUN **1.** a quicker way of getting somewhere than the usual route **2.** a quicker way of doing something: *Stencils have been used as a shortcut to hand-painting letters on signs.*

shorten shortens shortening shortened

VERB If you shorten something or if it shortens, it becomes shorter: *This might help to shorten the conversation.*

shortfall shortfalls

NOUN If there is a shortfall in something, there is less than you need.

shorthand

NOUN Shorthand is a way of writing in which signs represent words or syllables. It is used to write down quickly what someone is saying.

short list short lists

NOUN a list of people selected from a larger group, from which one person is finally selected for a job or prize

shortlist shortlists shortlisting shortlisted

VERB If someone is shortlisted for a job or prize, that person is put on a list of people selected from a larger group, from which one person is finally selected.

shortly

ADVERB **1.** Shortly means soon: *I'll be back shortly.* **2.** If you speak to someone shortly, you speak to that person in an abrupt and impatient way.

short-sighted

ADJECTIVE **1.** If you are short-sighted, you cannot see things clearly when they are far away. **2.** A short-sighted decision does not take into account the way things may develop in the future.

short-term

ADJECTIVE happening or having an effect within a short time or for a short time

shot shots

1. Shot is the past tense and past participle of SHOOT.

NOUN **2.** the act of firing a gun **3.** Someone who is a good shot can shoot accurately. **4.** In some sports, a shot is the act of kicking or hitting the ball or puck. **5.** a photograph or short film sequence: *I'd like to get some shots of the river.* **6.** *an informal use* If you have a shot at something, you try to do it.

shotgun shotguns

NOUN a gun that fires a lot of small pellets all at once

shot put

NOUN In athletics, the shot put is an event in which the contestants throw a heavy metal ball called a shot as far as possible.

shot putter NOUN

should

VERB **1.** You use *should* to say that something ought to happen: *He should have done better.* **2.** You also use *should* to say that you expect something to happen: *She should have heard from her friend by now.* **3.** *a formal use* You can use *should* to announce that you are about to do or say something: *I should like to express my thanks to my family.* **4.** *Should* is used in conditional sentences: *If they should discover the fact, what use would the knowledge be to them?* **5.** *Should* is sometimes used in *that* clauses: *It is inevitable that you should go.* **6.** If you say that you should think something, you mean that it is probably true: *I should think that's unlikely.*

shoulder shoulders shouldering shouldered

NOUN **1.** Your shoulders are the parts of your body between your neck and the tops of your arms.

VERB **2.** If you shoulder something heavy, you put it across one of your shoulders to carry it. **3.** If you shoulder the responsibility or blame for something, you accept it.

shoulder blade shoulder blades

NOUN Your shoulder blades are the two large, flat bones in the upper part of your back, below your shoulders.

shout shouts shouting shouted

NOUN **1.** a loud call or cry

VERB **2.** If you shout something, you say it very loudly: *He shouted something to me.*

shove shoves shoving shoved

VERB **1.** If you shove someone or something, you push that person or thing roughly: *She shoved her wallet into her coat pocket.*

NOUN **2.** a rough push

shove off

VERB **3.** *an informal use* If you tell someone to shove off, you are telling that person angrily and rudely to go away.

shovel shovels shovelling shovelled
  NOUN **1.** a tool with a long handle and a curved blade, used for moving earth or snow
  VERB **2.** If you shovel earth or snow, you move it with a shovel.

show shows showing showed shown
  VERB **1.** To show that something exists or is true means to prove it: *The survey showed that 29 percent would now approve the treaty.* **2.** If a picture shows something, it represents it: *The painting shows a crowd scene on a busy street.* **3.** If you show someone something, you let that person see it: *Show me your passport.* **4.** If you show someone to a room or seat, you lead that person there. **5.** If you show someone how to do something, you demonstrate it to that person. **6.** If something shows, it is visible. **7.** If something shows a quality or characteristic, you can see that it has it: *Her sketches and watercolours showed promise.* **8.** If you show your feelings, you let people see them: *She was flustered, but too proud to show it.* **9.** If you show affection or mercy, you behave in an affectionate or merciful way: *the first person who showed me some affection* **10.** To show a movie or television program means to let the public see it.
  NOUN **11.** a form of entertainment at the theatre or on television **12.** an exhibition: *an antiques show* **13.** A show of a feeling or attitude is behaviour in which you show it: *a show of optimism*
  PHRASE **14.** If something is **on show**, it is being exhibited for the public to see.

show off
  VERB **15.** *an informal use* If someone is showing off, that person is trying to impress people.

show up
  VERB **16.** *an informal use* If you show up, you arrive at a place where you are expected. **17.** If something shows up, it can be seen clearly: *The engraving on her ring barely shows up.*

show business
  NOUN Show business is theatre, movies, television, and music considered as a profession or industry.

showdown showdowns
  NOUN *an informal word* a major argument or conflict intended to end a dispute

shower showers showering showered
  NOUN **1.** a device that sprays you with water so that you can wash yourself **2.** If you have a shower, you wash yourself by standing under a shower. **3.** a short period of rain **4.** You can refer to a lot of things falling at once as a shower: *a shower of confetti*
  VERB **5.** If you shower, you have a shower. **6.** If you are showered with a lot of things, they fall on you or are given to you.

showing showings
  NOUN A showing of a movie or television program is a presentation of it so that the public can see it.

show jumping
  NOUN Show jumping is a horse-riding competition in which the horses jump over a series of high fences.

show-off show-offs
  NOUN *an informal word* someone who tries to impress people with his or her knowledge or skills

showroom showrooms
  NOUN a store where goods such as cars or electrical appliances are displayed

showy showier showiest
  ADJECTIVE large or bright and intended to impress people: *a showy house*

shrapnel
  NOUN Shrapnel consists of small pieces of metal scattered from an exploding shell.

shred shreds shredding shredded
  VERB **1.** If you shred something, you cut or tear it into very small pieces.
  NOUN **2.** A shred of paper or material is a small, narrow piece of it. **3.** If there is not

KNOWING WORDS: IDIOMS

BE WORD SHARP!

Idioms add colour to language by playing with the meanings of words.

show display

for show not practical, for effect only

goes to show you proves that something is true

run the show be in charge

show your face go somewhere despite embarrassment

steal the show take the attention away from others

NEL

a shred of something, there is absolutely none of it: *He was left without a shred of self-esteem.*

shrew shrews
NOUN a small, mouselike animal with a long, pointed nose

shrewd shrewder shrewdest
ADJECTIVE Someone who is shrewd is intelligent and makes good judgments.
shrewdly ADVERB
shrewdness NOUN

shriek shrieks shrieking shrieked
NOUN **1.** a high-pitched scream
VERB **2.** If you shriek, you make a high-pitched scream.

shrift
NOUN If you give someone or something short shrift, you pay very little attention to that person or thing.

shrill shriller shrillest
ADJECTIVE A shrill sound is unpleasantly high-pitched and piercing.
shrilly ADVERB

shrimp shrimps
NOUN a small, edible shellfish with a long tail and many legs

shrine shrines
NOUN a place of worship associated with a sacred person or object

shrink shrinks shrinking shrank shrunk
VERB **1.** If something shrinks, it becomes smaller. **2.** If you shrink from something, you move away from it because you are afraid of it.
shrinkage NOUN

shrivel shrivels shrivelling shrivelled
VERB When something shrivels, it becomes dry and withered.

shroud shrouds shrouding shrouded
NOUN **1.** a cloth in which a dead body is wrapped before it is buried
VERB **2.** If something is shrouded in darkness or fog, it is hidden by it.

shrub shrubs
NOUN a low, bushy plant

shrug shrugs shrugging shrugged
VERB **1.** If you shrug your shoulders, you raise them slightly as a sign of indifference.
NOUN **2.** If you give a shrug of your shoulders, you shrug them.

shrunken
ADJECTIVE *a formal use* Someone or something that is shrunken has become smaller than it used to be: *a shrunken elderly man*

shudder shudders shuddering shuddered
VERB **1.** If you shudder, you tremble with fear or horror. **2.** If a machine or vehicle shudders, it shakes violently.
NOUN **3.** a shiver of fear or horror

shuffle shuffles shuffling shuffled
VERB **1.** If you shuffle, you walk without lifting your feet properly off the ground. **2.** If you shuffle about, you move about and fidget because you feel uncomfortable or embarrassed. **3.** If you shuffle a pack of cards, you mix them up before you begin a game.
NOUN **4.** the way someone walks when he or she shuffles

shun shuns shunning shunned
VERB If you shun someone or something, you deliberately avoid that person or thing.

shunt shunts shunting shunted
VERB *an informal word* If you shunt people or things to a place, you move them there: *We were shunted from room to room.*

shut shuts shutting shut
VERB **1.** If you shut something, you close it.
ADJECTIVE **2.** If something is shut, it is closed.
shut down
VERB **3.** When a business or activity shuts down, it closes or ends.
shut up
VERB **4.** *an informal expression* If you shut up, you stop talking.

shutter shutters
NOUN Shutters are hinged wooden or metal covers fitted on the outside or inside of a window.

shuttle shuttles
ADJECTIVE **1.** A shuttle service is an air, bus, or train service that makes frequent journeys between two places.
NOUN **2.** a plane or vehicle used in a shuttle service

shuttlecock shuttlecocks
NOUN the feathered object used as a ball in the game of badminton

shy shyer shyest; shies shying shied
ADJECTIVE **1.** A shy person is nervous and uncomfortable in the company of other people.
VERB **2.** When a horse shies, it moves away suddenly because something has frightened it. **3.** If you shy away from doing something, you avoid doing it because you are afraid or nervous.
shyly ADVERB
shyness NOUN

sibling siblings
NOUN *a formal word* Your siblings are your brothers and sisters.

Ss

sick sicker sickest

ADJECTIVE **1.** If you are sick, you are ill. **2.** If you feel sick, you feel as if you are going to vomit. If you are sick, you vomit. **3.** *an informal use* If you are sick of doing something, you feel you have been doing it for too long. **4.** *an informal use* A sick joke or story deals with death or suffering in an unpleasantly frivolous way.

PHRASE **5.** If something **makes you sick**, it makes you angry.

sickness NOUN

sicken sickens sickening sickened

VERB If something sickens you, it makes you feel disgusted.

sickening ADJECTIVE

sickle sickles

NOUN a tool with a short handle and a curved blade used for cutting grass or grain

sickly sicklier sickliest

ADJECTIVE **1.** A sickly person or animal is weak and unhealthy. **2.** Sickly also means very unpleasant to smell or taste.

side sides siding sided

NOUN **1.** Side refers to a position to the left or right of something: *the two armchairs on either side of the fireplace* **2.** The sides of a boundary or barrier are the two areas it separates: *this side of the border* **3.** Your sides are the parts of your body from your armpits down to your hips. **4.** The sides of something are its outside surfaces, especially the surfaces that are not its front or back. **5.** The sides of a hill or valley are the parts that slope. **6.** The two sides in a war, argument, or relationship are the two people or groups involved. **7.** A particular side of something is one aspect of it: *the sensitive, caring side of human nature*

ADJECTIVE **8.** situated on a side of a building or vehicle: *the side door* **9.** A side road is a small road leading off a larger one. **10.** A side issue is an issue that is less important than the main one.

VERB **11.** If you side with someone in an argument, you support that person.

sideboard sideboards

NOUN a long, low cupboard for plates and glasses

sideburns

PLURAL NOUN A man's sideburns are areas of hair growing on his cheeks in front of his ears.

side effect side effects

NOUN The side effects of a drug are the effects it has in addition to its main effects.

sidekick sidekicks

NOUN *an informal word* Someone's sidekick is that person's close friend who spends a lot of time with him or her.

sideline sidelines

NOUN an extra job in addition to your main job

sideshow sideshows

NOUN Sideshows are small shows or displays at an exhibition, fair, or circus.

sidestep sidesteps sidestepping sidestepped

VERB If you sidestep a difficult problem or question, you avoid dealing with it.

sidewalk sidewalks

NOUN a paved path for walking on either side of a street

sideways

ADVERB from or toward the side of something or someone

siding sidings

NOUN a short railway track beside the main tracks, where engines and cars are left when not in use

sidle sidles sidling sidled

VERB If you sidle somewhere, you walk there cautiously and slowly, as if you do not want to be noticed.

siege sieges

NOUN a military operation in which an army surrounds a place and prevents food or help from reaching the people inside

sieve sieves sieving sieved

NOUN **1.** a kitchen tool made of mesh, used for sifting or straining things

VERB **2.** If you sieve a powder or liquid, you pass it through a sieve.

sift sifts sifting sifted

VERB **1.** If you sift a powdery substance, you pass it through a sieve to remove lumps. **2.** If you sift through something such as evidence, you examine it all thoroughly.

sigh sighs sighing sighed

VERB **1.** When you sigh, you let out a deep breath.

NOUN **2.** the breath you let out when you sigh

sight sights sighting sighted

NOUN **1.** Sight is the ability to see: *His sight was so poor that he could not read the print on the cover of the book.* **2.** something you see: *It was a ghastly sight.*

PLURAL NOUN **3.** Sights are interesting places that tourists visit.

VERB **4.** If you sight someone or something, you see that person briefly or suddenly: *He had been sighted in Charlottetown.*

⚠ **HEADS UP** The word **sieve** is pronounced SIV.

NEL

PHRASE **5.** If something is **in sight** or **within sight**, you can see it. If it is **out of sight**, you cannot see it.

sighted
ADJECTIVE Someone who is sighted can see.

sighting sightings
NOUN A sighting of something rare or unexpected is an occasion when it is seen.

sightseeing
NOUN Sightseeing is visiting the interesting places that tourists usually visit.
sightseer NOUN

sign signs signing signed
NOUN **1.** a mark or symbol that always has a particular meaning, for example in mathematics or music **2.** a gesture with a particular meaning **3.** A sign can also consist of words, a picture, or a symbol giving information or a warning. **4.** A sign is an event or happening that some people believe a divine power has sent as a warning or instruction to an individual or to people in general. **5.** If there are signs of something, there is evidence that it exists or is happening: *We are now seeing the first signs of recovery.*
VERB **6.** If you sign a document, you write your name on it: *He hurriedly signed the birth certificate.* **7.** If you sign, you communicate by using sign language.
sign on, sign up
VERB **8.** If you sign on or sign up for a job or course, you commit yourself to doing it.

signal signals signalling signalled
NOUN **1.** a gesture, sound, or action intended to give a message to someone **2.** A piece of equipment such as a light that tells vehicle or train drivers whether to stop or not.
VERB **3.** If you signal to someone, you make a gesture or sound to give that person a message.

signature signatures
NOUN If you write your signature, you write your name the way you usually write it.

significant
ADJECTIVE large or important: *a significant amount, a significant victory*
significance NOUN
significantly ADVERB

signify signifies signifying signified
VERB A gesture that signifies something has a particular meaning: *Her silence signified a desire to leave.*

sign language
NOUN Sign language is a way of communicating using your hands, used especially by deaf people.

signpost signposts
NOUN a road sign with information on it such as the name of a town and how far away it is

Sikh Sikhs
NOUN a person who believes in Sikhism, an Indian religion that separated from Hinduism in the fifteenth century and that teaches that there is only one God
Sikhism NOUN

silence silences silencing silenced
NOUN **1.** Silence is quietness. **2.** Someone's silence about something is that person's failure or refusal to talk about it.
VERB **3.** To silence someone or something means to stop that person from talking or making a noise.

silent
ADJECTIVE **1.** If you are silent, you are not saying anything. **2.** If you are silent about something, you do not tell people about it. **3.** When something is silent, it makes no noise. **4.** A silent movie has only pictures and no sound.
silently ADVERB

silhouette silhouettes
NOUN the outline of a dark shape against a light background
silhouetted ADJECTIVE

silicon
NOUN Silicon is an element found in sand, clay, and stone. It is used to make parts of computers.

silk silks
NOUN Silk is a fine, soft cloth made from a substance produced by silkworms.

silkworm silkworms
NOUN Silkworms are the larvae of a particular kind of moth.

silky silkier silkiest
ADJECTIVE smooth and soft

sill sills
NOUN a ledge at the bottom of a window

silly sillier silliest
ADJECTIVE foolish or childish

silt
NOUN Silt is fine sand or soil that is carried along by a river.

Instead of **SILLY** try...

an **absurd** joke

an **inane** remark

a **pointless** story

a **foolish** mistake

a **ridiculous** costume

silver

NOUN **1.** Silver is a valuable, greyish white, metallic element used for making jewellery and ornaments. **2.** Silver is also coins made from silver or from silver-coloured metal. ADJECTIVE OR NOUN **3.** greyish white

silverfish silverfishes

NOUN a small, silver insect with no wings that eats paper and clothing

silver wedding silver weddings

NOUN A couple's silver wedding is the twenty-fifth anniversary of their wedding.

silvery

ADJECTIVE having the appearance or colour of silver: *the silvery moon*

similar

ADJECTIVE **1.** If one thing is similar to another, or if two things are similar, they are like each other. **2.** In mathematics, two triangles are similar if the angles in one correspond exactly to the angles in the other.
similarly ADVERB

similarity similarities

NOUN If there is a similarity between things, they are alike in some way.

simile similes

NOUN A simile describes something by comparing it to something else, using like or as, for example, *She runs like a deer* or *He's as white as a sheet.*

simmer simmers simmering simmered

VERB When food simmers, it cooks gently at just below boiling point.

simple simpler simplest

ADJECTIVE **1.** Something that is simple is uncomplicated and easy to understand or do. **2.** Simple also means plain and not elaborate in style: *a simple coat* **3.** A simple way of life is uncomplicated. **4.** You use *simple* to emphasize that what you are talking about is the only important thing: *simple stubbornness, the simple truth*
simplicity NOUN

simple-minded

ADJECTIVE not very intelligent or sophisticated: *simple-minded pleasures*

simplify simplifies simplifying simplified

VERB To simplify something means to make it easier to do or understand.
simplification NOUN

simplistic

ADJECTIVE too simple or naive: *a rather simplistic approach to the subject*

simply

ADVERB **1.** Simply means merely: *It was simply a question of making the decision.* **2.** You

use *simply* to emphasize what you are saying: *It is simply not true.* **3.** If you say or write something simply, you do it in a way that makes it easy to understand.

simulate simulates simulating simulated

VERB To simulate something means to imitate it: *The wood has been painted to simulate stone.*
simulation NOUN

simultaneous

ADJECTIVE Things that are simultaneous happen at the same time.
simultaneously ADVERB

sin sins sinning sinned

NOUN **1.** Sin is wicked and immoral behaviour.
VERB **2.** To sin means to do something wicked and immoral.

since

PREPOSITION, CONJUNCTION, OR ADVERB **1.** Since means from a particular time until now: *I've been waiting patiently since half past three.*
ADVERB **2.** Since also means at some time after a particular time in the past: *She finished high school and has since been studying geography at university.*
CONJUNCTION **3.** Since also means because: *I should do well on the test, since I studied all week for it.*

sincere

ADJECTIVE If you are sincere, you say things that you really mean: *a sincere expression of friendliness*
sincerity NOUN

sincerely

ADVERB **1.** If you say or feel something sincerely, you mean it or feel it genuinely.
PHRASE **2.** You write **Yours sincerely** before your signature at the end of a formal letter. For example, if you began your letter *Dear Mr. Brown* you would use *Yours sincerely.*

sinew sinews

NOUN a tough cord in your body that connects a muscle to a bone

sinful

ADJECTIVE wicked and immoral

sing sings singing sang sung

VERB **1.** When you sing, you make musical sounds with your voice, usually producing words that fit a tune. **2.** When birds or insects sing, they make pleasant sounds.
singer NOUN

singe singes singeing singed

VERB **1.** To singe something means to burn it slightly so that it goes brown but does not catch fire.
NOUN **2.** a slight burn

SIMILE ▼×

a phrase that describes something by comparing it to something else, using **like** or **as**

"You looked just like a bird up there!"

Here is an example of a simile. It's a poetic way to describe how the man looked while he was in the air.

PHIL CRAVEN

Ss

single singles singling singled

ADJECTIVE **1.** Single means only one and not more: *A single leaf dropped to the ground.*
2. People who are single are not married.
3. A single bed or bedroom is for one person.
NOUN **4.** a recording of one or two short pieces of music on a small record or CD
5. Singles is a game of tennis, badminton, or squash between just two players.

single out

VERB **6.** If you single someone out from a group, you give that person special treatment: *He'd been singled out for some special award.*

single-handed

ADVERB If you do something single-handed, you do it on your own, without any help.

single-minded

ADJECTIVE A single-minded person has only one aim and is determined to achieve it.

singly

ADVERB If people do something singly, they do it on their own or one by one.

singular

NOUN **1.** In grammar, the singular is the form of a word that refers to just one person or thing.
ADJECTIVE **2.** *a formal use* unusual and remarkable: *her singular beauty*
singularity NOUN
singularly ADVERB

sinister

ADJECTIVE seeming harmful or evil: *There is something cold and sinister about him.*

sink sinks sinking sank sunk

NOUN **1.** a basin with taps supplying water, usually in a kitchen or bathroom
VERB **2.** If something sinks, it moves downward, especially through water: *A cargo ship sank in icy seas.* **3.** To sink a ship means to cause it to sink by attacking it.
4. If an amount or value sinks, it decreases.
5. If you sink into an unpleasant state, you gradually pass into it: *He sank into black despair.* **6.** To sink something sharp into an object means to make it go deeply into it: *The tiger sank its teeth into a piece of meat.*

sink in

VERB **7.** When a fact sinks in, you fully understand it or realize it: *The truth was at last sinking in.*

sinner sinners

NOUN someone who has committed a sin

sinus sinuses

NOUN Your sinuses are the air passages in the bones of your skull, just behind your nose.

sip sips sipping sipped

VERB **1.** If you sip a drink, you drink it by taking a small amount at a time.
NOUN **2.** a small amount of drink that you take into your mouth

siphon siphons siphoning siphoned

VERB If you siphon off a liquid, you draw it out of a container through a tube and transfer it to another place.

sir

NOUN **1.** Sir is a polite, formal way of addressing a man. **2.** Sir is also the title used in front of the name of a knight or baronet.

siren sirens

NOUN a warning device, for example on a police car, which makes a loud, wailing noise

sirloin

NOUN Sirloin is a prime cut of beef from the lower part of a cow's back.

sister sisters

NOUN **1.** Your sister is a girl or woman who has the same parents as you.
ADJECTIVE **2.** Sister means closely related to something or very similar to it: *Kentville, Nova Scotia is the sister city of Camrose, Alberta.*

sisterhood

NOUN Sisterhood is a strong feeling of companionship between women.

sister-in-law sisters-in-law

NOUN Your sister-in-law is the wife of your brother, the sister of your husband or wife, or the woman married to your wife's or husband's brother.

sit sits sitting sat

VERB **1.** If you are sitting, your weight is supported by your buttocks rather than your feet. **2.** When you sit or sit down somewhere, you lower your body until you are sitting.
3. *a formal use* When a parliament, law court, or other official body sits, it meets and officially carries out its work.

sitcom sitcoms

NOUN *an informal word* a television comedy series that shows characters in amusing situations that are similar to everyday life

site sites siting sited

NOUN **1.** a piece of ground where a particular thing happens or is situated: *a building site*
VERB **2.** If something is sited in a place, it is built or positioned there.

sitting sittings

NOUN **1.** one of the times when a meal is served **2.** one of the occasions when a parliament or law court meets and carries out its work

⚠ **HEADS UP** The word **siphon** is pronounced SIGH-fun.

NEL

situated
ADJECTIVE If something is situated somewhere, that is where it is: *a town situated 45 minutes from Kirkland Lake*

situation situations
NOUN **1.** what is happening in a particular place at a particular time: *the political situation* **2.** The situation of a building or town is its surroundings: *a beautiful situation on a hill*

six sixes
NOUN the number 6

sixteen
NOUN the number 16
sixteenth ADJECTIVE, ADVERB

sixth sixths
ADJECTIVE, ADVERB **1.** The sixth item in a series is the one counted as number six.
NOUN **2.** one of six equal parts

sixth sense
NOUN You say that someone has a sixth sense when that person knows something instinctively, without having any evidence of it.

sixty sixties
NOUN the number 60
sixtieth ADJECTIVE, ADVERB

sizable
ADJECTIVE fairly large: *a sizable amount of money*

size sizes
NOUN **1.** The size of something is how big or small it is: *the size of the audience* **2.** The size of something is also the fact that it is very large: *the sheer size of Canada* **3.** one of the standard graded measurements of clothes and shoes

sizzle sizzles sizzling sizzled
VERB If something sizzles, it makes a hissing sound like the sound of frying food.

skate skates skating skated
NOUN **1.** Skates are ice skates, roller skates, or inline skates. **2.** a flat, edible sea fish
VERB **3.** If you skate, you move about on ice or the ground wearing skates. **4.** If you skate around a difficult subject, you avoid discussing it.

skateboard skateboards
NOUN a narrow board on wheels that a person can ride in a standing or crouching position

skeleton skeletons
NOUN Your skeleton is the framework of bones in your body.

skeptic skeptics
NOUN someone who has doubts about things

that other people believe
skeptical ADJECTIVE
skepticism NOUN

sketch sketches sketching sketched
NOUN **1.** a quick, rough drawing **2.** A sketch of a situation or incident is a brief description of it. **3.** a short, humorous piece of acting, usually forming part of a comedy show
VERB **4.** If you sketch something, you draw it quickly and roughly.

sketchy sketchier sketchiest
ADJECTIVE giving only a rough description or account: *Details surrounding his background are sketchy.*

skew
ADJECTIVE in a slanting position, rather than straight or upright

skewer skewers skewering skewered
NOUN **1.** a long, metal pin used to hold pieces of food together during cooking
VERB **2.** If you skewer something, you push a skewer through it.

ski skis skiing skied
NOUN **1.** Skis are long pieces of wood, metal, or plastic that you fasten to special boots so you can move easily on snow.
VERB **2.** When you ski, you move on snow wearing skis, especially as a sport.

skid skids skidding skidded
VERB If a vehicle skids, it slides in an uncontrolled way, for example because the road is wet or icy.

skilful
ADJECTIVE If you are skilful at something, you can do it very well.
skilfully ADVERB

skill skills
NOUN **1.** Skill is the knowledge and ability that enables you to do something well. **2.** a type of work or technique that requires special training and knowledge

skilled
ADJECTIVE **1.** A skilled person has the knowledge and ability to do something well. **2.** Skilled work is work that can only be done by people who have had special training.

skim skims skimming skimmed
VERB **1.** If you skim something from the surface of a liquid, you remove it. **2.** If something skims a surface, it moves along just above it: *We saw seagulls skimming the waves.*

skim milk
NOUN Skim milk has had the cream removed.

Ss

skin skins skinning skinned
NOUN **1.** Your skin is the natural covering of your body. An animal skin is the skin and fur of a dead animal. **2.** The skin of a fruit or vegetable is its outer covering. **3.** a solid layer that forms on the surface of a liquid
VERB **4.** If you skin a dead animal, you remove its skin. **5.** If you skin a part of your body, you accidentally graze it.

skinny skinnier skinniest
ADJECTIVE extremely thin

skip skips skipping skipped
VERB **1.** If you skip along, you move along jumping from one foot to the other. **2.** If you skip something, you miss it or avoid doing it: *She never skips a meal.*
NOUN **3.** Skips are the movements you make when you skip.

skipper skippers
NOUN *an informal word* The skipper of a ship or boat is its captain.

skirmish skirmishes
NOUN a short, rough fight

skirt skirts skirting skirted
NOUN **1.** A woman's skirt is a piece of clothing that fastens at her waist and hangs down over her legs.
VERB **2.** Something that skirts an area is situated around the edge of it. **3.** If you skirt something, you go around the edge of it: *We skirted the town.* **4.** If you skirt a problem, you avoid dealing with it: *He was skirting the real question.*

skull skulls
NOUN Your skull is the bony part of your head that surrounds your brain.

skunk skunks
NOUN a small black-and-white animal from North America that gives off an unpleasant smell when it is frightened

sky skies
NOUN The sky is the space around the earth that you can see when you look upward.

slab slabs
NOUN a thick, flat piece of something

slack slacker slackest; slacks
ADJECTIVE **1.** Something that is slack is loose and not firmly stretched or positioned. **2.** A slack period is one in which there is not much work to do.
NOUN **3.** The slack in a rope is the part that hangs loose.
PLURAL NOUN **4.** Slacks are casual pants.
slackness NOUN

slacken slackens slackening slackened
VERB **1.** If something slackens, it becomes slower or less intense: *The rain had slackened to a drizzle.* **2.** To slacken also means to become looser: *Her grip slackened on his arm.*

slag slags slagging slagged
NOUN Slag is the waste material left when ore has been melted down to remove the metal: *a slag heap*

slalom slaloms
NOUN a skiing competition in which the competitors have to twist and turn quickly to avoid obstacles

slam slams slamming slammed
VERB **1.** If you slam a door or if it slams, it shuts noisily and with great force. **2.** If you slam something down, you throw it down violently: *She slammed the book down.*

> ⚠ **HEADS UP**
>
> A **slam dunk** (a basketball move where you slam the ball down through the net) is often shortened to **slam**.

slander slanders slandering slandered
NOUN **1.** Slander is something untrue and malicious said about someone.
VERB **2.** To slander someone means to say

KNOWING WORDS: WORD BUILDING

BE WORD SHARP!

To build a compound word, put two or more base words together.

sky the air above us

skydiving jumping out of a plane with a parachute

sky-high to a great height

skylight a window in a roof or ceiling

skyline the line where the sky meets buildings or ground

skyscraper a very tall building

NEL

untrue and malicious things about that person.
slanderous ADJECTIVE

slang
NOUN Slang consists of very informal words and expressions.

slant slants slanting slanted
VERB **1.** If something slants, it slopes: *The back can be adjusted to slant into the most comfortable position.* **2.** If news or information is slanted, it is presented in a biased way.
NOUN **3.** a slope **4.** A slant on a subject is one way of looking at it, especially a biased one.

slap slaps slapping slapped
VERB **1.** If you slap someone, you hit that person with the palm of your hand. **2.** If you slap something onto a surface, you put it there quickly and noisily.
NOUN **3.** If you give someone a slap, you slap that person.

slash slashes slashing slashed
VERB **1.** If you slash something, you make a long, deep cut in it. **2.** *an informal use* To slash prices or quantities means to reduce them greatly: *The music industry has been forced to slash prices on CDs.*
NOUN **3.** a diagonal line that separates letters, words, or numbers, for example in *kilometres/hour*

slat slats
NOUN Slats are the narrow pieces of wood, metal, or plastic in things such as blinds.
slatted ADJECTIVE

slate slates slating slated
NOUN **1.** Slate is a dark grey rock that splits easily into thin layers. **2.** a small, flat piece of slate used for covering roofs
VERB **3.** If an activity is slated for a certain time, it is scheduled to take place: *That building is slated for demolition next week.*

slaughter slaughters slaughtering slaughtered
VERB **1.** To slaughter a large number of people means to kill them unjustly or cruelly. **2.** To slaughter farm animals means to kill them for food.
NOUN **3.** Slaughter is the killing of many people. **4.** Slaughter is also the killing of animals for food.

slave slaves slaving slaved
NOUN **1.** someone who is owned by another person and must work for that person
VERB **2.** If you slave for someone, you work very hard for that person.
slavery NOUN

slay slays slaying slew slain
VERB *a literary or poetic word* To slay someone means to kill that person.

sleazy sleazier sleaziest
ADJECTIVE A sleazy place can be dirty, rundown, or not respectable.

sled sleds
NOUN a vehicle on runners used for travelling over snow

sledgehammer sledgehammers
NOUN a large, heavy hammer

sleek sleeker sleekest
ADJECTIVE **1.** Sleek hair is smooth and shiny. **2.** Someone who is sleek looks rich and dresses elegantly.

sleep sleeps sleeping slept
NOUN **1.** Sleep is the natural state of rest in which your eyes are closed and you are unconscious. **2.** If you have a sleep, you sleep for a while: *He'll be ready for a sleep soon.*
VERB **3.** When you sleep, you rest in a state of sleep.
PHRASE **4.** If a sick or injured animal is **put to sleep**, it is painlessly killed.

sleeper sleepers
NOUN **1.** You use *sleeper* to say how deeply someone sleeps: *I'm a very heavy sleeper.* **2.** a bed on a train, or a train that has beds on it

sleeping bag sleeping bags
NOUN a large, warm bag for sleeping in, especially when you are camping

sleeping pill sleeping pills
NOUN A sleeping pill is a pill that you take to help you sleep.

sleepover sleepovers
NOUN a gathering or party at which friends spend the night at another friend's house

sleepwalk sleepwalks sleepwalking sleepwalked
VERB If you sleepwalk, you walk around while you are asleep.

sleepy sleepier sleepiest
ADJECTIVE **1.** tired and ready to go to sleep **2.** A sleepy town or village is very quiet.
sleepily ADVERB
sleepiness NOUN

sleet
NOUN Sleet is a mixture of rain and snow.

sleeve sleeves
NOUN The sleeves of a piece of clothing are the parts that cover your arms.
sleeveless ADJECTIVE

sleigh sleighs
NOUN a sled, usually pulled by a horse or horses

Ss

⚠ **HEADS UP** The word **sleigh** is pronounced SLAY.

slender

Instead of **SLENDER** try...

ADJECTIVE
1. attractively thin and graceful
2. small in amount or degree: *the first, slender hopes of peace*

a **lean** body
a **slim** dancer
a **slight** figure
bony features
a **scrawny** teenager

sleuth sleuths
NOUN *an old-fashioned word* a detective

slew slews slewing slewed
1. Slew is the past tense of SLAY.
VERB **2.** If a vehicle slews, it slides or skids: *The bike slewed into the crowd.*

slice slices slicing sliced
NOUN **1.** A slice of cake, bread, or other food is a piece of it cut from a larger piece. **2.** In some sports, a slice is a stroke in which the player makes the ball go to one side, rather than straight ahead.
VERB **3.** If you slice food, you cut it into thin pieces. **4.** To slice through something means to cut or move through it quickly, like a knife: *The ship sliced through the water.*

slick slicker slickest; slicks
ADJECTIVE **1.** A slick action is done quickly and smoothly: *Slick passing and strong running are that football player's strengths.* **2.** A slick person speaks easily and persuasively but is not sincere: *a slick TV presenter*
NOUN **3.** An oil slick is a layer of oil floating on the surface of water.

slide slides sliding slid
VERB **1.** When something slides, it moves smoothly over or against something else.
NOUN **2.** a small piece of photographic film that can be projected onto a screen so that you can see the picture **3.** a small piece of glass on which you put something that you want to examine through a microscope **4.** In a playground, a slide is a structure with a steep, slippery slope for children to slide down.

slight slighter slightest; slights slighting slighted
ADJECTIVE **1.** Slight means small in amount or degree: *a slight dent* **2.** A slight person has a slim body.
PHRASE **3. Not in the slightest** means not at all: *This doesn't surprise me in the slightest.*
VERB **4.** If you slight someone, you insult that person by behaving rudely toward him or her.

NOUN **5.** A slight is rude or insulting behaviour.
slightly ADVERB

slim slimmer slimmest; slims slimming slimmed
ADJECTIVE **1.** A slim person is attractively thin. **2.** A slim object is thinner than usual: *a slim book* **3.** If there is only a slim chance that something will happen, it is unlikely to happen.
VERB **4.** To slim means to make something thinner: *an exercise to slim the thighs*
slimmer NOUN

slime
NOUN Slime is an unpleasant, thick, slippery substance.

slimy slimier slimiest
ADJECTIVE **1.** covered in slime **2.** Slimy people are friendly and pleasant in an insincere way: *a slimy business partner*

sling slings slinging slung
VERB **1.** *an informal use* If you sling something somewhere, you throw it there. **2.** If you sling a rope between two points, you attach it so that it hangs loosely between them.
NOUN **3.** a piece of cloth tied around a person's neck to support a broken or injured arm **4.** a device made of ropes or cloth, used for carrying or lifting things

slip slips slipping slipped
VERB **1.** If you slip, you accidentally slide and lose your balance. **2.** If something slips, it slides out of place accidentally: *One of the knives slipped from her grasp.* **3.** If you slip somewhere, you go there quickly and quietly: *She slipped out of the house.* **4.** If you slip something somewhere, you put it there quickly and quietly. **5.** If something slips to a lower level or standard, it falls to that level or standard: *The shares slipped to an all-time low.*
NOUN **6.** a small mistake **7.** A slip of paper is a small piece of paper. **8.** a piece of clothing worn under a dress or skirt

slipped disc slipped discs
NOUN a painful condition in which one of the discs in your spine has moved out of its proper position

slipper slippers
NOUN Slippers are loose, soft shoes that you wear indoors.

slippery
ADJECTIVE **1.** smooth, wet, or greasy, and difficult to hold or walk on **2.** You describe a person as slippery when he or she cannot be trusted.

Ss

slipstream slipstreams
NOUN The slipstream of a car or plane is the flow of air directly behind it.

slit slits slitting slit
VERB **1.** If you slit something, you make a long, narrow cut in it.
NOUN **2.** a long, narrow cut or opening

slither slithers slithering slithered
VERB To slither somewhere means to move there by sliding along the ground in an uneven way: *The snake slithered into the water.*

sliver slivers
NOUN a small, thin piece of something

slob slobs
NOUN *an informal word* a lazy, untidy person

slog slogs slogging slogged
VERB *an informal word* If you slog at something, you work hard and steadily at it: *We are still slogging away at our algebra homework.*

slogan slogans
NOUN a short, easily-remembered phrase used in advertising or by a political party

slop slops slopping slopped
VERB **1.** If a liquid slops, it spills over the edge of a container in a messy way.
NOUN **2.** a puddle of spilled or splashed liquid

slope slopes sloping sloped
NOUN **1.** a flat surface that is at an angle, so that one end is higher than the other **2.** The slope of something is the angle at which it slopes.
VERB **3.** If a surface slopes, it is at an angle.
4. If something slopes, it leans to one side rather than being upright: *sloping handwriting*

sloppy sloppier sloppiest
ADJECTIVE *an informal word* **1.** very messy or careless: *sloppy work, sloppy writing*
2. foolishly sentimental: *a sloppy love story*
sloppily ADVERB
sloppiness NOUN

slot slots slotting slotted
NOUN **1.** a narrow opening in a machine or container, for example for putting coins in
VERB **2.** When you slot something into something else, you put it into a space where it fits.

sloth sloths
NOUN **1.** *a formal use* Sloth is laziness. **2.** a South and Central American animal that moves very slowly and hangs upside down from the branches of trees

slouch slouches slouching slouched
VERB If you slouch, you stand or sit with your shoulders and head drooping forward.

slow slower slowest; slows slowing slowed
ADJECTIVE **1.** moving, happening, or doing something with very little speed: *His progress was slow.* **2.** Someone who is slow is not very clever. **3.** If a clock or watch is slow, it shows a time earlier than the correct one.
VERB **4.** If something slows, slows down, or slows up, it moves or happens more slowly.
slowness NOUN

slowly
ADVERB not quickly or hurriedly

slow motion
NOUN Slow motion is movement that is much slower than normal, especially in a movie: *It all seemed to happen in slow motion.*

sludge
NOUN Sludge is thick mud or sewage.

slug slugs
NOUN a small, slow-moving creature with a slimy body, like a snail without a shell

sluggish
ADJECTIVE moving slowly and without energy: *the sluggish waters*

sluice sluices sluicing sluiced
NOUN **1.** a channel that carries water, with an opening called a sluice gate that can be opened or closed to control the flow of water
VERB **2.** If you sluice something, you wash it by pouring water over it: *He had sluiced his hands under a tap.*

slum slums
NOUN a poor, run-down area of a city

slumber slumbers slumbering slumbered *a literary or poetic word*
NOUN **1.** Slumber is sleep.
VERB **2.** When you slumber, you sleep.

slump slumps slumping slumped
VERB **1.** If an amount or a value slumps, it falls suddenly by a large amount. **2.** If you slump somewhere, you fall or sit down heavily: *He slumped against the side of the car.*
NOUN **3.** a sudden, severe drop in an amount or value: *the slump in house prices* **4.** a time when there is economic decline and high unemployment

slur slurs slurring slurred
NOUN **1.** an insulting remark
VERB **2.** When people slur their speech, they do not say their words clearly.

slurp slurps slurping slurped
VERB If you slurp a drink, you drink it noisily.

Ss

slush

NOUN **1.** Slush is wet, melting snow. **2.** *an informal use* You can refer to sentimental love stories as slush.

slushy ADJECTIVE

sly slyer slyest

ADJECTIVE **1.** A sly expression or remark shows that you know something other people do not know: *a sly smile* **2.** A sly person is cunning and good at deceiving people.

slyly ADVERB

smack smacks smacking smacked

VERB **1.** If you smack someone, you hit that person with your open hand. **2.** If something smacks of something else, it reminds you of it: *Her tale smacks of fantasy.*

NOUN **3.** If you give someone a smack, you smack that person. **4.** a loud, sharp noise: *He landed with a smack on the ground.*

small smaller smallest; smalls

ADJECTIVE **1.** *Small* means *not large in size, number, or amount.* **2.** *Small* means *not important or significant: small changes*

NOUN **3.** The small

a **modest** apartment

a **miniature** model

a **petite** figure

a **dwarf** tree

Instead of **SMALL** try…

a **tiny** bit

a **minor** problem

a **meagre** amount

a **minuscule** droplet

of your back is the narrow part where your back curves slightly inward.

smallpox

NOUN Smallpox is a serious contagious disease that causes a fever and a rash.

small talk

NOUN Small talk is conversation about unimportant things.

smart smarter smartest; smarts smarting smarted

ADJECTIVE **1.** A smart person is clean and neatly dressed. **2.** Smart means clever: *a smart idea* **3.** A smart movement is quick and sharp: *to walk at a smart pace*

VERB **4.** If a wound smarts, it stings. **5.** If you are smarting from criticism or unkindness, you are feeling upset by it.

smartly ADVERB

smarten smartens smartening smartened

VERB If you smarten something up, you make it look neater and tidier.

smash smashes smashing smashed

VERB **1.** If you smash something, you break it into a lot of pieces by hitting it or dropping it. **2.** To smash through something such as a wall means to go through it by breaking it. **3.** To smash against something means to hit it with great force: *An immense wave smashed against the hull.*

NOUN **4.** *an informal use* If a play or movie is a smash, it is very successful. **5.** a car crash **6.** In tennis, a smash is a stroke in which the player hits the ball downward very hard.

smattering

NOUN A smattering of knowledge or information is a very small amount of it: *a smattering of Russian*

smear smears smearing smeared

NOUN **1.** a dirty, greasy mark on a surface: *a smear of pink lipstick* **2.** an untrue and malicious rumour

VERB **3.** If something smears a surface, it makes dirty, greasy marks on it: *The table was smeared with butter.* **4.** If you smear a surface with a greasy or sticky substance, you spread a layer of the substance over the surface.

smell smells smelling smelled

NOUN **1.** The smell of something is a quality it has, which you perceive through your nose: *a smell of damp wood* **2.** Your sense of smell is your ability to smell things.

VERB **3.** If something smells, it has a quality you can perceive through your nose, especially an unpleasant quality. **4.** If you smell something, you become aware of it through your nose. **5.** If you can smell something such as danger or trouble, you feel it is present or likely to happen.

smelly smellier smelliest

ADJECTIVE having a strong, unpleasant smell

smelt smelts smelting smelted

VERB To smelt a metal ore means to heat it until it melts, so that the metal can be extracted.

smile smiles smiling smiled

VERB **1.** When you smile, the corners of your mouth move outward and slightly upward because you are pleased or amused.

NOUN **2.** the expression you have when you smile

smirk smirks smirking smirked

VERB **1.** When you smirk, you smile in a sneering or sarcastic way: *The boy smirked and turned the volume up.*

NOUN **2.** a sneering or sarcastic smile

Ss

smith smiths
NOUN someone who makes things out of iron, gold, or some other metal

smitten
ADJECTIVE If you are smitten with someone or something, you are very impressed with or enthusiastic about that person or thing: *They were totally smitten with each other.*

smock smocks
NOUN a loose, coatlike garment used to protect clothing

smog
NOUN Smog is a mixture of smoke and fog that occurs in some industrial cities.

> ⚠ **HEADS UP**
>
> **Smog** is a blend of **smoke** and **fog**. Same goes for **brunch** (breakfast + lunch) and **motel** (motor + hotel).

smoke smokes smoking smoked
NOUN **1.** Smoke is a mixture of gas and small particles sent into the air when something burns.
VERB **2.** If something is smoking, smoke is coming from it. **3.** When someone smokes a cigarette, cigar, or pipe, that person sucks smoke from it into his or her mouth and lungs and blows it out again. **4.** To smoke fish or meat means to hang it over burning wood so that the smoke preserves it and gives it a pleasant flavour: *smoked bacon*
smoker NOUN
smoking NOUN

smoky smokier smokiest
ADJECTIVE A smoky place is full of smoke.

smooth smoother smoothest; smooths smoothing smoothed
ADJECTIVE **1.** A smooth surface has no roughness and no holes in it. **2.** A smooth liquid or mixture has no lumps in it. **3.** A smooth movement or process happens evenly and steadily: *smooth acceleration* **4.** Smooth also means successful and without problems: *staff responsible for the smooth running of the restaurant*
VERB **5.** If you smooth something, you move your hands over it to make it smooth and flat.
smoothly ADVERB
smoothness NOUN

smoothie smoothies
NOUN a thick type of drink made in an electric blender from milk, fruit, and crushed ice

smother smothers smothering smothered
VERB **1.** If you smother a flame or a fire, you cover it with something to put it out. **2.** To smother a person means to cover that person's face with something so that he or she cannot breathe. **3.** To smother someone also means to give that person too much love and protection: *She loved her own children, almost smothering them with love.* **4.** If you smother an emotion, you control it so that people do not notice it: *They tried to smother their glee.*

smothered
ADJECTIVE completely covered with something: *a spectacular trellis smothered in climbing roses*

smoulder smoulders smouldering smouldered
VERB **1.** When something smoulders, it burns slowly, producing smoke but no flames. **2.** If a feeling is smouldering inside you, you feel it very strongly but do not show it: *smouldering with resentment*

smudge smudges smudging smudged
NOUN **1.** a dirty or blurred mark or a smear on something
VERB **2.** If you smudge something, you make it dirty or messy by touching it or marking it.

smug smugger smuggest
ADJECTIVE Someone who is smug is very pleased with how good or clever he or she is.
smugly ADVERB
smugness NOUN

smuggle smuggles smuggling smuggled
VERB To smuggle things or people into or out of a place means to take them there illegally or secretly.

smuggler smugglers
NOUN someone who smuggles goods illegally into a country

snack snacks
NOUN a light, quick meal

snag snags snagging snagged
NOUN **1.** a small problem or disadvantage: *The only snag is that the story is not true.*
VERB **2.** If you snag a piece of clothing, you damage it by catching it on something sharp.

snail snails
NOUN a small, slow-moving creature with a long, shiny body and a shell on its back

snail mail
NOUN *an informal use* the conventional postal system, as opposed to e-mail

snake snakes snaking snaked
NOUN **1.** a long, thin, scaly reptile with no legs
VERB **2.** Something that snakes moves in long winding curves: *The lineup snaked out of the store.*

Ss

snap snaps snapping snapped
VERB **1.** If something snaps or if you snap it, it breaks with a sharp cracking noise. **2.** If you snap something into a particular position, you move it there quickly with a sharp sound. **3.** If an animal snaps at you, it shuts its jaws together quickly as if to bite you. **4.** If someone snaps at you, that person speaks in a sharp, unfriendly way.
NOUN **5.** the sound of something snapping
ADJECTIVE **6.** A snap decision or action is taken suddenly, without careful thought.

snapper snappers
NOUN a fish with edible pink flesh, found in waters around Australia and New Zealand

snapshot snapshots
NOUN a photograph taken quickly and casually

snare snares snaring snared
NOUN **1.** a trap for catching birds or small animals
VERB **2.** To snare an animal or bird means to catch it using a snare.

snarl snarls snarling snarled
VERB **1.** When an animal snarls, it bares its teeth and makes a fierce, growling noise. **2.** If you snarl, you say something in a fierce, angry way.
NOUN **3.** the noise an animal makes when it snarls

snatch snatches snatching snatched
VERB **1.** If you snatch something, you reach out for it quickly and take it. **2.** If you snatch an amount of time or an opportunity, you quickly make use of it.
NOUN **3.** If you make a snatch at something, you reach out for it quickly to try to take it. **4.** A snatch of conversation or song is a very small piece of it.

sneak sneaks sneaking sneaked
VERB **1.** If you sneak somewhere, you go there quickly, trying not to be seen or heard. **2.** If you sneak something somewhere, you take it there secretly.
NOUN **3.** *an informal use* someone who tells people in authority that someone else has done something wrong

sneaker sneakers
NOUN Sneakers are casual shoes with rubber soles, often used for playing sports.

sneaking
ADJECTIVE If you have a sneaking feeling about something or someone, you have this feeling rather reluctantly: *I had a sneaking suspicion that she was enjoying herself.*

sneaky sneakier sneakiest
ADJECTIVE *an informal word* Someone who is sneaky does things secretly rather than openly.

sneer sneers sneering sneered
VERB **1.** If you sneer at someone or something, you show by your expression and your comments that you think that person or thing is stupid or inferior.
NOUN **2.** the expression on someone's face when he or she sneers

sneeze sneezes sneezing sneezed
VERB **1.** When you sneeze, you suddenly take in breath and blow it down your nose noisily, because there is a tickle in your nose.
NOUN **2.** an act of sneezing

snicker snickers snickering snickered
VERB **1.** If you snicker, you laugh in a quiet, sly way: *They were snickering at her accent.*
NOUN **2.** a quiet, disrespectful laugh

snide
ADJECTIVE A snide comment or remark criticizes someone in a nasty and unfair way.

sniff sniffs sniffing sniffed
VERB **1.** When you sniff, you breathe in air through your nose hard enough to make a sound. **2.** If you sniff something, you smell it by sniffing. **3.** You can say that a person sniffs at something when that person does not think very much of it: *She sniffed at the household chore arrangements.*
NOUN **4.** the noise you make when you sniff **5.** A sniff of something is a smell of it: *a sniff at the flowers*

snip snips snipping snipped
VERB **1.** If you snip something, you cut it with scissors or shears in a single quick action.
NOUN **2.** a small cut made by scissors or shears

snippet snippets
NOUN A snippet of something such as information or news is a small piece of it.

snob snobs
NOUN **1.** someone who admires socially powerful people and looks down on people who are considered socially inferior **2.** someone who believes that he or she is better than other people
snobbery NOUN
snobbish ADJECTIVE

snooker
NOUN Snooker is a game played on a large table covered with smooth green cloth. Players score points by hitting differently coloured balls into side pockets using a long stick called a cue.

snoop snoops snooping snooped
VERB *an informal word* Someone who is snooping is secretly looking around a place to find out things.

snooper
NOUN a person who snoops

snooze snoozes snoozing snoozed
an informal word
VERB **1.** If you snooze, you sleep lightly for a short time, especially during the day.
NOUN **2.** a short, light sleep

snore snores snoring snored
VERB **1.** When a sleeping person snores, that person makes a loud noise each time he or she breathes.
NOUN **2.** the noise someone makes when he or she snores

snorkel snorkels
NOUN a tube you can breathe through when you are swimming just under the surface of the water
snorkelling NOUN

snort snorts snorting snorted
VERB **1.** When people or animals snort, they force breath out through their nose in a noisy way: *I snorted with laughter.*
NOUN **2.** the noise you make when you snort

snout snouts
NOUN An animal's snout is its nose.

snow snows snowing snowed
NOUN **1.** Snow consists of flakes of ice crystals that fall from the sky in cold weather.
VERB **2.** When it snows, snow falls from the sky.

snowball snowballs snowballing snowballed
NOUN **1.** a ball of snow for throwing
VERB **2.** When something, such as a project, snowballs, it grows rapidly.

snowdrift snowdrifts
NOUN a deep pile of snow formed by the wind

snowdrop snowdrops
NOUN a small white flower that appears in early spring

snowman snowmen
NOUN a large mound of snow moulded into the shape of a person

snub snubs snubbing snubbed
VERB **1.** To snub someone means to behave rudely toward that person, especially by making an insulting remark or ignoring him or her.
NOUN **2.** an insulting remark or an act of rude behaviour
ADJECTIVE **3.** A snub nose is short and turned up.

snuff
VERB To snuff a candle means to smother the flame of the candle.

snug
ADJECTIVE A snug place is warm and comfortable. If you are snug, you are warm and comfortable.
snugly ADVERB

snuggle snuggles snuggling snuggled
VERB If you snuggle somewhere, you cuddle up more closely to something or someone.

so
ADVERB **1.** *So* is used to refer back to what has just been mentioned: *Had he locked the car? If so, where were the keys?* **2.** *So* is used to mean *also*: *He laughed, and so did we.*
3. *So* can be used to mean *therefore*: *It's a bit expensive, so I don't think I will get one.*
4. *So* is used when you are talking about the degree or extent of something: *Why are you so cruel?* **5.** *So* is used before words like *much* and *many* to say that there is a definite limit to something: *There are only so many ways to answer that question.*
CONJUNCTION **6.** *So that* and *so as* are used to introduce the reason for doing something: *Work hard now so that you can spend time with your friends later.*

soak soaks soaking soaked
VERB **1.** To soak something or leave it to soak means to put it in a liquid and leave it there. **2.** When a liquid soaks something, it makes it very wet. **3.** When something soaks up a liquid, the liquid is drawn up into it.

soaked
ADJECTIVE extremely wet

soaking
ADJECTIVE If something is soaking, it is very wet.

soap soaps
NOUN Soap is a substance made of natural oils and fats and used for washing.
soapy ADJECTIVE

soap opera soap operas
NOUN a popular television drama in serial form about people's daily lives

soar soars soaring soared
VERB **1.** If an amount soars, it quickly increases by a great deal: *Property prices soared.* **2.** If something soars into the air, it quickly goes up into the air.
soaring ADJECTIVE

sob sobs sobbing sobbed
VERB **1.** When someone sobs, that person cries in a noisy way, breathing in short breaths.
NOUN **2.** the noise made when you cry

Ss

sober soberer soberest; sobers sobering sobered
ADJECTIVE **1.** If someone is sober, that person is not drunk. **2.** Sober also means serious and thoughtful. **3.** Sober colours are plain and rather dull.
VERB **4.** To sober up means to become sober after being drunk.
soberly ADVERB

sobering
ADJECTIVE Something that is sobering makes you serious and thoughtful: *the sobering lesson of the last year*

so-called
ADJECTIVE You use *so-called* to say that the name by which something is called is incorrect or misleading: *so-called environmentally friendly products*

soccer
NOUN Soccer is a game played by two teams of 11 players kicking a ball in an attempt to score goals.

sociable
ADJECTIVE Sociable people are friendly and enjoy talking to other people.
sociability NOUN

social
ADJECTIVE **1.** to do with society or life within a society: *people from similar social backgrounds* **2.** to do with leisure activities that involve meeting other people
socially ADVERB

socialism
NOUN Socialism is the political belief that the state should own industries on behalf of the people and that everyone should be equal.
socialist ADJECTIVE OR NOUN

socialize socializes socializing socialized
VERB When people socialize, they meet other people socially, for example at parties.

social work
NOUN Social work involves giving help and advice to people with serious financial or family problems.
social worker NOUN

society societies
NOUN **1.** Society is the people in a particular country or region: *a major problem in society* **2.** an organization for people who have the same interest or aim: *a debating society* **3.** a community of people living in a particular country or region who have shared customs, laws, and organizations

sociology
NOUN Sociology is the study of human societies and the relationships between

groups in these societies.
sociological ADJECTIVE
sociologist NOUN

sock socks
NOUN Socks are pieces of clothing for covering your feet and ankles.

socket sockets
NOUN **1.** a place on a wall or on a piece of electrical equipment into which you can put a plug or bulb **2.** Any hollow part or opening into which another part fits can be called a socket: *eye sockets*

sod
NOUN The sod is the surface of the ground, together with the grass and roots growing in it.

soda sodas
NOUN **1.** Soda is the same as SODA WATER. **2.** Soda is also sodium in the form of crystals or a powder, and is used for baking or cleaning.

soda water soda waters
NOUN Soda water is carbonated water used for mixing with other drinks such as fruit juice.

sodden
ADJECTIVE soaking wet

sodium
NOUN Sodium is a silvery-white chemical element that combines with other chemicals. Salt is a sodium compound.

sofa sofas
NOUN a long, comfortable seat with a back and arms for two or three people

soft softer softest

Instead of **SOFT** try...

ADJECTIVE
1. Something soft is not hard, stiff, or firm. **2.** Soft also means very gentle: *a soft breeze* **3.** A soft sound or voice is quiet and not harsh. **4.** A soft colour or light is not bright.
softly ADVERB

a fleecy fabric
a tender touch
a gentle landing
a pliable surface
a spongy mixture

soft drink soft drinks
NOUN any carbonated, non-alcoholic drink

soften softens softening softened
VERB **1.** If something is softened or softens, it becomes less hard, stiff, or firm. **2.** If you soften, you become more sympathetic and less critical: *Her tone softened as she spoke.*

software

NOUN Computer programs are known as software.

soggy soggier soggiest

ADJECTIVE unpleasantly wet or full of water

soil soils soiling soiled

NOUN **1.** Soil is the top layer on the surface of the earth in which plants grow.

VERB **2.** If you soil something, you make it dirty.

soiled ADJECTIVE

solace

NOUN *a literary or poetic word* Solace is something that makes you feel less sad: *I found solace in writing.*

solar

ADJECTIVE **1.** relating or belonging to the sun **2.** using the sun's light and heat as a source of energy: *a solar-powered calculator*

solar system

NOUN The solar system is the sun and all the planets, comets, and asteroids that orbit around it.

solder solders soldering soldered

VERB **1.** To solder two pieces of metal together means to join them with molten metal.

NOUN **2.** Solder is the soft metal used for soldering.

soldier soldiers

NOUN a person who serves in an army

sole soles soling soled

ADJECTIVE **1.** The sole thing or person of a particular type is the only one of that type.

NOUN **2.** The sole of your foot or shoe is the underneath part. **3.** a flat, seawater fish that you can eat

VERB **4.** When a shoe is soled, a sole is fitted onto it.

solely

ADVERB If something involves solely one thing, it involves that thing and nothing else.

solemn

ADJECTIVE Solemn means serious rather than cheerful or humorous.

solemnly ADVERB

solemnity NOUN

solicitor solicitors

NOUN a lawyer

solid solids

ADJECTIVE **1.** A solid substance or object is hard or firm, and not in the form of a liquid or gas. **2.** You say that something is solid when it is not hollow: *solid steel* **3.** You say that a structure is solid when it is strong and not likely to fall down: *a solid fence* **4.** You use *solid* to say that something happens for a period of time without interruption: *I cried for two solid days.*

NOUN **5.** a solid substance or object

solidly ADVERB

solidarity

NOUN If a group of people show solidarity, they show unity and support for each other.

soliloquy soliloquies

NOUN a speech in a play made by a character who is alone on the stage

solitary

ADJECTIVE **1.** A solitary activity is one that you do on your own. **2.** A solitary person or animal spends a lot of time alone. **3.** If there is a solitary person or object somewhere, there is only one.

solitary confinement

NOUN A prisoner in solitary confinement is being kept alone in a prison cell.

solitude

NOUN Solitude is the state of being alone.

solo solos

NOUN **1.** a performance or activity done by one person alone

ADJECTIVE **2.** A solo performance or activity is done by one person alone: *my first solo flight*

ADVERB **3.** Solo means alone: *to sail solo around the world*

soloist soloists

NOUN a person who performs a solo

solstice solstices

NOUN one of the two times in the year when the sun is at its furthest point south or north of the equator

soluble

ADJECTIVE A soluble substance is able to dissolve in liquid.

solution solutions

NOUN **1.** a way of dealing with a problem or difficult situation: *a quick solution to our problem* **2.** The solution to a riddle or a puzzle is the answer. **3.** a liquid in which a solid substance has been dissolved

solve solves solving solved

VERB If you solve a problem or a question, you find a solution or answer to it.

solvent solvents

ADJECTIVE **1.** If people or companies are solvent, they have enough money to pay all their debts.

NOUN **2.** a liquid that can dissolve other substances

solvency NOUN

Ss

sombre
ADJECTIVE **1.** Sombre colours are dark and dull. **2.** A sombre person is serious, sad, or gloomy.

some
ADJECTIVE **1.** You use *some* to refer to a quantity or number when you are not stating the quantity or number exactly: *There's some money on the table.* **2.** You use *some* to emphasize that a quantity or number is fairly large: *She had been there for some days.* ADVERB **3.** You use *some* in front of a number to show that it is not exact: *a farm some seven kilometres north*

somebody
PRONOUN Somebody means *someone*.

someday
ADVERB Someday means at a date in the future that is unknown or that has not yet been decided.

somehow
ADVERB **1.** You use *somehow* to say that you do not know how something was done or will be done: *You'll find a way of doing it somehow.* **2.** You use *somehow* to say that you do not know the reason for something: *Somehow it didn't feel quite right.*

someone
PRONOUN You use *someone* to refer to a person without saying exactly who you mean.

somersault somersaults
NOUN a forward or backward roll in which the head is placed on the ground and the body is brought over it

something
PRONOUN You use *something* to refer to anything that is not a person without saying exactly what you mean: *I have something to do before lunch.*

sometime
ADVERB **1.** at a time in the future or the past that is unknown or that has not yet been fixed: *He has to find out sometime.* ADJECTIVE **2.** *a formal use* Sometime is used to say that a person had a particular job or role in the past: *a sometime actress, dancer, and singer*

sometimes
ADVERB occasionally, rather than always or never

somewhat
ADVERB to some extent or degree: *The future seemed somewhat bleak.*

somewhere
ADVERB **1.** *Somewhere* is used to refer to a place without stating exactly where it is: *There has to be a washroom somewhere in this mall.* **2.** *Somewhere* is used when giving an approximate amount, number, or time: *somewhere between the winter of 1989 and the summer of 1991*

son sons
NOUN Someone's son is that person's male child.

sonar
NOUN Sonar is equipment on a vessel that calculates the depth of the water or the position of an underwater object using sound waves.

sonata sonatas
NOUN a piece of classical music, usually in three or more movements, for piano or for another instrument with or without piano

song songs
NOUN a piece of music with words that are sung to the music

songbird songbirds
NOUN a bird that produces musical sounds like singing

son-in-law sons-in-law
NOUN Someone's son-in-law is the husband of his or her daughter.

sonnet sonnets
NOUN a poem with 14 lines, in which lines rhyme according to a fixed pattern

soon sooner soonest
ADVERB If something is going to happen soon, it will happen in a very short time.

soot
NOUN Soot is black powder that rises in the smoke from a fire.
sooty ADJECTIVE

soothe soothes soothing soothed
VERB **1.** If you soothe someone who is angry or upset, you make that person calmer. **2.** Something that soothes pain makes the pain less severe.
soothing ADJECTIVE

sophisticated
ADJECTIVE **1.** Sophisticated people have refined or cultured tastes or habits. **2.** A sophisticated machine or device is made using advanced and complicated methods.
sophistication NOUN

soppy soppier soppiest
ADJECTIVE *an informal word* silly or foolishly sentimental

soprano sopranos
NOUN a woman, girl, or boy with a singing voice in the highest range of musical notes

⚠ **HEADS UP** The word **sombre** is pronounced SAWM-ber.

sorcerer sorcerers

NOUN a person who is supposed to perform magic by using the power of evil spirits

sorceress sorceresses

NOUN a female sorcerer

sorcery

NOUN Sorcery is magic that is supposed to be performed using the power of evil spirits.

sordid

ADJECTIVE **1.** dishonest or immoral: *a rather sordid business* **2.** dirty, unpleasant, or depressing: *a sordid motel*

sore sorer sorest; sores

ADJECTIVE **1.** If part of your body is sore, it causes you pain and discomfort. **2.** *a literary or poetic use Sore* is used to emphasize something: *I am in sore need of sleep.*
NOUN **3.** a painful place where your skin has become infected

sorely ADVERB

soreness NOUN

sorghum

NOUN a type of tropical grass that is grown for hay, grain, and syrup

sorrow sorrows

NOUN **1.** Sorrow is deep sadness or regret. **2.** Sorrows are things that cause sorrow: *the sorrows of this world*

sorry sorrier sorriest

ADJECTIVE **1.** If you are sorry about something, you feel sadness or regret about it. **2.** feeling sympathy for someone **3.** *Sorry* is used to describe people and things that are in a bad physical or mental state: *The abandoned puppy was in a pretty sorry state when we found it.*

sort sorts sorting sorted

NOUN **1.** a category of people or things with some common feature
VERB **2.** To sort things means to arrange them into different groups or sorts.

sort out

VERB **3.** If you sort out a problem or misunderstanding, you deal with it and find a solution to it.

SOS

NOUN An SOS is a signal that you are in danger and need help.

so-so

ADJECTIVE neither good nor bad: *The food is so-so.*

soufflé soufflés

NOUN a light, fluffy food, made from beaten egg whites and other ingredients, that is baked in the oven

sought the past tense and past participle of SEEK

soul souls

NOUN **1.** A person's soul is the spiritual part of that person that is supposed to continue after his or her body is dead. **2.** People also use *soul* to refer to a person's mind, character, thoughts, and feelings. **3.** *Soul* can be used to mean a person: *There was not a soul there.*

sound sounds sounding sounded; sounder soundest

NOUN **1.** Sound is everything that can be heard. **2.** A particular sound is something that you hear. **3.** The sound of someone or something is the impression you have of that person or thing: *I like the sound of your plan.*
VERB **4.** If something sounds or if you sound it, it makes a noise. **5.** To sound something deep, such as a well or the sea, means to measure how deep it is using a weighted line or sonar.
ADJECTIVE **6.** in good condition: *The builders will guarantee that the house is sound.*
7. reliable and sensible: *The logic behind the argument seems sound.*

soundly ADVERB

sound bite sound bites

NOUN a short and memorable sentence or phrase extracted from a longer speech, to be used later on a radio or television news program

sound effect sound effects

NOUN Sound effects are sounds created artificially to make a play, movie, or broadcast more realistic.

soundproof

ADJECTIVE If a room is soundproof, sound cannot get into it or out of it.

soundtrack soundtracks

NOUN The soundtrack of a movie is the part you hear.

soup soups

NOUN Soup is liquid food made by boiling meat, fish, or vegetables in water.

sour sours souring soured

ADJECTIVE **1.** If something is sour, it has a sharp, acid taste. **2.** Sour milk has an unpleasant taste because it is no longer fresh. **3.** A sour person is badtempered and unfriendly.
VERB **4.** If a friendship, situation, or attitude sours or if something sours it, it becomes less friendly, enjoyable, or hopeful.

source sources

NOUN **1.** The source of something is the person, place, or thing that it comes from: *the source of his confidence* **2.** The source of a river or stream is the place where it begins. **3.** any piece of writing or electronic file used to provide evidence in a report or piece of research

sour grapes

PLURAL NOUN You describe someone's behaviour as sour grapes when that person says that something is worthless but secretly wants it and cannot have it.

south

NOUN **1.** The south is the direction to your right when you are looking toward the place where the sun rises. **2.** The south of a place or country is the part that is toward the south when you are in the centre of that place or country.

ADVERB OR ADJECTIVE **3.** South means toward the south: *The taxi headed south. I met him at the south end of the park.*

ADJECTIVE **4.** A south wind blows from the south.

South America

NOUN South America is the fourth-largest continent. It has the Pacific Ocean on its west side, the Atlantic on the east, and the Antarctic to the south. South America is joined to North America by the Isthmus of Panama.

South American South Americans

ADJECTIVE **1.** belonging or relating to South America

NOUN **2.** someone who comes from South America

southeast

NOUN, ADVERB, OR ADJECTIVE Southeast is halfway between south and east.

southeasterly

ADJECTIVE **1.** Southeasterly means to or toward the southeast. **2.** A southeasterly wind blows from the southeast.

southeastern

ADJECTIVE in or from the southeast

southerly

ADJECTIVE **1.** Southerly means to or toward the south. **2.** A southerly wind blows from the south.

southern

ADJECTIVE in or from the south

South Pole

NOUN The South Pole is the most southerly point of the earth's surface.

southward

ADVERB **1.** Southward means toward the south: *the dusty road that led southward*

ADJECTIVE **2.** The southward part of something is the south part.

southwest

NOUN, ADVERB, OR ADJECTIVE Southwest is halfway between south and west.

southwesterly

ADJECTIVE **1.** Southwesterly means to or toward the southwest. **2.** A southwesterly wind blows from the southwest.

southwestern

ADJECTIVE in or from the southwest

souvenir souvenirs

NOUN something you keep to remind you of a holiday, place, or event

sovereign sovereigns

NOUN **1.** a king, queen, or royal ruler of a country

ADJECTIVE **2.** A sovereign state or country is independent and not under the authority of any other country.

sovereignty

NOUN Sovereignty is the political power that a country has to govern itself.

sow sows sowing sowed sown

VERB **1.** To sow seeds or sow an area of land with seeds means to plant them in the ground. **2.** To sow undesirable feelings or attitudes means to cause them: *You have sown discontent.*

sow sows

NOUN an adult female pig

soy

NOUN a sauce made from fermented soybeans; also used to refer to the soybean

soybean soybeans

NOUN a type of edible Asian bean

spa spas

NOUN a place that sells health and beauty treatments such as massages and steam baths

space spaces spacing spaced

NOUN **1.** Space is the area that is empty or available in a place, building, or container. **2.** Space is the area beyond Earth's atmosphere, surrounding the stars and planets. **3.** a gap between two things: *the space between the tables* **4.** Space can also refer to a period of time: *two incidents in the space of a week*

VERB **5.** If you space a series of things, you arrange them with gaps between them.

spacecraft

NOUN a rocket or other vehicle that can travel in space

⚠ **HEADS UP** The word **sovereign** is pronounced SAWV-run.

Ss

spaceman spacemen
NOUN an astronaut

spaceship spaceships
NOUN a spacecraft that carries people through space

space shuttle space shuttles
NOUN a spacecraft designed to be used many times for travelling out into space and back again

spacious
ADJECTIVE having or providing a lot of space: *the spacious living room*

spade spades
NOUN **1.** a tool with a flat metal blade and a long handle, used for digging **2.** Spades is one of the four suits in a pack of playing cards. It is marked by a black heart-shaped leaf symbol with a stem.

spaghetti
NOUN Spaghetti consists of long, thin pieces of pasta.

spam
NOUN unwanted e-mails, usually containing advertising

span spans spanning spanned
NOUN **1.** the period of time during which something exists or functions: *looking back over a span of 40 years* **2.** The span of something is the total length of it from one end to the other.
VERB **3.** If something spans a particular length of time, it lasts throughout that time: *a career that spanned 50 years* **4.** A bridge that spans something stretches right across it.

spangle spangles spangling spangled
VERB **1.** If something is spangled, it is covered with small, sparkling objects.
NOUN **2.** Spangles are small, sparkling pieces of metal or plastic used for decoration.

spaniel spaniels
NOUN a dog with long, drooping ears and a silky coat

spank spanks spanking spanked
VERB If a child is spanked, he or she is punished by being slapped, usually on the buttocks.

spar spars sparring sparred
VERB **1.** When boxers spar, they hit each other with light punches for practice. **2.** To spar with someone also means to argue with that person, but not in an unpleasant or serious way.
NOUN **3.** a strong pole that a sail is attached to on a yacht or ship

spare spares sparing spared
ADJECTIVE **1.** extra to what is needed: *What does she do in her spare time?*
NOUN **2.** a thing that is extra to what is needed
VERB **3.** If you spare something for a particular purpose, you make it available: *I can spare a few sheets of paper.* **4.** If someone is spared an unpleasant experience, that person is prevented from suffering it: *The city was spared the misery of an all-out transit strike.*

sparing
ADJECTIVE If you are sparing with something, you use it in very small quantities.
sparingly ADVERB

spark sparks sparking sparked
NOUN **1.** a tiny, bright piece of burning material thrown up by a fire **2.** a small flash of light caused by electricity **3.** A spark of feeling is a small amount of it: *that tiny spark of excitement*
VERB **4.** If something sparks, it throws out sparks. **5.** If one thing sparks another thing, it causes the second thing to start happening: *The tragedy sparked a wave of sympathy among students.*

sparkle sparkles sparkling sparkled
VERB **1.** If something sparkles, it shines with a lot of small, bright points of light.
NOUN **2.** Sparkles are small, bright points of light.
sparkling ADJECTIVE

sparrow sparrows
NOUN a common, small bird with brown and grey feathers

sparse sparser sparsest
ADJECTIVE small in number or amount and spread out over an area: *the sparse audience*
sparsely ADVERB

spartan
ADJECTIVE A spartan way of life is very simple with no luxuries: *spartan accommodation*

spasm spasms
NOUN **1.** a sudden tightening of the muscles **2.** a sudden, short burst of something: *a spasm of fear*

spasmodic
ADJECTIVE happening suddenly for short periods of time at irregular intervals: *spasmodic movements*

spastic spastics
ADJECTIVE **1.** A spastic person is born with a disability that makes it difficult for that person to control his or her muscles.
NOUN **2.** an offensive term for a person affected by muscle spasms

spate
NOUN A spate of things is a large number of them that happen or appear in a rush: *a recent spate of first novels from older writers*

spatial
ADJECTIVE to do with size, area, or position

spatter spatters spattering spattered
VERB **1.** If something spatters a surface, it covers the surface with drops of liquid. NOUN **2.** A spatter of something is a small amount of it in drops or tiny pieces.

spawn spawns spawning spawned
NOUN **1.** Spawn is a jelly-like substance containing the eggs of fish or amphibians. VERB **2.** When fish or amphibians spawn, they lay their eggs. **3.** If something spawns something else, it causes it: *The depressed economy spawned the riots.*

speak speaks speaking spoke spoken
VERB **1.** When you speak, you use your voice to say words. **2.** If you speak a foreign language, you know it and can use it.
speak out
VERB **3.** To speak out about something means to publicly state an opinion about it.

speaker speakers
NOUN **1.** a person who is speaking, especially someone making a speech **2.** a loudspeaker

spear spears spearing speared
NOUN **1.** a weapon consisting of a long pole with a sharp point
VERB **2.** To spear something means to push or throw a spear or other pointed object into it.

spearhead spearheads spearheading spearheaded
VERB If someone spearheads a campaign, that person leads it.

spec specs *an informal word*
NOUN **1.** a detailed description of something; a specification: *My father showed us the specs for our new house.*
PHRASE **2.** If you do something **on spec**, you do it hoping for a result but without any certainty: *He wrote the story on spec, hoping that a magazine would publish it.*

special
ADJECTIVE **1.** Something special is more important or better than other things of its kind. **2.** Special describes someone who is officially appointed, or something that is needed for a particular purpose: *We actually had to get special permission to go there.* **3.** Special also describes something that belongs or relates to only one particular person, group, or place: *the special needs of the chronically ill*

specialist specialists
NOUN someone who has a particular skill or who knows a lot about a particular subject: *a skin specialist*

specialize specializes specializing specialized
VERB If you specialize in something, you make it your specialty: *a store specializing in hockey gear*
specialization NOUN

specialized
ADJECTIVE developed for a particular purpose or trained in a particular area of knowledge: *a specialized sales team*

specially
ADVERB If something has been done specially for a particular person or purpose, it has been done only for that person or purpose.

specialty specialties
NOUN A person's specialty is something he or she is especially good at or knows a lot about: *Insects are her specialty.*

species
NOUN a class of plants or animals whose members have the same characteristics and are able to breed with each other

specific
ADJECTIVE **1.** particular: *specific areas of difficulty* **2.** precise and exact: *The teacher will ask for specific answers.*
specifically ADVERB

specification specifications
NOUN a detailed description of what is needed for something, such as the necessary features in the design of something: *I want to build it to my own specifications.*

specify specifies specifying specified
VERB To specify something means to state or describe it precisely: *In his will he specified that these documents were never to be removed.*

specimen specimens
NOUN A specimen of something is an example or small amount of it, which gives an idea of what the whole is like: *a specimen of your writing*

speck specks
NOUN a very small stain or amount of something

speckled
ADJECTIVE Something that is speckled is covered in very small marks or spots.

spectacle spectacles
NOUN **1.** a strange or interesting sight or scene: *a shocking spectacle* **2.** a grand and

Ss

impressive event or performance
PLURAL NOUN **3.** Someone's spectacles are that person's glasses.

spectacular spectaculars
ADJECTIVE **1.** Something spectacular is very impressive or dramatic.
NOUN **2.** a grand and impressive show or performance

spectator spectators
NOUN a person who is watching something

spectre spectres
NOUN **1.** a frightening idea or image: *the spectre of war* **2.** a ghost

spectrum spectrums
NOUN **1.** The spectrum is the range of different colours produced when light passes through a prism or a drop of water. A rainbow shows the colours in a spectrum. **2.** A spectrum of opinions or emotions is a range of them.

speculate speculates speculating speculated
VERB If you speculate about something, you think about it and form opinions about it.
speculation NOUN

speculative
ADJECTIVE **1.** A speculative piece of information is based on guesses and opinions rather than known facts. **2.** Someone with a speculative expression seems to be trying to guess something: *His mother regarded him with a speculative eye.*

speech speeches
NOUN **1.** Speech is the ability to speak or the act of speaking. **2.** a formal talk given to an audience **3.** In a play, a speech is a group of lines spoken by one of the characters.

speechless
ADJECTIVE Someone who is speechless is unable to speak for a short time because something has shocked that person.

speed speeds speeding sped
NOUN **1.** The speed of something is the rate at which it moves or happens.
2. Speed is very fast movement

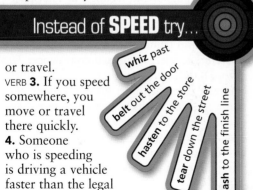

Instead of **SPEED** try...

whiz past

belt out the door

hasten to the store

tear down the street

flash to the finish line

or travel.
VERB **3.** If you speed somewhere, you move or travel there quickly.
4. Someone who is speeding is driving a vehicle faster than the legal speed limit.

speedboat speedboats
NOUN a small, fast motorboat

speed limit speed limits
NOUN The speed limit is the maximum speed at which vehicles are legally allowed to drive on a particular road.

speedway
NOUN a road or track for fast driving

speedy speedier speediest
ADJECTIVE done very quickly
speedily ADVERB

spell spells spelling spelled
VERB **1.** When you spell a word, you name or write its letters in order. **2.** When letters spell a word, they form that word when put together in a particular order. **3.** If something spells a particular result, it suggests that this will be the result: *This haphazard method could spell disaster for you.*
NOUN **4.** A spell of something is a short period of it: *a spell of rough weather*
5. a word or sequence of words used to supposedly perform magic
spell out
VERB **6.** If you spell something out, you explain it in detail: *Do I have to spell it out?*

spellbound
ADJECTIVE so fascinated by something that you cannot think about anything else: *She sat spellbound through the movie.*

spelling spellings
NOUN The spelling of a word is the correct order of letters in it.

spend spends spending spent
VERB **1.** When you spend money, you buy things with it. **2.** To spend time or energy means to use it.

spent
1. the past tense and past participle of SPEND
ADJECTIVE **2.** Spent describes things that have been used and therefore cannot be used again: *spent matches* **3.** If you are spent, you are exhausted and have no energy left.

sperm sperms
NOUN a cell produced in the sex organ of a male animal that can enter a female animal's egg and fertilize it

spew spews spewing spewed
VERB **1.** When things spew from something or when it spews them out, they come out of it in large quantities. **2.** *an informal use* To spew means to vomit.

sphere spheres
NOUN **1.** a perfectly round object, such as a ball **2.** An area of activity or interest can be referred to as a sphere of activity or interest.
spherical ADJECTIVE

Ss

sphinx sphinxes
NOUN In mythology, the sphinx was a figure with a person's head and a lion's body.

⚠ **HEADS UP**

The pronunciation of **sphinx** is unusual because it's taken directly from Greek: SFINGKS.

spice spices spicing spiced
NOUN **1.** Spice is powder or seeds from a plant added to food to give it flavour.
2. Spice is something that makes life more exciting: *Variety is the spice of life.*
VERB **3.** To spice food means to add spice to it. **4.** If you spice something up, you make it more exciting or lively.

spicy spicier spiciest

Instead of **SPICY** try...

ADJECTIVE
strongly flavoured with spices

a **tangy** taste
a **sharp** flavour
a **peppery** sauce
a **biting** aftertaste
zesty vegetable dip

spider spiders
NOUN a small, insect-like creature with eight legs that spins webs to catch insects for food

spike spikes
NOUN **1.** a long, pointed piece of metal
2. The spikes on a sports shoe are the pointed pieces of metal attached to the sole.
3. Some other long, pointed objects are called spikes: *beautiful pink flower spikes*

spiky spikier spikiest
ADJECTIVE Something spiky has sharp points.

spill spills spilling spilled
VERB **1.** If you spill something or if it spills, it accidentally falls or runs out of a container.
2. If people or things spill out of a place, they come out of it in large numbers.

spillage spillages
NOUN the spilling of something, or something that has been spilled: *an oil spillage in the Atlantic*

spin spins spinning spun
VERB **1.** If something spins, it turns quickly around a central point. **2.** When spiders spin a web, they give out a sticky substance and make it into a web. **3.** When people spin, they make thread by twisting together pieces

of fibre using a machine. **4.** If your head is spinning, you feel dizzy or confused.
NOUN **5.** a rapid turn around a central point: *a golf club that puts more spin on the ball*

spinach
NOUN a vegetable with large green leaves

spinal
ADJECTIVE to do with the spine

spine spines
NOUN **1.** Your spine is your backbone.
2. Spines are long, sharp points on an animal's body or on a plant.

spinning wheel spinning wheels
NOUN a wooden machine for spinning fibre, such as flax or wool

spinoff spinoffs
NOUN something useful that unexpectedly results from an activity

spinster spinsters
NOUN In the past, spinster was used to describe a woman who had never married.

spiny
ADJECTIVE covered with spines

spiral spirals spiralling spiralled
NOUN **1.** a continuous curve that winds around and around, with each curve above or outside the previous one
ADJECTIVE **2.** in the shape of a spiral: *a spiral staircase*
VERB **3.** If something spirals, it moves up or down in a spiral curve: *The aircraft spiralled down.* **4.** If an amount or level spirals, it rises or falls quickly at an increasing rate: *Prices have spiralled up recently.*

spire spires
NOUN The spire of a church is the tall, cone-shaped structure on top.

spirit spirits spiriting spirited
NOUN **1.** Your spirit is the part of you that is not physical and that is connected with your deepest thoughts and feelings. **2.** The spirit of a dead person is a non-physical part that is believed to remain alive after death. **3.** a supernatural being, such as a ghost **4.** Spirit is liveliness, energy, and self-confidence: *The school band is always full of spirit.* **5.** Spirit can refer to an attitude: *his old fighting spirit*
PLURAL NOUN **6.** Spirits can describe how happy or unhappy someone is: *in good spirits*
VERB **7.** If you spirit someone or something into or out of a place, you get that person or thing in or out quickly and secretly.

spirited
ADJECTIVE showing energy and courage

Ss

spirit level spirit levels

NOUN a device for finding out if a surface is level, consisting of a bubble of air sealed in a tube of liquid in a wooden or metal frame

spiritual spirituals

ADJECTIVE **1.** to do with people's thoughts and beliefs, rather than their bodies and physical surroundings **2.** to do with people's religious beliefs: *spiritual guidance*

NOUN **3.** a religious song originally sung by black people in the southern US

spiritually ADVERB

spirituality NOUN

spit spits spitting spat

NOUN **1.** Spit is saliva. **2.** a long stick made of metal or wood that is pushed through a piece of meat so that it can be hung over a fire and cooked **3.** a long, flat, narrow piece of land sticking out into a body of water

VERB **4.** If you spit, you force saliva or some other substance out of your mouth. **5.** When it is spitting, it is raining very lightly.

spite spites spiting spited

PHRASE **1. In spite of** is used to introduce a statement that makes the rest of what you are saying seem surprising: *In spite of all the warnings, they went boating without life jackets.*

VERB **2.** If you do something to spite someone, you do it deliberately to hurt or annoy that person.

NOUN **3.** If you do something out of spite, you do it to hurt or annoy someone.

spiteful

ADJECTIVE A spiteful person does or says nasty things to people deliberately to hurt them.

spitting image

NOUN If someone is the spitting image of someone else, that person looks just like the other person.

splash splashes splashing splashed

VERB **1.** If you splash around in water, your movements disturb the water in a noisy way. **2.** If liquid splashes something, it scatters over it in a lot of small drops.

NOUN **3.** A splash is the sound made when something hits or falls into water. **4.** A splash of liquid is a small quantity of it that has been spilled on something.

splatter splatters splattering splattered

VERB When something is splattered with a substance, the substance is splashed all over it: *the floor was splattered with paint*

spleen spleens

NOUN Your spleen is an organ near your stomach that controls the quality of your blood.

splendid

ADJECTIVE **1.** very good: *a splendid party* **2.** beautiful and impressive: *a splendid old mansion*

splendidly ADVERB

splendour splendours

NOUN If something has splendour, it is beautiful and impressive.

splint splints

NOUN a long piece of wood or metal fastened to a broken limb to hold it in place

splinter splinters splintering splintered

NOUN **1.** a thin, sharp piece of wood or glass that has broken off a larger piece

VERB **2.** If something splinters, it breaks into thin, sharp pieces.

split splits splitting split

VERB **1.** If something splits or if you split it, it divides into two or more parts. **2.** If something such as wood or fabric splits, a long crack or tear appears in it. **3.** If two people split something, they share it between them.

NOUN **4.** A split in a piece of wood or fabric is a crack or tear. **5.** A split between two things is a division or difference between them: *There is a split between those who agree and those who disagree with the plan.*

split up

VERB **6.** If two people split up, they end their relationship or marriage.

split second

NOUN an extremely short period of time

splitting

ADJECTIVE A splitting headache is very painful.

splutter splutters spluttering spluttered

VERB **1.** If someone splutters, that person speaks in a confused way because he or she is embarrassed. **2.** If something splutters, it makes a series of short, sharp sounds.

spoil spoils spoiling spoiled

VERB **1.** If you spoil something, you prevent it from being successful or satisfactory. **2.** To spoil children means to give them everything they want, with harmful effects on their character. **3.** To spoil someone also means to give that person something nice as a treat.

PLURAL NOUN **4.** Spoils are valuable things obtained during war or as a result of violence: *the spoils of war*

spoilsport spoilsports

NOUN someone who spoils people's fun

spoke spokes

1. Spoke is the past tense of SPEAK.

NOUN **2.** The spokes of a wheel are the bars that connect the hub to the rim.

spokesperson spokespersons
NOUN someone who speaks on behalf of another person or a group
spokesman NOUN
spokeswoman NOUN

sponge sponges sponging sponged
NOUN **1.** a sea creature with a body made up of many cells **2.** part of the very light skeleton of a sponge, used for bathing and cleaning **3.** a thing like a sponge: *a sponge cake*
VERB **4.** If you sponge something, you clean it by wiping it with a wet sponge.

sponsor sponsors sponsoring sponsored
VERB **1.** To sponsor something, such as an event or someone's training, means to support it financially: *The visit was sponsored by the Canadian Museum of Civilization.* **2.** If you sponsor someone who is doing something for charity, you agree to give that person a sum of money for the charity if he or she manages to do it. **3.** If you sponsor a proposal or suggestion, you officially put it forward and support it: *the MP who sponsored the bill*
NOUN **4.** a person or organization sponsoring something or someone
sponsorship NOUN

spontaneous
ADJECTIVE **1.** Spontaneous acts are not planned or arranged, but are done because you feel like it. **2.** A spontaneous event happens because of processes within something rather than being caused by things outside it: *a spontaneous eruption of the volcano*
spontaneously ADVERB
spontaneity NOUN

spoof spoofs
NOUN something such as an article or television program that seems to be about a serious matter but is actually a joke

spooky spookier spookiest
ADJECTIVE eerie and frightening

spool spools
NOUN a cylindrical object onto which thread, tape, or film can be wound

spoon spoons
NOUN an object shaped like a small, shallow bowl with a long handle, used for eating, stirring, and serving food

spoonful spoonfuls
NOUN the amount held by a spoon

sporadic
ADJECTIVE happening at irregular intervals: *a few sporadic attempts at keeping a diary*
sporadically ADVERB

spore spores
NOUN *a technical word* Spores are cells produced by bacteria and non-flowering plants such as fungi, which develop into new bacteria or plants.

sport sports sporting sported
NOUN **1.** A sport is a game or other enjoyable activity that needs physical effort and skill.
VERB **2.** If you sport something noticeable or unusual, you wear it: *He sported a bright orange scarf.*

sporting
ADJECTIVE **1.** relating to sport **2.** behaving in a fair and decent way

sports car sports cars
NOUN a low, fast car, usually with room for only two people

sportsman sportsmen
NOUN a man who takes part in sports and is good at them

sportswoman sportswomen
NOUN a woman who takes part in sports and is good at them

sporty sportier sportiest
ADJECTIVE **1.** A sporty car is fast and flashy. **2.** A sporty person is good at sports.

spot spots spotting spotted
NOUN **1.** Spots are small, round, coloured areas on a surface. **2.** Spots on a person's skin are small lumps or blemishes. **3.** A place can be called a spot: *the most beautiful spot in the garden*
VERB **4.** If you spot something, you notice it.
PHRASE **5.** If you do something **on the spot**, you do it immediately.

spot check spot checks
NOUN a random examination made without warning on one of a group of things or people: *spot checks by police officers*

spotless
ADJECTIVE perfectly clean
spotlessly ADVERB

spotlight spotlights spotlighting spotlighted
NOUN **1.** a powerful light that can be directed to light up a small area
VERB **2.** If something spotlights a situation or problem, it draws the public's attention to it: *a national campaign to spotlight the problem*

spotted
ADJECTIVE Something spotted has a pattern of spots on it.

spotter spotters
NOUN a person whose hobby is looking out for things of a particular kind: *a trend spotter*

Ss

spotty spottier spottiest
ADJECTIVE Someone or something that is spotty is marked with spots.

spouse spouses
NOUN Someone's spouse is the person he or she is married to.

spout spouts spouting spouted
VERB **1.** When liquid or flame spouts out of something, it shoots out in a long stream. **2.** When someone spouts what he or she has learned, that person says it in a boring way. NOUN **3.** a tube with a lip-like end for pouring liquid: *a teapot with a long spout*

sprain sprains spraining sprained
VERB **1.** If you sprain a joint, you accidentally damage it by twisting it violently. NOUN **2.** the injury caused by spraining a joint

sprawl sprawls sprawling sprawled
VERB **1.** If you sprawl somewhere, you sit or lie there with your legs and arms spread out. **2.** A place that sprawls is spread out over a large area: *a market that sprawls all over town* NOUN **3.** anything that spreads in an untidy and uncontrolled way: *urban sprawl*
sprawling ADJECTIVE

spray sprays spraying sprayed
NOUN **1.** Spray consists of many drops of liquid splashed or forced into the air: *The salt spray stung her face.* **2.** Spray is also a liquid kept under pressure in a can or other container: *hairspray* **3.** A spray of flowers or leaves consists of several of them on one stem. VERB **4.** To spray a liquid over something means to cover it with drops of the liquid.

spread spreads spreading spread
VERB **1.** If you spread something out, you open it out or arrange it so that it can be seen or used easily: *He spread the map out on his knees.* **2.** If you spread a substance on a surface, you put a thin layer on the surface. **3.** If something spreads, it gradually reaches or affects more people: *The news spread quickly.* **4.** If something spreads over a period of time, it happens regularly or continuously over that time: *The tournament was spread over two weeks.* **5.** If something such as work is spread, it is distributed evenly. NOUN **6.** The spread of something is the extent to which it gradually reaches or affects more people: *the spread of disease* **7.** A spread of ideas, interests, or other things is a wide variety of them. **8.** soft food put on bread: *cheese spread*

spreadeagled
ADJECTIVE Someone who is spreadeagled is lying with his or her arms and legs spread out.

spreadsheet spreadsheets
NOUN a computer program that is used for entering and arranging figures, used mainly for financial planning

spree sprees
NOUN a period of time spent doing something enjoyable: *a shopping spree*

sprig sprigs
NOUN a small twig with leaves on it

sprightly sprightlier sprightliest
ADJECTIVE lively and active

spring springs springing sprang sprung
NOUN **1.** Spring is the season between winter and summer. **2.** a coil of wire that returns to its natural shape after being pressed or pulled **3.** a place where water comes up through the ground **4.** an act of springing: *With a spring he had opened the door.* VERB **5.** To spring means to jump upward or forward: *She sprang to her feet.* **6.** If something springs in a particular direction, it moves suddenly and quickly: *The door sprang open.* **7.** If one thing springs from another, it is the result of it: *The failures sprang from three facts.*

springboard springboards
NOUN **1.** a flexible board on which a diver or gymnast jumps to gain height **2.** If something is a springboard for an activity or enterprise, it makes it possible for it to begin.

springbok springboks
NOUN a small antelope of southern Africa that moves in leaps

spring clean spring cleans spring cleaning spring cleaned
VERB To spring clean a house means to clean it thoroughly throughout.

sprinkle sprinkles sprinkling sprinkled
VERB If you sprinkle a liquid or powder over something, you scatter it over that thing.

sprinkling sprinklings
NOUN A sprinkling of something is a small quantity of it: *a light sprinkling of snow*

sprint sprints sprinting sprinted
NOUN **1.** a short, fast race VERB **2.** To sprint means to run fast over a short distance.

sprinter sprinters
NOUN an athlete who runs fast over short distances

sprite sprites
NOUN a type of elf or fairy

Ss

sprout sprouts sprouting sprouted
VERB **1.** When something sprouts, it grows.
2. If things sprout up, they appear rapidly: *Many new houses sprouted up in that region.*
NOUN **3.** a shoot of a plant

spruce spruces; sprucer sprucest; spruces sprucing spruced
NOUN **1.** an evergreen tree with needlelike leaves
ADJECTIVE **2.** Someone who is spruce is very neat and trim.
VERB **3.** To spruce something up means to make it neat and trim.

spunk spunks
NOUN *an informal word* Spunk is courage.

spur spurs spurring spurred
VERB **1.** If something spurs you to do something or spurs you on, it encourages you to do it.
NOUN **2.** Something that acts as a spur encourages a person to do something.
3. Spurs are sharp, metal points attached to the heels of a rider's boots and used to urge a horse on.
PHRASE **4.** If you do something **on the spur of the moment**, you do it suddenly, without planning it.

spurious
ADJECTIVE not genuine or real

spurn spurns spurning spurned
VERB If you spurn something, you refuse to accept it: *You spurned his last offer.*

spurt spurts spurting spurted
VERB **1.** When a liquid or flame

Instead of **SPURT** try...

surge from a hose
squirt from a tube
gush from a hydrant
spout like a fountain
spew blood from a wound

spurts out of something, it comes out quickly in a thick, powerful stream.
NOUN **2.** A spurt of liquid or flame is a thick, powerful stream of it: *a small spurt of blood* **3.** A spurt of activity or effort is a sudden, brief period of it.

spy spies spying spied
NOUN **1.** a person sent to find out secret information about a country or organization
VERB **2.** Someone who spies tries to find out secret information about another country or organization. **3.** If you spy on someone, you watch that person secretly. **4.** If you spy something, you notice it.

squabble squabbles squabbling squabbled
VERB **1.** When people squabble, they quarrel about something trivial.
NOUN **2.** a quarrel

squad squads
NOUN a small group chosen to do a particular activity: *the fraud squad, the volleyball squad*

squadron squadrons
NOUN a section of one of the armed forces, especially the air force

squalid
ADJECTIVE **1.** dirty, untidy, and in bad condition **2.** Squalid activities are unpleasant and often dishonest.

squall squalls
NOUN a brief, violent storm

squalor
NOUN Squalor consists of bad or dirty conditions or surroundings.

squander squanders squandering squandered
VERB To squander money or resources means to waste them: *They have squandered huge amounts of money.*

square squares squaring squared
NOUN **1.** a shape with four equal sides and four right angles **2.** In a town or city, a square is a flat, open place, bordered by buildings or streets. **3.** The square of a number is the number multiplied by itself. For example, the square of 3, written 3^2, is 3 x 3.
ADJECTIVE **4.** shaped like a square: *her delicate, square face* **5.** *Square* is used before units of length when talking about the area of something: *24 m^2* **6.** *Square* is used after units of length when you are giving the length of each side of something square: *a piece of fabric measuring a metre square*
VERB **7.** If you square a number, you multiply it by itself.

squarely
ADVERB **1.** Squarely means directly rather than indirectly or at an angle: *I looked squarely in the mirror.* **2.** If you approach a subject squarely, you consider it fully, without trying to avoid unpleasant aspects of it.

square root square roots
NOUN A square root of a number is a number that makes the first number when it is multiplied by itself. For example, the square roots of 25 are 5 and -5.

squash squashes squashing squashed
VERB **1.** If you squash something, you press it so that it becomes flat or loses its shape.
NOUN **2.** an edible gourd, the fruit of which may be cooked and eaten as a vegetable

Ss

3. Squash is a game in which two players hit a small rubber ball against the walls of a court using racquets.

squat squats squatting squatted; squatter squattest
VERB **1.** If you squat down, you crouch, balancing on your feet with your legs bent. **2.** A person who squats in an unused building lives there as a squatter.
NOUN **3.** a building used by squatters
ADJECTIVE **4.** short and thick

squatter squatters
NOUN a person who lives in an unused building without permission and without paying rent

squawk squawks squawking squawked
VERB **1.** When a bird squawks, it makes a loud, harsh noise.
NOUN **2.** a loud, harsh noise made by a bird

squeak squeaks squeaking squeaked
VERB **1.** If something squeaks, it makes a short, high-pitched sound.
NOUN **2.** a short, high-pitched sound
squeaky ADJECTIVE

squeal squeals squealing squealed
VERB **1.** When things or people squeal, they make long, high-pitched sounds.
NOUN **2.** a long, high-pitched sound

squeamish
ADJECTIVE easily upset by unpleasant sights or situations

squeeze squeezes squeezing squeezed
VERB **1.** When you squeeze something, you press it firmly from two sides. **2.** If you squeeze something into a small amount of time or space, you manage to fit it in.
NOUN **3.** If you give something a squeeze, you squeeze it: *She gave my hand a quick squeeze.* **4.** If getting into something is a squeeze, it is just possible to fit into it: *It would take four comfortably, but six would be a squeeze.*

squelch squelches squelching squelched
VERB **1.** To squelch means to make a wet, sucking sound.
NOUN **2.** a wet, sucking sound

squid squids
NOUN a sea creature with a long, soft body and many tentacles

squiggle squiggles
NOUN a wriggly line

squint squints squinting squinted
VERB **1.** If you squint at something, you look at it with your eyes screwed up.
NOUN **2.** If someone has a squint, that person's eyes look in different directions from each other.

squire squires
NOUN In the Middle Ages, a squire was a young man who assisted a knight before becoming a knight himself.

squirm squirms squirming squirmed
VERB If you squirm, you wriggle and twist your body about, usually because you are nervous or embarrassed.

squirrel squirrels
NOUN a small, furry animal with a long, bushy tail

squirt squirts squirting squirted
VERB **1.** If a liquid squirts, it comes out of a narrow opening in a thin, fast stream.
NOUN **2.** a thin, fast stream of liquid

stab stabs stabbing stabbed
VERB **1.** To stab someone means to wound that person by pushing a knife into his or her body. **2.** To stab at something means to push at it sharply with your finger or with something long and narrow.
PHRASE **3.** *an informal use* If you **have a stab** at something, you try to do it.
NOUN **4.** You can refer to a sudden, unpleasant feeling as a stab of something: *He felt a stab of guilt.*

stable stables
ADJECTIVE **1.** not likely to change or come to an end suddenly: *I am in a stable relationship.* **2.** firmly fixed or balanced and not likely to move, wobble, or fall
NOUN **3.** a building in which horses are kept
stability NOUN
stabilize VERB

staccato
ADJECTIVE consisting of a series of short, sharp, separate sounds

stack stacks stacking stacked
NOUN **1.** A stack of things is a pile of them, one on top of the other.
PLURAL NOUN **2.** *an informal use* If someone has stacks of something, that person has a lot of it.
VERB **3.** If you stack things, you arrange them one on top of the other in a pile.

stadium stadiums
NOUN a structure with rows of seats around it used for athletic events or concerts

staff staffs staffing staffed
NOUN **1.** The staff of an organization are the people who work for it.
VERB **2.** To staff an organization means to find and employ people to work in it. **3.** If an organization is staffed by particular people, they are the people who work for it.

stag stags
NOUN an adult male deer

Ss

stage stages staging staged
NOUN **1.** a part of a process that lasts for a period of time **2.** In a theatre, the stage is a raised platform where the actors or entertainers perform. **3.** You can refer to the profession of acting as **the stage.**
VERB **4.** If someone stages a play or event, that person organizes it and presents it or takes part in it.

stagecoach stagecoaches
NOUN a large carriage pulled by horses that used to carry passengers and mail

stagger staggers staggering staggered
VERB **1.** If you stagger, you walk unsteadily because you are ill or drunk. **2.** If something staggers you, it amazes you. **3.** If events are staggered, they are arranged so that they do not all happen at the same time.

staggering ADJECTIVE

stagnant
ADJECTIVE Stagnant water is not flowing and is unhealthy and dirty.

staid
ADJECTIVE serious and dull

stain stains staining stained
NOUN **1.** a mark on something that is difficult to remove
VERB **2.** If a substance stains something, the thing becomes marked or coloured by it.

stained glass
NOUN Stained glass is coloured pieces of glass held together with strips of lead.

stainless steel
NOUN Stainless steel is a metal made from steel and chromium that does not rust.

stair stairs
NOUN one of a series of steps going from one floor to another inside a building

staircase staircases
NOUN a set of stairs including the framework and walls

stairway stairways
NOUN a set of stairs

stake stakes staking staked
PHRASE **1.** If something is **at stake**, it might be lost or damaged if something else is not successful: *The whole future of the company was at stake.*
PLURAL NOUN **2.** The stakes involved in something are the things that can be lost or gained.
VERB **3.** If you say you would stake something valuable such as your money, life, or reputation on the success or truth of something, you mean you would risk it: *He is prepared to stake his own career on this.*
NOUN **4.** If you have a stake in something such as a business, you own part of it and its success is important to you. **5.** a pointed wooden post that can be hammered into the ground and used as a support

stale staler stalest
ADJECTIVE **1.** Stale food or air is no longer fresh. **2.** If you feel stale, you have no new ideas and are bored.

stalemate
NOUN **1.** A stalemate is a situation in which neither side in an argument or contest can win. **2.** In chess, a stalemate is a situation in which neither player can make any move permitted by the rules, so that the game ends and no one wins.

stalk stalks stalking stalked
NOUN **1.** The stalk of a flower or leaf is its stem.
VERB **2.** To stalk a person or animal means to follow or pursue that person or animal without being seen or heard. **3.** If someone stalks into a room, that person walks in a stiff, proud, or angry way.

stall stalls stalling stalled
NOUN **1.** a stand or booth for selling things in a market **2.** a compartment for an animal in a stable that is enclosed on three sides
VERB **3.** When a vehicle stalls, the engine suddenly stops. **4.** If you stall when someone asks you to do something, you try to avoid doing it until a later time.

stallion stallions
NOUN an adult male horse that can be used for breeding

SPELL-CHECK THIS!

A computer's spell-check won't catch wrong **homophones** (words that are spelled differently but sound the same).

He gave them a chillingly cold stair.

In this sentence, **stair** should be **stare**.
Stare means *a long, fixed look*.
A **stair** means *a series of steps*.

NEL

Ss

stamina

NOUN Stamina is the physical or mental energy needed to do something for a very long time.

stammer stammers stammering stammered

VERB **1.** When someone stammers, that person speaks with difficulty, repeating words and sounds and hesitating awkwardly.

NOUN **2.** Someone who has a stammer tends to stammer when he or she speaks.

stamp stamps stamping stamped

NOUN **1.** a small piece of paper with a sticky back that you stick on a letter or parcel before mailing it **2.** a small block with a pattern cut into it that you press onto an inky pad and make a mark with on paper; also the mark made by the stamp **3.** If something bears the stamp of a particular quality or person, it shows clear signs of that quality or of the person's style or characteristics.

VERB **4.** If you stamp a piece of paper, you make a mark on it using a stamp. **5.** If you stamp, you lift your foot and put it down hard on the ground.

stamp out

VERB **6.** To stamp out something means to put an end to it: *the battle to stamp out bullying in schools*

stampede stampedes stampeding stampeded

VERB **1.** When a group of animals stampede, they run in a wild, uncontrolled way.

NOUN **2.** a group of animals stampeding

stance stances

NOUN Your stance on a particular matter is your attitude and way of dealing with it: *He takes no particular stance on animal rights.*

stand stands standing stood

VERB **1.** If you are standing, you are upright, your legs are straight, and your weight is supported by your feet. When you stand up, you get into a standing position. **2.** If something stands somewhere, that is where it is: *The house stands alone on the top of a small hill.* **3.** If you stand something somewhere, you put it there in an upright position: *Stand the containers on bricks.* **4.** If a decision or offer stands, it is still valid: *My offer still stands.* **5.** You can use *stand* when describing the state or condition of something: *Youth unemployment stands at 35 percent.* **6.** If something can stand a situation or test, it is good enough or strong enough not to be damaged by it. **7.** If you cannot stand something, you cannot bear it: *I can't stand that movie.* **8.** If you stand in an election, you are one of the candidates. PHRASE **9.** When someone **stands trial**, that

person is tried in a court of law.

NOUN **10.** a stall or very small store outdoors or in a large public building

PLURAL NOUN **11. The stands** are a large structure where spectators sit to watch what is happening, especially at a sporting event. **12.** a piece of furniture designed to hold something: *an television stand*

stand by

VERB **13.** If you stand by to provide help or take action, you are ready to do it if necessary. **14.** If you stand by while something happens, you do nothing to stop it.

stand down

VERB **15.** If someone stands down, that person resigns from his or her job or position.

stand for

VERB **16.** If a letter stands for a particular word, it is an abbreviation for that word. **17.** If you say you will not stand for something, you mean you will not tolerate it.

stand in

VERB **18.** If you stand in for someone, you take that person's place while he or she is ill or away.

stand out

VERB **19.** If something stands out, it can be easily noticed or is more important than other similar things.

stand up

VERB **20.** If something stands up to rough treatment, it is not damaged or harmed. **21.** If you stand up to someone who is criticizing or attacking you, you defend yourself.

standard standards

NOUN **1.** a level of quality or achievement that is considered acceptable: *The work is not up to standard.*

PLURAL NOUN **2.** Standards are moral principles of behaviour.

ADJECTIVE **3.** usual, normal, and correct: *The practice became standard procedure for most car companies.*

standardize standardizes standardizing standardized

VERB To standardize things means to change them so that they all have a similar set of features: *We have decided to standardize our equipment.*

standby standbys

NOUN **1.** something available for use when you need it: *a useful standby*

ADJECTIVE **2.** A standby ticket is a cheap ticket that you buy just before a flight if there are any seats left.

stand-in stand-ins
NOUN someone who takes a person's place while the person is ill or away: *The meeting was run by a stand-in.*

standing
ADJECTIVE **1.** permanently in existence or used regularly: *a standing joke*
NOUN **2.** A person's standing is his or her status and reputation. **3.** *Standing* is used to say how long something has existed: *a friend of 20 years' standing*

standpoint standpoints
NOUN If you consider something from a particular standpoint, you consider it from that point of view: *from a military standpoint*

standstill
NOUN If something comes to a standstill, it stops completely.

stanza stanzas
NOUN a verse of a poem

staple staples stapling stapled
NOUN **1.** Staples are small pieces of wire that hold sheets of paper firmly together.
VERB **2.** If you staple sheets of paper, you fasten them together with staples.
ADJECTIVE **3.** A staple food forms a regular and basic part of someone's everyday diet.

star stars starring starred
NOUN **1.** a large ball of burning gas in space that appears as a point of light in the sky at night **2.** a shape with four, five, or more points sticking out in a regular pattern **3.** Famous actors, sports players, and musicians are referred to as stars.
VERB **4.** If an actor or actress stars in a movie or if the movie stars that person, he or she has one of the most important parts in it.

starboard
ADJECTIVE OR NOUN The starboard side of a ship is the right-hand side when you are facing the front.

starch starches starching starched
NOUN **1.** Starch is a substance used for stiffening fabric such as cotton and linen. **2.** Starch is a carbohydrate found in foods such as bread and potatoes.
VERB **3.** To starch fabric means to stiffen it with starch.

stare stares staring stared
VERB **1.** If you stare at something, you look at it for a long time.
NOUN **2.** a long, fixed look at something

starfish starfishes starfish
NOUN a flat, star-shaped sea creature with five limbs

stark starker starkest
ADJECTIVE **1.** harsh, unpleasant and plain: *the stark choice*
PHRASE **2.** If someone is **stark naked**, that person has no clothes on at all

starling starlings
NOUN a common bird with shiny, dark feathers

start starts starting started
VERB **1.** If something starts, it begins to take place or comes into existence: *When does the party start?* **2.** If you start to do something, you begin to do it: *My brother started to cry.* **3.** If you start something, you cause it to begin or to come into existence: *as good a time as any to start a business* **4.** If you start a machine or car, you operate the controls to make it work. **5.** If you start, your body suddenly jerks because of surprise or fear.
NOUN **6.** The start of something is the point or time at which it begins. **7.** If you do something with a start, you do it with a sudden jerky movement because of surprise or fear: *I awoke with a start.*

startle startles startling startled
VERB If something sudden and unexpected startles you, it surprises you and makes you slightly frightened.
startled ADJECTIVE
startling ADJECTIVE

starve starves starving starved
VERB **1.** If people are starving, they are suffering from a serious lack of food and are likely to die. **2.** To starve a person or animal means to prevent that person or animal from having any food. **3.** *an informal use* If you say you are starving, you mean you are very hungry. **4.** If someone or something is starved of a necessity, that person or thing is suffering because he or she is not getting enough of it: *The school was starved of cash.*
starvation NOUN

stash stashes stashing stashed
VERB *an informal word* If you stash something away in a secret place, you store it there to keep it safe.

state states stating stated
NOUN **1.** The state of something is its condition, what it is like, or its circumstances. **2.** Countries are sometimes referred to as states: *the state of Denmark* **3.** Some countries are divided into regions called states that make some of their own laws: *the State of Vermont* **4.** You can refer to the government or administration of a country as the state.
PHRASE **5.** If you are **in a state**, you are upset

Ss

and unable to control your emotions.

ADJECTIVE **6.** A state ceremony involves the ruler or leader of a country.

VERB **7.** If you state something, you say it or write it, especially in a formal way.

statement statements

NOUN **1.** something you say or write when you give facts or information in a formal way **2.** a document provided by a bank showing all the money paid into and out of an account during a period of time

statesman statesmen

NOUN a man who is an important and experienced politician

stateswoman stateswomen

NOUN a woman who is an important and experienced politician

static

ADJECTIVE **1.** never moving or changing: *The temperature remains fairly static.*

NOUN **2.** Static is an electrical charge caused by friction. It builds up in metal objects.

station stations stationing stationed

NOUN **1.** a building and platforms where trains stop for passengers **2.** A bus station is a place where some buses start their journeys. **3.** A radio or television station is the frequency on which a particular company broadcasts; also the place from which a broadcast originates. **4.** *an old-fashioned use* A person's station is the position or rank in society that he or she holds.

VERB **5.** Someone who is stationed somewhere is sent there to work or do a particular job: *She was stationed in Red Lake.*

stationary

ADJECTIVE not moving: *a stationary car*

stationery

NOUN Stationery is paper, pens, and other writing equipment.

statistic statistics

NOUN **1.** Statistics are facts obtained by analyzing numerical information. **2.** Statistics is the branch of mathematics that deals with the analysis of numerical information.

statistical ADJECTIVE

statistician statisticians

NOUN a person who studies or works with statistics

⚠ **HEADS UP**

Statistic is pronounced stuh-TIS-tik, but **statistician** is pronounced sta-tih-STISH-un.

statue statues

NOUN a sculpture of a person

stature

NOUN **1.** Someone's stature is that person's height and size. **2.** Someone's stature is also his or her importance and reputation: *the desire to gain international stature*

status statuses

NOUN **1.** A person's status is his or her position and importance in society. **2.** Status is also the official classification given to someone or something: *your legal status*

status quo

NOUN The status quo is the situation that exists at a certain time: *Keep the status quo.*

statute statutes

NOUN a law

statutory ADJECTIVE

staunch stauncher staunchest

ADJECTIVE A staunch supporter is a strong and loyal supporter.

stave staves staving staved

NOUN **1.** one of the curved pieces of wood forming the side of a barrel or other container

VERB **2.** If you stave something off, you try to delay or prevent it.

stay stays staying stayed

VERB **1.** If you stay in a place, you do not move away from it: *She stayed in bed until noon.* **2.** If you stay at a hotel or a friend's house, you spend some time there as a guest or visitor. **3.** If you stay in a particular state, you continue to be in it: *I stayed awake all night.*

NOUN **4.** a short time spent somewhere: *a very pleasant stay in Kingston*

stead

NOUN *a formal word* Something that will stand someone in good stead will be useful to that person in the future.

steadfast

ADJECTIVE refusing to change or give up

steady steadier steadiest; steadies steadying steadied

ADJECTIVE **1.** continuing or developing gradually without major interruptions or changes: *a steady rise in profits* **2.** firm and not shaking or wobbling: *He held out a steady hand.* **3.** A steady look or voice is calm and controlled. **4.** Someone who is steady is sensible and reliable.

VERB **5.** When you steady something, you hold on to prevent it from shaking or wobbling. **6.** When you steady yourself, you control and calm yourself.

steadily ADVERB

Ss

steak steaks
NOUN a thick slice of meat or fish, usually cooked by frying or broiling

steal steals stealing stole stolen
VERB **1.** To steal something means to take it without permission and without intending to return it. **2.** To steal somewhere means to move there quietly and secretively.

stealth
NOUN If you do something with stealth, you do it quietly and secretively.
stealthy ADJECTIVE
stealthily ADVERB

steam steams steaming steamed
NOUN **1.** Steam is the hot vapour formed when water boils.
ADJECTIVE **2.** Steam engines are operated using steam as a means of power.
VERB **3.** If something steams, it gives off steam. **4.** To steam food means to cook it in steam.
steamy ADJECTIVE

steam engine steam engines
NOUN any engine that uses the energy of steam to produce mechanical work

steamer steamers
NOUN **1.** a ship powered by steam **2.** a container with small holes in the bottom in which you steam food

steed steeds
NOUN *a literary or poetic word* a horse

steel steels steeling steeled
NOUN **1.** Steel is a very strong metal containing mainly iron with a small amount of carbon.
VERB **2.** To steel yourself means to prepare to deal with something unpleasant.

steel band steel bands
NOUN a group of people who play music on special metal drums

steep steeper steepest; steeps steeping steeped
ADJECTIVE **1.** A steep slope rises sharply and is difficult to go up. **2.** larger than is reasonable: *a steep price increase*
VERB **3.** To steep something in a liquid means to soak it thoroughly.
steeply ADVERB

steeped
ADJECTIVE If a person or place is steeped in a particular quality, that person or place is deeply affected by it: *an industry steeped in tradition*

steeple steeples
NOUN a tall, pointed structure on top of a church tower

steeplechase steeplechases
NOUN a long horse race in which the horses jump over obstacles such as hedges and ditches

steer steers steering steered
VERB **1.** To steer a vehicle or boat means to control it so that it goes in the right direction. **2.** To steer someone toward a particular course of action means to influence and direct that person's behaviour or thoughts.
NOUN **3.** a castrated bull

stem stems stemming stemmed
NOUN **1.** The stem of a plant is the long, thin central part above the ground that carries the leaves and flowers. **2.** The stem of a glass is the long, narrow part connecting the bowl to the base.
VERB **3.** If a problem stems from a particular situation, that situation is the original starting point or cause of the problem. **4.** If you stem the flow of something, you restrict it or stop it from spreading: *to stem bleeding*

stench stenches
NOUN a very strong, unpleasant smell

stencil stencils stencilling stencilled
NOUN **1.** a thin sheet with a cut-out pattern through which ink or paint passes to form the pattern on the surface below
VERB **2.** To stencil a design on a surface means to create it using a stencil.

step steps stepping stepped
NOUN **1.** If you take a step, you lift your foot and put it down somewhere else. **2.** one of a series of actions that you take in order to achieve something **3.** a raised, flat surface, usually one of a series that you can walk up or down
VERB **4.** If you step in a particular direction, you move your foot in that direction. **5.** If someone steps down or steps aside from an important position, that person resigns.

step-
PREFIX If a word like *father* or *sister* has *step-* in front of it, it shows that the family relationship has come about because a parent has married again: *stepfather, stepsister*

steppe steppes
NOUN a large area of open grassland with no trees

stepping stone stepping stones
NOUN **1.** Stepping stones are a line of large stones that you walk on to cross a shallow river. **2.** a job or event that is regarded as a stage in your progress, especially in your career

Ss

stereo stereos

ADJECTIVE **1.** A stereo recording or music system is one in which the sound is directed through two or more speakers.
NOUN **2.** a piece of equipment that reproduces sound from records, tapes, or CDs, directing the sound through two or more speakers

stereotype stereotypes stereotyping stereotyped

NOUN **1.** a fixed image or set of characteristics that people consider to represent a particular type of person or thing: *She fits the stereotype of the quiet, stern librarian.*
VERB **2.** If you stereotype someone, you assume that person is a particular type of person and will behave in a particular way.

sterile

ADJECTIVE **1.** Sterile means completely clean and free from germs. **2.** A sterile person or animal is unable to produce offspring.
sterility NOUN

sterilize sterilizes sterilizing sterilized

VERB **1.** To sterilize something means to make it completely clean and free from germs, usually by boiling it or treating it with an antiseptic. **2.** If a person or animal is sterilized, that person or animal has an operation that makes it impossible to produce offspring.

sterling

ADJECTIVE excellent in quality: *The volunteers are doing sterling work.*

stern sterner sternest; sterns

ADJECTIVE **1.** very serious and strict: *a stern father, a stern warning*

Instead of **STERN** try...

a steely gaze
a harsh lecture
a rigid outlook
a strict upbringing
a hard-nosed leader

NOUN **2.** The stern of a boat is the back part.

steroid steroids

NOUN Steroids are chemicals that occur naturally in your body.

stethoscope stethoscopes

NOUN a device used by doctors to listen to a patient's heart and breathing, consisting of earpieces connected to a hollow tube and a small disc

stew stews stewing stewed

NOUN **1.** a dish of small pieces of food cooked together slowly in a liquid
VERB **2.** To stew meat, vegetables, or fruit means to cook them slowly in a liquid.

steward stewards

NOUN **1.** a person who works on a ship or plane looking after passengers and serving meals **2.** a person who helps to direct the public at a race, march, or other event

stick sticks sticking stuck

NOUN **1.** a long, thin piece of wood **2.** A stick of something is a long, thin piece of it: *a stick of celery*
VERB **3.** If you stick a long or pointed object into something, you push it in. **4.** If you stick one thing to another, you attach it with glue or tape. **5.** If one thing sticks to another, it becomes attached and is difficult to remove. **6.** If a movable part of something sticks, it becomes fixed and will no longer move or work properly: *My gears keep sticking.* **7.** *an informal use* If you stick something somewhere, you put it there. **8.** If you stick by someone, you continue to help and support that person. **9.** If you stick to something, you keep to it and do not change to something else: *He should have stuck to the old ways of doing things.* **10.** When people stick together, they stay together and support each other.

stick out

VERB **11.** If something sticks out, it projects from something else. **12.** To stick out also means to be very noticeable

stick up

VERB **13.** If something sticks up, it points upward from a surface. **14.** *an informal use* If you stick up for a person or a principle, you support or defend that person or that principle.

sticker stickers

NOUN a small piece of paper or plastic with writing or a picture on it, that you stick onto a surface

stickhandle stickhandles stickhandling stickhandled

VERB **1.** In hockey, if you stickhandle the puck, you control it with your stick. **2.** If you stickhandle an issue or a problem, you manage it skilfully.

stick insect stick insects

NOUN an insect with a long, cylindrical body and long legs, which looks like a twig

sticky stickier stickiest

ADJECTIVE **1.** A sticky object is covered with a substance that can stick to other things: *sticky hands* **2.** *an informal use* A sticky situation is difficult or embarrassing to deal with. **3.** Sticky weather is unpleasantly hot and humid.

Ss

stiff stiffer stiffest

ADJECTIVE **1.** Something that is stiff is firm and not easily bent. **2.** If you feel stiff, your muscles or joints ache when you move. **3.** Stiff behaviour is formal and not friendly or relaxed. **4.** Stiff also means difficult or severe: *stiff competition for places on the team* **5.** A stiff breeze is blowing strongly.

ADVERB **6.** *an informal use* If you are bored stiff or scared stiff, you are very bored or very scared.

stiffly ADVERB

stiffness NOUN

stiffen stiffens stiffening stiffened

VERB **1.** If you stiffen, you suddenly stop moving and your muscles become tense: *I stiffened with tension.* **2.** If your joints or muscles stiffen, they become sore and difficult to bend or move. **3.** If fabric or material is stiffened, it is made firmer so that it does not bend easily.

> ⚠ **HEADS UP**
>
> The suffix **-en** can mean *make more so*: *soften, sweeten.* It can also mean *made of*: *woollen, wooden.*

stifle stifles stifling stifled

VERB **1.** If the atmosphere stifles you, you feel you cannot breathe properly. **2.** To stifle something means to stop it from happening or continuing: *I stifled a yawn.*

stifling ADJECTIVE

stigma stigmas

NOUN If something has a stigma attached to it, people consider it unacceptable or a disgrace: *a social stigma*

stile stiles

NOUN a step on either side of a wall or fence to enable you to climb over

stiletto stilettos

NOUN Stilettos are women's shoes with very high, narrow heels.

still stiller stillest; stills

ADVERB **1.** If a situation still exists, it has continued to exist and it exists now. **2.** If something could still happen, it might happen although it has not happened yet. **3.** *Still* emphasizes that something is the case in spite of other things: *Whatever you think of him, he's still your best friend.*

ADVERB OR ADJECTIVE **4.** Still means staying in the same position without moving: *Sit still. The air was still.*

ADJECTIVE **5.** A still place is quiet and peaceful with no signs of activity.

NOUN **6.** a photograph taken from a movie or video

stillness NOUN

stillborn

ADJECTIVE A stillborn baby is dead when it is born.

stilt stilts

NOUN **1.** Stilts are two long pieces of wood or metal on which people balance and walk. **2.** Stilts are also long, upright poles on which a building is built, for example on wet land.

stilted

ADJECTIVE formal, unnatural, and rather awkward: *a stilted conversation*

stimulant stimulants

NOUN a drug or other substance that makes your body work faster, increases your heart rate, and makes it difficult to sleep

stimulate stimulates stimulating stimulated

VERB **1.** To stimulate something means to encourage it to begin or develop: *to stimulate discussion* **2.** If something stimulates you, it gives you new ideas and enthusiasm.

stimulating ADJECTIVE

stimulation NOUN

stimulus stimuli

NOUN something that causes a process or event to begin or develop

sting stings stinging stung

VERB **1.** If a creature or plant stings you, it pricks your skin and injects a substance that causes pain. **2.** If a part of your body stings, you feel a sharp, tingling pain there. **3.** If someone's remarks sting you, they make you feel upset and hurt.

NOUN **4.** A creature's sting is the part it stings you with.

stink stinks stinking stank stunk

VERB **1.** Something that stinks smells very unpleasant.

NOUN **2.** a very unpleasant smell

stint stints

NOUN a period of time spent doing a particular job: *a three-year stint in the army*

stipulate stipulates stipulating stipulated

VERB *a formal word* If you stipulate that something must be done, you state clearly that it must be done.

stipulation NOUN

stir stirs stirring stirred

VERB **1.** When you stir a liquid, you move it around using a spoon or a stick. **2.** To stir means to move slightly. **3.** If something stirs you, it makes you feel strong emotions: *The power of the singing stirred me.*

NOUN 4. If an event causes a stir, it causes general excitement or shock: *two books that have caused a stir*

stirring stirrings
ADJECTIVE **1.** causing excitement, emotion, and enthusiasm: *a stirring account of the action*
NOUN **2.** If there is a stirring of emotion, people begin to feel it.

stirrup stirrups
NOUN Stirrups are two metal loops hanging by leather straps from a horse's saddle, which you put your feet in when riding.

stitch stitches stitching stitched
VERB **1.** When you stitch pieces of material together, you use a needle and thread to sew them together. **2.** To stitch a wound means to use a special needle and thread to hold the edges of skin together.
NOUN **3.** one of the pieces of thread that can be seen where material has been sewn **4.** one of the pieces of thread that can be seen where a wound has been stitched: *He had 11 stitches in his lip.* **5.** If you have a stitch, you feel a sharp pain at the side of your abdomen, usually because you have been running or laughing.

stoat stoats
NOUN a small wild animal with a long body and brown fur

stock stocks stocking stocked
NOUN **1.** A store's stock is the total amount of goods it has for sale. **2.** If you have a stock of things, you have a supply ready for use. **3.** The stock an animal or person comes from is the type of animal or person that he, she, or it is descended from: *She is of French Canadian stock.* **4.** Stock is farm animals. **5.** Stock is a liquid made from boiling meat, bones, or vegetables together in water. Stock is used as a base for soups, stews, and sauces.
PLURAL NOUN **6.** Stocks are shares bought as an investment in a company; also the amount of money raised by the company through the issue of shares.
VERB **7.** A store that stocks particular goods keeps a supply of them to sell. **8.** If you stock a shelf or cupboard, you fill it with food or other things.
ADJECTIVE **9.** A stock expression or way of doing something is one that is commonly used.
stock up
VERB **10.** If you stock up with something, you buy a supply of it.

stockbroker stockbrokers
NOUN A stockbroker is a person whose job is to buy and sell shares for people who want to invest money.

stock exchange stock exchanges
NOUN a place where there is trading in stocks and shares: *the Toronto Stock Exchange*

stocking stockings
NOUN Stockings are long pieces of thin clothing that cover the foot and leg.

stock market
another name for STOCK EXCHANGE

stockpile stockpiles stockpiling stockpiled
VERB **1.** If someone stockpiles something, that person stores large quantities of it for future use.
NOUN **2.** a large supply of something

stocktaking
NOUN Stocktaking is the counting and checking of all a store's or business's goods.

stocky stockier stockiest
ADJECTIVE A stocky person is rather short, but broad and solid-looking.

stoke stokes stoking stoked
VERB To stoke a fire means to keep it burning by moving it or adding fuel.

stomach stomachs stomaching stomached
NOUN **1.** Your stomach is the organ inside your body where food is digested. **2.** You can refer to the front part of your body below your waist as your stomach.
VERB **3.** If you cannot stomach something, you strongly dislike it and cannot accept it.

stone stones stoning stoned
NOUN **1.** Stone is the hard, solid substance found in the ground and used for building. **2.** a small piece of rock **3.** The stone in a fruit such as a plum or cherry is the large seed in the centre. **4.** You can refer to a jewel as a stone: *a diamond ring with three stones*
VERB **5.** To stone someone or something means to throw stones at that person or thing.

stony stonier stoniest
ADJECTIVE **1.** Stony ground is rough and contains a lot of stones or rocks. **2.** If someone's expression is stony, it shows no friendliness or sympathy.

stool stools
NOUN **1.** a seat with legs but no back or arms **2.** a lump of feces

stoop stoops stooping stooped
VERB **1.** If you stoop, you stand or walk with your shoulders bent forward. **2.** If you would not stoop to something, you would not disgrace yourself by doing it.

Ss

stop stops stopping stopped

VERB **1.** If you stop doing something, you no longer do it. **2.** If an activity or process stops, it comes to an end or no longer happens. **3.** If a machine stops, it no longer functions or it is switched off. **4.** To stop something means to prevent it. **5.** If people or things that are moving stop, they no longer move. **6.** If you stop somewhere, you stay there for a short while.

PHRASE **7.** To **put a stop to** something means to prevent it from happening or continuing.

NOUN **8.** a place where a bus, train, or other vehicle stops during a journey **9.** If something that is moving comes to a stop, it no longer moves.

stoppage stoppages

NOUN If there is a stoppage, a movement, activity, or supply is stopped.

stopper stoppers

NOUN a plug or cork that fits into the neck of a jar or bottle

stopwatch stopwatches

NOUN a watch that can be started and stopped by pressing buttons, which is used to time events such as races

storage

NOUN The storage of something is the keeping of it somewhere until it is needed.

store stores storing stored

NOUN **1.** a place where goods are kept for sale **2.** A store of something is a supply kept for future use. **3.** a place where things are kept while they are not used

VERB **4.** When you store something somewhere, you keep it there until it is needed.

PHRASE **5.** Something that is **in store for** you is going to happen to you in the future.

storeroom storerooms

NOUN a room where things are kept until they are needed

storey storeys

NOUN A storey of a building is one of its floors or levels.

stork storks

NOUN a very large white-and-black bird with long red legs and a long bill

storm storms storming stormed

NOUN **1.** When there is a storm, there is heavy rain, a strong wind, and often thunder and lightning. **2.** If something causes a storm, it causes an angry or excited reaction: *His words caused a storm of protest.*

VERB **3.** If someone storms out, that person leaves quickly, noisily, and angrily. **4.** To storm means to say something in a loud, angry voice: *He stormed at the players after they lost the game.* **5.** If people storm a place, they attack it.

stormy ADJECTIVE

story stories

NOUN **1.** a description of imaginary people and events written or told to entertain people **2.** The story of something or someone is an account of the important events that have happened to that person: *his life story*

stout stouter stoutest

ADJECTIVE **1.** rather fat **2.** thick, strong, and sturdy: *stout castle walls* **3.** determined, firm, and strong: *He can outrun the stoutest opposition.*

stoutly ADVERB

stove stoves

NOUN a piece of equipment for heating a room or for cooking

stow stows stowing stowed

VERB **1.** If you stow something somewhere or stow it away, you store it until it is needed. **2.** If someone stows away in a ship or plane, that person hides in it to go somewhere secretly without paying.

straddle straddles straddling straddled

VERB **1.** If you straddle something, you stand or sit with one leg on either side of it. **2.** If something straddles a place, it crosses it, linking different parts together: *The town straddles a river.*

straight straighter straightest

ADJECTIVE OR ADVERB **1.** continuing in the same

SPELL-CHECK THIS!

A computer's spell-check won't catch wrong **homophones** (words that are spelled differently but sound the same).

He gulped as the elevator stopped at the thirteenth story.

In this sentence, **story** should be **storey**. Storey means *one level of a building*. Story means *a retold account*.

direction without curving or bending: *The straight path will take you to the south entrance of the park. The woman stared straight ahead.* **2.** upright or level rather than sloping or bent: *Keep your arms straight.* **3.** honest, frank, and direct: *They wouldn't give me a straight answer. I told her straight that she should have been honest with them.*
ADVERB **4.** immediately and directly: *We always go straight home from school.*
ADJECTIVE **5.** neat and tidy: *Get this room straight.*

straightaway
ADVERB If you do something straightaway, you do it immediately.

straighten straightens straightening straightened
VERB **1.** To straighten something means to remove any bends or curves from it. **2.** To straighten something also means to make it neat and tidy. **3.** To straighten out a confused situation means to organize and deal with it.

straightforward
ADJECTIVE **1.** easy and involving no problems **2.** honest, open, and frank

strain strains straining strained
NOUN **1.** Strain is worry and nervous tension. **2.** If a strain is put on something, it is affected by a strong force that may damage it. **3.** You can refer to an aspect of someone's character, remarks, or work as a strain: *There was a strain of bitterness in his voice.* **4.** You can refer to distant sounds of music as strains of music. **5.** A particular strain of plant is a variety of it: *strains of rose*
VERB **6.** To strain something means to force it or use it more than is reasonable or normal. **7.** If you strain a muscle, you injure it by moving awkwardly. **8.** To strain food means to pour away the liquid from it.

strained
ADJECTIVE **1.** worried and anxious **2.** If a relationship is strained, people feel unfriendly and do not trust each other.

strait straits
NOUN **1.** You can refer to a narrow strip of sea as a strait or the straits: *the Strait of Canso*
PLURAL NOUN **2.** If someone is in a bad situation, you can say that person is in difficult straits.

straitjacket straitjackets
NOUN a special jacket used to tie the arms of a violent person tightly around his or her body

straitlaced
ADJECTIVE having a very strict and serious attitude to moral behaviour

strand strands
NOUN **1.** A strand of thread or hair is a single long piece of it. **2.** You can refer to a part of a situation or idea as a strand of it: *the different strands of the problem*

stranded
ADJECTIVE If someone or something is stranded somewhere, that person or thing is unable to leave.

strange stranger strangest
ADJECTIVE **1.** unusual or unexpected **2.** not known, seen, or experienced before: *alone in a strange country*
strangely ADVERB
strangeness NOUN

stranger strangers
NOUN **1.** someone you have never met before **2.** If you are a stranger to a place or situation, you have not been there or experienced it before.

strangle strangles strangling strangled
VERB To strangle someone means to kill that person by squeezing his or her throat.
strangulation NOUN

strangled
ADJECTIVE A strangled sound is unclear and muffled.

stranglehold strangleholds
NOUN To have a stranglehold on something means to have control over it and prevent it from developing.

strap straps strapping strapped
NOUN **1.** a narrow piece of leather or cloth, used to fasten or hold things together
VERB **2.** To strap something means to fasten it with a strap.

strapping
ADJECTIVE tall, strong, and healthy-looking

strata the plural of STRATUM

strategic
ADJECTIVE planned or intended to achieve something or to gain an advantage: *a strategic plan*
strategically ADVERB

strategy strategies
NOUN **1.** a plan for achieving something **2.** Strategy is the skill of planning the best way to achieve something.
strategist NOUN

stratum strata
NOUN a layer or series of layers of rock in the earth's surface

Ss

straw straws
NOUN **1.** Straw is the dry, yellowish stalks from cereal crops. **2.** a hollow tube of paper or plastic that you use to suck a drink into your mouth
PHRASE **3.** If something is **the last straw**, it is the latest in a series of bad events and makes you feel you cannot stand any more.

strawberry strawberries
NOUN a small red fruit with tiny seeds in its skin

stray strays straying strayed
VERB **1.** When people or animals stray, they wander away from where they should be. **2.** If your thoughts stray, you stop concentrating.
ADJECTIVE **3.** A stray dog or cat is one that has wandered away from home. **4.** Stray things are separated from the main group of things of their kind: *a stray piece of lettuce*
NOUN **5.** a stray dog or cat

streak streaks streaking streaked
NOUN **1.** a long mark or stain **2.** If someone has a particular streak, that person has that quality in his or her character. **3.** A lucky or unlucky streak is a series of successes or failures.
VERB **4.** If something is streaked with a colour, it has lines of the colour in it. **5.** To streak somewhere means to move there very quickly.
streaky ADJECTIVE

stream streams streaming streamed
NOUN **1.** a small river **2.** You can refer to a steady flow of something as a stream: *a constant stream of people*
VERB **3.** To stream somewhere means to move in a continuous flow in large quantities: *Rain streamed down the windshield.*

streamer streamers
NOUN a long, narrow strip of coloured paper used for decoration

streamline streamlines streamlining streamlined
VERB **1.** To streamline a vehicle, aircraft, or boat means to improve its shape so that it moves more quickly and efficiently. **2.** To streamline an organization means to make it more efficient by removing parts of it.

street streets
NOUN a road in a small or large community, usually with sidewalks and buildings along it

strength strengths
NOUN **1.** Your strength is your physical energy and the power of your muscles.
2. Strength can refer to the degree of someone's confidence or courage. **3.** You can refer to power or influence as strength: *The*

campaign against factory closures gathered strength. **4.** Someone's strengths are that person's good qualities and abilities.
5. The strength of an object is the degree to which it can stand rough treatment. **6.** The strength of a substance is the amount of other substances that it contains: *coffee with sugar and milk in it at the correct strength*
7. The strength of a feeling or opinion is the degree to which it is felt or supported.
8. The strength of a relationship is its degree of closeness or success. **9.** The strength of a group is the total number of people in it.
PHRASE **10.** If people do something **in strength**, a lot of them do it together: *The media are here in strength.*

strengthen strengthens strengthening strengthened
VERB **1.** To strengthen something means to give it more power, influence, or support and make it more likely to succeed. **2.** To strengthen an object means to improve it or add to its structure so that it can withstand rough treatment.

strenuous
ADJECTIVE involving a lot of effort or energy
strenuously ADVERB

stress stresses stressing stressed
NOUN **1.** Stress is worry and nervous tension. **2.** Stresses are strong physical forces applied to an object. **3.** Stress is emphasis put on a word or part of a word when it is pronounced, making it slightly louder.
VERB **4.** If you stress a point, you emphasize it and draw attention to its importance.
stressful ADJECTIVE

stretch stretches stretching stretched
VERB **1.** Something that stretches over an area extends that far. **2.** When you stretch, you hold out part of your body as far as you can. **3.** To stretch something soft or elastic means to pull it to make it longer or bigger.
NOUN **4.** A stretch of land or water is an area of it. **5.** A stretch of time is a period of time.

stretcher stretchers
NOUN a long piece of material with a pole along each side, used to carry an injured person

strewn
ADJECTIVE If things are strewn about, they are scattered about untidily: *The games were strewn all over the floor.*

stricken
ADJECTIVE severely affected by something unpleasant

strict stricter strictest
ADJECTIVE **1.** Someone who is strict controls

other people very firmly. **2.** A strict rule must always be obeyed absolutely. **3.** The strict meaning of something is its precise and accurate meaning. **4.** You can use *strict* to describe someone who never breaks the rules or principles of a particular belief: *a strict vegetarian*

strictly
ADVERB **1.** Strictly means only for a particular purpose: *I was in it strictly for the money.*
PHRASE **2.** You say **strictly speaking** to correct a statement or add more precise information: *Somebody pointed out that, strictly speaking, electricity was a discovery, not an invention.*

stride strides striding strode stridden
VERB **1.** To stride along means to walk quickly with long steps.
NOUN **2.** a long step; also the length of a step

strident
ADJECTIVE loud, harsh, and unpleasant

strife
NOUN *a formal word* Strife is trouble, conflict, and disagreement.

strike strikes striking struck
NOUN **1.** If there is a strike, people stop working as a protest. **2.** A hunger strike is a refusal to eat anything as a protest. **3.** a military attack: *the threat of air strikes*
VERB **4.** To strike someone or something means to hit that person. **5.** If an illness, disaster, or enemy strikes, it suddenly affects or attacks someone. **6.** If a thought strikes you, it comes into your mind. **7.** If you are struck by something, you are impressed by it. **8.** When a clock strikes, it makes a sound to indicate the time. **9.** To strike a deal with someone means to come to an agreement with that person. **10.** If someone strikes oil, gold, or minerals, that person discovers it in the ground. **11.** If you strike a match, you rub it against something to make it burst into flame.
strike off
VERB **12.** If a person is struck off, that person's name is removed from a list or group.
strike up
VERB **13.** To strike up a conversation or friendship means to begin it.

striker strikers
NOUN Strikers are people who are refusing to work as a protest.

striking
ADJECTIVE very noticeable because of being unusual or very attractive
strikingly ADVERB

string strings stringing strung
NOUN **1.** String is thin cord made of twisted threads. **2.** You can refer to a row or series of similar things as a string of them: *a string of islands, a string of injuries* **3.** The strings of a musical instrument are tightly stretched lengths of wire or nylon that vibrate to produce the notes.
PLURAL NOUN **4.** The section of an orchestra consisting of stringed instruments is called the **strings**.
string along
VERB **5.** *an informal use* To string someone along means to deceive that person.
string out
VERB **6.** If things are strung out, they are spread out in a long line. **7.** To string something out means to make it last longer than necessary.

stringed
ADJECTIVE A stringed instrument is one with strings, such as a guitar or violin.

stringent
ADJECTIVE Stringent laws, requirements, or conditions are very severe or are strictly controlled: *stringent rules for admission*

strip strips stripping stripped
NOUN **1.** A strip of something is a long, narrow piece of it. **2.** a long, narrow section of land or forest
VERB **3.** If you strip, you take off all your clothes. **4.** To strip something means to remove whatever is covering its surface. **5.** To strip someone of his or her property or rights means to take that person's property or rights away officially.

stripe stripes
NOUN Stripes are long, thin lines, usually of different colours.
striped ADJECTIVE

strive strives striving strove striven
VERB If you strive to do something, you make a great effort to achieve it.

stroke strokes stroking stroked
VERB **1.** If you stroke something, you move your hand smoothly and gently over it.
NOUN **2.** If someone has a stroke, that person suddenly loses consciousness as a result of a blockage or rupture in a blood vessel in the brain. A stroke can result in damage to speech and paralysis. **3.** The strokes of a brush or pen are the movements that you make with it. **4.** The strokes of a clock are the sounds that indicate the hour. **5.** A swimming stroke is a particular style of swimming.
PHRASE **6.** If you have **a stroke of luck**, then you are lucky and something good happens to you.

Ss

stroll strolls strolling strolled
VERB **1.** To stroll along means to walk slowly in a relaxed way.
NOUN **2.** a slow, pleasurable walk

stroller strollers
NOUN a folding chair on wheels for a baby or young child

strong stronger strongest
ADJECTIVE **1.** Someone who is strong has powerful muscles. **2.** You also say that someone is strong when that person is confident and has courage. **3.** Strong objects are able to withstand rough treatment.
4. Strong also means great in degree or intensity: *a strong wind*
5. A strong argument or theory is supported by a lot of evidence.
6. If a group or organization is strong, it has a lot of members or influence.
7. You can use *strong* to say how many people there are in a group: *The audience was about two dozen strong.* **8.** Your strong points are the things you are good at.
9. A strong economy or currency is stable and successful. **10.** A strong liquid or drug contains a lot of a particular substance.
ADVERB **11.** If someone or something is still going strong, that person or thing is still healthy or working well after a long time.
strongly ADVERB

Instead of **STRONG** try...
durable garbage bags
a **potent** chemical
a **forceful** push
a **mighty** wind
tough leather
a **muscular** athlete
a **powerful** argument
an **overpowering** odour

stronghold strongholds
NOUN **1.** a place that is held and defended by an army **2.** A stronghold of an attitude or belief is a place in which the attitude or belief is strongly held: *a stronghold of freedom*

structure structures structuring structured
NOUN **1.** The structure of something is the way it is made, built, or organized. **2.** something that has been built or constructed
VERB **3.** To structure something means to arrange it into an organized pattern or system.
structural ADJECTIVE
structurally ADVERB

struggle struggles struggling struggled
VERB **1.** If you struggle to do something, you try hard to do it in difficult circumstances. **2.** When people struggle, they twist and move violently during a fight.
NOUN **3.** Something that is a struggle is difficult to achieve and takes a lot of effort. **4.** a fight

strum strums strumming strummed
VERB To strum a guitar means to play it by moving your fingers back and forth across all the strings.

strut struts strutting strutted
VERB **1.** To strut means to walk in a stiff, proud way with your chest out and your head high.
NOUN **2.** a piece of wood or metal that strengthens or supports part of a building or structure

stub stubs stubbing stubbed
NOUN **1.** The stub of a pencil or cigarette is the short piece that remains when the rest has been used. **2.** The stub of a cheque or ticket is the small part that you keep.
VERB **3.** If you stub your toe, you hurt it by accidentally kicking something.

stubble
NOUN **1.** The short stalks remaining in the ground after a crop is harvested are called stubble. **2.** If a man has stubble on his face, he has very short hair growing there because he has not shaved recently.

stubborn
ADJECTIVE **1.** Someone who is stubborn is determined not to change his or her opinion or course of action. **2.** A stubborn stain is difficult to remove.
stubbornly ADVERB
stubbornness NOUN

stuck
ADJECTIVE **1.** If something is stuck in a particular position, it is fixed or jammed and cannot be moved: *His car is stuck in a snowdrift.* **2.** If you are stuck, you are unable to continue what you were doing because it is too difficult. **3.** If you are stuck somewhere, you are unable to get away.

stuck-up
ADJECTIVE *an informal word* proud and conceited

stud studs
NOUN **1.** a small piece of metal fixed into something **2.** A male horse or other animal that is kept for stud is kept for breeding purposes.

Ss

studded
ADJECTIVE decorated with small pieces of metal or precious stones

student students
NOUN a person studying at a school, college, or university

studied
ADJECTIVE A studied action or response has been carefully planned and is not natural: *She spoke with studied politeness.*

studio studios
NOUN **1.** a room where a photographer or painter works **2.** a room containing special equipment where recordings, movies, or radio or television programs are made

studious
ADJECTIVE spending a lot of time studying

studiously
ADVERB carefully and deliberately: *He was studiously ignoring me.*

study studies studying studied
VERB **1.** If you study a particular subject, you spend time learning about it. **2.** If you study something, you look at it carefully: *He studied the map in silence.*
NOUN **3.** Study is the activity of studying a subject: *the serious study of medieval archaeology* **4.** Studies are subjects that are studied: *media studies* **5.** a piece of research on a particular subject: *a detailed study of the world's most poisonous insects* **6.** a room used for writing and studying

stuff stuffs stuffing stuffed
NOUN **1.** You can refer to a substance or group of things as stuff.
VERB **2.** If you stuff something somewhere, you push it there quickly and roughly. **3.** If you stuff something with a substance or objects, you fill it with the substance or objects.

stuffing
NOUN Stuffing is a mixture of small pieces of food put inside poultry, meat, fish, or vegetables before they are cooked.

stuffy stuffier stuffiest
ADJECTIVE **1.** very formal and old-fashioned **2.** If it is stuffy in a room, there is not enough fresh air.

stumble stumbles stumbling stumbled
VERB **1.** If you stumble while you are walking or running, you trip and almost fall. **2.** If you stumble when speaking, you make mistakes when pronouncing the words. **3.** If you stumble across something or stumble on it, you find it unexpectedly.

stump stumps stumping stumped
NOUN **1.** a small part of something that is left when the rest has been removed: *the stump of a dead tree*
VERB **2.** If a question or problem stumps you, you cannot think of an answer or solution.

stun stuns stunning stunned
VERB **1.** If you are stunned by something, you are very shocked by it. **2.** To stun a person or animal means to knock that person or animal unconscious with a blow to the head.

stunning
ADJECTIVE very beautiful or impressive: *a stunning first novel*

stunt stunts stunting stunted
NOUN **1.** an unusual or dangerous and exciting action that someone does to get publicity or as part of a movie
VERB **2.** To stunt the growth or development of something means to prevent it from developing as it should.

stupendous
ADJECTIVE very large or impressive: *a stupendous amount of money*

stupid stupider stupidest
ADJECTIVE showing lack of good judgment or intelligence and not at all sensible

stupidity
NOUN a lack of intelligence or good judgment

sturdy sturdier sturdiest
ADJECTIVE strong and firm and unlikely to be damaged or injured: *a sturdy chest of drawers*

sturgeon
NOUN a large, edible fish, the eggs of which are also eaten and are known as caviar

stutter stutters stuttering stuttered
NOUN **1.** Someone who has a stutter finds it difficult to speak smoothly and often repeats sounds through being unable to complete a word.
VERB **2.** When someone stutters, that person hesitates or repeats sounds when speaking.

sty sties
NOUN **1.** a pen for pigs **2.** an infection in the form of a small red swelling on a person's eyelid

style styles styling styled
NOUN **1.** The style of something is the general way in which it is done or presented, often showing the attitudes of the people involved. **2.** A person or place that has style is smart, elegant, and fashionable. **3.** The style of something is its design: *new windows that fit in with the style of the house*
VERB **4.** To style a piece of clothing or a person's hair means to design and create its shape.

Ss

stylish
ADJECTIVE smart, elegant, and fashionable
stylishly ADVERB

suave
ADJECTIVE charming, polite, and confident: *a suave manner*

sub-
PREFIX **1.** The prefix *sub-* is used at the beginning of words that have *under* as part of their meaning: *submarine* **2.** The prefix *sub-* is also used to form nouns that refer to the parts into which something is divided: *subsection 2 of section 49, a particular subgroup of citizens*

subconscious
NOUN **1.** Your subconscious is the part of your mind that can influence you without your being aware of it.
ADJECTIVE **2.** happening or existing in someone's subconscious and therefore not directly realized or understood by that person: *a subconscious fear of rejection*
subconsciously ADVERB

subcontinent subcontinents
NOUN a large mass of land, often consisting of several countries, and forming part of a continent: *the Indian subcontinent*

subdue subdues subduing subdued
VERB **1.** If soldiers subdue a group of people, they bring them under control by using force: *It would be quite impossible to subdue the whole continent.* **2.** To subdue a colour, light, or emotion means to make it less bright or strong.

subdued
ADJECTIVE **1.** rather quiet and sad **2.** not very noticeable or bright

subject subjects subjecting subjected
NOUN **1.** The subject of writing or a conversation is the thing or person being discussed. **2.** In grammar, the subject is the word representing the person or thing doing the action expressed by the verb. For example, in the sentence *My cat keeps catching birds*, *my cat* is the subject. **3.** an area of study **4.** The subjects of a country are the people who live there other than its ruler: *They are subjects of the queen.*
VERB **5.** To subject someone to something means to make that person experience it: *She was subjected to constant interruption.*
ADJECTIVE **6.** Someone or something that is subject to something is affected by it: *He was subject to periods of depression.*

subjective
ADJECTIVE influenced by personal feelings and opinion rather than based on fact or rational thought

subjunctive
NOUN In grammar, the subjunctive or subjunctive mood is one of the forms a verb can take. It is used to express attitudes such as wishing and doubting.

sublime
ADJECTIVE Something that is sublime is wonderful and affects people emotionally: *sublime music*

submarine submarines
NOUN a ship that can travel beneath the surface of the sea

submerge submerges submerging submerged
VERB **1.** To submerge means to go beneath the surface of a liquid. **2.** If you submerge yourself in an activity, you become totally involved in it.

submission submissions
NOUN **1.** Submission is a state in which someone accepts the control of another person: *The dictator demanded total submission from the population.* **2.** The submission of a proposal or application is the act of sending it for consideration.

submissive
ADJECTIVE behaving in a quiet, obedient way

submit submits submitting submitted
VERB **1.** If you submit to something, you accept it because you are not powerful enough to resist it. **2.** If you submit an application or proposal, you send it to someone for consideration.

subordinate subordinates subordinating subordinated
NOUN **1.** A person's subordinate is someone who is in a less important position than that person.
ADJECTIVE **2.** If one thing is subordinate to another, it is less important: *Non-elected officials are subordinate to elected leaders.*
VERB **3.** To subordinate one thing to another means to treat it as being less important.

subordinate clause subordinate clauses
NOUN In grammar, a subordinate clause is a clause that adds details to the main clause of a sentence.

subscribe subscribes subscribing subscribed
VERB **1.** If you subscribe to a particular belief or opinion, you support it or agree with it. **2.** If you subscribe to a magazine, you pay to receive regular copies.
subscriber NOUN

⚠ **HEADS UP** The word **suave** is pronounced SWAHV.

NEL

Ss

subscription subscriptions
NOUN a sum of money that you pay to regularly attend a series of events or to receive regular copies of a magazine

subsequent
ADJECTIVE happening or coming into existence at a later time than something else: *My teacher plans to discuss volcanic eruptions and the subsequent damage they can cause to the environment.*
subsequently ADVERB

subservient
ADJECTIVE Someone who is subservient does whatever other people want that person to do.

subside subsides subsiding subsided
VERB **1.** To subside means to become quieter or less intense: *Her excitement suddenly subsided.* **2.** If water or the ground subsides, it sinks to a lower level.

subsidiary subsidiaries
NOUN **1.** a company that is part of a larger company
ADJECTIVE **2.** treated as being of less importance and additional to another thing: *Drama is offered as a subsidiary subject.*

subsidize subsidizes subsidizing subsidized
VERB To subsidize something means to provide part of the cost of it: *He feels the government should do much more to subsidize music programs.*
subsidized ADJECTIVE

subsidy subsidies
NOUN a sum of money paid to help support a company or provide a public service

substance substances
NOUN **1.** Anything that is a solid, a powder, a liquid, or a paste can be referred to as a substance. **2.** If a speech or piece of writing has substance, it is meaningful, important, or has a solid basis in fact: *a good speech, but there was no substance*

substantial
ADJECTIVE **1.** very large in degree or amount: *a substantial pay raise* **2.** large and strongly built: *a substantial stone building*

substantially
ADVERB Something that is substantially true is generally or mostly true.

substitute substitutes substituting substituted
VERB **1.** To substitute one thing for another means to use it instead of the other thing or to put it in the other thing's place.
NOUN **2.** If one thing is a substitute for another, it is used instead of it or put in its place.
substitution NOUN

subterfuge subterfuges
NOUN Subterfuge is the use of deceitful or dishonest methods.

subtitle subtitles
NOUN A movie with subtitles has a printed translation of the dialogue at the bottom of the screen.

subtle subtler subtlest
ADJECTIVE **1.** very fine, delicate, or small in degree: *a subtle change* **2.** using indirect methods to achieve something
subtly ADVERB
subtlety NOUN

subtract subtracts subtracting subtracted
VERB If you subtract one number from another, you take away the first number from the second.

subtraction subtractions
NOUN Subtraction is subtracting one number from another, or a question in which you do this.

suburb suburbs
NOUN an area of a town or city that is away from its centre

suburban
ADJECTIVE **1.** relating to a suburb or suburbs **2.** dull and conventional

suburbia
NOUN You can refer to the suburbs of a city as suburbia.

subversive subversives
ADJECTIVE **1.** intended to destroy or weaken a political system: *subversive activities*
NOUN **2.** A subversive person is one who tries to destroy or weaken a political system
subversion NOUN

subvert subverts subverting subverted
VERB *a formal word* To subvert something means to cause it to weaken or fail: *a cunning campaign to subvert the music industry*

subway subways
NOUN an electric railway that operates mostly underground in a city

succeed succeeds succeeding succeeded
VERB **1.** To succeed means to achieve the result you intend. **2.** To succeed someone means to be the next person to have his or her job. **3.** If one thing succeeds another, it comes after it in time: *The explosion succeeded the crash.*
succeeding ADJECTIVE

success successes
NOUN **1.** Success is the achievement of something you have been trying to do.
2. Someone who is a success has achieved an important position or made a lot of money.

HEADS UP The b in **subtle** is silent. It is pronounced SUT-uhl.

successful

ADJECTIVE having achieved what you intended to do

successfully ADVERB

succession successions

NOUN **1.** A succession of things is a number of them occurring one after the other. **2.** When someone becomes the next person to have an important position, you can refer to this event as that person's succession to this position: *his succession to the throne* PHRASE **3.** If something happens a number of weeks, months, or years **in succession**, it happens that number of times without a break: *He won the national figure-skating title five years in succession.*

successive

ADJECTIVE occurring one after the other without a break: *three successive victories*

successor successors

NOUN Someone's successor is the person who takes that person's job when he or she leaves.

succinct

ADJECTIVE expressing something clearly and in very few words

succinctly ADVERB

succulent

ADJECTIVE Succulent food is juicy and delicious.

succumb succumbs succumbing succumbed

VERB If you succumb to something, you are unable to resist it any longer: *She never succumbed to the temptation to order dessert.*

such

ADJECTIVE OR PRONOUN **1.** You use *such* to refer to the person or thing you have just mentioned, or to someone or something similar: *Inverness or Ingonish or some such place* PHRASE **2.** You can use **such as** to introduce an example of something: *herbal teas such as camomile* **3.** You can use **such as it is** to indicate that something is not great in quality or quantity: *The action, such as it is, is set in Hay River.* **4.** You can use **such-and-such** when you want to refer to something that is not specific: *Tell them I will be finished by such-and-such a date.* ADJECTIVE **5.** *Such* can be used for emphasizing: *I have such a terrible sense of guilt.*

suchlike

ADJECTIVE OR PRONOUN used to refer to things similar to those already mentioned: *shampoos, talcum powders, toothbrushes, and suchlike*

suck sucks sucking sucked

VERB **1.** If you suck something, you hold it in your mouth and pull at it with your cheeks and tongue, usually to get liquid out of it. **2.** To suck something in a particular direction means to draw it there with a powerful force. **3.** *an informal use* To suck up to someone means to do things to please that person in order to obtain praise or approval.

sucker suckers

NOUN **1.** *an informal use* If you call someone a sucker, you mean that that person is easily fooled or cheated. **2.** Suckers are pads on the bodies of some animals and insects that they use to cling to a surface.

suckle suckles suckling suckled

VERB When a mother suckles a baby, she feeds it with milk from her breast.

sucrose

NOUN *a technical word* Sucrose is sugar in crystalline form found in sugar cane and sugar beets.

suction

NOUN **1.** Suction is the force involved when a substance is drawn or sucked from one place to another. **2.** Suction is the process by which two surfaces stick together when the air between them is removed: *They stay there by suction.*

sudden

ADJECTIVE happening quickly and unexpectedly: *a sudden cry*

Instead of **SUDDEN** try...

an unexpected change

a hasty decision

an abrupt exit

a swift retreat

a startling noise

an impulsive twitch

an instant turnaround

immediate recognition

suddenly ADVERB
suddenness
NOUN

sudoku

NOUN a puzzle in which you have to enter numbers in a square made up of nine three-by-three grids, so that every column, row, and grid contains the numbers one to nine

sue sues suing sued

VERB To sue someone means to start a legal case against that person, usually to claim money from him or her.

Ss

suede

NOUN Suede is a thin, soft leather with a rough surface.

suffer suffers suffering suffered

VERB **1.** If someone is suffering pain, or suffering as a result of an unpleasant situation, that person is badly affected by it. **2.** If something suffers as a result of neglect or a difficult situation, its condition or quality becomes worse: *The bus service is suffering.*

sufferer NOUN

suffering NOUN

suffice suffices sufficing sufficed

VERB *a formal word* If something suffices, it is enough or adequate for a purpose.

sufficient

ADJECTIVE If a supply or quantity is sufficient for a purpose, there is enough of it available.

sufficiently ADVERB

suffix suffixes

NOUN a group of letters that is added to the end of a word to form a new word, for example *-ology* or *-itis*

suffocate suffocates suffocating suffocated

VERB To suffocate means to die as a result of having too little air or oxygen to breathe.

suffocation NOUN

suffrage

NOUN Suffrage is the right to vote in political elections.

suffragette suffragettes

NOUN a woman who, at the beginning of the twentieth century, campaigned for women to be given the right to vote

suffused

ADJECTIVE *a literary or poetic word* If something is suffused with light or colour, light or colour has gradually spread over it.

sugar

NOUN Sugar is a sweet substance used to sweeten food and drinks.

suggest suggests suggesting suggested

VERB **1.** If you suggest a plan or idea to someone, you mention it as a possibility for him or her to consider. **2.** If something suggests a particular thought or impression, it makes you think in that way or gives you that impression: *Your smile suggests that you are happy with the news.*

suggestion suggestions

NOUN **1.** a plan or idea that is mentioned as a possibility for someone to consider **2.** A suggestion of something is a very slight indication or faint sign of it: *a suggestion of dishonesty*

suggestive

ADJECTIVE **1.** Something that is suggestive of a particular thing gives a slight hint or sign of it. **2.** Suggestive remarks or gestures make people think about sex.

suicidal

ADJECTIVE **1.** People who are suicidal want to kill themselves. **2.** Suicidal behaviour is so dangerous that it is likely to result in death: *a mad, suicidal attack*

suicide

NOUN People who commit suicide deliberately kill themselves.

suit suits suiting suited

NOUN **1.** a matching jacket and pants or skirt **2.** In a court of law, a suit is a legal action taken by one person against another. **3.** one of four different types of card in a pack of playing cards. The four suits are hearts, clubs, diamonds, and spades.

VERB **4.** If a situation or course of action suits you, it is appropriate or acceptable for your purpose. **5.** If a piece of clothing or a colour suits you, you look good when you are wearing it. **6.** If you do something to **suit yourself**, you do it because you want to and without considering other people.

suitable

ADJECTIVE right or acceptable for a particular purpose or occasion

suitability NOUN

suitably ADVERB

suitcase suitcases

NOUN a case in which you carry your clothes when you are travelling

suite suites

NOUN **1.** In a hotel, a suite is a set of rooms. **2.** a set of matching furniture

suited

ADJECTIVE right or appropriate for a particular purpose or person: *He is suited for a job in the arts.*

suitor suitors

NOUN *an old-fashioned word* A woman's suitor is a man who wants to marry her.

sulk sulks sulking sulked

VERB Someone who is sulking is showing his or her annoyance by being silent and moody.

sulky sulkier sulkiest

ADJECTIVE showing annoyance by being silent and moody

sullen

ADJECTIVE behaving in a bad-tempered and disagreeably silent way: *a sullen and resentful workforce*

⚠ **HEADS UP** The word **suede** is pronounced SWADE.

Ss

sulphur
NOUN Sulphur is a pale yellow, non-metallic element that burns with a very unpleasant smell.

sultan sultans
NOUN In some Muslim countries, the ruler of the country is called the sultan.

sultana sultanas
NOUN **1.** a seedless raisin **2.** the wife of a sultan

sum sums summing summed
NOUN **1.** an amount of money **2.** In arithmetic, a sum is the total you get from adding two numbers together. **3.** The sum or sum total of something is the total amount of it that exists.
   sum up
   VERB **4.** If you sum something up, you briefly describe its main points.

summarize summarizes summarizing summarized
VERB To summarize something means to give a short account of its main points.

summary summaries
NOUN **1.** A summary of something is a short account of its main points: *I was asked to write a one-page summary of the book.*
ADJECTIVE **2.** A summary action is done without delay or careful thought: *a summary dismissal*
   summarily ADVERB

summer summers
NOUN Summer is the season between spring and autumn.

summit summits
NOUN **1.** The summit of a mountain is its top. **2.** a meeting between leaders of different countries to discuss particular issues

summon summons summoning summoned
VERB **1.** If someone summons you, that person orders you to go to him or her. **2.** If you summon up strength or energy, you make a great effort to be strong or energetic.

summons summonses
NOUN **1.** an official order to appear in court **2.** an order to go to someone: *The result was a summons to headquarters.*

sumptuous
ADJECTIVE Something that is sumptuous is magnificent and obviously very expensive.

sun suns sunning sunned
NOUN **1.** The sun is the star providing heat and light for the planets revolving around it in our solar system. **2.** You refer to heat and light from the sun as sun: *We need a bit of sun.*
VERB **3.** If you sun yourself, you sit in the sunshine.

sunburn
NOUN Sunburn is sore, red skin on someone's body due to too much exposure to the rays of the sun.
   sunburned ADJECTIVE

sundae sundaes
NOUN a dish of ice cream with flavoured syrup and sometimes other toppings

Sunday Sundays
NOUN Sunday is the day between Saturday and Monday.

sundry
ADJECTIVE **1.** *Sundry* is used to refer to several things or people of various sorts: *sundry journalists and lawyers*
PHRASE **2.** **All and sundry** means everyone.

sunken
ADJECTIVE **1.** having sunk to the bottom of the sea, a river, or lake: *sunken ships* **2.** A sunken object or area has been constructed below the level of the surrounding area: *a sunken garden* **3.** curving inward: *Her cheeks were sunken.*

sunlight
NOUN Sunlight is the bright light produced when the sun is shining.
   sunlit ADJECTIVE

KNOWING WORDS: WORD BUILDING

BE WORD SHARP!

To build a compound word, put two or more base words together.

sun the star in our solar system

sunshine/sunlight the bright light produced by the sun

sunbathe sit in the sunshine to get a tan

sundial a dial used for telling time by sunlight

sunflower a tall plant with large, sun-yellow flowers

sunglasses glasses with dark lenses to shade sunlight

NEL

Ss

sunny sunnier sunniest
ADJECTIVE When it is sunny, the sun is shining.

sunrise sunrises
NOUN Sunrise is the time in the morning when the sun first appears, and the colours produced in the sky at that time.

sunset sunsets
NOUN Sunset is the time in the evening when the sun disappears below the horizon, and the colours produced in the sky at that time.

sunstroke
NOUN Sunstroke is an illness caused by spending too much time in hot sunshine.

suntan suntans
NOUN If you have a suntan, the sun has turned your skin brown.
suntanned ADJECTIVE

super
ADJECTIVE very good: *a super party*

super-
PREFIX The prefix *super-* is used to describe something that is larger or more extreme than similar things: *a supercomputer, supersensitive*

superb
ADJECTIVE very good indeed
superbly ADVERB

supercilious
ADJECTIVE If you are supercilious, you behave in a scornful way toward other people because you think they are inferior to you.

superego
NOUN *a technical word* Your superego is the part of your mind that controls your ideas of right and wrong and produces feelings of guilt.

superficial
ADJECTIVE **1.** involving only the most obvious or most general aspects of something: *a superficial knowledge of music* **2.** not having a deep, serious, or genuine interest in anything: *a superficial and rather silly person* **3.** Superficial wounds are not very deep or severe.
superficially ADVERB

superfluous
ADJECTIVE *a formal word* unnecessary or no longer needed

superhuman
ADJECTIVE having much greater power or ability than is normally expected of humans: *superhuman strength*

superimpose superimposes superimposing superimposed
VERB To superimpose one image on another means to put the first image on top of the other so that they are seen as one image.

superintendent superintendents
NOUN **1.** a police officer of high rank **2.** a person whose job is to be responsible for a particular thing: *The superintendent of our apartment is very helpful.*

superior superiors
ADJECTIVE **1.** better or of higher quality than other similar things **2.** in a position of higher authority than another person **3.** showing too much pride and self-importance: *He smiled in a superior way.*
NOUN **4.** Your superiors are people who are in a higher position than you in an organization.
superiority NOUN

superlative superlatives
NOUN **1.** In grammar, the superlative is the form of an adjective that indicates that the person or thing described has more of a particular quality than anyone or anything else. For example, *quickest*, *best*, and *easiest* are all superlatives.
ADJECTIVE **2.** *a formal use* very good: *a superlative performance*

supermarket supermarkets
NOUN a store selling food and household goods arranged so that you can serve yourself and pay for everything at a checkout counter

supernatural
ADJECTIVE **1.** Something that is considered supernatural cannot be explained by normal scientific laws.
NOUN **2.** You can refer to supernatural things as the supernatural.

superpower superpowers
NOUN a very powerful and influential country such as the US

supersede supersedes superseding superseded
VERB If something supersedes another thing, it replaces it because it is more modern: *DVD players had superseded VCRs in most homes by 2002.*

supersonic
ADJECTIVE A supersonic aircraft can travel faster than the speed of sound.

superstar superstars
NOUN You can refer to a very famous entertainer or highly skilled athlete as a superstar.

⚠ **HEADS UP** The word **superfluous** is pronounced suh-PER-flew-us.

Ss

superstition superstitions
NOUN Superstition is a belief in things like magic and powers that bring good or bad luck.
superstitious ADJECTIVE

supervise supervises supervising supervised
VERB To supervise someone means to check and direct what that person is doing to make sure that he or she does it correctly.
supervision NOUN
supervisor NOUN

supper suppers
NOUN Supper is a meal eaten in the evening.

supplant supplants supplanting supplanted
VERB *a formal word* To supplant someone or something means to take that person's or thing's place: *By the 1930s the wristwatch had supplanted the pocket watch.*

supple
ADJECTIVE able to bend and move easily

supplement supplements supplementing supplemented
VERB **1.** To supplement something means to add something to it to improve it: *Many villagers supplemented their income by fishing for salmon.*
NOUN **2.** something that is added to something else to improve it

supplementary
ADJECTIVE added to something else to improve it: *supplementary doses of vitamin E*

supplier suppliers
NOUN a company that provides particular goods

supply supplies supplying supplied
VERB **1.** To supply someone with something means to provide it or send it to that person.
NOUN **2.** A supply of something is an amount available for use: *the world's supply of precious metals*
PLURAL NOUN **3.** Supplies are food and equipment for a particular purpose.

support supports supporting supported
VERB **1.** If you support someone, you agree with that person's aims and want him or her to succeed. **2.** If you support someone who is having difficulties, you are kind, encouraging, and helpful to that person. **3.** If something supports an object, it is underneath it and holding it up. **4.** To support someone means to prevent that person from falling by holding him or her. **5.** To support someone financially means to provide that person with money.
NOUN **6.** an object that is holding something up **7.** Moral support is encouragement given to someone to help that person do something

difficult. **8.** Financial support is money that is provided for someone or something.
supportable ADJECTIVE

supporter supporters
NOUN a person who agrees with or helps someone

supportive
ADJECTIVE A supportive person is encouraging and helpful to someone who is having difficulties.

suppose supposes supposing supposed
VERB **1.** If you suppose that something is the case, you think that it is likely: *I suppose that would be too obvious.*
PHRASE **2.** You can say **I suppose** when you are not entirely certain or enthusiastic about something: *Yes, I suppose he could come.*
CONJUNCTION **3.** You can use *suppose* or *supposing* when you are considering or suggesting a possible situation or action: *Supposing he were to miss the bus?*

supposed
ADJECTIVE **1.** *Supposed* is used to express doubt about something that is generally believed: *the supposed culprit* **2.** If something is supposed to be done or to happen, it is planned, expected, or required to be done or to happen: *You are supposed to report it to the police. It was supposed to be this afternoon.* **3.** Something that is supposed to be the case is generally believed or thought to be so: *When frozen, the Rideau Canal is supposed to be the longest skating rink in the world.*
supposedly ADVERB

supposition suppositions
NOUN something that is believed or assumed to be true: *the supposition that science requires an ordered universe*

suppress suppresses suppressing suppressed
VERB **1.** If an army or government suppresses an activity, it prevents people from doing it. **2.** If someone suppresses a piece of information, that person prevents it from becoming generally known. **3.** If you suppress your feelings, you stop yourself expressing them.
suppression NOUN

supremacy
NOUN If a group of people has supremacy over others, it is more powerful than the others.

supreme
ADJECTIVE **1.** *Supreme* is used as part of a title to indicate the highest level of an organization or system: *the Supreme Court of Canada* **2.** *Supreme* is used to emphasize

⚠ **HEADS UP** The word **supposed** is pronounced suh-POHZD.

NEL

Ss

the greatness of something: *the supreme achievement of the human race*
supremely ADVERB

surcharge surcharges
NOUN an additional charge

sure surer surest
ADJECTIVE **1.** If you are sure about

Instead of **SURE** try...

convinced of your honesty

certain that it's true

a definite answer

a clear goal

a decided opinion

an undeniable sign

guaranteed to please

confident that we'll win

something, you have no doubts about it. **2.** If you are sure of yourself, you are very confident. **3.** If something is sure to happen, it will definitely happen. **4.** *Sure* means *reliable* or *accurate*: *a sure sign that something is wrong*
PHRASE **5.** If you **make sure** about something, you check it or take action to see that it is done.
INTERJECTION **6.** Sure is an informal way of saying *yes*: *Can I come too? Sure.*

surely
ADVERB *Surely* is used to emphasize the belief that something is the case: *Surely these people here knew that?*

surf surfs surfing surfed
VERB **1.** When you surf, you go surfing.
2. When you surf the Internet, you go from website to website reading information.
NOUN **3.** Surf is the white foam that forms on the top of waves when they break near the shore.

surface surfaces surfacing surfaced
NOUN **1.** The surface of something is the top or outside area of it. **2.** The surface of a situation is what can be seen easily rather than what is hidden or not immediately obvious.
VERB **3.** If someone surfaces, that person comes up from under water to the surface.

surfboard surfboards
NOUN a long, narrow, lightweight board used for surfing

surfeit
NOUN If there is a surfeit of something, there is too much of it.

surfing
NOUN Surfing is a sport that involves riding toward the shore on the top of a large wave while standing on a surfboard.

surge surges surging surged
NOUN **1.** a sudden great increase in the amount of something: *a surge of panic*
VERB **2.** If something surges, it moves suddenly and powerfully: *The crowd surged forward.*

surgeon surgeons
NOUN a doctor who performs operations

surgery surgeries
NOUN Surgery is medical treatment involving cutting open part of a patient's body to treat the damaged part.

surgical
ADJECTIVE used in or involving a medical operation: *surgical gloves*
surgically ADVERB

surly surlier surliest
ADJECTIVE rude and bad-tempered
surliness NOUN

surmise surmises surmising surmised
VERB *a formal word* To surmise something means to guess it: *I surmised the delay was caused by a traffic jam.*

surmount surmounts surmounting surmounted
VERB **1.** To surmount a difficulty means to manage to solve it. **2.** *a formal use* If something is surmounted by a particular thing, that thing is on top of it: *The island is surmounted by a huge black castle.*

surname surnames
NOUN Your surname is your last name that you share with other members of your family.

surpass surpasses surpassing surpassed
VERB *a formal word* To surpass someone or something means to be better than that person or thing.

surplus surpluses
NOUN If there is a surplus of something, there is more of it than is needed.

surprise surprises surprising surprised
NOUN **1.** an unexpected event **2.** Surprise is the feeling caused when something unexpected happens.
VERB **3.** If something surprises you, it gives you a feeling of surprise. **4.** If you surprise someone, you do something that person was not expecting.
surprising ADJECTIVE

surreal
ADJECTIVE very strange and dreamlike

Ss

surrender surrenders surrendering surrendered
VERB **1.** To surrender means to stop fighting and agree that the other side has won. **2.** If you surrender to a temptation or feeling, you let it take control of you. **3.** To surrender something means to give it up to someone else: *The former owner surrendered his keys.* NOUN **4.** Surrender is a situation in which one side in a fight agrees that the other side has won and gives in.

surreptitious
ADJECTIVE A surreptitious action is done secretly or so that no one will notice: *a surreptitious glance*
surreptitiously ADVERB

surrogate surrogates
ADJECTIVE **1.** acting as a substitute for someone or something
NOUN **2.** a person or thing that acts as a substitute

surround surrounds surrounding surrounded
VERB **1.** To surround someone or something means to be situated all around that person or thing.
NOUN **2.** The surround of something is its outside edge or border.

surrounding surroundings
ADJECTIVE **1.** The surrounding area of a particular place is the area around it: *the surrounding countryside*
PLURAL NOUN **2.** You can refer to the area and environment around a place or person as that place's or person's surroundings: *very comfortable surroundings*

surveillance
NOUN Surveillance is the close watching of a person's activities by the police or army.

survey surveys surveying surveyed
VERB **1.** To survey something means to look carefully at the whole of it. **2.** To survey a building or piece of land means to examine it carefully in order to make a report or plan of its structure and features.
NOUN **3.** A survey of something is a detailed examination of it, often in the form of a report.

surveyor surveyors
NOUN a person whose job is to survey buildings or land

survival survivals
NOUN Survival is being able to continue living or existing in spite of great danger or difficulties: *There was no hope of survival.*

survive survives surviving survived
VERB To survive means to continue to live or exist in spite of great danger or difficulties: *Only a few people survived the shipwreck.*
survivor NOUN

sus-
PREFIX The prefix *sus-* is another form of SUB-.

susceptible
ADJECTIVE If you are susceptible to something, you are likely to be influenced or affected by it: *Elderly people are more susceptible to infection.*
susceptibility NOUN

suspect suspects suspecting suspected
VERB **1.** If you suspect something, you think that it is likely or is probably true: *I suspected that the report would be sent.* **2.** If you suspect something, you have doubts about its reliability: *He suspected her intent.* **3.** If you suspect someone of doing something wrong, you think that he or she has done it.
NOUN **4.** someone who is thought to be guilty of a crime
ADJECTIVE **5.** If something is suspect, it cannot be trusted or relied upon: *a rather suspect version of events*

suspend suspends suspending suspended
VERB **1.** If something is suspended, it is hanging from somewhere: *The light was suspended from the ceiling.* **2.** To suspend an activity or event means to delay it or stop it for a while. **3.** If someone is suspended from his or her job, that person is told not to do it for a period of time, usually as a punishment.

suspenders
PLURAL NOUN Suspenders are a pair of straps worn over the shoulders to hold up a pair of pants.

suspense
NOUN Suspense is a state of excitement or anxiety caused by having to wait for something.

suspension
NOUN **1.** The suspension of something is the delaying or stopping of it. **2.** A person's suspension is his or her removal from a job for a period of time, usually as a punishment. **3.** The suspension of a vehicle consists of springs and shock absorbers that provide a smooth ride. **4.** a liquid mixture in which very small bits of a solid material are contained and are not dissolved

suspicion suspicions
NOUN **1.** Suspicion is the feeling of not trusting someone or the feeling that something is wrong. **2.** a feeling that something is likely to happen or is probably true: *the suspicion that they were not being totally honest*

Ss

suspicious

ADJECTIVE **1.** If you are suspicious of someone, you do not trust that person. **2.** *Suspicious* is used to describe things that make you think that there is something wrong with a situation: *suspicious circumstances*
suspiciously ADVERB

sustain sustains sustaining sustained

VERB **1.** To sustain something means to continue it for a period of time: *Their teammates were unable to sustain the challenge.* **2.** If something sustains you, it gives you energy and strength. **3.** *a formal use* To sustain an injury or loss means to suffer it.

sustainable

ADJECTIVE **1.** capable of being sustained **2.** If economic development or energy resources are sustainable, they are capable of being maintained at a steady level without exhausting natural resources or causing ecological damage: *sustainable forestry*

sustenance

NOUN *a formal word* Sustenance is food and drink.

swab swabs swabbing swabbed

NOUN **1.** an absorbent pad used for cleaning a wound
VERB **2.** To swab something means to clean it using a large mop and a lot of water.
3. To swab a wound means to clean it or take specimens from it using a swab.

swag swags

NOUN *an informal word* goods or valuables, especially ones that have been gained dishonestly

swagger swaggers swaggering swaggered

VERB **1.** To swagger means to walk in a proud, exaggerated way.
NOUN **2.** an exaggerated walk

swallow swallows swallowing swallowed

VERB **1.** If you swallow something, you make it go down your throat and into your stomach. **2.** When you swallow, you move your throat muscles as if you were swallowing something, especially when you are nervous.
NOUN **3.** a bird with pointed wings and a long, forked tail

swamp swamps swamping swamped

NOUN **1.** an area of permanently wet land
VERB **2.** If something is swamped, it is covered or filled with water. **3.** If you are swamped by things, you have more than you are able to deal with: *She was swamped with calls.*
swampy ADJECTIVE

swan swans

NOUN a large, usually white, bird with a long neck that lives on rivers or lakes

swap swaps swapping swapped

VERB To swap one thing for another means to replace the first thing with the second, often by making an exchange with another person: *I swapped my apple for an orange.*

swarm swarms swarming swarmed

NOUN **1.** A swarm of insects is a large group of them flying together.
VERB **2.** When bees or other insects swarm, they fly together in a large group. **3.** If people swarm somewhere, a lot of people go there quickly and at the same time: *A crowd of students swarmed across the schoolyard toward the mall.* **4.** If a place is swarming with people, there are a lot of people there.

swarthy swarthier swarthiest

ADJECTIVE A swarthy person has a dark complexion.

swashbuckling

ADJECTIVE *Swashbuckling* is used to describe people who have the exciting behaviour or appearance of pirates.

swastika swastikas

NOUN a symbol in the shape of a cross with each arm bent over at right angles. It was the official symbol of the Nazis in Germany, but in India it is a good luck sign.

swat swats swatting swatted

VERB To swat an insect means to hit it sharply in order to kill it.

swathe swathes swathing swathed

VERB **1.** To swathe someone in something means to wrap that person up thickly in cloth or fabric: *He swathed the baby in a warm blanket.*
NOUN **2.** a long strip of cloth that is wrapped around something: *swathes of white silk*

sway sways swaying swayed

VERB **1.** To sway means to lean or swing slowly from side to side. **2.** If something sways you, it influences your judgment.
NOUN **3.** *a literary or poetic use* Sway is the power to influence people: *under the sway of more powerful neighbours*

swear swears swearing swore sworn

VERB **1.** To swear means to say words that are considered to be very rude or blasphemous. **2.** If you swear to something, you state solemnly that you will do it or that it is true. **3.** If you swear by something, you firmly believe that it is a reliable cure or solution: *Some people swear by taking extra vitamins.*

swearword swearwords
NOUN a word that is considered to be rude or blasphemous, which people use when they are angry

sweat sweats sweating sweated
NOUN **1.** Sweat is the salty liquid produced by your sweat glands when you are hot or afraid.
VERB **2.** When you sweat, sweat comes through the pores in your skin in order to lower the temperature of your body.

sweater sweaters
NOUN a knitted piece of clothing covering your upper body and arms

sweatshirt sweatshirts
NOUN a piece of clothing made of thick cotton, covering your upper body and arms

sweaty
ADJECTIVE covered or soaked with sweat

sweep sweeps sweeping swept
VERB **1.** If you sweep the floor, you use a broom to gather up dust or garbage from it. **2.** To sweep things off a surface means to push them all off with a quick, smooth movement. **3.** If something sweeps from one place to another, it moves there very quickly: *A gust of wind swept over the field.* **4.** If an attitude or new fashion sweeps a place, it spreads rapidly through it: *a phenomenon that is sweeping the country*
NOUN **5.** If you do something with a sweep of your arm, you do it with a wide curving movement of your arm.

sweeping
ADJECTIVE **1.** A sweeping curve or movement is long and wide. **2.** A sweeping statement is based on a general assumption rather than on careful thought. **3.** affecting a lot of people to a great extent: *sweeping changes*

sweet sweeter sweetest; sweets

Instead of **SWEET** try...

an engaging smile
a melodious voice
an adorable face
an angelic child
a darling idea
an agreeable nature
a charming thought
a mushy greeting card

ADJECTIVE
1. containing a lot of sugar: *a sweet dessert* **2.** pleasant and satisfying: *sweet success* **3.** A sweet smell is soft and fragrant. **4.** A sweet sound is gentle and tuneful.

5. attractive and delightful: *a sweet little baby*
PLURAL NOUN **6.** candies or other items that contain a lot of sugar
sweetly ADVERB
sweetness NOUN

sweet corn
NOUN a type of corn with a high sugar content that can be eaten as a vegetable

sweeten sweetens sweetening sweetened
VERB To sweeten food means to add sugar or another sweet substance to it.

sweetener sweeteners
NOUN a very sweet, artificial substance that can be used instead of sugar

sweetheart sweethearts
NOUN **1.** You can call someone whom you are very fond of *sweetheart*. **2.** A young person's sweetheart is that person's boyfriend or girlfriend.

sweet pea sweet peas
NOUN a plant with fragrant, climbing flowers

sweet tooth
NOUN If you have a sweet tooth, you like sweet food very much.

swell swells swelling swelled swollen
VERB **1.** If something swells, it becomes larger and rounder: *It causes the abdomen to swell.* **2.** If an amount swells, it increases in number.
NOUN **3.** The regular up and down movement of the waves at sea can be called a swell.

swelling swellings
NOUN **1.** an enlarged area on your body as a result of injury or illness **2.** The swelling of something is an increase in its size.

sweltering
ADJECTIVE If the weather is sweltering, it is very hot.

swerve swerves swerving swerved
VERB To swerve means to suddenly change direction to avoid colliding with something.

swift swifter swiftest; swifts
ADJECTIVE **1.** happening or moving very quickly: *a swift glance*
NOUN **2.** a bird with crescent-shaped wings
swiftly ADVERB

swig swigs swigging swigged *an informal word*
VERB **1.** To swig a drink means to drink it in large mouthfuls, usually from a bottle.
NOUN **2.** If you have a swig of a drink, you take a large mouthful of it.

swill swills swilling swilled
VERB **1.** To swill something means to pour water over it to clean it: *Swill the can out thoroughly.*
NOUN **2.** Swill is a liquid mixture containing waste food that is fed to pigs.

Ss

swim swims swimming swam swum
VERB **1.** To swim means to move through water using various movements with parts of the body. **2.** If things are swimming, it seems as if everything you see is moving and you feel dizzy.
NOUN **3.** If you go for a swim, you go into water to swim for pleasure.
swimmer NOUN

swimming
NOUN Swimming is the activity of moving through water using your arms and legs.

swimming pool swimming pools
NOUN an artificial pool for swimming in

swimsuit another name for BATHING SUIT

swindle swindles swindling swindled
VERB **1.** To swindle someone means to deceive that person to obtain money or property.
NOUN **2.** a trick in which someone is cheated out of money or property
swindler NOUN

swine swine
NOUN **1.** *an old-fashioned use* Swine are pigs. **2.** *an informal use* If you call someone a swine, you mean that person is nasty.

swing swings swinging swung
VERB **1.** If something swings, it moves repeatedly from side to side from a fixed point. **2.** If someone or something swings in a particular direction, that person or thing turns quickly or moves in a sweeping curve in that direction.
NOUN **3.** a seat hanging from a frame or a branch, which moves back and forth when you sit on it **4.** A swing in opinion is a significant change in people's opinion.

swipe swipes swiping swiped
VERB **1.** To swipe at something means to try to hit it making a curving movement with the arm. **2.** *an informal use* To swipe something means to steal it. **3.** To swipe a credit card means to pass it through a machine that electronically reads the information stored in the card.
NOUN **4.** To take a swipe at something means to swipe at it.

swirl swirls swirling swirled
VERB To swirl means to move quickly in circles: *The water swirled around his legs.*

swish swishes swishing swished
VERB **1.** To swish means to move quickly through the air making a soft sound: *The curtains swished back.*
NOUN **2.** the sound made when something swishes

switch switches switching switched
NOUN **1.** a small control for an electrical device or machine **2.** a change: *a switch in routine*
VERB **3.** To switch to a different task or topic means to change to it. **4.** If you switch things, you exchange one for the other
switch off
VERB **5.** To switch off a light or machine means to stop it working by pressing a switch.
switch on
VERB **6.** To switch on a light or machine means to start it working by pressing a switch.

switchboard switchboards
NOUN The switchboard in an organization is the place where all telephone calls are received.

swivel swivels swivelling swivelled
VERB **1.** To swivel means to turn around on a central point.
ADJECTIVE **2.** A swivel chair or lamp is made so that you can move the main part of it while the base remains in a fixed position.

swollen
ADJECTIVE Something that is swollen has swelled up.

swoon swoons swooning swooned
VERB *a literary or poetic word* To swoon means to faint as a result of strong emotion.

swoop swoops swooping swooped
VERB To swoop means to move downward through the air in a fast, curving movement: *A flock of pigeons swooped low over the square.*

sword swords
NOUN a weapon consisting of a very long blade with a short handle

swordfish swordfishes
NOUN a large sea fish with a long upper jaw

sworn
ADJECTIVE If you make a sworn statement, you swear that everything in it is true.

sycamore sycamores
NOUN a tree that has large leaves with five points

syllable syllables
NOUN a part of a word that contains a single vowel sound and is pronounced as a unit. For example, *book* has one syllable and *reading* has two.

syllabus syllabuses
NOUN An outline of subjects that are studied or taught for a particular course is called a syllabus.

Ss

symbol symbols
NOUN a shape, design, or idea that is used to represent something: *The maple leaf is a symbol of Canada. In this novel on life in Ontario, the pine is a symbol of strength.*
symbolize VERB

symbolic
ADJECTIVE Something that is symbolic has a meaning that is considered to represent something else: *a symbolic ceremony*

symbolism symbolisms
NOUN Symbolism is the use of symbols to represent ideas or qualities: *Storm symbolism is used throughout the movie whenever something bad is about to happen.*

symmetrical
ADJECTIVE If something is symmetrical, it has two halves that are the same, except that one half is like a reflection of the other half.
symmetrically ADVERB

symmetry
NOUN Something that has symmetry is symmetrical.

sympathetic
ADJECTIVE **1.** A sympathetic person shows kindness and understanding to other people. **2.** If you are sympathetic to a proposal or an idea, you approve of it.

sympathize sympathizes sympathizing sympathized
VERB To sympathize with someone who is having difficulties means to show that person understanding and care.

sympathizer sympathizers
NOUN People who support a particular cause can be referred to as sympathizers.

sympathy sympathies
NOUN **1.** Sympathy is kindness and understanding toward someone in difficulty. **2.** If you have sympathy with someone's ideas or actions, you agree with them.

symphony symphonies
NOUN a piece of music for an orchestra.

symptom symptoms
NOUN **1.** something wrong with your body that is a sign of an illness **2.** Something that is considered to be a sign of a bad situation can be referred to as a symptom of it: *a symptom of the racism in that area*
symptomatic ADJECTIVE

synagogue synagogues
NOUN a building where Jewish people meet for worship and religious instruction

synchronize synchronizes synchronizing synchronized
VERB **1.** To synchronize two actions means to

do them at the same time and speed. **2.** To synchronize watches means to set them to show exactly the same time as each other.

syncopation
NOUN Syncopation in rhythm is the stressing of weak beats instead of strong ones.

syndicate syndicates
NOUN an association of businesspeople formed to carry out a particular project

syndrome syndromes
NOUN **1.** a medical condition characterized by a particular set of symptoms: *Down syndrome* **2.** You can refer to a typical set of characteristics as a syndrome: *the syndrome of skipping from one wonder diet to the next*

synonym synonyms
NOUN If two words have the same or a very similar meaning, they are synonyms.

synonymous
ADJECTIVE **1.** Two words that are synonymous have the same or very similar meanings. **2.** If two things are closely associated, you can say that one is synonymous with the other: *Toronto is synonymous with the CN Tower.*

synopsis synopses
NOUN a summary of a book, play, or movie

syntax
NOUN The syntax of a language is its grammatical rules and the way its words are arranged.

synthesize synthesizes synthesizing synthesized
VERB When you synthesize, you combine ideas and information to form a complete new understanding.

synthetic
ADJECTIVE made from artificial substances

syringe syringes
NOUN a tube with a hollow needle at one end, used for injecting or extracting liquids

syrup syrups
NOUN a thick, sweet liquid made by boiling sugar with water

system systems
NOUN **1.** an organized way of doing or arranging something according to a fixed plan or set of rules **2.** People sometimes refer to the government and administration of the country as the system. **3.** You can also refer to a set of equipment as a system: *an old stereo system* **4.** In biology, a system is the set of organs that perform a certain function: *the immune system*

systematic
ADJECTIVE following a fixed plan and done in an efficient way: *a systematic study*
systematically ADVERB

SYMBOL

▼ ✕

a shape, design, or idea that is used to represent something

"Take the flag!"

Here is an example of a symbol. The knight passes on the flag because it is a symbol representing the whole kingdom.

NEL

SCOTT HEPBURN

Tt

tab tabs
  NOUN a small extra flap, loop, or piece that is attached to something, for example on a curtain so it can be hung on a pole

tabby tabbies
  NOUN a cat whose fur has grey, brown, or black stripes

table tables tabling tabled
  NOUN **1.** a piece of furniture with a flat, horizontal top supported by one or more legs **2.** a set of facts or figures arranged in rows or columns
  VERB **3.** If you table something such as a proposal, you say formally that you want it to be discussed.

tablecloth tablecloths
  NOUN a cloth used to cover a table

tablespoon tablespoons
  NOUN a large spoon used for serving food; also a measurement equal to 15 millilitres

tablet tablets
  NOUN **1.** any small, round pill made of powdered medicine **2.** a slab of stone with words cut into it

table tennis
  NOUN Table tennis is a game for two or four people in which you use bats to hit a small hollow ball over a low net across a table.

tabloid tabloids
  NOUN a newspaper with small pages, short news stories, and lots of photographs

taboo taboos
  NOUN **1.** a social custom that some words, subjects, or actions must be avoided because they are considered embarrassing or offensive: *We have a powerful taboo against boasting.* **2.** a religious custom that forbids people to do something
  ADJECTIVE **3.** forbidden or disapproved of: *a taboo subject*

tacit
  ADJECTIVE understood or implied without actually being said or written
  tacitly ADVERB

⚠ **HEADS UP**

Like the words **illicit** and **implicit**, **tacit** is pronounced with a soft c: TASS-it.

taciturn
  ADJECTIVE Someone who is taciturn does not talk very much and so seems unfriendly.

tack tacks tacking tacked
  NOUN **1.** a short nail with a broad, flat head **2.** If you change tack, you start to use a different method for dealing with something.
  VERB **3.** If you tack something to a surface, you nail it there with tacks. **4.** If you tack a piece of fabric, you sew it with loose stitches.

tackle tackles tackling tackled
  VERB **1.** If you tackle a difficult task, you start dealing with it in a determined way. **2.** If you tackle someone in a game such as football, you try to stop the ball carrier from moving forward, usually by knocking the person down. **3.** If you tackle someone about something, you talk to that person about it in order to get something dealt with.
  NOUN **4.** A tackle in sport is an attempt to stop the ball carrier. **5.** Tackle is the equipment used for fishing.

tacky tackier tackiest
  ADJECTIVE **1.** slightly sticky to touch: *The paint feels tacky to the touch.* **2.** an informal use badly made and in poor taste: *tacky furniture*

tact
  NOUN Tact is the ability to see when a situation is difficult or delicate and to handle it without upsetting people.
  tactless ADJECTIVE
  tactlessly ADVERB

tactful
  ADJECTIVE behaving with or showing tact
  tactfully ADVERB

tactic tactics
  NOUN **1.** A tactic is a method you use to achieve what you want.
  PLURAL NOUN **2.** Tactics are the ways in which troops and equipment are used in order to win a battle.
  tactical ADJECTIVE
  tactically ADVERB

tactile
  ADJECTIVE involving the sense of touch

tadpole tadpoles
  NOUN Tadpoles are the larvae of frogs and toads. They are black with round heads and long tails and live in water.

taffeta
  NOUN Taffeta is a stiff, shiny fabric that is used mainly for making women's clothes.

tag tags tagging tagged
  NOUN **1.** a small label made of cloth, paper, or plastic
  VERB **2.** If you tag along with someone, you go with that person or behind him or her.

Tt

tail tails tailing tailed
NOUN **1.** The tail of an animal, bird, or fish is the part extending beyond the end of its body. **2.** Tail can be used to mean the end part of something: *the tail of the plane*
VERB **3.** *an informal use* If you tail someone, you follow that person in order to find out where he or she goes and what he or she does.
PLURAL NOUN **4.** The side of a coin that does not have a person's head.

tail off
VERB **5.** If something tails off, it becomes gradually less.

tailor tailors tailoring tailored
NOUN **1.** a person who makes, alters, and repairs clothes
VERB **2.** If something is tailored for a particular purpose, it is specially designed for it.

tailor-made
ADJECTIVE suitable for a particular person or purpose, or specifically designed for that person or purpose

taint taints tainting tainted
VERB **1.** To taint something is to spoil it by adding something undesirable to it.
NOUN **2.** an undesirable quality in something that spoils it

take takes taking took taken
VERB **1.** *Take* is used to show what action or activity is being done: *I took a bath. She took her driving test.* **2.** If something takes a certain amount of time, or a particular quality or ability, it requires it: *He takes three hours to get ready.* **3.** If you take something, you put your hand around it and hold it or carry it: *Here, let me take your coat.* **4.** If you take someone somewhere, you drive that person there by car or lead him or her there. **5.** If you take something that is offered to you, you accept it: *He had to take the job.* **6.** If you take the responsibility or blame for something, you accept responsibility or blame. **7.** If you take something that does not belong to you, you steal it. **8.** If you take a pill or medicine, you swallow it. **9.** If you can take something painful, you can bear it: *We can't take much more of this.* **10.** If you take someone's advice, you do what that person says you should do. **11.** If you take a person's temperature or pulse, you measure it. **12.** If you take a car or train, or a road or route, you use it to go from one place to another. **13.** If you **take care of** someone or something, you look after that person or thing. **14.** If you **take care of** a problem or situation, you deal with it and sort it out.

take after
VERB **15.** If you take after someone in your family, you look or behave like that person.

take down
VERB **16.** If you take down what someone is saying, you write it down.

take in
VERB **17.** If someone is taken in, that person is deceived. **18.** If you take something in, you understand it.

take off
VERB **19.** When an airplane takes off, it leaves the ground and begins to fly.
takeoff NOUN

take over
VERB **20.** To take something over means to start controlling it.
takeover NOUN

take to
VERB **21.** If you take to someone or something, you like that person or thing immediately.

takeout
NOUN a hot cooked meal bought from a store or restaurant to be eaten elsewhere

takings
PLURAL NOUN Takings are the money that a business gets from selling its goods or services.

talc
NOUN a soft and smooth white, grey, or greenish mineral

talcum
NOUN Talcum or **talcum powder** is a soft, perfumed powder used for absorbing moisture on the body.

tale tales
NOUN a story

Instead of **TALE** try...
an unbelievable yarn
a brief anecdote
a sweeping epic
a heroic saga
a classic fable
a romantic drama
a thrilling cliffhanger
the story of how we met

talent talents
NOUN Talent is the natural ability to do something well.
talented ADJECTIVE

talisman talismans
NOUN an object that you believe has magic powers to protect you or bring luck

Tt

talk talks talking talked

VERB **1.** When you talk, you say things to someone. **2.** If people talk, especially about other people's private affairs, they gossip about them: *The neighbours might talk.* **3.** If you talk on or about something, you make an informal speech about it.
NOUN **4.** Talk is discussion or gossip. **5.** an informal speech about something

talk down

VERB **6.** If you talk down to someone, you talk to that person in a way that shows that you think you are more important or cleverer than him or her.

talkative

ADJECTIVE talking a lot

tall taller tallest

ADJECTIVE **1.** of more than average or normal height **2.** having a particular height: *a wall ten metres tall*
PHRASE **3.** If you describe something as **a tall tale**, you mean that it is difficult to believe because it is so unlikely.

tally tallies tallying tallied

NOUN **1.** an informal record of amounts that you keep adding to as you go along: *He ended with a reasonable goal tally last season.*
VERB **2.** If numbers or statements tally, they are exactly the same or they give the same results or conclusions.

talon talons

NOUN Talons are sharp, hooked claws, especially of a bird of prey.

tambourine tambourines

NOUN a percussion instrument made of a skin stretched tightly over a circular frame, with small, round pieces of metal around the edge that jingle when the tambourine is beaten or shaken

tame tamer tamest; tames taming tamed

ADJECTIVE **1.** A tame animal or bird is not afraid of people and is not violent toward them. **2.** Something that is tame is uninteresting and lacks excitement or risk: *The report was pretty tame.*
VERB **3.** If you tame people or things, you bring them under control. **4.** To tame a wild animal or bird is to train it to be obedient and live with humans.

tamper tampers tampering tampered

VERB If you tamper with something, you interfere or meddle with it.

tampon tampons

NOUN a firm, specially shaped piece of soft material that a female places inside her vagina to absorb the blood during her period

tan tans tanning tanned

NOUN **1.** If you have a tan, your skin is darker than usual because you have been in the sun.
VERB **2.** To tan an animal's hide is to turn it into leather by treating it with chemicals.
ADJECTIVE **3.** Something that is tan is of a light yellowish brown colour: *a tan dress*

tandem tandems

NOUN a bicycle designed for two riders sitting one behind the other

tang tangs

NOUN a strong, sharp smell or flavour: *the tang of lemon*
tangy ADJECTIVE

tangent tangents

NOUN **1.** A tangent of a curve is any straight line that touches the curve at one point only.
PHRASE **2.** If you **go off on a tangent**, you start talking or thinking about something that is not completely relevant to what has gone before.

tangerine tangerines

NOUN **1.** a type of small, sweet orange with a loose rind
NOUN OR ADJECTIVE **2.** reddish orange

tangible

ADJECTIVE clear or definite enough to be easily seen or felt: *tangible proof*

tangle tangles tangling tangled

NOUN **1.** a mass of things such as hairs or fibres knotted or coiled together and difficult to separate
VERB **2.** If you are tangled in wires or ropes, you are caught or trapped in them so that it is difficult to get free.

tango tangos

NOUN A tango is a ballroom dance using long, gliding steps and sudden pauses; also a piece of music composed for this dance.

tank tanks

NOUN **1.** a large container for storing liquid or gas **2.** an armoured military vehicle that moves on tracks and is equipped with guns or rockets

tankard tankards

NOUN a large metal mug used for drinking beer

tanker tankers

NOUN a ship or truck designed to carry large quantities of oil, gas, or liquid: *a gasoline tanker*

tannin

NOUN a brown or yellow substance found in plants and used in making leather

tantalizing

ADJECTIVE Something that is tantalizing makes

Tt

you feel hopeful and excited, although you know that you probably will not be able to have what you want: *a tantalizing glimpse of riches to come*

tantamount
ADJECTIVE If you say that something is tantamount to something else, you mean that it is almost the same as it: *That would be tantamount to treason.*

tantrum tantrums
NOUN a noisy and sometimes violent outburst of temper, especially by a child

tap taps tapping tapped
NOUN **1.** a device that you turn to control the flow of liquid or gas from a pipe or container **2.** the action of hitting something lightly; also the sound that this action makes
VERB **3.** If you tap something or tap on it, you hit it lightly. **4.** If a telephone is tapped, a device is fitted to it so that someone can listen secretly to the calls.

tap dancing
NOUN Tap dancing is a type of dancing in which the dancers wear special shoes with pieces of metal on the toes and heels that click against the floor.

tape tapes taping taped
NOUN **1.** Tape is plastic ribbon covered with a magnetic substance and used to record sounds, pictures, and computer information. **2.** a cassette or spool with magnetic tape wound around it **3.** Tape is a long, thin strip of fabric that is used for binding or fastening. **4.** Tape is also a strip of sticky material that you use for sticking things together.
VERB **5.** If you tape sounds or television pictures, you record them using a tape recorder or a video recorder. **6.** If you tape one thing to another, you attach them using adhesive tape.

tape measure tape measures
NOUN a strip of plastic or metal that is marked off in inches or centimetres and used for measuring things

taper tapers tapering tapered
VERB **1.** Something that tapers becomes thinner toward one end.
NOUN **2.** a thin candle

tape recorder tape recorders
NOUN a machine used for recording sounds onto magnetic tape, and for playing these sounds back

tapestry tapestries
NOUN a piece of heavy cloth with designs embroidered on it

tar
NOUN Tar is a thick, black, sticky substance that is used in making roads.

tarantula tarantulas
NOUN a large, hairy, poisonous spider

target targets
NOUN **1.** something that you aim at when firing a weapon **2.** The target of an action or remark is the person or thing at which it is directed: *He became a target for our teasing.* **3.** Your target is the result that you are trying to achieve.

tariff tariffs
NOUN **1.** a tax that a government collects on imported goods **2.** any list of prices or charges

tarmac
NOUN Tarmac is a material used for making road surfaces. It consists of crushed stones mixed with tar; also a runway made of this material.

tarnish tarnishes tarnishing tarnished
VERB **1.** If metal tarnishes, it becomes stained and loses its shine. **2.** If something tarnishes your reputation, it spoils it and causes people to lose their respect for you.

tarot
NOUN A tarot card is one of a special pack of cards used for telling fortunes.

tarpaulin tarpaulins
NOUN a sheet of heavy, waterproof material used as a protective covering

tarragon
NOUN a herb with narrow green leaves used in cooking

tarry tarries tarrying tarried
VERB *an old-fashioned word* To tarry is to wait, or to stay somewhere for a little longer.

tart tarts; tarter tartest
NOUN **1.** a pastry case with a sweet filling
ADJECTIVE **2.** Something that is tart has a sour or sharp taste. **3.** A tart remark is unpleasant and harsh.

tartan tartans
NOUN Tartan is a woollen fabric originating in Scotland with checks of various colours and sizes, especially to distinguish families or clans.

tartar
NOUN Tartar is a hard, crusty substance that forms on teeth.

task tasks
NOUN any piece of work that has to be done

Tasmanian devil Tasmanian devils
NOUN a black-and-white marsupial of Tasmania, which eats flesh

⚠ **HEADS UP** The word **tarot** is pronounced TAIR-oh.

573

Tt

tassel tassels
NOUN a tuft of loose threads tied by a knot and used for decoration

taste tastes tasting tasted
NOUN **1.** Your sense of taste is your ability to recognize the flavour of things in your mouth. **2.** The taste of something is its flavour. **3.** If you have a taste of a food or drink, you have a small amount of it to see what it is like. **4.** If you have a taste for something, you enjoy it: *a taste for publicity* **5.** If you have a taste of something, you experience it: *my first taste of defeat* **6.** A person's taste is his or her choice in the things he or she likes to buy or have around him or her: *His taste in music is great.* VERB **7.** When you can taste something in your mouth, you are aware of its flavour. **8.** If you taste a food or drink, you have a small amount of it to see what it is like. **9.** If food or drink tastes of something, it has that flavour.

taste bud taste buds
NOUN Your taste buds are the little points on the surface of your tongue that enable you to taste things.

tasteful
ADJECTIVE attractive and elegant
tastefully ADVERB

tasteless
ADJECTIVE **1.** vulgar and unattractive **2.** A tasteless remark or joke is offensive. **3.** Tasteless food has very little flavour.

tasty tastier tastiest
ADJECTIVE having a pleasant flavour

tatters
PLURAL NOUN Clothes that are in tatters are badly torn.
tattered ADJECTIVE

tattoo tattoos tattooing tattooed
VERB **1.** If someone tattoos you or tattoos a design on you, that person draws it on your skin by pricking little holes and filling them with coloured dye. NOUN **2.** a picture or design tattooed on someone's body **3.** a public military display of marching and music

tatty tattier tattiest
ADJECTIVE worn out or untidy and rather dirty

taught the past tense and past participle of TEACH

taunt taunts taunting taunted
VERB **1.** To taunt someone is to speak to that person about his or her weaknesses in order to make him or her angry or upset. NOUN **2.** an offensive remark intended to make a person angry or upset

taut
ADJECTIVE stretched very tight: *taut wires*

tavern taverns
NOUN a place where alcoholic drinks, especially beer, are sold and consumed

tawdry tawdrier tawdriest
ADJECTIVE cheap, gaudy, and of poor quality

tawny
NOUN OR ADJECTIVE brownish yellow

tax taxes taxing taxed
NOUN **1.** Tax is an amount of money that the people in a country have to pay to the government so that it can provide public services such as health care and education. VERB **2.** If a sum of money is taxed, a certain amount of it has to be paid to the government. **3.** If goods are taxed, a certain amount of their price has to be paid to the government. **4.** If people or companies are taxed, they have to pay a certain amount of their income to the government. **5.** If something taxes you, it makes heavy demands on you: *The dog's constant barking will be sure to tax your patience.*
taxation NOUN

taxi taxis taxiing taxied
NOUN **1.** a car with a driver that you hire to take you to where you want to go VERB **2.** When an airplane taxis, it moves slowly along the runway before taking off or after landing.

tea teas
NOUN **1.** Tea is the dried leaves of an evergreen shrub found in Asia. **2.** Tea is a drink made by brewing the leaves of the tea plant in hot water; also a cup of this. **3.** Tea is also any drink made with hot water and leaves or flowers: *peppermint tea*

tea bag tea bags
NOUN a small paper bag with tea leaves in it that is placed in boiling water to make tea

teach teaches teaching taught
VERB **1.** If you teach someone something, you give that person instructions so that he or she knows about it or knows how to do it. **2.** If you teach a subject, you help students learn about a subject at school, college, or university.
teaching NOUN

teacher teachers
NOUN a person who teaches other people, especially children

teak
NOUN a hard wood that comes from a large Asian tree

team teams teaming teamed
NOUN **1.** a group of people who work

Tt

together or play together against another group in a sport or game
VERB **2.** If you team up with someone, you join that person and work together with him or her.

teamwork
NOUN Teamwork is the ability of a group of people to work well together.

teapot teapots
NOUN a round pot with a handle, a lid, and a spout, used for brewing and pouring tea

tear tears tearing tore torn
NOUN **1.** Tears are the drops of salty liquid that come out of your eyes when you cry. **2.** a hole that has been made in something
VERB **3.** If you tear something, it is damaged by being pulled so that a hole appears in it. **4.** If you tear somewhere, you rush there: *He tore across the lawn and made it to the bus stop just in time.*

tearful
ADJECTIVE about to cry or crying gently
tearfully ADVERB

tease teases teasing teased
VERB **1.** If you tease someone, you deliberately make fun of that person or embarrass that person because it amuses you.
NOUN **2.** someone who enjoys teasing people

teaspoon teaspoons
NOUN a small spoon used for stirring drinks; also a standard unit of measurement equal to five millilitres

teat teats
NOUN a nipple on a female animal

tech techs
NOUN *an informal word* a high school that offers training in the trades and other practical subjects

technical
ADJECTIVE **1.** involving machines, processes, and materials used in industry, transport, and communications **2.** skilled in practical and mechanical things rather than theories and ideas **3.** involving a specialized field of activity: *I never understood the technical jargon.*

technicality technicalities
NOUN **1.** The technicalities of a process or activity are the detailed methods used to do it. **2.** an exact detail of a law or a set of rules, especially one some people might not notice: *The verdict may have been based on a technicality.*

technically
ADVERB If something is technically true or correct, it is true or correct when you consider only the facts, rules, or laws, but may not be important or relevant in a particular situation: *Technically, you are supposed to arrive at work ten minutes before your shift starts.*

technician technicians
NOUN someone whose job involves skilled, practical work with scientific equipment

technique techniques
NOUN **1.** a particular method of doing something: *new techniques of manufacture* **2.** Technique is skill and ability in an activity that is developed through training and practice: *her unique vocal technique*

techno-
PREFIX The prefix *techno-* means a *craft* or *art*: *technology*

technology technologies
NOUN **1.** Technology is the study of the application of science and scientific knowledge for practical purposes in industry, farming, medicine, or business. **2.** a particular area of activity that requires scientific methods and knowledge: *computer technology*
technological ADJECTIVE
technologically ADVERB

teddy teddies
NOUN A teddy or teddy bear is a stuffed toy that looks like a friendly bear.

tedious
ADJECTIVE boring and lasting for a long time: *the tedious task of cleaning my room*

tedium
NOUN the quality of being boring and lasting for a long time: *the tedium of unemployment*

tee tees teeing teed
NOUN **1.** the small wooden or plastic peg on which a golf ball is placed before the golfer first hits it
VERB **2.** To **tee off** is to hit a golf ball from the tee, or to start a round of golf.

teem teems teeming teemed
VERB **1.** If a place is teeming with people or things, there are a lot of them moving around. **2.** If it teems, it rains very heavily: *The rain was teeming down.*

teenage
ADJECTIVE **1.** aged between 13 and 19 **2.** typical of people aged between 13 and 19: *teenage fashion*
teenager NOUN

teens
PLURAL NOUN Your teens are the period of your life when you are between 13 and 19 years old.

teepee teepees
NOUN a cone-shaped tent of animal skins used by Aboriginal peoples

teeter teeters teetering teetered
VERB To teeter is to shake or sway slightly in an unsteady way and seem about to fall over.

teeth the plural of TOOTH

teethe teethes teething teethed
VERB When babies are teething, their teeth are starting to come through, usually causing them pain.

teetotaller
NOUN A teetotaller is someone who never drinks alcohol.
teetotal ADJECTIVE

tele-
PREFIX The prefix *tele-* means *at* or *over a distance*: *television*

telecommunications
NOUN Telecommunications is the science and activity of sending signals and messages over long distances using electronic equipment.

telepathy
NOUN Telepathy is the supposed direct communication between people's minds.
telepathic ADJECTIVE

telephone telephones telephoning telephoned
NOUN **1.** a piece of electrical equipment for talking directly to someone who is in a different place
VERB **2.** If you telephone someone, you speak to that person using a telephone.

telephone booth telephone booths
NOUN a small shelter in the street where there is a public telephone

tell tells telling told
VERB **1.** If you tell someone something, you let that person know about it. **2.** If you tell someone to do something, you order or advise that person to do it. **3.** If you can tell something, you are able to judge correctly what is happening or what the situation is: *I could tell he was scared.* **4.** If an unpleasant

or tiring experience begins to tell, it begins to have a serious effect: *The pressure began to tell on her.*

teller tellers
NOUN a person who receives or gives out money in a bank

telling
ADJECTIVE Something that is telling has an important effect, often because it shows the true nature of a situation: *a telling account of the war*

telltale
ADJECTIVE A telltale sign reveals information: *the sad, telltale signs of a recent accident*

temerity
NOUN If someone has the temerity to do something, that person does it even though it upsets or annoys other people: *She had the temerity to call her mom by her given name.*

temp temps
NOUN *an informal word* an office employee who works for short periods of time in different places

temper tempers tempering tempered
NOUN **1.** Your temper is the frame of mind or mood you are in. **2.** a sudden outburst of anger
PHRASE **3.** If you **lose your temper**, you become very angry.
VERB **4.** To temper something is to make it more acceptable or suitable: *curiosity tempered with some caution*

temperament temperaments
NOUN Your temperament is your nature or personality, shown in the way you react toward people and situations: *an artistic temperament*

temperamental
ADJECTIVE Someone who is temperamental has moods that change often and suddenly.

temperate
ADJECTIVE A temperate place has weather that is neither extremely hot nor extremely cold.

KNOWING WORDS: WORD BUILDING

BE WORD SHARP!

You can create new words by adding prefixes and suffixes to a base word.

tele- a prefix that means *at or over a distance*

telemarketing selling or advertising by telephone

telescope an object used to see things at a distance

television a device that receives broadcast signals

televise film and broadcast on television

telethon a charity marathon, broadcast on television

Tt

temperature temperatures
NOUN **1.** The temperature of something is how hot or cold it is. **2.** Your temperature is the temperature of your body.
PHRASE **3.** If you **have a temperature**, the temperature of your body is higher than it should be, because you are ill.

tempest tempests
NOUN *a literary or poetic word* a violent storm

tempestuous
ADJECTIVE violent or strongly emotional: *a tempestuous relationship*

template templates
NOUN a shape or pattern cut out in wood, metal, plastic, or card that you draw or cut around to reproduce that shape or pattern

temple temples
NOUN **1.** a building used for the worship of a god in various religions: *a Buddhist temple* **2.** Your temples are the flat parts on each side of your forehead.

tempo tempos
NOUN **1.** The tempo of something is the speed at which it happens: *the slow tempo of change* **2.** *a technical use* The tempo of a piece of music is its speed.

temporary
ADJECTIVE lasting for only a short time
temporarily ADVERB

tempt tempts tempting tempted
VERB **1.** If you tempt someone, you try to persuade that person to do something by offering him or her something that he or she wants. **2.** If you are tempted to do something, you want to do it but you think it might be wrong or harmful: *He was tempted to reply with sarcasm.*

temptation temptations
NOUN **1.** Temptation is the state you are in when you want to do or have something, even though you know it might be wrong or harmful. **2.** something that you want to do or have, even though you know it might be wrong or harmful: *There is a temptation to ignore the problem.*

ten tens
NOUN the number 10
tenth ADJECTIVE, ADVERB

tenacious
ADJECTIVE determined and not giving up easily
tenaciously ADVERB
tenacity NOUN

tenant tenants
NOUN someone who pays rent for the place he or she lives in, or for land or buildings that he or she uses
tenancy NOUN

tend tends tending tended
VERB **1.** If something tends to happen, it happens usually or often. **2.** If you tend someone or something, you look after that person or thing: *What is the best way to tend our cattle?*

tendency tendencies
NOUN a trend or type of behaviour that happens very often: *a tendency to be critical*

tender tenderer tenderest; tenders tendering tendered
ADJECTIVE **1.** Someone who is tender has gentle and caring feelings. **2.** If someone is at a tender age, that person is young and does not know very much about life. **3.** Tender meat is easy to cut or chew. **4.** If a part of your body is tender, it is painful and sore.
VERB **5.** If someone tenders an apology or resignation, that person offers it.
NOUN **6.** a formal offer to supply goods or to do a job for a particular price

tendon tendons
NOUN a strong cord of tissue that joins a muscle to a bone

tendril tendrils
NOUN Tendrils are short, thin stems that grow on climbing plants and attach them to walls.

tenement tenements
NOUN a rundown, low-rental building divided into apartments

tenet tenets
NOUN The tenets of a theory or belief are the main ideas it is based upon.

tennis
NOUN Tennis is a game played by two or four players on a rectangular court, in which a ball is hit by players over a central net.

tenor tenors
NOUN **1.** a man who sings in a fairly high voice **2.** The tenor of something is the general meaning or mood that it expresses: *The whole tenor of his poetry had changed.*
ADJECTIVE **3.** A tenor recorder, saxophone, or other musical instrument has a range of notes of a fairly low pitch.

tense tenser tensest; tenses tensing tensed
ADJECTIVE **1.** If you are tense, you are nervous and cannot relax. **2.** A tense situation or period of time is one that makes people nervous and worried. **3.** If your body is tense, your muscles are tight.
VERB **4.** If you tense, or if your muscles tense, your muscles become tight and stiff.
NOUN **5.** The tense of a verb is the form that shows whether you are talking about the past, present, or future.

tension tensions

NOUN **1.** Tension is the feeling of nervousness or worry that you have when something dangerous or important is happening. **2.** The tension in a rope or wire is how tightly it is stretched.

tent tents

NOUN a shelter made of canvas or nylon held up by poles and pinned down with pegs and ropes

tentacle tentacles

NOUN The tentacles of an animal such as an octopus are the long, thin parts that it uses to feel and hold things.

tentative

ADJECTIVE acting or speaking cautiously because of being uncertain or afraid

tentatively ADVERB

tenterhooks

PLURAL NOUN If you are on tenterhooks, you are nervous and excited about something that is going to happen.

tenuous

ADJECTIVE If an idea or connection is tenuous, it is so slight and weak that it may not really exist or may easily cease to exist: *a very tenuous friendship*

tenure tenures

NOUN **1.** Tenure is the legal right to live in a place or to use land or buildings for a period of time. **2.** Tenure is guaranteed permanent employment, especially as a teacher or lecturer: *His tenure ended in 1998.*

tepid

ADJECTIVE Tepid liquid is only slightly warm.

term terms terming termed

NOUN **1.** a fixed period of time: *her second term of office* **2.** one of the periods of time that each year is divided into at a school, college, or university **3.** a name or word used for a particular thing

PLURAL NOUN **4.** The terms of an agreement are the conditions that have been accepted by the people involved in it. **5.** If you express something in particular terms, you express it using a particular type of language or in a way that clearly shows your attitude: *The teacher spoke of her students in glowing terms.*

PHRASE **6.** If you **come to terms with** something difficult or unpleasant, you learn to accept it.

VERB **7.** To term something is to give it a name or to describe it: *He termed my performance memorable.*

terminal terminals

ADJECTIVE **1.** A terminal illness or disease cannot be cured and causes death gradually.

NOUN **2.** a place where vehicles, passengers, or goods begin or end a journey **3.** A computer terminal is a keyboard and a visual display unit that is used to put information into or get information out of a computer. **4.** one of the parts of an electrical device through which electricity enters or leaves

terminally ADVERB

terminate terminates terminating terminated

VERB When you terminate something or when it terminates, it stops or ends.

termination NOUN

terminology terminologies

NOUN The terminology of a subject is the set of special words and expressions used in it.

terminus terminuses

NOUN a place where a bus or train route ends

termite termites

NOUN Termites are small white insects that feed on wood.

tern terns

NOUN a small black-and-white seabird with long wings and a forked tail

terrace terraces

NOUN a flat, paved area next to a building where people can sit

terracotta

NOUN a type of brown pottery with no glaze

terrain

NOUN The terrain of an area is the type of land there: *the region's hilly terrain*

terrapin terrapins

NOUN a small, North American, freshwater turtle

terrestrial

ADJECTIVE involving the earth or land

terrible

ADJECTIVE **1.** serious and unpleasant: *a*

Instead of **TERRIBLE** try...

an atrocious smell
in a dreadful state
appalling neglect
vile crimes
a horrid mess
abysmal poverty
a frightful monster
a horrendous blizzard

terrible illness **2.** *an informal use* very bad or of poor quality: *a terrible haircut*

terribly

ADVERB very or very much: *I was terribly upset.*

Tt

terrier terriers
NOUN a small short-bodied dog

terrific
ADJECTIVE **1.** *an informal use* very pleasing or impressive: *a terrific movie* **2.** great in amount, degree, or intensity: *a terrific blow on the head*
terrifically ADVERB

terrify terrifies terrifying terrified
VERB If something terrifies you, it makes you feel extremely frightened.

territorial
ADJECTIVE involving or relating to the ownership of a particular area of land or water: *a territorial dispute*

territory territories
NOUN **1.** The territory of a country is the land that it controls. **2.** An animal's territory is an area that it regards as its own and defends when other animals try to enter it.

terror terrors
NOUN **1.** Terror is great fear or panic.
2. something that makes you feel very frightened

terrorism
NOUN Terrorism is the use of violence for political reasons.
terrorist NOUN OR ADJECTIVE

terrorize terrorizes terrorizing terrorized
VERB If someone terrorizes you, that person frightens you by threatening or tormenting you.

terse terser tersest
ADJECTIVE A terse statement is short and unfriendly.

tertiary
ADJECTIVE third in order or importance

test tests testing tested
VERB **1.** When you test something, you try it to find out what it is, what condition it is in, or how well it works. **2.** If you test someone, you ask that person questions to find out how much he or she knows.
NOUN **3.** a deliberate action or experiment to find out whether something works or how well it works **4.** a set of questions or tasks given to someone to find out what that person knows or can do

testament testaments
NOUN **1.** *a legal use* a will **2.** a thing that serves as a sign or evidence of a fact, event, or quality

test case test cases
NOUN a legal case that becomes an example for deciding other similar cases

testicle testicles
NOUN A man's testicles are the two sex glands that produce sperm.

testify testifies testifying testified
VERB **1.** When someone testifies, that person makes a formal statement, especially in a court of law: *She later testified at the Supreme Court.* **2.** To testify to something is to show that it is likely to be true: *a doctor's certificate testifying to her good health*

testimonial testimonials
NOUN a statement saying how good someone or something is

testimony testimonies
NOUN A person's testimony is a formal statement that he or she makes, especially in a court of law.

testis testes
NOUN A man's testes are his testicles.

testosterone
NOUN Testosterone is a male hormone that produces male characteristics.

test tube test tubes
NOUN a small, cylindrical glass container that is used in chemical experiments

tetanus
NOUN Tetanus is a painful infectious disease caused by germs getting into wounds.

tether tethers tethering tethered
VERB **1.** If you tether an animal, you tie it to a post.
PHRASE **2.** If you are **at the end of your tether,** you are extremely tired and have no more patience or energy left to deal with your problems.

text texts texting texted
NOUN **1.** The text of a book is the main written part of it, rather than the pictures or index. **2.** Text is any written material.
3. a book or other piece of writing used for study or an exam at school or college
4. Text is any piece of written, oral, or visual communication.
VERB **5.** If you text someone, you send that person a text message.
textual ADJECTIVE

textbook textbooks
NOUN a book about a particular subject for students to use

text feature text features
NOUN A text feature is a part of a text that helps a reader to navigate the text. Text features include title, headings, illustrations, labels, fonts, charts, table of contents, and glossary.

HEADS UP The word **tertiary** is pronounced TUR-she-air-ee.

Tt

text form text forms
NOUN A text form is a type of text that has a specific set of characteristics. For example, poetry, novels, comic strips, and posters are all different text forms.

textile textiles
NOUN a woven cloth or fabric

text pattern text patterns
NOUN A text pattern is the organizational structure of a text. Text patterns include cause and effect, compare-contrast, and sequence.

text feature text features
NOUN a text feature is a part of a text that helps a reader to navigate the text. Text features include title, headings, illustrations, labels, fonts, table of contents, and glossary.

texture textures
NOUN The texture of something is the way it feels when you touch it.

than
PREPOSITION OR CONJUNCTION **1.** You use *than* to link two parts of a comparison: *She was older than me.* **2.** You use *than* to link two parts of a contrast: *Players would rather play than train.*

thank thanks thanking thanked
VERB When you thank someone, you show that you are grateful for something, usually by saying *thank you.*

thankful
ADJECTIVE happy and relieved that something has happened
thankfully ADVERB

thankless
ADJECTIVE A thankless job or task involves doing a lot of hard work that other people do not notice or are not grateful for: *a thankless task*

thanks
PLURAL NOUN **1.** When you express your thanks to someone, you tell or show that person how grateful you are for something.
PHRASE **2.** If something happened **thanks to** someone or something, it happened because of that person or thing: *I'm as prepared as I can be, thanks to you.*
INTERJECTION **3.** You say *thanks* to show that you are grateful for something.

thanksgiving
NOUN **1.** Thanksgiving is an act of gratitude, especially in prayer or in a religious ceremony. **2.** In Canada and the United States, Thanksgiving is a public holiday in the autumn.

thank you You say *thank you* to show that you are grateful to someone for something.

that those
ADJECTIVE OR PRONOUN **1.** *That* or *those* is used to refer to things or people already mentioned or known about: *That man was waving.*
CONJUNCTION **2.** *That* is used to introduce a clause: *I said that I was coming home.*
PRONOUN **3.** *That* is also used to introduce a relative clause: *I followed her to a door that led inside.*

thatch thatches thatching thatched
NOUN **1.** Thatch is straw and reeds used to make roofs.
VERB **2.** To thatch a roof is to cover it with thatch.

thaw thaws thawing thawed
VERB **1.** When snow or ice thaws, it melts. **2.** When you thaw frozen food, or when it thaws, it returns to its normal state in a warmer atmosphere. **3.** When people who are unfriendly thaw, they begin to be more friendly and relaxed.
NOUN **4.** a period of warmer weather in winter when snow or ice melts

the
ADJECTIVE The definite article *the* is used when you are talking about something that is known about, that has just been mentioned, or that you are going to give details about.

theatre theatres
NOUN **1.** a building where plays and other entertainments are performed on a stage, or where movies are shown **2.** Theatre is work such as writing, producing, and acting in plays. **3.** An operating theatre is a room in a hospital designed and equipped for surgical operations.

theatrical
ADJECTIVE **1.** involving the theatre or performed in a theatre: *his theatrical career* **2.** Theatrical behaviour is exaggerated, unnatural, and done for effect.
theatrically ADVERB

thee
PRONOUN *an old-fashioned word* Thee means you.

theft thefts
NOUN Theft is the crime of stealing.

their
ADJECTIVE *Their* refers to something belonging or relating to people or things, other than yourself or the person you are talking to, which have already been mentioned: *It was their fault.*

theirs
PRONOUN *Theirs* refers to something belonging or relating to people or things, other than

yourself or the person you are talking to, which have already been mentioned: *The games were his, not theirs.*

them

PRONOUN *Them* refers to things or people, other than yourself or the person you are talking to, which have already been mentioned: *She picked up the pillows and threw them to the floor.*

theme themes

NOUN **1.** a main idea or topic in a piece of writing, painting, movie, or music: *the main theme of the book* **2.** a tune, especially one played at the beginning and end of a television or radio program

themselves

PRONOUN **1.** *Themselves* is used when people, other than yourself or the person you are talking to, do an action and are affected by it: *They think they've made fools of themselves.* **2.** *Themselves* is used to emphasize *they*: *He was as excited as they themselves were.*

then

ADVERB at a particular time in the past or future: *I'd left home by then.*

theologian theologians

NOUN someone who studies religion, especially the Christian faith and the nature of God

theology

NOUN Theology is the study of religion, especially the Christian faith and God.
theological ADJECTIVE

theoretical

ADJECTIVE **1.** based on or to do with ideas of a subject rather than the practical aspects of that subject **2.** not proved to exist or be true
theoretically ADVERB

theory theories

NOUN **1.** an idea or set of ideas that is meant to explain something: *the theory of evolution* **2.** Theory is the set of rules and ideas that a particular subject or skill is based upon.
PHRASE **3.** You use **in theory** to say that

although something is supposed to happen, it may not in fact happen: *In theory, prices should rise by two percent.*

therapeutic

ADJECTIVE **1.** If something is therapeutic, it helps you to feel happier and more relaxed: *Laughing is therapeutic.* **2.** In medicine, therapeutic treatment is designed to treat a disease or to improve a person's health.

therapy

NOUN Therapy is the treatment of mental or physical illness, often without the use of drugs or operations.
therapist NOUN

there

ADVERB **1.** in, at, or to that place, point, or case: *He's sitting over there.*
PRONOUN **2.** *There* is used to say that something exists or does not exist, or to draw attention to something: *There are flowers on the table.*

thereby

ADVERB *a formal word* as a result of the event or action mentioned: *The organization had recruited 200 new members, thereby making the campaign worthwhile.*

therefore

ADVERB as a result

thermal

ADJECTIVE **1.** to do with or caused by heat: *thermal energy* **2.** Thermal clothes are specially designed to keep you warm in cold weather.

thermometer thermometers

NOUN an instrument for measuring the temperature of a room or a person's body

thermostat thermostats

NOUN a device used to control temperature, for example on a central heating system

thesaurus thesauruses

NOUN a reference book in which words with similar meanings are grouped together

these the plural of THIS

SPELL-CHECK THIS!

A computer's spell-check won't catch wrong **homophones** (words that are spelled differently but sound the same).

Their they are! There getting away!

In the first sentence, **Their** should be **There**. In the second, **There** should be **They're**. **There** means *in that place*. **They're** is short for *they are*. **Their** means *belonging to them*.

thesis theses

NOUN **1.** the main idea or argument of an essay **2.** a long piece of writing, based on research, that is done as part of a university degree

they

PRONOUN **1.** *They* refers to people or things, other than you or the people you are talking to, that have already been mentioned: *They married two years later.* **2.** *They* is sometimes used instead of *he* or *she* where the sex of the person is unknown or unspecified. Some people consider this to be incorrect: *Someone could have a nasty accident if they tripped over that.*

thick thicker thickest

ADJECTIVE **1.** Something thick has a large distance between its two opposite surfaces. **2.** If something is a particular amount thick, it measures that amount between its two sides. **3.** Thick means growing or grouped closely together and in large quantities: *thick, dark hair* **4.** Thick liquids contain little water and do not flow easily: *thick soup* **5.** *an informal use* A thick person is stupid or slow to understand things.

thicken thickens thickening thickened

VERB If something thickens, it becomes thicker: *The clouds thickened.*

thicket thickets

NOUN a small group of trees growing closely together

thief thieves

NOUN a person who steals

thievery thieveries

NOUN Thievery is the act of stealing.

thigh thighs

NOUN Your thighs are the top parts of your legs, between your knees and your hips.

thimble thimbles

NOUN a small, metal or plastic cap that you put on the end of your finger to protect it when you are sewing

thin thinner thinnest; thins thinning thinned

ADJECTIVE **1.** Something that is thin is much narrower than it is long.

Instead of **THIN** try...

a narrow hallway
a slim margin
spindly legs
a rangy dog
a skinny cat
a lean athlete
a slender woman
fine facial features

2. A thin person has very little fat on his or her body. **3.** Thin liquids contain a lot of water: *thin soup*

VERB **4.** If you thin something such as paint or soup, you add water or other liquid to it.

thing things

NOUN **1.** an object, rather than a plant, an animal, or a human being

PLURAL NOUN **2.** Your things are your clothes or possessions.

think thinks thinking thought

VERB **1.** When you think about ideas or problems, you use your mind to consider them. **2.** If you think something, you have the opinion that it is true or the case: *I think she has a secret boyfriend.* **3.** If you think of something, you remember it or it comes into your mind. **4.** If you think a lot of someone, you admire that person or believe that he or she is good.

third thirds

ADJECTIVE **1.** The third item in a series is the one counted as number three.

NOUN **2.** one of three equal parts

Third World

NOUN The poorer countries of Africa, Asia, and South America can be referred to as the Third World.

thirst thirsts

NOUN **1.** If you have a thirst, you feel a need to drink something. **2.** A thirst for something is a very strong desire for it: *a thirst for money*

> **thirsty** ADJECTIVE
> **thirstily** ADVERB

thirteen

NOUN the number 13

> **thirteenth** ADJECTIVE, ADVERB

thirty thirties

NOUN the number 30

> **thirtieth** ADJECTIVE, ADVERB

this these

ADJECTIVE OR PRONOUN **1.** *This* is used to refer to something or someone that is nearby or has just been mentioned: *This is my mother.* **2.** *This* is used to refer to the present time or place: *this week*

thistle thistles

NOUN a wild plant with prickly-edged leaves and purple flowers

thong thongs

NOUN a long, narrow strip of leather

thorn thorns

NOUN one of many sharp points growing on some plants and trees

Tt

thorny thornier thorniest
ADJECTIVE **1.** covered with thorns **2.** A thorny subject or question is difficult to discuss or answer.

thorough
ADJECTIVE **1.** done very carefully and completely: *a thorough examination* **2.** A thorough person is very careful in what he or she does and makes sure nothing has been missed out.
thoroughly ADVERB

> **! HEADS UP**
> The word **thorough** is pronounced THUR-oh. Don't confuse it with **through**, pronounced THROO.

thoroughbred thoroughbreds
NOUN an animal that has parents that are of the same high-quality breed

thoroughfare thoroughfares
NOUN a main road forming a route between two places

those the plural of THAT

thou
PRONOUN *an old-fashioned word Thou* means *you.*

though
CONJUNCTION **1.** despite the fact that: *She stayed up late, even though she had to be up early the next morning.* **2.** if: *It looks as though you were right.*

thought thoughts
1. the past tense and past participle of THINK
NOUN **2.** an idea that you have in your mind **3.** Thought is the activity of thinking: *He was lost in thought.* **4.** Thought is a particular way of thinking or a particular set of ideas: *this school of thought*

thoughtful
ADJECTIVE **1.** When someone is thoughtful, that person is quiet and serious because he or she is thinking about something. **2.** A thoughtful person remembers what other people want or need, and tries to be kind to them.
thoughtfully ADVERB

thoughtless
ADJECTIVE A thoughtless person forgets or ignores what other people want, need, or feel.
thoughtlessly ADVERB

thousand thousands
NOUN the number 1000
thousandth ADJECTIVE, ADVERB

thrash thrashes thrashing thrashed
VERB **1.** To thrash someone is to beat that person by hitting him or her with something. **2.** To thrash someone in a contest or fight is to defeat that person completely.
thrash out
VERB **3.** To thrash out a problem or an idea is to discuss it in detail until a solution is reached.

thread threads threading threaded
NOUN **1.** a long, fine piece of cotton, silk, nylon, or wool **2.** The thread on something such as a screw or the top of a container is the raised spiral line of metal or plastic around it. **3.** The thread of an argument or story is an idea or theme that connects the different parts of it.
VERB **4.** When you thread something, you pass thread, tape, or cord through it. **5.** If you thread your way through people or things, you carefully make your way through them.

threadbare
ADJECTIVE Threadbare cloth or clothing is old and thin.

threat threats
NOUN **1.** a statement that someone will harm you, especially if you do not do what that person wants **2.** anything or anyone that seems likely to harm you **3.** If there is a threat of something unpleasant happening, it is very possible that it will happen.

threaten threatens threatening threatened
VERB **1.** If you threaten to harm someone or threaten to do something that will upset that person, you say that you will do it. **2.** If someone or something threatens a person or thing, that person or thing is likely to harm the other person or thing.

three threes
NOUN the number 3

three-dimensional
ADJECTIVE A three-dimensional object or shape is not flat, but has depth as well as length and width.

threesome threesomes
NOUN a group of three

threshold thresholds
NOUN **1.** the doorway or the floor in the doorway of a building or room **2.** The threshold of something is the lowest amount, level, or limit at which something happens or changes: *What is the cold temperature threshold of the human body? His boredom threshold was exceptionally low.*

thrice
ADVERB *an old-fashioned word* If you do something thrice, you do it three times.

thrift
NOUN Thrift is the practice of saving money and not wasting things.

thrifty thriftier thriftiest
ADJECTIVE A thrifty person saves money and does not waste things.

thrill thrills thrilling thrilled
NOUN **1.** a sudden feeling of great excitement, pleasure, or fear; also any event or experience that gives you such a feeling
VERB **2.** If something thrills you, or you thrill to it, it gives you a feeling of great pleasure and excitement.
thrilled ADJECTIVE
thrilling ADJECTIVE

thriller thrillers
NOUN a book, movie, or play that tells an exciting story about dangerous or mysterious events

Instead of **THRILLING** try...
an **electrifying** performer
an **exhilarating** ride
a **gripping** tale
a **wild** idea
a **riveting** plot
a **stirring** speech
a **spine-tingling** movie
a **rip-roaring** adventure

thrive thrives thriving thrived
VERB When people or things thrive, they are healthy, happy, or successful.
thriving ADJECTIVE

throat throats
NOUN **1.** the back of your mouth and the top part of the passages inside your neck **2.** the front part of your neck

throb throbs throbbing throbbed
VERB **1.** If a part of your body throbs, you feel a series of strong beats or dull pains.
2. If something throbs, it vibrates and makes a loud, rhythmic noise: *The engines throbbed.*

throes
PLURAL NOUN **1.** Throes are a series of violent pangs or movements: *death throes*
PHRASE **2.** If you are **in the throes of** something, you are deeply involved in it.

thrombosis thromboses
NOUN a blood clot that blocks the flow of blood in the body. Thromboses are dangerous and often fatal.

throne thrones
NOUN **1.** a ceremonial chair used by a king or queen on important official occasions **2.** The throne is a way of referring to the position of being king or queen.

throng throngs thronging thronged
NOUN **1.** a large crowd of people
VERB **2.** If people throng somewhere or throng a place, they go there in great numbers: *Hundreds of city workers thronged the scene.*

throttle throttles throttling throttled
VERB To throttle someone is to kill or injure that person by squeezing his or her throat.

through
PREPOSITION **1.** moving all the way from one side of something to the other: *a path through the woods* **2.** because of: *He had been exhausted through lack of sleep.* **3.** during: *He has to work through the summer.* **4.** If you go through an experience, it happens to you: *I don't want to go through that again.*
ADJECTIVE **5.** If you are through with something, you have finished doing it or using it.

throughout
PREPOSITION **1.** during: *I stayed awake throughout the night.*
ADVERB **2.** happening or existing through the whole of a place: *The house was painted brown throughout.*

throve a past tense of THRIVE

throw throws throwing threw thrown
VERB **1.** When you throw something you are holding, you move your hand quickly and let it go, so that it moves through the air. **2.** If you throw yourself somewhere, you move there suddenly and with force: *We threw ourselves on the ground.* **3.** To throw someone into an unpleasant situation is to put that person there: *It threw them into a panic.* **4.** If something throws light or shadow on something else, it makes that thing have light or shadow on it. **5.** If you throw yourself into an activity, you become actively and enthusiastically involved in it. **6.** If you throw a fit or tantrum, you suddenly begin behaving in an uncontrolled way.

throwback throwbacks
NOUN something that has the characteristics of something that existed a long time ago: *Everything about her was a throwback to the fifties.*

thrush thrushes
NOUN **1.** a small, brown songbird **2.** Thrush is a disease of the mouth and throat, caused by a fungus.

Tt

thrust thrusts thrusting thrust
VERB **1.** If you thrust something somewhere, you push or move it there quickly with a lot of force. **2.** If you thrust your way somewhere, you move along, pushing between people or things.
NOUN **3.** a sudden, forceful movement **4.** The main thrust of an activity or idea is the most important part of it: *the general thrust of his argument*

thud thuds thudding thudded
NOUN **1.** a dull sound, usually made by a solid, heavy object hitting something soft
VERB **2.** If something thuds somewhere, it makes a dull sound, usually by hitting something else.

thug thugs
NOUN a very rough and violent person

thumb thumbs thumbing thumbed
NOUN **1.** the short, thick finger on the side of your hand
VERB **2.** *an informal use* If someone thumbs a lift, that person stands at the side of the road and sticks out his or her thumb until a driver stops and gives him or her a lift.

thump thumps thumping thumped
VERB **1.** If you thump something, you hit it hard with your fist.
2. If something thumps somewhere, it makes a fairly loud, dull sound, usually when it hits something else. **3.** When your heart thumps, it beats strongly and quickly.
NOUN **4.** a hard hit: *a great thump on the back* **5.** a fairly loud, dull sound

thunder thunders thundering thundered
NOUN **1.** Thunder is a loud cracking or rumbling noise caused by expanding air that is suddenly heated by lightning. **2.** Thunder is any loud rumbling noise: *the distant thunder of the waterfall*
VERB **3.** When it thunders, a loud cracking or rumbling noise occurs in the sky after a flash of lightning. **4.** If something thunders, it makes a loud continuous noise: *The helicopter thundered low over the trees.*

thunderbolt thunderbolts
NOUN a flash of lightning, accompanied by thunder

thunderous
ADJECTIVE A thunderous noise is very loud: *thunderous applause*

Thursday Thursdays
NOUN Thursday is the day between Wednesday and Friday.

thus
ADVERB *a formal word* **1.** in this way: *I sat thus for nearly half an hour.* **2.** therefore: *Critics were thus able to denounce him.*

thwart thwarts thwarting thwarted
VERB To thwart a person or a person's plans is to prevent him or her from doing or getting what he or she wants.

thy
ADJECTIVE *an old-fashioned word* Thy means your.

thyme
NOUN a bushy herb with very small leaves

thyroid thyroids
NOUN Your thyroid, or **thyroid gland**, is situated at the base of your neck. It releases hormones that control your growth and your metabolism.

tiara tiaras
NOUN a semicircular crown of jewels worn by a woman on formal occasions

tic tics
NOUN a twitching of a group of muscles, especially the muscles in the face

tick ticks ticking ticked
NOUN **1.** a written mark to show that something is correct or has been dealt with **2.** The tick of a clock is the series of short sounds it makes when it is working. **3.** a tiny, blood-sucking, insect-like creature that usually lives on the bodies of people or animals
VERB **4.** To tick something written on a piece of paper is to put a tick next to it. **5.** When a clock ticks, it makes a regular series of short sounds as it works.
  tick off
  VERB **6.** *an informal expression* If you tick someone off, you annoy or irritate that person.
  ticking NOUN

ticket tickets
NOUN a piece of paper or card that shows that you have paid for a journey or have paid to enter a place of entertainment

tickle tickles tickling tickled
VERB **1.** When you tickle someone, you move your fingers lightly over that person's body in order to make him or her laugh. **2.** If something tickles you, it amuses you or gives you pleasure: *He is tickled by the idea.*

tidal
ADJECTIVE to do with or produced by tides: *a tidal estuary*

tidal wave tidal waves
NOUN another name for TSUNAMI

 **HEADS UP** The *h* in **thyme** is silent. It is pronounced TIME.

tide tides tiding tided

NOUN **1.** The tide is the regular change in the level of the sea on the shore, caused by the gravitational pull of the sun and the moon. **2.** The tide of opinion or fashion is what the majority of people think or do at a particular time. **3.** A tide of something is a large amount of it: *the tide of anger and bitterness*

tide over

VERB **4.** If something will tide someone over, it will help that person through a difficult period of time.

tidings

PLURAL NOUN *a formal word* Tidings are news.

tidy tidier tidiest; tidies tidying tidied

ADJECTIVE **1.** Something that is tidy is neat and arranged in an orderly way. **2.** Someone who is tidy always keeps his or her things neat and arranged in an orderly way. **3.** *an informal use* A tidy amount of money is a fairly large amount of it.

VERB **4.** To tidy a place is to make it neat by putting things in their proper place.

tie ties tying tied

VERB **1.** If you tie one thing to another or tie it in a particular position, you fasten it using cord of some kind. **2.** If you tie a knot or a bow, for example in a piece of cord or ribbon, you fasten the ends together to make a knot or bow. **3.** Something or someone that is tied to something else is closely linked with it: *Forty thousand jobs are tied to the project.* **4.** If you tie with someone in a competition or game, you have the same number of points.

NOUN **5.** a long, narrow piece of cloth worn around the neck under a shirt collar and tied in a knot or bow at the front **6.** a connection or feeling that links you with a person, place, or organization: *I had very close ties with the family.*

tied up

ADJECTIVE If you are tied up, you are busy.

tier tiers

NOUN one of a number of rows or layers of something: *Take the stairs to the upper tier.*

tiff tiffs

NOUN a small, unimportant quarrel

tiger tigers

NOUN a large meat-eating animal of the cat family. It comes from Asia and has an orange-coloured coat with black stripes.

tight tighter tightest

ADJECTIVE **1.** fitting closely: *The shoes are too tight.* **2.** firmly fastened and difficult to move: *a tight knot* **3.** stretched or pulled so as not to be slack: *a tight cord* **4.** A

tight plan or arrangement allows only the minimum time or money needed to do something: *Our schedule tonight is very tight.*

ADVERB **5.** held firmly and securely: *He held me tight.*

tightly ADVERB

tightness NOUN

tighten tightens tightening tightened

VERB **1.** If you tighten your hold on something, you hold it more firmly. **2.** If you tighten a rope or chain, or if it tightens, it is stretched or pulled until it is straight. **3.** If someone tightens a rule or system, that person makes it stricter or more efficient.

tightrope tightropes

NOUN a tightly stretched rope on which an acrobat balances and performs tricks

tights

PLURAL NOUN Tights are a piece of clothing made of thin, stretchy material that fits closely around a person's hips, legs, and feet.

tile tiles tiling tiled

NOUN **1.** a small, flat, square piece of something, for example slate or carpet, that is used to cover surfaces

VERB **2.** To tile a surface is to fix tiles to it.

tiled ADJECTIVE

till tills tilling tilled

PREPOSITION OR CONJUNCTION **1.** Till means the same as *until*.

NOUN **2.** a drawer or box in a store where money is kept, usually in a cash register

VERB **3.** To till the ground is to plough it for raising crops.

tiller tillers

NOUN the handle fixed to the top of the rudder for steering a boat

tilt tilts tilting tilted

VERB **1.** If you tilt an object or it tilts, it changes position so that one end or side is higher than the other.

NOUN **2.** a position in which one end or side of something is higher than the other

timber timbers

NOUN **1.** Timber is wood that has been cut and prepared ready for building and making furniture. **2.** The timbers of a ship or house are the large pieces of wood that have been used to build it.

time times timing timed

NOUN **1.** Time is what is measured in hours, days, and years: *What time is it?* **2.** *Time* is used to mean a particular period or point: *I enjoyed my time in Niagara Falls.* **3.** If you say it is time for something or it is time to do it, you mean that it ought to happen or be

Tt

done now: *It is time for a change.*
4. *Times* is used after numbers to indicate how often something happens: *I see them four times a year.* **5.** *Times* is used after numbers when you are saying how much bigger, smaller, better, or worse one thing is compared to another: *Our team jogged three times longer than your team.* **6.** *Times* is used in arithmetic to link numbers that are multiplied together: *Two times three is six.*
VERB **7.** If you time something for a particular point or period, you plan that it should happen then: *We could not have timed our arrival better.* **8.** If you time an activity or action, you measure how long it lasts.

timeless
ADJECTIVE Something timeless is so good or beautiful that it cannot be affected by the passing of time or by changes in fashion.

timely
ADJECTIVE happening at just the right time: *a timely appearance*

timer timers
NOUN a device that measures time, especially one that is part of a machine

timetable timetables
NOUN **1.** a plan of the times when particular activities or jobs should be done **2.** a list of the times when particular trains, boats, buses, or airplanes arrive and depart

timid
ADJECTIVE shy and having no courage or self-confidence
timidly ADVERB
timidity NOUN

timing
NOUN **1.** Someone's timing is his or her skill in judging the right moment at which to do something. **2.** The timing of an event is when it actually happens.

timpani
PLURAL NOUN Timpani are large drums with curved bottoms that are played in an orchestra.

tin tins
NOUN **1.** Tin is a soft, silvery-white metal. **2.** a small, metal container that may have a lid: *a cake tin*

tinder
NOUN Tinder is small pieces of dry wood or paper that burn easily and can be used for lighting a fire.

tinge tinges
NOUN a small amount of something: *a tinge of envy*
tinged ADJECTIVE

tingle tingles tingling tingled
VERB **1.** When a part of your body tingles, you feel a slight prickling in it.
NOUN **2.** a slight prickling feeling
tingling NOUN OR ADJECTIVE

tinker tinkers tinkering tinkered
NOUN **1.** a person who travels from place to place mending metal pots and pans or doing other small repair jobs
VERB **2.** If you tinker with something, you make a lot of small changes to it in order to repair or improve it: *All he wanted was to tinker with engines.*

tinkle tinkles tinkling tinkled
VERB **1.** If something tinkles, it makes a sound like a small bell ringing.
NOUN **2.** a sound like that of a small bell ringing

tinsel
NOUN Tinsel is long threads with strips of shiny paper attached, used as a decoration.

tint tints tinting tinted
NOUN **1.** a small amount of a particular colour: *a distinct tint of green*
VERB **2.** If a person tints his or her hair, he or she changes its colour by adding a dye to it.
tinted ADJECTIVE

tiny tinier tiniest
ADJECTIVE extremely small

KNOWING WORDS: IDIOMS

BE WORD SHARP!

Idioms add colour to language by playing with the meanings of words.

time what is measured in hours, days, and years

about time almost too late to be doing something

all the time very often

at a time in the same action

at the same time however

for the time being for the present moment

Tt

tip tips tipping tipped
NOUN **1.** the end of something long and thin: *a fingertip* **2.** If you give someone a tip, you give that person some money to thank him or her for providing a service. **3.** a useful piece of advice or information
VERB **4.** If you tip an object, you move it so that it is no longer horizontal or upright. **5.** If you tip something somewhere, you pour it there quickly or carelessly.
tipped ADJECTIVE

tipsy tipsier tipsiest
ADJECTIVE slightly drunk

tiptoe tiptoes tiptoeing tiptoed
VERB If you tiptoe somewhere, you walk there very quietly on your toes.

tirade tirades
NOUN a long, angry speech in which you criticize someone or something

tire tires tiring tired
VERB **1.** If something tires you, it makes you use a lot of energy so that you want to rest or sleep. **2.** If you tire of something, you become bored with it.
NOUN **3.** a thick ring of rubber fitted around each wheel of a vehicle and filled with air

tired
ADJECTIVE having little energy
tiredness NOUN

Instead of **TIRED** try...

haggard faces

weary travellers

easily fatigued

mentally drained

exhausted from hard work

tireless
ADJECTIVE
Someone who is tireless has a lot of energy and never seems to need a rest.

tiresome
ADJECTIVE A person or thing that is tiresome makes you feel irritated or bored.

tiring
ADJECTIVE Something that is tiring makes you tired.

tissue tissues
NOUN **1.** The tissue in plants and animals consists of cells that are similar in appearance and function: *scar tissue, dead tissue* **2.** Tissue is thin paper that is used for wrapping breakable objects. **3.** a small piece of soft paper that you use as a handkerchief

tit tits
NOUN a small songbird: *a blue tit*

titanic
ADJECTIVE very big or important

titillate titillates titillating titillated
VERB If something titillates someone, it pleases and excites that person.
titillation NOUN

title titles
NOUN **1.** the name of a book, play, or piece of music **2.** a word that describes someone's rank or job: *His official title is Design Manager.* **3.** the position of champion in a sports competition: *the Canadian featherweight title*

titled
ADJECTIVE Someone who is titled has a title such as *Princess*, *Lord*, *Lady*, or *Sir*.

titter titters tittering tittered
VERB If you titter, you laugh in a way that shows you are nervous or embarrassed.

TNT
NOUN TNT is a type of powerful explosive. It is an abbreviation for *trinitrotoluene*.

to
PREPOSITION **1.** *To* is used to indicate the place that someone or something is moving toward or pointing at: *They are going to Yellowknife.* **2.** *To* is used to indicate the limit of something: *goods to the value of 500 dollars* **3.** *To* is used in ratios and rates when saying how many units of one type there are for each unit of another: *This car only gets about 11 kilometres to the litre.*
ADVERB **4.** If you push or shut a door to, you close it but do not shut it completely.

toad toads
NOUN an amphibian that looks like a frog but has a drier skin and lives less in the water

toadstool toadstools
NOUN a type of poisonous fungus

toast toasts toasting toasted
NOUN **1.** Toast is slices of bread made brown and crisp by cooking at a high temperature. **2.** To drink a toast to someone is to drink in honour of that person.
VERB **3.** If you toast bread, you cook it at a high temperature so that it becomes brown and crisp. **4.** If you toast yourself, you sit in front of a fire so that you feel pleasantly warm. **5.** To toast someone is to drink an alcoholic drink in honour of that person.

toaster toasters
NOUN a piece of electrical equipment used for toasting bread

tobacco
NOUN Tobacco is the dried leaves of the tobacco plant that people smoke in pipes, cigarettes, and cigars.

Tt

toboggan toboggans
NOUN a long, light, narrow sleigh with a flat bottom and no runners, and with the front end curved up and back

today
ADVERB OR NOUN **1.** Today means the day on which you are speaking or writing. **2.** Today also means the present period of history: *the technology of today*

toddle toddles toddling toddled
VERB To toddle is to walk in short, quick steps, as a very young child does.

toddler toddlers
NOUN a small child who has just learned to walk

to-do to-dos
NOUN A to-do is a situation in which people are very agitated or confused: *It's just like him to make such a to-do about a baby.*

toe toes
NOUN **1.** Your toes are the five movable parts at the end of your foot. **2.** The toe of a shoe or sock is the part that covers the end of your foot.

toffee toffees
NOUN Toffee is a sticky, chewy candy made by boiling sugar and butter together with water.

toga togas
NOUN a long, loose robe worn in ancient Rome

together
ADVERB **1.** If people do something together, they do it with each other. **2.** If two things happen together, they happen at the same time. **3.** If things are joined or fixed together, they are joined or fixed to each other. **4.** If things or people are together, they are very near to each other.

togetherness
NOUN Togetherness is a feeling of closeness and friendship.

toil toils toiling toiled
VERB **1.** When people toil, they work hard doing unpleasant, difficult, or tiring tasks or jobs.
NOUN **2.** Toil is unpleasant, difficult, or tiring work.

toilet toilets
NOUN **1.** a large bowl, connected by a pipe to the drains, which you use when you want to get rid of urine or feces **2.** a small room containing a toilet

toiletries
PLURAL NOUN Toiletries are the things you use when cleaning and taking care of your body, such as soap and toothpaste.

token tokens
NOUN **1.** a flat, round piece of metal or plastic that can sometimes be used instead of money: *a subway token* **2.** If you give something to someone as a token of your feelings for him or her, you give it to that person as a way of showing those feelings.
ADJECTIVE **3.** If something is described as token, it shows that it is not being treated as important: *a token contribution to your fees*

told Told is the past tense and past participle of TELL.

tolerable
ADJECTIVE **1.** able to be put up with **2.** fairly satisfactory or reasonable: *a tolerable salary*

tolerance
NOUN **1.** A person's tolerance is his or her ability to accept or put up with something that may not be enjoyable or pleasant for him or her. **2.** Tolerance is the quality of allowing other people to have their own attitudes or beliefs, or to behave in a particular way, even if you do not agree or approve: *religious tolerance*

tolerant
ADJECTIVE accepting of different views and behaviour

tolerate tolerates tolerating tolerated
VERB **1.** If you tolerate things that you do not approve of or agree with, you allow them. **2.** If you can tolerate something, you accept it, even though it is unsatisfactory or unpleasant.
toleration NOUN

toll tolls tolling tolled
NOUN **1.** The death toll in an accident is the number of people who have died in it. **2.** a sum of money that you have to pay in order to use a particular bridge or road
VERB **3.** When a bell tolls, it rings slowly, often as a sign that someone has died.

tom toms
NOUN a male cat

tomahawk tomahawks
NOUN a small axe used by some First Nations and Native American peoples

tomato tomatoes
NOUN a small, round, red fruit, used as a vegetable, and often eaten raw in salads

tomb tombs
NOUN a large grave for one or more corpses, often built partly or completely above ground

tomboy tomboys
NOUN a girl who likes playing rough or noisy games traditionally associated with boys

HEADS UP The *b* in **tomb** is silent. It is pronounced TOOM.

tome tomes
NOUN *a formal word* a very large, heavy book

tomorrow
ADVERB OR NOUN **1.** Tomorrow means the day after today. **2.** You can refer to the future, especially the near future, as tomorrow.

ton tons
NOUN **1.** a nonmetric unit of weight equal to about 1016 kilograms
PLURAL NOUN **2.** *an informal use* If you have tons of something, you have a lot of it.

tonal
ADJECTIVE involving the quality or pitch of a sound or of music

tone tones toning toned
NOUN **1.** Someone's tone is a quality in that person's voice, which shows what he or she is thinking or feeling. **2.** The tone of a musical instrument or a singer's voice is the kind of sound it has. **3.** The tone of a piece of writing is the attitude the writer expresses, (for example, angry, passionate, loving), its style, and the ideas or opinions expressed in it: *I was shocked at the sarcastic tone of your movie review.* **4.** a lighter, darker, or brighter shade of the same colour: *The whole room is painted in two tones of orange.*
tone down
VERB **5.** If you tone down something, you make it less forceful or severe.

tone-deaf
ADJECTIVE unable to sing in tune or to recognize different tunes

tongs
PLURAL NOUN Tongs consist of two long, narrow pieces of metal joined together at one end. You press the pieces together to pick an object up.

tongue tongues
NOUN **1.** the soft part in the mouth that is used for tasting, licking and, in humans, speaking **2.** a language **3.** The tongue of a shoe or boot is the piece of leather underneath the laces.

tonic tonics
NOUN **1.** Tonic or tonic water is a colourless, carbonated drink that has a slightly bitter flavour and is often mixed with alcoholic drinks. **2.** a medicine that makes you feel stronger, healthier, and less tired **3.** anything that makes you feel stronger or more cheerful: *It was a tonic just being with her.*

tonight
ADVERB OR NOUN Tonight is the evening or night that will come at the end of today.

tonne tonnes
NOUN a unit of mass equal to 1000 kilograms

tonsil tonsils
NOUN Your tonsils are the two small, soft lumps in your throat at the back of your mouth.

tonsillitis
NOUN Tonsillitis is a painful swelling of your tonsils caused by an infection.

too
ADVERB **1.** also or as well: *You were there too.* **2.** more than a desirable, necessary, or acceptable amount: *He tried to carry too many books.*

tool tools
NOUN **1.** any handheld instrument or piece of equipment that you use to help you do a particular kind of work **2.** an object, skill, or idea that is needed or used for a particular purpose: *You can use the survey as a bargaining tool in the negotiations.*

toonie toonies
NOUN the Canadian two-dollar coin

toot toots tooting tooted
VERB If a car horn toots, it produces a short sound.

tooth teeth
NOUN **1.** Your teeth are the hard, enamel-covered objects in your mouth that you use for biting and chewing food. **2.** The teeth of a comb, saw, or zipper are the parts that stick out in a row on its edge.

toothpaste
NOUN Toothpaste is a substance that you use to clean your teeth.

top tops topping topped
NOUN **1.** The top of something is its highest point, part, or surface. **2.** The top of a bottle, jar, or tube is its cap or lid. **3.** a piece of clothing worn on the upper half of your body **4.** a toy with a pointed end on which it spins
ADJECTIVE **5.** The top thing of a series of things is the highest one: *the top floor of the building*
VERB **6.** If someone or something tops a poll or popularity chart, that person or thing does better than anyone or anything else on it: *Her book has topped the bestseller lists in almost every country.* **7.** If something tops a particular amount, it is greater than that amount: *The temperature topped 30°.*
top up
VERB **8.** To top something up is to add more of the same substance to it in order to keep it at an acceptable or usable level.

top hat top hats
NOUN a tall hat with a narrow brim that men wear on special occasions

THE WRITER'S EDGE

TONE

the attitude the writer expresses, the style, and the ideas or opinions expressed

"Don't make me break your teeth in half!"

Here is an example of tone. This sentence sets an angry and threatening tone, which isn't the best choice for a job application!

BRIAN MCLACHLAN

Tt

topic topics
NOUN a particular subject that you write about or discuss

topical
ADJECTIVE related to events that are happening at the time you are speaking or writing

topic sentence topic sentences
NOUN a sentence that states the main idea of the paragraph

topping toppings
NOUN food that is put on top of other food in order to decorate it or add to its flavour

topple topples toppling toppled
VERB If something topples, it becomes unsteady and falls over.

top-secret
ADJECTIVE meant to be kept completely secret

topsy-turvy
ADJECTIVE in a confused state: *My life was truly topsy-turvy.*

Torah
NOUN The Torah is Jewish law and teaching.

torch torches
NOUN a long stick with burning material wrapped around one end

torment torments tormenting tormented
NOUN **1.** Torment is extreme pain or unhappiness. **2.** something that causes extreme pain and unhappiness: *It's a torment to see them staring at me.*
VERB **3.** If something torments you, it causes you extreme unhappiness.

torn
1. Torn is the past participle of TEAR.
ADJECTIVE **2.** If you are torn between two or more things, you cannot decide which one to choose and this makes you unhappy: *torn between duty and pleasure*

tornado tornadoes
NOUN a violent storm with strong, circular winds around a funnel-shaped cloud

torpedo torpedoes torpedoing torpedoed
NOUN **1.** a tube-shaped bomb that travels underwater and explodes when it hits a target
VERB **2.** If a ship is torpedoed, it is hit, and usually sunk, by a torpedo.

torrent torrents
NOUN **1.** When a lot of water is falling very rapidly, it can be said to be falling in torrents. **2.** A torrent of speech is a lot of it directed continuously at someone: *torrents of abuse*

torrential
ADJECTIVE Torrential rain pours down very rapidly and in great quantities.

torrid
ADJECTIVE **1.** Torrid weather is very hot and dry. **2.** A torrid love affair is one in which people show very strong emotions.

torso torsos
NOUN the main part of your body, excluding your head, arms, and legs

tortoise tortoises
NOUN a slow-moving reptile with a large, hard shell over its body into which it can pull its head and legs for protection

tortuous
ADJECTIVE **1.** A tortuous road is full of bends and twists. **2.** A tortuous piece of writing is long and complicated.

torture tortures torturing tortured
NOUN **1.** Torture is pain that is deliberately caused to someone to punish that person or get information from him or her.
VERB **2.** If someone tortures another person, that person deliberately causes the other person great pain to punish him or her or to get information. **3.** To torture someone is also to cause that person to suffer mentally: *The memory of the event tortured him.*
torturer NOUN

toss tosses tossing tossed
VERB **1.** If you toss something somewhere, you throw it there lightly and carelessly.
2. If you toss a coin, you decide something by throwing a coin into the air and guessing which side will face upward when it lands.
3. If you toss your head, you move it suddenly backwards, especially when you are angry, annoyed, or want your own way.
4. To toss is to move repeatedly from side to side: *I tossed and turned and tried to sleep.*

tot tots totting totted
NOUN a very young child

total totals totalling totalled
NOUN **1.** the number you get when you add several numbers together
ADJECTIVE **2.** Total means complete: *a total failure*
VERB **3.** When you total a set of numbers or objects, you add them all together. **4.** If several numbers total a certain figure, that is the figure you get when all the numbers are added together: *Their debts totalled over 300 000 dollars.*
totally ADVERB

totalitarian
ADJECTIVE A totalitarian political system is one in which one political party controls everything and does not allow any other parties to exist.
totalitarianism NOUN

⚠ **HEADS UP** The word **tortuous** is pronounced TORE-chew-us.

tote totes toting toted
VERB *an informal word* If you tote something, you are carrying something that is heavy or awkward.

totem pole totem poles
NOUN a long, wooden pole with symbols and pictures carved and painted on it. Totem poles are made by some First Nations and Native American peoples.

totter totters tottering tottered
VERB When someone totters, that person walks in an unsteady way.

toucan toucans
NOUN a large tropical bird with a very large beak

touch touches touching touched
VERB **1.** If you touch something, you put your fingers or hand on it. **2.** When two things touch, their surfaces come into contact: *Their knees were touching.* **3.** If you are touched by something, you are emotionally affected by it: *I was touched by his thoughtfulness.* NOUN **4.** Your sense of touch is your ability to tell what something is like by touching it. **5.** a detail that is added to improve something: *finishing touches* **6.** a small amount of something: *a touch of mustard* PHRASE **7.** If you are **in touch** with someone, you are in contact with that person.

touchdown touchdowns
NOUN **1.** In football, a touchdown is the act of scoring points by reaching the opponents' goal line with the ball. **2.** Touchdown is the landing of an aircraft.

touching
ADJECTIVE causing feelings of sadness and sympathy

touchy touchier touchiest
ADJECTIVE **1.** If someone is touchy, that person is easily upset or irritated. **2.** A touchy subject is one that needs to be dealt with carefully, because it might upset or offend people.

tough tougher toughest
ADJECTIVE **1.** A tough person is strong and independent and able to put up with hardship. **2.** A tough substance is difficult to break. **3.** A tough task, problem, or way of life is difficult or full of hardship. **4.** Tough policies or actions are strict and firm: *tough measures against organized crime*
toughly ADVERB
toughness NOUN
toughen VERB

toupee toupees
NOUN a small wig worn by a man to cover a bald patch on his head

tour tours touring toured
NOUN **1.** a long journey during which you visit several places **2.** a short trip around a place such as a city or famous building VERB **3.** If you tour a place, you go on a journey or a trip around it.

tourism
NOUN Tourism is the business of providing services for people on holiday, for example hotels and sightseeing trips.

tourist tourists
NOUN a person who visits places for pleasure or interest

tournament tournaments
NOUN a sports competition in which players who win a match play further matches, until just one person or team is left

tourniquet tourniquets
NOUN a strip of cloth tied tightly around a wound to stop it from bleeding

tousled
ADJECTIVE Something that is tousled, such as hair, is untidy.

tout touts touting touted
VERB If someone touts something, that person tries to sell that thing or persuade someone of something.

tow tows towing towed
VERB **1.** If a vehicle tows another vehicle, it pulls it along behind it. NOUN **2.** To give a vehicle a tow is to tow it. PHRASE **3.** If you have someone **in tow**, that person is with you because you are looking after him or her.

toward
PREPOSITION **1.** in the direction of: *He turned toward the door.* **2.** about or involving: *My feelings toward this issue have changed.* **3.** as a contribution for: *a huge donation toward the new rink* **4.** near to: *We sat toward the back of the theatre.*

towel towels
NOUN a piece of thick, soft cloth that you use to dry yourself with

towelling
NOUN Towelling is thick, soft cloth that is used for making towels.

tower towers towering towered
NOUN **1.** a tall, narrow building, sometimes attached to a larger building such as a castle or church VERB **2.** Someone or something that towers over other people or things is much taller than them.
towering ADJECTIVE

Tt

town towns
NOUN **1.** a place with many streets and buildings where people live and work **2.** Town is the central shopping and business part of a town rather than the suburbs: *She has gone into town.*

township townships
NOUN In Canada and the US, a township is a division of a county with certain powers of government.

towpath towpaths
NOUN a path along the side of a canal or river used for towing barges

toxic
ADJECTIVE poisonous: *toxic waste*

toxin toxins
NOUN a poison, especially one produced by bacteria and very harmful to living creatures

toy toys toying toyed
NOUN **1.** any object made to play with VERB **2.** If you toy with an idea, you consider it without being very serious about it: *She toyed with the idea of calling him.* **3.** If you toy with an object, you fiddle with it: *He was toying with his glasses.*

trace traces tracing traced
VERB **1.** If you trace something, you find it after looking for it: *Police are trying to trace the owner.* **2.** To trace the development of something is to find out or describe how it developed. **3.** If you trace a drawing or a map, you copy it by covering it with a piece of transparent paper and drawing over the lines underneath.
NOUN **4.** a sign that shows you that someone or something has been in a place: *No trace of the treasure had been found.* **5.** a very small amount of something
tracing NOUN

Instead of **TRACE** try...

a **hint** of a smile
a **whiff** of springtime
no **evidence** of a crime
vanish leaving no **record**
a **remnant** of an older era

track tracks tracking tracked
NOUN **1.** a narrow road or path **2.** a strip of ground with rails on it that a train travels along **3.** a piece of ground, shaped like a ring, which horses, cars, or athletes race around
PLURAL NOUN **4.** Tracks are marks left on the ground by a person or animal: *the deer tracks by the side of the path*
ADJECTIVE **5.** In an athletic competition, the track events are the races on a running track.
VERB **6.** If you track animals or people, you find them by following their footprints or other signs that they have left behind.

track down
VERB **7.** If you track down someone or something, you follow the course or trail of that person or thing.

track record track records
NOUN The track record of a person or a company is that person's or company's past achievements or failures: *Your track record in getting new members to join the club is rather good.*

tracksuit tracksuits
NOUN a loose, warm suit of trousers and a top, worn for outdoor sports

tract tracts
NOUN **1.** A tract of land or forest is a large area of it. **2.** a pamphlet that expresses a strong opinion on a religious, moral, or political subject **3.** a system of organs and tubes in an animal's or person's body that has a particular function: *the digestive tract*

traction
NOUN Traction is a form of medical treatment given to an injured limb that involves pulling it gently for long periods of time using a system of weights and pulleys.

tractor tractors
NOUN a vehicle with large rear wheels that is used on a farm for pulling machinery and other heavy loads

trade trades trading traded
NOUN **1.** Trade is the activity of buying, selling, or exchanging goods or services between people, companies, or countries. **2.** Someone's trade is the kind of work he or she does, especially when it requires special training in practical skills: *a plumber by trade*
VERB **3.** When people, firms, or countries trade, they buy, sell, or exchange goods or services. **4.** If you trade things, you exchange them: *I traded seats with him.*

trademark trademarks
NOUN a name or symbol that a manufacturer always uses on its products. Trademarks are usually protected by law so that no one else can use them.

trader traders
NOUN a person whose job is to buy and sell goods: *a timber trader*

Tt

tradesman tradesmen
NOUN a person, for example a carpenter, who is engaged in a trade

trade union trade unions
NOUN an organization of workers that tries to improve the pay and conditions in a particular industry

tradition traditions
NOUN a custom or belief that has existed for a long time without changing

traditional
ADJECTIVE **1.** Traditional customs or beliefs have existed for a long time without changing: *traditional ceremony* **2.** A traditional organization or institution is one in which older methods are used rather than modern ones: *a traditional school*
traditionally ADVERB

traditionalist traditionalists
NOUN someone who supports the established customs and beliefs of his or her society, and does not want to change them

traffic traffics trafficking trafficked
NOUN **1.** Traffic is the movement of vehicles or people along a route at a particular time. **2.** Traffic in something such as drugs is an illegal trade in them.
VERB **3.** Someone who traffics in drugs or other goods buys and sells them illegally.

traffic light traffic lights
NOUN Traffic lights are the set of red, amber, and green lights at a road junction that controls the flow of traffic.

tragedy tragedies
NOUN **1.** an event or situation that is disastrous or very sad **2.** a serious story or play that usually ends with the death of the main character

tragic
ADJECTIVE **1.** Something tragic is very sad because it involves death, suffering, or disaster: *a tragic accident* **2.** Tragic movies, plays, and books are sad and serious: *a tragic love story*
tragically ADVERB

trail trails trailing trailed
NOUN **1.** a rough path across open country or through forests **2.** a series of marks or other signs left by someone or something as that person or thing moves along
VERB **3.** If you trail something or it trails, it drags along behind you as you move, or it hangs down loosely: *a small plane trailing a banner* **4.** If someone trails along, that person moves slowly, without any energy or enthusiasm. **5.** If a voice trails away or trails off, it gradually becomes more hesitant until it stops completely.

trailer trailers
NOUN an unpowered vehicle pulled behind a car that can be loaded with things, or a closed-in vehicle used as a place for living in

train trains training trained
NOUN **1.** a number of railway cars that are pulled by an engine **2.** A train of thought is a connected series of thoughts. **3.** A train of vehicles or people is a line or group following behind something or someone: *A train of clowns walked behind the marching band.*
VERB **4.** If you train someone, you teach that person how to do something. **5.** If you train, you learn how to do a particular job: *She trained as a serious actress.* **6.** If you train for a sports game or a race, you prepare for it by doing exercises.
training NOUN

trainee trainees
NOUN someone who is being taught how to do a job

trait traits
NOUN a particular characteristic or tendency: *a very common trait*

traitor traitors
NOUN someone who betrays his or her country or the group that he or she belongs to

trajectory trajectories
NOUN The trajectory of an object moving through the air is the curving path that it follows.

tramp tramps tramping tramped
NOUN **1.** a person who has no home, no job, and very little money **2.** a long walk: *I took a long, wet tramp through the forest.*
VERB **3.** If you tramp from one place to another, you walk with slow, heavy footsteps.

trample tramples trampling trampled
VERB **1.** If you trample on something, you tread heavily on it so that it is damaged. **2.** If you trample on someone or on that person's rights or feelings, you behave in a way that shows you don't care about that person or his or her rights or feelings.

trampoline trampolines
NOUN a piece of gymnastic equipment consisting of a large piece of strong cloth held taut by springs in a frame, on which a gymnast jumps to help him or her jump high

trance trances
NOUN a mental state in which someone seems to be asleep but is conscious enough to be aware of his or her surroundings and to respond to questions and commands

Tt

tranquil

ADJECTIVE calm and peaceful: *A lone canoe glided across the tranquil lake. I have a tranquil mind.*
tranquility NOUN

tranquillizer tranquillizers

NOUN a drug that makes people feel less anxious or nervous

trans-

PREFIX The prefix *trans-* means across, through, or beyond: *transatlantic*

transaction transactions

NOUN a business deal that involves buying and selling something

transcend transcends transcending transcended

VERB If one thing transcends another, it goes beyond it or is superior to it: *This sunset transcends all description.*

transcribe transcribes transcribing transcribed

VERB If you transcribe something that is spoken or written, you write it down, copy it, or change it into a different form of writing: *These letters were transcribed by his wife.*

transcript transcripts

NOUN a written copy of something that is spoken

transfer transfers transferring transferred

VERB **1.** If you transfer something from one place to another, you move it: *They transferred the money to a new account.* **2.** If you transfer to a different place or job, or are transferred to it, you move to a different place or job within the same organization. NOUN **3.** the movement of something from one place to another **4.** a piece of paper with a design on one side that can be ironed or pressed onto cloth, paper, or china
transferable ADJECTIVE

transfixed

ADJECTIVE If someone is transfixed by something, that person is so impressed or frightened by it that he or she cannot move: *He stood transfixed at the sight of the dinosaur display.*

transform transforms transforming transformed

VERB If something is transformed, it is changed completely: *The frown is transformed into a smile.*
transformation NOUN

transfusion transfusions

NOUN A transfusion or blood transfusion is a process in which blood from a healthy person is injected into the body of another person who is badly injured or ill.

transient

ADJECTIVE Something transient does not stay or exist for very long: *transient emotions*
transience NOUN

transistor transistors

NOUN **1.** a small electrical device in something such as a television or radio that is used to control electric currents **2.** A transistor or a transistor radio is a small, portable radio

transit

NOUN **1.** Transit is the carrying of goods or people by vehicle from one place to another. PHRASE **2.** People or things that are **in transit** are travelling or being taken from one place to another: *damage that had occurred in transit*

transition transitions

NOUN **1.** a change from one form or state to another: *the transition from war to peace* **2.** A transition word or phrase connects ideas within a sentence, paragraph, or story.

transitional

ADJECTIVE A transitional period or stage is one during which something changes from one form or state to another.

transitive

ADJECTIVE In grammar, a transitive verb is a verb that has an object.

transitory

ADJECTIVE lasting for only a short time

translate translates translating translated

VERB To translate something that someone has said or written is to say it or write it in a different language.
translation NOUN
translator NOUN

translucent

ADJECTIVE If something is translucent, light passes through it so that it seems to glow: *translucent petals*

transmission transmissions

NOUN **1.** The transmission of something involves passing or sending it to a different place or person: *the transmission of infectious diseases* **2.** The transmission of television or radio programs is the broadcasting of those programs.

transmit transmits transmitting transmitted

VERB **1.** When a message or an electronic signal is transmitted, it is sent by radio waves. **2.** To transmit something to a different place or person is to pass it or send it to the place or person: *the clergy's role in transmitting knowledge*
transmitter NOUN

transparency transparencies

NOUN **1.** a small piece of photographic film

⚠ **HEADS UP** The c in transcend is silent. It is pronounced tran-SEND.

Tt

that can be projected onto a screen
2. Transparency is the quality that an object or substance has if you can see through it.

transparent
ADJECTIVE If an object or substance is transparent, you can see through it.
transparently ADVERB

transpire transpires transpiring transpired
VERB **1.** *a formal use* When it transpires that something is the case, people discover that it is the case: *It transpired that he had gone on holiday.* **2.** When something transpires, it happens: *You start to wonder what transpired between them.*

transplant transplants transplanting transplanted
NOUN **1.** a process of removing something from one place and putting it in another: *a person who needs a heart transplant*
VERB **2.** When something is transplanted, it is moved to a different place.

transport transports transporting transported
NOUN **1.** Vehicles that you travel in are referred to as transport: *public transport*
2. Transport is the moving of goods or people from one place to another: *The prices quoted include transport costs.*
VERB **3.** When goods or people are transported from one place to another, they are moved there.

transportation
NOUN Transportation is the transporting of people and things from one place to another.

transvestite transvestites
NOUN a person who enjoys wearing clothes normally worn by people of the opposite sex

trap traps trapping trapped
NOUN **1.** a piece of equipment or a hole that is carefully positioned in order to catch animals or birds **2.** a trick that is intended to catch or deceive someone
VERB **3.** Someone who traps animals catches them using traps. **4.** If you trap someone, you trick that person so that he or she does or says something that he or she did not want to. **5.** If you are trapped somewhere, you cannot move or escape because something is blocking your way or holding you down.
6. If you are trapped, you are in an unpleasant situation that you cannot easily change: *She feels trapped in her job.*

trapdoor trapdoors
NOUN a small, horizontal door in a floor, ceiling, or stage

trapeze trapezes
NOUN a bar of wood or metal hanging from two ropes on which acrobats and gymnasts swing and perform skilful movements

trapezium trapeziums
NOUN a four-sided shape with two sides parallel to each other

trappings
PLURAL NOUN The trappings of a particular rank, position, or state are the clothes or equipment that go with it.

trash
NOUN **1.** Trash is garbage: *The trash is picked up on Mondays.* **2.** If you say that something such as a book, painting, or movie is trash, you mean that it is not very good.

trauma traumas
NOUN a very upsetting experience that causes great stress: *the trauma of his mother's death*

traumatic
ADJECTIVE A traumatic experience is very upsetting.

travel travels travelling travelled
VERB **1.** To travel is to go from one place to another. **2.** When something reaches one place from another, you say that it travels there: *Gossip travels fast.*
NOUN **3.** Travel is the act of travelling: *air travel*
PLURAL NOUN **4.** Someone's travels are the journeys that that person makes to places a long way from his or her home: *her travels in the Himalayas*
traveller NOUN
travelling ADJECTIVE

traveller's cheque traveller's cheques
NOUN Traveller's cheques are cheques for use when travelling in another country. You buy them at home and then exchange them when you are in another country for foreign currency.

traverse traverses traversing traversed
VERB *a formal word* If you traverse an area of land or water, you go across it or over it: *They have traversed the island from west to east.*

travesty travesties
NOUN a very bad or ridiculous representation or imitation of something: *That salad is a travesty of freshness.*

trawl trawls trawling trawled
VERB When fishermen trawl, they drag a wide net behind a ship in order to catch fish.

trawler trawlers
NOUN a fishing boat that is used for trawling

Tt

tray trays
NOUN a flat object with raised edges that is used for carrying food or drinks

treacherous
ADJECTIVE **1.** A treacherous person is likely to betray you and cannot be trusted.
2. The ground or the sea can be described as treacherous when it is dangerous or unreliable: *treacherous mountain roads*
treacherously ADVERB

treachery
NOUN Treachery is behaviour in which someone betrays his or her country or a person who trusts him or her.

tread treads treading trod trodden
VERB **1.** If you tread on something, you walk on it or step on it. **2.** If you tread something into the ground or into a carpet, you crush it in by stepping on it: *bubblegum that has been trodden into the pavement*
NOUN **3.** the sound made with the feet as a person walks: *his heavy tread* **4.** The tread of a tire or shoe is the pattern of ridges on it that stops it from slipping.

treadmill treadmills
NOUN Any task or job that you must keep doing even though it is unpleasant or tiring can be referred to as a treadmill: *My life is one constant treadmill of homework and chores.*

treason
NOUN Treason is the crime of betraying your country, for example by helping its enemies.

treasure treasures treasuring treasured
NOUN **1.** Treasure is a collection of gold, silver, jewels, or other precious objects, especially one that has been hidden: *buried treasure* **2.** Treasures are valuable items: *the finest art treasures in the world*
VERB **3.** If you treasure something, you are very pleased that you have it and regard it as very precious: *He treasures his friendship with her.*
treasured ADJECTIVE

treasurer treasurers
NOUN a person who is in charge of the finance and accounts of an organization

treasury
NOUN The treasury is the government department in some countries that deals with that country's finances.

treat treats treating treated
VERB **1.** If you treat someone in a particular way, you behave that way toward that person. **2.** If you treat something in a particular way, you deal with it that way or see it that way: *He treated his mistake*
as a joke. **3.** When a doctor treats a patient for an illness, he or she gives that person medical care and attention. **4.** If something such as wood or cloth is treated, a special substance is put on it in order to protect it or give it special properties: *The carpet has been treated with a stain repellent.* **5.** If you treat someone, you buy or arrange something special for that person that he or she will enjoy.
NOUN **6.** If you give someone a treat, you buy or arrange something special for that person that he or she will enjoy: *my birthday treat*
treatment NOUN

treatise treatises
NOUN a long, formal piece of writing about a particular subject

treaty treaties
NOUN a written agreement between countries in which they agree to do something or to help each other

treble trebles trebling trebled
VERB **1.** If something trebles or is trebled, it becomes three times greater in number or amount.
ADJECTIVE **2.** Treble means three times as large or three times as strong as previously: *Next year we can raise treble that amount.*

tree trees
NOUN a large plant with a hard woody trunk that supports branches and leaves at some distance from the ground

trek treks trekking trekked
VERB **1.** If you trek somewhere, you go on a long and difficult journey.
NOUN **2.** a long and difficult journey, especially one made by walking

trellis trellises
NOUN a frame made of horizontal and vertical strips of wood or metal and used to support plants

tremble trembles trembling trembled
VERB **1.** If you tremble, you shake slightly, usually because you are frightened or cold.
2. If something trembles, it shakes slightly.
3. If your voice trembles, it sounds unsteady, usually because you are frightened or upset.
trembling ADJECTIVE

tremendous
ADJECTIVE **1.** large or impressive: *It was a tremendous performance.* **2.** an informal use very good or pleasing: *tremendous fun*
tremendously ADVERB

tremor tremors
NOUN **1.** a shaking movement of your body

Tt

that you cannot control **2.** an unsteady quality in your voice, for example when you are upset **3.** a small earthquake

trench trenches
NOUN a long, narrow ditch dug into the ground

trenchant
ADJECTIVE Trenchant writing or comments are bold and firmly expressed.

trend trends
NOUN a change toward doing or being something different

trendy trendier trendiest
ADJECTIVE *an informal word* Trendy things or people are fashionable.

trepidation
NOUN *a formal word* Trepidation is fear or anxiety: *He saw the look of trepidation on my face.*

trespass trespasses trespassing trespassed
VERB If you trespass on someone's land or property, you go onto it without that person's permission.
trespasser NOUN

tresses
PLURAL NOUN *an old-fashioned word* A woman's tresses are her long, flowing hair.

trestle trestles
NOUN a wooden or metal structure that is used as a support for a table or a structure such as a bridge

tri-
PREFIX The prefix *tri-* means three: *tricycle*

trial trials
NOUN **1.** the legal process in which a judge and jury decide whether a person is guilty of a particular crime after listening to all the evidence about it **2.** an experiment in which something is tested: *Trials of the drug start next month.*

triangle triangles
NOUN **1.** a closed shape with three straight sides **2.** a percussion instrument consisting

of a thin, steel bar bent in the shape of a triangle
triangular ADJECTIVE

tribe tribes
NOUN a social division in a traditional society consisting of families or communities that are linked by social, economic, religious, or family ties and who have a common culture and language
tribal ADJECTIVE

tribulation tribulations
NOUN *a formal word* Tribulation is trouble or suffering: *the tribulations of a female soccer star*

tribunal tribunals
NOUN a special court or committee appointed to deal with particular problems: *an industrial tribunal*

tributary tributaries
NOUN a stream or river that flows into a larger river

tribute tributes
NOUN **1.** A tribute is something said or done to show admiration and respect for someone: *Police paid tribute to her courage.* **2.** If one thing is a tribute to another, it is the result of the other thing and shows how good it is: *His success has been a tribute to hard work.*

trice
NOUN If someone does something in a trice, that person does it very quickly.

trick tricks tricking tricked
NOUN **1.** an action done to deceive someone **2.** Tricks are clever or skilful actions done in order to entertain people: *magic tricks*
VERB **3.** If someone tricks you, that person deceives you.

trickery
NOUN Trickery is deception: *He accused his opponent of trickery.*

KNOWING WORDS: WORD BUILDING

BE WORD SHARP!

You can create new words by adding prefixes and suffixes to a base word.

tri- a prefix that means *three*

triad a group of three similar things

triathlon a sports contest with three different events

triceps a group of three muscles in your upper arm

trilogy a series of three books, movies, or plays

trillion a million million (million, billion, trillion)

trickle trickles trickling trickled
VERB **1.** When a liquid trickles somewhere, it flows slowly in a thin stream. **2.** When people or things trickle somewhere, they move there slowly in small groups or amounts.
NOUN **3.** a thin stream of liquid **4.** A trickle of people or things is a small number or quantity of them.

tricky trickier trickiest
ADJECTIVE difficult to do or deal with

tricycle tricycles
NOUN a vehicle similar to a bicycle but with two wheels at the back and one at the front

trifle trifles trifling trifled
NOUN **1.** A trifle means a little: *She seemed a trifle annoyed.* **2.** Trifles are things that are not very important or valuable. **3.** a dessert made of layers of sponge cake, fruit, jelly, and whipped cream or custard
VERB **4.** If you trifle with someone or something, you treat that person in a disrespectful way: *He was not to be trifled with.*

trifling
ADJECTIVE small and unimportant

trigger triggers triggering triggered
NOUN **1.** the small lever on a gun that is pulled in order to fire it
VERB **2.** If something triggers an event, it causes it to happen.

trigonometry
NOUN Trigonometry is the branch of mathematics that is concerned with calculating the angles of triangles or the lengths of their sides.

trill trills trilling trilled
VERB If a bird trills, it sings with short, high-pitched, repeated notes.

trim trimmer trimmest; trims trimming trimmed
ADJECTIVE **1.** neat, tidy, and attractive
VERB **2.** To trim something is to clip small amounts off it. **3.** If you trim off parts of something, you cut them off because they are not needed: *Trim off the excess crust.*
NOUN **4.** If something is given a trim, it is cut a little: *Some hairstyles need a trim every six to eight weeks.* **5.** a decoration on something, especially along its edges: *a fur trim*

trimming trimmings
NOUN Trimmings are extra parts added to something for decoration or as a luxury: *turkey with all the trimmings*

trinket trinkets
NOUN a cheap ornament or piece of jewellery

trio trios
NOUN **1.** a group of three musicians who sing or play together; also a piece of music written for three instruments or singers **2.** any group of three things or people together: *a trio of children's tales*

trip trips tripping tripped
NOUN **1.** a journey made to a place
VERB **2.** If you trip, you catch your foot on something and fall over. **3.** If you trip someone, you make that person fall over.

Instead of **TRIP** try...
a hiking **trek**
a long **journey**
a **voyage** by sea
an afternoon **outing**
an around-the-world **tour**

tripe
NOUN Tripe is the stomach lining of a pig, cow, or ox, which is cooked and eaten.

triple triples tripling tripled
ADJECTIVE **1.** consisting of three things or three parts: *a triple chocolate cake*
VERB **2.** If you triple something or if it triples, it becomes three times greater in number or size.

triplet triplets
NOUN Triplets are three children born at the same time to the same mother.

tripod tripods
NOUN a stand with three legs used to support something like a camera or telescope

trite
ADJECTIVE dull and not original: *his trite novels*

triumph triumphs triumphing triumphed
NOUN **1.** a great success or achievement **2.** Triumph is a feeling of great satisfaction when you win or achieve something.
VERB **3.** If you triumph, you win a victory or succeed in overcoming something.

triumphal
ADJECTIVE done or made to celebrate a victory or great success: *a triumphal return home after the tournament*

triumphant
ADJECTIVE Someone who is triumphant feels very happy because he or she has won a victory or has achieved something: *a triumphant shout*

trivia
PLURAL NOUN Trivia are unimportant things.

trivial
ADJECTIVE Something trivial is unimportant.

Tt

troll trolls
NOUN an imaginary creature in folklore that lives in caves or mountains and is believed to turn to stone at daylight

trolley trolleys
NOUN a small cart on wheels used for carrying heavy objects

trombone trombones
NOUN a brass wind instrument with a U-shaped slide that you move to produce different notes

troop troops trooping trooped
NOUN **1.** Troops are soldiers. **2.** A troop of people or animals is a group of them.
VERB **3.** If people troop somewhere, they go there in a group.

trooper troopers
NOUN a low-ranking soldier in a cavalry or armoured regiment

trophy trophies
NOUN **1.** a cup or other award given as a prize to the winner of a competition **2.** something you keep to remember a success or victory

tropical
ADJECTIVE belonging to or typical of the tropics: *a tropical island*

tropics
PLURAL NOUN The tropics are the hottest parts of the world between two lines of latitude, the Tropic of Cancer, 23.5° north of the equator, and the Tropic of Capricorn, 23.5° south of the equator.

trot trots trotting trotted
VERB **1.** When a horse trots, it moves at a speed faster than a walk, lifting its feet quite high off the ground. **2.** If you trot, you run or jog using small, quick steps.
NOUN **3.** When a horse breaks into a trot, it starts trotting.

trouble troubles troubling troubled
NOUN **1.** Troubles are difficulties or problems. **2.** If there is trouble, people are quarrelling or fighting: *There was more trouble after the game.*
PHRASE **3.** If you are **in trouble**, you are in a situation where you may be punished because you have done something wrong.
VERB **4.** If something troubles you, it makes you feel worried or anxious. **5.** If you trouble someone for something, you disturb that person in order to ask him or her for it: *Can I trouble you for some milk?*
troubling ADJECTIVE
troubled ADJECTIVE

troublesome
ADJECTIVE causing problems or difficulties: *a troublesome teenager*

trough troughs
NOUN a long, narrow container from which animals drink or feed

trounce trounces trouncing trounced
VERB If you trounce someone, you defeat that person completely.

troupe troupes
NOUN a group of actors, singers, or dancers who work together and often travel around together

trousers
PLURAL NOUN Trousers are a piece of clothing covering the body from the waist down, enclosing each leg separately.

trout
NOUN a type of freshwater fish

trowel trowels
NOUN **1.** a small garden tool with a curved, pointed blade used for planting or weeding **2.** a small tool with a flat blade used for spreading cement or plaster

truant truants
NOUN **1.** a child who stays away from school without permission
PHRASE **2.** If children **play truant**, they stay away from school without permission.
truancy NOUN

truce truces
NOUN an agreement between two people or groups to stop fighting for a short time

truck trucks
NOUN a large motor vehicle used for carrying heavy loads

truculent
ADJECTIVE bad-tempered and aggressive
truculence NOUN

trudge trudges trudging trudged
VERB **1.** If you trudge, you walk with slow, heavy steps.
NOUN **2.** a slow, tiring walk: *the long trudge home*

true truer truest
ADJECTIVE **1.** A true story or statement is based on facts and is not made up. **2.** *True* is used to describe things or people that are genuine: *She was a true friend.* **3.** True feelings are sincere and genuine.
PHRASE **4.** If something **comes true**, it actually happens.
truly ADVERB

truffle truffles
NOUN **1.** a soft, round, chocolate candy **2.** a round, mushroom-like fungus that grows underground and is considered very good to eat

trump trumps
NOUN In a game of cards, trumps is the suit with the highest value.

trumpet trumpets trumpeting trumpeted
NOUN **1.** a brass wind instrument with a narrow tube ending in a bell-like shape
VERB **2.** When an elephant trumpets, it makes a sound like a very loud trumpet.

truncated
ADJECTIVE Something that is truncated is made shorter.

trundle trundles trundling trundled
VERB If you trundle something or it trundles somewhere, it moves or rolls along slowly.

trunk trunks
NOUN **1.** the main stem of a tree from which the branches and roots grow **2.** the main part of your body, excluding your head, neck, arms, and legs **3.** the long, flexible nose of an elephant **4.** a large, strong case or box with a hinged lid used for storing things
PLURAL NOUN **5.** short pants worn by athletes, especially swimmers or boxers

truss trusses trussing trussed
VERB **1.** To truss someone or truss a person up is to tie that person up so that he or she cannot move.
NOUN **2.** the supporting framework of a roof, bridge, or other structure

trust trusts trusting trusted
VERB **1.** If you trust someone, you believe that he or she is honest and will not harm you. **2.** If you trust someone to do something, you believe that person will do it successfully or properly. **3.** If you trust someone with something, you give it to that person or tell it to him or her: *One member of the group cannot be trusted with the secret.* **4.** If you do not trust something, you feel that it is not safe or reliable: *I didn't trust my arms and legs to work.*
NOUN **5.** Trust is the responsibility you are given to deal with or look after important or secret things: *He had built up a position of trust.* **6.** a financial arrangement in which an organization looks after and invests money for someone
trusting ADJECTIVE

trustee trustees
NOUN someone who is allowed by law to control money or property he or she is keeping or investing for another person

trustworthy
ADJECTIVE A trustworthy person is reliable and responsible and can be trusted.

trusty trustier trustiest
ADJECTIVE Trusty things and animals are considered to be reliable because they have always worked well in the past: *a trusty black Labrador*

truth truths
NOUN **1.** The truth is the facts about something, rather than things that are imagined or made up: *I know she was telling the truth.* **2.** an idea or principle that is generally accepted to be true: *the basic truths in life*

truthful
ADJECTIVE A truthful person is honest and tells the truth.
truthfully ADVERB

try tries trying tried
VERB **1.** To try to do something is to make an effort to do it. **2.** If you try something, you use it or do it to test how useful or enjoyable it is: *She wanted me to try the soup.* **3.** When a person is tried, that person appears in court and a judge and jury decide if he or she is guilty after hearing the evidence.
NOUN **4.** an attempt to do something **5.** a test of something: *You gave it a try.*

> ⚠ **HEADS UP**
>
> In everyday speech, people often say *try and do something*. In writing, use **try to**: *Try to get some sleep.*

trying
ADJECTIVE Something or someone who is trying is difficult to deal with and makes you feel impatient or annoyed.

tryst trysts
NOUN an appointment or meeting, especially between lovers in a quiet, secret place

tsar another spelling of CZAR

tsarina another spelling of CZARINA

tsetse fly tsetse flies
NOUN an African fly that feeds on blood and causes serious diseases like sleeping sickness in people and animals

T-shirt T-shirts
NOUN a short-sleeved, cotton shirt with no collar

tsunami tsunamis
NOUN a large, often destructive sea wave, caused by an earthquake or volcanic eruption under the sea

tub tubs
NOUN a wide, usually circular, container

Tt

tuba tubas
NOUN a large brass musical instrument that can produce very low notes

tubby tubbier tubbiest
ADJECTIVE rather fat

tube tubes
NOUN **1.** a round, hollow pipe **2.** a soft, metal or plastic, cylindrical container with a screw cap at one end: *a tube of toothpaste*
tubing NOUN

tuberculosis
NOUN Tuberculosis is a serious infectious disease affecting the lungs.

tubular
ADJECTIVE in the shape of a tube

tuck tucks tucking tucked
VERB **1.** If you tuck something somewhere, you put it there so that it is safe or comfortable: *She tucked the letter into her backpack.* **2.** If you tuck a piece of fabric into or under something, you push the loose ends inside or under it to make it tidy. **3.** If something is tucked away, it is in a quiet place where few people go: *a little house tucked away in a valley*

tucker tuckers tuckering tuckered
VERB *an informal word* If you are tuckered out you are tired out.

Tuesday Tuesdays
NOUN Tuesday is the day between Monday and Wednesday.

tuft tufts
NOUN A tuft of something such as hair is a bunch of it growing closely together.

tug tugs tugging tugged
VERB **1.** To tug something is to give it a quick, hard pull.
NOUN **2.** a quick, hard pull: *He felt a tug at his arm.* **3.** a small, powerful boat that tows large ships

tug-of-war
NOUN A tug-of-war is a sport in which two teams test their strength by pulling against each other on opposite ends of a rope.

tuition
NOUN Tuition is the amount of money charged for instruction, especially at a college or university.

tulip tulips
NOUN a brightly coloured spring flower

tumble tumbles tumbling tumbled
VERB **1.** To tumble is to fall with a rolling or bouncing movement.
NOUN **2.** a fall

tumbler tumblers
NOUN a drinking glass with straight sides

tummy tummies
NOUN *an informal word* Your tummy is your stomach.

tumour tumours
NOUN a mass of diseased or abnormal cells that has grown in a person's or animal's body

tumultuous
ADJECTIVE A tumultuous event or welcome is very noisy because people are happy or excited.

tuna
NOUN Tuna are large fish that live in warm seas and are caught for food.

tundra
NOUN The tundra is a vast, treeless Arctic region.

tune tunes tuning tuned
NOUN **1.** a series of musical notes arranged in a particular way
VERB **2.** To tune a musical instrument is to adjust it so that it produces the right notes. **3.** To tune an engine or machine is to adjust it so that it works well. **4.** If you tune to a particular radio or television station, you turn or press the controls to select the station you want to listen to or watch.
PHRASE **5.** If your voice or an instrument is in tune, it produces the right notes.

tuneful
ADJECTIVE having a pleasant and easily remembered tune

tuner tuners
NOUN A piano tuner is a person whose job is to tune pianos.

tunic tunics
NOUN a sleeveless garment covering the top part of the body and reaching to the hips, thighs, or knees

tunnel tunnels tunnelling tunnelled
NOUN **1.** a long underground passage
VERB **2.** To tunnel is to make a tunnel.

turban turbans
NOUN a head covering worn by a Hindu, Muslim, or Sikh man, consisting of a long piece of cloth wound around his head

turbine turbines
NOUN a machine or engine in which power is produced when a stream of air, gas, water, or steam pushes the blades of a wheel and makes it turn around

turbot
NOUN a large European flatfish that is caught for food

turbulent
ADJECTIVE **1.** A turbulent period of history is

Tt

one where there is much uncertainty, and possibly violent change. **2.** Turbulent air or water currents make sudden changes of direction.

turbulence NOUN

tureen tureens

NOUN a large dish with a lid, for serving soup

turf turfs turfing turfed

NOUN **1.** Turf is short, thick, even grass and the layer of soil beneath it.

turf out

VERB **2.** *an informal expression* To turf someone out is to force that person to leave a place.

turgid

ADJECTIVE *a literary or poetic word* A turgid play, movie, or piece of writing is difficult to understand and rather boring.

turkey turkeys

NOUN a large bird kept for food; also the meat of this bird

turmoil

NOUN Turmoil is a state of confusion, disorder, or great anxiety: *That country is in a state of turmoil.*

turn turns turning turned

VERB **1.** When you turn, you move so that you are facing or going in a different direction. **2.** When you turn something or when it turns, it moves or rotates so that it faces in a different direction or is in a different position. **3.** If you turn your attention or thoughts to someone or something, you start thinking about that person or discussing him or her. **4.** When something turns or is turned into something else, it becomes something different: *A hobby can be turned into a career.*
NOUN **5.** an act of turning something so that it faces in a different direction or is in a different position **6.** a change in the way something is happening or being done: *Her*

career took a turn for the worse. **7.** If it is your turn to do something, you have the right, chance, or duty to do it.
PHRASE **8. In turn** is used to refer to people, things, or actions that are in sequence one after the other.

turn down

VERB **9.** If you turn down someone's request or offer, you refuse or reject it.

turn up

VERB **10.** If someone or something turns up, that person or thing arrives or appears somewhere. **11.** If something turns up, it is found or discovered.

turncoat turncoats

NOUN a person who leaves one political party or group for an opposing one

turning point turning points

NOUN the moment when decisions are taken and events start to move in a different direction

turnip turnips

NOUN a round root vegetable with white or yellow flesh

turnout turnouts

NOUN The turnout at an event is the number of people who go to it.

turnover turnovers

NOUN **1.** The turnover of people in a particular organization or group is the rate at which people leave it and are replaced by others. **2.** The turnover of a company is the value of the goods or services sold during a particular period.

turnstile turnstiles

NOUN a revolving mechanical gate at the entrance to some places, which allows people to pass through on foot, one at a time, and only in one direction

KNOWING WORDS: IDIOMS

BE WORD SHARP!

Idioms add colour to language by playing with the meanings of words.

turn change direction

turn against change from supporting to opposing

turn loose set free

turn on/off switch on/off

turn out result or end up

out of turn at the wrong time

NEL

Tt

turpentine
NOUN Turpentine is a strong-smelling, colourless liquid used for thinning paint.

turquoise
NOUN OR ADJECTIVE **1.** light bluish green
NOUN **2.** Turquoise is a bluish green stone used in jewellery.

> ⚠ **HEADS UP**
>
> **Turquoise** is from an old French word, and can be pronounced TUR-koyz or TUR-kwoyz.

turret turrets
NOUN a small, narrow tower on top of a larger tower or other building

turtle turtles
NOUN a large reptile with a thick shell covering its body and flippers for swimming. It lays its eggs on land but lives the rest of its life in the water.

tusk tusks
NOUN The tusks of an elephant, wild boar, or walrus are the pair of long, curving, pointed teeth it has.

tussle tussles
NOUN an energetic fight or argument between two people, especially about something they both want

tutor tutors tutoring tutored
NOUN **1.** a private teacher
VERB **2.** If someone tutors a person or subject, he or she teaches that person or subject.

tutorial tutorials
NOUN a teaching session involving a tutor and a small group of students

tutu tutus
NOUN a short, stiff skirt worn by female ballet dancers

TV TVs
NOUN **1.** TV is television. **2.** a television set

twang twangs twanging twanged
NOUN **1.** a sound like the one made by pulling and then releasing a tight wire **2.** A twang is a nasal quality in a person's voice.
VERB **3.** If a tight wire or string twangs or you twang it, it makes a sound as it is pulled and then released.

tweak tweaks tweaking tweaked
VERB **1.** If you tweak something, you twist it or pull it.
NOUN **2.** a short twist or pull of something

twee
ADJECTIVE sweet and pretty but in bad taste or sentimental

tweed tweeds
NOUN Tweed is a thick, woollen cloth.

tweet tweets tweeting tweeted
VERB **1.** When a small bird tweets, it makes a short, high-pitched sound.
NOUN **2.** a short, high-pitched sound made by a small bird

tweezers
PLURAL NOUN Tweezers are a small tool with two arms that can be closed together and are used for pulling out hairs or picking up small objects.

twelve
NOUN the number 12
twelfth ADJECTIVE, ADVERB

twenty twenties
NOUN the number 20
twentieth ADJECTIVE, ADVERB

twice
ADVERB Twice means two times.

twiddle twiddles twiddling twiddled
VERB To twiddle something is to twist it or turn it quickly.

twig twigs
NOUN a very small, thin branch growing from a main branch of a tree or bush

twilight
NOUN **1.** Twilight is the time after sunset when it is just getting dark. **2.** The twilight of something is the final stages of it: *the twilight of his career*

twin twins
NOUN **1.** If two people are twins, they have the same mother and were born on the same day. **2.** *Twin* is used to describe two similar things that are close together or happen together: *the little twin islands*

twine twines twining twined
NOUN **1.** Twine is strong, smooth string.
VERB **2.** If you twine one thing around another, you twist or wind it around.

twinge twinges
NOUN a sudden, unpleasant feeling: *a twinge of jealousy*

twinkle twinkles twinkling twinkled
VERB **1.** If something twinkles, it sparkles or seems to sparkle with an unsteady light: *Her green eyes twinkled.*
NOUN **2.** a sparkle or brightness that something has

twirl twirls twirling twirled
VERB If something twirls, or if you twirl it, it spins or twists around and around.

Tt

twist twists twisting twisted
VERB **1.** When you twist something, you turn one end of it in one direction while holding the other end or turning it in the opposite direction. **2.** When something twists or is twisted, it moves or bends into a strange shape. **3.** If you twist a part of your body, you injure it by turning it too sharply or in an unusual direction: *I've twisted my ankle.* **4.** If you twist something that someone has said, you change the meaning slightly.
NOUN **5.** a twisting action or motion **6.** an unexpected development or event in a story or movie, especially at the end: *Each day now seemed to bring a new twist to the story.*

twisted
ADJECTIVE **1.** Something twisted has been bent or moved into a strange shape: *a tangle of twisted metal* **2.** If someone's mind or behaviour is twisted, it is unpleasantly abnormal: *He's bitter and twisted.*

twit twits
NOUN *an informal word* a silly person

twitch twitches twitching twitched
VERB **1.** If you twitch, you make little jerky movements that you cannot control. **2.** If you twitch something, you give it a little jerk in order to move it.
NOUN **3.** a little jerky movement

twitter twitters twittering twittered
VERB When birds twitter, they make short, high-pitched sounds.

two twos
NOUN the number 2

⚠ HEADS UP

Many words are pronounced TOO. **To** means *toward.* **Too** means *also* or *too much.* **Two** means *the number 2.*

two-faced
ADJECTIVE A two-faced person is not honest in the way he or she behaves toward other people.

twofold
ADJECTIVE Something twofold has two equally important parts or reasons: *Their concern was twofold: personal and political.*

twosome twosomes
NOUN two people or things that are usually seen together

two-time two-times two-timing two-timed
VERB *an informal expression* If you two-time

your boyfriend or girlfriend, you deceive that person by having a romantic relationship with someone else without telling him or her.

tycoon tycoons
NOUN a person who is successful in business and has become rich and powerful

type types typing typed
NOUN **1.** A type of something is a class of it that has common features and belongs to a larger group of related things: *What type of dog should we get?* **2.** A particular type of person has a particular appearance or quality: *He is the type who likes to play safe.*
VERB **3.** If you type something, you use a typewriter or keyboard to write it.

typewriter typewriters
NOUN a machine with a keyboard with individual keys that are pressed to produce letters and numbers on a page

typhoid
NOUN Typhoid, or typhoid fever, is an infectious disease caused by dirty water or food. It produces fever and can kill.

typhoon typhoons
NOUN a very violent tropical storm

typhus
NOUN Typhus is an infectious disease transmitted by lice or mites. It results in fever, severe headaches, and a skin rash.

typical
ADJECTIVE showing the most usual characteristics or behaviour
typically ADVERB

typify typifies typifying typified
VERB If something typifies a situation or thing, it is characteristic of it or a typical example of it: *This story is one that typifies our times.*

typing
NOUN Typing is the work or activity of producing something on a typewriter or by using a keyboard.

typist typists
NOUN a person whose job is typing

tyrannosaurus tyrannosauruses
NOUN a very large, meat-eating dinosaur that walked upright on its hind legs

tyranny tyrannies
NOUN **1.** A tyranny is the cruel and unjust rule of people by a person or group: *The citizens hoped for an end to the tyranny.* **2.** You can refer to something that is not human but is harsh as tyranny: *the tyranny of drugs*
tyrannical ADJECTIVE

tyrant tyrants
NOUN a person who treats the people he or she has authority over cruelly and unjustly

Uu

ubiquitous
ADJECTIVE Something that is ubiquitous seems to be present or found everywhere: *the ubiquitous jeans and T-shirt*

udder udders
NOUN the baglike organ that hangs below a cow's body and produces milk

UFO UFOs
NOUN a strange object seen in the sky, which some people believe to be a spaceship from another planet. UFO is an abbreviation for *unidentified flying object.*

ugly uglier ugliest
ADJECTIVE very unattractive in appearance

ulcer ulcers
NOUN a sore area on the skin or inside the body, which takes a long time to heal: *stomach ulcers*

ulterior
ADJECTIVE If you have an ulterior motive for doing something, you have a hidden reason for doing it.

ultimate
ADJECTIVE **1.** final or eventual: *Olympic gold is the ultimate goal for many athletes.*
2. most important or powerful: *The ultimate ambition of any student should be to learn.*
NOUN **3.** You can refer to the best or most advanced example of something as the ultimate: *This hotel is the ultimate in luxury.*
ultimately ADVERB

ultimatum ultimatums
NOUN a warning stating that unless someone meets your conditions, you will take action against that person

ultra-
PREFIX The prefix *ultra-* is used to form adjectives describing something as having a quality to an extreme degree: *the ultra-competitive world of sport today*

ultramarine
NOUN OR ADJECTIVE bright blue

ultrasonic
ADJECTIVE An ultrasonic sound has a very high frequency that cannot be heard by the human ear.

ultrasound
NOUN sound that cannot be heard by the human ear because its frequency is too high. Ultrasound is used to create scanned images of the body.

ultraviolet
ADJECTIVE Ultraviolet light is not visible to the human eye. It is a form of radiation that causes your skin to darken after being exposed to the sun.

umbilical cord umbilical cords
NOUN the tube of blood vessels that connects an unborn baby to its mother and through which the baby receives nutrients and oxygen

umbrella umbrellas
NOUN a device that you use to protect yourself from the rain. It consists of a folding frame covered in cloth attached to a long stick.

umpire umpires umpiring umpired
NOUN **1.** In some sports, the umpire is the person who makes sure that the game is played according to the rules and who makes a decision if there is a dispute.
VERB **2.** If you umpire a game, you are the umpire.

umpteen
ADJECTIVE *an informal word* very many: *tomatoes and umpteen other plants*
umpteenth ADJECTIVE

un-
PREFIX The prefix *un-* is added to the beginning of many words to form a word with the opposite meaning: *This is an uncomfortable chair. He unlocked the door.*

> **⚠ HEADS UP**
>
> Un- is the most common prefix in English. It can be added to many parts of speech, even nouns!

unabashed
ADJECTIVE not embarrassed or discouraged by something: *He fell many times, but my brother continued skating unabashed.*

unabated
ADJECTIVE OR ADVERB continuing without any reduction in intensity or amount: *The noise continued unabated.*

unable
ADJECTIVE If you are unable to do something, you cannot do it.

unacceptable
ADJECTIVE very bad or of a very low standard

unaccompanied
ADJECTIVE alone

unaccustomed
ADJECTIVE If you are unaccustomed to something, you are not used to it.

unaffected
ADJECTIVE **1.** not changed in any way by a particular thing: *unaffected by criticism* **2.** behaving in a natural and genuine way: *She is the most down-to-earth, unaffected person I've ever met.*

unaided
ADVERB OR ADJECTIVE without help: *He was incapable of walking unaided.*

unambiguous
ADJECTIVE An unambiguous statement has only one meaning.

unanimous
ADJECTIVE When people are unanimous, they all agree about something.
unanimously ADVERB
unanimity NOUN

unannounced
ADJECTIVE happening unexpectedly and without warning

unarmed
ADJECTIVE not carrying any weapons

unassuming
ADJECTIVE modest and quiet

unattached
ADJECTIVE not fastened or connected to something

unattended
ADJECTIVE not being watched or looked after: *an unattended package*

unauthorized
ADJECTIVE done without official permission: *unauthorized parking*

unavoidable
ADJECTIVE unable to be prevented or avoided

unaware
ADJECTIVE If you are unaware of something, you do not know about it.

unawares
ADVERB If something catches you unawares, it happens when you are not expecting it.

unbalanced
ADJECTIVE **1.** with more weight or emphasis on one side than the other: *an unbalanced load, an unbalanced relationship* **2.** mentally or emotionally deranged **3.** made up of parts that do not work well together: *an unbalanced lifestyle* **4.** An unbalanced account of something is an unfair one because it emphasizes some things and ignores others.

unbearable
ADJECTIVE Something unbearable is so unpleasant or upsetting that you feel you cannot stand it: *The pain was unbearable.*
unbearably ADVERB

unbeatable
ADJECTIVE Something that is unbeatable is the best thing of its kind.

unbelievable
ADJECTIVE **1.** extremely great or surprising: *unbelievable courage* **2.** so unlikely that you cannot believe it
unbelievably ADVERB

unborn
ADJECTIVE not yet born

unbroken
ADJECTIVE continuous or complete: *ten days of almost unbroken sunshine*

uncanny
ADJECTIVE strange and difficult to explain: *an uncanny resemblance*

uncertain
ADJECTIVE **1.** not knowing what to do: *For a minute he looked uncertain.* **2.** doubtful or not known: *The outcome of the election is still uncertain.*
uncertainty NOUN

unchallenged
ADJECTIVE accepted without any questions being asked: *Our teacher will not let your disrespectful behaviour go unchallenged.*

uncharacteristic
ADJECTIVE not typical or usual: *My father reacted with uncharacteristic humour.*

uncivilized
ADJECTIVE unacceptable, for example by being very cruel or rude: *uncivilized behaviour*

uncle uncles
NOUN the brother of your mother or father or the husband of your aunt

unclean
ADJECTIVE dirty: *unclean water*

unclear
ADJECTIVE confusing and not obvious

uncomfortable
ADJECTIVE **1.** If you are uncomfortable, you are not physically relaxed and feel slight pain or discomfort. **2.** Uncomfortable also means slightly worried or embarrassed.
uncomfortably ADVERB

uncommon
ADJECTIVE **1.** not happening often or not seen often **2.** unusually great: *She had read her sister's last e-mail with uncommon interest.*
uncommonly ADVERB

uncompromising
ADJECTIVE determined not to change an opinion or aim in any way: *an uncompromising approach to life*
uncompromisingly ADVERB

Uu

unconcerned

ADJECTIVE not interested in something or not worried about it

unconditional

ADJECTIVE with no conditions or limitations: *a full three-year unconditional guarantee*

unconditionally ADVERB

unconscious

ADJECTIVE **1.** Someone who is unconscious is asleep or in a state similar to sleep as a result of a shock, accident, or injury. **2.** If you are unconscious of something, you are not aware of it.

unconsciously ADVERB

uncontrollable

ADJECTIVE If someone or something is uncontrollable, that person or thing cannot be controlled or stopped: *uncontrollable anger*

uncontrollably ADVERB

unconventional

ADJECTIVE not behaving in the same way as most other people

unconvinced

ADJECTIVE not at all certain that something is true or right: *Some critics remain unconvinced by the plan.*

uncouth

ADJECTIVE unpleasant and not well-mannered

uncover uncovers uncovering uncovered

VERB **1.** If you uncover a secret, you find it out. **2.** To uncover something is to remove the cover or lid from it.

undaunted

ADJECTIVE If you are undaunted by something disappointing, you are not discouraged by it.

undecided

ADJECTIVE If you are undecided, you have not yet made a decision about something.

undemanding

ADJECTIVE not difficult to do or deal with: *undemanding work*

undeniable

ADJECTIVE certainly true: *undeniable evidence*

undeniably ADVERB

under

PREPOSITION **1.** below or beneath **2.** You can use *under* to say that a person or thing is affected by a particular situation or condition: *The coastal region was under threat of a hurricane. Some animals are kept under unnatural conditions.* **3.** If someone studies or works under a particular person, that person is his or her teacher or boss. **4.** less than: *under five kilometres, children under the age of 14*

under-

PREFIX The prefix *under-* is used in words that describe something as not being provided to a sufficient extent or not having happened to a sufficient extent.

underarm

ADJECTIVE **1.** under your arm: *underarm hair*

ADVERB **2.** If you throw a ball underarm, you throw it without raising your arm over your shoulder.

undercarriage undercarriages

NOUN the part of an aircraft, including the wheels, that supports the aircraft when it is on the ground

underclothes

PLURAL NOUN Your underclothes are the clothes that you wear under your other clothes and next to your skin.

undercover

ADJECTIVE involving secret work to obtain information: *an undercover police officer*

undercurrent undercurrents

NOUN a weak, partly hidden feeling that may become stronger later

undercut undercuts undercutting undercut

VERB **1.** To undercut someone's prices is to sell a product more cheaply than that person does. **2.** If something undercuts your attempts to achieve something, it prevents you from being effective.

underdeveloped

ADJECTIVE An underdeveloped country does not have modern industries, and usually has a low standard of living.

underdog underdogs

NOUN The underdog in a competition is the person who seems likely to lose.

underestimate underestimates underestimating underestimated

VERB If you underestimate something or someone, you do not realize how large, great, or capable that person or thing is.

underfoot

ADJECTIVE OR ADVERB under your feet: *the icy ground underfoot*

undergo undergoes undergoing underwent undergone

VERB If you undergo something unpleasant, it happens to you.

underground

ADJECTIVE **1.** below the surface of the ground **2.** secret, unofficial, and usually illegal

undergrowth

NOUN Small bushes and plants growing under trees are called the undergrowth.

Uu

underhand
ADJECTIVE secret and dishonest: *underhand behaviour*

underlie underlies underlying underlay underlain
VERB The thing that underlies a situation is the cause or basis of it.
underlying ADJECTIVE

underline underlines underlining underlined
VERB **1.** If something underlines a feeling or a problem, it emphasizes it. **2.** If you underline a word or sentence, you draw a line under it.

underling underlings
NOUN someone who is less important than someone else in rank or status

undermine undermines undermining undermined
VERB To undermine an idea, feeling, or system is to make it less strong or secure: *You're trying to undermine my confidence again.*

underneath
PREPOSITION **1.** below or beneath
ADVERB OR PREPOSITION **2.** Underneath describes feelings and qualities that do not show in your behaviour: *I knew that underneath her laughter she was shattered.*
ADJECTIVE **3.** The underneath part of something is the part that touches or faces the ground.

underpants
PLURAL NOUN Underpants are a piece of clothing worn by men and boys under their pants.

underpass underpasses
NOUN a road or tunnel that goes under another road or railway

underpin underpins underpinning underpinned
VERB If something underpins something else, it helps it to continue by supporting and strengthening it: *The swim team's skill is usually underpinned by an immense team spirit.*

underprivileged
ADJECTIVE Underprivileged people have less money and fewer opportunities than other people.

underrate underrates underrating underrated
VERB If you underrate someone, you do not realize how clever or valuable that person is.

understand understands understanding understood
VERB **1.** If you understand what someone says, you know what that person means. **2.** If you understand a situation, you know what is happening and why. **3.** If you say that you understand that something is the case, you mean that you have heard that it is the case: *I understand that she's a lot better now.*

understandable
ADJECTIVE If something is understandable, people can easily understand it.
understandably ADVERB

understanding understandings
NOUN **1.** If you have an understanding of something, you have some knowledge about it. **2.** an informal agreement between people
ADJECTIVE **3.** kind and sympathetic

understatement understatements
NOUN a statement deliberately suggesting that something is smaller or less important than it really is: *To say he was a bit afraid was an understatement; he was terrified.*

understudy understudies
NOUN someone who has learned a part in a play so that he or she can act it if the main actor or actress is ill

undertake undertakes undertaking undertook undertaken
VERB When you undertake a task or job, you agree to do it.

undertaker undertakers
NOUN someone whose job is to prepare bodies for burial and arrange funerals

undertaking undertakings
NOUN a task that you have agreed to do

undertone undertones
NOUN **1.** If you say something in an undertone, you say it very quietly. **2.** If something has undertones of a particular kind, it indirectly suggests ideas of this kind: *There were undertones of sadness in her story.*

undervalue undervalues undervaluing undervalued
VERB If you undervalue something, you think it is less important than it really is.

underwater
ADVERB OR ADJECTIVE **1.** beneath the surface of the water
ADJECTIVE **2.** designed to work in water: *an underwater camera*

underway
ADJECTIVE Underway means already started: *The investigation into the crime is already underway.*

underwear
NOUN Your underwear is the clothing that you wear under your other clothes, next to your skin.

underwent the past tense of UNDERGO

UNDERSTATEMENT ▾×

a statement deliberately suggesting that something is smaller or less important than it really is

"Not really. Just a routine day, more or less."

Here is an example of understatement. The woman's refusal to brag shows her to be a modest hero.

STEVEN CHARLES MANALE

Uu

undesirable
ADJECTIVE unwelcome and likely to cause harm: *undesirable behaviour*

undid the past tense of UNDO

undisputed
ADJECTIVE definite and without any doubt: *the undisputed champion*

undivided
ADJECTIVE If you give something your undivided attention, you concentrate on it totally.

undo undoes undoing undid undone
VERB **1.** If you undo something that is tied up, you untie it. **2.** If you undo something that has been done, you reverse the effect of it.

undoing
NOUN If something is someone's undoing, it is the cause of that person's failure.

undoubted
ADJECTIVE You use *undoubted* to emphasize something: *The event was an undoubted success.*
undoubtedly ADVERB

undress undresses undressing undressed
VERB When you undress, you take off your clothes.

undue
ADJECTIVE greater than is reasonable: *undue violence*
unduly ADVERB

undulating
ADJECTIVE *a formal word* moving gently up and down: *undulating hills*

undying
ADJECTIVE lasting forever: *his undying love for his wife*

unearth unearths unearthing unearthed
VERB If you unearth something that is hidden, you discover it.

unearthly
ADJECTIVE strange and unnatural

uneasy
ADJECTIVE If you are uneasy, you feel worried that something may be wrong.
unease NOUN
uneasily ADVERB
uneasiness NOUN

unemployed
ADJECTIVE **1.** without a job: *an unemployed mechanic*
NOUN **2.** The unemployed are all the people who are without a job.

unemployment
NOUN Unemployment is the state of being without a job.

unending
ADJECTIVE Something unending has continued for a long time and seems as if it will never stop: *unending joy*

unenviable
ADJECTIVE An unenviable situation is one that you would not like to be in.

unequal
ADJECTIVE **1.** If a situation is unequal, it is not fair or it is unevenly balanced: *an unequal contest* **2.** Unequal things are different in size, strength, or ability.

uneven
ADJECTIVE **1.** An uneven surface is not level or smooth. **2.** not the same or consistent: *six lines of uneven length*
unevenly ADVERB

uneventful
ADJECTIVE An uneventful period of time is one when nothing interesting happens.

unexpected
ADJECTIVE Something unexpected is surprising because it was not thought likely to happen.
unexpectedly ADVERB

unfailing
ADJECTIVE continuous and not weakening as time passes: *his unfailing cheerfulness*

unfair

Instead of **UNFAIR** try...

ADJECTIVE not right or just
unfairly ADVERB

undue strain
an **unjust** system
a **biased** decision
unreasonable rules
a **wrongful** judgment

unfaithful
ADJECTIVE If someone is unfaithful to his or her lover or the person he or she is married to, that person has a sexual relationship with someone else.

unfamiliar
ADJECTIVE If something is unfamiliar to you, or if you are unfamiliar with it, you have not seen or heard it before.

unfashionable
ADJECTIVE Something that is unfashionable is not popular or is no longer used by many people.

unfavourable
ADJECTIVE not encouraging or promising, or not providing any advantage

Uu

unfit
ADJECTIVE **1.** If you are unfit, your body is not in good condition because you have not been getting enough exercise. **2.** Something that is unfit for a particular purpose is not suitable for that purpose.

unfold unfolds unfolding unfolded
VERB **1.** When a situation unfolds, it develops and becomes known. **2.** If you unfold something that has been folded, you open it out so that it is flat.

unforeseen
ADJECTIVE happening unexpectedly

unforgettable
ADJECTIVE Something unforgettable is so good or so bad that you are unlikely to forget it.
unforgettably ADVERB

unforgivable
ADJECTIVE Something unforgivable is so bad or cruel that it can never be forgiven or justified.
unforgivably ADVERB

unfortunate
ADJECTIVE **1.** Someone who is unfortunate is unlucky. **2.** If you describe an event as unfortunate, you mean that it is a pity that it happened: *an unfortunate accident*
unfortunately ADVERB

unfounded
ADJECTIVE Something that is unfounded has no evidence to support it: *unfounded allegations*

unfriendly
ADJECTIVE **1.** A person who is unfriendly is not pleasant to you. **2.** A place that is unfriendly makes you feel uncomfortable or is not welcoming.

ungainly
ADJECTIVE moving in an awkward or clumsy way

ungrateful
ADJECTIVE not appreciating the things you have

unhappy unhappier unhappiest
ADJECTIVE **1.** sad and depressed **2.** not pleased or satisfied: *I am unhappy at being left out of the game.* **3.** If you describe a situation as an unhappy one, you are sorry that it exists: *an unhappy state of affairs*
unhappily ADVERB
unhappiness NOUN

unhealthy
ADJECTIVE **1.** likely to cause illness: *an unhealthy lifestyle* **2.** An unhealthy person is often ill.

unheard of
ADJECTIVE never having happened before and therefore surprising or shocking

unhinged
ADJECTIVE Someone who is unhinged is mentally ill.

unhurried
ADJECTIVE Unhurried is used to describe actions or movements that are slow and relaxed.

unicorn unicorns
NOUN an imaginary animal that looks like a white horse with a straight horn growing from its forehead

unidentified
ADJECTIVE You say that someone or something is unidentified when nobody knows who or what that person or thing is.

uniform uniforms
NOUN **1.** a special set of clothes worn by people at work or school
ADJECTIVE **2.** Something that is uniform does not vary but is even and regular throughout.
uniformity NOUN

unify unifies unifying unified
VERB If you unify a number of things, you bring them together.
unification NOUN

unilateral
ADJECTIVE A unilateral decision or action is one made by only one of several people or groups involved in a particular situation.
unilaterally ADVERB

unimaginable
ADJECTIVE impossible to imagine or understand properly: *unimaginable beauty*

unimportant
ADJECTIVE having very little significance or importance

uninhabited
ADJECTIVE An uninhabited place is a place where nobody lives.

uninhibited
ADJECTIVE If you are uninhibited, you behave freely and naturally and show your true feelings.

unintelligible
ADJECTIVE *a formal word* impossible to understand

uninterested
ADJECTIVE If you are uninterested in something, you are not interested in it.

uninterrupted
ADJECTIVE continuing without breaks or interruptions: *an uninterrupted sleep*

Uu

union unions

NOUN **1.** an organization of people or groups with mutual interests, especially workers aiming to improve their pay and working conditions **2.** When the union of two things takes place, they are joined together to become one thing.

unique

ADJECTIVE **1.** being the only one of its kind **2.** If something is unique to one person or thing, it concerns or belongs to that person or thing only: *wildlife and vegetation unique to the Arctic region*

uniquely ADVERB

uniqueness NOUN

> ⚠ **HEADS UP**
>
> A thing is either unique or it isn't. In writing, don't use *most unique* or *very unique*.

unisex

ADJECTIVE designed to be used by both men and women: *unisex clothing*

unison

NOUN If a group of people do something in unison, they all do it together at the same time.

unit units

NOUN **1.** If you consider something as a unit, you consider it as a single, complete thing. **2.** a group of people who work together at a particular job: *the company's engineering unit* **3.** a machine or piece of equipment that has a particular function: *a remote control unit* **4.** A unit of measurement is a fixed standard that is used for measuring things.

unite unites uniting united

VERB If a number of people unite, they join together and act as a group.

United States

NOUN a country in southern North America

unity

NOUN **1.** Where there is unity, people are in agreement and act together for a particular purpose. **2.** If a piece of writing has unity, all sentences are on topic and each supports the main idea of a paragraph or the piece of writing as a whole.

universal

ADJECTIVE concerning or relating to everyone in the world or every part of the universe: *Music and sports programs have a universal appeal. Food and shelter are universal needs.*

universally ADVERB

universe universes

NOUN The universe is the whole of space, including all the stars and planets.

university universities

NOUN a place where students study for degrees

unjust

ADJECTIVE not fair or reasonable

unjustly ADVERB

unjustified

ADJECTIVE If a belief or action is unjustified, there is no good reason for it.

unkempt

ADJECTIVE untidy and not looked after properly: *unkempt hair*

unkind

ADJECTIVE unpleasant and rather cruel

unkindly ADVERB

unkindness NOUN

unknown

ADJECTIVE **1.** If someone or something is unknown, people do not know about or have not heard of that person or thing. NOUN **2.** You can refer to the things that people in general do not know about as the unknown.

unlawful

ADJECTIVE not legal: *unlawful entry*

unleaded

ADJECTIVE If something such as gasoline is unleaded, it contains no lead.

unleash unleashes unleashing unleashed

VERB When a powerful or violent force is unleashed, it is released.

unless

CONJUNCTION You use *unless* to introduce the only circumstances in which something will not take place or is not true: *We will go skating unless the ice starts to thaw.*

unlike

PREPOSITION If one thing is unlike another, the two things are different.

unlikely

ADJECTIVE **1.** If something is unlikely, it is probably not true or probably will not happen. **2.** strange and unexpected: *There are riches in unlikely places.*

unlimited

ADJECTIVE If a supply of something is unlimited, you can have as much as you want or need.

unload unloads unloading unloaded

VERB If you unload things from a container or vehicle, you remove them.

Uu

unlock unlocks unlocking unlocked
VERB If you unlock a door or container, you open it by turning a key in the lock.

unlucky
ADJECTIVE Someone who is unlucky has bad luck.
unluckily ADVERB

unmarked
ADJECTIVE **1.** with no marks of damage or injury **2.** with no signs or marks of identification: *unmarked police cars*

unmistakable
ADJECTIVE Something unmistakable is so obvious that it cannot be mistaken for something else.
unmistakably ADVERB

unmitigated
ADJECTIVE *a formal word* You use *unmitigated* to describe a situation or quality that is completely bad: *an unmitigated disaster*

unmoved
ADJECTIVE not emotionally affected: *He is unmoved by criticism.*

unnatural
ADJECTIVE **1.** strange and rather frightening because it is not usual: *There was an unnatural stillness.* **2.** artificial and not typical: *My voice sounded high-pitched and unnatural.*
unnaturally ADVERB

unnecessary
ADJECTIVE If something is unnecessary, there is no need for it to happen or be done.
unnecessarily ADVERB

unnerve unnerves unnerving unnerved
VERB If something unnerves you, it frightens or startles you.
unnerving ADJECTIVE

unobtrusive
ADJECTIVE Something that is unobtrusive does not draw attention to itself.

unoccupied
ADJECTIVE If a house is unoccupied, there is nobody living in it.

unofficial
ADJECTIVE without the approval or permission of a person in authority: *unofficial strikes*
unofficially ADVERB

unorthodox
ADJECTIVE unusual and not generally accepted: *an unorthodox theory*

unpack unpacks unpacking unpacked
VERB When you unpack, you take everything out of a suitcase or bag.

unpaid
ADJECTIVE **1.** If you do unpaid work, you do not receive any money for doing it. **2.** An unpaid bill has not yet been paid.

unpalatable
ADJECTIVE **1.** Unpalatable food is so unpleasant that you can hardly eat it. **2.** An unpalatable idea is so unpleasant that it is difficult to accept.

unparalleled
ADJECTIVE greater than anything else of its kind: *an unparalleled success*

unpleasant
ADJECTIVE **1.** Something unpleasant causes you to have bad feelings, for example by making you uncomfortable or upset. **2.** An unpleasant person is unfriendly or rude.
unpleasantly ADVERB
unpleasantness NOUN

unpopular
ADJECTIVE disliked by most people: *an unpopular idea*

unprecedented
ADJECTIVE *a formal word* Something that is unprecedented has never happened before or is the best of its kind so far.

unpredictable
ADJECTIVE If someone or something is unpredictable, you never know how that person or thing will behave or react.

unprepared
ADJECTIVE If you are unprepared for something, you are not ready for it and are therefore surprised or at a disadvantage when it happens.

unproductive
ADJECTIVE not producing anything useful

unqualified
ADJECTIVE **1.** having no qualifications or not having the right qualifications for a particular job: *dangers posed by unqualified doctors* **2.** total: *an unqualified success*

unquestionable
ADJECTIVE so obviously true or real that nobody can doubt it: *His devotion is unquestionable.*
unquestionably ADVERB

unravel unravels unravelling unravelled
VERB **1.** If you unravel something such as a twisted and knotted piece of string, you unwind it so that it is straight. **2.** If you unravel a mystery, you work out the answer to it.

unreal
ADJECTIVE so strange that you find it difficult to believe

Uu

unrealistic
ADJECTIVE **1.** An unrealistic person does not face the truth about something or deal with it in a practical way. **2.** Something unrealistic is not true to life: *an unrealistic picture*

unreasonable
ADJECTIVE unfair and difficult to deal with or justify: *an unreasonable request*
unreasonably ADVERB

unrelated
ADJECTIVE Things that are unrelated have no connection with each other.

unrelenting
ADJECTIVE continuing in a determined way without caring about any hurt that is caused: *unrelenting criticism*

unreliable
ADJECTIVE If people, machines, or methods are unreliable, you cannot rely on them.

unremitting
ADJECTIVE continuing without stopping

unrest
NOUN If there is unrest, people are angry and dissatisfied.

unrivalled
ADJECTIVE better than anything else of its kind: *an unrivalled collection of model airplanes*

unroll unrolls unrolling unrolled
VERB If you unroll a roll of something such as cloth or paper, you open it up and make it flat.

unruly
ADJECTIVE difficult to control or organize: *unruly children, unruly hair*

unsatisfactory
ADJECTIVE not good enough

unsaturated
ADJECTIVE If something is unsaturated, it is able to absorb or dissolve more. **Unsaturated fat** is made mainly from plants, fish, and vegetable oils and is considered to be healthier than saturated oils.

unscathed
ADJECTIVE not injured or harmed as a result of a dangerous experience

unscrew unscrews unscrewing unscrewed
VERB If you unscrew something, you remove it by turning it or by removing the screws that are holding it.

unscrupulous
ADJECTIVE willing to behave dishonestly in order to get what you want

unseemly
ADJECTIVE Unseemly behaviour is not suitable for a particular situation and shows a lack of control and good manners: *an unseemly squabble*

unseen
ADJECTIVE You use *unseen* to describe things that you cannot see or have not seen.

unsettle unsettles unsettling unsettled
VERB If something unsettles you, it makes you restless or worried.

unshakable
ADJECTIVE An unshakable belief is so strong that it cannot be destroyed.

unsightly
ADJECTIVE very ugly: *an unsightly scar*

unskilled
ADJECTIVE Unskilled work does not require any special training.

unsolicited
ADJECTIVE given or happening without being asked for

unsound
ADJECTIVE **1.** If a conclusion or method is unsound, it is based on ideas that are likely to be wrong. **2.** If something such as a building or organization is unsound, it is not safe, healthy, or in good condition.

unspeakable
ADJECTIVE very unpleasant

unspecified
ADJECTIVE You say that something is unspecified when you are not told exactly what it is: *The treasure was being stored in some unspecified place.*

unspoiled
ADJECTIVE If you describe a place as unspoiled, you mean it has not been changed and it is still in its natural or original state.

unspoken
ADJECTIVE An unspoken wish or feeling is one that is not mentioned to other people.

unstable
ADJECTIVE **1.** likely to change suddenly and create difficulty or danger: *an unstable political situation* **2.** not firm or fixed properly and likely to wobble or fall

unsteady
ADJECTIVE **1.** having difficulty in controlling the movement of your legs or hands: *unsteady on her feet* **2.** not held or fixed securely and likely to fall over
unsteadily ADVERB

unstuck
ADJECTIVE If something comes unstuck, it becomes separated from the thing that it was stuck to.

Uu

unsuccessful
ADJECTIVE If you are unsuccessful, you do not succeed in what you are trying to do.
unsuccessfully ADVERB

unsuitable
ADJECTIVE not right or appropriate for a particular purpose
unsuitably ADVERB

unsuited
ADJECTIVE not appropriate for a particular task or situation: *He's totally unsuited to the job.*

unsung
ADJECTIVE You use *unsung* to describe someone who is not appreciated or praised for his or her good work: *She is the unsung hero of the club.*

unsure
ADJECTIVE uncertain or doubtful

unsuspecting
ADJECTIVE having no idea of what is happening or going to happen: *His horse escaped and collided with an unsuspecting cyclist.*

untangle untangles untangling untangled
VERB If you untangle something, you undo the tangles.

untenable
ADJECTIVE *a formal word* A theory, argument, or position that is untenable cannot be successfully defended.

unthinkable
ADJECTIVE so shocking or awful that you cannot imagine it to be true

untidy untidier untidiest

Instead of **UNTIDY** try...

ADJECTIVE not neat or well arranged
untidily ADVERB

unkempt hair
a *cluttered* desk
rumpled clothes
a *jumbled* pile of shoes
a *dishevelled* appearance

untie unties untying untied
VERB If you untie something, you undo the knots in the string or rope around it.

until
PREPOSITION OR CONJUNCTION **1.** If something happens until a particular time, it happens before that time and stops at that time: *The store stayed open until midnight. He waited until she finished her dinner.* **2.** If something does not happen until a particular time, it does not happen before that time and only starts happening at that time: *It didn't rain until the middle of the afternoon. It was not until they arrived that they found out who he was.*

untimely
ADJECTIVE happening too soon or sooner than expected: *his untimely death*

unto
PREPOSITION *an old-fashioned word* Unto means the same as to: *I say unto you, we shall have peace.*

untold
ADJECTIVE You use *untold* to emphasize how great or extreme something is: *The emperor possessed untold wealth.*

untouched
ADJECTIVE **1.** not changed, moved, or damaged: *a small village untouched by tourism* **2.** If a meal is untouched, none of it has been eaten.

untoward
ADJECTIVE unexpected and causing difficulties: *no untoward problems*

untrue
ADJECTIVE not true

unused
ADJECTIVE **1.** not yet used **2.** If you are unused to something, you have not often done or experienced it.

unusual
ADJECTIVE Something that is unusual does not occur very often.
unusually ADVERB

unveil unveils unveiling unveiled
VERB When someone unveils a new statue or plaque, that person draws back a curtain that is covering it.

unwanted
ADJECTIVE Unwanted things are not desired or wanted, either by a particular person or by people in general: *He felt lonely and unwanted.*

unwarranted
ADJECTIVE *a formal word* not justified or not deserved: *unwarranted fears*

unwelcome
ADJECTIVE not wanted: *an unwelcome visitor, unwelcome news*

unwell
ADJECTIVE If you are unwell, you are ill.

unwieldy
ADJECTIVE difficult to move or carry because of being large or an awkward shape

unwilling
ADJECTIVE If you are unwilling to do something, you do not want to do it.
unwillingly ADVERB

Uu

unwind unwinds unwinding unwound
VERB **1.** When you unwind after working hard, you relax. **2.** If you unwind something that is wrapped around something else, you undo it.

unwise
ADJECTIVE foolish or not sensible

unwitting
ADJECTIVE Unwitting describes someone who becomes involved in something without realizing what is really happening: *She made an unwitting error.*
unwittingly ADVERB

unworthy
ADJECTIVE *a formal word* Someone who is unworthy of something does not deserve it.

unwrap unwraps unwrapping unwrapped
VERB When you unwrap something, you take off the paper or covering around it.

unwritten
ADJECTIVE Something that is unwritten is generally understood and accepted without being formally established or written down: *an unwritten law*

up
ADVERB OR PREPOSITION **1.** toward or in a higher place: *He ran up the stairs. There was snow high up in the mountains.* **2.** toward or in the north: *I'm flying up to Iqaluit.*
PREPOSITION **3.** If you go up a road or river, you go along it. **4.** You use *up to* to say how large something can be or what level it has reached: *traffic jams up to 15 kilometres long* **5.** *an informal use* If someone is up to something, that person is secretly doing something that he or she should not be doing. **6.** If it is up to someone to do something, it is that person's responsibility.
ADJECTIVE **7.** If you are up, you are not in bed. **8.** If a period of time is up, it is at an end.
ADVERB **9.** If an amount of something goes up, it increases.

up-and-coming
ADJECTIVE Up-and-coming people are likely to be successful.

upbringing
NOUN Your upbringing is the way that your parents have taught you to behave.

update updates updating updated
VERB If you update something, you make it more modern or add new information to it: *He had failed to update his will.*

upgrade upgrades upgrading upgraded
VERB If something is upgraded, it is raised to a higher standard: *She upgraded the software on her computer.*

upheaval upheavals
NOUN a big change that causes a lot of trouble

uphill
ADVERB **1.** If you go uphill, you go up a slope.
ADJECTIVE **2.** An uphill task requires a lot of effort and determination.

uphold upholds upholding upheld
VERB If someone upholds a law or a decision, that person supports and maintains it.

upholstery
NOUN Upholstery is the soft covering on chairs and sofas that makes them comfortable.

upkeep
NOUN The upkeep of something is the continual process and cost of keeping it in good condition.

upland uplands
ADJECTIVE **1.** An upland area is an area of high land.
NOUN **2.** Uplands are areas of high land.

uplifting
ADJECTIVE making you feel happy

upload uploads uploading uploaded
VERB If you upload a computer file or program, you transfer it from one computer into the memory of another computer.

upmarket
ADJECTIVE sophisticated and expensive

upon
PREPOSITION **1.** *a formal use* Upon means on: *I stood upon the platform.* **2.** You use *upon* when mentioning an event that is

KNOWING WORDS: IDIOMS

BE WORD SHARP!

Idioms add colour to language by playing with the meanings of words.

up toward a higher place

up against facing a difficulty

up and suddenly and for no apparent reason

up for ready to do something

up to doing

what's up what's going on

Uu

immediately followed by another: *Upon entering the hall she took a quick glance around.* **3.** If an event is upon you, it is about to happen: *The hockey season is upon us once more.*

upper uppers
ADJECTIVE **1.** referring to something that is above something else, or the higher part of something: *the upper arm*
NOUN **2.** the top part of a shoe

upper class upper classes
NOUN The upper classes are people who belong to a very wealthy or aristocratic group in a society.

uppermost
ADJECTIVE OR ADVERB **1.** on top or in the highest position: *The uppermost leaves receive the most sunshine.*
ADJECTIVE **2.** most important: *His family is now uppermost in his mind.*

upright
ADJECTIVE OR ADVERB **1.** standing or sitting up straight, rather than bending or lying down **2.** behaving in a very respectable and moral way

uprising uprisings
NOUN If there is an uprising, a large group of people begin fighting against the existing government to bring about political changes.

uproar
NOUN If there is uproar or an uproar, there is a lot of shouting and noise, often because people are angry.

uproot uproots uprooting uprooted
VERB **1.** If someone is uprooted, that person has to leave the place where he or she has lived for a long time. **2.** If a tree is uprooted, it is pulled out of the ground.

upset upsets upsetting upset
ADJECTIVE **1.** unhappy and disappointed
VERB **2.** If something upsets you, it makes you feel worried or unhappy. **3.** If you upset something, you turn it over or spill it accidentally.
NOUN **4.** A stomach upset is a slight stomach illness caused by an infection or by something you have eaten.

upshot
NOUN The upshot of a series of events is the final result.

upside down
ADJECTIVE OR ADVERB the wrong way up

upstage upstages upstaging upstaged
VERB If someone upstages you, that person draws people's attention away from you by being more attractive or interesting.

upstairs
ADVERB **1.** If you go upstairs in a building, you go up to a higher floor.
NOUN **2.** The upstairs of a building is its upper floor or floors.

upstart upstarts
NOUN someone who has risen too quickly to an important position and is too arrogant

upstream
ADVERB toward the source of a river: *They made their way upstream.*

upsurge
NOUN An upsurge of something is a sudden large increase in it.

uptake
NOUN You can say that someone is quick on the uptake if he or she understands things quickly.

uptight
ADJECTIVE *an informal word* tense or annoyed

up-to-date
ADJECTIVE **1.** being the newest thing of its kind **2.** having the latest information

up-to-the-minute
ADJECTIVE Up-to-the-minute information is the latest available information.

upturn upturns
NOUN an improvement in a situation

upturned
ADJECTIVE **1.** pointing upward: *rain splashing down on her upturned face* **2.** upside down: *an upturned bowl*

upward
ADVERB **1.** toward a higher place: *People stared upward and pointed.* **2.** to a higher level or point on a scale: *The world population is rocketing upward.*
upward ADJECTIVE

uranium
NOUN Uranium is a radioactive metal used to produce nuclear energy and weapons.

Uranus
NOUN Uranus is the planet in the solar system that is seventh from the sun.

urban
ADJECTIVE relating to a town or city: *urban development*

urbane
ADJECTIVE well-mannered, and comfortable in social situations

urge urges urging urged
NOUN **1.** If you have an urge to do something, you have a strong wish to do it.
VERB **2.** If you urge someone to do something, you try hard to persuade that person to do it.

Uu

urgent
ADJECTIVE needing to be dealt with right away
urgently ADVERB
urgency NOUN

urinal urinals
NOUN a bowl or trough fixed to the wall in a men's public toilet for men to urinate in

urinate urinates urinating urinated
VERB When you urinate, you go to the toilet and get rid of urine from your body.

urine
NOUN the waste liquid that you get rid of from your body when you go to the toilet

URL URLs
NOUN an abbreviation for *uniform resource locator*. It is a technical name for an Internet address.

urn urns
NOUN a decorated container, especially one that is used to hold the ashes of a person who has been cremated

us
PRONOUN A speaker or writer uses *us* to refer to himself or herself and one or more other people: *Why don't you tell us?*

US an abbreviation for *United States of America*

usage
NOUN **1.** the degree to which something is used, or the way in which it is used **2.** the way in which words are actually used: *The terms soon entered common usage.*

use uses using used
VERB **1.** If you use something, you do something with it in order to do a job or achieve something: *May I use your phone?* **2.** If you use someone, you take advantage of that person by making him or her do things for you.
NOUN **3.** The use of something is the act of using it: *the use of force* **4.** If you have the use of something, you have the ability or permission to use it. **5.** If you find a use for something, you find a purpose for it.
usable ADJECTIVE
user NOUN

used
VERB **1.** Something that used to be done or used to be true was done or was true in the past.
PHRASE **2.** If you are **used to** something, you are familiar with it and have often experienced it.
ADJECTIVE **3.** A used object has had a previous owner.

useful
ADJECTIVE If something is useful, you can use it in order to do something or to help you in some way.
usefully ADVERB
usefulness NOUN

useless
ADJECTIVE **1.** If something is useless, you cannot use it because it is not suitable or helpful. **2.** If a course of action is useless, it will not achieve what is wanted.

username usernames
NOUN a name that someone uses when logging onto a computer or website

usher ushers ushering ushered
VERB **1.** If you usher someone somewhere, you show that person where to go by going with him or her.
NOUN **2.** a person who shows people where to sit at a wedding or a performance

usual
ADJECTIVE **1.** happening, done, or used most often: *his usual seat*
PHRASE **2.** If you do something **as usual**, you do it in the way that you normally do it.
usually ADVERB

usurp usurps usurping usurped
VERB *a formal word* If someone usurps another person's job or title that person takes it when he or she has no right to do so.

utensil utensils
NOUN Utensils are tools: *cooking utensils*

uterus uteruses
NOUN *a formal word* A woman's uterus is her womb.

utility utilities
NOUN **1.** The utility of something is its usefulness. **2.** a service, such as water or gas, that is provided for everyone

utilize utilizes utilizing utilized
VERB *a formal word* To utilize something is to use it.
utilization NOUN

utmost
ADJECTIVE used to emphasize a particular quality: *I have the utmost respect for my coach.*

utter utters uttering uttered
VERB **1.** When you utter sounds or words, you make or say them.
ADJECTIVE **2.** Utter means complete or total: *scenes of utter chaos*
utterly ADVERB

utterance utterances
NOUN something that is said: *his first utterance*

Vv

v an abbreviation for VERSUS

vacant
ADJECTIVE **1.** If something is vacant, it is not occupied or being used. **2.** If a job or position is vacant, no one holds it at present. **3.** A vacant look suggests that someone does not understand something or is not very intelligent.
vacancy NOUN
vacantly ADVERB

vacate vacates vacating vacated
VERB *a formal word* If you vacate a place or a job, you leave it and it becomes available for someone else.

vacation vacations
NOUN **1.** a fixed period of time away from a job or school, usually for rest or travel: *the summer vacation* **2.** a holiday

vaccinate vaccinates vaccinating vaccinated
VERB To vaccinate someone means to give that person a vaccine, usually by injection, to protect him or her against a disease.
vaccination NOUN

vaccine vaccines
NOUN a substance made from the germs that cause a disease, which is given to people to make them immune to that disease

vacuum vacuums vacuuming vacuumed
NOUN **1.** a space containing no air, gases, or other matter
VERB **2.** If you vacuum something, you clean it using a vacuum cleaner.

vacuum cleaner vacuum cleaners
NOUN an electrical appliance that cleans by sucking up dirt

vagina vaginas
NOUN A woman's vagina is the passage that connects her outer sex organs to her womb.

vagrant vagrants
NOUN a person who moves from place to place, and has no home or regular job
vagrancy NOUN

vague vaguer vaguest
ADJECTIVE **1.** If something is vague, it is not expressed or explained clearly, or you cannot see or remember it clearly: *vague statements* **2.** If someone looks or sounds vague, that person is not communicating or thinking clearly.
vaguely ADVERB
vagueness NOUN

vain vainer vainest
ADJECTIVE **1.** A vain action or attempt is one that is not successful: *He made a vain effort to cheer her up.* **2.** A vain person is very proud of his or her looks, intelligence, or other qualities.
PHRASE **3.** If you do something **in vain**, you do not succeed in achieving what you intend.
vainly ADVERB

vale vales
NOUN *a literary or poetic word* a valley

valentine valentines
NOUN **1.** Your valentine is someone you love and send a card to on Saint Valentine's Day, February 14. **2.** A valentine is the card you send to the person you love on Saint Valentine's Day.

valet valets
NOUN a male servant who is employed to look after another man, particularly caring for his clothes

valiant
ADJECTIVE very brave
valiantly ADVERB

valid
ADJECTIVE **1.** Something that is valid is based on sound reasoning. **2.** A valid ticket or document is one that is officially accepted.
validity NOUN

validate validates validating validated
VERB If something validates a statement or claim, it proves that it is true or correct.

SPELL-CHECK THIS!

A computer's spell-check won't catch wrong **homophones** (words that are spelled differently but sound the same).

The nurse slowly pressed the needle into my vain.

In this sentence, **vain** should be **vein**. **Vein** means *a blood vessel*. **Vain** means *conceited*.

NEL

Vv

valley valleys

NOUN a long stretch of land between hills or mountains, often with a river flowing through it

valour

NOUN Valour is great bravery, especially in battle.

valuable valuables

ADJECTIVE **1.** having great importance or usefulness **2.** worth a lot of money
PLURAL NOUN **3.** Valuables are things that you own that cost a lot of money, especially small items.

Instead of **VALUABLE** try…

useful skills

invaluable advice

precious memories

helpful information

a priceless heirloom

valuation valuations

NOUN a judgment about how much money something is worth or how good it is

value values valuing valued

NOUN **1.** The value of something is its importance or usefulness: *information of great value* **2.** The value of something you own is the amount of money that it is worth.
PLURAL NOUN **3.** The values of a group or a person are the moral principles and beliefs that that group or person thinks are important: *the values of liberty and equality, family values*
VERB **4.** If you value someone or something, you think that person or thing is important or beneficial. **5.** When experts value something, they decide how much money it is worth.
valued ADJECTIVE
valuer NOUN

valve valves

NOUN **1.** a part attached to a pipe or tube that controls the flow of gas or liquid **2.** a small flap in your heart or in a vein that controls the flow and direction of blood

vampire vampires

NOUN A vampire is an imaginary being in folklore who is a corpse that comes out of its grave at night and sucks the blood of living people.

van vans

NOUN a covered vehicle larger than a car but smaller than a truck, used for carrying goods

vandal vandals

NOUN someone who deliberately damages or destroys things, particularly public property
vandalize VERB
vandalism NOUN

vane vanes

NOUN a flat blade that is part of a mechanism for using the energy of the wind or water to drive a machine

vanguard

NOUN If a person or group is in the vanguard of something, that person or group is leading the way in new developments or ideas.

vanilla

NOUN a flavouring for food, which comes from the pods of a tropical plant

vanish vanishes vanishing vanished

VERB **1.** If something vanishes, it disappears: *The moon vanished behind a cloud.* **2.** If something vanishes, it ceases to exist: *a vanishing civilization*

vanity

NOUN Vanity is a feeling of excessive pride about your looks or abilities.

vanquish vanquishes vanquishing vanquished

VERB *a literary or poetic word* To vanquish someone means to defeat that person completely.

vapour

NOUN Vapour is a mass of tiny drops of water or other liquids in the air, which looks like mist.

variable variables

ADJECTIVE **1.** Something that is variable is likely to change at any time.
NOUN **2.** In any situation, a variable is something in it that can change. **3.** In mathematics, a variable is a symbol such as x, which can represent any value or any one of a set of values.
variability NOUN

variance

NOUN If one thing is at variance with another, the two seem to contradict each other.

variant variants

NOUN **1.** A variant of something has a different form from the usual one, for example, in the United Kingdom *gaol* is a variant spelling of *jail*.
ADJECTIVE **2.** alternative or different

variation variations

NOUN **1.** a change from the normal or usual pattern: *regional variations of pronunciation, a variation in my diet* **2.** a change in level, amount, or quantity: *a large variation in demand*

Vv

varicose veins
PLURAL NOUN Varicose veins are swollen, painful veins in the legs.

varied
ADJECTIVE of different types, quantities, or sizes

variety varieties
NOUN **1.** If something has variety, it consists of things that are not all the same. **2.** A variety of things is a number of different kinds of them: *a wide variety of readers* **3.** A variety of something is a particular type of it: *a new variety of celery*

various
ADJECTIVE Various means of several different types: *trees of various sorts*
variously ADVERB

varnish varnishes varnishing varnished
NOUN **1.** a liquid that, when painted onto a surface, gives it a hard, clear, shiny finish
VERB **2.** If you varnish something, you paint it with varnish.

vary varies varying varied
VERB **1.** If things vary, they change: *Weather patterns vary greatly.* **2.** If you vary something, you introduce changes in it: *Vary your routine and you won't become bored.*
varied ADJECTIVE

vascular
ADJECTIVE relating to tubes or ducts that carry fluids within animals or plants

vase vases
NOUN an open container for flowers, often made of glass or china. A vase is usually taller than it is wide.

vasectomy vasectomies
NOUN an operation to sterilize a man by cutting the tube that carries the sperm

Vaseline
NOUN *a trademark* Vaseline is a soft, clear jelly made from petroleum

Instead of **VAST** try...

and used as an ointment or as a lubricant.

an **immense** field

a **colossal** fortune

a **massive** theme park

an **enormous** property

a **mammoth** undertaking

vast
ADJECTIVE extremely large
vastly ADVERB
vastness NOUN

vat vats
NOUN a large container for liquids

vault vaults vaulting vaulted
NOUN **1.** a strong, secure room, often underneath a building, where valuables are stored **2.** an arched roof, often found in churches
VERB **3.** If you vault over something, you jump over it using your hands or a pole to help.

VCR VCRs
NOUN an abbreviation for *videocassette recorder*. A VCR is a machine for recording and playing back programs from television.

VDT VDTs
NOUN a monitor screen attached to a computer or word processor. VDT is an abbreviation for *video display terminal*.

veal
NOUN Veal is the meat from a calf.

Veda Vedas
NOUN an ancient sacred text of the Hindu religion; also these texts as a collection
Vedic ADJECTIVE

veer veers veering veered
VERB If something that is moving veers in a particular direction, it suddenly changes course: *The aircraft veered sharply to one side.*

vegan vegans
NOUN someone who does not eat any food made from animal products, such as meat, eggs, cheese, or milk

vegetable vegetables
NOUN **1.** Vegetables are edible roots or leaves such as carrots or cabbage.
ADJECTIVE **2.** *Vegetable* is used to refer to plants in contrast to animals or minerals: *vegetable life*

vegetarian vegetarians
NOUN a person who does not eat meat, poultry, or fish
vegetarianism NOUN

vegetation
NOUN Vegetation is the plants in a particular area.

vehement
ADJECTIVE Someone who is vehement has strong feelings or opinions and expresses them forcefully: *He wrote a letter of vehement protest.*
vehemence NOUN
vehemently ADVERB

vehicle vehicles
NOUN **1.** a machine, often with an engine, used for transporting people or goods **2.** something used to achieve a particular purpose or as a means of expression: *The play seemed an ideal vehicle for his music.*
vehicular ADJECTIVE

Vv

veil veils
NOUN a piece of thin, soft cloth that women sometimes wear over their heads

vein veins
NOUN **1.** Your veins are the tubes in your body through which your blood flows to your heart. **2.** Veins are the thin lines on leaves or on insects' wings. **3.** A vein of a metal or a mineral is a layer of it in rock. **4.** Something that is in a particular vein is in that style or mood: *in a more serious vein*

velocity
NOUN *a technical word* Velocity is the speed at which something is moving in a particular direction.

velvet
NOUN Velvet is a very soft material that has a thick layer of fine, short threads on one side.
velvety ADJECTIVE

vendetta vendettas
NOUN a long-lasting, bitter quarrel that results in people trying to harm each other

vending machine vending machines
NOUN a machine that provides things such as drinks or snacks when you put money in it

vendor vendors
NOUN a person who sells something

veneer
NOUN **1.** You can refer to a superficial quality that someone has as a veneer of that quality: *a veneer of calm* **2.** Veneer is a thin layer of wood or plastic used to cover a surface.

venerable
ADJECTIVE **1.** A venerable person is someone you treat with respect because of that person's age, wisdom, or character. **2.** Something that is venerable is impressive because it is old or important historically.

venerate venerates venerating venerated
VERB *a formal word* If you venerate someone, you feel great respect for that person.
veneration NOUN

vengeance
NOUN **1.** Vengeance is the act of harming someone because that person has harmed you.
PHRASE **2.** If something happens **with a vengeance**, it happens to a much greater extent than was expected: *It began to rain again with a vengeance.*

venison
NOUN Venison is the meat from a deer.

venom
NOUN **1.** The venom of a snake, scorpion, or spider is its poison. **2.** Venom is a feeling of great bitterness or spitefulness toward someone: *He was glaring at me with venom.*
venomous ADJECTIVE

vent vents venting vented
NOUN **1.** a hole in something through which gases and smoke can escape and fresh air can enter: *air vents*
VERB **2.** If you vent strong feelings, you express them: *She wanted to vent her anger upon me.*
PHRASE **3.** If you **give vent** to strong feelings, you express them: *He gave vent to a lot of bitterness.*

ventilate ventilates ventilating ventilated
VERB To ventilate a room means to allow fresh air into it.
ventilated ADJECTIVE

ventilation
NOUN **1.** A ventilation system circulates fresh air in a building. **2.** Ventilation is the process of breathing air in and out of the lungs.

ventilator ventilators
NOUN a machine that helps people breathe when they cannot breathe naturally, for example if they are very ill

ventriloquist ventriloquists
NOUN an entertainer who can speak without moving his or her lips so that the words seem to come from a dummy
ventriloquism NOUN

KNOWING WORDS: WORD HISTORY

BE WORD SHARP!

Words are like living things. They grow and change.

The word **velocity** comes from the Latin word **velocitas**, meaning *swiftness*. Nobody is sure exactly where **velocitas** came from, but it may be related to the words **vigilant** and, oddly enough, **vegetable**. Both of these words were originally associated with being lively. New words like **velociraptor** (a swift-moving dinosaur) and **velodrome** (a speed-bicycling arena) make use of **velo-** as a prefix.

Vv

venture ventures venturing ventured
NOUN **1.** something new that involves the risk of failure or of losing money: *a successful venture in producing TV movies*
VERB **2.** If you venture something such as an opinion, you say it cautiously or hesitantly because you are afraid it might be foolish or wrong: *I would not even venture a guess.*
3. If you venture somewhere that might be dangerous, you go there.

venue venues
NOUN The venue for an event is the place where it will happen.

Venus
NOUN Venus is the planet in the solar system that is second from the sun.

veranda verandas
NOUN a platform with a roof that is attached to an outside wall of a house at ground level

verb verbs
NOUN In grammar, a verb is a word that expresses actions and states, for example *be*, *become*, *take*, and *run*.

! HEADS UP

Avoid boring, overused verbs like **ask**, **say**, and **walk**. Look up these words to find more descriptive synonyms.

verbal
ADJECTIVE **1.** You use *verbal* to describe things connected with words and their use: *verbal attacks on referees* **2.** *Verbal* describes things that are spoken rather than written: *a verbal agreement*
verbally ADVERB

verdict verdicts
NOUN **1.** In a law court, a verdict is the decision that states whether a prisoner is guilty or not guilty. **2.** If you give a verdict on something, you give your opinion after thinking about it.

verge verges verging verged
PHRASE **1.** If you are **on the verge** of something, you are going to do it soon or it is likely to happen soon: *on the verge of crying*
VERB **2.** Something that verges on something else is almost the same as it: *dark blue that verged on purple*

verify verifies verifying verified
VERB If you verify something, you check that it is true: *He admitted that none of his*

statements could be verified.
verifiable ADJECTIVE
verification NOUN

veritable
ADJECTIVE You use *veritable* to emphasize that something is really true, even if it seems as if you are exaggerating: *a veritable flood of e-mail*

vermin
PLURAL NOUN Vermin are small animals or insects, such as rats and cockroaches, which carry disease and damage crops.

vernacular vernaculars
NOUN The vernacular of a particular country or district is the language widely spoken there.

versatile
ADJECTIVE If someone is versatile, that person has skills that allow him or her to adapt to many different activities.
versatility NOUN

verse verses
NOUN **1.** Verse is another word for poetry.
2. one part of a poem, song, or chapter of the Bible or other scripture

versed
ADJECTIVE If you are versed in something, you know a lot about it.

version versions
NOUN **1.** A version of something is a form of it in which some details are different from earlier or later forms: *a newer version of the software* **2.** Someone's version of an event is that person's personal description of what happened.

versus
PREPOSITION *Versus* is used to indicate that two people or teams are competing against each other.

vertebra vertebras
NOUN A vertebra is one of a series of small bones that form a person's or animal's backbone.

vertebrate vertebrates
NOUN Vertebrates are any creatures that have a backbone.

vertex vertexes vertices
NOUN The vertex of something such as a triangle or pyramid is the point opposite the base.

vertical
ADJECTIVE Something that is vertical points straight up and forms a 90-degree angle with the surface on which it stands.
vertically ADVERB

Vv

vertigo
NOUN Vertigo is a feeling of dizziness caused by looking down from a high place.

verve
NOUN Verve is liveliness and enthusiasm.

very

Instead of **VERY** try...

remarkably different
intensely painful
unusually warm
terribly bitter
highly possible
deeply honoured
greatly surprised
profoundly affected

ADVERB **1.** to a great degree: *very bad dreams*
ADJECTIVE **2.** *Very* is used before words to emphasize them: *the very end of the book*
PHRASE **3.** You use **not very** to mean that something is the case only to a small degree: *He's not very nice to us.*

vessel vessels
NOUN **1.** a ship or large boat **2.** *a literary or poetic use* any bowl or container in which a liquid can be kept **3.** a thin tube along which liquids such as blood or sap moves in animals and plants

vest vests
NOUN a short, sleeveless piece of clothing worn over a shirt, especially under a suit coat

vestige vestiges
NOUN *a formal word* If there is not a vestige of something, then there is not even a little of it left: *They do not have a vestige of strength left.*

vet vets vetting vetted
NOUN **1.** a veterinarian
VERB **2.** If you vet people or things, you check them carefully to see if they are acceptable: *He refused to let them vet his speeches.*

veteran veterans
NOUN **1.** someone who has served in the armed forces, particularly during a war **2.** someone who has been involved in a particular activity for a long time: *a veteran of 25 political campaigns*

veterinarian veterinarians
NOUN a doctor for animals

veterinary
ADJECTIVE *Veterinary* is used to describe the work of a vet and the medical treatment of animals.

veto vetoes vetoing vetoed
VERB **1.** If someone in authority vetoes something, that person says no to it.
NOUN **2.** Veto is the right that someone in authority has to say no to something: *The president has the power of veto.*

vexed
ADJECTIVE If you are vexed, you are annoyed, worried, or puzzled.

VHF
NOUN VHF is a range of high radio frequencies. VHF is an abbreviation for *very high frequency.*

> ⚠ **HEADS UP**
> Ultra- is even stronger than **very**. **UHF** stands for *ultra-high frequency*, which is above **VHF**, *very high frequency.*

via
PREPOSITION **1.** If you go to one place via another, you travel through that place to get to your destination: *He drove to Kenora via Fort Frances.* **2.** Via also means done or achieved by making use of a particular thing or person: *to follow proceedings via newspapers or television*

viable
ADJECTIVE Something that is viable is capable of doing what it is intended to do without extra help or financial support: *a viable business*
viability NOUN

viaduct viaducts
NOUN a long, high bridge that carries a road or railway across a valley

vibrant
ADJECTIVE Someone who is vibrant is full of life, energy, and enthusiasm.
vibrantly ADVERB
vibrancy NOUN

vibrate vibrates vibrating vibrated
VERB If something vibrates, it moves back and forth very quickly but just by a tiny amount.
vibration NOUN

vice vices
NOUN **1.** a serious moral fault in someone's character, such as greed, or a weakness, such as smoking **2.** a tool with a pair of jaws that holds an object tightly while it is being worked on

Vv

vice-

PREFIX The prefix *vice-* is used before a title or position to show that the holder is next in rank to the person with that title or position: *vice-president*

vice versa *Vice versa* is used to indicate that the reverse of what you have said is also true: *She complimented him, and vice versa.*

vicinity

NOUN If something is in the vicinity of a place, it is in the surrounding or nearby area.

vicious

ADJECTIVE cruel and violent

viciously ADVERB

viciousness NOUN

victim victims

NOUN someone who has been harmed or injured by someone or something

victor victors

NOUN The victor in a fight or contest is the person who wins.

Victorian

ADJECTIVE Victorian describes things that happened or were made during the reign of Queen Victoria.

victory victories

NOUN a success in a battle or competition

victorious ADJECTIVE

video videos videoing videoed

NOUN **1.** Video is the recording and showing of films and events using a videocassette recorder, videotape, and a television set. **2.** a sound and picture recording that can be played back on a television set

VERB **3.** If you video something, you record it on magnetic tape for later viewing.

videocassette recorder the full name for VCR

vie vies vying vied

VERB *a formal word* If you vie with someone, you compete to do something sooner than or better than that person does.

view views viewing viewed

NOUN **1.** Your views are your personal opinions: *his political views* **2.** everything you can see from a particular place

VERB **3.** If you view something in a particular way, you think of it in that way: *They viewed me with contempt.*

PHRASE **4.** You use **in view of** to specify the main fact or event influencing your actions or opinions: *You may wish to study harder for math in view of your most recent test result.* **5.** If something is **on view**, it is being shown or exhibited to the public.

viewer viewers

NOUN A viewer is a person who watches, looks at, or inspects something: *a television viewer*

viewpoint viewpoints

NOUN **1.** Your viewpoint is your attitude toward something. **2.** a place from which you get a good view of an area or event

vigil vigils

NOUN a period of time, especially at night, when you stay quietly in one place, for example because you are making a political protest or praying

vigilant

ADJECTIVE careful and alert to danger or trouble

vigilante vigilantes

NOUN Vigilantes are unofficially organized groups of people who try to protect their community and catch and punish criminals without the legal right to do so.

vigorous

ADJECTIVE energetic or enthusiastic

vigorously ADVERB

vigour NOUN

Viking Vikings

NOUN The Vikings were sailors from Scandinavia who attacked and settled in many parts of northwestern Europe from the eighth to the eleventh centuries.

KNOWING WORDS: WORD BUILDING

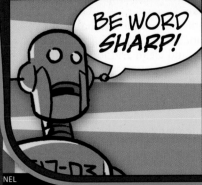

BE WORD SHARP!

You can create new words by adding prefixes and suffixes to a base word.

vice- a prefix that means *next lower in rank*

vice-chair a person next in rank to a chair

vice-consul a person next in rank to a consul

vice-principal a person next in rank to a principal

viceroy a person next in rank to a monarch

viceregal concerning a viceroy

Vv

vile viler vilest
ADJECTIVE unpleasant or disgusting: *a vile accusation, a vile smell*

villa villas
NOUN a house, especially a pleasant holiday home in a country with a warm climate

village villages
NOUN a collection of houses and other buildings in the country
villager NOUN

villain villains
NOUN someone who harms others or breaks the law
villainous ADJECTIVE
villainy NOUN

vindicate vindicates vindicating vindicated
VERB *a formal word* If someone is vindicated, that person's views or ideas are proved to be right: *My friend's instincts have been vindicated.*

vindictive
ADJECTIVE Someone who is vindictive is deliberately hurtful toward someone, often as an act of revenge.
vindictiveness NOUN

vine vines
NOUN a trailing or climbing plant that winds itself around and over a support, often one that produces grapes

vinegar
NOUN Vinegar is a sour liquid made from wine, beer, or cider, which is used in making salad dressings, pickles, and other foods.
vinegary ADJECTIVE

vineyard vineyards
NOUN an area of land where grapes are grown

vintage vintages
ADJECTIVE **1.** A vintage wine is a good quality wine that has been stored for a number of years to improve its quality. **2.** Vintage describes the time that something of quality was produced: *a vintage guitar*
NOUN **3.** a grape harvest of one particular year and the wine produced from it

vinyl
NOUN Vinyl is a strong plastic used to make things such as furniture and floor coverings.

viola violas
NOUN a musical instrument like a violin, but larger and with a lower pitch

violate violates violating violated
VERB **1.** If you violate an agreement, law, or promise, you break it. **2.** If you violate someone's peace or privacy, you disturb it.

3. If you violate a place, especially a holy place, you treat it with disrespect or violence.
violation NOUN

violence
NOUN **1.** Violence is behaviour that is intended to hurt or kill people. **2.** If you do or say something with violence, you use a lot of energy in doing or saying it, often because you are angry.

violent
ADJECTIVE **1.** If someone is violent, that person tries to hurt or kill people. **2.** A violent event happens unexpectedly and with great force. **3.** Something that is violent is said, felt, or done with great force: *violent language*
violently ADVERB

Instead of **VIOLENT** try...
a fierce hurricane
a savage beating
a fiery temper
a brutal attack
a vicious criminal
a furious outburst
a severe ice storm
murderous intentions

violet violets
NOUN **1.** a plant with dark purple flowers
NOUN OR ADJECTIVE **2.** bluish purple

violin violins
NOUN a musical instrument with four strings that is held under the chin and played with a bow
violinist NOUN

VIP VIPs
NOUN VIPs are famous or important people. VIP is an abbreviation for *very important person.*

viper vipers
NOUN a type of poisonous snake

virgin virgins
NOUN **1.** someone who has never had sexual intercourse
ADJECTIVE **2.** Something that is virgin is fresh and unused: *virgin land*
virginity NOUN

virginal virginals
ADJECTIVE **1.** Someone who is virginal looks young and innocent. **2.** Something that is virginal is fresh and clean and looks as if it has never been used.
NOUN **3.** a keyboard instrument popular in the sixteenth and seventeenth centuries

virile
ADJECTIVE A virile man has all the qualities

Vv

that a man is traditionally expected to have, such as strength and sexuality.
virility NOUN

virtual
ADJECTIVE Virtual means that something has all the characteristics of a particular thing, but it is not formally recognized as being that thing: *The country is in a virtual state of war.*
virtually ADVERB

virtual reality
NOUN Virtual reality is a situation or setting that has been created by a computer and that looks real to the person using it.

virtue virtues
NOUN **1.** Virtue is thinking and doing what is morally right and avoiding what is wrong. **2.** a good quality in someone's character **3.** A virtue of something is an advantage: *the virtue of neatness*
FORMAL PHRASE **4. By virtue of** means because of: *The article stuck in my mind by virtue of one detail.*

virtuoso virtuosos
NOUN someone who is exceptionally good at something, particularly playing a musical instrument

virtuous
ADJECTIVE behaving with or showing moral virtue

virus viruses
NOUN **1.** a kind of germ that can cause disease **2.** a program that alters or damages the information stored in a computer system
viral ADJECTIVE

visa visas
NOUN an official stamp, usually put in your passport, that allows you to visit a particular country

viscount viscounts
NOUN a British nobleman
viscountess NOUN

visibility
NOUN You use *visibility* to say how far or how clearly you can see in particular weather conditions.

visible
ADJECTIVE **1.** able to be seen **2.** noticeable or evident: *There was little visible excitement.*
visibly ADVERB

vision visions
NOUN **1.** Vision is the ability to see clearly. **2.** a mental picture, in which you imagine how things might be different: *the vision of a possible future* **3.** Vision is also imaginative insight: *a total lack of vision and imagination* **4.** an unusual experience that you have, in which you see things that other people cannot see, as a result of a dream or trance
visionary NOUN OR ADJECTIVE

visit visits visiting visited
VERB **1.** If you visit someone, you go to see that person and spend time with him or her. **2.** If you visit a place, you go to see it.
NOUN **3.** a trip to see a person or place
visitor NOUN

visor visors
NOUN a transparent, movable shield attached to a helmet, which can be pulled down to protect the eyes or face

visual
ADJECTIVE relating to sight: *visual problems*

visualize visualizes visualizing visualized
VERB If you visualize something, you form a mental picture of it.
visualization NOUN

vital
ADJECTIVE **1.** necessary or very important: *vital evidence* **2.** energetic, exciting, and full of life: *an active and vital life outside school*
vitally ADVERB

vitality
NOUN People who have vitality are energetic and lively.

KNOWING WORDS: WORD HISTORY

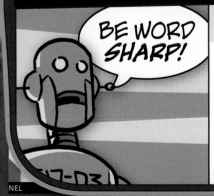

BE WORD SHARP!

Words are like living things. They grow and change.

The word **vital** originally comes from the Latin **vita**, meaning *life*. This root word is used in other modern English words, like *vitality* and *vitamin*. Advertisers often use related words like *vivify* and *vitalize* to give the effect of liveliness and energy. **Vitascope** was the name of the first movie projector that created lifelike images on screen.

Vv

vitamin vitamins
NOUN Vitamins are organic compounds that you need in order to remain healthy. They occur naturally in food.

vitriolic
ADJECTIVE *a formal word* Vitriolic language or behaviour is full of bitterness and hate.

vivacious
ADJECTIVE A vivacious person is attractively lively and high-spirited.
vivacity NOUN

vivid
ADJECTIVE very bright in colour or

Instead of **VIVID** try...

clear in detail: *vivid red paint*, *vivid memories*
vividly ADVERB
vividness NOUN

in **rich** detail
striking imagery
a **colourful** account
expressive language
a **graphic** description

vivisection
NOUN Vivisection is the act of cutting open living animals for medical research.

vixen vixens
NOUN a female fox

vocabulary vocabularies
NOUN **1.** Someone's vocabulary is the total number of words he or she knows in a particular language. **2.** The vocabulary of a language is all the words in it.

vocal
ADJECTIVE You say that someone is vocal if that person expresses his or her opinions strongly and openly.

vocation vocations
NOUN **1.** a strong wish to do a particular job, especially one that involves serving other people **2.** a profession or career

vocational
ADJECTIVE *Vocational* is used to describe the skills needed for a particular job or profession: *vocational training*

vociferous
ADJECTIVE *a formal word* Someone who is vociferous speaks a lot, or loudly, because he or she wants to make a point strongly: *vociferous critics*
vociferously ADVERB

vodka vodkas
NOUN a strong, clear, alcoholic drink

vogue
PHRASE If something is **the vogue** or **in**

vogue, it is fashionable and popular: *Colour photographs became the vogue shortly after their invention.*

voice voices voicing voiced
NOUN **1.** Your voice is the sounds produced by your vocal cords, or the ability to make such sounds.
VERB **2.** If you voice an opinion or an emotion, you say what you think or feel: *A range of opinions were voiced.*

void voids
NOUN **1.** a situation that seems empty because it has no interest or excitement: *The loss of her cat left a very large void in her life.* **2.** a large, empty hole or space: *His feet dangled in the void.*

volatile
ADJECTIVE liable to change often and unexpectedly: *The situation at work is volatile.*

volcanic
ADJECTIVE A volcanic region has many volcanoes or was created by volcanoes.

volcano volcanoes
NOUN a hill with an opening through which lava, gas, and ash burst out from inside the earth onto the surface

vole voles
NOUN a small mammal, like a mouse with a short tail, which lives in fields and near rivers

volition
NOUN *a formal word* If you do something of your own volition, you do it because you have decided for yourself, without being persuaded by others: *He attended the meeting of his own volition.*

volley volleys
NOUN **1.** A volley of shots or gunfire is a lot of shots fired at the same time. **2.** In tennis, a volley is a stroke in which the player hits the ball before it bounces.

volleyball
NOUN Volleyball is a game in which two teams hit a large ball back and forth over a high net with their hands. The ball is not allowed to bounce on the ground.

volt volts
NOUN a unit used to measure the force of an electric current

voltage voltages
NOUN The voltage of an electric current is its force measured in volts.

volume volumes
NOUN **1.** The volume of something is the amount of space it contains or occupies.

Vv

2. The volume of something is also the amount of it that there is: *a large volume of mail* **3.** The volume of a radio, TV, or stereo is the strength of the sound that it produces. **4.** a book, or one of a series of books

voluminous
ADJECTIVE very large or full in size or quantity: *voluminous skirts*

voluntary
ADJECTIVE **1.** Voluntary actions are ones that you do because you choose to do them and not because you have been forced to do them. **2.** Voluntary work is done by people who are not paid for what they do.
voluntarily ADVERB

volunteer volunteers volunteering volunteered
NOUN **1.** someone who does work for which he or she is not paid: *a volunteer at the library* **2.** someone who chooses to join the armed forces, especially during wartime
VERB **3.** If you volunteer to do something, you offer to do it rather than being forced into it.
4. If you volunteer information, you give it without being asked.

voluptuous
ADJECTIVE to do with luxury or giving pleasure to the senses: *voluptuous music*
voluptuously ADVERB
voluptuousness NOUN

vomit vomits vomiting vomited
VERB **1.** If you vomit, food and drink comes back up from your stomach and out through your mouth.
NOUN **2.** Vomit is partly digested food and drink that has come back up from someone's stomach and out through his or her mouth.

voodoo
NOUN Voodoo is a religion that combines Catholic ritual with traditional African charms and spells. It is mainly practised in the Caribbean, especially in Haiti.

vote votes voting voted
NOUN **1.** Someone's vote is that person's choice in an election, or at a meeting where decisions are made. **2.** When a group of people have a vote, they make a decision by allowing each person in the group to say what he or she would prefer. **3.** In an election, the vote is the total number of people who have made their choice: *The vote was higher than in the last election.*
4. If people have **the vote**, they have the legal right to vote in an election.
VERB **5.** When people vote, they indicate their choice or opinion, usually by writing on a piece of paper or by raising their hand.
6. If you vote that a particular thing should happen, you are suggesting it should happen: *I vote that we all go to a movie this Friday.*
voter NOUN

vouch vouches vouching vouched
VERB **1.** If you say that you can vouch for something, you mean that you have evidence from your own experience that it is true or correct. **2.** If you say that you can vouch for someone, you mean that you are sure that you can guarantee that person's good behaviour or support: *Her employer will vouch for her.*

voucher vouchers
NOUN a piece of paper that can be used instead of money to pay for something

vow vows vowing vowed
VERB **1.** If you vow to do something, you make a solemn promise to do it: *He vowed to do better in future.*
NOUN **2.** a solemn promise

vowel vowels
NOUN a sound made without your tongue touching the roof of your mouth or your teeth, or one of the letters a, e, i, o, u, which represent such sounds

> ⚠ **HEADS UP**
>
> Vowels are spoken with a continuous breath. Consonants are stalled by the tongue, teeth, or lips.

voyage voyages
NOUN a long journey on a ship or in a spacecraft
voyager NOUN

vulgar
ADJECTIVE showing a lack of taste or quality: *vulgar language, vulgar ambition*
vulgarity NOUN
vulgarly ADVERB

vulnerable
ADJECTIVE weak and without protection
vulnerably ADVERB
vulnerability NOUN

vulture vultures
NOUN a large bird that lives in hot countries and eats the flesh of dead animals

vying the present participle of VIE

Ww

wacky wackier wackiest
ADJECTIVE *an informal word* odd or unusual: *wacky clothes*

wad wads
NOUN **1.** A wad of paper or paper money is a thick bundle of it. **2.** A wad of something is a lump of it: *a wad of chewing gum*

waddle waddles waddling waddled
VERB When an animal, such as a duck, or a person waddles, that animal or person walks with short, quick steps, swaying slightly from side to side.

wade wades wading waded
VERB **1.** If you wade through water or mud, you walk slowly through it. **2.** If you wade through a book or document, you spend a lot of time and effort reading it because you find it dull or difficult.

waders
PLURAL NOUN Waders are long, waterproof rubber boots.

wafer wafers
NOUN a thin, crisp, sweet cookie

waffle waffles waffling waffled
VERB **1.** When someone waffles, that person talks or writes a lot without being clear or without saying anything of importance.
NOUN **2.** Waffle is vague and lengthy speech or writing. **3.** a thick, crisp pancake with squares marked on it, often eaten with syrup poured over it

waft wafts wafting wafted
VERB If a sound or scent wafts or is wafted through the air, it moves gently through it.

wag wags wagging wagged
VERB **1.** When a dog wags its tail, it shakes it repeatedly from side to side. **2.** If you wag your finger, you move it repeatedly from side to side as a warning or to show disapproval.

wage wages waging waged
NOUN **1.** A wage or wages is the regular payment made to someone each week for the work that he or she does, especially for manual or unskilled work.
VERB **2.** If a person or country wages a campaign or a war, that person or country starts it and carries it on over a period of time.

wager wagers
NOUN a bet

wagon wagons
NOUN a strong, four-wheeled vehicle for carrying heavy loads, usually pulled by a horse or tractor

waif waifs
NOUN a young, thin person who looks hungry and homeless

wail wails wailing wailed
VERB **1.** To wail is to cry loudly with sorrow or pain.
NOUN **2.** a long, unhappy cry

waist waists
NOUN the middle part of your body where it narrows slightly above your hips

wait waits waiting waited
VERB **1.** If you wait, you spend time, usually doing little or nothing, before something happens. **2.** If something can wait, it is not urgent and can be dealt with later. **3.** If you wait on people in a restaurant, it is your job to serve them food.
NOUN **4.** a period of time before something happens
PHRASE **5.** If you **can't wait** to do something, you are very excited and eager to do it.

waiter waiters
NOUN a man who works in a restaurant, serving people with food and drink

waiting list waiting lists
NOUN a list of people who have asked for something that cannot be given to them immediately, for example medical treatment

waitress waitresses
NOUN a woman who works in a restaurant, serving people with food and drink

waive waives waiving waived
VERB If someone waives something such as a rule or a right, that person decides not to insist on it being applied.

wake wakes waking woke woken
VERB **1.** When you wake or when something wakes you, you become conscious again after being asleep.
NOUN **2.** The wake of a boat or other object moving in water is the track of waves it leaves behind it. **3.** a gathering of people who have got together to mourn someone's death
PHRASE **4.** If one thing follows **in the wake of** another, it follows it as a result of it, or in imitation of it: *Floods followed in the wake of the hurricane.*

wake up
VERB **5.** When you wake up or something wakes you up, you become conscious again after being asleep. **6.** If you wake up to a dangerous situation, you become aware of it.

Ww

waken wakens wakening wakened
VERB *a literary or poetic word* When you waken someone, you wake that person up.

walk walks walking walked
VERB **1.** When you walk, you move along by putting one foot in front of the other on the ground. **2.** If you walk away with or walk off with something such as a prize, you win it or achieve it easily.
NOUN **3.** a journey made by walking: *We'll have a quick walk.* **4.** Your walk is the way you walk: *his rolling walk*
walk out
VERB **5.** If you walk out on someone, you leave that person suddenly. **6.** If workers walk out, they go on strike.

Instead of **WALK** try…

trudge through snow
saunter casually
march proudly
pace nervously
stagger blindly
stride confidently
wander aimlessly
plod through mud

walker walkers
NOUN a person who walks, especially one who walks in a particular way: *My sister is a slow walker and it always takes us ages to get to school.*

walking stick walking sticks
NOUN a wooden stick that people can lean on while walking

walk of life walks of life
NOUN The walk of life that you come from is the position you have in society and the kind of job you have.

walkover walkovers
NOUN *an informal word* a very easy victory in a competition or contest

walkway walkways
NOUN a passage, especially a raised structure between two buildings or a wide pathway in a park for people to walk along

wall walls
NOUN **1.** one of the vertical sides of a building or a room **2.** a long, narrow, vertical structure made of stone or brick that surrounds or divides an area of land **3.** a lining or membrane enclosing a bodily cavity or structure: *the wall of the womb*

wallaby wallabies
NOUN an animal like a small kangaroo

wallet wallets
NOUN a small, flat case made of leather or plastic, used for keeping money and sometimes credit cards

wallop wallops walloping walloped
VERB *an informal word* If you wallop someone, you hit that person very hard.

wallow wallows wallowing wallowed
VERB **1.** If you wallow in an unpleasant feeling or situation, you allow it to continue longer than is reasonable or necessary because you are getting a kind of enjoyment from it: *We're wallowing in misery.* **2.** When an animal wallows in mud or water, it lies or rolls about in it slowly for pleasure.

wallpaper wallpapers
NOUN Wallpaper is thick, coloured or patterned paper for pasting onto the walls of rooms in order to decorate them.

walnut walnuts
NOUN **1.** an edible nut with a wrinkled shape and a hard, round, light-brown shell **2.** Walnut is wood from the walnut tree, which is often used for making expensive furniture.

walrus walruses
NOUN an animal that lives in the sea, looks like a large seal, and has a tough skin, coarse whiskers, and two tusks

KNOWING WORDS: IDIOMS

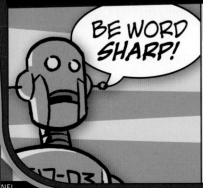

BE WORD SHARP!

Idioms add colour to language by playing with the meanings of words.

wall a vertical divider

a brick wall a person who does not listen or respond

a hole in the wall a small, dark store or restaurant

drive up the wall annoy

off the wall weird

wall to wall a large amount packed tightly

Ww

waltz waltzes waltzing waltzed
NOUN **1.** a dance that has a rhythm of three beats to the bar
VERB **2.** If you waltz with someone, you dance a waltz with that person. **3.** *an informal use* If you waltz somewhere, you do it in a relaxed and confident way: *She waltzed from person to person at the party.*

wan
ADJECTIVE pale and tired-looking

wand wands
NOUN a long, thin rod that magicians wave when they are performing tricks and magic

wander wanders wandering wandered
VERB **1.** If you wander in a place, you walk around in a casual way. **2.** If your mind wanders or your thoughts wander, you lose concentration and start thinking about other things.
wanderer NOUN

wane wanes waning waned
VERB If a condition, attitude, or emotion wanes, it becomes gradually weaker.

wangle wangles wangling wangled
VERB *an informal word* If you wangle something that you want, you manage to get it by being crafty or persuasive.

want wants wanting wanted
VERB **1.** If you want something, you feel a desire to have it. **2.** If something is wanted, it is needed or needs to be done. **3.** If someone is wanted, the police are searching for that person: *She was wanted for fraud.*
NOUN **4.** A want of something is a lack of it.

wanting
ADJECTIVE If you find something wanting or if it proves wanting, it is not as good in some way as you think it should be.

wanton
ADJECTIVE A wanton action deliberately causes unnecessary harm or waste: *wanton destruction*

war wars warring warred
NOUN **1.** a period of fighting between countries or states when weapons are used and many people may be killed **2.** a competition between groups of people, or a campaign against something: *a trade war, the war against crime*
VERB **3.** When two countries war with each other, they are fighting a war against each other.
warring ADJECTIVE

warble warbles warbling warbled
VERB When a bird warbles, it sings in a constantly changing manner.

ward wards warding warded
NOUN **1.** a room or group of rooms in a hospital, especially for people who need similar treatment **2.** an area or district that forms a separate part of a political constituency or local council **3.** A ward or a ward of court is a child who is officially put in the care of an adult or a court of law, because his or her parents have died or because he or she needs protection.
ward off
VERB **4.** If you ward off a danger or an illness, you do something to prevent it from affecting or harming you.

-ward
SUFFIX The suffix *-ward* forms adverbs or adjectives that show the way something is moving or facing: *homeward, westward*

warden wardens
NOUN **1.** a person in charge of a building or institution such as a prison **2.** an official who makes sure that certain laws or rules are obeyed in a particular place or activity: *a fire warden*

wardrobe wardrobes
NOUN **1.** a tall cupboard in which you can hang your clothes **2.** Someone's wardrobe is that person's collection of clothes.

KNOWING WORDS: WORD BUILDING

BE WORD SHARP!

You can create new words by adding prefixes and suffixes to a base word.

-ward a suffix that means *facing* or *toward*

backward facing the back

forward toward the front, or fore

downward toward the lower part

upward toward the upper part

skyward toward the sky

Ww

ware wares

NOUN **1.** Ware is manufactured goods of a particular kind: *kitchenware* **2.** Someone's wares are the things that person sells, usually in the street or in a market.

warehouse warehouses

NOUN a large building where raw materials or manufactured goods are stored

warfare

NOUN Warfare is the activity of fighting a war.

warhead warheads

NOUN the front end of a bomb or missile, where the explosives are carried

warlock warlocks

NOUN a man who claims to have magic powers and to be able to use them for good or evil

warm warmer warmest; warms warming warmed

ADJECTIVE **1.** Something that is warm has some heat, but not enough to be hot: *a warm day* **2.** Warm clothes or blankets

Instead of WARM try...

- a pleasant breeze
- a heated pastry
- balmy weather
- a flushed face
- tepid water
- a toasty fire
- a snug blanket
- a mild afternoon

are made of a material that protects you from the cold.
3. Warm colours or sounds are pleasant and make you feel comfortable and relaxed. **4.** A warm person is friendly and affectionate.
VERB **5.** If you warm something, you heat it up gently so that it stops being cold.
warmly ADVERB

warm up

VERB **6.** If you warm up for an event or an activity, you practise or exercise gently to prepare for it.

warmth

NOUN **1.** Warmth is a moderate amount of heat. **2.** Someone who has warmth is friendly and affectionate.

warn warns warning warned

VERB **1.** If you warn someone about a possible problem or danger, you tell that person about it in advance so that he or she is aware of it: *I warned him what it would be like.*
2. If you warn someone not to do something, you advise that person not to do it, in order to avoid possible danger or punishment: *I have warned her not to put weight on her ankle until it is healed.*

warn off

VERB **3.** If you warn someone off, you tell that person to go away or to stop doing something.

warning warnings

NOUN something said or written to tell people of a possible problem or danger

Instead of WARNING try...

- a chilling omen
- a police bulletin
- a friendly caution
- a neighbourhood alert
- a sign of things to come

warp warps warping warped

VERB **1.** If something warps or is warped, it becomes bent, often because of the effect of heat or water. **2.** If something warps someone's mind or character, it makes that person abnormal or corrupt.
3. The warp in a piece of cloth is the stronger lengthwise threads.

warrant warrants warranting warranted

VERB **1.** If something warrants a particular action, it makes the action seem necessary: *no evidence to warrant a criminal investigation*
NOUN **2.** an official document that gives permission to the police to do something: *a warrant for his arrest*

warranty warranties

NOUN a written guarantee promising to repair or replace a product if necessary: *a three-year warranty*

warren warrens

NOUN a group of holes under the ground connected by tunnels, which rabbits live in

warrior warriors

NOUN a fighter or soldier, especially in former times

warship warships

NOUN a ship built with weapons and used for fighting in wars

wart warts

NOUN a small, hard lump that can grow on someone's skin

wartime

NOUN Wartime is a period of time during which a country is at war.

wary warier wariest

ADJECTIVE cautious and on one's guard: *I was taught to be wary of strangers.*
warily ADVERB

Ww

was a past tense of BE

wash washes washing washed

VERB **1.** If you wash something, you clean it with water and soap. **2.** If you wash, you clean yourself using soap and water. **3.** If something is washed somewhere, it is carried there gently by water: *Wood is often washed ashore by the waves.*

NOUN **4.** The wash is all the clothes and bedding that are washed together at one time: *a typical family's weekly wash* **5.** The wash in water is the disturbance and waves produced at the back of a moving boat.

PHRASE **6.** If you **wash your hands of** something, you refuse to have anything more to do with it.

wash up

VERB **7.** If you wash up, you wash your hands. Wash up also means to wash the dishes, pans, and cutlery used in preparing and eating a meal. **8.** If something is washed up on land, it is carried by a river or sea and left there: *An old tire had washed up on the beach.*

washbasin washbasins

NOUN a deep bowl, usually fixed to a wall, with taps for hot and cold water

washer washers

NOUN a thin, flat ring of metal or plastic that is placed over a bolt before the nut is screwed on, so that it is fixed more tightly

washing

NOUN Washing consists of clothes and bedding that need to be washed or are in the process of being washed and dried.

washing machine washing machines

NOUN a machine for washing clothes

washroom washrooms

NOUN a room with a toilet and a sink, especially one in a public building

wasp wasps

NOUN an insect with yellow and

Instead of **WASTE** try...

blow a chance

misuse your time

fritter away your money

squander your education

try not to throw away food

black stripes across its body, which can sting like a bee

wastage

NOUN Wastage is loss and misuse of something: *wastage of resources*

waste wastes wasting wasted

VERB **1.** If you waste time, money, or energy, you use too much of it on something that is not important or necessary. **2.** If you waste an opportunity, you do not take advantage of it when it is available. **3.** If you say that something is wasted on someone, you mean that it is too good or too sophisticated for that person: *That joke was wasted on him.*

NOUN **4.** If an activity is a waste of time, money, or energy, it is not important or necessary. **5.** Waste is the use of more money or some other resource than is necessary. **6.** Waste is also material that is no longer wanted, or material left over from a useful process: *nuclear waste*

ADJECTIVE **7.** unwanted in its present form: *waste scraps of paper* **8.** not used or looked after by anyone

waste away

VERB **9.** If someone is wasting away, that person is becoming very thin and weak because of illness or from not eating properly.

wasted

ADJECTIVE unnecessary: *a wasted journey*

wasteful

ADJECTIVE causing waste by using something in a careless, extravagant, or inefficient way

wasteland wastelands

NOUN A wasteland is land that is of no use because it is infertile or neglected.

watch watches watching watched

NOUN **1.** a small clock usually worn on a strap on the wrist **2.** a period of time during which a guard is kept over something

VERB **3.** If you watch something, you look at it for some time and pay close attention to what is happening. **4.** If you watch someone or something, you take care of that person or thing. **5.** If you watch a situation, you pay attention to it or are aware of it: *I had watched her progress with interest.*

watch out

VERB **6.** If you watch out for something, you keep alert to see if it is near you: *My dad was watching out for deer as he drove.* **7.** If you tell someone to watch out, you are warning that person to be very careful.

watchdog watchdogs

NOUN **1.** a dog used to guard property **2.** a person or group whose job is to make sure that other organizations do not act illegally or irresponsibly

watchful

ADJECTIVE careful to notice everything that is happening: *the watchful eye of her father*

watchman watchmen

NOUN a person whose job is to guard property

Ww

water waters watering watered
NOUN **1.** Water is a clear, colourless, tasteless, odourless liquid that is necessary for all plant and animal life. **2.** You use *water* or *waters* to refer to a large area of water, such as a lake or sea: *the black waters of the lake*
VERB **3.** If you water a plant or an animal, you give it water to drink. **4.** If your eyes water, you have tears in them because they are hurting or you are sad. **5.** If your mouth waters, it produces extra saliva, usually because you think of or can smell something appetizing.
water down
VERB **6.** If you water something down, you make it weaker.

watercolour watercolours
NOUN **1.** Watercolours are paints that are mixed with water instead of oil, which are used for painting pictures. **2.** a picture that has been painted using watercolours

watercress
NOUN Watercress is a small plant that grows in streams and pools. Its leaves taste spicy and are usually eaten in salads or used as a garnish.

waterfall waterfalls
NOUN A waterfall is water from a river or stream as it flows over the edge of a steep cliff and falls to the ground below.

waterfront waterfronts
NOUN a street or piece of land next to an area of water such as a river, lake, or harbour

watering can watering cans
NOUN a container with a handle and a long spout, which you use to water plants

waterlogged
ADJECTIVE If something such as land is waterlogged, it is completely full of or soaked with water.

watermelon watermelons
NOUN a large, round fruit that has a hard, green skin and red, juicy flesh

waterproof waterproofs
ADJECTIVE **1.** not letting water pass through: *waterproof clothing*
VERB **2.** If something is made waterproof, water is not able to pass through it.

watershed watersheds
NOUN an event or period that marks a turning point or the beginning of a new way of life: *a watershed in Canadian history*

waterskiing
NOUN Waterskiing is the sport of skimming over the water on skis while being pulled by a boat.

water table water tables
NOUN The water table is the level below the surface of the ground at which water can be found.

watertight
ADJECTIVE **1.** Something that is watertight does not allow water to pass through. **2.** An agreement or an argument that is watertight has been so carefully put together that nobody should be able to find a fault in it.

waterway waterways
NOUN a canal, river, or narrow channel that ships or boats can travel along

waterworks
NOUN A waterworks is the system of pipes, filters, and tanks where the public supply of water is stored, cleaned, and distributed.

watery
ADJECTIVE **1.** pale or weak: *a watery smile*
2. Watery food or drink contains a lot of water or is thin like water.

watt watts
NOUN a unit of measurement of electrical power

KNOWING WORDS: IDIOMS

BE WORD SHARP!

Idioms add colour to language by playing with the meanings of words.

water a clear liquid

in hot water in trouble

keep your head above water stay out of difficulty

hold water make sense

like water freely and easily

water under the bridge old problems that are past

wattle wattles
NOUN a material for making fences or walls. It consists of stakes or sticks that are interwoven with twigs or branches.

wave waves waving waved
VERB **1.** If you wave your hand, you move it from side to side, usually to say hello or goodbye. **2.** If you wave someone somewhere or wave that person on, you make a movement with your hand to tell him or her which way to go. **3.** If you wave something, you hold it up and move it from side to side: *The doctor waved a piece of paper at him.*
NOUN **4.** a ridge of water on the surface of the sea caused by wind or by tides **5.** A wave is the form in which some types of energy such as heat, light, or sound travel through a substance. **6.** A wave of sympathy or panic is a steady increase in it that spreads through you or through a group of people. **7.** an increase in a type of activity or behaviour: *the crime wave*

wavelength wavelengths
NOUN **1.** the distance between the same point on two adjacent waves of energy **2.** the size of radio wave that a particular radio station uses to broadcast its programs

waver wavers wavering wavered
VERB **1.** If you waver or if your confidence or beliefs waver, you are no longer as firm, confident, or sure in your beliefs: *She has never wavered from her faith in him.* **2.** If something wavers, it moves slightly: *His hand wavered as he reached for the phone.*

wavy wavier waviest
ADJECTIVE having waves or regular curves: *wavy hair*

wax waxes waxing waxed
NOUN **1.** Wax is a solid, slightly shiny substance made of fat or oil and used to make candles and polish. **2.** Wax is also the sticky yellow substance in your ears.
VERB **3.** If you wax a surface, you treat it or cover it with a thin layer of wax, especially to polish it. **4.** If you wax eloquent, you talk in an eloquent way.

way ways
NOUN **1.** A way of doing something is the manner of doing it: *an excellent way of cooking meat* **2.** The ways of a person or group of people are their customs or their normal behaviour: *Their ways are certainly different.* **3.** The way you feel about something is your attitude to it or your opinion about it. **4.** If you have a way with people or things, you are very skilful at dealing with them. **5.** The way to a particular place is the route that you take to get there. **6.** If you go or look a particular way, you go or look in that direction: *She glanced the other way.* **7.** If you divide something a number of ways, you divide it into that number of parts. **8.** *Way* is used with words such as *little* or *long* to say how far off in distance or time something is: *They lived a long way away.*
PHRASE **9.** If someone or something is **in the way**, that person or thing prevents you from moving freely or seeing clearly. **10.** You say **by the way** when adding something to what you are saying: *By the way, I asked my sister to stop by.* **11.** If you **go out of your way** to do something, you make a special effort to do it.

wayside
PHRASE If people or things **fall by the wayside**, they fail in what they were trying to do, or they become forgotten.

wayward
ADJECTIVE difficult to control and likely to change suddenly: *wayward behaviour*

we
PRONOUN A speaker or writer uses *we* to refer to himself or herself and one or more other people: *We are going to see a movie.*

KNOWING WORDS: IDIOMS

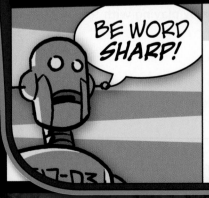

BE WORD SHARP!

Idioms add colour to language by playing with the meanings of words.

way path or manner

all the way to the limit

have a way with have special skill with

make way make room

no way absolutely not

under way in progress

NEL

weak weaker weakest
ADJECTIVE **1.** not having much strength: *weak from lack of sleep* **2.** If something is weak, it is likely to break or fail: *the weakest link in a chain* **3.** If you describe someone as weak, you mean that person is easily influenced by other people.
weakly ADVERB

weaken weakens weakening weakened
VERB **1.** If someone weakens something, that person makes it less strong or certain. **2.** If someone weakens, that person becomes less certain about something.

weakling weaklings
NOUN a person who lacks physical strength or who is weak in character or health

weakness weaknesses
NOUN **1.** Weakness is lack of moral or physical strength. **2.** If you have a weakness for something, you have a great liking for it: *a weakness for candy.*

wealth
NOUN **1.** Wealth is the large amount of money or property that someone owns. **2.** A wealth of something is a lot of it: *a wealth of information*

wealthy wealthier wealthiest
ADJECTIVE having a large amount of money, property, or other valuable things

wean weans weaning weaned
VERB To wean a human baby or a baby animal is to start feeding it food other than its mother's milk.

weapon weapons
NOUN **1.** an object used to hurt people in a fight or war **2.** anything that can be used to get the better of an opponent: *Surprise was his only weapon.*
weaponry NOUN

wear wears wearing wore worn
VERB **1.** When you wear something such as clothes, makeup, or jewellery, you have them on your body or face. **2.** If you wear a particular expression, it shows on your face. **3.** If something wears, it becomes thinner or worse in condition.
NOUN **4.** You can refer to clothes that are suitable for a particular time or occasion as a kind of wear: *beach wear* **5.** Wear is the amount or type of use that something has and that causes damage or change to it: *signs of wear*

wear down
VERB **6.** If you wear people down, you weaken them by repeatedly doing something or asking them to do something.

wear off
VERB **7.** If a feeling such as pain wears off, it gradually disappears.

wear out
VERB **8.** When something wears out or when you wear it out, it is used so much that it becomes no longer usable. **9.** If you wear someone out, you make that person feel extremely tired.

wear and tear
NOUN Wear and tear is the damage caused to something by normal use.

wearing
ADJECTIVE Someone or something that is wearing makes you feel extremely tired.

weary wearier weariest; wearies wearying wearied
ADJECTIVE **1.** very tired
VERB **2.** If you weary of something, you become tired of it.
wearily ADVERB
weariness NOUN

weasel weasels
NOUN a small wild animal with a long, thin body and short legs

weather weathers weathering weathered
NOUN **1.** The weather is the condition of the atmosphere at any particular time and the amount of rain, wind, or sunshine occurring.
VERB **2.** If something such as rock or wood weathers, it changes colour or shape as a result of being exposed to the wind, rain, or sun. **3.** If you weather a problem or difficulty, you come through it safely.
PHRASE **4.** If you are **under the weather**, you feel slightly ill.

weather forecast weather forecasts
NOUN a statement saying what the weather will be like the next day or for the next few days

weathervane weathervanes
NOUN a metal object on the roof of a building, which turns around in the wind to show which way the wind is blowing

weave weaves weaving wove woven
VERB **1.** To weave cloth is to make it by crossing threads over and under each other, especially by using a machine called a loom. **2.** If you weave your way somewhere, you go there by moving from side to side through and around the obstacles.
NOUN **3.** The weave of cloth is the way in which the threads are arranged and the pattern that they form: *a tight weave*

weaver weavers
NOUN a person who weaves cloth

Ww

web webs
NOUN **1.** a fine net of threads that a spider makes from a sticky substance that it produces in its body **2.** something that has a complicated structure or pattern: *a web of lies* **3.** The Web is the same as the WORLD WIDE WEB.

⚠️ **HEADS UP**

The **Internet** is a global computer network. The **Web** is a system of linked documents on the Internet.

webbed
ADJECTIVE Webbed feet have the toes connected by a piece of skin.

weblog weblogs
NOUN a person's online diary or journal that he or she puts on the Internet so that other people can read it. It is also shortened to blog.

website websites
NOUN a publication on the World Wide Web that contains information about a particular subject

wed weds wedding wedded
VERB If you wed someone or if you wed, you get married.

wedding weddings
NOUN a marriage ceremony

wedge wedges wedging wedged
VERB **1.** If you wedge something, you force it to remain there by holding it there tightly, or by fixing something next to it to prevent it from moving: *I wedged the shed door open with a piece of wood.*
NOUN **2.** a piece of something such as wood, metal, or rubber with one pointed edge and one thick edge, which is used to wedge something **3.** a piece of something that has a thick triangular shape: *a wedge of cheese*

wedlock
NOUN *an old-fashioned word* Wedlock is the state of being married.

Wednesday Wednesdays
NOUN Wednesday is the day between Tuesday and Thursday.

weed weeds weeding weeded
NOUN **1.** a wild plant that prevents cultivated plants from growing properly
VERB **2.** If you weed a place such as a garden, you remove the weeds from it.

weed out
VERB **3.** If you weed out unwanted things, you get rid of them.

week weeks
NOUN **1.** a period of seven days, especially one beginning on a Sunday and ending on a Saturday **2.** A week is also the number of hours you spend at work during a week: *a 35-hour week* **3.** The week can refer to the part of a week that does not include Saturday and Sunday: *They are working during the week.*

weekday weekdays
NOUN any day except Saturday and Sunday

weekend weekends
NOUN Saturday and Sunday

weekly weeklies
ADJECTIVE OR ADVERB **1.** happening or appearing once a week
NOUN **2.** a newspaper or magazine that is published once a week

weep weeps weeping wept
VERB **1.** If someone weeps, that person cries. **2.** If something such as a wound weeps, it oozes blood or other liquid.

weevil weevils
NOUN a type of beetle that eats grain, seeds, or plants

weft
NOUN The weft of a piece of woven material is the threads that are passed sideways in and out of the threads held in a loom.

weigh weighs weighing weighed
VERB **1.** If something weighs a particular amount, that is how heavy it is. **2.** If you weigh something, you measure how heavy it is using scales. **3.** If you weigh facts or

SPELL-CHECK THIS!

A computer's spell-check won't catch wrong **homophones** (words that are spelled differently but sound the same).

She was about to collapse, week from hunger.

In this sentence, **week** should be **weak**.
Weak means *not strong*. A **week** is *seven days*.

NEL

Ww

words, you think about them carefully before coming to a decision or before speaking. **4.** If a problem weighs on you, it makes you very worried.

weigh down

VERB **5.** If a load weighs you down, it stops you from moving easily. **6.** If you are weighed down by a difficulty, it is making you very worried.

weight weights weighting weighted

NOUN **1.** The weight of something is its heaviness. **2.** a metal object that has a certain known heaviness. Weights are used with sets of scales in order to weigh things. **3.** any heavy object **4.** The weight of something is its large amount or importance, which makes it hard to fight against or contradict: *the weight of the law*

VERB **5.** If you weight something or weight it down, you make it heavier, often so that it cannot move.

PHRASE **6.** If you **pull your weight**, you work just as hard as other people involved in the same activity.

weighted

ADJECTIVE A system that is weighted in favour of a particular person or group is organized in such a way that this person or group will have an advantage.

weightlifting

NOUN Weightlifting is the sport of lifting heavy weights in competition or for exercise.
weightlifter NOUN

weighty weightier weightiest

ADJECTIVE serious or important: *a weighty problem*

weir weirs

NOUN a low dam that is built across a river to raise the water level, control the flow of water, or change its direction

weird weirder weirdest

ADJECTIVE strange or odd
weirdly ADVERB

weirdo weirdos

NOUN *an informal word* If you call someone a weirdo, you mean that person behaves in a strange way.

welcome welcomes welcoming welcomed

VERB **1.** If you welcome a visitor, you greet that person in a friendly way when he or she arrives. **2.** If you welcome something, you approve of it and support it: *She welcomed the decision.*

NOUN **3.** a greeting to a visitor: *a warm welcome*

ADJECTIVE **4.** If someone is welcome at a place, that person will be warmly received there.

5. If something is welcome, it brings pleasure or is accepted gratefully: *a welcome rest* **6.** If you tell someone that he or she is welcome to something or welcome to do something, you mean you are willing for him or her to have or to do it.

INTERJECTION **7.** *Welcome* can be said as a greeting to a visitor who has just arrived.
welcoming ADJECTIVE

weld welds welding welded

VERB To weld two pieces of metal together is to join them by heating their edges and fixing them together so that when they cool they harden into one piece.
welder NOUN

welfare

NOUN **1.** The welfare of people is their general state of health and comfort. **2.** Welfare services are provided to help with people's living conditions and financial problems: *The main welfare program in Canada is called social assistance.*

welfare state

NOUN The welfare state is a system in which the government uses money from taxes to provide health care and other social services, and to give benefits to citizens in need.

well better best; wells welling welled

ADVERB **1.** If something goes well, it happens in a satisfactory way: *The test went well.* **2.** in a good, skilful, or pleasing way: *He draws well.* **3.** thoroughly and completely: *well established* **4.** kindly: *We treat our employees well.* **5.** If something may well or could well happen, it is likely to happen.

ADJECTIVE **6.** If you are well, you are healthy.

ADJECTIVE AND ADVERB **7.** You use *well* to emphasize an adjective, adverb, or phrase: *He was well aware of that.*

PHRASE **8.** As well means *also*: *She was a bus driver as well.* **9.** As well as means *in addition to*: *I have skates as well as skis.* **10.** If you say you **may as well** or **might as well** do something, you mean you will do it although you don't want to do it.

NOUN **11.** a hole drilled in the ground from which water, oil, or gas is obtained

VERB **12.** If tears well or well up, they appear in someone's eyes.

well-advised

ADJECTIVE sensible or wise: *You'd be well-advised to start studying early.*

well-balanced

ADJECTIVE sensible, sane, or properly balanced: *a well-balanced meal, a well-balanced individual*

well-being
NOUN Someone's well-being is that person's health and happiness.

well-earned
ADJECTIVE thoroughly deserved

well-heeled
ADJECTIVE *an informal word* wealthy

well-informed
ADJECTIVE having a great deal of knowledge about a subject or subjects

well-meaning
ADJECTIVE A well-meaning person tries to be helpful but is often unsuccessful.

well off
ADJECTIVE *an informal word* wealthy

well-to-do
ADJECTIVE wealthy

well-worn
ADJECTIVE **1.** A well-worn expression or saying has been used too often and has become boring. **2.** A well-worn object or piece of clothing has been used and worn so much that it looks old and shabby.

welt welts
NOUN a raised mark on someone's skin made by a blow from something like a whip or a stick

welter
NOUN A welter of things is a large number of them that happen or appear together in a state of confusion: *a welter of rumours*

wench wenches
NOUN *an old-fashioned or humorous word* a young woman or girl

wept the past tense and past participle of WEEP

were a past tense of BE

werewolf werewolves
NOUN In horror stories, a werewolf is a person who changes into a wolf.

west
NOUN **1.** The west is the direction in which you look to see the sun set. **2.** The west of a place or country is the part that is toward the west when you are in the centre: *British Columbia is in the west of Canada.* **3.** The West refers to the countries of North America and Europe.
ADVERB OR ADJECTIVE **4.** West means toward the west.
ADJECTIVE **5.** A west wind blows from the west.

westerly
ADJECTIVE Westerly means to or toward the west: *The Yukon is the most westerly territory.*

western westerns
ADJECTIVE **1.** in or from the west **2.** coming from or associated with the countries of North America and Europe: *Western cultures*
NOUN **3.** a novel or movie about life in the west of North America in the nineteenth century

westward
ADVERB Westward means toward the west: *He stared westward toward the horizon.*

wet wetter wettest; wets wetting wet
ADJECTIVE **1.** If something is wet, it is covered in water or another liquid. **2.** If the weather is wet, it is raining. **3.** If something such as paint is wet, it is not yet dry.
VERB **4.** To wet something is to put water or some other liquid over it. **5.** If people wet themselves or wet their beds, they urinate in their clothes or beds because they cannot control their bladders.
wetness NOUN

wetsuit wetsuits
NOUN a close-fitting rubber suit that a diver wears to keep his or her body warm

whack whacks whacking whacked
VERB If you whack someone or something, you hit that person or thing hard.

whale whales
NOUN a very large sea mammal that breathes out water through a hole on the top of its head

whaling
NOUN Whaling is the work of hunting and killing whales for oil or food.

wharf wharves
NOUN a platform beside a river, lake, or the sea, where ships load or unload

what
PRONOUN **1.** *What* is used in questions: *What time is it?* **2.** *What* is used in indirect questions and statements: *I don't know what you mean.* **3.** *What* can be used at the beginning of a clause to refer to something with a particular quality: *It is impossible to decide what is real and what is imaginary.*
ADJECTIVE **4.** *What* can be used at the beginning of a clause to show that you are talking about the whole amount that is available to you: *They try to save what money they can.* **5.** You say *what* to emphasize an opinion or reaction: *What nonsense!*
PHRASE **6.** You say **what about** at the beginning of a question when you are making a suggestion or offer: *What about a snack?*

whatever

ADJECTIVE OR PRONOUN **1.** You use *whatever* to refer to anything or everything of a particular type: *He said he would do whatever he could.* **2.** You use *whatever* when you do not know the precise nature of something: *Whatever it is, I don't like it.* ADVERB **3.** You use *whatever* to mean no matter what: *Whatever happens, you have to behave decently.* **4.** You use *whatever* to emphasize a negative statement or a question: *You have no proof whatever. Whatever is wrong with you?* INTERJECTION **5.** *an informal use* You use *whatever* to show that you have no interest in something: *Do you want to go to a movie? Whatever.*

whatsoever

ADVERB You use *whatsoever* to emphasize a negative statement: *I have no memory of it whatsoever.*

wheat

NOUN Wheat is a cereal plant grown for its grain, which is used to make flour.

wheel wheels wheeling wheeled

NOUN **1.** a circular object that turns on a rod attached to its centre. Wheels are fixed underneath vehicles so that they can move along. **2.** The wheel of a car is its steering wheel. VERB **3.** If you wheel something such as a cart, you push it. **4.** If someone or something wheels, that person or thing moves around in the shape of a circle: *She wheeled around to see what the noise was.*

wheelbarrow wheelbarrows

NOUN a small cart with a single wheel at the front, used for carrying things

wheelchair wheelchairs

NOUN a chair with wheels in which people who are injured or who have a disability can move around

wheeze wheezes wheezing wheezed

VERB If someone wheezes, that person breathes with difficulty, making a whistling sound, usually because he or she has a chest complaint such as asthma.
wheezy ADJECTIVE

whelk whelks

NOUN a snail-like shellfish with a strong shell and a soft, edible body

when

ADVERB **1.** You use *when* to ask what time something happened or will happen: *When are you leaving?* CONJUNCTION **2.** You use *when* to refer to a time in the past: *I met her when I was 16.*

3. You use *when* to introduce the reason for an opinion, comment, or question: *How did you pass the exam when you hadn't studied for it?* **4.** *When* is used to mean although: *He drives when he could walk.*

whence

ADVERB OR CONJUNCTION *an old-fashioned word* Whence means *from where.*

whenever

CONJUNCTION OR ADVERB Whenever means at any time, or every time that something happens: *I go to the movies whenever I can.*

where

ADVERB **1.** You use *where* to ask which place something is in, is coming from, or is going to: *Where is she?* CONJUNCTION, PRONOUN, OR ADVERB **2.** You use *where* when asking about or referring to something: *I hardly know where to begin.* CONJUNCTION **3.** You use *where* to refer to the place in which something is situated or happening: *I don't know where we are.* **4.** *Where* can introduce a clause that contrasts with the other part of the sentence: *A teacher will know each student's strengths, where a principal might not.*

whereabouts

NOUN **1.** The whereabouts of a person or thing is the place where that person or thing can be found. ADVERB **2.** You use *whereabouts* when you are asking more precisely where something is: *Whereabouts in Canada are you from?*

whereas

CONJUNCTION Whereas introduces a comment that contrasts with the other part of the sentence: *Her eyes are blue, whereas mine are hazel.*

whereby

PRONOUN *a formal word* Whereby means by which: *a new system whereby you get two report cards every term*

whereupon

CONJUNCTION *a formal word* Whereupon means at which point: *His enemies rejected his message, whereupon he tried again.*

wherever

CONJUNCTION **1.** *Wherever* means in every place or situation: *He heard the same thing wherever he went.* **2.** You use *wherever* to show that you do not know where a place or person is: *Go to the nearest police station, wherever that is.*

wherewithal

NOUN If you have the wherewithal to do something, you have enough money or other necessary resources to do it.

whet whets whetting whetted
PHRASE To **whet someone's appetite** for something means to increase that person's desire for it.

whether
CONJUNCTION You use *whether* when you are talking about two or more alternatives: *I don't know whether that's true or false.*

whey
NOUN Whey is the watery liquid that is separated from the curds in sour milk when cheese is made.

which
ADJECTIVE OR PRONOUN **1.** You use *which* to ask about alternatives or to refer to a choice between alternatives: *Which room are you in?*
PRONOUN **2.** *Which* at the beginning of a clause identifies the thing you are talking about or gives more information about it: *He went to the post office, which is next to the grocery store.*

whichever
ADJECTIVE OR PRONOUN You use *whichever* when you are talking about different alternatives or possibilities: *Make your pizzas round or square, whichever you prefer.*

whiff whiffs
NOUN **1.** a slight smell of something **2.** a slight sign or trace of something: *I caught a whiff of criticism in her remark.*

while whiles whiling whiled
CONJUNCTION **1.** If something happens while something else is happening, the two things happen at the same time. **2.** While also means but: *She had cold hands, while his were warm.*
NOUN **3.** a period of time: *a little while earlier*
PHRASE **4.** If an action or activity is **worth your while**, it will be helpful or useful to you if you do it.
while away
VERB **5.** If you while away the time in a particular way, you pass the time that way because you have nothing else to do.

whim whims
NOUN a sudden desire or change of mind

whimper whimpers whimpering whimpered
VERB **1.** When children or animals whimper, they make soft, feeble, unhappy sounds. **2.** If you whimper something, you say it in an unhappy or frightened way, as if you are about to cry.

whimsical
ADJECTIVE unusual and slightly playful: *an endearing, whimsical charm*

whine whines whining whined
VERB **1.** To whine is to make a long, high-pitched noise, especially one that sounds sad or unpleasant. **2.** If someone whines about something, that person complains about it in an annoying way.
NOUN **3.** A whine is the noise made by something or someone whining.

whinny whinnies whinnying whinnied
VERB When a horse whinnies, it neighs softly.

whip whips whipping whipped
NOUN **1.** a thin piece of leather or rope attached to a handle, which is used for hitting people or animals
VERB **2.** If you whip a person or an animal, you hit that person or animal with a whip. **3.** When the wind whips something, it strikes it. **4.** If you whip something out or off, you take it out or off very quickly: *She whipped off her glasses.* **5.** If you whip cream or eggs, you beat them until they are thick and frothy.
whip up
VERB **6.** If you whip something up, you prepare it or make it quickly: *He whipped up a meal for us after school.*

whiplash
NOUN a neck injury caused by your head suddenly jerking forward and then back again, for example in a car accident

whippet whippets
NOUN a small, thin dog used for racing

whir whirs whirring whirred
VERB **1.** When something such as a machine whirs, it makes a series of low sounds so fast that it sounds like one continuous sound.
NOUN **2.** the noise made by something whirring

whirl whirls whirling whirled
VERB **1.** When something whirls, or when you whirl it around, it turns around very fast.
NOUN **2.** You can refer to a lot of intense activity as a whirl of activity.

whirlpool whirlpools
NOUN a small, circular area in a river or the sea where the water is moving quickly around and around so that objects floating near it are pulled into its centre

whirlwind whirlwinds
NOUN **1.** a tall column of air that spins around and around very fast
ADJECTIVE **2.** more rapid than usual: *a whirlwind tour*

whisk whisks whisking whisked
VERB **1.** If you whisk someone or something somewhere, you take that person or thing there quickly: *We were whisked away into a*

Ww

private room. **2.** If you whisk eggs or cream, you rapidly stir air into them.
NOUN **3.** a kitchen tool used for quickly stirring air into eggs or cream

whisker whiskers
NOUN The whiskers of an animal such as a cat or mouse are the long, stiff hairs near its mouth.

whisky whiskies
NOUN Whisky is a strong alcoholic drink made from grain such as barley.

whisper whispers whispering whispered
VERB **1.** When you whisper, you talk to someone very quietly, using your breath and not your throat.
NOUN **2.** If you talk in a whisper, you whisper.

whistle whistles whistling whistled
VERB **1.** When you whistle a tune or whistle, you produce a clear musical sound by forcing your breath out between your lips.
2. If something whistles, it makes a loud, high sound: *The kettle whistled.*
NOUN **3.** A whistle is the sound something or someone makes when that person or thing whistles. **4.** a small instrument that you blow into to produce a whistling sound

whit
NOUN *a formal word* You say *not a whit* or *no whit* to emphasize that something is not the case at all: *The sick child is not a whit better.*

white whiter whitest; whites
NOUN OR ADJECTIVE **1.** White is the lightest possible colour. **2.** Someone who is white has pale skin and is usually of European origin.
ADJECTIVE **3.** If someone goes white, that person's face becomes very pale because he or she is afraid, shocked, or ill.
NOUN **4.** The white of an egg is the transparent liquid surrounding the yolk, which turns white when it is cooked.
whiteness NOUN

white-collar
ADJECTIVE White-collar workers work in offices rather than doing manual work: *Fraud is a white-collar crime.*

white lie white lies
NOUN a harmless lie, especially when told to prevent someone's feelings from being hurt

whitewash
NOUN **1.** Whitewash is a mixture of lime and water used for painting walls white.
2. an attempt to hide unpleasant facts: *The politician's speech was regarded as a whitewash.*

whither
ADVERB OR CONJUNCTION *an old-fashioned word* Whither means to what place: *Whither shall I wander?*

whittle whittles whittling whittled
VERB **1.** If you whittle a piece of wood, you shape it by shaving or cutting small pieces off it.
whittle away, whittle down
VERB **2.** To whittle away at something or to whittle it down means to make it smaller or less effective: *The 250 original competitors had been whittled down to 10 finalists.*

whiz whizzes whizzing whizzed
VERB *an informal word* If you whiz somewhere, you move to that place extremely quickly.

who
PRONOUN **1.** You use *who* when you are asking about someone's identity: *Who gave you that black eye?* **2.** Who at the beginning of a clause refers to the person or people you are talking about: *She is the one who runs marathons.*

> ⚠️ **HEADS UP**
>
> **Who, What, When, Where,** and **Why** are the 5 Ws—the questions that make a good news article.

whoa
INTERJECTION Whoa is a command used to slow down a horse, or to express surprise at something.

whoever
PRONOUN **1.** *Whoever* means the person who: *Whoever bought it for you has to return it.*
2. *Whoever* also means no matter who: *I pity him, whoever he is.* **3.** *Whoever* is used in questions to give emphasis to who: *Whoever thought of such a thing?*

whole wholes
ADJECTIVE **1.** indicating all of something: *Have the whole cake.*
NOUN **2.** the full amount of something: *the whole of Alberta*
ADVERB **3.** in one piece: *He swallowed it whole.*
PHRASE **4.** You use **as a whole** to emphasize that you are talking about all of something: *The country as a whole is in a very odd mood.* **5.** You say **on the whole** to mean that something is generally true: *On the whole, we should be glad they are gone.*
wholeness NOUN

Ww

wholehearted
ADJECTIVE enthusiastic and totally sincere: *wholehearted approval*
wholeheartedly ADVERB

wholesale
ADJECTIVE OR ADVERB **1.** Wholesale refers to the activity of buying goods cheaply in large quantities and selling them again, especially to stores: *We buy fruit and vegetables wholesale.*
ADJECTIVE **2.** Wholesale also means done to an excessive extent: *the wholesale destruction of wild plant species*
wholesaler NOUN

wholesome
ADJECTIVE positive and likely to improve your life, behaviour, or health: *a wholesome breakfast*

wholly
ADVERB completely

whom
PRONOUN Whom is the objective form of *who*: *my friends, two of whom are busy*

whoop whoops whooping whooped
VERB **1.** If you whoop, you shout loudly in a happy or excited way.
NOUN **2.** a loud cry of happiness or excitement: *whoops of delight*

whooping cough
NOUN Whooping cough is an acute infectious disease that makes people cough violently and produce a loud sound when they breathe.

whose
PRONOUN **1.** You use *whose* to ask to whom something belongs: *Whose pen is this?*
2. You use *whose* at the beginning of a clause that gives information about something relating or belonging to the thing or person you have just mentioned: *a person whose advice I respect*

> ⚠ **HEADS UP**
>
> Don't confuse **whose** and **who's**.
> **Whose** means *belonging to whom*.
> **Who's** is short for *who is*.

why
ADVERB OR PRONOUN You use *why* when you are asking or talking about the reason for something: *Why did you do it? He wondered why she suddenly looked happier.*

wick wicks
NOUN the cord in the middle of a candle, which you set alight

wicked
ADJECTIVE **1.** very bad: *a wicked thing to do*
2. mischievous in an amusing or attractive way: *a wicked sense of humour*
wickedly ADVERB
wickedness NOUN

wicker
ADJECTIVE A wicker basket or chair is made from twigs, canes, or reeds that have been woven together.

wicket wickets
NOUN a small window or opening used for activities like selling tickets. A wicket is often protected by a screen or grate.

wide wider widest
ADJECTIVE **1.** measuring a certain distance from one side to the other
2. If there is a wide variety, range, or selection of something, there are many different kinds of it: *a wide range of colours*
ADVERB **3.** If you open or spread something wide, you open it to its fullest extent.
widely ADVERB

Instead of **WIDE** try...

an **ample** bookcase
a **thick** tree trunk
a **baggy** sweater
a **open** meadow
broad shoulders
a **sweeping** view
an **extensive** tour
a **spacious** living room

wide-awake
ADJECTIVE completely awake

widen widens widening widened
VERB **1.** If something widens or if you widen it, it becomes bigger from one side to the other. **2.** You can say that something widens when it becomes greater in size or scope: *the opportunity to widen your horizons*

wide-ranging
ADJECTIVE extending over a variety of different things or over a large area: *a wide-ranging survey*

widespread
ADJECTIVE existing or happening over a large area or to a great extent: *the widespread use of chemicals*

widow widows
NOUN a woman whose husband has died

widowed
ADJECTIVE If someone is widowed, that person's husband or wife has died.

Ww

widower widowers
NOUN a man whose wife has died

width widths
NOUN The width of something is the distance from one side to the other.

wield wields wielding wielded
VERB **1.** If you wield a weapon or tool, you carry it and use it. **2.** If someone wields power, that person has it and is able to use it.

wife wives
NOUN A man's wife is the woman he is married to.

Wi-Fi
NOUN *a trademark* a system of accessing the Internet from machines such as laptop computers that aren't connected to a network by wires

wig wigs
NOUN a false head of hair worn to cover someone's own hair or to hide baldness

wiggle wiggles wiggling wiggled
VERB **1.** If you wiggle something, you move it up and down or from side to side with small, jerky movements.
NOUN **2.** a small jerky movement

wigwam wigwams
NOUN a dome-shaped hut or tent traditionally used by First Nations and Native American peoples, made by fastening mats, skins, or bark over a framework of poles

wiki wikis
NOUN a website (or page within one) that can be edited by anyone who looks it up on the Internet

wild wilder wildest; wilds
ADJECTIVE **1.** Wild animals, birds, and plants live and grow in natural surroundings and are not looked after by people. **2.** Wild land is natural and has not been cultivated: *wild areas of countryside* **3.** Wild weather or a wild sea is stormy and rough. **4.** Wild behaviour is excited and uncontrolled: *wild with joy* **5.** A wild idea or scheme is original and crazy.
NOUN **6.** The wild is a free and natural state of living: *These animals can only be found in the wild.* **7.** The wilds are remote areas where few people live, far away from towns.
wildly ADVERB

wilderness wildernesses
NOUN an area of natural land that is not cultivated

wildfire
NOUN If something spreads like wildfire, it spreads very quickly.

wild goose chase wild goose chases
NOUN a hopeless or useless search

wildlife
NOUN Wildlife means wild animals and birds.

Wild West
NOUN The Wild West was the western part of the United States when it was lawless and first being settled.

wiles
PLURAL NOUN Wiles are clever or crafty tricks used to persuade people to do something.

wilful
ADJECTIVE **1.** Wilful actions or attitudes are deliberate and often intended to hurt someone: *wilful damage* **2.** People who are wilful are stubborn and determined to get their own way: *a wilful little boy*
wilfully ADVERB

will
VERB **1.** You use *will* to form the future tense: *My mother will be quite annoyed.* **2.** You use *will* to say that you intend to do something: *I will not deceive you.* **3.** You use *will* when inviting someone to do or have something: *Will you have another coffee?* **4.** You use *will* when asking or telling someone to do something: *Will you do me a favour? You will do as I say.* **5.** You use *will* to say that you are assuming something to be the case: *They will be long gone by the time you wake up.*

will wills willing willed
VERB **1.** If you will something to happen, you try to make it happen by mental effort: *I willed the person in front of me to turn around.* **2.** If you will something to someone, you leave it to that person when you die: *Her uncle's farm is willed to her.*
NOUN **3.** Will is the determination to do something: *the will to win* **4.** If something is the will of a person or group, that person or group wants it to happen: *the will of the people* **5.** a legal document in which you say what you want to happen to your money and property when you die
PHRASE **6.** If you can do something **at will**, you can do it whenever or however you want.

willing
ADJECTIVE ready and eager to do something: *a willing helper*
willingly ADVERB
willingness NOUN

willow willows
NOUN A willow or willow tree is a tree with long, thin branches and narrow leaves that often grows near water.

Ww

wilt wilts wilting wilted

VERB **1.** If a plant wilts, it droops because it needs more water or is dying. **2.** If someone wilts, that person gradually loses strength or confidence: *The player visibly wilted under pressure.*

wily wilier wiliest

ADJECTIVE clever and cunning

wimp wimps

NOUN *an informal word* someone who is weak-willed and timid

win wins winning won

VERB **1.** If you win a fight, game, or argument, you defeat your opponent. **2.** If you win something, you succeed in obtaining it.

NOUN **3.** a victory in a game or contest

win over

VERB **4.** If you win someone over, you persuade that person to support you.

wince winces wincing winced

VERB When you wince, the muscles of your face tighten suddenly because of pain, fear, or distress.

winch winches winching winched

NOUN **1.** a machine used to lift heavy objects. It consists of a cylinder around which a rope or chain is wound.

VERB **2.** If you winch an object somewhere, you lift, lower, or pull it using a winch.

wind winds

NOUN **1.** a current of air moving across the earth's surface **2.** Your wind is the ability to breathe easily: *After the race, she took a while to recover her wind.* **3.** Wind is air swallowed with food or drink, or gas produced in your stomach, which causes discomfort. **4.** The wind section of an orchestra is the group of musicians who play wind instruments.

wind winds winding wound

VERB **1.** If a road or river winds in a particular direction, it twists and turns in that direction. **2.** When you wind something around something else, you wrap it around it several times. **3.** When you wind a clock or machine or wind it up, you turn a key or handle several times to make it work.

wind up

VERB **4.** When you wind up something such as an activity, you finish it. **5.** If you wind up in a particular place, you end up there.

windfall windfalls

NOUN a sum of money that you receive unexpectedly

wind instrument wind instruments

NOUN an instrument you play by using your breath, for example a flute, an oboe, or a trumpet

windmill windmills

NOUN a machine for grinding grain, generating electricity, or pumping water. It is driven by vanes or sails turned by the wind.

window windows

NOUN a space in a wall or in the side of a vehicle, usually with glass in it so that light can pass through and people can see in or out

window box window boxes

NOUN a long, narrow container on a windowsill in which plants are grown

windowsill windowsills

NOUN a ledge along the bottom of a window, either on the inside or outside of a building

windpipe windpipes

NOUN the tube that carries air into your lungs when you breathe

windshield windshields

NOUN the glass at the front of a vehicle through which the driver looks

windsurfing

NOUN Windsurfing is the sport of moving along the surface of a body of water standing on a board with a sail on it.

windswept

ADJECTIVE A windswept place is exposed to strong winds: *a windswept beach*

KNOWING WORDS: IDIOMS

BE WORD SHARP!

Idioms add colour to language by playing with the meanings of words.

wind moving air

get a second wind get a new burst of energy

get wind of hear about

in the wind likely to happen soon

run like the wind run very fast

throw caution to the wind take a risk

NEL

Ww

windy windier windiest

ADJECTIVE If it is windy, there is a lot of wind.

wine wines

NOUN Wine is the red or white alcoholic drink that is normally made from grapes.

wing wings

NOUN **1.** A bird's or insect's wings are the parts of its body that it uses for flying. **2.** An airplane's wings are the long, flat parts on each side that support it while it is in the air. **3.** A wing of a building is a part that sticks out from the main part or that has been added later. **4.** A wing of an organization, especially a political party, is a group within it that has a particular role or particular beliefs: *the left wing of the party*

PLURAL NOUN **5.** The wings in a theatre are the sides of the stage that are hidden from the audience.

winged ADJECTIVE

wink winks winking winked

VERB **1.** When you wink, you close one eye briefly, often as a signal that something is a joke or a secret.

NOUN **2.** the closing of your eye when you wink

winner winners

NOUN The winner of a prize, race, or competition is the person or thing that wins it.

winning winnings

ADJECTIVE **1.** The winning team or entry in a competition is the one that has won. **2.** attractive and charming: *a winning smile*

PLURAL NOUN **3.** Your winnings are what you have won in a competition or by gambling.

winter winters

NOUN Winter is the season between autumn and spring.

wintry

ADJECTIVE Something wintry has features that are typical of winter: *the wintry dawn*

wipe wipes wiping wiped

VERB **1.** If you wipe something, you rub its surface lightly to remove dirt or liquid. **2.** If you wipe dirt or liquid off something, you remove it using a cloth or your hands: *He wiped the tears from his eyes.*

wipe out

VERB **3.** To wipe out something is to destroy it completely.

wire wires wiring wired

NOUN **1.** Wire is metal in the form of a long, thin, flexible thread, which can be used to make or fasten things or to conduct an electric current.

VERB **2.** If you wire one thing to another, you fasten them together using wire. **3.** If you wire something or wire it up, you connect it so that electricity can pass through it.

wired ADJECTIVE

wireless

ADJECTIVE to do with devices or systems that need no wires, such as cellphones: *wireless communication*

wiring

NOUN The wiring in a building is the system of wires that supplies electricity to the rooms.

wiry wirier wiriest

ADJECTIVE **1.** Wiry people are thin but have strong muscles. **2.** Wiry things are stiff and rough to the touch: *wiry hair*

wisdom

NOUN **1.** Wisdom is the ability to use experience and knowledge in order to make sensible decisions or judgments. **2.** If you talk about the wisdom of an action or a decision, you are talking about how sensible it is.

wisdom tooth wisdom teeth

NOUN Your wisdom teeth are the four molar teeth at the back of your mouth, which grow in much later than other teeth.

wise wiser wisest

ADJECTIVE **1.** Someone who is wise can use his or her experience and knowledge to make sensible decisions and judgments.

PHRASE **2.** If you say that someone or some people are **none the wiser** or **no wiser**, you mean that they are unaware of a secret or know no more about something than they did before: *I replaced the broken window and they were none the wiser. I left the conference none the wiser.*

wisecrack wisecracks

NOUN a clever remark, often unkind, but intended to be amusing

wish wishes wishing wished

NOUN **1.** a longing or desire for something, often something difficult to achieve or obtain **2.** something desired or wanted: *That wish came true two years later.*

PLURAL NOUN **3.** Good wishes are expressions of hope that someone will be happy or successful: *best wishes on your birthday*

VERB **4.** If you wish to do something, you want to do it: *We wished to return.* **5.** If you wish something were the case, you would like it to be the case, but know it is not very likely: *I wish I were tall.*

wishbone wishbones

NOUN a V-shaped bone in the breast of most birds

Ww

wishful thinking

NOUN If someone's hope or wish is wishful thinking, it is unlikely to come true.

wishy-washy

ADJECTIVE *an informal word* If a person or a person's ideas are wishy-washy, then that person or his or her ideas are not firm or clear: *wishy-washy reasons*

wisp wisps

NOUN **1.** A wisp of grass or hair is a small, thin, untidy bunch of it. **2.** A wisp of smoke is a long, thin streak of it.

wispy ADJECTIVE

wistful

ADJECTIVE sadly thinking about something, especially something you want but cannot have: *A wistful look came into her eyes.*

wistfully ADVERB

wit wits

NOUN **1.** Wit is the ability to use words or ideas in an amusing and clever way. **2.** Wit means sense: *They haven't got the wit to realize what they're doing.*

PLURAL NOUN **3.** Your wits are the ability to think and act quickly in a difficult situation: *She kept her wits about her during the emergency.*

PHRASE **4.** If you are **at your wit's end**, you are so worried and exhausted by problems or difficulties that you do not know what to do.

witch witches

NOUN a woman claimed to have magic powers and to be able to use them for good or evil

witchcraft

NOUN Witchcraft is the supposed skill or art of using magic powers, especially evil ones.

with

PREPOSITION **1.** *With someone means in that person's company: He was at home with me.* **2.** *With is used to show who your opponent is in a fight or competition: next week's game with the Senators* **3.** *With can mean using or having: Apply the colour with a brush. He's the man with a moustache.* **4.** *With is used to show how someone does something or how that person feels: She looked at him with hatred.* **5.** *With can mean concerning: a problem with the telephone bill* **6.** *With is used to show support: Are you with us or against us?*

withdraw withdraws withdrawing withdrew withdrawn

VERB **1.** If you withdraw something, you remove it or take it out: *She withdrew the money from her bank.* **2.** If you withdraw to another place, you leave where you are and

go there: *He withdrew to his bedroom.* **3.** If you withdraw from an activity, you back out of it: *They withdrew from the science fair.*

withdrawal withdrawals

NOUN **1.** The withdrawal of something is the act of taking it away: *the withdrawal of troops, the withdrawal of support* **2.** The withdrawal of a statement is the act of saying formally that you wish to change or deny it. **3.** an amount of money you take from your bank account

withdrawal symptoms

PLURAL NOUN Withdrawal symptoms are the unpleasant effects suffered by someone who has suddenly stopped taking a substance to which he or she is addicted.

withdrawn

1. the past participle of WITHDRAW

ADJECTIVE **2.** unusually shy or quiet

wither withers withering withered

VERB **1.** When something withers or withers away, it becomes weaker until it no longer exists. **2.** If a plant withers, it wilts or shrivels up and dies.

withering

ADJECTIVE A withering look or remark makes you feel ashamed, stupid, or inferior.

withhold withholds withholding withheld

VERB *a formal word* If you withhold something that someone wants, you do not let that person have it.

within

PREPOSITION OR ADVERB **1.** *Within means in or inside.*

PREPOSITION **2.** *Within can mean not going beyond certain limits: Stay within the budget.* **3.** *Within can mean before a period of time has passed: You must write back within 14 days.*

without

PREPOSITION **1.** *Without means not having, feeling, or showing: She looked on without emotion.* **2.** *Without can mean not using: You can't get in without a key.* **3.** *Without can mean not in someone's company: He went without me.* **4.** *Without can indicate that something does not happen when there is a chance it will happen: He signalled the ship, again without response.*

withstand withstands withstanding withstood

VERB When someone or something withstands a force or action, that person or thing survives it or does not give in to it: *ships designed to withstand the North Atlantic winter*

witness witnesses witnessing witnessed

NOUN **1.** someone who has seen an event

Ww

such as an accident and can describe what happened **2.** someone who appears in a court of law to say what he or she knows about a crime or other event **3.** someone who writes his or her name on a document to show that another person's signature on the document is his or her real signature
VERB **4.** *a formal use* If you witness an event, you see it.

witticism witticisms
NOUN a clever and amusing remark or joke

witty wittier wittiest
ADJECTIVE amusing in a clever way: *this witty novel*
wittily ADVERB

wives the plural of WIFE

wizard wizards
NOUN a man in a fantasy story who has magic powers

wizened
ADJECTIVE having a wrinkled skin, especially with age: *a wizened old man*

WMD an abbreviation for *weapon(s) of mass destruction*

wobble wobbles wobbling wobbled
VERB If something wobbles, it shakes or moves from side to side because it is loose or unsteady: *a cyclist who wobbled into my path*

wobbly
ADJECTIVE unsteady: *a wobbly table*

woe woes *a literary or poetic word*
NOUN **1.** Woe is great unhappiness or sorrow.
PLURAL NOUN **2.** Someone's woes are that person's problems or misfortunes.

wok woks
NOUN a large, bowl-shaped metal pan used for Chinese-style cooking

woke the past tense of WAKE

woken the past participle of WAKE

wolf wolves; wolfs wolfing wolfed
NOUN **1.** a wild animal related to the dog. Wolves hunt in packs and kill other animals for food.
VERB **2.** *an informal use* If you wolf food or wolf it down, you eat it up quickly and greedily.

woman women
NOUN **1.** an adult female human being
2. Woman can refer to women in general: *the modern woman*

womanhood
NOUN Womanhood is the state of being a woman rather than a girl: *on the verge of womanhood*

womb wombs
NOUN A female's womb is the part inside her body where offspring are conceived and developed before birth.

wombat wombats
NOUN a short-legged, furry Australian animal that eats plants

wonder wonders wondering wondered
VERB **1.** If you wonder about something, you think about it with curiosity or doubt. **2.** If you wonder at something, you are surprised and amazed at it: *He wondered at the view.*
NOUN **3.** Wonder is a feeling of surprise and amazement. **4.** something or someone that amazes people: *the wonders of science*

wonderful
ADJECTIVE **1.** making you feel very happy and pleased: *It was wonderful to meet them.* **2.** very impressive: *Nature is a wonderful thing.*
wonderfully ADVERB

wondrous
ADJECTIVE *a literary or poetic word* amazing and impressive

wont
ADJECTIVE *an old-fashioned word* If someone is wont to do something, that person does it often: *a gesture he was wont to use while talking*

woo woos wooing wooed
VERB **1.** If you woo people, you try to get them to help or support you: *attempts to woo young voters* **2.** *an old-fashioned use* When someone woos another person, that person makes an effort to try to gain the other person's affection.

wood woods
NOUN **1.** Wood is the substance that forms the trunks and branches of trees.
PLURAL NOUN **2.** Woods are a large area of trees growing near each other.

wooded
ADJECTIVE covered in trees: *a wooded area nearby*

wooden
ADJECTIVE made of wood: *a wooden box*

woodland woodlands
NOUN Woodland is land that is mostly covered with trees.

woodpecker woodpeckers
NOUN a bird with a long, sharp beak, which it uses to drill holes into trees to find insects

woodwind woodwinds
NOUN Woodwinds are musical instruments such as flutes, oboes, clarinets, and bassoons, which were originally made of wood. They are played by being blown into.

⚠ **HEADS UP** The word **wizened** is pronounced WIZ-uhnd.

Ww

woodwork
NOUN **1.** Woodwork refers to the parts of a house, such as stairs, doors, or window frames, that are made of wood. **2.** Woodwork is the craft or skill of making things out of wood.

woodworm woodworm
NOUN **1.** Woodworm are the larvae of a kind of beetle. They make holes in wood by feeding on it. **2.** Woodworm is damage caused to wood by woodworm making holes in it.

woody woodier woodiest
ADJECTIVE **1.** Woody plants have hard, tough stems. **2.** A woody area has a lot of trees in it.

woof woofs
NOUN the sound that a dog makes when it barks

wool wools
NOUN **1.** Wool is the hair that grows on sheep and some other animals. **2.** Wool is also yarn spun from the wool of animals that is used to knit, weave, and make things such as clothes, blankets, and carpets.

woollen woollens
ADJECTIVE **1.** made from wool
NOUN **2.** Woollens are clothes made of wool.

woolly woollier woolliest
ADJECTIVE **1.** made of wool or looking like wool: *a woolly hat* **2.** If you describe people or their thoughts as woolly, you mean that they seem confused and unclear.

word words wording worded
NOUN **1.** a single unit of language in speech or writing that has a meaning **2.** a remark: *a word of praise* **3.** a brief conversation: *Could I have a word with you?* **4.** A word can also be a message: *The word is that we will be snowed in.* **5.** Your word is a promise: *He gave me his word.* **6.** The word can be a command: *I gave the word to start.*
PLURAL NOUN **7.** The words of a play or song are the spoken or sung text.

VERB **8.** When you word something, you choose your words in order to express your ideas accurately or acceptably: *the best way to word our invitations*

wording
NOUN The wording of a piece of writing or a speech is the words used in it, especially when these words have been carefully chosen to have a certain effect.

word processor word processors
NOUN a computer program designed to create documents using various features such as editing, formatting, and spell-checking

work works working worked
VERB **1.** People who work have a job that they are paid to do: *My mother works for a national newspaper.* **2.** When you work, you do the tasks that your job involves. **3.** To work the land is to cultivate it. **4.** If someone works a machine, that person controls or operates it. **5.** If a machine works, it operates properly and effectively: *The radio doesn't work.* **6.** If something such as an idea or a system works, it is successful: *The plan worked well.* **7.** If something works its way into a particular position, it gradually moves there: *The stitches had worked loose.*
NOUN **8.** People who have work have a job that they are paid to do: *She's trying to find work.* **9.** Work is the tasks that have to be done. **10.** something done or made: *a work of art* **11.** In physics, work is the transfer of energy. It is calculated by multiplying the force exerted by the distance moved. Work is measured in joules.
PLURAL NOUN **12.** A works is a place where something is made by an industrial process: *the old steel works*

work out
VERB **13.** If you work out a problem, you find the solution. **14.** If a situation works out in a particular way, it happens in that way. **15.** If you work out, you take part in physical exercise, especially at a gym.

KNOWING WORDS: IDIOMS

BE WORD SHARP!

Idioms add colour to language by playing with the meanings of words.

word a single unit of language

eat your words take back what you have said

in a word briefly

say the word give a signal to do something

spread the word tell other people a message

the last word something that ends a discussion

NEL

Ww

work up

VERB **16.** If you work up to something, you gradually progress toward it. **17.** If you work yourself up or work someone else up, you make yourself or the other person very upset or excited about something.

worked up ADJECTIVE

workable

ADJECTIVE Something workable can operate successfully or can be used for a particular purpose: *We need a workable solution. This plan simply isn't workable.*

workaholic workaholics

NOUN a person who finds it difficult to stop working and do other things

worker workers

NOUN a person employed in a particular industry or business: *a farm worker*

workforce workforces

NOUN The workforce is all the people who work in a particular place.

working workings

ADJECTIVE **1.** Working people have jobs that they are paid to do. **2.** Working can mean related to, used for, or suitable for work: *the working week, working conditions* **3.** Working can mean sufficient to be useful or to achieve what is required: *a working knowledge of French* PLURAL NOUN **4.** The workings of a piece of equipment, an organization, or a system are the ways in which it operates: *the workings of the provincial government*

working class working classes

NOUN The working class or working classes are the group of people in society who do jobs that involve physical rather than intellectual skills.

workload workloads

NOUN the amount of work that a person or a machine has to do

workman workmen

NOUN a man whose job involves using physical rather than intellectual skills or a person who is skilled in a trade or craft

workmanship

NOUN Workmanship is the degree of skill with which something is made or a job is completed.

workout workouts

NOUN a session of physical exercise or training

workplace

NOUN Your workplace is the building or company where you work.

workshop workshops

NOUN **1.** a room or building that contains tools or machinery used for making or repairing things: *a furniture-building workshop* **2.** a period of discussion or practical work in which a group of people learn about a particular subject: *a theatre workshop*

world worlds

NOUN **1.** The world is Earth, the planet we live on. **2.** You can use *world* to refer to people generally: *The eyes of the world are upon me.* **3.** Someone's world is the life that person leads and the things that person experiences: *We come from different worlds.* **4.** A world is a division or section of the earth, its history, or its people, such as the French-speaking world, or the ancient world. **5.** A particular world is a field of activity and the people involved in it: *the world of football* ADJECTIVE **6.** *World* is used to describe someone or something that is one of the best or most important of its kind: *a world power* PHRASE **7.** If you **think the world of** someone, you like or admire that person very much.

worldly worldlier worldliest

ADJECTIVE **1.** relating to the ordinary activities of life rather than spiritual things: *worldly pleasures* **2.** experienced and knowledgeable about life

world war world wars

NOUN a war that involves countries all over the world

worldwide

ADJECTIVE throughout the world: *a worldwide increase in skin cancers*

World Wide Web

NOUN The World Wide Web is a system on the Internet that people use to access stored, interlinked documents by using a computer.

worm worms worming wormed

NOUN **1.** a small, thin animal without bones or legs that lives in the soil or inside other creatures **2.** an insect such as a beetle or moth at a very early stage in its life **3.** a computer program that makes many copies of itself within a network, usually harming the system VERB **4.** If you worm an animal, you give it medicine in order to kill the worms that are living as parasites in its intestines.

worm out

VERB **5.** If you worm information out of someone, you gradually persuade that person to give you it.

Ww

worn

1. Worn is the past participle of WEAR. ADJECTIVE **2.** damaged or thin because of long use **3.** looking old or exhausted: *She looks frail and worn.*

worn out

ADJECTIVE **1.** used until it is too damaged to be of further use: *Those shoes are worn out. He wore a worn-out sweater.* **2.** extremely tired: *I was worn out after the drive.*

worried

ADJECTIVE unhappy and anxious about a problem or about something unpleasant that might happen

worry worries worrying worried

VERB **1.** If you worry, you feel anxious and fearful about a problem or about something unpleasant that might happen. **2.** If something worries you, it causes you to feel uneasy or fearful: *a question that had worried her all her life* **3.** If you worry someone with a problem, you disturb or bother that person by telling him or her about it: *She didn't want to worry the children with this.*

NOUN **4.** Worry is a feeling of unhappiness and unease caused by a problem or by thinking of something unpleasant that might happen: *the major source of worry* **5.** a person or thing that causes you to feel anxious or uneasy: *That bully is the least of our worries.*

worrying ADJECTIVE

worse

ADJECTIVE OR ADVERB **1.** Worse is the comparative form of **bad** and **badly**. **2.** If someone who is ill gets worse, that person becomes sicker than before.

PHRASE **3.** If someone or something is **none the worse** for something, that person or thing has not been harmed by it: *He appeared none the worse for the accident.*

worsen worsens worsening worsened

VERB If a situation worsens, it becomes more difficult or unpleasant: *My relationship with my best friend worsened.*

worse off

ADJECTIVE If you are worse off, you have less money or are in a more unpleasant situation than before: *There are people much worse off than me.*

worship worships worshipping worshipped

VERB **1.** If you worship a god, you show your love and respect for that god by praying or performing other religious acts. **2.** If you worship someone or something, you love or admire that person or thing very much.

NOUN **3.** Worship is the feeling of respect, love, or admiration you feel for something.

worshipper NOUN

worst

ADJECTIVE OR ADVERB Worst is the superlative of **bad** and **badly**.

worth

ADJECTIVE **1.** If something is worth a sum of money, it has that value: *a house worth 250 000 dollars* **2.** If something is worth doing, it deserves to be done.

NOUN **3.** A particular amount of money's worth of something is the quantity of it that you can buy for that money: *five dollars' worth of postage stamps* **4.** Someone's worth is the value or usefulness that person is considered to have.

worthless

ADJECTIVE having no real value or use: *a worthless piece of junk*

worthwhile

ADJECTIVE important enough to justify the time, money, or effort spent on it: *a worthwhile endeavour*

worthy worthier worthiest

ADJECTIVE If someone is worthy of something, that person deserves it: *a worthy champion*

would

VERB **1.** You use *would* to say what someone thought was going to happen: *We were sure it would be a success.* **2.** You use *would* when you are referring to the result or effect of a possible situation: *If you can help, I would appreciate it.* **3.** You use *would* when referring to someone's willingness to do something: *I wouldn't change places with him if you paid me.* **4.** You use *would* in polite questions: *Would you like some lunch?*

would-be

ADJECTIVE wanting to be or claiming to be: *a would-be pop singer*

wound wounds wounding wounded

NOUN **1.** an injury to part of your body, especially a cut to your skin

VERB **2.** If someone wounds you, that person damages your body using a weapon. **3.** If you are wounded by what someone says or does, your feelings are hurt.

wounded ADJECTIVE

wow

INTERJECTION *Wow* is an expression of admiration or surprise.

wrangle wrangles wrangling wrangled

VERB **1.** If you wrangle with someone, you argue noisily or angrily.

NOUN **2.** an argument that is difficult to settle

wrangling NOUN

Ww

wrap wraps wrapping wrapped

VERB **1.** If you wrap something or wrap something up, you fold a piece of paper or cloth tightly around it to cover or enclose it. **2.** If you wrap paper or cloth around something, you put or fold the paper around it. **3.** If you wrap your arms, fingers, or legs around something, you coil them around it. PHRASE **4.** If you are **wrapped up in** a person or thing, you give that person or thing all your attention.

wrap up

VERB **5.** If you wrap up, you put warm clothes on.

> ⚠ **HEADS UP**
>
> There are many words that begin with **wr-**: *wreck, wring, write*. In all of them, the *w* is silent.

wrapper wrappers

NOUN a piece of paper, plastic, or foil that covers and protects something that you buy: *candy wrappers*

wrapping wrappings

NOUN Wrapping is the material used to cover and protect something.

wrath

NOUN *a literary or poetic word* Wrath is great anger: *the wrath of the entire town*

wreak wreaks wreaking wreaked

VERB To wreak havoc or damage is to cause it.

wreath wreaths

NOUN an arrangement of flowers, leaves, or stems in the shape of a circle that is used as a decoration or placed on a grave as a sign of remembrance for the dead person

wreck wrecks wrecking wrecked

VERB **1.** If someone wrecks something, that person breaks it, destroys it, or spoils it completely. **2.** If a ship is wrecked, it has been so badly damaged that it can no longer sail. NOUN **3.** a vehicle that has been badly damaged in an accident **4.** If you say someone is a wreck, you mean that person is in a very poor physical or mental state of health and cannot cope with life.

wrecked ADJECTIVE

wreckage

NOUN Wreckage is what remains after something has been badly damaged or destroyed.

wren wrens

NOUN a small brown songbird

wrench wrenches wrenching wrenched

VERB **1.** If you wrench something, you give it a sudden and violent twist or pull: *She wrenched open the door.* **2.** If you wrench a limb or a joint, you twist and injure it. NOUN **3.** a metal tool with parts that can be adjusted to fit around nuts or bolts to loosen or tighten them **4.** a painful parting from someone or something

wrest wrests wresting wrested

VERB *a formal word* If you wrest something from someone else you take it from that person violently or with effort: *to try and wrest control of the government*

wrestle wrestles wrestling wrestled

VERB **1.** If you wrestle someone or wrestle with someone, you fight that person by holding or throwing, but not hitting, him or her. **2.** When you wrestle with a problem, you try to deal with it.

wrestler NOUN

wrestling

NOUN Wrestling is a sport in which two people fight and try to win by throwing or holding their opponent on the ground.

wretch wretches

NOUN *an old-fashioned word* someone who is thought to be bad or very unfortunate

wretched

ADJECTIVE **1.** very unhappy or unfortunate: *a wretched childhood* **2.** *an informal use* You use *wretched* to describe something or someone you feel angry about or dislike: *The wretched weather is going to spoil our day at the lake.*

wriggle wriggles wriggling wriggled

VERB **1.** If someone wriggles, that person twists and turns his or her body or a part of it using quick movements: *My brother always wriggles when he is restless.* **2.** If you wriggle somewhere, you move there by twisting and turning: *The snake wriggled across the road.*

wriggly ADJECTIVE

wring wrings wringing wrung

VERB **1.** When you wring a wet cloth or wring it out, you squeeze the water out of it by twisting it. **2.** If you wring your hands, you hold them together and twist and turn them as though you were washing your hands, usually because you are worried, nervous, or upset. **3.** If someone wrings an animal's neck, such as a bird, that person kills the animal by twisting and breaking its neck.

wrinkle wrinkles wrinkling wrinkled

NOUN **1.** Wrinkles are lines or folds in something, especially someone's skin as that

Ww

person grows old.

VERB **2.** If something wrinkles, folds or lines develop on it: *This fabric will not wrinkle.*

3. When you wrinkle your nose, forehead, or eyes, you tighten the muscles in your face so that the skin folds into lines.

wrinkled ADJECTIVE

wrinkly ADJECTIVE

wrist wrists

NOUN the part of your body between your hand and your arm that bends when you move your hand

writ writs

NOUN *a formal word* a legal document that orders a person to do or not to do a particular thing

write writes writing wrote written

VERB **1.** When you write something, you use a pen or pencil to form letters, words, or numbers on a surface. **2.** If you write something such as a poem, a book, or a piece of music, you create it. **3.** When you write to someone or write someone a letter, you express your feelings for that person in writing. **4.** When someone writes something such as a cheque, that person puts the necessary information on it and signs it. **5.** When you write data, you transfer it to a computer's memory.

write down

VERB If you write something down, you record it on a piece of paper.

write up

VERB If you write up something, you write a full account of it, often using notes that you have made.

writer writers

NOUN **1.** a person who writes books, stories, or articles as a job **2.** The writer of something is the person who wrote it.

writhe writhes writhing writhed

VERB If you writhe, you twist and turn your body, often because you are in pain.

writing writings

NOUN **1.** Writing is something that has been written or printed: *She wanted to get his promise in writing.* **2.** Your writing is the way you write with a pen or pencil.

3. Writing is also a piece of written work, especially the style of language used: *witty writing* **4.** An author's writings are his or her written works.

writing process

NOUN the stages involved in creating a piece of writing. They include brainstorming, drafting, revising, editing, proofreading, and publishing.

written

1. Written is the past participle of WRITE.

ADJECTIVE **2.** taken down in writing: *a written agreement*

wrong wrongs wronging wronged

ADJECTIVE **1.** unsatisfactory, or not working properly: *There was something wrong with the car.* **2.** not correct or truthful: *the wrong answer* **3.** bad or immoral: *It is wrong to kill people.*

NOUN **4.** an unjust action or situation: *the wrongs of the war*

VERB **5.** If someone wrongs you, that person treats you in an unfair or unjust way.

wrongly ADVERB

wrongful

ADJECTIVE A wrongful act is regarded as illegal, unfair, or immoral: *wrongful imprisonment*

wrought iron

NOUN Wrought iron is a pure type of iron that is formed into decorative shapes.

wry

ADJECTIVE A wry expression shows that you find a situation slightly amusing because you know more about it than other people.

wryly ADVERB

SPELL-CHECK THIS!

A computer's spell-check won't catch wrong **homophones** (words that are spelled differently but sound the same).

I stared at the paper, not knowing what to rite.

In this sentence, **rite** should be **write**. Write means *put on paper*. A **rite** is a ceremony.

NEL

Xx

x

1. The letter X is used to represent the name of an unknown or secret person or place: *The victim was referred to as Mr. X throughout Tuesday's court proceedings.* **2.** People sometimes write *X* on a map to mark a precise position. **3.** The letter *x* is used to represent a kiss at the bottom of a letter, a vote on a ballot paper, or the signature of someone who cannot write.

xenophobia

NOUN a fear or strong dislike of people from other countries

xenophobic ADJECTIVE

Xerox Xeroxes

NOUN *a trademark* a machine that makes photographic copies of sheets of paper with writing or printing on them; also a copy made by a Xerox machine

Xmas

NOUN *an informal word* Xmas is a shortened way to write Christmas.

X-ray X-rays X-raying X-rayed

NOUN **1.** a stream of radiation of very short wavelength that can pass through some solid materials. X-rays are used by doctors to examine the bones or organs inside a person's body. **2.** a picture made by sending X-rays through someone's body in order to examine the inside of it

VERB **3.** If you are X-rayed, a picture is made of the inside of your body by passing X-rays through it.

xylem

NOUN In botany, xylem is a plant tissue that conducts water and mineral salts from the roots and carries them through the plant. It forms the wood in trees and shrubs.

xylophone xylophones

NOUN a musical instrument made of a row of wooden bars of different lengths. It is played by hitting the bars with special hammers.

Xx

KNOWING WORDS: WORD HISTORY

BE WORD SHARP!

Words are like living things. They grow and change.

The **xylophone** was first created long ago in southeast Asia. After that, it became popular in Africa and central Europe, where it was used by amateur musicians. Though it was never connected to Greece, it got its name from the European tradition of naming things with Latin or Greek words. In Greek, **xylo** means *wood*, and **phone** means *sound*.

⚠ **HEADS UP** The word **xylem** is pronounced ZIGH-luhm.

Yy

-y

SUFFIX **1.** The suffix -y means *full of* or *with the quality of*: *watery* **2.** The suffix -y also means *a state, condition, or quality*: *jealousy, victory*

yacht yachts

NOUN a boat with sails or an engine, used for racing or for pleasure trips

yachting

NOUN Yachting is the sport or activity of sailing a yacht.

yachtsman yachtsmen

NOUN a person who sails a yacht

yak yaks

NOUN a type of long-haired ox with long horns, used mainly in Tibet as a pack animal and for its milk, meat, and hide

yam yams

NOUN A yam or sweet potato is a root vegetable that grows in tropical regions.

yank yanks yanking yanked

VERB **1.** If you yank something, you pull or jerk it suddenly with a lot of force.
NOUN **2.** a sudden, hard pull

yap yaps yapping yapped

VERB If a dog yaps, it barks with a high-pitched sound.

yard yards

NOUN **1.** a nonmetric unit of length equal to about 91.4 centimetres **2.** a piece of ground near or around a house or other building **3.** an enclosed area that is usually next to a building and is often used for a particular purpose: *a ship repair yard, a junkyard*

yardstick yardsticks

NOUN someone or something you use as a standard against which to judge other people or things: *High grades are not the only yardstick of success in school.*

yarn yarns

NOUN **1.** Yarn is thread used for knitting or making cloth. **2.** *an informal use* a story that someone tells, often with invented details to make it more interesting or exciting: *fishermen's yarns*

yawn yawns yawning yawned

VERB When you yawn, you open your mouth wide and take in more air than usual. You often yawn when you are tired or bored.

yawning

ADJECTIVE A yawning gap or opening is very wide.

ye

PRONOUN **1.** Ye is an old word used to mean *you*.
ADJECTIVE **2.** Ye is also an old spelling of *the*.

yeah

INTERJECTION *an informal word* Yeah means *yes*.

year years

NOUN **1.** a period of 12 months or 365 days (366 days in a leap year), which is the time taken for Earth to travel once around the sun **2.** a period of 12 consecutive months, not always January to December, on which administration or organization is based: *the current financial year*
PHRASE **3.** If something happens **year in, year out**, it happens every year: *a tradition kept up year in, year out*
yearly ADJECTIVE OR ADVERB

yearling yearlings

NOUN an animal between one and two years old

KNOWING WORDS: WORD BUILDING

BE WORD SHARP!

You can create new words by adding prefixes and suffixes to a base word.

-y a suffix that means *like*

creamy thick and milky, like cream

homey comfortable and warm, like a home

noisy loud, like many noises together

sugary sweet, like sugar

throaty husky, like a sound from your throat

Yy

yearn yearns yearning yearned
VERB If you yearn for something, you want it very much: *He yearned for sleep.*
yearning NOUN

yeast yeasts
NOUN Yeast is a kind of fungus that is used to make bread rise, and to make liquids ferment in order to produce alcohol.

yell yells yelling yelled
VERB **1.** If you yell, you shout loudly, usually because you are angry, excited, or in pain.
NOUN **2.** a loud shout

yellow yellower yellowest; yellows yellowing yellowed
NOUN OR ADJECTIVE **1.** Yellow is the colour of buttercups, egg yolks, and lemons.
VERB **2.** When something yellows or is yellowed, it becomes yellow, often because it is old.
ADJECTIVE **3.** *an informal use* If you say someone is yellow, you mean that person is cowardly.
yellowish ADJECTIVE

yellow fever
NOUN Yellow fever is a serious infectious disease that is found in tropical countries. It causes fever and jaundice.

yelp yelps yelping yelped
VERB **1.** When people or animals yelp, they give a sudden, short cry or bark.
NOUN **2.** a sudden, short cry or bark

yen
NOUN If you have a yen to do something, you have a strong desire to do it: *I had a yen to try sailing.*

yes
INTERJECTION You use *yes* to agree with someone, to say that something is true, or to accept something.

yesterday
NOUN OR ADVERB **1.** Yesterday is the day before today. **2.** You also use *yesterday* to refer to the recent past: *The fashions of yesterday often come back into style.*

yet
ADVERB **1.** If something has not happened yet, it has not happened up to the present time: *It isn't quite dark yet.* **2.** If something should not be done yet, it should not be done now, but later: *Don't switch the light off yet.* **3.** *Yet* can mean there is still a possibility that something can happen: *We may yet manage to get tickets for the play.* **4.** You can use *yet* when you want to say how much longer a situation will continue: *The show doesn't start for an hour yet.* **5.** *Yet* can be used for emphasis: *She changed her mind yet again.*

CONJUNCTION **6.** *Yet* means *but at the same time* or it introduces a fact that is surprising: *The soup is good, yet it could use more salt. She isn't a fan of that artist, yet she owns at least three of his paintings.*

yeti yetis
NOUN A yeti, or abominable snowman, is a large, hairy, apelike animal that some people believe exists in the Himalayas.

yew yews
NOUN an evergreen tree with bright red berries

yield yields yielding yielded
VERB **1.** If you yield to someone or something, you stop resisting and give in to that person or thing: *He yielded to temptation and opened his birthday gift one day early.* **2.** If you yield something that you have control of or responsibility for, you surrender it: *They refused to yield control of their territory.* **3.** If something yields, it breaks or gives way: *The handle yielded to her grasp.* **4.** To yield something is to produce it: *One season's produce yields food for the following year.*
NOUN **5.** A yield is an amount of food, money, or profit produced from a given area of land or from an investment.

yippee
INTERJECTION *Yippee!* is an exclamation of happiness or excitement.

yodel yodels yodelling yodelled
VERB When someone yodels, that person sings normal notes with high, quick notes in between. This style of singing is associated with the Swiss and Austrian Alps.

yoga
NOUN Yoga is a Hindu method of mental and physical exercise or discipline.

yogurt yogurts
NOUN Yogurt is a slightly sour, thick liquid made from milk that has had bacteria added to it and is often sweetened and flavoured.

yoke yokes
NOUN **1.** a wooden bar attached to two collars, which is laid across the necks of animals such as oxen to hold them together, and to which a plough or other tool may be attached **2.** If people are under a yoke of some kind, they are being oppressed: *under the yoke of slavery*

yokel yokels
NOUN someone who lives in the country and is regarded as being uneducated and old-fashioned

yolk yolks
NOUN the yellow part in the middle of an egg

(!) HEADS UP The *l* in **yolk** is silent. It is pronounced YOKE.

Yy

Yom Kippur

NOUN Yom Kippur is an annual Jewish religious holiday, which is a day of fasting and prayers. It is also called the Day of Atonement.

yonder

ADVERB OR ADJECTIVE over there: *There's an island yonder.*

yore

NOUN Yore means existing a long time ago: *nostalgia for the days of yore*

you

PRONOUN **1.** *You* refers to the person or group of people that a person is speaking or writing to. **2.** *You* also refers to people in general: *You can get a cellphone quite cheap these days.*

young younger youngest

ADJECTIVE **1.** A young person, animal, or plant has not lived very long and is not yet mature. NOUN **2.** The young are young people in general. **3.** The young of an animal are its babies.

youngster youngsters

NOUN a child or young person

your

ADJECTIVE **1.** *Your* means belonging or relating to the person or group of people that someone is speaking to: *I do like your name.* **2.** *Your* is used to show that something belongs or relates to people in general: *Your driving ability is affected by just one or two drinks.*

yours

PRONOUN *Yours* refers to something belonging or relating to the person or group of people that someone is speaking to: *His hair is longer than yours.*

yourself yourselves

PRONOUN **1.** *Yourself* is used when the person being spoken to does the action and is affected by it: *Why can't you do it yourself?* **2.** *Yourself* is used to emphasize *you*: *Do you yourself know the whole story?*

youth youths

NOUN **1.** Someone's youth is the period of that person's life before he or she is a fully mature adult. **2.** Youth is the quality or condition of being young and often inexperienced. **3.** a young person **4.** The youth are young people thought of as a group: *the youth of today* **youthful** ADJECTIVE

youth hostel youth hostels

NOUN a place where young people can stay cheaply when they are on holiday

yo-yo yo-yos

NOUN a round, wooden or plastic toy attached to a piece of string. You play by making the yo-yo rise and fall on the string.

yuppie yuppies

NOUN *an informal word* If you say people are yuppies, you think they are young, middle-class, and earn a lot of money, which they spend on themselves.

⚠ HEADS UP

Use **your** before the thing you own: *Is that your bag?* Use **yours** after: *Is that bag yours?*

SPELL-CHECK THIS!

A computer's spell-check won't catch wrong **homophones** (words that are spelled differently but sound the same).

If your going to bed, take you're pills first.

In this sentence, **your** and **you're** are mixed up. **Your** means *owned by you*. **You're** is short for *you are*.

NEL

Zz

zany zanier zaniest
ADJECTIVE odd or ridiculous in an amusing way: *zany humour*

zap zaps zapping zapped
VERB *an informal word* **1.** To zap something is to kill or destroy it. **2.** To move quickly between TV channels using a remote control.

zeal
NOUN Zeal is very great enthusiasm.
zealous ADJECTIVE

zealot zealots
NOUN a person who acts with very great enthusiasm, especially in following a political or religious cause

zebra zebras
NOUN a type of African wild horse with black and white stripes over its body

Zen
NOUN Zen is a form of Buddhism that concentrates on learning through meditation and intuition.

zenith
NOUN The zenith of something is the time when it is at its most successful or powerful: *the zenith of her career in engineering*

zero zeros zeroes zeroing zeroed
NOUN **1.** nothing, or the number 0 **2.** Zero is the freezing point, 0° Celsius.
ADJECTIVE **3.** Zero means there is none at all of a particular thing: *He has zero chance of winning the game.*
VERB **4.** To zero in on a target is to aim at it or to move toward it: *The headlines zeroed in on the major news stories.*

zest
NOUN **1.** Zest is a feeling of pleasure and enthusiasm: *zest for life* **2.** Zest is a quality that adds extra flavour or interest to something: *Her witty observations added zest to the discussion.* **3.** The zest of an orange or lemon is the outside of the peel, which is used to flavour food and drinks.

zigzag zigzags zigzagging zigzagged
NOUN **1.** a line that has a series of sharp, angular turns to the right and left in it, like a continuous series of Ws
VERB **2.** To zigzag is to move forward by going at an angle first right and then left: *Lightening zigzagged across the sky.*

zinc
NOUN Zinc is a bluish white metal used in alloys and to coat other metals to stop them from rusting.

zine zines
NOUN a self-published magazine

zing
NOUN *an informal word* Zing is a quality in something that makes it lively or interesting: *Salt and pepper add zing to a plain meal.*

zip zips zipping zipped
VERB When you zip something or zip it up, you fasten it using a zipper.

zipper zippers
NOUN a long, narrow fastener with two rows of teeth that are closed or opened by a small clip pulled between them

zodiac
NOUN The zodiac is an imaginary strip in the sky that contains the planets and stars, which astrologers think are important influences on people. It is divided into 12 sections, each with a special name and symbol. The signs of the zodiac are Aries, Taurus, Gemini, Cancer, Leo, Virgo, Libra, Scorpio, Sagittarius, Capricorn, Aquarius, and Pisces.

zombie zombies
NOUN **1.** *an informal use* If you refer to someone as a zombie, you mean that that person seems to be unaware of what is going on around him or her and seems to act without thinking about what he or she is doing. **2.** a dead person who has been brought back to life by witchcraft, especially in certain West African and Caribbean regions

zone zones
NOUN an area that has particular features or properties: *a school zone, an industrial zone*

zoo zoos
NOUN a place where wild animals are kept so that people can look at them

zoology
NOUN Zoology is the scientific study of animals.
zoological ADJECTIVE
zoologist NOUN

zoom zooms zooming zoomed
VERB **1.** To zoom is to move very quickly: *They zoomed to safety.* **2.** If a camera zooms in on something, it gives a close-up picture of it.

zucchini zucchini
NOUN a small vegetable with dark green skin

Zz

⚠ **HEADS UP** The word **zealot** is pronounced ZELL-uht.

INDEX OF SPECIAL FEATURES

BE WORD SHARP!